Praise for *Our Vietnam*

"A wonderful addition to the rich and diverse literature on the war. Langguth's firsthand experiences in Vietnam help infuse this anecdotally rich chronological narrative with a vividness and immediacy that propel the reader through nearly seven hundred pages of history. . . . Any book that becomes a vessel for meaningful reexamination of a national tragedy is exceptional and demands broad attention. And that is what Langguth's book is, and does."
—David Rudenstine, *The Nation*

"Powerful and enlightening."
—Chalmers Johnson, *The San Diego Union-Tribune*

"A thorough and vivid narrative . . . Langguth's narrations of battles are dramatic and compelling, and his sketches of his principal characters are wonderfully vivid and revealing."
—Jon Weiner, *LA Weekly*

"The detailed recounting of conversations and actions in Washington, Saigon, Paris, and Hanoi is so well wrought that I found myself carrying the book everywhere, hoping for just a few minutes to read what was going to happen next. This book will probably become a standard text for anyone engaged in serious study of the Vietnam War and that seminal period when America changed its battle strategies."
—Michael L. Ramsey, *The Roanoke Times*

"A grimly powerful procession of folly and tragedy."
—*Kirkus Reviews* (starred)

"A well-crafted and adroitly balanced account that tells a long, compelling story and sets itself apart from the Vietnam War pack."
—*Publishers Weekly* (starred)

"Compulsively readable and thoroughly researched."
—Marc Leepson, *The VVA Veteran*

Also by A. J. Langguth

A Noise of War: Caesar, Pompey, Octavian and the Struggle for Rome (1994)
Patriots: The Men Who Started the American Revolution (1988)
Saki: A Life of Hector Hugh Munro (1981)
Hidden Terrors (1978)
Macumba: White and Black Magic in Brazil (1975)
Marksman (1974)
Wedlock (1972)
Jesus Christs (1968)

A. J. Langguth

A TOUCHSTONE BOOK
PUBLISHED BY SIMON & SCHUSTER
NEW YORK • LONDON • TORONTO
SYDNEY • SINGAPORE

OUR
VIETNAM

The War
1954–1975

For NEIL DAVIS
(1934–1985)

 TOUHSTONE
Rockefeller Center
1230 Avenue of the Americas
New York, NY 10020

The Library of Congress has cataloged
the Simon & Schuster edtition as follows:

Langguth, A. J., date.
    Our Vietnam : the war, 1954–1975 /
A. J. Langguth.
        p. cm.
    Includes bibliographical references and index.
    1. Vietnamese Conflict, 1961–1975—United
States.   2. Vietnam—Politics and government—
1945–1975.   3. United States—History—1945–
I. Title.
DS558.L36 2000
959.704'3373—dc21   00-057384
ISBN 0-684-81202-9
        0-7432-1231-2 (Pbk)

Laos was never really ours after 1954.
South Vietnam is and wants to be.
—McGeorge Bundy,
Washington, D.C., 1961

The Americans thought that Vietnam was a war.
We knew that Vietnam was our country.
—Luu Doan Huynh,
Hanoi, 1999

CONTENTS

PART FOUR: LE DUAN AND GERALD R. FORD

CAST OF CHARACTERS

SOUTH VIETNAM

BAO DAI was crowned emperor by France in 1925 at age twelve. He collaborated with the Japanese during the Second World War, served Ho Chi Minh briefly as an adviser in 1945 and was restored as chief of state by the French. Never interested in governing, he was supplanted in 1955 by Ngo Dinh Diem. For nearly three decades, the former emperor was attended by a volunteer equerry, Bui Tuong Minh, nicknamed "Tommy."

BUI DIEM, son of a scholarly northern family, served as South Vietnam's ambassador to the United States from 1966 to 1972. During the 1968 election, he worked with Anna Chennault to persuade Thieu that Nixon would offer him better peace terms than Humphrey.

DUONG VAN MINH, known as "Big Minh" because he stood six feet tall, led the Revolutionary Military Council that overthrew Diem in November 1963. He himself was sent into exile after the January 1964 coup of Nguyen Khanh.

HOANG DUC NHA, educated in the United States, became an influential adviser to his cousin, Nguyen Van Thieu.

NGO DINH DIEM (1901–1963) returned to Saigon from self-imposed exile in the United States to become prime minister of South Vietnam in 1954 after the Geneva agreement divided the country. He replaced former emperor Bao Dai as head of government in 1955 and thwarted the planned unification elections of 1956. After U.S. complaints about his autocratic rule, he was deposed by a junta of his generals and murdered on November 2, 1963, along with Ngo Dinh Nhu, his brother and adviser.

NGO DINH NHU, Diem's younger brother, and his wife, Tran Le Xuan, became unpopular with the South Vietnamese people and with Americans in Washington and the U.S. embassy in Saigon for their influence over Diem. Madame Nhu was outspoken against the Buddhist protests of 1963 and the sympathy shown them by U.S. policymakers and the world press. Diem resisted repeated American efforts to limit the role of Nhu and his wife. Three of his other brothers were also influential in Diem's government: Ngo Dinh Can controlled the provinces around Hue with a lawless police force and was executed after the 1963 coup. Ngo Dinh Luyen, Diem's youngest brother, was his ambassador to Great Britain in the early 1960s. Ngo Dinh Thuc, the Ngo family's eldest son, was the Roman Catholic archbishop of Hue.

NGUYEN CAO KY, born in 1930, became prime minister of South Vietnam in 1965 and its vice president under Nguyen Van Thieu in 1967. Trained by the French military, he broke with Thieu in 1971 and fled the country in April 1975.

NGUYEN KHANH overthrew the leaders of the coup against Diem three months later in January 1964. He proved to be an inept leader and was sent into exile early in 1965.

NGUYEN VAN THIEU, a general trained in the United States who fought for the French, served as president of South Vietnam from 1967 until the Communists took the country in 1975.

TRAN KIM TUYEN, a Catholic with medical and law degrees from French schools in Hanoi, went south in 1954 and ran Nhu's secret police. Exiled and then jailed for plotting against Diem, he lived until 1975 under house arrest in Saigon before escaping to England.

TRI QUANG, a Buddhist dissident in South Vietnam, helped to bring down Diem in 1963. He was also a leader in the Struggle Movement against Ky in 1966, but when it was quelled, he withdrew to the An Quang pagoda in Saigon.

NORTH VIETNAM

BUI TIN, a fifty-year-old journalist who was also an officer in North Vietnam's PAVN, accepted Minh's surrender at the Independence Hall on April 30, 1975.

DANG VU HIEP, a veteran of Dien Bien Phu, was a political officer in the North Vietnamese army. He served as an adviser to the Vietcong in the Central Highlands, where he remained for ten years. In 1965, Hiep took part in the attacks on Pleiku on February 7 and the Qui Nhon barracks three days later.

HO CHI MINH (1890–1969) was born Nguyen Sinh Cung in the central Vietnamese province of Nghe Tinh. He joined the French Communist Party in 1920, and formed the Indochinese Communist Party in the early 1930s and a nationalist alliance called the Vietminh in May 1941. The founder of the Democratic Republic of Vietnam, Ho was revered in the North for his commitment to independence and unity.

LE DUAN (1908–1986) first enlisted in Ho's youth movement in 1928 and rose in the Communist ranks. He replaced Truong Chinh as acting general secretary of the Hanoi Politburo in 1956, the same year his pamphlet *The Path of Revolution in the South* inspired the resistance to Diem. Even before Ho's death, Le Duan had emerged as the driving force for southern independence.

LE DUC THO (1911–1990) became Hanoi's leading negotiator at the Paris peace talks. He declined the honor when he and Kissinger were awarded the 1973 Nobel Peace Prize because, he said, peace had not yet been established.

LUU DOAN HUYNH joined Giap's army as a seventeen-year-old and held posts in Hanoi's Foreign Ministry in Southeast Asia before becoming an intelligence analyst for the Department of U.S. Affairs. Huynh was a member of the five-person team that drafted documents for peace talks with the United States.

NGUYEN CHI THANH (1914–1967) commanded North Vietnamese operations in South Vietnam from 1965 until he died of a heart attack in July 1967.

NGUYEN HUU THO, a southerner, was named chairman of the National Liberation Front in December 1960 and took his orders from the Hanoi Politburo.

NGUYEN KHAC HUYNH, with his fellow high school classmates, tore down the Japanese flag in Hanoi in 1945. He carried the news of the French defeat to fellow troops in 1954 and took part in the Paris peace talks. When Communist soldiers entered Saigon in 1975, Huynh was an analyst in Hanoi with the Foreign Ministry.

NGUYEN MINH VY, who joined with Ho in 1945, governed the Fifth Zone during the war with France, overseeing the four coastal provinces south of Hue.

NGUYEN THI BINH, a granddaughter of the prominent advocate of independence Phan Chau Trinh, was jailed from 1951 to 1954 for resistance to the French. When the National Liberation Front became the Provisional Revolutionary Government in June 1969, Binh became foreign minister and second in rank at the Paris peace talks to Le Duc Tho.

NGUYEN THI DINH, who spent three years in the French Poulo Condore prison where her husband had died, led an early resistance to Diem in the Mekong Delta's Ben Tre province. In 1965, she became deputy commander of the South Vietnam Liberation Forces, the highest combat position held by a woman in the Vietcong.

NGUYEN THI NGOC DUNG, an effective speaker on behalf of the National Liberation Front throughout Europe, had run away in the mid-1940s to join the resistance to the French in the Mekong Delta. After marrying and having two children, she spent the next decades separated from her family as she worked for the Vietminh and then the Vietcong.

TA MINH KHAM (1926–1999), born in Ben Tre, joined Ho's forces before he was twenty, fought the French for nine years and became commander of a Vietminh battalion. After studying at the Beijing Military Institute from 1954 to 1957, Kham was sent to South Vietnam in 1961 to organize resistance to Diem and the Americans.

PHAM VAN DONG (1906–2000) was North Vietnam's premier from 1955 to 1975, the premier of the Socialist Republic of Vietnam until 1986. With Ho and Giap, he ruled the country until Le Duan became increasingly influential.

TRAN BACH DANG, ranking Communist political officer in Saigon, helped to plan the Tet offensive of 1968. His wife, Nguyen Thi Chon, had been captured and tortured by the South Vietnamese police the previous year.

TRAN QUANG CO, a twenty-six-year-old Vietminh at Dien Bien Phu, was assigned to the camp with Giap's prisoners of war. After the Geneva conference, Co joined the teaching staff of the Foreign Affairs College of the Foreign Ministry. From 1966 to 1968, he was also drafting Hanoi's negotiating terms to prepare for a possible peace conference.

TRAN VAN TRA, military leader of the National Liberation Front, was a lieutenant general in the North Vietnamese army. As chairman of the Central Office for South Vietnam (COSVN), he coordinated the assault on Saigon during the 1968 Tet offensive, although he later criticized it for being badly planned.

TRUONG CHINH (1907–1988) was born Dan Xuan Khu but took the name that meant "Long March" to show his solidarity with Mao. After making a bloody botch of Hanoi's land reform program, he was forced to step down as general secretary of the Indochinese Communist Party.

VAN TIEN DUNG, who replaced Giap as commander of the People's Army of Vietnam, was the commanding general who led the PAVN to victory in April 1975.

VO NGUYEN GIAP, born in 1911, was founder and commander of the People's Army of Vietnam (PAVN) until 1972. A member of the Communist Party from his mid-teens, Giap led the siege that defeated the French at Dien Bien Phu and advocated protracted guerrilla warfare against the Americans.

XUAN THUY (1912–1985) was Hanoi's foreign minister in the mid-1960s and then chief delegate to the Paris peace talks, although Le Duc Tho was the more powerful figure.

CAMBODIA

LON NOL (1913–1985), with Sirik Matak, organized the successful coup against Norodom Sihanouk in March 1970. His troops were defeated by the Khmer Rouge Communist rebels, and Lon Nol fled to Indonesia when the Communists took Cambodia on April 17, 1975.

POL POT, head of the Communist Khmer Rouge, was born Saloth Sar to a family connected to Sihanouk's royal line. His forces defeated Lon Nol in 1975, and as prime minister Pol Pot's policies were responsible for the death of 1.5 million Cambodians. His regime was overthrown by an army from the Socialist Republic of Vietnam in 1978.

NORODOM SIHANOUK, former prince of Cambodia, abdicated the throne in 1954 to form a popular political party. After his overthrow in 1970, Sihanouk went into exile in Beijing and supported the Khmer Rouge.

LAOS

KONG LE, a Lao army captain, headed the coup in August 1960 that overthrew the government backed by the United States and returned neutralist Prince Souvanna Phouma to power.

PHOUMI NOSAVAN (1920–1985) was a right-wing minister of defense supported in the late 1950s by the CIA.

SOUPHANOUVONG (1909–1995), younger half-brother of Prince Souvanna Phouma, became political leader of the Pathet Lao Communist movement.

SOUVANNA PHOUMA (1901–1984), prime minister of Laos at various times from 1951 to 1975, tried to steer a neutralist course but permitted U.S. bombing of Communist supply routes from 1963 to 1973.

UNITED STATES

CREIGHTON ADAMS (1914–1974), replaced William Westmoreland as commander of the Military Assistance Command, Vietnam (MACV) in July, 1968, and oversaw withdrawal of U.S. forces. Promoted to Army chief of staff in 1972.

DEAN ACHESON (1893–1971), appointed Truman's secretary of state in 1949, was a hardline adviser to both Kennedy and Johnson as one of the "Wise Men," but on March 26, 1968, reversed his policy and called for negotiation with North Vietnam.

GEORGE W. BALL, U.S. undersecretary of state from 1961 to September 1966, was the most outspoken dissenter from the escalations of Kennedy and Johnson.

CHESTER BOWLES (1901–1986), U.S. undersecretary of state in 1961 but dislodged from that job, was made a roving ambassador and then sent for his second tour as ambassador to India from 1963 until 1969. Bowles was punished by the Kennedy brothers for his public criticism of the Bay of Pigs invasion in Cuba.

McGeorge Bundy (1919–1996) was the president's assistant for national security affairs under Kennedy and, until February 28, 1966, under Johnson. A former dean of the faculty at Harvard College, Bundy was a major proponent of the Vietnam War.

William Bundy, older by two years than his brother McGeorge, he joined the Central Intelligence Agency in 1951, was assistant secretary of defense for international security affairs from 1961 to 1963 and then assistant secretary of state for Far Eastern affairs from 1964 to 1968.

William L. Calley, Jr., was a twenty-five-year-old second lieutenant from the 32nd Infantry Division (Americal) when he oversaw the massacre of Vietnamese civilians on March 16, 1968. Convicted by a court-martial of premeditated murder and sentenced to life in prison, Calley benefited from Nixon's intervention and was paroled in November 1974.

Clark Clifford (1906–1998), an attorney who advised Johnson privately, became secretary of defense in 1968 and almost immediately recommended disengaging from the war.

William Colby (1920–1996) was the CIA's Saigon station chief from 1959 to 1962, became involved in the late 1960s in civilian operations and also the Phoenix anti-guerrilla program. He was appointed CIA director in 1973.

Chester Cooper, a CIA analyst until 1964, when he moved to the White House as a member of the National Security Council. Working with Averell Harriman, Cooper repeatedly sought to end the war through negotiation.

Allen Dulles (1893–1969) was director of the CIA from 1953 until Kennedy replaced him after the Bay of Pigs.

John Foster Dulles (1888–1959), Allen Dulles's older brother, organized the Southeast Asia Treaty Organization during his years as Eisenhower's secretary of state. Dulles resisted the Geneva conference of 1954 but became an enthusiastic backer of Diem.

Elbridge Durbrow (1903–1997), a career foreign service officer, was appointed ambassador to South Vietnam by Eisenhower in 1957. Kennedy replaced him with Frederick Nolting in 1961.

Daniel Ellsberg went to South Vietnam in 1961 and returned from 1966 to 1967 as a senior liaison officer to the American embassy and the following year as assistant to the ambassador. Ellsberg turned against the war and leaked the documents known as the Pentagon Papers to the *New York Times*. Charged with conspiracy, theft and violation of espionage laws, Ellsberg was freed when the federal judge found the White House break-in of Ellsberg's psychiatrist's office to be government misconduct.

Michael Forrestal (1927–1989) was appointed by Kennedy to the staff of the National Security Council in 1962 and was involved in drafting the August 24, 1963, cable to Lodge that set off acrimonious debate in the White House.

J. William Fulbright (1905–1995), Democratic senator from Arkansas and chairman of the Senate Foreign Relations Committee, won approval for the Tonkin Gulf Resolution in August 1964, but by early 1966 chaired hearings to give a platform to antiwar spokesmen.

JOHN KENNETH GALBRAITH, a Harvard economist appointed as ambassador to India by Kennedy, was an early and witty critic of the Vietnam effort.

LESLIE GELB, as deputy director of the Defense Department's policy planning, was assigned by McNamara in June 1967 to write a history of the U.S. involvement in Vietnam.

ARTHUR J. GOLDBERG (1908–1990) was named secretary of labor and then associate Supreme Court justice by Kennedy. Johnson persuaded him to leave the Court in 1965 to replace Adlai Stevenson as ambassador to the United Nations.

ERNEST GRUENING (1887–1974), as a Democratic senator from Alaska, joined Wayne Morse of Oregon in casting the two votes against the Tonkin Gulf Resolution of 1964.

PHILIP HABIB (1920–1992), counselor for political affairs in the American embassy in Saigon in 1965, briefed the Wise Men at the March 1968 meeting that left most of them opposed to the war. In 1968, Habib went to Paris as part of Harriman's team and stayed on under Nixon until July 1970.

ALEXANDER M. HAIG was wounded while commanding a battalion in Vietnam in the mid-sixties. As Kissinger's military aide in the National Security Council, Haig was rapidly promoted by Nixon and finally named White House chief of staff in April 1973.

PAUL D. HARKINS (1904–1984) became the first commander of the U.S. Military Assistance Command, Vietnam (MACV) on February 13, 1962, when Kennedy expanded the U.S. military role in South Vietnam. His support for Diem was complete and uncritical.

W. AVERELL HARRIMAN (1891–1986), a former governor of New York, was appointed by Kennedy as ambassador-at-large and later in 1961 as assistant secretary of state for Far Eastern affairs; he moved on under Kennedy and Johnson to become undersecretary of state for political affairs and ambassador-at-large for Southeast Asia. Harriman negotiated the neutrality for Laos in Geneva in 1962 and headed the first Paris peace team in 1968.

ROGER HILSMAN, active in counterinsurgency in World War II, warned against reliance on only military solutions in Vietnam. From his posts in the State Department, Hilsman worked to replace Diem and drafted the August 24, 1963, memorandum that was seen as encouraging a military coup.

HAROLD K. JOHNSON (1912–1983) was jumped past forty-three senior generals by Lyndon Johnson to replace General Earle Wheeler in July 1964 as Army chief of staff. The following year, General Johnson was among those who recommended sending American combat troops to South Vietnam. General Westmoreland replaced him as Army chief in 1968.

LYNDON B. JOHNSON (1908–1973) succeeded to the presidency on the assassination of John Kennedy. He escalated the war in 1965 both by bombing North Vietnam and by introducing U.S. combat troops in the South. Antiwar sentiment led him to announce on March 31, 1968, that he would not be a candidate for reelection.

U. ALEXIS JOHNSON, a U.S. foreign service officer, went to Saigon as Maxwell Taylor's deputy ambassador in 1964.

JOHN F. KENNEDY (1917–1963), president of the United States from 1961 to 1963, expressed misgivings about the war, but his administration increased the number of American advisers in South Vietnam from 700 to 15,000.

ROBERT F. KENNEDY (1925–1968), John Kennedy's brother and his attorney general, was elected to the U.S. Senate from New York in 1964 and, before his assassination on June 5, 1968, declared his candidacy for president.

HENRY KISSINGER, born in Germany in 1923, was teaching international relations at Harvard University when Richard Nixon chose him as his national security adviser in 1969. After years of negotiation, Kissinger and North Vietnam's Le Duc Tho signed a peace agreement in Paris on January 27, 1973. In September 1973, Kissinger replaced William P. Rogers as secretary of state.

WILLIAM KOHLMANN, assigned to the CIA's Saigon station for much of the 1960s, cultivated Buddhists and other political leaders on behalf of the agency.

ROBERT W. KOMER, a senior analyst with the CIA, went to Saigon in 1966 as Johnson's special assistant for pacification. Before his departure in 1968, Komer oversaw the Phoenix program.

MELVIN R. LAIRD, a politically adept Wisconsin congressman, was Nixon's secretary of defense from 1968 to 1973. Laird named the U.S. effort to return the brunt of the fighting to the ARVN "Vietnamization."

EDWARD G. LANSDALE (1908–1987), a former advertising man, Lansdale worked for the CIA in the Philippines before going to South Vietnam in June 1954 to bolster Diem's government.

CURTIS LEMAY, the U.S. Air Force chief of staff from 1961 to 1965, was an early proponent of bombing in the North and said in late 1963 that the United States should bomb the country "back to the Stone Age." LeMay became George Wallace's vice presidential candidate in 1968.

LYMAN LEMNITZER (1899–1988), who predicted an invasion into the South by the North Vietnamese, was chairman of the Joint Chiefs of Staff from 1960 through 1962, when Kennedy named him NATO commander.

HENRY CABOT LODGE, JR. (1902–1985) replaced Frederick Nolting as ambassador to South Vietnam. After supporting the coup that led to Diem's murder, Lodge returned to the United States in 1964 to work against the Republican nomination of Barry Goldwater. He came back for a second stint as ambassador in 1965–1966. Nixon sent him in 1969 to replace Harriman as head of the U.S. delegation at the Paris peace talks.

GRAHAM A. MARTIN (1912–1990), replacing Ellsworth Bunker, became the last U.S. ambassador to South Vietnam. Martin's refusal to heed warnings about North Vietnamese intentions thwarted an orderly withdrawal of Americans and friendly Vietnamese from the country and led to the chaos of late April 1975.

EUGENE J. MCCARTHY, a Minnesota senator, challenged Johnson for the Democratic nomination in 1968 as an antiwar candidate. His strong showing in the New Hampshire primary encouraged Robert Kennedy to make the race.

JOHN MCCONE (1902–1991), director of the CIA from 1961 to 1965, strongly supported Diem and, arguing after the coup that a stable government in the South was unlikely, opposed retaliation bombing raids against North Vietnam.

GEORGE MCGOVERN, Democratic senator from South Dakota, was a leading critic of the Vietnam War. When he ran for president in 1972, McGovern was easily defeated by Nixon.

Robert S. McNamara, briefly president of the Ford Motor Company, served as secretary of defense from 1961 to 1968. Publicly optimistic, he slowly became convinced that the war could not be won.

John T. McNaughton (1921–1967), McNamara's influential assistant secretary of defense for international security affairs, backed the bombing of North Vietnam and increased American military involvement, but before his death in a plane crash in July 1967 he had decided losing South Vietnam would not jeopardize the U.S. position in the world.

John Mitchell (1913–1988) was Nixon's U.S. attorney general until he resigned to become chairman of his reelection campaign. In 1975, he served eighteen months in prison for his role in the Watergate break-in and cover-up.

Wayne L. Morse (1900–1974), a Democrat from Oregon, was the only senator to vote with Senator Ernest Gruening against the Gulf of Tonkin Resolution in 1964.

Frederick E. Nolting (1911–1989), ambassador to South Vietnam from 1961 to 1963, was heavily criticized for apologizing for Diem's shortcomings.

John H. Richardson went to Saigon as CIA station chief in 1962. Lodge had him recalled on October 5, 1963, for being too close to Diem and Nhu.

Franklin Delano Roosevelt (1882–1945), U.S. president from 1933 to 1945, spoke of making Indochina a trusteeship leading to independence but died before implementing his vision.

Walt W. Rostow worked on McGeorge Bundy's national security team from 1961 until he was named to head the policy planning office at the State Department. He replaced Bundy as chief adviser in 1966. He was an early and consistent advocate of bombing North Vietnam and increasing U.S. troop strength in the South.

Dean Rusk (1909–1994), assistant secretary of state for Far Eastern affairs during the Truman administration, Rusk as secretary of state ceded strategy for Vietnam to Robert McNamara at the Pentagon and continued to support policies aimed at a victory for South Vietnam.

James Schlesinger served as Nixon's CIA director until he replaced Elliot Richardson, who had briefly succeeded Laird as secretary of defense in 1973.

Ulysses S. Grant Sharp, Jr., deeply committed to the Vietnam War, succeeded Admiral Harry Felt in June 1964 as the Navy's Commander in Chief, Pacific, before retiring in 1968.

William H. Sullivan, a career foreign service officer, was Harriman's chief aide at the 1962 Geneva conference, which neutralized Laos. After serving as Johnson's ambassador to Laos, Sullivan became Kissinger's chief deputy during the Paris peace talks in 1972.

Maxwell D. Taylor (1901–1987), a four-star army general brought back from retirement by John Kennedy, chaired the Joint Chiefs of Staff before Johnson appointed him as ambassador to South Vietnam in 1964. The following year, he lost a debate with General Westmoreland over the proper role of U.S. troops in the war.

Cyrus R. Vance, secretary of the army from 1962 to 1963 and then McNamara's deputy secretary of defense until 1967, had become disillusioned with the war and went to Paris with Harriman in 1968 for the peace talks.

JOHN PAUL VANN (1924–1972), disgusted with the cautious approach of Diem's generals to fighting the Vietcong, was a senior U.S. Army official in the Mekong Delta who provided newsmen in the early 1960s with accurate accounts of ARVN failures. Vann retired in 1963, but Abrams appointed him to command all U.S. forces in the Central Highlands. He died in a helicopter crash during the North's Easter offensive of 1972.

WILLIAM WESTMORELAND replaced General Harkins and commanded U.S. forces in South Vietnam from 1964 to 1968, when he became U.S. Army chief of staff for the next four years. His policy for a war of attrition depended on increasing the number of U.S. combat troops at the expense of counterinsurgency. Westmoreland was followed by Creighton Abrams and in June 1972 by Frederick C. Weyand, the last American commander in South Vietnam.

EARLE G. WHEELER (1908–1975) was appointed U.S. Army chief of staff in 1962 by Kennedy. Two years later, Johnson appointed "Bus" Wheeler to the office of chairman of the Joint Chiefs, where he supported sending more American combat troops and increasing the bombing of the North.

CHINA

MAO ZEDONG (1893–1976), president of the People's Republic of China, broke with the Soviets in the 1960s and welcomed Richard Nixon to China on February 21, 1972.

ZHOU ENLAI (1898–1976), premier of the People's Republic of China for twenty-seven years from 1949 until his death, endorsed an unfavorable settlement for the North Vietnamese at the Geneva conference of 1954.

USSR

LEONID BREZHNEV (1906–1982) replaced Nikita Khrushchev as first secretary general of the Soviet Communist Party in 1964 and retained the position until his death. To offset China's military aid to North Vietnam, Brezhnev promoted an increase by the Soviet Union in such high-technology equipment as radar and surface-to-air missiles.

ANATOLY DOBRYNIN, Soviet ambassador to the United States from 1962 to 1986, was a go-between for Robert Kennedy and the Kremlin during the Cuban missile crisis of 1962.

NIKITA KHRUSHCHEV (1894–1971), secretary general of the Soviet Communist Party and premier of the USSR from 1958 to 1964, was removed and replaced by Brezhnev and Kosygin.

ALEXEI KOSYGIN (1904–1980), prime minister of the Soviet Union from 1964 to 1980, traveled to Hanoi early in 1965 to urge that the North Vietnamese negotiate with the United States, but the U.S. bombing of North Vietnam after the Vietcong attack on Pleiku led Kosygin to approve military aid for the North.

INDOCHINA, 1954–1975

CHINA

Nanning

DEMOCRATIC
REPUBLIC OF VIETNAM
(NORTH VIETNAM)

Dien Bien Phu

Hanoi

BURMA

Red River

Haiphong

Red River

N

LAOS

PLAIN
OF JARS

Gulf of
Tonkin

HAINAN

Mekong River

Vientiane

Vinh

Udorn (Udon Thani)

Dong Hoi

DMZ (1954)

Khe Sanh

Tchepone

Quang Tri

Hue

THAILAND

Mekong River

Da Nang

Kontum

Pleiku

Bangkok

CAMBODIA
(KAMPUCHEA)

Ban Me Thuot

U Tapao

FISHHOOK

An Loc

Cam
Ranh Bay

Gulf of Siam

Phnom Penh

PARROT'S BEAK

REPUBLIC OF VIETNAM
(SOUTH VIETNAM)

Sihanoukville
(Kompong Som)

Mekong River

Saigon

Mekong Delta

Area of Detail

South
China Sea

Saigon

Mekong River

My Tho

Vinh Long

Ben Tre

Vung Tau

Can Tho

N

0 Miles   50   100

Mekong Delta

0 Kilometers   150

0 Miles   100   200   300

0 Kilometers   300

© 2000 Jeffrey L. Ward

OUR VIETNAM

PART ONE

JOHN F. KENNEDY AND HO CHI MINH

ONE

KENNEDY AND HO
1960

Dwight Eisenhower was a minute or two early walking out the front door of the White House because he wanted to greet his successor as soon as he arrived. It was the morning of December 6, 1960, four weeks after the presidential election, and Eisenhower had interrupted a vacation in Georgia to come back to Washington for his first meeting with the president-elect, John Fitzgerald Kennedy. The crowd gathering on Pennsylvania Avenue agreed that Ike looked ruddy and beaming, but his staff understood that his public smile, while it won elections, did not always reflect his mood. Eisenhower was fretting as he waited, concerned that Kennedy would pull up in a car filled with smug young aides still congratulating themselves on beating the Republicans.

During the recent campaign, Kennedy had spared the president direct attacks, but Eisenhower saw no reason to be grateful. Ike might have been seventy, the oldest man ever to hold the presidency and the victim of a heart attack, ileitis and a stroke. Yet he knew that if the Twenty-second Amendment to the U.S. Constitution had not barred him from a third term and he had chosen to run again, he could have beaten Kennedy or any other Democrat. Kennedy's sharpest criticism had come in a campaign promise to "get the country moving again." Eisenhower might have resented the implication of stagnation and drift, but both he and Kennedy remembered the rancor between transition teams when Eisenhower succeeded Harry Truman in the White House and were determined to avoid any public show of hostility.

Jack Kennedy arrived promptly at 9 A.M. and made a good first impression

Dwight D. Eisenhower and John F. Kennedy before Kennedy's
inauguration as president *(Dwight D. Eisenhower Library)*

by showing up with only a driver at the wheel of his cream-colored Lincoln. And
he came hat in hand. Kennedy generally avoided headgear since none improved
his appearance more than his own thatch of reddish-brown hair. Today, however,
to show respect for the president, he was carrying a narrow-brimmed gray felt.

Kennedy climbed the six steps and shook Eisenhower's hand. To Ike's cordial welcome, he replied quietly, "It's good to be here." Although Kennedy, at
forty-three, was the youngest man ever to win the presidency, Ike detected no
youthful arrogance as they toured the White House kitchens and the swimming
pool. When they settled down to talk in the Oval Office, the president had to
admit that Kennedy displayed an impressive mastery of the topics they had
agreed to cover.

Their agenda had been prepared by George Ball, a State Department veteran, who had drafted a version for Kennedy and then revised it after the White House sent over its list of subjects Eisenhower wanted to discuss. Ike proposed nine items, opening with the question of sharing nuclear weapons with America's European allies. Laos, a small but irksome country in Southeast Asia, ranked second on the Eisenhower agenda. It hadn't appeared on Ball's list at all.

One key to Jack Kennedy's political effectiveness was his ability to listen attentively to an argument, ask probing questions and conclude a meeting by conveying his pleasure in the conversation—all the while giving no hint of what he might decide. It was a reserve that had protected him as a sickly youngster growing up in a household that celebrated rude good health. Kennedy had shielded his sensitivity from Joseph Kennedy, his overwhelming father, and young Joe, his older brother, until his reticence had become ingrained. By the time Jack Kennedy ran for president, he was adept at maintaining options and resisting decisions. Early in the 1960 campaign, he had called on a group of Harvard professors to develop platform promises that would win him votes without tying his hands once he was elected.

In private conversation, Kennedy could rely on an indefinable aura—journalists were labeling it "charisma," Greek for a power conferred by the gods—that left his companions convinced that an enduring bond had been forged. Older men took his close attention for deference; men of every age came to feel real affection for this rather remote young millionaire.

With women, his combination of detachment and ruffled good looks served Jack Kennedy even better. During the recent campaign, Eleanor Roosevelt had expressed misgivings about Kennedy's youth and about the influence of his father, whose isolationist views had alienated a generation of Roosevelt liberals. But even the Democrats' beloved dowager had paused in her attack to grant that young Kennedy had "an enormous amount of charm."

Kennedy's charm was working that morning on Dwight Eisenhower. After an hour and a half together, they were joined by Eisenhower's top cabinet officers for further discussion. Later in the day, Ike noted in his diary that his successor seemed to be "a serious, earnest seeker for information." But he couldn't be sure that this inexperienced Democrat was taking seriously enough Eisenhower's gravest concern—the drain on America's gold supply from too much overseas spending. "I pray he understands it," Ike wrote.

WORKING WITH Eisenhower's staff, a fifty-two-year-old Washington attorney named Clark Clifford was handling day-to-day matters for Kennedy's transition team. With the wavy blond hair and bland good looks of a minor movie actor, Clifford had come from St. Louis to transform himself into a Washington insider—arranging Harry Truman's weekly poker games, serving as an Eisenhower commissioner, defending a Republican secretary of the army against Joseph McCarthy. Although Clifford had backed a fellow Missourian, Stuart Symington, in the recent Democratic primary elections, Jack Kennedy continued to use him as his personal lawyer. After the election, Clifford urged Kennedy in a memorandum to stress publicly that he was going to appoint only those men with the highest qualifications for government service; he made no mention of female candidates. But Kennedy was having trouble assembling that first-rate cabinet. Moving through the salons of Georgetown, the president-elect lamented that for four years he had spent so much time seeking out people who could help him become president that he had met very few who could help him *be* president.

As his first appointments, Kennedy asked J. Edgar Hoover to continue as director of the Federal Bureau of Investigation and Allen Dulles to remain director of the Central Intelligence Agency. Liberal Democrats deplored that gesture of continuity and detected the influence of Kennedy's conservative father. But Hoover was too entrenched at the FBI to be fired by a new president who had been elected by a nationwide margin of only 120,000 votes—many of those disputed. Although Dulles kept his job for much the same reason, he was also an old friend. When Kennedy was recovering from serious back surgery in Palm Beach in 1958, Dulles often dropped by his bedside to pass the time with tales of international espionage. In return, the senator's wife, Jacqueline, introduced Dulles to the fictional hero of *To Russia with Love*, British agent James Bond. From then on, America's spymaster was always one of the first to buy Ian Fleming's latest thriller.

BESIDES STRIVING for excellence in his appointments, Kennedy intended to reward those politicians whose early support had been vital to his victory. Adlai Stevenson, twice the Democratic nominee, could have bartered successfully for secretary of state had he been willing to endorse Kennedy before the crucial spring primaries. But he had hesitated, hoping that the Democratic presidential nomination—worth something now that Eisenhower would not be running—might be thrust upon him for a third time. Stevenson's last chance for State vanished on the July evening at the Los Angeles Sports Arena when he let his name be placed in nomination for the presidency. The ensuing tumult saw Senator Hubert Humphrey lead a war dance around the convention floor, less on behalf of Stevenson than as revenge for Kennedy's shabby campaign against Humphrey in the West Virginia primary. There the Kennedy forces had brutally contrasted Humphrey's failure to serve in World War II with Jack Kennedy's heroism in the South Pacific.

But when the whooping died away and the Stevenson signs were hauled down, the nominee had been Jack Kennedy. Even Stevenson loyalists understood that if they wanted to win this time, the convention had made the right choice.

As JACK KENNEDY prepared for his inauguration, a frail seventy-year-old leader of an impoverished peasant nation watched from halfway around the world, won-

Ho Chi Minh
(AP/Wide World Photos)

dering what the election of this young Democrat would mean for his country. From Woodrow Wilson to Harry Truman, Ho Chi Minh had seldom succeeded in engaging Washington's sympathies. Now, frustrated but determined, he had just delivered a speech in Hanoi that amounted to a declaration of war against the United States. Eisenhower's policy-makers, preparing to leave office, found Ho's challenge easy to dismiss as the last cry of an old revolutionary. But had they looked past his stooped shoulders, they would have seen eyes that still glittered with visions of a united and independent Vietnam.

Ho was saddened that late in life he should be fighting America, since for decades it was France that had been his enemy. Not long before Ho's birth in 1890, the French had succeeded in a thirty-year campaign to claim all of Indochina as their colony. The conquerors set little value on Laos or Cambodia, the two other kingdoms that made up the Indochinese peninsula. It was Vietnam, with its fine seaports and a lively population, that became the center of French rule. Vietnam itself was made up of three territories—to the north, Tonkin, with Hanoi as its capital; to the south, Cochin China, with Saigon the capital. Ho had grown up in the middle sector, called Annam and governed by French appointees from the city of Hue.

But centuries before France coveted Indochina, China had already conquered Tonkin. Invading from the north in 111 B.C., the Chinese held the land for more than a thousand years. *Viet* was the Chinese word for a tribe of barbarians who had moved to the south—or *nam*—side of the Yangtze River. During their rule, the Chinese introduced the plow and other farming tools to the Red River Delta, where the city of Hanoi would one day rise. The delta's rich land was washed out each year by monsoon rains that flooded the rice paddies and ruined the crops. To survive, the Vietnamese built thousands of miles of dikes along the Red River and its tributaries. Besides its fertile soil, Vietnam had such luster that its poets claimed they could identify where China began by the heightened sheen to their side of the border. The shades of green alone seemed infinite— rice paddies of a green that melted across the horizon into a yellow haze. Sea- green palms rising above apple-green grasses, and rubber trees spreading oval leaves of pea-pod green. On distant hills, pine trees shimmered with needles that changed with the light from blue-green to the green that was almost black.

The Vietnamese themselves were smaller and more lithe than the Chinese, and yet the Chinese never succeeded either in absorbing or quelling them. Chil- dren of Ho's generation were taught about his nation's many uprisings for inde- pendence. As early as 39 A.D., the Trung sisters gathered enough troops to overwhelm the Chinese governor's residence and, for a brief time, proclaim themselves Vietnam's queens. After a dozen more failed rebellions, a revolt suc- ceeded in the year 939. Except for brief returns of Chinese rule in the fifteenth century and again late in the 1700s, Vietnam struggled along, independent, under several native dynasties—the Ngo, the Dinh, the Le. But the country was often convulsed by civil war until north and south were finally unified in 1802 under the Nguyen family. It was the Nguyens who resisted the French up to the day that Vietnam officially became a French protectorate in 1883.

With France's victory, a new class of Frenchmen arrived to run the country, taking over many of the positions that had been held by those Vietnamese public officials called mandarins. For centuries, education had been the path for an am- bitious Vietnamese to escape from his village. Examinations were given every three years, and the few who passed and became mandarins were provided an of- ficial residence, state-paid servants and the gilded trappings worthy of agents of their Imperial Majesty.

Ho's father had achieved mandarin status, even though he had been born to a second wife rather than a first. That misfortune usually restricted a man's op- portunities. But while tending water buffalo on a farm, he impressed the landowner with his intelligence and hard work and was allowed to marry a daughter of the household. She brought to the marriage the highly prized dowry of a rice paddy—the Chinese word for "happiness" included the symbol for a rice field. In heavily populated regions of Vietnam, entire families supported themselves on the yield from one-eighth of an acre.

With his new prosperity, Ho's father undertook studies to better himself. He moved the family to Hue for the mandarin examinations but was serving in a dis- tant province when he learned that his wife had died. Ho, a grieving ten-year-old, went to live with his mother's family. Although his father seldom saw his son, he followed tradition by sending him a new adult name. Ho would keep only the very common surname of Nguyen; otherwise, the boy born Nguyen Sinh Cung became Nguyen Tat Thanh—"he who will succeed."

Entering the mandarin class, Ho's father was appointed secretary to a government minister in Hue. Mandarins were no longer serving their Vietnamese emperor, however, and he chafed at being nothing more than France's educated lackey. "Being a mandarin," Ho's father complained, "is the ultimate form of slavery."

The degree of his contempt was exposed when he was discovered shielding Vietnamese who had broken French law. Removed from his post, he roamed throughout southern Vietnam and Cambodia for the next twenty years, until his death in 1930, earning his keep by writing letters for illiterate farmers. Although they were separated from him, their father's bitter courage inspired all three children. Ho's sister was suspected by the police of harboring dissidents who had rioted against the French, and Ho's brother, kicked by a French official, fought back and was sent to prison for treasonous activities.

Ho had grown up gifted in languages and greedy for books. In his mid-teens, he came to the attention of a rebellious mandarin, a man whose followers had once tried to seize control of several towns on Bastille Day, assuming that the French would be off their guard. The attempt failed, but the leader escaped and was now offering Ho a chance to study in Japan with other insurgent Vietnamese.

Ho chose instead to stay at a high school in Hue. He soon learned that his headmaster had served in the Foreign Legion and that the lessons were heavily biased toward the French. After four years of protesting that indoctrination, Ho drifted south to become a teacher himself. He ended up at a school for workers in a factory that produced *nuoc mam*, Vietnam's pungent fish sauce. Less than a year passed before a mutiny within the Chinese army in 1911 alarmed the French, who thought that the uprising across the border might threaten Indochina's stability. They shut down Ho's school. Since the French police already knew about Ho's political leanings, he dropped the name Thanh and sailed out of the port of Saigon on a French liner headed for Marseilles. He had become an assistant cook called Van Ba—"third child."

DURING THE NEXT few years, the young man docked in ports around the Mediterranean and North Africa. His voyage to the United States in 1912 fulfilled the dream of a boy who had grown up inspired by America's revolutionary war against England. After a stop in Boston, Ho reached New York, where he was thrilled to see the Statue of Liberty, his pleasure dimmed only by the fact that it had been the French who donated it. Otherwise, Ho was awed by the marvels of New York—the subway system; the great bridges spanning the East River; the skyline, dominated by the new Metropolitan Life Insurance Building.

Even more stirring was an excursion with a shipmate from the Hoboken docks to Chinatown, where Ho spoke in Cantonese with immigrant workers. The men told him that although they knew no English, they enjoyed equal protection under American law. Decades later, Ho could recall his trip to the United States in affectionate detail.

WHEN THE FIRST WORLD WAR broke out, Ho settled in London, shoveling snow and washing dishes, until Georges Escoffier, the chef at the Carlton House, took him on as an assistant pastry cook. Ho used his three years in the kitchens to learn English and to join an underground unit of Asian immigrants called the Overseas Workers. By the time he sailed to France, he had taken yet another name—Nguyen Ai Quoc, Nguyen the Patriot.

In Paris, Ho supported himself as an interpreter and by painting art works that were sold as "Chinese antiquities." The demands of Chinese calligraphy had made his fingers adept at retouching photographs, and Ho ran an advertisement in a working-class newspaper: "If you would like a lifetime memento of your family, have your photos retouched at Nguyen Ai Quoc's. A lovely portrait in a lovely frame for 45 francs."

As he scrambled for a living, Ho was reading widely in the teaching of Buddha, Confucius and Jesus and finding something to admire in each faith. But the religion that touched his heart, and promised the most for his country, was Marxism. Ho's upbringing in a French colony made him intriguing to prominent writers on the Left—Leon Blum; Karl Marx's nephew; the editors of France's Communist and Socialist journals. Before long, Ho had joined with another Vietnamese to publish a paper they called *Viet Nam Hon*, the "Soul of Vietnam." At the age of twenty-seven, he wrote his first serious manifesto, denouncing the injustice of conscripting Vietnamese to fight for France against Germany. Ho also assailed the French for selling distilled alcohol to his countrymen, who traditionally had drunk only small cups of rice wine. Ho argued that the resulting widespread drunkenness made liquor almost worse than opium since only 80,000 people in Vietnam used that drug, and most of them were Chinese.

Living among the French, Ho cast off any lingering sense that France might be ruling Indochina because of an innate superiority. "Whether soup salesmen or school caretakers," he wrote scornfully about the sort of Frenchmen who ended up in Vietnam, "once they get out to our colonies, our civilizers live like princes." Ho listed the battalion of Vietnamese servants a Frenchman could expect to command. "And madame enjoys: one dressmaker, one washer woman, one seamstress, one basket maker. The child has a special attendant who never leaves him."

Ho's indictment ran to 30,000 words. He railed against the fact that the rape of Vietnamese women went unpunished. He attacked French censorship of Vietnamese newspapers and branded the Catholic Church an accomplice in France's tyranny. Although his hundred-page polemic was meant to awaken his countrymen, Ho called for no specific action and the names of Marx and Lenin did not appear. Colonialism, not capitalism, was Ho's enemy.

But afterward, sitting alone in his room, Ho read for the first time Lenin's "Thesis on the National and Colonial Questions." He found the language dense and had to read passages several times, but he grasped its message—that revolution could not be separated from the fight against colonialism. He shouted out, as though addressing hordes of countrymen: "Dear martyrs, compatriots! This is what we need! This is the path to our liberation!"

IN 1919, HO HAD GONE with a few companions to Versailles to submit a plan for Indochina that would supplement Woodrow Wilson's Fourteen Points. Ho's eight demands included adding Vietnamese delegates to the French Parliament and establishing freedom of the press in Vietnam and the right to free association. Although Ho had rented a morning coat for a presidential audience, his unimposing figure was lost among the other colonial representatives from Africa and the Middle East, all clamoring to meet with Wilson. Not only was Ho denied an audience but, more discouraging, his agenda was dismissed by every political faction except the Socialists. Simply by making his demands, however, Nguyen the Patriot was becoming a hero to Vietnamese at home and throughout Europe. As the Soviet Communists consolidated their control of Russia, Ho concluded that they promised more for his country than the Socialists could offer and formally joined the French Communist party.

As he turned thirty, Ho was thin and pale with skin that one French writer described as the color of tea. He was taller than most of his countrymen, and his forehead rose high above his large and glowing eyes. Meeting him, however, men most often remarked on his gentleness. An early photograph, taken by French police suspicious of his political activity, conveyed a sense of wistfulness. The hat perched on Ho's head suggested less a dangerous revolutionary than Chaplin's little tramp.

Between the world wars, Ho wrote articles, edited a journal and represented Indochina at party congresses. In 1923, he entered Russia on a passport issued by the Chinese embassy in Paris. He claimed to be a Chinese citizen heading home by way of Moscow. Once in the Soviet Union, he was introduced to leading Bolsheviks—Leon Trotsky, Nikolai Bukharin and Joseph Stalin, whom Ho felt had a special sympathy for colonial causes. The next January, Ho was devastated when Lenin died before Ho could arrange a meeting, and he eulogized the Russian leader in an article for *Pravda*. "What are we going to do?" Ho asked. "That is the question the oppressed masses in the colonies are anxiously asking themselves. . . ."

Ho's answer was to embrace Lenin's warning that a revolution must never begin until all conditions favored its success. Ho's temperament preferred action to delay, but he understood the virtue of waiting. In Paris, he had once used the alias Nguyen O Phap—Nguyen Who Hates the French. Over the years, that hatred had been refined into an intellectual passion. He still denounced France's crimes against his people, but his spirit was free of resentment. Life in the Soviet Union had bestowed on him the gift of patience.

WHILE OTHER COMMUNIST leaders in Moscow were retreating into suspicious isolation, Ho still slept alongside his comrades on a mat on the floor, and his transparent decency won him a circle of Russian admirers. With age, Ho's manner grew only warmer, more avuncular, although some colleagues understood that his studied simplicity masked a sophisticated political mind.

The Soviets were monitoring developments in China, where a Western-educated doctor, Sun Yat-sen, had led a successful revolt against the Manchu dynasty. When Sun died in 1925, a young aide, Chiang Kai-shek, took up command of his forces and allied his troops with China's Communists. The Russians had backed Sun's Kuomintang party and had dispatched Mikhail Borodin, a high-ranking agent, to assist Chiang. Ho went along as Borodin's interpreter. Since Ho spoke Cantonese, the Russians hoped he could organize the many Vietnamese in China's southern provinces.

In Canton, Ho met a cosmopolitan young Chinese, Zhou Enlai, whose skill in languages matched his own. He also succeeded in recruiting several of his countrymen, most notably Pham Van Dong, the intense son of a mandarin from Hue. As Ho traveled to Shanghai, Bangkok and Hong Kong, he adopted new aliases, all the while spreading the gospel of revolution. He couched his message in words both cautious and concrete since, he said, "Peasants believe in facts, not theories."

In 1930, Ho met in Hong Kong with leaders of the many feuding nationalist factions. Afterward, legend had them convening in the Kowloon stadium during a soccer match so they could caucus undetected among the cheering crowd. Since Ho had warned by letter that he would have no confidence in any people except true Communists, the delegates agreed to become the Vietnamese Communist Party.

Despite his precautions, the French authorities tracked Ho to Hong Kong and persuaded the British police to arrest him. Ho's revolutionary energy had left him looking incandescent but alarmingly thin, and his jailers diagnosed him as tubercular. A sympathetic British lawyer arranged to send him to a sanitarium in England, but immigration authorities intercepted him in Singapore and took him back to a prison hospital. There friends engineered his escape and an obliging hospital employee reported that Ho was dead. The ruse tricked the French at Hanoi's Sûreté Bureau into closing their file on Nguyen Ai Quoc with the final notation: "Died in the Hong Kong gaol, 1933."

AS JACK KENNEDY pondered suggestions for his cabinet, one unfamiliar name kept surfacing—Robert Strange McNamara, a forty-seven-year-old systems analyst who had assumed the presidency of the Ford Motor Company the day after Kennedy's election. McNamara's promotion at Ford was noteworthy because he had become the company's first president who was not a member of the Ford family. Although Kennedy had never met the man, he was told that McNamara's was a mind of honed precision.

One persuasive sponsor was Robert Lovett, a Republican who had been Kennedy's first choice for secretary of the treasury. Over tea in Georgetown, Dean Acheson, Truman's acerbic secretary of state, warned Kennedy that Lovett, at sixty-five, had no interest in returning to government. But since Lovett's generation considered a direct request from a President almost a military command, Acheson predicted that Lovett would come armed with a stack of doctors' reports to prove that he was too sickly to serve.

When he and Kennedy met, Lovett did in fact produce medical affidavits that he was hemorrhaging severely and might soon face major surgery. Kennedy had to respect that excuse; neither he nor Lovett's doctors could know that their patient would live for another twenty-six years.

As consolation, Lovett put forward other cabinet candidates, with McNamara high on his list. The idea intrigued Kennedy. Like Lovett, McNamara would reassure the business and financial communities that had opposed his election. Kennedy's father often cursed the nation's business leaders but never underestimated their importance to the success of a presidency.

Five weeks after the election, Robert Kennedy, one of the president-elect's younger brothers, called McNamara to arrange a visit from a Kennedy representative. In 1946, timid and uncertain, Bobby Kennedy had entered Massachusetts politics to work on his brother's first campaign for the House of Representatives. Hearty Joe Kennedy, Jr., had not survived the war, and Bobby, almost a head shorter than either Jack or their youngest brother, Teddy, had seemed a born acolyte, a family member so accustomed to the shadows that any attention made him squirm. But during that first campaign, Bobby had taken three precincts as his sole responsibility and, away from the glare of publicity, working harder and longer than anyone else, had delivered them for Jack.

By 1952, Bobby had become the obvious choice to head Jack's uphill campaign for the U.S. Senate against the Republican incumbent, Henry Cabot Lodge. The victory that followed seemed to transform him. Fighting for his brother, Bobby could demand commitments and concessions that, asking for himself, would have left him flushed and stammering. By the time of the 1960 presidential campaign, the smallest of the Kennedy men was being denounced as a ruthless political operative and reveling in it. Now, speaking to the president of Ford Motors, Bobby asked McNamara to make time that same afternoon for an appointment with a Kennedy brother-in-law named Sargent Shriver.

The financial sacrifice that Jack Kennedy would be asking of McNamara impressed the president-elect. Except for his naval service and a couple of newspaper assignments cobbled together by his father with acquaintances in publishing, Jack Kennedy had never worked and seldom carried money. Bills for his expenses were sent, like those of his sisters, directly to his father's business office. As a result, money had little reality for him. He had teased his Boston political pals about their high new White House salaries until his father reminded him that $5,000 a year wasn't so grand, since Jack himself was spending between $400,000 and $500,000 on everything from his valet to his wife's designer gowns.

To the young Kennedys, a self-made man like McNamara commanded a certain respect, as their father did. But within the family, being a captain of industry or even a distinguished college professor could not compare with being a successful politician. Kennedy's maternal grandfather, John Fitzgerald, had been mayor of Boston, and Joseph Kennedy had considered challenging Franklin Roosevelt for the presidency in 1940. Jack Kennedy had inherited or acquired a zest for the struggle and glory of elective office. The same politicians his wife, Jackie, found dreary and self-serving intrigued him. He wanted to know everything about them — their families, their mistresses, their fiddling with campaign contributions.

SHRIVER ARRIVED in Detroit about three hours after Bobby's call. During the campaign, the Kennedys had often sounded out a man about a possible appointment, arousing pleasant expectations that could be deflated later. Several midwestern governors still found it hard to believe that the vice presidential nomination had gone to Senator Lyndon Baines Johnson of Texas when Bobby Kennedy had intimated that support for his brother all but guaranteed them a place on the ticket.

In putting together the cabinet, the brothers were being equally guarded. Jack Kennedy had broached the subject of secretary of state to a liberal like Chester Bowles by asking whom Bowles would appoint as his deputy. It was heady speculation, even for a man like Bowles, who had been a congressman from Connecticut. He came up immediately with the name of Dean Rusk, a former assistant secretary of state under Truman, who was currently heading the Rockefeller Foundation in New York. The amusing game had ended, however, with Bowles being thanked and sent away without an appointment.

Dealing with McNamara, Shriver dropped that coyness. He said that the president-elect was offering him the office of either secretary of the treasury or secretary of defense. Shriver added that he had been authorized to accept only a favorable reply. Otherwise, Mr. McNamara should plan to meet personally with the president-elect before he ruled out accepting a post. McNamara refused Treasury outright and seemed inclined to turn down Defense as well, but he flew to Washington the next day for an inconclusive introduction and agreed to return on Monday.

☐

McNAMARA KNEW he did not have the international expertise for Treasury, but he had developed methods of statistical control that should transfer effectively to Defense. After studying economics at the University of California at Berkeley, McNamara got his first and only glimpse of Asia by signing on with a friend as a hand aboard the passenger ship *President Hoover*. His father, a severe man with an eighth-grade education, had permitted the trip because a San Francisco dock strike had been settled and the crew would not have to cross a picket line. McNamara's youthful mother, Claranell Strange, doted on her firstborn son and honored her side of the family with his middle name.

As McNamara's ship reached Shanghai, Japanese planes bombed the city and, through a pilot's error, attacked their civilian ship. Several people were wounded and the lifeboats destroyed. Throughout the action, McNamara snapped photographs, and when he arrived the next fall at the Harvard Business School, he used the fragment of a Japanese bomb casing as a paperweight.

Studying for a master's degree, McNamara first encountered the theory of statistical control, which had been developed thirty years earlier at the E. I. duPont de Nemours Powder Company. The system allowed accountants to measure the earnings of each product against its specific cost in personnel and raw material. Manufacturing companies could compare the rate of return among their divisions and assess which managers were generating the largest profits. Above all, the new approach put an end to guesswork, be it inspired or impractical. Statistical control was eminently rational, as was Bob McNamara. His professors recognized that he had a remarkable gift for using statistics to solve practical problems.

During World War II, McNamara joined Charles "Tex" Thornton in teaching the Army Air Corps how to track its men and resources. At war's end, McNamara intended to return to the Harvard Business School as a faculty member. But in 1945, both he and his wife, Margy, contracted polio. McNamara's was a mild case, Margy's so severe that doctors said she would never walk again. She defied them and recovered, but in the first bleak days when McNamara expected to be caring for an invalid wife and raising their children, he gave up his dream of teaching and joined an ingenious collective that Tex Thornton had put together. Thornton was offering himself, McNamara and eight of their army colleagues as a management team. His target was any company farsighted enough to grasp that in postwar America the hunches of an Edison or Henry Ford no longer guaranteed success. Young Henry Ford II bought his argument that business decisions should be buttressed by demonstrable fact, and he signed up Thornton's Whiz Kids.

Thornton soon left for Hughes Aircraft and later founded Litton Industries, and McNamara became the team's star exponent of statistical control. His fourteen years at Ford proved highly successful, although he found neither the company nor its president especially congenial. For his part, Henry Ford regarded McNamara as a prized possession, a dependable performer crammed with data that Ford himself could not be bothered to remember. Ford had been generous in rewarding McNamara's efficiency, nicely set off as it was by his touches of deference. On becoming company president, McNamara's salary had risen to $410,000 a year. The job of Secretary of Defense paid $25,000.

Despite that disparity, the prospect of being sprung from Detroit's gilded confines appealed to McNamara. Polling Margy and their children, he found them willing to abide by his decision. After the years of adroit obeisance to Henry Ford, however, McNamara intended to insist on one ironclad condition before accepting the offer. He wrote it out and left a place for Kennedy's signature: McNamara must be guaranteed the freedom to appoint his own undersecretaries without political interference.

And yet, leaving Ford was a momentous decision. McNamara had been scheduled to meet Kennedy in Washington the following Monday. To buy time, he called Palm Beach to say that he had mailed off a letter with his terms. McNamara also explained that he could not reach the capital on Monday because a snowstorm in Michigan made flying impossible. Both were fibs. McNamara had not sent the letter, and air traffic had not been disrupted.

Kennedy was unperturbed by the delay. Fine, he said. Shall we make it Tuesday?

IN HIS ROLE as an automobile executive, McNamara had slicked back his hair until, with his blunt features, he looked rather like a snub-nosed bullet, and his clear-rimmed glasses could seem more a shield against the world than an aid to understanding it. In his private life at Ford, McNamara had set himself apart from the other executives with a relatively ascetic style of living that some colleagues took as a calculated reproach. He might strive mightily for power within the company, but McNamara still considered himself an idealist. That explained why he had been stirred by Jack Kennedy's *Profiles in Courage,* a nonfiction history of several uncompromising moments in the U.S. Senate. Kennedy had produced the book in Palm Beach in the mid-1950s during his long convalescence from back surgery. McNamara, a master of the art of gruff ingratiation, flew off for his second interview with Kennedy ready to pronounce *Profiles in Courage* the best book he had read in the last ten years.

Like most ambitious automobile men in Detroit, McNamara was a registered Republican. But studying at Harvard in 1940, he had voted in a straw poll for Franklin Roosevelt over Wendell Willkie—and then fretted that his conservative professors might trace the maverick vote to him. Twenty years later, he had voted for Kennedy in 1960, had even sent in a contribution, although nothing large enough to jeopardize his position at Ford or have come to the Kennedys' attention.

When McNamara arrived, Bobby was waiting with his brother in Jack's living room to size up his potential. If McNamara faltered, the Kennedys had considered asking Thomas Gates, Eisenhower's defense secretary, to stay on, with Bobby as his deputy. But McNamara had come to Georgetown wanting to be courted, not to be taken for granted. Opening the conversation with the skeptical belligerence he had perfected at board meetings, McNamara revived the rumor that *Profiles in Courage*, his favorite book, had been the work of a ghostwriter.

Despite fourteen years in public life, Jack Kennedy's poise could occasionally be shaken. When *Profiles* first appeared, questions about its authorship had infuriated him enough that he threatened to sue anyone who raised them. But two decades earlier, when Kennedy published another book—based on his Harvard undergraduate thesis and called *Why England Slept*—it had been clear that a *New York Times* columnist named Arthur Krock had done more than cosmetic editing of the manuscript. Whatever the contributions to *Profiles* by Ted Sorensen, Kennedy's talented Senate aide from Nebraska, the book had won the Pulitzer Prize for history, and by the time McNamara belatedly raised the issue, Kennedy had perfected his bland assurances of authorship.

Less easily resolved was McNamara's demand that he pick his own deputies. Certainly, that seemed to remove Bobby from consideration as his deputy. McNamara claimed to understand that potential employees did not bargain with the president of the United States but then went on to spell out his demands. The financial sacrifice he would be making allowed him to deal from strength, and Kennedy, not yet his boss, was fair game for bullying. McNamara pulled from his pocket a copy of the letter he said he had mailed from Michigan.

Later that day, David Bell, an economist being interviewed for the job of budget director, was left alone briefly in Kennedy's living room and saw McNamara's one-page letter lying open on a coffee table. Bell couldn't resist reading it and was struck by McNamara's confident tone. Not only did he set down his conditions, he ended with a pledge that if he and Kennedy reached an agreement, he would remain in Washington as long as Kennedy wished him to stay. Under Eisenhower, the Defense post had become a revolving door for businessmen willing to sacrifice only a year or two to the job. McNamara was signing on for the duration.

As they spoke, Kennedy did not respond directly to McNamara's contract but seemed more amused than offended by it. He said candidly that his campaign obligations were very heavy. A number of people had helped to elect him, and he would do his best to repay those obligations. But, he added, for three departments—State, Defense and Treasury—he was going to get the best Americans he could find, regardless of party or politics. With that, the deal was struck. McNamara would be returning to Detroit to tell his domineering boss, with carefully masked glee, that after a mere five weeks as president of Ford, he had accepted a higher calling.

First, though, Kennedy wanted to show off McNamara to the reporters waiting outside his townhouse. From their questions, members of the press were awed by the financial sacrifice McNamara would be making to come to Washington. Pressed for a dollar figure, McNamara finally estimated that over the next few years he would be losing at least $3 million dollars in salary and stock options.

He was adamant, though, in refusing to answer a different question: "Could you tell us whether you voted for Mr. Kennedy?"

Possibly, McNamara didn't want to confirm his apostasy to hostile colleagues back home. Perhaps he thought that telling the truth would look as though he were toadying to the president-elect. Or he may simply have resented the reporters' license to badger him.

Whatever his reason, McNamara replied, "I think my vote is my own affair."

FILLING THE TREASURY SPOT went smoothly. Douglas Dillon had been Eisenhower's undersecretary of state for economic affairs, and if he was not so well-known as Lovett, he had supported Richard Nixon in the campaign and would deflect criticism from the financial community. For his three priority appointments, Kennedy had now chosen two registered Republicans. He had taken soundings for the State Department with candidates like Bowles, but privately he was saying that he didn't want a Secretary as independent as John Foster Dulles had been under Eisenhower. Owing no political debt to Adlai Stevenson, Kennedy could ignore the fervent telegrams from Democrats across the country urging that he bestow State upon that most eloquent of liberals. Instead, Kennedy offered Stevenson the ambassadorship to the United Nations. After an hour of hand-wringing in the parlor of Walter Lippmann, Washington's foremost columnist, Stevenson choked back his very great disappointment and accepted.

From serving together in the Senate, Kennedy already knew J. William Fulbright, an Arkansas Democrat who chaired the Foreign Relations Committee, and for a time Kennedy seemed prepared to overlook the segregationist votes that Fulbright regularly cast to mollify white voters at home. Finally, however, the president-elect decided not to jeopardize the winning coalition that Robert Kennedy had forged with Negroes and southern whites, an alliance as diverse as Franklin Roosevelt's but far more fragile. During the campaign, Bobby had developed genuine affection for such unreconstructed southerners as James Eastland, and neither of the Kennedy brothers felt any urgency about extending civil rights legislation. But Kennedy's staff had pushed him to express concern over the jailing of a young Negro minister named Martin Luther King, Jr., and in Illinois the vote of King's grateful supporters had been as significant as any manipulation of ballots by the Chicago Democratic machine. Weighing Fulbright's liabilities once again, Kennedy decided they were simply too great.

When Kennedy called on Lippmann for other suggestions, the columnist floated an unlikely name—McGeorge Bundy, dean of the faculty at Harvard. Kennedy was aware of the man's nimble mind, which skipped where others plodded, but Bundy was barely past forty. Being young himself, the president-elect wanted to surround himself with grayer hair and longer résumés. He brought Bundy into the White House instead as his national security adviser, a job he kept deliberately amorphous. Bundy's range and influence would depend on how effectively the State Department functioned under whoever became its secretary.

EARLY IN DECEMBER, Dean Rusk, the Rockefeller Foundation president, was meeting with his board of trustees in Williamsburg, Virginia, when he got an urgent invitation to have breakfast with John Kennedy the next morning in Washington. Rusk had published an article in *Foreign Affairs* titled "The President" that called for a strong U.S. chief executive, served by a secretary of state who was content with an advisory role. The piece could be read as a reproach to Rusk's friend, Foster Dulles, now safely dead. Chester Bowles saw in it a troubling emphasis on routine procedure over creative thinking. As it happened, Rusk was spending the night as the guest of Bowles and his wife, and Bowles realized that Kennedy's call meant that he himself would not be tapped as Secretary. He managed to act enthusiastic on behalf of his protégé, however, and made Rusk promise to call him and report on the breakfast.

At ten-thirty the next morning, Rusk rang up with unexpected news. "I'm not going to become secretary of state," he announced, "because Kennedy and I simply found it impossible to communicate. He didn't understand me, and I didn't understand him."

Apparently, the two men, courteous and accomplished listeners, had sat with some awkwardness, each awaiting an initiative from the other. When Kennedy did speak, he still sounded prepared to offer the job to Fulbright. Rusk endorsed that idea. The conversation limped to a halt.

Bowles thought that Rusk hardly sounded disappointed. He was building a new house outside New York City, and he had been counting on his $60,000 Rockefeller salary to finance it. Like Defense, State paid $25,000. Friends had to assure him that his experience as Secretary of State would make him even more employable the next time he left government.

Another consideration was harder to resolve. Rusk had once served in the State Department and knew its political risks. Even Secretaries as self-assured as George Marshall and Dean Acheson had been vilified as weak in dealing with the Communists. Rather than confront his doubts about his judgment or self-confidence, Rusk told himself that he was somehow too young for the job. But since, at fifty-one, he was eight years older than the president-elect, that argument would scarcely persuade Kennedy. He might have been reassured to learn that, whoever got the job, Kennedy intended to act as his own secretary of state. Whatever his official title, Rusk would be expected to serve as the number-two man—the role that Bowles had envisioned for him.

Despite the unpromising breakfast in Georgetown, Kennedy called the next day to offer Rusk the job. Rusk insisted on a second meeting. He flew to West Palm Beach with a list of his misgivings, to which he added the fact that he had supported Stevenson at the Los Angeles convention. At that confession, Kennedy just laughed. In the end, Rusk succumbed, still fretting that the position was "so complex and so demanding."

MCNAMARA SOON tested Kennedy over their agreement on appointments when the president-elect rang up to ask whether McNamara was considering Franklin Roosevelt, Jr., as secretary of the navy. It was the post that had once launched Roosevelt's father on the national scene, and it was the younger Roosevelt's one request as repayment for his campaigning in West Virginia.

"I have heard his name mentioned," McNamara said, "but he's a playboy and totally unqualified."

"Well, have you met him?"

When McNamara admitted that he had not, Kennedy seized the high ground: "Don't you think you should meet him before coming to a final judgment?"

Trapped, McNamara agreed. Kennedy may have thought that Roosevelt's charm would soften any heart, but for McNamara more was at stake than this one appointment. He summoned Roosevelt, then working in Washington as a Fiat dealer, conducted a perfunctory interview and reported to Kennedy that he stood by his first impression.

Kennedy tried a ploy of his own: "Franklin Roosevelt, Jr., played a major role in my victory."

"Well, he's still not qualified to be Secretary of the Navy."

Kennedy said nothing. A pause that long and significant might have led another man to reverse himself. McNamara waited out his new boss.

At last, Kennedy sighed and said, "I guess I'll have to take care of him some other way."

SIXTEEN YEARS before Kennedy's election, a Chinese Communist named Mao Zedong had once angled for an invitation to Franklin Roosevelt's White House. The Roosevelt administration had not responded to Mao then, and he did not expect Kennedy to be more hospitable now. At sixty-seven, Mao was three years younger than Ho Chi Minh, and Ho enjoyed greater seniority within the Communist Party. But in the years since Washington's rebuff, Mao had grown in stature as leader of the mainland Chinese. His only rival in the Communist world was Nikita Khrushchev, Stalin's successor in Moscow.

In his youth, Mao had seemed an unlikely candidate for world prominence. Tall but slack and ill-coordinated, he was an esthetic provincial with a limp handshake, a high-pitched voice and an appetite for hot peppers and young women. Born in December 1893 on a three-acre farm in Hunan province, China's rice bowl, he had been named poetically Zedong, or "Anoint the East." But Mao, the family name, was the prosaic word for "hair," and the dissonance in his name pointed up contradictions in the boy's upbringing. Mao's mother was gentle and loving, his father a miserly brute. "The first capitalist I struggled against," Mao recalled, "was my father."

Like Ho, Mao loved books and poetry from an early age and was equally impressed by the American Revolution, especially George Washington's hard years of struggle against the British. But Mao harbored a fantastical strain different from Ho's intense practicality. When the headmaster of his school tried to convince the sixteen-year-old that his favorite book of Chinese history was romantic fiction and not the literal truth, Mao petitioned the mayor to have the man sacked.

Mao had been only a year old when Sun Yat-sen wrote his first revolutionary petition against the Manchu dynasty. By 1911, however, when Sun launched open warfare in Hankow, Mao was ready to join his revolutionary army. But in his eagerness to raise himself above his father's class, he disdained his fellow recruits as uncouth and dirty peasants and balked at doing the normal army chores. In time, he came to appreciate the strength and simplicity of his illiterate comrades and blamed his snobbery on the bourgeois education he had once admired.

Internal struggles wracked the Chinese revolution, and Sun Yat-sen fled to exile in Japan. Mao left the army and, rudderless, dropped in and out of schools—a police academy, a business course, law school, instruction in soap making. With a friend, he hiked across Hunan province, roughly the size of France, eating one sparse meal a day and toughening his body for the combat he saw coming. By age twenty-five, Mao was living in Beijing, reading the newly translated *Communist Manifesto* and pondering where the Chinese peasant fit into Marx's theory of capitalists and workers. He became an organizer and set up a cell of Communist revolutionaries devoted to turning China into a classless society. Although scrutiny by the secret police forced Mao underground, he managed to marry a professor's daughter and father two children.

The Moscow Comintern was dismayed by China's competing Communist cells—including one organized in Paris by Zhou Enlai—and sent a Dutch agent to meld them into one national party. Recruitment was slow, however, especially within the working class. By 1922, only thirty of the three hundred Chinese Communist Party members worked with their hands; the rest were writers and teachers.

When Sun Yat-sen died, Mao disapproved of a decision by Stalin and Mikhail Borodin, his agent in China, to make Chiang Kai-shek the generalissimo of all revolutionary forces, but he agreed to support Chiang against China's competing warlords. When the inevitable rupture came, Mao retreated to the countryside. There he received word that his wife, Yang Kaihui, and his younger sister had been executed by Chiang's nationalist party, the Kuomintang, in Changsha in 1930.

As Mao's forces grew in rural areas, Marxists in the cities denounced his reliance on the peasantry. Mao argued that the peasants might be ignorant and dirt-poor but they made up 70 percent of China's population. When they sneezed, Mao said, the other 30 percent of the people would be blown away.

AFTER THE JAPANESE seized Manchuria in 1931, Chiang Kai-shek's popularity fell sharply. Uncommitted Chinese wanted him to wage war against the Japanese rather than against China's Communists. Mao held his own convention and became the first chairman of a new rival government—the Chinese Soviet Republic. Because delegates trained in Moscow still considered Mao's theories too romantic, too dependent on the peasantry's raw courage, they named Zhou Enlai as the Red Army's political commissar. But their flag was Mao's design—a hammer and sickle within a red star.

For several years, Mao's forces recruited strenuously, but Chiang was not idle. Adopting tactics from a new German military adviser, Chiang surrounded Mao's forces in the south of Jiangxi province with a million troops and began to tighten the noose. He seemed on the verge of wiping out the entire Red Army. In desperation, Mao sent out suicide squads as a distraction and led his troops on a nighttime escape along forest trails. On October 16, 1934, with no fixed destination, some 86,000 men and a few hundred women set out on the march. Because Mao allowed only children old enough to walk, he had to abandon two infant sons born to him by his second wife, He Zizhen.

With Chiang's Nationalists in pursuit, Mao's soldiers hiked across 6,000 miles of China's roughest terrain. They crossed twenty-four rivers and—by Mao's poetic estimate—a thousand mountains. Wasted by fever, his matted hair hanging to his shoulders, Mao collapsed twice from malaria and had to be carried in a sedan chair. But as his troops passed through farms and villages, Mao insisted that they teach the peasants the six Chinese characters that meant "Divide the land."

One year after they began, a scant 4,000 survivors reached a sanctuary in Shanxi province, five hundred miles southwest of Beijing. It was only after the trek had ended—and was being compared in rigor and daring to Hannibal crossing the Alps—that it was called the Long March. Hannibal had been on the attack against Rome, Mao was in retreat, and yet from his new base in the ancient city of Yanan, Mao laid out a strategy for aggressive peasant warfare. Traditional Communist thinking still called for seizing cities. Mao's approach was more flexible. "Enemy advances, we retreat," he wrote. "Enemy halts, we harass. Enemy tires, we attack. Enemy retreats, we pursue."

In speeches and in *Basic Tactics*, his manual for officers, Mao set out maxims easy for his men to remember: "Political power grows from the barrel of a gun." And, to contrast with the looting and rape of other occupying armies, his Communist soldiers would live among the people "as fish lived in the water." Mao's command post was a cave in Yanan, a hole carved into a hill, with little more than a bed, a desk and—his one indulgence—a wooden bathtub. From his cave, Mao entertained a succession of Western writers who came away impressed with his vision for a reformed China. In *Red Star over China*, Edgar Snow, a journalist from Missouri, turned Mao into a heroic figure, not only for leftists in Europe and America but—in translation—for Chinese who had barely known Mao's name.

Speaking at an art academy during that period, Mao met a vivid young actress whose name translated as Blue Apple. To the dismay of the Chinese Central Committee, he put aside He Zizhen, the heroine of the Long March who had given him five children, to live with his new mistress. To mark their union, Blue Apple changed her name to Jiang Qing—Pure Waters.

Ho Chi Minh, navigating among the rival factions of international Communism, had traveled surreptitiously to China, but he found that Chiang Kai-shek had betrayed his former allies and instructed his secret police to round up the Communists. Ho slipped into Moscow, where his reception was not what he expected, either. Stalin's Comintern accused him of two offenses: he was more Nationalist than Communist, and he could only have been freed in Hong Kong by becoming a British agent.

Even Ho's association with Borodin worked against him since Stalin had ordered the man killed for being too ideological. But that does not describe me, Ho protested; I use theory only to achieve practical ends. Stalin remained suspicious, and although Ho escaped punishment, he could get no work. When he pleaded for a job, Soviet functionaries suggested manual labor. At last, he was entrusted with an assignment to lecture on Vietnamese history at the Institute for the Study of National and Colonial Questions. To make his lessons easier to remember, Ho wrote them in verse.

Ho would never speak of his ordeal in the Soviet Union and a surveillance that had seemed like house arrest. International Communism remained the best hope for liberating his people, and Moscow was its center. He might never feel the same warmth toward the Russians, but that would not stop him from using them when he must.

In the late thirties, Ho returned to more active organizing, and in 1940, disguised as a Mr. Tran, he went to a Chinese provincial capital near the border of Burma and Vietnam. He hoped to renew contact with Pham Van Dong, who had been arrested by the French for political activities but set free when Léon Blum's coalition government came to power in Paris. Ho also expected to meet for the first time a history teacher from Hanoi named Vo Nguyen Giap.

By January 1961, with his team in place, Kennedy welcomed a suggestion from Dwight Eisenhower that the two men meet once again before the inaugural, this time with Kennedy's chief cabinet officers. Ike seemed to be enjoying his final

Eisenhower at his last presidential news conference *(AP/Wide World Photos)*

days in office and was preparing a farewell address to the nation for 8:30 P.M. on January 17. Norman Cousins, the editor of the *Saturday Review of Literature* and a prominent campaigner against nuclear weaponry, had suggested that Eisenhower's final speech be a sweeping challenge to his countrymen. The idea appealed strongly to Eisenhower since George Washington had been his childhood hero, as much for his valedictory as for his victories at Princeton and Trenton. Eisenhower assigned the speech to his best writers, and the result was a warning that perhaps only a five-star general could make.

Eisenhower told his radio audience that the nation's military establishment, swollen to huge proportions by the Second World War, had joined with a thriving industry of arms manufacturers to create a force that was new to the American experience. "The total influence — economic, political, even spiritual," Ike went on, "is felt in every city, every statehouse, every office of the federal government."

To spell out the danger, Eisenhower employed a phrase that would resound long after he retired to his farm at Gettysburg: "In the councils of government, we must guard against the acquisition of unwarranted influence, whether sought or unsought, by the military-industrial complex."

The next day, savoring the acclaim for his speech, Eisenhower held his last presidential news conference. The sessions were always filmed, then edited for later viewing on television. Even so, they had exposed Eisenhower to taunts from the White House press corps because of his tendency to answer questions with false starts and digressions that defied parsing. For eight years, Eisenhower had suffered the suggestion that his erratic grammar proved him to be something of a dolt. On this last day, he took his revenge.

Robert Spivack, a columnist, tried to probe Eisenhower's mood by asking whether reporters had been fair to him over the years.

Ike treated the press corps to the grin that spoke so eloquently and meant so little.

"Well, when you come down to it," Ike said, "I don't see what a reporter could do much to a President, do you?"

AT 9 A.M. ON THURSDAY, January 19, John Kennedy arrived again at the White House. The schedule called for him to spend forty-five minutes alone with Eisenhower reviewing emergency military procedures. Then they would join cabinet members and aides to discuss the country's urgent problems. Kennedy was pleased to be seeing Eisenhower a second time, since the American public would be reassured by further evidence that the transition was harmonious. He also wanted to pursue the question of Laos. How would Eisenhower handle the problem and how prepared had Ike been to intervene militarily?

Ike's aide, General Wilton Persons, escorted Kennedy to the President. At his desk, Eisenhower impressed Kennedy as fit, pink-cheeked and unharassed, even though Eisenhower complained that he felt busier now, on his way out, than he had on entering the job. Ike was keen to show Kennedy how quickly the Oval Office could be evacuated. He called for his naval aide, picked up a telephone and said, "Opal Drill Three." The aide left, boarded a helicopter, circled overhead and returned just three minutes later. With that demonstration ended, Eisenhower urged Kennedy to name a top staff man to function the way Persons had done. "Only the tough problems get to you," Eisenhower said. Kennedy listened courteously but had already decided to immerse himself far earlier in the decision-making than Ike had done.

Eisenhower led Kennedy to the Cabinet Room where six White House officials, past and future, awaited them. Kennedy saw that Christian Herter, who had become secretary of state when Foster Dulles died, would do most of the talking. Taking up a crisis of leadership in Laos, Herter said that a negotiated settlement would bring Communists into the Lao government and they would end up controlling it.

A treaty signed in Geneva in 1954 had banned outside forces from Laos, but Herter claimed that an American military assistance group—called MAG—could be sent there without violating the agreement. Kennedy asked directly whether the United States should intervene if the unstable Lao government asked for protection. Yes, Herter said, and he provided one of the early metaphors for the strategic importance of Southeast Asia: Laos was the cork in the bottle.

Kennedy asked both Eisenhower and Thomas Gates, the outgoing secretary of defense, about the likely Communist response to U.S. action in Laos. Would they strike back with even greater force? Eisenhower speculated that the Chinese Communists did not want to provoke a major war but were playing poker with tough stakes. Gates cited a Pentagon survey that the United States might not be able to fight on two fronts around the world but could certainly handle one. With the right aircraft, the United States could cut the time it would take to move 12,000 troops to Laos to seventeen days, possibly even twelve. Deployment would be even quicker if the men came from Pacific bases and from Marine units based in Okinawa.

The conversation turned briefly to Cuba. Eisenhower said his administration was training guerrillas in Guatemala who opposed Fidel Castro. He urged that support for them be accelerated. Treasury Secretary Robert Anderson then spoke about stanching the flow of U.S. gold out of the country.

As the pragmatic discussions wound down, Eisenhower raised the only abstract question. When Herter remarked that morale was low among America's allies in the Royal Laotian Army, Ike broke in with a puzzled reflection: Why was it that the Communist soldiers in such countries always seem to have better morale than the soldiers representing democracy? Was there something about the Communist philosophy that gave their supporters a certain inspiration and dedication? The questions hung in the air as the meeting adjourned.

Immediately upon returning from the White House, Kennedy dictated his recollections of the session and asked his new cabinet officers to do the same. Impressed by Herter's urgency, Kennedy quoted him directly: "If Laos fell, then Thailand, the Philippines, and of course Chiang Kai Shek would go."

At that point, Kennedy had turned to Eisenhower for collaboration. Robert McNamara reported that Ike had disagreed with Herter about a coalition in Laos, suggesting that, even if it included Communists, such a government might be sustained indefinitely.

Clark Clifford had turned down an official appointment but had been present as a trusted aide, and his memorandum was the longest and most thorough. He recalled that Herter had explained that some U.S. allies considered the war in Laos a mere internecine battle among the Lao royal family and not the result of outside aggression. According to Herter, the British and French had both made it clear that they did not want to commit themselves to Laos. But Clifford also wrote that Eisenhower had been rigidly against including Communists in any future government, and he quoted Ike's glum conclusion that he would be willing "as a last desperate hope to intervene unilaterally."

None of the conflicting memoranda from the meeting referred to Laos's eastern neighbor. With his inauguration the next day, Kennedy would be inheriting America's problems around the globe, but apparently South Vietnam was not one of them.

☐

Vo Nguyen Giap, the man Ho expected to meet at the Chinese border in 1940, had been primed early to join Vietnam's struggle for independence. He had been born to a poor mandarin family in August 1911, in a village in Annam near the 17th parallel; the name Giap meant "armor." He was eight years old when his father was arrested for subversion and died in a French prison. Soon afterward, an older sister died the same way.

At fourteen, Giap read a pamphlet, *Colonialism on Trial*, by Nguyen Ai Quoc, the revolutionary leader living in Paris. That thrilling denunciation of colonial rule filled Giap with hatred for the French. A friend passed along a picture of Nguyen the Patriot wearing a fur hat, and the photograph was blurry enough that Giap imagined that his hero was hardly older than himself.

Giap studied at a Hue lycée run by a Catholic mandarin whose own son, Ngo Dinh Diem, had studied there ten years earlier. Although Giap's teachers found the boy pleasant and tractable in the classroom, his membership in a Vietnamese nationalist group led the French Sûreté to open a file on him. Arrested at eighteen for organizing a student demonstration, Giap was sentenced to three years in prison but released after a few months and allowed to transfer to a national academy in Hanoi to study philosophy and law. In 1937, Giap, at twenty-six, joined Ho's Indochinese Communist Party.

Political activities interfered with his law studies, and he failed to take the examination. By then, he was married to the daughter of a well-known Vietnamese writer. To support her and their infant girl, he began teaching history at a private school in Hanoi. One of his students, a well-born youth named Bui Diem, was transfixed by Giap's intensity. On the first day of class, Giap announced that he would not follow the course guide, which covered France from 1789 to the middle of the nineteenth century. "Look, there are a lot of books about this stuff," Giap said, as he paced in front of his students. "If you want to know about it, you can look it up. I'm only going to tell you about two things—the French Revolution and Napoleon."

Giap described Marie Antoinette's heedless indulgences with a scorn that made her fate seem justified, and Bui Diem delighted in his passionate accounts of the Paris Commune, the life of Robespierre, the death of Danton. Most engrossing of all were Giap's recreations of every one of Napoleon's campaigns. The class sat hypnotized as he described tactics, right down to skirmishes with dragoons and the Imperial Guard. To Bui Diem, Giap's lectures glowed with love and envy of Napoleon's career.

The sixteen-year-old was hardly a usual student himself. His father, Bui Ky, a leading poet, was working with his brother on a definitive history of Vietnam. Both father and uncle favored independence but lacked the temperament of revolutionaries. Bui Diem was the same. When Giap urged him to read Marx's *Das Kapital* in French and other Socialist tracts, they did not stir his soul.

Following the 1939 nonaggression pact between Stalin and Hitler, the Communist Party was banned in France and her colonies. Under a pseudonym, Giap wrote a two-volume guide to Communist policy for Vietnam's farmers. The French discovered the books and burned them. French agents in Hanoi identified Giap's wife and his sister-in-law as party members. Fleeing to Vinh with Giap's young daughter, the women were caught, put on trial and convicted of conspiracy. The sister-in-law was shot. Despite harsh pressure, Giap's wife did not betray the identity of another prisoner, Le Duan from central Vietnam, who had been a founding member of the Indochinese Communist Party. Sentenced to fifteen years in prison, Giap's wife died there in 1941; her child also did not survive.

It was after Giap escaped with Pham Van Dong to China that he finally met Nguyen the Patriot. Despite Ho's Western suit and gray felt hat, Giap instantly identified the slender older man as the renowned Paris revolutionary. At fifty, Ho was stooped and frail and called "Uncle" as a mark of respect. But his eyes shone with revolutionary fervor, and as they walked along a riverbank, Giap was captivated by conversation that was much livelier than he had anticipated from the hunching of Ho's shoulders.

Although Giap and Pham Van Dong had been ordered to study military tactics at a Chinese institute, their primitive bus broke down, and they stayed on with Ho at the border to evaluate the latest political developments. Hitler had crushed the French army, and Japanese soldiers were pouring into Indochina. For at least a decade, Japan had aspired to rule Asia, and as early as 1936, Japanese commanders had allied themselves with Germany against the Soviet Union. The next year, Japan invaded China's northern provinces. With the onset of World War II, the first Japanese troops landed in Indochina. Then Japan's attack on the U.S. naval base at Pearl Harbor on December 7, 1941, drew America into Asia's wars.

In that turmoil, Vietnamese nationalists waged uprisings in several areas of their country, including Ho's own province. He considered the rebellions premature, and yet there was the danger that if the French colonial rule collapsed, Japanese warlords would replace it. The time had come to return home. Taking the name Ho Chi Minh, he passed himself off as a Chinese journalist—Ho was a traditional Chinese name and Chi Minh could be translated as "Bringing Enlightenment." Slipping across the border by sampan, Ho set foot on Vietnamese soil for the first time in thirty years.

AT A BORDER AREA called Pac Bo, Ho set up headquarters in a limestone cave hung with stalactites. From there, in May 1941, he convened the Eighth Plenum of the Central Committee of the Indochinese Communist Party. Delegates sat on blocks of wood while Ho outlined a broad national front that would embrace not only workers but also farmers and even patriotic landowners. He called his movement Viet Nam Doc Lap Dong Minh Hoi, the League for Vietnamese

Independence. To make the name easier to remember, he shortened it to Viet-minh.

Using a flat rock as his desk, surrounded at all times by bodyguards, Ho wrote a series of pamphlets and manifestos about guerrilla warfare. First, the Vietminh would purge the country of the Japanese fascists and French imperial-ists. Then they would form the Democratic Republic of Vietnam. Ho already had its flag—one gold star on a red field.

Each day, Ho woke early on his bed of leaves and branches to rouse the oth-ers. His cave was cold, the mountain stream colder still, but Ho bathed there every morning. When he was not writing, he weeded the garden, gathered fire-wood, taught children to read and cooked meals of maize, wild bananas, and fish fresh from the river. At bedtime, Ho spun tales of Vietnam's past wars and revo-lutions. He predicted that in four or five years this war would enter a decisive phase and then Vietnam could once again be free. Around the campfire, his men listened night after night as Ho spoke their dream aloud.

The Vietminh training course began to draw 50 or 60 recruits each month. As the camp expanded, the men cleared more ground for dormitories, dining room, lecture hall and a field that could hold hundreds of trainees. To reach be-yond Pac Bo, Ho lithographed a small newspaper, *Independent Vietnam*, that re-ported news of the movement and denounced crimes by the French and Japanese. Ho charged cash for his newspaper since, he said, "he who pays for it will love it."

The paper was an immediate success, partly because Ho set a strict limit of fifty to a hundred words per article. Once Giap sent lengthy dispatches from an outlying area, and Ho chided him when he returned: "I didn't read them, and neither did the other comrades," Ho said, smiling. "Usually, they were long and unintelligible."

STIRRED BY RUMORS of a movement for Vietnam's independence, a twelve-year-old provincial boy ran away from home with a bundle of clothes and food, deter-mined to join Ho's crusade. His distraught mother appealed to the local Japanese commander, who alerted his men. When they found the child, Nguyen Cao Ky, hiding in a ditch, the Japanese officer scolded him and sent him home. "You are a very naughty boy," the officer said. "You made your mother cry."

HO LEFT PAC BO to cross back into China, expecting that Chiang Kai-shek would now welcome the Vietminh as allies against the Japanese. He walked the thirty miles to the Chinese frontier, where he was promptly arrested as a spy. For the next fourteen months, Ho was marched in chains from one to another of Chiang's prison camps. Any free time he spent composing poems—scraps of his impressions, lyrical tributes to the landscape. To reassure his jailers, he wrote in the classical Chinese, which they could read, rather than in Vietnamese.

After Wendell Willkie lost the 1940 U.S. presidential election to Franklin Roosevelt, he passed through China as Roosevelt's envoy to allied wartime leaders. Hearing that Willkie was being feted by the Chinese at a state dinner, Ho wrote a rueful poem from his cell:

Like you, I'm a visiting delegate.
Why then is the difference in treatment so great?

At other times, Ho consoled himself that his misery must have a purpose:

Under the pestle how terribly the rice suffers!
But it comes out of the pounding as white as cotton.
The same thing to a man in this world occurs:
Hard trials turn him into a polished diamond.

In Ho's absence, Giap studied guerrilla warfare at a Chinese military school in Yanan. Employing the tactics he learned fighting the Japanese, Giap continued to recruit and train a Vietminh army until it had grown to 10,000 soldiers. Then, at the Vietminh base camp, Giap got word that this time a report of Ho's death was no hoax. He had truly died in China. Like his comrades, Giap was all but paralyzed by grief, but he rallied to stage a memorial service.

A few months later, a scout smuggled a scrap of paper across the border, a five-line poem that ended, "I am thinking of my friends." His men recognized Ho's writing, and their joy swept through Pac Bo.

Ho never explained how he came to be released by the Chinese. He may have bribed his way out. But by mid-1944, he was back in Vietnam, where France's wartime government was sinking further into disarray. Even so, Ho warned Giap that a massive insurrection would be premature. "Stealth, continual stealth," Ho advised the Vietminh. "Never attack except by surprise. Retire before the enemy has a chance to strike back. . . ."

DURING THE MONTHS of Mao's Long March, Stalin had offered him no assistance. For that matter, Mao had not endured years of hardship in order to surrender his movement to foreigners, especially not to the Russians on his northern border. With the beginning of the Second World War, however, Mao looked for Western support in the common campaign against the Japanese. Although the United States seemed pledged to Chiang, Mao took heart from watching a sympathetic portrayal of America's destitute farmers in the film version of *The Grapes of Wrath*.

And the war did bring limited American attention to both Mao and Ho. The Vietminh rescued a Lieutenant Shaw, an American pilot shot down over the jungle, and sheltered him from the Japanese and their French collaborators. Ho traded on that good deed to ask for an audience with General Claire Chennault, the head of the U.S. Army Air Force in Asia. Chennault was famous for leading the Flying Tigers, volunteer American pilots who had turned back Japan's air attacks against China. Ho asked an American contact, Charles Fenn, to set up a meeting. Fenn worked for the Office of Strategic Services, which had been founded in 1942 to collect intelligence and support Allied resistance groups. The head of the OSS, William J. Donovan, had won the nickname "Wild Bill" during World War I for a succession of nervy schemes, including a proposal that the Allies end the war by kidnapping Germany's Kaiser Wilhelm.

Fenn said he would arrange a meeting with Chennault if Ho promised not to ask for anything. Ho agreed and, to make himself presentable, sewed a missing button on his sand-colored jacket. Chennault kept Ho waiting a mere five minutes before receiving him in a dress uniform laden with medals and seated behind a desk the size of a double bed. After listening to Chennault's exploits with the Flying Tigers, Ho reneged enough on his promise to beg one small favor: might he have a photograph of the general? Chennault had learned to anticipate that request. He opened a file with a choice of poses. "Take your pick," he said.

From then on, the photograph served Ho better than any visa. Brandishing it at Chinese officials and U.S. intelligence agents, Ho could prove that he enjoyed a close relationship with America. After all, the photo was signed, "Yours Sincerely, Claire L. Chennault."

GIVEN HIS LIFELONG ADMIRATION for Americans, Ho had reason to expect sympathetic support from Chennault's countrymen. And, in fact, when Franklin Roosevelt spoke with his son early in the war about Indochina, it was with an outrage that he usually masked with his thrusting smile. Unless the French pledged eventual independence for her colonies, Roosevelt said, the United States would not be justified in returning them "at all, ever." He added, "Don't think for a moment, Elliot, that Americans would be dying in the Pacific tonight if it hadn't been for the short-sighted greed of the French and the British and the Dutch."

Roosevelt expected that when China emerged from the war it would join a postwar United Nations organization as one of the world's four major powers — along with the United States, Britain and the Soviet Union. But so far, China's military performance had been disappointing, and the latest U.S. strategy of bombing Japan into submission was reducing the importance of China's contribution still further. When Winston Churchill met with Roosevelt for private talks on how to carve up the world when the war ended, he promised support for Roosevelt's China policy only if Britain was allowed to retain India.

Roosevelt sent out Major General Patrick Hurley, his swaggering ambassador to China, to meet with Mao and Zhou Enlai in Yanan and attempt to weld them into a united front with Chiang Kai-shek. Mao found Hurley something of a clown but agreed to integrate his Red Army on equal terms with Chiang's forces. When Chiang balked, however, Hurley returned to Washington and threw his backing to the generalissimo.

From Europe, the Free French were sending urgent requests that they be allowed to join the war in Asia. Roosevelt hoped to see Indochina become a postwar trusteeship and kept stalling. His warnings to Charles de Gaulle, the Free French leader, were couched in racial terms: the white man, Roosevelt said, must grant the yellow races their independence.

De Gaulle was not listening. In December 1943, he had gravely disappointed Ho and the Vietminh by asserting that France expected to reestablish her Indochinese colonies after the war. Meantime, if an Allied attack were to be launched in Southeast Asia, de Gaulle was determined that French troops fight and die there. "French blood shed on the soil of Indochina," he noted, "would constitute an impressive claim."

Roosevelt's rebuttal was terse. "France has milked it for one hundred years," he told his secretary of state. "The people of Indochina are entitled to something better than that."

Despite the president's personal feelings, the U.S. government was issuing contradictory statements about Indochina's future, even pledging that France's sovereignty would be restored to any territory or colony "over which flew the French flag in 1939." And Roosevelt himself seemed to prefer setting aside the troublesome issue until after the war had been won.

To stand beside him at his fourth inaugural in January 1945, the president called another of his sons home from active duty. James Roosevelt arrived to find his father haggard and drawn. The only subject that could rouse him from his crushing fatigue was a meeting with Churchill and Stalin scheduled for two weeks later at Yalta, a spa on the Black Sea. James Roosevelt returned to duty convinced that his sixty-three-year-old father would soon be dead.

The Roosevelt advisers who prepared his briefing papers for Yalta could not agree on Indochina. The secretaries of war and the navy argued that France must be treated once again as a great power and not penalized for her current weakness. From the State Department's Asian desk came a memorandum more attuned to Roosevelt's wishes. It urged that an attempt be made to persuade the colonial powers to behave as the United States had done in setting a firm date for liberating the Philippines. But internal politics within State prevented that paper from reaching Yalta.

At the conference, Roosevelt raised the question of Indochina, denounced French colonials for not improving life for the Indochinese, and proposed trusteeships for both Indochina and Korea. He got little support from Stalin, who contented himself with remarking that Indochina was a very important area.

Two days later, with Churchill present, Roosevelt tried again. Churchill said flatly that he would never "consent to forty or fifty nations thrusting interfering fingers into the life's existence of the British Empire." Afterward, speaking off-the-record to reporters, Roosevelt said Chiang Kai-shek and Stalin might agree to an Indochina trusteeship but "dear old Winston will never learn."

Like de Gaulle, Churchill did not have to bend. Within two months, the American president was dead. His successor, Harry Truman, pledged to follow Roosevelt's policies but accepted instead an interpretation of the Yalta agreements that permitted the French to control Indochina's fate. The new president's advisers saw America's priorities as the rebuilding of Europe and the curbing of Soviet influence. If stability in France required the return of her colonies, that price was not too high.

As THE SECOND WORLD WAR wound down, a twenty-year-old Vietnamese dandy named Bui Tuong Minh traveled south from Hanoi in the spring of 1945 at the invitation of his emperor. Bui had joined the Dai Viets upon their founding six years earlier. They were a political party that supported the emperor, called for independence from France and committed members to fight Communism. The Dai Viet founder—unlike Ho—had aligned himself with the Japanese occupation forces and against the United States and her allies.

At college, Bui had studied mathematics. But his passion was for American movies, especially Frank Capra's *Mr. Smith Goes to Washington*. His parents divorced when he was twelve, and he went to live with his mother, the dean of a Vietnamese high school for girls. Bui's father, a prominent Hanoi lawyer, was friendly with the man who became minister of youth under the Japanese. He was putting together an ambitious scheme to train postwar administrators: Vietnam's emperor would ask forty outstanding young men to join him at an academy in Hue, where they would be groomed for leadership. Vietnam would then be divided into forty provinces, and each cadet—trained, energetic and loyal to the emperor—would be sent to govern them.

That this cadre might be very young did not trouble their emperor since he had been only twelve when his father died and he assumed the throne as the latest heir to the Nguyen dynasty of 1802. The French allowed Vietnam's emperors to occupy their ceremonial palaces so long as they answered to Paris, and the boy had been educated there. Now, at thirty-two, Prince Nguyen Vinh Thuy was back to rule for himself under the name he had chosen—Bao Dai, Protector of Grandeur.

When Bui got to Hue, he sized up the emperor as a typical *tay con*, the dismissive Vietnamese phrase for a Frenchified countryman—literally, "a little European guy." Bui wondered whether Bao Dai even spoke Vietnamese. Still, he knew that the emperor had consistently pressed the French for greater independence for Vietnam, and the fact that France had refused him was hardly Bao Dai's fault. Bui was impressed, too, by the brilliance of his fellow cadets, although he and one classmate were the only Dai Viet members among them. The rest were Vietminh.

□

DURING THOSE SAME LAST DAYS of World War II, Archimedes Patti, an American agent from the Office of Strategic Services, heard about Vo Nguyen Giap from a U.S. Army major named Thomas. The OSS had not given the Vietminh much in the way of weapons until Japan took over Vietnam in March 1945. At that time, Major Thomas and a small contingent of Americans began to train two hundred elite Vietminh troops in using the machine guns, bazookas and mortars that were being dropped to Giap by air. Thomas had also met Giap's commander and praised the man's amiability, although in his reports he identified Ho Chi Minh variously as "Hoe" and "Hoo."

Patti watched the Americans working with Vietnamese units until the day that the Vietminh marched off to confront the Japanese. As they left, Patti had a premonition. Some day, he told himself, our American training and weapons may be used against the French.

ALTHOUGH HO CHI MINH could not compete in influence with de Gaulle, he could exploit his fresh opportunity at home. Soon after the Yalta conference, the Japanese had tightened their grip on Vietnam, but elsewhere in the Pacific their forces were collapsing. Ho was ready to gamble that if his Vietminh could wrest Hanoi from the Japanese, that victory would entitle him to a seat at future peace talks.

Chiang Kai-shek was tepidly endorsing the idea of Asian trusteeships, but he was distracted by his own battles with Mao's Red Army for control of China and seemed willing to let Indochina revert to the French. In mid-July 1945, President Truman met for the first time with the other Allied leaders at Potsdam, southwest of Berlin. Without telling the French, the Allies had already divided Vietnam into two sectors to prepare for whatever fighting with the Japanese might lie ahead. China would be responsible for Vietnam's north, Britain for the south.

Thirteen days after the Potsdam conference ended — and a week after America's atomic bombs devastated Hiroshima and Nagasaki — the Japanese surrendered. The Vietminh responded quickly with a manifesto that reflected Ho's patience. The French would be welcomed back to Indochina only as trading partners, it said, but a French governor could serve as president of Vietnam until the country was granted full independence "within no less than five years and no more than 10 years."

In a separate document, Ho and his colleagues called on the United States "as a champion of democracy" to keep the French colonists out of Indochina and to rein in the Chinese troops in the north. The statement also endorsed a ban on opium and appeared to expect U.S. economic aid.

With Ho's revolution poised to triumph, he knew he owed his victory to the nationalists in his ranks. The Vietminh had grown so quickly that its control by the Communists had been critically weakened. Accepting that reality, Ho decreed that his government would not be limited to Communists or even to Viet-minh cadres. Instead, he would reach out to a broad coalition of patriots. As Giap's troops marched toward the gates of Hanoi, they were calling themselves "the Viet-American Army." Along the Red River, Japanese sentinels did not fire on them as they swarmed over the largest bridge and prepared to take the city.

But inside Hanoi, young Vietminh were not waiting for Giap's army to arrive. As the defeated Japanese met in a final conclave on August 17, teenagers outside their meeting hall pulled down the government flag and ran up the revolutionary colors. Seventeen-year-old Nguyen Khac Huynh had dropped out of school in Hue earlier in the year to join the resistance in Hanoi. His heart leapt as he saw the banner of independence flying for the first time above the capital.

Two days later, Giap's troops made their victory official, and in a rush of patriotic fervor Huynh raced through the city, not eating, not sleeping, determined to remember every minute of the glorious day.

FOR BUI TUONG MINH, the emperor's academy during the final weeks of the Japanese occupation had been a waste of time, nothing more than a lot of horse-back riding and superficial courses in first aid. With the Japanese surrendering, and the French intending to come back, the academy was abruptly shut down. It was then that Bao Dai accepted an unlikely offer.

Through an emissary, Ho sent a message to the emperor: come to Hanoi and be the supreme adviser to my government. To the shock of his friends, Bao Dai accepted. He had no choice, he explained. He had studied French history and knew the fate of Louis XVI. Ho Chi Minh must either recruit me, the emperor said, or kill me.

BY SEPTEMBER 2, 1945, Ho's August Revolution was complete. In huge rallies, the people hailed Vietnam's independence with a rejoicing that was peaceful everywhere but in Saigon. There, the Vietminh did not have the same hold over the population that Ho exercised in Hanoi, and shooting broke out during a demonstration. The ensuing riot left a score of Vietnamese and Frenchmen dead. Ten days later, the first British and French troops arrived to enforce France's claim to the chaotic South.

In the North, however, Ho began an eloquent victory speech by invoking America's revolution of 1776. "All men are created equal," Ho said, quoting from the Declaration of Independence. "They are endowed by their creator with certain unalienable rights, among these are life, liberty and the pursuit of happiness." At that moment, Ho's supporters were claiming that his victory had been won with little bloodshed, although soon afterward numbers of his anti-Communist rivals were rounded up and executed.

As Ho set about building his nation, he counted on friendships he had forged within the OSS. He wrote to one OSS agent: "The war is finished. It is good for everybody. I feel only sorry that all our American friends have to leave us so soon."

DEAN RUSK had never met Ho Chi Minh, but he had been one of the Americans to aid Ho against the Japanese. As a deputy to General Joseph Stilwell in the China-Burma-India theater, Rusk authorized an air drop of U.S. arms and cigarettes to Ho's guerrillas. At the time, Rusk didn't care whether Ho was a nationalist or a Communist so long as he was trying to kill Japanese. And OSS agents like Patti were reporting enthusiastically about the Vietminh.

David Dean Rusk had grown up in Georgia, son of a man who had hoped to be a preacher but ended up delivering the mail. The boy hustled his way through Davidson College in North Carolina and during the early 1930s went to Oxford for three years as a Rhodes Scholar. Cecil Rhodes, the diamond merchant who endowed the scholarships, believed that the more the world was inhabited by Anglo-Saxons, the better for the human race. If Rusk never fully accepted that judgment, he did agree that the English seemed to have a special talent for leadership, a bias that later served him well among the Anglophiles in the State Department.

In his twenties, Rusk dropped his first name. As a result, before the Second World War, when he joined the administration at Mills, a women's college on the San Francisco Bay, he became Dean Dean Rusk. At Mills, Rusk broke the rules by courting a student who had concluded from his imposing forehead and high principles that Rusk was in his forties. Virginia Foisie discovered that he was only a very serious twenty-five, and the two were married three years later.

BESIDES HIS GLANCING CONTACT with Vietnam, Rusk played a role in shaping postwar Korea. For centuries, China and Russia each coveted the peninsula, but it was the Japanese who annexed it in 1910. During World War II, America and her allies had reached a vague agreement to set Korea free, possibly after several years of trusteeship. But when Japan abruptly surrendered, the Pentagon recommended that the United States accept the surrender on behalf of the southern part of Korea and let the Russians accept for the northern sector. Colonel Rusk, recently returned from his Asian posting, persuaded his military superiors that the 38th parallel would make a convenient division. As a result, Korea, like Vietnam, was divided into two nations. Kim Il Sung, a Communist trained in Moscow, was installed as head of a people's republic in the North. Syngman Rhee, educated in the United States, became president in the South.

WITH THE WAR'S END, Ho was quickly learning that he had few foreign friends. The Chinese troops, sent to supervise the Japanese withdrawal from North Vietnam, were ousting the Vietminh and plundering the countryside. To restore order in the south, Britain's commanding general was siding with the French —

and even with the Japanese survivors—against the Vietminh. Amid growing disorder, the commander shut down all Vietnamese newspapers and imposed martial law.

Nor, in his isolation, could Ho expect support from the international Communist Party. Moscow ignored his struggle and would not grant official recognition to his government. In France, even Communist voices were raised against him: "We cannot trust Ho," said the party's chief. "He is a Trotskyite at heart."

WHEN BAO DAI ARRIVED in Hanoi, Ho received him with an elaborate show of respect. But the emperor's very presence guaranteed tension from his supporters. After street demonstrators demanded Bao Dai's return to power, Ho looked for a way to get rid of him.

He asked whether the emperor would consent to undertake a special mission to China. General George Marshall was in Chungking, Ho explained, and it was vital that the Hanoi government contact him. Ho had sent repeated letters of friendship to President Truman and was getting no response. Would the emperor deliver in person another plea to Marshall for an alliance with the United States?

Aware of Ho's dilemma, Bao Dai was also looking for a way to resolve his status and invited young Bui Tuong Minh and Bui's father to accompany him to China. Bao Dai's wife, the Catholic daughter of wealthy landowners, preferred to remain in Hue. On the trip, Bui had a chance to study the emperor more closely and had to admit that his character had its attractive side. Years of pampered ease had left Bao Dai sheltered and naïve, but knowing that every political faction was trying to use him had also bred a cynicism and selfishness. Only his innate shyness saved him from arrogance. Bui found in the stars an explanation for what he saw as the emperor's tendency toward self-destruction. In Chinese astrology, Bao Dai was a Buffalo; in the West, a Scorpio.

Since their trip was an impromptu affair, neither Bui nor Bao Dai had any sort of papers. All the same, when they reached Chungking, General Marshall granted the emperor an audience and accepted Ho's latest overture. "I will take your letter to my government," Marshall said. "But I must tell you that I was assigned a different mission."

With that, Bui's father returned to Hanoi, but Bao Dai decided to take up residence in Hong Kong. Reports from North Vietnam indicated that the Communists were cracking down on Dai Viet Party members, and Bui's mother had disappeared into police custody. Bui decided to accompany Bao Dai and help in any way he could. The emperor might not be Hollywood royalty, but to a bored young man he exerted an irresistible combination of glamor and helplessness.

IN MARCH 1946, the French eased the Chinese out of northern Vietnam by giving up their claim to prewar leases in China. That same month, the British left the South, turning it over entirely to French troops. Ho felt he had no choice but to reach a settlement with France. He would retain control of Vietnam to a southern boundary at the 16th parallel, while the French would hold Cochin China—South Vietnam—the richest third of the country, with its rubber plantations, fertile rice fields and several gold mines. The French promised a referendum in the future that would allow the southerners to vote on unifying with Hanoi. To his associates, Ho drew on his barnyard upbringing to explain his willingness to compromise: "It is better to sniff French shit"—he used the Vietnamese word *cut*—"for a while than to eat Chinese shit all our lives."

As Ho was accepting those terms, the French negotiator, Jean Sainteny, expressed his pleasure that they had prevented fighting between their forces. Ho said, "You know very well that I wanted more than this. Still," he added, "I realize one can't have everything overnight."

Ho's CAPITULATION set off a wave of anger throughout North Vietnam. Getting the people to accept the agreement took all of Ho's pleading and prestige. With tears in his eyes, he addressed 100,000 Vietnamese in front of Hanoi's municipal theater and assured them that he would sooner die than sell out their country. "I swear I have not betrayed you," Ho said.

Giap found the settlement at least as galling. The French were responsible for the deaths of his wife, child and sister-in-law. But he, too, bowed to reality. Vietnam was not strong enough to wage a long war, and France was too strong to make it a short one. Speaking at the same rally, Giap called on the Vietnamese to submit.

Ho had acted in good faith and now, as president of his half of Vietnam, he flew to Paris to ratify the treaty. In the air over Damascus, however, he learned from the plane's radio that the rules had changed once again. A French admiral serving as high commissioner in Saigon—a former priest who regarded Ho as France's satanic enemy—had declared South Vietnam to be an entirely independent state within the French Union, "the Republic of Cochin China."

Ho protested that there must be a misunderstanding. The decree not only ignored the recent negotiations but would make uniting Vietnam all but impossible. By the time Ho's plane landed at Biarritz, he knew the report was accurate. His instinct was to fly home at once to protest the French high-handedness. Instead, he stayed on in the resort town to await the formation of a new French government. Nearly three weeks passed before Ho was allowed to proceed to Paris. Once there, he found the flags of France and Vietnam flying side by side above the throng that had turned out to hail this Asian ascetic as a modern-day Confucius or Buddha.

Ho saw himself more as Vietnam's Gandhi. His simple manner, his sandals and plain brown tunic, his artless answers, all combined to fascinate Parisian society in the way that Benjamin Franklin had once conquered the city. But Ho had paid a sterner price than Franklin for his revolution. When reporters asked whether he had been imprisoned long in his lifetime, Ho replied, "Time spent in jail is always long."

And he expected the same sacrifice from his countrymen. To a French government minister, Ho outlined the scenario if they could not avert war: "You would kill ten of my men for every one I killed of yours. But even at that rate, you would be unable to hold out, and victory would go to me. . . ."

When the conference was shifted from Paris to Fontainebleau, Ho was taken to live with the family of Raymond Aubrac, a young French official. Ho praised Aubrac's modest house and charmed his three children. But as negotiations continued, Ho learned that he could not reverse the decree of independence for South Vietnam. At most, the French would agree to a vague future settlement. On the Left, Communist leaders in Paris expected power to fall to them very soon and seemed no more interested than the capitalists in shearing off France's lucrative colonies.

"Don't let me go back empty-handed," Ho pleaded. He said he needed a concession to shield his moderate policies from the extremists in his own movement. But by the time he returned to Vietnam, it was Ho who had given all the ground. Giap prepared for the inevitable war to come by raising the strength of the Vietminh army to 100,000 men.

AT THE NORTH VIETNAMESE HARBOR of Haiphong on November 20, 1946, a French ship seized a Chinese junk, claiming it was carrying contraband arms. The Vietminh militia retaliated by boarding the French ship and taking prisoner its three-man crew. Fighting broke out around the harbor, which prompted the French high command to order that the North Vietnamese be taught "a harsh lesson." A French general traveled to Haiphong to spell out that lesson for the local French commanders: "If these dirty peasants want a fight," he said, "they shall have it."

A barrage of French artillery, tanks and naval guns killed about 1,000 civilians, but France went on to lose the propaganda war. When the Vietminh claimed that 20,000 Vietnamese had died, a French admiral countered by calling their figure inflated; it had been a mere 6,000, he said. Ho broadcast an appeal for calm, but turmoil wracked the country. In Saigon, the man who had been France's candidate as the first Vietnamese president of South Vietnam hanged himself from shame at collaborating with the French. Reluctantly, Ho accepted Giap's judgment that they must go back to waging war.

ON THE EVENING OF December 19, 1946, the Vietminh seized the offensive by attacking French barracks and civilian neighborhoods. The next afternoon, French troops surrounded Ho's residence, but Ho, Giap and their closest advisers had escaped to a rice field. Ho was suffering from a high fever and yet, hiding in the paddy, he drafted a vigorous call to the Vietnamese to fight for their country.

"Our resistance will be long and painful," Ho warned, "but whatever the sacrifices, however long the struggle, we shall fight to the end, until Vietnam is fully independent and reunified."

Ho's dream of achieving a peaceful independence had lasted little more than fifteen months.

GEORGE MARSHALL'S MISSION in China was clearly failing. Truman had sent him as his special envoy to fashion a truce between China's two factions, and Marshall seemed to expect that his Yankee integrity would somehow bind the two rivals together. Since his prestige had preceded him, both Chiang and Zhou Enlai, who represented Mao, paid tribute to Marshall's high character. But behind his back, Chiang criticized Marshall for his "policy of appeasement" toward Mao. In turn, Mao resented the American military aid to Chiang's forces. Marshall's shaky compromise soon broke down when Chiang sent his men to march against a Red Army stronghold. With Madame Chiang translating, an outraged Marshall accused the generalissimo of repeated bad faith and broken promises. "People have said you were a modern George Washington," Marshall concluded. "But after these things, they will never say it again."

Marshall left Asia as disillusioned with Chiang as Dean Rusk's commander, Vinegar Joe Stilwell, had been during his earlier service in China. Stilwell had referred to Chiang as "the Peanut" and suggested that the best way to cure China's corrupt and repressive regime might be to shoot him.

Marshall was flying home to become secretary of state in an administration committed to resisting the spread of Communism, and whatever his personal misgivings Marshall's State Department backed Chiang against Mao. Throughout the next four years of civil war, however, Mao's People's Liberation Army regularly outfought Chiang's Kuomintang army. The Communists destroyed thirty of Chiang's best divisions. In Manchuria alone, fifty of Chiang's generals and their troops defected to Mao. As the Red Army captured American-made jeeps, tanks and artillery, Mao laughed and called Chiang "our quartermaster."

With a Communist victory looking inevitable, Stalin worried that Truman might dispatch divisions of American troops to China, who might then push on to occupy the Soviet Union. To protect himself, Stalin urged Mao to be satisfied with the territory he already held. Insulted and infuriated, Mao complained that Stalin had never given the Chinese Communists anything but dull lectures and bad advice. Mao negotiated the surrender of Beijing and sent his troops on to decisive battles in Nanking and Shanghai.

Chiang escaped from the mainland with the remnant of his army and established a government in Taiwan. On October 1, 1949, Mao Zedong, chairman of the new People's Republic of China stood at the podium above the Gate of

Heavenly Peace and greeted the hundreds of thousands who had jammed into vast Tiananmen Square. Three million Chinese were dead, victims of the civil war. The survivors sang to Mao their marching song of victory:

> The Sun is rising red in the East,
> China has brought forth a Mao Zedong.

As Mao was pushing toward victory, Colonel Rusk followed George Marshall out of the army and into the State Department as head of the Office of Special Political Affairs, which oversaw the United Nations delegation in New York. At State, Rusk supported the Marshall Plan for rebuilding Europe and backed a ban on all nuclear weapons. When the question arose of recognizing the state of Israel, Rusk clashed with Truman's legal counsel, Clark Clifford, who won the argument and persuaded the president to recognize the new nation. Marshall had also opposed recognition, but when friends urged him to resign on principle, he explained that a cabinet officer did not resign when the man with the constitutional responsibility to make a decision decided to exercise it. Rusk agreed with him and sometimes quoted Truman's blunt description of his powers: "The President makes foreign policy."

When Dean Acheson replaced Marshall in 1949, he named Rusk his undersecretary of state. But Rusk decided that he was the department's senior Asian expert and requested a demotion to overseeing State's Far Eastern affairs desk.

Rusk subscribed to the Washington consensus that World War II might have been avoided if the Allies had acted against the Japanese when they marched on Manchuria or against Hitler when he occupied the Rhineland. Now he saw the Soviet Union as an antagonist rather than as a former ally, and he shared the president's dislike of Mao—Truman called him "Mousie Dung." Rusk considered Chiang Kai-shek's defeat that year a tragedy for China, but he admitted that Chiang's cause had become hopeless and approved of Truman's decision not to challenge Mao's victory by landing U.S. troops on the Chinese mainland.

In his third-tier job, Rusk was quiet and uncontentious. He leaned toward Roosevelt's conclusion that colonialism was dead and the United States would be wrong to try to revive it. But Acheson, an avowed North Atlantic man, was committed to the ambitious and expensive Marshall Plan for rebuilding Europe, which also meant allowing France back into Vietnam. When Acheson told Rusk to muzzle his views, Rusk reminded himself who was the boss and shut up.

Not that Truman was showing much interest in Vietnam, even after the French began diverting Marshall Plan money to finance their colonial presence there. Despite the promises made to Ho in 1946, France's forces in Vietnam had gradually risen from the agreed-upon 20,000 troops to 150,000—a third of France's postwar army. But the French soldiers controlled only Vietnam's cities; the countryside belonged to the Vietminh. Ho reproached the pessimists in his ranks with a prediction: "Today the locust fights the elephant," he said. "But tomorrow the elephant will be disemboweled."

IN THE MEKONG DELTA in the mid-1940s, a dreamy schoolgirl, Nguyen Thi Ngoc Dung, saddened her mother by running away to join the resistance movement against the returning French. "Going to the jungle," the rebels called it, though they were only camping out in marshland near a fruit grove. Miss Dung's name was written without a bar through the D, which caused it to be pronounced "Zung," just as the name of Le Duan, emerging these days as the top Vietminh leader in the South, became "Le Zwan."

Young Miss Dung had first been converted to the revolution by a song, not a manifesto. Studying at a French school in Saigon, she heard fellow students singing about their ancestors' war against the Chinese and realized that her own education had been designed to ensure her loyalty to the French. She asked herself bitterly why she should be studying Charlemagne while she was being deceived about her own history.

When Dung joined the resistance and was sent to the countryside, her romantic spirit soared. It was her first time away from the comforts of city life, and she was hearing stories from farmers in the villages of Kim Son and Long Hung about parents who had died in Poulo Condore prison and their bodies tossed into the sea. To Dung, the poverty of peasant life was a revelation. These were people who had nothing and yet seemed happy to give her the best of what little they did have.

Since Miss Dung was a Vietminh and her hosts often were not, she felt obliged to make sure they understood the danger in harboring her. "Why do you let me stay?" she asked one old woman. "I don't care about the risks," the woman said. "A lot of people have been killed here, and I thought that meant the end of the revolution. But seeing you, I see that the revolution goes on."

The woman's passion surprised and shamed Dung, who had seen herself as the educated liberator come to instill moral values. Then, when she joined the village women in going barefoot, she couldn't walk after an hour or two. She didn't know how to chop wood or cook a meal, and she shrank from the sight of earthworms in the dirt. But Dung persevered, going out with Vietminh women at night to dig up a road until it was impassable for the French soldiers. Ho had written that since the French had the use of cars, the people must make them blind and lame. If no one told the French where the Vietminh were hiding, they could not find them. Since their cars required roads, if the roads were cut, the French would be left limping. And if each farmer contributed a mere handful of rice to a common village barrel, the result would be enough to feed the Vietminh hiding nearby. Ho said that every villager could support the revolution in one of three campaigns—against illiteracy, against hunger, against foreign invaders.

Dung opened reading classes. She worried that if the others knew she spoke

French, they would hate her, and she told no one. But her class in Vietnamese was an instant success among the village women and children. After working all day in the fields, the women lighted coconut palm leaves as torches to guide them through the marshes and across the monkey bridges. They showed up at class each night eager to learn, often with a baby under their arm, and studied under rows of poon, a fruit with a flammable oil that they strung together and burned for light. Since the classes were also a social event, the women insisted on singing before they settled down to study. Miss Dung taught them "Who Loves Ho Chi Minh More Than Children?" But her students knew Ho only by name, and Dung couldn't supply many details about him. She had only read Ho's writing about the cynical way the French kept 90 percent of the people in their colonies illiterate and persuaded the rest to be grateful to France for bringing civilization to Vietnam, an accusation that her own experience bore out.

Dung first learned about Ho as a man on the day at a Vietminh provincial camp when she found artisans using a wooden board to make lithographs of his face. When they gave her one, Dung was impressed by Ho's high forehead but had not expected his wispy goatee. She took the picture back to the villagers and found that they venerated it.

When the house next door to Dung's family in My Tho was commandeered as a French jail, her mother began to hear the cries of men and women being tortured. All four sons, like Dung, had joined the Vietminh, and their mother prayed to Buddha for them and became a vegetarian, hoping that her sacrifice might somehow spare their lives.

As the years wore on, the family returned to a semblance of normal life. The brothers married, and Miss Dung helped their wives get to a Vietminh stronghold in Dong Thap province where the French could never penetrate. In that fastness, the Vietminh built thatched houses that allowed families to live together and where the sick or wounded could come to recover. Dung's older sisters also came to the base, and a younger sister became a midwife to the revolutionaries. In 1950, Dung married a former student at the Polytechnic in Hue who had been imprisoned in Poulo Condore for anti-French activities, then released with Le Duan in 1945. Giving birth to three children in the early 1950s, Dung had to surrender them almost at once. Each infant was sent away from the rebel camp, to be raised by a sister in My Tho.

A FEW MONTHS after Rusk moved to the Far Eastern affairs desk at State, Acheson tried to convince reporters at the National Press Club that it was not leftists in Washington who had lost China to Mao. He explained that a political vacuum had opened and that the Red Army had ridden to power on a new revolutionary spirit. Then, in an omission he would regret, Acheson defined the U.S. defensive perimeter across the Pacific in a way that seemed to omit South Korea.

In North Korea, Kim Il Sung was twenty-two years younger than Ho and far less patient. Unwilling to wait for an eventual unification of the two Koreas, Kim went to Moscow in 1949 and received Stalin's approval for an invasion across the 38th parallel and into the South. But Stalin proved to be a duplicitous ally. Before the scheduled invasion, he ordered all Russian advisers removed from North Korea's army divisions. Stalin knew those withdrawals would weaken Kim's capability, but he did not want to give the United States proof of Soviet involvement.

About that time, Ho also fell victim in a minor way to Stalin's sly self-preservation. At a conference in Moscow, Ho took a Soviet magazine from his briefcase and asked Stalin to autograph it. Stalin obliged him but sent his secret police to steal the magazine back from Ho's quarters. More suspicious than Chennault, Stalin didn't want his signature brandished around Vietnam to show Ho's intimacy with the leader of world Communism.

During that secret trip to Moscow, Ho also asked that the Soviet Union officially recognize his government and supply arms and other aid. Stalin agreed to diplomatic ties but otherwise treated Ho rather disdainfully. When Ho asked for quinine to fight malaria among his troops, Stalin outraged his own aides by directing them to send only half a ton. They took his miserliness as a sign that Stalin expected Ho to fail.

ON JUNE 25, 1950, Kim Il Sung launched his attack on South Korea and plowed easily through the countryside to seize its capital at Seoul. But when the southerners made a stand near Pusan, Kim's soldiers could not clinch their victory. Across the Pacific, Harry Truman thought he saw history repeating a recent lesson. He told a Boy Scout jamboree at Valley Forge, Pennsylvania, that the Communist imperialists now were behaving like Hitler and Mussolini. With that, Truman led the United States into war, pledging to unify Korea under a United Nations flag.

At first, all went well for the West. Douglas MacArthur, hero of the war against Japan, retook Seoul, and Truman gave him permission to lead U.N. troops drawn from eighteen countries across the parallel and into the North, as far as the Yalu River, which divided Korea from China. At a meeting on Wake Island in October 1950, MacArthur assured Truman that the Chinese would not enter the fray. As for the Russians, an American general told reporters, "If the Russkies come down, we'll fight the Russkies."

The U.N. forces drove the North Koreans back above the 38th parallel, and in retreat Kim became hysterical, sobbing that the Americans would end up occupying all of his country. But the Chinese had massed a reserve army of half a million men along their Korean border. China's leaders were convinced that the United States intended to use Kim's adventure as a pretext for invading China. Their own victory was scarcely a year old, and Mao's council knew that the China Lobby in the United States—conservatives led by Senator William Knowland of California—were arguing that China should be returned to Chiang Kai-shek.

Mao's Communist leadership was nervous enough to launch a preemptive strike. While Stalin remained aloof, 300,000 Chinese crossed over into Korea and sent the United Nations's forces flying. For the second time in six months, Kim's men held Seoul.

MacArthur asked Truman for twenty or thirty nuclear bombs to drop on targets inside China. But G-2, the Army's intelligence office, advised Truman that atomic bombs would be taken as a sign of desperation and would weaken U.S. support among other Asian allies. When the president refused MacArthur's request, the five-star general challenged Truman's policy of containment and, in April 1951, was very publicly relieved of his command.

Truman's action intensified the debate at home. He got support from General Omar Bradley, who called carrying the war into China "the wrong war, at the wrong place, at the wrong time and with the wrong enemy." MacArthur's backing came from the China Lobby, from Henry Luce's *Time* and *Life* magazines and, for one bizarre evening, from Dean Rusk. In May 1951, Foster Dulles invited Rusk to join him and Senator Paul Douglas of Illinois, both strongly committed to MacArthur, at a dinner given by like-minded members of the China Institute. Rusk perhaps did not count on the publicity his appearance would receive. Despite his guarded language, columnists read the text, which Rusk had not cleared with the department, as a commitment to overthrow Mao's government. Walter Lippmann, in a column titled "Bradley vs. Rusk," wrote that Rusk seemed to be ruling out a negotiated settlement in Korea and was announcing instead that the American terms in the conflict were unconditional surrender. Acheson was forced to hold a news conference to deny that the Truman administration had shifted from its limited aims in Korea.

Foster Dulles came to Rusk's rescue. Later in the year, he used his position as chairman of the Rockefeller Foundation to get Rusk hired as its president.

WITH THE KOREAN WAR dragging on, a third-term Congressman paid a fleeting visit that same year to Indochina. Since Representative John Kennedy intended to run for the Senate in 1952, a familiarity with foreign policy would enhance his credentials, and he was making the trip with his brother, Bobby, and their sister, Patricia. During a stopover in Japan, however, Kennedy ran a fever so high that he was flown to a U.S. hospital in Okinawa. His entourage passed off the episode as a recurrence of the malaria they said he had contracted as a naval officer in the South Pacific. In fact, Kennedy had been diagnosed as suffering from Addison's disease, which could be fatal—to the victim and to his political aspirations.

When Kennedy recovered and resumed his fact-finding tour, he spent time in Vietnam with Edmund Gullion, an American embassy official who believed that only an independent Vietnam government could withstand the Vietminh.

Kennedy also stopped by the Saigon apartment of Seymour Topping, the Associated Press's first reporter in Vietnam. He wanted to talk over the war with Topping and his wife, the daughter of Chester Ronning, a Canadian diplomat based in China. Audrey Topping was a day away from giving birth to her first child, and Kennedy brightened her spirits by comparing her to a Botticelli madonna. After two hours of absorbing the Toppings' pessimism about French prospects in Vietnam, Kennedy said he intended to raise the issue when he got home. But he predicted that it would give him trouble with his constituents.

Back in the United States, Kennedy challenged Truman's Vietnam policy, telling a national radio audience, "In Indochina, we have allied ourselves to the desperate effort of a French regime to hang on to the remnants of Empire." Kennedy warned against sending U.S. soldiers to fight alongside the French in Vietnam. Perhaps, he suggested, "some people of colored origin" could be recruited, since the Communists were capitalizing on the history of white Frenchmen oppressing the Vietnamese. But Kennedy added that the true answer was for the West to recognize "that every country is entitled to its independence."

The congressman's attitude represented a surprising reversal for him over the past two years. When Mao gained control of China, Kennedy had risen in the House of Representatives to excoriate the policies of his fellow Democrat in the White House. Blaming two China experts by name—Owen Lattimore and John Fairbank—Kennedy had called on Congress to prevent "the onrushing tide of Communism from engulfing all of Asia." Now Kennedy's latest speech caused a different rumbling in foreign policy circles; Dean Acheson considered his criticism of France an unwarranted attack on America's oldest ally.

By then, however, Acheson was engaged in a more explosive battle. Already troubled by Mao's takeover in China, the American public was becoming impatient with the long negotiations over Korea. Despite the 33,000 American deaths, any treaty seemed likely to do no more than restore the prewar border along the 38th parallel. Truman's policy of containing Communism was being attacked by politicians who urged that the West retake China and Eastern Europe, possibly even the Soviet Union. To avoid the appearance of weakness, Acheson's diplomatic language grew harsh. He denounced "Soviet imperialism" while he increased Marshall Plan aid to the point that France could finance her Indochinese war openly. Even so, Acheson remained vulnerable to attacks from the Republicans, especially a claim by Senator Joe McCarthy of Wisconsin that Acheson was shielding government officials who were either outright Communists or friendly to Communist causes. Investigations and purges within the government were aimed at discrediting several leading Asia experts—John Service, John Paton Davies, O. Edmund Clubb. One of the men Congressman Kennedy had singled out, Owen Lattimore of Johns Hopkins University, was also attacked, even though Lattimore had never served in the State Department.

Acheson's Ivy League hauteur made him an irresistible target for fervid anti-

Communists from farm states and the West Coast. Even though the various hearings had uncovered no Communists in government, many Americans were concluding that where there was smoke there must be fire. When Acheson joked that serving in the navy had taught him that where there was smoke, there was usually a smoke machine, the quip was cited as one more proof that he was not taking the Communist threat seriously.

As cries of treason rang out across the country, a State Department official named Alger Hiss was accused of spying for the Soviets in the 1930s. Hiss was protected by the statute of limitations, but when he denied the charge under oath, he was convicted of perjury. Richard Nixon, the California senator running in 1952 as Dwight Eisenhower's vice presidential candidate, fashioned a campaign phrase that played on voter distrust of Democratic nominee Adlai Stevenson's erudition and their frustration with merely holding the line against Communism, not defeating it decisively. "Stevenson," Nixon told a Los Angeles audience, "holds a Ph.D. degree from Acheson's College of Cowardly Communist Containment."

After Eisenhower's election, Washington's hostility toward the Communist bloc became even more unrelenting. Republican gains in the Congress resulted in McCarthy being named chairman of a Senate investigative subcommittee, and Foster Dulles was bringing to his appointment as secretary of state a religious sense of mission. He gave the world to understand that there could be no compromise between virtue—represented by the United States—and the wickedness of the Soviet Union and its allies. To Dulles, such nationalist leaders as Pandit Nehru of India became even more suspect, and Ho Chi Minh's ties to China automatically branded him as an enemy. Eisenhower, vividly recalling his party's campaign slogans, warned his new cabinet officers that they must prevent the Democrats from retaliating with the cry "Who lost Vietnam?"

Vice President Nixon shared Dulles's zeal. During an Asian trip in 1953, Nixon saw at first hand the French contempt for their Vietnamese subjects but remained convinced that France must fight on. Toasting his French hosts in Hanoi, Nixon pledged continued U.S. aid and predicted France's eventual victory against the Vietminh.

Once home, Nixon spoke out against any attempt to convene an Indochina peace conference. Explaining the war to the American public, he borrowed a metaphor that both Eisenhower and Dulles had already embraced: South Vietnam was the first in a line of dominoes, Nixon said. If it fell to Communism, the rest of Asia would soon be lost. He added that both the French and the British might soon seek peace in Vietnam—"unfortunately"—since their defection would leave the duty of saving Asia squarely with the United States. Privately, Nixon argued that if success in Vietnam required the use of nuclear weapons, so be it.

☐

UPON EISENHOWER'S ELECTION, Dean Rusk had left the State Department, but he had known Service and Davies from his days with Stilwell and testified, to no avail, at their loyalty hearings. Rusk also assured colleagues that he could recall no instance of Alger Hiss trying to subvert his staff. Rusk's friendship with Foster Dulles spared him a congressional investigation of his own.

Rusk had learned from the China Institute episode that speaking out, whether from the Left or the Right, could jeopardize a man's career. When Virginia Rusk said that her husband had developed an "infinite capacity to adjust to the inevitable," Rusk took her remark as a compliment.

DURING HO'S YEARS of inconclusive battles with the French, he issued regular communiqués from a hut deep in the Vietnam jungle, exhorting his countrymen to fight on while he and his international supporters—Nehru of India was one of the few—pressed for a new peace treaty. Ho understood that Vice President Nixon and others were urging the French to resist a conference because a coalition government was sure to mean Vietminh participation. But French public opinion had turned against the war. A thirty-seven-year-old deputy, François Mitterrand, complained in a speech, "We have granted Vietnam 'full independence' eighteen times since 1949. Isn't it about time we did it just once, but for good?"

By January 1954, international pressure had forced a meeting in Berlin that included delegates from the United States, the Soviet Union, Britain and France. They agreed to a spring conference in Geneva that would try, at last, to reach an accord on Korea and Indochina. But Foster Dulles still opposed a Vietnam treaty. When a reporter asked if he planned to meet with the Chinese delegates in Switzerland, Dulles replied, "Not unless our automobiles collide."

Then, as the date approached, France's bargaining position was dramatically undercut. According to alarming reports from Vietnam, 13,000 French soldiers were trapped under siege by General Giap's troops at a mountain outpost called Dien Bien Phu.

WHILE GIAP WAS FIGHTING the Japanese in 1944, Ho named him commander in chief of the army. Giap, then thirty-two, was young enough to be Ho's son, was almost certainly his heir and, during Ho's fruitless talks with the French at Fontainebleau, had become the unofficial head of state. At about that time, Archimedes Patti, the OSS officer, finally met Giap face-to-face and found him self-confident but deadly serious. Giap had appeared good-humored in his youth. Now smiling seemed to come hard to him.

As Giap fought the French throughout the early 1950s, he had pursued his four-step theory of war—maneuver, large movement, positioning, victory. In a notable example of maneuvering, he thwarted French strategy by moving his troops to the Laotian border, covering 180 miles in six weeks. To outsiders, that

General Vo Nguyen Giap
(Vietnam News Agency)

rate of progress might have seemed leisurely except that Giap forbade his men to travel on the exposed roads. Lacking both vans and trucks, he ordered three divisions of Vietminh to hack their way on foot through jungle that was all but impenetrable.

In 1953, Giap launched his second stage by marching through Laos to the royal capital of Luang Prabang, where he installed a leftist prince named Souphanouvong as his deputy and declared creation of the Government of the Free Laotian, the Pathet Lao.

In France, Giap's successes were provoking shuffles in the military high command. When the latest French commander, General Henri Navarre, arrived in Vietnam, he came with the full backing of Foster Dulles and a surefire plan for victory. But Navarre also confronted the prospect of peace talks, which were starting to look inevitable. Since he could not let Giap go on picking off small pockets of French soldiers at will, Navarre decided he would provoke a full-scale battle sometime in 1954. The French would either crush the Vietminh or fight them to such an obvious stalemate that France could negotiate an honorable peace.

Dien Bien Phu, three hundred miles west of Hanoi in mountains along the Laotian border, seemed the right place to mass enough French soldiers to disrupt the Vietminh supply routes from China and Laos. In November 1953, Navarre sent in elite battalions of French paratroopers to seize the large plain—eleven miles long and about five miles wide. Navarre calculated that, to fire on his camp, Vietminh gunners would have to move into exposed positions, where his own guns and planes could wipe them out. Expecting to annihilate the Vietminh main force, Navarre promised Paris victory by the end of 1955.

The French counted on supplying their troops by land, even though many roads were not secure from guerrilla attack. The only other option was to provide reinforcements and supplies by air, which would require skirting a mountain rim that dominated the plain. But the need for that alternative seemed unlikely. An American general, John "Iron Mike" O'Daniel, inspected Dien Bien Phu and agreed with Navarre that it was impregnable.

A classic Chinese military manual might have changed their minds. "Never fight on a terrain which looks like a tortoise turned upside down," a Chinese tactician had once written. "Never camp there for long." Giap had anticipated Navarre's strategy and expected the French to occupy the plain when the rainy season ended in late October. Before that time, Giap had begun moving a Vietminh division toward Dien Bien Phu.

For the past four years, modern-day Chinese strategists had been traveling to Vietnam to offer advice. From his own war in Korea, Mao had diverted thousands of tons of 75-millimeter Russian and Chinese cannon, ammunition and hand grenades, along with tens of thousands of Skoda rifles.

As Giap prepared for a showdown, Ho flew secretly to Beijing, where he stayed at the house of one of Mao's ablest commanders, Chen Geng, who had advised the Vietminh four years earlier during their northern border campaign. Ho requested even more Chinese help to blunt the expected French offensive, and Mao sent Chen to Vietnam with six hundred trucks, many driven by Chinese soldiers.

To those reinforcements, Giap added tens of thousands of Vietnamese porters. Transporting equipment on the backs of ponies or of the Vietminh themselves, Giap forged a ring of destruction. Heavy guns and rocket launchers would make it impossible to escape from the camp and turn resupplying by air into a lethal gamble. And Navarre had been wrong in calculating the range of Giap's artillery. They could hit the French airfield from hills only three miles away.

ON THE WESTERN SIDE of the mountains, Tran Quang Co, a twenty-six-year-old Vietminh, was assigned to the camp where Giap intended to house his prisoners of war. By enrolling with the resistance in 1945, Co had followed a family tradition. His parents were dead, but his five older brothers had already joined Giap. Co's own motive was simple. "I don't want to be a slave," he had said then, and he reminded himself of that sentiment whenever he regretted the fact that he was trained for nothing but warfare.

For five months, Co waited with his propaganda unit while other of Giap's troops broke down their artillery into pieces small enough to carry up the mountainside. Co knew the work was grueling but exhilarating since the French remained unaware of the range of Vietminh artillery that could be arrayed along the mountain crest. The job was scarcely done, however, when Giap delayed the attack, and the artillery had to be broken down again and lugged back to safety. Then, mere days before the siege, the whole grinding chore was repeated. From his vantage point, Co admired Giap's logistics and marveled at the way one man on a small bicycle could pedal over the trails balancing large stores of food.

A city boy, Co hated the constant rain and the leeches that sucked blood from his legs. Waiting for the battle to begin, Co's unit received only a few stray prisoners picked up by Vietminh patrols, usually Africans from Morocco, Tunis and Angola. Co tried to make them realize that they should not be fighting against Ho. "You are mercenaries," he lectured them. "We are all victims of the French colonists, but we are trying to emancipate our people. When you go home, you must do the same."

ON THE FIGHTING SIDE of the mountain, another young Vietminh, Dang Vu Hiep, was also impatient for the attack to begin. Like Co, Hiep had joined the Vietminh in 1945, right out of secondary school, in a town north of Hanoi. For the next seven years, he had emerged unscathed from occasional skirmishes, but during a battle in 1952, he had been lightly wounded in the thigh and arm by a French shell.

Men and women like Co, who would have pursued some other career in peacetime, made up the majority of Vietminh recruits, with the result that the bravest soldiers might have a poet's soft hands. That was not true of Hiep, whose blunt and determined features were those of a soldier from any age or culture. When his colleagues were sent for military training to China, Hiep was kept at home to study political lessons. Beginning at the company level, each Vietminh unit had a political officer who shared command with the military officer and was expected to know equally as much about command and tactics. By 1954, Hiep had become the political officer for the 102nd Regiment of the Vietminh's 308th Division. Although he himself had joined the Communist Party the year after he entered the Vietminh, Hiep's lectures to the men played down Marxism. He reminded them instead why they were fighting and assured them that patriotism was a noble virtue, a religion. He drilled into them a need to respect the local population, which would sharpen the contrast between the Vietminh and the supercilious French.

Soldiers spent the dry season from October to April in tactical training, and Hiep sometimes heard the men of his regiment worrying that they did not have enough experience for the battle they were facing. They had fought well so far against the French but had never conducted a siege. As they waited, Hiep kept them studying Giap's plan until they were clear and confident about its goal. "We must be determined," Hiep reminded them. "If we have doubts, we cannot fight."

FROM NOVEMBER through February, Giap had been launching diversionary attacks around Vietnam, forcing Navarre to tie up his troops in minor skirmishes. The French, impatient for a showdown, dropped leaflets over the roads around Dien Bien Phu with a taunting challenge: "What are you waiting for? Why don't you attack if you are not cowards? We are waiting for you."

By holding back, Giap had amassed 800 Russian trucks, each capable of carrying two-and-a-half tons, and the Chinese had scraped together for him another 200 U.S. trucks of the same size, built by General Motors and captured in Korea.

A major engineering feat was widening a mule track into a stretch of road for thirty-five miles, from Dien Bien Phu back to the Vietminh supply dump. For the job, Giap conscripted two engineer regiments, an infantry regiment, 7,000 army recruits and 10,000 civilian farmers. By now, Giap's combat troops at Dien Bien Phu were approaching 50,000. He estimated the French total at 16,000.

On Saturday, March 13, 1954, Giap sprang his trap.

Vietminh commandos slipped onto the Dien Bien Phu air base, poured water into the fuel tanks of the fighter planes, set off explosive charges to tear up the landing strip, and left behind pamphlets written in French and German: "Dien Bien Phu will be your grave." At 5 P.M., enough Vietminh artillery rained down to shake the floors of the French command posts and send earth flying into the trenches. The camp's lights went out, the telephone lines were cut. A French chaplain began to count the incoming shells—fifteen to eighteen per minute.

Giap calculated that the French troops had enough supplies on hand to last eight days. After that, they would require a daily minimum of 200 tons of food and ammunition. As the siege continued, aircraft—including U.S. planes from the CIA—began dodging through the treetops to drop parachutes with supply canisters. Each day, French soldiers crawled out from the camp under Giap's machine-gun and cannon fire to drag in the containers.

Giap's own supply problems were at least as vexing. French planes were showering the area with "butterfly bombs," small grenades slowed in their descent by a pair of wings. Touching down lightly, they exploded when stepped on. Their targets were the thousands of Vietnamese men, women and children who were stretched through the underbrush in a human chain and made contact only by tiny oil lamps that glimmered through the heavy curtain of trees and vines.

The Vietminh and their supporters had redoubled their efforts since the Communist Party announced a new policy of land reform with the slogan "Land to the Tillers." Along narrow paths, sheltered by the jungle canopy, the Vietnamese passed ammunition from hand to hand. The only food was rice. On that human conveyer belt, men and women ate nine-tenths of the rice as they moved shells and equipment. The final tenth was saved for the Vietminh troops manning the guns.

Vietminh near Giap's base knew that Chinese soldiers had joined the battle wearing North Vietnamese insignia, but they did not hear the bickering over strategy between Giap and General Chen. Even at this climactic moment, Giap could not forget the threat that China had once posed, and he reminded himself that the Vietnamese had beaten back three massive invasions from the north, always against greater odds than they faced now.

Given that history, Giap felt confident that he could ignore Chen's advice that he send his troops against the French fortress in a vast human wave, a tactic called "Pointed Head, Long Tail." It required a great massing of troops for the first assault and then extended ranks of soldiers to continue the battle. Giap disapproved of the number of casualties that the Chinese had been willing to sustain in Korea and decided that using their tactic would lead to unacceptable losses. He intended to save lives by digging tunnels to move his troops and to cover his bunkers with undetectable camouflage.

Chen complained to Mao's high command that not only was Giap an inept tactician, he was also hogging the credit that should go to his Chinese allies. In Beijing, however, Chen's superiors understood the damaging international repercussions if their presence in Vietnam could be proved. Chen was told that since the battle of Dien Bien Phu was being fought on Vietnamese soil, Giap must be seen as the victor.

As FRANCE'S POSITION became untenable, the Eisenhower administration was weighing the use of atomic bombs to save the garrison. Throughout the month of April, Vice President Nixon recommended rescuing the French troops with two or three atomic bombs, and several of Eisenhower's military advisers agreed. But General Matthew Ridgway, MacArthur's replacement as commander in Korea and now representing the army among the Joint Chiefs of Staff, argued that intervention would lead to the sending of U.S. ground troops and a stalemate like the one in Korea. Ridgway was an articulate exponent of what the Pentagon was calling the "Never Again Club"—officers who resisted any attempt to commit American troops to a land war in Asia.

For eight years, under both Truman and Eisenhower, the United States had accepted French assurances that their war was going well. Now Eisenhower refused to pay a further installment on the American investment. To French pleas that he send U.S. troops, Ike said he would commit them only with congressional approval—and that, he knew, he would never get. Too many senators were insisting there be no more Koreas.

Ike was also sensitive to the scant time that had passed since Hiroshima and Nagasaki. He lashed out at hard-line advocates like Air Force Chief of Staff

Nathan Twining and Admiral Arthur Radford, chairman of the Joint Chiefs. "You boys must be crazy," Eisenhower said. "We can't use those awful things against Asians for the second time in less than ten years. My God!"

To pressure Washington, the French claimed that the Chinese were about to march on Vietnam, and Foster Dulles urged Ike to announce that such an invasion would be the equivalent of a declaration of war against the United States. Eisenhower responded by raising the stakes: if he were going to war against China, he said, he should ask Congress for the authority to go to war against Russia as well.

The president challenged his Joint Chiefs to picture the result of a preventive nuclear strike. "I want you to carry this question home with you. Gain such a victory, and what do you do with it? Here would be a great area from Elbe to Vladivostok . . . torn up and destroyed, without government, without its communications, just an area of starvation and disaster. I ask you what would the civilized world do about it? I repeat, there is no victory except through our imaginations."

FOR EIGHT WEEKS, two hundred Vietminh big guns pounded down on the French camp. As the French artillery emplacements were destroyed, so was the French will to fight on. On the afternoon of May 7, Giap ordered an all-out attack and watched as white flags sprung up at several French outposts. From Hanoi, Navarre told a deputy to reach the camp's command headquarters by phone and order that its white flag be hauled down. "Look, man," General Christian de Castries was told, "naturally you've got to call it quits. But one thing is certain is that everything you've done so far is superb. You mustn't spoil it all now by hoisting the white flag. You're overwhelmed, but there must be no surrender, no white flag."

At 5:30 P.M., Giap's men overran the headquarters building and captured its officers. That night the Vietminh charged the one garrison still holding out and took prisoner its last 2,000 soldiers.

Vo Nguyen Giap had reversed three hundred years of military history. For the first time in the annals of Western colonialism, Asian troops in fixed battle had defeated a European army.

WHEN THE FIGHTING ENDED, Dang Vu Hiep emerged unscathed, but in his fastness on the Lao side of the mountain Tran Quang Co's skull had been grazed by a bomb fragment. He dismissed it as a mere nick and went on processing the flood of prisoners driven into his camp by the final battle. "You see, the French can be beaten," Co told the newly arriving Africans. "Go home and do the same."

In Thanh Hoa province, south of Dien Bien Phu, Nguyen Khac Huynh, the teenager who had thrilled in 1945 to the raising of Vietminh colors in Hanoi, was now a twenty-six-year-old company commander. By radio, Huynh got the news that Giap's forces had prevailed. Over the past nine years, Huynh had learned considerably more about Karl Marx than when his only motive had been to drive the foreigners from his country. But independence had remained his sacred goal, and today had finally brought it.

Because communication was unreliable, Huynh ran from unit to unit to report that the French fortress had fallen, telling himself over and over that this was another great day in his life.

IF HO'S ONLY ENEMY had been France, his delegation to the Geneva conference might have dictated terms that would force the French to slink away. But Ho understood that the fist within the French puppet force was American and that any settlement must appease the United States.

In Beijing, China's leadership was proving at least as cautious as Eisenhower had been, and when Zhou Enlai went to Geneva, it was to represent his own country's interests, not Ho's. Partitioning Vietnam and giving Ho only the northern sector might ensure that U.S. troops would never again be massed along the Chinese border. Dining with a French delegate, Zhou remarked that he had come to Geneva to make peace, not to back the Vietminh.

Nor did the Soviets want Ho to press hard at Geneva. America's intervention in Korea had ended up strengthening Chinese authority in Southeast Asia. A wider war in Vietnam might lead to Russia's tenuous influence in the region evaporating altogether. With both the Russians and Chinese backing away from direct confrontation with the United States, the Vietminh, despite holding four-fifths of the country, arrived in Geneva once again as supplicants.

Zhou's maneuvering produced a general agreement that Vietnam should be divided, and dickering began over which parallel should serve as the border. Intent on salvaging what he could, Pham Van Dong, Vietnam's chief negotiator, suggested the 13th parallel. That would draw the line at Qui Nhon in central Vietnam and give the Vietminh two-thirds of the country.

The French called for a border at the 18th parallel, about eighty miles south of Vinh. The eventual compromise settled for the 17th parallel. The two Vietnams would be roughly the same size—63,360 square miles in the North, 65,726 in the South—and each would have a population estimated at 15 million.

The French had fared better as negotiators than as warriors. Under the terms of the agreement, neither the Pathet Lao nor the Cambodian resistance movement retained control over any territory in their countries. And an election aimed at unifying the two halves of Vietnam would be deferred for two years—not held within six months, as Pham Van Dong had urged. To preside over South Vietnam, the Vietminh were forced to accept the return of Bao Dai, their former emperor.

Officially, the treaty was no more than a cease-fire, and France and Ho's government were the only two signatories. But Britain and the Soviet Union, as cochairs of the conference, assumed responsibility for upholding the partition of

Vietnam, pending the 1956 elections. Other nations at the conference—China, Laos and Cambodia—endorsed the conditions verbally. An international commission was set up to monitor violations of the agreement, with Canada representing the West, Poland the Communists and India the neutral nations. They were to guarantee that the French withdrew from the south, that the Vietminh went north and that no outside powers interfered in the region.

By underwriting more than 75 percent of France's military expenses, the United States had spent as much as $2 billion to keep the French in Indochina. All the same, Foster Dulles would not sign the treaty. He agreed only to "note" its terms. Dulles committed the United States to diplomatic relations with Bao Dai's government in the south but refused the same recognition to Ho. And he made headlines around the world by refusing to shake the hand extended to him by Zhou Enlai.

The Vietminh delegates looked on sourly, aware that Dulles should have grasped Zhou's hand and wrung it in gratitude. Pham Van Dong summed up their view of Zhou's performance at Geneva: "He has double crossed us."

TWO

DIEM
1960

B AO DAI WOULD BE no match in skill or character for Ho Chi Minh, and the Americans knew it. For Vietnam's former emperor, the eight years since he left Hanoi had been barren and humiliating. Early in his exile in Hong Kong, he told his volunteer equerry to get a job to support himself. Young Bui had acquired the nickname "Tommy." He went to work in a local bank, and the two men shared an apartment in a neighborhood called Happy Valley. The American satirist S. J. Perelman, on a world tour, reported an encounter with Bao Dai in a Hong Kong nightclub. Perelman was also introduced to Bui, whom he described as "a silky party," and he ridiculed Tommy's attempts to present the emperor as a man of substance. "Backbiters were saying that he went to the movies every afternoon," Perelman wrote, quoting Bui. "If he did, it was only in an attempt to improve his English."

As their war had dragged on, the French lured Bao Dai back to Vietnam with promises of greater independence but never fulfilled them. By the 1950s, Bui had moved to Saigon and gone to work for the Paramount Pictures distributor and then for a government minister's import-export business. Bao Dai heard that he was in Saigon and summoned him to Gia Long Palace, named for the founder of the Nguyen dynasty. Their reunion did not go well.

Bao Dai asked, in French, "What are you doing these days?"

"Working for a living, sire."

Bao Dai proposed commissioning Bui as a captain in the French army.

"For what, sire?"

"To crush the enemy—the Communists."

"I don't see any enemy right now, sire, except the French."

As he left, Bui was sure that his remark had made Bao Dai feel more guilty than angry. The emperor retreated to his estate in the mountains of Ban Me Thuot, where he hunted tigers and dallied with young women. When he overheard one of them being mocked as a prostitute, Bao Dai objected. "She is only plying her trade," the emperor said. "I'm the real whore."

By the time of the 1954 conference, Tommy Bui and Bao Dai had reconciled and gone together to Geneva for the duration of the talks. Every day, they shared a taxi to the conference room, but once inside, Bao Dai remained a passive observer. When he bought a house in Cannes, nothing luxurious, word spread that he was living in a château, on the scale of Egypt's deposed King Farouk. Bui also moved to Cannes after studying law in Paris and spent his evenings with the former emperor. By then, they shared a new bond—Bao Dai had taken up with Bui's father's former mistress. The emperor's wife and five children lived in his two-story home, but he preferred the nearby villa where he had installed his mistress. Nights, Bao Dai went to the Cannes casino and allowed the manager to point him out to other patrons. With money scarce, Bao Dai chain-smoked, drank coffee but never liquor, and put down $2 bets at the roulette table. Occasionally, he would meet with a French or Vietnamese politician and afterward seemed to have a bit of spending money, but he never wanted Bui present during those transactions.

Foreign pressure led Bao Dai to appoint a nationalist named Ngo Dinh Diem as his prime minister. That done, the former emperor withdrew even further from politics. When journalists visited him in Cannes, he turned the talk to soccer. Tommy Bui occasionally challenged him on the way Diem in Saigon was usurping his power. Bao Dai retreated further into an unbreachable silence.

WITH BAO DAI a weak reed, Washington had to invest its hopes in Prime Minister Diem. Although their temperaments were incompatible, the two men had known each other for more than two decades, from the time Diem once served as Bao Dai's minister of the interior. Vietnam's emperors were always Buddhists, but for three hundred years French and Portuguese missionaries had been converting Vietnamese commoners to the Roman Catholic religion, not without resistance. In 1864, Emperor Tu Duc had been worldly enough to suggest exchanging emissaries with Abraham Lincoln in Washington, and yet he denounced Catholicism as nothing more than a cloak for Western infiltration of his kingdom. Diem's family had been among the Catholic converts, and he grew up as the third of six sons in a devout northern family. When he left Bao Dai's government in his early thirties, it was because he was as frustrated as the emperor by France's refusal to permit reform. But as Bao Dai retreated to the Côte d'Azur, Diem's nature steered him to a different kind of exile.

Ngo Dinh Diem visits Ban Me Thuot as premier in 1955 *(AP/Wide World Photos)*

A portly and retiring bachelor, Diem did not feel a religious calling, although the monastic life held a strong attraction for him. Before the Japanese occupation, he had lived in Hue with his mother and a younger brother, going to mass every morning and passing his days in hunting or developing photographs in his darkroom. Diem had met with Giap for private talks before Giap joined the Communist Party, but their ideological chasm was already too wide for them to unite against the French.

Over the years, as the French and later the Japanese used Bao Dai to give a show of legitimacy to their regimes, the emperor made new and futile overtures to Diem. While Bao Dai's standing sank from his willingness to collaborate, the decades of foreign occupation left Diem's reputation unscathed.

By the end of the Second World War, Ho could attest personally to how unshakable Diem's anti-Communism had become. At the time the French were shutting down Bao Dai's academy in September 1945, the Vietminh captured Diem and sent him to a camp just south of the Chinese border. During his six months as a prisoner, Diem contracted a near-fatal case of malaria and survived only to learn that the Vietminh had shot to death an older brother and a nephew. When Diem was brought to Hanoi as part of Ho's attempt to recruit respected

Vietnamese nationalists for his government, Diem's grief formed the backdrop for their interview.

Arriving under guard, Diem was indignant when Ho offered him a high position. "You are a criminal who has burned and destroyed the country," Diem said, "and you have held me prisoner."

Ho apologized. In a war for independence, he said, mistakes were sometimes made. But the welfare of the people outweighed those errors. "You have grievances against us, but let's forget them."

Diem asked how he could forget his brother's death at the hands of the Vietminh.

"I knew nothing of it," Ho said. "I had nothing to do with your brother's death. I deplore such excesses as much as you do."

Diem said that his brother and his son were only two of the hundreds killed by the Communists and the hundreds more betrayed by them. "How can you dare to invite me to work with you?"

Ho responded with the philosophy that had sustained him through his own years of privation and pain. "Your mind is focused on the past," he chided Diem. "Think of the future—education, improved standards of living for the people."

Diem revealed the stubbornness he masked with a bland formality. He, too, would work toward those goals, he said, but not because of pressure from the Vietminh. "I am a free man," Diem told Ho. "I shall always be a free man. Look me in the face. Am I a man who fears oppression or death?"

"You are a free man."

Ho proved it. The next morning, he allowed Diem to rise at 6 A.M. and walk out of Hanoi. Other Vietminh leaders disapproved of Ho's impulsive clemency. They sentenced Diem to death in absentia and made attempts to assassinate him. When Diem appealed to the French authorities for protection, he was told that no police were available to guard him. In August 1950, he chose exile.

Diem traveled through Europe, stopping in Rome for an audience with the pope before alighting at various Maryknoll seminaries along America's East Coast. Wesley Fishel, a Michigan State University professor familiar with Vietnam, introduced Diem to New York's Francis Cardinal Spellman, who in turn brought him together with politicians in Washington. Two were fellow Catholics—Senator Mike Mansfield and Representative John Kennedy.

Diem was not the only candidate for prime minister under Bao Dai, and the French considered him hostile to their business interests, which they expected to survive the change in government. The names the French put forward could be dismissed as collaborators, however, and the one serious alternative to Diem, Dr. Nguyen Ngoc Bich, had his own liabilities. Although not a Communist himself, Bich had fought with the Vietminh, and his father was prominent in the Cao Dai, an eclectic sect that revered Confucius, Buddha, Jesus, Joan of Arc and Victor Hugo. Despite a medical degree, Bich could seem so mystical that Diem looked hard-headed and practical to the Vietnamese colony in Paris and to Foster Dulles, who saw that he would be dependably anti-Communist.

DESPITE THEIR BITTERNESS over the Geneva agreement, the members of Hanoi's Politburo were taking its terms seriously. As the French withdrew, the Communists called many of the Vietminh troops north, past the 17th parallel, to wait out the two years until the elections for unification. Some veterans of Dien Bien Phu, including Dang Vu Hiep, the regimental political commander during the siege, were sent directly to Moscow to study at the military institute named for Lenin. Going to the Soviet Union had been his dream and Hiep was ecstatic.

Other Vietminh faced the more prosaic prospect of leaving their families behind in Hue or the Mekong Delta and going off to a kind of exile in North Vietnam until after the promised elections. Partings were often tearful, with dutiful husband and grieving wife each holding up two fingers, not in a victory salute but as a reminder that they would be separated for only two years.

Each sector in the Delta was told to send a number of its regular troops to the north, but the local leadership could choose which Vietminh would make the trip. When one of Miss Dung's brothers was selected, his wife could have joined him, but their son was only three years old and she decided to wait out the two years until her husband returned. Dung, who believed in the good faith behind the accords, went to Hanoi, where she was assigned to buoying up the refugees' morale until they could go home again.

The resettlement was especially bitter for a man named Nguyen Minh Vy, another member of the revolutionary class of 1945. Vy had spent the last six years living in the Fifth Zone, those four coastal provinces south of Hue that were controlled by the Vietminh. French troops had been stationed at bases in the mountains to the west, but Ho's support among the civilian population ran so high that the soldiers seldom contested the whole vast area. Occasionally, Vietminh troops in the zone might shoot down a French plane, but for the most part the French were safe in their highland camps, attended by the montagnards. On paper, Pham Van Dong in Hanoi was responsible for the zone, but Vy gradually assumed more duties until he became its unofficial governor.

Despite the fighting elsewhere in the country, Vy had found the early 1950s rewarding. He governed what amounted to a country within a country—arranging to supply civilians with food, waging campaigns against illiteracy, overseeing the crops and keeping the trains running through the 300 kilometers of railroad in his zone. Vy's family, old and proud, had always resisted the French, and he felt that now he was giving his countrymen a taste of independence.

Vy was miserable when he learned that his zone would be required to ship 100,000 Vietminh—including some women and children—from the 3 million population in the four provinces. Staying behind until the last day of the time limit imposed in Geneva, he faced a barrage of questions from his constituents: "If we won the war, why must we be the ones to leave?" "Why should we give in to Diem? Who can believe in him?" That last was a particular challenge to Vy. As a teenager during Diem's brief service under Bao Dai before World War II, Vy had been captured and imprisoned by government police.

All the same, he argued against his heart and assured the doubters that the entire world would uphold the accords. Farewell followed painful farewell until the morning when he himself had to make the one-day boat trip north. Setting out on a final inspection, he found the early morning streets eerily quiet. Most people who would be sailing on the Polish ship *Kilinski* were staying indoors to weep and pray. A girl of ten appeared, caught at Vy's elbow, threw her arms around him and begged him to stay. He chided her mildly. "Don't you understand yet?"

"I can't accept it," the child said. "I have seen the years of resistance when the elders didn't leave. But if you go now, the enemy will come."

Vy promised her that the enemy had all returned to France. Then he pulled away and headed for the ship. It was already August 15, 1955. He told himself that he would be back in even less time than the two fingers being raised along the pier.

LIKE FOSTER DULLES, Ngo Dinh Diem had distanced himself from the Geneva agreement. He considered its terms a betrayal of his life's struggle and, as prime minister, refused to commit his new government to honoring them. Dulles went further. He had decided that the threat posed by China and North Vietnam must be met by an alliance of anti-Communist nations. NATO—the North Atlantic Treaty Organization—was effectively checking Soviet expansion in Europe. Now a Southeast Asia Treaty Organization would unite several unlikely allies— Great Britain and France from Europe, Pakistan and the Philippines in the East. Australia and New Zealand were also invited to join, even though their immigration policies barred Asians from their shores. SEATO's sole representative from Southeast Asia was Thailand.

Dean Rusk was by then president of the Rockefeller Foundation, but, looking on from New York, he considered the new pact a mistake. Only half-joking, Rusk said he could analyze U.S. policy by charting Dulles's travels. Whenever Dulles left Washington, Eisenhower's native caution reined in any American adventurism. But when Dulles came home, U.S. policy went on the offensive again. Rusk did agree with Dulles that Southeast Asia was strategically important to the United States. And since Rusk also considered Ho a Communist dedicated to controlling Laos and Cambodia as well as Vietnam, he favored sending both military and economic aid to Indochina. But the SEATO treaty involved more than aid. Its terms pledged the United States to defend South Vietnam, Laos and Cambodia against armed attack, and Rusk thought that commitment went too far. He watched disapprovingly as the treaty, with scant debate, cleared the Senate by a vote of 82 to 1.

At the Pentagon, support for the new treaty was more guarded. The Joint Chiefs did not want to assume responsibility for training South Vietnam troops until they were convinced that Diem had created a sound government. But Dulles, not traveling at the time, persuaded Eisenhower that the best way to make South Vietnam stable was first to build up Diem's army.

ONCE DIEM WAS NAMED prime minister, he threw together a staff, scooping up educated anti-Communists wherever he found them. One of his early recruits was a tiny man hardly larger than a child, with a child's bashful smile but a coroner's eyes. Dr. Tran Kim Tuyen, not yet thirty, was a northern Catholic with both law and medical degrees from the French faculties in Hanoi. Although he was keenly ambitious, Tuyen was all too aware of his provincial accent and the way he stumbled over long and unfamiliar words. As a student, he had demonstrated against France's control over Vietnam's Catholic clergy, which got him in trouble with the police. But his religion inoculated him against Ho's nationalist appeal.

While Tuyen was still in school, one of Diem's younger brothers sought to travel secretly from Hanoi to a safely Catholic district along the Laotian border. To avoid the Vietminh, a priest asked Tuyen to lead the way on his bicycle while the brother, Ngo Dinh Nhu, followed over the jungle paths in a cyclo, a seat attached to the front of another bicycle. When they reached the enclave, Tuyen was impressed by how warmly the local Catholic hierarchy greeted this member of the Ngo family. That had been 1946, and Tuyen began to wonder whether he might have a career in politics, leading the way for men more glib and wellborn than he.

By mid-June 1954, the Geneva agreement left many Vietnamese Catholics with no heart for fighting the Communists any longer. Not equipped to challenge the Vietminh, they began moving south, where they could join Prime Minister Diem. Tuyen at the time was serving in an outlying province as a military surgeon, but each weekend he left his post to go courting in Hanoi. He was at his sweetheart's apartment—French nuns at her school called her "Jackie"—when her brother-in-law burst in to say that if Tuyen would leave at that very moment, he could fly south on the prime minister's plane.

A calculating young man, Tuyen resented the rash decision being forced on him. He would be leaving with the clothes on his back and one change of trousers. All the same, he hurried to the door and turned to ask Jackie, "If I go south now, will you join me there?" Her family included many members of the Vietminh, but Jackie accepted that oblique marriage proposal.

As Tuyen climbed onto an old military plane, he was dazzled by how formally Diem's entourage was dressed. The prime minister himself wore a white sharkskin suit, and Tuyen crept aboard feeling like a schoolboy. During the flight to Saigon, however, Diem left his seat and asked Tuyen to slide over so he could join him. Groping for words, the prime minister struck Tuyen as awkward at small talk but painfully sincere. Diem got quickly to the point. "My brother, Mr. Nhu, is already working in South Vietnam to create an organization to help me in my mission," Diem said. "I have heard that you know a lot of intellectuals in the north."

Tuyen explained that he had given up political organizing years ago. Diem overrode that objection and asked if he would help in South Vietnam.

Tuyen said, "Yes, Prime Minister."

When they reached Saigon, Tuyen was invited to live in the prime minister's palace, which sounded grand but reflected no luxury. Along with Diem's private secretary and a few army officers, Tuyen slept each night on the carpet of an antechamber. Diem's office and bedroom were nearby, and from time to time he dropped by to offer stilted greetings.

On July 7, 1954, Diem officially took over a government that did not, in fact, exist. His cabinet appointees were inexperienced, and the French were undercutting him, hoping to install a leader less hostile to their colonial history. Bao Dai retained for himself the power to appoint men to high office but still refused to come to Saigon. The head of the South Vietnamese army was reported to be planning a coup d'état, and three powerful and well-armed religious sects were threatening to bring down Diem with a civil war.

AGAINST THAT FORMIDABLE ARRAY of enemies, Prime Minister Diem could boast only one new friend, but because that man was a U.S. Air Force officer named Edward Lansdale, the odds on his survival improved considerably. Lansdale, at forty-eight, had already promoted himself into something of a spy-business legend. Born in Ohio, raised in Los Angeles, he had scraped along before World War II as a clever but erratic advertising executive in Manhattan, handling the Levi Strauss account. After the Japanese attacked Pearl Harbor, the army was slow in activating Lansdale's ROTC commission from UCLA since he was already thirty-five and suffering from an enlarged thyroid. When he was finally assigned to military intelligence, Lansdale's file was marked "For limited service only."

But he ingratiated himself with "Wild Bill" Donovan, who arranged for Lansdale to serve officially in the army but work for the OSS. At the war's end, Lansdale was sent as an intelligence officer to the Philippines. "Filipinos and I fell in love with each other," Lansdale recalled.

Lansdale had none of a spy's traditional skills. He never managed to qualify as a marksman on an army rifle range, and he was tone deaf to foreign languages. But the islands proved to be hospitable to his freewheeling manner. Under a beaky nose, Lansdale's black brush mustache waggled in a seemingly artless grin, and he charmed villagers by playing his harmonica. *The Ugly American*, a popular novel of the 1950s based on his career, gave the same talent to its hero, barely disguised as Colonel Edwin Hillendale, and glorified him as exactly the sort of American who should be administering overseas aid.

In life, however, Lansdale's assignment was to help the Philippine government put down a rebellion by the Hukbalahaps. Washington considered the Huks, like Ho, a threat to U.S. security. Since he couldn't speak his new allies' language, Lansdale got across his message by acting out charades and drawing pictures in the sand. Soon he was claiming that his shortcoming had proved to be an asset. A bilingual interpreter, he said, often lacked empathy, whereas "the look in your eyes and your shoulders and your hands tell a lot when you're really concentrating."

With his closest local contact, Lansdale didn't need sign language. He had singled out Ramón Magsaysay, a Philippine congressman who spoke English, as the man to beat the Huks, and Lansdale sold him both to his nominal army boss and to the man Lansdale actually worked for—Frank Wisner of the Office of Policy Coordination, a U.S. dirty tricks operation developed by the OSS that would soon be folded into the newly created CIA.

When Magsaysay was named secretary of national defense, he and Lansdale became inseparable. Lansdale's wife had tired of his lust for adventure and stayed in Georgetown with their children. After the Huks tried to assassinate Magsaysay, he sent his own wife and children to safety in Bataan and moved into Lansdale's bachelor quarters at the U.S. military compound. The two men worked effectively at reforming a corrupt central government while their guerrilla teams launched military assaults against Huk strongholds in the hills.

Those patrols allowed Lansdale's flair for showmanship to run free. Once, when Filipino soldiers cut off the head of a Huk prisoner, Lansdale snatched it up by the hair and began shouting questions about Huk hideouts. Getting no answer, he slapped its face until the soldiers looking on thought he had gone mad.

"Colonel, Colonel," an officer protested, tugging at Lansdale's sleeve, "it is dead. It cannot talk to you."

"No, you stupid son of a bitch!" Lansdale shouted at him. "Of course, it can't! But it could have, if you hadn't been so fucking stupid as to sever the head from the body."

Using black propaganda, Lansdale persuaded villagers that the Huks planned to massacre all the women and children in any village they overran. More significantly, he and Magsaysay used the Philippine army to oversee the next national election. Filipinos in record numbers rejected their despised government and swept in reform candidates. Little by little, Lansdale and Magsaysay were taking the revolution away from the Huks. "It's not enough to be *against* Communism," Lansdale said regularly. "You have to be *for* something."

Two years later, with the backing of Foster Dulles and his brother, Allen, the

CIA's first director, Ramón Magsaysay was elected president of the Philippines in a landslide. The grateful Dulles brothers dispatched Ed Lansdale to Vietnam, expecting him to accomplish for Ngo Dinh Diem what he had just achieved so spectacularly in Manila.

LANSDALE KNEW that doing his new job well meant forging close ties with the prime minister, even though Diem's circling enemies had made him suspicious of everyone but his immediate family. His first meeting with Diem started awkwardly. Searching through the corridors of the chaotic palace, Lansdale turned in desperation to a rotund man in a white suit, sitting placidly alone. "Where might I find Prime Minister Diem?" Lansdale asked.

The man replied, "I am Diem."

Lansdale had come prepared with notes on ways to help Diem govern more effectively. Since Diem didn't speak much English and Lansdale spoke nothing else, an information officer from the American embassy translated Lansdale's suggestions into French. Diem listened and nodded.

Within three weeks, Diem found Lansdale congenial enough to ask that he move into the palace. Bacause Lansdale remained officially a colonel in the Air Force, he had to refuse. But he responded at night to Diem's frequent summons to the palace for long, one-sided conversations and sympathized, more than Tuyen did, with Diem's craving for formality. However late the hour, Lansdale arrived at the palace in full uniform.

By then, legions of U.S. experts were flying to Saigon to offer Diem conflicting advice on how to pull together his inchoate country. The night before their audience with him, they often denigrated Diem at a Saigon dinner party. Or afterward they commiserated in bars and restaurants about the excruciating boredom of his monologues. Diem might command only tenuous loyalty throughout his nation, but he had an abundance of spies. The disparagement by American visitors reached him promptly, and he observed that it never came from Lansdale. Indeed, Lansdale's liking for Diem went beyond any instructions from Washington. He had concluded that Diem was a gentle man with, if you listened for it, a subtle humor. He might talk until dawn but only because his interests were so broad—not merely politics but education, agriculture, philosophy.

Gradually, Lansdale met Diem's relatives. With their oldest brother slain by the Vietminh, Confucian tradition anointed Ngo Dinh Thuc as the head of the Ngo family; Thuc was also Vietnam's Catholic archbishop. But Lansdale realized that Diem depended most heavily on a younger brother, Ngo Dinh Nhu, and Nhu's glamorous wife. Another brother, Ngo Dinh Can, who lived with their mother in Hue, treated central Vietnam as his fiefdom. The youngest and most worldly of Diem's brothers, Ngo Dinh Luyen, was abroad, representing Vietnam in London. Diem tended to keep ambassadorships in the family.

Madame Nhu's father headed the embassy in Washington, and her mother served as South Vietnam's observer at the United Nations.

Lansdale's weeks of listening to Diem with mute sympathy had won him Diem's trust or, at the least, had neutralized his distrust. When the prime minister invited Lansdale to a family dinner with the Ngos, the political wizard of the Philippines seemed poised for another triumph.

By now, TRAN KIM TUYEN had spent nearly two months in the palace with no job, taking his meals in the kitchen and alternating his two pair of trousers. Diem's secretary of state worked at a small table in a nearby corridor, and he looked up one day as Tuyen walked by.

"The prime minister has asked me to find a job for you," the man said. "There's the Ministry of Education and Information. Could you go there?"

"That's okay," Tuyen said, pleased at a chance to improve the government's propaganda.

By that time, more than 800,000 North Vietnamese, most of them Catholic, had fled to the south, assisted by the U.S. Seventh Fleet. Tuyen's first assignment at the ministry was to get them settled, often against their will. Once they arrived in Saigon, the refugees were insisting on staying even though they were clogging the city. Diem's government could not persuade them to spread out to undeveloped areas in the countryside. The northerners argued that they had made a great sacrifice in leaving their homes and now Diem should house and feed them amid the comforts of Saigon. After marveling for years at the effectiveness of Communist propaganda, Tuyen was eager to experiment with tricks of his own. He shipped several old people to a Saigon refugee camp and directed the police to arrest them very noisily. Tuyen then printed their photographs on posters and pamphlets throughout the south, labeling them Communist agents who had been sent to South Vietnam to campaign against being evacuated from Saigon.

It was entirely Tuyen's concoction. The old folk had no Communist connections. But the ruse served to break up the resistance. Soon Diem's agents could label anyone who insisted on staying in Saigon either a Communist or a dupe, and refugees heeded the exhortation to launch their new life in the countryside.

Tuyen's next target was a clandestine nationalist magazine circulating anti-American sentiments among Saigon's intellectuals. When a few readers were caught with the magazine, Tuyen took their copies to the Ministry of Education's printing service, where he duplicated the magazine's format, substituting articles with Communist propaganda written in turgid Marxist jargon. The same undercover agents who had been suppressing the magazine then went to work distributing Tuyen's version. After two of Tuyen's fake issues, the magazine was tarred as Communist, and its true editors stopped publication.

□

IN SOUTH VIETNAM's fragmented society, however, the threat to Diem's authority was coming less from the Communists than from the religious sects that had flourished under French rule. In the 1920s, lower-ranking civil servants had flocked to the new religion that looked to a spirit named Cao Dai as a guide to the universe. The French Sûreté had kept Cao Daists under surveillance, along with followers of another new religion, the Hoa Hao. But neither group had seemed to attract active rebels against France, and the Hoa Hao resented the Vietminh for assassinating their leader in 1947. Yet, both groups, along with gangsters from the Binh Xuyen sect, wanted to wrest power from Diem and his Catholic followers. At one point, Tuyen was ousted from his job when Cao Daists succeeded in taking over his ministry. By that time, Jackie had come south with her savings from teaching in Hanoi, and the newlyweds could scrape by while Tuyen finagled to get back on the government payroll.

In the meantime, he took to hanging about the offices of a magazine called *Xa Hoi*, or "Society," published by Diem's brother Nhu and his wife. With her delicate features, flirtatious manner and tiny but voluptuous figure, Madame Nhu's Vietnamese name seemed to suit her—Tran Le Xuan, or "Beautiful Spring."

Mme. Nhu's family had made its fortune under the French and sent her to a lycée in Hanoi where she perfected her French but never learned to write in Vietnamese. Married for ten years, she and Nhu were working together to spread their alternative to either French colonialism or Ho's Vietminh. An offshoot of Christianity, it was called *nhan vi*, which translated as "personalism." While studying in France, Nhu had embraced the philosophy, which emphasized the dignity of the individual above any claim by the state. Nhu was convinced that personalism could be an appealing alternative to Communism, but whenever he tried to explain it, his convoluted and mystical language baffled potential converts.

Tuyen found Nhu more sympathetic than his brother, although Diem had the greater energy. Tuyen saw a look of depletion in Nhu's triangular face, as though he were worn out by the ideas constantly doing battle in his brain. Nhu, at fifty, was twenty years older than Tuyen, who turned him into an idealized older brother, one he would work strenuously to please.

Besides editing his magazine, Nhu had formed a worker's party—the Revolutionary Personalists—with a long Vietnamese name that got shortened to Can Lao. Nhu kept it a secret organization, and because the Ngo family trusted only their fellow religionists, Catholics dominated the Can Lao leadership. Tuyen was put to work writing the party's rules.

ED LANSDALE WAS IRRITATED by Diem's support for his brother's Can Lao party, since its clandestine nature worked against the open democracy Lansdale envisioned for South Vietnam. Yet in fighting Hanoi, Lansdale could tolerate any

Ngo Dinh Nhu
(AP/Wide World Photos)

number of secret operations. He ordered his deputy, Major Lucien Conein, to develop a paramilitary cadre in the north. As a cover, Conein, who had fought with the French resistance in Tonkin against the Japanese, enrolled his agents in a French refugee program. Their true mission was to destroy Hanoi's printing presses and to contaminate the oil supply of the city's buses. Even though none of Lansdale's saboteurs had much success, he trumpeted their effectiveness to Washington with an adman's fervor.

Lansdale was also using U.S. funds to bribe the South's religious sects into supporting Diem. In civilian clothes, he went to the mountain hideout of the Cao Dai military leader and persuaded him to accept a brigadier general's commission in Diem's regular army. In return for switching sides, the new general received $3.6 million. Reasonable estimates put Lansdale's total outlay to the sects at $12 million, but he shrugged off the accusations of bribery. The money, he said, was simply "back pay."

Lansdale's resourcefulness did not end with his checkbook. When he heard that Diem's army chief of staff, General Nguyen Van Hinh, was plotting a coup. Lansdale invited Hinh's two top aides on a junket to the Philippines and found ways to keep them amused until the danger passed.

Quelling the Binh Xuyen gang—swollen with profits from gambling, prostitution and extortion—posed the hardest test. For years, Bao Dai had protected its leaders and allowed them to carry weapons. When Diem declared war on the cult, most Americans on the scene were betting he would lose. But Lansdale backed the crackdown, and after several days of fierce gunplay in downtown Saigon, Diem's army routed the Binh Xuyen troops. Until that success, Eisenhower had been poised to replace Diem with a more forceful nationalist. The outcome convinced him that Diem might rise to his challenge.

Lansdale's admiring dispatches to Washington about Diem omitted one point. So far, none of his military victories had been against Communist troops. They had all come at the expense of anti-Communist factions in South Vietnam. All the same, Diem's triumphs emboldened him and his American advisers to force a showdown with the absentee emperor. On October 23, 1955, the South Vietnamese were presented ballots with a clear choice: monarchy under Bao Dai or a republic with Diem as president.

Ngo Dinh Nhu indicated he was ready to stuff the ballot boxes. Lansdale cautioned against any irregularities but drew on his advertising expertise to recommend that Diem print his own ballots in red, the color of happiness, and Bao Dai's in green, the color of a cuckold. While Diem accepted that scheme, he also turned his brother loose at the polls. Nhu's agents told voters to throw away the green ballots. Those who disobeyed by remaining loyal to the emperor were often beaten.

The referendum provided Diem with an epic victory. Nationally, his total reached 98 percent. In Saigon, he did even better. His 605,025 votes were one-third more than the number of the city's registered voters. Three days after the election, Diem announced the creation of the Republic of Vietnam with himself as its president.

WHEN HO HAD SET ABOUT redistributing North Vietnam's farmland in 1954, he looked to his powerful northern neighbor as a model, even though revolutions in the two countries had been as different as the men who led them. Mao Zedong had come to power without being imprisoned or starved by his enemies, and he claimed to oppose torture. Yet his followers had swept over China's farmland with a vengeance. Calling their crusade the "settling accounts movement," they seized farms from China's 35 million landowners and turned them into cooperatives. Within two years of the early 1950s, at least 2 million landlords had been executed—possibly twice that number. Nor was Mao's cadre always satisfied with confiscation. They might heat iron rods over open fires and sear a landlord until he revealed where he had hidden his gold.

To oversee land redistribution in North Vietnam, Ho appointed the Politburo's most ardent Maoist, Dang Xuan Khu, who had fought alongside the Chinese and had adopted a name to reflect that proud achievement. He became Truong Chinh, which meant "Long March." A small man, Chinh was conspicuous among fellow revolutionaries for his fastidious appearance and for theoretical writings that were severe, even pompous. Colleagues considered him impractical, with little political acumen. The striking contrast of his neat appear-

Truong Chinh in the early 1950s
(Vietnam News Agency)

ance with the disheveled southern leader Le Duan seemed to confirm which of them was the man of action.

In the early days of World War II, when the party was being devastated, Chinh had become acting secretary general and moved Communist headquarters to a village near Hanoi, where the French police network was ineffectual. By the time of the land reform, Ho was nominally in charge, but, despite his temperamental shortcomings, Chinh became its actual chief. As his Chinese advisers steered him down their own violent path, Chinh was initially reluctant but gave in. At his direction, the Vietminh treated landowners brutally and swelled the flow of refugees to Diem in the South. After the more than 800,000 northerners had gone, Chinh was finding their departure a mixed blessing. They had left behind land that he could now parcel out to the Vietminh. But the exodus had also cut badly into rice production and produced much the same shortages that the Vietminh had faced during their brief exercise of power in 1945. This time, Chinh averted famine only by importing Burmese rice that was underwritten by the Soviet Union.

Chinh's rules for land redistribution were complicated but inflexible. He spurred on his *can-bo*, or cadres, to be ruthless in dividing the population into five categories from landlord down to "agricultural worker," a euphemism for "peasant." Every village felt Chinh's repression, even when the difference between its biggest and smallest tract of land was no more than a quarter of an acre.

Chinh's lieutenants trained thousands of young Communists in sessions ending with the shout "Down with the landlords!" Students whose parents owned land were forced to write sixty-page confessions of the ways their families had abused peasants. If they couldn't recall examples, they invented histories of flogging and rape. Meanwhile, Chinh's tribunals sentenced to death many farmers who scarcely qualified as landlords. Even supporting the Vietminh in the past offered no sure protection.

Many farmers who had taken up arms for independence balked at having their small farms absorbed into state cooperatives. When chores they had once done willingly for themselves—spreading manure, shoring up dikes—were neglected, production declined further. A party newspaper described a "Comrade Chiem," who had fought bravely against the French but was reluctant to join his local cooperative. Rather than accept the low government prices, men like Chiem were peddling rice and meat on the black market. Still others were selling off their family paddies and water buffalo before they could be seized by the state. By 1956, with the July 20 deadline approaching for the referendum to unite the country, North Vietnam was in turmoil.

IN THE SOUTH, Diem's land program had also misfired. His government tried to win support by lowering to 25 percent the maximum that landlords could take from the crops as rent; the traditional figure had been 50 percent. But in the years before 1954, the Vietminh had distributed land in the south to hundreds of thousands of farmers. Those families, who had become tenant farmers again, did not regard Diem's law as relief but as inflicting an old burden. Worse, Diem's law required them to pay back rent for the past ten years on land they had been farming for nothing.

When Diem refused to hold the 1956 referendum, Washington supported his decision. Senator John Kennedy blamed Hanoi: "Neither the United States nor Free Vietnam," he said, "is ever going to be a party to an election obviously stacked and subverted in advance, urged upon us by those who have already broken their own pledges under the agreement they now seek to enforce."

Britain and the Soviet Union, as cochairmen in Geneva two years earlier, agreed that maintaining the cease-fire in Vietnam was the ranking priority and that elections could be postponed. As for the International Control Commission, Diem ignored its protests; he had already accused its members of spying for Hanoi.

In Hanoi, the Politburo saw Diem's decision as Geneva's final betrayal. But while the Communist world painted Diem and Foster Dulles as the villains, some northerners admitted that their regime was poorly prepared to absorb South Vietnam with its many competing loyalties. Even in Ho's birthplace, farmers had risen up to protest the land policies of their native son. Giap's troops cracked down by opening fire and killing farmers by the thousands.

The bloodshed was a particular reproach to Truong Chinh, since it came at a time when China was enjoying a brief political relaxation. In Beijing, the party's propagandists quoted Mao's poetry to signify an end to intellectual repression. "Let a hundred flowers bloom," wall posters proclaimed. "Let a hundred scholars contend." But in North Vietnam's cities, an urban protest called the Intellectuals' Revolt was crushed instantly, and writers were arrested, their journals shut down. People were made to plead guilty to such crimes as reading the French newspaper Le Monde or listening to jazz broadcasts on the Voice of America.

As early as 1957, Ho was forced to launch a campaign called "Rectification of Errors," an acknowledgment that party leaders should have depended upon persuasion rather than brute strength to launch the cooperative farms. Hanoi's newspapers began to warn that Socialism could not be sold "by sincerity alone" and that workers in the fields were right to expect the state's ideology to produce a better income for them.

One small landowner, speaking for many, reported that he had given up his own farm and returned to the government program because meat coupons were distributed only to members of the cooperatives. Even so, he was now content. "I love living in this village," he said. "My family has lived here for generations. In accordance with ancient custom, my umbilical cord was cut off and buried in local soil, and my father's body is buried here, too. How can anyone leave his native village without regrets?"

By the end of 1959, the worst of the land revolts had ended, and three-fourths of North Vietnam's farmers had joined cooperatives. Ho's admirers absolved him of the killing and imprisonment and blamed instead the cadre who surrounded him. As penance, Ho required Chinh to resign from his post as the party's general secretary and become simply a Politburo member. He also saw to it that Chinh's confession of errors was widely publicized. Even though Giap had distrusted the Chinese methods, he, too, was compelled to apologize publicly for the behavior of his troops. Because the soldiers had seen enemies everywhere, Giap said, they had resorted to cruel methods: "Worse still, torture came to be regarded as a normal process."

Ho had decided that Le Duan, as a southerner, should become the party's general secretary, but there was a complication: besides the wife taken in his youth, Le Duan had married again during his long service in the South. Ho told him that he did not want to see two wives turning up in Hanoi, and Le Duan left the second woman to fight on in the resistance without him.

Gentle, self-effacing, never more ruthless than he needed to be, Ho knew that the men in his government would obey his orders, even when it meant humbling themselves. As he once observed, "What could they possibly do without me? It was I who made them."

☐

As Ho GRAPPLED with securing the north, Tran Kim Tuyen was helping the Ngo family to tighten its grip over the south, proving a loyalty that would soon be generously rewarded. In the spring of 1956, Madame Nhu sought out Tuyen to order him to report to her brother-in-law's office. There, Tuyen found Diem as courteous and aloof as ever.

Looking the young man over from his open shirt to cheap sandals, Diem said: "Try to be better dressed. In a few days, I may be introducing you to the American ambassador."

For a week, Tuyen went everywhere in a pressed jacket and new shoes until the day when Diem called him in to meet Frederick Reinhardt. The American ambassador had prodded Diem into setting up an intelligence service along the lines of the CIA, and Diem had named an elderly mandarin as its nominal head. But that man refused to deal with Americans, and Tuyen was being drafted as his go-between.

After a ceremonial exchange of greetings, Reinhardt said that someone from the embassy would get in touch with Tuyen, and soon the CIA station chief came to call, with an agent named Philip Potter in tow. From then on, Tuyen and Potter met at a CIA safe house, and Tuyen was told to report any decisions they made directly to Ngo Dinh Nhu. Almost at once, the new agency—called Social and Political Services, or SEPES—ran afoul of its American parent. The CIA wanted to prepare for an extended conflict with North Vietnam by sending in agents to infiltrate Ho's government. Nhu and Tuyen sought quicker results by recruiting men for sabotage and propaganda. In the youthful and good-humored Potter, Tuyen felt he had found both ally and friend. But when Potter left Vietnam Tuyen bickered over tactics with his replacement so heatedly that the American stopped working with Tuyen and turned instead to Vietnamese military intelligence officers. As it happened, both approaches at infiltration failed despite the money allotted to them. Whatever their mission, agents who got into North Vietnam were immediately identified and imprisoned or killed.

Ed Lansdale was not part of the debate. He had been recalled to Washington early in 1957, assigned to staff duty at Air Force headquarters in the Pentagon, and Lou Conein had gone to work with a special warfare unit at Fort Bragg. When Magsaysay died in a plane crash in March, Lansdale mourned his friend and the end of his Asian career. But he was pursued by a literary remnant of his Vietnam years: readers who knew of Lansdale assumed incorrectly that he had inspired the title character in a novel set in Saigon during the Eisenhower years. To be identified as Graham Greene's *Quiet American* was no compliment since Pyle, the undercover agent, was smug and dangerous in his ignorance.

Tuyen had not met Lansdale nor had he been briefed on restrictions that the CIA's charter imposed against agency activities within the United States. Tuyen intended to use his expanding network of informants to shape South Vietnam's political life, and when William Colby arrived in 1959 as deputy CIA station chief, he endorsed Tuyen's approach. Tuyen found Colby smoothly polite, if not as expansive as Potter had been.

Colby also proved generous with the funds at his disposal. Tuyen received CIA money to send artists and writers to conferences abroad and to help his political friends in Saigon. The infusion of American money came at a welcome time because Saigon's intelligence operations had become fragmented and competitive. Nhu's critics claimed that he had created thirteen different internal security units, including the Vietnamese Special Forces, who became his personal shock troops. Besides Tuyen's office and the Vietnamese military officers working with the CIA, Nhu set up special sections of the national police to root out Communist infiltration wherever they found it.

One of those police agencies was proving more industrious than the others—the office in Hue run by Diem's brother, Ngo Dinh Can. Its police claimed to have uncovered a honeycomb of Communist cells in central Vietnam and began making massive arrests. Can warned Diem that the Vietminh had infiltrated the south in vast numbers and that only his agents could uproot them. He persuaded Diem and Nhu to allow his agents to set up headquarters in Saigon, but Can refused to let them report to the capital's police since he claimed that their ranks were already riddled with Communists. Tuyen worried that Can was jealous of his growing power and seemed ready to provoke a showdown over whose security agency would prevail. As Tuyen knew, no outsider would ever win against a member of the Ngo family. He responded with a show of obsequious cooperation, arranging office space for Can's men in a former French compound and rounding up cars and typewriters for their use.

FROM THE NORTH, Ho's Politburo watched in alarm as agents of the Ngo brothers set out on a campaign of torture and terror in southern cities. The Vietminh who stayed in the Mekong Delta after 1954 had wrapped their weapons in plastic and buried them in the paddies. Now Diem's men were persecuting those veterans and their families. As early as 1956, Nguyen Minh Vy in Hanoi was hearing of atrocities by Diem's soldiers, who bragged over government radio and in the Saigon newspapers about their crackdown on Vietminh survivors. The details could be gory, including boasts by Diem's troops that they were cutting off Communist heads.

Former Vietminh were not the only victims. In 1943, at the age of seventeen, Dr. Tran Bach Dang had joined the Communist Party but was presently living quietly in the South as a nonpartisan historian. Traveling in Vinh Long province, Dang saw a farmer arguing with soldiers from the local military post. As Dang watched, the soldiers seized the man, cut off his head and demonstrated their contempt by playing soccer on the grass with the head as their ball.

That sort of cruelty, combined with indiscriminate arrests and torture, were driving uncommitted Vietnamese into a new resistance against Diem. His officers were labeling as Communist sympathizers any family that had fought the French or was related to a Vietminh. In the Delta, rape became a commonplace, broken legs the price for resisting interrogation. After what he had seen in Vinh Loc, Dang could believe other lurid stories that were circulating in the South—that a policeman had cut out a woman's gall bladder, for example, to prove somehow that he had killed a Communist.

With Diem treating the Vietminh routinely as traitors, they turned for help to the North. One old farmer summed up his dilemma to a foreign journalist: "If a son is mistreated by his father, he may adopt another." As that adopted father, Ho was being pushed to respond by insistent calls from South Vietnam's Communist chief. Three or four years older than Giap, Le Duan had spent seven years in French jails before joining Ho in China in the 1940s. Although he stayed behind in the South, he had no confidence in the Geneva accords. Watching families make the two-finger gesture of quick unification, Le Duan muttered, "Two years? More like twenty!"

Most of Hanoi's leaders were educated men and often from wealthy families. Among themselves, they mocked Le Duan for his central Vietnamese accent, which they considered coarse and often unintelligible. They also ridiculed him for an early job as a railway attendant. But in the South, his commitment had made his rugged physique as familiar and nearly as revered as Ho's frail one, and southerners were calling him the soul of their resistance. Marshaling the unorganized Vietminh left behind in the South, Le Duan's Delta cadre formed them into fighting squads.

At its Fifteenth Plenum in January 1959, the Politburo heard Le Duan's impassioned plea on behalf of his fellow southerners: Our people are suffering terribly. They can no longer stand by and let Diem's army hunt them down and murder them. They must rise up. And if we do not lead them, they will form their own resistance and we will become irrelevant.

The Politburo responded with Resolution 15, which raised the military struggle in the South to the same status as the existing political effort. The leadership authorized a secret mission to the South to bring arms and other supplies for waging war. Called Group 559 and led by a North Vietnamese colonel, its 40 volunteers had to be physically fit and preferably unmarried. They traveled down the Truong Son Route, which Westerners called the Ho Chi Minh Trail, and came back convinced that the southerners were ready to fight.

While that inspection tour was under way, Diem approved measures that guaranteed his subjects would continue to suffer. In May 1959, he signed Law 10/59, which restored the French guillotine to Vietnam. Diem's men roamed the countryside with mobile equipment for beheading Communists and those accused of stealing farm equipment or water buffalo. Diem's law denied the right of appeal to anyone convicted by those traveling military courts.

Le Duan in 1950
(Vietnam News Agency)

ON JANUARY 26, 1960, three companies of the newly formed rebel army attacked Diem's 32nd Regiment. About to become officially the Politburo's party secretary, Le Duan was willing to take the risk that too many setbacks for the Saigon government might lead the Americans to intervene with their own troops.

The resistance forces did not yet have a name, and they were led by Nguyen Huu Xuyen, a former Vietminh with no official rank. The battle site he chose was seven kilometers north of the Delta's Tay Ninh City, on the way to the Cambodian border. Since this was to be the rebels' first engagement, Xuyen called the site by its old French name, "Two Tour Base." Xuyen's men attacked at 12:30 A.M. while most of the Saigon troops were asleep. Three hours later, they withdrew, taking with them the post's weapons and ammunition. To the rebels, those hours had transformed the struggle against Diem from political to military.

Xuyen's companies — the 60th, 70th and 80th — added up to fewer than 300 men, against almost 1,700 of Diem's troops. But the casualty ratio was the opposite: fifteen of the revolutionaries killed and 20 wounded, compared with scores killed among the Saigon troops and as many as 500 wounded, 200 seriously. Xuyen released his captives as his unit withdrew; he had no capacity to hold prisoners.

The element of surprise had been important but did not entirely explain Xuyen's victory. More significantly, he had been informed about every detail of the post's security measures by the 200 of Diem's men who were also Xuyen's double agents.

□

BUOYED BY THAT MILITARY SUCCESS, southerners in March 1960 called for the anti-Diem forces to rise up at once and overthrow him. That was moving too fast for Hanoi. On March 28, the Politburo's Regional Committee for the South, which had been set up to oversee all resistance activity in South Vietnam, denounced the recent forays as unauthorized by Resolution 15. Southerners were told to avoid terrorism and violence, which could drive non-Communist Vietnamese into the camp of Diem and his American backers.

But the optimism of Group 559 had led to creation of two more units— Group 759 to send the southerners supplies by sea, and Group 959 to furnish new equipment to the Communists in Laos. Since the north wanted to appear to be respecting the six-year-old Geneva agreement, Hanoi's participation had to be secret. And Ho was once again insisting on patience. The time was not ripe, he said, for a full-scale uprising against Diem.

Without advocating total insurrection, however, Le Duan stepped up the campaign to attack Diem's soldiers and police. With his blessing, the rebels assassinated Diem's provincial officials, often the Catholic appointees considered especially cruel, or effective.

FOR THE POLITBURO to direct the struggle in the South, more control was required than the Regional Committee was providing. On December 10, 1960, Hanoi formed the National Liberation Front and issued a ten-point declaration that called on South Vietnam to overthrow Diem and his colonial masters from the United States and unify the two halves of the country.

As chairman of the NLF, the Politburo selected Nguyen Huu Tho, a dedicated Communist but never identified as a party member. Son of the manager of a French rubber plantation in the Mekong Delta, Tho had studied in France at Aix-en-Provence, where he was remembered principally for his skill at poker. After serving an apprenticeship with a Vietnamese law firm in the 1930s, Tho married a girl from his Delta province and raised a family of eight children. But by 1949, he had drifted leftward, joining a group of 900 Vietnamese intellectuals who petitioned the French to negotiate with Ho. The next year, he demonstrated against the three U.S. warships from the Seventh Fleet sent to Saigon to show support for the colonial government. The French arrested Tho and packed him off without a trial to two years in a prison north of Dien Bien Phu. He was released after a hunger strike, only to be arrested again in 1954 during a demonstration against Diem. That time, Tho either escaped or was set free by Vietminh guerrillas.

His new Front started small, recruiting revolutionaries like Dr. Dang, the historian, as its political strategist. The Politburo did not expect the CIA or any informed observer to believe the fiction that the NLF was independent. But the Communists had struggled for decades by following a precise formula and would not abandon it now. Its traditional three divisions were the Communist Party itself, its leadership the driving force; a people's army, christened in South Vietnam the PAFL, the People's Armed Forces of Liberation; and a National Unity Front that would attract a broad alliance of workers and peasants. The Communists found intellectuals more brittle than strong, but the party needed them, too.

In running the military, the Communists believed as strongly as McNamara at the Pentagon in civilian control, whether it was over the Front's PAFL or over PAVN, Giap's People's Army of Vietnam. Each of Giap's proposals had to pass before the Politburo, where it would almost certainly be approved, but not before extensive debate and possible changes. Ho trusted Giap, but he would not surrender ultimate power to him.

The name of the southern guerrillas, even abbreviated to PAFL, was unwieldy. Diem's American advisers congratulated themselves on coming up instead with a derogatory term for their new enemy. They called Tho's soldiers "Vietcong"—Vietnamese Communists. Rather than being abashed, however, the guerrillas cheerfully adopted the catchy name and then scored a more telling propaganda stroke. They labeled their enemy the My-Diem clique—"My" meaning "American"—which identified Diem with white foreigners and stirred memories of the recent war against the French. Throughout the Mekong Delta, bitter survivors of Diem's crackdown against the Binh Xuyen, Hoa Hao and Cao Dai sects seemed likely recruits for Tho's Front.

The Vietcong duplicated Ho's training camps of twenty years earlier, down to the outdoor tables with logs for seats and lessons drawn in charcoal on boards of polished wood. For many farm boys, it was their first time in a classroom. Those considered fit to be political cadres were tutored in the writings of Marx, Mao and Ho. Sometimes, the Front's recruits were sent to join the South Vietnamese army for training in the use of artillery guns. When they defected, they were told to come away with their uniforms and rifles.

In the forests around Cu Chi, twenty miles northwest of Saigon, the Vietcong reopened tunnels dug during the French war. The people aboveground had stayed loyal to the Vietminh, which meant that the NLF's larger rallies of farmers in their black trousers and conical straw hats could be staged safely at a nearby French rubber plantation. Below the earth, soldiers and civilians had carved out 125 miles of tunneling, sometimes three stories deep, using only short-handed shovels and wicker baskets to carry away the dirt. Narrow even for the slim-hipped Vietnamese, the tunnels stretched west to the Cambodian border. The Vietcong fashioned trap doors near the roots of rubber trees and spread the milky white sap across the wood panels to glue on grass and leaves as camouflage. With air vents disguised as snake holes, the chambers were designed so that one level could be sealed off quickly if the enemy resorted to chemical weapons.

In case Diem's troops uncovered a tunnel and lowered themselves inside, corridors were fitted with booby traps—sometimes bombs, more often punji sticks, sharpened bamboo points that stuck up through a loose cover of grass and could maim a foot.

The Vietminh's digging had revealed underground wells for water, and NLF soldiers lighted the tunnels with candles, flashlights and oil lamps. Neighboring farmers brought the rebels food, usually rice wadded in a handkerchief. Cooking was done over what the Vietcong called Dien Bien Phu stoves, their underground chimneys carrying smoke far from the fires. Each Vietcong soldier dug his own foxhole. When it was safe to sleep outside, men who had found a parachute cut it into a two-layer hammock with the top mesh for mosquito netting.

The Vietcong had also designed their own flag, different from Giap's. Theirs was a gold star on a divided field: the red background on top stood for the liberated North, the blue at the bottom for the occupied South.

UNTIL THE FORMATION of the NLF, Tuyen had hoped that Diem's appointees could reason with their critics or bribe them into dropping their opposition. But, besides suspected Communists, Can's men were now making blanket arrests of known nationalists. As their files passed Tuyen's desk, he tried to shield the small percentage he considered part of a patriotic opposition. He endorsed Can's harsh methods against the others, however, those men and women he regarded as a genuine threat to the state.

As he signed the flood of requisitions on behalf of Can's men, Tuyen did not want to hear about their methods, preferring to concentrate on those prisoners he had personally set free. But Can's men had come to regard Tuyen as an ally and dropped by his office expecting to be congratulated on their effectiveness. As the widespread crackdown spread, Tuyen could not avoid hearing details of arbitrary torture and assassination.

As a result, Tuyen may have disarmed Can's hostility, but he himself was developing a reputation as the overlord of the nation's secret police. The American embassy regarded him as a sinister figure, and while Tuyen maintained formal relations with Colby, neither man mentioned Can's operation. In his own mind, Tuyen still considered himself a political strategist, although he enjoyed the way his presumed power let him cut through the bureaucracy to protect an occasional opposition figure. He heard, however, that agents within the CIA were calling him Vietnam's Goebbels, likening him to the Nazis' notorious propagandist. Tuyen concluded that most CIA agents were like the American journalists who flew into Saigon for a few days: they might contact a number of Vietnamese sources, but they lacked the background to evaluate what they heard.

When a back-slapping career officer, Elbridge Durbrow, was named U.S. ambassador, he was appalled by the influence that Nhu and his wife seemed to exert over Diem. Durbrow had not met Tuyen, but he had heard the embassy rumors and called on Diem to urge strongly that Tuyen be fired.

Diem took up the matter with Nhu, who claimed it was all a misunderstanding. Tuyen had no power to arrest anyone. When he came to the palace, it was to release an opposition figure, not to jail him. Diem was unwilling to cross his brother or to appear to be taking orders from the Americans. When Tuyen was allowed to stay on, Durbrow took the rebuff as one more proof that Diem had lost touch with South Vietnam's political realities.

With Nhu's support, Tuyen's unit grew to 500 people, dwarfing Can's section of about 60, and Tuyen could step up his effort to protect legitimate politicians from the police hard-liners. Whenever Tuyen got a man released to his custody, he set him free with the same admonition: express your opinion if you must, but don't try to overthrow the government.

By 1960, Nhu also endorsed that approach, and Tuyen was arranging secret meetings in the palace between Nhu and opposition leaders. Nhu had come to regard Tuyen as his fixer, a man with enough contacts in every corner of Vietnamese society to succeed with any project, large or small.

ALTHOUGH WASHINGTON regarded Hanoi as cunningly subverting the Geneva accords, it was the Politburo members who considered themselves betrayed again on every side. They especially resented their two most powerful Communist allies for urging them to delay the attempt at unification. Beijing advised Ho to expect a long wait and in the meantime to avoid open warfare. Moscow offered similar outdated advice: Hanoi should limit the struggle between South and North to economic competition. Ho's colleagues, especially those from the South, read that caution as evidence that the larger powers were acting from self-interest and cared only about improving their own relations with the West.

AS THE VIETCONG slowly coalesced, Miss Dung, now living in Hanoi, heard stories about an impatient woman in the Delta who was calling on local Vietminh veterans to dig up their weapons and resist Diem's persecution. When they did, they often found that the alkaline marsh water had rusted the rifles beyond repair. All the same, they staged uprisings in Ben Tre and My Tho in January 1960. When those collapsed, most male Vietminh fled their villages. Mrs. Nguyen Thi Dinh was left with only women and children, and Diem's propagandists were claiming that the brief revolt was dead. Mrs. Dinh would prove them wrong.

She had been a revolutionary from the time, as an eighteen-year-old girl, that she married an older Vietminh in 1938. Soon after their son was born, her husband was arrested and died in Poulo Condore. Mrs. Dinh sent the child to be raised in the North; a few days later, she, too, was arrested and spent the next three years in prison.

Freed by 1945, she led the takeover of Ben Tre's provincial capital in the

Mrs. Nguyen Thi Dinh
(Ta Minh Kham family)

name of Ho Chi Minh, then went underground during the French War and the early years of the Diem regime. In taking up the cause of independence again, Mrs. Dinh preached that within all of Diem's soldiers was a true Vietnamese, and they must be given an opportunity to change their allegiance. She told Vietminh mothers who sold food in the villages to carry photographs of their sons and tell the government soldiers that their boys were serving in Diem's army in other provinces. When soldiers were about to tear up a house because of the family's Vietminh affiliations, the women were to beg, "Don't punish us for the past." If a shamefaced captain blamed his commander, the mothers learned to join together and say, "All right, let's go to see your commander." Confronting that officer, they said, "You have claimed to be here for the common people, but your soldiers are destroying our villages as they search for Vietminh." "It's not me," an intimidated officer was likely to reply. "The Americans make us do it."

Mrs. Dinh organized protest rallies with witnesses to testify about the devastation of their villages. In the front rank, she put the sharpest-tongued old women and instructed them to call each of Diem's soldiers "son" before they unleashed their invective. She taught protesters the signals for when to disperse and when to sit down in the village square. Medics were on hand in case the soldiers opened fire.

As they set out for a protest, the women wound their long tresses high on their heads until each hairdo looked like an onion. "We're not afraid of the Vietminh," Diem's soldiers joked. "But we're afraid of those big-haired women."

Mrs. Dinh was not receiving help from the North, and when the Regional Committee urged caution, she ignored its rebuke. She stationed women holding palm leaves cut to look like rifles where Diem's men could make out their profiles by moonlight and worry that the Vietminh had returned to the province. She taught the women to collect food wrappers and cigarette butts and dump them to make the site look like a Vietminh encampment. At night, women reported to Diem's men that they had seen Vietminh nearby and would then go to the paddies and explode hollowed bamboo shoots with rocks inside, which produced the sound of bombs.

In town, Mrs. Dinh's women posted declarations signed "The People's Justice Committee," promising to execute the most brutal officials. When possible, they made good on the threat. Their victims were among the 700 assassinations of Diem's village appointees in the twelve months up to May 1958. To get weapons, rebel women opened outdoor food stalls and lulled government soldiers into laying down their rifles while they ate. Since the soldiers tended to believe Saigon's propaganda that the revolution had been scotched, they were easy to distract while teenagers ran off with their weapons. More aggressive vendors pushed a soldier down and, as other women pretended to help him up, grabbed his rifle. Women trained others in the tactic. They called it "pull the legs."

DIEM HAD ORGANIZED a sham legislative election in August 1959, which he hoped would satisfy his critics. The following April, however, he received a petition from a group of South Vietnamese with credentials as lifelong nationalists, several of them his former cabinet ministers. Bui Diem, the student who had admired Giap but resisted his proselytizing, was living in Saigon and helped to draft the document in the dining room of the Caravelle Hotel. Respectfully, it called on Diem to guarantee basic civil rights and recognize political opposition. If he did, the people of the South could contrast their system with that of Hanoi and gladly make the sacrifices that would preserve their liberty.

In Hanoi, the leadership was jubilant at the distinguished protest and expected newspaper coverage to convince Washington that Diem was not worth supporting. But Vietnam remained on the periphery of America's vision, and any press reports were few and brief.

Rather than heed the appeal, Diem lashed out. He shut down newspapers and arrested dozens of men he considered disloyal. One well-known writer responded by killing himself and leaving behind a note that he could not go on living under Diem. Although Bui Diem had been one of the men who had helped prepare the petition, he had been too junior to sign it and, for the time, was safe from the crackdown. He had known Tuyen from their days in the North and felt he would protect him. But as Tuyen went about the city trying to get others from the Caravelle group released, he found his own political loyalties being increasingly tested.

☐

NEAR THE END OF THE YEAR, Ngo Dinh Nhu awoke to a crisis that seemed beyond Tuyen's ability to fix. At 2:30 A.M. on November 11, 1960, Nhu spotted suspicious movements outside his window. Through the gloom, he made out a number of troops surrounding the presidential palace. Nhu called Tuyen at once and told him to find out what was afoot. Soon afterward, Tuyen got another call, this one from Pham Xuan An, a Vietnamese reporter for the Reuters news agency. An told him that he and Robert Shaplen, the Asia correspondent for the *New Yorker* magazine, had picked up rumors that sent them hurrying to Saigon's central post office. There, they confirmed that a military coup against Diem was already under way, led by Colonel Nguyen Chanh Thi, whose paratroopers ringed the palace. Before An could say more, soldiers burst in and cut the telephone lines.

A few minutes passed and then, startlingly, Tuyen's phone rang for a third time. The post office director was calling from an emergency system in the basement that the rebels had overlooked. Not long before, the director had nearly been fired as a suspected Dai Viet, but he was nearing retirement age and Diem allowed him to stay on. Tuyen let the man think that he was the one who had saved his job. Now he was offering to patch Tuyen through to the palace and also to any troops outside Saigon who might have remained loyal to Diem.

Speaking to the bases that surrounded the city, Tuyen got instant pledges of support. Then he rang the palace to talk with the captain responsible for its security. "I will need at least twelve hours to bring military units from the countryside," Tuyen told him. "Tell me whether you can resist that long."

"I can hold out that long," the captain said, "but probably no longer."

"What is the state of mind there?"

"Mrs. Nhu is very tough," the captain answered. "She wants to fight even if she dies. Mr. Nhu is quiet. He doesn't seem to know what to do."

"What about President Diem?"

The captain said that Vo Van Hai, the president's private secretary, had turned out to be in league with the rebels and was urging Diem to negotiate with them. Colonel Thi was demanding that either he or a fellow officer be named as prime minister. Diem must also agree to remove Mrs. Nhu from the palace. That second condition seemed to come from Hai, who had long disliked her.

Saigon radio was already broadcasting a manifesto from Thi's revolutionary committee that claimed the president was being removed for corruption and for his suppression of Vietnamese liberties. When Tuyen heard the names of the plotters, he recognized that one, Phan Quang Dan, had the most direct stake in the coup's success. Educated at Harvard, Dan had received the largest plurality the previous year in the bogus elections for the National Assembly. The Diem regime charged that Dan's votes had come from Communists and Communist sympathizers and refused to seat either him or another opposition candidate. Both men had then been tried and convicted of electoral fraud.

Hai left the palace to confer with the coup leaders, taking with him Diem's word that he was ready to compromise. Diem had been shaken by the challenge and wanted to believe that if he met the rebel demands he could stay on as president. By that time, however, Tuyen had contacted Bien Hoa, the base of both the Fifth and Seventh Divisions, and commanders there had promised to head for Saigon. The Seventh was headed by a Catholic convert named Nguyen Van Thieu.

As he went on marshaling support, Tuyen sent Jackie and their children to the nearby house of a British friend. Reports of the coup had spread during the early morning hours, and the deputy U.S. ambassador dispatched a messenger to offer Tuyen sanctuary. He declined, sure that only he could save the nation. At 5 A.M., Tuyen called William Colby, the CIA station chief. Colby's public position had been that his agency should not try to influence events but merely gather information for the embassy. Given the close contact that CIA agents maintained with several coup leaders, however, Tuyen suspected they had supplied active encouragement, and now Colby's reaction convinced him that the Americans had known about the revolt ahead of time. When Tuyen told him that troops were on their way to rescue Diem, Tuyen thought Colby sounded wary and possibly disappointed. "Are you sure about the units outside Saigon?" Colby asked. "Are you sure they're loyal to the government?"

Aware that he was marked for arrest, Tuyen bolted for a friend's home and was gone by the time a military police captain arrived for him. Five hours later, the first loyalist troops rode into the city. But moving in enough men to retake the palace would require more time than Tuyen had estimated. As negotiations with Thi went back and forth, one voice rang out against compromise. Pacing the palace floor, Madame Nhu challenged Diem in grandiloquent language. He must act as the president he was destined to be, she insisted, and reject the threats of this ambitious rabble. Diem had been chosen to save his country. He must hold firm.

Was Diem listening? Tuyen could not guess what the president was thinking, but Diem issued a proclamation to be read over Saigon radio that promised to dissolve the current regime. His new government would include the rebellious officers and other dissidents. "Be calm," Diem counseled his audience, "and have confidence in the patriotism of the president and in his unlimited love for the people."

As the hours wore on and more loyalist troops drew closer to Saigon, Thi and his colleagues were losing heart. Some of the rebel officers had told their men that they had only marched on the palace to save Diem from a Communist attack. Now the paratroopers realized they had been duped and were threatening to mutiny.

Inconclusive negotiations went on for hours until word reached the palace that Thi had fled to Cambodia in a plane supplied by the head of the Air Force

Transport Command, a young pilot named Nguyen Cao Ky. As news spread that the coup was collapsing, crowds of well-wishers flocked to the palace to cheer their president. When Diem was assured that he was safe, he renounced his earlier promises to the coup leaders and ordered his men to fire on any rebellious stragglers.

His pride prevented Tuyen from rushing to claim his share of credit. Finally, thirty-six hours after the coup began, Nhu invited him to the palace, where Tuyen found the Ngo brothers seated together. As Nhu explained Tuyen's role in aborting the coup, Diem barely seemed to listen. Tuyen knew there was no danger of thanks from a man both shy and slow in bestowing praise.

Diem soon rose and left the room. When they were alone, Nhu asked Tuyen whether he had known about the coup in advance and seemed to believe his denial. But Nhu was enraged by the CIA's link to the rebels and would have been still angrier if he had known the agency's continuing role. While Nhu's men were arresting coup sympathizers around Saigon, Colby was hiding one of them in an empty CIA apartment. And when Colby met with Nhu, he lied about the role of another CIA agent in encouraging the plotters. Nhu had his own sources, however, and warned Colby sternly that his brother's government would not accept more American interference.

Otherwise, Nhu was elated that danger had been averted and asked Tuyen to suggest who should be rewarded. "Just one person," Tuyen said. As a result, Vietnam's highest decoration was duly awarded to the director of the post office. "Bao-Quoc Huan Chuong," his medal read—Protector of the Nation.

Although Thi's military plot had failed, power in South Vietnam had shifted all the same. Alone with his family, Diem was not the mandarin whose maddening composure had frustrated a succession of American diplomats. When crossed in private, Diem fumed and shouted in rages that were short-lived and best ignored. Should he detect an insult from a political opponent, Diem might cry, "Shoot him dead!" But he forgot that order almost at once and might soon be instructing Nhu to help the man and his family.

Nhu understood that when they disagreed over policy, he, as a younger brother, could never contradict Diem. He had learned to keep silent and rely on his network of agents to bypass the president's intemperate instructions. As for his wife, Nhu's response remained fawningly romantic. At fifty-five, Nhu smoked too much and worked past too many midnights. Frail and ashen-skinned, he looked older than Diem, while Madame Nhu, fifteen years younger than her husband, was undeniably flowering. She had given birth to their fourth child shortly before menopause, and Nhu was besotted anew with the baby's mother. When aides reported political meddling by his wife, Nhu waved away their criticism. "Oh," he would say, "she's a little girl."

Diem's monkish nature guaranteed that he could never be at ease with his sister-in-law, but she made a lively hostess for the official receptions he hated, and he had come to accept that she was being called the First Lady of South Vietnam. In the wake of the attempted coup, however, Tran Le Xuan would never again be merely the little girl his brother had married. At a moment of high peril, while the men around her dithered and debated, Madame Nhu had risen operatically to the challenge. After that night, her voice would be impossible to silence.

THREE

BOWLES
1961

O<small>N JANUARY 20</small>, 1961, a cold bright morning in Washington, John F. Kennedy delivered a truculent inaugural address that promised aggressive support for America's friends and vehement resistance to her foes. Kennedy's tough rhetoric particularly suited the strong anti-Communist sentiments of Walt Whitman Rostow, an economic historian from the Massachusetts Institute of Technology. One of Kennedy's many Cambridge advisers during the presidential campaign, Rostow took credit for his potent campaign pledge to "get the country moving again." That alone seemed to guarantee a job in Washington. But it had been long in coming. Kennedy first intended to appoint Rostow as chairman of the State Department's Policy Planning Council, but Rusk, who had been pliant about accepting the political nomination of Chester Bowles as undersecretary, took a cue from McNamara at Defense and said no. "That's all right," Rostow told Kennedy blithely. "I already have a fine job on the campus. Don't worry about me."

But Kennedy was determined to find a place for Rostow, who had just published a well-received study, *The Stages of Economic Growth,* and seemed to possess the intellectual rigor the new president hoped would distinguish his administration. Rostow radiated as well a bluff good cheer straight from the pages of Dickens. His years in the classroom had left him impervious to twitting, and he never lost his beaming smile or his professorial aplomb. Rusk had also vetoed McGeorge Bundy for a job at State before Kennedy brought him into the White House as his special assistant for national security affairs. With Rostow, the presi-

Walt W. Rostow testifying before the Senate Foreign Relations Committee
(©Bettmann/Corbis)

dent had no better idea than to appoint him as Bundy's deputy. Whatever his feelings about sharing duties with a rival academic, Bundy was a gracious host. He divided responsibility for the crises the administration could expect to face, reserving Cuba, the Congo and Berlin for himself and leaving to Rostow the problems of Southeast Asia.

During Eisenhower's last weeks as president, Ed Lansdale had been sent to Saigon to prepare a report for the Pentagon, and Rostow received a copy of his findings a few days before Kennedy's first national security meeting on Saturday, January 28. He found the news alarming. Lansdale warned that the United States must awake to the crisis in South Vietnam and "treat it as a combat area of the Cold War." He sounded the usual themes—the widespread dissatisfaction with the Ngo family, especially with Nhu and his wife; the inadequacy of Diem's forces to repel troops from the North or put down rebels already in the South; the red tape and corruption that spread from Saigon to the countryside.

Alarmed, Rostow took the report to his first private briefing with the president. Kennedy had slotted him for half an hour, but rather than paraphrase Lansdale, Rostow handed him the entire report and said, "You ought to read this."

Kennedy considered its heft. "All of it?"

"Yes," said Rostow. "All of it."

Kennedy had taken lessons in speed-reading and boasted wryly about the number of words he could read in one minute. Now, however, Kennedy took his time. When he finished, he looked up and asked, "This is the worst one we've got, isn't it? You know, Eisenhower never uttered the word 'Vietnam.' "

Wanting to judge the pessimistic messenger for himself, Kennedy invited Lansdale to the January 28 meeting of the highest officers of his new government—Rusk, McNamara and his assistant Paul Nitze, Allen Dulles and another CIA official, and General Lyman Lemnitzer, chairman of the Joint Chiefs of Staff. Lansdale waited outside until the others had finished discussing a plan drafted under Eisenhower for invading Cuba with anti-Castro forces. He was then led into the Cabinet Room along with J. Graham Parsons, the assistant secretary of state for Far Eastern affairs. A career officer, Parsons had served as Eisenhower's ambassador to Laos and negotiated a truce the previous autumn between the Lao neutralist leader, Souvanna Phouma, and the anti-Communist Lao general the United States was funding. That general immediately violated the agreement, and the day before Kennedy's inaugural Souvanna Phouma had denounced Parsons as "the ignominious architect of the disastrous American policy toward Laos." The attack wounded Parsons because he considered Souvanna the most impressive of the Laotian leaders and had only been carrying out Eisenhower's policies. Now he was being presented to Kennedy's advisers as the State Department's authority on Vietnam.

When Lansdale entered the room, Kennedy greeted him with a compliment on his Vietnam report. Rusk derailed that cordiality by asking whether the president wouldn't prefer to begin with Parsons's presentation of a counterinsurgency plan that had just been wired to Washington from the embassy in Saigon. Parsons explained that so far the proposal had been approved only at the low level of the Far Eastern desk but soon they could expect an additional 220 pages to justify boosting the South Vietnamese army by 20,000 men; that would bring its total to 170,000 troops. The plan would also accelerate the training of Vietnam's 30,000-man civil guard by MAAG—the U.S. Military Assistance Advisory Group. The new costs would run to about $40 million.

Kennedy immediately had questions: If the crisis was so urgent, what good were new troops who could be ready for action only a full year or two later? And if there were only 10,000 Communist guerrillas, why did Diem need 170,000 soldiers? Wasn't the crisis facing Vietnam less military than political? Parsons explained that a larger army in the south would deter a conventional attack across North Vietnam's border by General Giap's 300,000 troops.

When Kennedy suggested sending southern guerrillas into the north, Allen Dulles spoke up: four teams of eight men had been organized to harass the Communists, he said, but Diem was not enthusiastic about the idea. That gave Lansdale his chance to step in and take over the briefing. He explained that Diem resisted any American plan that required him to delegate authority. According to

Diem, only three men in the country could make a tough decision and not simply pass it back to him. Diem asked for the 20,000 increase because the Communists expected to bring him down with the political front they had recently formed in the South.

Kennedy asked for an estimate of the odds on Diem's surviving. Lansdale explained that the Communists expected 1961 to be their big year, but an all-out U.S. effort could frustrate them and pave the way for an offensive by Diem's troops in 1962. He also repeated his favorite themes: Americans in Vietnam must be infused with high morale and get closer to the Vietnamese. Diem must permit legitimate opponents to speak out rather than imprisoning or killing them. But Diem believed that the Americans had been involved the previous year in the plot to depose him, and even Lansdale could not dissuade him.

Lansdale said he had tried to get Nhu to take a public role that would make him look less sinister than he did on the sidelines, but Diem depended on having his brother close at hand in the palace. Kennedy, who had recently weathered criticism for bringing his brother Bobby into the cabinet as attorney general, made no comment.

But the president did repeat his wish that anti-Communist guerrillas infiltrate the north, despite Dulles's warning that even if the North Vietnamese were unhappy, Ho's government was well entrenched. At his turn to speak, Rusk defended the performance of State's diplomats in Saigon from Lansdale's implied criticism. On the one hand, they were supposed to pressure Diem to make reforms that he resisted. Yet they were also called upon to reassure a touchy and suspicious mandarin of America's unwavering support. Rusk said that Durbrow, as U.S. ambassador for the past three-and-a-half years, had played that difficult role energetically but should be replaced soon. When Kennedy volunteered to write a letter of support to Diem, Rusk assured him that a response to Diem's congratulations on Kennedy's election was already making its way through the State Department. It could be revised to emphasize America's backing.

The session broke up with Kennedy dissatisfied. He had already set up a special task force to deal with the nettlesome question of Cuba. Now he was thinking of a similar task force for Vietnam. And he wanted a decision on whether Lansdale, still officially an Air Force brigadier general, should go as ambassador to South Vietnam in place of a career State Department officer. Bundy and Rostow had stayed behind after the meeting, and Kennedy told them that within three months he expected his administration to be better off than it was now in four regions—Vietnam, Laos, the Congo and Cuba.

Rusk was also unhappy with the session but for another reason. He fretted to McNamara that these new task forces might interfere with State's normal workings. McNamara was already aware that normalcy at State was exactly what annoyed Kennedy, and he sympathized only fleetingly before reminding Rusk that a crisis might call for new measures.

Back in his office that evening, Rusk hashed over the meeting with Graham Parsons. Who, he asked, is this Lansdale? Parsons explained that he had inspired *The Ugly American* but did not add that Parsons himself always referred to the novel as "that horrible book." Parsons granted that Lansdale had performed ably in Manila, and later had become close to Diem. But he was also a lone wolf, flamboyant, tagged by the State Department as an operator.

"How 'tagged'?" Rusk asked.

"Not a team player," Parsons said. Lansdale seemed to resent the other Americans in Vietnam, especially those in the foreign service. As for "Durbie"— Ambassador Durbrow—it was the Pentagon's view that he pushed Diem too hard. Parsons rejected Lansdale's suggestion that a non-Communist opposition party, guided by the United States, be allowed to emerge in South Vietnam. Rusk asked whether the situation would soon become critical. It was near-critical now, Parsons said, but not hopeless. And Diem remained the best fellow for the job.

ED LANSDALE left the White House eager to let Diem know how his briefing had gone. "Dear Friend," he began, President Kennedy had been warmly interested and had asked many questions. "I am sure you can count on him as an understanding friend." That said, Lansdale attempted once again to goad Diem to action. "Your country needs to rouse its spirit right now, the way Winston Churchill did for Britain at a dark hour." Lansdale offered specific tactics, including a meeting of province chiefs at which Diem would call for more honest data. He also recommended that Diem meet with his political critics and urge them to unite in one unfettered but loyal opposition movement. "You might talk to them, too, the way you did to me in 1955 and 1956—that your dream for Vietnam was to have two strong political parties."

But Lansdale was not writing to the Diem of 1955. The day after that letter, Durbrow cabled from Saigon that the "Vietnamese people lack the necessary sophistication and understanding, as well as the necessary sense of political responsibility, to make a two-party democratic system work at this time."

The American ambassador and President Diem often differed, but they agreed in their low opinion of Diem's countrymen.

TWO DAYS AFTER the Lansdale briefing, Kennedy authorized an increase in the U.S. budget of $28.4 million to expand the South Vietnamese army by 20,000 men and another $12.7 million to improve the quality of the Vietnam Civil Guard. Lansdale learned, however, that he would not be carrying the good news to Diem in person. The State Department had decided—with the agreement of ranking CIA officials—that he was too independent to be an effective ambassador. Kennedy, who had liked Lansdale, was surprised to have him rejected. State's official excuse was that if it became known that the new ambassador had

Ambassador Frederick Nolting *(AP/Wide World Photos)*

once worked for the CIA, the embassy would be compromised. Rostow tried to convince Kennedy that passing over Lansdale was for the best. "He may have been good," Rostow wrote in a memo. "I believe so, but Diem never had to deal with him when he bore the full burden of an Ambassador, with all the awkward inevitable problems of negotiation."

The State Department toyed with other candidates, but in the end Rusk chose Frederick Nolting, the consul general in Paris with no experience in Asia. Fritz Nolting's chief duty in Saigon would be to maintain good relations with Diem and with the American military, both of whom had mistrusted Durbrow as insufficiently committed to the struggle. "We must go with Nolting, whom I know well personally," Rostow told Kennedy. "You will find him a man of rare strength and character."

Nolting had only one qualm about accepting the assignment, and it was not his lack of grounding in Asia. His four daughters were either at college or approaching college age, and Nolting didn't want to be separated too long from his family. He asked Rusk if a two-year tour of duty didn't seem about right. "Yes," Rusk replied, "this seems quite satisfactory."

Then, with a rueful chuckle, Rusk added, "Perhaps the way things are going, we'll be lucky if we have a mission there for six months."

GRAHAM PARSONS was also heading for a new assignment. Even though Rusk had announced that the new administration had full confidence in holdovers from the Eisenhower years, Parsons was not surprised to be shuffled off to Europe as ambassador to Sweden. During a White House lunch, the Swedish prime minister asked what Kennedy saw as America's problems in the world. "Well, Mr. Prime Minister, of course there is Laos," Kennedy replied. "Laos is a great problem."

Gesturing down the table to Parsons, Kennedy said, "Perhaps I shouldn't talk about Laos because the greatest expert on Laos in our government is sitting just two, three places down from me, and I ought to be pretty careful."

As the laughter died away, Kennedy added dryly, "You know, he *is* our great expert on Laos, and perhaps it's for that reason that I'm sending him to you as ambassador to Sweden."

KENNEDY'S INCREASED FUNDS for Vietnam gratified Walt Rostow, but he considered money alone no answer to the crisis Lansdale had identified. Rostow blamed the Pentagon for regarding Vietnam as part of the Laotian problem rather than the other way around. Now Lansdale had at least alerted Kennedy to a guerrilla war underway in the Mekong Delta for which the United States was badly prepared. Rostow had left the briefing with a new assignment—to gather information about this new style of warfare.

Earlier in the month, Nikita Khrushchev in Moscow had made an ominous promise to support wars of liberation wherever they might occur. China's rulers understood that he was warning them that the Soviet Union was still the leader of the Communist bloc. But in Washington, Khrushchev's speech had been taken as a declaration of war against the West by the man who had predicted two years earlier that "we will bury you." To accomplish that goal, the Communists' tactic seemed to be guerrilla warfare.

Rostow put together a briefing kit with Khrushchev's speech, along with writings from Mao and from Che Guevara, the Argentinean fighting at Fidel Castro's side in Cuba. The packet gave Kennedy his first exposure to Mao's literary style—"Guerrillas must move among the people as fish swim in the sea"—and he amused Jackie Kennedy with his own satiric variations.

Consulting the Special Warfare Center at Fort Bragg, North Carolina, Rostow learned that fewer than 1,000 men were studying guerrilla warfare. In case of a Third World War, the army saw them as saboteurs and spies behind enemy lines. But Kennedy envisioned a far grander mission. The army must train men to meet the insurgent challenges throughout Southeast Asia and Latin America. At Rostow's suggestion, the president appointed a major general to turn Bragg

W. Averell Harriman *(AP/Wide World Photos)*

into a center for teaching guerrilla combat. Training would stress the need for soldiers to assume the same tasks as the new Peace Corps that Kennedy was also creating. Besides fighting rebels, they would build bridges, village markets, schools, field hospitals.

The concept of a cadre called Special Forces was not entirely new. Organized in 1952, the first unit had sent men to South Vietnam in 1957 to train Vietnamese commandos at Nha Trang. Members of that original squad had designed for themselves a green beret, a variation on the red berets worn by U.S. paratroopers. At the time, the Pentagon had vetoed that bit of flash, but Kennedy, despite his own aversion to headgear, thought the green berets would create esprit and authorized their return.

RICH, TART-TONGUED, boasting three decades of public service, Averell Harriman at seventy had burned to join the New Frontier far more ardently than the Kennedy brothers cared to enlist him. Harry Truman had argued before the election that American voters in 1960 were not ready to elect a Catholic president. Because Harriman was devoted to Truman, he had been slow in endorsing

Kennedy, to the disgust of his earthy second wife, Marie. "He's making a god-damned ass of himself," she complained to a Kennedy fund-raiser. "You've got to do something about it or he's going to lose absolutely everything."

Harriman was finally pried loose from a $30,000 campaign contribution, and Kennedy let the elderly former governor of New York second his nomination at the Los Angeles convention. But when cabinet jobs were being doled out, Harriman was considered well past his prime, and Bobby Kennedy opposed any appointment as merely a sentimental gesture.

Jack Kennedy believed, however, that Harriman could be salvaged if one infirmity of age was remedied. As president-elect, he attended a small luncheon during which Harriman harshly denounced an aide for a remark that another guest had made. Afterward, Kennedy told Michael Forrestal, a Harriman protégé, "Averell's hearing is atrocious. If we're going to give him a job, he has to have a hearing aid, and I want you to see that he does." Marie Harriman promptly got a device for her husband's right ear, and Kennedy gave him the ambiguous title of roving ambassador.

During the first weeks, Harriman toured world capitals, chatting with old friends from World War II days, when he had been Franklin Roosevelt's lend-lease administrator in London and later ambassador to Moscow. Calling on Nehru in New Delhi, Harriman also arranged to meet Souvanna Phouma, the Lao prince admired by Graham Parsons but considered unreliable by factions in State, the Pentagon and the CIA. Souvanna's offense was establishing a neutralist government in the mid-fifties that included his half-brother, Prince Souphanouvong, the leader of the Pathet Lao forces backed by Ho and Giap.

Convinced that Souvanna would take Laos into the Communist camp, the Dulles brothers had encouraged a fierce-talking anti-Communist named Phoumi Nosavan to seize the capital and install a regime friendly to the West. The two princes fled—Souvanna Phouma to Paris, Souphanouvong to Hanoi.

The Americans were soon embarrassed when Kong Le, a diminutive captain in the Lao paratroopers, threw out the anti-Communists and invited Souvanna Phouma to come home. Although Washington agreed to deal with Souvanna's regime, the CIA continued to arm Phoumi Nosavan, who retook the Lao capital, Vientiane, and once again exiled Souvanna. As Harriman drank tea with Souvanna in Delhi, he decided that his American critics had misjudged him. The prince seemed sincere about keeping his country neutral, a logical policy since Laos was surrounded by China and Burma to the north, Thailand to the west, Cambodia to the south, and both halves of Vietnam to the east.

Souvanna also shared his countrymen's aversion to bloodshed. Dean Rusk had been amused and frustrated to learn that two opposing Lao forces had once left the battlefield to attend a water festival, relaxing together for ten days before returning to resume their hugely ineffectual combat.

The long, feathery names of its leaders imbued Laotian warfare with the soft sounds of a pillow fight, and during those years when they had been largely ignored by the French, the Lao had enjoyed a sunny agrarian society. Warfare, especially over ideology, struck them as an aberration, although Communist and U.S. artillery and land mines continued to kill and maim them. Their American advisers joked that Phoumi Nosavan's troops scored a victory every time they remembered not to drop their rifles as they ran away. But the Pathet Lao, stiffened by North Vietnamese cadres and Soviet arms, were proving more determined. Even at that, John Kenneth Galbraith observed from his position as ambassador to India that the Lao simply did not share the civilized world's passion for killing.

After his meeting with Souvanna Phouma, Harriman concluded that the United States should take a risk and back this practical man, who had been trained as a civil engineer. At least, unlike the CIA's creatures, Souvanna seemed genuinely brave and independent. The problem was that Phoumi Nosavan, whom even his supporters considered a corrupt rogue, still enjoyed the favor of the CIA's crew on the scene, as well as backing from the U.S. general in Vientiane. Harriman decided to bide his time.

FOR ROBERT MCNAMARA, the first weeks of 1961 had represented a cram course in Washington politics. His success in blocking the appointment of Franklin Roosevelt, Jr., seemed to indicate that a brisk manner combined with an air of utter self-assurance would serve as well with Jack Kennedy as it had with Henry Ford. A mere three weeks into the job, however, McNamara was jolted to learn that he could be as vulnerable as the lowliest of the so-called Irish Mafia, those cronies Kennedy had brought with him from Boston.

Soon after Lansdale's briefing on Vietnam, McNamara spent hours reviewing hundreds of photographs of Soviet missile sites. He had barely finished when he was urged by his newly appointed press secretary, Arthur Sylvester, to introduce himself over drinks to the Pentagon press corps. McNamara protested that he wasn't prepared, but Sylvester, a former reporter for a New Jersey daily paper, said, "Don't worry. They're a fine bunch and will treat you well."

McNamara's first, protective instinct had been sound. Among the gaps in his political education was the distinction between a briefing "on background"—which meant reporters could publish what they were told if they didn't attribute the information—and "off the record," which meant they agreed to write nothing at all. And the first question he was tossed was a grenade.

"Mr. Secretary, you have been here now for three weeks. What do you have to say about the missile gap?"

For the past two years, the Democrats had charged that Eisenhower was weakening America's defenses by not stepping up production of nuclear intercontinental ballistic missiles. Congressional Democrats had quoted predictions that by 1961 the Soviet Union could have as many as 200 such missiles against a mere 54 available to the United States. Kennedy repeated the accusation during his televised debates with Nixon, and the "missile gap" became an emotional and potent issue in his campaign. At Harvard, a young professor, Henry Kissinger, weighed in for the Democrats. "There is no doubt the missile gap exists," he said.

The morning after McNamara's session with the Pentagon reporters, the *New York Times* ran a front-page story under the headline "Kennedy Defense Study Finds No Evidence of a 'Missile Gap.' " The reporter, Jack Raymond, had respected the background rules but revealed that the Soviet Union had not engaged in the crash program to build missiles that the Democrats had been predicting, and the United States still held a comfortable lead. As his source, Raymond did not mention McNamara; he relied instead on the phrase "it is said." In Washington, who had said it was unmistakable. The Republicans immediately accused Kennedy of knowingly campaigning on a falsehood. The waggish Senate minority leader, Everett Dirksen of Illinois, not only called on McNamara to resign but demanded that the presidential election be voided and held again.

For McNamara, his imposing pride built on foundations of insecurity, the gaffe was shattering. He went at once to Kennedy and offered his resignation. "Oh, come on, Bob, forget it," the president said. McNamara heard no anger in his voice but might have missed a tinge of amusement that his stiff-necked secretary of defense had been taught a political lesson. "We're in a hell of a mess," Kennedy added, "but we all put our foot in our mouth once in a while. Just forget it. It'll blow over."

It did, but not before Kennedy needled McNamara the next week at his press conference. A reporter asked how the president viewed background briefings, and with a broad smile Kennedy replied, "Well, they are hazardous in many cases, and I believe Mr. McNamara might agree with me."

AFTER HIS BLUNDER with the press, McNamara reverted to his corporate methods of secrecy and disinformation. During a closed session of the Senate's Armed Services Committee, he spelled out that policy. The senators were weighing the Zeus project, which had been designed to protect against intercontinental ballistic missiles. More than $900 million had been spent on Zeus with no success, and McNamara admitted to the panel that it had been a costly disappointment. But, he added, neither the Russians nor the American public should ever find that out.

"What we should be saying," McNamara testified, "is that we have the most perfect anti-ICBM system that the human mind will ever devise." He deplored the news reports already circulating about Zeus's failure. "I think it is absurd to release that kind of information to the public."

RETURNING HOME, Harriman was not briefed on the adventure that the CIA was planning for Cuba, but he did receive word that the agency's military operation in Laos was about to collapse. Shortly before Eisenhower left office in January, he had sent Phoumi Nosavan's anti-Communist troops six AT-6 planes—fighters armed with bombs and rockets—together with American advisers called "White Star" teams. But on March 9, 1961, the Pathet Lao combined forces with Kong Le to seize an open Laotian field called the Plain of Jars.

Its name was literal. Hundreds of four-foot jars of solid rock with fitted lids had been carved there, perhaps as prehistoric burial urns. The Lao said that when tribes of their earliest ancestors were driven out of Thailand, jars already covered the plain.

Confronted by the Pathet Lao, Phoumi Nosavan's troops once again ran away, and the Communists seemed poised to overrun both Vientiane and the royal city of Luang Prabang. Kennedy's White House had to turn its attention from the pending Cuban operation to deal with its first world crisis.

Meeting with the president, McNamara presented top-of-the-head advice with boardroom bravura. Each of the CIA's AT-6s, he said, should be armed with 200-pound bombs. When McNamara finished, Dean Rusk spoke to the room at large. Rusk hated these brainstorming sessions, offended that his soft-spoken and carefully hedged arguments might be lost in a contentious uproar. He much preferred to linger afterward and speak privately with the president, even though Kennedy enjoyed the parry and thrust of debate and was already growing impatient with Rusk's diffidence.

In this case, however, Rusk could draw on his own military experience in the Chinese-Burma theater, where the landscape was also mountainous jungle. Bombing was not effective when used alone, he said, although it might assist soldiers on the ground. And how badly could a mere six planes hurt the Communist troops?

For a moment, McNamara looked unprepared, but he recovered quickly. During earlier briefings on Laos, he had come to see that the Joint Chiefs, behind their braid and epaulets, were men of uneven ability, not so different from the rivals he had bested at Ford. At one session, the Chiefs had raised the prospect of sending U.S. forces into Laos to blunt the Pathet Lao offensive. A military briefer showed Kennedy a map of the two Lao airports where U.S. soldiers could be landed. Their presence, he assured the president, would make a significant difference.

"Well, how many troops?" Kennedy asked.

A thousand troops a day could be landed, although the airports could be used only during daylight hours.

Kennedy nodded. "How many troops do the Pathet Lao have?"

"Five thousand, Mr. President."

"Well, what happens if the Pathet Lao allow you to land troops for two days at both airports, and then they bomb the airports? Then what are you going to do?"

The Chiefs admitted that they hadn't thought about that possibility.

On another occasion, a briefing officer suggested that single-engine trainers flown by Lao pilots might disrupt the supply flights that the Soviet Union was making to the Pathet Lao. Kennedy asked whether those training planes were as fast as the Russian aircraft. No one from the military contingent could answer him.

Now the idea was being floated that a division of U.S. Marines be parachuted directly onto the Plain of Jars to hold it until Phoumi Nosavan's troops could be prodded back to fight.

"We can get them in, all right," General Lemnitzer said. "It's getting them out again that worries me." Walt Rostow argued for sending a smaller number of American soldiers into the Mekong Valley on the Laotian side of the border, not to fight but simply as bargaining chips at a future peace conference. But like many military strategists in Washington—and in Beijing—Lemnitzer recalled vividly the cost of the Korean War and was loathe to wage another land war in Asia. He was a holdover from the Eisenhower administration and loyal to the policy of nuclear deterrence over the more flexible response advocated by retired Army general Maxwell Taylor. At the Pentagon, the Never Again Club vowed to demand political guarantees from their civilian bosses. If U.S. troops were sent again to the Far East, the Pentagon wanted to be promised an all-out war, with no weapons denied to them. Kennedy had paid a courtesy call on Douglas MacArthur, in retirement at the Waldorf-Astoria Hotel in New York, and found that the general endorsed that policy.

Now Lemnitzer raised the specter of Chinese troops swarming over the Lao border and spelled out the Pentagon's condition for approving a deployment of American troops: "If we are given the right to use nuclear weapons," he said, "we can guarantee victory."

Kennedy did not feel obliged to comment on every observation made at these sessions. When Lemnitzer finished, the president said nothing for longer than usual and then dismissed the meeting.

AFTER THAT SORT of discussion, Kennedy found the prospect of a neutral Laos increasingly appealing. He would use the crisis to alert the American public and, in the process, nudge Moscow back to the conference table. Kennedy hoped that Khrushchev shared his distaste for open warfare over such insignificant real estate.

As his press conference opened, Kennedy was standing in front of three maps of Laos that had been color-coded to show the gains of Communist forces from August 1960, to the present time, eight months later. He announced that "Soviet planes, I regret to say" had made more than one thousand sorties in the region and that the Pathet Lao were being joined by combat troops from North Vietnam.

Choosing to ignore the years of CIA activity in Laos, Kennedy claimed that the United States unreservedly respected the country's neutrality and endorsed a recent British recommendation for new peace talks. But if those negotiations were to fail, Kennedy raised the possibility of retaliation by SEATO.

A reporter asked a basic question that had been ignored during the feverish White House brainstorming: "Mr. President, there appears to be some national unawareness of the importance of a free Laos to the security of the United States and to the individual American." Would the president spell out that importance?

Kennedy mentioned the proximity of Laos to Thailand and South Vietnam, "to which the United States has very close ties." After that, he indulged in a bit of boilerplate about "the cause of freedom around the world, that quite obviously affects the security of the United States."

To reporters, Kennedy's remarks were familiar Cold War rhetoric. To Secretary McNamara, untutored in international affairs, the president was stating an important truth: losing Indochina to the Communists would jeopardize the security of the West. That was the best judgment of the experts—Acheson, Lovett and the rest—and McNamara would carry out their policy.

WITHIN A MONTH, Kennedy was back on television addressing the American public. This time, he spoke not about distant Laos but about a calamity closer to home. Backed by the CIA, Cuban refugees had failed ignominiously in their attempt to overthrow Fidel Castro by invading Cuba at a cove called Bahía de Cochinos, the Bay of Pigs.

Planning for the assault had been a badly kept secret, and yet at the same moment the rebels were dying or surrendering, Rusk had told a press conference that "the American people are entitled to know whether we are intervening in Cuba or intend to do so in the future. The answer to that question is no."

The U.S. role was instantly exposed, but Kennedy disarmed the nation by taking full responsibility for the fiasco. Privately, he blamed bad advice from the CIA and concluded that he must replace Allen Dulles. Kennedy reminded his advisers that only Senator William Fulbright had come out forcefully against the attack. "The Castro regime is a thorn in the flesh," a Fulbright memorandum had observed. "But it is not a dagger in the heart."

Another voice opposing the invasion had also been raised, then muffled. Planning the coup had been limited to a select group that excluded Chester Bowles, the undersecretary of state, but Bowles had heard that Cuban exiles were training at a camp in Guatemala. Alarmed, he sent a memo to Rusk in late March, detailing his objections. A covert operation would not only violate the charter of the Organization of American States, Bowles wrote, but would also undercut Kennedy's stature as a new president committed to high principle in his foreign policy. Washington should not proceed with the invasion merely because a lot of time and money had already been spent on it.

Chester Bowles
(*AP/Wide World Photos*)

Bowles's political credentials were stronger than Rusk's. Before he was thirty, he had founded a successful advertising agency, Benton & Bowles, and had gone on to serve the Democrats in major ways—as Franklin Roosevelt's director of the wartime Office of Price Administration; as governor of Connecticut in 1949; as ambassador to India two years later. Bowles had even won a term in Congress but left the House in hopes of becoming Kennedy's secretary of state. Although he had been the first nationally known liberal to endorse Kennedy during the recent campaign, Bowles's commitment had seemed halfhearted and his gabby idealism made Kennedy impatient. Once, when Bowles had just left the Oval Office, the president remarked to Ken Galbraith, "Chet tells me there are six revolutions going on in the world. One is the revolution of rising expectations. I lost track of the other five."

Although Kennedy still called his secretary of state "Mr. Rusk," Bowles knew that their lack of intimacy did not deprive Rusk of the heft of his position. He ended his warning about Cuba with a plea: if Rusk agreed with him that the plan was a blunder, "I suggest that you personally and privately communicate your views to the President. It is my guess that your voice will be decisive." Bowles added that if the administration was determined to go ahead, he wanted to be informed at once so he could take his objections directly to Kennedy.

Rusk did not pass along Bowles's memorandum to the president. He justified withholding it on the grounds that Kennedy had once said he didn't like having a bunch of memos shoved at him. A few days after receiving the memo, Rusk assured Bowles that the Cuban operation had been greatly scaled down and reminded him that the CIA had run minor guerrilla operations in the past without attracting much attention. Bowles asked whether the newly modified Cuban invasion would end up on the front page of the *New York Times.* Rusk said he doubted that it would, adding that he did not feel it was necessary for Bowles to see the president.

Rusk said long afterward that his experience as chief of war plans in the China-Burma-India theater had convinced him that the small brigade of Cuban exiles "did not stand a snowball's chance in hell." But Rusk explained that since he was no longer in the army, he had not passed along that military judgment to Kennedy. When the *New York Times* published reports that both Rusk and Bowles had advised against the invasion, the president called Rusk to remind him pointedly that he had done no such thing.

The disaster left everyone in the White House feeling miserable. At one session, Bobby Kennedy burst out with a sentiment that his brother may have shared and depended upon Bobby to express. "Goddam all of you!" Bobby shouted. "You're supposed to be so bright, and you helped get the President elected, and now you got us into this situation, and the Russians will think we're a paper tiger!"

Bowles especially was punished for being indiscreet about being right. He had shared enough of his misgivings with friends in the press to be considered a traitor by a demoralized White House that saw loyalty as the prime virtue. Cued by the president and Bobby, *Time* magazine reported that Bowles had behaved "somewhat deviously" in the affair. The next week, the magazine assessed Bowles's influence at the White House as "way, way down."

Being defeated by Castro, bearded and brash in his combat fatigues, led to outbreaks of machismo around the capital. When Allen Dulles did not shrink from admitting his agency's culpability, Bobby Kennedy offered his highest tribute: "Dulles is a man." Tweaking the Kennedys' vulnerability, Thruston Morton, the Republican National Committee chairman, announced that "the time has come for our government to sing basso in world affairs."

A WEEK AFTER the Bay of Pigs, Khrushchev spared Kennedy further international distress by agreeing to press the Pathet Lao to accept a cease-fire and to reconvene the Geneva negotiations, seven years after the last conference. In Moscow, Khrushchev told American Ambassador Llewellyn Thompson that he saw no need to risk war over Laos when it would fall into his lap like a ripe apple.

But before the conference could open, it looked as though the capital, Vientiane, might still be overrun. The Communists were simply pursuing the same strategy that had worked well against the French—score one last military victory to send their negotiators to the bargaining table with a strong hand.

Rusk and Harriman were boarding a flight for a routine conference in Ankara, Turkey, when Rusk said that since the administration hoped to launch negotiations in Geneva in May, Harriman should travel to Laos for a firsthand evaluation. Harriman sighed to himself; he had packed no tropical clothes. But at the Ankara Post Exchange he found one thin suit that fitted him and flew off in the direction of Laos. From the days of Franklin Roosevelt, Harriman was accustomed to making decisions without elaborate instructions from Washington. On his way to Asia, he chose to call in at other capitals as far away as New Delhi—seven cities in eleven nights. Since Souvanna Phouma was also traveling, the two men's paths crossed only in Cambodia, where they met again briefly in the Phnom Penh airport's VIP lounge.

Arriving in Saigon, Harriman conferred with General Lemnitzer, whom Kennedy had sent out for a military analysis. They agreed that the Western powers would be seriously weakened in Geneva if the United States did not send in troops to secure Vientiane—preferably as part of SEATO but alone if necessary. The hard choices that Eisenhower had posed barely three months earlier were no longer theoretical.

And then, with their own goals met, the Pathet Lao stopped fighting. The Communists accepted April 24 for a cease-fire, May 3 for an opening session in Geneva. Lemnitzer could fly home to take up membership in the Never Again Club, and Harriman could hope that his call for military intervention would not be leaked to Laos's neutralist leaders.

IN WASHINGTON, it was no secret that Lyndon Johnson was enjoying the office of vice president as little as his predecessors had. When Johnson campaigned against him in the Democratic primaries, Kennedy had been careful not to offend his older, more powerful Senate colleague. Forced to explain to the many runners-up after the convention why they had not been chosen for the second spot, Bobby Kennedy sometimes suggested that his brother had offered Johnson the job as a courtesy and had been dismayed when he accepted. But during the primaries, Jack Kennedy had told friends that while Johnson would be his first choice as a running mate, he would never give up his power as Senate majority leader.

Once in office, Kennedy was conspicuously solicitous of his running mate, who had delivered Texas's crucial electoral votes. England's prime minister, Harold Macmillan, once told Kennedy that Eisenhower had never permitted Nixon into the living quarters of the White House. With that in mind, Kennedy saw to it that Johnson appeared on every official guest list and was sometimes invited with his wife to dine informally with the Kennedys. Bored as Jacqueline

Kennedy was by politics, she observed Lady Bird Johnson's active partnership in her husband's career with an appalled fascination.

Soon after the inauguration, Kennedy joked with Kenneth O'Donnell, an aide from Boston, that henceforth O'Donnell would be in charge of the care and feeding of Lyndon Johnson. Over a drink, Kennedy tried to plumb that outsized psyche. "I just want you to know one thing," he told O'Donnell. "Lyndon Johnson was a majority leader of the United States Senate. He was elected to office several times by the people. He was the number-one Democrat in the United States, elected by us to be our leader.

"I'm President of the United States. He doesn't even like that. He thinks he's ten times more important than I am—he happens to be that kind of a fellow. But he thinks you're nothing but a clerk. Just keep that right in your mind. You have never been elected to anything by anybody, and you are dealing with a very insecure, sensitive man with a huge ego. I want you literally to kiss his fanny from one end of Washington to the other."

If Kennedy appreciated Johnson's complexity, his administration included East Coast liberals who regarded Johnson as something of a galoot. They tended to forget that he had been the Senate's master manipulator because beneath a rancher's exterior lay delicate calibrators attuned to the sensitivities around him. Johnson suffered the amused disdain at the White House and blamed the president's brother for much of it. But he had to admit that the president himself treated him with only kindness and courtesy. Since Jack Kennedy preferred to be seen as coolly pragmatic rather than as compassionate, however, he had concluded his lecture to O'Donnell with a practical consideration. "I can't afford to have my Vice President, who knows every reporter in Washington, going around saying we're all screwed up. So we're going to keep him happy. *You're* going to keep him happy."

In May, when Kennedy proposed sending Johnson on a fact-finding mission to seven Asian countries, the vice president gave his detractors fresh ammunition to disparage him. During the recent campaign, Johnson's physical courage had provoked snide gossip about his performance in World War II. As a young congressman, he had wangled a commission as a lieutenant commander in the navy and sought a brief assignment to the Pacific theater. Once there, however, his plane was attacked by Japanese Zeros during a routine inspection flight. For the thirteen minutes until the aircraft could return to its base in New Guinea, Johnson had shown notable composure. But a second B-26 bomber on the same mission was shot down, and the next day Johnson flew back to Texas to regale voters with harrowing stories of his ordeal under fire. General MacArthur did his part for the young politician by awarding him the military's third-highest honor, the Silver Star medal for gallantry, a decoration that was not bestowed on the plane's pilot or crew.

Now Johnson resisted being sent to a war zone, even though the skirmishes in Vietnam villages were remote from any place he was likely to visit. But once he was persuaded to go, Johnson began looking for ways to exploit the minimal risk he was taking. Stopping over in Taiwan, he heard from Ray Cline, the CIA station chief, that when Eisenhower had visited the previous year, the Chinese on the mainland fired 140,000 rounds against the island of Quemoy to show their contempt for his presence on Chinese soil. "If they fire on Quemoy," Johnson said, "I want to know it immediately."

Like most people meeting Johnson for the first time, Cline was impressed equally by his sharp attentiveness and by his flair for theatrics. Even after Cline assured him that he would be in instant communication with the vice president's motorcade, Johnson called four or five times en route: "What are the Chinese doing at Quemoy?" When Cline had nothing to report, he could sense the vice president's disappointment.

Drama did mark Johnson's departure from Taiwan for Vietnam, however, when his parting statement was momentarily misplaced. The vice president fussed and stewed and finally turned on Carl Rowan, a veteran black journalist who had recently signed on as the State Department's deputy for public affairs. "I'll tell you this, goddamit," Johnson shouted in front of an entourage that included Lady Bird, Kennedy's sister Jean and her husband, Stephen Smith. "If the Foreign Service and the USIA people don't perform, the next time I make a trip, the whole goddam staff that's with me is going to go home with their peckers in their pocket." At that, he stomped away, and Rowan laughed until tears came to his eyes.

When Johnson reached Saigon on the evening of May 11, his party was welcomed by carefully coached Vietnamese rounded up by Nhu's private guard. They waved Vietnamese and American flags and shouted, "Van tue! Long life!" Diem put up the visitors in the government guest house and scheduled Johnson's audience for the next morning. At 8 A.M., Johnson was driven to Gia Long Palace, accompanied by the new ambassador, Fritz Nolting, who had arrived in the country only two days earlier. The luxury and high ceilings of the president's salon on the second floor, together with Diem's reserved air, seemed to subdue the vice president, and Johnson was formal as he handed over a ceremonial gift with a subliminal message—a set of books from American Heritage. Johnson also passed Diem a letter from Kennedy and sat back while he read it.

Diem's response was in character. He set aside Kennedy's detailed suggestions and, smoking one cheap Vietnamese cigarette after another, treated Johnson to a lesson in his nation's history. When he reached the current situation, he noted that several years had passed since he had proposed that the Eisenhower administration pay to increase his Civil Guard by 20,000 men.

Johnson had been sent to get Diem's agreement on the letter's key proposals, and he tactfully steered the conversation back to them. Lansdale had warned

Kennedy against any pressure that would suggest that the Vietnamese president be "a good boy." Offending Diem guaranteed that Nolting would encounter the same resistance that had made Durbrow ineffectual. Kennedy had heeded that advice; in effect, his letter thanked Diem for allowing the United States to underwrite his government. Diem seemed to find no disrespect in that approach.

Warning signs emerged, however, that, despite today's cordial atmosphere, Diem's intransigence would surface again as soon as Johnson left the country. When the vice president raised Kennedy's point that political and economic actions were as important as military measures, Diem agreed so long as those civilian actions were appropriate to his beleaguered nation. That judgment, he did not need to add, rested entirely with his family.

Responding to Kennedy's appeal for better relations with Cambodia, Diem laid any blame on Prince Norodom Sihanouk. And he balked at a proposal that the United States send fiscal experts to monitor the effectiveness of various joint projects. Americans would not be impartial, Diem said. Eventually, Johnson won him over.

As he was leaving, Johnson asked for a prompt answer, in writing, to Kennedy's proposals. Diem had promised a response to a previous counterinsurgency plan within two weeks and then had taken two-and-a-half months to deliver it. Today, Diem said he would produce his answers before Johnson left Saigon. Then he presented the bill for his cooperation: Johnson should tell Washington that South Vietnam would require another $30 million next year, above the amount the United States was already contributing.

Their business done, Johnson could relax with purely ceremonial duties. Meeting the exotic Madame Nhu, he reacted with the lecherous gallantry she appreciated, and each of them felt that a rapport had been achieved. During a sightseeing tour, Johnson leaped from his car to demonstrate Texas-style campaigning to the curious crowds. He bellowed praise for Diem as a leader "who would fight Communism in the streets and alleys, and when his hands are torn, he will fight it with his feet." Even in bemused translation, that message may have been lost on his audience, but Johnson's goodwill was not. The crowd cheered, and his Vietnamese escort murmured, "C'est magnifique!"

In all, Johnson could consider his mission a success. At a state dinner that evening, he toasted Diem as "the Winston Churchill of Asia," praise that quickly reached Tran Kim Tuyen and grieved him to hear. Tuyen had hoped that the new team in Washington would find ways to make Diem more responsive to his people. Instead, it looked as though the Vietnamese themselves would have to reverse Diem's disastrous policies.

Tuyen would have been no more reassured to overhear Johnson's conversation during the plane ride back to the United States. Stanley Karnow, a reporter for *Time* magazine, asked him incredulously about the comparison with Churchill. "Did you really mean it?"

In a sentence, Johnson laid out America's options as he saw them: "Shit," the vice president said, "Diem's the only boy we got out there."

WHEN THE RUSSIANS ANNOUNCED that their foreign minister, Andrei Gromyko, would attend the opening session of the Geneva conference on Laos, Rusk felt he should be there as well. The mood around the White House was still downcast because of the Cuban fiasco, and Rusk's report on the first round of talks did nothing to lighten spirits. Never an optimist about dealing with the Communists, Rusk predicted that the negotiations would probably fail.

Harriman set off for Switzerland more hopefully. He was to stay on for the substantive work ahead when, after a week or so, Rusk returned to Washington. Both men knew that the president wanted a settlement that would remove Laos as a domestic political issue. As Kennedy told his advisers, "If we have to fight for Southeast Asia, we'll fight in South Vietnam." With that in mind, Rusk agreed to let representatives from the Pathet Lao be seated and the talks begin.

On his return to government service, Harriman had become a believer in Parkinson's Law. Advanced four years earlier by a British civil servant, that thesis held that the amount of work expanded with the time allotted to it. Rusk's delegation numbered 126, and Harriman feared that many hours would be wasted in tedious meetings. The staff had already produced a mountain of reports that Harriman did not intend to read, and he was sure Kennedy wouldn't read them, either.

Although he deplored that glut of assistants, Harriman requested one more man, someone to coordinate the sprawling mission. The State Department sent William Sullivan—low-ranked and, despite prematurely gray hair, only thirty-eight years old. Harriman took to him immediately and ordered Sullivan to cut the delegation to a manageable size. He came back with a list that labeled one-third of the delegation as extraneous. "That's not enough," Harriman said. "I want it cut by half."

Sullivan made good on that assignment, and Harriman wired Washington that he intended to name the newcomer his chief deputy. Rusk's State Department replied that no one would accept Sullivan in that role because he was only a Class 3 officer. Harriman argued that the British, the Russians and the rest would accept anyone he introduced as his deputy. "Nobody will know, nobody will care, what his rank is," Harriman wrote.

State explained that it was the other members of Harriman's staff—the Class 1 and Class 2 officers—who would not accept Sullivan. At that, Harriman went down the list, identified every higher-ranking man likely to make trouble and sent him home.

But in other negotiations with his own government, Harriman remained stymied. Chen Yi, the Chinese foreign minister, had stayed in Geneva after Rusk left, and Harriman wanted to talk with him informally. He made the mistake of telling State that he planned to arrange a meeting, and Rusk grew alarmed that if the press found out, China's prestige would soar and the United States would look anxious and weak. He sent a wire denying permission and advising Harriman to maintain only a "correct attitude" toward the Chinese.

In a rage, Harriman threatened to quit. Franklin Roosevelt had sent him on more vital missions with only a line or two of instructions. Who was this Rusk? When his second request to meet Chen Yi was also rejected, Harriman complained to Ken Galbraith in India, who passed along his protest to Kennedy. The president ruled for Harriman, but by then Chen Yi, who had been receiving broad hints about a possible meeting, had become chagrined by the delay and returned to Beijing.

Gromyko also left the talks, with a jibe at their slow pace. "One cannot sit indefinitely on the shores of Lake Geneva, counting swans," he said. After one stormy session, his replacement, a deputy foreign minister named Pushkin, gave Harriman an insight into the growing rift between China and the Soviet Union, a rupture that some State Department officials were still discounting. The Chinese had loudly denounced the United States for supporting Phoumi Nosavan, and Harriman delivered a quiet but bitter rebuttal, citing Chinese aid to the Pathet Lao. The next day, when Harriman saw Pushkin, the Russian said, "You did the Chinese a great injustice."

"What do you mean?"

"They're not helping the Pathet Lao," Pushkin said. "All the arms and ammunition are coming from us."

Harriman understood that, despite State's misconceptions about Chinese and Soviet solidarity, the Russians in Geneva were embracing neutralism for Laos as a way to block Chinese expansion in Indochina. Khrushchev's interest in Laos might be minimal, but he could spare a few planes for an airlift that would remind the North Vietnamese that he, not Mao, was their dependable ally.

In Hanoi, Politburo members were content to let the great powers work out an accord, since they cared only about their continued access to the jungle roadway becoming known worldwide as the Ho Chi Minh Trail. Slogging over primitive paths from the North's panhandle down the several hundred miles to South Vietnam could take more than a month. Hanoi planned to expand its network of roads until they were wide enough to move trucks and artillery into the South. Support bases and fuel storage tanks would be built underground, like the tunnels of Cu Chi. For the construction, the Vietnamese had already commandeered Soviet supplies meant for Laos, including bulldozers.

China and Russia hoped a neutral government in Laos might mean the withdrawal of U.S. aid. But whether or not Laotian Communists joined a coalition, Hanoi was firm on one point: Pathet Lao troops must be allowed to hold what they already occupied, since that territory contained the Ho Chi Minh Trail.

□

AS HIS FIRST HAPLESS SPRING in the White House neared an end, Kennedy suffered another foreign policy debacle less public than the Bay of Pigs but personally humiliating. It came about when Khrushchev agreed to a summit meeting in Vienna in early June. The president and his wife made the trip by way of France, where Jacqueline Kennedy conquered Parisians with her bright smile, fluent French and white Givenchy gown. In talks with de Gaulle, Kennedy established an edgy détente by exercising his usual diffidence with his elders. De Gaulle advised strongly against getting bogged down in Indochina and warned Kennedy that France would not honor SEATO commitments there. No French soldier would ever go to Southeast Asia, de Gaulle said. He doubted afterward that Kennedy would heed his advice.

A few weeks before the European trip, the president had further strained his weak back while planting a ceremonial tree in Canada. To ease his pain, he had brought along on his plane Max Jacobson, a New York doctor known for his amphetamine treatments. During the presidential campaign, Kennedy had found that the doctor's weekly syringe gave him relief, with the welcome side effect of a euphoria induced by Jacobson's mix of chemicals that included "speed" and steroids.

Arriving in Vienna, Jacqueline Kennedy made Khrushchev as giddy as she had de Gaulle. When he claimed that the Soviet Union had sent more teachers to the Ukraine than the tsar had done, Mrs. Kennedy protested, "Oh, Mr. Chairman, don't bore me with statistics." Khrushchev exploded with laughter and went back to trying to amuse her.

During two days of talks with her husband, however, the Soviet premier was decidedly less jovial, and Kennedy's dependable charm could not seem to melt the unyielding Bolshevik. To a friend, Kennedy compared Khrushchev to his hard-dealing father, who expected "all give and no take." His son knew how to jolly Joe Kennedy out of a stern mood, but with Khrushchev none of Kennedy's quips were working.

The Russian intended his intransigence to serve as a test. During his tour of America two years earlier, Khrushchev had met Kennedy and liked the senator's good-natured smile. He had been pleased in November when Kennedy beat Nixon, whom Khrushchev regarded as an unprincipled capitalist puppet. Still, Kennedy now represented the Soviet Union's foremost adversary, and the time for smiling was over.

With the atmosphere already chilly, Kennedy let himself be trapped into an ideological debate he could not possibly win. In his airy way, he had once studied at the London School of Economics, but Khrushchev had devoted his life to the Marxist dialectic. He batted away Kennedy's jejune sallies about democracy and freedom with the assurance of a Jesuit debating dogma. Worse for Kennedy, their unequal exchange was being witnessed by Charles Bohlen of the State Depart-

Soviet Premier Nikita Khrushchev in East Berlin *(Archive Photos)*

ment and by Llewellyn "Tommy" Thompson, the U.S. ambassador to Moscow. The president could predict, correctly, that although both men were reasonably loyal, his rout would be the talk of Georgetown dinner parties.

When they got down to specifics, Khrushchev agreed readily to a negotiated settlement for Laos. Let the people there decide what government they wanted, he said, without the great powers interfering. Without mentioning North Vietnam, Khrushchev went on to observe, however, that the United States could do nothing more hopeless than wage a guerrilla war against a nation whose government Washington might disapprove but which enjoyed the support of its people.

The second day of talks, during a fruitless debate over a ban on nuclear testing, Khrushchev raised the issue Kennedy had been anticipating since February. From hints out of Moscow, the president knew that the Russians were ready to squeeze the United States over Berlin. Khrushchev began by noting that it was now sixteen years since the end of World War II and time to make peace with Germany. The Soviet Union was ready to sign a treaty with East Germany, which would end American access to its sector of Berlin.

Kennedy said firmly that they were not talking about a secondary problem like Laos. He had spent two days arguing against any shift in the balance of power between their two countries, and now Khrushchev was suggesting a cataclysmic upheaval. Khrushchev replied that he was willing to give Kennedy until the end of the year to make a red-carpet withdrawal from Berlin. But he would definitely sign the treaty. If the United States wanted to go to war over Berlin, the blame would lie with Washington. Kennedy asked for one final session with only interpreters present and pleaded with Khrushchev to rescind his ultimatum. Khrushchev said his decision was final. He would sign in December.

Glumly, Kennedy said, "It will be a cold winter."

KHRUSHCHEV WAS BLUFFING. He faced a drain of skilled workers from East Germany that amounted to 10,000 a week, a flow difficult to stanch since Germans could cross into West Germany through the open city of Berlin. In debating with a capitalist, Khrushchev might be full of bombastic confidence about the ultimate triumph of Communism, but to himself he admitted that the material riches of West Germany were dazzling the East German people. Khrushchev discounted the abstract appeal of liberty; he thought most people measured their freedom in terms of meat and potatoes and what kind of boots they could buy for a ruble. He did not underestimate the lure of owning a Mercedes-Benz, and East Germany could not meet that desire.

As the bargaining sessions ended, Khrushchev's blunt energy had left Kennedy shaken as seldom before in his life. He took the threat over Berlin entirely seriously and sought out James Reston, a *New York Times* columnist skilled at cosseting powerful men. Reston relayed to the world the mood Kennedy wished he had felt—"solemn, although confident." Reston added that Kennedy had come through his baptism in Cold War diplomacy very well, and that the president "rates more highly in the estimation of the men who watch these exchanges than'he has at any time since he entered the White House." Reston did not identify those observers, nor did his article include one of Kennedy's asides to him: "Now we have a problem in making our power credible, and Vietnam is the place."

BACK IN WASHINGTON, Kennedy asked Rusk and Ted Sorensen to draft written replies to Khrushchev's formal aide-mémoire with its December deadline. Rusk was inclined to keep negotiations going and hope the Russian ultimatum could be talked to death, and his staff produced a dry response. Sorensen's draft was deemed too filled with ringing—but inappropriate—phrases. Looking for a way to convince Khrushchev that he was underestimating the wrong man, Kennedy brought Dean Acheson back to the White House and learned that Acheson saw Berlin as a test of wills. Vice President Johnson agreed, and Walt Rostow called the U.S. commitment to Berlin absolute, even if the city were militarily untenable. Another academic, Arthur M. Schlesinger, Jr., disagreed. A Harvard history professor brought to Washington so that he might one day write an authorized version of the Kennedy years, Schlesinger had been blaming himself for his silence during Bay of Pigs briefings. He had been intimidated by the confident generals and admirals, chests heavy with combat ribbons. This time, he would speak up against Acheson's hard line.

The issue, Schlesinger wrote to the president, was "to put it crudely: Are you chicken or not? When someone proposes something which seems tough, hard, put-up-or-shut-up, it is difficult to oppose it without seeming soft, idealistic, mushy, etc."

Kennedy took Schlesinger's point but went ahead and called together the National Security Council to consider declaring a state of national emergency, a drastic measure that Acheson strongly supported. A few minutes before joining with the full council, Kennedy met privately with his closest advisers. Ted Sorensen, who would be drafting the president's speech, sat in with Rusk, Bundy and McNamara. As he listened, Sorensen was awed by the brilliance of McNamara's arguments in favor of declaring a national emergency. Speaking without notes but rapping out each point in its logical sequence, the defense secretary presented the military and political benefits of the declaration in a way that struck Sorensen as irrefutable.

When he finished, Kennedy said quietly, "No, I think it's a bad idea."

The small group then moved to the Cabinet Room where the full security council awaited them. Kennedy called on McNamara, who launched into a second brilliant argument, again without notes but entirely precise and informed, to prove conclusively that declaring a state of national emergency was a bad idea. As he watched the performance, Sorensen's admiration was tinged with disbelief.

The president instructed McNamara to prepare a military plan for Berlin that excluded the use of nuclear weapons and yet would give the Russians second thoughts. In the meantime, Kennedy went on television to reassure the American public that the Vienna summit had been a very sober two days but that there had been "no threats or ultimatums by either side."

To signal his resolve, Kennedy asked Congress to expand the military budget by $3.25 billion and to double the draft calls, increasing the armed forces by 217,000 men. He also called up units of the Reserves and National Guard. That call-up resulted in a massive disruption of civilian lives, and street demonstrations broke out against the unfair burden being imposed on some reservists. At a press conference, Kennedy responded to the criticism with a rare expression of his innate fatalism: "Life," he told reporters, "is unfair."

IN ANNOUNCING his military buildup to the nation, Kennedy added an alarming recommendation: American families should build and stock underground shelters against the possibility that nuclear weapons would be launched because of Berlin. Although the speech also called for further negotiations, reporters in Washington—and Khrushchev in Moscow—took it as Kennedy hoping to demonstrate toughness. Khrushchev retaliated by putting a hard-line army marshal in command of the Soviet troops in Berlin. But he kept the man in Moscow.

In the end, Khrushchev hit upon a simple strategy for keeping East Germany's workers at home, one that Kennedy had half-expected. Walking with Rostow near the White House one day, the president had said: "You know, Khrushchev is going to build a wall. And I won't be able to do a damned thing. I can barely hold NATO together."

On August 13, East German troops strung barbed wire around East Berlin and then constructed a concrete wall, all within East German boundaries. Kennedy responded by sending Lyndon Johnson to read a speech to West Berliners with a phrase that Rostow cribbed from Jefferson, pledging to defend the city with American lives, fortunes and sacred honor. Schlesinger's game of chicken then ensued. Fifteen hundred men from the U.S. 8th Infantry drove down the autobahn into West Berlin. Khrushchev made no attempt to stop them. He had his wall and could announce to the Soviet Congress that, since the Western powers were showing sufficient understanding of the situation, he would not be signing the threatened treaty with East Germany. Kennedy's victory, if it was one, hardly erased his Cuban debacle, and he anticipated further testing during the negotiations over Laos.

As HARRIMAN LABORED in Geneva to force Phoumi Nosavan into a coalition with the Pathet Lao, South Vietnam's secretary of state, Nguyen Dinh Thuan, arrived in Washington with a letter for the president. Kennedy read the message slowly and went over its contents with Walter McConaughy, the assistant secretary of state for Far Eastern affairs who was representing Rusk. Diem was now asking the United States to fund 100,000 more South Vietnamese troops, which would bring his army's strength to 270,000. The cost would be another $175 million over the next two-and-a-half years and an annual $20 million a year after that.

Courteously, Kennedy asked Thuan the questions Vietnam always seemed to raise, including how much of the Communist strength in the South came from local citizens. Thuan acknowledged that the French had never held more than the cities and main roads and that the Vietcong now occupied the countryside and controlled most of the population. But he stressed that former Vietminh were coming down from the North to join the struggle. In that, Thuan was not wrong, although his estimate of 7,000 every month since February was far too high.

Kennedy spoke frankly with him about his domestic problem with Diem's request. He forwarded the letter immediately to McNamara, who would be testifying that same day before a Senate committee. Kennedy also suggested that Thuan call on several Republican senators, especially Minority Leader Dirksen, to commit them to a budget increase. The president was even more candid about the inadequate size of the U.S. Military Assistance and Advisory Group in South Vietnam. He warned, though, that any increase in American advisers would have to be handled quietly. Under an already strained interpretation of the 1954 Geneva agreement, the number was currently about 700 men. Since Harriman in Geneva was pledging that Washington would honor any new accord, Kennedy didn't want it known that he was about to violate the earlier terms.

THROUGHOUT THE SUMMER OF 1961, Kennedy kept postponing decisions on Vietnam and letting the policy memoranda pile up. He had appointed Maxwell Taylor to head an inquiry into what had gone wrong in Cuba and was increasingly looking to Taylor, who held the nebulous title of the president's military representative, for the sort of crisp analyses that the Joint Chiefs seemed incapable of providing. Passing Taylor in a White House corridor one day, Kennedy pressed into his hand Diem's letter requesting more soldiers.

"What do I do about this?" Kennedy asked.

Taylor set about collecting information for a reply and included a recent memo from Ed Lansdale. After consulting two Pentagon colonels Lansdale considered reliable, he said, he had concluded that an agreement to boost Diem's strength to 270,000 men could be delayed for as long as eighteen months, since troops from an earlier increase were still being trained. But Lansdale made the point that South Vietnam had been fighting for fifteen years—eight years during the French war, one year against the sects, six years against a growing guerrilla movement. Diem's government was "badly in need of a breathing spell." He did not add that Ho's troops had been fighting for that same period, plus another six years against the Japanese and their French collaborators during World War II.

Lansdale offered detailed plans for how Diem's fifteen divisions should be deployed if he was eventually granted the increase. For now, the Vietcong controlled 20 percent of South Vietnam's 66,000 square miles and could launch hit-and-run attacks throughout another 40 percent, Lansdale said. In spite of those figures, he doubted that Diem's army required even 220,000 men to produce a "breakthrough"—a sharp setback for the Communists that would provide a fighting chance for the south.

Taylor and Walt Rostow sent a memo of their own directly to Kennedy that listed three courses of action: Graceful disengagement. An attack on Hanoi under a convenient political pretext. Or—the only option they were presenting seriously—a continued buildup of South Vietnam's army while standing ready to intervene with U.S. troops if the Chinese Communists came across the border.

It was the ground that every White House meeting on Vietnam plowed over, always concluding that Diem must somehow do better. When Rusk went to Paris, Maurice Couve de Murville, France's foreign minister, tactfully took a share of the blame: we all have failed to turn Diem's government into a popular one, he said. Speaking for Britain, Lord Home said he didn't know how to improve Diem's popularity, either.

CHESTER BOWLES did have an idea, which he intended to set forth in another memorandum to Rusk. His last attempt at influencing policy had not only failed to prevent the Bay of Pigs but had led to his being ostracized. Bowles was never asked to join any of the shifting, often overlapping, committees that were discussing Vietnam. Then in June, with Rusk overseas and Bowles the acting secretary of state, he antagonized Bobby Kennedy still further when he opposed sending American soldiers to the Dominican Republic after its dictator, Rafael Trujillo, was assassinated. Behind his back, Kennedy called Bowles a "gutless wonder."

Bowles blamed the State Department for the continued sniping against him in the press and agreed with Ken Galbraith's maxim: "Never underestimate the power of the bureaucracy." To Bowles, it was clear that entrenched lower-level officials at State were resisting any departure from the Dulles policies of the 1950s. But Bowles's problems didn't stem entirely from underlings. Rusk had twice asked if he wouldn't be happier as a roving ambassador, and Kennedy himself called Bowles to the White House, ostensibly for a swim. At the pool, Kennedy began by saying that he might have made a mistake in not appointing Bowles secretary of state in the first place. As it was, the new initiatives he had expected from the department were not forthcoming. The president said he didn't blame Bowles for those shortcomings, but Bowles seemed to have become a focus for the discontent. Would he like to go to Chile as ambassador?

Bowles said no, but he asked for time to consider other options.

Articles by Joseph Alsop and other Washington insiders quickly had Bowles on his way out, first for his tendency to harbor only "big thoughts," but also because of his behavior during the Bay of Pigs. On the morning of Bowles's next meeting with Kennedy in mid-July, Reston reported in the *Times* that the president intended to ask for his resignation.

But Bowles had been busy in the meantime, marshaling the Democratic liberals who had never entirely welcomed Kennedy to their wing of the party. If he was to go, Bowles decided, Kennedy would have to fire him and offer a public explanation. As their meeting opened, Bowles took the initiative by showing Kennedy two memoranda that Rusk had not forwarded to the White House. One was Bowles's warning against the Cuban invasion, the other concerned a reorganization of the State Department. Recognizing Bowles's challenge to fire him, Kennedy backed away and agreed that he should stay on as undersecretary, at least until after Labor Day. But the White House leaks did not end. Pierre Salinger, Kennedy's bouncy press secretary, told reporters off the record that Bowles might not be around much longer.

Undeterred by his conspicuous lack of influence, Bowles was ready to urge that Kennedy admit that the U.S. position was rapidly deteriorating in all of Southeast Asia. To challenge the Communists militarily would involve "our prestige and power in a remote area under the most adverse circumstances," Bowles wrote. He called for an alternative political approach that might "save us from having to choose between diplomatic humiliation or a major military operation." Bowles noted that Thailand had stayed independent for centuries by bending to the prevailing winds. If South Vietnam were lost, the Thai leaders would accommodate themselves to the Chinese.

So far, everything Bowles was saying supported the domino theory. But rather than conclude that the United States must fight all the harder to hold South Vietnam, he presented a sweeping alternative: Don't stop with neutralizing Laos. Join with China, the Soviet Union, India and Japan to create a neutralist belt throughout the entire region—Burma, Thailand, South Vietnam, Cambodia and Malaya.

Bowles spelled out the many snags and complications in his approach, including the effect such a policy might have on U.S. allies in Taiwan and the Philippines. But Andrei Gromyko was currently attending the U.N. General Assembly, and Bowles urged Rusk to explore his idea with the Soviet foreign minister when they met the next day.

Bowles sent copies of his proposal to his allies—Stevenson at the United Nations, Harriman and George Ball at State—and all of them agreed that his idea had merit. In a covering memo to Schlesinger at the White House, Bowles said that unless a political settlement were worked out soon the United States might face the choice of "a major commitment of U.S. troops, with a rapid and disadvantageous escalation, or a precipitous retreat."

The proposal was pure Bowles—grandiose, idealistic, more than a little impractical. The secretary of state's response was pure Rusk. He did not raise the suggestion with Gromyko, and he did not reply to Bowles's memorandum.

THE CORE WEAKNESS in Bowles's grand plan was that, like most of his colleagues in Washington, he underestimated Hanoi's will and overestimated the Soviet capacity to bend it. Even at that, however, some members of Ho's Politburo would have embraced a neutralist solution. Since 1954, Hanoi's goal had been to get the Americans out of Vietnam. That done, they were sure the South inevitably would swing to them. Until that time, the Hanoi foreign office was promoting a rather tricky strategy: They would apply enough military pressure in the South to frustrate Washington and end support for Diem. But not so much that Kennedy would dispatch U.S. troops. The North Vietnamese understood China's position: Beijing would not send Chinese troops to them unless Diem or his allies marched across the 17th parallel. Hanoi was less sure about the unpredictable West.

As Kennedy fretted, Ho was leading the serene life of a secular saint. China's military attaché in Hanoi saw him often and was impressed by Ho's indifference to the passage of time. Although he was already seventy-one, he didn't seem concerned whether the struggle for unification took another twenty years. When Ho dropped in to chat at the Chinese embassy, the topic was always the small details of daily life, never politics. Once inside the compound, Ho sent away his body-

Ho Chi Minh in Beijing
(*Vietnam News Agency*)

guards with a smile. "The Chinese embassy is the safest place in the world," he said.

Ho had learned early the propaganda value of simplicity. At a lavish dinner during his 1946 trip to France, he had turned aside all offers of food and wine, accepting only a single apple. And he had presented the apple to a child as he walked out of the Hôtel de Ville, where a crowd had gathered to cheer him. In an early essay, Ho had praised collectivism as the opposite of individualism. Morality for a Communist Party member, he wrote, consisted of "putting the Party's interests above everything else, in all circumstances."

By now, Ho's personal sacrifices were deeply ingrained. He typed his own articles on an old typewriter. He drank only tea. At any gathering, he headed for the plainest chair. He often wore a cotton coat given him by Zhou Enlai's wife, one of the rare gifts from the Chinese that he had accepted. Chinese officials living in Hanoi felt a greater liking for Ho than for Mao and wanted to believe the tale that one of Ho's recent ancestors had been a Chinese tutor who seduced his student; that would make Ho half-Chinese.

Within the Politburo, Ho let subordinates contend over policy. The previous autumn, Le Duan, with his southern biases, had become party secretary. His dislike for the policy of peaceful coexistence guaranteed that North Vietnam would not tilt toward the Soviet Union if the rift widened between Hanoi's two giant allies. In the south, the Vietcong ranks were growing steadily at about 1,500 a month, and that number, edging toward 20,000, did not include hundreds of thousands of friendly villagers. Vietcong attacks grew in daring, with sizable victories in Phuoc Thanh and Darlac provinces. But one statistic was distressing. Ho did not have exact figures, but the number of Americans in South Vietnam, under the flimsy pretext of advising Diem's army, had risen from 700 to something approaching 3,000. That increase had come during the first nine months of the Kennedy administration. Ho asked his colleagues why the young American president was turning out to be a Truman or Eisenhower when it was so much more in his interest to be a Roosevelt.

HIS LIFETIME of liberal pursuits made Bowles's attitudes easy to predict, but Rusk remained enigmatic, even to the men who saw him every day. With a showdown looming between the two men, Bowles's staff tried to figure out how the secretary of state managed to combine passivity and belligerence. Veterans at State claimed that because Rusk had not foreseen the Chinese intervention in Korea, he had been deeply shocked. Taking the invasion as a personal failure, he was determined never again to offer an optimistic prediction of Communist behavior. Or was Rusk's apparent hostility toward Bowles simply that of a self-made man rankled by an East Coast snobbery he ascribed to Bowles? Men quoted the remark of Bowles's plainspoken wife upon first meeting Rusk: "I was told you look like a bartender, and you do."

The Bay of Pigs had convinced Bobby Kennedy that to protect his brother he must dig deeper into foreign policy and advise him more aggressively. Rusk had moved in the other direction. When McNamara took his cue from the president and began to challenge the Joint Chiefs, Rusk was content to let the defense secretary lead the questioning. McNamara continued to be scrupulous about deferring to Rusk's right to speak first, as senior cabinet officer. But Rusk always replied, "No, that's all right, Bob. You go ahead." Mac Bundy joked to colleagues about Rusk's reticence. He claimed that Rusk was alone with the president when Kennedy asked for his opinion on a policy matter. In Bundy's version, Rusk replied, "If there weren't so many people in the room, I would tell you."

That sort of criticism may have reached Rusk, but he did not seem fazed by it. Privately, he said that if McNamara wanted to take over Vietnam policy, it was fine with him. But Bowles and his fellow liberals in the State Department considered any solution for Vietnam more political than military and were appalled to watch Rusk fading before their eyes. They were further disheartened when the president decided he needed another on-site inspection and chose to send his two most militant advisers, Maxwell Taylor and Walt Rostow. Among the Bowles loyalists, Rostow was considered a bit barmy.

WHEN KENNEDY ANNOUNCED the Taylor-Rostow mission at his October 11 press conference, a reporter asked whether sending Taylor confirmed rumors that the president might dispatch U.S. troops to South Vietnam, Thailand or Laos. "Well, we are going to wait till General Taylor comes back and brings an up-to-date description of the situation," Kennedy replied, "particularly in Vietnam."

Taylor had written his own instructions for the trip, expecting the president to sign off on them. But because Kennedy wanted to squash speculation over U.S. combat forces, he rewrote the charge and eliminated Taylor's suggestion that he evaluate what American soldiers could accomplish in Vietnam. Kennedy explained that if he decided against sending them, there could well be a "damaging letdown in Vietnamese morale." The president also deliberately misled the New York Times into running a story that Taylor—and the Joint Chiefs—were reluctant to send U.S. combat troops.

But in a top-secret telegram to Admiral Harry Felt, the U.S. commander in the Pacific, Lemnitzer wrote, "However, you should know (and this is to be held most closely) General Taylor will also give most discreet consideration to introduction of U.S. Forces if he deems such action absolutely essential." Lemnitzer added that Joseph Alsop and the other reporters would be aboard Taylor's plane but stressed that they were not part of the mission. "They are merely being given a ride to Saigon as a courtesy." To Rostow, Kennedy gave an impossible assignment: In four days, he was to plumb the hearts of the South Vietnamese people. Did they really want to be independent of Hanoi? Would they fight to save themselves from Communism?

Boarding the plane on October 16, Rostow loosened his tie and joined Taylor in getting to know the nine junior members of their team. Taylor instructed them to fan out across the countryside and prepare individual evaluations under their own names, which he would append to his report. Brigadier General Lansdale was aboard, although the other delegates were not sure which agency he was representing.

To his friend General Sam Williams, Lansdale had written disconsolately that Taylor "had a mob going" and "I think you know my feelings at being part of a big showy deal with a lot of theorists." On the other hand, "maybe I can snatch a few minutes alone with Diem and others, and make it pay off." Any meeting would have to be just that casual. In Washington, Taylor had made it clear that Lansdale would not be going to the palace for the official visits. "You'll simply be 'working party,' " Taylor said. Once aloft, Taylor dashed the rest of Lansdale's limited enthusiasm by ordering him to investigate the cost and effectiveness of building an immense fence across the entire western border of South Vietnam to stop infiltration down the Ho Chi Minh Trail. "That's not my subject," Lansdale protested, to no avail. "I'm no good at that."

In Honolulu, the task force was briefed by Admiral Felt, who recommended continued support for Diem but no U.S. troops at the present time. As the delegation stayed overnight in Hawaii before flying on to Saigon, Tran Kim Tuyen and a handful of other top Vietnamese officials met secretly to plot ways they could influence its members. Tuyen planned to argue that no amount of U.S. aid could save South Vietnam unless Diem immediately declared a national emergency and appointed a special council that would reform his government from the top down. Diem had to purge the incompetents who were being retained either because he hated to fire them or because of their flattery and false optimism. As a fellow Catholic, Tuyen was in a position to add that such men often held their posts only because they shared Diem's religion. As for the Nhus, Tuyen was ready to defend them, although Nhu inspired complaints about nepotism and his wife was an easy target for Communist propaganda. Tuyen argued, however, that Nhu was the only person Diem would trust to head an emergency council. Tuyen's cabal could agree on what must be done, but none of them dared to approach Diem with any aspect of their plan except, possibly, declaring a state of emergency. And without reorganization such a declaration would be worthless.

THE NEXT DAY, about the time the Washington visitors set down at Tan Son Nhut airport, Diem did in fact declare a state of national emergency, but it had nothing to do with a crisis in leadership. He was responding to rains in the Mekong Delta that had created the worst flooding in many decades. As they flew into Saigon, Taylor's delegation saw the devastation from the air with only a few rooftops rising above the ruined crops and drowned livestock.

Politics in South Vietnam were roiling as well. After months of study, Kennedy had approved giving Diem's air force six T-33 jet aircraft and U.S. personnel for training and maintenance. And on October 16, the day Taylor's group left Washington, Nolting cabled that Diem had reversed his long-standing opposition to introducing U.S. troops and would now accept them "ostensibly for guard duty, not for combat unless attacked."

When Taylor's plane landed, Lansdale hung back and let the others get swallowed up by reporters waiting on the tarmac. When he finally stepped out, one of Diem's aides sidled up and murmured, "The President would like to see you immediately." Lansdale caught Rostow's eye and told him about the invitation. "I might be there for dinner, I don't know," Lansdale said happily. "Would you please tell the boss this isn't a protocol call? I'm just going to see an old friend."

☐

AT THE PALACE, Lansdale found Diem and Nhu chain-smoking and primed with anxious questions. Diem had met Taylor twice in the past but now he wanted Lansdale's evaluation. What did Taylor want? What was he going to ask of them? Although Lansdale considered Taylor a cold and shortsighted autocrat with a manipulative charm, he told Diem not to worry. Taylor had only come to learn how the Americans could better help him. Diem knew that Lansdale opposed his asking for U.S. troops on the grounds that they would be as ineffectual as France's soldiers had been. But he confessed that he had agreed recently to accept American combat units. Trying to sound merely mournful, Lansdale was angry. "Have you reached the point in your affairs that you're going to need them to stay alive?"

When Nhu started to reply, Lansdale cut him off sharply. "I asked your brother, not you."

The Ngos were desperate enough to accept the rebuke. Diem said finally, "You mean I shouldn't ask for troops?"

"Do you *need* them?"

Again, Diem sat for moments before answering. "No."

Calmer now, Lansdale said, "Stay with that, then."

When Lansdale gave Taylor a laundered report of his evening, he was sure that the general was missing the nuances of Vietnamese politics. Taylor was keener to kill Vietcong, Lansdale concluded, than to probe their motivation.

THE NEXT DAY, Diem met with Taylor, Rostow, Nolting and Sterling J. Cottrell, who came along as the chairman of Kennedy's task force on Southeast Asia. When Taylor asked for a briefing on the situation, Diem delivered a four-hour monologue in French, allowing Taylor to make only an occasional aside. The change in time zones put Saigon twelve hours ahead of Washington, and Diem's lulling voice, combined with clouds of tobacco smoke, were making Taylor drowsy. But he snapped to attention when a brief pause let him ask about sending U.S. combat troops or SEATO forces. Why had Diem dropped his opposition?

Because of Laos, Diem said. The Communists were trying to infiltrate enough troops through Laos that even by building up his own army Diem could not compete with them. He added that the presence of American soldiers would not trouble the South Vietnamese people, since they already saw their war as an international one. But if troops were to be introduced, the United States and South Vietnam must sign a bilateral treaty. Without that, the troops could be withdrawn at any time. As for SEATO forces, that meant relying on France and Britain, and Diem did not consider them dependable allies. Because Diem spoke by indirection, the Americans were not sure afterward what he expected from them. But apparently Lansdale's disapproval had impressed Diem, and for the moment he was not asking for American combat troops.

☐

WITH NO IDEA about how to gauge Vietnamese attitudes, Rostow was delighted when Nolting proposed a way to establish their political sentiments. A military officer named Nguyen Khanh would go with Rostow to several South Vietnamese jails and translate for him the opinions of captured Vietcong. Fellow officers considered Khanh more ambitious than able, but Rostow was pleased to have his assistance and saw nothing strange in questioning prisoners about their feelings toward Hanoi. Khanh, in serviceable English, assured Rostow that he could point out which of the men were sincere and which were only telling the Americans what they wanted to hear. On the basis of a random sampling—and limited interviews with people who were not in jail—Rostow could report good news to Kennedy: the overwhelming majority of the South Vietnamese did not want their country ruled by Hanoi.

Meantime, Taylor was paying a courtesy call on Duong Van Minh, the Vietnamese general nicknamed "Big Minh" for his comparatively hulking size. Diem and his family distrusted the attraction Minh seemed to hold for visiting Americans and had given him the illustrious title of commanding general but no troops to command. Minh filled his days playing tennis and raising hothouse orchids. When Taylor asked Minh to tell him, soldier-to-soldier, whether the Communists were gaining strength, Minh answered obliquely. He seemed to be saying that the population was unhappy and felt strongly that Diem favored Catholics over the nation's other religions. Province chiefs who were appointed with no qualifications but their loyalty to the palace often arrived at their post speaking a northern dialect the people could barely understand. Those chiefs commanded all of the province's troops except during a very occasional military operation. Minh described one young palace favorite, already a major, whom Minh considered hardly fit to be a corporal.

As he left, Taylor tried to buck up Minh's spirits and urged him not to be discouraged. Minh reminded him morosely that Taylor had never had to confront the sort of war being fought in Vietnam and that he had been able to retire when political decisions had gone against him. But Minh added that he appreciated having had a chance to speak frankly. Other officers would do the same, but only individually or in a very small group. In South Vietnam these days, they felt as though they were in a diving airplane—either they would have to level off or it would be too late.

While Taylor met with Big Minh, Lansdale was back at the palace with Nhu, who had forgiven his outburst at their last meeting and had invited him to call. This time, Nhu took the offensive. The real problem in Vietnam, he said, was the way the United States was selling out the anti-Communist forces in Laos. To the Asian man in the street, the situation in Laos meant the end of SEATO and proof that the United States was ready to abandon all other anti-Communists. As a result, Asians were becoming demoralized. They hoped General Taylor's visit would produce a psychological shock in both South and North Vietnam.

Nhu lectured Lansdale on the inflated value that Westerners placed on liberty. His underdeveloped country was unfairly criticized, he said, and made to feel that it was somehow responsible for being attacked by Communists. Sardonically, Nhu noted that American reporters were labeling as corrupt the anti-Communist Lao leaders, and yet not a single journalist would expose the fact that Souvanna Phouma, the neutralist, controlled Laos's national bank and airline or that the Pathet Lao's ally, Kong Le, maintained several wives and a Chinese concubine. No, Western reporters went after only the supposed corruption of Phoumi Nosavan. And President Diem. "People say that I am responsible for the bad things, never the good things," Nhu concluded. "I'm afraid that I've let myself become paralyzed by fear of criticism."

Late in the trip, Diem suggested that Rostow also call on Nhu. During their three-hour interview, Nhu played the pragmatic younger brother praising Diem as a virtuous and courageous man but too soft and not modern in his methods. What the country needed was a highly centralized structure to hold its fragments together. Unimpressed, Rostow left the palace convinced that Nhu was blatantly power-hungry. He summed him up with professorial scorn as nothing more than a librarian — and a fascist one.

TAYLOR AND ROSTOW left Saigon for a two-day tour of the countryside, one day traveling near the Demilitarized Zone that separated the two halves of the country, the other flying over the flood-ravaged Mekong Delta. When they returned to the capital and prepared for a final call on Diem, Taylor used those last hours to alienate the American general who would have to implement whatever military plans Taylor recommended to Kennedy. Lieutenant General Lionel McGarr, chief of the Military Assistance Advisory Group, had already annoyed Taylor by questioning Taylor's scheme to smuggle U.S. combat troops into Vietnam as flood relief workers. McGarr also challenged Taylor's proposal that MAAG evaluate South Vietnamese officers for Diem but not exercise control over them. McGarr said that would put the Americans in an intolerable position; Taylor did not bother to answer.

As Nolting left for the farewell meeting, McGarr said that he would meet him at the palace. Well, no, the ambassador replied. Taylor had decided to keep the meeting small and — a jibe — they would be speaking French.

The general protested to Taylor. "As representative of the Joint Chiefs of Staff in Vietnam," McGarr said, "I recommend that I attend."

Taylor answered that it would be a personal meeting with Diem. McGarr was not to go.

"It is your decision, General."

Taylor considered that response huffy, but he relented and let McGarr tag along, reminding himself that McGarr's tour of duty would end soon and someone more suitable could replace him.

At the palace, Taylor spelled out his ruse for introducing U.S. combat forces into Vietnam without publicly violating the Geneva accords. The devastating floods would provide a humanitarian excuse. Army units from Engineering, Medical, Signal and Transportation could arrive in the Delta to help the villagers. Combat soldiers would be sent along to protect them. Obviously, Taylor said, if the military crisis got worse in the South, those American soldiers would constitute a reserve.

At one point, Diem asked Rostow how he ranked South Vietnam as a developing nation. Rostow said he had met able men throughout the South and offered a few names. "These men you have met talk well," Diem said. "But they cannot do the job." He picked up his telephone receiver and brandished it. "The job can only be done with this." As the meeting adjourned, Diem seemed to welcome Taylor's idea about U.S. troops, but the specifics were left to further negotiation.

Taylor preferred not to fly directly back to Washington but to have his team members draft their findings away from the city's political infighting. After a stopover in Bangkok, he intended to take them to the mountain town of Baguio in the Philippines and give them two days to compose their reports. Since sending combat troops would require quick action, Taylor cabled a brief overview of his proposal to the State Department, asking that it be passed along to Mac Bundy in the White House, McNamara and Lemnitzer in the Pentagon, and Allen Dulles, in his last days at the CIA.

Before he even left Bangkok, however, Taylor learned that his recommendation was a dud. Rusk broke away from a conference he was attending in Japan to wire that the flood control ruse was too transparent. He hadn't decided whether to support sending troops, Rusk said. But if they went, he wanted the administration to be straightforward about them.

Since that response seemed to paint Taylor as a conniver, he cabled back that his suggestion in no way had been a ruse. The flood damage was a real emergency. Rather, his proposal was a way to meet Diem's changeable attitude about U.S. troops without committing the large numbers that Taylor predicted would be required to put down the rebels—three U.S. divisions for a total of 60,000 to 75,000 men.

Rusk might be undecided about sending troops. The president had no doubts at all. He couldn't let South Vietnam fall to Ho Chi Minh, but with the future of Berlin still uncertain and negotiations over Laos only inching forward, Kennedy did not want to send any American soldiers. But what to do about Joe Alsop, who had gone along for the ride? He was already criticizing Kennedy's foreign policy for its lack of firmness.

AT THE PENTAGON, the Joint Chiefs supported sending U.S. troops to demonstrate America's commitment. Once back at the White House, Rostow recommended stationing 25,000 SEATO forces along the demilitarized zone to bottle up Giap's men. Rostow kept making the point that a guerrilla war would never end if reinforcements could be supplied as they were needed. Kennedy had expected to defang the clamor for U.S. troops by dispatching his hard-line aides to Saigon, one a highly respected general, the other known to advocate military action. The president thought he had been clear in letting Taylor understand that he did not want him returning with a recommendation to send troops. Why, then, was he cabling that unwelcome advice even before he got home? During the Eisenhower years, Taylor had called for innovative thinking about future wars. Yet now, confronted by a guerrilla war, he was turning out to be one more hidebound army officer.

At their farewell session, Diem had asked that Lansdale be assigned again to Vietnam. Although Taylor disapproved of Lansdale's unconventional approach, he wired Diem's request from Bangkok. In the margin of Taylor's cable, however, someone at State immediately scribbled, "No. No. NO!"

Since it would be several days before Kennedy could stifle Taylor in person, he had Bundy send a top-secret, eyes-only telegram to Bangkok. "The President requests that your conclusions on Vietnam, especially those relating to U.S. forces, not be discussed outside your immediate party in terms which would indicate your own final judgment. He is most concerned that you and he should have firm common ground when decisions are taken, and rumors of your conclusions could obviously be damaging."

But the inevitable rumors were loud enough to reach Mike Mansfield. Writing to Kennedy as a friend as well as Senate majority leader, Mansfield lobbied for his own solution. Calling the situation delicate and dangerous, he strongly opposed sending U.S. troops. Mansfield recalled Diem's earlier determination to rid his country of French influence and found it hard to understand why he should now be asking for foreign troops to shore him up.

Mansfield called instead for uniting Vietnam "by means other than the sword" and for implementing the reforms that the United States had repeatedly pressed Diem to make. Mansfield also recommended appointing an ambassador who was not a State Department veteran because the post was "one of high career risk."

Summing up, Mansfield listed the obvious dangers—including intervention by the Chinese, which would play into Russia's hands—and added a final caution against sending U.S. troops, even if they could defeat Giap's men: "We will have achieved a 'victory' that would cost billions of dollars in military and aid expenditures over the years into the future."

THE NEXT DAY, November 3, 1961, Kennedy welcomed the Taylor-Rostow delegation at the White House and met privately with the general for more than an hour to review his final report. Its preamble deplored the Communist aggression against "a new country only seven years old" but did not acknowledge that South

Vietnam had not been designed to celebrate even its third birthday. The summary also offered Rostow's usual solution: in time, the United States would have to make Hanoi pay by attacking North Vietnam, the source of the guerrilla war. The report estimated the maximum voluntary support for the Communists in South Vietnam at 200,000, or less than 2 percent of the population—a Vietnamese guess that the team had picked up in Saigon. "There is no need for fatalism that, somehow, Southeast Asia will inevitably fall into Communist hands," the report continued. "We have the means to make it otherwise." Then, ignoring Kennedy's wishes, Taylor set out in writing his proposal to introduce a U.S. task force into South Vietnam of 6,000 to 8,000 soldiers. The argument was advanced for the first time that a chief purpose in committing those troops would be to raise national morale among Diem's countrymen. The report acknowledged that the policies it recommended would shift America's relationship with Vietnam "from advice to limited partnership." But if Vietnam went, so would Southeast Asia. "What will be lost is not merely a crucial piece of real estate, but the faith that the U.S. has the will and the capacity to deal with the Communist offensive in their area."

The report presented McNamara with a quandary. He knew that the Bay of Pigs had left White House civilians dubious about the Joint Chiefs, and the debacle had produced a flicker of self-doubt in McNamara as well. He told Kennedy afterward that he had tried to persuade the Chiefs to change their invasion plans for Cuba—in what way, McNamara did not say. But when the Chiefs reminded him of their success in Guatemala in 1954, he had voted for the invasion. In retrospect, McNamara concluded that the Cuban failure was his fault, too. In his first months of service, he had failed the president both politically over the missile gap and militarily in Cuba. At a press conference, he then compounded the problem by imitating his president's style and trying to share the blame for the Cuban failure. As the chief executive at the Defense Department, McNamara told reporters, "any errors, therefore, are my errors." To the Joint Chiefs, who felt that their plans had been emasculated from political motives, McNamara's gesture was patronizing and unfair.

Now McNamara saw a chance to win back favor with his Chiefs. He circulated the Taylor report among them and on November 8 signed off on a reply in which the Chiefs supported Taylor's recommendations. McNamara passed along their warning that 8,000 troops might be only the beginning. So small a force would probably not deter the Communists unless the United States made it clear that North Vietnam would be punished for continuing to support the Vietcong.

McNamara predicted that, at worst, Hanoi and Beijing might intervene directly in the South, which would require a maximum force of 205,000 men. Even if Berlin were to erupt, that number was still manageable. McNamara's only reservation was that Kennedy first agree to a long-range commitment before troops were actually sent.

After McNamara signed that recommendation, however, he got word that the president was displeased with Taylor's report and had called back all copies. Once again, Kennedy was leaking his version of the deliberations by telling favored reporters that Taylor had returned from Vietnam recommending against the dispatch of U.S. troops. Given that unmistakable signal, McNamara joined with Rusk, who had been reading the portents from the White House more adroitly. By November 11, Rusk had helped McNamara back away from his hasty agreement with the Chiefs, and the two of them joined in urging that the United States commit itself to "the clear objective of preventing the fall of South Vietnam to Communists." But although the time might come for introducing American soldiers, that time was not yet. Better to encourage Diem to strengthen his political base.

At meeting after meeting, the agenda now concerned only questions of how. How could Diem be made popular? How could the Vietcong be resisted? But no one asked why South Vietnam was essential to U.S. security, and no one recommended getting out entirely. Chester Bowles was not consulted. At the CIA, the new director was John McCone, a Republican who had been Eisenhower's chairman of the Atomic Energy Commission. To his last day, Allen Dulles had played down any rift between the Soviets and the Chinese and warned that they might fight together to protect Communist interests.

With Bowles's influence in decline, George Ball, the undersecretary of state for economic affairs, had become the administration's foremost skeptic on Vietnam. He first objected to sending troops in meetings that included McNamara and his deputy, Roswell Gilpatric, but not the president. The only debate that mattered, however, was going on at the White House, where Mac Bundy was urging Kennedy to commit in advance one division—20,000 to 25,000 soldiers—but send it only when needed. Bundy's memo reflected the possessive attitude toward Asia reflected in that earlier question, "Who lost China?"

"Laos was never really ours after 1954," Bundy wrote. "South Vietnam is and wants to be."

Since Ball was not included in Kennedy's meetings, he was disturbed enough to raise the issue with the president directly. If you agree to send troops, Ball warned, "within five years, we'll have three hundred thousand men in the paddies and jungles and never find them again. That was the French experience. Vietnam is the worst possible terrain both from a physical and political point of view."

Jack Kennedy was usually receptive to differing views and tolerant about hearing them out. This time, he was annoyed. "George, you're just crazier than hell. That just isn't going to happen."

Afterward, brooding over the president's rebuke, Ball wondered whether Kennedy wasn't plagued by his same forebodings. Still, being called crazy rankled him. Back in his office, Ball told an aide: "We're heading hell-bent into a mess, and there's not a goddamn thing I can do about it. Either everybody else is crazy, or I am."

IN A SHOWDOWN before the National Security Council on November 15, Kennedy found himself the least militant man in the room. He began by saying that he could make a rather strong case against intervening in an area 10,000 miles away, against 16,000 guerrillas who were fighting a government army of 200,000, in a country where millions of dollars had been spent for years with no success.

After the Bay of Pigs, Kennedy had quoted the adage "Victory has a thousand fathers. Defeat is an orphan." In that case, he had been compelled to adopt the Cuban defeat and wanted no more like it. When Rusk suggested that Vietnam was like the crisis in Berlin, Kennedy disagreed. When McNamara outlined a possible assault on North Vietnamese bases, Kennedy picked his plan to pieces. When Rusk assured him that a number of countries would support U.S. action, Kennedy expressed his doubts. And when Lemnitzer spoke up for stemming the Communist onslaught, Kennedy asked how he could justify acting in Vietnam while they were ignoring Cuba.

Lemnitzer replied that, even seven months after the Bay of Pigs, the Joint Chiefs still wanted to invade Cuba.

The meeting was getting testy. Comfortable with dissent only when coolly expressed, Kennedy found an excuse for ending the session without a decision. He wasn't sure, he said, whether Congress, even with a Democratic majority, was prepared to support the action proposed for South Vietnam. He wanted to get the opinion of that master tactician, the vice president. But this meeting had been called so hastily that Johnson, traveling in Michigan, could not get back for it. Kennedy did not add that he knew Johnson would be strongly in favor of sending troops. The delay simply gave him a chance to let the contentious mood dissolve. He ended the meeting by saying that no action would be taken at the present time. That was just after 11:30 A.M.

Kennedy's agitation did not end when his aides left the room. He had a sinking feeling that no one was giving enough attention to Vietnam, and he spoke immediately with Taylor and with Harriman, who was in Washington briefly from Geneva. Rusk had not said much after the president disputed his few observations, and Kennedy sent Bundy to the State Department to brief him on what he would be asked later in the day. Kennedy intended to head off Rusk's customary protest that a matter needed further thought before he could commit himself.

At their 4:15 P.M. meeting, Rusk learned that the president had accepted his argument that Nolting was doing a good job and should remain in Saigon. But the session smoked Rusk out on two key points. He acknowledged that he was against bombing Hanoi to punish the North's support for the Vietcong. And, even though Diem might fall, Rusk thought it imperative that Washington show its determination to hold on there. If the United States didn't confront

Dean Rusk
(AP/Wide World Photos)

Khrushchev over Vietnam—Rusk was speaking with surprising passion—it would mean a terrible defeat. He suggested that the present policy of increased aid for Diem be called the Rusk-McNamara Plan. Then the president could fire both of them if it didn't work.

Brave words. But Kennedy knew that if the American people punished anyone for defeat in Vietnam, it would not be the secretaries of state and defense.

ALTHOUGH McNAMARA had changed his advice about sending troops, his reversal had been nimble enough not to jeopardize his standing at the White House. Kennedy approved most of his other recommendations, and on November 22, in National Security Action Memorandum 111, the president authorized shipment of helicopters, light planes and transports, along with small ships to be manned by Americans.

At the many meetings, Rostow had argued long and genially for bombing Vietcong sanctuaries within both Laos and North Vietnam. Such bombing was also the heart of SEATO Plan 5, a contingency scenario drafted the past April for maintaining troops in Laos. As he signed off at last on the Pentagon's recommendations, Kennedy joked, "If this doesn't work, perhaps we'll have to try Walt's Plan Six."

The president was only making a courteous bow to Rostow and any other aides disappointed by his caution. To Schlesinger, Kennedy was less generous about Taylor's original report. He was especially irked by the argument that U.S. troops would raise morale in South Vietnam. "The troops will march in, the bands will play, the crowds will cheer," Kennedy said. "And in four days everyone will have forgotten. Then we will be told we have to send in more troops. It's like taking a drink. The effect wears off, and you have to take another."

Even though Kennedy had settled on half-measures, he expected even those to be kept secret. Having muffled the demand for firmer action in Vietnam, he didn't want to confront the issue again soon. And there remained the matter of the 1954 Geneva accords. State Department lawyers, headed by Abram Chayes, reminded Rusk that if the United States did not abide by the accords, it could scarcely then accuse Hanoi of violating them. Loopholes might justify sending advisers, but Rostow's desire to punish Hanoi with attacks deep inside the North "would go beyond permissible self-defense under general international law and would be contrary to the United Nations charter."

WITH CUBA A BOTCH and Vietnam adrift, Kennedy could no longer put off changing his staff to eliminate the weaknesses uncovered during his first eleven months in office. Chet Bowles chose that inopportune moment to tell Rusk that the administration was accepting the same mistaken assumptions in Asia that had misled Foster Dulles. Bowles recommended several appointments at State, including Harriman for the Far Eastern desk. Rusk gave him no hint that he was discussing with the White House much greater changes than that. He said only that Harriman's appointment would not be fair to Walter McConaughy, who had been designated for the job, since he had just bought a new house in Washington.

Then, after Thanksgiving, Rusk insisted that Bowles come to his office the next Sunday, where Rusk handed him a press release stating that Bowles was out, to be replaced by George Ball. State's third-ranking post would go to George McGhee, rather than to another career officer, U. Alexis Johnson, who had lobbied for the job. Rostow and a young Kennedy campaigner, Richard Goodwin, were moving from the White House to State, Rostow to take the planning position for which Rusk had blocked him in January. For Bowles, the only bright spot was Harriman's appointment to Far Eastern affairs. McConaughy, so recently unmovable for compassionate reasons, was being shipped overseas. Bowles would assume Harriman's nebulous title of roving ambassador.

When Bowles finished reading the release, Rusk said that within a few hours Pierre Salinger would announce the changes to reporters at the Kennedy family's compound in Hyannis Port, Massachusetts. Offended and mortified, Bowles said that until he could talk with his wife and friends he would neither quit government—Rusk's clear preference—or take the new job. Kennedy had foreseen that reaction and told Ted Sorensen to be standing by at the White House. Sorensen had recruited Bowles for the Kennedy campaign and admired him. "Hold his hand a little," the president said, "one liberal to another."

When Rusk told him to come over, Sorensen had been authorized to negotiate with Bowles until they arrived at something acceptable to him. Bowles immediately turned down the roving position. Sorensen asked what else would keep him in Washington. After considerable haggling and a call to Kennedy in Hyannis Port, they agreed that Bowles would consider new foreign policy responsibilities if they included direct access to the president. Bowles left the State Department to be consoled by family and friends and to review what had gone wrong. He wondered especially why Rusk had behaved so underhandedly. The answer seemed to lie in a snide talk that Dean Acheson had given to a gathering of foreign service veterans. Rusk's State Department was like a medieval court, Acheson said, in which the king reigned but did not rule, and feudal barons wielded almost total power. Bowles concluded that the image had offended Rusk, and when he saw Bowles's influence slipping with the Kennedy brothers, he had relieved himself of his most assertive baron.

Kennedy created a clumsy new title for Bowles — the president's special representative and adviser on Asian, African and Latin American affairs — and threw in a pay raise and a White House car. Even at that, it took an hour of Kennedy's low-keyed flattery to get Bowles to accept. During the interview, Bowles offered his explanation for the breakdown in their relationship since Kennedy entered the White House. I am not one of the tough, terse, yes-or-no types you apparently find it easiest to work with, Bowles said, and there's nothing I can do to become one.

The president politely rejected that analysis, but Bowles had accurately described Bobby Kennedy and the men whose standing had risen at the White House: Bundy, with his memoranda reduced to lists of one-paragraph options. McNamara, who had reversed his troop recommendation with dexterity and conviction. Taylor, obdurate in ignoring Kennedy's instructions but with a bearing that commanded respect. Compared to their brisk confidence, a man like Bowles could indeed seem vain, wordy, self-involved.

As the year drew to an end, Kennedy faced one more disagreeable chore. He had to call in Ed Lansdale to tell him he would not be replacing Fritz Nolting as ambassador in Saigon. With Bowles gone, the president hoped that Rusk would become more decisive and was not going to overrule him on the appointment. Kennedy told Lansdale that he was needed more urgently as the executive officer of a new panel on Cuba called the Special Group. He would serve with Taylor, McCone, Bobby Kennedy and other top aides, and his new assignment was the kind Kennedy had once mocked: the American who knew Ngo Dinh Diem best was being moved to advise about a country he had never seen.

A last Vietnam detail remained. Kennedy wanted one cabinet officer to be responsible for monitoring progress there. The logical person was the secretary of state, but Rusk knew too well the bureaucratic risks in the job. His apologists at State said that Rusk had been scarred by the period when Acheson and Truman's secretary of defense, Louis Johnson, were not on speaking terms, and the workings of government had suffered. That view presented Rusk as a selfless man determined never to challenge Kennedy's hard-charging defense secretary. The truth may have been simpler. McNamara was still an innocent in the ways of Washington. On November 27, when Kennedy asked for a supervisor for Vietnam, McNamara ignored the collective wisdom of soldiers throughout history and volunteered for the job.

In Saigon, no one was happy with the results of the Taylor-Rostow mission. Between consulting with Kennedy and Bundy, Rusk had also met with the French and British ambassadors to Washington to fill them in on the deliberations. As a result, when William Trueheart, the deputy chief of the Saigon embassy, paid a courtesy call on the new British ambassador to South Vietnam, that man read to him what Trueheart had not yet heard: Kennedy had decided to send hardware and advisers but not combat troops. Nolting wired Rusk to complain that it was "naturally embarrassing and discouraging to have these results conveyed to us first by the British." Particularly since their embassy would leak the decision immediately to the Vietnamese.

At the palace, however, Diem was seething about more than protocol. He compared Taylor's visit to George Marshall's trip to China, when Marshall had insisted that Chiang Kai-shek share his power with a few intellectuals who called themselves the Liberal Party. Where was Chiang now?

And Kennedy had asked Ken Galbraith, another of those hectoring Americans, to stop by Saigon on his way back from India. Galbraith warned Kennedy that "we are now married to failure" and recommended in a flippant phrase that Diem be replaced—"nothing succeeds like successors." Diem was convinced that many Americans shared that view and might be ready to act on it. He was especially furious about lectures from the Americans because none of them appreciated the obstacles he faced—the Communist rebels, certainly, but also the shortage of loyal and efficient politicians. Whenever he would consult with Phan Huy Quat, a physician born in the North, Quat meandered on about "freedom" but clearly did not understand the realities of governing or why wartime required stern police methods. Quat was too busy ingratiating himself with the American embassy.

As for the American aid, where was it? In June, with much fanfare, the United States had promised funds for the first 20,000-man buildup of the South Vietnamese army. The money had not arrived. And Diem had carefully laid the groundwork with his cabinet and the National Assembly for the arrival of the U.S. troops. Now he had to go back and tell them that American soldiers were not needed after all.

As for the American press! Diem understood that their influence was powerful in their own country. But shouldn't they exercise some responsibility and remind their readers that South Vietnam was under a Communist siege? His own experience with American journalists had been insulting. If he didn't grant an interview, they called him aloof. If he did, those same reporters ridiculed him for how long he spoke with them.

FOUR

BIGART
1962

WHEN DIEM COMPLAINED about the journalists who bedeviled him, he would single out François Sully from *Newsweek* magazine, a curly-haired former French paratrooper who laughed his way through each day until he sat down at the typewriter to excoriate Diem. Like Jerry Rose, his opposite number at *Time*, Sully was what editors called a stringer, not a full-time staff member but a useful body kept on a retainer and paid by the number of stories he filed. Both the Associated Press and United Press International had sent regular staff to Saigon, but because their stories went to newspapers with widely different editorial positions, wire service copy was kept relentlessly dispassionate. The newsmagazines preferred more vivid accounts and allowed more interpretation. At *Time*, the opinions were supplied by editors in New York, at *Newsweek* by Sully in the field.

Throughout the 1950s, *Time* had portrayed Diem as a resilient, deeply religious Vietnamese nationalist. Henry Luce, the magazine's owner, had been born to missionaries in China and had never lost his family's zeal for converting Asia to the American way. *Newsweek*, on the other hand, regularly enumerated Diem's weaknesses, along with ongoing speculation that he might be replaced. After the attempted coup in 1960, *Newsweek* had urged Diem to treat the failed rebellion as "a grim signal of the extent of opposition to his authoritarian regime."

The *New York Times* had been depending on quick visits to Saigon by correspondents stationed elsewhere in Asia, but the Taylor mission stirred its foreign desk to send out the paper's reporter with the strongest credentials for covering a war. Homer Bigart had won Pulitzer prizes for his reporting in World War II and

Korea when he wrote for the *New York Herald Tribune*. He had moved over to the *Times*, and by early 1962 he was fifty-five, with an appreciation for Scotch whiskey that had added a banker's bulk to his dark suits and thick glasses. Fighting a life-long stutter, he had learned to carve his speech into bursts of bitter wit.

Because Bigart had passed up many offers to become an editor, his bosses were often younger or less talented than he. "Clarks," he called them, drawling out the word "clerks" in the English manner. No more proficient in languages than Ed Lansdale, Bigart claimed to get along by responding to anything said to him in French with a shrug and "*C'est drôle.*" And, like Lansdale, Bigart offered a rationale for being monolingual. "It's n-n-not how m-m-many languages you speak," he would tell younger reporters. "It's w-w-what you s-s-say in any one of them."

Bigart had first visited Vietnam in 1945 to report on the French struggle to reclaim their colony. Six years later, the *Herald Tribune* sent him back for another look, and it was then that he encountered Congressman John Kennedy making his tour of Asia. In an informal briefing, Bigart had contributed to Kennedy's pessimism about the prospects of French success. Now, a full decade later, Bigart was returning again. For this tour he had agreed to stay only six months and almost at once began counting the days.

Bigart's writing style had been neutered considerably when he moved to the *Times*, where editorial policy required that reporters efface themselves nearly off the page. All the same, few readers of a Bigart article could miss his opinions. It was Kennedy's bad luck that, just as he was trying to shore up Diem's regime with the least public attention, one of America's keenest reporters should materialize in Saigon.

Nor was the White House penchant for secrecy congenial to another fresh arrival. The new AP bureau chief, Malcolm Browne, was half Bigart's age but matched his drive and dedication. Trained in chemistry at Swarthmore, Browne had been won over to journalism during a stint in Korea with the military newspaper *Stars and Stripes*. Arriving in Saigon, he was as charmed by the city as Bigart was repelled by it.

Most journalists dropping into South Vietnam for short jaunts were at the mercy of the embassy for contacts and transportation. Joe Alsop had been steered to Kien Hoa province because of its successes in agriculture and was content to linger there with its province chief. Lieutenant Colonel Pham Ngoc Thao freely admitted that he had once been with the Vietminh and claimed that the experience had taught him how to run the Vietcong off his territory.

Noting the favorable coverage Thao was getting, Mal Browne chose Kien Hoa for his first look at the Army of the Republic of Vietnam, or ARVN; Americans pronounced the acronym "Arvin." When Browne arrived, Thao's soldiers were hoping to box in a Vietcong battalion between two hamlets, but Browne found that the ARVN were hardly the fighters Alsop had painted. After hours

Homer Bigart
during World War II
(AP/Wide World Photos)

spent wading through rice paddies, Thao's troops had killed only one unarmed farmer, who was living with his wife and children in a hut painted with antigovernment slogans. A Vietnamese officer told Browne, "It looks as though the Vietcong got away again." Their escape would have been less surprising had his American advisers and the newsmen known that Colonel Thao remained a Communist officer.

In 1945, as Albert Thao, he had been a middle-class Hanoi teenager mad for his motorcycle and for Ho's revolution. Quick, slim and mocking, with a disarming walleye, Thao went south during the French War and stayed on when other Vietminh heeded the call to return to Hanoi. Thao's Catholic family vouched for him with Ngo Dinh Thuc, the archbishop, who put him in touch with Tran Kim Tuyen. With that backing, Thao rose steadily in the ARVN. Nhu sent him to study counterinsurgency techniques in Malaysia and depended on him to investigate fellow officers suspected of disloyalty. Thao capped his service to Diem by helping to thwart the 1960 coup. Rewarded by being named province chief of Ben Tre, Thao worked covertly with Mrs. Nguyen Thi Dinh and her resourceful women and Vietcong guerrillas to ensure the tranquility Alsop had found so impressive.

Even without knowing of Thao's duplicity, however, Bigart was increasingly disgusted with the miasma of falsehoods and menace spreading across Vietnam. Not only did Nhu and his secret police spin webs of deceit, but Nolting and his underlings at the embassy struck Bigart as scarcely more truthful, and clumsier in their lies. Soon after Kennedy authorized the military buildup, Stanley Karnow, the experienced reporter for *Time*, was drinking coffee on the Saigon riverfront with a U.S. Army press officer. From their table on the terrace of the Majestic Hotel, Karnow was startled to see an American aircraft carrier hove into view. The vessel was delivering the first shipment of American helicopters strapped to its deck. Karnow grabbed the officer's arm. "Look at that carrier!"

His companion pretended to squint. "I don't see nothing," he said.

KARNOW'S OFFICER was only following the lead of his commander in chief. At a January press conference, Kennedy was asked a direct question: "Mr. President, are American troops now in combat in Vietnam?"

"No," said Kennedy, turning gratefully to a question about his Food for Peace program.

Testifying in executive session before the Senate Foreign Relations Committee, Ambassador Nolting also assured listeners that no Americans were engaged in combat. He added the qualification "as of now" but did not say that the first combat flights were scheduled to begin only hours after his testimony.

Two days before Kennedy's press conference, pilots from the U.S. Air Force's covert Jungle Jim unit had been given a new mission. No longer were they merely training Vietnamese pilots. So long as one Vietnamese flew in their six-man crew, they could provide close support for ARVN ground troops. High on the list of qualifications to become a Jungle Jim was expendability. A volunteer for the flights, called "Farmgate," had to be a bachelor willing to sign a statement that if captured in Country 77—code for Vietnam—he agreed that his government would deny any knowledge of him.

As part of the buildup, the U.S. military group was adopting an expansive new title—Military Assistance Command, Vietnam, or MACV. In February, the Pentagon sent to lead it Paul Harkins, a fifty-seven-year-old four-star general. An aide to George Patton in World War II, Harkins hardly represented the new counterinsurgency era of Green Berets and Jungle Jims. But he was Max Taylor's choice, and Kennedy continued to believe that, because Taylor had once challenged Pentagon policy, he remained the man to oversee MACV in its guerrilla war. Horst Faas, a photographer newly arrived in Mal Browne's AP bureau, arranged to take Harkins's picture for the wires, but when he arrived at the general's office he found him in his dress whites. Faas suggested that he change to fatigues for a photograph in the field; he did not understand yet that the White House wanted no American general in combat gear spread across the world's newspapers. "Forget that kind of picture," Harkins told him. "I'm not that kind of general."

As that remark circulated among Saigon's press corps, reporters judged the new arrival to be not only vain but also likely to report to the Pentagon without troubling to make on-the-spot investigations. If that conclusion was unfair, Harkins did not improve matters when he outlined his approach to his job: "I am an optimist, and I am not going to allow my staff to be pessimistic."

PRESIDENT DIEM was grateful for his excellent hearing. Since assassination was a constant threat, he could count on hearing the sound of a match being struck while he slept, and the breathing of another person in his bedroom was enough to rouse him. Yet, when he heard the first explosions on the morning of February 27, Diem was sure that the noise was coming from ten or twelve miles away. It took him moments to realize that his palace was being bombed, and longer still to recognize that the attack was coming from his own air force.

That morning, a discontented young bomber pilot, Sublieutenant Nguyen Van Cu, had taken off from the Bien Hoa airbase with orders to support ARVN ground troops on their operation. Instead, Cu swerved his American-built Skyraider and headed for Saigon with a second plane behind him. Cu had persuaded its pilot, Lieutenant Phan Phu Quoc, that bombing the palace was the signal that would touch off a general uprising of South Vietnam's military. Cu assured Quoc that all the armed services, and even the Americans, were in on the plot. As proof, Cu quoted from a recent *Newsweek* article critical of Diem.

A little before 7 A.M., Nhu's children were playing in the garden when Cu flew overhead, low enough to frighten the deer on the palace lawn. The children ran to an elaborate shelter of tunnels beneath the palace, and their father and their uncle, Archbishop Ngo Dinh Thuc, soon joined them. They listened as a bomb fell on the verandah near Diem's office that would have demolished his stairs to the shelter. It was a dud, however, and Diem reached safety underground. Madame Nhu was the last to arrive. As she lingered in her apartment, taking time to dress properly, flying glass had cut her arm slightly. Within the shelter, she fretted about permanent scarring.

During the fifty-minute raid, the planes did not empty their full load of rockets and napalm, which could have leveled the palace. Quoc's plane was shot down by Vietnamese navy antiaircraft guns and crash-landed outside Saigon. Captured and taken to jail, he complained that he had been stupid to listen to Cu, who landed in the Cambodian capital of Phnom Penh, 145 miles to the west. He was immediately arrested by Cambodian police while he was telling reporters on the scene that Diem's family was hated by the military and the Vietnamese people. But there had been no coup. Cu was disgruntled because he had learned that pilots in the United States and France enjoyed more benefits than Diem was granting them.

The danger had barely passed when Tran Kim Tuyen got a call that Diem wanted to see him. This time, Tuyen looked at the many people surrounding the president and realized that he had not been summoned for congratulation. Diem's first question was pointed. "Did you know about this in advance?"

Tuyen said meekly, "No, Mr. President."

Nor did he know that one of the pilots was the son of a man Tuyen had once released from police custody. But the order to set him free had come from Diem himself. "He's an old man," Diem had said at the time. "He's not dangerous. When I was under arrest by the Communists in North Vietnam, this man came to look after me." Diem had forgotten that directive and was consulting a dossier with the damning notation that the father had been released "due to the intervention of Dr. Tuyen." It took a thorough investigation to convince Diem that there had been no coup and to lift the cloud from over Tuyen.

As BIGART AND BROWNE filed stories about the bombing, each found it necessary to define "napalm" for their readers. It was jellied gasoline, they explained, and the palace had first denied it had been dropped because the Vietnamese were sensitive on the subject since the French had used napalm against them. One palace servant had died in the attack, and 10 soldiers wounded. An American civilian working for a contracting firm was also killed when he climbed to the top of his four-story apartment to watch the excitement and fell from the roof.

Another unlikely casualty of the bombing was a training program that Diem once warmly embraced. In 1950, Wesley Fishel, the assistant professor at Michigan State University who had met Diem in Japan during Diem's exile, had persuaded his university to sponsor Diem's first trip to the United States. As a founding member of a lobby called American Friends of Vietnam, Fishel arranged a contract five years later between MSU and the Diem regime to train a new generation of Vietnamese administrators, especially the police.

Fishel's team included about sixty scholars, but they often ended their Vietnam tours despairing of any real change, and several Michigan professors had recently attacked the Diem government in the *New Republic* magazine. Outraged, Diem said that if the articles had appeared while the authors were still in Vietnam, he would have put them on trial for fomenting insurrection. As it was, even before the bombing, the Ngo family had become convinced that the Michigan team was plotting against them. When Diem notified the university that he would not be renewing its contract, Fishel wrote to Michigan State's president that for the first time in seven-and-a-half years he had become pessimistic about the fate of South Vietnam. Fishel said that the "evil influences" around Diem began with Nhu and his wife—"brilliant, vivacious, bitchy and brutal in her Borgia-like fashion."

DISSATISFIED with the information he was getting from Saigon, Kennedy kept asking travelers to call in whenever they were in that part of the world and report their impressions to him. During an Asian tour in February, Bobby Kennedy made an hour's refueling stop at Tan Son Nhut airport and took reporters' questions. The attorney general was caught up at home in an epic constitutional challenge by Negro civil rights leaders. It was a confrontation with southern segregationists that neither he nor his brother had encouraged, but they were prepared to resolve the crisis with federal troops. Not long before Kennedy's Asian trip, Stan Karnow, on leave in Washington, tried to discuss Vietnam with the attorney general and had been waved off impatiently. "We've got 20 Vietnams a day to handle," Bobby Kennedy said then.

He was paying more attention on this impromptu second visit. Bobby had accompanied his brother on Jack Kennedy's first trip to Saigon in 1951, and, as a rather callow twenty-six-year-old, had been much taken with the toughness of the French Foreign Legion. But he had also written home to his father that the French were "greatly hated" and that U.S. aid to them had made "us quite unpopular." In a plebiscite, Bobby had added, Ho Chi Minh would get 70 percent of the vote.

On this trip, Kennedy assured the correspondents that the United States was in Vietnam to win. But he tripped himself up when a reporter asked him to define just what it was the United States would be winning. A war? No, said Kennedy, not a war; a struggle. "What is the semantics," the reporter persisted, "of war and struggle?"

Before he thought better of it, the nation's ranking lawyer tried to explain. "It is a legal difference." Bobby paused. "Perhaps it adds up to the same thing. It is a struggle short of war."

ALTHOUGH THE SAIGON foreign press had been an irritant for years, Bigart's presence and Browne's aggressive reporting began to reverberate throughout Washington until Carl Rowan and Arthur Sylvester were pondering ways to curb their former colleagues' influence.

In approving the U.S. buildup the previous November, Kennedy had also agreed that a joint message be sent by State, Defense and the U.S. Information Agency ordering all American personnel to restrict any help to reporters covering the war to "routine cooperation." Three months later, Admiral Felt banned Saigon reporters from going along on helicopter assault missions with American pilots, and reporters complained loudly about being excluded from the flights. But while the ban was galling, many of the Vietcong raids were in the Delta, within driving distance of Saigon. Reporters could get to a battle site, gather information and be back in their offices in time to file for New York's deadlines. Even more infuriating than Felt's order, then, were the exceptions being made to it. Howard Sochurek of *Life* magazine was regularly given special access, and Bigart was enraged when Alsop from the *New York Herald Tribune* boarded a helicopter within two days of his arrival in Saigon. Bigart had been waiting weeks for the same permission. "If the NY Times cannot safeguard its correspondents against this kind of favoritism," Bigart wired his foreign desk in cablese, "eye want to quit."

From Washington, Sterling Cottrell, directing the task force on Southeast Asia, recommended that Nolting be freer in helping reporters to cover the war but told the ambassador to explain that the Kennedy administration did not want coverage of Vietnamese civilian casualties. Harriman had assumed his new role as assistant secretary for Far Eastern affairs, and as a lifelong Democrat he was enough disturbed by Cottrell's approach to send Rowan a memo marked "Burn This." The press, Harriman wrote, would treat the expanded assistance to Vietnam "as our participation in this war—a new war under President Kennedy—the Democratic War Party, so skillfully avoided by the Republican President Eisenhower. The press do not belong in these aircraft but can be kept fully informed by briefings in Saigon by our military or embassy."

Rowan disagreed. He predicted a major domestic furor over the "undeclared war" in South Vietnam and challenged any restrictions that invoked national security: the administration claimed to want to avoid tipping off the enemy, which suggested that reporters were lax about security, perhaps even disloyal; that charge was sure to infuriate them. Writing in confidence, Rowan could acknowledge the real reason for the attempted blackout: "We do not want news reports to build up a detailed record that might be cited as evidence of our violation of the Geneva accords."

Since Sochurek had agreed to submit his *Life* magazine copy for embassy review, Rowan was able to brief Alexis Johnson at State on what he had written before it appeared in print. Rowan found "proof enough that the press boys already have enough detailed information about troops and material to paint a disturbing picture of U.S. involvement." *Life*'s story would also be highly critical of Diem, Nolting and embassy and military personnel.

Hoping to soften those judgments, Lansdale went to New York for a leisurely lunch with *Life*'s editors. He pointed out that Karnow had also been criticizing Diem from his Hong Kong office and reminded the editors that Karnow had opposed aid to Chiang Kai-shek in the struggle against Mao. Launching into a wholehearted defense of Diem, Lansdale said fervently that if the editors suggested replacing him, they would be playing God.

To END THE CONFUSION over press policy, Rowan drafted for Rusk's signature Cable 1006, with new instructions for the Saigon embassy. Reporters were not to be provided with the number of Americans involved in an operation. They were not to be allowed on combat missions if "undesirable dispatches" were likely to result. Rowan ended with a reminder that during World War II the press had voluntarily accepted broad and effective censorship.

As a veteran correspondent, Bigart was willing to make certain concessions. When he finally got his helicopter ride, he boarded a cumbersome H-21

Shawnee—crews called it the Flying Banana—to cover an ARVN offensive at Cai Ngai, a jungle outpost south of Saigon. That day, American pilots fired the .30-caliber machine guns from their helicopters, and three men were killed. The Americans labeled them as Vietcong. Otherwise, ARVN troops refused to pursue the fleeing enemy and settled down instead for lunch. Bigart reported on the ignominious episode without noting that the killing had been done by Americans. In New York, Bigart's editors cut out most of his other damning details.

Sometimes, Bigart could feel that he was fighting a war on two fronts. Not only was Nolting increasingly hostile, but his own editors favored an uninflected reporting he found irresponsible. The *Times* might run both Bigart's version of a skirmish and the official Saigon account, even though the stories were diametrically opposed. Bigart considered New York's editing evasive—"clarkish"—and advised young reporters to remember their stories as they wrote them and never read the edited version. One day, he was denouncing to Mal Browne the folly of publishing two divergent accounts. "How ca-ca-can a fact and a lie both be correct?" Bigart demanded. "Aren't we supposed to choose?" Without waiting, Bigart answered his own question: "Yes."

To relieve his frustrations, Bigart wrote amusing complaints to Betsy Wade, his one confidante on the newspaper's foreign desk. Telling of Madame Nhu's increasingly bombastic speeches, Bigart concluded: "It's a queer set-up, but our leader in Washington has decided we must live with it. I am composing a song, to be sung to the tune of 'I'm an Old Cowhand,' that runs:

"*We must sink or swim*
With Ngo Dinh Diem.
We will hear no phoo
About Madame Nhu.
Yippee-i-aye, i-aye, etc."

The joke was too good not to share with his readers. A few days later, Bigart described U.S. policy on the front page of the *Times* as "Sink or swim with Ngo Dinh Diem." The irresistible jingle somehow slipped past his editors and lived on in Saigon long after Bigart had made his getaway.

SOON AFTER THE PALACE BOMBING, Nhu showed his undiminished confidence in Tuyen by assigning him to a new pet project. They would deprive the Communist fish of their water—the farmers they lived among—by moving those farmers into secure enclaves. Tuyen was to work out the details, collaborating with that province chief of demonstrated efficiency, Colonel Pham Ngoc Thao.

A similar scheme called "agrovilles" had collapsed three years earlier, but this time there would be British expertise and American money behind it. About the time of the Taylor-Rostow mission, Robert G. K. Thompson of the British colonial service visited Saigon to expound upon his success in beating back guerrillas in Malaya. He recommended adopting his Malayan "new villages" but calling them perhaps "strategic hamlets." Rather than fighting battles, Diem's regime would seize administrative control of the country's 16,000 hamlets. The guerrillas' clandestine support network would then wither away.

The plan required skill and caution. Diem's police must first identify the Vietcong in each community before the people could be moved, for their own protection, into the larger settlements and issued weapons. Thompson envisioned the first armed villages as an oil blot that would spread gradually across the country until the South Vietnamese were linked from ocean to mountains. Diem had abolished local elections in the villages, but in these strategic hamlets the farmers would once again vote, forging a bond among themselves that they could never feel for faraway Saigon. Max Taylor met with Thompson and endorsed the plan, as did Nolting and the CIA.

Roger Hilsman, a brash survivor of the war against the Japanese in Burma, was also visiting Saigon for another report to Kennedy, and he found Thompson's idea a workable alternative to the more conventional tactics that mesmerized the Pentagon. During his trip, Hilsman had witnessed a traditional ARVN attack—with support from the Farmgate B-26s—against 300 Vietcong near the Cambodian border west of Saigon. The government's assault had been telegraphed so clumsily that the guerrillas escaped. But through a map-reading error five Cambodians were killed, including three children. Back in Washington, Hilsman described the botch to Kennedy, who shook his head and mused, "I've been President for over a year. How can things like this go on happening?"

Hilsman's briefing left Kennedy more determined to send greater numbers of Green Berets to Vietnam and to herd more South Vietnamese into the strategic hamlets.

NHU RESENTED THE PRAISE heaped on the British Thompson because he saw a crucial difference between his country and Malaya: Thompson's "new towns" of Malayans had been under attack by ethnic Chinese. That was not the same as protecting a hamlet filled with brothers and nephews of the Vietcong. Nhu told Tuyen that their plan must reflect Vietnamese culture.

Once again, Tuyen began by studying Communist methods. Although his agents had often seized secret directives from Hanoi, no one had bothered to read them. Tuyen scooped up an armful and sat down to learn from the enemy. Hanoi's instructions to the cadres in the south tended to be badly printed and dense with jargon, but Tuyen found their insights shrewd. One pamphlet informed the Vietcong that although Ho was revered as a god in the north, treating him that way would not work with southerners. They should circulate instead stories that stressed Ho's ordinary qualities, that made him sound like a very good uncle.

Tuyen saw the trap he and his fellow propagandists had fallen into. Remembering the way Communists idolized Ho, they had been trying to inspire an equal reverence for their president, grinding out such slogans as "Diem, Beloved Leader of His Country." Tuyen prepared new material for the countryside with neither Diem's photograph nor his messages. Downplaying the president, Tuyen found, was coming easily to him.

Although Hilsman and others had recommended patience, Colonel Thao was the man overseeing the villagers, and they resisted being torn from their ancestral land in the name of freedom and shut up behind barbed wire. When scouts told Thao that the strategic hamlets were provoking rebellion, he urged even greater speed, and Nhu and Tuyen agreed. They must create as many of the armed hamlets as possible. If mistakes were made, they could review the results after six months.

For another aspect of the program, however, Tuyen favored less enterprise, not more. He urged farmers to placate the Vietcong when the rebels burst upon their hamlet by offering no resistance. To avoid giving offense, they should listen attentively to the Communist propaganda and allow the guerrillas plenty of time to disperse. A hamlet's goal should be nothing more than satisfying the Vietcong from midnight to dawn and sending them away convinced they had won over the people to their cause. Such a tactic would let the villagers return to their daily routine. The result would be limited government casualties, and the conflict could drag on until the Vietcong lost heart.

Meantime, to explain the strategic hamlet program to farmers, Nhu brought leaders from throughout South Vietnam to a ten-day series of lectures at a newly built camp outside Saigon on the road to Bien Hoa. At the inauguration, Nhu served up an hour of his unintelligible Personalist philosophy. To recover the audience, Tuyen put aside lifelong misgivings about the poor public figure he cut and launched into a hard-sell of the hamlet concept. Over the next weeks, more than 2,000 local officeholders were indoctrinated at the camp and, to his surprise, Tuyen found that his enthusiasm was igniting them. But his success came at a price. Through his spies, reports of Tuyen's effectiveness reached Nhu. As a double agent reported back to Tuyen, "This is very serious. When I told Mr. Nhu that his suspicions were groundless, he got angry and said, 'Tuyen wants to be president.'"

Nhu's evaluation was not accurate. Tuyen was becoming convinced that Diem must be replaced, but he did not want to occupy the palace. He only wanted to choose the man who did.

MADAME NHU was throwing her prodigious energy into building support for her family and alienating her countrymen in the process. She cast herself as the latest of Vietnam's female crusaders for independence and organized what she called the Women's Solidarity Movement. Coercing the wives of Vietnam's generals and high officials to join, Madame Nhu decided to inspirit women by erecting a memorial to the legendary Trung sisters. From a local sculptor, she ordered a statue that would cost about 6 million piasters—some 20,000 U.S. dollars at the official exchange rate—and cajoled a Saigon theater owner to kick off her fund-raising with a benefit movie screening.

A few wives dared to demur. "Madame Nhu," one said, "this is not appropriate for the time being. The people are poor. Millions spent on a statue will make good propaganda for the Communists. Please cancel the project and use the money for social services." But most of the women were as adept as their husbands in saying what the Ngo family wanted to hear. "No, no!" they cried. "It will be a symbol of our movement. We must do it as quickly as possible." Madame Nhu soon had her statue, massive and ungainly but with the features of one Trung sister unmistakably her own.

President Diem was required by law to clear his decrees with his ministers; Madame Nhu had no such restriction. From the palace, she announced a ban on dancing, claiming that soldiers in the countryside resented Saigon's indulgences. Besides, she added, the population was already "dancing with death," and that should be enough.

By contrast, Ho in Hanoi was keeping his austerity to himself. He refused a Chinese gift of a Panda-brand short-wave radio because the giant receiver would have overwhelmed the small house he had built for himself on the grounds of the former French governor's mansion. Ho donated the radio to the Chinese embassy for weekend dances, although he would not be joining in them. At a banquet in Beijing, he had once been pulled to the dance floor by one of Mao's more aggressive female companions. After an uncomfortable turn, Ho had excused himself and retired for the evening. "Dancing is for young people," he said apologetically.

Madame Nhu was also proving less tolerant than Ho about predicting the future. When a young aide mocked astrology as mere superstition, Ho said, "Wait until you're thirty-five, and see what you think then." He himself was enough of a believer to keep his actual birth date a secret; astrologers claimed that revealing the day exposed a person to death or defeat. Instead, Ho celebrated April 19, the day he had founded the Vietminh.

In Saigon, however, Madame Nhu outlawed every form of fortune-telling, together with boxing matches and beauty contests. When she banned contraceptives, adultery, prostitution and divorce, the South Vietnamese offered various explanations for the crackdown. Some claimed that Madame Nhu's motives were mercenary, that her family would lose a fortune if her sister divorced a rich husband in favor of her French lover. Others saw blatant hypocrisy since it was widely believed that Madame Nhu herself had taken many lovers. But Tuyen's spy network had never turned up evidence that she was unfaithful. He took her latest excesses as another sign of an innate prudery but one that would hinder the anti-Communist cause. Tuyen began to meet with a cluster of former Diem supporters who were also troubled by Madame Nhu's behavior. Tuyen felt enough protected by past services to Nhu that he considered addressing him candidly.

He wrote a long letter that began with extravagant praise for the First Lady and segued into a few paragraphs of very mild criticism. Madame Nhu was an excellent lady, Tuyen wrote, motivated only by patriotism and good will. But because she was somewhat new to politics, the Communists had been able to exploit her innocent mistakes. Tuyen suggested a number of cosmetic changes that would present the Ngo family as more approachable. Madam Nhu should dress more simply. She might get into her car and sit next to the driver without waiting for bodyguards to open her door or always demanding a police escort. Having grown up in a simple family himself, Tuyen could explain that visiting a poor household would win popular support. Her hosts might not have a spare cup for tea, and she should not expect one. To put the family at ease, it would be up to her to begin the conversation.

Gentle as his letter was, Tuyen had second thoughts and kept it locked in his desk for a week. When he showed it to his most trusted allies, they encouraged him, but Tuyen did not tell Jackie what he was contemplating. Her participation in the women's movement had created a crisis because Madame Nhu suspected her of trying to build a popular following for herself. She had sent Jackie a deliberately insulting note, informing her that she could never be a candidate for political office.

At last, Tuyen overcame his hesitation and handed Nhu his letter. For many days afterward, they spoke by phone and Tuyen detected no change in his manner. But Madame Nhu had often rung with minor chores for Tuyen—pick up the children at school, organize an impromptu street fair—and she stopped calling. Somewhat later, a chambermaid in the palace explained to Tuyen what had happened. Unwilling to confront his wife directly, Nhu had pretended to leave Tuyen's letter inadvertently on a bedside table. Still later, Nhu told Tuyen in passing, "I don't know how it happened, but my wife read your letter, and she's not happy with you."

NOR WAS MADAME NHU HAPPY with Bigart of the *Times*. He had ended one innocuous column on Saigon's first USO show with a bit of palace gossip: "Mme. Ngo Dinh Nhu will be going abroad soon. However, reports that she will be absent for several months have been discounted as wishful thinking by Government sources." The *Times* did not run the story, but censors at the palace brought their carbon copy to Nhu's attention, and the South Vietnamese Department of Information ordered Bigart to be on the next plane out of Saigon. Sully of *Newsweek* was to be expelled with him.

Nolting might have happily banished the two reporters himself—and Madame Nhu in the bargain, since her statements about the Americans were becoming increasingly disagreeable. But Washington wanted to avoid the publicity sure to result from the ouster of reporters from two major U.S. publications. The State Department instructed the ambassador to intervene on their behalf, and Nolting protested the expulsion at the palace. Diem looked embarrassed and said that his sister-in-law's recent remarks had been emotionally understandable but politically stupid. He quickly agreed to overrule the expulsion of Bigart—who would not be grateful for the reprieve—but the mention of Sully's name resurrected Diem's old resentments. Nhu's police had spread stories about Sully as a Communist spy, French agent, inveterate womanizer. Nolting explained that he was not defending the Frenchman as a person but had been explicitly directed to point out that expelling *Newsweek*'s correspondent could damage both American public opinion and support for Vietnam in the U.S. Congress. To that, Diem replied that Sully had been insulting his family for years. Would President Kennedy allow a foreign correspondent to remain in the United States who publicly questioned his personal integrity?

Nolting sidestepped that chance for a civics lesson and accepted Diem's compromise: Sully could stay until his visa expired in June or July. After that, Nolting hoped to be dealing with Robert Elegant, a *Newsweek* correspondent who had visited Saigon recently. The ambassador passed along to Washington Elegant's judgment that "Sully has been here too long."

IN MAY 1962, McNamara flew to Vietnam for his first look at the war he was conducting. He took along Lemnitzer and Sylvester, his press spokesman, flying on what was called the Poor Man's 707—a cargo plane refitted on the cheap—that required only one stop between Washington and Saigon. Since McNamara had insisted that no more than $20,000 be spent to reconfigure the plane, no money had been left for soundproofing. The resulting noise eliminated both social chat and last-minute briefings.

In Saigon, Nolting and Harkins had been busy restricting what their staffs could tell the brusque and demanding defense secretary. They knew that the Joint Chiefs were already concerned that negative evaluations of the war's progress might undermine the president's resolve. Ken Galbraith was particularly lethal because he presented his views with the wit Kennedy relished. From the New Delhi embassy, Galbraith wrote that Diem had 170,000 troops and he couldn't beat 20,000 rebels. By that measure, the American people were not safe from the Sioux. "Incidentally," Galbraith added, "who is the man in your administration who decides what countries are strategic? I would like to have his name and address and ask him what is so important about this real estate in the Space Age."

With years of corporate infighting behind him, McNamara wasn't alarmed or even much interested in a letter like Galbraith's. Anybody could write a critique, but until it had been run through layers of vetting at State and Defense,

McNamara knew it had no chance of being translated into policy. So far, Kennedy had suggested only that Galbraith inform Hanoi's representative in New Delhi that if the Politburo ever wanted to send a secret message to the White House, the Communists could use Galbraith as a back channel. McNamara took that to mean that the president was still unwilling to accept a neutral Vietnam but wanted to keep the option open.

In Saigon, MACV was determined that McNamara's forty-eight hours in Vietnam should leave him with a strongly positive impression. Harkins was counting on his chief of intelligence, Air Force Colonel James Winterbottom, who had already been exposed to McNamara's statistical ferocity. At a Honolulu conference in February, the Secretary had interrupted Winterbottom's confusing presentation of charts and figures to observe that the Vietcong seemed to have grown from 17,000 in December 1961, to a force estimated between 18,500 to 27,000—all in a single month. When Harkins tried to explain away the discrepancy, Lemnitzer cut in to say that Winterbottom's numbers could even make it look as though the U.S. side was losing. McNamara instructed Winterbottom to come up with one accurate statistic against which they could gauge future progress.

While Harkins continued to be optimistic, McNamara was receiving from the CIA and the rest of the intelligence community reports that the Vietcong were supported by at least 100,000 part-time guerrillas and their sympathizers. Before he left Washington, McNamara cabled ahead to order a province-by-province analysis of what territory Diem's government controlled and what was held by the Vietcong. As Winterbottom struggled to meet his deadline, the pressure began to tell. At a Saigon officers' club, he fought with a deputy and knocked him down; and he was almost sent back to the United States when he fondled a general's wife at a party. As the date of McNamara's tour grew closer, Winterbottom began to base his estimate of enemy casualties on his intuition. When one U.S. air strike in the Delta produced no enemy bodies, Winterbottom wrote down "36 KIAs"—killed in action. George Allen, an analyst on loan from the Defense Intelligence Agency, asked where the figure had come from. "Well, ah," Winterbottom said, "it was a platoon that ran into the goddamned tree line, wasn't it?"

"Yeah," Allen agreed.

"Well, Christ, they, you know, they napalmed the goddamned place! They must have killed them all."

ALLEN'S TEAM ESTIMATED that the local Communist battalions and identifiable guerrilla units now ran to more than 40,000 men. Winterbottom called that figure unacceptable and insisted it be lowered. The team tightened its criteria for confirming a Vietcong presence and brought down the number to between 20,000 and 25,000. That figure still did not indicate that the war was being won, and Harkins protested that he couldn't tell McNamara that there were that many

Vietcong in the country. Winterbottom took Allen and another civilian off the project and went to work with two military aides he expected to be more tractable. Major Sam Dowling and Captain Jimmy Harris felt wretched about the assignment but did as they were told. They cut back the figure to 17,500. By the time McNamara got to Saigon, it was the more authoritative-sounding 16,305.

Winterbottom had prepared the sort of map that McNamara had specified in Honolulu. Six feet high, three feet wide, it showed all of South Vietnam up to the Demilitarized Zone. Red acetate overlays with blue stripes represented the areas controlled by the Vietcong; blue overlays indicated areas controlled by the GVN, the government of Vietnam. The two other categories were plain red for "VC in ascendancy," yellow for "GVN in ascendancy." So much red dotted the map that Harkins's staff called it "the measle map," but it was not shown to Harkins himself until the night before McNamara was due to land. At a rehearsal of his briefing, Harkins was appalled. "Oh, my God!" he said. "We're not showing that to McNamara!" With Harkins supervising, Winterbottom peeled off red acetate until he had removed about one-third of the enemy-controlled areas and returned half of the contested areas to government control.

McNamara had sent ahead his questions so the briefing held no surprises. But the Secretary was proving less adept than Kennedy at asking follow-up questions. He did not comment, for example, when Harkins's briefer cooked the statistics by comparing ARVN offensives from March 21 with Vietcong activity from April 14, a discrepancy that made the ARVN seem commendably aggressive. McNamara was told that during the previous three weeks there had been no operations involving a battalion — at least 300 men — but he did not ask about earlier or smaller skirmishes. Had he done, McNamara would have been forced to take back the bad news that the Vietcong had initiated 3,000 clashes since March 21, including 200 actual offensives. Most of them had been minor, but at least 7 had indeed been of battalion size.

The ARVN desertion rate was also presented attractively, down each month from six per thousand soldiers to four. Doing the arithmetic, McNamara might have realized that, given 170,000 ARVN troops, desertions were running 680 each month. And had he asked and received a truthful answer about how that compared with Vietcong desertions, he would have learned that ARVN desertions were three times higher. Harkins had anticipated that McNamara might grow suspicious when he saw the estimate of 16,305 Vietcong, since it was lower than any of the figures at the Honolulu briefing three months earlier. Harkins explained away the discrepancy by saying that MACV could now depend upon more accurate reporting. McNamara seemed gratified by the proof that the American buildup had produced results so quickly. According to a Pentagon summary, the ARVN forces — "doubtless because of dynamic guidance by U.S. advisers" — were managing to keep the Vietcong off balance.

To see those advisers at work, McNamara was whisked by helicopter with Lemnitzer and Harkins to inspect strategic hamlets in Binh Duong province. Sully of *Newsweek* had published photographs of more than 800 villagers from Ben Cat being marched at gunpoint by Diem's men to their new and unwelcome strategic hamlet while soldiers burned down their former houses. Other reporters found that the forcible evictions fostered Communist sympathies among previously neutral villagers, and Harkins admitted that some of the resettlement had been done under duress. But he could assure McNamara of the program's solid benefits.

Pressing on to Dalat, McNamara met Diem for the first time and heard out his request for more U.S. artillery and aircraft. Colonel Thao was traveling with the defense secretary, which may have explained why each of McNamara's stopovers was punctuated by a bloody Vietcong attack on an ARVN regiment. During McNamara's briefing at Binh Duong, five government troops were killed. When he flew north from Dalat to Danang near the demilitarized zone, the Communists blew up a troop train ten miles north of Danang, killing 27 of Diem's civil guard and wounding 30 more.

McNamara flew next to the rice paddies of An Xuyen at the southern end of the Mekong Delta. Its people had fought the French vehemently and considered Diem's soldiers no more than French collaborators. Bigart had coerced John Mecklin, the embassy's new press officer, into providing a helicopter so that he and Charles Mohr of *Time* could serve as the press pool for McNamara's junket. At each stop, Bigart heard McNamara being told that the surrounding countryside was now secure.

In April, Saigon's press corps had welcomed a newcomer to the UPI bureau. Neil Sheehan, a twenty-five-year-old Harvard graduate, scored an immediate scoop against Browne's AP when he reported the slaughter of 200 Vietcong in a battle forty miles south of Saigon. The information had come from an American adviser at an officers' club bar, where Sheehan, at least, had been entirely sober; he had learned early to avoid alcohol. When the UPI story was splashed across the *New York Times*, an embarrassed Bigart rousted Sheehan from bed so they could drive together to the battle site and count the bodies for themselves. They found fifteen. Correcting the story was humiliating for Sheehan, but the episode made him distrust any number he could not verify.

McNamara, on the other hand, was exhilarated by his quick tour and its unconfirmed statistics. Before departing from Saigon, he agreed to brief the resident press corps in Nolting's living room. Long before he went to the Pentagon, McNamara's favorite vacation pastime was climbing mountains in Colorado, and he arrived at the ambassador's residence unshaven and in dusty khakis and hiking boots. His plane was waiting, McNamara explained, to take him back to Washington for his first field report to the president.

McNamara had filled notebooks with his observations during his inspection, which he summarized for the reporters: "I've seen nothing but progress and hopeful indications of further progress in the future." Asked if he might feel differently if he were to stay more than two days, McNamara said, "Absolutely not!" His positive feelings would only be reinforced, he said, and offered specifics—a Colonel Tong had particularly impressed him, and he had met an ARVN major, only twenty-one, who had cleared a large territory of Vietcong and was now protecting 11,000 people. The Secretary said he knew of no U.S. officer that age who could do as well. Was force being used to move farmers into the strategic hamlets? Yes, McNamara granted. Some of the cleared areas had been controlled by the Vietcong for fifteen years, and older people did not like to move. Communists might try to infiltrate the new hamlets, but they would be identified through security checks.

When Bigart asked him to remove the ban on reporters going on helicopter missions, McNamara replied that the United States was not at war and that no large-scale military actions involved thousands of young Americans being sent out to die. National security considerations sometimes prohibited publicity, he added, and he blamed the press corps for blowing occasional setbacks out of proportion, which, in turn, caused "grave problems for U.S. policies at home." McNamara accused the reporters of writing too much about American casualties, those twenty U.S. servicemen who had been killed in Vietnam.

Bigart provided the only light moment when he complained again about MACV's restrictions. "Mr. Secretary," he said, "we're not getting enough news."

McNamara laughed mirthlessly. "Well, Mr. Bigart," he said, "that's not my impression. My impression in Washington every morning is that you're getting a great deal of news—a very great deal."

"Yes," Bigart agreed sourly. "But I'm having to work too hard for it."

McNamara was asked off-the-record what he thought of Diem. By now, he knew that nothing was ever off-the-record. "One of the advantages of my job," he replied, "is that it has given me the privilege of meeting some of the great men of the world. And I want to tell you that President Diem will rank with the two or three greatest I have been privileged to meet."

Sheehan had been in the country less than a month and already was sure that almost everything McNamara had said was wrong. Recalling the Secretary's reputation for brilliance, he followed him to his waiting car.

As McNamara settled into the back seat, Sheehan said rather plaintively, I am not writing this. But how can a man of your caliber be so optimistic about a war we've barely begun to fight?

McNamara fixed him with his look of absolute assurance and answered, "Every quantitative measure we have shows that we're winning this war." With that, a Marine guard shut the car door, saving Secretary McNamara the trouble.

☐

WHEN AVE HARRIMAN took over the Far Eastern affairs desk in Washington, he left Bill Sullivan in Geneva to negotiate the terms for Laos's neutrality. Sullivan didn't consider Laos a country with rigid boundaries, and if the Communists controlled the Lao borders with China and North Vietnam, he was inclined to shrug off that violation of the 1954 accords. He had accepted Harriman's judgment that the neutralist Souvanna Phouma should head a coalition government and had maneuvered the recall of the CIA chief in Laos, who was still backing the right-wing Phoumi Nosavan.

Sullivan asked Harriman to make a stopover in Vientiane on his next trip to persuade Phoumi to accept a lesser ministry in Souvanna's coalition rather than the powerful Ministry of Defense. Harriman, at his crankiest and most calculating, shook his finger at Phoumi and at delegates from Thailand who had come to protest a Communist state on their border. Michael Forrestal, Harriman's protégé from Mac Bundy's staff, was along to translate Harriman's tirade into French.

You're destroying your state, Harriman told Phoumi angrily, and you'll destroy yourself with it. By the time he finished, Harriman had offended everybody in the room, especially the Thai foreign minister. But they agreed to gamble on a neutral Laos. Soon afterward, Phoumi lost any residual status when he sent a tenth of his army, about 5,000 men, to reinforce a provincial capital in the Laotian northeast. On May 6, two days before McNamara touched down in Bangkok on his way to Saigon—and one year and three days after the Lao cease-fire—the Pathet Lao seized the town of Nam Tha and sent Phoumi's men racing in panic toward the Thai border. Phoumi tried to save face by claiming that the troops had come from the North Vietnamese army and were marching on Thailand. Sullivan had never trusted Phoumi with his perpetually damp eyes, and he asked a diminutive American general, Reuben Tucker, to drive near Nam Tha and check on Phoumi's claims. Tucker not only found no North Vietnamese, he sent back word that Phoumi "couldn't lead a squad around a corner." Tucker's quip got forwarded to Washington, where Kennedy enjoyed repeating it.

THE LATEST MEETING of a sullen National Security Council replayed themes from the preceding year. Harriman and Roger Hilsman called for a show of force to bolster Sullivan's position in Geneva. With McNamara and Lemnitzer off in Saigon, the Joint Chiefs resisted using U.S. troops as political pawns. They would agree to moving the Seventh Fleet into the Gulf of Siam. But if more U.S. troops were to be sent to Thailand and moved near the Lao border, the Chiefs wanted the guarantees from Kennedy that he had already refused to give them. Rostow weighed in with a recommendation that the Jungle Jims bomb a railroad in North Vietnam; other council members ignored him.

Kennedy approved moving the fleet since that option was agreeable to all sides. But as they rode back to the State Department, Harriman and Hilsman worried that the Communists might read so mild a response as proof that the United States had written off Laos and would not pursue a neutralist solution if they thought they could have the country outright. Hilsman called Bundy, who caught Kennedy just as he was leaving for dinner and laid out Hilsman's objections. Kennedy told Bundy to stop the fleet. Hilsman reached Lemnitzer in Saigon and relayed that order. Then, an hour later, Kennedy had third thoughts. Forrestal and John McCone, the new CIA chief, had gone to consult with Eisenhower at Gettysburg. They returned to say that Ike favored a strong response in Laos.

When Kennedy called the State Department, he got Bill Sullivan, home for consultations. "What the hell is going on over there?" Kennedy demanded.

"What do you mean?" Sullivan asked.

"Do you know that Roger Hilsman has just stopped the fleet in the middle of— Let me talk to Hilsman."

Kennedy told Hilsman he would be sending troops, at least as far as Thailand, and the fleet should proceed as well. "But try to impress on everyone," the president added, "the importance of avoiding a leak to the press." The next day, the *New York Times* reported that Kennedy had written off Phoumi's right-wing soldiers as hopeless but was trying to salvage the Geneva conference with a show of force.

In Hanoi, Politburo analysts were grimly amused by Western predictions that the attack on Nam Tha meant renewed warfare. Like their earlier assaults during negotiations with the French, the offensive had been intended only to strengthen the Communist position at the bargaining table. North Vietnam persuaded the Pathet Lao not to enter the royal capital of Luang Prabang or even alarm Washington by showing themselves on the banks of the Mekong.

Le Duan, aware that the subtlety of Hanoi's approach might look like weakness to the Vietcong, justified his tactics in a letter to the Communist leadership in the South. Had the Pathet Lao raised the stakes, he wrote, "the war would not involve only the Phoumi Nosavan forces, but also the American forces." Hanoi's strategy remained unchanged: persuade Washington that its puppet armies could not win but do it without provoking the Americans into coming to their aid.

The previous February, the Politburo had sent the NLF secret instructions to compile a list of South Vietnamese political figures who were not identified with Hanoi's cause but sympathetic to it. In case the United States was thinking of neutrality for South Vietnam as well as Laos, the Politburo wanted to propose reliable but untainted men and women to serve in a coalition government.

McNAMARA HAD ABSORBED most of his briefers' optimism during his Vietnam visit, but he had stumped them with the question of Laos. He said to Lemnitzer: Let's assume the worst, that the enemy drives straight down the Mekong Valley through Laos toward Cambodia? What do we do?

Lemnitzer had to leaf through his briefing book for an answer. "SEATO Plan Five," he read aloud, the contingency plan for sending U.S. troops to Laos.

Acting the regular guy, McNamara turned to Admiral Felt—whose friends called him Don—and said, Well, Harry, suppose we do what Lem says and put divisions in the country? Impressively, McNamara rolled out the names of several Laotian towns where U.S. troops might be sent. What would the Americans do next? Stay at the landing field? Move into the countryside? If so, where?

Felt was no more glib in discussing Laos than Lemnitzer had been. He picked up on McNamara's mention of a specific Laotian town and replied, "We can wipe Tchepone off the face of the earth in forty-eight hours." But that had not been McNamara's question. He turned next to Harkins to ask how that Laotian strategy would affect Vietcong positions in South Vietnam. Harkins did not know. Nolting tried to rescue him with a homily about Thailand and South Vietnam being the pillars of U.S. policy and Laos the keystone.

Having made his point, McNamara instructed the commanders to prepare a response for a Communist push down the Mekong. His brief question-and-answer session guaranteed that he would not be recommending that Kennedy commit troops to Laos.

LATE IN MAY, Khrushchev criticized Kennedy for sending American units into Thailand on a maneuver but said he would continue to back a neutralized Laos. Souvanna, agreeing to talk, set a deadline of June 12, which the negotiators managed to meet. On the eleventh, Souvanna could announce the creation of a coalition government. The agreements to neutralize Laos were signed a few weeks later, nearly fifteen months after Rusk and Harriman first went to Geneva.

Harriman predicted to Kennedy that North Vietnam would keep using the Ho Chi Minh Trail but for the time being would probably let Laos remain neutral. He urged that the United States back Souvanna and his neutralists and obey the agreement so scrupulously that any violations by the Communists would damage their standing elsewhere in Asia and Africa. That would be far more favorable to American interests than past policy had been. If Souvanna declared that Laos no longer wanted SEATO's protection, the Pentagon should pull out its military advisers, the White Star teams. Not every member of the National Security Council was happy about what Harriman had accomplished, but neither was there strong dissent. Grinning, Kennedy turned to him and said, "Well, we'll go along with the Governor."

HAVING EASED KENNEDY past the crisis in Laos, Harriman went back in late July to Switzerland, where he had a chance to apply the same diplomacy to South Vietnam. Two days before McNamara convened his sixth conference on Vietnam in Hawaii, a Burmese official approached Harriman at a reception in Geneva to ask whether he would like a chance to talk privately with the North

Vietnamese. Harriman remembered that to request permission from Rusk ensured a refusal. He drew instead on his growing influence with Kennedy and obtained the president's approval personally.

One Sunday morning, Harriman and Sullivan parked on a side street to avoid attention, walked to the Hôtel Suisse, entered through a service door and went up the back stairs to the Burmese suite. The North Vietnamese foreign minister, Ung Van Khiem, and two aides had already arrived.

Harriman opened the conversation with a heartfelt recollection of Roosevelt's dream of an independent Vietnam guaranteed by international treaty. He personally had heard Roosevelt express his strong feelings on the subject. What might have happened, Harriman mused, if President Roosevelt had lived to carry out that policy? Through his interpreter, Khiem let the elderly American know that Hanoi's leadership was well aware of Roosevelt's intentions, which was why they were all the more surprised when the United States underwrote France's attempt to take back her colonies. Cutting through the nostalgia, Khiem said that the intervening years represented a great tragedy, one that had caused the people of Vietnam much suffering.

The two men soon found they could agree only on the past and not much else. Khiem brought up Washington's connivance in canceling the 1956 elections. Now, he said, American forces were ruthlessly killing South Vietnamese. With the White House backing a neutral Laos, how could Kennedy justify his military intervention in South Vietnam? Harriman countered with recent ICC findings that Hanoi was directing the guerrillas in the South. Stop supporting them, Harriman said, and Vietnam will have peace. Khiem was dismayed to find that even Harriman regarded North and South as two separate countries, not as a two-year aberration after the 1954 conference, and he launched into a lecture on the war, as viewed from above the 17th parallel.

One of Khiem's aides, on hand to translate, was troubled by his chief's rigidity. To him, Harriman's message had been clear enough: Respect the accords in Laos and Washington might rethink the future of South Vietnam. But Khiem had brought no specific instructions from Hanoi and was ill equipped to improvise, even though that same month Politburo members had agreed that neutralizing the South was a possibility. Nor did Khiem's aide expect him to be quick-witted enough to propose opening a back channel to pursue the matter. He saw Khiem as very similar to what he had heard about Khiem's American counterpart, Dean Rusk—unimaginative, insecure, chained to the past. Khiem had been a Communist Party leader in the South before being named foreign minister in 1960. Unlike most of his predecessors, he had never headed the ministry's American desk.

The aide admitted, in fairness, that Khiem faced a technical problem. The North Vietnamese had no direct line from Geneva. Every message went out from their embassy to Beijing and was then forwarded to Hanoi. Under those circumstances, Khiem could not report anything that would upset the Chinese. The aide wondered whether anyone in the West understood just how poorly equipped his foreign ministry was. The budget often did not provide for the Western newspapers and magazines that might offer insights into America's thinking. All the same, Khiem's aide waited for Harriman's response with a sense that in this room on this day a chance for peace was being lost.

Harriman did not choose to debate Khiem. He said merely that U.S. military aid would continue so long as northern aggression continued against South Vietnam. The session ended with mutual thanks to their host. The Burmese had provided a forum for each side to state its case disingenuously and demand from the other an unconditional surrender.

AFTER SIX MONTHS as an undercover CIA man in Saigon, William Kohlmann was often lonely. The agency had arranged for him to work out of the USAID office, and, while officials there were pleasant enough, the secrecy to his assignment kept him isolated. Kohlmann's job was handling assets—those Vietnamese who agreed to report to the CIA—but his slot had been empty after his predecessor was kicked out of the country for being too friendly with potential coup plotters. Kohlmann had inherited only three Vietnamese.

He was a conspicuous figure around town, his handsome head with its classic features joined to a badly damaged body. During World War II, Kohlmann had left Yale to spend three years in the infantry. He returned to New Haven for a history degree in 1948 and then a year of dabbling in graduate courses. The State Department attracted him as a gentlemanly career, and he took the Foreign Service examination before going off to study in France. In Paris, however, Kohlmann contracted poliomyelitis, which meant a month in an iron lung and then two-and-a-half years of recovery at home in Louisiana.

Kohlmann had done very well in State's written tests, but when he showed up in Washington for the oral examination—stooped over a cane, limping badly and dragging a useless right arm—the interviewer explained that a Foreign Service officer had to be prepared on five minutes' notice to leap on a camel and ride across the Sahara. Since it could take Bill Kohlmann almost that long to cross a Parisian boulevard, he considered it entirely reasonable that he was rejected.

But the interviewer looked again at Kohlmann's test scores and, with the trace of a wink, suggested that he apply at the Government Printing Office. In 1952, the GPO was one front for recruiting for the CIA, which was not yet five years old. Kohlmann took the hint and signed on with the agency for a desk job writing short biographies of political figures. After three years, he wangled a transfer to clandestine operations, where he discovered that several Yale classmates were also in the CIA—moderate Republicans, men from the Social Register. As a Jew, Kohlmann had never felt himself in a ghetto in New Haven, but these were men he had not met there.

Kohlmann had been sent to Vietnam only because he spoke good French, not for any expertise about the country. After a hurried orientation in Washington, he flew across the Atlantic trying to remember whether it was Saigon or Hanoi that was America's ally. When he arrived and glanced around Saigon, Kohlmann found the street life cramped and dirty and scoffed at the notion of the city being called the Paris of the Orient. But he settled into a downtown apartment across from the Continental Hotel, hired a maid and went by taxi each morning to his USAID office for 10 piasters, about 12 cents, including tip.

Kohlmann soon decided that the receptions and parties given by the Vietnamese were more congenial than those of his countrymen. Individual Vietnamese were likely to take him as an exotic foreigner rather than as a disabled spook. But after Paris, Vietnamese culture seemed arid, and the Confucian emphasis on family loyalty simply bizarre. Although John Richardson, the CIA station chief, was praising Diem lavishly in his reports, Kohlmann and the other agents were expected to make discreet contact with Diem's opponents, and Kohlmann saw that one agent was unusually skilled at ingratiating himself— Lucien Conein, Lansdale's deputy in the futile harassment of Hanoi and currently assigned to work with the South Vietnamese military.

Nicknamed Lou, Conein had been born in Paris in 1919 but raised in Kansas City. Other agents warmed to his brash bonhomie, and Conein was a regular presence in Saigon's bars where, tall and dark, a drink in one hand, an arm slung over his companion's shoulder, he poured out stories from a life of unlikely adventure. The two fingers missing from his right hand, for example, had been lost during a caper in Germany; that made a better story than his accident with a car's fan belt. Kohlmann's reserve kept him from joining Conein's circle, but he granted that Lou had a knack for winning the confidence of the Vietnamese generals who shared his riotous nights on the town. When Conein announced that he was off to a popular hookers' bar "for a free feel," the fastidious Kohlmann, although no prude, was gratified to be assigned to Vietnam's ascetic Buddhists.

Certainly, no one else in the agency was paying much attention to the complaints from Buddhist priests, called bonzes, that Diem was constantly discriminating against them, even though they represented the overwhelming religion of his country. The Buddhists welcomed their access to this clever American, so courageous in surmounting his handicap, and tended to overestimate Kohlmann's influence within the mission. As relationships developed, CIA policy encouraged putting any local asset on a small retainer, but Kohlmann was disappointed whenever a Vietnamese took his money. It was a better game to influence those high-minded opposition leaders through persuasion.

By mid-1962, Kohlmann's widening contacts had convinced him that Diem was both hated and ineffectual. At the U.S. embassy, however, his CIA superiors disliked Kohlmann's Buddhist assets for the threat they posed to a stable government.

□

Ta Minh Kham in 1949 as
Vietminh battalion deputy chief
(Ta Minh Kham family)

TA MINH KHAM took up life in South Vietnam about the time Bill Kohlmann did and was building up assets of his own. Born in Ben Tre, Kham had joined the Vietminh before he was twenty. During nine years of fighting the French, he had risen to the rank of captain and commander of a battalion. After the 1954 accords, Kham went north to Hanoi, where he was chosen to be one of the fifteen Vietnamese sent to study at the Beijing Military Institute. All lectures were given in Chinese, and Kham picked up the language quickly. Many other foreigners were studying at the institute, most notably Mongolians and North Koreans. Their three-year course was aimed at preparing them to direct a unit of any size—battalion to division level, and they learned how to use artillery effectively in supporting ground troops. But among themselves, Kham and his Vietnamese classmates agreed that they would have to modify their Chinese training to fit the realities at home. Vietnam could never accept the rate of casualties that China had sustained in Korea or the Soviets in World War II.

At the end of 1961, Kham was one of the officers sent down the Ho Chi Minh Trail to recruit farm boys for the next stage in the war for independence. The first time McNamara flew over the Delta, Kham, a Vietcong lieutenant colonel, was hiding in the jungle of Song Be province with his new command, the 2nd Regiment. Kham considered his men too green yet for battle, but they were safe for now since Diem's lethargic troops would never come looking for them.

☐

IF KHAM'S REGIMENT was not yet prepared to fight, other Vietcong units were already creating havoc around the country. In one massive ambush ninety miles from Saigon on June 5, two trains were destroyed and looted while the security teams on board fled to safety. By the end of the month, seventeen trains had been damaged or destroyed in the first six months of 1962.

U.S. antiguerrilla manuals maintained that the Communist units only blocked convoys from the front and did not set land mines along the flanks of an ambush. But the Vietcong had begun to use teleguided mines against the first vehicles and then others to prevent retreat by the last cars and trucks. That done, they covered the ground at either end of the convoy with additional mines and prepared to mow down the troops rushing to the convoy's rescue. Later, U.S. helicopters might deliver reinforcements to a trapped convoy, but the first strike belonged to the Vietcong.

On June 16, about twenty miles north of Saigon, the Vietcong laid an ambush at 7 A.M. in full view of villagers who saw no reason to alert the ARVN at nearby Ben Cat. When a civilian truck drove down the road ahead of the convoy, a Vietcong soldier in hiding detonated a land mine, and his company sprayed the convoy's two armed cars with 57-mm recoilless rifles. An American captain and lieutenant riding in an open jeep were killed, along with at least 27 Vietnamese riding in the convoy's seven vehicles. It took three hours for reinforcements to arrive by road. Helicopter pursuit teams finally lifted off from Saigon at 3 P.M., but the Vietcong were long gone.

Kennedy's Special Forces could not stem that sort of assault. Prodded by Rostow, the army had hurriedly enlarged the Special Warfare Center at Fort Bragg and opened the first Green Beret base in the Central Highlands in late 1961. Its mission was to keep the Rhade tribesmen of Darlac province from falling under Vietcong control. At home, American volunteers who were not already paratroopers went through airborne school at Fort Benning, Georgia, and returned to North Carolina for a course in guerrilla warfare. They camped out in the swamps, field-stripped their weapons blindfolded, trained with garrotes for silent strangulation; they were expected to make their kill in the first thirty seconds of hand-to-hand combat.

Colonel Kham had fought the French for nine years and studied warfare for another three years in Beijing. The Special Forces could not spare the time for that degree of preparation. Their course ran three months.

Early in 1962, the U.S. Army began to send members of its 2,000 Green Berets to train the Vietnamese mountain people who had been formed into units called the Civilian Irregular Defense Group. The Americans were to act only as advisers, command being left to South Vietnam's officers. But many in the ARVN showed contempt for these montagnards—the rough-hewn, often illiterate mountain people they were supposed to lead. As for the 200,000 montagnards themselves, they had been content to be ignored by Saigon until Diem's resettlement of the northern Catholics, which had driven 80,000 refugees into their mountains. When the montagnards protested that influx of strangers, Diem's men confiscated their spears and crossbows, which the tribes used every day in foraging for food, seldom in battle.

The U.S. Special Forces troops were authorized to return the weapons if tribesmen signed up for a new security program. But the methods for weeding out the Vietcong and their sympathizers from the mountain settlements were primitive. Recruits who arrived for training had to vouch for the man standing next to them in line. The village chief attested to the loyalty of the rest. Men chosen to be trail watchers were flown across Vietnam to the port of Danang, where they spent eight weeks learning how to identify and report Vietcong movement along the border. Although the rest of the training remained officially under the Vietnamese Special Forces, on patrol the Americans tended to take charge. Their initiative suited the ARVN officers, who had no faith in the skill of their irregular units.

From Saigon, Diem and his political generals had watched developments in the highlands suspiciously. By mid-1962, at least 10,000 montagnards had received rudimentary military training and had been issued weapons. Since the area around the pilot project in the town of Buon Enao was not dense with Vietcong, Diem's commanders ordered a sharp reduction of arms within the forty-village complex. The American Green Berets were as irate as the montagnards by the order and refused to help in collecting the arms again. Vietnamese soldiers did the job instead, often roughly.

As more Special Forces camps sprang up near the Ho Chi Minh Trail, they were plagued by a problem first seen at Buon Enao: Vietnamese recruits from the farmlands hated life in the mountains. Hoping to be taken home, they clung to the landing struts of visiting helicopters, jumping to earth only moments before they would break a leg. At night, they waited for dark and sneaked back to their villages.

Green Berets who endured life in those same isolated outposts were rewarded by American helicopters ferrying in steaks, beer and tapes from home to play on the new portable cassette players. The Americans drilled the irregular recruits, doled out medicine and led fruitless patrols through jungle so thick it could take eight hours to hack forward one mile. They learned to ignore the occasional harassing shots fired from outside their perimeter.

Tough and devoted, the kind of young soldiers who made their president proud, the Green Berets also knew—long before their first camp was overrun on January 3, 1963—that any time Colonel Kham or another Vietcong commander cared to do it, their Special Forces camp could be wiped out overnight.

With McNamara speaking optimistically in Washington, and with the Saigon embassy resisting reporters' demands for more accurate information, the guerrilla war had faded from the headlines. To mutual relief, Homer Bigart was leaving

Vietnam and would be replaced by David Halberstam, a twenty-eight-year-old correspondent recently based in Africa; Halberstam was certain to be less cantankerous than Bigart had been. By August 22, Kennedy could hold a news conference without the subject of Vietnam even being raised.

Soon afterward, with the 1962 congressional elections approaching, Ted Sorensen arranged to meet privately with Russia's ambassador, Anatoly Dobrynin. Sorensen asked that the Soviet Union not heighten tensions in ways that would help the Republicans. Dobrynin passed the request to Khrushchev and got back a reassuring message: there would not be another crisis over Berlin before November. Khrushchev did not tell his ambassador about the surprise he was planning in Cuba.

The Soviet premier had listened to the Kennedys' stern words against Castro and concluded that the only way to preserve Cuba's Communist government against another invasion was to send missiles to the island with nuclear warheads. He might have moved even faster had he heard about Operation Mongoose, a series of dirty tricks that Lansdale was running with the CIA; they included the option of using a Mafia hit man to assassinate Castro. As it was, Khrushchev felt stealth was essential since the missiles had to be in place and ready to fire before Washington discovered them. The Pentagon currently boasted 5,000 nuclear warheads around the world to Russia's 300, and 273 land-based and Polaris missiles to an estimated 75 Soviet missiles. Moving the Soviet missiles closer to the United States would help to offset those lopsided numbers, and Khrushchev relished treating the Americans to their own medicine. The United States had already ringed the Soviet Union with nuclear bases in Turkey, Italy and West Germany. The previous March, meeting with Dobrynin before he left for Washington, Khrushchev complained that the U.S. nuclear superiority had made the Americans arrogant. Without confiding his intentions, Khrushchev added, "It's high time their long arms were cut shorter."

That logic persuaded a reluctant Castro to accept the missiles. The Soviets cleared an area near several Cuban ports and used their own men to unload the hardware—intermediate-range missiles, launching equipment, obsolete IL-28 bombers for coastal defense. Flying fourteen miles above Cuba, a U-2 spy plane alerted Washington to some of the 85 Russian ships that were making the 183 deliveries, but CIA analysts took the heavy traffic as no more than a buildup of conventional weapons.

On October 14, Mac Bundy, appearing on a Sunday television interview program, denied that there were offensive missiles in Cuba. About that time, a U-2 pilot was taking the first photographs of Soviet medium-range ballistic missiles, each 60 feet long. Khrushchev had assured Castro that he would send enough of them that even if some were crippled or disabled, New York and Chicago could be destroyed. Also marked for obliteration would be the nation's capital, which Khrushchev disparaged as "the little village of Washington."

Late Monday afternoon, CIA photographic specialists called two of the agency's deputy directors with new findings from the San Cristóbal area of western Cuba. John McCone had recently returned from a European honeymoon but was out of town again, burying a stepson killed accidentally in California. Because Kennedy's Washington was highly social, notifying his staff required deciding which dinner parties to break up. That evening, McNamara had hosted Bobby Kennedy's regular discussion group and wasn't informed of the findings until nearly midnight. CIA deputies did reach Max Taylor, who recently had been named chairman of the Joint Chiefs. He was giving his own dinner party with guests that included McNamara's deputy, Ros Gilpatric, and Rusk's deputy, Alexis Johnson.

Roger Hilsman, no favorite of Rusk's, had been alerted to the new data in his role as State's director of intelligence and research. He called Rusk out of a dinner for the German foreign minister. A CIA deputy, Ray Cline, rang his friend Mac Bundy to say guardedly, "Those things we've been worrying about—it looks as though we've really got something." Kennedy was due to return to Washington after midnight from a fund-raising tour in New York State. Bundy decided against disturbing him until the next morning, when all of the intelligence reports could be assembled.

Before 9 A.M. on Tuesday, October 16, Bundy called on the president while Kennedy was still in robe and slippers. Kennedy looked over the reports and called a secret meeting of the National Security Council's executive committee.

In the first discussions, McNamara tended to shrug off the threat. The Soviets already had nuclear weapons on their own soil aimed at the United States. "It makes no great difference whether you are killed by a missile fired from the Soviet Union or from Cuba," McNamara said. Bombing the sites or invading the island were raised as possible responses, but McNamara recommended the milder alternative of a naval blockade.

Rusk suggested a diplomatic protest. When that was talked down, he withdrew into silence and then concocted an excuse to skip further meetings: his absence from his customary routine might set off a national panic, Rusk said. He went about his daily chores, leaving George Ball to represent State. As the debate proceeded, Ball argued in a memo against an unannounced air attack on the missile positions and joined McNamara in urging a blockade. Ball pointed out, "We tried Japanese as war criminals because of the sneak attack on Pearl Harbor."

The growing sense of crisis was making the meetings rancorous, and labels had emerged of "hawk" and "dove." On Friday, October 19, when the Joint Chiefs had their audience with Kennedy, they didn't know that he had activated the White House tape recorder. Curtis LeMay from the Air Force pushed for air strikes. He denounced a blockade as politically inspired and seemed to take glee in baiting Kennedy for entertaining such a weak response. "And I'm sure a lot of our citizens would feel that way, too," LeMay added. "You're in a pretty bad fix, Mr. President."

Kennedy was not sure he had heard correctly. "What did you say?"

LeMay repeated, "You're in a pretty bad fix."

Kennedy was not going to quarrel with the Air Force chief and only said, with a laugh, "You're in with me."

After the president left the room, David Shoup, the crusty Marine Corps commandant, congratulated LeMay: "You pulled the rug right out from under him. Goddamn!"

As Kennedy's tape kept turning, Shoup reflected the rage that persisted at the Pentagon almost a year and a half after the Bay of Pigs. "Somebody's got to keep them from doing the goddamn thing piecemeal," Shoup exclaimed. "That's our problem. Go in there and friggin' around with the missiles. You're screwed. Go in there and friggin' around with the lift. You're screwed. You're screwed, screwed, screwed, screwed. Some goddamn thing, some way, that they either do the son of a bitch and do it right, and quit friggin' around."

Still grousing, the Chiefs left the room just before the tape ran out. But their argument had made some converts. McCone, Max Taylor and Paul Nitze were now calling for air strikes to destroy the missiles. Dean Acheson, brought in again for consultation, pressed strenuously for them, as did Treasury Secretary Dillon. The problem was that McCone's CIA, which had been slow in detecting the weapons in the first place, could not say for sure where they had been hidden. That led McNamara to repeat that a naval blockade was the most decisive action America could take with the least risk of nuclear war.

The prospect of warheads aimed at the White House had concentrated Kennedy's attention on the Soviet Union and its leaders in a way that even the Berlin scare had not done. Charles "Chip" Bohlen, a State Department Russian specialist, was in Paris as U.S. ambassador. But Tommy Thompson was on hand as the diplomat with the freshest firsthand knowledge. Kennedy bombarded him with questions about Khrushchev and his comrades until the president and his advisers had absorbed more Russian history and culture than they had previously cared to know.

Kennedy's family understood better than his advisers the degree to which Jack Kennedy was haunted by the specter of nuclear war. One Soviet missile exploding over one U.S. city could kill 5 million people—the same proportion of the population that had been killed during the entire Civil War. Throughout his sickly boyhood, Kennedy had tried to purge himself of any debilitating softness or sentimentality. But his mother had seen him cry after the botched Cuban invasion, and his sisters knew that scenes of nuclear devastation occupied the most terrifying corner of his imagination. Bobby Kennedy understood as well, and as the argument grew more tense he seized upon Ball's reference to Pearl Harbor and announced loudly, "I don't want to see John F. Kennedy go down in history as the American Tojo."

McNamara also sensed the president's preference and was holding firm against air strikes. Considering how to announce his decision, Kennedy got a ruling from State that the word "quarantine" should be substituted for McNamara's more menacing "blockade." On Friday, October 19, Kennedy tried to tamp down press speculation about a crisis by campaigning for Democrats in Cleveland and Chicago. A reporter asked Arthur Sylvester that day if there were, in fact, missiles in Cuba. Sylvester consulted with McNamara and lied in the name of national security. No, Sylvester said, there were not.

On Saturday, Kennedy pleaded a respiratory infection and flew back to Washington. In Moscow, Khrushchev was aware that the Americans now knew of the shipments, but he expected them not to protest until after the U.S. elections, and by then his missiles would be fully operational. Instead, the White House announced that on the evening of Monday, October 22, Kennedy would address the nation. At a final meeting Sunday night, Rusk recommended that everyone get as much rest as possible. "By this time tomorrow, gentlemen," he said portentously, "we will be in a flaming crisis." McNamara spent the night on a cot in his office.

The Pentagon had prepared for 500 air sorties to hit the missiles in case Kennedy could be induced to change his mind, and certainly the president's address to the nation was as bellicose as the Chiefs could wish. He warned Khrushchev that any nuclear attack against the United States from Cuba would be answered by retaliation directly against the Soviet Union.

The quarantine was to take effect at 10 A.M. on Wednesday, October 24. Late Tuesday night, nervous and so exhausted that he kept repeating himself, Bobby Kennedy called on Ambassador Dobrynin to complain about Khrushchev's deceit. Dobrynin didn't much care for Bobby—he found him hot-headed and lacking in humor—but in this instance he had to admit that the Kennedys were right. He was embarrassed about misleading the president and said little. As Bobby Kennedy calmed down and prepared to leave, he asked the ambassador what instructions the captains of Soviet ships on their way to Cuba had received after his brother's speech. Dobrynin said they had been told not to bow to unlawful demands for a search on the high seas.

Shaking his head, Bobby Kennedy left. Dobrynin immediately reported the visit to the Kremlin word for word to let Khrushchev see for himself how agitated the Americans had become.

U.S. TELEVISION NETWORKS trained their cameras on the imaginary line of the quarantine so the world could watch as a Soviet submarine approached. But Kennedy ordered the navy destroyers not to make a submarine their first interception. Although the Soviets had officially rejected Kennedy's ultimatum, the Pentagon was reporting that late Wednesday five Soviet ships large enough to be carrying missiles had changed their course, and a smaller cargo ship had stopped dead in the water. Rusk was unmistakably gloating when he told a reporter, "We were eyeball to eyeball, and the other fellow just blinked."

The first contact with a Soviet ship came twenty-two hours after the submarine sighting. Heeding the advice of Harriman and Tommy Thompson, Kennedy wanted to give Khrushchev a graceful way of backing down. American ships hailed the *Bucharest*, a tanker, but made no attempt to go aboard.

The debate, however, was not over. At 4 P.M. on Saturday, October 27, Max Taylor arrived at the White House with news that a U-2 plane had been shot down over Cuba, giving the Joint Chiefs a renewed reason for a preemptive strike. At 6 P.M., the president joined his tautly wound advisers and lowered the room's temperature by crisply sharing his nightmare. "It isn't the first step that concerns me," he said, "but both sides escalating to the fourth and fifth step—and we don't go to the sixth because there is no one around to do so."

At 7:45 P.M., Bobby Kennedy invited Dobrynin to his office at the Justice Department. The attorney general told the ambassador that a lot of American generals and others were "spoiling for a fight" over Cuba. Russia's missiles had to be removed. If Khrushchev agreed, the United States would pledge not to invade Cuba and would also reciprocate by scrapping its obsolete missiles in Turkey. He added that President Kennedy could not admit to the deal publicly and that getting permission from Turkey and NATO for the removal could take months.

It was the concession Khrushchev needed. His speech the next day was full of self-praise for his own restraint. Privately, Bobby Kennedy had impressed on Dobrynin the need for absolute silence about their conversation. Who knows? Bobby said. I might run for president, and my prospects would be damaged if this secret deal about the missiles in Turkey were to come out.

WITH THE RUSSIAN nuclear missiles removed, McNamara was seeing himself as a vital counterweight to the unimaginative and bellicose Joint Chiefs. The president agreed. It was lucky for us, he told Arthur Schlesinger, that McNamara was Defense Secretary. The president was receptive, then, when McNamara recommended replacing at least two of the Chiefs. Another crisis is likely to arise, McNamara said, and you don't want to go through that same wrangling. Kennedy was more sensitive than his Secretary to the politics of removing a chief in midterm; neither of them could recall it ever having been done.

"Which two would you get rid of?" the president asked.

"LeMay and Anderson."

Admiral George Anderson, chief of naval operations, was nearing completion of his first two-year term. He had already been handed one indignity: next in line to be chairman of the Joint Chiefs, he had been shoved aside to put Max Taylor in the job. Anderson had argued strenuously for stronger military action against Castro, and at the height of the tension had told McNamara to leave the Naval Operations Room, go back to his office and let the navy run things. At that, McNamara ordered Anderson to acknowledge his express instructions that the navy was not to employ force without McNamara's direct permission.

Kennedy pondered the uproar that was certain to spread from the Pentagon to the Congress. "All right," he said at last. "You can fire one. Which one will it be?"

"Anderson."

McNamara left the Oval Office and was not consulted again before the announcement came that Kennedy had appointed Admiral Anderson as ambassador to Portugal.

BY THE FALL OF 1962, General Harkins was impatient to wind up the war quickly and thought he had the solution. The South Vietnamese army would sweep across the countryside in one vast nationwide offensive while Diem's air force flew saturation raids against Vietcong sanctuaries. That would be followed by a sudden explosion of fighting by every loyal Vietnamese under arms—the Army, Navy Rangers and Marines, combined with the Popular Forces and Regional Forces in the villages, montagnard scouts and the other paramilitary units. The total number would approach half a million. And that did not include the thousands of women training with Madame Nhu or the Catholic youth groups that could be pressed into service.

Harkins went to the palace to sell the idea to Diem, and for once the Vietnam president was compelled to do the listening. Pulling out his notebook, Harkins explained with mounting excitement how to push for instant victory.

Diem bridled. Examining Harkins's estimate of the Vietcong, he protested that the figures of 20,000 hard core and 100,000 local guerrillas were too low, especially in the western mountains and near the demilitarized zone. Harkins admitted he did not know the number of sympathizers but said that VC guerrilla units often included local men who had been forced to join, and they would not fight willingly. Overall, Harkins insisted, the ratio was very favorable for the government.

Secrecy was the key. To prepare, everyone would have to work far into the night for the next four months. When all available intelligence had been gathered, Diem, as supreme commander, would give the order and the Vietcong would be annihilated. Okay, Harkins allowed, maybe instead of killing off the Vietcong, his explosion would only drive them underground. Even that would be a plus. The government could use the breathing space to complete the strategic hamlets and move the economy forward. Harkins granted that he might be optimistic—he always was. But within one year, the Communists could be destroyed, and he didn't know why, when he had presented the idea to McNamara in Honolulu, the Secretary had not been enthusiastic.

The mention of McNamara's resistance gave Diem the out he wanted. In principle, he said, the plan was very good. But his first reaction was that one had better be thinking about three years from now, not next year. And—Diem seemed to be weighing the scheme carefully—the Vietcong would not accept that sort of defeat.

Harkins answered boldly: They would have to accept it.

We don't know the enemy's viewpoint, Diem said.

Harkins was giddy with impending victory. His philosophy in war, he said, was not to worry about the enemy but to let the enemy worry about him.

Fine, said Diem. In principle. But we have to expect the Vietcong to reinforce their ranks.

If the Vietcong brought in more forces, Harkins vowed, there would just be more of them to defeat. And if they go into hiding, that will convince the population that the average V.C. was not 12 feet high, after all. Harkins suggested a bounty system to reward villagers who turned in the Vietcong in their midst.

Nothing about Harkins's plan appealed to Diem. It would take away troops who defended him against palace coups and give new authority to Vietnamese generals he didn't trust. Persuaded by Nhu's conviction that a prolonged stalemate was preferable to heavy casualties, Diem was promoting his most cautious colonels, replacing overly zealous officers and threatening the promotions of those commanders who did not hold down their losses.

Harkins deplored that approach and criticized it obliquely. He had heard the same story twice, he began, once in Saigon, once in Bac Lieu: An ARVN battalion commander had taken up a position along a riverbank. When his American adviser pointed out that across the stream seemed a better place to camp, the officer had said that the area was already occupied by V.C. The adviser asked, "Why don't you go after them?"

"As long as we don't bother them," the ARVN commander replied, "they won't bother us."

Harkins said that if some commanders did not want to fight, they should tell Diem and let the president find more aggressive replacements. Meantime, Harkins wanted Diem to focus again on his nationwide explosion. The president need only say "go" and planning would begin.

Better to take three years, Diem repeated. Smiling, he added that if the strategy were tried and failed, people would charge General Harkins with inefficiency.

Harkins said he was ready to take that risk.

At that, Diem agreed halfheartedly that Harkins could begin exploring his idea. But Diem warned that the Vietcong was not a worm that could be crushed under one's heel.

Among the Americans, McNamara was not alone in resisting Harkins's proposal. When Harriman heard about it, he saw the risks and threw his new prestige with Kennedy into sabotaging it. Impressed by the way Harriman had salvaged Laos, the president was speaking admiringly of him these days, and others at the White House admitted that they had been too quick to write him off as a New Deal relic. Basking in that approval, Harriman indulged the churlish side of his nature, and Kennedy looked on amused as Harriman ostentatiously turned off his hearing aid while opponents argued their case. During one debate over Laos, Harriman was cursing the "goddamned generals" who were so ready to send troops to Indochina. Then he seemed to remember that General Earle Wheeler was sitting across the table. "Oh, excuse me, Wheeler," Harriman said without even trying to look discomfited.

Because Kennedy had been adroit at maintaining a high level of civility in the White House, Harriman's outbursts became legendary around Washington. When Bundy compared him to an old crocodile who seemed to be sleeping before he flashed his jaws, Harriman embraced the image and displayed in his office the crystal, brass and silver crocodiles that friends were showering on him.

To squelch Harkins's plan, Harriman wrote to Nolting to demand more realistic reporting and to warn against overoptimism. Harriman was sure the Vietcong would be tipped off about Harkins's offensive long before it took place and would go into hiding. The result would be chaos and the loss of many civilian lives. Harkins's explosion would only weaken the government forces while the Communists slipped back into their tunnels and jungle camps. Don't approve Harkins's plan, Harriman concluded his cable, without consulting the State Department.

Harriman's concern for civilian casualties was rare among his colleagues. The Pentagon had drafted a plan to poison mountain rice fields if they could be feeding the Vietcong, even though the paddies belonged to local montagnards. McNamara approved the idea on the grounds that the montagnards had already deserted the province where the crops were to be destroyed. It was left to Harriman to shoot down the plan in a letter to Gilpatric at Defense. He quoted a Saigon embassy report that very few refugees had actually left the Phu Yen Mountains. The montagnards who were still there would suffer from the aerial spraying, and since the Vietcong and the general population were closely intertwined, the State Department could not approve the poisoning.

At the Pentagon, Lemnitzer viewed Harriman's concern incredulously. Strange, the general complained, that we can bomb, kill and burn people but are not permitted to starve them.

WHILE HARKINS WAS PROMOTING his grand military stroke, a different sort of explosion was already brewing within the Saigon press corps. Complaints about restricted access and deceitful MACV information had built up until Mal Browne wrote to Harkins in August to protest the number of touchy subjects that photographers were forbidden to shoot—prisoners, battle casualties, Americans flying Vietnamese planes. Browne reminded Harkins of the traditions of the American press and noted that at Little Big Horn an AP correspondent had died in an ambush very similar to those in Vietnam. The protest was ignored until two weeks later when Sully at Newsweek quoted remarks by a professor just back from Hanoi.

Born in France but teaching at Howard University, Bernard Fall had published *Street Without Joy*, an account of the errors of his countrymen in Vietnam. During his recent trip, Fall said, Truong Chinh, the North Vietnamese theorist from the days of agrarian reform, had reminded him that military actions succeeded only when the politics behind them were popular. But the U.S. advisers insisted on fighting a conventional war that was doomed.

Madame Nhu struck back at Sully with an open letter issued by her paramilitary women's group, demanding his expulsion in the name of the women tortured or murdered by the Communists. Tran Kim Tuyen cornered the new U.S. press officer at dinner one night to inform him that Sully was a French agent who was soon to be ousted. John Mecklin had been brought to Saigon on leave from Time, Inc. He knew and liked Sully from the time they had covered the fall of Dien Bien Phu together and didn't believe Sully was anyone's agent. Mecklin regarded him as merely a French chauvinist who ignored the evidence that America was succeeding where France had failed.

Once more, Nolting made a direct appeal to Diem on Sully's behalf, but four days later Sully was ordered to leave. A dozen irate resident reporters and stringers caucused on the matter until the early hours at the Caravelle Hotel. Some wanted to issue a strong protest; others worried that such a manifesto might get them expelled as well. To a few colleagues, Sully's nationality made him suspect, and he was obliged to swear that he was working for neither the French nor the Communists.

The next day, the more militant reporters sent a protest to the palace and to President Kennedy signed by Browne, Sheehan and the representatives of CBS, NBC, and *Time* magazine. Halberstam, the correspondent who had lately replaced Bigart for the *New York Times*, signed as well. The letter made the point that the United States was spending $1 million a day in South Vietnam, where it had "stationed ten thousand of its finest young men."

Diem ignored the protest entirely. In Washington, a spokesman brushed it off with an expression of Kennedy's appreciation for the reporters' concern and praise for their "all-important task." After a hero's sendoff at Tan Son Nhut, Sully flew to Hong Kong to compose his farewell to Diem and the Nhus. The resulting article got *Newsweek* permanently banned from South Vietnam.

When Diem proved he could expel Sully with no reprisals from Washington, the attacks on foreign journalists by Saigon's tame local press grew louder. Madame Nhu explained to an American reporter that her country was not compelled to respect "your crazy freedoms." In late October, James Robinson of NBC was expelled. The charge was a minor visa infraction, but his actual offense was unforgivable. Emerging from one of Diem's three-hour monologues, Robinson told his interpreter that the interview had been a waste of his time.

When nine reporters lined up to sign a statement on Robinson's behalf, Nolting and his deputy, William Trueheart, drove again to the palace but could

David Halberstam
(Horst Fass, AP/Wide World Photos)

win Robinson only a three-day reprieve. At a state dinner before he left, Madame Nhu arrived, subdued and charming. Reporters complained to her about the latest expulsion. She murmured that they must understand that conditions were unusual because her country was at war. Watching her performance, Mecklin agreed with the correspondents that the palace now knew it could safely overrule the embassy on press policy.

IN THE WEEKS after David Halberstam succeeded Homer Bigart, embassy officials congratulated themselves on the improvement. Standing more than six feet tall, powerfully built, with horn-rimmed glasses and a wary, lopsided grin, Halberstam seemed committed to objective reporting, and the embassy was sure he would celebrate the progress being reported from the field. Nolting and his aides did not know that as managing editor of the *Harvard Crimson*, the undergraduate newspaper, Halberstam had engaged in a weekly competition to see which editor could offend the most readers.

On graduation, Halberstam had gone south to Mississippi and then to Nashville, covering the civil rights struggle of American blacks and despising both racial discrimination and the official lies from county courthouses. Hired for the *New York Times* Washington bureau, he had proved too stormy and rough-hewn for Scotty Reston's genteel clubhouse. Halberstam's editors hoped that an assignment in the Third World might hone his talent and put the brakes on his compulsive drive.

In the Congo, Halberstam came to respect Horst Faas, the AP photographer, and swapped information in casual talks with Edmund Gullion, the country's American ambassador. Gullion had been stationed in Vietnam at the end of the French War and reminisced with the young reporter about the challenges confronting a Western power in Indochina.

Getting to know Bigart at the *Times*, Halberstam had recognized a kindred spirit, and he arrived in South Vietnam aware that Homer would be reading his stories in New York. That hardly meant he would slant his dispatches; both men considered that a betrayal of trust. But when Halberstam made up his mind about Nhu and Diem, about America's involvement in this war and about the tactics being used to win it, his readers would know what he thought.

Halberstam had been in South Vietnam for less than three months when John Mecklin got a glimpse of the rage that deceit or incompetence could provoke in him. On Thanksgiving Day, General Harkins had launched the largest combat helicopter operation in history—forty-five U.S. helicopters ferrying Vietnamese troops to assault a Vietcong base north of Saigon. Even though about 200 American pilots and infantry advisers were aboard the helicopters, Harkins had neither alerted the American reporters nor invited them along. Once again, the Vietcong had received ample warning and suffered few losses, but the damage to neighboring villages was ruinous.

When he learned of the operation, Halberstam burst into Mecklin's office at the Information Agency, shaking with fury, and threw on his desk a letter addressed to Nolting. He waited as Mecklin read Halberstam's warning that the news blackout had converted him from "a neutral bystander to an angry man." The letter noted that 200 Americans had risked their lives in the operation, from which reporters had been banned. "The reason given is security," Halberstam wrote. "This is, of course, stupid, naive and indeed insulting to the patriotism and intelligence of every American newspaperman and every American newspaper represented here."

Halberstam pointed out that, from the minute helicopters landed, "You can bet the V.C. knew what was happening. You can bet Hanoi knew what was happening. Only American reporters and American readers were kept ignorant. . . ."

Halberstam's letter was intemperate, insulting and—Mecklin had to admit—entirely justified. To him, it was clear that the palace had banned reporters and that Nolting, still under orders to maintain good relations with Diem, had been forced again to go along. But Mecklin felt that Washington shared in the blame. The Kennedy White House had approved Cable 1006, with its permission for the U.S. mission to bar reporters from those operations likely to provoke negative coverage.

FIVE

LODGE
1963

SHEEHAN OF UPI had inherited the 7th ARVN Division from Bigart. Since Vietnam was too big for one reporter to cover, especially with the embassy's restrictions on helicopter travel, Bigart had found that he could travel easily by car to the Delta and monitor progress there with the American advisers. Taking Sheehan along to the 7th Division headquarters just outside My Tho, Bigart had introduced him to the colonel who was the chief U.S. adviser. When Bigart and that man returned to the United States, Sheehan went on making the trip and checking in with the colonel's successor, a hardscrabble Virginian named John Paul Vann. At first, Sheehan was put off by Colonel Vann's cheerleading for the ARVN and by the way he tried to paint Huynh Van Cao as a legitimate leader. Colonel Cao, a Catholic principally distinguished by his loyalty to the palace, was no soldier, and Sheehan soon caught on to the game. Cao was acting on what Diem had said to his favorite officers and then, to the Americans, denied saying: Don't incur casualties by fighting the Vietcong. Your job is to protect me against coups.

In case even Cao proved disloyal, Diem appointed a distant cousin to command the province's crucial armored regiment. Vann realized that Cao had no stomach for battle but was hoping that a somewhat transparent stratagem would improve his performance. No matter how often Cao shied away from pursuing the Vietcong troops within his grasp, Vann lauded him to reporters as a great warrior. The tactic failed since Cao basked in the praise but went on letting the enemy slip away. On one occasion, he agreed to pursue a rugged Communist

Colonel John Paul Vann (© *Hulton Getty/Liaison Agency*)

battalion, then reneged at the last moment and blamed his lower echelons. When he inflated the number of Vietcong casualties, the result was a hero's parade in Saigon and a promotion from Diem to the rank of general.

Speaking to reporters and visiting dignitaries from Washington, Vann kept up the charade of Cao's aggressiveness. To MACV headquarters, he filed more honest accounts, but Harkins shrugged off Vann's warnings of the persistent problems in ARVN leadership. As Cao became steadily more obdurate — "I make the decisions," he would say — Vann retired to his quarters, cursing Cao and the mother who bore him.

Although nine months of Vann's one year in South Vietnam had passed in frustration, he hoped to redeem his tour with the biggest operation of the war. The attack looked especially promising because Vann would be working with a new counterpart. Cao's promotion had put him in charge of a newly created command — IV Corps, with headquarters at Can Tho and responsibility for the entire Mekong Delta. Vann's new partner, Bui Dinh Dam, was a northern Catholic loyal to Diem but realistic about his limitations as a strategist and open to Vann's advice. The assault was scheduled to begin at 4 A.M. on the first day of 1963. When Colonel Dam postponed it one day, it was not from nerves but because he thought the American helicopter pilots might need time to recover from their New Year's Eve.

The plan itself was simple enough to ensure success. Vann had obtained ten

H-21 Shawnee troop-carrying helicopters. Each would make four trips, landing waves of ARVN at a village thirty-five miles southwest of Saigon. Their landing site was beside a canal that was shielded by coconut trees. Those 330 ARVN soldiers would be joined by two battalions of Civil Guards marching up from the south with a company of thirteen M-113 amphibious armored personnel carriers. The carriers would bring another infantry company.

The target was a radio transmitter being guarded by a reinforced company of Vietcong regulars. ARVN intelligence indicated that the enemy numbered 120 men, although the American advisers thought that the number, as usual, might be exaggerated. The government was sending in a force of nearly 2,000 men. Against such odds the Vietcong were unlikely to fight back. The ARVN could trap them and score a legitimate victory. Vietcong prisoners were admitting—often after being tortured—that the helicopters terrified their comrades and that the American advisers loomed up as far more formidable than the French. An ARVN success this day could be trumpeted throughout the Delta.

From a spotter plane, Vann watched the first landing at 7 A.M. But as a ground fog deepened, the helicopter pilots refused to fly. The second and third lifts would have to be delayed for at least two hours until the sun burned the fog away. Instead of an ARVN battalion moving out first against the guerrillas, it was the hapless Civil Guard, approaching on foot, who provoked the Vietcong to react. The Communists opened fire on those government forces from a hiding place in the tree line 30 yards away. Almost at once, the Civil Guard's two top officers were killed, and their men ran for cover behind a mud dike. During the next two hours, until 10 A.M., ARVN artillery fired occasional salvos at the guerrillas but always overshot their position.

The Dinh Tuong province chief, Major Lam Quang Tho, Diem's political appointee to head the armored regiment, had set up field headquarters two miles from the ambush. But Tho did not head for the site himself or direct the second Civil Guard battalion to reinforce the men under attack. And since he notified neither Vann nor Dam, the opening battle of the operation was all but over before they heard about it.

Vann cruised in his L-19 over Ap Bac—*ap* was Vietnamese for "hamlet"—to find a place to land the ten H-21s bringing in a reserve company. They would be accompanied by five of the new Bell helicopter gunships. The manufacturer called them HU-1 Iroquois, their pilots called them Hueys. Vann chose a spot to the west that was 300 yards from the tree line. That would put the landing zone nearly out of range of where he suspected the Vietcong were hiding with their .30-caliber rifles. But the U.S. Army pilots resented Vann's know-it-all attitude and took that moment to assert themselves. Disregarding his radio message, they flew instead toward a location only 200 yards from the trees.

For months, Vietcong commanders had been tempering their men's fear of

Ap Bac battlefield, January 3, 1963 *(© Bettmann/Corbis)*

the frightening machines that roared down at them from the sky. They called the H-21s "angleworms" and taught their men to shoot ahead of their target by two-thirds the length of a fuselage. That way, the helicopter would fly into the bullet. Gunners of the 514th Vietcong Regiment now proved they had mastered that lesson. As the ungainly helicopters came in to land, Vietcong machine-gun fire ripped through their aluminum skins. All of the H-21s were riddled with bullets, and three of them dropped from the sky. Overhead, the Hueys unleashed their rockets and machine-gun fire. For months, American advisers had been complaining that the guerrillas did not fight fair, that they attacked by night and then only when they had superior numbers. After a raid, they slipped away without standing up to fight.

At the hamlet of Bac, the Vietcong stood up.

In five fateful minutes, they shot down a fourth helicopter, one of the heavily armed Hueys that the Vietcong called "Dippers." Its pilot had followed a code of gallantry by trying to pick up survivors from the downed H-21s, but he lost his main rotor blade and crashed. At the scene, an awed American, Captain Joel Steine, marveled at the guerrillas' determination. "After napalm, rockets, machine-gunning and artillery," he said, "they came right back."

The ARVN displayed the result of their own brand of training—months of avoiding casualties, clomping loudly on patrol to alert the Vietcong and let them slip away, making a priority of pleasing the palace, not fighting the war. ARVN soldiers cowered in muck behind the dikes, and their American advisers could not rouse them. Overhead, John Vann was thrashing about in anger. Risking Vietcong fire, he ordered his pilot to fly low enough over the scene that he could check positions. Then he radioed for Captain Ly Tong Ba, commander of the M-113 armored unit, to get to Ap Bac at once with his thirteen vehicles. In Vietnam, the M-113 was the closest vehicle to a tank, and each held a dozen infantrymen. His U.S. adviser radioed back that Ba refused to move. "I don't take orders from Americans," Ba was saying. When Vann got Colonel Dam to repeat the command, Ba claimed that the high banks of a canal had immobilized his 10-ton carriers, and he refused to search for another crossing point. Instead, he asked headquarters to send the infantry.

Ba was immobilized by politics, not cowardice. Unless Tho gave the order, Ba couldn't be sure that Diem approved. As a Buddhist among largely Catholic officers, Ba felt especially exposed. But, for now, he had to face Vann's fury. Over a field telephone that allowed for no privacy, he could hear Vann asking Ba's American adviser whether he could get the M-113s to Ap Bac. The adviser said he could. "Then shoot that rotten cowardly son-of-a-bitch right now," Vann screamed, "and move out!"

It didn't come to that. Ba agreed to double back and find another way to cross the canal. More than three hours after Vann's first call, the carriers reached Ap Bac, where they ran into a volley of Vietcong machine-gun fire. The carriers' gunners, who were exposed on top of their vehicles, dove to safety inside, but from there they could fire only aimlessly. In the confusion, Captain Ba was struck by the barrel of an untended .50-caliber gun and left dazed and out of commission for twenty minutes.

When the battle resumed, one intrepid Vietcong squad leader jumped from his foxhole and threw a grenade onto an M-112. His example set off a volley of grenades from his squad and sent Ba into retreat.

By MIDAFTERNOON, the Saigon press corps had heard reports that a major battle was under way. Halberstam of the *Times* and Peter Arnett of the AP began calling their military contacts and then drove to Tan Son Nhut to talk with angry helicopter pilots as they flew back from the operation. UPI's Sheehan and Nick Turner of Reuters gathered up Sheehan's Vietnamese reporter, Nguyen Ngoc Rao, and drove through the night at 70 miles an hour in Turner's Triumph sedan. Reaching Tan Hiep and piecing together details of the Vietcong victory, they learned that General Cao had planned to drop the Saigon paratroopers behind the Civil Guard and the armored carriers, rather then put them in open rice fields to the east where they could block the escape route the guerrillas were sure to take once darkness fell. Vann jabbed at the map to show where the troops should land, but Cao kept repeating, "It is not prudent, it is not prudent."

Brigadier General Tran Thien Khiem, chief of the Vietnamese Joint General Staff, had flown to the scene, and he backed up his general. Since General Harkins had not come to the site where, by now, five helicopters had been lost, Sheehan saw that Lieutenant Colonel Vann was clearly outranked by the ARVN officers.

At Ap Bac, the Vietcong had been alerted by other guerrillas at nearby Tan Thoi, where they were intercepting ARVN radio signals, and they hurried out to make the paratroopers' landing a lethal one. Cao had lied to Vann by saying he had ordered the drop for 4 P.M., when it would still be light. He had ordered it for dusk. But then a mistake—either by the American pilots flying the transport planes or by the Vietnamese jumpmaster—sent the paratroopers dropping directly in front of the guerrillas, after all, rather than in the sanctuary Cao had chosen for them. The paratroopers took heavy casualties, and two of their American advisers were killed. Cao still hoped that the Vietcong would melt away without further losses to his troops, and he forbade dropping flares to light up their line of escape.

The Vietcong survivors obliged him by vanishing. Despite thousands of rounds from ARVN rifles and machine guns on the ground, and 8,400 rounds of gunfire and 100 rockets from the Hueys, the Vietcong had suffered only 18 men killed and 39 wounded. ARVN casualties were four times as high, although by the time the numbers got to Saigon, they had been substantially reduced.

VIETCONG CADRES, schooled in propaganda techniques, were exploiting their victory even as they retreated from Ap Bac. As a unit passed through neighboring villages, four men carried a makeshift stretcher with a large shape hidden beneath blue cloth. Pausing for water, the guerrillas silently set down their burden. Villagers came to stare and speculate about what was under wraps, but the Vietcong commander shooed them away. "Under this blue cloth," he said, "is a new secret weapon. By means of it, we have shot down dozens and dozens of the enemy's helicopters at Bac." Then his men picked up their intriguing burden and moved on to the next hamlet.

THEIR SENSE OF DRAMA served the Vietcong again that same week when they released a thirty-one-year-old American sergeant named Roque Matagulay. He had been taken five months earlier when he wandered into the jungle to hunt game. The Vietcong assembled 400 villagers to witness their generosity as they put Matagulay on a bus back to freedom. Once in Saigon, he acknowledged that he had not been tortured except for being forced to listen to world news broadcasts on Radio Hanoi and take tests on what he heard.

In his Communist camp, Colonel Ta Minh Kham was annoyed to hear that

Matagulay, who had lost forty-five pounds in captivity, was complaining that his diet had been rice, salt, oil and leaves, relieved only by an occasional rat or barbecued gopher. We gave him what we ourselves eat, Kham thought. Although deer often ran through the trees, the Vietcong were forbidden to waste ammunition by shooting at them.

DURING THE BATTLE of Ap Bac, an extended printers' strike had shut down New York newspapers, but the *New York Times* kept printing its Western edition, which was flown to Washington each day and distributed at the White House. The paper usually ran Halberstam's stories on an inside page, but the catastrophe at Ap Bac put Vietnam on the front page, above the fold. The headline noted that five helicopters had been downed and another nine hit. The subhead was uncompromising: "Defeat Worst Since Buildup Began—Three Americans are Killed in Vietnam." The story ran beside a photograph of General Lemnitzer, smiling widely as he assumed command of the NATO forces. Kennedy had appointed Max Taylor to succeed him as chairman of the Joint Chiefs.

The next morning's edition brought the president no better news. Colonel Vann had arranged for Halberstam and Arnett to be flown over the battlefield on January 4, which the *Times* report called "a slow and bitter day." The sole action had come in the morning when ARVN soldiers accidentally trained their howitzers on their own troops, killing 3 and wounding 12.

Sheehan had been nearby during that miscalculation, and he dove into the mud with Brigadier General Robert York, the only one of the twelve general officers stationed in Vietnam to visit the battle site. When frightened ARVN soldiers refused to touch their dead, Sheehan helped to carry the bodies to helicopters. He told Halberstam later that when he saw the blankets "with their little feet sticking out, I did something I hadn't done in years. I crossed myself."

Back at the base camp, Halberstam ran into Harkins, who was accompanied by Cao's honor guard, resplendent in white helmets. He asked the general what had happened. "We've got them in a trap," Harkins said, "and we're going to spring it in half an hour." At the scene, General York gave Sheehan a more realistic answer: "What the hell's it look like happened, boy? They got away—that's what happened."

WITH HIS AP STAFF to rely on, Mal Browne could stay in Saigon, churning out copy from Arnett's reports and beating Sheehan's UPI decisively in the number of papers that carried their reports. Keeping his distance also prevented Browne from falling under the influence of John Vann. Browne had sized up Vann as a cocky little squirt whose taste in civilian clothes ran to cheap shirts with matching ties. But to Halberstam and Sheehan, Vann was a ready source of accurate information, brave in battle, equally brave in bucking MACV's press restrictions. In a dispatch, Sheehan quoted Vann's summation of the past two days: "a miserable damn performance." Exhausted and furious, Vann went on, "These people won't listen. They make the same goddam mistakes over and over again in the same way." Sheehan did not identify Vann by name, but when the story reached Vann's home in Rochester, New York, his mother-in-law instantly recognized the source, as did Harkins in Saigon. He was going to remove Vann until an aide pointed out that the reporters would crucify him.

When Cao made Vann his scapegoat for the defeat, Madame Nhu picked up his excuses and retailed them to the complaisant Vietnamese press. She said that an American colonel flying above the battle in a light plane had overruled the orders of ARVN's more knowledgeable commanders.

The *Honolulu Star-Bulletin* printed Sheehan's account of the battle, which allowed Admiral Felt to read the unwelcome news in vivid detail. Next, the *Washington Post* ran Sheehan's long postmortem, leading Kennedy to wonder whether Sheehan's pessimism about the war might be more reliable than Harkins's weekly "Headway" reports to the Pentagon.

A week after the battle, Felt flew to Saigon to reassure the president that the U.S. effort was still on track. When the admiral arrived at the airport, Sheehan crowded to the front of the reporters and asked for Felt's assessment of Ap Bac. "I'd like to say that I don't believe what I've been reading in the papers," Felt answered. "As I understand it, it was a Vietnamese victory—not a defeat, as the papers say."

Felt looked to Harkins, who said, "Yes, that's right. It was a Vietnamese victory. It certainly was."

As the officers walked away, Harkins murmured to Felt the name of the reporter who had asked the question, and the admiral came back to confront him. "So you're Sheehan," Felt said. "You ought to talk to some people who've got the facts." Sheehan could not erase the image of Harkins in his pressed suntans and spotless shoes viewing the aftermath of the fighting from far in the rear.

"That's right, Admiral," said the twenty-five-year-old former army pay clerk. "That's why I went down there every day."

Looking toward Harkins, Sheehan added, "You might try sending your own people down."

THE VIETCONG did not cooperate in supplying Felt with good news. While the admiral was in Saigon, the Vietcong battalion commander returned to Ap Bac, raised his flag over the hamlet and challenged General Cao to a rematch. It was a challenge Cao could resist. Leaving Vietnam, Felt scheduled a press conference to apply balm to the hurt pride of Vietnamese like Cao who had been stung by criticism from the American advisers. "There are times in your own family when you have disappointments with your wife," the admiral explained. "Generally, we understand each other. It is only the exception when we become a little bit angry."

Felt was asked whether he still considered the operation a success. He repeated his earlier answer and turned again for corroboration to Harkins, who had been doodling on a pad. "Yes," said the startled general. "I consider it a victory. We took the objective."

Halberstam and the others were jolted that his answer could miss the point so badly. Control of territory was not the purpose of guerrilla war. As the reporters noted, the ARVN may have taken the objective, but they took it twenty-seven hours late, when the enemy was long since gone.

WITH REPERCUSSIONS from Ap Bac troubling the White House, two more Washington visitors were in Saigon, trying to make sense of Vietnam for Kennedy. Roger Hilsman from the State Department had been there the previous year, but his companion, Michael Forrestal, would be collecting first impressions, and Forrestal's judgments could count heavily with the president.

Forrestal's highly developed sense of irony let him see the macabre side to his joining Mac Bundy's staff. As Truman's secretary of the navy, his father, James Forrestal, had devised the first National Security Council because he was concerned that the Pentagon was not represented at the White House during policy decisions. When the Departments of Navy and War merged to become the Department of Defense, the elder Forrestal became its first Secretary. Bouts of depression led him to take his life in 1949, the year that his son graduated from Princeton. Averell and Marie Harriman all but adopted Michael and watched fondly as he graduated from Harvard Law and developed a thriving international law practice as a partner at Sherman & Sterling in New York. Curly-headed and chubby, Mike Forrestal exuded charm and social ease.

By accepting Walt Rostow in the White House, Bundy had shown that he was flexible about the men Kennedy wanted to add to the NSC staff. On his own, Bundy had recruited Carl Kaysen, a Harvard economist he had known and liked from the time they were in their late twenties at Harvard. But Bundy vetoed a job for Henry Kissinger, whom he had also known at Harvard, because of his unrelenting self-promotion. Whether to take on Mike Forrestal had been a trickier decision. Bundy was generous about providing his junior staff with access to Kennedy when the president needed their expertise. But Forrestal and Kennedy were both avid weekend sailors, and Forrestal's sardonic attitude toward Washington's power scramble appealed to the president. As a result, Forrestal had his own channel to the Oval Office. Both Bundy and McNamara were bothered by that easy access and tried to rein Forrestal in. When he disputed a point with McNamara, the Secretary would chide him: "Mike, you're talking well, but where are your facts? You state things so glibly. What percent of territory has the government lost in the last month? What percent does it have and what percent does it not have? Where are your statistics? Don't give me poetry."

And if Forrestal went through Bundy to see the president, he compared the ordeal to a sterilizing bath. Bundy wanted to know precisely what Forrestal intended to say and then hectored him about it with variations of "Have you thought that out?" Forrestal found Bundy the least creative thinker on the NSC, always two cautious steps to the rear of a discussion. He suspected that Kennedy felt the same and kept Bundy out of his political decisions. Forrestal's own assignment upon joining the NSC had come directly from the president: "You will be my emissary to that special sovereignty, Averell Harriman."

During Forrestal's stay in Saigon, Halberstam was astonished at how openly cordial he was to him and Sheehan. It was a time when the embassy staff refused to speak to either of them, and Halberstam had reason to believe background checks were being run on his past affiliations. Forrestal seemed to assume that being agreeable to the Saigon press corps was part of his assignment.

THE PRESIDENT was frankly puzzled by the hostility between Harkins and Nolting and the reporters in Saigon. Kennedy had always liked journalists well enough, and before he went into politics his few civilian jobs had been newspaper assignments arranged by his father. He felt close to Charles Bartlett, the *Chattanooga Times* Washington correspondent, and a rising reporter at *Newsweek*, Ben Bradlee, had become something of a pal. The Bradlees were invited occasionally to the White House for an impromptu private dinner.

Growing up, Kennedy had seen the political advantages of a tame press corps. He had watched as his father all but reduced the *New York Times* columnist Arthur Krock to the role of family retainer, and in Congress, Kennedy had worked at establishing that same sway with his generation of newsmen. Hugh Sidey, for example, a reporter in *Time* magazine's Washington bureau, had been easily won over while Kennedy was still in the Senate. Sidey was grateful that Kennedy never acted snobbishly toward him, and to please the dashing senator he would deliver an advance copy of *Time* each week to the Capitol. If the issue mentioned Kennedy, Sidey waited in the press gallery until the senator scanned the item and gave him a thumbs up.

Once Kennedy was elected president, Sidey became his chronicler for the magazine and suffered an occasional rebuke. When *Time* reported that Kennedy had posed for a men's fashion magazine, Kennedy became the angriest Sidey had ever seen him. "People are going to remember me because I posed for the cover of *Gentlemen's Quarterly*," he said, pacing back and forth. A similar outburst against the *New York Herald Tribune* led Kennedy to cancel the twenty-two copies of the paper delivered to the White House each morning. But those squalls were rare. Kennedy liked sparring with reporters, and his live television news conferences allowed him direct access to the electorate. Kennedy spoke well extemporaneously, and he knew how to turn away tough questions with a quip and his dazzling smile.

But with Ap Bac, the era of charm and easy deceit seemed to be coming to an end. Newspapers around the country were being highly critical. The *Chicago Daily News*, the *Baltimore Sun*, and the *Washington Daily News* ran editorials about "humiliation" and "disorganization." In a widely syndicated column, Hanson Baldwin, the *New York Times* military analyst, deplored the overreliance on helicopters in South Vietnam. Machines bearing troops who descended briefly from the sky could never control the countryside, he wrote. In a phrase Giap would have endorsed, Baldwin added that "legs are a soldier's chief weapon."

MACV went on blaming reporters for the ruinous publicity, but civilians in Washington were not so sure. In a message of strained tact, Harriman called on Nolting and Harkins to increase their informal contacts with the American journalists. By early February 1963, Kennedy was meeting regularly with his senior advisers to consider the questions "Why do we have such a bad press from South Vietnam?" and "Should we be more forthcoming with the U.S. press in Saigon despite Vietnamese government objections?"

In mid-May, Kennedy's dissatisfaction with the war's progress led to a policy change and an embarrassing leak. Max Taylor informed McNamara in a memo that the Joint Chiefs no longer wanted Farmgate helicopter pilots restricted from shooting at the Vietcong unless they had been fired upon. When the *Washington Daily News* ran Sheehan's story about the change under the headline "Shoot First," a State Department official called the Pentagon to ask why such a significant restriction had been eliminated without Rusk being consulted. He was told that Bobby Kennedy had sent the change directly to the president for a quick decision. The order had been circulated among helicopter pilots in Vietnam and leaked immediately to Sheehan.

The White House instructed Mecklin to analyze the quality of reporting coming out of Saigon, and he prepared a cable for Nolting's signature that characterized it "probably as good as the average reporting of stateside story like earthquake or Hollywood divorce." The difference was Vietnam's complexity. The cable acquitted the reporters of actively trying to undercut the U.S. war effort, but Mecklin emphasized that their average age was twenty-seven. They had "approximately the same experience to cover Vietnam as they do routine stateside police beat." During his visit, Forrestal had also asked Mecklin for a candid appraisal that he could take directly to Kennedy, and Mecklin unburdened himself about the frustrations of brokering between a remote ambassador with a policy of limited disclosure and a press corps whose reporting had sometimes been "irresponsible, sensationalized and astigmatic."

That harsh judgment promptly reached its victims. Soon afterward, reporters heard with little sympathy that Mecklin had to fly to the Philippines for chest surgery. Merton Perry, a stringer for *Time*, said, "I hope the son-of-a-bitch dies."

But Mecklin survived. As he recovered, he debated returning to Saigon, where an unforgiving press corps was calling him "Meck the Knife."

☐

AFTER HIS FIRST TRIP TO SAIGON in seven years, Mike Mansfield released a Senate report that alarmed the White House and outraged the Ngo family. At Kennedy's request, Mansfield and three other senators had made their tour in December 1962, and their findings were devastating: Mansfield found Diem no nearer than he had been in 1955 to coping with his challenges. At best, U.S. aid would be required for years to come.

The American embassy reported that Nhu was interpreting Mansfield's report as a prelude to a United States pullout. In that, he was correct about Mansfield's recommendation but not about Kennedy's response to it. On his return from Saigon, Mansfield had flown to Palm Beach, where the Kennedy family was gathered for the Christmas holidays. Alone with the president, Mansfield recommended withdrawing U.S. troops from a hopeless civil war. Kennedy seethed at such bleak advice from a man he respected, but he did not argue with him. Afterward, he told his scheduling secretary, Kenny O'Donnell, "I got angry with Mike for disagreeing with our policy so completely, and I got angry with myself because I found myself agreeing with him."

For the present, however, Kennedy intended to go on bolstering Diem, and by the time Mansfield made his findings public, he had toned them down. He no longer called for American withdrawal, but he did list the host of problems and warned against converting the struggle into an American war. Kennedy invited him to the White House for another talk, this time with O'Donnell sitting in.

The president confessed to second thoughts about their earlier conversation. He had come to accept the wisdom of a complete military withdrawal from South Vietnam. "But I can't do it until 1965," Kennedy added, "after I'm reelected."

Even though Kennedy had seemed to face down Khrushchev over the Cuban missiles, he was sure that Republican conservatives could raise enough protest over abandoning Vietnam to jeopardize his second term. When Mansfield left, Kennedy told O'Donnell that withdrawal in 1965 would make him one of the most unpopular presidents in history. He would be damned everywhere as a Communist appeaser. "But I don't care," Kennedy said. "If I tried to pull out completely now from Vietnam we would have another Joe McCarthy red scare on our hands, but I can do it after I'm reelected. So we had better make damned sure that I *am* reelected."

The subject remained on Kennedy's mind when he was speculating about the future with Charles Bartlett, his trusted friend in the press corps. "We don't have a prayer of staying in Vietnam," Kennedy told him. "Those people hate us. They are going to throw our asses out of there at almost any point. But I can't give up a piece of territory like that to the Communists and then get the people to reelect me."

To Ted Sorensen, Kennedy made a remark that his father would have found even more heretical. Early in the 1960 campaign, Joe Kennedy had shared a convivial dinner with Henry Luce, the publisher of *Time, Life* and *Fortune*. Luce liked Jack Kennedy and had agreed some years earlier when his father asked him to write the introduction to *Why England Slept*. Both men knew that Luce's influential *Life* magazine would endorse Nixon, but Joe Kennedy hoped to protect Jack from *Time's* skewering in its news columns.

For his part, Luce was prepared to be tolerant. "On domestic affairs," he said, "of course Jack will have to be left of center."

Joe Kennedy erupted. "How can you say that? How can you think that any son of mine would ever be a fucking liberal?"

Luce assured him that it was entirely permissible for Jack to veer leftward at home. But foreign policy was different. If Jack Kennedy showed any sign of weakness toward the anti-Communist cause, Luce warned, "why then we'll certainly be against him."

"Well, there's no chance of that," Joe Kennedy said. "You know that."

As secretary of state, Rusk remained as obdurate as Luce against recognizing Communist China, but Hilsman and others at State were urging a reexamination of U.S. policy, and Sorensen raised the question with Kennedy.

"That's for the second term." Kennedy said it so lightly that even Sorensen, who had been divining his moods for some eight years, was not sure whether he was serious.

Kennedy could confide his doubts about Vietnam to Mansfield and O'Donnell, since their political fortunes also hung on a Democratic victory in November 1964. But to keep Americans fighting, and dying, in order to ensure his second term was not a decision to share widely. Kennedy would plug along instead with the unsatisfactory status quo until January 1965. Less partisan advisers like Rusk never heard him express doubts about staying the course in South Vietnam. To McNamara, malleable and discreet, Kennedy said only that he would be out of the war in 1965, no matter how it was going.

The president had plans for the coming months that could alter the international mood enough that a Communist victory in Vietnam would seem less catastrophic at home. Throughout the spring, Sorensen had been working on a speech that would convey Kennedy's strong commitment to peace and possibly move Khrushchev toward a treaty banning nuclear tests.

Adopting Sorensen's words, Kennedy was asking the Soviet leaders to rise above their Cold War attitudes. "But I also believe that we must examine our own attitudes—as individuals and as a Nation—for our attitude is as essential as theirs." Sorensen's draft touched upon Kennedy's greatest apprehension: if nuclear war should come, "all we have worked for would be destroyed in the first twenty-four hours."

WHEN JOHN MECKLIN decided to return to Saigon, he used a round of courtesy calls in Washington to try to change the press policies of Rowan's Cable 1006. Pierre Salinger heard him out and suggested that he present his views directly to the president. Mecklin went back to the White House on April 29, worried about criticizing his Saigon bosses. "If you don't level with the President," Salinger said, "he doesn't want to talk to you at all."

In the Oval Office, Mecklin was disarmed when Kennedy called him by name and asked about his health before coming to the point. "Why are we having so much trouble with the reporters out there?"

Mecklin had spent his weeks in the Philippines regretting what he had said to Forrestal, and he gave Kennedy a more generous description of the Saigon newsmen. They compared favorably with any, he said, but they were bitter at Diem's regime and at the embassy. Washington should change its press policy. When Kennedy asked for specifics, Mecklin said the U.S. mission should take reporters into its confidence since they were always going to find out about defeats and deceptions anyway. As it was, they took our secrecy as an affront to their patriotism. We should prove them wrong by extending our trust.

Mecklin thought the president looked skeptical but willing to try. Kennedy told Salinger later that the conflict in Saigon appeared to be so intense that he doubted that any policy would work, but he called for a draft of new instructions. Soon afterward, a classified cable went out to the embassy advising cooperation with U.S. correspondents and urging against overly optimistic statements about the war's progress. After three months away from South Vietnam, Mecklin returned to Saigon, hoping for a new dawn in press relations.

AT ABOUT THE TIME of Mansfield's inspection tour, Tran Kim Tuyen was lecturing about the strategic hamlets to a group of new cadres. Most visiting Americans were more enthusiastic than Mansfield about the program, although many hamlets were little more than chicken wire and a few rifles. Tuyen got his usual warm applause from the carefully selected men who would be in charge of the latest settlements. But as he stepped from the dais, a colonel approached to say that President Diem had summoned him to the palace.

Since Tuyen hadn't seen Diem in four or five months, he wondered at the urgency. At the palace, he found Diem especially formal and hesitant, smoking steadily to avoid speaking. At last, Diem said, "A big movement against our government has begun at the United Nations, led by the African countries. We need someone to go abroad to counter that propaganda."

Tuyen knew then that Diem had learned about his clandestine meetings with officers and politicians who shared his disillusion with the Ngo family. Trapped, he said, "If you wish it, I can go."

Diem was instantly relieved, then conciliatory. "Go home now and rest," he said, adding that instructions would be forthcoming. From that moment, Tuyen was out of work. Nhu no longer called. Days passed, then weeks, until another of Nhu's aides was announced as Tuyen's successor. With that, Tuyen gave into a petty revenge that estranged him further from the palace. Since most of his staff and equipment had been cajoled from other offices, he sent his aides back to their army jobs and returned nine of the ten cars he had been lent. The new man found only three typewriters and a heap of useless documents. It was sabotage. Hearing that accusation, Tuyen gave his high-pitched giggle and reminded friends that his job had depended upon personal relationships. It wasn't his fault that he had been replaced by an unimaginative civil servant. Then in early May, Tuyen had a chance to prove his point by rendering one last service to the Diem regime.

The issue seemed trivial. As part of his crackdown against religious sects in the mid-fifties, Diem had ordered that only South Vietnam's flag—yellow with red stripes—could be flown in public. At first, he tried to enforce the ban even-handedly, and when Catholics hung out Christmas flags later in the decade, Diem ordered them removed. Since his retinue knew that his angriest instructions were usually best ignored, the Catholics flew their flags anyway and the controversy soon died. In the spring of 1963, however, papal flags had flown again to honor the fifth anniversary of the ordination of Diem's brother, the archbishop. Buddhists in Hue planned a celebration of their own for May 8 to mark Buddha's 2,578th birthday. As part of the festivities, they set out their own flags.

In Hue, Vietnam's center of Buddhist scholarship, opposition to the government had become increasingly bold. Diem heard that at Hue University, antigovernment slogans were being splashed across buildings, always with meticulous diacritical marks. So when the monsignor reported seeing Buddhist flags, Diem became enraged and called in his chief of staff, a man Tuyen considered one of those mandarins with no political sense. Diem told him, "Send an official telegram, telling the local authorities to take down the Buddhist flags." Another man might have waited out the president's mood, but this time Diem was obeyed.

Hue's Buddhists defied the ban, and the city's officials hesitated to enforce it. With the authorities wavering, the Buddhists staged a huge birthday celebration with unmistakable political overtones. Ngo Dinh Can took the outpouring as an insult to his family, but even his tough cadre couldn't break up the demonstration. The province chief, a Catholic, sent troops to the scene in armored carriers and ordered them to open fire. When the smoke cleared, 9 civilians were dead and 14 wounded. Two children had been crushed to death by carrier tracks.

In Saigon, the panicked palace staff tried to shift the blame to the Vietcong: a Communist agent had thrown a grenade, they said, and the victims were crushed as they fled the scene. But bystanders had taken home movies of government soldiers shooting into the crowd. The next day, more than 10,000 residents of Hue marched through the streets in protest.

Although the Buddhists had never been tightly organized, the crisis was uniting them. On May 10, a prominent Buddhist issued a manifesto demanding punishment for the men who had fired, compensation for their victims and equality with the Catholic Church, including the right to fly Buddhist flags. At the same time, a Buddhist priest, Thich Tri Quang, urged the crowd to be alert for any Vietcong attempts to exploit the unrest. Follow the example of Gandhi, Tri Quang told them. Fly your flags—he would take responsibility—but carry no weapons, even though each protester must be prepared to die.

Diem was enough rattled by events to overlook his suspicions about Tuyen. Summoning him to his private chambers, Diem asked for help. Tuyen thought for a moment. "The trouble started in Hue," he said, "so you must get in touch with the leading Buddhists there. Get them on a special plane to Saigon for talks." Diem nodded and sent Tuyen home. The bonzes soon arrived in the capital with their elderly and ineffectual Buddhist pope and their spokesman, Thich Thien Minh. Tuyen considered Tri Quang, who had stayed behind in Hue, a demagogue, but he was the only one who seemed able to control the crowd.

To resolve the crisis, Diem's advisers offered to set up a committee with the three monks among its members. In return, the Buddhists were to stop further demonstrations. Thuan, Diem's chief minister, conducted the public negotiations, then met secretly with Thien Minh to untangle any snags. Within several days, they had drafted a communiqué to be signed by Diem and the Buddhist pope, and Diem seemed satisfied with its provisions: freedom to fly religious flags; equality among Catholics, Buddhists and other faiths; an end to arbitrary arrests in Hue; government compensation for the May 8 victims.

With Diem about to approve the agreement, his sister-in-law broke in upon him late on the evening before the ratifying ceremony. She scanned the document and told Diem flatly that he could not sign it. You are the president of this nation, she said. Who is this Buddhist monk to sign on the same line beside you?

When Diem hesitated, Madame Nhu stormed from his room. Thuan tried to convince him that she had been wrong and that he should honor his commitment. Finally, Diem agreed, but he wrote in the margin next to the terms: "All these things I already do for the Buddhist Church and will continue to do them."

Thuan called on Tuyen to explain Diem's notation to the Buddhists, who were predictably outraged. Tuyen managed to persuade them that the essence of the text had not been compromised, and the meeting broke up with the understanding that the communiqué would be published the next day. Tuyen went home feeling smug. The palace still needed him.

The next morning, June 7, Thuan sent the final draft to the Office of Information Services and told its clerks to release it to the public. Before they could act, however, Madame Nhu called and ordered them to stop. Her shouting scared the staff. They apologized to Thuan but said they did not dare to defy her. At the palace, Thuan found Diem in a funk. He looked miserable and clearly had no thought of how to resolve his dilemma. While he hesitated, Madame Nhu called a special meeting of her women's organization and issued a statement of her own that insulted the Buddhists and repudiated in advance any agreement with them.

Her proclamation charged that the protesting Buddhists were "exploited and controlled by Communism and oriented to sowing of disorder and neutral-ism." It also called on the government to expel all foreign agitators "whether they wear monk's robes or not" and, in passing, slammed the American mission as "inclined to take Vietnam for a satellite of a foreign power or organization." Af-terward, Madame Nhu explained her reasoning to her brother-in-law: if the Bud-dhist delegation was entitled to have a political position as a group of private citizens, her women's organization deserved the same right to take a stand.

Nonsense, said Thuan. Madame Nhu wasn't a private citizen. She was the president's sister-in-law, living in the palace. The Buddhists can rightly say that we cannot trust a man who signed a pact one day and reneged the next. Thuan did say all of that. But he said it only to Tuyen, not to Diem or his family.

Nor was Nhu prepared to contradict his wife. A military officer rode with him to the airport for a flight to Dalat, where Nhu intended to spend the week-end. The man found Nhu furious with his wife's female cadre. "A silly mistake," Nhu said, fuming, "and silly people to insult the Buddhists."

Nhu's weekends were supposedly spent hunting in a secure forest near the re-sort city. But he usually went into the woods alone and stayed there, smoking silently and seldom firing his rifle. After three days of brooding, Nhu drove back from the airport with the same aide, who found him still irate, but now with the Buddhists. After Thuan met with Nhu, he told Tuyen there was nothing more to be done. Madame Nhu was accusing anyone who had negotiated with the Buddhists of appeasement, and Tuyen found himself even more isolated from the palace.

FROM HIS USAID OFFICE, Bill Kohlmann watched with keen interest as the drama unfolded. Although he had widened his circle of Buddhist contacts, he felt somewhat restricted by his embassy's antipathy to them. Tempers were run-ning high, and Kohlmann felt obliged to counsel the Buddhists to act with re-straint. But he could not maintain his tenuous friendships if he repeated Nolting's line that they should wait the two years until the next elections and show their displeasure at the polls.

One young Buddhist Kohlmann had cultivated was a lapsed bonze named Tran Quang Thuan—who shared a name but nothing else with Diem's chief minister. Kohlmann's Thuan, now twenty-nine, had been sent by his pagoda to schools in Hanoi, Sri Lanka and Great Britain. A slight burr reflected five years of studying sociology at Edinburgh University. Returning to Vietnam, Thuan was dismayed by the low level of Buddhist scholarship and by his elders' lack of am-bition. In 1961, he asked to be released from his orders and married the daughter of a wealthy family. But the favoritism that Diem extended to Catholics rankled him, and he retained his ties to the few politically minded Buddhists in Hue and Saigon.

Thuan met Kohlmann at a British embassy reception and was pleased when Kohlmann sought him out afterward. They stayed in touch as Thuan con-fided his increasing dissatisfaction with Diem. But their conversations remained guarded. Kohlmann did not reveal his CIA connection, and Thuan did not tell him when, on June 10, a Buddhist acquaintance called to borrow Thuan's old Austin sedan. Thuan suspected the reason for the request, but he owed much to the Buddhists. If they asked him for a favor, he would not question it.

WITH DIEM WAVERING over negotiations, Buddhists in Saigon and Hue mounted new antigovernment rallies. The crowd came by bus and pedicab from different directions to prevent Diem's police from breaking up their protest before the American newsmen arrived; Buddhist leaders were proving adept at timing their demonstrations for maximum press coverage in the United States. On June 11, a Buddhist contact called to tell Bill Kohlmann to go at once to a nearby intersection. Heading out the door, Kohlmann was willing to bet that the American newsmen had got the same call before he did.

The Buddhist spokesman, Duc Nghiep, had been even more diligent than Kohlmann suspected. The previous night, he told a monk to ring Mal Browne and say that an "important event" would be taking place at the pagoda. Nghiep alerted other journalists as well, but demonstrations against Diem had become old news, and no other reporter was willing to get up before dawn to check out the tip. Browne, however, remembered Nghiep's earlier announcement that two monks had volunteered for a martyr's death to protest the Diem regime—one offering to disembowel himself, the other choosing fire. Browne took those pledges seriously, even though he was not aware of recent tests that the Buddhists had been conducting. They had found that gasoline was easily ignited but burned itself out too quickly. Mixing equal parts of gasoline and diesel fuel produced a more intense and longer-lasting flame.

At Xa Loi pagoda, Browne and a Vietnamese translator found crowds of monks in their yellow robes, along with Buddhist nuns dressed in gray. The nun who served him tea was weeping, and Nghiep pressed through the throng to recommend that Browne stay until the very end. After half an hour of fervent chanting, the leaders gave a signal that silenced the congregation and moved everyone to the street. A column of marchers formed behind Thuan's Austin. Five monks were crowded inside. By now, the Saigon police were as blasé as the reporters about these marches and sent a white jeep to clear the way. At the corner of Phan Dinh Phung and Le Van Duyet Streets, the procession stopped and fanned out in a circle to block the intersection. Two Buddhists emerged from the car and assisted a third monk, frail and old, as he walked to the center of the circle. Browne raised his camera.

The younger Buddhists laid a cushion on the pavement and helped the aged bonze—Browne learned that his name was Thich Quang Duc—as he settled into the lotus position. In a hurry now, they raced back to the car for a large plastic gasoline can and doused Quang Duc with pink fluid. As they stepped back, Duc struck a match and let it fall onto his oil-soaked robe. In a second, he disappeared

Malcolm Browne with his photograph of
Thich Quang Duc *(AP/Wide World Photos)*

behind a wall of black and yellow fire. When a breeze blew the flames from his face, Browne saw that his eyes were pressed shut, his features distorted with pain. The smell of his charred flesh was reaching the spectators. Duc neither moved nor cried out, but the crowd began to moan, and women screamed.

Two monks had come with a banner that confirmed which audience they intended to witness Duc's sacrifice. In English, it read A BUDDHIST PRIEST BURNS FOR BUDDHIST DEMANDS. A bonze with a portable microphone repeated over and over, also in English, "A Buddhist priest becomes a martyr."

Shocked as he was by the scene, Browne kept shooting film, capturing the moment when a fire truck showed up and monks threw themselves in front of its wheels to prevent the crew from putting out the fire. Duc's body burned for another ten minutes. As the flames died away, the twitching corpse fell forward. Monks had brought a coffin, but Duc's charred limbs could not be bent to fit inside. Browne's last view was of an arm sticking out from the wooden box, still smoking.

□

BROWNE'S PHOTOGRAPHS of Duc's immolation went out on the AP wire and set off a worldwide chain of shock and recriminations. Mecklin understood that the pictures would instantly become a symbol of the intolerable situation in South Vietnam. At the palace, even Diem saw that he must now offer to negotiate with the moderate Buddhists. Only his sister-in-law remained implacable. Tuyen heard a popular rumor that at lunch she had denounced Diem as a coward and hurled a tureen of soup across the table. Even if the story were not true, Madame Nhu found ways to express her feelings. She called Duc's death a barbecue and offered to furnish the gasoline and matches for other priests inclined to emulate him. "Let them burn!" she exulted. "And we shall clap our hands."

At the U.S. embassy, the acting ambassador, William Trueheart, was coping as best he could. Just as the Buddhist protests exploded in May, Fritz Nolting had left for a long cruise with his family through the Greek islands. Trueheart felt genuine affection for Nolting but thought that his constant yielding to the palace had hurt America's interests. He resolved to be tougher.

Savvy and unsentimental, the Buddhist leaders had removed what they said was Quang Duc's heart from his ashes and placed it in a jar at Xa Loi pagoda. They assured the faithful that since the heart had not burned, their martyr's restless spirit would find peace only when Diem accepted the Buddhist demands. Reparations remained the problem. Negotiating on Diem's behalf, Thuan said that each family of the Buddhists killed in Hue had already received 10,000 piasters and might be paid more. But the government wanted to investigate further before admitting responsibility. In Washington, the State Department found the Buddhist terms reasonable and wired Trueheart to urge Diem to accept them. The cable added an FYI: "If Diem does not take prompt and effective steps to reestablish Buddhist confidence in him, we will have to reexamine our entire relationship with his regime."

Tri Quang and other Hue Buddhists announced that they would fly to Saigon, but were they coming to negotiate or to agitate? Trueheart used their arrival to press Diem harder than any U.S. diplomat had done since Durbrow. His threat of an American public disavowal finally convinced Diem of the depths of Washington's displeasure. Jubilant, Thuan called the embassy to say that negotiations with the Hue contingent were going well. On June 16, a joint statement from the monks and the Vietnamese government blurred the Buddhist demands enough to produce an agreement. But Trueheart heard that rumors of coups and countercoups were continuing unabated throughout South Vietnam, even though he considered Diem, with his flaws, to be better than any alternative.

BEING AN IRISH CATHOLIC in Massachusetts had won elections for Jack Kennedy. By serving as Boston's mayor and a congressman, his grandfather and namesake, John Fitzgerald, had left him a sturdy political legacy. But in running for president, Kennedy had to allay his party's fears that his religion could fatally damage his chances. To show he could carry a Protestant state, he entered the West Virginia primary, and he won more ground by appearing before a Baptist convention in Dallas. But his youthful ailments and his father's money had shaped Kennedy's character to a greater degree than his religion, and he wore his faith lightly.

Even in Massachusetts, being Catholic could have certain drawbacks. Kennedy's parents had been blackballed at the Brookline Country Club, and Jack was kept out of Harvard's leading social clubs. But by the time he reached the White House, he had sailed over every social gulf and was unperturbed that Mac Bundy's mother, for example, was one of the entrenched Boston Lowells. All the same, Kennedy knew that his father took gleeful satisfaction in triumphing over the aristocracy that had shunned him. He had particularly relished the symbolism of Jack's 1952 Senate victory over Henry Cabot Lodge—his very name a parody of Yankee pretension.

In that race, both candidates had been smoothly photogenic, but Kennedy was fifteen years younger, with a father supplying the cash and a mother and sisters determined to take tea with every female voter in the state. Lodge lost by 68,700 votes at the same time Eisenhower was sweeping Massachusetts. He took his defeat in good part and agreed to represent the Republican administration at the United Nations. There he developed a reputation for arrogant independence, but he was rarely challenged by Foster Dulles, since Lodge had been instrumental in securing the Republican nomination for Ike. From New York, Lodge defended the U.N. and the State Department against Joe McCarthy's attacks, and he guided Khrushchev during his tour of the United States in 1959. Lodge became such a highly visible figure that Nixon chose him the following year as his vice presidential candidate. Conservative Republicans, who had not forgiven Lodge for thwarting the 1952 presidential hopes of Robert Taft, passed along stories of Lodge's lethargic campaigning and blamed him for the narrow loss to Kennedy and Johnson.

THE TIME HAD COME to replace Nolting in Saigon. Kennedy was considering Ed Gullion, the ambassador Halberstam had admired in the Congo, but Rusk vetoed that appointment and recommended Lodge instead. The idea of embroiling his former adversary in Vietnam was irresistible, and Kennedy soon had an opportunity to sound out Lodge in person. Defeat at the polls had turned Lodge into a private citizen for the first time in almost three decades. When an institute devoted to Atlantic studies opened in Paris, Lodge signed on there and in mid-June brought its first report to the White House. As they talked, Kennedy said, "Cabot, I'd like to persuade you to go to Vietnam."

Lodge responded in the way his generation and social class answered a president: "If you need me, of course I want to do it."

But he asked for time to consult with his wife and with Eisenhower at his

Henry Cabot Lodge
(AP/Wide World Photos)

Gettysburg farm. Emily Lodge proved enthusiastic, Eisenhower less so. Wasn't it clever, Ike remarked sourly, how Kennedy recruited Republicans for his most potentially damaging jobs—McNamara at Defense, Dillon at Treasury, McCone at the CIA. Now he was ready to sacrifice another GOP leader.

It's my duty, Lodge replied, and called the White House to accept. Before the appointment was announced, Lodge met with Roger Hilsman and acknowledged the political risk of becoming a Republican scapegoat for a Democratic administration. "I want you to know that if it will serve the United States, I am expendable," Lodge said. "Just don't do it for unimportant reasons."

Fritz Nolting was on a ship in the mid-Atlantic when he heard a news bulletin that Lodge would replace him. Nolting was scheduled to return to South Vietnam until August 21, when another Honolulu conference would be followed by the change in ambassadors. In the meantime, however, Nhu was unleashing his police on the troublesome foreign reporters as never before. As Peter Arnett of the AP was covering a Buddhist demonstration north of Saigon, he was punched in the face and knocked to the ground, and his camera was smashed. He was rescued by Halberstam, who stood eight inches taller than the plain-clothes police. Wading in, swinging his arms, Halberstam shouted, "Get back, get back, you sons of bitches, or I'll beat the shit out of you." Not waiting for a translation, Nhu's men ran away. Mal Browne had climbed a power pole for a shot of Arnett's bleeding face, which became another photograph to fuel outrage across America.

But not at the embassy. Since the Vietnamese were claiming that one of the reporters had thrown the first punch, Trueheart refused to make an official protest. He wired Washington to explain that, given the reporters' intense hatred of the Saigon government, he didn't feel he could refute the police testimony. Trueheart did agree to Browne's request that a U.S. consular officer accompany him and Arnett the next day when they obeyed a summons and reported to police headquarters. After a four-hour interrogation, the two reporters were charged with assault. They in turn filed charges against their attackers and demanded compensation for Arnett's camera.

Parties on all sides felt aggrieved. Browne, Halberstam, Sheehan and Peter Kalischer of CBS News sent a telegram to the president describing the melee and asking that Kennedy personally insist that Diem's government end the harassment. State Department spokesmen called the correspondents' home offices in New York and read their editors a portion of Trueheart's cable. By deleting his criticism of the journalists' behavior, they could suggest that the embassy shared their outrage.

At Xa Loi, a monk used the attack on Arnett to request that the embassy send a unit of the U.S. advisers already in Vietnam to protect the pagoda's priests from assassination; Trueheart sent back word that the United States could not honor the request. In her tame English-language newspaper, the *Times of Vietnam*, Madame Nhu resurrected charges that the United States had backed the failed coup of 1960. And down the hall in the palace, Diem harangued Nolting, who had returned to Vietnam only to endure hours of reproach until Diem agreed to drop the charges against the AP reporters. To Washington, Nolting described Diem as being in a martyr's mood but again recommended forbearance.

The ambassador's last days on the job were a waking nightmare. Ignoring Nolting's expressed wishes, Nhu named a strategic hamlet for him. The day before the dedication ceremony, an American helicopter mistook the hamlet for one controlled by the Vietcong and wounded six of its residents. The next day, an ARVN jeep struck a boy from the same village, and rumors flew that the ambassador's car had killed him. Around the country, four more monks burned themselves to death.

But Nolting achieved one final success. As the ambassador was leaving for Honolulu, Diem promised to reject his brother's plan to stage a police raid on the Buddhist pagodas.

On August 21, Nolting was meeting with Roger Hilsman in Honolulu when the wire services reported that Diem had declared martial law and that men from his army had burst into Xa Loi and pagodas in Saigon, Hue and other provincial cities. They had tossed grenades and teargas canisters and shot at priests who tried to resist. To prevent the Americans from interfering, the raid's planners had cut off telephones in the offices and homes of all senior U.S. officials in Saigon, except for one line to General Harkins's headquarters. Even so, two Buddist priests managed to take shelter in the nearby USAID office where Bill Kohlmann kept his desk. Tri Quang also eluded the secret police and went into hiding.

Hilsman looked on as Nolting scanned the tickers and thought he read despair in the ambassador's face. From Honolulu, Nolting sent Diem a personal message: "This is the first time that you have ever gone back on your word to me."

IN SAIGON, the American journalists at Xa Loi pagoda were convinced that with Nhu's men shooting at monks, reporters might be next. At 4 A.M., Sheehan and Halberstam showed up at the embassy, insisting that they see Mecklin. A coolness lingered between him and the reporters, but he was sympathetic to their appeal for sanctuary. Eight years earlier, one of Mecklin's friends working for the UPI in Singapore had been beaten to death by a mob. Mecklin was miffed, though, that these two seemed to be demanding his protection, rather than asking for it. He also knew that opening his house to them would be a catastrophic career move. But Trueheart gave permission and Mecklin said yes. Almost immediately, sniping began from embassy colleagues who detested both reporters. In Washington, Rusk and McCone agreed that Mecklin was surely leaking stories to his guests.

BEFORE CABOT LODGE left Washington, Kennedy gave him one specific instruction: "I suppose that these are the worst press relations to be found in the world today," the president said, "and I wish you, personally, would take charge of them." At first report of the assault on the pagodas, the State Department reached Lodge in Tokyo and asked him to cut short his leisurely approach to Saigon and fly there immediately. At 9:30 P.M. on August 22, less than two nights after the pagoda raids, Lodge landed at Tan Son Nhut to be met by Trueheart, Harkins and forty reporters. Because he arrived half an hour after Diem's new curfew, the reporters had been brought to the airport in a bus, escorted by police jeeps. Turning away from the official party, Lodge raised his voice to ask, "Where are the gentlemen of the press?"

Gathering reporters into an admiring audience, Lodge spent five minutes praising the role of a free press in a democracy and pledging to help the reporters do their jobs. After months of insults from the embassy, the soft words were balm to his listeners. Halberstam considered Lodge the handsome image of a perfect American ambassador. But the journalists also detected a reassuring toughness. Looking forward to Lodge's inevitable showdown with Diem, they boasted to their Vietnamese friends, "Our old mandarin can lick your old mandarin."

When Lodge arrived at the ambassador's residence, a staff member warned him that Nhu planned to have him killed and make it look like a Vietcong assassination. Lodge brushed aside the warning and went to bed.

Getting up earlier than usual the next morning, he took the official Checker limousine to the embassy on Ham Nghi Boulevard. Then, as his first official act, Lodge walked to the USAID office to greet the two Buddhists who had taken shelter there. Learning that they were vegetarians, Lodge ordered a supply of fresh fruit and vegetables.

WITH LODGE'S ARRIVAL, the prospect of an impending coup seized Saigon's imagination. To furnish Washington with a reading of the political mood, the CIA included a report that Tri Quang had pledged to keep agitating until Diem's government fell. By the agency's reckoning, three plots might achieve that goal—one headed by Tuyen; another by Lieutenant Colonel Pham Ngoc Thao, still undetected as a Communist officer; and a third by an even more shadowy military cabal. The CIA report was correct about Tuyen, although these days he was forced to do his plotting from a distance. As the Buddhist unrest continued to spread, he had been summoned again to the palace. Tuyen found Diem seated at a round table with an open file before him. He spoke even more deliberately than usual. In the past, he had addressed Tuyen with the friendly *anh*. Today it was *ong*, or Mister. Diem did not mention a coup. Instead, he reminded Tuyen about the agitation of the African countries against South Vietnam at the United Nations. Tuyen must go to Cairo immediately—within forty-eight hours—since it was Egyptians who were leading the campaign. "I will go if I can do anything," Tuyen said.

With Jackie five months pregnant, Tuyen was nervous about leaving her. But since Madame Nhu's young brother, a Saigon wastrel who was gaining in influence, had been heard threatening to kill Tuyen, Diem was letting him off easy. Until he could board a plane, however, Tuyen worried that he might still be arrested.

He made it out of Tan Son Nhut and, after a stopover in Bangkok, was landing at the Cairo airport when the pilot announced that Egypt had just extended diplomatic relations to North Vietnam. Left without instructions, Tuyen holed up in a hotel room for two weeks, pondering his next move. He couldn't return to Saigon, and the Paris embassy was sure to distrust him. His best bet seemed to be Hong Kong. Tuyen flew there and checked into a cheap hotel. Within ten days, British intelligence agents tracked him down and repaid past favors by moving Tuyen to more comfortable and secure quarters in Kowloon. Tuyen stayed in touch with his fellow rebels as best he could but realized that the leadership of any successful coup had moved up a rung beyond him.

The CIA report had missed other anti-Diem activity as well. Thuan, whose car drove Duc to his martyrdom, was meeting regularly with Buddhists in a room over a pharmacy to plot more street protests. Downstairs, a woman was told to ring a bell if Nhu's police showed up; the plotters would escape through the attic. And within the palace, Nhu was dreaming up a phony coup, one he would then crush and use to justify even more sweeping powers for his family.

But despite the nonstop intriguing in South Vietnam, the first attempted coup against Diem came not in Saigon but in Washington.

IN JULY, James Thomson, who had been working contentedly as an aide to Chet Bowles until Bowles was forced out, was assigned to Roger Hilsman after he moved from State's Bureau of Intelligence to replace Harriman as head of Far Eastern affairs. Thomson liked his new boss well enough but after Bowles's gentlemanly style, he found Hilsman a strange hybrid, very much a straight arrow and yet an aggressive bureaucratic infighter. A graduate of West Point, Hilsman had served ten years in the army, then earned a Yale Ph.D. But what defined him seemed to be his years in Burma during World War II as a jungle guerrilla with the unit called Merrill's Marauders. Thomson summed up Hilsman as a Boy Scout with brass knuckles.

Hilsman could act as though no one else understood counterinsurgency, and he didn't hesitate to override the Joint Chiefs about guerrilla warfare. During a Lemnitzer presentation on strategy in Laos, Kennedy noticed Hilsman squirming and grimacing. "I don't think Roger agrees with you, General," Kennedy said. "Perhaps we can hear from him." Lemnitzer surrendered his place before the map and handed Hilsman his pointer. The story soon circulated that Hilsman had snatched it from the general's hand.

Hilsman was inclined to treat the vice president with the offhand disdain of the aides who took their cue from Bobby. In return, Johnson disliked Hilsman for his brashness and for his constant attacks on Diem. Monitoring Diem's behavior during the Buddhist crisis, Hilsman concluded that the Vietnamese president was fighting on too many fronts—the Buddhists; the high school and college students who were rallying to support them; the U.S. embassy; the foreign press corps. These days, the Vietcong seemed low on Diem's list of enemies. Harriman and Mike Forrestal shared Hilsman's conclusion that Diem could not win the war. Because Mac Bundy had never taken much interest in Vietnam, Forrestal as his deputy was becoming an influential voice at the White House.

Americans had agreed for years that Diem should be separated from the Nhus, but increasingly he was looking like their puppet. Diem surely had endorsed Nhu's raids on the pagodas, and it was now apparent that Nhu's police and Special Forces—not the army—had carried them out. Even the high-ranking ARVN officers most loyal to Diem were complaining to their CIA contacts and to the American journalists that they had played no role in the raids and accused Nhu of planting the false version to suggest that he had the army's backing. The generals described his mood as both triumphant and dangerous. As for Madame Nhu, Diem's relationship with her remained intense but complicated.

For years, she had known when to coo at him and when to bite. But sources at the palace said that Diem had found no way to strike back at her except with the empty threat that he might take a wife.

WITH DIEM ENJOYING the support of Kennedy's senior advisers, replacing him would take a drastic change in U.S. policy. Then, on August 24, a Saturday, those senior men were providentially gone from Washington. Rusk had left for the United Nations and stayed on for a ballgame at Yankee Stadium. McNamara was rock climbing in the Wyoming Tetons, and McCone was also on vacation. The president was in Hyannis Port. Hilsman, Harriman and Forrestal had remained in Washington.

Hilsman drafted two cables. The first was an unclassified bit of guidance for the world's press: the State Department was admitting what Halberstam and his colleagues had been reporting for the past two days—U.S. officials had clear evidence that Nhu's secret police and Special Forces had attacked the pagodas, some of them dressed in ARVN uniforms. That cable was intended to soothe the Vietnamese generals and expose Nhu's deceit to the world. Taken alone, it would have sailed past even Rusk and McNamara.

Hilsman then drafted a second cable for Lodge, which, despite its shaded wording, sent the new ambassador an unambiguous message: The United States government could not tolerate a situation in which power rested with Nhu. If Diem would not replace him, perhaps Diem himself could not be preserved in office. The embassy should tell Vietnam's key military leaders that Washington would support Saigon neither militarily nor economically until the Nhus—and, if he remained obdurate, Diem—were removed.

With Rusk in New York, George Ball was State's ranking man in Washington. Saturday afternoon promised to be uneventful, and Ball had left the office for a round of golf in Maryland at the Falls Road course. He and a colleague, Alexis Johnson, got as far as the ninth green, where they found Harriman and Hilsman waiting for them. Everyone drove back to Ball's house.

As he read through the incoming cables from the CIA in Saigon with feelers from the Vietnamese generals about a coup, Ball knew that any reply would be explosive, but he was a willing collaborator with Harriman and Hilsman. He had believed for some time that national self-respect required Washington to stand up to the Nhus. He told himself that America should not be in the business of abetting coups, but how legitimate was Diem, an American creation, in the first place? Ball suggested a few changes in the cable's wording, which were quickly accepted.

The decision now rested with the president, and Ball put in a call to Hyannis Port. Kennedy sounded agreeable about sending the message, although he reminded Ball that if the generals did stage their coup, Washington might not find his replacement an improvement. When Ball read to him the cable's final line—

"We shall continue to assist Vietnam to resist Communist aggression and maintain its independence"—Kennedy did not want to be so explicit. "I don't know about that last sentence," he said. "Why don't you leave the last sentence out?"

Ball agreed that it undercut the severity of Washington's warning and drew a line through it. With that, Kennedy said, "If Rusk and Gilpatric agree, George, then go ahead."

They had been talking over the secure telephone line that always accompanied the president. When Ball got through to New York, however, Rusk was nervous about discussing so sensitive a matter over an open line. Nor did Rusk feel he could debate the cable's substance since Kennedy had already approved it. But he added one sentence that, however he may have intended it, read as unmistakable encouragement for a coup. The amended cable now read, "You may also tell appropriate military commanders we will give them direct support in any interim period of breakdown of central government mechanism."

That expanded text was dispatched to McNamara's deputy, Ros Gilpatric, at his farm in Maryland. He sent back his approval. Ball wondered afterward—with the secretary of defense unreachable and the president and secretary of state already signing off—whether Gilpatric had felt that he had little choice. McCone also being unavailable, the same sense of dealing with an accomplished fact may have influenced Richard Helms, the deputy at the CIA. Ball tried to contact Max Taylor as chairman of the Joint Chiefs, but Taylor was dining out. His deputy, Marine General Victor Krulak, gave his approval. When Taylor returned from dinner, he saw the cable and raised no objections.

Mike Forrestal called Kennedy again to report total agreement, but now the president was sounding dubious. He asked, "Are you sure you are all right?" Forrestal reassured him, and DEPTEL 243 left Washington at 9:36 P.M.

WHEN THE CABLE reached Lodge in Saigon, he was dissatisfied. Given the twelve-hour time difference, his reply could still arrive in Washington on Sunday, asking that his instructions be modified. He did not want to ask Diem to remove the Nhus. Not only would Diem refuse, but he would be alerted in time to block whatever action his dissident generals were planning. Lodge wanted to go instead to those generals directly and tell them that "we are prepared to have Diem without Nhus but it is in effect up to them whether we keep him." Ball agreed with Lodge's reasoning and cleared the change with Forrestal, who was acting on Mac Bundy's behalf. With that, Washington sent off permission for Lodge to bring down the government of South Vietnam.

SUNDAY FOUND HILSMAN BUSY with the press. Lodge had agreed to permit a Voice of America broadcast that would absolve the South Vietnamese army of guilt for the pagoda raids, and Hilsman wanted to brief reporters in Washington on the statement that the VOA would be beaming overseas. He called the AP's senior

State Department correspondent, but neither he nor the *New York Times* reporter were available. Unwilling to wait longer, Hilsman called to the house of UPI's correspondent, Stewart Hensley, who copied down the text and asked what the United States was prepared to do next. Hilsman considered Hensley a friend as well as a journalist. He mentioned that Washington might cut off South Vietnam's aid. But he told the reporter to label that part of the story as Hensley's own speculation.

At the Voice of America, however, the staff released the UPI story rather than the State Department's more guarded version. As a result, Lodge was preparing to present his credentials to Diem at Gia Long Palace on Monday morning when the VOA announced, in both English and Vietnamese, that Lodge's government might sharply reduce its aid to Vietnam unless Diem got rid of the secret police officials responsible for the pagoda attacks.

Mecklin planned to accompany Lodge to the palace, and he raced to the ambassador's residence with the VOA transcript. He arrived at the same time as Harkins and his military contingent, all dressed in white for the 11 A.M. ceremony. They waited around a coffee table while Lodge read the transcript. Furious, he threw it back on the table. "Jack Kennedy would never approve of doing things this way," he said.

As the hour approached for them to leave, Mecklin wondered whether Diem might be sufficiently offended to cancel their audience. Lodge saw a more ominous possibility. "Paul," he said to Harkins at the residence door, "perhaps you better not come. If they try any funny business, it might be better if one of us were on the outside."

The precaution was unnecessary. Diem greeted Lodge affably and listened to the new ambassador's complaints about Madame Nhu and the persecution of the Buddhists. He responded with a two-hour defense of his policies and a request that Lodge stop the United States from meddling in Vietnamese affairs. From Diem's remarks, it could seem that he knew about Hilsman's cable. If so, would that dampen the generals' enthusiasm for their coup?

IN WASHINGTON, the sense of urgency, even euphoria, that had swept Hilsman's cable past every weekend barrier had given way to a cold-eyed Monday morning reckoning. General Krulak had felt queasy enough about Saturday's haste to draft a memorandum for the record that detailed the frenzied consultations. He included Max Taylor's private response when he finally read the cable: It was not explicit enough, it didn't give Diem a chance to do what Washington wanted and, worst, it reflected "the well-known compulsion of Hilsman and Forrestal to depose Diem." Had Mac Bundy been in town, Taylor concluded, he would not have approved the cable, which he called "an aggressive end run."

McNamara arrived at a noon meeting at the White House annoyed at being bypassed and ready to light into the anti-Diem faction. If McNamara singled out

Hilsman, it would be for Hilsman's pessimism over Vietnam and because an assistant secretary of state was a safer target than Averell Harriman or Bundy's man Forrestal.

The president opened the session by calling for a full discussion. He said it wasn't too late to pull back the go-ahead that the Saigon generals had been given and to tell them that Washington wanted to continue supporting Diem, and even Nhu. With Cuba never far from the president's thoughts, he wanted assurances that the *New York Times* stories out of Saigon were not a repetition of those by Herbert Matthews for the *Times* in the late 1950s, which Kennedy thought had swung public sentiment behind Fidel Castro. Now were the Vietnam dispatches influencing foreign policy in that same way? Kennedy described Halberstam as a twenty-eight-year-old kid who was running a political campaign in South Vietnam. He didn't want a reporter's biases to be shaping American policy, the president said. Hilsman assured him that they were not.

Trying to orchestrate the debate, Harriman pointed out that before the pagoda attacks the embassy had no way of assessing the depth of the anti-Diem sentiment among the Vietnamese. To that, Kennedy replied by reminding his advisers that Diem and Nhu might be somewhat repugnant, but they had carried out a great deal of U.S. policy. If his administration moved to overthrow them, it should not be to oblige the *New York Times*.

Taylor spoke for the Joint Chiefs, making a strong appeal for Diem as the only man who could hold together his badly fragmented military. As the debate wore on, recriminations threatened to break through the veneer of civility. But the heat was focusing Kennedy's attention on South Vietnam, much as Soviet missiles in Cuba had led to Tommy Thompson's briefings on Russia. Kennedy suddenly wanted to know about Saigon's personalities—about Khiem, Khanh and Minh, and which officers remained loyal to Nhu. Hilsman said the only one was Colonel Le Quang Tung, head of the Vietnamese Special Forces—and, possibly, the commanders of a few Vietnamese Marine battalions.

To rebut the Pentagon's arguments, Hilsman reported that he had received a call from Admiral Felt in the Pacific, and Felt advised against delay. Hilsman enjoyed watching Max Taylor's angry disbelief when he heard that Felt had ignored protocol and contacted a junior State Department official.

Biding his time, McNamara now raised objections to the vagueness of Hilsman's cable. When Kennedy commented that he did not believe Diem would let Nhu be ejected from the scene, Rusk was bold enough to disagree. Hilsman undercut him by saying that, according to the Saigon embassy, the brothers would rise or fall together.

They were weighing the several scenarios when Kennedy asked what would happen if they found they had to live with Diem and Nhu, after all. Hilsman said that outcome was horrible to contemplate. Only once did anyone raise an underlying question. That man was Rusk, and he did it tentatively. Unless a change could be engineered in South Vietnam, Rusk said, Washington might have to decide whether to pull its resources out or to move U.S. troops in. No one chose to discuss pulling out.

Kennedy suggested holding another meeting that same afternoon, and Taylor recommended inviting former Ambassador Nolting, who was back in Washington. Hilsman tried to scotch the idea by remarking that Nolting's views were colored by being emotionally involved in the situation. To that, Kennedy replied, "Maybe properly."

The president's dry comment was an indication that Hilsman's Saturday night victory was not yet a certainty.

As HILSMAN PREPARED for the 4 P.M. meeting, Harriman called to get his reading of its likely mood. Hilsman said he thought he could bring Nolting around to the inevitability of a coup. Harriman asked, Are some people getting cold feet?

I'm afraid of Max Taylor, Hilsman said. But we have to make this work.

Meantime, Forrestal was doing his part to keep Kennedy committed to a change in Saigon. He drafted a memo recommending that the president end the next session by restating the terms of the August 24 cable. Getting that sort of suggestion to the president was one advantage of working in the White House, but McNamara had a method of his own. For meetings with Kennedy, he often arrived early and used the time to bring around Rusk and the others to his thinking. On this day, before the president joined them, McNamara laid out his position: they should not press Kennedy for a decision. He knew he could expect a private meeting with the president after the sixteen other participants—who included Nolting, Bobby Kennedy and Edward R. Murrow from USIA—had retired from the scene.

The formal session opened with Colby reporting that CIA agents in Saigon had met recently with two South Vietnamese generals. One predicted a coup within the week, the other had given what Colby described as "a jumpy answer." Harriman had not come to the meeting, an absence that lowered the temperature when Nolting offered a heartfelt defense of Diem. The Vietnamese president was not a liar, Nolting said, but a man of integrity.

Kennedy asked whether Diem had ever explained why he had not kept his promise about the raids, and Hilsman broke in to remind Nolting of the shock the ambassador had felt in Honolulu. Nolting assured Kennedy that—after he had time to think over the events—he had concluded that Diem had not lied. It was new Buddhist agitation that had changed Diem's mind that a reconciliation was possible. Nolting also defended Nhu as an able man who was not anti-American. At fifty-four, he was eight years younger than his brother, and Nolting saw him replacing Diem one day. The Vietnamese people respected Nhu's gift for command, Nolting said.

When Kennedy remarked that he saw no point in abetting a coup unless it stood a chance of success, Nolting claimed that no military support currently existed for a coup. But if the United States indicated its support for one, the generals might rally to oust Nhu. And if that happened, Diem might choose to go down with his brother in the palace. Nolting noted that events had come nearly full circle during the past three years. Ambassador Durbrow had told Diem that Nhu must go, but it had been Durbrow who left Saigon. "The way things are going," Kennedy said, smiling, "we may be forced to have Lodge tell Diem just that. If you're right, Lodge's tour will be the shortest round trip in history."

Since the second meeting had resolved nothing, a third was scheduled for the following noon, four days after Hilsman's cable had reached Saigon. Harriman sensed that the anti-Diem faction was being routed, and he arrived for the next round prepared to add to his abrasive reputation. Before the meeting, Forrestal took him aside to say he was upset about the criticism of his own role in the cable affair. He was ready to quit Washington and go back to practicing law in New York. Harriman told him to "quit being a goddamned fool." That was Harriman talking to a young man who had been like a son to him.

As the meeting started, Harriman was intentionally rude to Krulak, a man so short he was called sardonically "Brute." Harriman then told Max Taylor that Taylor had been wrong on every issue since World War II. Turning his glare on Nolting, Harriman said he was sorry to have to be blunt but he had been too soft on Diem. When Nolting started to defend himself, Harriman advised him to keep his mouth shut. "No one cares what you think," he said.

That was too much for Kennedy. He said pointedly that the president, for one, was interested in whatever Ambassador Nolting had to say. Nolting replied that he was surprised to hear that General Harkins favored a coup. During Nolting's absence from Saigon, the behavior of Trueheart—his deputy and friend—had wounded him deeply. Now it seemed that even Harkins had lost faith in the Nolting strategy. All the same, the honor of the United States was involved. Supporting a coup would set a bad precedent.

George Ball disagreed. Diem's actions negated any obligation for good faith, and his supporters had started down an anti-American path. Diem and Nhu had badly damaged the U.S. position in the eyes of the world, and Washington could not back off from its all-out opposition to them. A failed coup would be failure for Washington as well. There was no possibility that the war could be won by Diem's government and no acceptable alternative to his being deposed.

McNamara sensed that Kennedy was leaning toward a coup but only if its success could be guaranteed. He asked for a list of ways the United States could help the rebels to win over any of their reluctant fellow generals. Still not stifled, Nolting insisted that only Diem could hold the fragmented country together, which provoked another outburst from Harriman. Kennedy abruptly adjourned the meeting; the group would reconvene at 6 P.M.

☐

MAX TAYLOR was now the one to worry that his position had been undercut, and only Paul Harkins could salvage it. He cabled the general in Saigon to pass along Kennedy's request for his candid opinion and added a bit of guidance of his own. FYI, Taylor wrote, Hilsman's memo had been prepared without the participation of the Joint Chiefs. "Authorities are now having second thoughts."

Harkins took the hint and wired back that he had entertained doubts about the memo but assumed it represented a coordinated policy between Washington and Admiral Felt. Harkins agreed the Nhus had to go but hoped Diem could be retained. He said he hadn't had a chance to discuss the matter with the new ambassador. He seemed unaware that Lodge, never a team player, was dodging both Harkins and his resistance to a coup.

Before the White House meeting reconvened, Kennedy took Rusk, McNamara, Bundy and Taylor to another room for a private discussion. When they emerged, Kennedy suggested that Lodge and Harkins be asked again for their frank views. We thought Harkins favored the coup, Kennedy explained, but he apparently thought a decision had already been made in Washington and that it was his task to carry it out.

Harriman knew that his belligerence at the noon meeting had disturbed Kennedy. As this session was breaking up, he wielded his shiv more adroitly. "Mr. President, I was very puzzled by the cable from General Harkins," he said, "until I read the outgoing from General Taylor." Kennedy knew that Taylor had leaned on Harkins, and now Harriman was sparring in a style Kennedy could enjoy. He looked about to laugh but contained himself until only Hilsman remained at his side. Then the president chuckled and said, "Averell Harriman is one sharp cookie."

THE CABLE EPISODE had served to make Mac Bundy suspect that he might have been delegating Vietnam's affairs too freely to Mike Forrestal. However much the cable's instigators denied it, the flap looked exactly like what Taylor had called it—an end run around Kennedy's senior advisers. Publicly, Bundy brushed off the controversy, remarking that it only proved that one should not do business on the weekend. But it could look as though Forrestal's loyalties lay more with Averell Harriman than with Bundy's NSC. To serve Kennedy properly, Bundy had better school himself on the unappetizing choices over Vietnam.

Earlier in the year, Newsweek had noted that Rusk "was not known for force and decisiveness" and reported that Washington observers were calling Mac Bundy "the real Secretary of State." The magazine bestowed the title in a cover story on Bundy with the tag line "Cool Head for the Cold War." The photograph showed him looking pink-cheeked and quizzical, with a furrowed brow that seemed to crowd his sandy hair to the back of his head. The clear plastic frames

McGeorge Bundy (UPI/Corbis-Bettmann)

to his glasses suggested a man with no affectations, and his neat blue suit, white shirt and unexceptionable necktie were equally utilitarian. Nothing about the picture distracted from the unsparing intelligence in Bundy's eyes.

His precise mind, always revved up to outstrip a challenger, had won Bundy first place at Groton. During the college entrance examination, he took a gamble and ridiculed the test's English section. "This question is silly," Bundy wrote. "If I were giving the test, this is the question I would ask, and this is my answer." The next September, Yale's dean announced to the freshman class that, for the first time in university history, a student had scored three perfect scores on the college boards.

Bundy majored in mathematics and slashed his way to victory in debates at the Yale Political Union. During his junior year, he was elected to Phi Beta Kappa and tapped for Skull and Bones, Yale's most exclusive club. But life was preparing a comeuppance. After graduation in 1939, Bundy offered himself for public service by running for the Boston City Council in a safely Republican district. He lost to a Democratic unknown.

As Hitler rose in Germany, Bundy advocated American intervention to stop him. "Though war is evil," Bundy wrote at the age of twenty-one, "it is occasionally the lesser of two evils." He went through World War II as an aide to a family friend, Rear Admiral Alan R. Kirk, and watched the Normandy invasion from the flag bridge of the USS *Augusta*. When the war ended, Bundy began to coauthor Henry Stimson's memoirs, *On Active Service in Peace and War*. He also worked briefly on the Marshall Plan and joined Douglas Dillon, Christian Herter and the Dulles brothers as a junior member of the team that advised Thomas Dewey on foreign policy during his campaign for the presidency in 1948. Four years earlier, Roosevelt had defeated Dewey, the governor of New York, but this time Dewey was running against Harry Truman, and, like most Americans, Bundy did not doubt the outcome. Again, however, voters made their own judgment.

After Truman's reelection, Bundy went to Harvard as an instructor of government. He had no doctorate; his credential was to be the Stimson book. When people mentioned his older brother William, who had received a law degree before he joined the CIA, Bundy referred to Bill wickedly as "my learned brother."

Their father had served as assistant secretary to Stimson, first at State and then at the War department, and that intimacy with Washington guaranteed that the Bundy house on Boston's Beacon Street would be filled with political figures. Mac Bundy edited Dean Acheson's papers; Bill Bundy married Acheson's daughter. But Bundy's mother, a niece of A. Lawrence Lowell, the fabled president of Harvard, was one of the city's social fixtures as well. When Nathan Pusey from a small college in Wisconsin was named as Harvard's president in 1953, the East Coast trustees prevailed on him to choose Bundy for the number-two position, dean of the faculty of arts and sciences. Bundy's reviews as dean were mixed. Although his own writings were scant and seldom theoretical, most professors found him respectful of their scholarship. Men like Rostow at MIT admired Bundy's mental agility but thought he seemed content to glitter at faculty meetings and on the lecture platform.

In the days when the Kennedy family lived near Boston, Jack Kennedy and Mac Bundy had gone to the same debutante parties, but the two men got to know each other only after Senator Kennedy was elected, on his second try, to the Harvard Board of Overseers. Bundy's practical approach to issues appealed to Kennedy, who was usually ill at ease with abstractions. Both men took a mechanic's approach to the engine of government: Find out what was broken, fix it and keep the ship of state aloft. Leave to others the mysteries of aerodynamics.

When Bundy arrived in Washington, his value as an ally had been quickly apparent to a man as attuned as McNamara to corporate politics. McNamara presided over the largest of the cabinet posts, with millions of military and civilian employees; Bundy had whittled down his staff from 74 to 49. But McNamara was anchored in the Pentagon, and Bundy could pop into Kennedy's office several times a day. As a result, Bundy was where he knew he belonged, at the center of international power. To reach Stimson's level, he gladly put in the long hours at low pay. As he sat through interminable meetings, Bundy drew long, perfectly straight parallel lines a hair's breadth apart—graphic evidence of his self-control. No matter how complex an issue, Bundy could reduce it to a page or two that spelled out the president's options. Unlike Rusk, however, Bundy was not reticent about promoting his own views, and now Kennedy deserved his thinking on

Vietnam. Bundy had resisted efforts to get him to Honolulu or Saigon. But the next time he was invited, he would clear time for the junket.

For *Newsweek*'s article, the editors asked Kennedy to evaluate Bundy. The president's reply began with the asset he ranked even above loyalty: "First," Kennedy said, "you can't beat brains—"

AFTER ONE particularly fractious session over Vietnam, Jack Kennedy had said in mock despair, "My God, my administration is coming apart." But in Saigon, Ngo Dinh Nhu saw something worse—an end not only to his power but to his life. Even Tuyen, his former right hand, went on plotting against him, although he watched Nhu's dilemma from Hong Kong with remnants of sympathy. Tuyen said to himself that Nhu was on the back of a tiger and had no way to get off. But Nhu thought he might have discovered a way, although it was one that Tuyen would have bitterly opposed. Nhu was considering secret talks with Hanoi.

ON THE SUNDAY EVENING of Hilsman's frantic cable, Lodge attended his first diplomatic party in Saigon. Also on hand were members of the International Control Commission, the relic from 1954 that was charged with enforcing the Geneva accords. Mieczyslaw Maneli, the Polish member, was an affable lawyer who had survived Auschwitz to become a member of his country's Communist Party. Watching Lodge arrive, Maneli was annoyed by his superior air and the way ambassadors from smaller countries were fawning over him. When Maneli was introduced, Lodge asked only about the time difference between Warsaw and Saigon, then drifted away without waiting for an answer.

Had Lodge lingered, he might have found the Pole worth his attention. For months, the French and Indian ambassadors had been trying to set up a meeting between Maneli and Nhu, who was also attending this reception. Maneli guessed that the motives of the two diplomats were different. The Indian genuinely admired Nhu, whose occasional anti-American remarks appealed to his neutralism. As for the Frenchman, Maneli reported to Warsaw that with the United States poised to reject the Diem regime, France wanted to buy in at a bargain price and somehow connect Diem to North Vietnam. The French ambassador seemed to expect Maneli to broker an agreement between Ho and Diem that would force out the Americans and restore France's prestige in Indochina.

The rapprochement had already begun not long ago when Maneli flew to Hanoi and met with the North's leadership. Ho sat silently as Maneli asked Pham Van Dong how to react if Nhu were to approach him. Dong advised him to go to any meeting and listen intently. Let Nhu know that the Americans must leave Vietnam. After that, we can negotiate everything else. Maneli asked if Dong were suggesting some sort of federation. "We can come to any agreement with any Vietnamese," Dong replied. "We are realists."

Maneli left the interview convinced that if talks did occur, Hanoi wanted to guarantee that this time they would not include Moscow or Washington, and

Pham Van Dong
(Vietnam News Agency)

definitely not China. Maneli also suspected that earlier peace feelers had been extended between Ho and Diem. But calling on China's ambassador in Hanoi, Maneli found him far more inflexible than Dong had been. He insisted that Diem and Nhu must be thrown on the scrap heap of history.

Those had been the developments before Lodge arrived in Saigon. On this night, he left the diplomatic reception early, and after he had gone, the French and Indian ambassadors and two other guests formed a circle around Nhu and edged him as unobtrusively as they could to Maneli's side. As they shook hands, Nhu said he had heard a great deal about the Pole from mutual friends, adding the unlikely claim that, except for France, Poland was the foreign country the Vietnamese knew best since they shared hundreds of years of fighting for independence from powerful neighbors—Germany and Russia in Poland's case, China in Vietnam's. Assuring Maneli that he wanted nothing more than peace, Nhu arranged for a private meeting later in the week.

At 6 P.M. the next evening, Maneli was invited to the French embassy, where the ambassador warned him that his scheduled meeting with Nhu would never take place because the Americans were carrying out a coup that very night.

THE FRENCH DELEGATION had been misinformed. But tense days passed until the afternoon of August 30, when Nhu called in those generals he knew were plotting against him and treated them to a masterful performance. Suavely conciliatory, he told them about a vast American conspiracy that involved the CIA, the foreign press and members of the U.S. mission. They all wanted him out of the way, Nhu said. But they were working against the welfare of the Vietnamese people, and President Kennedy agreed with him.

His guests listened attentively, trying to betray neither shock nor guilt. A CIA contact at the meeting reported that afterward several generals seemed to have accepted Nhu's assurances that the U.S. government would soon be publicly announcing its approval of Diem's policies. Nhu added that he could manage Lodge; as the ambassador got a better grasp of the situation, he would come to endorse Nhu's actions. Big Minh asked Nhu how he should answer when Americans asked what the generals thought about the current state of affairs. Say "No comment," Nhu suggested. Or say you don't have enough information.

The next day, the Saigon CIA station began its cable to Washington, "This particular coup is finished." The generals did not feel ready. They had even discussed recommending to Diem that he make Nhu his prime minister.

SEEING THAT THE NGO family had weathered the coup scare, Maneli kept his appointment at the palace. Nhu received him in a room piled so high with books, letters, documents and newspapers that Maneli was sure nothing could ever be found there. Seating his guest at a small table, Nhu launched his monologue: The war was a spiritual one, and if he seemed to be fighting Communism—Nhu was aware that he was talking with a party member—his crusade was actually aimed at putting an end to materialistic capitalism. Both the Americans and his own Vietnamese allies misunderstood the purpose of the strategic hamlets. They were actually the basis for a direct democracy that one day would, as Karl Marx had predicted in a different context, cause the state to wither away.

Maneli was sure he had misheard, but Nhu repeated the remark and added, "The sense of my life is to work so that I can become unnecessary."

Nhu made no protestation of loyalty to the Americans, but neither did he take up Maneli on his offer to convey a message to Hanoi. Puzzled, Maneli went away wondering whether Nhu considered negotiations with Ho no more than a life preserver should the Americans one day bail out.

NHU MET THAT SAME DAY with Cabot Lodge to make it clear who had just won their test of nerve. Lodge already knew. A few days earlier, with coup planning at its height, he had received an extraordinary message from Kennedy—seen by only Rusk, McNamara and Bundy—that reflected the president's determination not to authorize another Bay of Pigs. "When we go, we must go to win," Kennedy wrote, "but it will be better to change our minds than to fail."

Lodge sent back a halfhearted acknowledgment granting that, of course, Kennedy had the right to call off a coup at any time. But Lodge still wanted to get rid of Nhu and despaired at the Vietnamese generals' lack of spine. Urging them forward, he complained to Washington, "puts me in the position of pushing a piece of spaghetti." Now that those generals had capitulated to Nhu, Lodge—like Durbrow and Nolting before him—seemed trapped in one-sided negotiations with the palace.

Nhu's language was fustian and indirect, but his message was clear: Lodge must force the U.S. agents who were promoting a coup against the Ngo family to leave Vietnam. Just that morning, the *Times of Vietnam* had run a list of the family's American enemies, which allowed Nhu to add, "Everybody knows who they are." Nhu also demanded that the U.S. radio broadcasts end their attacks and that Lodge accept the fact that the Diem government would soon be tightening visa controls over the Americans already on the scene.

After listing his terms, Nhu offered a few concessions. His wife would be leaving on a European trip, possibly followed by a speaking tour in the United States. Nhu himself planned to resign from government and move his family to Dalat. He could not leave at the moment, however, because his extensive contacts with dispirited Vietcong commanders were about to lead soon to mass defections from the Communist ranks.

Nhu told Lodge that he had met with Maneli earlier in the day and rejected any contact with Hanoi. His loyalty, Nhu said, remained unshakably with the Americans.

YEARS EARLIER, when Paul Kattenburg had been a young foreign service officer in Saigon, he had admired Diem. Now, as chairman of Kennedy's Interdepartmental Working Group on Vietnam, he went back on a fact-finding trip at about the time Lodge arrived and spoke again with Vietnam's embattled president. The interview left Kattenburg shaken. Diem might be technically sane, but his neuroses, once mild, were strangling him. As the two men spoke in French—Kattenburg had been raised in Belgium—Diem mumbled and offered up only irrelevant statistics and anecdotes. He praised his brother Thuc, the archbishop, as a holy man and said it was criminal that the American journalists should be impugning him. As for Nhu—he was a pure intellectual who asked nothing for himself.

The meeting ended inconclusively. Diem was evasive about holding elections or going before the National Assembly to justify his actions. As Kattenburg broke free after three hours, Diem pleaded with great emotion, "Try to help us!"

"Please do the same for us," Kattenburg replied. But he saw no hope and left the palace dejected.

In that mood, he arrived in Washington past midnight on August 31 to learn that he had been summoned to the State Department the next morning for an 11 A.M. meeting. The participants were the regulars, minus the president but with the addition of Lyndon Johnson. Rusk had assured the vice president that the crisis had passed and he could skip the meeting, but Johnson had come anyway.

Johnson knew—as they all did—that Hilsman and his allies had taken a daring risk and, at least for now, had lost. When Harriman heard that Kennedy would not be on hand for this postmortem, he stayed away, too.

Kattenburg slipped into the conference room, took a seat behind Hilsman and listened while Rusk laid out the problem: now that a coup was no longer likely, how could Diem be persuaded to follow Washington's orders? Rusk sounded reluctant to continue making the removal of Nhu Washington's first priority. McNamara instantly agreed. Relations now must be reestablished between the two governments, McNamara said, especially between Lodge and Diem. Rusk asked whether anyone in the room doubted that the coup was really off. He seemed to be inviting a moment of discreet gloating from the men who had objected all week to Hilsman's cable.

Even though Kattenburg had missed the earlier harsh words, an instinct told him to keep quiet. But his was an ebullient temperament and he spoke up anyway: I have some doubts, he said. The Voice of America broadcast suggesting that aid might be suspended had boosted the morale of the anti-Diem faction. It was an enormous pity that the effect had been undercut the next day by the too-rapid pullback. The Vietnamese generals remained very, very suspicious of the United States, and it was tragic that Harkins had not given them reassurances about U.S. support even after they claimed the plotting had stopped.

Hilsman had first met Kattenburg when they were doctoral candidates at Yale and had brought him into the Far East bureau. Today he wanted to protect him from his own vehemence. As he took the official notes for the meeting, Hilsman wrote himself a reminder to change the phrase "it was tragic" to "it should be noted."

Kattenburg's heresy roused both Rusk and McNamara. Given what Harkins had been told about Big Minh losing heart, they said, Harkins had been absolutely right not to commit the United States. Hilsman offered the tactical concession that Harkins should not have acted differently but then explained that what Mr. Kattenburg really meant was that the generals had needed an authoritative assurance that the United States was behind them. Rightly or not, many of them believed that junior CIA men had encouraged the 1960 coup and then jettisoned it. This time, they had been contacted once again by only two low-level agents while Nhu was assuring them that President Kennedy backed his policies.

The mood was turning prosecutorial. When Hilsman said that middle-level Vietnamese officers and bureaucrats remained disaffected, McNamara demanded to know what evidence he had. Hilsman replied that his information came from conversations between those people and our embassy officials. But he did not feel that he was bearing up well under McNamara's stern questioning. Certainly, he added lamely, we have no statistics.

Kattenburg chimed in to agree about the dissatisfaction with Diem's government but was forced to admit that he had talked personally to only three Vietnamese. He then made another political blunder by defending the Saigon journalists to men who considered the reporters almost as harmful to South Vietnam's stability as the Vietcong. In fact, the journalists might have been worse since they had the capacity to damage the administration at home. Now here was Kattenburg telling them that they must consider the judgment of such seasoned newspapermen as Robert Trumbull of the *New York Times* and Keyes Beech of the *Chicago Daily News*, both of whom were reporting Diem's unpopularity.

McNamara was not going to accept newspaper reports as evidence. What Kattenburg was claiming, he said, only proved that the unhappy people were limited to Saigon. Kattenburg saw that he was simply too junior to be taken seriously. Nothing he could say would shake McNamara's opinion. All that mattered in this room was who dominated the meeting.

Kattenburg studied the men in the front tier of seats around the table, appalled by their collective ignorance. These senior officials know nothing, he thought. They have all the answers, but they know nothing.

And yet Kattenburg spoke up once more, this time effectively sabotaging his career, although he stayed in government for another decade in a variety of unexalted posts. If the United States acquiesced in the assault on the Buddhists, Kattenburg said, or even acquiesced to such halfway measures as applauding Diem for his negotiations with a few tame bonzes, the United States would be butted out of the country within six months to a year. It would be better, Kattenburg concluded, to withdraw now in a dignified way.

Mac Bundy called on Kattenburg to justify that bombshell.

Kattenburg explained that Diem had turned into a petty dictator inseparable from Nhu. In South Vietnam, the people expected the Vietcong to win. We might be able to paper over the discontent with Diem and Nhu and survive a few months, and with so many guns on the street the people could do nothing right now. But the discontent would crescendo.

That's speculation, Rusk said.

Kattenburg had lost their attention. He had spoken the unthinkable to those who believed in the Vietnam crusade. And he had advocated withdrawal fourteen months before Jack Kennedy's reelection. If no one in the room voiced that crass political consideration, it was not far from the mind of Vice President Johnson, who spoke for the first time: We must decide that we are not going to pull out of Vietnam, he said, and that we will not undertake a coup. Johnson said he hadn't known about Hilsman's Saturday cable until the following Tuesday and had never agreed that Washington should be plotting with the Vietnamese generals. Now that they had failed to organize a coup, we should reestablish ties to the Diem government and stop playing cops and robbers. Johnson added that there was certainly a bad situation in South Vietnam, but there were bad situations in the United States, too. Shrinking the international dilemma to the dimensions of the U.S. Congress, where he had ruled supreme, Johnson concluded, "It's difficult to live with Otto Passman"—a ranking Democrat who had often challenged his leadership—"but we can't pull a coup on him."

AFTER YEARS of condensing world events to a fifteen-minute broadcast, the CBS television network was expanding its nightly news to half an hour. To trumpet that new seriousness, Walter Cronkite, the program's anchorman, went to Hyannis Port on the morning of September 2 to film an exclusive interview with President Kennedy. In the course of their conversation, Cronkite observed that Vietnam was the only hot war the United States was fighting and asked about the difficulties there. Kennedy's reply was aimed less at American viewers, who were showing little interest in the conflict, than at an audience of two men and a woman in Gia Long Palace. Unless Diem's government made a greater effort to win popular support, Kennedy said, he didn't think the war could be won.

"In the final analysis," Kennedy added, "it is their war. They are the ones to win it or lose it." The United States was prepared to go on assisting South Vietnam, but "in my opinion, in the last two months the government has gotten out of touch with the people." The Buddhist repression had been unwise, the president continued, but with changes in policy—and perhaps personnel—the government could regain popular support.

Cronkite protested that, from every indication out of Saigon, Diem had no intention of changing. Kennedy replied that the decision was Diem's and noted that the Vietnamese president had been counted out many times before. Kennedy added that he did not agree with those who said America should withdraw. Even though 47 Americans had been killed in South Vietnam, and even though the country was far away, the struggle was important. The interview ended with Kennedy praising Lodge for putting the job of ambassador ahead of his political career.

"Sometimes," the president said genially, "politicians do those things, Walter."

BUT AT OTHER TIMES politicians delayed, vacillated and clung to the options that would protect their careers. Since his inauguration, Kennedy's Vietnam policy had been haphazard but simple: Defeat the Vietcong. Or, if that was impossible, keep Diem afloat through the reelection campaign in 1964. Or, if even that modest goal could not be met, replace Diem swiftly and quietly, with no telltale links between the conspirators and Washington. But the years of stealth and inattention had led to chaos, and Kennedy was being forced to spend much of every working day confronting Vietnam.

Bobby Kennedy had begun to sit in on the interminable meetings, offering loyal if simplistic advice. After listening to cabinet members as they spun their wheels, Bobby asked whether the war could be won with Nhu and Diem. No, said Rusk, unless the Nhus changed their line. Bobby persisted: Will they

President John F. Kennedy *(UPI/Corbis-Bettmann)*

change? Wasn't Diem now reading press reports that Washington could live with him and his family? Didn't that speculation reduce our bargaining power? We have to be tough, said Bobby as a recognized master of political hardball. Lodge must do more than say that our president is unhappy. Tell Diem he must do as we say, Bobby concluded, or American public opinion will force us to cut down our effort. Bobby had missed the session with Kattenburg but arrived at the same question: "And if we've concluded that we are going to lose with Diem, why do we not grasp the nettle now?"

To such rashness, Rusk offered an avuncular tut-tut. First of all, Diem would not be relying on newspaper stories to fathom the U.S. government's views. And threatening to pull out of Vietnam would be very serious. If the Vietcong took over in Vietnam, we would be in real trouble. Take things slowly was Rusk's advice. Let Lodge talk to Diem before deciding on the next move.

Mac Bundy agreed that this was not the moment for a decision. Max Taylor pointed out that only three weeks ago they had believed the war could be won with Diem. Why had they now changed that judgment? Frustrated, Bobby asked again what Washington should do if they decided they couldn't win with Diem.

McNamara explained that they could not answer that question because they didn't have enough information. He suggested sending General Krulak to Saigon on another fact-finding mission. This meeting had been convened at

10:30 A.M. on Friday, September 6. McNamara proposed that Krulak get to Vietnam immediately and return on Monday, September 9.

Hilsman spotted the danger in sending only a military man, and the president agreed that a State Department official should also make the trip. Once the meeting ended, however, McNamara tried to get Krulak on a plane within ninety minutes. Alerted to that ploy, Hilsman had the plane held until his man could get to the airport. It was a suitable beginning to the most antic of Washington's many fly-by attempts to gather information.

Accompanying Krulak would be Joseph Mendenhall, a State Department adviser who had once been stationed in the Saigon embassy. During the flight, Brute Krulak barely spoke to his civilian counterpart. Once on the ground, they raced off to canvass their conflicting sources. Despite a frenzied schedule, they missed McNamara's deadline by a day and were not back at the White House until Tuesday, September 10.

Before he left Washington, Krulak had known what he would find. The previous February, he had persuaded his golfing partner, John McCone, to reverse the CIA's National Intelligence Estimate 53–63, "Prospects in South Vietnam." The draft had explained that the struggle would be long and costly, and it pointed to the host of problems Saigon faced. Krulak scoffed at its warning about a lack of trust between the ARVN soldier and the farmer. He said it was a given in Asia that "the soldier will kick the peasant as he goes by." When McCone finished with the Estimate in April, it read, "We believe that Communist progress has been blunted and that the situation is improving."

In July, Krulak had intervened again, this time to block John Vann from briefing the Joint Chiefs. Vann, favorite source of the Saigon press corps, had been back in Washington and looking forward to the chance to challenge Harkins and Krulak, who had been touting the success of the strategic hamlet program. They claimed that all 11,246 hamlets would be completed by the end of 1963, and the Vietcong would be left thrashing about outside their perimeters. In a tactful rebuttal, Vann planned to debunk that approach and urge that the war be fought more aggressively.

As he waited outside the Joint Chiefs' office in a freshly pressed uniform, Max Taylor's aide rang up the clerk at the desk. The man put down the phone and said, "Looks like you don't brief today, buddy."

On this day, however, Mendenhall could not be shut off so neatly. After Krulak assured Kennedy that the war was being won, Mendenhall spoke of a virtual breakdown of government in Saigon, a police reign of terror and the mass arrest of students who sided with the Buddhists. He had found that same mood of fear and hatred when he traveled to the coastal cities of Hue and Danang, where students were saying that a Vietcong victory would be better than continuing with Diem. The war, already going badly, could not be won if Nhu remained in Vietnam.

The president regarded Krulak and Mendenhall and asked, "The two of you did visit the same country, didn't you?"

But Kennedy seemed to be the only person who wanted to smooth over their differences. When Mendenhall suggested that Trueheart, Nolting's Judas, agreed with his assessment, Nolting reminded the group caustically that Mendenhall had been predicting since 1961 that the Vietcong were about to defeat Diem. How, Nolting demanded, could a government so doomed have survived and even made headway? Before Mendenhall could answer, the president interrupted to ask again, more seriously, how two people observing the same terrain could come back with such different reactions.

No one spoke. The honest answer was that one side or the other was deluded, but Kennedy clearly wanted to resolve their differences, not exacerbate them. At last, Krulak offered the president a self-serving rationale. Mr. Mendenhall had presented the urban conditions in Vietnam, he said, while his own had been a nationwide perspective. Krulak's tactfulness evaporated when Rufus Phillips, home from the Saigon embassy, sketched his own gloomy picture. Krulak snapped that Phillips, a former CIA agent in charge of Vietnam's AID program, was putting his judgment over that of General Harkins. Krulak said that he, for one, would take Harkins's opinion.

Rusk called for time to digest these latest reports. Kennedy agreed and dismissed the company with his usual warning to keep their disagreements out of the papers. Twelve days passed. Then Kennedy sent McNamara and Taylor back to Saigon for yet another attempt to chart the whirlwind.

To HANOI, the turmoil in the South was deeply gratifying. Although Pham Van Dong encouraged overtures from Nhu, he had never trusted Diem's brother and had no intention of negotiating seriously with him. In the first months of organizing the National Liberation Front, a few of the Politburo's dozen members had worried that Nhu might succeed in winning away non-Communist NLF members. But the majority believed that Tho's NLF would prove steadfast, and by late 1962 any concern over mass defections had passed.

As for a neutral South Vietnam, northerners like Truong Chinh favored the idea, but his prestige had never recovered from the bloody botch he had made of land ownership. Le Duan dominated the Politburo, and he did not intend to let diplomacy once again subvert the South's independence. As he saw it, after the Laotian settlement, the United States had dug its claws into South Vietnam and was not interested in another neutralist solution. That, too, was the reading of other Communists who had studied U.S. policy most intently. Since 1954, almost every North Vietnamese who became foreign minister had first headed Hanoi's American desk. As their country's experts on Washington, they found no evidence that Rusk and McNamara would even consider neutralism.

But the Politburo could still enjoy Nhu's deep game and the distrust he was

Ho Chi Minh with Le Duan *(Vietnam News Agency)*

spreading. Diem might claim that Tri Quang and other Buddhists were being run by the Communists. Hanoi knew better. Some Vietcong had joined in the anti-Diem demonstrations, but Tri Quang himself was far too headstrong to be a dependable Communist ally. For the North, the Buddhist upheaval was only a welcome diversion, and the comedy became richer when Tri Quang appealed for refuge at the U.S. embassy, and Lodge took him in and refused to surrender him to the Vietnamese authorities.

Lodge was ignoring Washington's advice to heal the rift with Diem, and he had cut off Harkins and John Richardson, the CIA station chief, from embassy decisions. But while the ambassador was charming Saigon's reporters with lunches and private interviews, a pro-Diem element within the U.S. press was bringing up its own artillery in the form of Joe Alsop, Marguerite Higgins and Henry Luce. All three knew Asia better than their younger antagonists in the press corps. Alsop had served most of World War II in China and left the service as a captain on Chennault's staff. Both Higgins and Luce had been born in China to missionary parents. At the age of six months, Higgins had been taken from Hong Kong to Vietnam in the hope that Dalat's high mountain air would cure her malaria. Along with their sense of personal investment in Asia went a professional competitiveness. Luce's *Time* magazine, aiming for an aura of omniscience, took whacks at most other news operations. And both Alsop and Higgins wrote for the *New York Herald Tribune* at a time when the *New York Times*, first with Bigart, now with Halberstam, was dominating the Vietnam reportage.

Halberstam made a tempting target—still under thirty, more than a little self-righteous and vocal about his conviction that the American mission was invariably lying. At the embassy's last Fourth of July party, Halberstam had refused to shake hands with Harkins. Over dinner with friends, he regularly denounced the general for issuing glowing reports while he went on wasting American and Vietnamese lives. Although Halberstam drank temperately, his wrath could be intoxicating. Once, slamming his fist on a restaurant table, he shouted, "Paul D. Harkins should be court-martialed and shot!"

Maneli, the Polish ICC member, had run into Halberstam at the Cercle Sportif, Saigon's version of a country club, and was impressed by his outspoken hostility to the embassy. While in Hanoi, Maneli urged Pham Van Dong to grant Halberstam and Sheehan visas and let them enter North Vietnam. Dong refused. "We are not interested in building up the prestige of American journalists," he said. Maneli suspected that Hanoi's leadership worried that accurate reports from the North would help the Pentagon to improve its strategy. He knew that Giap had described the American Joint Chiefs as even less expert in fighting Vietnam's kind of war than the French had been, and slower to learn from their mistakes. The United States could be defeated sooner if it got no tips from its journalists.

WHEN MAGGIE HIGGINS reached Saigon, she fired her first salvo by calling the young American reporters "typewriter strategists" who seldom went into battle. Before she left Washington, Brute Krulak had briefed her and, over dinner with Charles Mohr of *Time*, Higgins was indiscreet enough to reveal the bias she had brought with her. "Reporters here," she told Mohr—and soon denied saying, "would like to see us lose the war to prove they're right." When her stories impugned both the Buddhists and the Saigon press corps, nervous *New York Times* editors began to challenge Halberstam. Since his reporting of the pagoda raids had proved more accurate than the State Department's first version, he was near the end of his patience. After one tweaking by the foreign desk, Halberstam wired back, "If you mention that woman's name to me one more time I will resign repeat resign and I mean it repeat mean it."

Given Alsop's social standing in Washington, his assaults were potentially even more damaging. As a congressman, Jack Kennedy had stayed at Alsop's comfortable house on Dumbarton Road while he recovered from a bout of Addison's disease. On inauguration night, the new president had dropped in there for a nightcap. Now Alsop proved his fealty with a column that denounced the Saigon press corps as the same sort of crusaders who had undercut Chiang in China and Batista in Cuba. Alsop claimed that reporters were depending on the one U.S. adviser out of ten who thought all foreigners fought badly, and they were ignoring the majority of Americans who admired the South Vietnamese as soldiers. To Alsop, the constant press criticism had reduced Diem, once a courageous leader, to a man who saw plots in every corner.

Without naming Halberstam, Alsop singled him out for an attack that might have been more damning except for the columnist's curious choice of phrase when he spoke of Vietnam's "fighting front." Every resident reporter knew that Vietnam had no World War II fronts, that the American frustration arose from looking constantly to the rear for an ambush or a hit-and-run raid. Halberstam considered Alsop's charges much like those of Joe McCarthy, reckless attempts to stifle dissent. But Alsop's columns provoked irksome new cables from Halberstam's New York office. One read, "Assume you keeping material balanced."

The worst assaults against the press corps were coming from Luce's *Time*, until finally one of them ricocheted and inflicted unintended casualties. Charlie Mohr could generally expect massive rewriting from his editors. In August, his dispatch calling Madame Nhu a destructive influence had appeared in the magazine as a tribute to "a fragile, exciting beauty." A month later, Mohr's file began "The war in Vietnam is being lost." Otto Fuerbringer, *Time*'s managing editor, turned it into another attack on the Saigon reporters for deliberately slanting their coverage. That was too much for Mohr. He resigned, along with his stringer, Mert Perry.

Editors at the *New York Times* were not the only ones concerned that their reporters had become part of the story. Browne's AP office in New York demanded that he take a vacation, and Sheehan was resisting that same pressure from UPI.

SENDING MCNAMARA and Taylor to Vietnam was part of Kennedy's plan to nurse along the American effort for the next fourteen months. Eisenhower had allowed the French to collapse in Vietnam during his first term. But even after the successful outcome of the missile crisis, Kennedy's stature would not let him accept that kind of major defeat. A further complication also involved domestic politics. In the spring, Kennedy had endorsed a civil rights bill that, given southern opposition in Congress, had scant chance of passing. All the same, the president asked Negro leaders to put off a massive demonstration they were planning to hold in Washington. They refused his request. On August 28, almost a quarter of a million marchers heard the Reverend Martin Luther King, Jr., share his dream of racial harmony. Many Americans found King's eloquence to be thrilling, but Kennedy worried that being linked to the burgeoning Negro movement was politically damaging. Polls showed the president's approval rating had dipped from 60 to 47 percent—one more reason to relegate a divisive issue like Vietnam to his second term.

In the meantime, Kennedy was torn about Diem's fate and the obligation he felt to him. Big Minh, the likeliest general to lead a coup, had dropped hints that if Diem were to be overthrown, he must also be killed; clemency would expose the plotters themselves to danger. As Kennedy weighed his unattractive choices, he decided to make one last effort to eject the Nhus from Gia Long Palace, and he turned to the only American who might cajole Diem into doing it.

For Ed Lansdale's meeting at the White House, McNamara invited him to ride along in the Secretary's limousine. Lansdale knew that Bobby Kennedy was furious because Castro had not been toppled, and he suspected that the president shared that impatience. But when they got to Kennedy's office, the topic was not Cuba but Vietnam. The president said he was ready to send Lansdale back to Saigon, with the assignment of persuading Diem to ship his brother and sister-in-law out of the country. Would you be willing to go? Kennedy asked. Yes, Lansdale said.

Kennedy put one more question to him. "But if that didn't work out—or I changed my mind and decided we had to get rid of Diem—would you be able to go along with that?"

Lansdale hesitated. He understood that with Diem the choice would not be exile but death. Lansdale had no moral qualms about assassination as a policy tool; during the Mongoose planning, he had discussed killing Castro. But Kennedy seemed to understand that Diem was different for him. Was he asking whether Lansdale would oversee Diem's execution or asking that he simply not warn Diem what was coming? With the president's language deliberately ambiguous, Lansdale did not feel he could violate CIA etiquette by asking him to be more precise.

Slowly, he shook his head. "No, Mr. President, I couldn't do that. Diem is my friend."

Kennedy covered the moment with sympathetic tact, but the interview was over and Lansdale understood that he would not be returning to Saigon. McNamara had been the only witness to the exchange. Lansdale knew that the Secretary had never approved of him, but he was unprepared for McNamara's anger during the ride back to the Pentagon. "You don't talk to the President of the United States that way," McNamara said. "When he asks you to do something, you don't tell him you won't do it."

That was the attitude of the man Kennedy was now sending back to Vietnam to set the stage for getting out of the war at the right political moment, and McNamara would have to bring around Max Taylor to the idea of withdrawal. Taylor might not be able to placate all of the Joint Chiefs, but his prestige would weigh heavily against their protests.

LODGE HAD FIRST RESISTED this latest McNamara trip. When Kennedy overruled him, the ambassador allowed Harkins to take charge of the guests for the early days of their tour, and the general assured them that the upheaval in Saigon had not affected the war effort. At home, McNamara had seemed to side with Krulak. In South Vietnam, he pulled out Rufus Phillips's report and demanded to know why Harkins's briefing officers would not admit that the strategic hamlet program was failing.

His new belligerence was a sign that McNamara was ready to give his president the kind of report Kennedy wanted. On this trip, he was meeting with the sort of civilian experts he had shunned in the past. McNamara identified one of them in his report as "Professor Smith" from a leading American university. In fact, the man was P. J. Honey, a highly regarded lecturer on Vietnam at the University of London. Bill Bundy, Mac Bundy's older brother, was along on the trip and saw that Honey impressed McNamara because he had been one of Diem's earliest advocates and spoke fluent Vietnamese. These days, Honey was predicting that Diem could not last twenty-four hours without his brother. It was Nhu's bribes and network of informers and secret police that allowed Diem his lofty isolation. With his own back to the wall, Nhu was sure to stop Diem from making any changes. Kennedy must choose: either support Diem totally or expect a coup within four weeks.

Lodge was committed more firmly than ever to that coup and hoped to unnerve the palace by keeping his distance. In the meantime, however, one of Diem's few concessions had unexpectedly turned sour. Madame Nhu had finally left the country, but only to seek an international platform for her invective. While McNamara was in Saigon, she said in Rome on September 25 that America's junior officers—men like Colonel Vann—were "acting like little soldiers of fortune."

At that, Lodge broke his tactical silence and denounced the remark as cruel. "These men should be thanked, not insulted," he said, adding that some had been killed at the side of their Vietnamese comrades. His angry retort put Madame Nhu temporarily on the defensive, but she recovered neatly. Kennedy's aides had been debating for months what to do if she accepted a speaking engagement in the United States but had reached no decision about giving her a visa. When she left Saigon, her itinerary had called for her to attend only a conference in Belgrade. Now Madame Nhu announced that she already had a valid U.S. visa and was heading for New York to tell her story.

BECAUSE THE KRULAK TRIP had been so hectic, Kennedy specified that McNamara's entourage should take ample time. That turned out to be ten days. Mecklin watched as McNamara's brusque questioning exposed the holes in his briefers' arguments, but since the Defense Secretary was traveling everywhere with Harkins, he did not hear the despair from younger officers that they unloaded on Halberstam, Sheehan and Peter Arnett. When McNamara and Taylor went for their interview with Diem, Lodge and Harkins went along. Although Nhu did not join them, his intelligence service had accurately calculated McNamara's weakness, and Diem was armed with maps and charts. Delivering a two-and-a-half-hour monologue, he chain-smoked as usual but jumped up repeatedly to point to graphs that proved the war was being won. When McNamara was permitted to speak, Diem rejected his protests about the political repression. If anything, Diem said, he had been too kind to the Buddhists.

Taylor briefed Diem on his own findings. Two years after Taylor botched his first assignment by talking of combat troops, his latest report was guaranteed to please Kennedy. He had talked with scores of Vietnamese and American officers, Taylor said, and become convinced that the Vietcong rebellion in the northern and central sectors of South Vietnam could be reduced by late 1964 to sporadic gunfire. The Delta would take longer to subdue, but even there the insurrection could be quashed by the end of 1965. Those predictions, however, depended on Diem's meeting the American demands for change.

Escorted as he was by Diem's soldiers, Taylor had only managed to meet with Big Minh over a game of tennis in the muggy heat; McNamara went along to watch. During breaks in the game, Minh let each of Taylor's pointed remarks go unreturned. When he paid a farewell call two days later, Taylor spoke more openly about removing Nhu, but even then Minh did not reveal a plan of action. "In summary," Taylor concluded his account to Kennedy of their dispirited conversation, "General Minh sees his country in chains with no way to shake them off."

FLYING BACK to Washington, McNamara, Taylor and Bill Bundy drafted the policy statement Kennedy was expecting, and the president unveiled it on October 2 before the National Security Council. He said the report now provided his administration with a unified approach to Vietnam, which everyone in the room should carry out with a good heart. And without talking to reporters. Kennedy had achieved unity by adroitly widening the gulf between the two camps of his advisers. Privately, the administration would go on nagging Diem. But its public statements would endorse Harkins's position that America's sound military strategy was showing progress. In fact, the White House would go further and claim that the brunt of U.S. training would be done by 1965; only a limited number of advisers should be required past that date. Indeed, so well had the MACV succeeded that 1,000 U.S. military personnel could be withdrawn by the end of the current year—which meant within three months.

McNamara himself had drafted that language on the flight from Saigon. He knew the ground rules. Of course, the war was not going well, but with congressional hearings coming up, Senators William Fulbright, Frank Church and others who were raising questions would be lulled by a show of disengagement. Kennedy did not want to be accused later of having been too optimistic, and he worried that the simple logistics of withdrawal might require more time. To protect himself, he decided to attribute the two predictions about specific dates for troop withdrawal to McNamara and Taylor.

McNamara anticipated Pentagon resistance to the pledge to withdraw a thousand troops by the end of 1963 and was determined to have it announced publicly—as he put it, "set in concrete."

When Pierre Salinger announced the new Vietnam policy, most Americans in Saigon were bitterly disappointed. The first paragraph committed the United States to go on working with the hated South Vietnamese government, and the promise to bring back a thousand advisers suggested that Kennedy was still buying the Harkins fantasy of an early victory. At the USIS, Mecklin was sickened by the news before he realized that the announcement was only the public face of a private strategy. His first clue came with the transfer of John Richardson, the CIA station chief. Arriving in Saigon with the same instructions as Nolting, Richardson had worked to ingratiate himself at the palace. But Nhu remembered William Colby's deceit, knew that Lou Conein was the CIA's conduit to the dissident generals and never trusted Richardson. Nor did the generals, who thought he would betray their plans to Diem. And Lodge saw Richardson as a remnant from the failed policy of appeasement.

A CIA station chief's identity and his transfer would not normally make the newspapers, but nothing in Saigon these days was normal. To cover himself, Lodge wired Mac Bundy that Sheehan had been checking the story at the embassy. The reporter was being told nothing, Lodge said, but he would bet that someone would talk. In fact, within hours Sheehan was reporting that Richardson was leaving Saigon and would not return.

In their report, McNamara and Taylor had drafted a weaseling and confidential paragraph about coup planning: the United States should not actively encourage one, but the Saigon mission should urgently identify and build contacts with potential coup leaders—"alternative leadership" was the sanitized phrase. Kennedy directed Hilsman to come up with possible cuts in Diem's aid package that would not damage the war effort, and Hilsman and Bill Bundy identified several, including loans for water and electrical power projects and reductions in the Commodity Import Program aimed at stemming inflation in Vietnam. The sternest reprisal would be recognized only by the Ngo brothers—a cutback in CIA funding for the 1,840-man Special Forces led by Lieutenant Colonel Le Quang Tung, a Diem loyalist. Washington would agree to resume support for Tung's troops only if they were sent to fight Communists along the Lao border.

In the distant hope that Diem might still follow orders, the aid cutbacks were not made public. But the palace, determined to show that the Ngo family could not be blackmailed, sneered at that discretion. On October 7, the *Times of Vietnam*, the regular conduit for Nhu and his wife, ran a furious story, with an eight-column headline, that the United States mission had frozen its economic aid. With that leak, Diem and Nhu signed their own death warrants.

NO READER of the *Times of Vietnam* could doubt what message the United States was sending. Two days later, Kennedy underlined it when he began his press conference by defending the CIA. Richardson's American opponents had been leaking stories that the agency was a rogue operation with its own agenda of keeping Diem in power. The *Times of Vietnam* had taken the opposite tack, accusing the CIA of plotting Diem's overthrow. Kennedy told reporters that the CIA had done a good job in Vietnam but that Washington still faced the same problems in Saigon as it had a month earlier. The *Times of Vietnam* took Kennedy's remarks as a blessing on those who were intriguing against the regime.

By now, the president was increasingly troubled by the prospect of messy and unpredictable results in Saigon. He simply wanted Diem to behave like the reasonable political bosses he knew—Richard Daley in Chicago or David Lawrence in Philadelphia. While Washington waited and wondered, Jim Thomson at the State Department drew a wan smile from the president with his parody of the interminable White House debates over Vietnam. Mike Forrestal passed along the gibes to Kennedy, whom Thomson had quoted as saying, "We must not lose sight of our ultimate objective, and in no state was the Vietnamese vote worth very much."

Nhu showed his own awareness of American domestic politics by circulating a broadsheet among the Vietnamese armed forces. In it, Nhu argued that there was no difference between the Buddhist crisis in Vietnam and the Negro crisis in the United States. Just as John Kennedy was ordering his brother to enforce integration in the South, so had President Diem called upon his brother to discipline the Buddhists. In fact, Nhu concluded, the Vietnamese response had been less extreme. At least the palace had not used dogs against the Buddhists, or cattle prods.

IN WASHINGTON, Kennedy sensed that he had lost control of circumstances in Vietnam. Through cables signed by Rusk, he hounded Lodge to keep the Vietnamese generals on their tether and not let them move unless they could guarantee a swift victory. The president had another concern: Lodge was due back in Washington for routine consultations, and a coup might be attempted in his absence. If so, Kennedy wanted Harkins, not Trueheart, designated as the mission's acting chief. Lodge blithely rejected both directives. On October 3, he cabled that the coup was too far advanced to abort in any way except by betraying its leaders to Diem and that "would make traitors out of us." As for Harkins, he was "a splendid general and an old friend of mine to whom I would gladly entrust anything I have." Except, it turned out, the Saigon embassy. Lodge argued that it would not be sensible to put a military man in charge of an affair so profoundly political.

For his own reasons, Kennedy had shown Lodge every deference, but his ambassador seemed to be plunging down a path that Kennedy's senior advisers considered perilous. Bobby Kennedy had also come out against a coup, although his influence was undercut by his way of popping in and out of the debate and then granting that he had not read all the cables and reports. No one had risen to Bobby's earlier suggestion that they consider getting out of Vietnam entirely, and during a full-scale review on October 29, he admitted that he could make no sense out of what was going on. Washington appeared to be ready to put the future of Southeast Asia in the hands of a man whose identity none of them even knew. Hearing that stark truth from his brother, the president directed Mac Bundy to make one last attempt to rein Lodge in. "We do not accept as a basis for U.S. policy that we have no power to delay or discourage a coup," Bundy wired. But Kennedy had to face the possibility that a coup might occur while Lodge was away. If so, Bundy added, Harkins should take command.

TRAN QUANG THUAN, the lapsed bonze with the notorious Austin sedan, had been held in Nhu's prison since early September. Meeting at the pharmacy with eleven other Buddhists, he had been caught when police seized the downstairs clerk before she could sound her warning bell. The police tied Thuan's hands together, blindfolded him and led him to a room with two pleasant surprises: it was air-conditioned, and the captain in charge had once been his father's bodyguard. He promised to protect Thuan against torture and to supply him with regular meals.

After three days, however, Thuan was taken across the hall and blindfolded again. For three hours, he was stretched out on a wooden cross while a water-soaked cloth was placed over his mouth and nose every ten or fifteen minutes. He was sure he would suffocate. Each time the cloth was lifted, Thuan was asked the same two questions: Why do you demonstrate against the government? Which U.S. personnel are helping you? Thuan answered that his group had tried to publish their grievances in newspapers, which was forbidden, and to schedule an audience with Diem, which was refused. That was why they had taken to the streets. And since their banners required only 20 meters of cloth, they had no need for American support. Thuan was led back to a cell, with one small hole in the wall. For two weeks, he was awakened at midnight by guards trying to addle him by disturbing his sleep.

Next, Thuan was blindfolded and taken outside to a place where he could hear running water. "Confess," a guard said, "or we're going to shoot you." Thuan was sure they were ready to dump his body in the Mekong. He prayed silently but did not speak.

When that bluff failed, Thuan was taken next to state police headquarters. Once again, he found a friend from his past; the chief of the interrogation center had taught him French in Hanoi. "I've been given instructions by Mr. Nhu," the man said. "You will be sent to Con Son." Thuan's heart sank. On the island that the French had named Poulo Condore, the prison was composed of tiny cells called tiger cages. They had once held Pham Van Dong, Le Duc Tho and other prominent Vietminh. "Meantime," the chief continued, "is there anything I can do for you?"

He assigned Thuan to a large cell with two young monks. A U.N. team was due any day to probe charges of abuse, and a guard instructed Thuan to testify that he had been involved with the CIA and the Cambodian government in an attempt to overthrow Diem. At 2 P.M. on Friday, November 1, as Thuan was beginning his third month in prison, a clamor arose from the street outside and then a gate slammed shut. Thuan and his fellow prisoners thought perhaps the U.N. team had arrived. But they heard gunshots and the gate being forced open. A voice cried, "We have come to liberate you from prison!"

Thuan told the others, "Don't applaud. It could be a trick. Don't say anything."

Troops rushed through the building, shouting that they had come from their base at Binh Hoa to rid the country of repression. The prisoners asked for a radio to confirm the news and found that Armed Forces Radio, the American station, was reporting a "civil disturbance" under way. The rebel leader announced that he intended to release all the captives, but Thuan and the others dissuaded him. "Some are thieves," Thuan said, "and some are really Vietcong." He and nine other political prisoners volunteered to stay in the prison, reviewing each case individually. It was 4 P.M. the next day before they finished and Thuan could go home. His wife welcomed him with the latest rumors about the fate of President Diem and Counselor Nhu.

AT THE PALACE, the morning of November 1 had begun with a courtesy call by an American delegation. Admiral Felt had arrived in Saigon the previous day on an overnight visit. Before leaving, he went with Lodge to see Diem. The previous day, Madame Nhu in Los Angeles had charged that Lodge had "become more mysterious than an Asian." It was not meant as a compliment, but Felt might have agreed with her. He saw Lodge's cables only because Max Taylor insisted on forwarding them to Hawaii. Otherwise, the ambassador had cut off the entire Pacific military command from the plotting against Diem.

Nor were the Vietnamese generals more forthcoming. Harkins complained that during a parade the previous Saturday he had sat for two hours in the reviewing stand with Big Minh and General Tran Van Don. The word "coup" had been spoken only once, when Don assured Harkins there would be none. Now, from his belated reading of embassy cables, Harkins learned that Don had told the CIA's Conein that the coup would happen before November 2.

When Felt left for the airport, Diem asked Lodge to stay on for a few minutes. Aware that Lodge would be returning soon to Washington, Diem made a pointed joke: "There's an old saying here that every time the American ambassador leaves, there is a coup against the government."

Diem knew the identities of the various dissidents, and Big Minh topped the list, which explained why Minh commanded no troops and could fill his days with tennis and hothouse orchids. But the coup that Diem expected to prevail

General Duong Van (Big) Minh (© *Bettmann/Corbis*)

was the one being mounted by his brother. Loyal troops pretending to be neutralists would seize Saigon and invite all anti-Diem commanders to join them. As the generals fell into Nhu's trap, he would pick them off one by one. Within a few days, the opposition would be annihilated and U.S. aid would resume.

Lodge parried Diem's reference to a coup by mentioning rumors that Lodge himself had been marked by the regime for assassination. Genially, he added that such transparently false reports had in no way affected his feelings of friendship for President Diem. In parting, Diem put in a good word for Paul Harkins, took a slap at John Vann as very imprudent and urged Lodge to assure Kennedy that he was a good and frank ally. He was taking the president's suggestions seriously and wanted to carry them out. It was a question of timing.

ALTHOUGH GENERAL DON had promised Conein a forty-eight-hour notice before the coup began, he didn't trust Harkins with that much time. On Friday morning, Don rode with Harkins to the airport to speed Felt on his way. When Harkins returned to his office, Don went directly to the Vietnamese Joint General Staff headquarters. Conein was waiting there with Don's fellow conspirators. The junta had also rounded up six Diem loyalists, including Colonel Tung of Nhu's special forces. Diem's Navy commander had been killed earlier that morning.

At 1:45 P.M., with the coup safely launched, Don telephoned Major General

Richard Stilwell to ask that Harkins be notified. Harkins relayed the news to Lodge but found that the ambassador already had more up-to-date information. According to Conein, the rebel generals would guarantee safe passage for Diem and Nhu if they resigned immediately. The generals wanted to give Diem no chance to play on old loyalties or stall until reinforcements could arrive. Diem must say yes or no. That would end the conversation. If it was no, they would attack the palace.

At 4:30 P.M., aware now that the coup was genuine and not his brother's concoction, Diem telephoned Lodge at the embassy. Lodge had been expecting the call. If Diem asked for asylum, the ambassador felt he could hardly refuse since he was still harboring Tri Quang. "Some units have made a rebellion," Diem said in French, "and I want to know: What is the attitude of the United States?"

Lodge answered in French, "I do not feel well-informed enough to be able to tell you. I have heard the shooting, but I'm not acquainted with all the facts. And it is 4:30 A.M. in Washington. It's impossible for me to get any opinion from our government at this hour."

"But you must have some general idea," Diem persisted. "After all, I am a Chief of State. I have tried to do my duty. I want to do now what duty and good sense require. I believe in duty above all."

But Madame Nhu was in Los Angeles and not able to define his duty for him. Major General Ton That Dinh, the lightweight military governor of Saigon, had now joined the coup out of wounded vanity from past slights. Major General Nguyen Khanh, whose first allegiance was always to himself, had not gone to the coup headquarters, but Khanh said he endorsed the conspiracy.

Diem was left with only Lodge's empty praise: "You have certainly done your duty." The ambassador reminded him that he had praised Diem's courage and contributions that very morning. No one could take away the credit for all Diem had done. "Now I am worried about your physical safety," Lodge went on. "I have a report that those in charge of the current activity offer you and your brother safe conduct out of the country if you resign. Have you heard this?"

"No." It was final proof—if more were needed—that Lodge was in league with his enemies. After a decade as America's partner, Diem could expect no help from the embassy. "You have my telephone number," Diem said. It was not a question. It was goodbye.

"Yes," Lodge said. "If I can do anything for your physical safety, please call me."

"I am trying to reestablish order," Diem said.

LODGE PUT DOWN THE RECEIVER and listened to the guns going off throughout the city. He drafted a cable for the State Department setting out his brief conversation with Diem and then ate dinner. Afterward, the lower volume of gunfire suggested that the coup leaders were mopping up pockets of resistance. During his many political campaigns, Lodge had learned that when he got tired, he invariably got testy. His opponents derided his regular naps, but Lodge insisted on plenty of sleep. At 9 P.M., with shells still exploding not far from his residence, Lodge went to bed.

AT 2 P.M. on November 1, Bill Kohlmann was in a taxi, heading back from lunch to his desk at the U.S. AID office, when he heard the first explosions. At the office door, he found the staff being sent home, and he assumed that the thirty or forty CIA employees had also gone to their houses. A friend from USIA lived across the street from the palace and chose to return instead to Kohlmann's apartment, out of the line of fire. His Vietnamese contacts had not supplied Kohlmann with the details of the coup, but like everyone in Saigon he had been expecting it. Influenced by the Buddhists he was recruiting, he was convinced that if Diem stayed in power the country would go to the Communists. So, although Kohlmann regarded himself as a conservative and averse to change, the advent of the coup gratified him. As cannon roared and afternoon lengthened into evening, Kohlmann poured his guest a drink and put on a recording of Schubert's *Trout* Quintet.

AT THE JOINT GENERAL STAFF headquarters, Big Minh got through to the palace by phone at 5 P.M. and issued his ultimatum to Nhu. To convince him that the brothers could not expect deliverance this time, one rebel trained a pistol on Tung of Special Forces and forced him to tell Nhu that he had been captured. Diem himself took Minh's next call and refused to resign. Using the palace radio, he tried to reach loyal commanders around the country, but he had no Tuyen to coordinate his rescue.

At 4 A.M. on November 2, insurgent troops laid siege to Gia Long Palace with cannon and machine guns, burning down several nearby buildings. Inside the palace, Diem's last dedicated troops held out for more than two hours, but at dawn they flew a white flag of surrender over the palace. When the rebels moved into the open, however, their captain was shot and killed. At that, the rebels stormed the palace, only to find that Diem and Nhu had fled.

ACROSS THE INTERNATIONAL DATE LINE, November 1 began at the White House with Mac Bundy's 8 A.M. staff meeting. Unlike Lodge, he and Forrestal had stayed up all night, reading cables as they came in from the embassy. Bundy had worried that prolonged civil strife would complicate the war against the Vietcong, but now he could report that, except for the palace guard, the South Vietnamese army seemed firmly behind its rebel generals. The White House expected the coup leaders to be more tractable than Diem and was ready with instant political advice. Hilsman and Bundy drafted a wire urging the generals to stress repeatedly that "Nhu was dickering with the Communists to betray the anti-Communist cause." Lodge assured them wearily that the point was already being made. Next, Hilsman and Bill Sullivan sent detailed instructions on how to deal with Tri Quang. According to Conein, the generals wanted the monk to join their government, but the State Department preferred not to see him in any new cabinet. And the generals were warned to expect a delay of a few days before their government was recognized. Anything hasty might give the impression that they had been manipulated by the Americans. Certainly, the generals should avoid calling on Lodge in a large group, which could look as though "they were reporting to headquarters."

Amid the jubilation, only Paul Harkins sounded a somber note with a telegram to Max Taylor that began, "We are no longer a republic."

FRIDAY EVENING, not long before Lodge went to bed, Diem and Nhu left the palace through a door on Cong Ly Street and slipped past the guards posted there. With them were a servant, a military aide and a resident of Cholon, Saigon's Chinese quarter. To protect his business interests, the man had organized Chinese units of Nhu's Republican Youth. He drove the brothers now to his clubhouse and helped them get through by telephone to the Taiwan embassy. The fugitives asked for asylum and were refused. They stayed throughout the night at the clubhouse, placing other calls. When they spoke again with the rebel generals, they indicated they were still inside the palace.

At 6:20 A.M., Diem called General Don to say he realized he must surrender but wanted a ceremony with full military honors. Don said that after the treachery with the white flag, his colleagues would not hear of extending Diem any honors at all. At 6:45 A.M., Diem called another general to say that he and his brother had taken refuge at the Cha Tam Catholic Church in Cholon. They would surrender there.

Big Minh assigned a cadre of officers to pick them up, including at the last minute his own bodyguard. Minh had once told Conein that he favored killing both Diem and Nhu, but most of the other generals wanted to spare their lives. Even so, just two weeks earlier, Minh had assigned sharpshooters to kill Nhu as he drove back to the palace from the general staff headquarters. That attempt was aborted when Nhu invited General Don to ride with him. Now, as the officers left to arrest Diem and Nhu, Don was arranging for someplace to hold them until they could be put on a plane for the Philippines and their eventual exile in Rome.

PRESIDENT KENNEDY called a meeting of his chief advisers for 9:30 A.M. It was to be entirely off-the-record, with Rusk, McNamara, McCone, Bobby Kennedy and the others encouraged to speculate freely on U.S. policy now that Diem was deposed and in hiding. Forrestal interrupted the session to bring Kennedy a telegram that was stamped with the designation used only on messages that could affect national survival.

"Best estimate this time is that Diem and Nhu dead. Radio announcement reporting they committed suicide by poison." The brief bulletin noted that the suicides took place on the way from Cholon to the general staff headquarters. The bodies were either inside that office or the armored personnel carrier that had been sent to transport them.

Kennedy scanned the page and bolted from the room. His look of shock and dismay was one Max Taylor had never seen, although others remembered his same appalled response to the failure at the Bay of Pigs. But Kennedy shielded the breaks in his composure. From childhood, he knew that shows of emotion led to taunts and jeers. And scorn over displays of softness were not limited to Kennedy's family. Maggie Higgins had tried to embarrass Halberstam by circulating the story that a photograph of dead soldiers had moved him to tears. And, earlier in the year, during a Senate investigation of McNamara's role in awarding questionable contracts for the TFX aircraft, the Secretary's usual tamped-down emotionalism had burst free. McNamara told the committee that his twelve-year-old son had asked how long it was going to take him to prove his honesty. At that, McNamara began to cry. Hearing about the scene, Kennedy was disturbed enough to contact the committee's chairman in hopes he could deny that such a display of weakness had occurred.

With his regret or guilt under control, Kennedy returned to the meeting and spoke about the serious effect the deaths would have in America and abroad. He, for one, doubted that the two men—as Catholics—would have killed themselves. Hilsman disagreed; even given their religion, he didn't find suicide difficult to imagine since the Ngos would have seen the coup as Armageddon. Kennedy adjourned the meeting until the afternoon, when more accurate information might be available.

DIEM AND NHU had been standing on the church steps when a convoy of several jeeps and an armored personnel carrier pulled up. Diem asked if they could stop at the palace for the personal items he would need for the flight out of Vietnam. The officers were nervous and wanted to get back to the safety of their headquarters. General Mai Huu Xuan, the ranking officer, said that his orders were to take Diem directly to headquarters. As the convoy was turning around for the return trip, one young officer asked permission to shoot Nhu but was told that both men were to be delivered safely, as ordered.

Big Minh had sent another order, however, with his bodyguard. Captain Nguyen Van Nhung waited in the personnel carrier's turret while Diem and Nhu had their hands tied behind their backs. A colonel was also inside. During the ride to Saigon, the prisoners were shot point-blank by a submachine gun. They were also shot in the back of the head and stabbed, Nhu repeatedly.

By the time the last jeep arrived at headquarters, the bodies already had been lifted from the personnel carrier and laid out on the ground. Expecting the cap-

Madame Ngo Dinh Nhu
in Los Angeles
(Archive Photos)

tives to arrive in passenger cars, General Don went outside to investigate, found the corpses and instructed a fellow general to tell reporters that the deaths had been accidental. Don then went to Big Minh. "Why are they dead?" he demanded.

Don considered Minh's reply haughty: "And what does it matter that they are dead?"

When General Xuan arrived, he did not see Don standing by the door and reported to Minh laconically in French, *Mission accomplie.*

THE COUP'S MANEUVERS had gone forward with an efficiency rarely seen in ARVN operations against the Vietcong. Colonel Tung of Special Forces was taken outside the headquarters building and shot. The Diemist General Cao had been effectively bottled up in the Delta, still convinced that the troop movements were part of Nhu's false coup. The political aftermath of the assassinations, however, was turning out to be messier than Minh and Xuan anticipated. Madame Nhu learned of the coup at the Beverly Wilshire Hotel in Los Angeles, where she had gone for minor cosmetic surgery on her eyes. She put through a call that night to her strongest sympathizer in the Washington press corps. "Do you believe they are dead?" she asked Maggie Higgins.

"I am afraid so."

"I could spit upon the world," Madame Nhu said. Her teenage daughter had been traveling with her, but three other children were at the family estate in Dalat. "Are they going to kill my children, too?"

Higgins assured her that Kennedy would never permit it. Madame Nhu began to sob and asked why the Americans weren't helping to get her children out. Higgins promised to contact the State Department. Since it was 2 A.M., she called Hilsman at home. "Congratulations, Roger," Higgins began. "How does it feel to have blood on your hands?"

"Oh, come on now, Maggie," Hilsman replied. "Revolutions are rough. People get hurt."

But he arranged for the three Nhu children to fly to Rome, where they could join their mother and her brother-in-law Thuc, the archbishop. Another uncle, Ngo Dinh Can, the potentate of central Vietnam, had been reduced to begging for asylum from the U.S. consul in Hue. The consul refused, saying he could not guarantee Can's safety. Can was promised instead a safe haven in Saigon, which he took to mean the U.S. embassy. Tri Quang was still living there, along with Ann Gregory of the *Times of Vietnam*. With her husband out of the country, Mrs. Gregory had feared that she would be attacked for her friendship with the Nhus and had applied successfully for sanctuary. Can flew to Saigon on a U.S. plane sent up to Hue by the embassy. At Tan Son Nhut, however, he was arrested by the Vietnamese authorities and led to jail. The Americans had betrayed his trust, but they had also imposed conditions on Can's enemies: he was not to be mistreated or executed without a public trial. In due course, Can was tried and shot by a firing squad. His will left his personal fortune, held in foreign banks, to Catholic charities.

As Can was being seized, the generals released most of the country's 20,000 political prisoners from Diem's fifty jails. Many had been held for months, some for years. Student demonstrators told of being stripped naked and tortured; young women had been marked for harsh and sadistic treatment. Word of those abuses had filtered through all levels of Vietnamese society, which accounted for the jubilation in the streets. Revelers tied ropes to the statue of Madame Nhu posing as a Trung sister and smashed it to the ground. Army officers accustomed to looks of nervous suspicion now received bouquets of flowers from grateful civilians.

In the Oval Office, an aide received news of the jubilant outpouring in Saigon and crowed, "Lodge is so popular he could be elected to any office!"

"Don't bet on it," Jack Kennedy said dryly, setting off hoots of laughter among his staff. "In Vietnam, Mr. President!" they cried. "Only in Vietnam!"

THROUGH KENNEDY'S unwitting assistance, Halberstam had managed to stay on to watch the ending of the Ngo family drama. From Bernard Kalb, a CBS reporter visiting Saigon, Halberstam heard about Kennedy's lunch some ten days before the coup with the new publisher of the *New York Times*, thirty-seven-year-old Arthur Ochs Sulzberger. The president did not mention Halberstam by name. He merely suggested that it could be time for a change in the *Times'* Saigon personnel.

In the past, the paper might have obliged him. Nine years earlier, the *Times* had obeyed when Allen Dulles asked Sulzberger's father to keep another correspondent, Sydney Gruson, out of Guatemala, where the CIA was engaged in overthrowing the leftist president. And Kennedy remembered that the *Times* had also bowed to the White House by printing less than its reporters knew about the planned invasion at the Bay of Pigs. This time, however, young Sulzberger and his editors balked. To demonstrate their independence, they even canceled the leave for which Halberstam had been scheduled.

Hearing Kalb's account did not ignite Halberstam's temper. To him, everything in Washington seemed faded and distant compared to the vividness of life in Vietnam. The reporters who received regular death threats were far more worried that they might somehow miss the coup. In October, the AP had sent Browne on leave. Before he left, he devised a code with his wife's name that would yank him back from Tokyo once a coup began. His phrase was, "Le Lieu is in the john." The message referred to a time when random gunplay in front of his office had led Browne to send her for protection to the toilet, where the walls were thickest. Browne whiled away his days in Japan waiting for a message that did not come and was back in Saigon before the generals acted. But Sheehan was not. UPI also insisted that he take a breather in Tokyo during the last week of October. When he protested, his editor said, "Come up here and take a rest, Neil. Or stay down there and wait for your last paycheck."

Sheehan had also worked out a private alert. An ARVN contact would send a coded message to either Halberstam or the UPI office. One or the other would then cable him in Tokyo: "Please buy Blue Lotus two geisha dolls, Kyoto style." Blue Lotus was Sheehan's Vietnamese girlfriend. Since Nhu's spy network knew of every romantic entanglement, the message was plausible.

Despite the turmoil in Saigon, Sheehan's system at first worked smoothly. An officer's son delivered the message to Sheehan's colleague at the UPI, who immediately sent a cable about the dolls to the Tokyo bureau. There, however, it lay buried for nineteen hours before Sheehan finally saw it.

Journalists in Saigon and New York knew that the coup would not end the rancorous debate over the reporting out of Saigon. At the AP and the *New York Times*, editors saw a way to inoculate their embattled reporters with the profession's highest honor and undertook successful campaigns to win the Pulitzer Prize for Browne and Halberstam. Sheehan, missing the coup, missed the prize.

☐

TWO DAYS AFTER the coup began, Lou Conein called the generals to say that Lodge was ready to receive them. Minh sent Don and Don's brother-in-law, Brigadier General Le Van Kim, telling them to explain to the ambassador that he was tied up in a conference with Tho, the vice president. On the way to the embassy, Don speculated about what Lodge would have to say. He thought that the junta would be asked to name as prime minister a strongly pro-American civilian named Dr. Phan Huy Quat. At least Conein had ordered a special plane to rush Quat back to Saigon from Can Tho in the Delta.

When the generals arrived, Lodge came out grinning to congratulate them on their success. He advised issuing a statement that would absolve the military from the murders of Diem and Nhu. Make it clear, Lodge said, that you offered them safe passage and that you deplore their unfortunate deaths but, after all, that's the kind of thing that can happen in a coup d'état. When his visitors agreed, Lodge asked if they had ideas for future relations between their two countries.

"Certainly," Don said, smiling, "and we would like to start getting milk and flour for free sale immediately. And, of course, the restoration of economic aid."

Trying to seem respectful of their independence, Lodge asked what kind of government they had in mind. But when they said they would probably name Tho as prime minister, Lodge could not restrain himself. Why not as president? Doing that would make the transition from Diem seem less abrupt.

No, "president" was to be held as a ceremonial title for Big Minh. The generals expected to continue their provisional government for at least six months while they wrote a new constitution. Certainly, the process wouldn't take more than two years.

Looking grave, Lodge asked, "Will you stay united and win the war?"

Yes, the generals nodded. They knew from bitter experience the costs of being divided.

THE COUP was three days old when Stanley Karnow met with Tran Kim Tuyen in Hong Kong. Tuyen had been a good source, but Karnow was wary of him, although he did sometimes repeat Tuyen's observation that Vietnam might be underdeveloped economically but was highly developed politically. Now Karnow urged Tuyen to return with him to Saigon. Tuyen was dubious; besides, the airport was still closed. But he agreed to go as far as Singapore with Karnow and twenty other foreign reporters. From there they might pick up more reliable information. On landing, Tuyen contacted the local CIA station chief and got from him Conein's list of the new ruling junta. Looking it over, Tuyen found no enemies and a number of officers for whom he had done favors. He saw no reason for any of them to hurt him. With Jackie now in her seventh month of pregnancy, Tuyen decided to take the risk.

After Tuyen's first night at home, Colonel Pham Ngoc Thao came to call the next morning. Despite Tuyen's reputation for collecting intelligence, he had not yet discovered Thao's ties to Hanoi. "Had I known in advance that you were coming," Thao said, "I'd have advised against it. Everything has gone wrong. If Minh had sent me to find Diem in Cholon, he and Nhu would still be alive. Now we have Minh, who is not a leader, and a lot of very biased men in the junta. It's too bad you came back."

Tuyen was away later that morning when soldiers appeared at his house to arrest him. Jackie tried to call him, but they had cut the telephone lines. When he returned, they took him to jail. Tuyen told himself, I know too much about the junta. I know about their corruption and the way they groveled before Nhu for so many years. They would like to kill me.

Instead, the generals tried Tuyen for corruption and abuse of power and sentenced him to five years in prison.

AT THE MORNING STAFF MEETING on November 4, Mac Bundy announced that the United States would recognize Saigon's military government within the next day or two. Bundy had been impressed by photographs of the citizens of Saigon throwing garlands of roses at ARVN tanks. The Kennedy administration was contemplating a military coup against the leftist president of Brazil, and Bundy joked that the generals of Latin America should learn to organize similar spontaneous shows of support. Bundy's analysts agreed that cutting off the commodity support program to Vietnam had been the decisive factor in moving Minh and the others to act. Bundy warned that photographs might soon appear showing Diem and Nhu in a pool of blood with their hands tied behind their backs. With his air of unflappable amusement, Bundy added that this was not the preferred way to commit suicide. He regretted that the coup leaders insisted on sticking to that story.

The following day, Ambassador Charles Bohlen called on de Gaulle in Paris and found that the French premier was also unperturbed about the deaths of Diem and Nhu. The Ngo brothers had never supported French interests in Vietnam, de Gaulle said. But he predicted that the junta would now press for increased assistance that Washington would find hard to refuse. Eventually, an increase in the fighting would make these Vietnamese generals as unpopular as Diem had been.

As de Gaulle was prophesying disaster, Rusk was assuring a closed session of the Senate Foreign Relations Committee that the new government in Saigon would be effective and largely civilian. He played down U.S. involvement in the coup, pointing out that the many rumors since 1960 had left him skeptical that an uprising would ever occur. Rusk did not share with the Fulbright committee the cable Lodge sent directly to Kennedy describing the American role—it was "certain that the ground in which the coup seed grew into a robust plant was prepared by us and that the coup would not have happened when it did without our preparation." Kennedy responded by thanking Lodge for a fine job and assuring him how much he looked forward to Lodge's visit to Washington when the two men could review the situation face-to-face.

FOR MCNAMARA AND TAYLOR, traveling to Honolulu for Vietnam briefings had become a routine shuttle, but Mac Bundy was not blasé. Events since the Hilsman telegram in August had convinced him that he must apply to Vietnam the brains that Kennedy valued so highly. Expecting rigorous days ahead, Bundy was grateful to be able to sleep on the plane and arrive in Hawaii rested and ready to reexamine Indochina policy. Mike Forrestal had warned him that past meetings had consisted of 100 observers in the commander's conference room watching the military briefers unveil "a dazzling display of maps and charts, punctuated with some impressive intellectual fireworks from Bob McNamara." Bundy asked whether there could be fewer briefings. Or did candid talk occur only during the private dinners? Forrestal said that McNamara had found one way to disrupt the military's agenda: when a briefer became mechanical and unpersuasive, McNamara loudly interrupted. But to be so openly rude was not Bundy's style. Chester "Chet" Cooper, on loan to the White House from the CIA, had observed the two men and concluded that Bundy's mind was a scalpel, McNamara's an ax.

A week earlier, Forrestal had called Robert Kleiman of the New York Times editorial board to complain about a Halberstam story that he thought denigrated Harkins. Forrestal claimed that the dispatch reflected the reporter's personal animus against the general, although Forrestal knew very well that Lodge held Harkins in the same low esteem. Kleiman took the opportunity to suggest that the White House reconvene the Geneva conference and negotiate a settlement to the war. He argued that the south would never be stronger than it was after the coup. Don't wait until another deterioration, which would lead to a ten-year war like the one in Malaya. Forrestal assured Kleiman that his idea was folly. At some point, South Vietnam would be able to approach the north as equals. Until that time, the South Vietnamese would consider another conference a sell-out.

A few days later, Forrestal might have sounded less convincing. Kennedy asked him to stay behind after a staff meeting and told him that Forrestal would be going with Bundy to Honolulu, then on to Cambodia. His mission was to soothe Prince Sihanouk, who had become alarmed by the coup next door. When Forrestal got back, Kennedy said, he was to start a complete review of the U.S. involvement in Vietnam and what could be done about it. "I even want to think about whether or not we should be there," Kennedy added. Meantime, his review must remain secret for one more year.

In Honolulu, Bundy saw that events in Vietnam might not accommodate the president's campaign timetable. Only a week earlier, Lodge had been pressing Diem to make political reforms. Now that the generals were in charge, Lodge was saying that the embassy should not insist on a democratic regime or even on early elections. Sounding like Nhu, Lodge said that Vietnam was not ready to change its government at the ballot box; he would count himself lucky if the generals could get through the next six months without a falling out. Don't push them too hard, Lodge repeated.

Harkins spoke, shedding his usual optimism and giving a bleak summary of government weakness in the Mekong Delta. The Vietcong were stronger than they had been a year earlier. When his turn came, Trueheart admitted that 70 percent of the strategic hamlets in the Delta were substandard. The embassy officials did agree to one change that would please Kennedy. Since he entered the White House, the president had been pressing for more guerrilla action in Cuba and in North Vietnam. The political benefits were obvious. Guerrillas were cheap and covert. If their raids did not always go undetected, they could always be denied. So far, the CIA had been in charge of the harassing missions in North Vietnam but—as Tuyen had learned years earlier—they were not working. Now, led by McNamara, the Pentagon was complaining that the CIA's use of a few agents in worn-out planes had guaranteed failure. Only the Defense Department could beef up the operation until Hanoi's leadership felt the pain.

Bill Colby, who had overseen those missions, knew their shortcomings. Even if agents survived in the North long enough to blow up railroad tracks, the enemy would have them repaired the next day. Colby broke in to say, "Mr. Secretary, it isn't gonna work. It's just not gonna work." But McNamara knew his president. He heard Colby out with impatient coldness and then transferred the program to his department and instructed the military to prepare a year-long campaign of graduated intensity against the North. Colby asked himself whether turning covert operations over to the Pentagon wasn't the first step toward direct U.S. action against the North.

But that was hardly Jack Kennedy's objective. His enthusiasm for sabotage in the North presumed that it would be carried out by the South Vietnamese. In speeches and press conferences, the president still defined his objective as maintaining an independent South Vietnam and fostering democracy there. But lately, Kennedy had begun listing as his very first goal the bringing home of American advisers. As for the 1,000-man troop reduction by December, Kennedy would meet that deadline only because of a slowdown in sending replacements to Vietnam. Max Taylor was not withdrawing entire units.

The Honolulu meeting broke up, leaving Bundy with a challenge as he headed back to Washington. The other participants had convinced him that the military appraisals, for once, had been realistic. How was he to reconcile their gloomy predictions with the past assurances that the South Vietnamese could cope on their own in little more than a year?

Bundy set aside that conundrum to concentrate on what to tell his staff, who would expect a pithy summation of his trip. Bundy decided to say that McNamara's briefings tended to be sessions in which people tried to fool him, and he tried to convince them that they could not.

☐

JOHN CONNALLY, the Texan appointed by McNamara as secretary of the navy after he rejected Franklin Roosevelt, Jr., had served less than two years before he resigned in 1962 to run successfully for the governorship of Texas. In Austin, Connally sided with the conservative Democrats who had been battling for a quarter of a century with liberals led by Senator Ralph Yarborough. Lyndon Johnson had managed to straddle the two factions, although the liberals suspected that his heart was with Connally. As the 1964 election approached and Kennedy's civil rights bill strained the party loyalty of white southern Democrats, the president could not afford a divided party in Texas. He agreed to a trip that he hoped would raise campaign funds and stitch together the two blocs, at least through his re-election. On November 20, Kennedy celebrated his brother Bobby's thirty-eighth birthday and flew the next morning to San Antonio.

The president's Texas hosts did not hide the depth of their antagonism for each other. Although Kennedy had brought Yarborough with him, Connally seemed intent on snubbing the senator, even to excluding him from a gala at the governor's mansion in Austin the night of Friday, November 22, that would mark the end of Kennedy's trip. Equally touchy, Yarborough refused to ride in the same open car with Johnson in motorcades through San Antonio and Houston. Kennedy saw how drastically the years as vice president had reduced Johnson's power in his home state, even if the breach could be papered over and the sniping kept from public view. Members of Kennedy's entourage remained nervous, however, about the third city he was to visit. Editorials in the *Dallas Morning News* constantly attacked the president, and during a recent speech in the city Adlai Stevenson had been spat upon and hit with a picket sign. Some of Kennedy's staff recommended canceling the Dallas engagement, but that would be admitting that the president was afraid of his own constituents.

The hostility that Kennedy expected in Dallas set him to musing. He told his wife and Kenny O'Donnell, "If anybody really wanted to shoot the President of the United States, it was not a very difficult job—all one had to do was get on a high building someday with a telescopic rifle, and there was nothing anybody could do to defend against it."

By 12:30 P.M., Central Standard Time, the presidential motorcade was winding through Dallas from the airport to the convention center. The president and Mrs. Kennedy were sharing their car with Governor and Mrs. Connally, who rode in the jump seats facing them. A Secret Service agent was driving the convertible with another agent seated beside him. Kennedy had forbidden agents to ride on the small running boards at the rear.

Nellie Connally gestured to the applauding crowds and raised her voice to say, "Mr. President, you can't say Dallas doesn't love you."

Kennedy said, "That is very obvious."

☐

THAT SAME FRIDAY AFTERNOON, Mac Bundy had gone to McNamara's conference room at the Pentagon to review the next defense budget. Kermit Gordon from the Budget Bureau was also on hand, along with Kennedy's science adviser, Jerome Wiesner. After the meeting, McNamara planned to fly to Hyannis Port with Max Taylor to meet with Kennedy when he returned from Texas. Taking his place at the end of the long table, McNamara sat with his back to his office door. Officials from Defense and Budget had begun their presentations when McNamara's military aide came through the door and tapped the Secretary's shoulder.

McNamara got up and disappeared into his office. A call from Bobby Kennedy was waiting. After hanging up, McNamara went back to the meeting and beckoned for Bundy and Ros Gilpatric to join him. His door closed again, and time passed as the other officials waited, mystified. Then Bundy returned with Gilpatric.

"I think we better share with the rest of you what has happened," Gilpatric said. "We have to report that the President has been shot. We are not sure how serious it is."

Bundy added, "Ken O'Donnell is with the President, and he hasn't given up hope."

"It looks very bad," Gilpatric said.

McNamara returned, fighting to control his emotions. Taking his seat, he began straightening papers, his usual signal for a session to resume. The scheduled presentations limped along for another forty-five minutes until Robert Kennedy called again to report that his brother was dead. Bundy said, "I think we better get over to the White House."

The meeting broke up in an air of disbelief. McNamara lent Bundy his Pentagon car and chauffeur, then went to locate Taylor and the Joint Chiefs. Before Jack Kennedy recalled him to active duty, Taylor had been hired to oversee construction of the Lincoln Center for the Performing Arts in Manhattan. During that civilian interlude, he had taken to napping every day after lunch. When he returned to the Pentagon, Taylor ordered his staff never to disturb him when his door was closed.

He had barely stretched out on his sofa when a general disobeyed him and called from the military command center to say that the president was dying. Taylor summoned the Chiefs to his office to discuss whether the murder was part of a plot to overthrow the U.S. government. Orders went to the nine ranking commanders around the world to raise their level of readiness.

Rusk had intended to fly from the Honolulu conference to a meeting in Japan, along with six members of Kennedy's cabinet. Instead, the captain brought him a wire service bulletin about the assassination. Rusk asked Pierre Salinger to call the White House for confirmation. Then Rusk announced Kennedy's death over the plane's loudspeaker. "We have a new president," Rusk said. He added, "God bless our new president and our nation."

For the next fifteen minutes, no one on the plane spoke. Turning back to land in Hawaii, the pilot found a full military alert and orders for him to fly non-stop to Washington.

AT THE WHITE HOUSE, Bundy had made the arrangements for Rusk's plane to return. That done, he paced the Oval Office, shocked and numb. Robert Kennedy had gone home to his family in Virginia; Ted Kennedy was in Hyannis Port. Bundy made a halfhearted attempt to collect Kennedy's papers. They belong to his heirs now, he told himself.

Ted Sorensen stopped by, looking for solace. "He had only three years," Sorensen said. "The president was my life."

Alone again, Bundy found himself sobbing as he had rarely done. Kennedy had been so much more alive than any of the rest of them, Bundy thought. Then, realizing that he would never be seeing him, Bundy cried again. At 6:30 P.M., a military aide came to fetch him for the helicopter ride to Andrews Air Force Base. Bundy would meet the plane that was bringing Kennedy's body, and the new president.

MCNAMARA ACCEPTED Robert Kennedy's invitation to drive with him to Andrews but begged off from joining Jackie Kennedy and the late president's aides in *Air Force One*. Instead, he waited while the Kennedy entourage left the plane with the coffin and while Johnson made an appeal to God and the nation for their help. Then McNamara cut through the crowd and took Johnson's hand in a prolonged clasp. After a hug for Lady Bird, McNamara guided them to a helicopter, where Bundy, Max Taylor and George Ball, standing in for Rusk, were waiting to return to the White House. Later that night, McNamara went out to Bethesda Naval Hospital to help Jackie make decisions: A closed coffin, given Kennedy's hideous wounds. Burial at Arlington Cemetery, rather than at the Kennedy family plot in Boston.

McNamara's instinctive response on the tarmac had been intended to reassure a new president who had few illusions about the feelings of his countrymen. Three years of boredom and frustration had left Johnson feeling useless, his belly ballooning as he ate and drank and picked at his wounds. Bobby Kennedy had been his worst tormenter. Every time I reached out to him, Johnson complained, he kicked me in the groin. Now the entire Kennedy family would be bathed in a nation's compassion, and Johnson had to rise above his past resentments to act as the country's first mourner. With outsize emotion, he appealed to all of the Kennedy appointees to remain in their jobs, not just during a transition period but as long as he was president. "I need you more than he did," Johnson kept repeating to cabinet officers and White House staff. He meant it. As a southerner distrusted by the country's Negroes, as a caricature of the backroom politician, as a graduate from a Texas teacher's college in a town awash with Ivy League alumni, Johnson had to prove himself worthy of the job he owed to an assassin's bullet.

Mac Bundy had always behaved correctly to the vice president, but his memo to Johnson concerning his first cabinet meeting reflected the degree to which Kennedy's men thought Johnson needed a hasty polish. "My own hunch," Bundy began, "is that this meeting should be very short. . . ." He reminded Johnson that many cabinet officers were "quite numb with personal grief" and urged that "in keeping with your own instinct of last night you will wish to avoid any suggestion of over-assertiveness." Bundy predicted that Rusk would offer the resignations of the entire body, Johnson would ask them to stay on and would solicit their suggestions for the speech he was planning before the joint Houses of Congress. "I think this is all there is to it," Bundy concluded briskly, "except for a few words about President Kennedy, and perhaps a moment of silence in his memory at the beginning or end of the meeting."

For the moment, Johnson accepted those patronizing cues and did as he was told. After the meeting, he went down to Bundy's suite. He had rarely visited there, except for briefings in the windowless Situation Room during the Cuban missile crisis. Bundy had arranged for a CIA report, and Johnson was relieved to hear that the world, rather than erupting at Kennedy's death, seemed to have been stilled by it.

Lodge had come back to Washington to meet with Kennedy. Instead, two days after the assassination, his reception from Johnson was scarcely congratulatory. Johnson had never approved of Lodge's enthusiasm for deposing Diem, but he had been restrained at whatever meetings he attended. When Kennedy went around the room soliciting opinions, Johnson had always hoped that he would not be the first to be called upon.

Lodge's audience with the president was restricted to the Vietnam insiders—Rusk, McNamara, Ball, Bundy and McCone. Lodge assured Johnson that his embassy had not been responsible in any way for the deaths of Diem and Nhu. The day before, Johnson had heeded Bundy's warning that he should rein in his assertiveness. But now he treated his new inner circle to a more typical performance, filled with sorrowful reproaches. He had never been happy with the U.S. operation in Vietnam, the president said, and strong voices in Congress were calling for us to get out altogether. A great many people throughout the country questioned the overthrow of Diem, and Johnson was not at all sure that Washington had taken the right course in unseating him. It had not been his decision, but it was a fait accompli. Now all that mattered was achieving the U.S. objectives.

Johnson warned Lodge that the bickering within the U.S. mission must end at once. As ambassador, Lodge was in complete charge, and Johnson would hold him personally responsible for creating harmony. When McNamara recommended that Washington give the junta members generous economic aid but

President
Lyndon Baines Johnson
(Yoichi R. Okamoto/LBJ Library Collection)

not ask that they do the impossible, Johnson spelled out his philosophy: We did not have to reform every Asian into our own image. He wanted less effort placed on so-called social reforms and more on winning the war. McCone listened, pleased that Johnson was unwilling to send Americans abroad as do-gooders.

After the advisers filed out, a Johnson aide named Bill Moyers came in to hear how the meeting had gone. Moyers, in his mid-twenties, had studied for the ministry before he was taken up as a surrogate son by the Johnsons, who had two teenage daughters. Moyers found the new president leaning back in his chair, feet propped on a wastepaper basket and clinking the ice cubes in a glass of Scotch. Moyers asked what the ambassador had to say.

Johnson mixed together the bleak assessments of Lodge and McCone and exaggerated both of them for maximum effect: "He said it's going to hell in a handbasket out there. He says the army won't fight. . . . Says the people don't know whose side to be on. If we don't do something, he says, it'll go under any day."

"So?"

Johnson regarded his glass. "So they'll think with Kennedy dead, we've lost heart. So they'll think we're yellow and we don't mean what we say."

Moyers asked who would think Johnson was yellow.

"The Chinese," Johnson said, with no irony. "The fellas in the Kremlin. They'll be taking the measure of us." Johnson had not been at the center of Kennedy's foreign policy, but he had seen the Soviet probing over Berlin and Cuba. "They'll be wondering just how far they can go."

"What are you going to do?"

"I'm going to give those fellas out there the money they want," Johnson said. "This crowd today says a hundred or so million will make the difference."

Johnson added that he had told them they would have more if they needed it. "I told them I'm not going to let Vietnam go the way of China. I told them to go back and tell those generals in Saigon that Lyndon Johnson intends to stay by our word. But, by God, I want them to get off their butts and get out in those jungles and whip hell out of some Communists. And I want them to leave me alone, because I've got some bigger things to do right here at home."

Moyers knew what those bigger things were—the Civil Rights Act, Medicare, the antipoverty program, pending bills that could transform America. Johnson would try to use Kennedy's murder to persuade Congress to pass the social legislation he cared about at least as much as his predecessor had. Ever since Roosevelt's New Deal, Democrats had been coining two-word slogans to sum up their vision. Kennedy had campaigned on the New Frontier, but it had died with him. Johnson would enter history by building the Great Society.

BUNDY HAD DRAFTED National Security Action Memorandum 273 for Kennedy after the Honolulu conference, but when Johnson reviewed it, he made one significant change. Much as Kennedy favored undercover raids against Hanoi, he had not wanted them undertaken by Americans. Bundy knew that and specified that a plan of guerrilla sabotage be drawn up for "Government of Vietnam resources." Johnson struck out that restriction.

As vice president, he had distrusted the official reports from Vietnam but did not blame McNamara or Harkins for them. Johnson believed that Diem's flunkies had given him the misinformation he desired and that the embassy had passed it along uncritically. McNamara would be heading to Europe for a NATO conference in early December, and Johnson told him to return by way of Saigon with a more accurate estimate of the war's progress. Barely two months before, McNamara had handed Kennedy a report that foresaw an American pullout by 1965. Now, with a new president's agenda to satisfy, McNamara was prepared to jettison his previous optimism.

He would not make his reversal public. Arriving in Saigon on December 19, McNamara gave reporters his routine expression of confidence in progress during the coming year. Meeting with Minh's junta, McNamara made no effort to ingratiate himself. General Don thought he stared at him coldly as they met again and avoided looking him in the eye. Puzzled, Don assumed that McNamara was still angry over the double murder of Diem and Nhu and did not know which officers to blame.

At the first of McNamara's two meetings, Don reviewed the war's status for an audience that included the Vietnamese generals and much of the American mission. The next day, the delegations were smaller—only McNamara, Lodge and the CIA's McCone, along with Big Minh, Prime Minister Tho, and Generals Don and Kim. McNamara looked the four Vietnamese over and asked abruptly, "Who's in charge here?"

His hosts responded with nervous smiles. Don expected Minh to say "I am." But that was not Minh's way. He looked to the others and said nothing. Don noticed McNamara's irritation. He knew the Americans were already dubious about Minh. Lodge had asked Don to prod Minh to act faster, or at the very least meet more often with Lodge. Don thought McNamara had decided that Minh's lethargy was infecting the rest of them. The defense secretary criticized Don and others for taking too many titles and, presumably, accomplishing too little. Don tried to explain that he was both defense minister and chief of the army only temporarily, but McNamara seemed to resent his explanation.

McNamara also urged Minh to make speeches that would rally the people. McCone chimed in to say how effectively Johnson had done just that in the days after Kennedy's assassination. The Vietnamese tried to make the Americans understand that their two peoples were very different. If Minh made too many speeches, he would be considered a dictator. Better to accomplish results, solve problems province by province and not talk too much. In time, Minh's government would be appreciated.

For this trip, spending two days in Vietnam was ample since McNamara already knew what Johnson wanted. In his report, he summed up the situation as "very disturbing. Unless the current trends were reversed in the next two or three months, they would lead to neutralization at best and more likely to a Communist-controlled state."

Assessing enemy strength, McNamara sounded curiously like Halberstam, who had lately returned to New York. "Vietcong progress has been great during the period since the coup, with my best guess being that the situation has in fact been deteriorating in the countryside since July to a far greater extent than we realized because of our undue dependence on distorted Vietnamese reporting."

McNamara estimated that the Vietcong currently controlled much of the population in key provinces, especially directly south and west of Saigon. He also confirmed Halberstam's account of friction between Lodge and Harkins but was inclined to blame the ambassador. "Lodge simply does not know how to conduct a coordinated administration," McNamara wrote, pointing out that Rusk, Mc-

Cone and he himself had spoken to the ambassador about that shortcoming. In a judicious aside, McNamara added that he didn't think Lodge was consciously rejecting their advice—"he has just operated as a loner all his life and cannot readily change now." Nor was McNamara reassuring about the generals who now led South Vietnam's government. "Indecisive and drifting," he called them, six weeks after the coup. Big Minh and his colleagues were not showing any talent for administration, although McNamara assured Johnson that he had spoken strongly to them about what they should be doing. He might have been even blunter if he had heard Minh tell journalists that he preferred tennis and cultivating orchids to presiding over the boring meetings of his fellow generals.

McNamara estimated that 1,000 to 1,500 North Vietnamese soldiers had entered South Vietnam through Laos during the first nine months of the year to bolster the Vietcong, and heavier weapons were coming in by way of the Mekong River. McNamara was ordering a U-2 spy plan to map the Lao and Cambodian borders so that plans could be laid for operations across them. But the infiltration—McNamara called it "serious and annoying"—was less damaging than the lethargy of the generals and the discord within the American embassy.

Perhaps he was overly pessimistic, McNamara concluded, but he advised the White House to "watch the situation very carefully, running scared, hoping for the best, but preparing for more forceful moves if the situation does not show early sign of improvement."

In the interim, Brute Krulak was drafting sabotage and propaganda campaigns against the North. He could expect a skeptical hearing in the Oval Office, since Johnson had little respect for the Chiefs even before the Bay of Pigs. As Senate majority leader, he had watched their predecessors come before the appropriations committees in squabbling disarray and admired McNamara's ability to bring them to heel. But Johnson knew that many of his southern colleagues held the Chiefs in great esteem and that leaks to reporters from a disgruntled Pentagon would give the Republicans damaging ammunition. For that reason, Johnson made a point of seeking out the Chiefs during a reception on his first Christmas Eve in the White House. "Just let me get elected," he joshed with them, "and then you can have your war."

ON JANUARY 2, Krulak submitted a list of proposals—including patrols called DeSoto missions—for U.S. destroyers in the Tonkin Gulf. The missions' goal would be to gather intelligence about Hanoi's infiltration of the South Vietnamese coast. The Navy had been carrying out such activities since 1950 against China, North Korea and the Soviet Union, using electronic intelligence ships to monitor enemy radar. The *Craig* was authorized to go within four nautical miles of the North Vietnamese mainland, carrying South Vietnamese commandos to harass radio broadcasting locations. American personnel would stay on board to measure frequencies and search out other targets. DeSoto patrols would begin in late February.

MORE EVEN THAN KENNEDY, President Johnson tended to regard American reporters as employees of his own public relations machine. He took anything faintly critical as a personal affront and was particularly galled by editorial cartoonists who pictured him wearing a string necktie; he swore he had never owned one in his life. And yet, as he went about trying to charm Washington's influential journalists, those people Kennedy had attracted so effortlessly, Johnson was inclined to play up his Texas folksiness. Early in December, he rang Walter Lippmann to ask, "Could I drop by and bum a drink from you?"

Lippmann, wholly at ease with men like Kennedy and Mac Bundy, was startled by Johnson's approach. "What's that?"

"Could I drop by and bum a drink off of you?"

When Lippmann graciously assented, the president then had to ask for his Cleveland Park address.

During that same media campaign, Johnson spoke with Katharine Graham, whose husband had died in a tormented suicide and left Mrs. Graham controlling the *Washington Post.* Johnson began, "I just hear that sweet voice on the telephone"—inflated gallantry meant more often to amuse than seduce—"and I would like to break out of here and be like one of those young animals down on my ranch, jump a fence."

Mrs. Graham laughed prettily and played along: "Now that's going to set me up for a month."

Johnson could expect those established Washington figures to respond to his new title. But he had one more target, and that man would never regard his title as legitimate. Bobby Kennedy was taking offense often in the days since his brother's murder. When Johnson moved into the Oval Office, Bobby considered him pushy, even after Johnson explained that McNamara had advised it. When Rusk and Adlai Stevenson made brief statements of support for the new president at the first cabinet meeting, Bobby, who arrived late, jeered that Johnson only valued toadies. When Johnson scheduled his address to the Congress for the Tuesday after the assassination, Bobby complained that it would follow too closely upon his brother's funeral and got Bundy to move the speech back a day. When Johnson said, "I need you more than the President ever needed you," Bobby took his appeal for insincere hokum.

Despite the tension between them, Johnson considered it vital that Kennedy stay on as attorney general through the 1964 election, but he was receiving no assurances. After his second week in office, Johnson asked Clark Clifford to call on Bobby and get him to divulge his plans. Later that evening, Clifford reported that he and Kennedy had spent two hours together, and he could give Johnson the answer he needed: "He's going to stay."

PART TWO

Vo Nguyen Giap
and
Lyndon B. Johnson

SIX

KHANH
1964

IN LATE JANUARY 1964, Major General Nguyen Khanh passed along a disturbing rumor to Colonel Jasper Wilson, the Hue region's senior U.S. adviser. Khanh claimed that another coup was being planned, this time by generals who favored joining with the North in a neutralist coalition. Among the plotters Khanh accused were Big Minh, Tran Van Don and Le Van Kim. Surely the United States would not accept neutrality for South Vietnam?

As his answer, Wilson quoted Cabot Lodge's recent statement opposing that solution. Wilson's reply had the effect of Hilsman's August 24 telegram—Khanh was satisfied that he could expect U.S. backing. He would do his duty, travel the next day to Saigon, and thwart the traitors.

If Khanh succeeded, the North Vietnamese would have to reassess their policy for the second time in six weeks. The Communist Party's Ninth Plenum had ended a debate in December over the impact of Diem's assassination, agreeing finally with Le Duan that Hanoi must now support an all-out offensive by their General Nguyen Chi Thanh in the South. Thanh must unseat the Saigon government before Washington could decide to intervene even more aggressively. Although it was important to topple Minh quickly, the North would not be sending its own troops at this time. The Vietcong must do the job or interest the Saigon junta in a neutralist solution. But while Hanoi had authorized overtures to the ARVN leadership, Khanh was wrong. Minh's junta had rejected them.

All the same, Khanh's suspicions struck a nerve with Lodge. The ambassador had just criticized de Gaulle for publicly proposing neutrality for all of In-

Premier and Major General
Nguyen Khanh
(AP/Wide World Photos)

dochina and for his willingness to recognize Communist China. Lodge passed along Khanh's rumors to Washington—that Kim and Don, as former French officers, were "rabidly pro-French," that Big Minh had bought a house in France. Lodge's own instincts told him that Don and Kim were patriots, but Khanh's reputation as a shrewd observer gave him pause. In his cable, Lodge noted that he hardly knew Khanh but had been told that he was the ablest commander in South Vietnam.

To obey Johnson's ban on feuding within the U.S. mission, Lodge promised to share Khanh's information with Harkins and Peer De Silva, who had replaced Richardson as CIA station chief. Before the assassinations, Kennedy had been offended by the attacks on Harkins and extended his tour to avoid any appearance that he was coming home because of pressure from the embassy or the *New York Times*. But early in January, Bundy had sent an eyes-only memo to Johnson that began, "I do not know anyone, except perhaps Max Taylor, in the top circle of government who believes that General Harkins is the right man for the war in Vietnam now."

Bundy's indictment repeated Halberstam's criticism in language even less temperate: Harkins had been "unimpressive in his reporting and analyzing, and has shown a lack of grip on the realities of the situation." Bundy added that he was not trusted by the new Vietnamese regime. All that was protecting Harkins's job was a good past record and antagonism from the press and Lodge and Hilsman. "In the Pentagon," Bundy wrote, "Lodge and Hilsman are dirty words, so the defensive reaction is fierce."

Bundy reported that McNamara was engaged in a long-range scheme to ease Harkins out over Max Taylor's opposition. He planned to appoint William Westmoreland as Harkins's deputy, break the news gradually to Taylor and promote Westmoreland several months later. But Bundy wanted faster action. The case was "much too important to be decided by Bob McNamara's reluctance to offend Max Taylor." Bundy explained to Johnson that he had raised his objections with McNamara and could do it again, more forcefully. "But he has much more direct experience of Vietnam than I, and I doubt if my words can be decisive. You, on the other hand," Bundy assured the president, "can give him a direct order to do what in his heart he knows he should. He is a soldier."

Bundy's clumsy attempt to circumvent McNamara showed how little he knew the president he had been serving for the past six weeks. To Johnson, Bundy—Yale and Harvard, inherited money, social standing—would always be suspect as a Kennedy man. McNamara—Harvard, to be sure, but only the Business School, wealthy by his own hand, California by way of Detroit—was more congenial. And McNamara was the more adroit courtier, quicker at deducing Johnson's inclinations, smoother at advancing the president's ideas as his own.

THE CIA'S SKETCHY DOSSIER on Nguyen Khanh was no help to Lodge in assessing the man. Son of a wealthy planter, Khanh at thirty-six was a 1947 graduate of the Dalat Military Academy. He had then trained in French airborne and infantry schools and, in 1957, at the Command and General Staff College, Fort Leavenworth, Kansas.

As early as 1954, Khanh had supported coups against Diem but had been restored to favor when Big Minh appointed him deputy commander in Hue. Tuyen's agents had investigated Khanh after captured documents seemed to link him with Communist intelligence. Like many Vietnamese, including Big Minh, Khanh did have family ties to northern Communists, but Tuyen pronounced the evidence against him inconclusive. Later, transferred to Can Tho south of Saigon, Khanh had ingratiated himself with Diem by supporting him against the 1960 coup attempt.

After the successful coup in November, Khanh was posted again to Hue. What the CIA report did not observe—although his fellow generals did—was Khanh's resentment at not being better rewarded. The agency missed other colorful details: Khanh had been raised in Saigon by his father's mistress, a Vietnamese actress, which may have explained his penchant for theatrics. At sixteen, Khanh had joined the Vietminh, then switched to the French when he saw a grander stage for his ambitions. General Don considered Khanh slippery and self-serving and had distrusted him since his role in preserving Diem in 1960. During the planning of the past November, Khanh had been informed of the generals' timetable only the day before they launched their coup.

Another quirk in Khanh's personality might have alerted Lodge to his current intentions: Whenever he was on the verge of a new undertaking, Khanh grew a goatee. Now, flying south in civilian clothes, Khanh sported a smudge of hair on his receding chin. David Nes, a State Department officer recently assigned to the embassy, read reports coming from Hue and guessed why Khanh was headed for Saigon. But when Lodge left for his residence that afternoon, he told Nes that—coup or no coup—he was not to be disturbed until 8 A.M. the next morning.

Khanh's fellow conspirator, the Saigon commander General Tran Thien Khiem, matched Lodge's indifference. Khanh slipped away from Jasper Wilson in Saigon, claiming a dental appointment but going instead to a friend's house. He waited there until early on the morning of January 30, when he expected to lead a band of paratroopers that would occupy the general staff headquarters. At the same moment, Khiem would surround the houses of the ruling junta. Each of them was to move at 4 A.M.

The hour came and went with no sign of Khiem. Khanh called him. "Oh," Khiem said, "I must have forgotten to set my alarm, and I overslept." He assured Khanh that despite the delay there would be no problem.

IT WAS STILL before dawn when an aide warned Tran Van Don that members of the Vietnamese Civil Guard were trying to break into Don's house. Don't fire on them, Don said. He got up, washed, dressed and called Kim, who said that his house was also ringed with troops. No one seemed to know who was commanding them since the minister of the interior denied all knowledge. Big Minh speculated that it was a few junior officers being ridiculous. The matter could all be settled at headquarters, Minh said.

A few minutes later, however, a car came for Don and he was ordered inside. As he was being driven past Minh's residence, he saw that it, too, was surrounded. At airborne brigade headquarters, several of Don's colleagues were led in and told to wait with him. Finally, a colonel announced that Khanh would be arriving in a few minutes. Instead, the generals were taken under guard to My Khe beach, near the port of Danang.

The sea air was cold. Since Don and the others had brought no warm clothes, their guards bought sweaters for them. Night came, but Don could not sleep. He kept thinking that only three months ago he and his cabal had been deciding Diem's fate. Tonight, Khanh held that same power over Don and his fellow generals. Khanh could have them all killed and, as it turned out, was weighing that option.

One of Khanh's first acts had been to send a man to shoot Major Nguyen Van Nhung, promoted recently from captain for his role in murdering Diem and Nhu. Aside from his family, the brutal Nhung went unmourned. But did his execution suggest that Khanh would once again favor Diem's Catholic clique? Tri Quang canceled a planned pilgrimage to India and went instead to Hue to prepare for a new resistance.

LODGE'S REPORT about coup rumors in Saigon had barely reached Washington before Khanh took the generals into custody. Rusk wired back instructions to make sure the world knew that the United States had not supported this new coup. And if Big Minh could be kept as a figurehead, Rusk thought that he seemed the best bet for rallying the people. Minh, however, would agree to that role only if Khanh released his fellow generals, which Khanh refused to do. After two days, Joe Mendenhall at State recommended that Rusk stress two arguments in Khanh's favor: he would be more efficient than Big Minh's generals, and he was adamant against neutralism.

Lodge met with Khanh to inform him that he would rise or fall in American opinion—in other words, Johnson's estimation—by how quickly he moved against the Vietcong. No more rhetoric. No more reorganization. Results. Khanh agreed emphatically and asked that Lodge recommend a prime minister. He also wanted Lodge to pick up the financial losses if Khanh attacked neutralization by severing relations with France. Lodge reminded him that there were 450 French schoolteachers in South Vietnam and that during the last ten days alone French doctors had given a million free cholera shots. Hasty action would be imprudent.

At about that time, President Johnson was conferring with McNamara over the confusion Khanh had sown. McNamara had no suggestion except to make the South Vietnamese military more aggressive. At Johnson's news conference the next day, he announced that Khanh would be stepping up the military pace against the Vietcong. To questions about neutralization, the president spelled out his differences with de Gaulle: "If we could have neutralization of both North Vietnam and South Vietnam, I am sure that would be considered sympathetically."

But Hanoi would not renounce Communism. A spokesman there explained that since there were no foreigners in the North the question of neutrality did not apply to them. De Gaulle's proposal concerned only the South.

Over the next few days, Washington sent Khanh more detailed directives: He should see that farmers got a good price for their rice. At the same time, he should carry out land reform. He should revitalize the amnesty program for repentant Vietcong. His government should include those same Hoa Hao and Cao Dai sects that Diem had once suppressed. Most importantly—certainly to Don and his confined fellow generals—Khanh "should treat deposed members of preceding government humanely in order to preserve his international image."

Lodge wanted to believe that Khanh's action had been more than a crude power grab. As a lifelong politician, he drew a comforting comparison: Often the men who managed a successful American primary campaign were not the same ones suited to handling the runoff, and they in turn would not be the ones to hold elective office. Big Minh's generals may have cleared out the dry rot of the Diem regime, but now a new man must win the war. General William Westmoreland, not yet announced as Harkins's successor, had arrived in the country. Touring the Delta, he looked for disaffection among the ARVN officers there and found none.

LYNDON JOHNSON was facing disturbing prospects a mere nine months before the election that would make his presidency legitimate. De Silva's CIA office now predicted that if Khanh faltered, the next government was likely to negotiate the neutrality that Johnson wanted to avoid. The president met with Mike Mansfield, who called de Gaulle's approach "a faint glimmer of hope." Since Johnson felt differently, however, Mansfield agreed to put Democratic Party unity above his misgivings and not speak out publicly again about Vietnam. Johnson had another Senate ally in Fulbright of Arkansas, who also ruled out a negotiated settlement. Fulbright saw only two choices — continuing to support Saigon or invading the North with U.S. troops.

By March, determined that Khanh succeed, Johnson recalled his own round of handshaking in Saigon and decided that an old-fashioned stumping tour would boost Khanh's popularity. To show how it was done, the president proposed to send over his secretary of defense. "Bob," Johnson said as he briefed McNamara before he left, "I want to see about a thousand pictures of you with General Khanh, smiling and waving your arms and showing the people out there that this country is behind Khanh all the way."

McNamara was game. In the first heady days of Kennedy parties, he had practiced in front of a mirror to master a new dance called the Twist. Now he would bring that same diligence to his attempts at stem-winding oratory. Flying with Khanh from the Delta to Hue, McNamara assured the Vietnamese at every stop that their new leader had America's full backing.

From his Vietcong headquarters hidden near the village of Binh Gia in Quang Ngai province, Colonel Kham heard with mixed feelings about the spectacle McNamara was making of himself. The Vietcong were trying to prove that the struggle was unwinnable and persuade Washington to withdraw. But McNamara's blatant commitment to another coup master suggested that the United States was going to be difficult to dislodge. On the other hand, the photographs of McNamara looming over General Khanh made the Communists' anti-Diem slogan of past years even more effective. Now the people must rise up and overthrow the My-Khanh clique.

General Curtis E. LeMay, General Maxwell D. Taylor, and
General Earle G. Wheeler *(© Hulton Getty/Liaison Agency)*

Tran Van Don and the generals still under house arrest in Dalat credited
McNamara for their one bright moment in the weeks since Khanh rounded
them up. By radio, they had listened to McNamara arrive at Tan Son Nhut and
shout the rousing endorsement Johnson was demanding from him. "You have
the best possible leader in General Nguyen Khanh," McNamara assured the
general's loyalists at the airport. "Long live Vietnam!"

McNamara had been coached to proclaim that last phrase in Vietnamese,
much as Jack Kennedy had once practiced phonetically to dazzle the Germans
with "Ich bin ein Berliner." But Mac Bundy, who had drilled Kennedy, spoke no
Vietnamese, and in any case its intonations were elusive for a Westerner. With a
show of unmistakable sincerity, McNamara had shouted, "Vietnam, go to sleep!"
Don and the others laughed every time they thought about it.

McNAMARA CAME BACK to Washington unconvinced that his magnetism alone
would sustain Khanh in office. He had seen blank faces in every village—mask-
ing indifference or hostility—and was not sure that Khanh could control the
army. David Nes, Lodge's Saigon aide, prepared a report for the ambassador of
unrelieved gloom, the most optimistic note being that, if the Vietcong could be
deprived of all outside support, they might wither away in five to ten years.

The Joint Chiefs were pushing to take the war secretly across the borders of

Cambodia and Laos while launching air attacks against the North. Walt Rostow, who had moved to State as chairman of policy planning, agreed. To "make it somewhat easier to keep Mao out of the act," Rostow recommended that U.S. planes provide high cover while South Vietnamese aircraft did the actual bombing of selected northern targets. Rostow proposed starting with a radio station at Vinh, but he warned that Washington would have to be prepared for escalation.

The Pentagon had prepared a top-secret schedule for a day-by-day countdown until the first air strike was launched against Hanoi, probably in late June. The plan included a stipulation that bombing would start only after Congress had pledged its support. Meantime, peace talks must be staved off until Hanoi had a good taste of America's military might. Bombing, at least initially, would be done by South Vietnamese planes, not Farmgate or other U.S. aircraft. The Pentagon planners intended to launch what they called "D-Day" by mining North Vietnamese ports and bombing bridges and trains in order to keep men and supplies out of the South. They would then step up bombings against targets that had "maximum psychological effect on the North's unwillingness to stop the insurgency." Those targets would include petroleum storage tanks, airfields, barracks and training areas, ports and communication sites.

Pressure to act was bearing down on Johnson, not only from within his own administration but from the Republicans. At Dirksen's suggestion, Johnson invited to the White House a group of ranking Republicans, including Bourke Hickenlooper, an Iowa conservative who used the forum to urge a hard line against the North. As Johnson summarized the session the next day, "Hickenlooper said they had to stand and show some force and put our men in there and let come what may, and no one disagreed with him."

BY PHONE, Johnson spoke with Robert Kennedy about his Vietnam dilemma, agreeing readily with every suggestion Kennedy made for keeping the focus on the political struggle. "I think that's good thinking," the president said, "and that's not any different from the way I have felt about it." The United States had to come up with "some diplomatic programs and political programs, Johnson said, "instead of just sending out twenty extra planes." He also welcomed Kennedy's suggestion for an emergency council on Vietnam and invited him to be a member.

"I'd be glad to," Kennedy said. "I'd be glad to."

"I just think it's the hottest thing we've got on our hands," Johnson said, "and the most politically dangerous."

For all their attempts at good will, conversation between them was never going to be easy. Kennedy faltered as he tried to explain that he never wanted to push himself on Johnson. In turn, the president was all hearty reassurance. "You're even needed more than you were," he concluded. "They're never gonna separate us as far as I'm concerned."

Bobby murmured, "Thank you."

And if any of Johnson's people ever tried to create a rift, Johnson added, "Why, I'll get rid of any one of 'em if we can put the finger on it."

Two weeks later, reporting on the meeting about Vietnam, Kennedy warned the president against trying to get a congressional resolution of support for the war. "It seems likely," Kennedy said, "that they'll start asking somebody to spell out exactly what's going to happen if you—we—drop bombs there, and then they retaliate, until we eventually bomb Hanoi, and all that kind of business, and the answers to those questions are so difficult to give, particularly if you're giving them to a lot of people that are antagonistic."

Johnson asked his attorney general whether he could declare war by executive order. Kennedy admitted that he had not looked into the question, but he guessed that, constitutionally, approval by Congress was not essential.

JOHNSON NEXT CALLED Senator Richard Russell of Georgia for a long bout of commiseration. "Oh, I've got lots of trouble," the president began. "What do you think about this Vietnam thing?"

"It's the damned worst mess I ever saw." Russell sounded even more dejected than Johnson. "I don't see how we're ever getting out without fighting a major war with the Chinese and all of them down there in those rice paddies and jungles. I just don't see it. I just don't know what to do."

"Well," said Johnson, "that's the way I've been feeling for six months."

If the Chinese entered the war, Russell said, the United States would be doing them a favor by killing their excess coolies. He was both chairman of the Senate Armed Services Committee and one of the Senate's staunchest segregationists. He doubted that the American people were ready to send in U.S. troops. So if it came down to a choice, he would get out—preferably by installing a new leader in Saigon who would ask the Americans to leave.

Johnson did not pursue that approach. "How important is it to us?" he asked.

"Not important a damned bit."

Johnson raised the issue of SEATO obligations. Russell reminded him, "We're the only ones paying attention to it." Other than keeping America's word or saving face, he added, no one would expect the United States to be the only one of fourteen signatories to stay in.

The previous day McNamara had been to Capitol Hill, and Russell had been troubled by his testimony. "I'm not sure he's as objective as he ought to be in surveying the conditions out there." McNamara might be a can-do guy, "but I'm not sure he understands the history and background of those people out there as surely as he should."

Russell, in fact, sounded wary about all of Johnson's advisers. "You'd better get some brains from somewhere to apply to this thing. I don't know what to do with it."

"Well, I spend all my days with Rusk and McNamara and Harriman and Vance and all those folks that are dealing with it, and I would say it pretty well adds up to them now that we've got to show some power and some force and that they do not believe—they're kind of MacArthur in Korea—they don't believe that the Chinese Communists will come into this thing. But they don't know. Nobody can really be sure. But their feeling is that they won't. And, in any event, we don't have much choice, that we're treaty-bound and we're there, that this will be a domino that will kick off a whole lot of others, that we've got to prepare for the worst."

Johnson said he had avoided heeding that advice because he doubted that the American public would support him. "I don't think the people of the country know much about Vietnam, and I think they care a hell of a lot less," he said.

Recent Gallup poll results bore him out. Sixty-three percent—almost two-thirds of those interviewed—said they were paying little or no attention to the fighting in Vietnam. Another survey indicated that a quarter of the public had not even heard that fighting was under way. The small fraction of the people who knew much about Vietnam thought the president should take stronger action.

Johnson observed that he had already been catching hell because 35 Americans had been killed in Vietnam so far in 1964. Russell pointed out that more than that number had died from automobile accidents in Atlanta.

Just the same, Johnson complained, the Republicans were making Vietnam a political issue.

"It's the only issue they've got," Russell said contentedly.

Counting noses, Johnson had found only three senators who wanted the United States to pull out—Mansfield, Wayne Morse of Oregon and Ernest Gruening of Alaska. Russell warned him that young Frank Church of Idaho should be added to the list, although Church was not going to make his sentiments public.

Russell tried again to tell Johnson that his advisers were too firmly committed to expanding the war, but the president defended them. "Rusk has tried to pull back, tried to hold back on everything," Johnson said. "But he's about come to the conclusion that Laos is crumbling, Vietnam is wobbly—"

"Laos, Laos, Laos," Russell broke in scornfully. "Hell, it ain't worth a damn." Some Vietnamese would actually fight, Russell said, but Laos was just a rathole.

Johnson's complaints about Cabot Lodge set off an indignant exchange of stories about Lodge's arrogance and ineffectiveness. In a cable five days earlier, Lodge had suggested that the advisory phase of the war may have come to an end and that the time was approaching for the United States to take over the fighting. Lodge speculated that South Vietnam might need a U.S. high commissioner, someone who really gave the orders.

"He thinks he's dealing with barbarian tribes out there," Russell said angrily. "And he's the emperor and he's just going to tell them what to do. There's no doubt in my mind that he had ol' Diem killed out there."

"That was a tragic mistake," Johnson said, "and we've lost every—" Russell, too worked up to be polite, broke in: "He was going to get someone more pliant to Lodge, who'd do exactly what he said, right quick. He's living up on Cloud Nine. It's a bad mistake. I don't know. I think perhaps the best thing you could do would be to ask Lodge if he don't think it's about time that he was comin' home."

"Well," said Johnson glumly, "he'd be back home campaigning against us on this issue every day."

Exactly, Russell said. So why not recall him now. That way, voters would dismiss his criticism as retribution for being fired. It had worked for Truman against MacArthur.

Johnson seemed intrigued by Russell's suggestion that he recruit an outsider—someone "not scared to death of McNamara"—to visit Vietnam and smell the air, get the atmosphere. Someone with no prejudgments. The natural choice would be a distinguished general from World War II. Russell offered the name of Omar Bradley and assured the president that Bradley was "not in his dotage by a hell of a lot." On the other hand, Bradley might be too humble. Johnson asked about Lucius Clay, and Russell said he would accept Clay's judgment. He commanded a lot of respect, had no predilections about Asia and would stand up to Lodge. All the same, Russell added, he was sick at heart about the choices. "It's a tragic situation. It's just one of those places where you can't win. Everything you do is wrong."

Johnson read him Mansfield's latest memorandum, making disparaging asides about each recommendation. Johnson considered Mansfield a Milquetoast with no spine, and he snorted when he reached the proposal for an international conference. "Conferences ain't going to do a damn bit of good," the president said.

In that, at least, the Politburo's leadership agreed with him. After the disastrous results of 1954, Le Duan was resisting another international meeting.

"They ain't going to take back and give us the territory and behave," Johnson said. "We tell 'em every week, we tell Khrushchev, and we send China and Hanoi and all of 'em word that we'll get out of there and stay out of there if they'll just quit raiding their neighbors, and they just say, 'Screw ya.' "

"That's right," Russell said.

The conversation was becoming circular. Russell said the American people could understand going in—sending troops, punishing Hanoi with bombs—but that would lead to war with China, and America would be worse off than it was now. And, truthfully, why should the Russians help out Washington? "We keep pouring money in and not even getting good will in return."

A month before, McNamara had demonstrated why Russell thought he was no longer objective about the war. At a Pentagon news conference, a reporter asked for his response to Senator Morse calling it "McNamara's War." McNamara had noted that the war was being waged by the U.S. government in accordance with the president's policy. But he didn't object to it being named for him. "I think it is a very important war, and I am pleased to be identified with it and do whatever I can to win it."

Now Russell came back to his misgivings: "McNamara is the smartest fella any of us know. But he's got so much—he's opinionated as hell—and he's made up his mind. I don't think—"

Johnson would not hear it. "I think he's a pretty flexible fellow." After all, on his latest trip to Saigon, McNamara had talked Khanh out of any adventurism in the North until his own government was more stable.

McNamara was also holding at bay the commandant of the Marine Corps, Wallace Greene, and Air Force Chief LeMay. Since March, Greene had protested against what he called half-measures in the South, and LeMay had pressed for attacking Vietcong sanctuaries in Cambodia and supply lines in Laos. At the CIA, McCone was ignoring a thousand years of Vietnamese hostility and recommending that Khanh ask Chiang Kai-shek to send two or three Taiwanese divisions to the southern tip of the Mekong Delta. Roger Hilsman, although aware that he had no future in Johnson's regime, suggested that Washington prove its commitment to Southeast Asia by stationing U.S. troops in Thailand.

Johnson told Russell that McNamara's idea was to buy time that would get the president past his November elections. "But these politicians got to raising hell, and Scripps-Howard writing these stories, and all the Senators, and Nixon, Rockefeller and Goldwater—let's move, let's go in the North—" And now, Johnson added, his own advisers were recommending bombing selective targets in North Vietnam—an oil plant or refinery and supply points on the Ho Chi Minh Trail.

"Aw, hell," Russell said. "That's not worth a hoot." He and Johnson traded stories from Korea when LeMay's Air Force had bombed heavily with a spectacular lack of results. Russell told of American pilots dropping shells worth $7 million to collapse an entire mountain onto the tracks of a North Korean railroad. The next morning, reconnaissance flights showed the trains running smoothly. We controlled the sea and the air in Korea, Russell concluded, "and we never did stop 'em. Not going to stop these people, either."

"Well," Johnson said hopelessly, "they'd impeach a president that runs out, wouldn't they? Outside of Morse, everybody says you've got to go in."

They both agreed that Nguyen Khanh, with his ferocious rhetoric about taking the war north, was not the man to solve their problem. Khanh would not follow the script, Russell said, and announce, "You damn Yankees, get out. I'm running this government now."

Johnson protested. "Wouldn't that pretty well fix us in the eyes of the world? Make us look mighty bad?"

"Well, I don't know." Russell permitted himself a dry chuckle. "We don't look too good right now."

☐

AFTER THAT DASH of cold realism, Johnson needed reassurance from his staff. Mac Bundy called soon afterward, and Johnson complained to him about staying awake all night, worrying that Vietnam was becoming another Korea. "I just don't think it's worth fighting for, and I don't think we can get out. It's just the biggest damn mess." Johnson spoke about his personal aide in the White House, an army sergeant with six small children. He said he kept that man's face in mind whenever he heard talk of sending U.S. troops. How could he justify asking a man like that to make the sacrifice of going to Vietnam?

Bundy was not attuned to Johnson's pauses. He took a momentary silence as an invitation to respond, but Johnson had not finished and overrode him. " 'Course, you start runnin' from the Communists, they just might chase you into your own kitchen." The Communists wanted to be seen as unbeatable—"that's what that half of the world is going to think if this thing comes apart on us."

The prospect of widening the war drained the energy from Johnson's voice. "But this is a terrible thing we're getting ready to do—"

In contrast, Bundy's reply came in clipped, metallic tones. "Mr. President, I just think it's the *only* big decision, in one sense. This is the one we have a need to reach up and get it, or we let it go by. And I'm not telling you today what I'd do in your position; I just think the most we have to do is pray with this another while."

Johnson raised Russell's suggestion of a fresh evaluation. Bundy shot down each name. Bradley? "No good." Clay? "Wouldn't add anything." Johnson asked what Bundy's brother was advising. Bill favored "touching things up," Bundy said, and Forrestal was "ready to move a little bit." Mac Bundy himself did not expect much from air attacks against the North. They would be "more to galvanize action against the center of this infection." Bundy's feeling was that they needed to study the proposed targets more closely. "The main object is to kill as few people as possible," Bundy said, "while creating an environment in which the incentive to react is as low as possible. But I can't say to you that this is a small matter."

Bundy then lofted a proposal of his own. What if the president announced that only volunteers would go to Vietnam, men enthusiastic about combating the Vietcong terror. He granted that the Joint Chiefs would oppose the idea, however, and Johnson let it die. He knew that Bundy had seen Walter Lippmann lately and asked for the columnist's views. Bundy explained that Lippmann favored a diplomatic approach, although it would lead to eventual control of South Vietnam by Hanoi. At least, it would give the United States time to walk away.

Taken aback, Johnson pressed for details, but Bundy begged off. He wasn't the one to expand on Lippmann's thinking, he said, because he didn't agree with it. He did know that Lippmann had been talking to George Ball. Johnson had an inspiration. How about getting Lippmann to the White House? That very day. "I'd like to hear McNamara and Lippmann debate it."

Bundy agreed to set up an appointment for 4 P.M. that afternoon and signed off, as he often did, with a chipper, "Aye, aye, sir."

JOHNSON'S COURTING of Washington's journalism establishment had reaped high returns in favorable coverage. After Bundy and his wife spent a weekend at Kay Graham's estate, Bundy could report to Johnson that, although the *Washington Post* never made a formal endorsement for president, Mrs. Graham had said that if anyone at the White House could not tell whom the *Post* was for, "then it must be because we can't read."

Until now, Lippmann had proved equally obliging. Just three days earlier, his column had scolded former aides of Jack Kennedy—whom he did not name—for attempting to usurp Johnson's choice of a running mate in the 1964 election. He urged Robert Kennedy to repudiate that effort by men who hoped to advance themselves by restoring a Kennedy to the White House. "What John F. Kennedy started," Lippmann wrote, "will be measured in the cold calculus of history, not by his intentions but by the outcome. The outcome is now the business of the Johnson Administration."

Lippmann did not restrict his defense of the president to his columns. Making his customary spring tour of Europe earlier in the month, he encountered a guest at a Parisian dinner party who mocked Johnson's backwoods manners. Lippmann surprised the table with his heated rebuttal, and the host tried to soothe him by remarking, "Isn't it true he's called Ol' Corn Pone?"

"Not by me," said Lippmann sternly.

Lawrence O'Brien was certainly no part of the cabal that Lippmann saw pushing Robert Kennedy for the 1964 ticket. As Johnson's chief congressional liaison, O'Brien checked in often from Capitol Hill, relishing his job far more these days than when he worked for Jack Kennedy. O'Brien and Johnson could talk in political shorthand and were equally skilled in projecting how a subcommittee might vote. While Kennedy had preferred to immerse himself in foreign policy, Johnson was fuming regularly about all the ambassadors and other overseas visitors Mac Bundy kept running through the Oval Office. But Johnson had unlimited time for calling a congressman if O'Brien thought the man was wavering on the Civil Rights bill.

Under duress, Kennedy had supported the most comprehensive rights legislation since the end of the Civil War. New laws would open up to Negroes the nation's restaurants, movie theaters and every public accommodation. They would end discrimination in hiring and commit the federal government to integrating the nation's colleges. Johnson could listen without protesting when an unreconstructed friend like Dick Russell assailed Negroes in ugly terms, and Johnson himself could lapse into segregationist language when it suited his listeners. But Johnson's heart was in the Civil Rights bill. If, to get it past his southern cronies, he had to say from time to time that "President Kennedy is watching from heaven," it was corn pone in the service of a heartfelt commitment.

Johnson would get the Civil Rights bill passed, however, not as a tribute to Jack Kennedy but as a guarantee that East Coast liberals could never again deny his presidential stature. He would pass his ambitious program, run for president on a ticket without Robert Kennedy and sweep to victory on his own merits. A simmering war in Vietnam must not derail that agenda.

That was why Lippmann's potential defection to de Gaulle's position was disturbing, and Bundy could have warned Johnson that the discussion was likely to get acrimonious. Just back from Europe, Lippmann had called on Bundy the previous week and had taken instant offense when Bundy greeted him by asking abruptly, "Well, what's the French plan? I can't seem to find out, and you presumably know what it is, so tell me."

Lippmann replied that he did not answer questions put to him in that tone of voice and that, in any case, Bundy did not seem in a mood to listen to an explanation. From the time Lippmann first raised Bundy's name with Jack Kennedy, he had hoped to see him one day as secretary of state. But now Lippmann was wondering whether Bundy's years in the White House hadn't coarsened his approach to issues.

After Bundy made an apology of sorts, the two men calmed down. But Bundy kept harking back to de Gaulle's call for neutralization and finding fault with it. When he described the plan as no more than a way to deliver South Vietnam to the Communists, Lippmann chided him. "Mac, please don't talk in such clichés." He spoke of Marshal Tito, the Yugoslav who was a nationalist first, Communist second. That was the best the United States could hope for in Vietnam, Lippmann said. The next day, he wrote a column supporting de Gaulle's position: Let the United States go on backing Saigon while pressing both North Vietnam and China for neutrality. Otherwise, the Johnson administration had "no credible policy for winning the war or ending it."

On this afternoon, Lippmann would be coming back to the White House so that McNamara could set him straight. When he arrived, he found not only the defense secretary but also Bundy and George Ball, sitting in for Rusk. If Johnson's goal was to neutralize Lippmann, his strategy worked. They argued for two-and-a-half hours, with Johnson insisting on a guarantee that South Vietnam would not fall to Ho and Lippmann admitting that there might be no such guarantee but no alternative, either.

Reporting back to Rusk, Ball said the session had not converted Johnson to Lippmann's view, but at least it seemed to slow down his willingness to adopt the Pentagon's scenario. Ball hoped another meeting could be devoted to examining the assumptions of America's Vietnam policy rather than simply to ratifying an escalation there. Since Johnson had agreed to send Ball to consult with de Gaulle in Paris, Lippmann could be pardoned for leaving the White

House convinced that the president was at least considering a negotiated settlement.

WHILE BALL PREPARED for his trip, the administration was priming another emissary. J. Blair Seaborn, the Canadian member of the ICC inspection team, was going to Hanoi at Washington's request, and Bill Sullivan had prepared an ambitious agenda for him: Seaborn was to explore any split between the Soviets and the Chinese and to estimate the degree of war weariness in the North. He was also to identify the opposing factions within the Politburo. That done, Seaborn should warn the Hanoi leadership that Washington's patience was wearing thin and remind them of America's vast military resources for punishing the North. Not surprisingly, after all of that, the North Vietnamese took Seaborn as a crude apologist for the United States—possibly even a spy—and ignored his message.

The Politburo did worry that Johnson was determined to expand the war. But its members, isolated and inexperienced on the international stage, had not prepared a plausible alternative. They had discussed neutralizing the South but still had not drafted a position. The Communists would have been surprised to hear Johnson's stewing aloud about being dragged into a broader war. He also fretted that he had no formal approval from Congress for the escalation that its members seemed to be favoring. Johnson quoted Arthur Vandenberg, the Michigan Republican who had led the bipartisan foreign policy consensus for Truman. "If you want us on the landing," Vandenberg had said, "we sure as hell better be in on the takeoff."

To put Congress firmly on the record, Bill Bundy at State drafted a resolution that could be introduced at an appropriate time. Blaming the hostilities on North Vietnam, with Chinese assistance, it concluded, "Now, therefore, be it resolved by the Senate and House of Representatives of the United States in Congress assembled: That the United States regards the preservation of the independence and integrity of the nations of South Vietnam and Laos as vital to its national interest and to world peace."

The resolution would pledge backing for the president if he sent U.S. troops to protect either South Vietnam or Laos. It also authorized spending a certain amount—the totals were left blank for 1964 and 1965—to pursue those objectives. And it stipulated that more money could be authorized as needed.

THE DAY AFTER Lippmann's command appearance at the White House, Khanh convened a special tribunal at Dalat to decide the fate of Generals Don, Mai Huu Xuan, Le Van Kim and Ton That Dinh. Big Minh was being loosely held under house arrest in Saigon, but since he was still serving as chief of state, he flew up to join the judges. For reasons Don did not understand, the proceedings began at 1 A.M., with Khanh presiding. As Don looked around the room, he saw childhood friends and his fellow conspirators in the coup against Diem. The irony of being forced to face them as a prisoner was a bitter one.

The generals were interrogated separately for five-and-a-half hours. None of the questions involved the original charge of promoting neutralism. Instead, Khanh seemed to be building some sort of exoneration for himself, demanding details about the coup against Diem that most men in the room already knew. Khanh even questioned the generals' decision to reunite Madame Nhu with her children.

The court deliberated for more than nine hours. When the defendants were brought back for the verdict, Khanh phrased it obliquely. We ask, he said, that once you begin to serve again in the army, you not take revenge on anybody. With that, the tribunal's members gathered around the four defendants to congratulate them. But although their full liberty was restored, the hearing had not ended in acquittal. The four were found guilty of lax morality, insufficient qualification for command and "lack of a clear political concept." They were suspended from commanding troops for various terms — Kim for six years, Don for eighteen months. Minh said he would have offices set up for them in Saigon so that they could work on research and planning until the ban was lifted. In the meantime, he advised them to remain in Dalat.

In Saigon, Bill Kohlmann watched with dismay the name-calling and finger-pointing that Khanh had set off. Hardly better than McCarthyism, Kohlmann thought, with any political enemy smeared as being a "pro-French neutralist." Kohlmann did not detect much French influence anywhere in the country and considered the crude attacks on the four generals as pro-Communist to be sheer nonsense. Kohlmann granted that General Don was Frenchified, a smart dresser and, with his good looks and smooth manner, probably a womanizer, but Kohlmann had no doubts about Don's loyalty to South Vietnam's cause. He saw signs, though, that some American colleagues had succumbed to the prevailing hysteria. One CIA man believed rumors that Kohlmann's friend, Tran Quang Thuan, was a double agent for the French. Annoyed, Kohlmann heard out the accusations that Thuan was meeting regularly with a French officer from the Sûreté.

"I don't believe the reports, but all right—put a tail on him." Kohlmann intended that tired cliché to convey his weary disbelief. After a period of surveillance, the evidence was in. Thuan and the Frenchman could not be conspiring since they had never met.

The incident showed how widely CIA officers differed in their approach to the Vietnamese. A few wanted full-fledged agents with their signature on a payroll contract. Other Americans believed with Kohlmann that it was more effective to pick sympathetic Vietnamese and contribute to their favorite publications or political factions.

Kohlmann had no illusions that dribs and drabs of money, a few hundred dollars here and there, bought either loyalty or obedience. Using Thuan as his contact, Kohlmann was now sending small amounts to Tri Quang at the pagoda for the monk to use in his public causes. But should American policy again outrage the Buddhists, Kohlmann knew they would take to the barricades once more. Around the CIA, there were labels for the Vietnamese assets—witting collaborators, paid witting collaborators, even unwitting collaborators. Money alone motivated a few of them. For the others, patriotism and anti-Communism were more dependable levers.

WITH JOHNSON'S BLANK CHECK not yet endorsed by Congress, McNamara flew to Honolulu to meet with William Westmoreland, who was succeeding Harkins at last as COMUSMACV—Commander of the U.S. Military Assistance Command, Vietnam. Two days after the Dalat interrogation, Khanh sent instructions that the four generals were not to return to Saigon without his explicit permission. While they waited, Khanh went off to join the Americans in Honolulu.

Westmoreland was withholding final judgment on Khanh, but for now he saw him as cocky, young and short. Given Westmoreland's own unbending presence—McNamara considered him a casting director's dream of a general, all ramrod posture and craggy good looks—he had looked on sympathetically when the defense secretary forced himself to embrace Khanh during their campaigning together. But Khanh, despite his bold words, seemed to be worrying more about his own safety than about pursuing the war. He had devised an escape route in case he was threatened by either the Vietcong or his fellow officers—down the Saigon river by boat to the beach resort of Vung Tau and by plane from there to France. One night, the arrival of a shipment of U.S. tanks triggered Khanh's alarm system, and he prepared to evacuate. Khanh's wife tripped on the way to the boat and bruised herself severely. Khanh himself disappeared. Late the next day, he was traced to Vung Tau. Westmoreland went there in person to assure him it was safe to return to Saigon.

But in Honolulu, Khanh claimed to have the full support of the South's generals. Adroit at belittling his opponents, Khanh told Lodge in strictest confidence that when Diem was killed he had been holding a briefcase containing 1 million U.S. dollars. Realizing belatedly how bulky that sum would have been, Khanh added that the money had been "in the largest denominations." According to Khanh, Big Minh had confiscated the briefcase and never turned it over to the government. At the same time, Khanh added, Minh had pocketed 40 kilograms of gold bars. Lodge cautioned Khanh against making the story public. It would only shake civilian faith in all generals. Khanh said he hoped that Big Minh would go quietly.

Before he left Hawaii, Westmoreland bowed to election-year realities and agreed that air attacks against North Vietnam could be deferred, even though a recent Special National Intelligence Estimate suggested that the bombing might

General
William C. Westmoreland
(AP/Wide World Photos)

cause Hanoi to reduce its support for the Vietcong. McNamara could return to Washington with the recommendation his president wanted.

Mac Bundy had sounded out his friend Ray Cline at the CIA to ask—in strictest confidence—whether the South Vietnamese could hold out through the November elections, and Cline had not said they couldn't. At the Capitol, Fulbright argued against bringing Bill Bundy's resolution to the Senate. "It would create a kind of war fever on the Hill," Fulbright said. Johnson worried that the delay might cause him problems later, and he told his aides what he, as Senate majority leader, would have done to a president who tried to slip a war past him. But the Republican candidate looked certain to be the bellicose Barry Goldwater, and the Civil Rights bill was still in committee. Better to wait. Looking on from the sidelines, Jim Thomson cracked that Johnson had spent the first three months learning to be president and would now spend the next nine months running for the office.

WITH HIS CIVIL RIGHTS legislation overcoming the southern resistance in Congress, two other intertwined problems faced the president: rejecting Robert Kennedy as his vice presidential running mate and settling on an alternative. Describing the perfect candidate, Johnson drew on a favorite castration image. "Whoever he is, I want his pecker in my pocket." The president often added his definition of loyalty: a man who would kiss Johnson's ass—sometimes he specified in Macy's window at high noon—and announce that it smelled like a rose.

If possible, Johnson preferred a running mate with the Kennedy aura but not the name. He dangled the job in front of McNamara, who was coming to understand the layers of cunning and guile to his new boss. To accept Johnson's highly tentative offer would be to betray political ambitions, and from that day forward McNamara would become an object of suspicion. Then, too, no matter how pleased Johnson might claim to be by McNamara's accepting, he might easily withdraw the offer the next day.

Sargent Shriver, a Catholic from Illinois and a Kennedy brother-in-law, would have effectively blocked Robert Kennedy. But the Kennedy family vetoed the idea, and it fell to Kenny O'Donnell to tell the president that if he wanted a Catholic running mate he should take the obvious choice and not an in-law. That was not going to happen. Johnson was saying about Robert Kennedy, "I don't need that little runt to win." In private, Kennedy returned the invective. Johnson was "mean, bitter, vicious—an animal in many ways."

Johnson turned next to Hubert Humphrey, and most of his advisers favored the Minnesota senator, although Johnson worried that Humphrey's ebullience caused him to talk too much. And if Humphrey were anointed too early, the Democratic convention in late August would be short on suspense. Johnson kept his choice to himself, bothered that he was leaving an ambiguity for Robert Kennedy and his circle to exploit.

Meantime, Lodge's growing involvement in Republican politics meant that Johnson would soon have to name a new ambassador. On June 18, Lodge wired Rusk that he must return home to campaign for William Scranton, a moderate Pennsylvania Republican. Otherwise, Lodge wrote, his party's leadership might fall into hands that were "imprudent and impulsive." Lodge quoted Rusk's words back at him: "I remember well your saying here how vital it is that both major parties nominate men who could be trusted with the atomic bomb." Lodge recommended that his deputy, Alex Johnson, replace him.

Expecting the resignation, the president had already begun a whirl of calls and consultation. Bundy, McNamara and Robert Kennedy all volunteered for the job. When Scotty Reston endorsed Kennedy, Johnson was immediately on the phone, explaining that he wanted to avoid the suspicion that he was somehow banishing Kennedy. Plus, there was the physical danger involved. And, Johnson added guardedly, "Bobby's a very controversial man in this country."

IT WAS MAC BUNDY's bad timing to call with his own candidate as ambassador not long after Johnson had exploded at the head of the Secret Service over newspaper leaks about an upcoming Johnson trip to New York. The president had scarcely finished his scolding when Bundy came on the line to propose that Johnson send to Saigon McNamara's former deputy secretary of defense. Roswell Gilpatric had been caught in the crossfire between General Dynamics and Boeing over contracts for the TFX aircraft. Although he had not been charged with wrongdoing, Gilpatric had left the Pentagon the previous January, replaced by Cyrus Vance. With his unquenchable self-confidence, Bundy said, "I think you will find at lunch tomorrow that everybody—Dean, Bob and I—all think your best bet is, in fact, Gilpatric. And that maybe he's—"

Johnson cut in. "No doubt," he said laconically. "I couldn't name him at all. I can't name Gilpatric."

Bundy was stunned. "You're sure of that, Mr. President?"

"Yeah. Yeah. I'm not going to name him."

"Well, then, we have to go back to the boards," Bundy said, trying to recover from Johnson's finality. "We had assumed that whatever might have been his political troubles before, any man losing a very fat and fancy practice for the most dangerous job in government would get more cheers than groans."

For Johnson, the issue was closed. "I'm pretty confident it's going to be Taylor."

Having been swatted down so unexpectedly, Bundy was cautious. "Rusk and McNamara think that would be a mistake."

But naming Gilpatric would be hari-kari, Johnson replied. Political suicide.

"Well," said Bundy, with more candor than their relationship usually allowed, "I'm astonished at your decision." Unwisely, he began to catalog his objections to Max Taylor. The general was too old and physically weary. He had a bum heart, or at least had experienced a warning. Bundy seemed to forget that he was talking to a man less than six years younger than Taylor who had survived a far more serious heart attack.

Johnson said firmly, "I just have a feeling that the people of this country have more confidence in Taylor out there than any man who's going to be available to us that I have heard of." He observed that the public didn't consider Taylor an aggressive warrior like LeMay. But putting Taylor in Saigon would show that Washington meant business. Johnson would be having dinner that night with Fulbright and would sound him out about Taylor.

Bundy said tartly, "Then it's going to leak."

He had invoked the one word to give Johnson pause. When the president pressed for details, however, Bundy backed down. "He'd keep his mouth shut for you. For the length of time you need."

With that opening, Bundy tried to resurrect Gilpatric, and then returned forcefully to his objections about Taylor.

"On the real merit, I would say this is a tired man with an uncertain health problem, and I myself do not believe that, in fact, he has ever understood that war. I think this is just the painful truth."

"Well," said Johnson indulgently, "it's a good place for him to get to understand it, then."

"Mr. President, men of sixty-two and a half who are tired are not an easy bet for that. I think what you're getting is great protection and no harm." Getting nowhere, Bundy tried a small joke: perhaps his advisers should consider the president himself for the assignment.

If Johnson was amused, he concealed the fact. Life in Saigon would be less stressful than Taylor's constant round of international conferences, Johnson said, citing his own experience with flights to Los Angeles that left him fatigued and constipated. "I believe he'll be easier there," Johnson concluded, "than fighting LeMay."

THE NEXT MORNING, Johnson called the Pentagon. When he told McNamara that he wanted to give every possible consideration to Taylor, the defense secretary agreed immediately. "I would lean to Max on this issue," McNamara said. "I think Mac leans to Ros."

"He does, very much," Johnson said, "and he says that he thinks you and Rusk do."

"No," McNamara assured him. "I lean to Max with one qualification—his health." McNamara segued into emotional praise for Taylor as a patriot and concern that the general not give his life for his country. He was still in that rhetorical mood when Johnson mused again about being pushed out of Southeast Asia.

"I don't believe we *can* be pushed out," McNamara said stoutly. "We just can't allow it. You wouldn't want to go down in history as—"

Johnson would not let him finish that unthinkable phrase. "How are we going to avoid it?"

McNamara had the answer: "By continuing to show some signs of firmness."

AS ONE SUCH DISPLAY of firmness, Johnson had signed National Security Action Memorandum 288, authorizing South Vietnamese troops to cross into Laos for operations along the border. Johnson also wanted to entice other countries to aid Saigon militarily, although the Pentagon was cool to the idea. The allied command in Korea had struck the Joint Chiefs as too much trouble for too limited results. Max Taylor, in accepting the ambassadorship, shared that resistance, but a Gallup poll showed that 58 percent of the American people wanted to see a United Nations army coping with Southeast Asia.

Late in June, the president asked Rusk to provide a legal basis for sending U.S. troops to Vietnam. As his answer, Rusk invoked that same SEATO treaty he had deplored when Foster Dulles won Senate approval for it. Rusk brought up SEATO again that week during an evening visit with Hervé Alphand, the French ambassador. Rusk pressed Alphand for the French definition of neutrality—

would it apply to both halves of Vietnam? It should, of course, Alphand replied. But first apply it to South Vietnam. He reminded Rusk of de Gaulle's approach to his Algerian problem: embrace a negotiated settlement; work out the details later.

Rusk wanted Alphand to understand the depth of Washington's commitment. The United States was a Pacific power as well as an Atlantic one, Rusk explained. "To us, the defense of South Vietnam has the same significance as the defense of Berlin."

Alphand found the comparison outlandish. "The stakes in Europe are enormous," he protested. "The loss of Berlin would shake the foundations of Western security. On the other hand, if we were to lose South Vietnam, we would not be losing much." Rusk said that it was all part of the same struggle—to prevent an extension of Communist influence.

At the *New York Times*, the fact that Johnson was exploring his authority to send troops would have puzzled Scotty Reston, since the president had recently assured him, "We won't abandon Saigon, and we don't intend to send in U.S. troops." In his campaigning, Johnson was giving the electorate that same assurance. He would not call on American boys to fight a war that Vietnamese boys must fight for themselves.

DENYING ROBERT KENNEDY second place on the Democratic ticket required a face-to-face meeting. On July 27, Johnson brought Kennedy to the White House and predicted that he had a great role to play in their party. Perhaps Kennedy would manage Johnson's campaign as he had run his brother's? Declining that sop, Kennedy said regretfully, "I could have helped you, Mr. President."

Johnson knew better. Democratic liberals already backed him because Congress was likely to enact his ambitious domestic agenda. But a Harris poll showed that 33 percent of southern Democrats would not vote for a ticket with Robert Kennedy's name on it. His zeal as attorney general in protecting civil rights demonstrators had made his name anathema in white Dixie.

The forty-five-minute talk in the Oval Office might have ended the matter on a subdued but not entirely sour note except for the question of how to announce Johnson's decision. The president wanted Kennedy to withdraw his candidacy and, after he had gone, told Bundy to convey his wishes. Kennedy replied he would not try to overturn Johnson's decision, but felt no need to make it easier for him. "A large part of the reason I was at all interested in the Vice Presidency was because of the interest of others," Kennedy said. "If I suddenly withdraw my name without discussing it with them, it would be impossible for them to understand."

Bundy pressed the point. Kennedy resented him as a turncoat and became more determined not to oblige Johnson. As the story of Johnson's decision spread throughout the capital, he had to make some sort of statement and called back to

Robert F. Kennedy *(AP/Wide World Photos)*

the Oval Office Clark Clifford, who had drawn up the talking points Johnson had used in facing Kennedy. Johnson explained his problem: he had to dump Kennedy without appearing to do it.

Clifford said, "Why don't you reach a policy decision that, after careful consideration, you've decided that you're not going to select anyone from your cabinet?"

Johnson thought it over. "That's pretty thin, isn't it?"

"Well, it *is* pretty thin, but it's a lot better than nothing."

The announcement was made to reporters and columnists, who were primed to explain to their readers Johnson's real motive. Kennedy sent telegrams to the other cabinet officers—including McNamara, Rusk and Adlai Stevenson: "Sorry I took so many of you nice fellows over the side with me." That wire was also methodically leaked. Relieved that he had "that damned albatross" off his neck, Johnson began to treat the matter lightly. Inviting three political reporters to lunch at the White House, he described the confrontation, mimicking what he called Kennedy's funny voice and claiming that his Adam's apple had bounced up and down like a yo-yo. Almost immediately Kennedy heard about that performance and taxed Johnson with it. The president denied the whole story. "He tells so many lies," Kennedy wrote in an angry memorandum to himself, "that he convinces himself after a while he's telling the truth. He just doesn't recognize truth or falsehood."

ON THE SUNDAY MORNING of August 2, 1964, Thomas Hughes, the State Department's director of intelligence and research, was among the aides who called on the president with puzzling news. Six or seven hours earlier, North Vietnamese high-speed patrol boats had fired torpedoes at an American destroyer, the USS *Maddox*, as it moved along the North Vietnamese coastline in the Gulf of Tonkin. The *Maddox* had fired back, joined by aircraft from the USS *Ticonderoga*, which was stationed nearby. Two North Vietnamese PT boats had been damaged as they retreated. A third was left dead in the water.

Hughes had taken the news to Rusk's house at 5:30 A.M., soon joined there by Ball, Cy Vance and Earle Wheeler, the new chairman of the Joint Chiefs. The Bundy brothers were away for the weekend, but a couple of CIA analysts had been summoned. The group pored over maps, trying to make sense of the attack. Everyone knew about the stepped-up DeSoto patrols against the North that Johnson had authorized the past December in Plan 34A, but they did not connect them to the *Maddox*.

When they convened in the Cabinet Room at the White House, the president was also incredulous. Why would the North Vietnamese risk a confrontation they were bound to lose? He was reminded about the DeSoto patrols and that Air Vice Marshal Nguyen Cao Ky had been boasting to reporters in Saigon that his planes had dropped combat troops into North Vietnam for sabotage. In the early hours of July 31, an OPLAN 34A harassing raid had been launched against Hon Me and Hon Nieu, two islands off the North's coast. Perhaps the Communists had concluded that the *Maddox* was part of that operation.

After five minutes, Johnson broke off the discussion. He compared what had happened to a man sitting with a girl in a movie theater and moving his hand slowly up her leg until she turned and slapped him. Johnson knew the arguments for and against retaliation and did not want to debate them now. To underscore how unflappable he was, he made an absurd change of subject. Turning to Wheeler, he said: "General, you are my chief strategic adviser. If you saw that postal pay bill marching down Pennsylvania Avenue, how would you handle it?"

As Wheeler stumbled and fumbled, the other men in the room relaxed and enjoyed his discomfort. If the president was so little troubled, the nation was not confronted by a momentous decision.

"The bill is already passing Eleventh Street," Johnson went on ragging Wheeler. "Come on, General, I need your advice."

Johnson's lack of concern over Tonkin seemed matched in the Politburo.

Max Taylor had wired from the Saigon embassy, asking to be allowed to tell Nguyen Khanh about the attack before Hanoi broadcast what Taylor assumed would be a "falsified version." But Radio Hanoi was silent.

Washington's instant communication and rigid chain of command made it impossible for the Americans to fathom what had happened in the Gulf. The Politburo had recently come to several conclusions: Taylor's appointment as ambassador was proof that Washington was preparing to widen the war. Since Westmoreland was already on the scene, why send another general—rather than someone like Harriman—unless an expanded war was in the offing? With that in mind, Hanoi found the patrolling of its shores by American warships particularly sinister. As part of a preventative policy, the Politburo approved its navy's right to attack, and Giap had instructed ship captains to guard against foreign vessels violating North Vietnamese waters. If an emergency arose, commanders were to use their own discretion.

On August 2, the result had turned out badly. The attack on a U.S. ship was deplorable. Although Giap would not reprimand the men responsible, he would give orders to ensure that the provocation was not repeated.

BEFORE THE ATTACK, the *Maddox* had been restricted to eight nautical miles from North Vietnam and fifteen miles from China's coast. At a press conference on Monday, the president announced that the U.S. patrols would continue and that any attacking Communist ship would not only be turned back but destroyed. He did not reveal that he had just pushed back the limits for the patrols to eleven miles from the North Vietnamese mainland. The Pentagon was not protesting that restriction because, even from eleven miles at sea, the 5-inch guns of its destroyers could reach beyond the coastline.

In Saigon, Taylor drafted an aggrieved cable about Johnson's mild response. "Such an attitude would immediately be construed in Saigon as indication that U.S. flinches from direct confrontation with North Vietnamese," Taylor wrote.

Monday afternoon, Mac Bundy called Rusk to discuss a small White House meeting set for early that evening to review the rules of engagement. Since aides would not be included, Bundy asked Rusk to bring along any documents that would help them in drafting an answer to Taylor. Rusk reported that Khanh was already "kicking up, saying we should retaliate," but Bundy predicted that the entire affair would soon pass.

He seemed to be right. The only flap over the Tonkin Gulf arose when Hubert Humphrey spoke on television about the covert OPLAN 34A raids and was as candid as Ky about their purpose. The raids, hardly a secret to the North Vietnamese, were still undisclosed to the American public, and Johnson was furious at Humphrey's indiscretion: "The damned fool just ought to keep his goddamned big mouth shut, at least until reelection is over." Johnson warned one of Humphrey's friends that he could be talking himself out of the vice presidential nomination. "He just yak yak yak yak," Johnson complained. "Just dancing around with the bald head."

But for the next twelve hours, the crisis seemed over. Then, at 7:40 A.M. on August 4, the *Maddox* reported an imminent attack by unidentified vessels. About 9 A.M., McNamara and Wheeler got copies of that message. Following Johnson's directive from the previous day, fighter aircraft from the *Ticonderoga* were launched to protect the *Maddox* and another destroyer, the *Turner Joy*. While McNamara was reading the first message, the *Maddox* reported that the unidentified ships had now disappeared from its radar screen. A few minutes later, McNamara called the president to say that the *Maddox* was on alert again, and then he convened three Pentagon staff members and his deputy, Cy Vance. They began studying possible targets for retaliatory air strikes—PT boats and bases, petroleum storage tanks, but also airfields, bridges and factories. It was approaching midnight in Vietnam—twelve hours ahead of Washington time—when Lieutenant General David Burchinal told McNamara that retaliation could begin at dawn. McNamara reported to Johnson that he was preparing options that would include a set of one-time targets—PT boats or bridges—as well as such long-term tactics as the mining of major ports along North Vietnam's coastline.

Before noon, McNamara called Rusk with news that Admiral Ulysses Grant Sharp in the Pacific said the destroyer was under torpedo attack and that the Pentagon was working on retaliation. Meetings continued throughout the afternoon, although James Stockdale, a pilot from the nearby *Ticonderoga*, had flown over the two destroyers that day and seen no sign of North Vietnamese boats. But Admiral Sharp in Honolulu was not polling the pilots on the scene.

At 1:27 P.M., Captain John Herrick, the DeSoto patrol commander on board the *Maddox*, sent a flash message to Sharp and to Washington: "Review of action makes many reported contacts and torpedoes fired appear doubtful. Freak weather effects on radar and overeager sonar men may have accounted for many reports. No actual visual sighting by *Maddox*. Suggest complete evaluation before any further action taken."

But Johnson, although running on a peace platform, had seen the advantage to a stinging slap if it could be presented as a limited response. Accepting the Republican nomination for president in San Francisco, Goldwater had accused McNamara of misleading the American people on Vietnam and Johnson of refusing even to say "whether or not the objective over there is victory." An air strike against the North would prove Goldwater wrong about the weakness of the president's policy. And a fresh Communist attack on August 4 could also provide the opportunity to present the congressional resolution Bill Bundy had drafted. There was yet another plus: Talking with Larry O'Brien, Johnson weighed the effect on his antipoverty bill of "bombing the hell out of the Vietnamese." Johnson hoped the crisis would make congressmen more reluctant to vote against him on domestic legislation. He planned to meet with leaders from the Hill later in the afternoon and get them committed to his policy before the first bombs fell.

Once again, the military chain of command gave the president what he wanted to hear. After a call from McNamara, Admiral Sharp reached General Burchinal to say that, whatever Herrick might be reporting, Sharp had no doubt that the second attack had occurred. That exchange took place at 2:08 P.M. Forty minutes later, Herrick sent a second message: "Certain that the original ambush was bona fide."

At a National Security Council meeting that afternoon, Rusk reacted with the same wound-up excitement he had brought to the crisis over Cuban missiles. He said that as an indication of Hanoi's intentions, this second attack was more serious than the first one.

Johnson asked whether the North Vietnamese wanted a war, and the CIA's McCone got the answer half-right. No, he said, they were responding out of pride and defending against U.S. attacks on their off-shore islands. But he went on to say that they were raising the ante.

Carl Rowan's information agency would have to justify the retaliation, and he asked whether the administration knew for a fact that the North Vietnamese provocation had taken place. Rowan said the administration had to be prepared for charges that Washington had fabricated the incident. McNamara replied that they would know definitely in the morning. But that would be after U.S. planes had already bombed in the North. Meantime, Rusk suggested asking the congressional leaders whether the White House should finally seek a resolution of support for the war. When McNamara called for another DeSoto patrol to show that the United States could not be intimidated, the others seemed to agree with him until George Ball broke the silence: "Mr. President, I urge you not to make that decision. Suppose one of the destroyers is sunk with several hundred men aboard. Inevitably, there'll be a Congressional investigation. What would your defense be?"

Since planes and small ships could carry out the DeSoto missions with far less risk, Ball said, the evidence would indicate that Johnson had used American boys as decoys. "Just think what Congress and the press would do with that!" They would say that Johnson had thrown away lives just to have an excuse to bomb the North.

Ball ended with an emotional appeal: "Mr. President, you couldn't live with that."

As silence lengthened in the room, Johnson seemed torn. Then he said to McNamara, "We won't go ahead with it, Bob. Let's put it on the shelf."

At 6:07 P.M., McNamara released his final authorization for a strike of 64 sorties launched from U.S. aircraft carriers against four North Vietnamese PT boat bases and a petroleum storage area. At 6:45 P.M., unaware that McNamara had already given the order, eighteen congressmen from both parties arrived at the White House in a somber mood. Johnson greeted them with a dramatic plea for secrecy.

"It is dangerous to have the leaders come here," the president began. "The reporters see they are coming and they go back and report all over the Hill. Some of our boys are floating around in the water. The facts we would like to present to you are to be held in the closest confidence and are to be kept in this room until announced."

Charles Halleck, a Republican unintimidated by Johnson, bristled at the lecture. "I did not tell a damn person," he said.

"I know no one did," said Johnson unconvincingly, "but it is on both tickers anyway. We have to be very careful."

McNamara briefed the group on the second attack, and Rusk warned that it should not be seen as an accident.

Russell of Georgia, who had been fretting to Johnson less than three months earlier about Vietnam as quicksand, now argued that giving up the right to sail through the Tonkin Gulf would psychologically affect U.S. prestige in Hanoi's eyes and mislead the Communists about what steps Washington was willing to take.

Rusk said, "We are trying to get across two points—one, leave your neighbor alone and, two, if you don't we will have to get busy." He added that Hanoi's radio broadcasts were highly inaccurate because they had been denying the second attack. "They have not talked about what did happen but what did not happen," Rusk said.

Some congressmen worried about the reaction of the Chinese. McNamara predicted that there would be no reprisal. And he assured them that the bombers from two carriers would supply enough airpower to do the job in the North.

Hickenlooper, the Iowa Republican, said he was opposed to quarreling for weeks over whether Johnson had authority for the strikes. The president must have the right to send the armed forces into action. Johnson, at his most statesmanlike, agreed but assured them that he needed their advice. If he did offer forth a resolution asking for their support, it would be very damaging not to get it passed.

Mike Mansfield had not been swept up in the prevailing war fever, and he tried to distinguish between the negotiations with Russia over Cuba and the current crisis. You may be getting involved with a minor third-rate state, he warned Johnson. The Communists won't be faced down, and it would take a lot of lives to mow them down.

The president asked Mansfield for a formula apart from what the Joint Chiefs were recommending. Call the attacks isolated acts of terror, Mansfield suggested, and involve the United Nations.

Rusk said that would not be practical, and Johnson returned to the congressional resolution: "I have told you what I want from you."

Fulbright said, "I will support it." And George Aiken from Vermont said, "By the time you send it up, there won't be anything for us to do but support you."

JOHNSON INTENDED to inform the American people of his air strikes against the North but could not risk the lives of the pilots by making a premature announcement. Awaiting word from Admiral Sharp, Johnson watched irritably as television's prime evening hours slipped away. It was 11:30 P.M. before Sharp called McNamara to say that the *Ticonderoga*'s planes had been launched at 10:43 P.M., Washington time. It would take almost two hours for them to reach their targets. Seeing Johnson's impatience, McNamara assured him that once the planes had left the carrier, he could make his announcement. The North Vietnamese would get the news simultaneously but would not know which targets were being attacked.

Johnson continued to fret. "I'd sure as hell hate to have some mother say, 'You announced it and my boy got killed.' "

McNamara soothed his jitters. "I don't think there's much danger of that, Mr. President."

Unwilling to see his address slip past midnight on the East Coast, Johnson went on television and radio from the White House at 11:36 P.M., with news that the air action was underway.

"Aggression by terror against the peaceful villages of South Vietnam has now been joined by open aggression on the high seas against the United States of America," Johnson said. Although he was a gifted mimic, he had never mastered a persuasive impersonation of the public Lyndon Johnson. To sound solemn, he slipped into such dolorous tones that he seemed to be mocking his audience. "We Americans know, although others appear to forget, the risk of spreading conflict. We still seek no wider war."

The response to the president's speech was all he might have wished. He had shown firmness without the disturbing signs of recklessness that voters feared in Goldwater. In the *New York Times*, Scotty Reston said that even men who had wondered how Johnson would act under fire "were saying that they now had a commander-in-chief who was better under pressure than they had ever seen him."

The strongest dissenting voice in the press was raised by I. F. Stone in his weekly newsletter. Izzy Stone had begun his publication in the 1950s, when his contentious left-wing politics made him unemployable by major U.S. publications unwilling to take on Joe McCarthy. Based in Washington, Stone turned his deafness, near blindness and outcast status to his advantage. He sought no exclusive interviews with politicians, as Lippmann and Reston did, but rather scoured committee reports and official white papers, looking less for what they announced than for what they concealed.

Stone now reminded readers of the League of Nations Covenant, the Kellogg Pact and the United Nations Charter, all of which outlawed reprisals in peacetime. He wrote, *"Hackworth's Digest,* the State Department's huge Talmud of international law, quotes an old War Department manual, *Rules of Land Warfare,* as authoritative on the subject. This says reprisals are never to be taken 'merely for revenge' but only as an unavoidable last resort 'to enforce the recognized rules of civilized warfare.' " And they should not exceed the degree of violence committed by the enemy. Stone cited the damage that the 64 sorties had done to North Vietnam's bases. "Why did we have to shoot from the hip?" he asked. "Who was Johnson trying to impress? Ho Chi Minh? Or Barry Goldwater?" Stone's *Weekly* had a circulation of 5,000 subscribers.

AT THE WHITE HOUSE, Bundy was upbeat, although he acknowledged that the evidence of a second attack was less than they had thought the day before. During the incident, Bundy had been sharply reminded again of the reduced role he played with this president. With Bill Bundy on vacation, Johnson had gone to Mac Bundy's office. That in itself was unusual. Early on, Johnson had upbraided Mac for dropping into the Oval Office as casually as he had done with Kennedy, and Johnson was even less given to impromptu visits to his staff.

"You know that resolution your brother's been talking about for the past few months?" Johnson asked. "Well, now's the time to get it through the Congress."

"Mr. President," Bundy said, "that seems too fast to me."

"I didn't ask you that question," Johnson said. "I want you to do it."

At his next staff meeting, Bundy had a chance to pass along that snub. Douglass Cater, a liberal journalist recently added to the White House staff, was attending his first meeting with Bundy, and Cater also questioned the resolution, which was set to go before the Senate the following day.

How did an attack on U.S. forces specifically justify a resolution in favor of the maintenance of freedom in Southeast Asia? Cater said that the logic troubled him and he'd like to think the matter through.

Bundy treated him to his arctic smile. "Don't," he said.

TO GEORGE BALL, Johnson slyly assigned the job of guiding through Congress the Southeast Asia Resolution—quickly termed the Tonkin Gulf Resolution. Despite Fulbright's pledge of support at the White House, he might be inclined, as chairman of the Senate's Foreign Relations Committee, to probe and analyze its terms. Since Fulbright had sponsored Ball for an appointment with Jack Kennedy, Ball's reputation for honesty would reassure him.

For his part, Ball believed that serving the president loyally outside the White House protected his ability to argue positions that involved a cause he cared far more about than Vietnam—promoting the European Economic Community. Ball had been impressed in the 1950s by Jean Monnet's grand design to integrate European and American economic institutions. The respect was mutual. Monnet found Ball different from his countrymen, who often did not "see things in their complexity."

In the new version of the resolution that Ball and Rusk took to Congress on August 6, however, the language was not complex. Ball considered it "a terrifyingly open-ended grant of power" but was counting on Fulbright and other senators to temper its broad language.

In a cover letter, Johnson asked for authority not merely to respond to attacks on U.S. forces or even to carry out treaty obligations to South Vietnam. He wanted Congress to approve in advance whatever he saw as America's responsibilities in all of Southeast Asia. Johnson was also asking for a roll-call vote so that, three months before the presidential elections, every congressman would be on the record.

To save time, Johnson had recommended joint hearings of the Senate and House committees on Foreign Relations and the Armed Services. During the discussion, the sweeping nature of the resolution was spelled out unmistakably when John Sherman Cooper, Republican from Kentucky, asked Fulbright, "Are we now giving the President advance authority to take whatever action he may deem necessary respecting South Vietnam and its defense, or with respect to the defense of any other country included in the treaty?"

Fulbright answered, "I think that is correct."

Cooper persisted: "Then, looking ahead, if the President decided that it was necessary to use such force as could lead into war, we will give that authority by this resolution?"

Fulbright was unfazed by Cooper's implication. "That is the way I would interpret it," he said.

Some congressional aides watched Fulbright ramming through the resolution and thought they knew the reason for his commitment. Whether the secretary of state was Rusk or Foster Dulles, Fulbright tended to view them with disdain, and it was widely understood that he considered himself more able than any Secretary who testified before him. Now, with a fellow southerner in the White House, prospects were bright that, after the coming election, the lackluster Rusk could be removed and Fulbright could at last assume his rightful title.

THE VOTE CONFIRMED Johnson's instinct for timing. In their committee votes, two Republican representatives, H. R. Gross of Iowa and Edward Derwinski of Illinois, voted "present," which did not commit them to the legislation but allowed them to avoid a nay vote. The next day, August 7, no one on the House floor was willing to vote against a presidential call to arms in an election year. The vote was unanimous, 416 to 0. In the Senate, Johnson had the satisfaction of forcing Goldwater to vote for his resolution. With ninety senators voting, the only two defectors came from his own party—Wayne Morse of Oregon and Ernest Gruening of Alaska.

Morse had argued strenuously that the resolution violated Article I, Section 8, of the U.S. Constitution, which vested the right to declare war in the Congress, not in the president. "War cannot be declared speculatively," Morse said on the Senate floor. "War cannot be declared to meet hypothetical situations yet to arise on the horizons of the world."

When House Speaker John McCormack called the White House to congratulate Johnson, the president denounced Morse as undependable and erratic. Gruening, on the other hand, was simply ungrateful: "He's just no good. I've spent millions on him up in Alaska." But Johnson's wrath was focused for the moment on Representative Edgar Foreman, a Republican from Johnson's home state. Foreman had observed that the Democrats were calling Goldwater trigger-happy, but how responsible had it been for Johnson to announce the Hanoi raids an hour and a half before the planes were over their target? Johnson was always aware that his telephone conversations were being recorded—although the other party seldom knew—and his language was usually decorous. But the congressman had gone too far. Johnson assured the Speaker that Foreman was a "little shitass."

On August 10, 1964, the president signed the resolution into law. With Congress safely in his pocket, Johnson could take a more relaxed attitude about the Tonkin affair and express his doubts about whether the second attack on August 4 had actually occurred. "Hell," Johnson told Ball, "those dumb, stupid sailors were just shooting at flying fish."

Walt Rostow shared his skepticism. Lower-level policy-makers were surprised that Rostow, although normally ebullient, was these days—as Jim Thomson put it—bouncing off the walls with enthusiasm. "The second attack probably hadn't happened," Rostow told Thomson and others, "but it was the chance to do what we should have been doing all along."

Back at the White House, Thomson described the scene to Mac Bundy, who directed Thomson to call over to the State Department and "tell Rostow to button his lip." Thomson begged off. He felt a little too junior, he explained, to be conveying that message to the chairman of the State Department's Policy Planning Council.

A WEEK AFTER the raids in the North, an American general named Alden Sibley, back in South Vietnam after a three-year absence, asked Nguyen Khanh what he thought the retaliation had accomplished.

"The men in the streets of Hanoi reacted to this attack with smiles on their faces," Khanh said.

When Sibley asked how he could gauge the mood in the North, Khanh claimed that his infiltration efforts were giving him accurate intelligence. The people of the North were disenchanted, Khanh said. Given the hardships of the Communist regime, they would welcome unification under his leadership. Khanh would become a kind of Tito.

Had General Sibley checked with Blair Seaborn, Washington's Canadian go-between, he would have found that at least one man in Hanoi was not smiling. Seaborn met again with Pham Van Dong on August 12 to pass along the warning that if the Communists persisted on their present course, they could expect to go on suffering the consequences. Dong angrily accused the United States of escalating the war.

NOT FACING ELECTIONS himself, Khanh was less reluctant than Johnson to provoke either Hanoi or Beijing. He declared a "state of urgency," which he used to impose press censorship and curbs on foreign travel; ban demonstrations and strikes; search private homes at will; and jail "elements considered dangerous to national security." Terrorists and financial speculators were to be put to death. Khanh was also reorganizing the government, replacing Big Minh in the top position and forming a new legislature. When he reported those changes to Max Taylor, the ambassador expressed concern over renewed instability. Khanh said he had no choice.

But Buddhist leaders saw Khanh heading down Ngo Dinh Diem's path less than a year after the same crackdowns had proved fatal to his regime. Tri Quang demanded withdrawal of the new decree, which Khanh was calling the Vung Tau Charter in honor of his hideaway. When Buddhists took to the streets, Khanh felt he owed his position to them and permitted no interference with their rallies. But as fervor mounted, Khanh became unstrung. On the night of August 25, his defense minister, Tran Thien Khiem, and Nguyen Van Thieu, the ARVN's ambitious commander, sought out Big Minh and urged him to oppose Khanh in a hasty election for president that a council of generals had called for the next day. Taylor got word of the scheming and sent De Silva from the CIA to Khiem. Taylor himself called on Big Minh. Both Americans conveyed the same message: Washington wanted no more changes in government. "Our candidate is Khanh."

Late the next night, Khanh's men pulled Khiem from bed and charged him with the plot. The following day, however, Khanh offered his own resignation — for reasons of health — and turned the government over to Nguyen Xuan Oanh, a Ph.D. from Harvard, who had been out of Vietnam for the sixteen years before Diem was overthrown. Oanh was so Americanized that Paul Harkins had called him Jack Owen.

With the total breakdown of authority, rampaging gangs of young Catholics and Buddhists tore through the streets of Saigon, hacking at each other with clubs and machetes. At Da Nang, nine of every ten houses in a Catholic refugee community were set on fire, and three Catholics were lynched. Rioting entered its third day, with 2,000 students staging a sit-down strike in front of Khanh's Saigon office. Leaders of the protest claimed that Khanh, despite his resignation, remained "too tricky." The next day, it was Catholics who took control of the streets, attacking every Buddhist student they saw and shouting pro-Khanh slogans and "Down with neutralism!"

Saigon's panicky police fired into the crowd, killing 6 demonstrators and wounding 12. Khanh was not on hand to watch as anarchy overtook his capital. He had fled to safety in Dalat. Oanh described him to reporters as "unwell," adding the undiplomatic phrase "more sick mentally than physically." Oanh went on, "I was told he will need quite a long period of medical treatment."

Taylor and his deputy, Alex Johnson, flew to Dalat to see for themselves and found a rested Khanh enjoying the sunshine and annoyingly complaisant about getting his government to function again. He was not "fou," or mad, as Oanh had suggested, Khanh complained to Taylor. Rather, he was being treated for high blood pressure and hemorrhoids.

Taylor gave Khanh tips on how to prevent the other generals from staging a coup, but Khanh had more devious plans. Returning to Saigon, he announced that he was yielding to Buddhist demands that he finally release General Don and the others from detention in Dalat. Khanh ordered them flown to his stronghold in Vung Tau and offered them various positions in his government. But at 9:15 A.M. on September 13, as the four generals waited on the tarmac, they learned that a coup was under way. From Dalat, Khanh called Big Minh and asked him to put down the uprising. Minh refused. Khanh must fly back to Saigon and deal with it himself. Don was puzzled by Khanh's reluctance until he found that this latest coup had been a ruse worthy of Ngo Dinh Nhu. Or, at least, it had started that way. Khanh intended to use loyal forces to create a temporary crisis that would let him get rid of Khiem and Big Minh.

What Khanh did not foresee was that General Lam Van Phat, whom he had recently sacked as interior minister, would hear of his plot, hurry to the Saigon radio station and denounce Khanh's chicanery. Listening to the broadcast and ever fearful, Khanh suspected that the brash Nguyen Cao Ky, until now a dependable ally, might have fallen in with Phat. If so, he would be dispatching fighter bombers to attack Khanh. He sent his family out of the Dalat palace for safekeeping and ordered that it be ringed by an antiaircraft battalion. Khanh also called Alex Johnson to ask whether Washington would send American Marines ashore to preserve him in power. After a teletype conference, Rusk, Ball and Bill Bundy answered no. But they agreed not to recognize Phat.

Khanh's suspicion of Ky was unfounded. He remained loyal. And since other troops did not rally to Phat, he was easily foiled. General Duong Van Duc, an ally in the Delta, had been put out of commission when his American adviser, Colonel Samuel Homan, brought a bottle of Scotch and drank with him until both men were harmless.

Khanh promised no immediate reprisals against the few rebels, although he did later relieve them of their command. With the danger passed, Khanh took

Ky's advice and returned to Saigon. Before the flap, he had shaved his goatee to mark the beginning of a bold new phase.

Max Taylor had returned from consultations in Washington to meet for the first time with Big Minh and Khanh together. The ambassador stressed that they should not expect indefinite U.S. support if they could not settle the differences among their senior officers. Taylor told Washington that when he learned that Khanh intended to return to Vung Tau "as a parting shot, I reminded him that things always seemed to go better when he stays in Saigon."

Taylor's role had moved from banker and writer of checks to personal confessor. Over the next days, he tried to lighten Khanh's dark moods and temper his bitterness against his enemies. Taylor reported that as Khanh left a meeting "he said that his only consolation was that only 41 days more remained in his present tenure of office. I tried to cheer him up, but this was one of his black days."

AT THE TIME Khanh was snapping up power with his Vung Tau Charter, Lyndon Johnson was preparing to receive his party's nomination for president in the most carefully crafted convention in recent memory. His one fear had been that Robert Kennedy—possibly in league with sister-in-law Jacqueline—would stampede the delegation at the last moment with nostalgia for the New Frontier and force himself onto the ticket. Or was Kennedy going to run instead for the Senate from New York? That possibility would present other pitfalls. A week before the convention, Johnson and Rusk commiserated about the young man—Robert Kennedy was thirty-eight—who had made his disdain for both of them apparent during his brother's days in office. Rusk's detractors claimed that since Johnson became president, his Georgia accent had deepened until few traces remained of his years in Larchmont. Rusk suggested to Johnson that Kennedy's run for the Senate would be "a drag on your own position in New York State." But they agreed that Kennedy was almost freakishly ambitious.

"Mr. President," said Rusk, "I just can't wrap my mind around that kind of ambition. I don't know how to understand it." Johnson replied, "I don't, either."

On August 25, Kennedy ended the uncertainty by declaring his candidacy for the Senate from New York. It was his first run for public office, and his hands trembled as he made the announcement. His candidacy was not universally hailed. A *New York Times* editorial painted him as a carpetbagger from Massachusetts and attacked him as harshly as Rusk had done for his unbecoming ambition. "In characteristic fashion," the newspaper said, "he did not wait to be asked." Instead, he set in motion a steamroller that flattened the New York State leadership. But polls showed that Kennedy was the only Democrat who could beat the moderate Republican incumbent, Kenneth Keating. In Washington, Johnson overcame his personal distaste, endorsed Kennedy's candidacy and persuaded New York Mayor Robert Wagner to accept it.

☐

EXCEPT FOR JOHNSON'S UNCERTAINTY over Robert Kennedy's intentions, the only cloud over the convention was an attempt by sixty-eight delegates and alternates from the Mississippi Freedom Democratic Party to be seated in place of the official delegation, which was all white and led by an outspoken racist. Johnson's commitment to civil rights ran deep but not at the expense of his election. The president coerced Humphrey and Walter Reuther of the AFL-CIO into calling the lawyer representing the Freedom Party and complaining that if its black delegates were seated, the backlash among white voters would elect Goldwater. The credentials committee came up with a compromise that seated two of the Freedom delegates and invited the others to sit on the convention floor as "honored guests."

Johnson was also fussily enmired in less explosive issues—picking the forty-foot photograph of himself as a stage backdrop, naming the horde of Democrats to nominate him or second the nomination, approving the convention theme song from the Broadway musical *Hello, Dolly!* Its star, Carol Channing, was coming to Atlantic City with new lyrics for "Hello, Lyndon!"

When the nominating speeches ended and the roll of states was called, Johnson let the applause go on at numbing length, then strode to the podium, thanked the delegates briefly and put forth Humphrey as his choice for vice president. His official acceptance speech was to come on August 27, his fifty-sixth birthday, followed by a $1,000-a-ticket party for 4,000 guests. In an uninspired speech, Johnson lauded American military strength but said nothing about Vietnam.

Afterward, the president wanted reassurance from his aide, Walter Jenkins, that the speech had gone well. For days before the convention, Johnson's moods had swung between antic activity and a showy depression that he expected to be coaxed out of. Sometimes he threatened to renounce the presidency and retreat to his ranch. He counted on Lady Bird to jolly him out of those moods; when she obliged him, it was often in writing. Earlier in the year, Mrs. Johnson had written that as a private citizen he would become restless and "look for a scapegoat. I do not want to be it. You may drink too much for lack of a higher calling."

Now with the prize in his grasp, Johnson remained insecure and asked Jenkins how long he had spoken. Told it had been forty-two minutes, Johnson asked, "How many applauses did I get?"

"Practically every sentence," Jenkins assured him.

The president had enjoyed a triumph, but the convention's high point was yet to come. Johnson was not in the hall when Robert Kennedy came onstage to introduce a filmed testimonial to his brother called *A Thousand Days.* The tribute had been scheduled for the convention's first day, but Johnson had it delayed until he and Humphrey were safely nominated.

When Kennedy appeared at the rostrum, the convention hall exploded with cheers and applause. Arthur Schlesinger stood on the convention floor, moved by the depth of emotion. He listened for the organ music that usually quieted the crowd, but after a few futile attempts the organist stopped playing. Kennedy, looking small and alone in the spotlight, smiled sadly and raised his hand to end the tumult. The delegates only cheered louder. Senator Henry Jackson from Washington State was presiding, and when Kennedy tried again for silence, Jackson whispered that he should let the applause go on. "Let them get it out of their system," he said.

It took twenty-two minutes before Kennedy could deliver his brief remarks. He concluded them with a verse from *Romeo and Juliet*, chosen by Jacqueline Kennedy. Given the high emotion of the moment, few in the audience reflected on the choice she had made. But John Kennedy's widow also grieved over the usurpation that had followed her tragedy. The last line Robert Kennedy quoted rendered her judgment on the man the Democrats had just nominated to succeed her husband.

"When he shall die," Kennedy read from the slip of paper she had given him, "take him and cut him out in little stars,

> "And he will make the face of heaven so fine
> That all the world will be in love with night,
> And pay no worship to the garish sun."

THE AMERICAN BOMBINGS after Tonkin Gulf roused Mao to devote September and early October to reassuring leaders from all three Indochinese states about China's backing. Members of the Pathet Lao's political front were the first to arrive in Beijing. "Your struggle is heroic," Mao told them. They were fighting on the front line against U.S. imperialism, and "it is certain that you will win." But Mao worried that these Lao intellectuals were not forging close enough ties with the masses. "Are you their friends or their enemies? They are not clear about this." He reminded them that their side must be scrupulously honest and not "take a single needle and thread from the masses."

Mao complimented the delegation on avoiding mistakes his party had made, twice by leaning too far to the political right, three times too far to the left. As for today, Chinese culture still harbored too many bourgeois intellectuals in the press, the movies, the stage, the universities. But that would change. "I will be happy to see that in the coming year or two, bourgeois intellectuals will not sleep well as a result of the rectification campaign."

In a ham-handed way, Mao tried to bolster Lao self-esteem. "You should not look down upon yourself because your country is a small one," he said. After all, the chairman of the Indonesian Communist Party came from an ethnic minority on a small island southwest of Sumatra. "Marx was from a minority race," Mao continued. "He was a Jew. Jesus was also a Jew." And Confucius, from a thinly populated state in China, was eventually recognized as a sage.

Mao asked that the Lao warn their Central Committee members about Soviet revisionism of Marxist doctrine but also assure them that hope was on China's side. "Khrushchev is not a good person," Mao said. "But he also helped us. He has helped us to understand the Soviet Union—how the first socialist country has deteriorated into revisionism."

When Sihanouk of Cambodia came to Beijing some three weeks later, Mao could not assume that he shared Marx's philosophy or even understood it. "The last time I met you," Mao said, "I asked you to read a book, that is, a part of Engels's 'Socialism: From Utopian to Scientific.' "

"Yes, I have read the book."

"If you are interested, you may want to read another book. It is called 'The Communist Manifesto.' This is the first book of Marxism."

"I know the book," Sihanouk replied blandly.

"You know it," Mao said. "But you must make the determination to stand on the side of the majority."

To convince the prince to join with the Communists, Mao flattered him on his support of Hanoi. "Some socialist countries are not so good as you are," Mao said. "They make friends with the Americans, as well as talk about friendship with them. You are struggling against the Americans. Only by struggling will you be able to survive." Mao assured Sihanouk that "the Americans have done all kinds of stupid things. Probably it will take nine or ten years before they are forced to expel Chiang Kai-shek's representative from the United Nations."

Those two audiences were rehearsals for Pham Van Dong's parley on October 5. The North Vietnamese might never forgive Beijing's 1954 betrayal at Geneva. But in the ten years since then, aid from China had totaled some half a billion in U.S. dollars, and North Vietnam might soon be needing considerably more. Le Duan had arrived in Beijing earlier than Pham Van Dong, landing shortly before the Tonkin retaliation. He told Mao that Hanoi intended to send a division of troops into South Vietnam. Now Mao warned Dong about the timing of those reinforcements. He said Washington had not decided whether to attack North Vietnam. If it did, America may need to "fight for one hundred years, and its legs will be trapped there." He deciphered recent statements out of Washington as meaning that the White House did not want to fight that expanded war.

Pham Van Dong agreed. They should try their best not to let the U.S. imperialists carry the war to the North. "We must adopt a very skillful strategy, and should not provoke it," he said. But if the United States dared to enter the war, the North Vietnamese would fight and win.

"Yes," said Mao, approvingly, "you can win it." He noted that the United States had a total of eighteen army divisions, of which half must be kept at home. Of the remaining nine, half were in Europe, the others in the Asia-Pacific region. "It is impossible for the United States to send many troops to South Vietnam," Mao said. If the Americans should dare to bring the war to the North, however, he recommended building defenses that would stop them from penetrating too far. But do not engage your army in a head-to-head confrontation with the Americans.

Dong said that his Politburo agreed with the Chairman.

Mao explained that the more thoroughly a Communist nation beat a Western army, the more comfortable the West felt about peace talks. "For example," he said, "you beat the French, and they became willing to negotiate with you." The Algerians defeated the French badly, and the same French willingness resulted. All the same, Mao added, "It is not completely a bad thing to negotiate. You have already earned the qualifications to negotiate. It is another matter whether or not the negotiation will succeed." After all, Beijing had been negotiating with Washington in Warsaw over the fate of Taiwan, talks that had lasted more than nine years. As Mao paused, Zhou Enlai supplied a statistic: "More than 120 meetings have been held."

Mao reminisced about one occasion when the Americans withdrew their representatives, and Beijing had responded with a deadline for returning to the talks. Some of Mao's advisers had urged that China not give an ultimatum but, Mao concluded, we did. And the Americans returned to the talks.

KHRUSHCHEV HAD BEEN preparing a showdown with China over leadership of the Communist bloc at a world party conference in December. The bad feeling went back to Stalin's day, when the Russians resented Mao's uncooperative attitude about trade. As for ideology, Khrushchev had been sure from his first meeting that Mao could not accept Soviet superiority within international Communism. Khrushchev considered the Chinese unbelievably courteous, remarkably ingratiating and thoroughly hypocritical. He was embarrassed by the Chinese claim that America was a paper tiger since it was so clearly untrue, and he thought Mao had no real grasp of the devastation of nuclear war. But worst of all, even after Khrushchev had denounced Stalin's cult of personality in 1956, he saw Mao following the same path.

But Mao also rejected the Soviet concept of peaceful coexistence with the West. After receiving Khrushchev in China in 1958, Mao had complained to his physician, "Chiang Kai-shek wants the United States to use the bomb against us. Let them use it. Let's see what Khrushchev says then."

Two years later, Khrushchev attacked Mao publicly by name and withdrew all Soviet aid and technical advisers from Mao's ambitious strategy of an agricultural and industrial Great Leap Forward. To launch his vision, Mao had challenged doubters in his ranks to dream beyond their mundane statistics. Robert McNamara was still working at the Ford Motor Company when Mao scoffed at the idea that anything could be resolved by discussing only numbers, without politics. "The relationship between politics and numbers is like that between officers and soldiers," Mao explained. "Politics is the commander."

Within a few months of Khrushchev's withdrawal, however, the worst drought of the century struck China, and famine killed many millions of Chinese, perhaps thirty million in all. The next year, Albania's leaders broke with Khrushchev over his denunciation of Stalin and turned instead to Mao, providing China's one ally among the Eastern European Communist bloc.

Le Duan watched the rift between the Soviets and China becoming wider and measured its impact on his country. At the time Hanoi first agreed to back southern resistance to Diem, Khrushchev had also endorsed Le Duan's call to action but declined to send weaponry. Le Duan saw that China had started sending military aid to the NLF as early as 1961, and the Cuban missile episode had persuaded him that China, after all, was the more revolutionary of his two giant partners. The next year, he convinced his Central Committee to tilt toward Beijing, but Ho abstained from the vote and managed to pull Hanoi's policy back to neutrality. The ideological combat grieved Ho personally, but he understood its diplomatic possibilities.

By the time of the Gulf of Tonkin bombings, Hanoi's Politburo saw that neither ally was rushing to its defense. Le Duan came to agree with Ho that North Vietnam's only rational course was to stay friendly with both nations.

But ten days after Pham Van Dong met with Mao, the Soviet Union's Central Committee removed Khrushchev as first secretary of the Communist Party and as premier. Leonid Brezhnev was named to the party post, Alexei Kosygin as premier. Domestic failures, including a ruinously bad harvest, had contributed to Khrushchev's ouster, but in Hanoi the leadership could only wait anxiously to see what the changes meant for them.

GEORGE BALL'S WIFE, RUTH, had grown accustomed to the routine. All day, her husband would labor as Rusk's deputy at the State Department on alarms in Europe or Cyprus, then come home and brood over Vietnam. She would hear him bound out of bed before dawn to dictate his arguments into a tape recorder. From the time Congress mindlessly passed the Tonkin Gulf Resolution, Ball had been obsessed with getting his forebodings on paper. He knew that what he was recommending was too sensitive to let McNamara or the Joint Chiefs hear of it before he had finished the entire memorandum. Only a few trusted colleagues and his aide, George Springsteen, knew what was afoot.

On October 5, 1964, it was ready: a single-spaced sixty-seven-page analysis of the options the United States faced in Vietnam. When Ball sent copies to Rusk, McNamara and Bundy, he addressed them as "Dean, Bob and Mac," an indication that these were still informal thoughts. Ball did not send a copy to the president.

Those who knew their middle names sometimes joked that Robert Strange McNamara lived up to his in a way that George Wildman Ball decidedly did not. Born in Iowa, with a law degree from Northwestern, Ball had gone to Washing-

Undersecretary of State
George W. Ball
(AP/Wide World Photos)

ton in 1934 to work for Roosevelt's New Deal in the Farm Credit Administration. During the last days of World War II, Ball joined a presidential commission studying the effects of Allied bombing on Germany, then gravitated to Jean Monnet's circle, working toward European unity.

Perhaps because Ball, like Chet Bowles, had been an adviser to Adlai Stevenson, he had never established a rapport with Jack Kennedy, but his transparent loyalty disarmed any suspicions that Johnson might have harbored about him. It did not hurt Ball's standing, either, that he had long considered Robert Kennedy spoiled and petulant and would remind people about Kennedy's early friendship with Joe McCarthy.

Genial, somewhat plump, with wavy silver hair and black-framed glasses, Ball was a reassuring presence at meetings, however provocative his opinions. Rusk trusted him to be a team player and did not worry that Ball would try to undercut him, even if Johnson would have tolerated the attempt. The president himself once paid Ball a two-edged compliment about his loyalty: Ball was like the small-town schoolteacher applying for a job in Texas, Johnson said. When school board members asked whether he taught that the world was flat or round, the eager applicant replied, "Oh, I can teach it either way."

"That's you," the president told Ball. "You can argue like hell with me against a position but I know outside this room you're going to support me. You can teach it flat or round."

Ball had titled his memo, "How Valid Are the Assumptions Underlying Our Vietnam Policy?" In it, he pointed out how little time the president's advisers had given to considering a political way out of the war and called for a study in depth without further delay. Until that was done, the United States faced four choices:

- Continue what it was doing and expect a neutralist coup in Saigon.
- Or, given the hopelessness of the current policy, accept a deeper involvement—which meant taking over the war with American ground troops. The world would regard that choice as an embracing of the French policy that had collapsed a decade ago.
- Or launch further air attacks against the North to improve the U.S. bargaining position. That would provoke the North into sending its army into South Vietnam and would also lead to committing U.S. ground forces.
- Or, Ball's choice, Washington might try for a political settlement, one without a U.S. military commitment but one that would delay the Communists from taking over South Vietnam.

Ball dismissed any comparisons with Korea, where 100,000 troops had crossed an established border. In Vietnam, the infiltration had been so gradual that some of America's allies considered the war an internal rebellion. And Ball warned against assuming that Washington could somehow control the risk or halt the escalation. It was in the nature of escalation, Ball wrote, "that each move passes the option to the other side, while, at the same time, the party which seems to be losing will be tempted to keep raising the ante." Ball summed up with an image appropriate to Asia: "Once on the tiger's back, we cannot be sure of the place to dismount."

Ball had written with a sense of urgency because he was picking up signals from colleagues and from the U.S. mission in Saigon that, behind the soothing campaign rhetoric, fateful decisions lay ahead. To argue that because Khanh was on the verge of collapse the United States must bomb the North to improve southern morale—"a form of political therapy," Ball called it—stood logic on its head.

The response to Ball's heresy was quick and angry. Ball watched McNamara fingering his copy as though it were a poisonous snake. The defense secretary was absolutely horrified, Ball noted, and seemed to think that even setting down such thoughts was akin to treason. Rusk could more easily shrug off Ball's memo. He knew that the president would always defer to the hierarchy, and it was Rusk who held the title of Secretary. Mac Bundy finished reading the memo unconvinced.

He had already supplied Johnson with his own memorandum refuting comparisons between the French and the American roles in Vietnam. Not only were the American people more reconciled to the U.S. role in the conflict than the French had been, Bundy argued, but Washington also had military might beyond anything available to France in the early 1950s.

All the same, Bundy prided himself on fairness. Two weeks later, he sent Ball's paper to Johnson with his own cover note. "George Ball has sent this over as a personal memorandum." Bundy said he had "reservations about it, especially as a proposal in the height of the campaign." Bundy was more aware than Ball how thoroughly the presidential campaign was shaping every decision at the White House. As the campaign began, Bundy had offered to change his registration to Democratic if it would help, the same proposal he had once made to Kennedy. Like Kennedy, Johnson preferred a nominal Republican as his national security adviser and vetoed the idea.

Unwelcome as Ball's memo was, its three recipients agreed to discuss its specifics, even though Ball thought they seemed more concerned with leaks to the press than with the merits of his case. Their apprehension had some basis. Ball had known Reston of the *Times* for more than thirty years. They lived at opposite ends of Woodley Road in Washington, and Ball considered him more friend than journalist. When Reston wrote a column about "a high-level parley" on Vietnam at which a "Devil's Advocate" had expressed views opposing Johnson's policy, it was not hard to deduce his source. Ordinarily, that kind of leak would have unleashed Johnson's fury, but campaign demands were keeping him from his White House paperwork. He had not seen Ball's memo at all.

If Mac Bundy was unmoved by Ball's arguments, his brother in the State Department was more receptive. Bill Bundy retained ties with the CIA, and its recent Special National Intelligence Estimate—abbreviated to the bureaucratic SNIE—predicted such a paralysis of leadership in Saigon that the South's leaders would seek some sort of accommodation with Ho, accompanied by "a general petering out of the war effort." Given that possibility, Bill Bundy studied Ball's analysis and found most of it hard to disagree with. He was irked, though, by Ball's comparisons with the French. Like the president and his other aides, Bundy found de Gaulle too annoying a figure on the world scene to admit that he might be right.

But on October 19, Bill Bundy produced his own forty-two-page paper titled "The Choices We Face in Southeast Asia." It summed up the current liabilities—a bad colonial heritage; a nationalist movement taken over by Communists who ruled half of what had historically been a united country; the fact that Ho had inherited the better military force and more talented leaders. War games conducted by the Pentagon earlier that autumn had indicated that, even without Chinese intervention, the war would escalate to the point that the Joint Chiefs would call for tactical nuclear weapons.

Bill Bundy concluded with a formula: Bomb North Vietnam harshly for a few days, even a week, then bow to international outrage, start negotiations and accept that the South would go Communist in a year or two. Use that time to shore up defenses in Thailand. The domino theory had always been much too pat, Bundy wrote. And if a negotiated coalition did lead to a Communist government, at least it would be a Vietnamese solution that excluded China from participating in it. A Communist Vietnam could even become a buffer against the further spread of Chinese influence.

Even though Bundy understood that no policy changes would be made before the election, he sent his memo not only to his brother, Rusk and McNamara but also to Mike Forrestal and McNamara's deputy, John McNaughton. Again, the president was tied up with campaigning.

But the Vietcong were not willing to respect Johnson's priorities. Early on November 1, sappers armed with mortars attacked a large airfield that the United States had constructed just outside the city of Bien Hoa, about twenty miles north of Saigon. In fifteen minutes, four Americans were killed. The losses were especially stunning to the American people because the Pentagon had never revealed the vast size of the base.

It was not the first attack against Americans in the South; the *Card*, the ship used to ferry helicopters, had been sunk in Saigon harbor in early May. But it was the war's boldest and most destructive assault against a U.S. installation. From Taylor in Saigon, it brought a demand for immediate retaliation. He cabled that a reprisal against a North Vietnamese airfield, preferably Phuc Yen near Hanoi, would reduce the likelihood of a second attack against the crowded U.S. bases at Tan Son Nhut or Danang. A raid would also offset the depressing effect the attack was having on the latest Saigon government, created when Khanh turned power over to a civilian chief of state named Phan Khac Suu. Unhappy with the choice of Suu, Taylor described him to Washington in much the terms Mac Bundy had used in trying to block Taylor's own appointment: "Old beyond his years" — Suu was sixty-three — "and clearly lacking in physical stamina." But Taylor was gratified that Suu had called the American embassy to seek guidance on his cabinet choices. When Tran Van Huong, also in his sixties and frail, had reluctantly agreed to be Suu's prime minister, the *New York Times* relegated his appointment to page 9. Bien Hoa put Vietnam back on the front page.

At the Pentagon, the Chiefs told McNamara that Taylor's tit-for-tat approach was not enough. They urged actions over the next three days that would include air strikes, landing U.S. forces and evacuating American dependents from the South. But, as Rusk admitted in a cable for only Taylor to read, the American elections in forty-eight hours were influencing Washington's decision. After Johnson received his mandate, Rusk wrote, there could be "a more systematic campaign of military pressure on the North with all implications we have always seen in their course of action."

☐

ON NOVEMBER 3, 1964, Johnson got his mandate. He carried 44 states and took the electoral college by 486 to 52. Goldwater won his own Arizona and Alabama, Georgia, Louisiana and South Carolina, where voters rejected Johnson's civil rights legislation. It was the greatest sweep of the electoral college since 1936, when Franklin Roosevelt held Alf Landon to the eight votes of Maine and Vermont. That was not the end to Johnson's triumph. His popular vote of more than 43 million to Goldwater's 27 million represented 61 per cent, the largest margin in American history. The president also carried with him the highest congressional majorities since 1936—68 Senate Democrats, including Robert Kennedy in New York—and 295 Democrats in the House, a gain of 37 seats. On the state level, the Johnson sweep cost the Republicans more than 500 seats in legislatures and assemblies.

Johnson went to his ranch to recover from the campaign, leaving Bill Bundy in Washington as head of a new interagency working group to confront again U.S. policy on Vietnam.

THE SUCCESS at Bien Hoa brought renewed energy and cohesion to the National Liberation Front. With Khanh blundering around the country in the spring and summer, some members of the Front who were not Communists had thought perhaps they could topple his regime without direct intervention by North Vietnam. They even spoke of pulling away from Hanoi. But the Tonkin Gulf retaliation had made it clear to the Hanoi Politburo that America was committed to war. For months, the CIA had been reporting movement into the South by regular troops from the North. The White House, unwilling to set off a new debate during an election year, had played down the infiltration. By autumn, however, Hanoi began to send more troops to counter what the Communists saw as an inevitable U.S. buildup. Even mavericks within the NLF were now accepting their new northern partners.

In October, Dang Vu Hiep, the political officer of Vietminh Regiment 102 at Dien Bien Phu, put on the farmer's traditional dark shirt and trousers—Americans called them "black pajamas"—and made his way down the Lao trails into the South. Poets among the Vietcong compared the stretches of rough roads to veins connecting the trunk of Vietnam's body.

When he reached the Fifth Zone—the Communist stronghold in the center of South Vietnam that Nguyen Minh Vy had left so reluctantly nine years earlier—Hiep changed into a khaki uniform with no indication of rank. His commander in chief, Major General Nguyen Don, wore the same unadorned outfit. Within their ranks, the Vietcong were willing to overlook a man's civilian past so long as he was now committed to independence and unity. They joked that probably their most skilled sappers, the men who had attacked Bien Hoa, had been thieves and robbers before they became soldiers; that was why they pos-

William P. Bundy
(© *Bettmann/Corbis*)

sessed the needed degree of stealth, and why they knew how to neutralize the American guard dogs. These fresh Communist troops were blurring the distinction between North Vietnamese army officers sent south and the local NLF commanders. And neither of them distinguished between the ARVN units—all were the "puppet troops" of the Americans. Hiep considered it his assignment to make the puppets and their masters pay for their crimes against the Vietnamese people.

BILL BUNDY'S new Vietnam Working Group convened on election day and met for the next two weeks every day and through the weekends. "Hawk" and "dove" now described whether a man favored an expanded war or quick negotiations. Ball might be the most despairing dove, but his doubts about the war—if not his conclusions—were shared privately by Harriman, Forrestal, Robert Johnson from State's Policy Planning Council, Allen Whiting, Tom Hughes, State's intelligence officer, and Harold Ford of the CIA. Also included in the Working Group were two of Mac Bundy's other assistants, Jim Thomson and Chet Cooper, the long-time CIA official transferred to the White House. John Mc-Naughton, another member, had lately taken as an aide a clever young Harvard

OUR VIETNAM

disarmament scholar named Daniel Ellsberg. The group's leading hawk was Admiral Lloyd Mustin, representing the Joint Chiefs. McNamara, Rusk and Mac Bundy joined the discussion only when the most basic issues arose.

Bill Bundy outlined the familiar choices: more of the same; massive bombing of the North; a series of gradually harsher bombings that would force Hanoi to negotiate. He favored the third course, Option C, the calculated escalation of bombing, which Bundy described in language that could sound either witty or chilling: "It seems to me," he said, "that our orchestration should be mainly violins, but with periodic touches of brass."

He was able to convince most of the group, but the ambiguities in his own proposal troubled him. A few days before his paper was due to go to Johnson, Bundy decided on a more forthright conclusion: accept a Communist takeover in South Vietnam—and probably Laos and perhaps Cambodia—and redouble U.S. efforts in Thailand and Malaysia. After a weekend of making what he considered a "mild view" as strong as he could, Bill Bundy sent the result to McNamara and Rusk. McNamara recognized that Ball's poisonous snake was poised to strike again. He went at once to consult with Rusk at the State Department, and Rusk sent for Bill Bundy to come to his office on the seventh floor.

"It won't wash," Bundy was told, and, with that, all of his own doubts resurfaced. In his heart, he knew that he had not bought his own argument. The domino theory might be too simplistic, but a Communist South Vietnam? That would pretty well doom current U.S. policy in all of Asia.

Soon after Bundy left Rusk's office, he sent his assistant, Jonathan Moore, to McNaughton's office at the Pentagon. "I've got to collect every copy of that memo," Moore told Dan Ellsberg.

"Admiral Mustin didn't like it, right?"

Ellsberg had guessed correctly. Mustin had immediately written a vehement rebuttal. By the time the Working Group's conclusions were distributed, Bill Bundy was recommending a slow buildup in the bombing of the North. His weekend apostasy had ended, leaving him with only violins and brass. His brother favored more intense bombing. But as Mac Bundy wrote in the margin of his copy of Bill's memo, there was "no hurry."

WHEN MAX TAYLOR spent most of his days in combat with a hostile army, they were Nguyen Khanh's men, not Giap's. To Taylor, the ARVN generals seemed determined to pull their country apart, but for the moment Khanh looked stable, both politically and personally. Big Minh had gone willingly to Thailand and Khiem to Washington as ambassador. Even though Khanh would remain head of the armed forces, he had indulged the Americans by naming Huong as prime minister. But neither Buddhists nor Catholics trusted Huong, a former Saigon mayor, and they swarmed into the streets again to protest. Honest enough but rigid, Huong declared another round of martial law.

Taylor came back from consultations in Washington in early December with Johnson's demand that the Saigon generals unite before Washington took any stronger action against the North. Conveying that message was especially urgent because Khanh had tried lately to cover his weakness with a new stridency about carrying the war to the North. And Westmoreland had met with the flashy and impulsive Nguyen Cao Ky, who had helped preserve Khanh in September. Now, less than three months later, Ky was saying that Khanh had to be replaced by another general, Nguyen Van Thieu. Westmoreland made Ky promise to give Khanh and Huong three more months. As he agreed, Ky gave the American general a bit of advice: Never pay attention to what a Vietnamese tells you. Judge only by his actions.

To impress the ARVN generals with Johnson's seriousness, Taylor asked Westmoreland to give a dinner at his villa on December 8 for some twenty senior South Vietnamese officers, including Ky, Thieu and the commanders of the country's four military corps. They constituted an armed forces council, created to monitor Khanh's behavior, and Taylor wanted to warn them against further upheaval. Don and the other Dalat generals, freed but relegated to meaningless jobs, were on hand for the steaks Westmoreland was serving.

As the meal ended, Taylor looked down the long table and addressed the guests in his serviceable French. The latest political chaos, he said, had "completely dismayed the staunchest friends of South Vietnam." If the United States was going to increase its aid, there must be stability. Bundy had worried that Taylor might not have the energy to be effective, but on this night it was his vigor that was raising tempers. When Taylor said his country was losing patience with so many coups, Don considered his tone condescending. The ambassador sounded like a schoolmaster lecturing a class of unruly students. Don was sure that the suave Cabot Lodge would never have made such a gaffe.

Taylor did not report the details of his dinner. He only assured Washington that his comments about the need for a durable government "have had an effect and are receiving wide currency in Vietnam circles." But Tri Quang had launched a hunger strike, floods were devastating areas north of Saigon and Khanh was flailing about for a way to assert himself. Within two weeks of the dinner, he had arrested journalists and opposition politicians. Although the High National Council had been established as a buffer against military dictatorship, Khanh now asked its members to require that all officers with twenty-five years of service retire from the army. That would get rid of Big Minh, Don and the other Dalat generals. Khanh was trying to ingratiate himself with officers like Thieu and Ky, who were being called, predictably, the Young Turks. When its members balked, Khanh dissolved the High Council and went at 2 A.M. with ten of the Turks to wake up Premier Huong and give him the news. The next day, Huong sought advice from Ambassador Taylor, who told him to defy Khanh. Taylor then sent for the four leading Turks.

If the ambassador had been less than diplomatic at Westmoreland's house, he now assumed the role of their commanding officer. "Do you understand English?" he demanded. Ky, Thieu and the others nodded. Obviously, Taylor began, it had been a wasted dinner. He launched into a furious attack on their irresponsible behavior. Their actions were suicidal nonsense, and the United States would not stand for it again. As he finished, Taylor said that he regretted having to speak so bluntly — later he wrote off losing his temper as "calculated asperity" — and everyone shook hands.

But once outside, the generals complained loudly that Taylor had treated them like puppets, and their anger fed Khanh's confidence. He rejected Taylor's call that he go to the embassy and insisted that Taylor come instead to his office. The next morning, Taylor and Alex Johnson found him alone with a large notepad on his desk. Taylor reverted to French. The Young Turks had blamed Khanh for dissolving the national council, he said. Who, in fact, had been responsible?

Khanh hedged. It was an army decision, he said, but "it is not my army." He granted, though, "*Je suis responsable.*" He was responsible.

What was his authority?

"*Ces gens ne sont pas bons,*" Khanh replied. The fellows on the council were not good.

Taylor asked if his action meant that the South Vietnamese army was injecting itself once again into politics.

"*Reste dans son rôle.*" It would remain in its role.

Taylor reminded Khanh of their conversation after the ambassador had returned from Washington earlier in the month. Now the recent actions had created a military government with the merest civilian façade. It would be difficult, if not impossible, for the United States to cooperate with such an arrangement. "You *have* to punish the Young Turks," Taylor said.

Khanh was calm but unyielding. Since he had always thought the Americans favored Big Minh, he reminded Taylor that loyalty was a reciprocal matter. More pointedly, Khanh said that Vietnam was not a vassal of the United States.

Given the American blood shed in the country, the jibe stung. Taylor replied that he could not but say that he had lost confidence in General Khanh.

Still matter-of-fact, Khanh reminded Taylor to keep to his place as an ambassador. It was really not appropriate, he said, for Taylor to be speaking that way on a political matter with the commander in chief of the armed forces. Nor should Taylor have summoned the younger generals to the embassy the previous day.

Taylor pointed out that Khanh had not shown the courtesy of informing him before he dissolved the council.

Khanh said that he had not wanted to disturb the ambassador in the middle of the night.

After accusations back and forth, Khanh said abruptly, "I am ready to quit." He added, Would that be helpful?

Yes, Taylor replied.

Khanh had not expected that answer. To recover, he began musing aloud. Possibly, he would take command of an army corps. Or quit the service entirely and stay on in South Vietnam as a civilian. What would Taylor think of those ideas?

That was up to General Khanh and his government, Taylor said, but he had heard that Khanh was thinking of taking a trip abroad. Was he considering that possibility?

Khanh said that he was not. He raised the specter of Ngo Dinh Diem. The United States had not been very loyal to Diem, Khanh remarked. It was the more telling shot since Taylor had opposed Diem's overthrow. The ambassador said mildly that some Americans may perhaps have done things that they had no authority to do.

Testing Taylor's firmness, Khanh reversed himself and said he was attracted by the idea of leaving South Vietnam. But what would the embassy think if his generals didn't agree? Or the prime minister refused to accept his resignation?

Taylor pulled back to his role as diplomat. That was entirely between Khanh and his government, he said.

Khanh asked how long he had to reach a decision.

Taylor said he was certainly not setting time limits, but Khanh should give serious consideration to resolving the problem that had been created.

The ambassador left the South Vietnamese general staff office and went to wire Washington for travel funds for Khanh. Bill Bundy, replying on Rusk's behalf, endorsed the line that Taylor had taken and speculated about Khanh's successor. But Khanh had tape-recorded the confrontation, and he was not going anywhere.

BY PLAYING HIS TAPE for the Young Turks, Khanh presented them with a quandary. Taylor's high-handedness had to offend them, at least according to any public response they might make. But their jobs depended on continued U.S. support. Khanh was demanding that they sign a manifesto that they would "take appropriate measures to preserve the honor of all the Vietnamese Armed Forces and to keep national prestige intact." Four of the young generals signed the document. Thieu and Ky, anticipating a long and prosperous affiliation with the Americans, did not. But neither was Ky ready to sever all ties with Khanh, after helping to install him in office. He complained to a reporter that Taylor had insulted Khanh by saying that he had been a general while Khanh was still a cadet.

Khanh took his crusade public. He told reporters that the Vietnamese military could not fight "to carry out the policy of any foreign country." If that were not clear enough, a day later, on December 24, he issued a declaration of independence from foreign manipulation. Speaking to the younger generals, he was specifically anti-American, urging them to criticize U.S. policy openly and often. American aid was not necessary, Khanh told them. He recommended that the military begin preparing anti-American demonstrations.

Ed Lansdale used the turmoil in Saigon to urge that Mac Bundy call upon those Americans who had worked well with the Vietnamese—including Rufe Phillips and John Vann—even if Rusk's State Department had misgivings about them. Make Lou Conein the official liaison to Khanh, for example. Lansdale was not putting himself forward, he said, lest he be accused of self-promotion. Bundy did not act on the suggestion, but Conein was able to resurrect his friendship with Khanh informally. Lansdale remained a consultant to the White House on its Food for Peace program.

Convinced that the American embassy would soon stage a coup against him, Khanh sent out frantic signals to the National Liberation Front. He had a number of channels, including a brother-in-law who sided with the rebels. Tri Quang was encouraging Khanh to travel to Laos and get in touch with the Vietcong there. But because Khanh's wife was friendly with Conein's wife, Conein heard about Khanh's plans and took Khanh on a helicopter ride over a recent battle site. Pointing to the devastation below, Conein said, Look at that! The United States must get out of here. Conein looked into Khanh's eyes and said earnestly, And when we do, we will take you and your family to safety.

It was a test, and Khanh failed it. Although he said nothing, Conein sensed that he welcomed the idea. From that moment, Khanh was finished. Conein liked him well enough, but Conein's loyalty was to the war effort. Khanh had begun to exhibit the least appealing traits of the Nhus—Madame Nhu's public excoriation of U.S. policy and her husband's overtures to the Communists.

SEVERAL WEEKS BEFORE Khanh's manifesto, a Vietcong sapper named Nguyen Thanh Xuan and a colleague had been ordered to stage a raid on December 24. Their target was the Brink, a large hotel in the center of Saigon. When it had been converted to house U.S. officers, the Americans had renamed the building in honor of General Francis G. Brink, the first U.S. commander in Vietnam and an early casualty. Overcome by depression during a visit to Washington, General Brink had killed himself.

The two Vietcong bought black market ARVN uniforms and insignia and studied the way the South Vietnamese soldiers talked to people, got in and out of cars and smoked their cigarettes. Disguised as an ARVN major and his chauffeur, they loaded the trunk of one of their two cars with explosives set to detonate at 5:45 P.M. on Christmas Eve. From a Vietcong informant, they had the name of an American colonel who had recently returned to the United States.

The Vietcong posing as an officer caused a scene at the Brink's desk, insist-

ing that the U.S. colonel was still in the country and planned to join him for dinner. The major said he would return home in his own car and his chauffeur,
Xuan, would wait to escort the American to the major's house.

Pulling into a parking lot below the hotel, Xuan approached a Vietnamese
policeman guarding the front gate. He was hungry, Xuan said. If the American
colonel arrived, would the policeman say that his chauffeur would be right back?
The cop agreed. Despite their training by Michigan State University and the
CIA, the Saigon police in their white uniforms were not imposing figures. From
the time of the anti-Diem demonstrations, American reporters dismissed them as
"white mice."

Xuan walked a prudent distance, found a café and sat down to wait. He was
gratified when the hotel blew up exactly on time. Two Americans were killed and
53 persons wounded, 43 of them Vietnamese.

The next evening, Max Taylor asked Johnson to retaliate against the North
as he had done after the Gulf of Tonkin episode. Drafting the wire himself, Taylor presented two advantages: "Hanoi will get word that, despite our present
tribulations, there is still bite in the tiger they call paper, and U.S. stock in this
part of the world will take sharp rise. Some of our local squabbles will probably
disappear in enthusiasm which our action would generate." Given the tension
between him and Khanh's generals, Taylor recommended excluding South Vietnamese aircraft from any reprisal.

And yet the ambassador had to admit, given Saigon's poisonous political atmosphere, that he could not prove that it was Vietcong who had bombed the
Brink. He hoped the National Liberation Front would take credit for the raid and
rule out the possibility that a hysterical Khanh was now bombing his American
allies.

Johnson was at his Texas ranch. Mac Bundy flew there with a packet of cables and his own summation of the pros and cons of another strike against the
North. By that time, it was December 28. Before a strike could be mounted, six
days would have passed. That, Bundy thought, would "give this signal a very
mixed meaning to Vietnamese and to the world." But Bundy gave only five reasons for resisting a strike and nine reasons for going forward with it. Number one
was that the Pentagon recommended hitting the North's Vit Thu Lu barracks, a
fitting choice since the Brink had been a bachelor officers' quarters. Because full
contingency plans for future bombings had already been drawn up, Bundy could
identify the North Vietnamese barracks as Target 36. General Wheeler, chairman of the Joint Chiefs, had recommended 40 air strikes by U.S. planes at that
site and 12 sorties by the South Vietnamese. No napalm was to be used.

Bundy cited the lift in spirits that a firm reprisal would give Saigon poli-
tics—it was also one that "will do wonders for the morale of U.S. Personnel in
South Vietnam." He reminded Johnson that the point of retaliation was to slow
Vietcong escalation in the South. Taylor and his entire team favored an air strike,

and they were the people on the spot. But Bundy's memo concluded with an urbane caution:

"It was Winston Churchill who said you should never trust the judgment of the man on the spot.

"Or, to put it another way, it is easy for advisers to be brave, but it is the President who must live with the decision."

On December 30, Ambassador Taylor got his answer. Johnson had been feeling oppressed by the choices he was being given. With the Saigon military in such disarray, America's allies were no match for General Giap. As the president put it, he didn't want to send a widow woman to slap Jack Dempsey. And he was sure the conservatives in Congress would seize on Vietnam as a reason to block his Great Society programs.

"They hate this stuff," Johnson said, "they don't want to help the poor and the Negroes, but they're afraid to be against it at a time like this when there's all this prosperity. But the war—oh, they'll like the war."

That same day, Joe Alsop's column stepped up the pressure by contrasting Johnson's hesitation over Vietnam with John Kennedy's resolve during the Cuban missile affair. The implication was that Johnson lacked his predecessor's guts.

The president may not have met Alsop's definition of manliness but, in his cable to Taylor, Johnson stood up for a moment to his Joint Chiefs, General Westmoreland and the entire Saigon mission. McNamara and Rusk had made a recommendation more to his liking, and he agreed with them that there be no retaliation.

That did not mean, however, that Johnson was ready to confide in the American electorate that had just provided his landslide. He would not explain to them the long odds in Vietnam or expect their support for an American pullout. Instead, Johnson took the occasion to spell out only for Taylor his long-term strategy as it was evolving.

First, the ambassador must get all U.S. families out of South Vietnam. Given the likelihood of actions by Washington that would provoke the Vietcong to further attacks on Americans, Johnson said, "I simply do not understand why it is helpful to have women and children in the battle zone, and my own readiness to authorize larger actions will be very much greater if we can remove the dependents and get ourselves into real fighting trim." Johnson also suggested that both the Bien Hoa and Brink attacks suggested carelessness on the American side.

The president's next point indicated that Lansdale may not have written his memo in vain. Was the United States making full use of the kind of Americans who had shown an ability to get along with the South Vietnamese leadership? Reading the cable, Taylor had to realize that Johnson's description of such men—"the most sensitive, persistent and attentive Americans that we can find"—hardly described his own performance in recent weeks.

With those preliminaries attended to, Johnson left little doubt what 1965 would bring. "Every time I get a military recommendation, it seems to me that it calls for large-scale bombing." He had never felt that this war would be won from the air, Johnson said. Instead, it required more Rangers, Special Forces and Marines on the ground.

"I am ready to look with great favor on that kind of increased American effort, directed at the guerrillas and aimed to stiffen the aggressiveness of Vietnamese military units up and down the line. Any recommendation that you or General Westmoreland make in this sense will have immediate attention from me, although I know that it may involve the acceptance of larger American sacrifice. We have been building our strength to fight this kind of war ever since 1961, and I myself am ready to substantially increase the number of Americans in Vietnam if it is necessary to provide this kind of fighting force against the Vietcong."

Johnson's response owed more to his instinctive reaction to a challenge than to the carefully drawn memoranda of his advisers. As he said, his thinking had been consistent since 1961. But he had muzzled himself for the first three years out of deference to Jack Kennedy, and he had dissembled throughout 1964 in order to win the election. Now that he could be his own man, that man would be the commander in chief who won America's latest war.

Taylor replied to Johnson's call to arms with a long analysis of the unsatisfactory situation in Saigon but enthusiasm for the "Phase II operations" against Hanoi. Buried at the end of his cable, however, was a cheerless suggestion that six months earlier Taylor would have been shocked to hear, much less to be making: Shrink down the American presence, support the South only with planes and ships and thereby "disengage ourselves from an unreliable ally and give the GVN" — the government of Vietnam — "the chance to walk on its own legs and be responsible for its own stumbles."

The president was ready to send troops, the ambassador to withdraw them. For McNamara, there was no choice. He brushed aside Taylor's heresy and focused on the military buildup.

LIEUTENANT COLONEL TA MINH KHAM and his Communist units had been ready since November for their most ambitious assault. A year earlier, his 2nd Regiment had shattered the 32nd Battalion of the Black Tiger Special Forces that had been formed under Diem. After that battle in the Ben Cat district, northwest of the Bien Hoa airbase, Kham's regiment withdrew inland to Binh Gia, east of Saigon and well north of Khanh's stronghold at Vung Tau. Enough Vietcong had reached the area that the NLF forces now had two regiments there, including some troops from the PAVN — northerners who had come down the trail like Hiep but had not stopped in the highlands.

Kham's battle plan had to be approved by General Tran Van Tra, military affairs chairman of the Communist headquarters in the South. Located in Tay

Ninh province, the base was across the country from Binh Gia and hidden among the jungle's oldest trees near the Cambodian border. Tra invited to join him only the Vietcong commanders who would be taking part in the action. For sending information over any distance, Tra transmitted coded radio messages, always changing the cipher. To communicate at closer range, the Vietcong used walkie-talkies—American-made PRC 25s bought on the Saigon black market with U.S. dollars. The ARVN had the same model, but the Vietcong laughed at their laziness. Their simple code seldom changed; an ARVN message of "crabs crawling to area" always meant that tanks were on the way.

At Tra's headquarters, more than a dozen officers debated Kham's plan. Some men wanted bolder action; others counseled greater caution. When a compromise was achieved, specific duties were parceled out. Only the commanders leading troops were shown the plan. No one else was given any details. The intense secrecy explained why Vietcong plans were rarely disclosed ahead of time.

Back at his camp, Kham and his political cadres briefed the three regiments about their mission's importance and the need for discipline. The men already knew the lessons of *dau tranh*, the struggle movement to liberate their country. The doctrine stressed two aspects. Political action included organizing protests, promoting riots and drawing out any diplomatic initiatives long enough to sap the enemy's will. Now, however, Kham's men were moving to armed struggle— *dau tranh vu trang*—which was always coordinated with the political offensives. Since they were entering this new and violent phase, they were offered a choice. Anyone who was confident of success could join in, the cadres said. Any others could remain at the camp. Afterward, the men who fought would evaluate the battle.

Seven or eight of the new recruits in each battalion asked to stay behind. They were assigned to guard military equipment and not chided for their decision.

On December 2, 1964, Kham's men began shelling ARVN troops at a base once used by the French. American advisers called for eight fighter planes and for fifteen helicopters to lift in ARVN Task Force Battalion 38. The Vietcong were expecting them and destroyed the helicopters as they landed. From Ap Bac, Kham and his officers had learned the trick of aiming for where a helicopter would be a second or two later and letting it fly into their gunfire.

After that skirmish, Kham's troops waited a week and then seized and held the town of Binh Gia. Kham had chosen the site carefully, since he knew his troops were not yet strong enough to fight without every natural advantage. Binh Gia offered the right terrain for luring the Americans into bringing in troops by helicopter, but it also provided ground cover for the Vietcong waiting to attack. To retake the town, the Saigon command sent its 3rd Armored Battalion. Kham's men shot up that battalion badly, then withdrew under a heavy rain of bombs.

Saigon's 30th Battalion succeeded in capturing Binh Gia again. Kham considered the U.S. bombers of limited value against the Vietcong's forest strongholds, but he respected the damage they could do to an exposed position. At their first approach, he had moved his men back to take cover among the thick trees.

Kham delayed the next assault until December 27. Then he sent men to encircle the ARVN's 30th Battalion and threw in his three infantry battalions—each unit numbering 350 to 400 men. To those 1,200 troops, he added companies of artillery and reconnaissance, another 120 men. Kham moved alongside his soldiers, coordinating positions on his PRC 25.

Saigon headquarters dispatched a special task force to the scene to relieve the pressure on its 30th Battalion. Kham knew that those units, supplied with armor, were considered the best the ARVN had to offer. Two U.S. advisers were directing the South Vietnamese from a helicopter. Kham's men shot it down. Kham saw that one dead American was a lieutenant colonel, his own rank, and knew that more troops would soon be arriving to recover the bodies. When the ARVN's 33rd Special Task Force appeared, it was repelled. But Kham knew the battle was not over.

On December 30, after three days of fighting, Saigon dropped in the 4th ARVN Marine Battalion in another attempt to get the American bodies. The next day, Kham's men waited until 11 A.M., when the ARVN Marines moved toward the downed helicopter. At that, the Vietcong opened fire from the protection of a nearby rubber plantation. On January 1, 1965, Saigon marked the new year by dropping in 2,000 paratroopers. Kham's men mowed down many of them.

Vietcong machine-gun fire ignited dried grass at the landing site and sent it up in flames. Kham was grimly amused to hear Saigon radio claim that the fire had been his diabolical strategy. He did not object to taking credit for a lucky accident.

The battle escalated on January 3, with the ARVN sending in sixteen General Motors military carriers, two tanks and a third special task force. Again, they were annihilated and another U.S. adviser killed. A total of five Americans had died during the campaign, and 11 were wounded. A UPI dispatch underscored for American readers what Kham's men had achieved: the guerrillas "showed they were capable of striking at will in government-held territory."

When the fighting ended and the Communist troops retreated to their base, Kham estimated that 2,000 ARVN troops had been killed or wounded. Because Kham's men had no food for prisoners, another 1,000 had been captured and released. The Vietcong lost between 70 and 80 men, with another 200 wounded. Vietcong medical treatment could not match what the Americans provided for the ARVN, and a higher percentage of their wounded always died.

Summing up the battle for the White House, Taylor assured Johnson that "we have not suffered a Dien Bien Phu as some describe it." Taylor blamed the piecemeal commitment of government forces, which had allowed the Vietcong to pick off reinforcements. He reported only one-quarter of the number of ARVN casualties that Kham had estimated but twice as many dead Vietcong. Taylor added cautiously that his figures were what Saigon was claiming.

Before Kham left the battlefield, he had surveyed the dead with a pang of loss and no elation at the sight of ARVN corpses strewn across the field. When the Vietcong survivors gathered on January 4 to analyze their strategy and dole out medals, it was a muted celebration.

Perhaps, Kham thought, their show of strength at Binh Gia would prove to the Americans that they should withdraw from his country. But Washington seemed determined to persist. Kham and the other commanders formed their regiments into the Communists' 9th Division. When the American soldiers landed, they would be ready for them.

SEVEN

BALL
1965

MAC BUNDY was finally going to Vietnam. In late January, he handed Johnson a troubled memo and requested a discussion with the president limited to McNamara and himself. "What we want to say to you is that both of us are now pretty well convinced that our current policy can lead only to disastrous defeat."

America's best friends among the South Vietnamese had become discouraged by Washington's inactivity, Bundy continued. "They feel that we are unwilling to take serious risks. In one sense, all of this is outrageous, in light of all that we have done and all that we are ready to do if they will only pull their socks up."

Bundy deplored the current stance of the United States, which he described as "essentially passive." Ruling out the middle path—muddling along and hoping for stability in Saigon—Bundy narrowed Johnson's choices to two alternatives and presented them with a conscientiously even hand.

"The first option," he wrote, "is to use our military power in the Far East and to force a change of Communist policy. The *second* is to deploy all our resources along a track of negotiation, aimed at salvaging what little can be preserved with no major addition to our present military risks. Bob and I tend to favor the first course, but we believe that both should be carefully studied and that alternative programs should be argued out before you."

Bundy stressed the gravity of the questions and the fact that the responsibility rested with the president, not with him or McNamara. But they were convinced that the time had come for hard choices. Bundy added, "You should know that Dean Rusk does not agree with us." Rusk admitted that the situation was un-raveling, but since the consequences of either escalating or withdrawing were so bad, the United States simply had to make its present policy work. "This would be good if it was possible," Bundy added. "Bob and I do not think it is."

Bundy's warning was unwelcome. Earlier in the month, Johnson had barely touched on the war in his State of the Union message to Congress. He had spoken instead of funding a new program of national health care for the elderly to be called Medicare. Johnson also pledged to create a Department of Housing and Urban Development that would oversee the rebuilding of America's cities. He would make federal aid available to students in preschool—through a new Head Start program—and in college, through sixty education bills; their cost would total several billion dollars. His aides were not surprised by Johnson's em-phasis on education. One of them joked that the president's respect for it was so abnormal, even superstitious, that he probably thought education cured chilblains.

Since Johnson's libido rivaled his predecessor's, he found it natural to pre-sent his dilemma over Vietnam as though it were a soap opera: If he left the Great Society, the woman he loved, for that bitch of a war in Vietnam, he would lose everything at home. But Vietnam, an unprincipled seductress, had allies in Con-gress. If Johnson abandoned her, it would set off a destructive debate that could shatter his presidency. Johnson would stay faithful to his domestic dreams and pay just enough for Vietnam to silence his opponents.

But Johnson was coming to realize that he could wait no longer for the South Vietnamese to meld themselves into a dependable ally. Perhaps bombing the North would hasten the process. When Johnson authorized a resumption of the DeSoto patrols in Tonkin Gulf, Taylor cabled that a new attack by the North, followed by strong retaliation, would "offer a priceless advantage" to the cause of stability in Saigon.

For his meeting with McNamara and Bundy, Johnson also included Rusk. Bundy had deliberately presented the president with a fork in the road, and John-son was likely to choose escalation. Yet he seemed to be resisting. Rusk, after all, wanted to muddle along, and his word carried increasing weight. Since the most challenging advice was coming from Bundy, Johnson wanted him to go out for one last evaluation before more bombs fell on the North. It was a familiar exer-cise, usually entrusted to McNamara. President and adviser both knew what con-clusions they could expect.

To ensure that no crisis arose during Bundy's absence, DeSoto patrols were delayed until February 7. As Bundy flew to Saigon on February 2, Premier Kosy-gin left Moscow and headed for Hanoi.

DANG VU HIEP had spent the month of January integrating the NLF local guer-rillas with northern troops that had come lately to the highlands in the South. All of them reported to Major General Nguyen Don, and Don authorized the planning in late January for another major strike against the Americans and their puppet army. Thirty of the Communists' bravest sappers were briefed for an attack on a U.S. air base. As a political officer, Hiep was based at regional headquarters, west of Danang and about 125 miles north of the intended target. Neither he nor his fellow officers knew that Kosygin would be in North Vietnam during this latest assault on the Americans. Nor did they know about Bundy's inspection tour. In fact, they had never heard of McGeorge Bundy.

Traveling with Bundy were John McNaughton, McNamara's deputy; Leonard Unger from State; William Gaud from USAID; Bill Colby from the CIA; and Chet Cooper. A native of Boston and graduate of MIT, Cooper had spent enough time in New York to develop a distinctive rasp. He had found the prospect of being an engineer unappealing and switched to economics in the doctoral program at Columbia. During World War II, Cooper had been snapped up by the OSS. After serving in Burma and China, he found himself, to his mystification, regarded as an expert Asian analyst by the fledgling CIA. He worked with Bill Bundy in the Office of Reports and Estimates and went to London in the late 1950s. Finally, when Mac Bundy grew dissatisfied with the quality of information coming from the CIA, he persuaded Cooper to leave the agency and work in the Kennedy White House. Cooper drafted Bundy's itinerary for four days in Saigon with a minimum of ceremonial affairs. He suggested meeting with Tri Quang, if Taylor approved, and spending at least half a day out of Saigon as "useful, and even refreshing." Cooper also volunteered one bit of information from his prior visits: "I know a damn good Chinese restaurant."

Cooper's light tone was quickly dispelled when the visitors landed in Saigon on the Vietnamese holiday of Tet and learned that only an hour earlier Gustave Hertz, a senior AID official, had been kidnapped by the Vietcong. They also found Nguyen Khanh's position looking shakier than ever. Dissident officers were agreeing with Lou Conein's hunch that Khanh intended to join forces with the NLF.

The downfall of Diem and Nhu had convinced Washington not to underestimate the political power of Tri Quang's Buddhists, and although Bill Kohlmann could monitor their thinking, they remained independent and headstrong. The leadership had been supporting Khanh, but his high-handed tactics were causing a rift. Since the Buddhists would figure in any political solution, Bundy intended to sound them out during his trip.

First, though, Bundy had to call on Khanh. He spoke with him at noon on February 5 for ninety guarded minutes, covering three main issues. Khanh asked about going north; Bundy said the United States would consider bringing pressure on the North if the Saigon government were stable and reasonably popular. When Khanh returned again to "liberating the North," Bundy corrected him:

That was not U.S. policy. Measures against the North would only be undertaken to win the war in the South.

Khanh asked whether Washington would accept a military man to head the government or would insist upon a civilian. Bundy replied that the United States was looking only for results from a person with enough popular support to stay in power for a reasonably long time. Lastly, Khanh asked that Bundy explain to him the U.S. policy objectives. Bundy cited South Vietnamese independence and freedom, seguing into the litany that the Americans were only there to help, that the South Vietnamese must bear the main burden.

Without informing the embassy, Khanh had assembled twenty of his fellow generals in an adjoining room so that he could present Bundy to them as proof of his continuing American support. Taylor took the tactic as one more of Khanh's tricks, but Bundy agreed to see the group and gave the officers a brief pep talk. He neutralized any favorable impact for Khanh by never mentioning his name.

WHEN BUNDY INVITED the Buddhist leader Thich Thien Minh to call on him at the ambassador's residence on Saturday, February 6, the monk asked Tran Quang Thuan to go along as his translator. The fifteen months since Thuan's release from Diem's prison had been hectic. He had disapproved of the murders of Diem and Nhu but knew that the palace had kept dossiers to show the corruption among almost all of the generals; Thuan thought Don might have been the one exception. Otherwise, to preserve the junta's reputations, the Ngo brothers had to die.

Although Khanh named Thuan as his minister of social welfare, their relations had been clouded. Thuan quit in protest over Khanh's arbitrary rule; Khanh refused to accept his resignation. Thuan had stayed on through the summer's anarchy, trying to mediate between Buddhists and Catholics and often insulted for his efforts. As for Khanh personally, Thuan deplored his constant manipulating but found him intelligent, even fair-minded.

But like Colonel Thao, Pham Xuan An, the Saigon journalist, had a secret commission in the North Vietnamese army. An had been collecting information about Khanh's overtures to the Vietcong and knew about Tri Quang's urging that he get to Laos and open negotiations from there.

Escorting Thich Thien Minh into the embassy, Bundy conducted the interview, pausing to let Thuan translate. Thuan found Bundy obviously bright and quite nice. Taylor seemed less arrogant than Lodge but not as sharp-witted. When Bundy asked what Thien Minh saw as the ideal government for South Vietnam, the monk replied, "One based on principles of equality and justice."

Asked to elaborate, the priest turned to Thuan, who spoke at length about the South's inequities in education and within the ARVN. Bundy had left Washington favoring a "sharp confrontation" with the Buddhists, but nearly two hours of opaque meandering about South Vietnamese politics were tiring him, and he made only cursory notes. As it happened, in less than twelve hours most of his briefings would be out of date, anyway.

Bundy intended to follow Chet Cooper's advice and get out of Saigon on Sunday, February 7. His open itinerary for the day might include a stop at Pleiku, a dusty marketplace high in South Vietnam's central mountains.

But that morning, Pleiku was also the destination of thirty Communist sappers. At 2 A.M., as Bundy's party slept in Saigon, the Vietcong fired American mortars captured in earlier skirmishes into U.S. Camp Holloway and its nearby airstrip. Their aim was deadly. Eight Americans were killed, 126 wounded, and 10 U.S. planes destroyed. When the news reached Colonel Hiep at Communist headquarters, he felt no particular sense of triumph. His men were already planning other raids, and Pleiku did not seem especially memorable.

But in Saigon, the impact reverberated throughout the American mission. Bundy hurried to the operations room at Westmoreland's headquarters, accompanied by Taylor and Alex Johnson. As Bundy took charge, Westmoreland considered his manner understandably intense but also abrupt and at times slightly arrogant. To Westmoreland, Bundy was one more civilian who smelled a whiff of gunpowder and fancied himself a field marshal. As the others debated what response to recommend to Washington, Westmoreland held back, speaking only when asked a question. Better than anyone in the room, he appreciated how vulnerable every U.S. base was to surprise attack, and yet, as commander, the ultimate responsibility for security rested with him.

The idea of retaliating while Kosygin was still in Hanoi disturbed Bundy, but the others reminded him that any bombing targets would be far south of the capital. And the Pleiku attack was too provocative to ignore.

Given the time difference, Johnson could convene his advisers, along with Mike Mansfield and Speaker John McCormack, before 8 P.M. on Saturday evening. General Wheeler admitted that the attack had been a surprise and that the Vietcong had slipped away with no casualties. He recommended that U.S. planes bomb three barracks in the North. Pilots could be over their targets by 3 P.M., Sunday afternoon, and the South Vietnamese would be authorized to hit a fourth barrack.

Johnson read aloud intelligence estimates of the North Vietnamese casualties that could be expected from U.S. strikes: At Dong Hoi barracks, 3,600 military killed or wounded out of 6,000 troops stationed there, and another 40 civilian casualties. Ninety out of 150 troops at Vit Thu Lu barracks; no civilian casualties. Seven hundred and twenty of the 1,200 men at Chap Le barracks; 30 civilian casualties. The president had received no firm estimate of losses at Vun Con, the target that was being assigned to the South Vietnamese.

George Ball was hearing a cry for vengeance that he considered overwhelming. To oppose it would be futile and, he thought, tactically unwise. If Johnson could not be dissuaded, all Ball would have accomplished by protesting would be to antagonize his fellow advisers. At that point, Cyrus Vance, McNamara's deputy, left the room and came back with a recommendation from Bundy in Saigon that strikes begin at once.

Johnson went around the room, forcing each man to speak aloud. Ball said that everyone agreed the strikes were necessary and the targets appropriate. But disingenuously he suggested that the raids be held off until Kosygin had left North Vietnam. Mansfield and Vice President Humphrey sided with him, as did Ambassador Llewellyn Thompson, on leave from Moscow. Thompson said the Soviet Union would conclude that we were deliberately insulting its premier.

McNamara saw through Ball's delaying tactic. You're trying to prevent a retaliatory raid, he said, not postpone it. We have to show immediately that we are responding to the Pleiku attack. There will always be an objection about timing.

Ball listened, impressed as always by McNamara's ability to bull his way past any obstacle. As Ball gave in, only one other man tried to defuse the enthusiasm for striking back. Facing Johnson directly across the table, Mansfield said: "We are not now in a penny-ante game. It appears that the local population in South Vietnam is not behind us or else the Vietcong could not have carried out the surprise attack." We might be getting into a war with China, Mansfield continued, and we might be healing the split between Moscow and Beijing.

Bill Bundy was sure Mansfield wished he were alone with Johnson and not forced to air his disagreement in front of a room filled with men who opposed his views. Johnson seemed to wish the same. Impatiently, he said, "We have kept our gun over the mantel and our shells in the cupboard for a long time now, and what was the result? They are killing our men while they sleep in the night.

"I can't ask our American soldiers out there to continue to fight with one hand tied behind their backs."

As HIS DELEGATION worked over its recommendations in Saigon, Mac Bundy kept being called away to the secure KY-9 line in order to update Washington on the events at Pleiku. Remembering how often Bundy's staff had pestered the Saigon embassy for the latest developments, Chet Cooper was amused to hear Bundy grumble after the fourth interruption, "If those guys would only leave us alone for an hour, perhaps we could work things out."

When the embassy learned that retaliation had been approved, Westmoreland invited Bundy to fly with him to Pleiku to assess the damage and asked Khanh to join them. Khanh was too pleased by the prospect of punishing the North to object that he had been told only after the decision was made.

Once they reached the base and moved among the wounded men, Bundy showed that he was no automaton. Westmoreland noticed how disturbed he was by the sight of dead and dying Americans, and a reporter for the *Washington Star* wrote that Bundy looked stricken as he spoke quietly with a wounded enlisted man, a mere teenager. When Bundy returned to Saigon, Chet Cooper also saw the change. For a day or so, Bundy's self-control remained shaken, and Cooper thought that, unnerved, he seemed more human.

Bundy was annoyed, however, when colleagues speculated that the sight of blood had influenced his recommendations. He was far too rational for that, and indeed his advice to Johnson had not changed from his memo of two weeks earlier. That was what he meant when he quipped afterward that Pleikus were like streetcars—if you don't catch one, another will be along soon.

From the White House, the president insisted that all American wives and children be evacuated from Vietnam within a week or ten days. Cy Vance reported that U.S. planes had left their carrier Sunday morning at 1:05 A.M., Washington time, and would be over their targets fifty-five minutes later. Johnson ordered Vance to call him throughout early morning hours as the Pentagon received results of the raids. Vance took him at his word and called at 3:40 A.M., 4:10, 4:55 and 5:10.

In military terms, the raids were not successful. Of the four targets, three were protected by bad weather and the U.S. pilots could not see clearly enough to unload their bombs. The extent of the damage to Dong Hoi, the fourth target, was not immediately apparent.

McNamara announced the disappointing results when Johnson convened the National Security Council at 8 A.M. Since the raids—called Flaming Dart for their ability to sting—had been limited to retaliation, Council members agreed that U.S. planes should not return for a second attack on targets they had not hit. Several congressional leaders were sitting in on the meeting, and when Representative Gerald Ford did not grasp their reasoning, the others explained that a delayed attack would be seen as the sort of provocation they wanted to avoid.

For Nguyen Cao Ky, the strikes had been a chance to avenge himself with Max Taylor. At his dressing down of the Young Turks, Taylor had singled out Ky, informing him that he could not return to his airborne unit because the putsch against Big Minh had revealed his true ambitions. "You are now up to your neck in politics," the ambassador had told Ky, who swallowed his angry retorts. Now here Ky was, flying again—and on a bombing run over a North Vietnamese barracks.

BUNDY LEFT SAIGON on Sunday evening to draft his report on the trip home. Canceling a stopover in Honolulu, he changed planes at Clark Field in the Philippines and, given the time difference, arrived in Washington at 10 P.M. He went straight to the White House with the eight-page memorandum and its five-page addendum that he and McNaughton had drafted. Johnson read them before he went to bed.

The gist was familiar. Bundy was making arguments that the Joint Chiefs had put forth in August and that had been rejected in September and December.

But Bundy now put the case in precise language that Johnson found hard to refute.

"The situation in Vietnam is deteriorating," Bundy began, "and without new U.S. action defeat appears inevitable—probably not in a matter of weeks or perhaps even months, but within the next year or so. There is still time to turn it around, but not much."

Considering the limited time he had spent—all of it in South Vietnam—Bundy's conclusions were sweeping: "The stakes in Vietnam are extremely high, the American investment is very large, and American responsibility is a fact of life which is palpable in the atmosphere of Asia, and even elsewhere. The international prestige of the United States, and a substantial part of our influence, are directly at risk in Vietnam." The burden could not be unloaded on the Vietnamese themselves, he wrote, and there was no way to negotiate an exit.

According to Bundy, the time had come for "graduated and continuing" bombings against the ninety-four possible targets that had first been identified the previous year. He was sure he spoke for the task force that had accompanied him and for the American mission in Vietnam.

The memo offered a few hopeful notes: Vietcong casualties the past January had been the highest of any month of the war; the South Vietnamese, although war-weary, were tough and resilient. Yet "it remains a stubborn fact that the percentage of the countryside which is dominated or threatened by the Vietcong continues to grow." The population seemed to believe that "the Vietcong are going to win in the long run."

Bundy acknowledged that General Khanh took a "highly tactical view of the truth," but he argued that Khanh "with all his faults, is by long odds the outstanding military man currently in sight—and the most impressive personality generally." Bundy shrugged off Taylor's view that Khanh had to be removed from the scene.

As Bundy pressed the case for continued bombing of the North, even without a specific provocation, he presented a new caveat to the president:

"A final word. At its very best the struggle in Vietnam will be long. It seems to us important that this fundamental fact be made clear and our understanding of it be made clear to our own people and to the people of Vietnam. Too often, in the past, we have conveyed the impression that we expect an early solution when those who live with this war know that no early solution is possible. It is our own belief that the people of the United States have the necessary will to accept and to execute a policy that rests upon the reality that there is no shortcut to success in South Vietnam. McG. B."

Bundy, the former college debater, was calling upon a president—who played his cards from inside the vest—to go before the American people and confess to them that the campaign promises he had made only three months earlier were suddenly invalid.

On February 8, Johnson convened his usual cast, minus Rusk, who was suffering from influenza. By then, Johnson had received a supplement to Bundy's report that estimated the success of continued bombing of the North at "somewhere between 25 per cent and 75." Quixotically, the analysis suggested that even if the policy failed, it would have been worth the price. "At a minimum, it will damp down the charge that we did not do all that we could have done, and this charge will be important in many countries, including our own." In other words, Americans and their allies would feel better about failing than about not putting U.S. power to the test.

When Johnson met next with his closest aides, McNamara advised him that one raid each week against the North would be enough to keep up morale in the South. Johnson authorized an expanded strike plan but told his advisers to keep quiet about it.

George Ball had marveled at the ingenious contortions of logic in his opponents' arguments. He regarded McNamara and the Bundy brothers as gifted dialecticians who were arguing that the crumbling of the South Vietnamese government was not a signal to cut U.S. losses and get out but rather as proof that America must bomb the implacable North to strengthen the will of the corrupt South. Four years earlier, Joseph Heller, the American novelist, had published a satire on the convolutions of the military mind. As Ball listened to the current debate, he recognized Catch-22 in its purest form.

TIMING OF THE ESCALATION did not rest entirely with Washington. Three days after the Pleiku attack, the Vietcong struck again. Their target was a hotel that housed American enlisted men in the town of Qui Nhon, and the raid was ghoulishly effective. Since Westmoreland remained unaware of the North's loose control over Vietcong attacks and how far in advance they were planned, he assumed that the bomb that exploded at Qui Nhon was a reprisal for the air strike against the northern barracks. Again, the Vietcong planning had been deadly. The explosive was detonated at 8 P.M., when most of the soldiers were resting after dinner but before they went out for the evening. The entire building collapsed in on itself, killing 23 men, wounding 21 and trapping other Americans under beams and plaster—the largest number of U.S. casualties from a single attack.

Cries and moaning could be heard from beneath the rubble, and one GI's broken leg lay buried beneath tons of debris. The only opening into the ruined building was too small for any American on the scene, but Johnson's wheedling for support from other nations had led South Korea to send a unit of medics. A Korean captain volunteered to slip inside with an electric saw and a syringe of morphine. Despite the drug, the boy's screams echoed from the wreckage while the doctor sawed off his leg.

FOUR HOURS AFTER the hotel collapsed, Westmoreland was notifying the Pentagon and Admiral Sharp in Hawaii which targets the 2nd Air Division intended to hit in North Vietnam. Almost at once, the Joint Chiefs sent back a different list. During a confused night, Westmoreland received contradictory messages and was instructed not to confide in the South Vietnamese, a warning that came too late since Vietnamese pilots had been involved in the planning. The raids at dawn on February 11 were named Flaming Dart II, but they were more significant than that. They were a preview of a major change in Washington's tactics, an unrelenting bombing campaign to be called Operation Rolling Thunder.

The muddle over targets had arisen because Johnson did not want to call attention to his escalation. Dong Hoi was hit again, and U.S. and South Vietnamese planes struck at the North Vietnamese barracks at Chap Le. Meeting with congressional leaders, Johnson gave them no clue that the United States had embarked on a campaign of sustained air strikes against the North. Nor did a White House announcement mention either Qui Nhon or reprisals. The latest strikes were simply due to "further direct provocations by the Hanoi regime" and its "continued acts of aggression."

George Ball and the Bundy brothers drafted an explanation that they assumed Johnson would want to make to Congress and the American people. They were dismayed when the president rejected giving that honest explanation of a policy change. Instead, several days later he tacked on a few unrevealing paragraphs to an unrelated speech.

If the American public remained unaware of the shift, close observers of Johnson's policies were alarmed by it. To soothe Moscow's fears, Tommy Thompson invited Anatoly Dobrynin to his house and assured him that, despite the attacks on the North, Johnson still hoped for an exchange of visits with Soviet leaders. Dobrynin said he would inform his government, but in Moscow the Soviets quickly rejected America's justification for the strikes.

Harold Wilson, the British prime minister, was even more agitated. He proposed flying to Washington immediately to discuss what he saw as a crisis in Vietnam. Mac Bundy told the British ambassador that such a visit would be unhelpful, but Wilson persisted until Johnson himself had to get on the line to scotch the trip. The president's phone call was brutal. There was nothing to get upset about, he said, any more than Johnson should be alarmed over Britain's troubles in Malaysia. He brushed aside Wilson's complaints about the hectoring his Labor Party was giving him in the House of Commons. Johnson said that he had plenty of problems with his own Congress but did not see "what was to be gained by flapping around the Atlantic with our coattails out." If the prime minister had any troops to spare, Johnson would be glad to have them in South Vietnam. Otherwise, "why don't you run Malaysia and let me run Vietnam?"

CLOSER TO HOME, Mac Bundy was facing a mild revolt among his own staff. Jim Thomson was much impressed by his new boss and appreciated Bundy's rational approach to issues. Despite his affection for Chester Bowles, Thomson had considered him like a four-year-old in his whims and mercurial enthusiasms. As for Bill Bundy, Thomson pegged his emotional age at fourteen, with the inevitable mood swings of an adolescent. After only one day in Mac Bundy's office, Thomson had returned home to tell his wife, "I'm finally working for a grown-up."

Reading Mac Bundy's latest memo, however, Thomson felt deep misgivings and took them up with Chet Cooper in a memorandum of his own. What had happened to the idea of negotiation? Thomson asked. Look at the way the Kennedy administration's bright promise had been dulled by the Bay of Pigs. The United States should not pay an even higher price for Vietnam. "I know that these are not new questions," Thomson concluded, "but I would feel utterly negligent if I did not raise them again at this time."

When Senator Thomas Dodd, the Connecticut Democrat, and Republican Minority Leader Dirksen made hawkish speeches on Vietnam, Thomson worried that they seemed to be equating the option of negotiation with appeasement, even treason. Encouraged by Chet Cooper, Thomson reworked his memo, labeled it "One Dove's Lament" and sent it to Bundy. As usual, Bundy heard out Thomson's concerns and thanked him for airing them, but Bundy's advice to the president remained unchanged.

FROM HANOI, it was easy to assume that because Westmoreland had been Max Taylor's protégé, the two men agreed on how to win the war. As ambassador, Taylor represented the final authority inside South Vietnam, but Westmoreland had now been in the country for more than fourteen months and had received his fourth star when he officially took command. As he traveled the country, Westmoreland was formulating a strategy of his own.

Taylor had first encountered Westmoreland in Sicily during World War II and had been impressed by the younger man's Eagle Scout qualities. Westmoreland never smoked, seldom drank and limited his cursing to "dad gum." He had entered military life at seventeen at the Citadel in Charleston, South Carolina, going on to West Point in 1932 and returning to the academy as its superintendent in 1960. One of his first requisitions for the South Vietnamese army had been bugles and whistles to improve training and morale.

On taking command, Westmoreland had also informed the 22,000 U.S. servicemen that he would expect them to put in a sixty-hour week. In his rare press interviews, he held to Johnson's campaign line: "For us to shoulder the full burden I think would be disastrous." And until the rash of raids on Brink, Pleiku and Qui Nhon, he had seemed to regard Vietnam as merely a training ground for future wars. "Any true professional," he told a reporter in Saigon, "wants to march to the sound of gunfire."

Pushing for sustained bombing, Max Taylor argued that attacking the North would persuade Ho's government to end its support of the Vietcong, and

General Westmoreland and Ambassador Maxwell Taylor
(*Agence France Presse/Archive Photos*)

the Joint Chiefs had prepared a schedule of four northern targets to be hit each week over an eight-week period. All targets would be below the nineteenth parallel, which would keep them well south of Hanoi and the port at Haiphong. The bombing would be done by fighter-bombers—F-100s and F-105s—rather than the Strategic Air Command's B-52s. The selected targets did not warrant the big and expensive bombers, and there was too great a chance of losing them. The Chiefs argued that destroying the targets would convince Hanoi that the cost of insurgency had become too high. In case it did not have that effect, they were prepared to recommend more bombing.

But Westmoreland did not share Taylor's confidence that the Chiefs were right, and he mocked State Department predictions that the bombing could produce results within months. Graduated response might raise morale in the South very briefly, Westmoreland concluded, but it would never affect the will of the North Vietnamese.

As WESTMORELAND GRAPPLED with a strategy for victory, the Communists had their own plan for avoiding a head-on collision with the United States. Early in February, Le Duan sent it to General Nguyen Chi Thanh, who had lately assumed command of Hanoi's forces in the South. Le Duan exhorted Thanh to speed up the pace of infiltration from the North. The victory at Binh Gia had shown that the northern forces, when properly armed, could meet the American challenge, but their numbers in the South were still too small to defeat the ARVN.

Le Duan recommended drawing the ARVN away from their bases and wiping them out. When that was accomplished, Thanh should prepare an uprising throughout the South so massive that Washington would bow to the people's will and withdraw its troops. The Americans would then settle for a neutral South Vietnam, which would be acceptable to Hanoi. In the meantime, Thanh should limit the NLF forces to the countryside. Once neutrality was achieved, the NLF leaders could move into the cities to guarantee a new government friendly to Hanoi. Would his plan succeed in preventing Washington from making it a wider war? Le Duan quoted Napoleon: "Let's act, then see."

ROBERT KENNEDY was troubled by his brother's legacy in Vietnam. He lamented to Edwin Guthman, his press spokesman, that members of Jack Kennedy's executive committee had never given to Vietnam the same serious attention they had devoted to Cuba during the missile crisis. "We were just getting to it," Kennedy said ruefully. As he took his seat in the Senate, Kennedy heard an erroneous rumor that Johnson might be considering pulling out of South Vietnam altogether. Alarmed, Kennedy resolved to make Vietnam the subject of his maiden speech in the Senate.

He wanted to call for keeping the effort at its current level — no withdrawal, no escalation. Sure that counterinsurgency could still work, he told Guthman to collaborate on the speech with Roger Hilsman, who had left State and joined the faculty at Columbia University. Together, the two men went through several drafts to ease Kennedy's concern that he would look disloyal to Johnson or seem brash after so short a time in the Senate. In early February, a text was delivered that Kennedy found satisfactory.

Harking back to Tonkin Gulf, the speech disparaged the effectiveness of bombing. "We must understand that while bombing targets in North Vietnam may induce more caution in Hanoi, it will not bring peace in South Vietnam. In the last analysis, the way to defeat the terrorists is to increase our capability to fight their kind of war."

Before he could deliver those remarks, the Vietcong struck Pleiku and Johnson began the retaliatory bombing. Kennedy put the speech aside and kept quiet.

ROLLING THUNDER was scheduled to begin officially on February 20. But Saigon politics got in the way, and the air strikes had to be postponed since Nguyen Khanh was in trouble again. This time, the coup against him was being plotted by a Catholic professor, Nguyen Van Kiem, with military muscle supplied by General Lam Van Phat.

Ky went to warn Khanh that his divisive tactics were only weakening his position. You can't play off the Catholics against the Buddhists the way the colonialists might, Ky said. As prime minister, you must unite the country. The Young Turks still support you, but you must stop playing politics and crack down on further demonstrations.

"If you can't get tougher," Ky concluded, "you should resign. Otherwise, the country will blame you—and your children will be ashamed of you." Family sentiments were much on Ky's mind; not long before, he had divorced the French mother of his five children to marry an Air Vietnam stewardess. Khanh showed Ky out of his office with a smile. "I know what you mean, Ky. But remember, you are young and impetuous."

Realizing that his warning would not be heeded, Ky began to plot with Thieu, the ARVN commander in the Delta. When Khanh went on a routine visit to Can Tho, Ky planned to fly down and arrest him. Others of the Young Turks balked and told Ky he was acting too rashly. Just as Ky canceled his coup, however, General Phat struck. For the first twenty-four hours, that putsch, too, seemed doomed. But on February 19, Khanh called Ky to say, "I think something has happened. There are a lot of tanks on the move."

In past coups, Vietnamese air force planes had been decisive. This time, Ky's pilots reported that tanks were blocking access to their hangars. Ky jumped into a jeep and headed for Tan Son Nhut. If anyone were going to overthrow Khanh, he would do it, not Phat.

Phat's men chased Khanh's Mercedes through the streets of Saigon. At the airport gates, Ky intercepted Khanh's driver. Get out of the car, Ky shouted to Khanh, and walk toward me. Slowly, Khanh obeyed. None of Phat's men tried to stop him.

When he reached Ky's jeep, Khanh said, "Phat is practically in control of Saigon. Can you help me get out of here?"

"I don't think I can." Ky explained that his pilots could not take off. "Where do you want to go?"

Khanh seemed dazed. "The Mekong," he said. "Anywhere, but let's get out of here."

Ky always kept an emergency plane ready for takeoff. He motioned Khanh into his jeep and took a back road to its hangar. With Phat's tanks heading toward the runway, the two men boarded the DC-3, and Ky revved up. As the tanks moved to block his takeoff, Ky opened up the plane's engine and lifted above them. Airborne, Khanh admitted that he did not know what to do. He asked to be taken to his mother's house in Dalat. To Ky, he said, "You have my full authority to handle the problem."

Ky dropped Khanh off, flew back to Saigon and found the airport still ringed with tanks. He flew instead the twenty miles north to Bien Hoa, where he pronounced himself temporary commander. When he reached forty cabinet members and Young Turks by telephone, they agreed that Ky's authority might be shaky but it trumped Phat's. Those with planes flew to Bien Hoa; the rest came by car. With the generals converging, Ky sent a plane for Khanh. On his arrival, Khanh was overwhelmed by the clamor in the room. Some voices were shouting for him to resign, others for him to stay. Mopping his brow, he said, "I would like to go back to Dalat."

Ky walked him back to the runway and shook his hand at the plane's door. "Well, Ky," Khanh said, "if you want to do something I can't stop you. But don't be rash, and don't forget our friendship, all the good times we have had together."

Back in the conference room, Khanh's departure had brightened the mood. Taking charge, Ky demanded that any change in government be legal. Given the confusion of the past year, legality weighed on all of them. Ky insisted that they get rid of Phat somehow, return to Saigon and call on Dr. Suu, as chairman of the High National Council, to bless their new government.

General Robert Rowland, the adviser to South Vietnam's air force, arranged to bring in Phat and Pham Ngoc Thao to bargain with Ky; Thao had not been exposed as a Communist. Meantime, Ky sent observation planes to drop leaflets over Phat's troops. "Do not resist," they read, "or Ky will bomb you."

With rebel soldiers defecting, Phat and Thao fled to a Catholic village and hid there undetected while Ky consolidated his position. Khanh was the most easily disposable. The Turks named him a roving ambassador. Chester Bowles could have told him how much the title was worth, but Khanh accepted gratefully. As he left Saigon, he spoke candidly to General Don about his intentions: "I think the time has come for me to cause a sensation or two on the world political stage, just for fun." Khanh also handed over a dossier with documents that cleared Don and the other Dalat generals of the charges against them.

At a grand farewell ceremony at the airport, Khanh played his final scene on Vietnamese soil with unabashed flair. He dropped down, scooped up dirt near the runway and announced that he was taking away a part of his native land, the country he so dearly loved.

The comedy was ended. After Khanh's departure, Thao managed to stay in hiding for some weeks until his luck ran out and he was found and killed. His instructions from Hanoi had always been vague: Rise in the ARVN and cause what trouble you can. A fellow Communist and friend from his youth wrote an admiring epitaph that credited Thao with a major role in destroying the credibility of two Saigon governments.

Determined now to restore some legitimacy, the ARVN generals agreed to keep the aged and compliant Suu as chief of state, and ratified Phan Huy Quat as temporary premier; Quat was the man many of the generals suspected the Americans had favored all along. At the embassy, Taylor was disturbed by suggestions from Washington that perhaps the time had come for sending American troops to South Vietnam, with the limited assignment of protecting the U.S. airfield at Da Nang.

The man who had proposed committing U.S. troops three-and-a-half years earlier had reversed his position. He sent back a cable explaining his reservations about receiving them. It would be a step "in reversing long standing policy of avoiding commitment of ground combat forces" in South Vietnam. "If Danang needs better protection," Taylor went on, "so do Bienhoa, Tan Son Nhut, Nhatrang and other key base areas."

Taylor predicted that once the Saigon government saw that Washington was willing to take over that responsibility, it would unload other military chores on the Americans. That, in turn, would increase friction with ARVN commanders and with South Vietnamese civilians. Taylor granted that U.S. Marines would be effective in guarding Da Nang's perimeters, but he came back to a consideration Kennedy had raised as a junketing congressman: "White-faced soldier, armed, equipped and trained as he is, is not suitable guerrilla fighter for Asian forests and jungles. France tried to adapt their forces to this mission and failed; I doubt that U.S. forces could do much better."

When Taylor and Westmoreland disagreed about the usefulness of bombing the North, Taylor had prevailed. Now because he admitted that Da Nang might need more protection, Taylor lost the first round over ground troops. The same day he spelled out his objections, Westmoreland sent a wire of his own. Taylor had reluctantly agreed to ask for a Marine battalion—up to 1,900 men. Westmoreland requested a brigade—6,000 to 7,000.

ALEXEI KOSYGIN'S VISIT to Hanoi pointed up a decision in Soviet policy that dated from the time Khrushchev was ousted the previous October. His opponents had removed him but were continuing his policy toward Vietnam. In China, Mao had blocked access by land for the Soviet hardware that Giap's army needed, and the Soviets had been compelled to send the weaponry by sea. The Chinese protested publicly that they were not undercutting their North Vietnamese allies by blocking Soviet aid. But the Soviet RPG-2 antitank weapons that the Vietcong had used with such deadly effect at Binh Gia had come on ships.

Pro-Soviet members of China's leadership included Deng Xiaoping, and they responded tepidly that the Vietnam War posed a threat to China. Khrushchev had complained that the schism between his country and China only benefited the United States, but his comrades did not support his recommendation that defense spending be cut and North Vietnam's aid be limited because China was making delivery too difficult. Khrushchev had proposed concentrating instead on consumer goods for Soviet citizens, but the leadership preferred to pursue his earlier policy and increase the Soviet supplies sent by ship. At the same time, they stressed that they would continue Khrushchev's policy of peaceful coexistence with the West.

Since Khrushchev had become a symbol of the rift with Mao, his ouster was a concession to the Chinese. The Soviets were alarmed that if the fissure became a chasm, China might end up allied with America against her Socialist ally.

Edgar Snow, a reliable channel for Mao in the past, interviewed him at the end of 1964, when Mao made it clear that in the decade since the Geneva accords, China had not veered from its policy of putting self-interest first. The Vietcong could win in South Vietnam, Mao said blandly, by relying on their own resources. And if the United States did expand the war now that Johnson had won the election, that alone would not bring China into the conflict "as long as China itself was not attacked." Mao also predicted that China and the United States would one day enjoy friendly relations.

CONFRONTED BY Westmoreland's pressure and Max Taylor's resistance, Johnson had sided with his ambassador and sent two battalions—fewer than 2,000 men—for guard duty at Da Nang. In that, Johnson had Eisenhower's backing. During a two-and-a-half-hour talk at the White House, Ike, who had been so cautious when he had the power to act, was as bellicose as Rostow and LeMay. He quoted Napoleon as calling morale in war three times as important as material and added that he would put the ratio even higher. Although the air strikes after the Tonkin Gulf incident had raised South Vietnamese morale, it was sinking again because there had been no follow-up.

But Ike remained a realist. McCone had told him that the Vietcong continued to get many of their weapons by capturing them from the ARVN. The people of the South must want to be saved, Eisenhower said. Otherwise, nothing could be done for them. And the French had never recognized the importance of a desire for independence.

Eisenhower seemed to have picked up complaints from the Pentagon about Johnson's control over every military decision. He said pointedly that it was essential to trust and back a commander, and he quoted an adage: "Centralization is the refuge of fear." That said, Ike offered very specific military advice of his own. Don't destroy the Soviet-built MIG aircraft in Hanoi right away. But do leave Hanoi in no doubt about the price of continued aggression.

Johnson asked about negotiating. Ike served up a story about Abraham Lincoln, who had the Emancipation Proclamation ready long before he issued it. Lincoln had waited for a military success, so that the edict would be seen as a sign of strength. Don't negotiate from weakness, Eisenhower said.

Johnson put forward a worst-case scenario: what if the Chinese came south, which would require eight to ten U.S. divisions to stop? Again, Ike's answer was more cold-blooded than his responses as president. Use any weapons necessary, including tactical nuclear bombs. He was sure that using them would not lead to further escalation.

FROM THE PENTAGON, John McNaughton, assistant secretary for international security affairs, sent a paper to McNamara, Bundy and a few others that spelled out the U.S. aims in South Vietnam more crisply and cynically than was usually considered good form. "U.S. aims," McNaughton began:

70%—to avoid a humiliating U.S. defeat (to our reputation as a guarantor).

20%—to keep SVN (and then adjacent) territory from Chinese hands.

10%—to permit the people of SVN to enjoy a better, freer way of life.

Also—to emerge from crisis without unacceptable taint from methods used.

NOT—to "help a friend," although it would be hard to stay if asked out.

His paper broke no new ground about tactics, dealing principally with the image the United States must project: "It is essential—however badly Southeast Asia may go over the next 2–4 years—that U.S. emerge as a 'good doctor.' We must have kept promises, been tough, taken risks, gotten bloodied and hurt the enemy very badly."

AT 9 A.M. ON MARCH 8, ready to get bloodied, two U.S. Marine battalion landing teams reached Da Nang, each with 800 infantrymen. McNaughton had tried at the last minute to replace the Marines with army airborne troops stationed in Okinawa as a way to lower public awareness of the new commitment. But Westmoreland argued that the Marines were better trained for maintaining themselves on South Vietnam's beaches.

In hiding, Dang Vu Hiep had received his second star as a North Vietnamese colonel. To him, the distinction between soldiers and Marines scarcely mattered. He was on hand to watch the Americans land, and the fact that they had arrived so quickly after the attack at Pleiku and Qui Nhon proved to him that they had been in the pipeline for months. He did not doubt that more U.S. troops would soon be following. For Colonel Hiep, it was essential to attack the Americans as soon as they got to their new base. He and his fellow officers were already planning a battle that would demoralize them.

BUT FOR TODAY, all was cloudless. General Thi, commander of the ARVN first corps, staged elaborate welcoming ceremonies with young Vietnamese women who smiled and draped leis around the necks of Marines in full battle regalia. The local U.S. Army advisory group held up a derisive sign painted on a sheet: "Welcome to the gallant Marines."

Alex Johnson, up from Saigon for the landing, was troubled to see that the battalions had brought along 8-inch howitzers that could fire atomic warheads. Westmoreland assured him that since the U.S. planes in Vietnam already had a nuclear capability, and since the Marines had brought no atomic shells, neither Hanoi nor Western reporters would conclude that nuclear weapons were about to be used. Westmoreland did ease one embassy misgiving, however, and changed the name of the battalions from the Marine Expeditionary Force to III Marine Amphibious Force. Embassy staff had worried that the Vietnamese would connect the earlier name to the French expeditionary corps they had fought for so long.

Taylor was already touchy about being overridden and further annoyed that the amount of heavy equipment, tanks and artillery was far greater than he had expected. Learning that Westmoreland had word of the landing before he did, the ambassador pulled rank. "Do you know my terms of reference," he chided Westmoreland, "and that I have authority over you?"

Westmoreland turned away that rare show of anger with assurances that he understood completely. He was already having his own doubts about the Marines he had requested. They had been trained for amphibious assaults, not for digging in for an extended defense. And, for now, their orders limited them to defending Da Nang.

TEN DAYS after the first two Marine battalions landed, Westmoreland asked Taylor to approve a third battalion that would defend the base at Phu Bai. Against his better judgment, Taylor would accept the idea of a full U.S. division for Vietnam, but he wanted the Pentagon to be clear about the hazards. Either the division could go to the highlands and cut off infiltration through the jungle—that would put the Americans in highly exposed areas with poor logistics—or the Americans could be stationed in such coastal enclaves as Quang Ngai, Qui Nhon and Nha Trang. But, Taylor pointed out, "they would be engaged in a rather inglorious static defensive mission unappealing to them and unimpressive in the eyes of the Vietnamese." The ambassador recommended further study.

Meantime, the president had authorized—along with the air strikes against the North—U.S. bombing of South Vietnam. For citizens of the South—the men and women America had come to protect—it was a fateful decision. Past policy had limited bombing in the South to the support of a ground action. Now American planes could attack suspected Vietcong installations, in a war that guaranteed many villages could qualify. The Farmgate aircraft were stripped of their deceptive Vietnamese colors and flown as U.S. planes, and their raids sent terrified families streaming into new refugee centers.

In Beijing, Mao was also changing policy. On March 30, three weeks after the first U.S. Marines landed at Da Nang airstrip, Mao opened China's railroads to Soviet weaponry and supplies for Hanoi.

THE AMERICAN MISSION soon learned that Marines near the Demilitarized Zone did nothing to deter Vietcong in Saigon. At 10 A.M. on March 30, while Taylor was in Washington for consultation, two men pretended to have engine trouble in front of the riverfront hotel the Americans were renting as their embassy. Vietnamese guards shouted to the men and, as they ran, shot them dead. But their car bomb exploded, killing a U.S. Navy petty officer, an American secretary and 20 Vietnamese clerks and workers. Fifty-four other Americans were wounded from flying glass. Secretaries limped from the building with blood seeping through their skirts and blouses. The darkened office of Peer De Silva, the CIA chief, had seemed impenetrable; the bomb blew away its flimsy façade and partially blinded him.

Given the latest provocation in Saigon, the mood at the White House was martial. The president's advisers met on April 1 to sort out the various requests for troops. Back from an inspection tour, Army Chief of Staff Harold Johnson recommended a U.S. division of 16,000 men, either around Saigon or in the Central Highlands. General Johnson, who had survived the Bataan Death March of World War II and three years in a Japanese prison, was not given to false optimism. He startled McNamara and his fellow Chiefs by predicting that victory in South Vietnam would take five years and 500,000 men. No one else had presented so bleak a picture.

Besides Westmoreland's request for a third Marine battalion, Admiral Sharp wanted still another. And the Joint Chiefs asked for an army division for the highlands and a Marine division near the South's northern border. The three leading civilians—Rusk, McNamara and Mac Bundy—argued successfully that so many U.S. troops might very well set off new anti-American demonstrations against Ky's shaky military government. But the president approved the two battalions and made the decision Colonel Hiep had confidently expected: U.S. troops no longer would be locked into a defensive role. From now on, they could launch their own attacks against the Vietcong. Mac Bundy spread the word, however, that Johnson wanted to minimize any suggestion that this new turning point in the war represented a departure from the policy he had sold to American voters four months earlier. The change "should be understood as being gradual and wholly consistent with existing policy."

JOHNSON COULD WAVE AWAY most of the protests that Rolling Thunder set off around the world, claiming they were propaganda instigated by Hanoi, Beijing and Moscow. But some demands that the bombing be stopped were coming from countries that were not Communist—France, Sweden, India—and from within the United States. The same day that Johnson approved more combat troops for Vietnam, Rusk received an appeal from ambassadors representing four nonaligned nations who asked for negotiations "as soon as possible, without posing any preconditions."

Johnson hit upon the ideal forum for delivering his response. Ike's brother, Milton Eisenhower, the president of Johns Hopkins University in Baltimore, had asked Johnson to speak there on April 7. The White House arranged for the 9 P.M. speech to be televised live across the country.

This would be Johnson's bow to aides like Mac Bundy, who had been encouraging him to take the American people into his confidence, explain what Vietnam represented and how his administration was responding. By then, Johnson had at last seen George Ball's long memo from the previous October. At lunch in late February, Ball had given a copy to Bill Moyers, who handed it to Johnson that same day. Two days after that, Johnson had called a meeting to discuss Ball's approach. The president had read and digested Ball's argument, even referring from memory to specific page numbers. But McNamara smothered Johnson's spark of interest with a deluge of statistics, and Rusk was surprisingly ardent in opposing Ball's position. Ball saw that he was being shunted into the role of devil's advocate. If his very real opposition was leaked, it would seem as if he were merely taking a debater's stance while remaining wholeheartedly on the team. All the same, Ball had raised questions that Johnson intended to lay to rest at Johns Hopkins.

The president was also ready to endorse Mac Bundy's pet idea. Since the Great Society programs seemed popular with the American public, Johnson should propose a Southeast Asia Development Corporation and pledge billions of dollars for projects throughout the area. Bundy's example was a huge dam for the Mekong River—"bigger and more imaginative than TVA, and a lot tougher to do."

The scattered and muted voices of the peace movement had been complaining that Johnson's policy toward the North was all punishment, no reward. As an increasingly critical voice, Lippmann was summoned again to the anteroom off the Oval Office the night before the Johns Hopkins speech. "Walter," said the president, "I'm going up to Baltimore tomorrow to give a speech, and I'm going to hold out that carrot you keep talking to me about. Now Mac here is going to show you the speech, and I want to know what you think of it."

Before he surrendered the text, however, Johnson wanted Lippmann to understand the political pressures the president was facing: Wayne Morse favored withdrawal, but that would turn South Vietnam over to the Communists. "I'm not just going to pull up my pants and run out on Vietnam," the president declaimed to his captive audience. "Curtis LeMay wants to bomb Hanoi and Haiphong. You know how much he likes to go around bombing. Now I'm not going to do that." Lippmann raised the possibility of negotiating. Johnson claimed there was no one to negotiate with. "So the only thing there is to do is to hang on. And that's what I'm going to do."

When Lippmann was allowed to read the speech, he saw that it was just one more demand that the North surrender, sweetened this time with development money. He told Bundy that if Johnson expected Hanoi to negotiate, he must offer an unconditional cease-fire. Lippmann left the White House once again hoping that Bundy could persuade the president to modify his approach.

But Lippmann had not witnessed the way Johnson had recently been thrashing about, trying to extricate himself from a policy he felt was doomed. To Harold Johnson, the army chief, Johnson had exploded: "Bomb, bomb, bomb! That's all you know. Well, I want to know why there's nothing else." He added a nasty crack. "You generals have all been educated at taxpayers' expense and you're not giving me any ideas and any solutions for this damn little piss-ant country."

Meeting with his usual advisers, Johnson acted as though their elite educations mocked his helplessness. He railed at Bundy, Rusk and McNamara, demanding "more ideas and more horsepower and more imagination." Get every South Vietnamese under forty into uniform and killing Communists. "Get off that gold watch, Phi Beta Kappa key," Johnson exhorted them. "Let's get going!"

But when Robert Kennedy came to the White House to propose one way to get fresh thinking, Johnson dismissed his idea instantly. Kennedy, who had not heard Johnson telling friends "I love that Dean," suggested replacing Rusk with Bill Moyers. Johnson stared at him, then asked if he was really serious.

"Oh, yes," Kennedy said, going on to list Rusk's shortcomings.

Johnson reminded him that his brother had chosen Rusk. "I can't understand your feeling this way," the president said.

Kennedy replied that Jack Kennedy had been planning to get rid of Rusk.

"I like Bill Moyers," Johnson said. "But I'm not about to remove Rusk."

When realism overtook frustration, Johnson did not blame his generals or his advisers. "If I were Ho Chi Minh," he said in those moments, "I would never negotiate." Scoffing at an optimistic phrase being floated by the embassy in Saigon, Johnson said: "Light at the end of the tunnel? Hell, we don't even have a tunnel. We don't even know where the tunnel is."

None of those doubts were on display when Johnson took the microphone at Johns Hopkins. To his young audience, he insisted that he was only doing what every American president had done since 1954 to help South Vietnam defend its independence. How many students knew that Johnson was invoking a spurious independence, never intended to last more than two years? Perhaps not many. Mac Bundy had astonished Lippmann during one of their discussions by having no clear grasp of when the nation called South Vietnam had come into being.

If America withdrew from Vietnam, Johnson said, it would only be to fight a wider war in other countries. "We must stay in Southeast Asia—as we did in Europe—in the words of the Bible: 'Hitherto shalt thou come, but no further.' "

Speaking past his campus audience, Johnson assured Hanoi that American "patience and our determination are unending." Since he would not falter, Johnson called on Hanoi to blink. Start peace talks, he said, before thousands more were killed and before bombers destroyed in North Vietnam what the Communists had built. Then Johnson produced his carrot: "The vast Mekong River can provide food and water and power on a scale to dwarf even our own TVA. The wonders of modern medicine can be spread throughout villages where thousands die each year from lack of care. Schools can be established to train people in the skills that are needed to manage the process of development."

All of those wonders were available if Ho, Giap and Le Duan gave up their vision of a unified and independent Vietnam. They must settle instead for a South Vietnam guided by the United States and acting through such former employees of the French as Nguyen Cao Ky and Nguyen Van Thieu.

Exulting afterward about his offer, Johnson told Moyers, "Ho will never be able to say, 'No.' "

Ho HAD GONE to Beijing, and it was Pham Van Dong who seemed to be responding the next day to Johnson's speech. But he was not making a direct rejoinder; his government did not move so quickly. Instead, Dong was spelling out a bargaining position that the Politburo had been fashioning for weeks. In an address to the National Assembly, the prime minister set out Hanoi's conditions:

"The United States must observe the Geneva Agreements by withdrawing all troops, dismantling its bases, canceling its military alliance with Saigon and ending its acts of war against the North.

"Pending the peaceful reunification of Vietnam, the two zones must refrain from alliance with foreign countries.

"The South Vietnamese people must settle their own internal affairs in accordance with the program of the South Vietnamese National Front for Liberation."

To underscore the first three conditions, Dong's fourth point read, "The peaceful reunification of Vietnam is to be settled by the Vietnamese in both zones, without foreign interference."

Johnson seized on Hanoi's insistence on adopting the NLF program as a way to escape from negotiations that he and his advisers considered premature. In Hanoi, the Four Points had been considered an opening ploy for further bargaining, although two conditions were not negotiable: Washington had to stop bombing the North and had to withdraw its troops from the South. After the sacrifices that the Vietcong had made, the NLF demands certainly had to be considered. But there were differences within the Politburo about how rigidly to interpret that third point. There was room for compromise.

ON APRIL 8 AND 9, 1965, Ho met secretly with Mao in Beijing to coordinate their response to recent developments. They agreed on a central premise: China would send no combat troops unless Washington expanded the land war into North Vietnam. Mao did, however, promise whatever material support Ho needed. The Soviet Union was still claiming philosophical and economic leadership of world Communism, but China had exploded its first atom bomb in October 1964, and Chinese leaders had sometimes discussed the possibility of war with Russia.

Although Mao did not want to commit his men to combat, he was prepared to send support troops, and by May they were ready to move. First, though, Ho had to overcome vehement protests within his Politburo against welcoming Chinese military forces onto Vietnamese soil. A compromise was reached that limited what the Chinese could build. For the moving of supplies, roads were permitted; in case of a Chinese invasion, they could be flooded. On their side, the Chinese offered a concession: North Vietnamese fighter pilots could take off and land from airstrips on the Chinese side of the border. That would shield them from hot pursuit by American planes.

FOR THE MOMENT, the Johns Hopkins speech was a public relations success. Chet Cooper reported that letters and telegrams about Vietnam had gone from five to one against Johnson's policies to four to one in favor. George Ball had found Pham Van Dong's Four Points promising, but publicly he only repeated that the aggression lay with Hanoi. Radio Beijing denounced Johnson's speech as "full of lies and deceptions." Moscow called it "noisy propaganda," and Hanoi spokesmen rejected Johnson's Mekong River project as no more than an attempt to bribe them. Johnson shrugged off the accusations. Having offered unconditional discussions, he could now direct his attention to building up U.S. military strength in South Vietnam.

JOHNSON'S VIETNAM SPEECH had not won over everyone at home. Tom Hayden, a shaggy twenty-six-year-old idealist, had been protesting the war for two years and considered it a deliberate diversion from the inequalities in American society. As editor of the University of Michigan student daily earlier in the decade, Hayden had become disillusioned with the National Student Association, although he did not yet know that it was funded by the CIA. Even so, its agenda did not meet his need for a break with the pragmatic liberalism of the past. Hayden assessed America from the perspective of John Stuart Mill, Albert Camus and C. Wright Mills, and no current politician spoke for the kind of nation Hayden envisioned. He followed Al Haber into an organization that Haber was calling Students for a Democratic Society, and after college Hayden went to Atlanta to take part in the struggle against segregation. In 1962, he became a principal author of a new SDS manifesto. Because the group held its national convention in a small town ninety miles north of Detroit, the seventy-five-page document was named for the site—the Port Huron Statement. Achingly romantic, unmistakably American, the manifesto described SDS members as "the people of this generation, bred in at least modern comfort, housed now in universities, looking uncomfortably at the world we inherit. . . ." It specifically renounced Communism—"the Communist movement has failed"—and picked up the lambent phrase from the *Pacem in Terris* encyclical of Pope John XXIII that men must be regarded as "infinitely precious. . . ."

SDS was only the most ambitious among a growing number of student organizations. In October 1964, students had swarmed over the University of California's Berkeley campus to protest the arrest of a civil rights recruiter. Out of that demonstration, the Free Speech Movement was born. In Massachusetts, a Harvard group called Tocsin had joined forces with Brandeis students opposed to nuclear testing. Hayden now proclaimed that "issues arise together and need to be addressed together," and by 1965 no issue was more urgent than Vietnam.

The SDS had been divided over how to end the war. One member reminded its current president, Paul Potter, that "we must tread deliberately on the Vietnam question because a lot of SDS people are far from being for withdrawal." But as SDS began to organize a "March on Washington to End the War in Vietnam," Potter was spelling out the country's choices with more rigorous clarity than George Ball.

We must admit, Potter wrote, that neutralizing South Vietnam was only sugar coating to cover a bitter pill, that ending the war meant that in all likelihood South Vietnam would go Communist. SDS members must accept those consequences. "I must say to you," he continued, "that I would rather see Vietnam Communist than see it under the continuous subjugation of the ruin that American domination has brought."

Even after that declaration, SDS remained too cautious to support the "We Won't Go" petitions being circulated by a U.S. Communist splinter group that vowed to spurn the draft until the United States pulled out of Vietnam.

Hayden left his job as a community organizer in Newark to go to Washington for the march. SDS had provided a list of approved slogans for placards, including "Freedom Now in Vietnam," along with the somewhat contradictory "Withdraw Now" and "Negotiate." Senator Gruening, one of the two votes against the Tonkin Gulf resolution, agreed to address the marchers, as did I. F. Stone, the independent journalist. Frictions within the peace movement became clear at the Washington Monument, when Phil Ochs, the folksinger, sang sardonic verses titled "Love Me, I'm a Liberal." One couplet ran, "And I'll send all the money you ask for, but don't ask me to come along."

Irked, Izzy Stone told the crowd that he had been a liberal for years. "I've seen snot-nosed Marxists and Leninists come and go," Stone added. But it was Potter—lean, debonair and unassailably midwestern—whose lofty call for action sent the marchers home to organize and march again.

"I do not believe," Potter cried, "that the President or Mr. Rusk or Mr. McNamara or even McGeorge Bundy are particularly evil men. If asked to throw napalm on the back of a 10-year-old child, they would shrink in horror. But their decisions have led to the mutilation and death of thousands and thousands of people. What kind of system is it that allows good men to make those kinds of decisions?"

Potter then set out the challenge facing the SDS: "We must name that system. We must name it, describe it, analyze it, understand it and change it." In the audience, red-diaper babies—students whose parents had been members of the American Communist Party—knew that the system's name was Capitalism. But that was the tired bogeyman invoked by their families in the 1930s. For now, the young would rebel simply against "the system."

As a former Harvard dean, Bundy became a logical target for those academics who had supported Johnson in November and now saw him heading down Goldwater's trail. About the time of the SDS march, professors at the University of Michigan organized what they called a teach-in. A prominent government official would be invited to make the case for U.S. involvement, then antiwar spokesmen would rebut him. In replying to his invitation, Bundy denounced their letter as a piece of propaganda and went on to remark gratuitously that "if your letter came to me for grading as a professor of government, I would not be able to give it high marks."

The professors were stung to action. Bundy's next invitation came signed by four hundred University of Michigan faculty members. Bundy had been urging the president to make the case for the U.S. role, but Johnson had resisted that sort of disclosure. Now Bundy would do the job. He would explain the imperative of Vietnam to the campus and the world. In accepting the challenge, he ruled out debating Hans Morgenthau, a University of Chicago professor who had recently criticized both Bundy and McNamara for lacking sound judgment and an understanding of foreign policy. Nor would he debate Senator Wayne Morse. But he did agree to the name of George M. Kahin, an Asia expert from Cornell. Seven hundred tickets were sold for the debate on May 15 in Washington, D.C. Television crews and 130 radio stations prepared to broadcast it.

Then, on April 24, a coup d'état much closer than those in Saigon commanded Johnson's attention. The State Department had been supporting a pro-American dictatorship in the Dominican Republic. Now rebels fighting to restore the nation's constitution had risen up, and it looked as though they might prevail. To quell them, the U.S. ambassador urged Washington to send in American Marines. On April 28, Johnson spoke with congressional leaders in the company of the CIA director, now Admiral William Raborn, to assure them that the coup was headed by men trained by Castro. Johnson then sent the Marines, announcing that they were needed to protect American citizens in the Dominican Republic. Mac Bundy agreed that another country coming under Castro's control would be the worst possible political disaster for the administration and urged Johnson to spell out the choice—"freedom vs. Castro."

By May 2, Johnson had a pat story to silence doubters like Fulbright, who questioned whether the coup leaders were in fact Communists. The embassy staff was in peril, the president insisted. "We are trying to stop murder," he said, even though it was the rebels who had appealed unsuccessfully to the U.S. ambassador to mediate the crisis. For reporters, Johnson conjured up a gallery of horrors: 1,500 innocent people had been murdered and their heads cut off; the U.S. ambassador had been cowering under his desk in Santo Domingo while rebels shot up the embassy. But when the embassy released a list of fifty-four Communists or Castroites among the rebels, several of the names turned out to be well-known conservatives. His exaggerations exposed, Johnson blamed irresponsible reporting.

THE DOMINICAN CRISIS passed quickly. Heeding appeals from the Organization of American States, the factions signed a cease-fire on May 5 and agreed to democratic elections. The flap did, however, provide an excuse for blocking Bundy from taking part in a debate that the president had not authorized. Three hours before the national teach-in was to begin, its moderator was informed that Bundy would not be participating. Johnson had abruptly ordered him onto a plane for the Dominican Republic, although the White House did not announce that fact. Throughout the day, television cameras panned to the empty chair where Bundy should have been sitting.

From Johnson's standpoint, the affair was bad enough, and Bundy's presence would have been intolerable. Other historians showed up to speak, including Hans Morgenthau, and even Schlesinger appeared, criticizing the bombing of North Vietnam as ineffectual. At day's end, Barry Commoner, a University of Washington biologist, rose to revenge the Michigan contingent for Bundy's earlier snideness. Bundy might give other professors bad marks, Commoner began, but he "has turned in a terrible record on attendance." He said that the antiwar protesters would have to give Bundy a makeup exam.

AFTER MORE THAN TWO MONTHS of Rolling Thunder, Senator Robert Kennedy arranged to meet privately with Johnson at the White House. He had not publicly voiced his doubts about bombing the North, but now in the small study next to the Oval Office, Kennedy broached the idea of a brief pause—only a few days, even one or two. It would do no harm, Kennedy said, and maybe something useful would come of it.

Johnson already had an interagency group exploring the idea of a pause and could assure Kennedy truthfully that his idea was being considered. The president was skeptical, however. Wouldn't it convince Hanoi that he was too eager for a settlement? Wouldn't the North Vietnamese use it to rush more equipment to the South? And yet a pause was politically attractive, and if Johnson risked it, Kennedy could not say later that his advice had been spurned. Bus Wheeler and the Joint Chiefs assured him that if the pause were short enough no real harm would be done.

On May 10, Johnson informed Moscow of the impending hiatus and asked the Russians to tell the North Vietnamese. Unwilling to be seen as brokers for America, the Russians refused. When a U.S. courier left a message at the North

Vietnamese embassy in Moscow, it was returned the next day in a plain envelope. The White House had no idea that the North Vietnamese had been offended because the envelope was marked simply "Hanoi" and not with the formal name of the "Democratic Republic of Vietnam." Johnson had committed the same gaffe in his Johns Hopkins speech, and the Politburo took his calling their country "Hanoi" as a deliberate slight, a sign that he did not accept their right to exist. As for making contact through Moscow, the North Vietnamese worried that China would suspect collusion, and that would hurt the North's cause.

Although he had no confidence that a pause would produce results, Johnson stopped the bombing on Wednesday, May 12, at noon, Washington time. Politburo members did not, as Johnson feared, take the pause for weakness. They saw it instead as a propaganda ploy that indicated harsher measures would be coming their way. They already knew that on May 4 the president had requested a supplemental $700 million for the military in Vietnam. Johnson asked that this not be a routine appropriation but rather a vote of confidence for his Vietnam policy. Robert Kennedy griped privately that Johnson already had enough funding and only wanted to box the Congress into supporting him. Kennedy threatened not to vote for the resolution. But he did. Once again, Morse and Gruening held out—joined by a third senator, Gaylord Nelson of Wisconsin.

FOR JOHNSON, May was proving to be a month of shouting and deliberate snubs. The Johnsons' social secretary remembered the praise showered on Jacqueline Kennedy for White House evenings with Pablo Casals and Leonard Bernstein. She called Eric Goldman, a Princeton history professor, to ask that he arrange a "White House Festival of the Arts." The Johnsons approved Goldman's guest list, and invitations went out to painters, writers, dancers and musicians. At first only two declined—Edmund Wilson, the critic, and E. B. White, the essayist—and their refusals were courteous. Robert Lowell, the poet, first accepted and then sent a note praising Johnson's domestic programs but expressing "the greatest dismay and distrust" of his foreign policy. Declining to take part in the festival, Lowell warned that "we are in danger of imperceptibly becoming an explosive and suddenly chauvinistic nation, and may even be drifting on our way to nuclear ruin."

The New York Times ran Lowell's letter on its front page. Other refusals followed, including one from Alexander Calder, creator of the mobile. White House organizers made it clear to John Hersey that his scheduled reading should not include passages from his Hiroshima reportage, but Hersey ignored them and introduced the excerpt by saying, "Let these words be a reminder. The step from one degree of violence to the next is imperceptibly taken and cannot be taken back."

Dwight Macdonald, a dependable provocateur of the Left, had supported a boycott of the event until his own invitation arrived. He appeared bearing a petition to explain that having come to the White House did not lessen one's dismay at the president's actions in Vietnam and the Dominican Republic. Johnson retaliated by letting reporters overhear him say of his guests, "Some of them insult me by staying away, and some of them insult me by coming."

ED LANSDALE, officially retired from the Air Force, was playing every angle to get back to Vietnam. In position papers and memoranda, he was lecturing the government on the mistakes being made in the war, and he hoped to channel his ideas through Hubert Humphrey. But Lansdale's antagonists within the Washington bureaucracy were not going to let him dazzle Johnson as he had Kennedy, and they successfully shut him out. In desperation, Lansdale offered to go to Saigon as a standby tourist on the Military Air Transport Service. To a friend, Lansdale wrote that he would "just be available to Vietnamese who needed an American to talk things over with (which they obviously can't with Taylor, Johnson, etc.)." But when Lansdale sounded out his Vietnamese contacts, he found they were afraid that being seen with him would endanger their relations with the embassy, and Lansdale dropped the idea.

ABOUT THE TIME bombing resumed on May 18, Mai Van Bo, the chief of North Vietnam's delegation in Paris, called several French officials to ask urgently that they see him. Pledging the Frenchmen to the strictest confidence, Bo said that Pham Van Dong's Four Points should not be considered prior conditions but rather "working principles for a negotiation." If Washington recognized those principles, it could lead to a Geneva conference like the one in 1954. Bo added a major concession: the North would not expect U.S. troops to leave until after the negotiations were successful. Within two days, the Frenchmen passed along Bo's message to Washington. Bo waited almost a month and then asked his French contacts at the ministry of foreign affairs what had happened. They said that Rusk's State Department had not responded.

MAX TAYLOR'S YEAR as ambassador had been an unmitigated failure, but not for the reasons Bundy had predicted. Rather than being listless and spent, Taylor had charged onto the political scene in a manner that alienated the Vietnamese he had to work with. And the same man who had recommended U.S. ground troops in 1961 — and was told to change his mind — had not been able to overrule Westmoreland's request for Marines four years later. From his Senate office, Robert Kennedy sent him a handwritten note, warning that Taylor was being blamed for the lack of progress in South Vietnam. "And I don't think," Kennedy added, "there is anyone back here who defends you or who speaks up on your behalf."

As early as March, Mac Bundy had urged Johnson to recall Taylor and leave Alex Johnson in charge. "Max has been gallant, determined and honorable to a

Air Force Vice Marshal
Nguyen Cao Ky
(AP/Wide World Photos)

fault," Bundy wrote—preparing for the inevitable "but"—"but he has also been rigid, remote and sometimes abrupt." Although Johnson refused to embarrass the ambassador with an early recall, he was waiting out the weeks until Taylor's year commitment was up. Taylor's warnings that bombing alone would not persuade the North to end the war were ignored, as was his conviction that U.S. troops should not go on the offensive in the South. Nor was Taylor consulted about his successor. He was displeased to learn that Cabot Lodge—lethargic in all things but overthrowing Diem—would be returning as ambassador. Taylor wrote to ask Bundy that he be allowed to leave Saigon as soon as Lodge arrived.

For a time in the spring of 1965, it looked as though Taylor might be able to point to one success. More than either McNamara or Lodge, he had been committed to civilian rule in Saigon. With Khanh gone and Phan Khac Suu installed as chief of state and Phan Huy Quat as prime minister, Taylor had devised protective coloration to pretend that the Saigon government was more than a military cabal. Then, on the evening of June 12, Quat summoned his ministers and military commanders to his office. Nguyen Cao Ky did not know what to expect, but he was glad to see beer and a cold buffet laid out in one corner of the room.

When Quat appeared, he complained that Suu was opposing his every move; Suu responded with vague platitudes about the rule of law. Ky felt contempt for Suu, doddering and hardly cogent even at his best. Quat heard Suu out, struck his desk and declared, "I resign." Since the military council had named him premier, Quat said, he was handing power back to the armed forces.

The next step was to persuade Suu to sign over Quat's authority so that Nguyen Van Thieu, a soft-spoken general with the fewest enemies, could legally assume command. But Suu was not to be hurried and persisted in rehashing past problems. Half an hour past midnight, Ky sent two colleagues into the next room to write out Quat's resignation and hunt up a tape recorder. They left with Suu wailing, "Why is my dear friend Quat deserting me?"

Ky made himself another sandwich and waited. When his men returned, he took Quat's declaration and the tape machine to Suu's place at the table. "Please, Mr. Chief of State, would you read this message? We don't have any more time to discuss things."

Without protest, Suu read Quat's resignation and the meeting broke up. The next morning, Ky nominated Thieu to the fifty-member Armed Forces Council. But to Ky's astonishment, Thieu refused the position. He did not want the responsibility, he said.

The meeting turned into another marathon. Ky suggested General Nguyen Huu Co, whose name provoked hours of debate before he too refused. Beds were provided, and the officers ate in their mess. The next morning, Ky suggested Brigadier General Nguyen Chanh Thi, the flashy I Corps commander. Like Westmoreland, Thi was a paratrooper who often jumped with his men. Now, however, he would not budge. "No, no, no!" Thi cried. "Never!"

At the next coffee break, the three reluctant generals collared Ky and told him he was their choice. Ky granted that if the military did not decide soon, the civilians would start ridiculing them. With a few rhetorical flourishes—"I am ready to accept as I've always accepted any job, even the hardest, that the armed forces has assigned to me"—Ky agreed. His fellow generals cheered their choice.

That action had been taken while Taylor was in Washington for consultation. He returned to Saigon to find not only a military government but one headed by the officer he had most grievously insulted.

WHEN HE HEARD in early July that Max Taylor was leaving Saigon, Lansdale hoped for a moment that his contacts with the vice president might win him the ambassadorship. Humphrey had sacrificed his influence with Johnson by expressing doubts over Vietnam, but he did urge Lodge to take Lansdale on his staff. More usefully, Senator Thomas Dodd of Connecticut, who blamed Lodge for Diem's murder, threatened to block his appointment unless Lansdale had an official title.

To heal the breach, Lodge invited Lansdale to lunch and they ran through possible jobs for him. "Go with me," Lodge said finally. "You'll be my assistant and take over the pacification programs in Vietnam. I'll take care of you."

As a result, Lansdale was back in Saigon late in August, his arrival the subject of considerable press attention. *Newsweek* expected him to oppose the permission recently given to U.S. pilots to bomb South Vietnamese villages suspected of harboring Vietcong. Reporters also observed, however, that the war had changed irrevocably since Lansdale's last tour of duty. One correspondent hailed him as a miracle worker but said it would take 300,000 Lansdales to make a difference in present-day South Vietnam.

Lansdale began collecting his old team, including Lou Conein, who had been on indefinite leave from the CIA. He also signed up Daniel Ellsberg, who agreed to leave McNaughton's staff in the Defense Department. Ellsberg had been to Vietnam once before. After he earned a summa cum laude degree at Harvard and served three years in the Marines, he first went to Saigon in the fall of 1961, a few weeks before the Taylor-Rostow mission, as a RAND Corporation member of a high-level Pentagon task force.

Ellsberg came back sure that the Communists would defeat Diem. He advised his RAND bosses to steer clear of Vietnam research and returned to his own studies on how to guard against surprise nuclear attacks by the Soviet Union. But Ellsberg considered himself a Cold War professional, and three years later he moved to the Pentagon, drafting speeches for McNamara in support of the war. It was more as a reserve Marine officer, then, and less as a detached analyst that Ellsberg prepared to pick up a rifle and return to Vietnam.

Conein appreciated his enthusiasm but thought he seemed to be playing at cowboys and Indians. Ellsberg's naïveté about life in a poor Asian country amused Lansdale, who taught him such survival tricks as not brushing his teeth with Saigon's tap water. Apart from his inexperience, however, Lansdale found him both brilliant and compassionate. For his part, Ellsberg admired the respect that Lansdale showed the Vietnamese. Where other Americans could be condescending, Lansdale would listen—not, perhaps, always understanding—but listening in a way that achieved rapport.

One of Lansdale's few complaints about his young volunteer was Ellsberg's loose treatment of classified documents. He would carry top-secret papers in a pants pocket, oblivious to the danger they could pose if they were lost or stolen.

PRESIDENT JOHNSON may have thought he had kept his options open after the Tonkin reprisal raids, but Politburo members had anticipated the decisions he would make. They dreaded, but expected, that he would keep bombing them. Communist strategists had assumed that when the United States saw it was losing the war in the South, bombing of the North would begin. Six months before the onset of Rolling Thunder, Hanoi's Foreign Ministry set up boardinghouses around the country for city children and their mothers.

Once the first bombs fell, Ho called on all Vietnamese to fight for the liberation of their entire country. For the displaced youngsters, being evacuated was alarming, but the city-bred children found an openhearted welcome in the countryside, and any sense of superiority quickly disappeared. With their country cousins, they were now facing a common enemy. As the American bombs dropped, the people of North Vietnam were united as never before.

No one in Hanoi knew of the debate within the White House that Dong's Four Points for Peace had been provoking since April. Richard Goodwin on the White House staff read the points in the spirit that Hanoi had intended and wrote to Johnson that they had not been presented as conditions but rather as a statement of ultimate objectives — "just as we say any settlement has to provide for an independent South Vietnam, tied to no alliance, etc." Goodwin guessed accurately that the rigid language had been included as a guarantee to the NLF that it would not be sold out at a future conference. The United States says the same kind of thing to reassure Saigon, Goodwin concluded. But Johnson saw Goodwin as a Jack Kennedy man, recruited for the White House from the Alliance for Progress programs Goodwin had helped to launch. Compared to the judgment of his secretary of state, Goodwin's opinion counted for little.

And Rusk was telling Johnson that Dong's statement was simply Communist deception because "the third of those four points required the imposition of the National Liberation Front upon all South Vietnam." To Rusk, the points were proof that Hanoi was not interested in talking seriously about peace. He did not seem to know that the NLF's program included the setting up of a neutral coalition in the South. Nor had he heard that some NLF members were predicting that to reunify the country would take a long time, perhaps decades. In the North, the Politburo had a much shorter timetable. But if the slower NLF approach would stop the Americans from expanding the war, Hanoi would not contradict its Front.

Watching Vietcong victories against the ARVN at Ba Gia and Dong Xoai that spring, Westmoreland was frustrated. He had been getting nonstop advice from Washington, often contradictory, usually trivial, always annoying: use U.S. techniques to jazz up ARVN recruiting; put 50 or so U.S. soldiers in ARVN battalions to stiffen their backbone; provide food directly to ARVN soldiers and their families rather than through the chain of command. Fed up, Westmoreland asked Admiral Sharp to define his authority, and Sharp replied that, as the man on the ground, Westmoreland's word was final. But the admiral added, "I'm sure you realize that there would be grave political implications if sizable U.S. forces are committed for the first time and suffer a defeat."

Westmoreland soon allowed American troops to accompany the ARVN on offensive patrols, and reporters on the scene saw that U.S. Marines and paratroopers were no longer limited to guarding the coastal bases. Pressed to admit to the change in their role, Johnson's spokesman told Washington reporters that there had been none. He did go on to say that Westmoreland had the authority to support ARVN forces facing an aggressive attack. Westmoreland was too disciplined to call that hedging a lie, although he was unhappy that it was misleading. His next recommendations, however, would face Johnson with the decision he had been ducking.

Westmoreland was convinced that the Communists were now ready to move into the third stage of Giap's strategy. Because they would end isolated guerrilla attacks and move to standing battles, he was calling for forty-four more battalions. During McNamara's next inspection tour, Westmoreland confided to the defense secretary that he would need yet another twenty-four battalions as well. That meant he was calling for 175,000 U.S. troops, to be followed by another 100,000. And that total, he said, would only put the United States in a position to begin to win the war. McNamara told him to ask for whatever troops he needed and leave the political and public relations aspects to him.

In Washington, Ball was determined to make a last attempt to halt the rush toward turning Vietnam into an American war. Because he understood the president's obsession with being in control of events, he titled his June 18, 1965, memo, "Keeping the Power of Decision in the South Vietnamese Crisis" and opened with Emerson's apocalyptic line: "Things are in the saddle and ride mankind." Ball outlined his familiar objections against waging a white man's war in Asia, and once again used Moyers as his conduit for reaching the president. Moyers called the following Monday to say that Johnson had read the memo over the weekend. He agreed with its substance—with "one or two slight changes possibly."

Ball had pointed out that the French lost to Giap despite fielding 205,000 Vietnamese soldiers and 250,000 of their own battle-vetted troops. Moyers took notes on Johnson's reaction and read them back to Ball: "I don't think I should go over one hundred thousand," the president had commented, "but I think I should go to that number and explain it." Johnson wanted Ball to spend the next ninety days making projections of military activity in South Vietnam after the monsoon season ended. The president assured Ball that he did not intend to ride off in the wrong direction.

"I told McNamara that I would not make a decision on this," Johnson added, "and not to assume that I'm willing to go overboard on this. I ain't. If there is no alternative, the fellow who has the best program is the way it will probably go."

With few illusions, Ball got to work. To persuade Johnson, he had to budge Rusk, McNamara or Bundy, which looked impossible. With Rusk, their differences had degenerated into routine banter. "Look," Deputy Secretary Ball would say about Saigon to Secretary of State Rusk, "you've got no government. It's impossible to win in a situation where you've got this totally fragile political base. Those people"—Thieu and Ky—"are clowns."

To which Rusk would respond good-naturedly: "Don't give me that stuff. You don't understand that at the time of Korea we had to go out and dig up Syngman Rhee out of the bush where he was hiding. There was no government in Korea, either. We're going to get some breaks, and this thing is going to work."

With McNamara, the exchanges were edgier. As a cabinet officer, he was always aware that Ball's rank did not match his own, and Ball found McNamara's reliance on statistical arguments both intriguing and suspect. Once, after McNamara had rattled off the odds for the success of various military operations—65 percent for this one, 30 for that—Ball had joked that perhaps the figures were actually 64 percent and 29 percent. He saw that such teasing did not amuse the defense secretary.

That left Mac Bundy. Distressed by the public criticism, Bundy was making professorial attempts to defend his position, at least within the Ivy League. Earlier in the year, an editorial in the *Harvard Crimson* advised getting out of Vietnam. Since one of the editors was Kay Graham's son, Donald, Bundy took time to draft an eleven-page rationale for the war. Bundy lectured Graham on how appeasing Hitler in 1938 had led to World War II. His analogy presumed that either China or the Soviet Union was bent on conquering all of Asia. And that Ho would allow his country to be their staging area.

Bundy had realized belatedly that Johnson had shipped him to Santo Domingo only to keep him from the teach-in. Bridling at the ploy—and without consulting Johnson—Bundy arranged for a chance to redeem himself. He contacted Fred Friendly, a CBS television producer, and agreed to a live debate; he also withdrew his objection to Hans Morgenthau. The confrontation was set for June 21, about the time Ball expected to finish a new memo for the president called "Cutting Our Losses in Vietnam."

When Johnson read in the press that Bundy was going to appear, he exploded to Moyers. "Do you see this? Bundy is going on television—on national television—with five professors. That's an act of disloyalty. He didn't tell me because he knew I didn't want him to do it."

Johnson instructed Moyers to tell Bundy that the president would be pleased—mighty pleased—to accept his resignation. Before Moyers could respond, Johnson said, "On second thought, maybe I should talk to him myself." With Moyers still taken aback, Johnson said, "No, you go do it." Moyers hesitated. Johnson muttered to this, his most loyal aide, "That's the trouble with all you fellows. You're in bed with the Kennedys."

Deeply disturbed, Moyers called Richard Goodwin that night to say that Johnson's behavior had him extremely worried, that he didn't feel he was even talking to a human being. Goodwin agreed that Johnson's monologues these days suggested paranoia. The president's irritation with the White House arts festival had left him vowing, "I am not going to have anything more to do with the liberals. They won't have anything to do with me. They just follow the Communist line—liberals, intellectuals, Communists." Johnson told Goodwin that since he couldn't trust anyone anymore, he was going to get rid of everybody who didn't agree with his policies.

THAT WAS THE BACKGROUND when Mac Bundy showed up at his office on the morning of the debate. He repeated to his staff a tip from his wife that indicated Bundy was well aware of his instinct to go for the jugular. He quoted Mary Bundy as saying, "Try to be tonight the man I married and not the man I almost didn't marry." Bundy might appreciate that insight but could he act on it?

CBS had given the debate a portentous title—"Vietnam Dialogue: Mr. Bundy and the Professors"—and assigned as moderator its political commentator, Eric Sevareid. The black-and-white telecast could not capture Bundy's scrubbed pink aura, and with the clear plastic frames of his glasses he looked especially young and unformed next to the weathered Morgenthau. Bundy began by quoting long passages from the Johns Hopkins speech. From Morgenthau's rebuttal, Bundy saw that neither he nor his two academic colleagues were prepared to recommend abandoning the South entirely. As they entered the hour's last segment, Bundy went for a knockout. He accused Morgenthau of congenital pessimism in foreign affairs and quoted from his past prediction that the Marshall Plan would fail. Reading Morgenthau's words in doleful tones, Bundy noted that four years earlier he had also seen Communist domination of Laos as a foregone conclusion.

"I may have been dead wrong on Laos," Morgenthau responded plaintively, "but it doesn't mean I am dead wrong on Vietnam."

Bundy would not let up. He next quoted Morgenthau as praising Diem in 1956 for the "miracle" he had wrought. The judgment had little bearing on a debate nine years later, but that scarcely mattered. Most viewers saw the brilliant Mr. Bundy eviscerating his opponent. As one University of Michigan professor wrote to the colleagues who first invited Bundy to debate, "I am forced to conclude that we pursued McGeorge Bundy until he caught us."

Within the White House, however, Bundy had won no victory. Moyers spared him most of Johnson's invective but let him know that the president opposed the debate. In defying him, Bundy knew his term as national security adviser was coming to an end. But he was not yet ready to quit. He could endure the president's coolness and the new and belittling nickname he called Bundy behind his back—"my debater."

Not long afterward, Moyers was in the presidential bedroom when Johnson asked if he would mind getting his pajamas from the next room. "Of course not," Moyers replied.

"And after you've got my pajamas," Johnson said, "go downstairs and fire Bundy."

A story in that day's *Washington Post* had displeased Johnson and he was sure Bundy was responsible. Moyers protested, but he went to the basement office and found, to his relief, that Bundy had gone for the night.

The next morning, Johnson said, "You didn't fire Bundy, did you?"

Moyers said that he had not been available. "I knew you didn't," Johnson said. "He called this morning and didn't say anything about it. Go down and do it now."

This time, Bundy was at his desk. Moyers said, "The president sent me down to fire you."

Bundy looked up briefly from his papers. "Again?" he asked and went back to work.

But Bundy sympathized with Johnson. He called it a lousy way to run a war when the president did not have a number-one aide he trusted. Bundy contacted President Pusey at Harvard and asked, "Suppose I wanted to get out of government, would you have a place?"

Pusey said, "You know you're not the easiest piece of goods to sell in the community, but I can find a way, and I'll work on it."

ONLY MAC BUNDY, at the lowest point of his influence with Johnson, seemed to see any virtue in Ball's argument, but he called to warn Ball that Johnson had decided to approve a new reprisal raid. The Vietcong had recently killed a prisoner of war, Sergeant Harold Bennett, in retaliation for Saigon's execution of a convicted Vietcong terrorist. The Vietcong had also bombed a Saigon riverboat restaurant on the Mekong, killing 12 Americans and 32 Europeans and Vietnamese. And NLF radio was announcing that Max Taylor, Alex Johnson and Westmoreland were on a Vietcong death list. Taylor wired Washington to suggest immediate bombing in the populated Haiphong and Hanoi areas, which had been off limits to Rolling Thunder. He described the riverboat bombing as the bloodiest atrocity the United States had endured and said—in an aside that would have infuriated the Hanoi leadership—that the Vietcong were "well aware that we place higher value on human life than they do."

Rusk, McNamara and Bundy all disagreed with Taylor's recommendation. They did not want to tie an important bombing escalation like hitting Haiphong and Hanoi to any single espisode. But, as Bundy told Ball, Johnson was siding with Taylor. A dreadful decision, Ball said. Bundy said it was not yet firm, but he felt he should warn Ball that Johnson thought the country would react strongly to the latest provocation since the casualties were even higher than they had been at Pleiku. For himself, Bundy added, his personal judgment still ran with Ball's.

Bundy had also received McNamara's June 26 outline for boosting U.S. support for South Vietnam. Although the president was ready to approve a level of

95,000 U.S. troops, McNamara was arguing that the figure had to be higher still. He wrote that "the tide almost certainly cannot begin to turn in less than a few months and may not for a year or more; the war is one of attrition and will be a long one."

McNamara had been convinced by Westmoreland's argument that Hanoi was moving to the third stage of conventional war. He expected the change to make it "easier to identify, locate and attack the enemy." For McNamara, Americanizing the war would shift the balance in Washington's favor and lead to negotiations. Unaware of the Politburo's delicate relations with both China and the Soviet Union, McNamara urged that the United States "press the Chinese to bring the aggression against the South to an end."

McNamara had no doubt that the United States would win the struggle. "Even though casualties will increase and the war will continue for some time, the United States public will support this course of action because it is a combined military-political program designed and likely to bring about a favorable solution to the Vietnam problem."

McNamara's proposal was a first draft and had not yet gone to the president. Mac Bundy tore into it with emotion he rarely displayed on paper or in person.

"My first reaction is that this program is rash to the point of folly," Bundy wrote. He rejected the argument that the war was becoming a conventional one. "In particular, I see no reason to suppose that the Vietcong will accommodate us by fighting the kind of war we desire." He added, "I think the odds are that if we put in 40–50 battalions with the missions here proposed, we shall find them only lightly engaged and ineffective in hot pursuit."

Bundy pointed out that McNamara was not asking anything from the South Vietnamese government before Washington committed 200,000 men. "But this is a slippery slope toward total U.S. responsibility and corresponding fecklessness on the Vietnamese side." As long as he was allied with Bundy against Ball, McNamara had been spared the precision of Bundy's mind. Now he received its full brunt. Bundy was questioning him the way Jack Kennedy had probed bellicose recommendations from his Joint Chiefs.

"The paper also omits examination of the upper limit of U.S. liability," Bundy continued. "If we need 200 thousand men now for these quite limited missions, may we not need 400 thousand later? Is this a rational course of action? Is there any real prospect that U.S. regular forces can conduct the anti-guerrilla operations which would probably remain the central problem in South Vietnam?"

Finally, Bundy asked McNamara to explain the point of a troop buildup. "If it is to get to the conference table, what results do we seek there? Still more brutally, do we want to invest 200 thousand men to cover an eventual retreat? Can we not do that just as well where we are?"

The aggressive tone of Bundy's memo came after he had been denounced on national television as an architect of America's Vietnam policy. He was not fully converted to Ball's policy of withdrawal, which explained why he was sending this heretical memo to McNamara, not to Johnson. Aware of his own ebbing influence with the president, Bundy wanted McNamara to stop Johnson from escalating.

Not that any confrontation was likely to sway Johnson now. The previous month, Clark Clifford, ubiquitous adviser to presidents, had volunteered his doubts in a letter to the White House. "This could be a quagmire," Clifford wrote. He got no answer.

As Mac Bundy punctured McNamara's assumptions, his brother was still seeking that elusive middle way between escalation and withdrawal. Bill Bundy recommended holding on in the South with the 85,000 U.S. troops already committed there.

The stakes were high enough for Rusk to make one of his rare commitments in writing. Without informing McNamara or Ball and Bill Bundy in his own State Department, Rusk wrote to Johnson that if America faltered in Vietnam "the Communist world would draw conclusions that would lead to our ruin and almost certainly to a catastrophic war."

By now, Johnson had four proposals on his desk, and Mac Bundy sensed that pulling out of South Vietnam was not an option. Since McNamara had not revised his memo to meet Bundy's objections, Bundy seized on his brother's middle way and used his role as doorkeeper to nudge Johnson as best he could.

The day before the policy session scheduled for July 2, Bundy wrote to the president, "I find that both Rusk and McNamara feel strongly that the George Ball paper should not be argued with you in front of any audience larger than yourself, Rusk, McNamara, Ball and me. They feel that it is exceedingly dangerous to have this possibility reported in a wider circle. Moreover, both of them feel great reticence about expressing their own innermost thoughts to you in front of any larger group. So they both would prefer a meeting limited to the five of us in the morning."

Bundy's suggestion played to Johnson's penchant for secrecy and guaranteed that Ball would be the only one recommending withdrawal. Less than an hour later, Bundy produced another memorandum that would mute even that lone voice before it could be heard.

"The positions within the government are roughly as follows," Bundy explained. "McNamara and Ball honestly believe in their own recommendations, though Bob would readily accept advice to tone down those of his recommendations which would move rapidly against Hanoi by bombing and blockade.

"Dean Rusk leans toward the McNamara program, adjusted downward in this same way."

The Joint Chiefs were strongly in favor of going even further than McNamara, Bundy continued, wanting specifically to take out the Surface-to-Air Missile sites, but along with the SAMs also the Soviet aircraft, the IL-28 light bombers and the MiGs in the Hanoi area. But what Bundy termed "second level men" in both State and Defense—the assistant secretaries—were not optimistic about South Vietnam's future. They were reluctant to see a forty-four-battalion increase with a call-up of the reserves and wanted to watch developments over the summer before going in more deeply. "So they would tend to cluster around the middle course suggested by my brother."

As he had done from his first memo to Johnson as president, Bundy attempted to stage-manage his responses: "My hunch is that you will want to listen hard to George Ball and then reject his proposal," Bundy wrote. "Discussion could then move to the narrower choice between my brother's course and McNamara's."

Bundy helpfully spelled out the questions Johnson should ask, leading off with an imponderable. "What are the chances of our getting into a white man's war with all the brown men against us or apathetic?"

Bundy himself had already provided Johnson with a partial answer in a paper he called "France in Vietnam, 1954, and the U.S. in Vietnam, 1965—A Useful Analogy?" Preparing for the Morgenthau debate had cleared up some of Bundy's misconceptions about the South's history, and he granted that without U.S. military and economic support South Vietnam "would quickly succumb to Communist domination." But the reason for France's failure and why America could expect success lay in their respective homefronts. Bundy underlined in his text— "the war's accute unpopularity" in France and "French political instability."

He explained to Johnson that "France was never united or consistent in her prosecution of the war in Indochina. The war was not popular in France itself, was actively opposed on the left and was cynically used by others for domestic political ends." The Vietminh had often made good use of France's domestic divisions.

By comparison, Bundy reported, the American public generally supported the war. The most articulate critics—academics and church groups—were a minority within their own organizations, but "they have stimulated extensive worry and inquiry in the nation as a whole." With the academic year over, the protest movement had temporarily subsided. The latest Harris poll showed 62 percent of Americans approving Johnson's handling of Vietnam, but when only those with a firm opinion were separated from the undecideds, almost 80 percent approved of the bombing and more than 60 percent called for sending more troops.

Those were the percentages in Johnson's pocket as he sat down to hear George Ball plead again for U.S. withdrawal.

AT 11 A.M. ON JULY 2, 1965, Johnson met in the Cabinet Room with the small number of men Bundy had recommended. No minutes were kept, but Bill Bundy soon heard what Johnson had decided—to buy himself the time to build a global consensus, he was dispatching representatives around the world. Harriman, using as a cover story that he was on a sightseeing trip, would head for Moscow to sound out the Soviets about U.S. escalation. Ball should refine his proposals for negotiation and seek direct contacts between private Americans and the NLF and with the North Vietnamese in Paris, perhaps through Mai Van Bo. Ball cabled the embassy in Saigon that the United States was not immediately willing to recognize Ho's government, but that it might be possible much later, if fruitful negotiations were underway.

McNamara was to go to Saigon in the middle of the month with Cabot Lodge and Wheeler of the Joint Chiefs to evaluate plans from Westmoreland that would commit the United States through 1966.

To DISCUSS HIS OPTIONS still further, Johnson instructed Mac Bundy to assemble in Washington the dozen-and-a-half former government officials whom the president called his "Wise Men." Dean Acheson, with his bristling gray mustache, was the ranking member, and Robert Lovett would be there, five years after his perilous health led him to reject Jack Kennedy's cabinet offer. Eugene Black and John McCloy, two former presidents of the World Bank, were invited, along with Ros Gilpatric, General Omar Bradley and Arthur Larson, a Duke University professor who had served presidents since Franklin Roosevelt.

Many of those distinguished elders were members of the Council on Foreign Relations. Bill Bundy had maintained close relations with the council's board long before he was appointed to the Far Eastern desk at State, and Lodge, Taylor and Mac Bundy had already briefed council members in New York. Most of Johnson's guests shared the Bundy brothers' esteem for Henry Stimson. McCloy called Stimson his "hero-statesman" and regarded the men on Johnson's guest list as being cast from Stimson's admirable mold.

The Wise Men were taken to the seventh floor of the State Department for new briefings by Rusk, McNamara and Tommy Thompson, who spoke to them about Russia. They were then assigned to specific task forces. When they met again as a group, McCloy took the lead. Simply blunting the Vietcong's monsoon offensive might not force Hanoi to the bargaining table, he said. Addressing Rusk and McNamara directly, McCloy added, "We are about to get our noses bloodied, but you got to do it. You've got to go in."

Arthur Larson, hardly the assembly's richest man or the possessor of the loftiest credentials, was a dissenting voice. Even if Hanoi could somehow be forced out, he said, the United States might never get a stable and democratic South Vietnam. Larson could not derail the support for escalation, and when Paul Hoffman, an industrialist who had once headed the Marshall Plan, suggested negotiating, Acheson and Arthur Dean came down hard on him. Dean, Eisenhower's negotiator for the Korean armistice, said this was no time to turn U.S. policy over to the United Nations.

Late that afternoon, a few visitors were invited to the White House to let them argue the president into a decision he had already made. Over highballs, Johnson treated his guests to an imposing display of self-pity. Everyone and everything was against him—Congress, the press, the intellectuals, fate itself. No one was supporting him on Vietnam. The Wise Men were not as accustomed as Johnson's staff to those lamentations, and Acheson blew up at him. You're entirely right on Vietnam, the former secretary of state said impatiently, and you have no choice except to press on. Successful action will be far more important than any explanations.

At that, the other Wise Men joined in. McCloy had never considered Vietnam vital to American security, and Acheson had drafted a memorandum with Ball on ways to reach a political settlement. But now they were detecting signs of doubt in the president when they thought a show of strength was essential. Forgetting their own qualms, they swamped Johnson with evangelical advice. Mac Bundy afterward gave Acheson most of the credit. "The mustache," he told his staff, "was voluble."

Their visit ended with the East Coast policy patricians urging Johnson to follow his inclination, but other elements of the equation remained to be added to his consensus. As he prepared to send McNamara to Saigon, Johnson sought to buck up his defense secretary against any ethical qualms. "We know ourselves," Johnson said, aware—as McNamara was not—that their telephone conversation was being recorded, "that when we asked for this Tonkin Gulf Resolution, we had no intention of committing this many ground troops."

"Right," said McNamara dutifully.

"And we're doin' so now and we know it's goin' be bad, and the question: do we just want to do it out on a limb by ourselves?"

McNamara said that if Johnson accepted his recommendation for sending large numbers of troops, the administration should also call up the Reserves. "Almost surely," McNamara continued, "if we called up Reserves, you would want to go to the Congress to get additional authority. This would be a vehicle for drawing together support."

McNamara sketched out examples of dialogue that the president might use in winning over the congressmen. Johnson, who had been coping with Congress since McNamara was a graduate student, heard him out and said blandly, "Well, that makes sense."

IN JULY, China's first contingent of engineers arrived in North Vietnam's Tay Nguyen province. A two-star general, Hoang Phuong, went to greet the Chinese at their camp some forty miles north of Hanoi. The engineering troops prepared antiaircraft bases and stored ammunition in caves, preparing against massive U.S. bombing. In time, 60,000 to 70,000 Chinese arrived; with rotation, as many as 300,000 eventually served in North Vietnam. At first, the pragmatic Vietnamese applauded as Chinese trucks rolled by, and some held up Mao's Little

Red Book of Communist aphorisms. But when the Chinese quickly built a well-guarded compound, it was at least as much to protect themselves from their allies as from American bombs. Friction arose regularly between the hosts and guests, and at every opportunity the local Vietnamese stole Chinese equipment and supplies. The Chinese retaliated by shouting insults at Vietnamese citizens in the street.

Since Ho wanted Washington to be aware of the deterrent he had invited in, he encouraged early antiaircraft strikes against the U.S. bombers in order to call attention to the Chinese presence. As a result, Communist casualties ran high in those first days because the Chinese had not yet dug trenches for their guns.

IN MOSCOW, meanwhile, Harriman was having a frank talk with Premier Kosygin. "Speaking in human terms, between ourselves," the Soviet leader asked, did Washington seriously believe that there was a real legal government in South Vietnam? "You just cannot believe this," Kosygin added. "Yet the United States, for this so-called government, sheds the blood of its own soldiers and kills defenseless Vietnamese."

Harriman said he wanted to raise another question: did the Soviet Union really believe that without the support and direction of the North Vietnamese there would be a serious problem in the South?

I am thoroughly familiar with Vietnam, Kosygin answered, and I know that the South Vietnamese would fight with bamboo sticks, if necessary, against the current regime.

Harriman responded with a defense of U.S. policy that would have made Walt Rostow proud. When he finished, Kosygin laughed and said, "You don't believe what you are saying."

Harriman countered that the premier had to accept that what he had just said was the genuine belief of the president, his advisers, Congress and the American people. Since Johnson had said that the honor of the United States was involved, why not accept his invitation to discuss the situation?

Kosygin replied that he was not authorized to negotiate. But how could the United States claim that it was helping the South Vietnamese? "This is a monstrous statement," he added. "You are killing South Vietnamese. History will never forgive the United States for this crime. This will always be a blot on the United States."

Kosygin turned the discussion to his country's problems with China. He claimed that Johnson was aiding China by turning all of Asia against America and proving China's point that war was inevitable. Kosygin added that he had never said as much to anyone else, but he hoped Harriman would pass along that thought to the president.

As Harriman continued to argue for the justice of Johnson's policies, Kosygin lost patience. I could buy these Saigon puppets of yours tomorrow for 1 million dollars, he said. And it is for those marionettes that you sacrifice the people of Vietnam and your own people as well. The United States should not think that making an overture to Hanoi would be seen as weakness, Kosygin added. Nor should Washington make the mistake of equating Beijing with Hanoi. Kosygin had known Ho Chi Minh for thirty years and could assure Harriman that Ho was a heroic figure, loved and admired by his countrymen. Fighting him for many years will not help.

Harriman complained that Hanoi was showing no interest in talks. Kosygin reminded him that "people with the noise of bombs in their ears are not anxious to negotiate."

BEFORE LEAVING for Saigon, McNamara had sent the embassy a list of two broad questions and twenty-five more specific ones that he expected Westmoreland and the civilian staff to answer. For example, what assurance could the American mission give that, if Westmoreland got his troop increase, it would prove to the Vietcong that they could not win?

When they sat down together, Westmoreland explained that it was impossible to furnish the Secretary with meaningful statistics. He could only predict that besides the forty-four battalions under consideration, he would need another twenty-four battalions, plus combat support and logistical troops. And that would merely put Westmoreland at the beginning of his strategy's "win phase." As he had already mentioned, that meant 175,000 U.S. troops at the start, with another 100,000 to come. But Communist actions could cause those figures to be revised upward. Westmoreland predicted that the new U.S. troops could halt the losing trend by the end of 1965, take the offensive in phase two during the first six months of 1966 and then defeat the enemy and destroy his bases in a period of one year to eighteen months later. That timetable presumed that phase two could in fact be achieved in 1966, although Westmoreland was careful not to offer any guarantee. Calculating by presidential elections, however, the general's figures suggested a reassuring prospect: the war could be won and peace declared before the 1968 election.

In June, General Thieu had agreed to serve as chief of state, with Ky as prime minister. Ky had undercut his own reputation by citing Adolf Hitler as the kind of leader South Vietnam required. When McNamara called on the Saigon generals, he found Thieu full of optimism after three weeks of his partnership with Ky. But when McNamara asked whether 200,000 U.S. troops would guarantee a stable South Vietnamese government, Thieu spelled out what he expected from the Americans. "If U.S. troops were to relieve the ARVN," he said, his troops could then turn to pacification. Thieu seemed to be admitting that the ARVN preferred defensive measures to going after a more deadly and expanding Vietcong.

McNamara appeared willing to jump up the next increase in troops from Westmoreland's twenty-four battalions to the twenty-seven battalions that the

Joint Chiefs were recommending. He also differed with Westmoreland over whether or not the National Guard and the Reserves should be activated, as Jack Kennedy had done when he expected a face-off over Berlin. McNamara endorsed the idea; Westmoreland considered it premature. Without congressional legislation, a call-up could last for only one year, and Westmoreland foresaw a longer war than that.

Before they could resolve their differences, McNamara received a cable from his deputy, Cy Vance, reporting a decision by the "highest authority"—cablese for "the president"—to give Westmoreland his battalions. What's more, Vance told McNamara that Johnson would not ask Congress for a supplemental budget for Vietnam of more than $300-to-$400 million since the president believed that any higher request would kill his domestic programs. The Voting Rights Act, for example, was just then being written into final form by a congressional committee.

In the past, McNamara had gone to Saigon on a fact-finding mission with his conclusions all but drafted. This time, Johnson had not gone through the motions of waiting for him to return. But although the president's mind was made up, he wanted to strengthen his consensus. He held several large gatherings and listened attentively while advisers, military chiefs and congressmen debated what he should do; some of them may have thought they were influencing his decision. On July 21, McNamara passed around copies of his top-secret recommendations. At first, Ball welcomed the president's seemingly searching questions: "What has happened in the recent past that requires this decision on my part? What are the alternatives? Also, I want more discussions on what we expect to follow from this decision."

Johnson asked whether Washington had wrung every single soldier out of every allied country. "Are we the sole defenders of freedom in the world?" Running through possible actions, Johnson concluded, "Let's look at all our options so that every man at this table understands fully the total picture."

McNamara was ready with a map that compared current allied holdings in the South with those of the previous year. The American mission calculated that the Vietcong now controlled 25 percent of the South, the Saigon government 50 percent, with the remainder of the country in dispute. Areas where the Vietcong predominated were marked in red, and the president remarked that it looked dangerous to put U.S. soldiers in those red territories. McNamara agreed but noted that American troops would protect themselves by keeping their backs to the sea. "Our mission would be to seek out the V.C. in large-scale units," he said, an assignment that sounded like Thieu's recent proposal in Saigon.

After a brief discussion of Vietcong tactics, Johnson asked if anyone disagreed with McNamara's memo. Looking directly at Ball, he added, "If so, I'd like to hear from them." By now, Ball had his speech rehearsed, but he delivered it with no real hope of converting his audience of one. Instead, he volunteered a pledge of fealty that undercut what little leverage he might have had. Ball said that he foresaw a perilous voyage and had great apprehension that the United States could win. Then—in Johnson's graphic phrase—Ball cut off his own pecker and put it in the president's pocket. "But let me be clear," Ball said. "If the decision is to go ahead, I'm committed." With that concession, Ball guaranteed that he could always speak and could always be ignored.

Ball suggested letting the Saigon government fall apart and accepting a Communist takeover. "Can we make a case for this?" Johnson asked. "Discuss it fully?"

"We have discussed it," Ball granted. "I have had my day in court."

Johnson tried to coax him back on the offensive. "We haven't always been right," he said. "We have no mortgage on victory." But, the president added, unless Ball came up with a specific plan for disengagement, "I feel we have very little alternative to what we're doing." He did call, however, for another meeting to wring Ball's objections dry.

Rusk harked back to 1961 and said Washington probably should have committed itself more heavily then. Lodge dismissed the current Saigon regime. "I don't think we ought to take this government seriously," he said. "We have to do what we think we ought to do, regardless of what the Saigon government does." For Lodge, this new phase "gives us the right and duty to do certain things with or without the government's approval."

Johnson called on Ball to outline a specific course of action, but as Ball began to respond, Johnson interrupted: "We'll have another meeting this afternoon where you can express your views in detail. Now let Bob tell us why we need to risk 600,000 lives."

McNamara estimated there would be 200,000 more American troops in Vietnam by the first of the year, with the Reserves called up to fill out that figure. Then, in mid-1966, he would call up 235,000 more, replacing the Reserves with regulars, for a total of approximately 600,000 additional men. Of that number, 75,000 men would be sent immediately simply to protect the existing bases.

The president argued that the more men he sent, the greater number he would lose.

General Wheeler jumped in to reassure him. "The more men we have, the greater likelihood of smaller losses."

But if you put in 100,000 men, Johnson persisted, what makes you think Ho Chi Minh won't put in another 100,000?

"That means greater bodies of men," Wheeler said, "which will allow us to cream them."

The president asked what the chances were of more North Vietnamese going South.

Wheeler put the odds at fifty-fifty. "He would be foolhardy to put one-fourth of his forces in South Vietnam. It would expose him too greatly in the North."

It troubled Johnson that he was not getting intelligence out of North Vietnam. Raborn could only assure him that the CIA had a task force at work on the problem.

When the meeting resumed at 2:45 P.M., Ball had brought his own chart to enhance his presentation. Polls being Johnson's favorite political currency, Ball brought figures to show the correlation during the Korean War between casualties and public support. As the number of dead and wounded rose from 11,000 in 1950 to 40,000 two years later, the percentage of Americans who thought Truman had been right to intervene fell from 56 percent to 30 percent.

Ball tried to minimize the president's dread of looking weak. "No great captain in history ever hesitated to make a tactical withdrawal if conditions were unfavorable to him," he said. "I have grave doubts that any Western army can successfully fight Orientals in an Asian jungle."

Johnson's resolve could not be changed, but it could be shaken. "That's the key question," he remarked. "Can Westerners, deprived of accurate intelligence, successfully fight Asians in the jungle and rice paddies?"

Ball said, "I think we have underestimated the seriousness of this situation. What we are doing is giving cobalt treatment to a terminal cancer case." He reviewed the neighboring countries, offering vague predictions about Thailand, South Korea, Taiwan, Indonesia and Japan. Johnson raised U.S. credibility and the taunt that America was a paper tiger.

"The worse blow would be that the mightiest power in the world is unable to defeat guerrillas," Ball replied. He speculated on Europe's reaction to a pullout of American troops: France could hardly blame Washington, the British had retired from their own empire and were realistic about the United States doing the same, even though they might get a bit of mischievous pleasure—Ball used the German word *Schadenfreude*—from the withdrawal.

Mac Bundy granted that Ball had raised truly important questions but complained that he had given no weight to the losses Hanoi was suffering. Any incipient doubts Bundy might have entertained during the past month had been firmly tamped down again. "The world, the country and the Vietnamese people would have alarming reactions if we got out," he said.

With the others all lined up against Ball, the meeting was adjourned until the next day.

AT NOON ON JULY 22, Johnson met with an array of military advisers; he also invited Clark Clifford. Speaking first, and forcefully, Admiral David McDonald, chief of naval operations, said that putting in more men would turn the tide, and he wished Washington had done it long before. He viewed the choices starkly: "Get out now or pour in more men."

The Pentagon's experts disagreed over whether to give Westmoreland even more troops than he was requesting. Secretary of the Navy Paul Nitze said yes.

Air Force Chief of Staff John McConnell said no because he preferred to strike more targets in the North. Wallace Greene, the Marine commandant, recommended adding 72,000 Marines to the 28,000 already in Vietnam—those would be over and above Westmoreland's request. Harold Johnson, the Army's chief of staff, guessed that the U.S. buildup would not bring in either China or the Soviet Union.

The president asked, "But China has plenty of divisions to move in, don't they?"

"Yes," said General Johnson, "they do."

"*Then* what would we do?" The president's persistence set off the same long silence among the Joint Chiefs that Jack Kennedy's questions had done.

"If so," said General Johnson at last, "we have another ball game."

The president was the only one in the room to raise the question of civilian casualties. "Are we killing civilians along with V.C.?"

General Wheeler granted that some were dying. They were "accompanying the V.C.," he explained. "It can't be helped."

But Johnson had obtained more precise figures. "The Vietcong dead is running at a rate of 25,000 a year," he said somberly. "At least 15,000 have been killed by air—half of these are not part of what we call Vietcong. Since 1961, a total of 89,000 have been killed. The South Vietnamese are being killed at a rate of 12,000 a year."

Stanley Resor, secretary of the army, strove to focus the discussion on the president's options. He recommended the McNamara plan since Washington could not renege on its commitment and America's allies were watching carefully.

The president asked, "Do all of you think the Congress and the people will go along with 600,000 people and billions of dollars 10,000 miles away?"

Resor said the Gallup poll showed people favoring the commitment.

"But if you make a commitment to jump off a building," Johnson said, "and you find out how high it is, you may withdraw the commitment." He then called on Mac Bundy to spell out the opposing view. "Some Congressmen and Senators think we are going to be the most discredited people in the world," the president said. "What Bundy will now tell you is not his opinion or mine—I haven't taken a position yet—but what we hear."

Bundy ran down the damning list of U.S. military failures in South Vietnam and noted that "after twenty years of warnings about war in Asia, we are now doing what MacArthur and others have warned against." It was a pro forma performance, with Bundy making arguments he did not believe. McNamara assured the group that the Pentagon could refute most of Bundy's points.

The president observed that Gerald Ford in the House had demanded that Johnson testify before the Congress and tell why the administration was compelled to call up the Reserves. Ford seemed ready to oppose the decision.

☐

SINCE BALL WAS NOT ASKED to attend the military session, Bundy had summarized his position concisely and coolly. When the generals and admirals left the White House, Ball and other civilians were called back to hear how the meeting had gone. The president was chiefly concerned that calling up the Reserves not be seen as a change in policy. But Ball was heartened by Clifford's candid displeasure with the Pentagon briefing.

On his side, Clifford was finding the meetings the most remarkable since he had challenged George Marshall over whether to recognize the new nation of Israel in 1948. On that occasion, Clifford had carried the day, and Truman had promptly extended recognition to the Jewish state. Clifford knew the predictable styles of the men around the Cabinet Room table — Ball, deep voiced and impassioned; Mac Bundy, crisp; Rusk, calm and methodical; McNamara, precise and certain; Lodge, never an intellect, but heard out as a Republican and the man who would be returning to Saigon as ambassador. Clifford had said little during the session with the generals. But his notes were acute: he noticed how annoyed McNamara became when Nitze proposed giving Westmoreland even more troops than he had asked for, and he saw that McNamara's apocalyptic version of the domino theory now stretched well past Laos and Cambodia to affect the futures of Pakistan, Greece, Turkey, the nations of Africa.

When the civilians filed in after lunch, Clifford thought the president sounded frustrated by the lack of a concrete peace plan from the State Department. "This war is like a prize fight," Johnson said. "Our right hand is our military power, but our left must be peace proposals. Every time you move troops forward, you should move diplomats forward, too. I want this done. The generals want more and more from me. They want to go farther and farther. But State has to supply me with something too." Rusk sat by silently.

Listening to Clifford, Ball sensed that he might have found a potential ally. As the meeting broke up, he whispered that he wanted to speak to him privately and led Clifford a few yards down the hall to the Roosevelt Room.

Am I correct, Ball began, in assuming that you have deep doubts about the war and McNamara's proposals?

Not only do I have such doubts, Clifford replied, but I sent a letter in May to the president spelling out my concerns.

Ball became animated. "I have been looking for support for a long time," he said, adding that Clifford's influence with Johnson was tremendously important. Ball wanted to give Clifford his series of memoranda. "Can you handle them?" he asked. "They are highly classified."

Clifford said that, as a chairman of the president's Foreign Intelligence Advisory Board, he had the proper clearances and a safe at his house. If Ball had the memos hand-delivered, he would take care of them.

A guard stopped Clifford as he was leaving the White House to say that

Johnson was looking for him. In the anteroom of the Oval Office, he found the president waiting with Mac Bundy. Johnson was eager to hear Clifford's reactions, and Clifford obliged by ridiculing General Wheeler's mindless optimism. "The way the military acted today reminded me of the way they dealt with President Truman during the Korean War," Clifford said. He doubted that the Pentagon was being straight with Johnson.

"I know what pressure you're under from McNamara," Clifford added, "but if you handle it carefully you don't have to commit yourself and the nation." He concluded by raising two questions: Could a military victory be won? And if you did win, what would you have?

Johnson heard him out in silence and said he wanted to talk again after Clifford had more time to reflect on the meetings. Later that day, Clifford received Ball's memos at his office, took them home and stayed up until 2 A.M. reading them. Although he found Ball's logic persuasive, he doubted whether, after so many months and even years, Johnson was paying much attention to him.

When Clifford telephoned the next day to congratulate him, Ball was exhilarated. But Clifford had already received a call from Moyers warning him that Johnson had made up his mind to back McNamara and Westmoreland. As press secretary, Moyers felt barred from speaking out, although he agreed with Ball. But he could read Johnson well enough to know that he would not overrule Rusk, McNamara and Bundy. Their minds would have to be changed first. Clifford promised Ball a long, hard talk with the president but reminded him—as Dick Russell had told Johnson sixteen months before—that the president's advisers might by now have a personal stake in the decisions they were promoting.

Coaching Clifford for his moment with Johnson, Ball explained whose opposition the president feared most. He had told Ball: "George, don't pay any attention to what those little shits on the campus do. The great beast is the reactionary elements in this country. Those are the people we have to fear."

JOHNSON CALLED to invite Clifford and his wife to Camp David on Saturday and mentioned that Bob and Margaret McNamara would also be there. Clifford knew McNamara would be a formidable opponent in the private debate that Johnson was setting up. He acknowledged McNamara's skillful marshaling of facts but felt he had come to a wrong conclusion. And yet his forceful personality was carrying the argument against the more perceptive voices.

Among the other weekend guests was Arthur Goldberg. When Adlai Stevenson died in June, the president had persuaded Goldberg to resign from the U.S. Supreme Court to head the United Nations delegation. Since Goldberg's sacrifice was a large one, Johnson held out the possibility that in 1968 he could become the first Jewish vice presidential candidate.

The president called a meeting on Vietnam for 5 P.M. Sunday at Aspen Lodge, with its vistas of the Catoctin Mountains. Johnson sat at the head of the dining room table, Clifford on his right, McNamara on his left. Goldberg and Horace Busby found other seats, and Jack Valenti, an aide, was there to take notes.

Clifford had prepared a lawyerly brief against the war but, launching into it, he was surprised by his own passion. "I hate this war," Clifford said. "I do not believe we can win."

If, against the odds, the United States did prevail, America would face a long occupation with constant harassment. "And if we don't win, after a big buildup, it will be a huge catastrophe. We could lose more than 50,000 men in Vietnam. It will ruin us. Five years, 50,000 men killed, hundreds of billions of dollars—it is just not for us."

Clifford called for a probing for an honorable way out after the monsoon season at the end of the year. "Let the best minds in your administration look for a way out, not ways to win this unwinnable war. I can't see anything but catastrophe for my country."

McNamara's rebuttal added no new insights. Clifford was prepared to challenge his optimism point by point, but Johnson cut off the debate, saying only that no one wanted peace more than he. As his guests returned to their cottages, Johnson drove around the camp by himself for an hour, then walked for another hour in the summer dusk.

Discussions, repetitive and unproductive, went on for another day. By the second evening, Clifford saw that the meeting had become a council of war. The president had committed himself—put his stack in, he would say—and when the question arose of bombing newly installed Russian surface-to-air missile sites in North Vietnam, Clifford argued strongly for taking them out. He was on board.

DESPITE JOHNSON'S RESISTANCE to giving another major speech on Vietnam, both Mac Bundy and McNamara assumed that he would go to the American public to explain the escalation of troops and his calling up of the Reserves. Instead, at a routine midday press conference, Johnson said that he was approving another 50,000 troops, bringing the total to 125,000, and would be sending more later, as requested. He was not calling up Reserve units now, although he did not rule out that action in the future. He was, however, doubling the draft call gradually from 17,000 per month to 35,000.

In not calling up the Reserves—but only in that—Johnson was taking the advice of Ken Galbraith, who had recently proposed several ways to lower the political heat over Vietnam. One was a presidential order to "instruct officials and spokesmen to stop saying the future of mankind, the United States and human liberty is being decided in Vietnam. It isn't; this merely builds up a difficult problem out of all proportion. It is also terrible politics."

Secretly, the president had approved an increase of 100,000 men by the end of 1965, with the prospect of another 100,000 in 1966. But he insisted to reporters that his decision did "not imply any change in policy whatever." As for financing the buildup, Johnson knew that McNamara had estimated the added expenditures for the war at $10 billion through 1966, but he said only that he was asking $300-to-$400 million until January "when the figures would be firmer."

McNamara had tried to persuade Johnson to call for increased taxes to stave off inflation as defense spending rose. He drafted a memorandum so tightly held that neither the secretary of the treasury nor the chairman of the Council of Economic Advisers got a copy.

Johnson read the proposal skeptically. "What's your vote count?"

McNamara had not polled the relevant members of Congress and said so. "I know it will be difficult," he said. "But that's what you have legislative liaison people for."

"You get your ass up to the Hill," Johnson said, not unpleasantly but in a way he would not have spoken to his defense secretary a year earlier. "And don't come back till you have the vote count."

McNamara did as he was told and reported that Johnson's suspicions had been correct. A tax increase would fail. But with the bravado that explained his reputation for integrity, McNamara added, "I would rather fight for what's right and fail than not try."

Exasperated, Johnson said, "Goddammit, Bob, that's what's wrong with you—you aren't a politician." He lectured him again about the way Franklin Roosevelt's effectiveness with Congress had dropped after he tried unsuccessfully to pack the Supreme Court.

Listening to Johnson's evasions at his next press conference, McNamara understood that Johnson thought he was protecting his Great Society programs. In fact, the president was saying as much: he would not allow his domestic goals to be "drowned in the wasteful ravages of cruel wars." Joe Alsop also watched Johnson meet with reporters and explained to his readers that the "press conference came alive, it carried absolute conviction, when he began to talk of all his hopes of making America a better place to live in during his Presidency." Unlike Johnson's campus critics, Alsop faulted the president for favoring political measures in Vietnam ahead of military action. But, Alsop added, "it must be said there is a genuine element of pathos (and pray God, the pathos does not turn into tragedy) in the spectacle of this extraordinary man in the White House wrestling with the Vietnamese problem. . . ."

To play down the importance of Vietnam at his press conference, Johnson had announced two high-profile appointments—Abe Fortas to replace Goldberg on the Supreme Court and John Chancellor, a well-known television newsman, to be director of the Voice of America. The president may have been as tormented as Alsop suggested by the decisions he was making in Vietnam, but that did not stop him from boasting later about the way he had slipped the troop escalation past his press conference: "If you have a mother-in-law with only one eye and she has it in the middle of her forehead, you don't keep her in the living room."

ON AUGUST 5, Morley Safer brought the war back to the living room. A thirty-three-year-old Canadian working for CBS News, Safer sent a report that a squad of U.S. Marines operating out of Da Nang had recently burned down the nearby brick-and-straw village of Cam Ne. CBS Radio aired his account, but his film had to be flown from Saigon to Los Angeles and on to New York. It was not until television viewers could watch American Marines setting fire to the thatched roofs that the events at Cam Ne caught their attention.

On the soundtrack, Safer described the scene as a microcosm of the Vietnam War. American firepower could win military victories, Safer said, "but to a Vietnamese peasant whose house meant a lifetime of backbreaking labor, it will take more than Presidential promises to convince him that we are on his side."

Early the next morning, Frank Stanton, president of CBS News, was awakened by a roaring voice on the phone: "Frank, are you trying to fuck me?"

"Who is this?" Stanton asked.

"Frank, this is your President, and yesterday your boys shat on the American flag."

As a man who always kept on three television sets in his office, Johnson knew that Safer's voice now outweighed the most eloquent printed reports. He ordered Safer investigated for Communist connections and, when none were found, convinced himself that Safer had paid the Marine commander to set the fires and had that man investigated as well. At the Pentagon, Arthur Sylvester demanded that CBS fire Safer, along with his South Vietnamese cameraman, Ha Thuc Can, although Can had persuaded the Marines not to point their flamethrower down a hole where village women and children were hiding. By the time the uproar died away, Defense Department officials were monitoring the network evening news as assiduously as their commander in chief.

Johnson was also under attack these days from an unlikely antagonist. Art Buchwald, a syndicated satirist, began a column, "Every once in a while, when I have nothing better to do, I wonder what the country would be like if Barry Goldwater had been elected President of the United States." The result, Buchwald wrote, was frightening to imagine, and he listed the trigger-happy actions Goldwater would have taken in Vietnam: he would have bombed the North, refused to negotiate, sent in battalions of Marines with Hawk missiles to protect American airfields and gone on supporting the Saigon generals, no matter how shaky their regime.

Buchwald conceded that his scenario seemed far-fetched and that surely Goldwater would not have gone that far. "But fortunately, with President Johnson at the helm, we don't even have to think about it."

☐

DESPITE HAVING BEEN REBUFFED in May, Mai Van Bo in Paris continued to make overtures to Washington. In July, the president of the Dreyfus Fund, an investment banker named Urah Arkas-Duntov, arranged through a French journalist to meet with Bo, who gave him Hanoi's softer line from May and did not seem concerned about the U.S. bombing in the North. Arkas-Duntov defied U.S. State Department objections and scheduled a second visit. Bo offered to talk with any American official if Washington would accept the Four Points as he had interpreted them. At that, the State Department called Ed Gullion out of retirement to make the contact. For security, Bo would be termed "R," Gullion "X" and two other Americans, if they joined the process, would be "Y" and "Z." The overture was called XYZ.

Gullion was sent off to meet Bo with unpromising terms. He was allowed to say that any settlement could be compatible with the Four Points, but he was also told to add that there was growing pressure in the United States to widen the war, and the government was finding it increasingly difficult to resist. Gullion should add that prolonging the war was bound to lead to China's long-term control of Vietnam.

Gullion's report on his first contact went to Mac Bundy, who suggested to the president how the next secret meeting in Paris should unfold. "Let R do the talking this time," Bundy suggested, "and see if there is any give in his position."

But at the second meeting on August 15, Bo was more rigid, perhaps because of Ho's recent interview in *Le Monde*, which seemed to indicate that only the NLF could represent the South since the Saigon government was entirely an American creation. Three days later, however, Bo was amiable again, assuring Gullion that reunification of North and South Vietnam "could wait some time."

Then, on September 3, Bo appeared to be taking his cue from a speech by Pham Van Dong that complained about the Americans intensifying both their bombing in the North and their ground action in the South. "Bombings must stop unilaterally, immediately, totally and definitively," Bo said. "Then there would be a possibility for negotiations."

Why had Bo become cold and formal? During the hiatus in his meetings with Gullion, U.S. air strikes had hit new and critical targets—the Ban Thach hydropower plant, a lock at Bich Phuong and, according to Pham Van Dong's speech on August 31, densely populated areas and many hospitals.

The two negotiators agreed to meet on September 7. Gullion showed up. Bo did not. Officials at his office said he was sick. The XYZ channel was closed.

THE COMMUNISTS BELIEVED their battle for independence had entered a third phase. First the French War, then the Special War against the ARVN and its American advisers and now, in 1965, the American War. In Hanoi, a senior North Vietnamese general, Chu Huy Man had been preparing to seize the Central

Highlands. Hearing that Johnson was sending the U.S. 1st Cavalry Division, however, Man changed his plan. He would still attack the Special Forces camp at Plei Me and ambush the ARVN who came to relieve it. But now he hoped to draw in U.S. troops as well. The Vietnamese knew that their Chinese comrades mocked the Americans as "paper tigers," but Man and his officers considered them a formidable threat. Even Mao had admitted privately that the Americans might be paper tigers but they had real teeth. Man told his officers that he wanted to lure the tiger out of the mountains.

Johnson had specifically mentioned sending the 1st Cav, but the Communists did not know the division's history. It had absorbed the 7th Cavalry, led in 1876 by General George Custer and all but wiped out by Sioux warriors at Little Big Horn. The division, with its black-and-gold shoulder patch, redeemed its reputation with notable bravery in the Pacific in both World War II and Korea. Now—and this the Communists did know—they were being supplied with helicopters. As the U.S. Army's first airmobile unit, the Cav could drop from the sky wherever General Man attacked.

There was one hitch, however, and it troubled the division's commander, Major General Harry Kinnard. At Fort Benning, he had learned from the president's televised speech that his men were being sent to Vietnam without Johnson's declaring a national emergency. That meant that the 50 percent of his troops whose enlistments were ending would not be going with him. Half of Kinnard's 1st Air Cavalry would be facing combat with no airmobile training.

The division sailed on August 16 by troop ship from Charleston, South Carolina. Before the troops reached Vietnam a month later, Lodge was back at the Saigon embassy and advising Johnson against a settlement with Ho. Despite Lodge's lackluster reputation at the White House, he had seemed a safe choice for a second round as ambassador since Westmoreland would be in actual charge of the country.

About the time the 1st Cav shipped out, General Man's troops left North Vietnam, walking down the Ho Chi Minh trail in rubber sandals cut from worn truck tires. They carried ankle-high combat boots supplied by the Chinese and 22 pounds of food to last for their two-month trek. Packhorses and porters on bicycles brought cans of cooking oil, rice and peanuts for the Communist base that Man was building along the Ia Drang—"Ia" means "river" in Vietnamese. Protected by the jungle roof of leafy branches, the base was close to the sanctuary that Cambodia could provide.

Colonel Ta Minh Kham, as a veteran now of earlier skirmishes with the ARVN, compared the two deployments of men. The North Vietnamese were insinuating themselves through the trees, the Americans were landing on his country with a thud. He decided that the Communist propaganda was true enough: our army moves as lightly as cats; the Americans move like elephants. Kham wondered why the Americans, who seemed to think of themselves as brave cow-

Lieutenant Colonel
Robinson Risner
(AP/Wide World Photos)

boys, were instead arriving in Vietnam as Don Quixotes, ready to fight a war they could not win.

LIEUTENANT COLONEL ROBINSON RISNER, an ace pilot during the Korean War, had been averaging one raid every day over North Vietnam, but he had been taking too many hits. After he bailed out from one plane and then had a second close call, the Air Force sent him to cool off with three days of golf in the Philippines. Returning on September 9 to Korat Air Force Base in central Thailand, Risner found a note from the commander of the Pacific Air Force: "Robbie, be careful. Don't get shot down again. I have plans for you."

Soon afterward, Risner was flying over North Vietnam toward a SAM site about ten miles north of the provincial capital of Thanh Hoa. Risner loved flying. He believed in the U.S. cause in Vietnam and took pride in destroying his given targets. This morning's assignment was to drop napalm on the control tower. A second pilot would follow to dive-bomb the missiles with 750-pound bombs.

As he flew over Highway 1, however, Risner's cockpit exploded from ground fire and filled with smoke. Another flight commander radioed that Risner's plane was burning and kept shouting, "Get out!" Risner had always promised himself he would never be captured. He was heading for the ocean, two or three miles away, when his stick pitched into his lap and threw him against the canopy. He ejected and plummeted to earth. He could see that he would be landing in a rice field and watched as people ran toward him.

Risner had not had time to jettison the 45 pounds of survival equipment in the plane's seat. Hitting the ground with it, he pulled the ligaments of his right knee. He squeezed the quick-release switch on his parachute, rose and tried to run, got tangled in parachute cords and slashed his leg trying to cut free. He grabbed his pistol, but a North Vietnamese already had a rifle trained on him.

Risner threw down the pistol and let the Vietnamese tie his hands. A few old women tried to beat him with sticks, but the village chief stopped them. Risner was stripped, washed down with water from a well and handed ragged but clean clothes to wear. The Vietnamese led him to a wooden bed, covered him with mosquito netting and left him to sleep. It was noon on September 15, 1965.

When he awoke, Risner could hear the pilot of an SA-16 flying boat—the duckbutt, pilots called it—circling in hopes of rescuing him. The villagers blindfolded Risner and hurried him to a thicket where he could not be seen. When the rescue squadron gave up, villagers took him back to a house and gave him a bowl of sugar and a can of Czechoslovakian condensed cream. Risner found it too sweet. In pantomime, he asked for rice, which they brought him.

At dusk, he was escorted along roads and trails, his guides doubling back to keep him away from hostile villagers. Risner's knee throbbed with every step. He thought of his wife and five sons, who would have to pack now and return to Oklahoma City from their quarters in Okinawa. The Vietnamese reached a truck, put him inside and bounced over rough roads throughout the night. At about 9 A.M., they arrived in downtown Hanoi.

Risner was led inside the Hoa Lo prison; he found later that Americans called it the Hanoi Hilton. Inside its twenty-two-foot walls, Risner considered his new responsibilities. As a lieutenant colonel, he assumed he was the North's ranking prisoner. A friend had been captured in Korea, but Risner had never asked him about the experience or whether he had been tortured.

Risner was taken to a room where a North Vietnamese officer in his midforties was waiting at a table. He offered Risner a cigarette; Risner said he did not smoke. The man asked questions about American strategy and logistics. Risner told him he could give only his name, rank, serial number and date of birth. The man persisted. When Risner did not answer, he simply went on to the next question. Risner thought he seemed very pleasant and that things might be okay.

Other interrogators came and went. Some of them threatened him with execution as a war criminal, but he passed his first days without torture. Although talking to other prisoners was forbidden, Risner learned that each of six cells housed an American, most of them friends from the Air Force.

After two weeks, Risner was sent to another prison, a dilapidated French motel that its inmates called the Zoo. As senior officer, he was able to negotiate outdoor exercise time for the prisoners and lightbulbs for each dark cell. Guards occasionally brought magazines but only to point out the race riots sweeping across America. One day, the camp commander pulled out the April 23, 1965, issue of *Time* with Risner's picture on the cover. The editors had chosen his earlier rescue from the ocean to dramatize America's new air war. At the time, Risner had considered the cover an honor, but the commander's tone was caustic. The only Americans we would rather capture than you, he said, are Johnson, McNamara and Rusk. With heavy sarcasm, he noted that Risner seemed to be a hero in America for murdering the Vietnamese people and blowing up their houses. "Are you sorry?" he demanded.

Risner would not respond to him, but cautiously he was communicating with a growing number of American prisoners. They broke holes in cell walls, left notes in the shower room, brushed up on Morse code. When guards caught them at it—some six weeks after he was shot down—Risner was the one made to pay. Blindfolded, newspapers stuffed in his mouth, he was driven back to the Hanoi Hilton and slapped into leg irons too tight to let him stand. For three days, with neither food nor water, he was left to lie in his own filth while outside his window a loudspeaker blared toneless music. Risner had been raised in a religious family. Now he found himself praying with new urgency. "Lord," he said, "I have been in long enough."

He was released only to be blindfolded with his wrists painfully bound and pushed outside to march around a courtyard. He kept falling down from hunger and diarrhea. Next, he was wrapped with ropes so tight that his right shoulder popped from its socket. His feet, stretched behind him, were tied to his neck in a way that choked him if he did not keep his back arched. Now he was praying, "Lord, let me faint."

The guards tied him to a post, and he heard himself screaming in agony. After several hours, he shouted, "Okay, I'll talk." The head guard told him to be quiet, but Risner could no longer control his screaming. When he was beaten, he already ached so badly he could not feel the blows.

Because Risner had always believed that he would not give an enemy more than the Geneva conventions required, he hated himself when a new interrogation began and he answered the questions—his type of aircraft, the base he had flown from. When the Vietnamese produced a pencil and paper, he used fingers with no feeling left in them to copy what they dictated: an apology to the Vietnamese people for grave and heinous crimes against them.

That done, the ropes were untied and he was taken to a room without leg irons. For the first time in thirty-two days, he could lie on his stomach. He felt wretched about what he had done. Against every resolution he had made, he had talked. He had not given away anything of value. But to Risner, that was not the point. He had talked.

The next morning, guards brought him a normal food ration—half a bowl of soup made from a leafy vegetable, three spoonfuls of cabbage, a small loaf of bread. From then on, Risner was interrogated each day about every aspect of his life. His neighbor in the next cell was Navy Commander Jim Stockdale, the pilot who had been flying over Tonkin Gulf at the time of the reputed second attack. They agreed they were sure to be freed by June of 1966.

Screams from the torture room became routine. When the North Vietnamese asked Risner to broadcast the day's news over the camp radio, he refused and considered killing himself. He tried to damage his larynx by eating his ration of lye soap. By the third day, he could not so much as whisper. Then he coughed and his voice came back. Risner read the text he was given, but he stumbled often and tried to mimic a German accent.

His captors knew his tapes were unusable for propaganda, but they had a better idea. Forty-eight of the prisoners were marched two miles through the center of Hanoi, while the North Vietnamese jeered and cursed them. "You have seen with your own eyes the hatred of the Vietnamese people," the guards said to the men they had not yet broken. Confess your crimes, and your treatment will be humane and lenient. "If you do not, you will be put on trial and probably put to death."

As a senior officer, Risner modified the Code of Conduct to make it realistic. Do not give up anything willingly, he told the new men. Make them torture you. But do not risk permanent physical damage or a mental breakdown. He was coming to understand the range of men's tolerance for pain. Burly athletes were no more likely to withstand torture than less imposing men. One navy officer confessed to Risner that he had never been able to bear any sort of unpleasantness. He said that when the Communist interrogator slammed down his hand in anger against the table, "I shrivel up inside."

JOHNSON WAS SENSING that the Pentagon might have been wrong about the effect of the bombing and the buildup of troops, and he asked Clark Clifford to go to Saigon and return with firsthand observations. Delighted by the president's show of confidence after overruling him in the spring, Clifford got to South Vietnam late on October 26 and was driven to Lodge's villa. Saigon's tree-lined boulevards charmed him, but he could see the impact of the American buildup—congested military traffic, slapdash construction and off-duty GIs prowling the dozens of new bars.

Although Clifford liked Lodge's upbeat disposition, he thought the ambassador had learned little about Vietnam and its people. Since Lodge's wife had been evacuated with the other dependents, he seemed grateful to have houseguests and introduced Clifford to Henry Kissinger, the Harvard professor who was also staying at the residence as a visiting consultant. Lodge had given Kissinger royal treatment, even flying him up to Nha Trang where Ky and his wife spent every Sunday at Bao Dai's former beachfront villa. Ky appreciated Kissinger for his adroit use of chopsticks and for his attempts to ingratiate himself with Ky's family. When Kissinger asked dozens of questions but took no notes, Ky credited him with having a prodigious memory.

Clifford's own mission was limited to gauging the value of U.S. intelligence operations, and he found them badly coordinated. Although Saigon's politics remained volatile and little progress was being made in winning over the countryside, Lodge seemed entirely confident. He had held a reunion lately with Tri Quang, his former houseguest, who had proved surprisingly docile. The monk had asked Tran Quang Thuan once again to translate, and when Thuan stopped by the pagoda he discovered that Tri Quang had borrowed a Mercedes convertible for the ride to Lodge's residence. Thuan suggested that a less flashy car might be more appropriate, but from behind the wheel Tri Quang shook his head and said, Let's go. When the ambassador came out to the curb to welcome them, Thuan thought he looked amused.

As they talked, Lodge asked for Tri Quang's reaction to the bombing of North Vietnam, and the monk clearly had been weighing the question. Do it over a shorter period of time, he said, and make the North beg. Don't prolong it.

He cited the reaction of Germany during the last days of World War II. Hitler by that time was unpopular with young Germans, and yet they still defended their country. If you continue to prolong the bombing, the people will rally and unite. So, Tri Quang repeated, get it finished quickly. To what degree was he telling Lodge what the Americans wanted to hear? The ambassador could not be sure, but for the moment the monk was not in the streets.

Westmoreland was equally encouraging. He claimed that enemy casualties had now risen to the point that the Communists would not be able to replace them.

Clifford flew to the huge new U.S. Army headquarters at Bien Hoa, where planning was underway for helicopters to deliver a full Thanksgiving dinner with cranberries and yams to every GI in South Vietnam, no matter how remote or hostile the territory around his base. He returned to Washington enthusiastic about the skill and energy of the young soldiers and CIA agents he had met.

But before he could report to Johnson, a *Los Angeles Times* article described Thieu and Ky as immature and selfish and suggested that the judgment had come from Clifford and Kissinger. Moyers called Clifford to warn that Johnson was furious. He suggested that, rather than come to the White House, Clifford explain himself in writing. A letter did not help. When they finally met about a week later at Johnson's ranch, the president berated Clifford, who said again that the story was untrue and that he deeply resented Johnson's questioning of his word. The unexpected counterattack shut Johnson up.

Kissinger did not have the privilege of confronting the president in person.

He wrote to Clifford, admitting to a meeting with journalists but insisting that he had said almost nothing and certainly not what he was quoted as saying.

"I am depressed and shaken," Kissinger concluded, "that my offer to be helpful to the administration and to Ambassador Lodge has ended so ignominiously. I have tortured myself these past few days to decide what I could have done otherwise and I still cannot understand what happened."

The explanation was one McNamara would have understood. The reporter, Jack Foisie, had come late to a press luncheon and had not heard that Kissinger's remarks were off-the-record. It was Kissinger's misfortune that Johnson read the story with particular interest because Foisie's sister, Virginia, was married to Dean Rusk.

Kissinger had a chance to convey publicly his esteem for Johnson when *Time* called in mid-November for a quote to use because the number of Americans killed in Vietnam had risen above 1,000. Johnson had to make "difficult and lonely decisions," Kissinger said, and compared the president to Gary Cooper playing a sheriff in the film *High Noon.*

THE COMMUNISTS were determined to attack the 1st Cav before the Americans could get their bearings. The battle was meant to be a bloody initiation, a warning that even with the Cav's terrifying firepower the United States would not prevail. Communist officers had heard an ARVN general boast about the strong defenses at the Special Forces base at Plei Me, which was why General Man chose it as his first target. He attacked on October 19 with two northern regiments. The siege went on for four days and nights. On the fifth day, an ARVN armored task force came down a dirt road grandly labeled Route 7 and ran into a Communist ambush. But General Man did not have enough soldiers to spring his trap properly, and pulverizing strikes by U.S. planes drove them off. In Saigon, Westmoreland guessed correctly that the Communists intended to return. Flying to the highlands, he ordered General Kinnard to pursue the attackers and wrest away the initiative.

On their side, the North Vietnamese saw one way to hold down their losses. They must get as near to the Americans as possible — "cling to their belts," the political officers told the troops — because then the U.S. aircraft would be reluctant to strafe and bomb. As it happened, General Man's troops would get closer than they anticipated.

EVER SINCE his CBS debate, Mac Bundy knew his usefulness to Johnson had ended, but he wanted to disengage from the White House in a way that did not suggest a break with the president's Vietnam policy. Bundy's wife, sister and other members of his family disapproved of the war, but Bundy's reasons to leave, being personal, were not to be made public. The example of his father's government service under Stimson shaped his decision. In Bundy's view, when you accepted an appointment, the president was also handing you a pistol; you did not quarrel and then turn his own weapon against him. Loyalty might not be the highest virtue, but betrayal was an unforgivable sin. Much about Johnson galled Bundy, but he retained some affection for the man. Even when he considered Johnson a posturing and self-pitying ham actor, he knew how deeply Vietnam troubled him.

Bundy's restlessness sent signals to his friends. He turned down Kay Graham's offer to become editor of the *Washington Post*'s editorial pages, but when John McCloy, the chairman of the Ford Foundation, sounded him out about the presidency of that giant philanthropy, Bundy expressed interest. Now seventy, McCloy shared Bundy's ambiguous feelings about Johnson. Just before Max Taylor went as ambassador to South Vietnam, McCloy had turned down a feeler from the president about the assignment. In frustration, Johnson called him "yellow," and McCloy had bolted from the room. Later, after much lobbying by Bundy, he had joined a bipartisan panel that backed Johnson in the 1964 election.

McCloy raised the issue of the Ford presidency on November 7. The next day, Bundy acted forthrightly. He wrote a note about the offer and sent it to Johnson's ranch. As Bundy weighed his future, McCloy sent Bundy's friend, Charles Wyzanski, a federal judge and a Ford trustee, to persuade him. Bundy met with Wyzanski and his wife for breakfast, and the judge suggested that a foundation presidency, after seven or eight years, could lead to more exciting prospects—secretary of state, for example, or the presidency of Harvard. The money involved was appealing in two ways: The foundation spent some $200 million a year to promote social progress around the world. And its director received $75,000, compared to Bundy's current $30,000. Wyzanski said that his board had considered McNamara for the job but had been put off by his "dominating personality." Bundy speculated about whether his own manner was too abrasive as well. He did not always suffer fools gladly, Bundy admitted, but he never got credit for all the fools he *did* suffer.

Bundy was inclined to take the job. His wife liked New York. The foundation, the world's largest, presented a challenge. And he could slip out of the administration with no public notice of his disagreement with Johnson over being more forthcoming with Congress and the public about the war's looming costs. The day after his breakfast with Wyzanski, Reston reported the offer on the *Times'* front page. Johnson had not responded to Bundy's note, but the article enraged him. Within the week, Bundy said that he intended to take the job but would stay on until the end of next February. To Johnson, those who served him were great patriots. Those who left could expect inventive invective. Bundy went from being "my debater" to "a smart kid, period."

IN THE LATE AFTERNOON of November 2, with Washington traffic at its heaviest, Norman Morrison, a thirty-one-year-old Quaker, went with his infant daughter,

Emily, to the Pentagon. In a parking lot forty feet from McNamara's fifth-floor window, he set himself on fire. Witnesses disagreed about whether he had dropped the child or handed her to someone in the crowd, but she survived, with traces of kerosene on her blue coveralls.

By the time McNamara was told of the commotion below, he could see only a crowd, smoke and two ambulances. Morrison's wife, Anne, released a statement that he had been protesting "the great loss of life and human suffering caused by the war in Vietnam." McNamara knew that Margy and their three children shared many of Morrison's sentiments, but he did not want to talk about the suicide with them or anyone else.

Five days after Morrison's immolation, McNamara sent Johnson the finished draft of a memo he and his staff had been preparing. McNamara noted what he called the "substantial loss of American lives" through the current policy. To justify those sacrifices, he focused as seldom before on the menace that China presented. The February decision to bomb North Vietnam and the sending of U.S. troops "make sense only if they are in support of a long-run United States policy to contain Communist China," which McNamara claimed was as dangerous as Germany in 1917, Germany and Japan in the late 1930s and the Soviet Union in 1947. To contain China would require "American attention, money and, from time to time unfortunately, lives."

AFTER THE PLEI ME ATTACK, General Kinnard sent out Lieutenant Colonel Harold G. Moore, Jr., and his 1st Battalion, 7th Cavalry Regiment, to go by helicopter to a landing zone and track down the Communists. Soon after arriving in Vietnam, Moore had taken a jeep down Route 19 to visit the site at which the Vietminh had ambushed a French mobile group. At the time, Moore was carrying Bernard Fall's *Street Without Joy*, which described the battle, and he found a six-foot stone obelisk inscribed in French and Vietnamese: HERE ON JUNE 24, 1954, SOLDIERS OF FRANCE AND VIETNAM DIED FOR THEIR COUNTRIES. Bone fragments, shell casings and the burned frames of destroyed vehicles still littered the spot, but Moore found a rough beauty to the highlands. Chu Pong Mountain rose 2,400 feet to the west, its limestone ridges extending into Cambodia.

As Moore walked the old battlefield, he thought, "This is a tough enemy we're up against. We'd better watch our ass." And then, for an instant, he wondered if Vietnam was the right place for America to be fighting, or the right time. He quickly put aside that wisp of doubt. America's policy was to contain Communism, and he had already fought in Korea to carry it out.

Headquarters gave Moore's mission the code name Silver Bayonet, and Moore let his operations officer pick the name for the site near the base of the mountain where the battalion would land. The man chose "X"—in the NATO alphabet, "X-Ray." To disguise their 66th Regiment, the North Vietnamese had also chosen the letter "X."

Early on Sunday morning, November 14, Moore's reconnaissance helicopter pilots reported that X-Ray was large enough for eight, even ten, helicopters to land. The pilots had spotted evidence of enemy activity, however, and Moore briefed his men on tracking and destroying the Communists. At his order, Alpha and Bravo Companies would move to the northwest while Charlie Company moved southeast toward the mountain. Delta Company would man the mortars, firing artillery at other areas for eight minutes to distract the enemy. Then X-Ray's surrounding terrain would be pounded for twenty minutes to prepare for the helicopter landings. Moore set 10:30 A.M. for them to touch down, but when artillery was slow in getting into position, he shoved the time back one hour.

Moore and his men flew in from 2,000 feet on Huey helicopters with their doors open. Morning fog was burning off, and from the sky the Americans could watch their 105-mm artillery shells crashing down on trees around the landing zone. Timing the landing was nerve-wracking. The guns had to be stilled at the last minute so that the Communists were still at bay but the Hueys took no hit. Once on the ground, Moore found the site smaller than he expected, no larger than a football field. But it was the only suitable spot between the mountains and the Drang River. He assumed that, at least, the landing had achieved total surprise.

But General Man had been expecting them. Although trees and brush lower down Chu Pong Mountain blocked the Communists from seeing X-Ray, they had posted scouts at the peak to signal when the Americans arrived.

At 11:30 A.M., helicopters brought in Alpha Company and the rest of Bravo. The soldiers met only an unexpected silence and opened C-rations to eat a hurried lunch. Moore jogged into the brush where his men were holding their first prisoner, a skinny young Vietnamese who was unarmed, barefoot and scared nearly speechless. Quaking, he told the translator that there were three Communist battalions on the mountain that very much wanted to kill Americans. Moore called for a helicopter to take the prisoner back to the base at An Khe.

The informant had deprived General Man of his element of surprise but not his superior numbers. Fifteen minutes past noon, Moore heard rifle shots, and then confusion exploded around him. One of his lieutenants took his men charging off after a few North Vietnamese, quickly losing contact with the rest of the platoon and surrounded by the enemy. Adding to the oddness of the scene were huge mounds like anthills on every side. Termites had processed wood and laterite dirt into red towers as strong as concrete. Rising twelve to fifteen feet in the air and covered with grass and scrub, they provided the Communists with foxholes in the air that let them shoot down at the Americans.

From the low bursts of machine-gun fire, snapping of automatic rifles, booming of mortars and bursts of rocket, Moore knew the enemy had made full contact before his own battalion had even landed. And now he had to deal with a platoon stranded between North Vietnamese units. Moore said to himself, "Shit!"

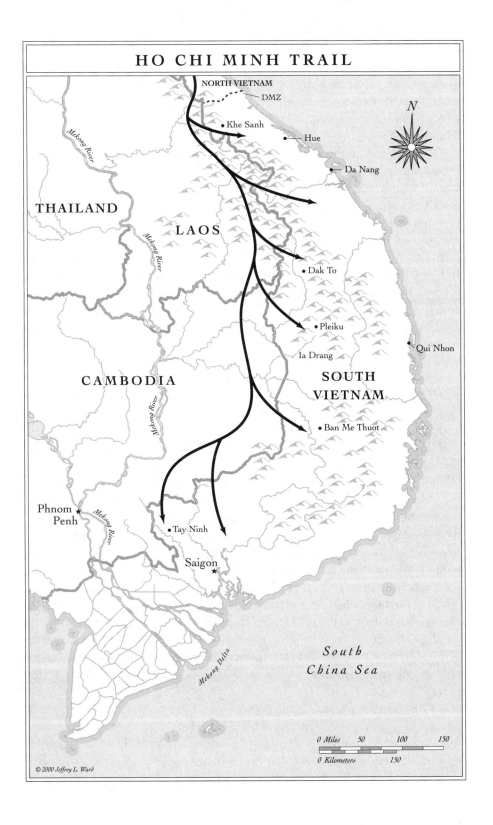

HO CHI MINH TRAIL

NORTH VIETNAM

DMZ

Khe Sanh

Hue

Da Nang

N

THAILAND

LAOS

Mekong River

Mekong River

Dak To

Pleiku

Qui Nhon

Ia Drang

CAMBODIA

SOUTH
VIETNAM

Mekong River

Ban Me Thuot

Phnom
Penh

Mekong River

Tay Ninh

Saigon

Mekong Delta

South
China Sea

0 Miles   50   100   150

0 Kilometers   150

© 2000 Jeffrey L. Ward

A Cav captain, who had spent a year with the Special Forces, spotted 150 of General Man's soldiers dropping from trees and rushing his position. He recognized that they were not Vietcong but North Vietnamese from the People's Army of Vietnam. Over the battalion radio, the captain shouted, "They're PAVN! They're PAVN!"

The Americans threw off their packs and began trotting across the elephant grass to the tree line. Many were mowed down. In only five minutes, every American in the advance squad had been hit; one of them described it as running into a wall of lead. Deafening noise drowned out the officers' commands and the screams of their dying men.

General Man's soldiers were being shot, too, as they rushed down the mountain. His snipers had tied themselves by rope to upper branches along the tree line, and as they were picked off, their corpses fell and dangled in the air. On the ground, the North Vietnamese were hearing a single order: Attack! But even with their practice since Ap Bac, the Communists were not destroying the American helicopters. Several were hit, but none crashed or had to be abandoned. Moore ordered the fifth wave of eight Hueys to return to Plei Me and wait there until he got control of X-Ray.

As the battle wore on, Moore required ammunition and water, and there were wounded to evacuate from among the termite mounds. He turned to Major Bruce Crandall, a thirty-four-year-old college baseball all-American. Crandall commanded a group of pilots who, until today, had no combat experience. He and Captain Ed Freeman, a veteran of Pork Chop Hill in Korea, flew into the blizzard of fire, dropped off ammo boxes and picked up thirteen wounded GIs. With that, other Hueys risked landing and pulled out more of the wounded.

Moore saw that, as of today, none of Vietnam's past lessons applied to the war he was fighting. The North Vietnamese were not going to quit and fade away. They were carrying the action to the Americans with all of their firepower and determination. By 3 P.M., Charlie Company had turned aside a Communist attempt to penetrate the American left flank, and Moore could bring in the rest of his troops, one or two Hueys at a time. Forty-five minutes later, Moore had assembled his men when he got word that an American company of reinforcements was heading up the road toward them. But the second platoon, further up the slope, remained cut off by the Communists. Moore coordinated an attack by Alpha and Bravo Companies to rescue them. They moved out at 4:20 P.M. but got only 50 yards before running into North Vietnamese troops streaming down the mountain.

Captain Tony Nadal, Alpha's commander, had told his men to fix bayonets for an attack, and now he saw one of his sergeants stabbing a North Vietnamese soldier through the chest. Looking on, another GI thought, It's like practice against straw dummies—forward, thrust, pull out, move on. But the two American companies got barely 75 yards toward the isolated platoon when a North

An American casualty in the Ia Drang Valley *(AP/Wide World Photos)*

Vietnamese soldier killed an American gunner and captured his weapon. From the sound, the GIs knew they were now taking fire from their own gun.

By 5 P.M., with dirt and smoke obscuring the X-Ray landing zone, Major Crandall flew in reinforcement troops from Bravo's 2nd Battalion. The fighting went on until 5:40 P.M., when darkness began to cloak the scene. Moore ordered his men to pull back, drag out the dead and wounded to the landing zone and re-supply for the night ahead. To cover their withdrawal, Captain Nadal requested a smoke run that would drop shells almost directly on top of his men, but the Fire Direction Center reported that no smoke was available. Moore asked instead for white phosphorus—the men called it "Willy Peter"—and those shells were soon releasing clouds of dazzling white smoke and scattering fragments of phosphorus that ignited when they hit the air. White phosphorus had been used in Korea, but Moore calculated correctly that it would be an unnerving novelty for the North Vietnamese. As the sky turned bright white, the Communist guns went silent. Alpha Company retrieved its wounded without further injury to its men, and the two companies set up their nighttime perimeter.

Alpha had lost 3 officers and 31 enlisted men killed or wounded, Bravo one officer and 46 enlisted men killed or wounded. And the isolated Bravo platoon remained trapped outside the American perimeter. Moore's men had been fighting for eight hours, yet as he walked through their ranks he found morale high. "We'll get 'em, sir," the men said. Each company had 15 to 20 soldiers with less than two weeks left before they were due to go home. After today, some would be making the trip in body bags. At 7:15 P.M., Moore returned to his command post near a termite nest.

Joe Galloway, a UPI reporter, had already impressed Moore with his willingness to share in the dangers of battle. When he called from a nearby landing zone for permission to fly in, Moore said that if he was crazy enough to come, he could. Approaching X-Ray, Galloway saw pinpoints of light moving down the mountain in a constant stream three hundred yards wide and half a mile long. The North Vietnamese were coming down to fight. They stopped half a mile from the American perimeter and took up positions for a morning attack. The Communist main force remained quiet, but three times during the night some fifty men probed the isolated 2nd Platoon. Each time, American artillery and rifle fire drove them back.

The North Vietnamese had intended to begin Monday's attack at 2 A.M., but U.S. air strikes disrupted their ranks and scattered a part of one battalion. It was 6:30 A.M. before the 7th Battalion of the Communists' 66th Regiment charged the American perimeter, aided by the H-15, a local Vietcong main force battalion. They burst through the U.S. line wearing helmets covered with netting and laced with grass. To one GI, they looked like a hundred little trees.

Moore decided that he had been preoccupied with rescuing his trapped platoon and not with evaluating the enemy's tactics. He found that the North Vietnamese had moved so close that he could not use his artillery. Rifles were trading heavy fire, but in the afternoon the Americans broke through to the stranded unit and got out the dead and wounded on stretchers. Lieutenant Dennis Deal came upon the body of one dying North Vietnamese soldier who was clasping a grenade in a way that would activate it if anyone pushed his corpse aside to get his weapon. Pondering that degree of dedication, Deal told himself, We are up against an enemy who is going to make this a very long year.

Day and night passed, then again, as the Americans watched their friends dying in agony. They took cheerless satisfaction in cries of pain whenever their shells landed on a North Vietnamese enclave. It was no time for keeping score, but the Americans were sure they were killing hundreds of the enemy. About midnight on Wednesday morning, Moore got a message that astonished him: Westmoreland wanted him to leave X-Ray early that morning and fly to Saigon to meet with the headquarters staff.

Moore, who had briefed Westmoreland in Korea, was sure that he would never issue such a stupid order. He suspected that Westy had mentioned casually that he would want to get Moore's report on the battle and then some staff puke back in Saigon had passed along the remark as a direct and immediate order. The North Vietnamese were probing his perimeter as Moore radioed his refusal: he had been the first man into the engagement and intended to be the last man out.

The matter was dropped.

Moore ordered a sweep beyond the perimeter and called for all available aerial firepower. Four A-1E Skyraiders materialized overhead with bombs and napalm and unloaded them on the North Vietnamese to the southeast. A flight of jet fighter-bombers joined the attack. Peter Arnett of the AP had caught a helicopter into the landing zone for the final bombardment. As the North Vietnamese fled, they were pursued by 250-pound and 500-pound bombs, by napalm and by 20-mm cannon. Moore called for the last 500-pound bombs to drop as close as he dared, and the earth shook thirty yards away from the Americans. Sometime after 10 A.M., the battle was over.

Two battalions of a relief column reached X-Ray later in the morning to find North Vietnamese corpses stacked like firewood in piles six feet high. Moore hated estimating enemy casualties but knew that Saigon would be pressing him for figures. When his company commanders reported 834 PAVN dead by body count, Moore knew they had not literally counted every fallen man. Cutting back their figure by 200, he passed along to headquarters an even more problematical estimate of 1,215 killed or wounded by artillery, air and rocket attacks. Those enemy casualties lay beyond his perimeter and would be hauled away by the Communists for treatment or burial. His own losses could be measured more precisely: 79 Americans killed, 121 wounded, none missing.

But to Moore, the significance of the engagement could not be quantified with numbers. The war was no longer guerrillas sniping at ARVN. For the first time since Dien Bien Phu, the North Vietnamese had sent out a division to stand and fight.

As MOORE'S MEN prepared to return to Camp Holloway, Specialist Fourth Class Jack Smith, a young member of the reinforcement team, was sobered by the sight of them. The men were the color of red clay and their eyes had widened until the pupils, lost in an expanse of white, were focused on nothing at all. Veterans called it the thousand-yard stare.

Smith's father, Howard K. Smith, was a well-known network television newsman. The son had been raised in London during his father's assignment there and had gone back to America at the beginning of his teens. Loafing through school and a couple of years at a military institute, young Smith had enrolled at Georgia Tech but spent his days instead with the civil rights protesters who were changing the South. Withdrawing from college before he flunked out, Smith volunteered for the army to get his military service out of the way. At age twenty, he was on a Liberty ship headed for Qui Nhon.

On landing, Smith anticipated a life in the jungle punctuated by sniping and an occasional ambush. He knew light combat was as much as his company could handle since officers and men were greener than the grass they would be marching through. On one of their first operations, a GI heard a noise from a village bunker, caught sight of black silk and whirled around, opening fire. When he saw he had shot a young woman carrying a baby, he sank down, crying and vomiting. A medic tried to work on the woman but his hands trembled too violently. What a mess, Smith thought, resenting the news camera crew determined to get the whole episode on film.

Not too long afterward, Smith's company was sent out on foot to Ia Drang. It was the third day of the battle, and Smith considered Moore's 1st Battalion, fighting since Sunday, the filthiest troops he had ever seen. The worst of the wounded were bandaged with dirty shirts and whimpering as they were pumped full of morphine. Others smoked cigarettes or lay in a coma with plasma bottles on hooks above their stretchers. When an occasional shell whistled in, Smith instinctively ducked, but the men of the 1st Battalion could estimate within 50 to 75 feet where a shell would land and kept standing. Then all at once a burst of gunfire had even those veterans running for cover.

The North Vietnamese leaders had remembered Giap's order as they set out for Ia Drang: "You must win the first battle." For them, the engagement was not over. They would attack the American column and split it into many pieces, then mingle closely with the enemy until airpower was useless. That would mean hand-to-hand fighting, but North Vietnam's 8th Battalion was fresh and ready to avenge the defeat of the last three days.

Smith had been a radio operator until he was made a supply clerk a few days before Charlie Company, 2nd Battalion, 7th Cavalry, was sent to relieve X-Ray. Smith had learned one army lesson well: if you were going to kill the enemy, you had to make him less than human; he was already referring to the Vietnamese as "gooks." Smith watched gratefully as Skyraiders dropped antipersonnel charges that sparkled in the sunlight like green confetti before they exploded on the ground. When another plane dropped napalm on the enemy's front line, Smith couldn't see the North Vietnamese, but he heard them screaming as their skin burned.

Another Communist attack, easily repelled, came at 3 P.M., followed by hours of steady firing. It was Smith's first night in combat, and with the sky lighted dazzlingly by flares, he couldn't sleep. The next morning, his commanders considered the threat ended and marched the men out of their perimeter and past Communist corpses, some fresh, some rotting, ants everywhere.

The plan was to head six miles to another LZ named Albany and be flown out by helicopter. But the battalion commander was providing security only at the head of the column, not at the sides or rear. Watching the man for the last three days, Smith had already judged him incompetent, and he questioned now whether they should be simply strolling through the site of a major battle. By the time the head of the column reached the landing zone, Smith and his company were still struggling through the high elephant grass.

The day was very hot, and sweat fogged Smith's glasses. Setting down his gear and ax for a smoke, he had taken several puffs when he heard rifle shots directly in front of his column. Smith flopped down and grabbed his M-16 rifle. When they had first been issued, the rifles had looked to Smith's company like plastic toys after the heavier M-14s, but they were proving themselves in combat. A bullet slammed into the dirt near Smith's side, and others went over his head. As bullets exploded around them, the battalion commander fell apart. He dove into a foxhole, muttering, "What should I do? What should I do?"

Smith's executive officer sprang to his feet and took command. He shouted, "Follow me! Let's get the hell out of here!"

Smith's company and the 1st Platoon crouched low and ran to the right, away from the landing zone. Their officer was following a strategy of aggressive action by charging directly into the ambush. Smith looked back at a radio operator named Richards just as the man moaned and slumped to the ground. Kneeling over his body, Smith felt him shudder and heard blood bubbling up from a hole through his heart. His eyes bulged, his tongue flicked out and Richards was dead. He was the first man Smith had seen die.

Smith shouted for a medic before he realized that the men around him had stopped moving. There was a moment of silence and then four hundred North Vietnamese mortars and automatic weapons opened fire from behind the huge termite mounds. The noise was overpowering. Smith's fellow soldiers were dropping and hit. He was sure at least 20 were dead or dying. As the firing grew louder, Smith dug into the dirt. He was counting on the officer who had led them into this place to get them out. But that man had been struck in the back and was moaning with pain. As Smith tried to bandage his wound, a bullet ripped through the man's boot and tore away his toes. Nearby, another GI was in shock, bleeding in spurts from an internal wound and cursing at the enemy and at his pain.

The head and shoulders of a Communist soldier arose from the elephant grass. As though in a dream, Smith grabbed his rifle, put it on automatic, shoved it into the man's face and pulled the trigger. He watched the face disappear. The scene was growing hazy, but Smith knew that, from the first shot until this bloodbath around him, only a minute or two had passed. The officer beside him was almost dead. He told Smith that his wife's name was Carol and asked Smith to write and tell her that he loved her. Then, mustering his last strength, he crawled away to find his troops. The sight of that determination broke through Smith's shock and forced him forward.

Now images overwhelmed him. One American looked covered from head to toe with red paint. Skyraiders flashed overhead, and Smith could watch the tall grass curling from the heat of their napalm. With the raids hitting both North Vietnamese and Americans, Smith heard cries from both armies. In that first chaotic hour, most of his battalion's casualties seemed to have come from other Americans shooting blindly at anything that moved.

Smith caught himself repeating "Oh, God, oh, God." During training at Fort Benning, Georgia, he had met one sergeant's wife and four children. Now the man was dying, struck three times in the chest. Smith squeezed his hand and lied to him that he was going to make it. The man had survived World War II and Korea, yet now, Smith thought, this little war had got him. As North Vietnamese soldiers entered the woods where Smith was crouching, he heard them talking. Their voices sounded like children to him. Cruel children. The most frightening sound Smith had ever heard. The soldiers were looking for wounded GIs. When they found one, they shot him. Smith told his sergeant to play dead and willed himself to stop shaking.

The ten or twelve North Vietnamese who came upon him took Smith for dead. One lay on top of him to set up his machine gun, his head between Smith's feet. The man was shaking so badly himself that he didn't feel the life in the body beneath him. When the North Vietnamese opened fire, Smith's platoon returned it and killed about half of the squad. Sure that all the other GIs were dead, the Americans lobbed in grenades from an M-79 launcher. Scared, the soldier on top of Smith jumped up and ran, but grenades cut him down. One grenade landed near Smith, but his dead sergeant's body took most of its shrapnel. Smith felt a blow to the head, waves of something hot and a stinging in his left leg. He passed out. When he came to, blood was running down his forehead and filling the lenses of his glasses. He bandaged the side of his face and wrapped a cloth around his head. He felt numb but better.

The day wore on with the men of both armies killing and being killed. Smith saw mangled corpses from his platoon—a man with only one bone and shredded skin sticking out from his sleeve where his arm had been. But Smith was not hearing the pounding of artillery and air strikes anymore, and he was past being horrified by what he was seeing. Then three Communist machine-gun crews crawled to the American mortar platoon and opened fire, and Smith's hearing returned. He heard a different man scream every few seconds as he was hit. The American platoon was nearly wiped out.

Most of the Americans seemed to get hit in the belly. Smith could identify those strangled cries that never stopped and sounded different from the others. Fifteen or twenty men lay around him all screaming that way until they went hoarse and passed out. When they revived, they screamed again until they died. Smith had begun to cry.

That day, wounded men killed themselves with their pistols rather than endure the pain. One man who had not been hit could no longer bear the scene around him and killed himself with his grenade. At dusk, the enemy turned their captured U.S. mortars against the American survivors. Shrapnel hit Smith in the right thigh, and now he, too, was screaming, "My legs! God, my legs!" He tore the bandage off his face and wound it tight around his thigh, but he could still feel his blood spurting. For the first time that day, he knew he was going to die.

A flare saved him. When U.S. planes lighted up the sky again, the North Vietnamese drew back. In a daze, his throat parched but with no water, Smith risked a cigarette. He tore off the ends where the tobacco was soaked with his blood and cupped the flame so it would not be seen. When the last of the rifle fire died away, he crawled to a spot where a few men from his unit were gathering and drank from the canteen of a fallen GI. The man must have been hit in the face, Smith thought, because the contents seemed one-third blood. He drank deeply and passed the canteen around.

With night, the temperature had dropped to 50 degrees, and Smith was shivering from cold. He heard movement in the grass and took out his grenade. He was past caring, but he would not be taken alive. The noise came from fifteen Americans patrolling for survivors. They gave a low whistle and entered the clearing, where the wounded men crawled toward them, crying. Smith seized hold of one GI, but other men were hurt more badly, and Smith was left behind until the patrol could return.

Before the Americans got back, North Vietnamese machine gunners had located Smith and the others, but U.S. artillery zeroed in and quickly killed them off. Beyond artillery range, however, the Communists were moving through the grass, killing wounded GIs. Smith could hear, "No, no, no, please!" and then the bullets.

As dawn broke, the rifle shots Smith was now hearing came from Americans not sure where the enemy was hiding. What a waste that would be, he thought. To have survived so long and then be killed by one of our bullets. He had thought that all the blood had been drained from his body, but he began to bleed again.

With orange light spreading across the sky, Smith could take in the scene. He had been resting his head on a buddy's corpse. The man, a professional saxophone player with two weeks left in the army, was so shot up that Smith barely recognized him. He looked down at his own bleeding wound and saw ants crawling inside. Smith took over a dead lieutenant's radio and reached battalion headquarters. After an eternity, a circling helicopter asked Smith to mark his spot with a smoke grenade. He took one from the dead lieutenant's gear.

Smith's captain ran up with the first sergeant and two radio operators. "Sorry, Sir," Smith said, "I lost my fucking ax."

"Don't worry, Smitty," the captain said. "We'll get you another one."

LIKE SMITH, Thomas Bird, another young rifleman, was airlifted into Ia Drang. In the months that followed, he did not talk with other soldiers about what had happened to him there. Only after he got home did Bird begin to tell his story, and it proved to be a harrowing one.

The weather had changed, and a drizzling sky turned the red clay to mud. Bird's unit set off at 6 A.M. and marched for nine hours, breaking only for ten minutes to eat. They were carrying a three-day supply of C-rations, nine cans, in black socks strapped to their packs. Bird estimated that he was carrying about 40 pounds, including his M-16 rifle, sixteen clips of bullets and two grenades. His company had reached a mountain ridge line, halfway between its peak and the valley.

As the Americans came down to the valley for the night, they took rifle fire from the right. Bird had never been in combat. He froze, then dropped behind a spindly tree. Rain kept the Huey gunships from providing air support, but Bird had recovered and was firing off rounds. Too fast. He was running out of bullets.

Helicopters finally got through and dropped boxes of ammo, which fell too far from their perimeter for the Americans to retrieve them. By night, everyone was out of ammunition. Because flares were lighting the sky, the North Vietnamese were not attacking. But through bullhorns they were yelling, "Kill GI! Kill GI!" Bird was frightened until he heard Staff Sergeant Starkweather, a Korean vet, yell back, "Fuck you! Fuck you, you bastards! Come and get me!"

Bird decided Starkweather was the man to follow. But as Bird's unit entered a clump of trees, the Communists burst out at them, shooting steadily. To Bird, the mayhem blurred his vision, but he kept following Starkweather. Out of ammo again, he was ready to use his rifle as a baseball bat when he heard Starkweather calling, "Put your weapons down and don't resist! Don't resist!"

Forty North Vietnamese materialized in brown uniforms camouflaged with twigs and leaves and took the twelve GIs prisoner. They pulled off the Americans' gear, bound their wrists with twine and led them in a column up a hill to the PAVN base camp. In a clearing, they ordered the Americans to strip and kneel while they tied their wrists to their ankles. The position ground the prisoners' knees into the dirt. For relief, Bird fell over on his side.

In the morning, their guards kept the prisoners apart and slapped around anyone who tried to speak. Bird was not thinking of that violation of the Universal Code of Military Conduct. At that moment, he felt no loyalty to anything.

Early on the morning of November 16, an American company patrolled the area and found them, still tied up. The North Vietnamese had slipped away while they were sleeping. The company's lieutenant suspected a trap and demanded that Starkweather, bound and naked, prove his identity. When other GIs let the lieutenant know he was making a fool of himself, he ordered the prisoners untied. Bird's knees and neck were covered with scabs, his chest covered with blood. The GIs wrapped the prisoners in their own ponchos and called for medical evacuation teams—called Dustoffs—to come and fetch them. Since the Pleiku hospital was full, the men were flown to Qui Nhon for five days, then returned to Cav headquarters.

Bird found the Cav's morale low. The men had gone from a gung-ho naïveté to a shock that was slow in lifting. Mostly, his ordeal had left Bird skeptical about helicopter warfare. If the choppers couldn't go in because it was too humid or they were carrying too much weight, that left the Americans stranded in the jungle where the enemy was king. Bird thought, We were indoctrinated in counterinsurgency, we were trained with helicopters, but we were never schooled in Che Guevara.

Mustered out of the army, Bird was disappointed by his reception back in the United States. That hometown indifference was changed to awe, however, when he began to concoct the thrilling account of his capture.

As in all wars, many Vietnam veterans refused to talk about what they had seen and done. Others found relief in describing their experience. A few, for reasons of their own, manufactured a role for themselves that they had not played.

Impressed civilians could not have known that Bird had indeed been at Ia Drang but only as part of a relief column of the 2nd Battalion, 5th Cavalry that arrived at the landing zone after the battle had ended. When an editor later compiled a book of Vietnam war stories, Bird felt that his ficiton had become sufficiently well known that he was trapped into repeating it.

The deceit troubled him, but Bird consoled himself by thinking that at least his lies—unlike those of the government—had not killed anybody.

IN SAIGON, WESTMORELAND ADDED up the casualties from the battle at Ia Drang and declared victory. The North Vietnamese had killed 305 American men in those four days of fighting. But the 1st Cav and the 1st Battalion of the 7th Cavalry had killed 3,561 Communists—or so the figure was being reported. A ten-to-one kill ratio certainly spelled success.

And yet, less than a week after the battle, Westmoreland cabled Washington requesting another 200,000 troops. That was double what he had predicted he would need only last July. By his earlier estimate, 275,000 U.S. servicemen would be in Vietnam by 1966. Now the figure would rise to an alarming 410,000, with no apparent end. Flying to Vietnam with Wheeler to judge for himself, McNamara got even worse news. Westmoreland raised the possibility of requiring still another 200,000 in 1967.

ALTHOUGH JOHNSON'S HEART ATTACK of 1955 seemed safely behind him, when he underwent surgery in October to remove his gall bladder and a kidney stone, his medical history slowed his recovery. With the public coming to doubt Johnson's candor, rumors arose that his problem had actually been another heart attack. To Johnson, the natural way to rebut the speculation was to pull up his shirt and show his scar. Never squeamish about his body, he had seemed to enjoy swimming naked in the White House pool and compelling fastidious aides like Mac Bundy to conduct business while the president was on the toilet. But photographs of the presidential belly struck some viewers as vulgar or at least unesthetic, and in a caricature for the New York Review of Books, where editors were increasingly opposed to the war, David Levine drew the scar with the contours of Vietnam. This latest criticism plunged Johnson into self-pity and talk of resigning.

Vietnam continued to dominate his thinking on December 7, when Johnson summoned his advisers to the ranch to debate whether he should authorize a pause in the bombing of the North over Christmas. Despite the failure of the halt in May to promote talks, the president had been edging toward another try. The month before, he had declared himself 60 percent for a pause at Thanksgiving, although it would only be "preparatory to knocking hell out of 'em." But Johnson waited for McNamara to come back from his seventh trip to Vietnam before deciding on another temporary bombing halt.

His latest trip had shaken McNamara badly. Westmoreland was asking huge troop increases, and yet the evidence was persuasive that, despite the bombing, the North Vietnamese could move 200 tons of supplies into the South every day. For once, McNamara was subdued as he spoke with reporters on leaving Saigon. "We have stopped losing the war," he said, but Hanoi was raising the level of the conflict. McNamara added that the Communists' decision to stand and fight at Ia Drang could lead to only one conclusion: "It will be a long war."

Home in Washington, McNamara told Johnson he had the choice of compromise, which meant no longer guaranteeing the independence of the South, or of giving Westmoreland his troops and bombing even more strenuously in the North. McNamara recommended a Christmas bombing pause. Since the United States would soon be escalating the war, the president should try to prove to the country that he had done his best to negotiate.

Johnson had brought to the ranch his usual three advisers—McNamara, Rusk, Mac Bundy, plus Robert Komer from Bundy's staff. Moyers and Joseph Califano, another White House aide, came in from Austin. They found Johnson morose. He had little time for Fulbright, whose criticism of the war was growing more insistent, but neither did Johnson see any light in Vietnam. "We're getting deeper and deeper in," the president complained. "If I bog my car down, I don't want a bulldozer to come and get me." He said he would gladly trade back to the place America had been in when he entered the presidency thirteen months earlier.

Although McNamara favored a Christmas pause, he doubted that it would win over Fulbright. "He wants to let the Commies in," the defense secretary said. Johnson reminded them that another U.S. election was coming up for a third of the senators and all of the representatives. Vietnam was a priority problem, the president said. "It comes ahead of poverty and education. It's a new ball game."

While Johnson was debating with himself over a bombing pause, the National Liberation Front stole the initiative by proclaiming a unilateral cease-fire in the South for twelve hours. A radio broadcast announced that they were acting so that Catholic soldiers in the various armies could celebrate Christmas Eve and attend mass.

When Rusk met the next day with Dobrynin, the Soviet ambassador repeated what Rusk had heard at the U.N. in October from Hungary's foreign minister: Hanoi would not negotiate so long as the North was being bombed. The United States must stop its bombing unconditionally if talks were to begin. Dobrynin added that he could not understand the American stubbornness. The only argument for bombing he had heard was that a suspension would be a sign of weakness. But he warned against a short pause combined with an ultimatum. That had happened the previous May and only made matters worse.

The president had McNamara on the phone polling congressmen. Since neither chamber was in session, many were traveling and unavailable. But McNamara was getting more questions than pledges of support. Senators John Pastore and Mike Monroney were worried about reaction from the voters. "The American public won't take the war for long," Pastore said. Leverett Saltonstall of Massachusetts said the increasing number of casualties was beginning to stir up his constituents.

Speaker John McCormack took a hard line, however, and Gerald Ford wanted to mine Haiphong Harbor. Senator Sam Ervin said, "We ought to bomb North Vietnam out of existence." Thomas Kuchel, a moderate Republican, reported that "the people of California want us to get on with the war." He favored more ground troops and expanded bombing and saw no need to seek further approval from Congress.

Mike Mansfield, who was reached as he traveled in South Vietnam, recommended extending the Communist cease-fire from twelve hours until Tet, the Vietnamese New Year, which would begin on January 21. Even to his friend McNamara, Robert Kennedy was not encouraging when McNamara called. He said that he could not give a worthwhile judgment on the basis of a three-minute discussion, but he had a few political suggestions before any new military buildup—a cease-fire, a longer bombing pause, contacts through Algeria with the NLF.

Since McNamara said a step-up in the bombing of the North was inevitable, Johnson's other advisers were edging toward a pause, and Ball proposed ending the bombing of the North altogether. It was no longer needed to raise morale in the South, he said; the arrival of American troops had done that. And rather than break the will of the North Vietnamese, it was uniting the country against the United States. Ball expanded on that point at a December 17 meeting in the Cabinet Room. "I was in charge of bombing surveys in World War Two," he recalled, "and bombing never wins a war. We are driving the North Vietnamese to a greater dependency on China—and boxing in the Soviets. We are also making plans for negotiation more difficult."

That his recommendation might sound less defeatist, Ball suggested conducting the war in South Vietnam with redoubled vigor, and Johnson seized on that scheme: "The problem is the Chiefs go through the roof when we mention the pause."

"I can take on the Chiefs," McNamara said, adding that during the pause Washington would move to increase its forces in the South.

Valenti was taking notes. When Johnson paused, he wrote, "President thinking—thoughtful, quiet, obviously concentrating deeply." Johnson asked McNamara if he wanted to explore strategy with the Joint Chiefs.

"No, I need to know what you want," McNamara said. "The Chiefs will be totally opposed. We decide what we want and impose it on them." Since they saw Vietnam as exclusively a military problem, he added, nothing would change their views.

"I know exactly what the arguments of the Chiefs are," McNamara concluded. "Before you decide, I cannot deliver. After you decide, I can deliver."

Johnson seemed ready to order a pause. "The weakest link in our armor is public opinion," the president said. "Our people won't stand firm—and will bring down the government.

"We're going to suffer political losses," he went on. "Every President does in off years. But it is because of damn fool liberals who are crying about poverty—which funds I doubled in one year. But we need money for all these programs. How do you divide up this money? Every hangover Kennedy columnist is sniping about Johnson cutting off Great Society programs."

WHEN JOHNSON CONVENED his advisers the next day, he began by resurrecting a criticism made by Adlai Stevenson from beyond the grave. Eric Sevareid, the television commentator, had interviewed him two days before Stevenson's death and published the result in the November 30 issue of *Look* magazine. Stevenson had complained that U.N. Secretary General U Thant had won agreement from the North Vietnamese in early October 1964 to send an emissary to Rangoon, Burma, to discuss peace terms with the United States. Stevenson said someone in Washington had delayed the session until after the presidential elections. Then, with a meeting still possible, McNamara had turned it down. When the article appeared, Rusk assured Johnson that the account was surely false and that Sevareid had "probably received a very substantial fee" for writing it. McNamara had in no way been involved, Rusk said, but he himself had worried that news of a meeting would leak to the South Vietnamese and look as though Washington "was dickering for a settlement behind the backs of Saigon."

Now, when the matter came up again, Rusk defended himself by explaining to Johnson that in diplomacy "there is a difference between rejecting a proposal and not accepting it." He said that distinction had apparently been lost on U Thant.

Before they considered the bombing pause, Johnson turned to Clifford, who had joined the regulars, along with Abe Fortas and Alex Johnson, Taylor's former deputy. The president asked Clifford whether he should deliver his State of the Union message in person. Clifford said that, given Johnson's surgery, he must appear. The president agreed and settled on the date of January 19.

As Johnson polled his aides, Rusk described the American people as isolationists at heart. "You must think of the morale of the American people if the other side keeps pushing." But Rusk put the chances of a pause leading to a settlement as one in twenty.

Bundy said that Johnson should not alert Gerald Ford in the House about his decision. "He will denounce us," Bundy said.

McNamara ticked off reasons—one through six—for the pause, concluding again that a military solution in Vietnam was not certain—"one out of three or one in two. Ultimately, we must find a solution. We must find a diplomatic solution."

Johnson asked him, "Then no matter what we do in the military, there is no sure victory?"

"That's right," McNamara said. "We have been too optimistic. One in three or two in three in my estimate."

Clifford observed to himself that even McNamara's doubts were offered with crisp authority.

"I'm more optimistic," Rusk said, "but I can't prove it."

Clifford had overcome his own misgivings about the bombing and was surprised that McNamara now should be the one expressing doubt. Why consider these massive troop buildups, Clifford asked, if military victory was so unlikely.

"What you are saying is," Ball coached McNamara, "they quit and come to the conference table."

McNamara was not accustomed to bearing bad news. "Right," he agreed readily. "This seems a contradiction. I come to you for a huge increase in Vietnam—400,000 men." But, at the same time, that increase could lead to escalation by the North Vietnamese and to what McNamara termed "undesirable results." He suggested they look for alternatives.

As the meeting broke for lunch, Johnson issued a particularly strong warning against leaks, a theme McNamara took up with fervor. "The greatest danger of leaks," McNamara said, "is right in this room. You simply cannot discuss this with your wife. I can see stories about this, and I am embarrassed. Please let us check ourselves and discuss this with no human being."

After a forty-five-minute lunch, Johnson asked Clifford for his views. This time, Clifford played hawk to McNamara's dove and was no ally for Ball. Since the president clearly was not going to consider Ball's option, Clifford did not bother with it. He predicted that North Vietnam expected to outlast the United States and must be shown that it could not win. This was no time for a bombing pause.

Johnson appreciated the clarity of Clifford's summation and passed him a note across the table: "Magnificent—to sum up—As Abraham Lincoln said—'You can't fertilize a field by farting through the fence.'"

But just before the meeting adjourned at 5:20 P.M., Johnson fixed each adviser with a penetrating look and said to McNamara, almost as an afterthought, "We'll take the pause."

Four days later, a joint bulletin from Saigon and the White House announced a cease-fire beginning on Christmas Eve and lasting for thirty hours. The bombing of North Vietnam would stop for the same period. Johnson flew to his ranch, and McNamara took his family to Colorado for a skiing vacation.

Christmas morning, McNamara heard from Washington that Johnson seemed to be extending the pause for another day or two. He decided to do what he had accused Roger Hilsman of attempting during the weekend cable episode of August 1963. He would cut out Rusk and the others and argue his case for a longer pause directly with the president. Johnson agreed that he could come to the ranch, and McNamara arranged for an Air Force jet to pick him up on December 27.

He landed at the ranch airstrip at 6:20 P.M., had dinner with Johnson, Lady Bird and their daughter Luci and then withdrew with the president for three hours of pleading for prolonging the bombing halt. At last, Johnson agreed but wanted to link the pause to a show of diplomatic activity, and McNamara informed Rusk, who still opposed the extension but realized that the president had made up his mind. The next morning, McNamara wrote cables from Johnson's ranch office that would send Harriman to Eastern Europe, Arthur Goldberg to the Vatican and to U Thant at the United Nations. Ball was put in charge of overseeing the diplomatic offensive—Humphrey to the Philippines and India; G. Mennen Williams, Jack Kennedy's assistant secretary of state to capitals in Africa; State's Thomas Mann to Latin America. Rusk issued a fourteen-point program to send with them that proposed negotiations with Hanoi without preconditions.

IN HANOI, the Politburo viewed the rush of American envoys around the globe as proof that Washington had already decided to send more troops and was trying to soften world opinion. Johnson might even intend to try to invade Vietnam north of the 17th parallel. Certainly, he was attempting to install a permanent puppet government in Saigon.

Ho was not taking an active part in formulating the North's response. As he felt his health deteriorating, he had called together the Politburo and relinquished his power to its members. "I'll be your flag," Ho said. He could still be an icon to rally the people. But they would make the decisions.

That show of confidence did not mean that Ho felt secure about his political heirs. He saw how authoritarian Giap had become from his years of heading the army. His nature was now a marked contrast with that of Pham Van Dong, who tried to be everyone's friend. As for Le Duan, Ho saw a growing megalomania and disapproved of his hostility to the Chinese. But unity with the South demanded that the other members get along with Le Duan, and Ho hoped that, acting together, Giap and Dong could rein him in. The problem was that Le Duan was strong-willed and Dong was a bureaucrat. Dong had never challenged Ho's rulings—which was good—but neither would he take on Le Duan. In the power vacuum that Ho was creating, Le Duan was certain to dominate the Politburo. And of its members, he remembered most keenly how North Vietnam had been betrayed by the negotiations of 1954.

Lately, Le Duan had seemed to go out of his way to exacerbate Hanoi's problems with Beijing. During this year's trip to Moscow, he had criticized Chinese policies in a talk to Vietnamese embassy staff and students studying in the Soviet Union. Some of those students were outraged and sent his remarks home. When their letter disappeared, they accused Le Duan of intercepting and burning it. But he was equally outspoken on Chinese territory. Stopping over in Beijing on his way from Moscow, he spoke to Vietnamese embassy personnel there for three hours, criticizing the Chinese for relying too heavily on peasant farmers in maintaining their revolutionary government. At home, Le Duan's rivals said that such outspoken criticism of a Communist ally was forbidden unless approved by the Central Committee. Unrepentant, Le Duan said North Vietnam's ambassador in Beijing agreed with his every word.

To A DEGREE that Washington did not understand, all of the Politburo members saw the bombing of their country as a serious challenge to their sovereignty and were sure that their people felt as they did—ashamed to enter into talks with bombs falling around them. Nor was a pause, a cessation, enough incentive to negotiate. Bombing of the North had to stop unconditionally.

As for Johnson's array of envoys, flying everywhere but Hanoi, did Washington still believe that Moscow or Beijing made decisions for North Vietnam? And the North's leadership was even less impressed by the Fourteen Points that Rusk had issued lately, under prodding from Johnson. Rusk called them "U.S. Contributions to the Basket of Peace." But they contained phrases sure to cause the North to reject them: Hanoi must decide "to cease aggression" and the bombing of the North could stop "as a step toward peace, although there has not been the slightest hint or suggestion from the other side as to what they would do if the bombing stopped."

As for Pham Van Dong's Four Points of the previous spring, the American statement said that "Hanoi's Four Points could be discussed along with other points which others might wish to propose." Rusk's proposal ended with an unbending summation: "In other words, we have put everything into the basket of peace except the surrender of South Vietnam."

The response in English over Radio Hanoi was one of fiery defiance. Titled "Johnson Puts Everything into the Basket of Peace but Peace," it denounced Rusk's exercise as a smoke screen for the expanded war to come. But beneath the rigid tone, a clarification was being offered. Washington seemed to balk at Pham

Nguyen Duy Trinh
(Vietnam News Agency)

Van Dong's third point about the South following the program of the NLF, but the Front controlled four-fifths of the South's territory and 10 million of its people. Its program called only for independence, democracy, neutrality and, eventually, the peaceful reunification of North and South. Since Washington claimed to respect the Vietnamese people's right to self-determination, how could it justify objecting to that third point?

To STRENGTHEN HANOI'S WILL to resist, Zhou Enlai met with the NLF's ranking delegate in Beijing to warn him that the U.S. peace offensive was a ruse. The Americans may speak of unconditional negotiations, Zhou said, but consider the conditions they are actually laying down: Hanoi must give up its support for you in the South, and you in the South must lay down your weapons and surrender to the Saigon government. The United States is hatching a plot to expand the war, possibly to all of Indochina, Zhou added, and even to China. If that happened, "the Chinese people will face it and accept it and will fight the war until the end."

But Hanoi did not altogether rule out negotiations. In April, a southerner, Nguyen Duy Trinh, had been named as the first foreign minister who was also a member of the Politburo. Since that time, Hanoi's strategy had been threefold: to endure the U.S. air strikes, to exhaust the American troops in the South and to erode the will of America's people to fight on.

Although Washington did not discuss those goals, they were hardly secret. They had even been set to music as a popular song that was being sung throughout the country. But U.S. intelligence coming out of the North had not improved since the days of Lansdale and Conein.

EIGHT

SALISBURY
1966

As Mac Bundy's influence with Johnson waned, he reverted to a role he found congenial. Rather than offering advice, he was reporting information to the president and laying out options. With the New Year, he could relay news from Johnson's far-flung emissaries: Beijing denounced the peace offensive as a sham. The Hungarians were more optimistic, although they reminded Washington how hard it was to communicate with men living in a jungle. Tito of Yugoslavia urged the White House to let the differences within Hanoi's Politburo ripen a little longer.

Both Britain and Canada were assuring Russia that the United States was serious about wanting talks. The Algerians had agreed to meet with the NLF. As for de Gaulle, Bundy said he privately praised the bombing pause but, speaking to the British ambassador, had sneered at America's peace feelers. Vice President Humphrey had calmed Taipei's nervousness about U.S. intentions; Rusk had done the same in Bangkok. But Bundy had to conclude that "the lines are nearly all out but we have no diplomatic answers back."

Bundy did not mention the fruitless attempt to exhume the XYZ connection. In November, Gullion had written to introduce to Bo another retired foreign service officer, Paul Sturm, whose code name was to be "Y." Bo was still "R" in cables to Washington. He met with Sturm but was puzzled when he seemed to have no new message from Washington. Sturm was told to return after the bombing had stopped and tell Bo that a clear reduction in Vietcong attacks would be a welcome response to the U.S. pause. But when Sturm tried to reach Bo on New Year's Day, he was told that, once again, Bo was ill.

From Lodge in Saigon came a barrage of bad news about the way the pause had affected the South. Vietcong attacks in the week beginning December 26 had risen to 1,133, Lodge said, "the highest totals of incidents since the Communist aggression began." Lodge added that Ky said that during the pause the number of people entering Chieu Hoi camps for villagers escaping from Vietcong control had dropped, and Saigon's newspapers were also critical of the hiatus.

As were the U.S. Joint Chiefs. They urged resuming operations against the North immediately since the pause placed American troops "under serious and progressively increasing military disadvantage." But it was McNamara's pause and he was fighting for it tenaciously. He challenged the Chiefs: Show me how the U.S. effort in the South was being hurt, and I will advise the president to resume the bombing. The Pentagon did not respond, but by January 10, Johnson had also soured on the pause and seemed to be siding with the Chiefs. When McNamara repeated that there was no disadvantage in waiting through the Tet holiday near the end of January, the president disagreed. "Every day makes a difference," Johnson said, yet he did not give the order to resume bombing.

As Johnson fretted, Mac Bundy urged him to be more open with the American people about the choices he faced and to give Congress a chance to reconsider the broad license they had issued seventeen months earlier in the Tonkin Gulf Resolution. But Bundy was at the nadir of his influence with the president.

At one point, Johnson permitted Jack Valenti to draft a presidential statement explaining America's vital interests in the war. Before that was completed, George Ball returned from a meeting with Fulbright's Foreign Relations Committee to say that although members questioned the wisdom of Johnson's policies, they did not see any other course to follow. Fulbright's committee also invited Johnson to discuss Vietnam with them, but he declined. He already knew how the congressional leaders stood. Mansfield and Fulbright wanted to scale back military action to avoid confronting China; Dirksen wanted the president to do anything necessary to win. And Dick Russell, who had warned Johnson against involvement in Vietnam less than two years before, now said he was willing to kill any number of Vietnamese civilians if that would spare American boys from dying. Johnson decided that if he went back to Congress now, he would be denounced as a warmonger by the liberals and as a weakling by the conservatives. The polls were no help. As the bombing pause stretched past Tet, 42 percent of the people wanted it prolonged, but 44 percent called for the bombing to resume.

On January 28, Johnson invited Clark Clifford back to the White House, along with other Wise Men—John McCloy, Allen Dulles and Arthur Dean, who had been the U.S. negotiator in Korea. By that time, McNamara had shared his doubts about Vietnam policy with a number of Georgetown friends. At a New Year's Eve party, he had spoken of the war with Toni Bradlee, whose husband Ben had left Kay Graham's *Newsweek* to become deputy managing editor of her

Washington Post. Mrs. Bradlee shared Margy McNamara's opposition to the war, and as other guests laughed and sang, she questioned McNamara about America's role. For two hours, he responded with a torrent of words, and tears streaming down his cheeks. A week later, at a dinner party in Cambridge given by Arthur Schlesinger, McNamara told Ken Galbraith, Dick Goodwin and Carl Kaysen that he no longer believed a victory could be achieved in Vietnam. His only hope was a withdrawal with honor.

Among the Wise Men, however, McNamara shed that defeatism and called for a resumption of the bombing so long as it was carefully controlled. The American people, he said, would not support a policy that did not back up the large number of troops that Washington intended to put in Vietnam. McNamara now doubted that bombing alone would influence the Politburo, since Pentagon estimates indicated that even with heavy bombing, the North Vietnamese could infiltrate 4,500 men every month into the South. And yet, in the month before the pause, the United States had dropped 50 percent more tonnage on the North than the United States had dropped on Korea in the heaviest month of bombing. Still, McNamara concluded, doubling Westmoreland's men over the next six months might break Hanoi's will.

Clifford disagreed that the bombing was not effective. "We must fight the war where we are strongest," he told Johnson. "In the air." As the meeting was breaking up, Johnson reminisced about his days in the House. "I was the first Congressman to speak up for the Truman Doctrine," he said. "I am not happy about Vietnam, but we cannot run out. We have to resume bombing."

The next day, Johnson and McNamara began selecting targets. At 10 A.M. on January 31, Johnson announced that U.S. Air Force planes were once more bombarding North Vietnam.

ALTHOUGH JOHNSON'S SQUADRON of flying envoys had returned home, the publicity given their travels had put Vietnam near the top of the American agenda. Felix Greene, a former official of the British Broadcasting Corporation now living in Northern California, offered to fly to Hanoi. Greene had been well received in China when he filmed an interview with Zhou Enlai, and Ho had said in the past that he would accept Greene as a messenger. Vice President Humphrey, gradually rehabilitating himself after a year's exile from Vietnam meetings, noted that Greene apparently had a good deal of sympathy with Ho's regime "even though, from what I hear, a non-Communist himself." Johnson wrote, "Get this to Rusk immediately." The overture withered at the State Department.

Valenti met with John Steinbeck, who had been awarded the Nobel Prize for literature four years earlier, and described him as a fascinating man with an "imaginative flair for war and its weapons," but Mao would have been disillusioned with the author of *The Grapes of Wrath.* Steinbeck advised one huge bombing strike against the North and then another pause. "You see, I was in the blitz in London," he explained. "People get used to anything, except what they don't expect. It's when the pattern is broken that they get uneasy." Steinbeck ridiculed the use of rifles, recommending instead "an open-bore 12-gauge or, if you are man enough, a 10-gauge automatic shot gun." Johnson forwarded that memo to McNamara. But Westmoreland was already complaining that the Pentagon was not supplying him with enough M-16 rifles, and Steinbeck's advice went unheeded.

Harder to ignore was the increasing interest that Fulbright's Senate committee was taking in Vietnam. On February 4, the senators held the first of five televised hearings on the president's request for a $400 million increase in aid for Vietnam during the current fiscal year. Rusk and Max Taylor were among the dependable voices of support, but they were challenged by James Gavin, a retired lieutenant general and former ambassador to France. Gavin had written a letter to *Harper's* magazine proposing a radical change in Westmoreland's search-and-destroy policy of attrition. Gavin recommended holding U.S. troops to defensive enclaves, stopping the attacks on North Vietnam and seeking a political settlement in Geneva or at the U.N. Earle Wheeler and the Joint Chiefs assured McNamara that Gavin's enclave theory was certain to fail. Although the Chiefs' language was guarded, it translated to one conclusion: The ARVN could not survive outside of the protected U.S. bases. But if the ARVN joined the Americans within their zones of safety, the Communists would take over the countryside — 90 percent of the south's land, 60 percent of its people.

Johnson had no intention of adopting Gavin's plan. Nor would he listen to George Kennan, who cited recent events in Indonesia as refuting the domino theory. What enraged the president was the fact that his war strategy was being debated live on national television. The Senate hearings were provoking more opposition to the war than Bundy's CBS appearance had done.

Wayne Morse had lately tried and failed to rescind the Tonkin resolution, which only he and Gruening of Alaska had opposed originally. Now millions could watch Morse's debating skill. He told Max Taylor, "I happen to hold to the point of view that it isn't going to be long before the American people, as a people, will repudiate our war in Southeast Asia."

Taylor responded, "That, of course, is good news to Hanoi, Senator."

Morse was no ARVN general, compelled to hold his tongue. He said, "I know that that is the smear that you militarists give to those of us who have honest differences of opinion with you, but I don't intend to get down in the gutter with you and engage in that kind of debate, General."

Morse's reputation for being mercurial made his criticism easier to slough off. Dean of the law school at the University of Oregon, he had been elected to the Senate as a Republican, supported Adlai Stevenson's first campaign for president and switched to the Democratic Party. Fulbright's growing discontent had to be taken more seriously. Despite his domestic votes to placate Arkansas segregationists, he was considered a well-informed student of foreign policy. After World War II, Fulbright had sponsored a plan to use foreign monies owed to the United States to finance an exchange of professors and students from countries around the world. The Senate had named those scholarships for him.

As Senate majority leader in the 1950s, Johnson had called Fulbright "my secretary of state," in contrast to Ike's Foster Dulles. Now Fulbright was saying publicly that he regretted supporting the Tonkin resolution and that the Vietcong should be invited to new peace talks in Geneva. Around the White House, Johnson had taken to calling him "Senator Halfbright."

In questioning Taylor, Fulbright showed that his years in Washington had not diminished his folksy qualities. He was trying to get Taylor to equate the U.S. firebombing of Tokyo in World War II with what was going on in Vietnam— "millions of little children, sweet little children, innocent pure babies who love their mothers, and mothers who love their children, just like you love your son, thousands of little children, who never did us any harm, being slowly burned to death." Taylor could respond only that the United States was not deliberately attacking civilian populations in South Vietnam.

Early on the morning after the first hearing, Johnson called Larry O'Brien, his chief congressional liaison, to complain that the hearings were "a very, very disastrous break." He instructed Lodge in Saigon to leak a rebuttal to Johnson's senate critics. Working through Barry Zorthian, the mission's chief information officer, the ambassador settled on Ward Just, a highly regarded reporter for the *Washington Post.* "Senior U.S. officials," Just's story began, "are dismayed and angered by Congressional criticism of the war in Vietnam. This view is shared, it is understood, by virtually every top official in the U.S. civilian and military command." Valenti assured Lodge that Johnson had read the story with delight: "Tell Barry, he did an excellent job, and we are grateful."

But Johnson could not rely on an occasional jab at Fulbright's committee. He decided to upstage the hearings by joining his advisers on their upcoming trip to Honolulu. There he would meet personally with Westmoreland, Thieu and Ky. Johnson confided to Rusk that he especially wanted to get to know Thieu so that "if something happened to Ky, well, we wouldn't necessarily be tied to Ky too much."

Johnson's arrival in Honolulu late on February 5 marked the first time Westmoreland had seen him since they met at West Point when Johnson was vice president and the general was the academy's superintendent. Westmoreland thought Johnson seemed fretful, even overwhelmed, by the burden of the war. "General," he told Westmoreland, "I have a lot riding on you." At another point, Johnson touched on his concern about public dissent from the field. "I hope you don't pull a MacArthur on me," he said. Westmoreland preferred to take the observation as rhetorical and say nothing.

As the delegations prepared to sit down, Ky was gleeful to find himself directly across from the president, with only Thieu to one side, and his defense minister, General Nguyen Huu Co, on the other. Better still, Max Taylor had been relegated to the back of the room. Magnanimously, Ky walked over and shook his hand.

Johnson wanted to use the occasion to press for the domestic reforms in South Vietnam; he understood them better than military strategy. Bui Diem, who had assisted in drafting the Caravelle Manifesto that once enraged President Diem, was put to work on a speech for Ky to deliver before the assemblage. Bui Diem had reconciled himself to working under a military government and considered that Thieu and Ky, despite their jockeying for position, meant well at heart. Writing the speech was a way to put Ky on record as favoring democracy, and Bui Diem drafted a call for creating a constitution and returning to civilian control; he knew that the ringing phrases would appeal to Ky's taste for heroics. Thieu was more cautious about commitments, however, and struck out the loftier passages. Even so, President Johnson listened intently and concluded that, whatever Ky's other qualities, he certainly knew how to talk.

As the conference was ending, Johnson treated the delegates to his own bravura performance, running down a list of civilian objectives and assigning responsibility for each of them. "In paragraph two," Johnson read, " 'larger outputs, more efficient production to achieve credit, handicraft, light industry, rural electrification.' Are those just phrases, high-sounding words, or have you coonskins on the wall?"

The idiom puzzled several Vietnamese seated near Bui Diem, and they leaned over to ask, "*Ong ay noi cai gi the?*"—Just what is the gentleman talking about?

When he came to the great number of refugees in the South being created by the war, Johnson said, "That is just as hot as a pistol in my country. You don't want me to raise a white flag and surrender, so we have to do something about that. . . ." Johnson explained that he had specifically not talked about the battlefield because "we want to be able honestly and truthfully to say that this has not been a military buildup conference here in Honolulu."

That night, Johnson invited Ky and Thieu to have a drink with him and Westmoreland. The talk was desultory until Johnson whispered to Ky, "Come into my bedroom for a moment." Puzzled, Ky followed the president who, it turned out, wanted to roust Humphrey from Washington and send him to Saigon with Thieu and Ky. It was another sign that Humphrey's year of isolation for wobbling on Vietnam might be ending.

Johnson assembled a number of old hands to accompany the vice president—Harriman, Mac Bundy, Chet Cooper, Lansdale and Valenti. Until one of Valenti's cables fell into Humphrey's hands, the vice president was not aware that Valenti had been told to report back to Johnson on Humphrey's actions every day. Jim Thomson, along on the trip, talked to reporters in Saigon who were critical of the war's conduct, but Lansdale got Thomson together with Dan Ellsberg, who was far more optimistic.

In all, Johnson's euphoria proved contagious. Humphrey, enthusiasm always at full throttle, pronounced himself impressed and heartened by his brief glimpse of Vietnam. Mac Bundy, days away from escaping from government altogether, called the changes since his trip a year ago "fantastic."

But Johnson found that the Senate hearings had taken the toll he feared. George Reedy, his latest press secretary, warned that deep divisions were arising among the voters. It was no longer hawks versus doves but vultures versus chickens. And Reedy said that the public was taking the unanimity among Johnson's advisers as proof that the president was listening only to men already so committed to war that they had no alternative. Reedy recommended inviting to the White House both Gavin and Kennan, but Johnson continued to worry about giving his critics legitimacy and invited neither. Senator Church of Idaho went on television's *Today* show to warn about the dangers that Vietnam posed. Monitoring his three television sets, Johnson had to admit that Church had been effective.

The president's leading foreign and domestic foes all seemed to be weighing in at the same time. On February 15, a statement signed by Ho flatly rejected Johnson's offer to end the bombing and hold back new American troops if the Politburo would stop its infiltration by land and sea. Ho restated the Four Points in more impassioned language and noted that Hanoi's cause enjoyed worldwide support, "including broad sections of the American people."

Robert Kennedy learned of Hanoi's softer private messages relayed through Italy's foreign minister, and he was angry that the State Department had bungled that overture. Blaming Rusk, Kennedy was lining up with the advisers—Ball, Harriman, even McNamara—who wanted to negotiate. As a conciliatory gesture, Kennedy had sent Johnson *Never Call Retreat*, Bruce Catton's account of Abraham Lincoln's search for a peaceful solution during Lincoln's crisis. But when the pause ended, Kennedy had told the Senate on January 31, "If we regard bombing as the answer in Vietnam, we are headed straight for disaster." Two weeks later, Kennedy issued a statement, drafted by Dick Goodwin, that the NLF should share in power under any negotiated settlement. Kennedy had cleared Goodwin's draft with McNamara, Taylor and others. He told reporters that he had also shown the statement to Moyers and found that he did not disagree.

He was asked, "Do you speak for the White House?"

Kennedy's grin, more wolfish than Jack's, could also convey more mischief. "I don't think anyone has ever suggested," he said, "that I was speaking for the White House."

Reporters deduced that it was the opposite. The *New York Times* called the statement a break with Johnson, and the conservative *Chicago Tribune* labeled him "Ho Chi Kennedy." For an even more damning way to strike back, Johnson turned to television. On *Meet the Press*, Mac Bundy quoted Jack Kennedy's opposition to popular front governments—Kennedy had been speaking in Berlin in 1963—and on ABC's *Issues and Answers*, George Ball equated coalitions with Communist governments. From New Zealand, where Humphrey was trying to enlist greater support for the war, the vice president was quoted as saying that Kennedy's recipe for peace included "a dose of arsenic."

To redeem himself, Kennedy also took to television, granting on the *Today* show that his position was "a little confusing." As Kennedy backed down, Johnson backed off. Neither Democrat wanted to split the party, and Kennedy was displeased when he heard that war protesters were cheering his name. "I'm not their Wayne Morse," he said. By February 23, Johnson and Kennedy were flying together to New York on *Air Force One* with the state's other congressmen to watch Johnson receive an award from Freedom House. In accepting, Johnson vowed again that the American goal was not conquest in South Vietnam while Kennedy gnawed on a cigar and offered minimal applause.

Bundy had not warned Kennedy about the rebuttal he made on *Meet the Press*. It was his final official service to Lyndon Johnson. Preparing to leave government, Bundy wrote a memorandum for his own files, assuring himself that although the price of the Vietnam War might be high, the "danger to one man's life, as such, is not a worthy guide. Casualties and costs must be accepted if basic questions of a nation's interest, right and power were to be answered."

Overcoming any hurt feelings, Robert Kennedy and his wife, Ethel, showed up for Bundy's farewell party in Georgetown. Joe Alsop was one of the hosts, and Valenti and Moyers represented the White House. As early as January 1965, Bundy had recommended Moyers as his eventual successor. Lately, he had put a new date on the same memo and sent it back to the president. Bundy was dumbfounded when Johnson chose instead Walt Rostow, Bundy's former deputy and currently State's chairman of policy planning. Equally stunned were colleagues who considered Rostow's optimism about the war to be misguided, even infernal. Rostow did nothing to reassure them. He predicted to Harriman that the bombing of the North would go on escalating, probably until Washington and Moscow reached a nuclear confrontation. Only from extreme crises, Rostow explained, do some settlements come.

SPECIALIST JACK SMITH had spent the past three months at a U.S. military hospital outside of Tokyo. The battle at Ia Drang had cracked his jaw, and shrapnel had slashed a vein, but none of his organs had been hit. He limped in both legs, however, and took pills for his nerves—a tic in his face and trembling hands he could not control. Then an officer appeared to say that Smith would be rejoining his unit at An Khe on Route 19.

"They're saying this is the Yalu River all over again," the officer said, referring to the Korean battle that had brought in Chinese troops. "They want everyone we can send them. Even one-legged men are going back."

There was an exception. After the battalion commander who broke down at Ia Drang botched his next operation, Hal Moore got him removed. Smith was outraged that the man was not court-martialled and regarded his quiet transfer as an army whitewash.

By that time, Smith himself had lost any taste for heroism. He did not think about whether the war was right or wrong, only about the lessons he had learned: Dig deep holes. Don't be curious; when you hear a bullet, look down, not up. Kill the bad guy before he kills you. And the lesson that haunted him every day of his recovery: "I've used up all my luck. If I go back, I'll die."

Against his every instinct—except for self-preservation—Smith wrote to his father for help. His lackluster academic performance had somewhat estranged them, and Smith knew he must be insane with fear to be writing the letter. Howard K. Smith responded like a father. I happened to bump into a general I know, he wrote, and he needs you in his public information office.

But when he was discharged from the hospital, Jack Smith tore up the letter and decided to return to his unit. He persuaded himself that he owed it to his buddies. Except that, arriving back in Vietnam, he found that his buddies were all dead.

WHEN LE DUAN LED a delegation to Beijing in late March, Zhou Enlai warned him that the purpose of Kosygin's trip to Hanoi had been to split North Vietnam from China and to betray the North's struggle by improving relations with the United States. He cautioned against accepting Russian pilots or volunteers. "You will be in trouble," Zhou said. "The Soviets may disclose secrets to the enemy."

The Chinese interpreter was relieved whenever Mao did not appear at a session, since the Chairman tended to turn his back and speak very softly. Zhou appreciated the value of an accurate translation and would often repeat more distinctly what Mao had just said.

Le Duan returned two weeks later, and Zhou was joined by Deng Xiaoping, who addressed North Vietnam's great fear. "Do the Chinese want to take control over Vietnam? We would like to tell you frankly that we don't have any such intention." Perhaps, Deng added, the very enthusiasm that he, Zhou Enlai and others had shown for aiding Hanoi had been misinterpreted. Comrade Mao had once warned that it might be.

Deng touched on the Chinese troops lent to North Vietnam for construction. "We don't know whether it is good for the relations between two parties and two countries or not when we sent 100,000 people to Vietnam. Personally, I think it's better for our military men to come back home right after they finish their work."

Deng and Zhou raised their own grievance about Chinese ships being denied entry to Vietnamese ports. They quoted a Vietnamese commander as saying, "It is our sovereignty. You can only come when you are allowed to." If the Vietnamese were that suspicious, China would withdraw its men at once. "We have a lot of things to do in China," Deng said.

Le Duan responded with a dignified defense. None of the Vietnamese in the room had heard of such incidents at the ports, he said, and they did not represent Hanoi's policy or attitude. But the true problem concerned the Soviet Union. "You are saying that the Soviets are selling out Vietnam, but we don't say so." With reformist movements under way in Socialist countries around the world, Le Duan said, there should be countries like China to criticize them but also to cooperate in keeping them on the revolutionary path. "It is not our concern that China is trying to take control over Vietnam," Le Duan concluded. "If China were not a Socialist country, then we would be really concerned."

SINCE DIEM'S ASSASSINATION, the Buddhists of Hue and Da Nang had responded to each change of government with demands and street demonstrations. Bill Kohlmann's best source, Tran Quang Thuan, had flown on occasion to central Vietnam to dampen the protests—often successfully, sometimes not. Max Taylor had lectured Khanh about the anti-American protests in Hue but accepted Khanh's assurances that Tri Quang and another troublesome monk would be leaving the country. Returning to South Vietnam, Lodge took a different approach. "The Buddhists are crucial in Vietnam," he wrote to Johnson. "Among the Buddhist clergy are the only Vietnamese with genuine political talent." Lodge was sure his former houseguest could be reasoned with, and he recommended bringing the Dalai Lama to Saigon to show Tri Quang a living embodiment of the way the Communists treated Buddhist clergy.

Ky's success at Honolulu had persuaded him of Johnson's backing, however, and he resolved to force a showdown with Tri Quang, whom he considered a power-hungry humbug. Ky had watched Tri Quang forge an alliance between the two chief Buddhist sects—the South's Hinayana, or Smaller Wheel, which held that enlightenment was restricted to an elite, and central Vietnam's Mahayana, or Greater Wheel, which believed that it could be achieved by anyone.

Tri Quang counted on support from his friend Cabot Lodge but found that other Americans now valued stability above his complaints. When Buddhist demonstrations erupted again in I Corps, the embassy became even less sympathetic. Ky blamed the I Corps commander, General Nguyen Chanh Thi, who had fled to Cambodia after the failed coup against Diem in 1960. Ky had watched suspiciously as Thi first helped to bring Khanh to power and then contributed to his ouster. Flying to Da Nang, Ky stripped Thi of his command, offering a cover story that Thi would soon be leaving for treatment at a U.S. hospital. When Thi rejected that ruse, Ky put him under house arrest.

The Buddhists sent an appeal to Washington. Johnson ignored it. YANKEE GO HOME graffiti started appearing around Hue, and Ky heard rumors of White House meetings over his future. In Saigon, young Buddhists in white shirts tore through the streets, breaking windows and turning over American jeeps. In addition to solemn torchlight parades through Hue, the Buddhists burned down the U.S. Information Service building. Tri Quang's strategy seemed aimed at exasperating Washington into pulling out its troops from the South. "And if the Americans do leave," he said, "I will have achieved passively what the Vietcong have been unable to do by killing people."

To avoid Khanh's fate, Ky had to act. On May 14, he held a secret meeting at 3 A.M. with only his most trusted officers. He did not confide his plans to Thieu and certainly not to the Americans. At 5 A.M., he dispatched ARVN troops into Da Nang, supported by the fighter-bomber wing he had commanded. Vietnamese paratroopers and Marines encountered no opposition when they seized the radio station and set out for the army headquarters, where the division commander had sided with the Buddhists.

The opposition they did meet, however, came not from renegade ARVN units but from General Lewis Walt, commander of the U.S. Marines. On hearing of Ky's action, he called an ARVN officer, who in turn reached Ky at his Saigon office. "General Walt has asked me to stop the operation," the man said. "If we continue to use air cover, he has threatened to send up American planes to shoot them down."

Ky called Lodge with his own threat. If Walt's ultimatum represented U.S. policy, Ky would fly to Da Nang and lead his planes himself. Even though Lodge promised to countermand Walt, Ky flew to Da Nang, lined up the largest ARVN guns and trained them on the U.S. Marine base across the river.

"If Americans start to shoot down our planes, destroy the Marine base," he told the local commanders. "That is an order."

By that time, Walt had heard from Lodge. He asked Ky to come to see him. Ky said he was too busy and turned down a second request as well. Walt asked if he could come to Ky instead. Again, Ky refused. But when Walt sent yet another message, Ky relented. "All right," he said. "I can spare you five minutes."

Walt appeared, saluted smartly and asked why Ky had sent the troops.

"Is it really any business of yours, General?" Ky asked.

"Well," said Walt, "I'm in command of the American Marines here, and I'm the adviser to the Vietnamese command. I think in view of my position, I might have been told about it."

Ky was revenging himself for every American slight and snub he felt he had endured. He lectured to Walt until finally Walt protested. "But you know Danang is quiet," he said. "My Marines can go into the bars for a drink. I don't see why you had to send in troops."

Ky said sarcastically that he was glad Walt's Marines could have a drink. But he was the prime minister, trying to restore order against a Buddhist rebellion. Wouldn't Walt do the same?

Walt asked mildly whether Ky also intended to occupy Hue and was visibly relieved when Ky said no. Instead, Ky blockaded the roads out of Da Nang. Without food, gasoline or other essentials, the rebel ARVN general capitulated. Ky sent in police to restore order, seized Tri Quang and locked him up in a Saigon hospital. With the crisis past, Lodge congratulated Ky on his decisiveness, and Walt found a way to patch up their relationship. He learned that Ky liked Tabasco sauce and told him that the man who bottled it was his best friend. "I'll see that you're never short of Tabasco as long as you live." Walt kept his word, and every month Ky got a case of sauce.

THROUGHOUT THE SPRING and early summer, the CIA reported that the American bombing of North Vietnam, while destructive, had not stopped Hanoi from maintaining—and perhaps even stepping up—its support of the Communist troops in the South. If that intelligence discouraged Johnson, he did not change course, despite new attacks on his policy from Robert Kennedy and Barry Goldwater. Robert Kintner, a retired network executive, monitored the television news shows Johnson missed, and he relayed Goldwater's call for a greater all-out effort in the war along with Kennedy's speech attacking the escalation as unwise. Kintner noted that Kennedy had not mentioned Johnson by name but had effectively portrayed him as too dependent on military force.

According to the polls Moyers was forwarding to Johnson, 67 percent of New York voters rated the president's job performance favorably, down only 2 percent from the percentage of votes he had received eighteen months earlier. But his approval rating among liberals had dropped to 47 percent compared with Robert Kennedy's 65 percent. Given Johnson's general popularity, he could indulge Ken Galbraith, who was teaching again at Harvard but still trying to influence the White House. The latest Buddhist upheavals had given Johnson "an opportunity only the God-fearing deserve and only the extremely lucky get," Galbraith wrote on April 3. If Ky's government fell, Washington should pick up and get out. On June 16, Galbraith tried again, offering to write a speech for Johnson that would set the stage for an orderly withdrawal. He received a reply drafted by Rostow for Johnson's signature. "I have never doubted your talent for political craftsmanship," the letter began, "and I am sure you could devise a script that would appear to justify our taking an unjustifiable course in South Vietnam." Galbraith made one last attempt on June 28, pointing out that he had been right about Vietnam from the time Kennedy first sent him there five years earlier. He warned Johnson that his advisers were plodding down a road that could lose him his place as one of the country's greatest presidents.

"The people who want to invest more and more in this war have nothing to lose," Galbraith wrote tartly. "They will end up working for a foundation."

□

GALBRAITH HAD ASSURED Johnson that 1966 was a time of opportunity for America, partly because of the cataclysm that was overtaking China. During an extended stay in Shanghai, Mao and his wife, Jiang Qing, read about a 1961 play that seemed to criticize Mao for removing his defense minister, Peng Zhen, who was now mayor of Beijing. Mao used the newspaper item as a pretext to form a committee to guide what he termed a Cultural Revolution. When Peng was named a member, he tried to limit the committee's role to discussion, but Mao wanted action.

He saw Peng—indeed Beijing itself—much as Johnson saw East Coast liberals—pretentious, effete, harboring feelings of superiority toward his lowly origins. And, like Johnson, Mao derided his opponents for being squeamish about bodily functions. "If you have to fart," he exhorted a Communist meeting, "fart! You will feel much better for it."

During his sojourn in Shanghai, Mao had shunned publicity so thoroughly that he was rumored to be dead. Now at seventy-five, Mao was ready to take on Peng, the nation's capital and anyone who did not share his hostility toward the Soviet Union. For the benefit of television cameras, he went to the town of Wehan and swam the Yangtze River, then ordered his current minister of defense, Lin Biao, to send troops into Beijing. They secured all government buildings and set up checkpoints at main intersections.

Having established his vigor, Mao returned to Beijing. He wrote out a wall poster urging the young to overthrow their tired and corrupt elders. Mao's first 100,000 recruits ranged in age from fourteen to twenty-two, plucked by army recruiters from high schools and universities. To deceive Mao's enemies, the young people were said to be training for a mass educational campaign. Instead, they were being worked into a rebellious frenzy.

Three hundred million Chinese had been born since Mao came to power in 1949, and he was determined that they not be soft. Mao and his comrades had been about twenty-three years old when they made their revolution. Let the young now make another. "Knock down the old," Mao challenged his cadres— the Hung Wei Ping, or Red Guards. It was as though Johnson had authorized Students for a Democratic Society to terrorize Wall Street, Yale and the Dallas Chamber of Commerce.

From Hanoi, Ho watched with disapproval as the Red Guards adopted a moral code more stringent than Madame Nhu's. Not only was dancing outlawed but kissing was denounced for being a waste of time and for spreading the hepatitis B virus. "Adults and children," a newspaper warned, "we must rid ourselves of the kissing habit." The North Vietnamese depended too heavily on China's aid to protest the excesses of the Red Guards, who burst in on Peng Zhen, pulled him from his bed and dragged him downtown to face a barrage of criticism.

Posters that had been rigidly controlled since the brief era of blooming flowers were now plastered across public buildings like garish wallpaper. Mao produced one promising that great beauty would arise from the present chaos. But for now, "Hats are flying in the air and cudgels are roaming the land." Mao appeared at the Gate of Heavenly Peace in Tiananmen Square wearing army fatigues and a cap with the red star. Millions of young people came to receive his benediction, each wearing khakis with red armbands and waving Mao's book of homilies.

The new revolution was no respecter of veterans from the past. The son of Mao's colleague Deng Xiaoping was paralyzed when he was pushed from a fifth-floor window. A young woman named Ding joined the Red Guards and turned on her mother, a teacher denounced by her students as a "bad element." She had worked for the Communists against the Japanese, but that was not enough to spare her. When her school was set upon and a secretary beaten to death, Ding's mother was denounced and then—in the euphemism for torture—"struggled against." She was beaten with bats studded with nails, and her back was broken. When her older children spirited her away to a hospital, only the soles of her feet were not bloody. Doctors at first refused to risk their careers by treating her until a former student protested that even prisoners of war deserved medical care.

When Ding's mother thought she might die, she appealed to her children not to blame the Communist Party. "This is a big revolution," she said, "and any revolution has its casualties."

WITH THE LATEST Buddhist crisis defused, Ed Lansdale had spent the summer of 1966 making the rounds of South Vietnamese politicians and relaying their opinions to an indifferent ambassador. The old complaints about Lodge were growing louder. He had forbidden his deputy, William Porter, to speak to Thieu or Ky but was not meeting with them, either. He was at the embassy only five or six hours each day, bored, tired and aware, as Lansdale was not, that South Vietnam was now the property of MACV and the Pentagon. In his discursive memoranda, Lansdale clearly pined for the days when Saigon's cabinet ministers were worth cultivating. But every topic the civilians raised was either trivial or impossible to realize. One of them asked that one hundred tapes of Vietnamese music be donated to American universities and Walter Reed Hospital. Another spoke about reactivating a Farmer's Union, although in the countryside the farmers tended to believe, as they had since 1960, that the Communists would eventually win. A politician in Gia Dinh province was predicting that the Politburo would simply abandon the cities of Hanoi and Haiphong and move to the countryside. Lansdale passed on that observation to Lodge, with his own summation: "Quite an unusual enemy we are up against."

☐

THE PRESIDENT was scrutinizing the results of his party's primary elections, labeling any candidate who opposed his Vietnam policies a "Peacenik." Over all, Johnson found the results encouraging: In Massachusetts, Maryland and New Jersey, the doves had been trounced. Peace candidates did somewhat better in Rhode Island and New Hampshire, but the Republican winner in New Hampshire had campaigned for all-out bombing of Vietnam.

DAN ELLSBERG had interrupted a home leave in the United States to go again to Vietnam on a brief fact-finding mission. He departed from Saigon on the secretary of defense's plane, and near the end of the flight he watched Bob Komer, a friend from their days together at the RAND Corporation, arguing with McNamara at the rear of the aircraft. Komer had left Rostow's staff to take charge of the pacification effort in the South.

Their plane was nearing Andrews Air Force Base in Washington when McNamara beckoned to Ellsberg to join them. "Dan, you're the one who can decide this." It was a favorite McNamara gambit for drawing another person into a discussion. "Komer here is saying that we've made a lot of progress in pacification. I say that things are *worse* than they were a year ago. What do you say?"

"Well, Mr. Secretary," Ellsberg began, "I'm most impressed with how much the *same* things are as they were a year ago. They were pretty bad then, but I wouldn't say it was worse now, just about the same."

McNamara said, "That proves what I'm saying! We've put more than a hundred thousand more troops into the country, and there's been no improvement! Things aren't better at all! That means the situation is really *worse!* Isn't that right?"

"Well, you could say that." The pilot was telling passengers to take their seats for landing. "It's an interesting way of seeing it," Ellsberg added.

On the ground, McNamara strode to a podium set up near the runway and addressed the reporters and television cameras. "Gentlemen," he said, "I've just come back from Vietnam, and I'm glad to be able to tell you that we're showing great progress in every dimension of our effort. I'm very encouraged by everything I've seen and heard over there. . . ."

McNamara's agility impressed Ellsberg as deeply as it had Ted Sorensen five years earlier. To himself, Ellsberg murmured, "Wow!"

COLLEGE CAMPUSES held a nostalgic allure for McNamara as intellectual havens, but Vietnam was denying him their sanctuary. He had learned the dimensions of college discontent the previous year at Amherst College's graduation ceremonies. Many students were wearing black armbands to protest the war, and as their honors were announced, McNamara was startled to find that students graduating summa cum laude wore the highest percentage of black bands.

Next he had been jeered when his younger daughter graduated from Chatham College in Pittsburgh. And going to work for Robert Kennedy, she became friendly with Sam Brown, a notable antiwar activist. Away at St. Paul's preparatory school in Connecticut, McNamara's son, Craig, was not only geographically distant. The boy was going into Boston each Wednesday for counseling with a psychiatrist, and one week he stayed on to attend a meeting of Quakers who denounced the war.

Shaken, he called McNamara at the Pentagon and asked him to send documents that defended America's policy. In the press of business, McNamara sent a few routine pamphlets. He became aware of his son's distress only when he found an American flag hanging upside down in the boy's room.

In November 1966, McNamara agreed to fly up to Harvard to address the classes given by Henry Kissinger and those of Richard Neustadt at a new public policy school named for John F. Kennedy. McNamara's jaunt began with a placid reunion at Harvard's business school, followed by an impromptu debate with undergraduates at Quincy House, a student residence. Like Mac Bundy, McNamara enjoyed intellectual fencing when his data and stature gave him the greater reach. His adrenaline pumping agreeably, he left for Kissinger's class in a station wagon provided by Harvard. A campus policeman was at the wheel. As they started down a narrow brick lane, some 800 students surrounded the car and forced the driver to stop. When they began to rock the car, McNamara sprang out to confront them.

"Okay, fellas," he shouted. "I'll answer one or two of your questions. But remember two things: We're in a mob and someone might get hurt and I don't want that. I also have an appointment on the other side of the river in five minutes."

McNamara asked who was in charge. Michael Ansara, the president of Harvard's Students for a Democratic Society, pushed forward with a microphone. McNamara got the two of them up on the car's hood so they could be seen by the students at the end of the lane and began recalling his happy days as a student protester at Berkeley. That reminiscing only provoked loud insults and renewed jostling from the crowd. A voice asked why Washington accused Hanoi of causing the war with its aggression after 1957, and McNamara could score a debater's point. The aggression, he shouted, started in 1954, not 1957. The government knew that "because the International Control Commission wrote a report that said so," McNamara continued. "You haven't read it, and if you have, you obviously didn't understand it."

The voice shouted that he had, in fact, read the report. McNamara taunted him: "Why don't you guys get up here since you already seem to have all the answers."

The din grew louder. Afterward, McNamara rationalized his next remark as an attempt to avert violence by showing he could not be intimidated. "I was tougher than you then," he yelled, about his Berkeley days, "and I'm tougher today! I was more courteous then, and I hope I'm more courteous today!"

It was not the remark to quell a crowd. McNamara jumped from the hood and ducked back into Quincy House, where an undergraduate named Barney Frank led him through a maze of underground tunnels that connected several Harvard buildings. They surfaced in Harvard Yard in time for McNamara to meet with Kissinger's graduate class. But the hatred he had faced left him disturbed, and it took half an hour of browsing in a Harvard Square bookstore to restore his composure. Later at dinner with Neustadt and other professors, McNamara confided what he would never have said from the hood of a car: the war was going badly.

The discussion turned to research that Neustadt had published on a rift between London and Washington after the Cuban missile episode. McNamara knew the controversy well. Eisenhower had promised to let the British buy a new air force nuclear missile called the Skybolt, but when it failed five tests, McNamara scrubbed further development. He had not been entirely candid with his British counterpart, however, and bad feelings developed. To ease the strain, Kennedy had been forced to offer Prime Minister Macmillan the new Polaris submarine and missile as a consolation, which, in turn, complicated America's relations with other European allies. One of Neustadt's colleagues said that an examination of the origins of the Vietnam War might have similar scholarly interest.

McNamara seemed receptive to the idea. Possibly an attempt could be made to document—only for the use of future scholars—what was going wrong for America in Vietnam.

BUNDY HAD AGGRESSIVELY defended Johnson's policies on television. Now Rostow in his memoranda was proving even more combative. Let a group of Democratic congressmen propose a peace conference, and Rostow lectured them about the folly of pressing for talks and a cease-fire. "I would like to keep in touch on the matter," Rostow concluded, "which concerns us all, and our President more than anyone."

But other cracks were appearing in the Democrats' united facade. Missouri Senator Stu Symington called Rostow to say, "You and I have been hawks on Vietnam since 1961. I am thinking of getting off the train soon. If I do, the first one to know will be the President. But we are old friends, and I wanted to give you this warning.

"It looks to me that, with the restraints on the use of airpower, we can't win. We are getting in deeper and deeper, with no end in sight. In 1968, Nixon will murder us. He will become the biggest dove of all times. There never has been a man in American public life that could turn so fast on a dime."

Rostow gave Johnson a summary of Symington's call and got back a note that showed that Robert Kennedy was seldom far from the president's mind: "I know at least one more fellow who can turn faster on a dime than Nixon. Guess who?"

FOR EIGHTEEN MONTHS, Harrison Salisbury, a New York Times editor, had been applying for a visa to enter North Vietnam. Writing to Pham Van Dong, he got no response, but the silence did not discourage him. In the early 1950s, Salisbury had been the paper's Moscow bureau chief and knew that Communist regimes often favored indirection. He contacted Soviet newspapermen, peace activists, anyone he thought might intercede with Hanoi on his behalf. By the spring of 1966, he was ready to try another approach. Traveling to Asia, he circled the countries that surrounded China, filing stories from each stop but also applying for a visa wherever the North Vietnamese maintained an embassy. Still, he received no word from Hanoi.

Back in New York, Salisbury speculated that, with Christmas approaching, both sides might call a truce and that the Communists could consider it a good time to show off the results of the American bombing to an American reporter. Norman Morrison, the Quaker who incinerated himself at the Pentagon, had become a martyred hero in North Vietnam, and his widow, Anne, wrote a letter to Hanoi on Salisbury's behalf.

On December 15, a cable arrived at the Times informing Salisbury that he could pick up his North Vietnamese visa in Paris. The day before, Hanoi had accused Washington of sending bombers the farthest yet into the capital. For two days, the Communists said, planes had been bombing the city's center rather than its industrial suburbs. The State Department denied the accusation, and the Pentagon claimed that any damage must have come from a misfiring of Hanoi's own surface-to-air missiles.

For Salisbury, the timing was awkward since his older son, Michael, was being married on New Year's Eve. But no one in his family would expect Salisbury to pass up the chance to be the first U.S. journalist to report from the North. Getting into Hanoi would be the scoop of his career. Salisbury apologized to his son and boarded Air France.

Thin, white-haired, wading into action like an angry stork, Salisbury was a driven newsman, quick and impatient but also cerebral and prescient. In the days when Washington saw only a Communist monolith, Salisbury in Moscow had detected splintering in the alliance between China and the Soviet Union. Time magazine had reviled his reporting as softheaded.

Salisbury's bristling contempt for mediocrity had stalled his rise at the Times, where suave manners and Southern gentility were rewarded. Salisbury was arguably the paper's most accomplished newsman, but his title was assistant managing editor. The managing editor was Clifton Daniel, a North Carolinian married to Harry Truman's daughter, Margaret.

In Paris and then Phnom Penh, glitches almost prevented Salisbury from catching the International Control Commission plane that would take him to North Vietnam by way of Vientiane. After forty-eight hours of uncertainty, Salisbury got at last to Hanoi, shivering in the winter chill and aware suddenly that he had only the vaguest idea of how America had become enmired in Vietnam. It was probably France's fault, he decided, for not releasing its colonies as pragmatically as the British had done.

Salisbury's stolid upbringing in Minnesota had not entirely smothered a helpless romanticism. From the time his plane touched down, he was thrilled to be—as he kept telling himself—"behind enemy lines." He had been booked into Thong Nhat, or the Reunification, a hotel the French had called the Metropole. At 6 A.M. on his first morning, Salisbury's hosts took him to the Museum of the Revolution and gave him a quick briefing on their country's history—the Trung sisters and Tran Hung Dao, who had defeated 300,000 Mongols in 1288. Salisbury was struck by how contemporary the stories seemed as his guides told them.

He was driven next to Pho Nguyen Thiep Street, five minutes from his hotel, where a bomb had fallen earlier that month. Through interpreters, Salisbury spoke to residents who told him that a bomb or rocket had exploded, collapsing thirteen houses, killing five civilians and injuring eleven more. The people on the street were sure that their neighborhood had been singled out for the destruction, but looking 150 yards down the street, Salisbury saw the Long Bien railroad bridge. He concluded that an American pilot, flying at 1,200 miles an hour, had simply missed his target. Salisbury had covered London for UPI at the end of the German blitz and later had seen the rubble that had once been Stalingrad and Sevastopol. The loss of life on Pho Nguyen Thiep saddened him as an American, but he did not consider the destruction especially dramatic.

As he was escorted around the city, Salisbury found other places that had suffered greater damage. In the village of Phuc Xa, outside of Hanoi, the North Vietnamese told him that 24 persons had been killed and 23 wounded. The target seemed to have been a nearby dike along the Red River. Salisbury found that he and the villagers each admired the efficiency of the other's culture. Phuc Xa had been struck in mid-August and rebuilt in thirty-six days with help from surrounding villagers, which impressed Salisbury. But the villages were awed by the loading date stamped on one bomb fragment. "Imagine!" one survivor exclaimed. "The bomb was loaded in July and within a month it fell here in this village."

Salisbury's tour was making him increasingly skeptical about the bombing targets selected with such precision by the Pentagon and then painstakingly reviewed by the president and his defense secretary. In Washington, for example, the Van Dien truck park had been touted as a major target of the bombing on December 13. Salisbury found a half-dozen loading sheds, with the wreckage of twelve or fourteen buses and trucks that were being repaired at the time. Pilots had also struck—again accidentally, Salisbury was sure—the Polish Friendship School half a mile away up the road. Before he left New York, Salisbury had looked up the statistics: That month, just under 400,000 U.S. servicemen were in South Vietnam, up from 15,500 at the time of Kennedy's assassination. That was more men than the United States had sent to Korea. As for bombs, 300,000 tons had fallen in 1966. It was true that more had been dropped in South Vietnam than in the North, but the gap was narrowing every month. What was the point, Salisbury asked himself, in using $2 million aircraft and highly trained American pilots to bomb a handful of trucks already needing repair? And in the process destroying a school supported by the Poles?

Bigart and Halberstam had incensed the U.S. government by reporting from the South. Now Salisbury's dispatches from the North, which the *Times* was promoting heavily, were even more damaging to the White House. Salisbury could not be dismissed as a foreigner, which was the charge against Morley Safer and Peter Arnett. Nor as young and untried, the grounds for criticizing Sheehan and Halberstam. Nor as a radical. Salisbury, who had begun reporting during the New Deal, believed as fervently as Johnson in government's capacity to improve men's lives.

From the Pentagon, Arthur Sylvester denounced the *Times*'s exposé. Was Salisbury belittling the military importance of the targets? He should walk down the main street of Nam Dinh, the country's third-largest city, where he would find a large antiaircraft installation protecting the railroad. It had been struck three times between late April and the first of June.

But Salisbury had already made that trip and found no guns, only a textile factory. Its operators said the plant had been hit nineteen times. The 24,000 children of Nam Dinh had been evacuated to the countryside, but the dike that protected the city from the Dao River had been struck repeatedly. Salisbury watched a thousand men and women working to repair it.

Turning to the war's political side, Salisbury spent four hours with Premier Pham Van Dong, who assured him that North Vietnam was prepared to fight for twenty years or longer in what Dong called its "sacred war." He also emphasized that his Four Points should not be seen as conditions that must be met before Hanoi entered into peace talks.

In a later dispatch, Salisbury introduced readers to Le Duan, although he had not met with him. "The party secretary's name is not well known outside of North Vietnam," Salisbury wrote. "But there it is regarded as quite possibly even more important in party circles than that of Premier Pham Van Dong." Salisbury added that some observers believed that if Ho died, either Le Duan or Truong Chinh would succeed him.

On Christmas evening, Salisbury returned to Hanoi and sent more dispatches to the *Times*. He anticipated attacks on his credibility, and they quickly materialized. Sylvester made them personal by referring to him publicly as "Harrison Appallsbury" and to the newspaper as "*The New Hanoi Times*." Sylvester himself was leaving the Pentagon, but his public affairs office sent letters to congressmen and foreign officials admitting that some of Salisbury's observations might prove correct but charging that many others had come, without attribution, from North Vietnamese propaganda tracts. Bill Bundy forwarded the Pentagon's rebuttal directly to officials in London, and the State Department sent its embassies a seven-page cable that made that same point, although adding that Salisbury's reports could not "be dismissed out of hand." Salisbury wished he could ask his critics one question: if he didn't rely on casualty figures from local officials, who else would supply them in a Communist country?

Yet the administration's counteroffensive was making converts among other journalists. With a son who had been severely wounded in Vietnam, Howard K. Smith told his ABC television audience that Salisbury's dispatches were "careless, erratic and misleading." The *Washington Post* repeatedly challenged Salisbury's reliability, while the *Times* itself ran on its front page a dissenting view of Salisbury's conclusions by Hanson W. Baldwin, the paper's military affairs analyst. Baldwin quoted Pentagon sources as calling Salisbury's reports of civilian casualties "grossly exaggerated." Clifton Daniel privately instructed *Times* editors to "do everything we can in the coming weeks to balance the Salisbury reports." A *Times* editorial called for an end to the bombing but said there was no shred of evidence that the United States was deliberately targeting civilians.

Salisbury filed a total of fourteen reports from Hanoi and another eight from Hong Kong. Despite his paper's queasiness, their impact galvanized the peace movement and led to more aggressive challenging of government statistics.

When the Pentagon announced that 400 U.S. planes had been shot down over the North, Hanoi responded that, with robot planes and drones, the figure was closer to 1,600. Baldwin checked with his sources and reported that when the losses were calculated throughout Southeast Asia—including damaged planes and planes that failed on takeoff or from accidents—the tally rose to 1,700.

In his independent weekly, I. F. Stone threw back at Baldwin another of his facts. Stone noted that the *Times*'s story had disclosed that more bombs were being dropped on North and South Vietnam in one year than had been dropped in the entire four years of warfare against Japan throughout the Pacific. Stone added that Salisbury was practicing freedom of the press in the best Jeffersonian tradition, and every newsman, whatever he felt about the war, should applaud him. Instead, the response to his stories "has looked as mean, petty and unworthy a reaction as I have ever seen in the press corps."

Salisbury's reportage had been the most significant of 1966, but the editors who bestowed Pulitzer Prizes were not prepared to insult a president whose wrath was notorious. When the award went elsewhere, Salisbury claimed to be untroubled. As he told his sons, if reporters didn't upset people, they were not doing their job.

NINE

McNamara
1967

Salisbury's reports particularly disturbed McNamara because they revealed how misleading his own description of the bombing raids had been. From the beginning, he had convinced himself that precision was possible, and since he, together with the president and General Wheeler, chose the sites to keep clear of the Chinese border or heavily populated areas, McNamara felt justified in playing down the inevitable civilian casualties. Even before the *Times* articles appeared, however, McNamara himself was expressing doubts about the strikes' effectiveness. The number of sorties—one mission by one plane—now added up to 13,200 a month. McNamara was resisting Pentagon demands for a greater number of raids and for permission to hit more sensitive targets.

Admiral Sharp sent Wheeler a bitter cable from Honolulu: "Our air strikes on the railyard and the vehicle depot were hitting the enemy where it was beginning to hurt. Then, Hanoi complains that we have killed a few civilians, hoping they would get a favorable reaction. And they did, more than they could have hoped for."

Sharp concluded, "The restrictions should be removed. And then when Hanoi screams in anguish we should hit them again."

Rostow, who shared the admiral's frustration, thought he knew the reason for McNamara's growing reluctance. Rostow's own family stoutly believed in his policies, but he wondered what dovish influence McNamara's wife and children might be having.

□

General Nguyen Chi Thanh *(Ta Minh Kham family)*

IN JANUARY 1967, Hanoi's ranking commander in the South, General Nguyen Chi Thanh, came out of the jungle in Cambodia, changed to civilian clothes and flew with a false passport from Phnom Penh to Hong Kong and on to Hanoi. The war might not be going as well for the Americans as Westmoreland was claiming, but the U.S. troops had succeeded in taking control of some rural areas and driving Communist main force units toward the South's borders. Thanh worried that one day Johnson would give in to Westmoreland's pleas and let him send troops into Laos to cut off the Ho Chi Minh Trail. To avoid that, Thanh had been consulting with Le Duan and was now ready to present his plan to the Politburo. It involved a gambit Paul Harkins would have recognized.

On one given day, preferably tied to a holiday when the enemy was either at home or befuddled from celebrating, the Vietcong would rise up in every province of South Vietnam in a show of force that would startle the world. Afterward, America—a country Thanh considered wealthy but irresolute—would give up. But one Politburo faction turned out to be as wary of Thanh's grand stroke as Diem had been about the ARVN dealing a similar death blow.

Giap was especially outspoken against it. Such an ambitious plan would be coming much too early in the war, he said, and would cost their forces too many lives. For some time, Giap had been urging that Thanh's forces revert to guerrilla warfare. But Thanh, the only military man who shared Giap's rank, had persisted in engaging the Americans in large-scale battles. Giap worried that, no matter who won those engagements, Johnson might yield to the Pentagon, invade Vietcong sanctuaries in Laos and Cambodia and perhaps even send ground troops to carry the war into the North.

A harsher bombing policy out of Washington could also be ruinous. Humanitarian concerns seemed to have spared the dikes of the Red River. But should that policy change, hundreds of square miles of farmland could be destroyed and the farmers drowned. By one estimate, Hanoi itself would be submerged beneath eleven feet of water.

Le Duan argued strenuously that they must not overrate American strength in the South. During their debate, he remained unfailingly considerate of Giap and his opinion. Besides Giap's stature, Le Duan would never forget that his late wife had once protected him from the French. But he was determined that his strategy prevail.

The leadership agreed that Thanh's idea must be given further study.

In the South, 1967 was shaping up as the fiercest year of the war, with U.S. ground troops pushing forward with their search-and-destroy operations. But optimists in the Politburo agreed with Thanh that the American people were fatigued from the seeming stalemate. One decisive Communist victory would have them demanding that Johnson negotiate an end to the war. The Politburo debated a resolution that the "situation allows us to shift our revolution to a new stage, that of decisive victory." Some members called for Thanh's General Offensive to be followed by a General Uprising as well. The Politburo had to weigh three possible results: An overwhelming victory that would force the enemy to accept Hanoi's terms; healthy wins at many sites but none of them decisive enough to prevent America from regrouping and going on with the war; or that the United States would make up for its losses by sending in large reinforcements and step up the war in North Vietnam and Cambodia. Politburo members considered that third contingency the least likely but had to discuss how to prepare for it.

Thanh waited in the South for the resolution that would authorize his General Offensive. Meanwhile, he could start moving ammunition into the province capitals. And in the forests of Cu Chi, Vietcong were constructing a mock-up of the new compound that the Americans had built to house their embassy. But no final planning by the party's Central Office for South Vietnam—the Americans called it COSVN—and the Regional Command (B2) could begin until Hanoi's Political Bureau passed its resolution.

BY MID-FEBRUARY, when Cabot Lodge was ready to end his second tour as ambassador, his standing with the Vietnamese who had once praised him was sorely diminished. Lodge planned to take Lansdale back to the United States with him and bluntly told him so. "L.B.J. wanted you out here with me," the ambassador said, "but you've failed on that, and you better come with me." Lansdale drew on his Washington contacts and won permission to stay on.

On McNamara's trip the previous fall, he had hinted to Westmoreland that he might expect expanded duties, and ever since, the general had been lobbying for the ambassadorship. He told Bus Wheeler that he should also have the title of Commander in Chief, U.S. Forces, Vietnam, which would give him the military and civilian control that MacArthur once exercised in Japan. To Westmoreland, the advantage to centralized control was obvious, but his euphoria was short-lived. Wheeler told him in early March that Johnson had been talked out of the idea. After the debacle with Max Taylor, Rusk would not concede the civilian post to another general. Instead, Johnson chose seventy-three-year-old Ellsworth Bunker to head the mission while Komer oversaw the pacification program. Johnson brought his new team to Guam on March 20 to introduce them to Thieu and Ky.

At the conference, Ky proudly presented Johnson with a copy of a new constitution for South Vietnam that had been patched together in the year since their Honolulu conference. It provided for both a president with broad powers and a prime minister who would lead a Congress divided into two chambers. The document's American influences were explained by the fact that John Roche in the White House had helped to draft it. One provision required that the president be born in Vietnam. That was not only a bow to the U.S. constitution, but it also eliminated men like Tran Van Don, who had been born in France.

Besides containing a bill of rights, the new document promised land reform, union organizing and welfare benefits. Ky pledged himself to national elections for president and the new Senate; they would be followed by voting for a house of representatives. Accepting South Vietnam's document, Johnson said that he looked upon it "just as proudly as I looked at Lynda, my first baby."

In other matters, Westmoreland took the opportunity to warn Johnson against further bombing pauses in the North. He also gave what was, by far, his most pessimistic forecast. If the Vietcong did not disintegrate—and Westmoreland saw no reason that they should—the war could go on indefinitely. As Westmoreland sat down, he noticed a disbelieving look from McNamara's deputy, John McNaughton.

The meeting's principal goal had been to reorganize the many agencies at work in South Vietnam. Komer emerged as Westmoreland's top civilian deputy in a military chain of command. Cabot Lodge had nicknamed Komer "Blow Torch," and Westmoreland also found him abrasive but tried to appreciate his maniacal drive. The chimera of winning South Vietnamese hearts and minds was now called CORDS—Civil Operations and Revolutionary Development Support—this year's version of the agroville and strategic hamlet programs.

Komer would oversee Saigon's attempt to bring education, medical care and economic benefits to islands of security that would eventually spread across the country. That approach had not worked for at least fifteen years, but Westmoreland threw his prestige behind it. To guard the model hamlets, he assigned militia from the Regional and Popular Forces. He also gave Komer command of a heightened attempt to seek out and kill Vietcong leaders. Called "Phoenix," it would be run by Colby of the CIA, back again in South Vietnam.

IF THE WAR had become tidier on the organizational charts, on the battlefield it was even messier than Westmoreland had reported. That explained why he was now asking for another 200,000 U.S. troops. If granted, his request would raise the total to 670,000 men. But that was not all Westmoreland wanted. He again urged going into Laos and Cambodia, stepping up bombing raids in the North and mining its harbors. He also raised the possibility of landing an amphibious unit north of the Demilitarized Zone. That would put U.S. troops on North Vietnam's soil.

The total Pentagon budget was currently $71 billion, with $25 billion going to Southeast Asia. Westmoreland's requests would add another $10 billion annually. Ambassador Bunker, whose military experience had begun and ended fifty years earlier in Yale's ROTC, endorsed invading Laos and Cambodia.

Johnson asked Westmoreland to return to the United States, ostensibly to address a luncheon of AP executives. The general had declined the previous year when a similar invitation was relayed through McNamara. This time, Johnson made his appearance an order. Besides its political benefits, the speech would provide a cover for their consultation over the requested large troop increase. Speaking at the Waldorf-Astoria Hotel on April 24, Westmoreland warned the editors that the end was not in sight. America was fighting a war of attrition, he explained, which was the only alternative to a war of annihilation. Since the word "annihilation" suggested the use of nuclear weapons, Westmoreland's strategy sounded reassuring. But leaving the hotel, he was jolted to see an effigy of himself being burned by antiwar demonstrators.

To McNamara, Westmoreland had described the 200,000 new troops as his "optimum" force, and with them he could wind down U.S. involvement in two years. He also submitted a "minimum essential" plan for 80,500 men; that included two-and-a-third new divisions and four tactical fighter squadrons. With them, the winding down would take three years. If he got no new forces above the 470,000 already approved for 1967, he estimated that it would require five more years before America could safely disengage. Westmoreland went to plead his case at the White House on April 27, the day before he was booked to address a joint session of Congress. Pentagon speechwriters were already at work on his remarks.

At their meeting, the president kept his counsel, although Westmoreland thought he was leaning toward calling up the Reserves and supplying the 200,000 men. But Johnson asked pointedly, "When we add divisions, can't the enemy add divisions? If so, where does it all end?"

Westmoreland assured him that the Communists would be hard-pressed to support twelve divisions in South Vietnam; currently, they had eight. They did not touch on a debate simmering in Saigon, where a young CIA analyst was challenging the army's estimates of enemy strength. Samuel Adams had been in South Vietnam since mid-1965, keeping track of the number of Vietcong and North Vietnamese soldiers. He was protesting that Westmoreland's intelligence officers were beginning to drop some paramilitary Communist forces—the 120,000 self-defense militia and secret self-defense militia—from the order of battle. Adams claimed the deletion suggested that more progress was being made in the war than the accurate figures could substantiate.

With Westmoreland, however, Johnson raised another concern: "At what point does the enemy ask for volunteers?"

"That is a good question," Westmoreland said. But with the current program of 470,000 men, "we would be setting up a meat grinder. We would do a little better than hold our own."

Bus Wheeler did not seem to be backing Westmoreland's call for harsher bombing in the North. "The bombing campaign," Wheeler said, "is reaching the point where we will have struck all worthwhile fixed targets except the ports."

Westmoreland saw that Rostow was his only ally in the room for moving into Laos and Cambodia. Rostow also favored some spectacular use of the new troops—landing north of the DMZ, for example.

Westmoreland left the White House knowing that he would not get quick approval of his optimum figure. But in reviewing the next day's speech, he also knew that his words would get back to the men who were doing the fighting, and he did not want to dishearten them. Westmoreland thought he must surely be the first commander to address Congress while a war was still going on. Since he did not want to mislead his audience, he hoped to be inspiring without ever using the word "victory."

Those qualms hardly mattered. Senators and representatives cheered when Westmoreland paid tribute to America's fighting men—"the finest ever fielded by our nation"—and their applause followed after him as he saluted smartly and strode from the chamber. Even Fulbright admitted it had been a good speech. "From the military standpoint, it was fine," Fulbright told Westmoreland. "The point is the policy that put our boys over there."

Westmoreland celebrated at a White House luncheon while Rusk briefed guests on the status of the latest diplomatic overtures to the North. The comic Martha Raye, one of Westmoreland's favorite performers, was on hand from New York to entertain.

Westmoreland's appearance set off a flurry of new memoranda to the president. Mansfield nominated himself to go to China as Johnson's representative for talks with Zhou Enlai. He also thought it was worth pursuing an expensive scheme to string an electronic barrier down the Ho Chi Minh Trail to deter North Vietnamese traffic. Mansfield reminded the president that, as Johnson's deputy in the Senate, he had sometimes tugged on Johnson's coattails when it was time to stop talking and sit down. He was figuratively tugging now, Mansfield wrote, and "the hour is growing very, very late."

Rostow drafted the answer to Mansfield's letter, quoting Rusk's reasons for opposing a visit to China. Mansfield must remember that as a senator he was "an officer of the United States Government," Rusk said, and therefore his appearance in China would lead to "great confusion among our friends in free Asia, including the fear that we were about to sell them out."

From the Ford Foundation, Mac Bundy recommended that Johnson limit the bombing in the North. He thought American opinion was uneasy because there were no defined limits to the levels of force or the dangers that might arise. Bundy shied away from the issue of troop increases: "All that I can say is that I think there should be a limit and that it should be stated and understood fairly soon." Bundy cited the 1968 election as one reason Hanoi would not negotiate now. But he predicted that American voters would appreciate that South Vietnam had not been lost and was not going to be. "An articulate minority of Eastern intellectuals (like Bill Fulbright)," Bundy concluded, playing to Johnson's phobia, "may not believe in what they call the domino theory, but most Americans (along with nearly all Asians) know better."

Johnson was as dissatisfied as Jack Kennedy had been with the performance of the State Department, but getting rid of its Secretary was out of the question. With support for the war curdling, Johnson relied more than ever on Rusk's stalwart backing. To improve matters, however, he instructed McNamara to persuade Nicholas Katzenbach to give up the cabinet post he had inherited when Robert Kennedy left the administration. Katzenbach was to trade the title of attorney general for the lesser one of undersecretary of state. McNamara hardly relished the assignment, but Katzenbach made it easy for him by promptly agreeing.

WESTMORELAND FLEW BACK to Saigon, concerned that opposition from McNaughton and another Pentagon civilian, Alain Enthoven, might be swaying McNamara against his optimum figure. Both men were targets of resentment among the Joint Chiefs for meddling in military matters they could not comprehend. The Chiefs mocked McNaughton, who loved gadgets, for posting lights outside his office—red to ward off visitors, green to indicate that he was available. And Enthoven, a systems analyst, was seen as dependably hostile to the Chiefs' budget requests. But McNamara did not need prompting from his subordinates to question Westmoreland's analysis of the war. He went home every

Robert S. McNamara
in September 1967
(*AP/Wide World Photos*)

night to a wife who had stopped talking about Vietnam but whose disapproval was intensifying doubts in her husband that were the more potent for being six years late.

On May 19, McNamara wrote his own version of the three skeptical memos he had eviscerated or ignored in recent years—those of George Ball and Bill Bundy in October 1964; and Mac Bundy's description in February 1965 of Mc-Namara's troop proposals as "rash to the point of folly."

As he finally gave expression to his own misgivings, McNamara could see a way out of Vietnam—for himself, if not for the country. The past April, George Woods, the president of the World Bank—officially, the International Bank for Reconstruction and Development—had asked to meet with McNamara. In December, Woods would be ending his five-year term, and the bank's charter provided that the U.S. president nominate an American for the post, since Washington contributed most of the funds. In McNamara's private dining room at the Pentagon, Woods asked whether he would be interested in the job. Doing good works around the globe certainly looked preferable to pulverizing one small portion of it, and McNamara called the offer "appealing." But he had once promised a president to serve as long as he was needed, and this particular president relinquished aides with bitter reluctance. McNamara reported the overture to Johnson, who accepted the news impassively and did not mention it again.

Given that prospect on the horizon, however, McNamara could write his memo with new fervor. He began by noting that Hanoi would probably not negotiate until after next year's presidential elections. He did not need to add that even Westmoreland's optimum prediction saw the war continuing past 1968. His memorandum did, however, go on to another point that Johnson hardly needed made, either. "The Vietnam war is unpopular in the country," McNamara informed a president whose White House was often ringed with protesters chanting, "Hey! Hey! LBJ! How many kids did you kill today?"

McNamara added, "Most Americans do not know how we got where we are, and most, without knowing why, but taking advantage of hindsight, are convinced that somehow we should not have gotten this deeply in. All want the war ended and expect their President to end it. Successfully. Or else."

McNamara reviewed the situation in the South in much the mixed terms of Harkins and Lansdale earlier in the decade. After staving off defeat in 1965, the military side was going well. The political war was not: "Corruption is widespread. Real government control is confined to enclaves. There is rot in the fabric." Bombing the North had not reduced Hanoi's will to resist or its ability to supply aid to the South.

In McNamara's opinion, the Soviets did not want Vietnam to jeopardize their relations with America, and the Chinese were preoccupied with their Cultural Revolution, although they would join the war to preserve the Communist government in the North. At home, giving Westmoreland his 200,000 men would mean finally calling up the Reserves and would encourage the hawks to demand even sterner measures—bombing the North's lifeline of locks and dikes, mining its harbors against Soviet ships, waging major battles in Laos and Cambodia. And—if U.S. losses were running high—tactical nuclear or bacteriological weapons.

Summing up, McNamara wrote in language the antiwar movement would have cheered: "The picture of the world's greatest superpower killing or seriously injuring 1,000 noncombatants a week, while trying to pound a tiny backward nation into submission on an issue whose merits are hotly disputed, is not a pretty one."

For the first time, McNamara took note of Indonesia, where General Suharto had seized the government in the fall of 1965 and massacred hundreds of thousands of suspected Communists. The region's largest domino had fallen, bloodily, but into the Western camp. McNamara argued that "the trend in Asia was now running in America's favor, which reduced the importance of South Vietnam." McNamara had been among Ball's critics for stating a problem without offering a solution. Now he did marginally better. McNamara could not bring himself to recommend unilateral withdrawal, but he suggested eliminating what he termed "ambiguities" from U.S. objectives.

Washington would remain committed to seeing that the people of South Vietnam determined their own future, but "this commitment ceases if the country ceases to help itself." He recommended against Westmoreland's approach, which "could lead to a major national disaster," and called instead for bombing the North only to interdict NVA troops below the 20th parallel. McNamara wanted a firm cap on the increase in U.S. ground troops at 30,000 and more flexibility in negotiating a political settlement. Otherwise, "the war in Vietnam is acquiring a momentum of its own that must be stopped."

The Joint Chiefs were quick to protest McNamara's version of the war, and he dutifully forwarded their rebuttal to the president. They wanted to mine Haiphong Harbor, even though Helms at the CIA endorsed McNamara's view that none of the military's options would affect either the war in the South or Hanoi's determination. Bill Bundy, forgetting his earlier moment of clarity, called McNamara's memo "a figleaf for withdrawal." Rostow's contribution was to offer a middle way. Not so long ago, it had been McNamara and the Bundy brothers steering a path between Ball and the hawks. Now Rostow interposed himself between McNamara and the Chiefs. Continue bombing the North, Rostow suggested, but more selectively. Send more troops, less than Westmoreland requested but still enough to require calling up the Reserves, whatever the domestic repercussions. Indeed, Rostow considered the call-up a potent tool: "Nothing you could do would more seriously impress Hanoi that the jig was up."

When at last he made his decision, Johnson cut even Westmoreland's minimum request almost in half. He authorized 47,000 more troops and imposed a ceiling of 525,000. Although very disappointed, Westmoreland thrust out his jaw and did not protest when Johnson told reporters that the new figures were acceptable to the general.

IN EARLY JULY, before Hanoi's debate could be resolved over the wisdom of staging a general uprising, its leading advocate was silenced. General Nguyen Chi Thanh's unexpected death led to rumors that he had been killed by bomb fragments from a B-52 raid or even murdered for opposing Giap. The prosaic truth was a heart attack. Thanh fell ill in the South on July 4, was flown to Hanoi for treatment and died two days later.

Thanh was gone, but Le Duan remained committed to his strategy and was winning over the Central Committee. Giap had stopped arguing. He developed stomach problems, flew to consult doctors in Hungary and prolonged his convalescence there. When the time came, he would sign off on the general uprising. His army had become a bureaucracy, and the forms must be observed. Ho, too, had counted the votes. He agreed with Giap that the general offensive was premature, but he would not contest Le Duan and the Central Committee. When the roll was called, he abstained.

□

IN HIS SWELTERING HANOI CELL, Robbie Risner was being beaten regularly for minor infractions. When handcuffs bit into his wrists until he could no longer stand the pain, Risner wrote out a new confession of war crimes against the Vietnamese people. The guards collected similar statements from every prisoner in the Zoo and printed them in a North Vietnamese newspaper.

Risner developed kidney stones, which the guards treated with pain pills and a shot intended to dilute them. But Risner's agony remained hideous, and he could not eat. Guards brought him bananas and sugar with canned cream. He turned away. When the stone finally passed, the Vietnamese brought him a full pound of sugar and encouraged him to eat it. Risner decided he must be valuable enough to be kept alive.

He soon understood why. The North Vietnamese had begun running foreign delegations through the prisons, and Risner became a prize exhibit, although it took the threat of the rope torture to get him to agree to meet with them. For the first visitors, an East German camera crew, his interrogators supplied the questions he would be asked and the answers he was to give. Risner at first balked at saying that the United States should withdraw its troops, dismantle its bases and cut off aid to Thieu's puppet government. But he relented and was rewarded with two photographs of his family that his wife had sent to Hanoi.

Risner tried to convey to the East German journalists the duress under which he was performing. One crew member said only, "Wipe the sweat off. You've looked terrified the whole time."

The Germans asked to use the photos of his family that Risner had just received. He stalled, got back to his cell, tore up the pictures and buried them in a bucket brimming with his excrement. That show of defiance earned him two more bindings of his knees to his throat, this time with nylon, since rope left permanent scars.

Convinced that his back had become paralyzed, Risner gave up. He plunged his hands into the bucket, retrieved the pieces and handed them over. But his guards had lost face. He was left handcuffed and in leg irons, a relief at first after the nylon straps. But as the handcuffs cut deeper into the bone, Risner asked God for endurance. By the time a North Korean delegation arrived, his hands had swollen to balloons, and he had to take shots against blood poisoning from the boils on his wrists. To the Koreans he said truthfully that he had never bombed their country. Then he let them know that he had shot down eight North Korean planes in air-to-air combat. The Vietnamese made him sign an apology for his insolence.

Risner's third visitor was an American woman, and the Vietnamese were clearly worried about her. They told Risner, Do not slander our country to her, or you will regret it for the rest of the time you are here. They moved him three miles away to a better-looking prison called the Plantation and brought him a needle and thread to sew on his buttons and look more respectable. Then he was ushered into a room with Mary McCarthy, a prominent American writer living in Paris.

They were permitted to chat. Miss McCarthy described Senator Eugene McCarthy's campaign for the presidency on a peace platform. Although she and the senator were not related, Risner thought she seemed optimistic about his chances. When she asked what he missed most, Risner said, "A Bible."

"Don't they give you Bibles?"

"No."

Risner found the woman large and forceful. Turning that energy on the North Vietnamese, she demanded the right to send Risner a Bible. In fact, she would send Bibles for everyone. The Vietnamese seemed panicked and consulted among themselves.

That would cause problems, she was told at last. When she volunteered to send Risner a cake, his guard said quickly, "He does not need that. We give him plenty of wholesome foods." He turned to his prisoner. "Isn't that right?"

"Yes," Risner said.

As Mary McCarthy was leaving, she mentioned her hopes for an early end to the war. "We had better knock on wood," she said, and rapped three times on the table between them. When she was gone, Risner was interrogated for hours by guards trying to discover the coded message in her knocking.

After that visit, another forty or so Americans from the antiwar movement began arriving for a week or two in North Vietnam. Susan Sontag, a New York writer influential in the movement, made the trip and, at Hanoi's Historical Museum, learned about the Trung sisters, the Chinese occupations, the victory at Dien Bien Phu. She did not call on Robbie Risner, but when she returned to New York, she wrote, "The North Vietnamese genuinely care about the welfare of the hundreds of captured American pilots and give them bigger rations than the Vietnamese population gets 'because they're bigger than we are,' as a Vietnamese officer told me, 'and they're used to more meat than we are.'"

If WESTMORELAND SUFFERED in silence about being overruled by the president, congressmen were defecting noisily and in alarming numbers from Johnson's team. On July 25, he called the Senate's ranking committee chairmen to the White House, thanked them for years of friendship and said, "I want to give you a chance to make any comments you wish." Some of his guests focused on the domestic programs stalled in Congress, but Fulbright cut through to what was on all their minds. "Mr. President, what you really need to do is stop the war. That will solve all your problems."

The Vietnam War was a hopeless venture that no one liked, Fulbright continued. "Vietnam is ruining our domestic and our foreign policy. I will not support it any more." To prove that he was serious, Fulbright threatened to renounce a lifetime of internationalism and vote against the foreign aid bill. He might even bottle it up in his committee.

Johnson came back swinging. If the Congress wanted to tell the rest of the world to go to hell, that was its prerogative, the president said. For a country like the United States, with a gross national product of $800 billion and a budget of $175 billion, a request of $3 billion in foreign aid was minimal. "Maybe you don't want to help the children of India, but I can't hold back."

Looking to sow dissent in their ranks, Johnson said he wasn't going to argue his position on Vietnam because "I understand all of you feel like you are under the gun when you are down here, at least according to Bill Fulbright."

"Well," Fulbright responded, "my position is that Vietnam is central to the whole problem. We need a new look. The effects of Vietnam are hurting the budget and foreign relations generally."

The president made the debate personal. "Bill, everybody doesn't have a blind spot like you do. You say, 'Don't bomb North Vietnam' on just about everything. I don't have the simple solution you have." Aggrieved, Johnson said Ho had turned down his every overture. As for bombing the North, "I am not going to tell our men in the field to put their right hands behind their backs and fight only with their lefts." Westmoreland had told him that the bombing was America's offensive weapon.

"If you want me to get out of Vietnam," Johnson concluded, "then you have the prerogative of taking the resolution under which we are out there now"—the Tonkin Gulf Resolution steered through the Senate by Fulbright almost three years earlier. "You can repeal it tomorrow. You can tell the troops to come home. You can tell General Westmoreland that he doesn't know what he is doing."

At that, gentle Mike Mansfield pulled on Johnson's coattail by suggesting that the discussion turn to government operations.

TWO WEEKS LATER, Senator John Stennis of Mississippi, a staunch ally of the Joint Chiefs, opened hearings on U.S. air policy in Vietnam and called the Pentagon's senior commanders as his first witnesses. For McNamara, the timing added to his stress. His wife had been hospitalized in July with an ulcer while McNamara was in Saigon, dickering with Westmoreland over troop strength. Margy McNamara checked into Johns Hopkins University Hospital under an assumed name so that her husband's absence would not add to his reputation for being unfeeling. When he got back to Washington, McNamara made the hour's trip each night to see her and still appeared as early as ever at his Pentagon office. But he looked exhausted and sometimes he had not shaved. He would often say, "Margy got my ulcer."

One night, while he was visiting the hospital, McNamara got word that John McNaughton had been killed in an airplane collision, along with McNaughton's wife and younger son. McNamara seemed to take the loss of his protégé stoically, but the president soon heard that, from exhaustion or grief, McNamara's jaw was quivering uncontrollably. Johnson called to wish Margy McNamara a quick recovery, and when he hung up, he said to an aide: "You know, he's a fine man, a wonderful man, Bob McNamara. He has given everything, just about everything, and, you know, we just can't afford another Forrestal."

McNamara would have granted that his strain was increased by a sense that, with his own doubts about Vietnam mounting, he could not carry the president with him. But McNamara was not tempted to kill himself as James Forrestal had done. And in Paris, a new initiative was underway that might yet end his nightmare.

HENRY KISSINGER, his gaffe from the previous year forgiven, had met in Paris in June for a drink with Herbert Marcovitch, a French doctor, to talk about the Vietnam War. Marcovitch said a close friend, Raymond Aubrac, had long and warm ties to Ho Chi Minh. Not only had Ho stayed with Aubrac's family twenty-one years before, when his 1946 agreement with France collapsed, he was godfather to one of Aubrac's sons. If Washington was interested, Marcovitch was prepared to explore that old friendship.

The State Department told Kissinger that he must make it clear he was not acting in an official role. But he could urge the two Frenchmen to go to North Vietnam and explore the possibilities. In late July, Aubrac, who had fought in the French resistance during World War II, arrived in Hanoi with his friend and was received by Ho, Premier Dong and other northern officials. Returning to France, they contacted Kissinger through an elaborate code to say they had something of interest for him. Their new channel was being called "Pennsylvania."

At State, Rusk viewed with cynicism, even resentment, the outsiders who tried to broker an agreement with Hanoi. "Eight months pregnant with peace," he sneered, and all of them hoping to win the Nobel Peace Prize. Whatever Kissinger's motives, he went back to Paris, where he learned that the North Vietnamese had strongly suggested that a bombing halt could soon lead to negotiations.

Earlier in the year, Foreign Minister Nguyen Duy Trinh had told Wilfred Burchett, a sympathetic Australian journalist, that talks could start if the bombing ended "unconditionally"; in the past, Hanoi's phrase had been "finally and unconditionally." That apparent concession had been enough to keep Harriman's aide, Chester Cooper, exploring new avenues through London and Moscow during the latest bombing pause. Finally, acting for the president, Rostow told him that even a forty-eight-hour extension of the pause would be impossible. Cooper had been dealing with British Prime Minister Harold Wilson and the Soviet's Kosygin, who was visiting London, and both men were disappointed and angry. But as Cooper thought it over, he concluded that Washington had never shown much interest in his efforts.

That experience again left both Harriman and Cooper badly disillusioned. Grousing to each other, they had once agreed that Cooper would draft a protest for Harriman that was strong enough to carry the threat of resignation. Cooper sat up through the night working on language that was respectful but implacable. In the morning, he brought the result to Harriman, who read it through aghast. When he finished, he handed it back to Cooper.

"I can't send this," Harriman said. "It would be all right for you to send. You're expendable."

Deeply offended, Cooper marched off and did not speak to Harriman for three days. Even the Crocodile knew he had gone too far. He sent Cooper a note of apology and a case of Calon Segur, an excellent red Bordeaux.

But "Pennsylvania" might be different. The Frenchmen said Hanoi seemed understanding about Washington's domestic political concerns. After the bombing stopped, North Vietnamese representatives would meet in secret to discuss everything except South Vietnam's internal affairs.

During his stay in Hanoi, Aubrac went alone to call on Ho and was surprised by how old he had become. He was dressed in a Chinese robe and walked with a cane, but his eyes retained their sparkle and his mind was keen. Ho said he regretted hearing that Aubrac had sold his former house. "Where shall I live when I next come to Paris?" he asked, and then wondered whether he would be welcome in Paris.

After fifty minutes, Premier Dong walked Aubrac to his car. "We try to spare President Ho as many details as we can," Dong said. "He is an old man. We want him to live to see his country unified." But during the talks Dong had said again that the Communists would not expect U.S. troops to withdraw until an agreement had been reached, nor would they press for immediate unification of North and South.

The United States had also softened its position. In June, at a summit meeting with Kosygin in Glassboro, New Jersey, Johnson had budged slightly on infiltration into the South. Now he would accept assurances that the North not send its regulars. By August, the president was going further still. He allowed Kissinger to tell the Frenchmen that North Vietnam need pledge only not to take "military advantage."

Chet Cooper accompanied Kissinger to a Left Bank hotel to underscore that the message came from the president and to stress the significance that, for the first time, Washington was not insisting on substantial reciprocity. But two weeks earlier, the Pentagon had launched a major bombing campaign to isolate Hanoi and Haiphong from their supply routes, and the Frenchmen asked how they could convince the North that Washington was serious about peace with the bombing just raised to a new level. They agreed to make another trip to Hanoi but asked that Cooper get the bombing reduced again as a signal of good faith. Cooper could only promise to try.

In Hanoi, some Politburo members had taken the overture as another attempt to get them to lower their guard, and the intense bombing confirmed their suspicions. On August 22, Aubrac and Marcovitch were denied visas on the disingenuous grounds that bombing had made Hanoi too dangerous for visitors. They were told to deal in Paris with Mai Van Bo, who received their message but did not get back to them. By the time McNamara was due to testify before the Stennis committee, the latest road to peace was leading nowhere.

SHORTLY AFTER 10 A.M. on August 25, McNamara took the witness chair in front of Senator Stennis and his committee. Johnson thought the Chiefs' testimony the previous day had badly undercut his bombing policy. The generals were murdering me, he complained. Now it was up to McNamara to undo the damage, and Johnson tried to warn him of the heat he would be facing.

"I am not worried about the heat," McNamara replied, "as long as I know what we are doing is right." By now, Johnson no longer tried to tone down the priggish qualities of his defense secretary. He merely looked at him.

To counteract the hearings' impact, Johnson had recently overruled McNamara and permitted strikes again on several new targets in the North. American planes bombed Hanoi's Paul Doumer Bridge, which had been off-limits, and also a zone at the Chinese border that McNamara had been keeping back as a buffer so that Beijing would not miscalculate U.S. intentions. At the time, McNamara accepted Johnson's freer bombing, but now he was ready to speak his mind. For the first time, he would let the American public know what friends and antagonists in government already knew. He had prepared an eight-page statement for the press.

He had seen no evidence, he began, "that would lead me to believe that a less selective bombing campaign would change the resolve of North Vietnam's leaders or deprive them of the support of the North Vietnamese people."

McNamara had to rebut the thrust of the generals' testimony—that civilians like him and his analysts should get out of the way and let U.S. pilots hit every target on the Pentagon's list. In the past, McNamara might have relished the challenge. He was prepared to demonstrate why every one of the fifty-seven exempted targets were either worthless or carried the risk of hitting Soviet ships. Sounding like Harrison Salisbury eight months earlier, McNamara pointed out that one target was a plant that produced a mere thirty tires a day. Nine others were depots that contained less than 6 percent of North Vietnam's fuel supply.

For six hours, senators pummeled McNamara in closed session with questions prompted by testimony from the Chiefs. Senator Howard Cannon, a Nevada Democrat, reminded McNamara that the targets he denigrated had been recommended by the military. Why had not their advice been followed? "I am wondering whether or not you have confidence in the members of the Joint Chiefs," Cannon said. McNamara responded with a lecture on the U.S. Constitution, which awarded control over the military to a civilian president who might at times disagree with his generals. With a trace of his old spirit, McNamara added that if he did not have confidence in the Chiefs, "they wouldn't be Chiefs."

McNamara's roughest moments came from Strom Thurmond of South Carolina, the Republican who had bolted from the Democratic Party in 1948 to run against Truman on the segregationist Dixiecrat ticket. After remarking that he was disappointed in McNamara's statement, Thurmond reproached him in the same way that the White House had tried to discredit Robert Kennedy. "I think it is a statement of placating the Communists," Thurmond said. "It is a statement of appeasing the Communists. It is a statement of no-win."

McNamara sat quietly, thinking that Thurmond was an ass but determined to give answers that were reasonable if not entirely candid. He denied that his was a no-win policy but quickly shifted the focus to the judgment of others. "I think from what you have heard from General Westmoreland and General Wheeler and the other chiefs . . . each of them firmly believes that we are winning and will continue to win."

When the committee broke for lunch, McNamara braced himself to face reporters with a confident grin. One quoted Senator Symington to him: "He says if you are right, we should get out of Vietnam."

McNamara called that conclusion completely wrong. "My policies don't differ with those of the Joint Chiefs," he said, "and I think they would be the first to say it." McNamara maintained that any apparent disagreement was only a misunderstanding. His differences with the Chiefs were very narrow.

AT THE PENTAGON, the Chiefs were furious. McNamara had defended the policy of gradualism that they knew was not working and then claimed that they agreed with him. Bus Wheeler seemed to be the most enraged, even though he owed his position to McNamara. When Max Taylor left for Vietnam in 1964, McNamara had skipped past senior officers to give Wheeler the job. Having watched the services quarreling among themselves, the new Chief was determined to end the bickering before it reached McNamara. Because Wheeler admired McNamara and was himself considered deftly political, other officers blamed him for going along with gradual escalation and not arguing more strenuously for the dramatic strokes that Rostow and Westmoreland were advocating. To those senior officers, the United States must either take an unambiguous position on Vietnam—or get out.

Now at last Wheeler was prepared to make public his unhappiness. He called the Chiefs to his office, told an aide that he would take calls only from the president and laid out his idea for redressing their years of pliant acquiescence. The next morning, at a press conference, the Chiefs would all resign together.

Wheeler finished his pitch and waited. Only the army chief endorsed the idea. Harold Johnson said he wished he had resigned two years earlier when the president and McNamara overrode the Chiefs and refused to call up the Reserves. General Johnson did not know that the decision had been entirely Lyndon Johnson's, that McNamara had put aside his own doubts in order to support him. Air Force Chief John McConnell seemed willing to go along with whatever the majority decided. Greene of the Marines was not ready for such drastic action.

Nor, as it turned out, was Bus Wheeler. He had been suffering chest pains throughout the week—a warning of a heart attack that lay in store for him the following month. He decided the next morning that his oath to uphold his commander in chief must outweigh the satisfaction of letting America know that the military was being blamed for strategies they detested.

But the Stennis subcommittee members did not need resignations from the Chiefs to draw their own conclusions. Their report announced that McNamara had "shackled" the bombing effort. That forced the president to deny publicly that his administration was divided and fueled his anger over the problems his defense secretary was causing. Johnson had always known that McNamara felt more at ease with the Kennedys and kept in regular contact with them. But he had tested McNamara often enough to be convinced that he could be loyal to him as well. Until lately, the trade-off had been satisfactory. But these days Robert Kennedy was distancing himself from the White House over Vietnam, and McNamara was visibly fraying. Given Johnson's fear of leaks, he now discussed Vietnam each week at a Tuesday luncheon restricted to his senior aides—Rusk, McNamara, Rostow and Helms from the CIA. After the Senate testimony, he began including General Wheeler—or another of the Chiefs after Wheeler suffered his heart attack. Johnson was speaking with McNamara less often, and now on Tuesdays, McNamara's would not be the only voice representing the Pentagon.

As Saigon's September 3 elections approached, both Thieu and Ky announced that they would run for president. With worldwide attention focused on the voting, the elections had to appear less contrived than when Diem once won so spectacularly. But in honest elections, an army general and an air vice marshal could split the military vote and result in a civilian victory. Rumors already spread through Saigon that the Americans would back any candidate but Thieu. Fanciful stories even had the embassy supporting a Saigon lawyer named Truong Dinh Dzu, who was running a vigorous peace campaign. Dzu had outwitted the restrictions against candidates considered pro-Communist or neutralist by concealing his views until he had been certified for the ballot. Then he unveiled a dove as his campaign symbol and called for negotiations with the NLF.

What Washington did want badly was a show of legality. Komer's pacifica-

South Vietnam President Nguyen Van Thieu *(AP/Wide World Photos)*

tion teams were urging the South Vietnamese to vote, and although Bill Kohlmann was back in Virginia grappling with Vietnamese classes at the CIA's language school, his assets had been split among other free-spending agents.

To avoid dividing the military vote, the forty-eight generals of the Armed Forces Council assembled to hash over their dilemma. The council's answer was for Thieu to resign his commission and run as a civilian. Ky might have only limited respect for Thieu, but he knew he was too smart for that. Thieu said, "I still belong to the armed forces, and you cannot retire me."

Ky tried a threat. He would drop from the race, he said, and go back to the air force. Another general raised the stakes. If Ky were willing to make such a sacrifice to avoid a split among the armed forces, why not go further and run as Thieu's vice president? Ky embraced the idea, made a fervent plea for unity and got a standing ovation from his fellow officers. Immediately afterward, he launched a campaign to subvert the new constitution, which gave Vietnam's vice president as little power as his American counterpart. Ky organized a secret military cabal to set national policy and oversee the promotion of all military and civilian officials. Whoever was elected president would be bound by the decisions of this council, which guaranteed that, as council chairman, Ky would hold more power than Thieu. Ky described his creation as an "underground Politburo" and considered it adequate consolation for sacrificing the title of president.

Despite the machinations, the Thieu-Ky ticket won only 33 percent of the vote. Dzu, the peace candidate, ran second with 17 percent. Tran Van Don, disqualified for president by his French birth, won the largest number of votes for the Senate. Thieu reacted to Dzu's showing by having him arrested for illegal currency transactions, even though changing money on the black market was routine at all levels of Vietnamese society. When Thieu went on to jail other opposition figures, the American embassy reacted as Tuyen had once done under Diem and quickly got them released.

Ky hailed the meager support for his ticket as proof that the elections had not been rigged. If he had wanted to cheat, Ky said, he could have won 60 percent of the vote, even 70.

LATE IN SEPTEMBER, Johnson returned to his home state and on the twenty-ninth gave a speech in San Antonio that said clearly that the United States would stop the bombing if the North agreed to "productive discussions." But he reverted to the demand that Hanoi not take advantage of the "cessation or limitation." Those last words were a sop to hawks who claimed that a halt in bombing jeopardized American lives in the South. Four days later, back in Washington, the president hashed over the lack of progress toward talks with his senior men. McNamara these days was outnumbered by Rusk and Rostow, who judiciously professed their willingness to meet with Hanoi while at the same time closing ranks against any promising overtures. Rusk said that Bo in Paris had finally responded to the Kissinger letter and added that "Bo said something like talks will start after the cessation of bombing."

Rostow broke in: "To correct that, it was that talks *could* start but no other assurances were given."

Johnson was clearly resisting another bombing halt, but McNamara tried anyway to change his mind. He repeated his judgment that past pauses had not hurt the U.S. effort, to which Rusk replied ironically, "If the bombing isn't having that much effect, why do they want to stop the bombing so much?" His question ignored Hanoi's willingness to endure the bombing for two-and-a-half years rather than agree to Washington's terms.

Of more immediate concern to the president was an antiwar demonstration planned for Washington on October 21. McNamara reported that a lawyer named Warren Christopher was heading a task force to devise the government's defensive strategy. McNamara asked whether the president would be in the capital.

"Yes," Johnson said, "I will be here. They are not going to run me out of town."

McNamara, alert for so long to Johnson's moods, no longer cared about agreeing with him. He observed that the president's presence in Washington might do more to stimulate disorder than to calm it.

Francis Bator, as an economic adviser on the National Security Council, was not invited to meetings on Vietnam, but he could have predicted Johnson's next response. Like the Bundy brothers, Professor Bator was a product of Groton and the Ivy League, but as the son of a Hungarian émigré family, he did not bring to the White House any Puritan reservations about Johnson's behavior. When he was included in a meeting, Bator made a point of going early to the Cabinet Room and positioning himself in the second tier of chairs directly in front of the president. From there, he could watch with real pleasure when Johnson exploded with profanity or lapsed into lachrymose self-pity. To Bator, when the president played to his audience like an old vaudevillian, it was phase one of his decision-making process. But when he entered phase two, the theatrics fell away and Johnson made crisp and logical choices.

What effect would it have on the war, he asked now, if he announced that he was not going to run for another term? Johnson assured them that if he had to make the decision today, it would be not to run. His small audience understood that the president was still in his first phase and that they had a role to play.

Rusk spoke for them: "You must not go down. You are the Commander-in-Chief, and we are in war. This would have a very serious effect on the country."

McNamara said brusquely, "I don't think you should appear too cute on this."

To prove his sincerity, the president asked again what his leaving office would do to the war effort, and again McNamara did not supply the answer he was angling for. No effect on men and funding, McNamara said, and he would not speculate on the psychology of America, the morale of the GIs or the effect on Hanoi. He seemed to be saying that Johnson's decision would be irrelevant to all of them. "But I do think that they would not negotiate under any circumstances," McNamara added, "and they would wait for the 1968 elections."

THE NEXT DAY, when the question of responding to Bo in Paris came up again, Rusk urged delay. "We ought not to hurry," he said. "We need our scenario. It's best to do it on a steady basis. We should keep the dialogue going and not let the matter come to a head quickly."

At the State Department, Bill Bundy had been concerned about Rusk's behavior for several months. Johnson's attention—with prompting from Rostow—had been focused on the changes in McNamara. But McNamara himself had been jolted to call on Rusk at State early one afternoon and have the Secretary pull open a drawer, take out a bottle and offer him a drink. Bill Bundy saw Rusk moving through his days like a zombie until late afternoon when his senior staff came by for informal talks. Then, a couple of stiff scotches seemed to bring Rusk back to life. But the men closest to him were fond enough of Rusk not to gossip about his condition. At the Pentagon and the Johnson White House, McNamara had not generated that protectiveness.

As the discussion of "Pennsylvania" went on, Johnson was frustrated by the conflicting way Bo's message was being taken by Rostow and Rusk and by Mc-Namara. "Who exactly are M and A?" Johnson asked. For security reasons, Marcovitch and Aubrac were being discussed only by their initials. "They aren't our people, are they?"

"No," said Rusk, getting the Frenchmen confused. "A is a scientist. M is a Communist."

To counteract that disparaging summation, McNamara put in a word for Kissinger as a shrewd negotiator, the best he had seen in his seven years in Washington.

Trusting to his hopes more than to McNamara's newly suspect data, Johnson said, "I know this bombing must be hurting them. Despite any reports to the contrary, I can feel it in my bones. We need to pour the steel on," he said. "Let's hit them every day and go every place except Hanoi."

McNamara answered that his office had already authorized all but 5.8 percent of the Joint Chiefs' targets.

"Hit all you can." Johnson gave it as an order.

McNamara replied wanly, "You will never get it down to zero."

To THE WHITE HOUSE, the demonstration planned for Saturday, October 21, looked well organized and menacing. Within the peace movement, planning was marked by tension and discord. SDS opposed any march at all since it would only delude the protesters that they could influence government policy. Its national secretary, Greg Calvert, identified his group with Che Guevara, Castro's Argentinean ally recently killed in Bolivia. Deriding other groups for working within the system, Calvert told reporters that SDS was actively organizing sedition.

But as the date approached, SDS backed down and joined in, along with many intentionally outrageous figures from America's growing counterculture. Only marginally political, legions of hippies had dropped out of the middle class to smoke marijuana and drop tablets of the hallucinogen called LSD. Timothy Leary, a Harvard researcher, had become a zealous promoter of the acid, and although he would not be going to Washington, Abbie Hoffman, his antic spiritual heir, would be there. Hoffman was promising to stop the war by meditating so intently that the Pentagon would rise ten feet off the ground and shed its evil spirits.

The rally started peacefully with at least 50,000 demonstrators gathered at the Lincoln Memorial. Most in the crowd were students, but more than 150 organizations were carrying banners—church groups, peace groups, New York radicals calling themselves the Revolutionary Contingent. Dr. Benjamin Spock, author of a popular book on caring for babies, denounced Lyndon Johnson for betraying everyone who had believed his 1964 campaign promises. John Lewis from the Student Nonviolent Coordinating Committee, one of the small number of blacks in the audience, led a chant against the draft, "Hell, no! We won't go!" He then asked for a moment of silence in Che's memory.

The rally ended, and marchers moved toward the Pentagon, taking a back road that the government insisted they use. Some members of the National Mobilization Committee—shortened to "Mobe"—wanted to defy the order, but walking down the highway might have made them easier to block. Well-known writers had joined the march. Near the front was Robert Lowell, who had declined to come to Johnson's garden party, and Norman Mailer, the novelist, who saw a book in the offing. When they reached the Pentagon's north parking lot, a band of the most impassioned protesters rushed the building. About two dozen got inside before they were beaten and arrested.

To Rusk, it was obvious that the Communists were behind the demonstration. Johnson tended to agree and directed Helms to prove it. Helms's report drew on CIA sources and the rest of the country's security apparatus—the FBI, the National Security Agency, the many military agents. They found "no significant evidence that would prove Communist control or direction of the U.S. peace movement or its leaders." Rusk called the report naïve and said the CIA had not looked hard enough.

But at his office, McNamara thought he understood what was inflaming the protesters below his window. He watched 5,000 militants line up directly in front of the National Guardsmen protecting the building. Hippie girls were jamming flowers down the barrels of the guardsmen's unloaded rifles, but those conciliatory gestures did not register with McNamara. Instead, he saw a hellish scene of girls flaunting naked breasts and spitting in guardsmen's faces. As had happened at Harvard, McNamara grew competitive about the demonstrators, recalling again his days at Berkeley when he sometimes moderated between hostile students and the university president. McNamara told himself that these people were doing it all wrong. The demonstrators should follow the example of Gandhi. They needed discipline. By God, he could have shown them. Had he been leading them today, he would have shut the Pentagon down.

VERY SOON AFTERWARD, McNamara had the chance to thrust himself to the forefront of the peace movement and provide the leadership he thought it lacked. Ten days after the March, Johnson met with the customary Wise Men, summoned back to Washington. The president was troubled by the growing protests, although they still seemed manageable. Robert Kennedy had edged further toward open dissent, but he was finding himself uncomfortably in front of most Senate colleagues and was not ready to make a final break.

For McNamara, his judgments were no longer detached or calculated. At the Tuesday Lunch on October 31, he said he had concluded that to continue the administration's present course in Vietnam "would be dangerous, costly in lives and unsatisfactory to the American people." On November 1, the day Clark Clifford convened the Wise Men, McNamara handed Johnson the only copy of his most desperate attempt yet to change the course of the war. In a cover note to his recommendations for the next fifteen months, McNamara acknowledged that his views "may be incompatible" with Johnson's. On its surface, the memo's impersonal language was no different from what McNamara had been churning out for the past seven years, but now his sense of failure shone through: No military action was likely to break Hanoi's will, he wrote. The demands at home for America's withdrawal would increase. U.S. casualties would rise to 30,000 dead, approaching the Korean War's total of 33,000.

Rather than face that future, McNamara pleaded with Johnson to stop the bombing of the North completely. He should not increase U.S. ground troops. He should not call up the Reserves. He should not expand the war into North Vietnam, Cambodia or Laos. Or mine the North's harbors or bomb its dikes and largest cities. What the president should do instead was gradually transfer the burden of fighting back to the South Vietnamese.

Had McNamara seen his memorandum after the president finished with it, he would have known his personal war was lost. Objections had been scrawled in the margins — "How do we get this conclusion?" "Why believe this?" "I agree" had been added to only one paragraph — McNamara's prediction that talks with the North would start with propaganda rather than serious bargaining.

THAT EVENING, the Wise Men met for drinks and dinner with Rusk and McNamara at the State Department. Except for Lovett and McCloy, who sent regrets, the evening included the same men Johnson had relied upon throughout his presidency — Acheson, Harriman, Omar Bradley, Arthur Dean, Abe Fortas and Max Taylor. Mac Bundy, who had been sending Johnson cheery notes since he left the White House, was there, along with Douglas Dillon and George Ball, both also out of government. McNamara noted ruefully which three participants were missing from the session in July 1967. They were Arthur Larson, George Kistiakowsky, a Harvard chemistry professor and policy adviser, and Paul Hoffman, who once headed the Marshall Plan to rebuild Europe — men known to oppose Johnson's policies. On hand to give the briefings were Bus Wheeler for the Chiefs and George Carver from the CIA.

McNamara had come to discount Carver's optimism as no more reliable than Rostow's. The previous spring, when Carver had not been available for McNamara's regular agency briefing, George Allen, with experience in Saigon that went back to 1954, had come instead. Allen was prepared to follow agency policy and deliver Carver's briefing, but McNamara cut him off and asked to talk informally. Allen protested that he could get in trouble with his director. Don't worry,

McNamara answered with his old confidence, I'll take care of Helms. For the next hour, he heard the pessimism that was rife within the agency but bleached from its official briefings.

Speaking to the Wise Men on this night, the briefers exuded confidence. McNamara thought: Typical of Johnson to treat the event as a poker game and not put all the cards on the table. Johnson certainly would not show them McNamara's memo, and he would not give them a recent evaluation from Helms that minimized the political consequences of withdrawing from Vietnam. When the evening ended, Bill Bundy thought another factor, besides the official optimism, had contributed to keeping the affair congenial but scarcely tough-minded. We fed them too well, Bundy concluded. And everyone had one more drink than led to hard thinking at night.

When Johnson met with the group the next day, they were still docile. Only Ball favored restricting the bombing to the area around the DMZ, and even he said, "No one in the group thinks we should get out of the war." Harriman might have contradicted him, but he would not argue publicly for negotiations. Despite his persistent efforts to ingratiate himself—he had given elaborate wedding parties for each of Johnson's daughters—the president considered Harriman a Kennedy man, and at first he had not invited him to Glassboro to meet with the Soviet premier. Harriman longed to be back in the presidential inner circle and said nothing throughout the meeting.

McNamara had not done anything so bold as distributing his confidential memo to this senior group, but he had been indiscreet at dinner, and Clifford made sure the president knew it. "No matter what we do, this will never be a popular war," Clifford began. "No wars have been popular, with the possible exception of World War Two. But we must go on because what we are doing is right.

"Secretary McNamara said last night that perhaps his and Rusk's efforts since 1961 have been a failure. This is not true. Their efforts have constituted an enormous success." Clifford said history books would look very favorably on both Kennedy and Johnson because they had not waited for public opinion to catch up with them.

The Wise Men left the White House united behind the president. They urged him to play down the bombing and bloody loss of life and stress instead that Americans were reaching, as Mac Bundy termed it, "the end of the road."

With his visitors gone, Johnson returned to McNamara's memo. He wanted to keep McNamara on the team through the 1968 elections. He especially did not want him drifting into the camp of Robert Kennedy, who was sounding like a possible challenger. But Johnson was not prepared to change a policy that had just been endorsed by a conclave of the nation's most respected elders. Without informing McNamara, Johnson told Rostow to poll six men on the memo's contents without telling them who had written it. Nick Katzenbach at State agreed almost completely with McNamara's thinking; Abe Fortas thought the writer had seen one too many protest demonstrations. Rostow was less barbed but equally dismissive. Hanoi's leaders now realized that they could not take over the South, Rostow said, and that they would have to accept the 17th parallel for some time to come.

By now, the president and his defense secretary agreed on only one point: it was time for McNamara to leave. Six days after the Wise Men departed, George Woods of the World Bank rode with McNamara through the streets of Washington and pressed him to accept the bank's presidency. "You're still my horse," Woods said.

Johnson was adept at guessing which tantalizing job might keep a man loyal when he left Johnson's employ. Or, if not loyal, quiet. After Roger Hilsman announced his resignation, the prospect was dangled before him of becoming ambassador to the Philippines. Hilsman had grown up there and loved the country, but he declined and instead wrote *To Move a Nation*, the first dissenting book on Vietnam by a policy-maker. With McNamara, the World Bank suited Johnson's purpose even better than an ambassadorship, since the bank's president was specifically barred from involving himself in domestic politics. Henry Fowler, Dillon's replacement at the Treasury, had hoped to head the Bank himself until Johnson called to tell him his choice: "McNamara, McNamara, McNamara."

Eight days after their talk, Woods learned that Johnson was nominating McNamara for the job. McNamara was not told immediately, but as polling the 107 member nations got underway, Woods called to say that the nomination was creating controversy but would be approved.

On November 27, Woods was informed by cable that the *Financial Times* in London had printed a story about the nomination. When McNamara heard, he went at once to the Oval Office to negotiate the terms of his departure. He agreed to stay on through the next budget cycle; that would keep him at the Pentagon through the coming February. As Johnson and McNamara spoke, the White House press corps downstairs was in turmoil. Johnson's press secretary, who knew nothing about the appointment, was assuring reporters that McNamara was staying at Defense.

Once back in his Pentagon office, McNamara closeted himself with Robert Kennedy. A slogan often derided in Vietnam called on the Saigon government to win the hearts and minds of the South Vietnamese. Robert Kennedy had won McNamara's heart years ago, and Kennedy's arguments against the war had won over his mind. Now Kennedy wanted more: he wanted McNamara's reputation.

He urged McNamara to resign with a blast at Johnson's policies and join the growing ranks of war protesters. For Kennedy, the decision had been easier. Disliking Johnson for years, he had found a way to define his brother's war—Americans in Vietnam only to advise their counterparts—as being different from Johnson's bombing and mounting casualties. But McNamara had been at the center of both wars. Whether Johnson had ever genuinely wavered or only wanted to be persuaded to follow a course he had already chosen, McNamara had stiffened his spine and urged on him the policies that even Bundy had called rash. He could not simply walk away from the war as Kennedy was doing.

McNamara had always had to fight back tears—his welling up over Vietnam was nothing new to him—and he used the word "love" often and without self-consciousness. He had loved Jack Kennedy, and he still loved Bobby. He claimed to love Lyndon Johnson, too, and believed that his love was requited. But Johnson had fed on the stories that McNamara was on the brink of a breakdown and sometimes confided that he was shuffling McNamara to a less stressful job in order to save his sanity, possibly his life. Did Johnson love McNamara? Not as much as he detested Robert Kennedy.

When Kennedy saw that McNamara was not going to denounce Johnson's policies, he asked next that he leave the Pentagon quietly, if he must, but turn down the Bank presidency. That would leave him able to speak out later. Kennedy thought he knew his man. Free of responsibility to Johnson, McNamara would listen exclusively to Kennedy. If Kennedy challenged Johnson in the presidential election less than a year away, McNamara would be out stumping for him. As he left the Pentagon, Kennedy was persuaded that McNamara would reject the Bank.

Meantime, rumors of McNamara's departure were spurring other friends to action. Bill Moyers reported that Kay Graham had called in tears. "It is absolutely horrible how the President is treating Bob McNamara," Moyers quoted her as saying. "It's the worst thing that ever happened in this town."

On November 29, the World Bank's executive board was read a statement from McNamara: "I've told the President as long as Vietnam remains a serious problem and he wishes me to remain, I shall do so." But, he went on, if the requirements of the bank could be reconciled with that obligation, he would give thoughtful consideration to any offer.

The board met on and off from noon to 6:15 P.M. before voting to offer McNamara the position. Woods and five directors went to the Pentagon to tell him, and he accepted at once. Since Johnson had never told him about the nomination, McNamara could say later that he never knew whether he had quit or been fired. But McNamara had quit. The November 1 memorandum had been his letter of resignation.

Since their initial discussion of McNamara leaving Defense, Johnson had not reached out to him in the way Kennedy was doing. The president knew that, for all the personal loyalty McNamara professed to feel for him—and McNamara called at one point to say he was sitting in his Pentagon office with tears in his eyes—Robert Kennedy had prior claim. Johnson had played his best card by getting McNamara the one job he wanted most, a chance to achieve the Great Society on a global scale without the dead weight of Vietnam on his shoulders. If that boon did not keep McNamara in the fold, no mere words from Johnson would do it better.

The night of the twenty-ninth, Robert Kennedy met Arthur Schlesinger, Pierre Salinger and others at the King Cole Bar in Manhattan. Kennedy gave the group McNamara's highly selective version of events: that apart from a vague conversation with the president in the spring, he first heard he was leaving government from a leak out of London. That seeming callousness gave Schlesinger a new reason to dislike Lyndon Johnson and ask whether any self-respecting person wouldn't have his resignation on the president's desk within half an hour. Why was McNamara letting Johnson silence him?

Kennedy said he thought McNamara would do as Kennedy had urged him: resign from government and reject the Bank. If so, Kennedy could have the ally best equipped to change America's view of the war. When Kennedy's group left the bar at 1 A.M., the early edition of the New York Times was on the street. A front-page headline read, "McNamara Takes World Bank Job."

Schlesinger thought Kennedy looked surprised, then sad.

As 1967 DREW TO AN END, a female NLF official named Nguyen Thi Chon hoped she might be about to regain her freedom. Early in the year, Mrs. Chon had seen men following her at the Saigon market. She was the wife of Tran Bach Dang, but living together was too dangerous for them. Dang had also risen in the NLF from the days when he watched ARVN soldiers playing soccer with a farmer's head. He now headed the Front's political committee. Dang's comrades admired his brilliance, although the way his eyes narrowed could suggest coldness. His wife had been dedicated to the resistance since the French retook her country from the Japanese, but she had a wide smile and laughed easily. Her job was working with the Front's women's union.

Returning from the market, Mrs. Chon opened the door to her house, and ten Saigon policemen pushed in with her. They accused her of smuggling and took her identification card to a Vietcong defector waiting in a police car. He confirmed that Mrs. Chon was an officer of the women's union.

At first, she took her arrest calmly, worrying only that she might be used to track down her husband. But as they led her to the police car, she realized that they might kill her. She vowed to find the self-control to tell them nothing.

At Ngo Quyen prison, police took her to a small room and brought in the man who had betrayed her. He began to apologize, "Lady—" She cut him off. Who else had he identified? Two other leaders, he admitted, Le Chi Rieng and Duy Lien, deputy chairman of the People's Committee of Saigon. Had either of them confessed to anything? No, said the man.

Nor would she. When Mrs. Chon refused to admit to her activities, the policemen tied her hands, laid her on a small table and put a strip of cloth across her mouth. They did then what Diem's agents had done to Thanh four years earlier, pouring water on the cloth until she felt she was drowning. "When you are willing to talk," a policeman told her, "nod your head."

To end the suffocation, Mrs. Chon nodded. The guards found that she was only stalling. Tying her to a chair, they fastened clamps to her elbows, neck and nipples. When she was securely wired to a field generator, they cranked the handle until she fainted from pain.

Over the next month, there were many more sessions. No matter which Vietnamese agents oversaw the torture, Mrs. Chon was sure their questions had been prepared by American advisers.

When the torture ended, Mrs. Chon was taken to the central police station. She saw no torture there, only clerks busy with paperwork. CIA agents released her from Vietnamese custody and took her to a safe house somewhere in Saigon. Mrs. Chon could not identify the neighborhood, but from children's voices she knew it was near an elementary school. A man who called himself "Mr. Lewis" brought a doctor to check on her health.

"I don't need a doctor," Mrs. Chon said bitterly. "Why did you let the Saigon police torture me?"

The American brought in two other prisoners and said they were all going to be released. Mrs. Chon knew them as senior officials in the Front—Tran Van Kieu, who was bloodied, and a woman named Lien, with scars where her fingers had been burned.

"Many others are being held," Mrs. Chon protested. "Why choose to release me?" She knew the answer: they hoped she would lead them to her contacts. She told the two others, "You can go. I'm staying here. But if our friends want me released, I will agree."

Mrs. Chon remained at the CIA house for two months. During that time, American agents came often to talk with her. She parried their questions with lectures on why the Vietnamese people longed to be independent. The meetings became informal, even intimate; a female CIA agent complained to her about an unrequited love.

One day, a man came to say that the Front wanted her released. Mrs. Chon heard later that he had slipped away to COSVN to get those instructions.

Her release was handled like a military operation. Mrs. Chon was flown by helicopter to Cu Chi and put down in a landing cleared for parachute jumps. She was led close to the tree line and allowed to walk away. Friendly villagers guided her to the Front's encampment, where she picked up several bits of information: Speaking for the Front, her husband had warned the CIA that if she were not released alive, a high-ranking U.S. official would be killed in retaliation. After much haggling, Tran Bach Dang had agreed to trade her and another Front official for two American prisoners, U.S. Marine Corporal José Agosto-Santos and Army Private Luis Ortiz-Rivera.

Mrs. Chon also learned that with 1968 approaching, preparations were underway in Cu Chi for an event that would shock the world like nothing that had come before it.

WITH HIS DEFENSE SECRETARY irretrievably lost to him, Johnson wanted an authoritative show of optimism and called Westmoreland back to Washington for congressional briefings. "We have got our opponents almost on the ropes," Westmoreland testified. U.S. troops were grinding down the Communists and building up the ARVN so that South Vietnamese soldiers could take over a progressively greater share of the fighting. The American people could finally expect "some light at the end of the tunnel," Westmoreland said.

Meeting with reporters, the general found them less receptive to his message than most congressmen had been. Shortly after Westmoreland had left Saigon, Communist troops attacked and held the area surrounding a Special Forces camp at Dak To in the mountains of Kontum province. When it took five days to dislodge them, both Washington and Hanoi claimed victory. Neil Sheehan was now working in the Washington bureau of the *New York Times*, and he had reacted to reports from Dak To with an instinct that Westmoreland did not seem to share. Although the general mentioned a captured document that mentioned a "concentrated offensive," he seemed to take the information lightly.

"Let me clear up one point," Sheehan said. "You don't think that the battle of Dak To is the beginning or the end of anything particular for the enemy?"

Westmoreland answered, "I think it's the beginning of a great defeat for the enemy."

TEN

CLIFFORD
1968

WHILE WESTMORELAND was making that prediction, feverish activity was underway among the Vietcong. Late in the fall, the Politburo let COSVN know that a date finally had been approved for the General Offensive, General Uprising. In Vietnamese, the phrase was Tong Cong Kich, Tong Khia Nghia, abbreviated to TCK-TKN. The new lunar year began January 31, 1968. On that day, Tet Mau Than, the people of every southern province would rise up and throw off the Thieu-Ky government.

The heavy defenses around Saigon and its surrounding Gia Dinh province posed the greatest challenge. The Communists needed to draw away ARVN troops from the capital. At the same time, they would have to rush in Vietcong cadres from the Delta to make sure the main targets could be hit and held. The regional command, B-2, was responsible for toppling Saigon's government and paralyzing the American nerve center. Even before receiving formal authorization, B-2 commanders had drawn up plans for an effective assault. They listed as their five main targets the offices of the ARVN general staff, the Vietnamese Special Forces and the National Police, along with Tan Son Nhut airport and the presidential palace. A second cluster of objectives included Saigon's post office and radio station, Bien Hoa airbase and a large city prison. The earliest plans dated from as far back as 1964, and, despite the shift to the battlefield in recent years, they had not been updated.

Tran Bach Dang was now the Communists' chief political planner in Saigon, and the torture of his wife the previous year made him even more ardent for success. Dang himself had escaped from a French prison in the late 1940s, an experience that taught him to value stealth and nerve. For years, he had been living undisturbed in one of Saigon's better neighborhoods. His next-door neighbor was Deputy Ambassador William Porter, a career diplomat who had come to Vietnam from Algeria. Dang boasted to his comrades that between Porter's house and his own was only one wall, although admittedly it was a high wall topped with barbed wire. "Porter should thank me," Dang said, "because there will never be a Vietcong bomb or land mine on our street."

Dang was coordinating with Tran Van Tra, the two-star general who had succeeded Nguyen Chi Thanh, but the men disagreed over tactics. Tra was going along with the General Uprising; Dang said, "We only need to show the Americans that if they still think they can win, they are wrong." To the list of vital targets, Dang added the U.S. embassy. He explained to his fellow officers, "Let us say to the world that we can attack anywhere, in a place the United States could never expect."

To prepare for the offensive, the Vietcong had brought thousands of land mines into the city and stored them with friendly families. In Saigon alone, Dang estimated that he had hidden weapons and ammunition at four hundred houses. The Communists had planted Vietcong on the American embassy staff, who gave them detailed descriptions of the compound's layout. For the embassy attack, commanders sought volunteers, warning that they must be prepared to die. Ten men of varied backgrounds were chosen, among them a taxi driver, a government official, a dockworker, an electrician, a man who sold noodles on the street. The recruits were sent to Cu Chi to practice getting inside of the rough mock-up of the embassy compound. Over and over, half of them rushed from the ground while the others climbed trees and dropped inside the walls.

By MID-JANUARY, Westmoreland was receiving vague hints that the Communists were planning a new military initiative. He could not be sure whether it would come before or after the Tet ceasefire for the New Year, but he asked Thieu to cancel the scheduled forty-eight-hour break in the fighting. Thieu argued that the cancellation would damage ARVN morale and agreed only to cutting the truce back to thirty-six hours. When McNamara was warned in Washington about a possible Communist attack on Hue, he eased the complete bombing halt for Tet by giving U.S. bombers permission to strike as far north as Vinh.

Westmoreland predicted in a television interview that recent shelling of the U.S. Marine base at Khe Sanh, near the Demilitarized Zone, meant the Communists were trying for what he called "a spectacular battlefield success" before the Tet cease-fire. Westmoreland had now been in South Vietnam through three previous Tets and knew how completely the holiday absorbed the country. Firecrackers, for example, were normally banned in South Vietnam, but Thieu's government was permitting them for four days. Even though Westmoreland an-

General Tran Van Tra
(Ta Minh Kham family)

ticipated other signs of government laxness, he was appalled to learn that Thieu's scaling back of the cease-fire had never been announced; no one was on duty at the Vietnamese press office to do it. Vietcong activity in the past had been limited, and this year the NLF had announced a seven-day Tet cease-fire. As a result, the ARVN had granted widespread leaves.

To CELEBRATE the Year of the Monkey, George Jacobson, the U.S. mission coordinator, gave a reception the night before Tet at his house within the embassy compound. The party was a decorous affair, marked by a massive fireworks display on the embassy lawn. Barry Zorthian, the ranking U.S. information officer, left quite early, looking forward to a peaceful Tuesday. But he was awakened after a few hours by telephone reports of attacks underway throughout II Corps, the mountainous region north of Saigon. The province capitals being hit included Da Nang and Pleiku—names familiar to the American public—but also Nha Trang, Kontum and Ban Me Thuot, a montagnard stronghold.

If Zorthian was surprised by the attacks, General Tran Van Tra was furious. The uprising in II Corps had started twenty-four hours too soon, and all because of a stupid error. Tra's B-2 command was using the traditional lunar calendar. But the highlands were under the direct supervision of the party Central Committee, and leaders there had consulted a newly revised calendar being used in Hanoi.

Acting on that warning, the Saigon government canceled even the shorter cease-fire. But most ARVN soldiers had already gone home, and only 25 of Saigon's military police remained on duty. Tra may have lost the valuable advantage of surprise, but since the Americans seemed to think fighting was restricted to the highlands, his offensive could still succeed.

On Tuesday, January 30, Dang's ground team waited until after midnight to blow a hole in the eight-foot wall of the U.S. embassy compound. Once past the wall, they killed two of the five Marine guards and attacked the embassy itself with bazookas, but they could not get inside it.

At home, Zorthian was hearing more noise than Tet celebrations could explain. He called MACV's Office of Combat Operations and got a few scraps of news. There seemed to be an attack on the palace, and it might be only one of several around the capital. Next, Combat Operations relayed reports of an attack on the embassy. Zorthian had every modern means of military and civilian communications available to him, but he could not get through to the embassy on any of his lines. The Marine guards had tied them all up with their calls for reinforcement. Zorthian remembered George Jacobson and dialed his number on a regular Saigon line. Jacobson picked up the phone. From his second-story window, he had a clear view of the courtyard. He described the first shots and the Vietcong attempt to get inside the embassy itself. Zorthian kept the line open and listened while Marine guards patrolled the compound, looking for Vietcong. After 2 A.M., there seemed to be no more movement, but Jacobson agreed to stay locked inside his house while Zorthian began to call reporters.

FOR CLARK CLIFFORD, January 30 had begun auspiciously with a unanimous Senate vote confirming him as secretary of defense. Clifford was attending Johnson's Tuesday Lunch, where the latest reports had the Communists shelling the U.S. Marine outpost near Khe Sanh. Bus Wheeler explained an intricate ruse that Westmoreland had devised to lift the siege: He recommended moving U.S. ships close to the North Vietnamese coast and telling the ARVN generals that America was planning to invade. After that, Westmoreland would simply wait. Communist spies within the ARVN would pass the warning to Hanoi. Giap would instantly withdraw his troops from Khe Sanh in order to defend the North, ending his siege against the Marines.

Clifford found the proposal astonishing and was doubly amazed to hear McNamara endorse it. Clifford protested that the scheme made no sense to him and got the feeling that Johnson agreed but was reluctant to veto a plan put forth by the military and supported by the man who would still be defense secretary for one more month. Johnson told Wheeler to let Westmoreland go ahead with the planning. As Clifford was wondering how to jettison the idea, Walt Rostow was called away and came back to say that heavy shelling had hit Saigon. Vietcong targets seemed to include the American embassy.

Johnson spoke first. "This could be very bad."

Rusk said, "I hope that it is not Ambassador Bunker's residence."

Wheeler played down the danger. "This same type of thing has happened before," he assured the others. "In a city like Saigon, people can infiltrate easily." Wheeler called that sort of attack "about as tough to prevent as a mugging in Washington," and McNamara commented that it sounded like a public relations problem, not a military one.

THE MARINE GUARDS at the U.S. embassy shared Rusk's concern for the safety of Ellsworth Bunker, Lodge's replacement as ambassador, but their solution would not have pleased the secretary of state. They took him to Ed Lansdale.

Lansdale had been in Washington for two months, dejected about the election of Thieu and Ky, men he considered unsuited for leadership. But he had been easily lured back to Saigon when Bunker seemed to want him there. Lansdale arrived just before Tet and returned to his house on Cong Ly Street. To make the property safe, he had tried to persuade families within three blocks of his walls to report to him any stranger they might spot.

So far, the precaution seemed to be working. When the Marines arrived with Bunker, Lansdale gave up his bedroom to the ambassador and put on his pair of black pajamas to scout the neighborhood. As the scope of the offensive became clearer, however, the Marines worried that Lansdale lived too near the road to the airport and moved Bunker to a more distant location.

AT 4:30 A.M., Peter Arnett got through by phone to Jacobson at his house and found him rather jaunty. Arnett quoted him as saying, "The Vietcong sent in a few sapper units to celebrate Tet in their own inimitable way." He told Arnett that he had a hand grenade and was ready to make a stand. Jacobson, who had served nine years in Vietnam, most of them as an army colonel, speculated about the Vietcong motive: "They are calculating a big splash all over the world with their activities."

As reporters came rushing into the AP bureau with their stories, Arnett was amazed at the audacity and scope of the Communist attack. To see for himself, he ran toward the embassy, past Saigon's red-brick Catholic Cathedral in a square the Vietnamese had named for Jack Kennedy, until he reached Hai Ba Trung Street. There he crouched behind a fence. U.S. military police had taken over the upper floor of an apartment building across from the American compound and were shooting down into the grounds. Dang's men were returning fire from behind the walls. The American rescue team had radioed the embassy staff to hold out as best they could. Trying to reach them in the darkness was too risky.

At first light, a cluster of Huey helicopters flew low toward the embassy roof.

Peter Arnett
(AP/Wide World Photos)

Before the lead pilot could touch down on the landing pad, Communist gunfire drove it away. On the street, the American MPs massed and rammed open the compound's gate, but they were forced back by Dang's men firing from above them. As Arnett prepared to run to a nearby office building to call in his story, he asked an American officer whether the Vietcong had got inside the embassy itself. "My God, yes," the distracted man said. "We're taking fire from up there."

The AP bulletin reached the East Coast newspapers in time for their first morning edition: "The Vietcong seized part of the U.S. Embassy in Saigon early Wednesday and battled Americans who tried to recapture it."

When Arnett got back to his vantage point, the number of reporters had grown: Peter Braestrup and Lee Lescaze from the *Washington Post*; Tom Buckley and Charlie Mohr, now reporting for the *New York Times*; François Sully, who had outlasted the Ngo family and was back in Saigon for *Newsweek*. By the time of a second helicopter assault, soldiers from the U.S. 101st Infantry Division could jump onto the embassy roof and move down through the building's corridors. After a military police squad broke through the front gate, reporters trailed after them and witnessed the carnage—Vietcong bodies in green or brown uniforms and dead Americans, their blood on the walls.

One wounded Vietcong had slipped into Jacobson's house and was spotted hiding in a bathroom. An MP threw up a gas mask and a .45 pistol to Jacobson's second-floor window. The Vietcong raised his M-16. Jacobson killed him with two shots.

By 10 A.M., the compound was quiet. Westmoreland arrived in khakis to tell reporters that "the enemy's well-laid plans went afoul." He stressed that the Communists had not got inside the embassy itself. But since American television would show a Vietcong inside Jacobson's bathroom, Westmoreland's distinction struck viewers as no more than a quibble. When the general claimed that the enemy was on the run, Arnett remembered Paul Harkins using that phrase after Ap Bac. And another veteran of Ap Bac once again was less politic than his commander. "Christ," John Vann told Arnett, "we knew the V.C. were up to something, but this extensively, nothing."

The day went on, revealing the full scale of the Communist General Offensive. Following their long-standing plan, the North Vietnamese and Vietcong had struck Tan Son Nhut and Bien Hoa airbases, the presidential palace, the headquarters of the South Vietnamese Joint General Staff and the U.S. command post for III Corps. In all, the Communists had hit 39 of South Vietnam's 44 province capitals, 71 of its 242 district centers and scores of other military and civilian targets. To Arnett, the offensive was a tidal wave crashing over the country.

The General Uprising, however, was not going according to plan. Saigon's 4 million people had barricaded themselves inside their houses and refused to obey when the Vietcong banged on their doors and told them to come out. No number of assurances that Saigon was now liberated from Thieu and the Americans could persuade them. For three days, ARVN and U.S. soldiers struggled to regain control of the city, which remained shut down under a round-the-clock curfew. Prowling the streets, Arnett found a mass grave that was a full block long, with corpses stacked five bodies high. He estimated the number at six hundred — mostly dead Vietcong, he was told. He found two other mass graves, however, filled with women and children. The sheer competence in coordinating so daring an assault had impressed Arnett, but he knew that his editors in New York would not welcome reports praising the Communists for their superb training and devotion to their cause. Westmoreland's evaluation, on the other hand, was being widely quoted.

A week after the offensive began, Arnett went to the province capital of Ben Tre, the Delta town where Mrs. Nguyen Thi Dinh had rallied resistance to Diem ten years earlier. Arnett had been there just before Tet and found it quiet and appealing. Now all was desolation — the marketplace in ruins, office buildings hollowed and black from shelling, two miles of thatched-roof houses burned to the ground. An American major told Arnett that hundreds of bodies lay buried in the rubble of houses and apartments. Arnett cajoled the man into telling him what had happened. The Vietcong had infiltrated Ben Tre, the major said, and by the first morning controlled the market and the residential districts. When the Communists threatened the American military compound, there had been no choice, the major explained. The ARVN chief of staff had ordered in air strikes, and Arnett was looking at the result. Sadly, the major said, "It became necessary to destroy the town to save it."

The day Arnett's story hit Washington, Johnson demanded that Zorthian find out the name of the indiscreet officer. When that proved impossible, military commanders assured other reporters that Arnett had fabricated the quote as a metaphor for the entire war. Joe Alsop, for one, chose to believe them. At an embassy dinner sometime later, Alsop inspected Arnett across the table and asked, "You're the fellow who makes up quotes, aren't you?" Arnett sprang toward him, fists clenched, before Ambassador Bunker pressed on his shoulder and said, "Peter, go back and sit down. And Joe—tut tut and shut up."

As widely circulated as the major's quote was a picture by Eddie Adams, an AP photographer on his third tour in Vietnam. Adams was touring the Cholon district with the country's national police commander, Brigadier General Nguyen Ngoc Loan, who had inherited the police force that survived Nhu. Vietnamese Marines captured a Vietcong officer and led him to Loan with his hands tied behind his back. Adams and an NBC camera crew watched Loan raise his pistol and shoot the man in the head. Adams clicked his camera at the same instant.

Loan lowered his pistol and smiled grimly. "They killed many Americans and many of my people," he said and walked away.

Back in the AP darkroom, Horst Faas inspected the film strip through a magnifying glass. "Damn," he muttered. To the left of the frame, Loan stood in profile, his black hair ruffled into a pair of small horns. Fully extended, his arm protruded from the rolled-up sleeves of his fatigue jacket. Loan's pistol gleamed against a dim background of city buildings. Six inches from the barrel, a man in a plaid shirt grimaced in pain and fear and died with his eyes half shut, his mouth twisted in a sob.

The horror of the picture transcended politics. The New York Daily News, which strongly supported the war, ran it on page 1. So did the New York Times, although editors paired the Adams photograph with one of an ARVN colonel holding the body of a child killed by the Vietcong.

Americans and the ARVN were snuffing out the resistance around the country except in Hue, where fighting went on ferociously. The secretary of the city's Communist Party, a man named Hoang Van Vien—called Ba—had been organizing for months, helped along by a complete breakdown of U.S. intelligence. The small CIA unit in Hue seldom traded information with the American advisory team, and neither stayed in regular contact with South Vietnamese intelligence. By the time of radio reports about suspicious movement around a

THE TET OFFENSIVE, 1968

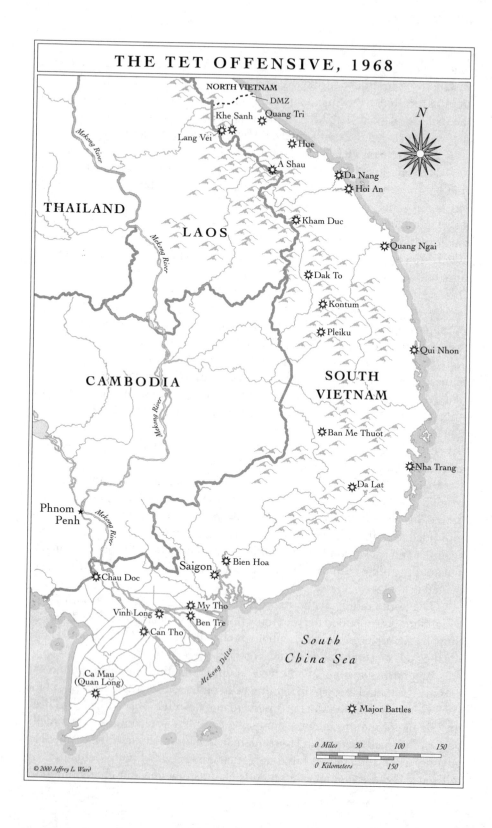

NORTH VIETNAM

DMZ

Quang Tri

Khe Sanh

Lang Vei

Hue

A Shau

Da Nang
Hoi An

THAILAND

LAOS

Kham Duc

Quang Ngai

Dak To

Kontum

Pleiku

Qui Nhon

CAMBODIA

SOUTH
VIETNAM

Ban Me Thuot

Nha Trang

Da Lat

Phnom
Penh

Bien Hoa

Saigon

Chau Doc

My Tho

Vinh Long
Ben Tre

Can Tho

Ca Mau
(Quan Long)

*South
China Sea*

☼ Major Battles

0 Miles   50   100   150

0 Kilometers   150

© 2000 Jeffrey L. Ward

U.S. base at Phu Bai, eight miles to the southwest on Route 1, the Communists had already taken most of Hue.

Ba's men carried lists of the Vietnamese military and political figures marked for capture or death. No American or other foreigner, except for the French, was to be spared. They seized the senior U.S. adviser, Philip W. Manhard of the State Department, at his residence, and he was not seen again. Stephen H. Miller from the U.S. Information Agency was led to a field behind a Catholic seminary and shot with his hands tied behind his back.

Breaking through their door to reach two Jesuit priests, a Spaniard and a Belgian, the Vietcong told them in halting English to come out with their hands in the air. The rebel leader wore a khaki shirt and shorts, and a medal with Ho's likeness. His clipboard held copies of identity cards from residents in the neighborhood. He ordered the priests tied up and taken to Manhard's house, which the Vietcong were using as their interrogation center. Since the priests knew that Frenchmen were to be spared, the Spaniard said he was from "south of France" and the Belgian said he was from "north of France." They were written a safe conduct pass and set free.

Their escape was a fluke that reflected the prevailing chaos. Other Roman Catholics had been marked as reactionary leaders to be destroyed, and priests who were genuinely French-born were buried alive. On the fifth day of fighting, Vietcong raided the Phu Cam Cathedral and led away the 400 men and boys who had taken refuge there. Some were called forward by name, others because they were of military age. The Vietcong officer told them not to worry; they were only being taken to a nearby pagoda to reconcile past enmities with Buddhist leaders. Two days later, the Vietcong came back to the cathedral and instructed the Catholic women to pack food and clothing for their sons and husbands. The Communists collected the packages and marched off again toward the pagoda.

But the prisoners were already dead. Four hundred and twenty-eight had been killed—about 100 South Vietnamese servicemen, 100 students, the rest government officials or Catholic males. They had been shot or clubbed to death with axes and shovels.

The savagery was due in part to conflicting orders out of Hanoi. First, the Communist troops were told to stand firm and resist the Americans as they tried to retake the city. Soon afterward, another order arrived, telling northerners and the Vietcong to withdraw into the mountains to the west. But American bombing raids panicked the retreating Communist forces, and the prisoners left behind were killed in an attempt to cover up the brutality of the month-long occupation. Thousands of people died, their bodies clumsily concealed in mass graves. Tran Van Quang, the ranking Northern general on the scene, and his subordinates were criticized in Hanoi but allowed to keep their positions.

Shelling from both sides had wracked the handsome city, but after twenty-five days of house-to-house fighting, the Communists were driven out of Hue on February 24.

LYNDON JOHNSON had not been at the White House briefing in 1961 when Eisenhower wondered aloud at the superiority of Communist forces, but seven years later he raised the same question with his senior advisers. "What makes the North Vietnamese fight so well," he asked, "with so much more determination than the South Vietnamese?"

The others looked to Helms. "I think it is a combination of good training and good brainwashing," the CIA director said. "There is a certain heroism about dying for the cause." Helms praised North Vietnamese training and discipline, adding, "Their system eliminates all doubt from their mind."

As he waited to assume office, Clifford regularly attended meetings with Johnson, and he summarized them with a disconcerting clarity that stressed the difference between what the administration was saying and what it was doing. On the one hand, Washington was assuring the American people that the Tet offensive was not a Communist victory and that it had cost the enemy between 20,000 and 25,000 combat soldiers. And yet the Pentagon was calling the situation more dangerous today than before Tet and recommending that Westmoreland be sent many more troops. Clifford called it a "very strange contradiction."

He thought that Johnson had compounded the problem by calling the Communist offensive a complete failure. Clifford suspected that George Aiken, the Republican senator from Vermont, had spoken aloud what most Americans were thinking: "If this is a failure, I hope the Vietcong never have a major success."

IN THE DAYS BEFORE TET, Khe Sanh had assumed a misleading symbolism because of Dien Bien Phu. It was another mountain base, the closest to North Vietnam in the northwestern corner of the South. In Hanoi, Giap had counted on the similarity to panic Westmoreland into draining troops away from Saigon and giving Tran Bach Dang and General Tra a better chance there. Rostow contributed to the growing jitters in Washington by telling reporters—in background sessions where he could not be quoted directly—that the Communists would probably try "a Dien Bien Phu" at Khe Sanh. Johnson became so alarmed that he had Max Taylor, back at the White House as a military consultant, set up a special White House Situation Room with an immense aerial photograph of the base and a scale model of the terrain so the president could keep track of American and enemy movements.

Johnson was suspicious of Westmoreland's assurances that the base could be held, and he demanded from Bus Wheeler a written endorsement of Westmoreland's position signed by the Joint Chiefs. On February 2, Wheeler explained to Westmoreland in a cable that Johnson was afraid Khe Sanh might become so imperiled that "he could be confronted with a decision to use tactical nuclear weapons to redress the balance—a decision he does not want to be forced to make."

Westmoreland's reply was hardly encouraging. B-52 strikes and America's other weaponry would prevent another Dien Bien Phu, he said. But looking over the entire northern I Corps area, a massive North Vietnamese attack across the DMZ would change the equation dramatically. In that event, the United States should be prepared to use weapons of maximum effectiveness against a massing of enemy troops. "Under such circumstances," Westmoreland added, "I visualize that either tactical nuclear weapons or chemical agents would be active candidates for employment."

AT KHE SANH ITSELF, three North Vietnamese divisions had pinned down the five U.S. Marine battalions but were themselves taking heavy casualties during their siege. Whatever Johnson might fear, Giap's focus from the first salvo in early January had remained centered on the Tet offensive at the end of the month. One clue was the Marines' water supply area. It lay outside the American perimeter, and yet Giap's troops did not try to cut it off.

William Tuohy of the Los Angeles Times was among the reporters to risk dropping into Khe Sanh on a supply plane. The NVA had cut Highway 9, the road from Khe Sanh to the coast, and all supplies had to be brought in by air. The aircraft flew low through heavy clouds, skirting the mountains and ducking NVA fire. The base's unflappable Marine commander, Colonel David Lownds, estimated the NVA regulars at 20,000, against his 5,000 troops, which included a battalion of ARVN rangers. The Communists already occupied the town of Khe Sanh, three miles south of the base, and had overrun a U.S. Special Forces camp to the west. In that assault, the NVA had used tanks for the first time.

Inside Khe Sanh, losses had been intense. During the first three weeks of the siege, more than half of Bravo Company of the 3rd Reconnaissance Battalion had been killed or wounded. To Tuohy, a debonair survivor of three years in Vietnam, the shell-pocked countryside looked like a red-dirt moonscape, with heavy ground mist wafting across the camp and enveloping the base each night. Tuohy learned that the Marines called their airstrip the H Zone—for "Hit." The NVA were knocking out so many aircraft that the Marines had set up a bunker for medics who had to pull wounded men from burning planes. The area around that wooden bunker was called Downtown. A Marine told Tuohy that going Downtown was like playing Russian roulette. Nothing might hit you, but a few hundred meters away another Marine would be cut down by artillery fire.

Tuohy crouched low, ran to a squad with several black Marines and wrote down their barrage of jokes that punctuated the shelling. Tuohy had heard the GI names for the enemy grow increasingly respectful—from "VC" to "Victor

Charlie" to "Mr. Charles." These Marine grunts knew him well enough from this siege to call him simply "Vic."

A lance corporal from Brooklyn recited for Tuohy the squad's defiant motto: "Yea, though we walk through the Valley of the Shadow of Death, we fear no evil—for we are the meanest motherfuckers in the Valley."

IN WASHINGTON, Lyndon Johnson abruptly faced a second Asian crisis. On January 23, the North Koreans captured the USS *Pueblo*, an American intelligence ship, in the international waters of the Sea of Japan. The ship was not armed but was stocked with electronic listening devices. The North Koreans fought their way aboard, killing one American sailor. Now Johnson was being urged by bellicose congressmen to mine another harbor—not only Haiphong, but Wonsan in North Korea. Resisting, Johnson told reporters he was sure that military force would not bring the men home. But he did call up 14,000 Reserves. The swell of support for a freshly beleaguered president quieted the antiwar protests momentarily and gave Robert Kennedy new doubts about his political future. Since last year, Senator Eugene McCarthy of Minnesota had been gearing up to challenge Johnson in the Democratic primaries. Gene McCarthy was neither related to Joe McCarthy, who had died in 1957, nor a political ally of the Kennedys. But listening to McCarthy nominate Stevenson for president in 1960, Jack Kennedy was detached enough to call his speech the best of the convention and had sent him twice on missions abroad. Galbraith considered McCarthy better educated than either Jack or Robert Kennedy, and McCarthy himself had ridiculed Bob Kennedy's strenuous quest for self-improvement.

Even so, as McCarthy's misgivings about Vietnam grew, he had urged Robert Kennedy to run against Johnson. Kennedy held back, fretting that his candidacy would be seen as a personal vendetta that would split the party. On the eve of Tet, Kennedy assured journalists off the record that he "would not oppose Lyndon Johnson under any conceivable circumstances." McCarthy did not seem to pose much of a threat, either. Because it was the nation's first primary, New Hampshire had an inflated importance, and polls there showed Johnson leading McCarthy 76 percent to 6 percent. But that was before Tet. By mid-February, American casualties had reached the highest one-week total of the war—543 killed, 2,547 wounded. For the first time, the proportion of American casualties was running higher than that of the ARVN.

BUS WHEELER had urged Westmoreland to ask for as many troops as he needed but to keep his request off the record and use instead Wheeler's back channel. The president was speeding to Vietnam the 10,500 Airborne and Marine troops he had already authorized, but Westmoreland wanted many more than that.

On Sunday, February 11, Johnson called his senior people to the White House family dining room to evaluate Westmoreland's latest cable. Earlier, the general had taken Wheeler's advice and requested troops obliquely enough that a leak would not force Johnson's hand. But Westmoreland was stung by Washington's reaction to Tet. He resented having to suggest that he needed more troops simply to stave off collapse. He wanted to explain that he was asking for them so he could seize the initiative.

Then Wheeler wired back, advising him that the first message had lacked urgency and suggesting that he make his request explicit. The second cable called for six more battalions to go on the offensive, and on Sunday at the White House, Rusk recommended sending them. McNamara agreed. But both men stipulated that the new troops should be sent only temporarily. They should not represent a permanent rise in the ceiling of 525,000 men. Johnson was annoyed: "Westy said he *could* use troops one day last week. Today he comes in with an urgent request for them."

The president went around the table asking, "Do all of you feel that we should send troops?" McNamara was the first to answer yes. Rusk, Helms, Wheeler, Taylor and Rostow fell into line. Clifford had decided not to vote until he was sworn in at Defense.

"Is there any objection?" Johnson asked. There was none. Still dissatisfied, Johnson sent Wheeler to Vietnam the next day to talk with Westmoreland in person.

CLIFFORD HAD COME to share McNamara's respect for Bus Wheeler. He appreciated the general's self-effacing modesty and his lack of the bluster that men like LeMay wore like another combat ribbon. Given his own political gifts, Clifford appreciated Wheeler's skill in negotiating with the other Chiefs, keeping the more obstreperous in line and avoiding damaging confrontations with the White House.

Wheeler arrived in Saigon on February 23 and told Westmoreland that the president faced a hard decision, which he was deferring until Wheeler's return. Westmoreland thought Wheeler, less than a year past his heart attack, looked exhausted. He had also come trailing gloom, which Westmoreland blamed on the Tet reporting. He set about assuring Wheeler and his chief aide, Bill DePuy, that the ARVN had recovered its morale in the past three weeks and had begun to draft men as young as eighteen. But on Wheeler's first night, the Vietcong launched a rocket attack near his quarters, and Wheeler asked to move into Westmoreland's residence.

The next day, the two generals explored Westmoreland's desire to expand the war. In the past, Westmoreland had opposed calling up the Reserves because they would serve for only one year, and if that term were extended, he foresaw a clamor to bring them home. Now he said he could deal "telling blows" within that one-year limit.

To achieve his goal, Westmoreland needed 200,000 more troops—the opti-

mum number he had set at the White House in 1967. He wanted a first incre-
ment of 108,000 in May, slightly more than half of the total increase. The others
would be held in reserve until the North Vietnamese won more significant victories. Or until Johnson changed course and permitted an invasion of Laos and
Cambodia; Wheeler warned him that the chances of that happening were no
better than fifty-fifty. Without comment, Wheeler endured the roseate briefings
Westmoreland had lined up for him and did not reveal his own conclusions before he left Saigon.

Westmoreland soon found out why. Wheeler's report called for the new
troops to forestall failure, not to ensure success. "The offensive has by no means
run its course," he wrote. Wheeler questioned ARVN stamina, predicted high casualties and described Westmoreland's troop margin as paper-thin. "For those
reasons he is asking for additional forces as soon as possible during this calendar
year." Wheeler recommended 205,719 additional troops in three phases.

JOHNSON TOOK A BREAK from the quarreling over numbers to fly to Fort Bragg and
address units that were already approved and on their way to Vietnam. Talking
with paratroopers of the 82nd Airborne Division, Johnson noticed that 50 percent
of the men were black and asked why. They had volunteered because of the Airborne's high morale, the president was told. And because of the extra jump pay.

The president flew next to El Toro Marine Base in Southern California to
spend the night on the *Constellation*, a carrier that would soon be sailing for the
South China Sea. The next morning, eating breakfast with twenty-five of the
ship's sailors, he asked for questions, but the men were young and shy. "Nobody
likes to go to war, or die," Johnson told them. "I was scared to death when I told
my mother goodbye. I was shaking, but I did not want the fella next to me to
know it."

Prodded to speak up, one sailor finally asked about the hippies and war protesters. "Practically every period in our history, beginning with the Revolutionary
War, there were hippie and beatnik types then," Johnson assured him. "And the
War of 1812 and 1846 and the Civil War, World War One and Two—we had zoot
suiters and appeasers and isolationists."

Back at the White House, Johnson told aides that he was not surprised that
none of the men were happy about going to Vietnam. But he was troubled that
once they had overcome their diffidence they had challenged his conduct of the
war. He tried to explain that he wanted to keep Russia and China from sending
troops. The North Vietnamese, he told them, "have two big brothers that have
more weight and people than I have." But even then some of the men protested
that Johnson's way of fighting wasn't effective.

GENE MCCARTHY'S CAMPAIGN was drawing young people by the thousands,
many of them under the voting age of twenty-one. Early on, his daughter at Rad-

cliffe had urged him to oppose the war, but McCarthy was no firebrand. He looked as bored in Congress as Jack Kennedy had been, and his support for liberal causes was spotty. Only the Vietnam War had rattled his detachment. Long before declaring his candidacy, he had called for a national debate over bombing the North.

The college students heading for New Hampshire bowed to pragmatism, shaved their beards and shed the colorful clothes that might brand them as drug-addled hippies. They called their sacrifice getting "Clean for Gene." Amused or derisive, observers labeled the swarm of 10,000 students from more than a hundred campuses the "Children's Crusade."

His young volunteers seemed to have more appetite for campaigning than McCarthy did. They paid three visits to the house of every Democratic voter in the state and followed up with two phone calls. McCarthy seemed to find plunging into a sea of outstretched hands somehow demeaning. But his very reluctance to snatch after power made him attractive to the youthful idealists who shuddered at the spectacle of a president who grabbed at it with both hands.

McCarthy's appeal included his alienated irony. "The Democratic Party in 1964 promised 'no wider war,' " McCarthy said after Tet. "Yet the war is getting wider every month. Only a few months ago, we were told that 65 percent of the population was secure. Now we know that even the American Embassy is not secure."

And, despite Johnson's mania for secrecy, voters were learning that the war might get wider still. On March 8, as Clifford began his second week as defense secretary, he got an urgent note from Phil Goulding, the Pentagon press aide who had replaced Arthur Sylvester. Goulding had heard that both Neil Sheehan and Hedrick Smith of the New York Times had discovered that Westmoreland was requesting a large buildup of troops. Sheehan even had the precise figure of 206,000, and his story, which appeared two days later, sent Johnson into a rage.

On March 12, the day of the New Hampshire primary, Rusk was completing a second day of testimony before Fulbright's Senate committee. It was his first appearance in two years. Rusk had wanted to testify the previous year in order to bolster support for the war, but Johnson forbade it for the same reason he had opposed television appearances by Bundy and McNamara. The president did not want his advisers debating his policies in public. That first year, Rusk had accepted Johnson's ban, but he worried that if he refused to appear again Fulbright would hold up the State Department's appropriation.

Fulbright appeared in front of the cameras wearing a necktie festooned with doves and olive branches, and Rusk noted sourly that half of the committee members were wearing pancake makeup. Church of Idaho told the television audience that he worried that the Asian crocodile was being fed with American lives. Symington said he was concerned that America's fiscal security was being undermined by the Vietnam budget. Still smarting over the Tonkin Gulf Resolution, Fulbright pushed Rusk to promise there would be more consultation with Congress in the future. The Secretary replied noncommittally that if more troops were to be sent to Vietnam "appropriate members of Congress" would be consulted.

Over two days, Rusk answered hostile questions with laconic calm, rousing himself only when Senator Claiborne Pell raised what he called a moral question: was the suffering in Vietnam worth the effort? Appearing angry or at least ruffled, Rusk denounced "moral myopia" and said the United States had undertaken "the endless struggle for freedom." The hearings ended, and Rusk was relieved to adjourn for a congenial drink with his adversaries in a Senate back room.

That night in the New Hampshire Democratic primary, Gene McCarthy did not win, but Lyndon Johnson lost decisively. McCarthy's vote of 42.2 percent stunned the president's partisans and thrilled his critics. Johnson's vote was only 7.2 percent larger, and 500 Republicans had written in McCarthy's name on their ballots. What was generally overlooked was that Johnson had not entered his name for the balloting, nor had he campaigned or organized in the state. Each of his 49.4 percent had come from a voter who had to write in his name. On election day itself, Johnson's politicking had been limited to a statement praising the Senate for passing the Civil Rights Act of 1968. But McCarthy's sharp-witted staff had taken advantage of the primary rules, and their candidate took twenty of the twenty-four delegates to the convention.

Johnson made no comment about New Hampshire, but the night before, he had called the results accurately, predicting that McCarthy would get at least 40 percent. "Every son-of-a-bitch in New Hampshire who's mad at his wife or the postman or anybody is going to vote for Gene McCarthy," Johnson said. A poll after the election found that more than half of the Democratic voters had not known McCarthy's position on Vietnam. They described themselves as simply "dissatisfied" with the war.

Robert Kennedy was speaking in the Bronx while the New Hampshire votes were being tallied, and he asked Schlesinger to meet him later at "21," the Manhattan nightclub. Once again, Kennedy was dejected. He thought McCarthy would feel that he had given Kennedy his chance and now had earned the right to press on to the convention. If so, Kennedy said, "I can't blame him."

Schlesinger proposed a gambit. Endorse McCarthy now and let him prove to the Democratic leadership that Johnson must go. At that point, the same leaders would realize that McCarthy was a weak candidate and turn to Kennedy at the Chicago convention. Kennedy said no, he could not pretend, even through the primaries, that he favored McCarthy for president. At that, Schlesinger gave him McCarthy's phone number in New Hampshire, and Kennedy left the table to congratulate him. Their talk was brief but amiable.

Although the evidence of Johnson's vulnerability had whetted Kennedy's competitive instincts, Schlesinger was one of his few senior advisers who favored his running. McNamara strenuously opposed it, arguing that he would be staining his record against a year when he could actually win. Since he left the White House, Moyers had drifted toward the Kennedy camp, and he also opposed the idea, as did Ted Sorensen.

The day before the primary, Sorensen had met with Johnson for two hours, most of the time given over to a presidential monologue about the schisms within the country. At last, Johnson paused and asked, What can I do? Sorensen recommended appointing a commission to analyze what had gone wrong in Vietnam.

There was a precedent for the proposal but not a promising one. After the rioting among black Americans in 1967, Johnson had appointed Illinois Governor Otto Kerner to head a commission investigating the crisis. Kerner concluded that America was "moving toward two societies, one black, the other white—separate but unequal," and Johnson had refused to accept the report. Despite that background, Johnson gave Sorensen vague encouragement about forming a commission. He also let drop an unexpected insight into a debate continuing among his advisers, even with McNamara gone. "Clifford is not the hawk that he had been painted to be," Johnson said, "and his critics would be surprised at the position he is taking."

The president said he worried that a Vietnam commission might undercut Rusk or suggest to Hanoi that he was throwing in his hand. But he and Sorensen tossed back and forth the names of possible commission members before Johnson said, "You know, maybe Robert Kennedy should be chairman." Neither man needed to say that the appointment might keep Kennedy out of the primaries.

Sorensen reported his talk to Kennedy, who suspected a trick. Still, the overture could not be ignored. Picking up on Johnson's hint about Clifford, Kennedy asked his brother Ted to set up an 11 A.M. meeting the next day at the Pentagon.

Clifford could encompass many loyalties, but a president would always outrank the others. He stopped by the White House before his meeting and listened as Johnson unleashed his own distrust. Be on guard, Johnson warned him. This could be a trick.

On the way to Clifford's office, Kennedy still had qualms and asked Sorensen, "But how do I know that the announcement of a commission would really mean any change in policy?" Once they got to the Pentagon, Kennedy immediately set out his conditions. To Clifford, they amounted to a barely disguised threat. Kennedy said there were two ways he could correct Vietnam policy. One was by being elected president. The other was to convince Johnson that he must change course.

For the last forty-eight hours, Kennedy's strongest impulse had been telling him to run. Now he emphasized that this commission idea had come entirely from Sorensen. It was Sorensen's last-ditch effort to keep Kennedy out of the race, and he laid out the deal even more baldly: if Johnson made a public statement that his policy had proved to be in error and appointed a committee to recommend action, then Kennedy would agree not to enter the race.

Clifford cut him off impatiently. "Ted, you know as well as I do that the President could not issue a statement saying that the country's policy was a failure."

Kennedy became conciliatory. The statement need not go that far, he said. Johnson need only say that he was reevaluating, in its entirety, the nation's policy on Vietnam and then appoint the commission members Kennedy recommended.

Clifford was sufficiently suave that Sorensen thought, for a moment, that he was endorsing the idea. He asked whom they would like to see on the commission and waited while both Kennedy and Sorensen threw out names: Edwin Reischauer, Kingman Brewster, Ros Gilpatric, Carl Kaysen, General Lauris Norstad and General Matthew Ridgway, Senators Mansfield, John Sherman Cooper and George Aiken. And Robert Kennedy.

As they offered nominees, Kennedy sensed that Clifford was cool to them and asked directly for his reaction. Clifford said that Kennedy's chances of defeating Johnson for the nomination were zero. He reminded them about 1948, when Truman was deserted by angry southerners while liberals were backing Henry Wallace and Democrats were trying to persuade Eisenhower to run on their ticket. Truman had won. Clifford also warned Kennedy not to assume that when the convention opened in August the situation in Vietnam would be the same as it was now. He expected an improvement over the next five months, Clifford said, although he was deliberately vague about whether it would come on the battlefield or through negotiations. And, he concluded, if Kennedy did manage to get the nomination, it would be worthless. The party would be split, and a Republican would be elected.

Kennedy said he had considered those points and still felt he would have to run unless Johnson agreed to his proposal. Without saying so, Kennedy was demanding from Johnson the surrender that Johnson was demanding from Hanoi.

Clifford said he would take up the matter with the president and call them with his answer. That same afternoon, Clifford repeated the conversation in the small lounge off the Oval Office. Johnson listened with Humphrey and Abe Fortas and then ticked off his objections: it would look like a political deal; it would give comfort to Hanoi; it was an attempt to usurp presidential authority; and the men Kennedy proposed were all known opponents of the war. Clifford called to pass along that reaction, and Sorensen asked if he might put Kennedy on an extension. Johnson, without asking, had picked up a line in his office. He wanted to hear how Kennedy took another rejection.

Kennedy asked whether it would make a difference if he were not a commission member. Clifford said it would not change Johnson's mind. After they hung up, Johnson decided he had better protect himself against Kennedy's version of the incident, and he had DeVier Pierson, the White House counsel, call to assure Sorensen that the president wanted to consult with anyone—in government or out—who had good ideas about Vietnam. That included Reischauer, Ridgway, both Kennedy brothers, George Ball and Sorensen himself—whose visit to the White House Johnson had enjoyed. But a commission would undercut advisers at State and Defense. "We both know," Pierson continued dutifully, "the President won't play politics on Vietnam."

In the Senate Caucus Room on March 16—four days after New Hampshire, four years after he first considered the challenge—Robert Kennedy declared himself a candidate for president.

JOHNSON HAD WATCHED Clifford operate for more than two decades and knew how canny he could be. The president had also learned from the Tuesday Lunches that Clifford was not the true believer Johnson had thought he was sending to the Pentagon. But when Clifford proposed calling the Wise Men together again for a postmortem on the Tet offensive, Johnson had no reason to suspect a trap. As Clifford went down the guest list, he characterized the leanings of several of them—Cabot Lodge, for example, was "hawkish," Douglas Dillon a dove. Clifford did not put a label to his own name, and when he termed Acheson a hawk, he knew better.

Johnson may have known better, too. Acheson had been restive since the last Wise Men's session, feeling that his reputation was being used as the façade for policies that were never being satisfactorily explained. Determined to learn more, he scheduled what he expected to be a candid meeting with Johnson, but when he showed up for it, the president only ranted on about Khe Sanh. In the midst of Johnson's tirade, Acheson excused himself and walked back across Lafayette Park to his law office. As he arrived, the phone was ringing. It was Rostow asking why he had walked out on the president. Acheson explained: "You tell the President—and you tell him in precisely these words—that he can take Vietnam and stick it up his ass."

Listening in, Johnson ordered Acheson, as his president and commander in chief, to return to the Oval Office. Men who had been through World War II did not refuse that direct order. Once back at the White House, however, Acheson told Johnson that his Joint Chiefs did not know what they were talking about, and he demanded more realistic briefings. As a result, Philip Habib from State paid a visit to Acheson's Georgetown house. Brooklyn-born and outspoken, Habib had once served as political counselor in Saigon. After a bit of probing, he was convinced that Acheson sincerely wanted an accurate evaluation, and Habib confided his doubts.

No matter what Westmoreland was saying, Tet had been a serious setback for the United States, Habib said. North Vietnam and the Vietcong had taken heavy losses, but Tet made the war a new ball game. Acheson was deep in research about the Korean War for his memoirs and was regretting all over again that he had not warned Truman forcefully against MacArthur crossing the Yalu River into North Korea. This time, he would serve his president better.

As the Wise Men were being rounded up, Westmoreland learned that he, at least, would be getting out of Vietnam. Bus Wheeler called to say that the president had just announced at a news conference that he was naming Westmoreland U.S. Army chief of staff. Johnson had not informed him, although—like McNamara with the World Bank—Westmoreland had known that the assignment was a possibility.

On paper, Westmoreland was being promoted, and Wheeler said the president advised him to ignore the inevitable rumors that he was being kicked upstairs. Then Wheeler flew out to meet with Westmoreland in person and inform him that there was no possibility of his getting a large contingent of GIs. Westmoreland knew that decision was final. Making his last official troop request from Vietnam, Westmoreland asked for 13,500 men. Once again, Johnson could say that he was giving his commander everything he had requested.

At 6 p.m. on March 25, the Wise Men—called, for the record, the Senior Advisory Group—came together in the secretary of state's dining room, a smaller room down the hall from the department's banquet hall. The president was in the building for a speaking engagement, his announced topic farm policy. But every speech, no matter how unrelated, seemed to come back to Vietnam, which alarmed Clifford. Addressing the National Alliance of Businessmen the previous week, Johnson had seemed to say that he was going to win the war no matter what the cost in American lives. And one phrase had left his opponents convinced that he had called them traitors. Campaign workers told Johnson that the speech had hurt him badly in Wisconsin, where the presidential primary was only days away, and Mac Bundy was troubled enough to warn the president, "If we get tagged as mindless hawks, we can lose both the election and the war." Bundy added that Johnson must call a bombing halt within the next six months—well before the November election—and it had to last a good long time. Harry McPherson, one Texas aide who could talk straight to Johnson, told him that his present policy would result in the nomination of Robert Kennedy for the Democrats, Nixon for the Republicans and very possibly Nixon's election.

Tonight at the State Department, the president did not dine with his guests but simply shook hands and promised to see them the next day. After dinner, the group moved to the Operations Center that had been set up in the Kennedy years to deal with crises twenty-four hours a day. Bill Bundy had chosen the briefers, counting on them to offer hardheaded analyses and not promise drastic improvement any time soon. But the first of the three, General Bill DePuy, now the Joint Chiefs' officer for counterinsurgency, followed Westmoreland's line and hailed

Tet as a U.S. victory. Arthur Goldberg challenged DePuy's figures: Hadn't the general just said that the Communists had lost 80,000 men killed in action? Yes, DePuy said.

What was the usual ratio of men wounded to those killed? About three to one would be a conservative estimate, DePuy said.

How many effective troops do you estimate the Communists now have?

Perhaps 230,000 or 240,000, DePuy said.

Goldberg did the math. Well, he remarked, with 80,000 killed and a ratio of three to one, that comes to some 320,000 Communists killed or wounded. He paused. "Who the hell is there left for us to be fighting?"

George Carver, although still supporting the war, was candid about problems in pacification. He granted that achieving the program's objectives would take far longer than the CIA's previous estimates. Phil Habib spoke last and, to Clifford, his was the decisive judgment. Repeating much of what he had told Acheson, Habib estimated that real progress in the South could take five to seven years.

When he finished, Clifford deliberately put him on the spot. "Phil," he asked, "do you think a military victory can be won?" Clifford knew what Habib was saying privately. Now he wanted him to say it in front of his unreconstructed boss; Rusk was awaiting his reply.

Habib knew the damage an honest answer might do to his career. He gave it anyway. "Not under present circumstances."

Clifford was implacable: "What would you do if a decision was yours to make?"

Habib paused, then plunged ahead: "Stop the bombing and negotiate."

When the meeting broke up after 11 P.M., Clifford went back to his Pentagon office. Like McNamara during the Cuban missile debate, he intended to sleep there overnight. Tomorrow's crisis might not involve nuclear weapons, but it could be crucial to a president's survival. So far, Clifford was pleased with the impact the briefings seemed to be having, particularly on Cy Vance, McNamara's former deputy. Vance suffered from a painfully bad back that had forced him to leave government in 1966, but he had known the president since Johnson's Senate days and his opinion carried weight. Even so, Clifford worried that dawn's second thoughts might dissipate the late-night pessimism.

The Wise Men met again after breakfast, but Clifford had to leave for a White House briefing with Creighton Abrams, Westmoreland's successor. Clifford took an immediate liking to Abrams, a World War II tank commander, because he was short and stocky, plainspoken, free of posturing and political ambition; because he was nothing like Westmoreland.

Johnson was determined to counter whatever griping Abrams might have heard from Westmoreland about the limit on troops. To make his point, the president pressed Bus Wheeler into a two-man vaudeville routine.

General Creighton Abrams
(AP/Wide World Photos)

JOHNSON: Didn't we tell General Westmoreland that we would let him do what he wants to do and we would support him?

WHEELER: Yes. General Westmoreland is there in South Vietnam. He has complete authority. He can't go across the DMZ. There are limits in Laos and Cambodia.

JOHNSON: Whose strategy is used?

WHEELER: It is completely from Westmoreland.

JOHNSON: Do we handicap him?

WHEELER: No.

The president had been informed that the previous evening's briefings had shaken confidence among his visitors. Rostow told him that he smelled a rat, that the session had seemed rigged to demoralize the guests. Johnson asked Abrams and Wheeler to stay on to provide the civilians with their hopeful projections. First, however, he broke into a long justification for not sending the troops that Westmoreland had requested. In recent days, Johnson was looking as frazzled and spent as McNamara before he was shuffled out of the Pentagon, and the pallor of the president's skin pointed up the red sties breaking out along his eyelids.

He told the generals that Gene McCarthy, Robert Kennedy and the political Left all had planted informants in his State and Defense Departments. Then he removed any lingering doubt that domestic political concerns were dominating his thinking.

"We need more money—in an election year," Johnson said. "We need more taxes—in an election year. We need more troops—in an election year. And we need cuts in the domestic budget—in an election year.

"And yet I cannot tell the people what they will get in Vietnam in return for those cuts. We have no support for the war. This was caused by the 206,000-man request and the leaks, by Teddy Kennedy and Bobby Kennedy. I would have given Westy the 206,000 men if he said he needed them, and if we could get them."

Hearing the rant, Clifford felt sad for Johnson but also buoyed by the sense that the president finally knew he must change his policy. When the Wise Men arrived for lunch at the White House, Johnson sent away most government officials in order to talk only with his guests. Harriman simply ignored the restriction, showed up at the dining room and called for the stewards to set another place for him. Again, however, Harriman had not come to speak. His presence would simply remind Johnson that if the time was approaching for negotiation, the president need look no further for his representative.

As the guests got to business, they turned to Mac Bundy, not yet fifty and the youngest of the group but also the most deft at preparing a summary. Johnson asked him for the consensus.

"Mr. President," Bundy began, "there has been a very significant shift in most of our positions since we last met." In November, they had found reasons to hope for steady progress. The briefings last night had dashed that hope. "Dean Acheson summed up the majority feeling when he said that we can no longer do the job we set out to do in the time we have left, and we must begin to take steps to disengage."

Bundy went on, "That view was shared by George Ball, Arthur Dean, Cy Vance, Douglas Dillon and myself." Scrupulously, Bundy named the three men who took a different position, two of them generals—Omar Bradley and Max Taylor, and Robert Murphy, a former ambassador and president of Corning Glass International. Clifford thought Johnson seemed more uneasy than angry as he started around the table for comments. When Acheson said that military victory was impossible, General Wheeler made the mistake of correcting him. We are not seeking a military victory in Vietnam, Wheeler said, only helping the southerners to ward off a Communist victory. Acheson had come a long way to reach his new position on the war and would not be diverted by a quibble.

"Then what in the name of God are five hundred thousand men out there doing—chasing girls? This is not a semantic game, General. If the deployment of all those men is not an effort to gain a military solution, then words have lost all meaning."

Earlier in the month, Arthur Goldberg had sent Johnson an eight-page argument for a complete halt to the bombing. At the time, the president had been enraged. "Let's get one thing clear!" he had lectured his aides. "I'm telling you now that I am not going to stop the bombing! Now I don't want to hear anymore about it. Goldberg has written me about the whole thing, and I've heard every argument, and I'm not going to stop it. Now is there anybody here who doesn't understand that?"

That was twelve days ago. Now Johnson was equally forceful when Rostow tried to rescue Bus Wheeler by saying that the military did have an option that could alter the struggle: the United States could invade North Vietnam. Johnson brusquely warned him off: "No, no, no! I don't want to talk about that."

Max Taylor pronounced himself dismayed by what he was hearing from Bundy and the others. "The picture I get is a very different one from that you have," he said. Rather than simply despair that the American public was disillusioned by Tet, Taylor exhorted them, "Let's do something about it."

Abe Fortas argued against Acheson's position. Acheson came back hard. "The issue is not that stated by Fortas," he said. "The issue is, can we do what we are trying to do in Vietnam. I do not think we can."

Arthur Dean mentioned that last night's briefings had led the group to conclude reluctantly that the United States had to get out of Vietnam. Johnson tried to sound blithe: "The first thing I'm going to do when you all leave is find those people who briefed you last night." But it was no joke. Johnson slipped a note to Clifford asking that he and Rusk join him outside for a moment. Promising to return shortly, the president led his two Secretaries to the hallway and exploded. "Who poisoned the well with these guys? I want to hear the briefings myself." He sent Rusk and Clifford to their offices and went back to cope with the unwelcome judgments.

It appears to me, Johnson told the group, that six advisers favored some form of disengagement, one was in between and four were opposed. Mac Bundy said it was not that clear-cut. Rather, everyone should wait to see if more of the fighting could be shifted to the ARVN and what the effect of a bombing pause might be.

Johnson thanked the men and sent them home. Walking with him to the Oval Office, Humphrey commiserated. "Tet really set us back," he said. But Johnson was thinking that if his Wise Men, steady and balanced, had been so badly shaken by Tet, what was the average citizen thinking? Within a week, Wisconsin's voters would let him know.

FOR THE PAST TEN DAYS, Johnson's staff had been preparing a national television address. Clifford read the first draft and was appalled. He understood that he had three options: Change the president's mind 180 degrees, which George Ball had never been able to do. Or carry out Johnson's policies despite his own misgivings, the path McNamara had chosen. Or resign quietly, as Mac Bundy had done. But, Clifford reminded himself, he faced their choices after less than three weeks in his job.

Johnson's instructions to his speechwriters had been uncompromising. "Let's get 'peace' out of the speech except that we're ready to talk," he told Harry McPherson. "We're mixing up two different things when we included peace initiatives in this speech. Let's make it troops and war." Looking on, Clifford knew that McPherson shared his doubts and watched sympathetically as he kept his eyes on his notebook and said nothing.

On March 28, two days after the Wise Men left the White House, three days before the president's speech and five days before the Wisconsin primary, Clifford met with Rusk and Rostow at the State Department and told them candidly what bothered him. "What the President needs is a speech about peace," he said. "We must change it. We must take the first step toward winding down the war and reducing the level of violence."

For the first time, neither Rusk nor Rostow challenged him. To nudge Rusk further along, Clifford suggested letting McPherson prepare a softer speech with a bombing pause and let Johnson choose between them. McPherson worked late into the night on the alternate speech. When the president called to request changes, McPherson could deduce which of the drafts Johnson was preparing to deliver. Immediately upon hanging up, he rang Clifford at the Pentagon. "We've won!" he exclaimed. "The President is working on our draft."

But Johnson was also working on an addendum of his own. Three months earlier, he had asked White House aide Horace Busby for a brief personal statement that he could add to his State of the Union address. At the time, Lady Bird Johnson read the result and made one small change to strengthen the language. That night, Johnson had carried Busby's paragraphs to the Capitol, but they stayed in his pocket.

On March 31, Johnson again faced the American people, determined to convey his desire for peace in the one way that might convince them of his sincerity. Speaking from the Oval Office at 9:01 P.M., he first described the results of the Tet offensive, then announced that to deescalate the war he was stopping all bombing of North Vietnam except in an area above the DMZ where Hanoi's soldiers could threaten American troops. With the world's hopes for peace in the balance, Johnson said, he did not want to devote one hour of the coming days to partisan causes.

"Accordingly, I shall not seek, and I will not accept, the nomination of my party for another term as your President."

To THE WORLD, the president's announcement was scarcely believable. When his speech ended, Johnson's own glee over the surprise he had sprung diluted for

President Johnson addressing the nation, March 31, 1968
(Yoichi R. Okamoto/LBJ Library Collection)

the moment whatever regret he was feeling. He had shown all those journalists that they had never understood him—Tom Wicker at the *New York Times* who wrote that Johnson retiring was as unlikely "as it is that Dean Rusk will turn dove"; Carl Rowan, who had returned to journalism as a columnist and was sure that the odds against Johnson not running "can't be better than a million to one."

The clues that Johnson had sometimes thrown out had been easily taken as self-pity or an invitation to talk him back into running. But Johnson vividly recalled his heart attack in 1955 and the operations he had undergone as president. He had grown up around his father's mother, who had been paralyzed by a stroke as devastating as the one suffered by Joe Kennedy. Besides his health and the war in Vietnam, however, Johnson's immediate future gave him little incentive for clinging to power. He would soon have to ask for a tax increase, and Hoover at the FBI was predicting new and violent race riots in the coming months.

With the cameras turned off, Johnson was more buoyant than Clifford had seen him in months. He paced the White House gnawing at a big slab of chocolate cake and taking calls of congratulation and commiseration while he watched television commentators struggling to cope with his bombshell. At 11 P.M., Johnson held a short press conference to emphasize that his decision was final.

Back with family and friends, he wanted to be sure that they appreciated the magnitude of his sacrifice. "I was never surer of any decision I ever made," he declared, "and I have never made any more unselfish one. I have 525,000 men whose very lives depend on what I do, and I can't afford to worry about the primaries. Now I will be working full time for those men out there."

For public consumption, his two Democratic rivals agreed with him. Robert Kennedy called Johnson's withdrawal "truly magnanimous." Gene McCarthy said Johnson deserved the "honor and respect of every citizen." On April 2, Wisconsin voters were less charitable. McCarthy won 56 percent of the vote, Johnson little more than one-third. When Richard Nixon lost the race for the California governorship in 1962, he had told reporters bitterly that they wouldn't have Nixon to kick around anymore because it was his last press conference. With nine months left to serve in the White House, Johnson could not make the same threat, but he did tell the press corps, "You fellows won't have me to pick on any more. You can find someone else to flog and insult."

WHEN RONALD RIDENHOUR was drafted out of Arizona State College and sent as an army private to Hawaii, he expected to wind up in Vietnam. For two-and-a-half months, he trained in an island jungle with a unit of 30 men. Then their group was split up, 15 of his new buddies going off to Charlie Company of the 11th Infantry Brigade. Ridenhour was assigned instead to a light observation helicopter company. He would be flying over Vietnam's treelines, spotting Vietcong and shooting at them with machine guns mounted on the chopper doors.

Getting from Hawaii to Da Nang took thirteen days by troopship. To pass the time, Ridenhour had made the mistake of bringing along books by Bernard Fall, and the more he read, the less enthusiasm he felt for what lay ahead. Oh, my God, he thought, this is a civil war. What have I got myself into?

His misgivings intensified on his first mission. Providing light air cover for the 2nd Infantry, Ridenhour's chopper flew over a village of 150 hooches. No one saw anything suspicious until one young man dressed in black ran out of a hut and into a rice paddy. The pilot brought their helicopter down. The crew chief was on the right door, Ridenhour on the left. They flew low enough to shout at the Vietnamese to stop. When he kept running, the crew chief fired a burst in front of him. It was meant to urge him back. Instead, the bullets hit the man in the hip. For the first time, Ridenhour saw real gunfire at real people. He was badly shaken, and the lieutenant who had fired the shots sounded hysterical as he radioed the commander of the line company on the ground that he must help the wounded man. He kept insisting until finally a voice said, "I'm coming."

As the helicopter crew watched, infantrymen ran up to the Vietnamese as he lay in a pool of his blood. Their lieutenant pulled out his .45 and shot the man through the head. He radioed up to Ridenhour's chief, "This man no longer needs help, sir."

They understood the message: You new men, you cherries—the infantry officer was saying to them—this is what Vietnam is all about.

Ridenhour spent the next four months flying missions and watching half a dozen Vietnamese killed in the same way. According to the army, they were all enemy kills. Ridenhour saw them as people flat-out murdered before his eyes. By mid-April 1968, his sergeant was sick of his complaining and gave him a choice: out of the unit or time in jail. Ridenhour packed his bags and headed for brigade headquarters. When he arrived, the base reminded him of a small American city with maybe 10,000 residents.

He had not been there long when he ran into one of the GIs from Hawaii who had gone to Charlie Company. They got a beer, found an empty tent and sat down to swap war stories.

After a minute or two, Charles Gruver said, "Hey, man, did you hear what we did at Pinkville? We killed all those people. We massacred a village."

"What do you mean?" Ridenhour was not entirely surprised. In his hooch, he had listened one night from three bunks away as one man told another, "We killed 'em—fifty or sixty." "How do you do that?" his friend had asked. "You just close your eyes and pull the trigger." When Ridenhour asked later what they had been talking about, they told him, "Nothing, man. You didn't hear anything."

Now Butch Gruver seemed to want to talk. "We lined them up—men, women and children. Like a bunch of Nazis," he said. "We mowed 'em down."

Ridenhour knew the cluster of villages. Their pink color on GI maps indicated both their density and the degree of their Vietcong sympathy. As Gruver told about his four hours in Pinkville, Ridenhour had an epiphany: If I know about this and do nothing, I'm as guilty as they are. He promised himself that he would track the story down and piece together a factual account of what had gone on last March 16. He already knew that the hamlet's Vietnamese name was My Lai.

ON MARCH 14, on patrol along Highway 1, a booby trap had killed U.S. Sergeant George Cox of Charlie Company and mutilated two of his squad. Cox was highly regarded for the way he looked after his men, and, in their grief, the surviving squad members shot a Vietnamese woman working in a nearby field. When they found her still alive and unarmed, they shot her again, pulled off a ring she was wearing and stomped her to death. Angry villagers saw the murder and went to the American camp to complain. Captain Ernest Medina told them that the woman had been holding the detonator of a land mine. Looking on, another U.S. officer, Second Lieutenant William Calley, admired the way Medina handled the situation.

The next afternoon, officers of Charlie Company were briefed for an operation on March 16. In the three months since the company arrived in country, 5 of its men had been killed and 23 wounded, but none of those casualties had come in combat. They were due to snipers, land mines and booby traps. Captain Carl Creswell, a chaplain, stopped by the briefing to greet the survivors from the company, which was down now to 105 men. He heard a major saying, "We're going in there, and if we get one round out of there, we're gonna level it."

"You know," said Creswell, "I didn't really think we made war that way."

Creswell never got the major's name. He only remembered the way the man looked at him and said, "It's a tough war, Chaplain."

Later that day, Charlie Company held a memorial service for Sergeant Cox. The men reminisced about training with him and about meeting Cox's wife in Hawaii. Afterward, Captain Medina gathered everyone together for a rally. Tomorrow, he told them, they would be outnumbered more than two to one by the 250 to 280 men from the 48th Vietcong Battalion. But their helicopter gunships would even the odds. Medina picked up a shovel and drew a map of their target in the dirt. Four settlements, labeled My Lai 4, spread across a broad valley along the Tra Khuc River. U.S. intelligence had established that My Lai was entirely controlled by the enemy. Tomorrow would be Charlie Company's chance to avenge George Cox.

Many villagers might be at market, Medina said, but Lieutenant Colonel Frank Barker had given permission to treat My Lai as a Vietcong stronghold. The men should kill the pigs and other livestock and drop them down the wells to contaminate the water. As they moved through the villages, they should cut down the banana trees and burn the hooches. They were to take no prisoners. Those were Barker's orders. Medina took them to mean that no Vietnamese should leave My Lai alive.

AT DAWN, the men of Charlie Company were lifted the eleven miles to My Lai 4 by the 174th Helicopter Assault Company. Photographing their takeoff was Ron Haeberle, a draftee assigned to public information at the brigade headquarters in Duc Pho. To boost troop morale, he and a reporter, Jay Roberts, were to join the mission and produce a story for the armed forces newspaper, *Stars and Stripes*. That sort of dispatch sometimes got picked up by the AP and generated support for the war. Just before 7:30 A.M., American artillery used map coordinates to shell the village. The gunfire sent the Vietnamese running for shelter or for the tunnels beneath their houses. Haeberle came in with the second lift of troops and shot the approach to the landing zone with Ektachrome color film in his 35-mm Nikon.

One of the GIs, Michael Bernhardt, had trained from the age of thirteen at the La Salle Military Academy in Long Island, New York. Lately, he had volunteered for Vietnam as a paratrooper. Until Medina's pep talk the night before, Bernhardt had not worried about his tour. But once on the ground, he saw that his unit was receiving no return fire, and yet the Americans were shooting everywhere. Any Vietnamese male who was spotted was shot down, wounded or killed. At 8 A.M., Medina radioed the operation center that his men could confirm 15 VC dead.

Lieutenant William L. Calley *(AP/Wide World Photos)*

Lieutenant Calley took Charlie Company through My Lai 4; the Vietnamese who lived there called the hamlet Tu Cung. Rusty Calley stood only 5 feet 4 inches tall. At first, he had been turned down by the army for being tone deaf. But as the widening war boosted draft calls, he was reevaluated and allowed to enlist. Calley graduated from Officers Candidate School and then Jungle Warfare School. There the Vietnamese were routinely described as "gooks," "slants," or "dinks." As part of the training, Calley was ordered to give a talk titled "Vietnam Our Host." It consisted of such advice as "Don't assault the women" and "Be polite." He considered the lecture a farce, since the real lesson of his training was that you could never trust a Vietnamese. Any one of them might do you in.

Moving through the village, Charlie Company's platoons split into squads and then into groups of two and three to move among the bamboo and banana trees. Calley's 1st Platoon shouted at villagers to come out of their houses. Although they had no interpreter, they gathered up about sixty old men, children and women carrying babies. Some of the Vietnamese had already been wounded by machine-gun fire that had raked their houses before the Americans advanced.

One old woman had been struck by an M-79 grenade that did not explode but lodged in her belly.

Men in Calley's unit were beginning to act in ways that shocked a few of them. Allen Boyce from New Jersey stabbed a middle-aged farmer with the bayonet fastened to his rifle. He shot another man in the neck, threw him down a well and dropped a grenade in after him. "That's the way you've got to do it," he told Varnado Simpson, a rifleman who had considered Boyce a good friend.

Dennis Conti, as he rounded up villagers, saw other GIs shoving women and children into bunkers and tossing in grenades. The whole platoon seemed crazed with blood. When Conti found a Vietnamese woman with a four-year-old, he dropped his pants, pointed his gun at the child's head and gestured to the woman until she knelt before him. Just then, Calley arrived on the scene and ordered Conti to pull up his pants and get back to work.

Overhead, Lieutenant Colonel Frank Barker was checking from his helicopter on how the firefight was progressing. Medina reported that at 8:30 A.M. the body count was up by another 69 enemy dead, to a total of 84. Even though no Americans had been killed or wounded, Charlie Company kept on firing at anything that moved. Floyd Wright and Max Hutson, the weapons squad leader, came upon a middle-aged woman climbing out of a tunnel. They shot her, and she fell back dead. When Charlie Hutto's M-60 machine gun got heavy for him, he traded weapons with Esequiel Torres. Hutto took Torres's rifle, and they went on shooting Vietnamese.

Gary Crossley shot an old man in the arm, almost severing it. Still, the man tried to raise his hand in the air and shout, "No VC! No VC!" A woman carrying a baby came out of her house and pulled the man inside.

Thomas Partsch asked Crossley why he had not finished the old man off. Crossley said he had only wanted to know what it felt like to shoot someone. He could not bring himself to do it another time. At that, Hutson and Wright burst into the house after the old man and opened fire on him and on the woman who had tried to protect him.

From a neighboring hamlet, Medina called on his radio to demand that Calley's men keep moving. Medina had no respect for Calley and did not buy his excuse that the large number of civilians they had collected were slowing them down. Get rid of them, Medina said.

Calley went back to Conti and Paul Meadlo and said, "Take care of them."

"We are," Meadlo said. "We're watching over them."

Calley said, "No, I want them killed."

He moved to stand beside Meadlo and Conti. "We'll get in line and fire into them." When the other two held back, Calley got angry. "Come here! Come here!" he ordered them. "Come on, we'll line them up. We'll kill them."

Conti concocted an excuse about a fault in his grenade launcher and moved away.

Calley said to Meadlo, "Fire when I say, 'Fire.' "

Conti watched as they planted themselves ten feet from the Vietnamese and shot in a spray, back and forth. The Vietnamese screamed as the bullets tore through their bodies and ripped into their heads. Meadlo kept his rifle on automatic. He reloaded a magazine of bullets, fired on semiautomatic and paused to reload again. Instead, he stopped. Tears running down his cheeks, he pressed his rifle on Conti. "You shoot them." Conti shoved the rifle away and pointed at Calley. "Let him do it," he said.

By then, it hardly mattered. Only a few children had survived, sheltered by their mothers. As the dazed children tried to stand, Calley picked them off one by one. When all were dead, he turned away. To Conti, he looked calm. "Okay," Calley said, "let's go."

They moved with other men from the platoon toward the far end of the village, gathering up Vietnamese on the way. Calley halted his prisoners by an irrigation ditch and sat down. Meadlo trotted up, still with tears in his eyes. Forty or fifty villagers were lined up along the ditch. "We've got another job to do," Calley told the ten GIs standing around him. He approached an old Vietnamese in white robes and demanded that he tell them where the Vietcong had gone. The man shook his head helplessly. Calley hit him in the mouth with the butt of his rifle, then broke off the interrogation long enough to retrieve a two-year-old who had climbed from the ditch. Calley picked up the boy, threw him back into the ditch and shot him.

Harry Stanley, who knew some Vietnamese phrases, asked the old man the questions Calley had been putting in English but got the same answers: no Communist soldiers in the village, no weapons. Calley seized him, pushed him into the ditch and shot him with Meadlo's M-16. An elderly woman tried to get to her feet and Calley killed her.

As more Vietnamese prisoners arrived, herded by Calley's men, he ordered them shoved into the ditch. Most GIs obeyed, but James Dursi had been playing with the children, and when he heard that Calley intended to kill the villagers, Dursi said he would not join in. He was already devastated from opening fire on a fleeing villager and then seeing that he had killed a woman and her baby.

Calley told Robert Maples, "Load your machine gun and shoot these people."

Maples shook his head. "I'm not going to do that." Calley pointed his M-16 at Maples. The others protested, and Calley backed down and started firing by himself. Tears or not, Meadlo joined him. Again, mothers tried to shield their babies as other platoon members began to shoot. As Meadlo went on pulling the trigger, he was sobbing. He screamed at Dursi, "Why aren't you firing? Fire! Why don't you fire?" Scraps of bone and flesh were flying out of the ditch.

Ron Haeberle had caught up with Calley's platoon and took pictures as the

GIs burned houses, killed pigs and water buffalo and threw grenades into bunkers. He saw American soldiers rounding up villagers and shooting them. Like Mal Browne and Eddie Adams, Haeberle kept on taking pictures.

Medina's 2nd Platoon was racing through nearby Binh Tay, raping and murdering. Gary Roschevitz lined up seven women between the ages of eighteen and thirty-five and ordered them to strip. He intended to rape all of them. But the first woman became hysterical, the others screamed and Roschevitz opened fire on their naked bodies with his M-79 grenade launcher.

Not every man joined in the carnage. Ridenhour discovered that the day had even produced one act of gallantry. Hugh C. Thompson, a twenty-five-year-old helicopter pilot from the 123rd Aviation Battalion, was hunting out possible enemy targets when he flew over the treetops and found no hostile fire coming at him. Spotting wounded villagers on the ground, he dropped green smoke to bring them help. But when he refueled and returned, they were all dead. Flying as low as five feet over clear ground, Thompson came to a ditch filled with wounded Vietnamese. He set his helicopter down and got out.

Calley trotted up. Thompson asked what was going on. It's none of your business, Calley told him. He was in charge of the ground troops. "I'm the boss here," Calley said.

When Thompson took off again, his crew chief, Glenn Andreotta, told him that Calley's sergeant was shooting the Vietnamese in the ditch. Thompson had served as a Navy Seabee for three years in the early 1960s. He returned to his native Georgia, married and fathered two sons. But managing a funeral home had proved too tame. He signed up for army flight training and made it to Vietnam the last week of 1967. Thompson did not balk at exchanging fire with the enemy or scooping up Vietcong suspects in his chopper for interrogation. But what was happening beneath him was no better than what the Nazis had done.

Flying low over the northern end of the village, he saw a band of Vietnamese—as many as ten, including the children—bolting toward a rough bunker. They were being chased by Americans from the 2nd Platoon returning from Binh Tay.

Thompson landed his helicopter between the villagers and the GIs. He radioed to the gunships overhead that he needed help and instructed his second crewman, an eighteen-year-old door gunner named Lawrence Colburn, to swing his machine gun around until it was trained on the Americans. Above the noise of the rotors, Thompson shouted that if they began to shoot the villagers, Colburn should stop them. "Open up on 'em!" Thompson told him. "Blow 'em away!"

Colburn wondered whether he could bring himself to shoot fellow Americans, but he kept his gun aimed at them.

Thompson jumped out and ran over to Stephen Brooks, the lieutenant in charge. I want to get those people out of here, Thompson said. The only way to do it, Brooks said, was with grenades.

"Just hold your men right where they are," Thompson shouted, "and I'll get the kids out."

Overhead, the gunships heard Thompson's voice breaking as he shouted obscenities at them to land and get the Vietnamese to safety. Two pilots, Danny Millians and Brian Livingston, took the chance. They landed, scooped up two men, two women and several children and flew them away from the carnage.

After twenty minutes on the ground, Thompson was about to fly away for re-fueling. But first he went back to the spot where he had encountered Calley. As they flew over the ditch, Andreotta saw something move. Thompson covered his crewmen as they went to investigate. Andreotta lowered himself four feet into the ditch to step among a hundred bloody corpses. Cowering among the bodies was a three-year-old boy covered in filth and torn flesh. One of Thompson's sons was about his age. He saw the shock on the child's face and flew his limp body to an ARVN hospital. Colburn watched his boss crying as he prepared to land in Quang Ngai.

To RIDENHOUR, it was like lancing a boil. His former buddies from Charlie Company seemed compelled to open up to him. Four of the six men in his new unit had been at My Lai that day, and they all needed to share their sense of guilt and horror. The greatest puzzle was Mike Terry. A devout Mormon, he had impressed Ridenhour in Hawaii as being an unusually decent man.

Now they were together on a new mission as night fell. They found a bunker and settled down under a sky bright with stars. Terry began to tell his story. Ridenhour gave no sign that he had already heard the worst of it. Terry said he and a buddy, Billy Doherty, had stopped for lunch fifteen or twenty feet from the ditch where Calley murdered the villagers.

But as they ate, too much noise was coming from the ditch—the sound of moaning and limbs flopping around disturbed them. Doherty and he got up, walked to the edge and divided up the wounded. "Then we finished them off," Terry told Ridenhour. "Pow, pow. When it was quiet, we sat back down and finished our lunch."

Ridenhour found himself in a rage he did not understand. He had seven months to go in Vietnam, and he would be out on more patrols with these men from Charlie Company. For now, he had to control himself. But if he got home alive, someone was going to pay.

He asked mildly, "Mike, don't you see that it was wrong?"

"I don't know, man." Terry shrugged. "It was just one of those things."

He rolled on his side and went to sleep.

BEFORE JOHNSON'S BROADCAST on March 31, Rusk had called Harriman to say that, in the unlikely event Hanoi responded to his peace overture, the president would be asking Harriman to represent the United States. Watching the broadcast, Harriman heard himself described as "one of our most distinguished Americans," but he was as surprised as everyone else when Johnson took himself out of the campaign. At that, Harriman began pushing so aggressively for a full bombing halt that Max Taylor became nettled and told Johnson that he should replace Harriman with Clifford.

Just as Hanoi's Four Points had been mistaken for a direct answer to Johnson's Johns Hopkins speech, Hanoi Radio's broadcast on April 3 seemed another prompt response to a presidential address. But the Politburo seldom reacted so quickly. The government had been preparing for months to follow up the Tet offensive by relaxing its conditions for beginning talks. Now, before they could send out delicate signals, Johnson was capitulating. News could sometimes be slow in reaching Hanoi, but his statement spread through the capital within minutes. Hanoi's cool radio announcement three days later scarcely reflected the glee the leadership was feeling. While the U.S. government had not fully met the North's legitimate demands, the broadcast noted, and had not satisfied "progressive public opinion in the United States and the world," Ho's government would send representatives to meet with American officials. If they could agree to stop the bombing unconditionally and halt all other acts of war against the North, then genuine peace negotiations could begin.

The day after Hanoi accepted Johnson's offer, Martin Luther King, Jr., the conscience of the civil rights movement, was shot to death in Memphis, Tennessee. The grief and rage of black Americans set off riots, arson and looting in Washington and in more than a hundred other cities across the nation. With 75,000 National Guardsmen and regular army troops on the streets to restore order, Clifford compared the uprising to Vietnam; it was America's domestic Tet. The president canceled a conference planned for Honolulu and summoned Westmoreland to Washington instead.

The general arrived with his usual reassurances. Clifford had noted wryly the portentous way Westmoreland enunciated every word when reporting to the president. "In the negotiations," he assured Johnson now, "Governor Harriman will have a hand with four aces, and the enemy will have two deuces."

Clifford was less amused by Westmoreland's answer when he was asked about the acceptable conditions for a cease-fire. "I do not see any acceptable cease-fire," the general said. "We would just like the North Vietnamese to go home and turn in their weapons."

In Beijing, Zhou Enlai spent the week of April 13 scolding Pham Van Dong. Zhou complained that North Vietnam's agreeing to hold talks amounted to the surrender Westmoreland was seeking. Hanoi's Politburo had made a fatal compromise, he said. In the past, its leaders had insisted on a complete end to bombing in the North. Now they were going to meet, even though bombs continued to fall south of the 20th parallel. And Dong's government had also buckled over the site for a conference. Johnson had said the Americans would go anywhere, yet when Hanoi's leaders proposed Phnom Penh—a clever move, Zhou conceded, to win over Sihanouk—they let Johnson veto their choice. Frankly, Zhou concluded, the world's people were disappointed.

He listed for Dong the several dilemmas facing the American president—Westmoreland's request for another 200,000 troops, which Johnson was refusing; Democratic primary elections that had sharply diminished Johnson's prestige; a crisis in the value of the dollar. Zhou said that the only event the Chinese had not anticipated was the murder of Martin Luther King.

Johnson's March 31 statement was "a wicked and deceitful scheme," Zhou went on. "In fact, he doesn't want to give up the war. The statement is only a means for them to overcome the difficult time. As it turned out, your April 3 statement solved his difficulties." Hanoi had been wrong to compromise. Negotiations were fine but only from a stronger position.

As Zhou continued to belabor the same points, Pham Van Dong protested only once, when Zhou quoted him as saying that North Vietnam would stop sending troops to the South. "No, I have never said that," Dong said. "Never, ever."

Zhou granted that he might have received a mistranslation.

Otherwise, Zhou continued on the offensive. At the end of their talks, Dong assured him that the North was not going soft. "This will of ours is like iron and stone," he said, "which is unshakable."

HARRIMAN FRETTED as a month dragged on with no agreement on where the talks should be held. It was after Washington suggested Geneva that Hanoi countered with Phnom Penh and then rejected Vientiane in Laos as a compromise. In each case, the objection to a site was political but cloaked by technical excuses: Cambodia did not have sufficient communications equipment. Despite the undeniable capacity of the Ho Chi Minh Trail, Hanoi claimed that Laos lacked adequate transportation connections. Washington would have accepted Indonesia's offer to anchor its one Russian-built cruiser off the coast of Vietnam for the conference; Hanoi said the ship lacked sufficient press facilities.

When North Vietnam nominated Warsaw, Harriman called Rostow to urge that the president not turn it down. Too late, Rostow said; a rejection had already been prepared. Harriman got through to Johnson and found that the president's euphoria immediately after renouncing his office had given way to a sullen mood. He would not agree to any East European capital and brushed aside Harriman's argument that a site within the Soviet sphere would undercut China's influence.

Harriman persisted. "I would like to be able to tell you how I feel."

"You have, you see." Johnson hung up as Harriman was saying into the dead line, "I am a soldier. I obey orders."

Xuan Thuy
(Vietnam News Agency)

Rusk had downplayed the likelihood of Paris, but on May 3, Hanoi told Bill Sullivan, now U.S. ambassador in Vientiane, that its delegation could be in Paris within a week. The next morning, Johnson announced his agreement. He was sending Cy Vance, McNamara's former Pentagon deputy, to ensure that Harriman's eagerness to sign a treaty did not blind him to the objections of Rusk and Rostow. Hanoi's delegation would be headed by Xuan Thuy, a plump and cheery member of Hanoi's Central Committee. Harriman had met him six years ago in Geneva.

Not the best educated of Hanoi's officials, Xuan Thuy had been trained in herbal medicine, and he spoke no language but Vietnamese. He had been an early recruit to the Vietminh, however, writing as a journalist for underground newspapers. Over the years, he had moved effectively through various Communist front groups, always persuasive and likable. The Politburo could be sure that Xuan Thuy had a good grasp of its strategy and, whatever the American provocations, would not lose his temper.

Ambassador Bunker had flown to Washington to join in the preparations, although he was even less enthusiastic about the talks than Rusk. Bunker wanted to know why they could not be delayed for another five or six months to let the

South recover more fully from Tet? Clifford thought to himself that, given the respect inspired by Bunker's manner and his seventy-four years, he could present a real obstacle to ending the war.

As negotiations became inevitable, Rusk was evasive about discussing their terms. In the middle of a discussion of the next bombing halt, he would tell again about his various negotiations with the Soviets since the end of World War II. Rusk's lesson was always the same: from Korea to Berlin, Communist negotiators could not be trusted.

With Harriman and Vance preparing to leave for Paris, Rusk grew even more obdurate and refused to draft any fallback positions for them, insisting that they stick to a hard-line opening statement and await further instructions. Harriman held his tongue but shared his anger with Clifford. He had negotiated with Russian leaders going back to Trotsky, he complained. When he had gone to Moscow in 1943, Roosevelt had simply told him to explain America's position to Stalin. "I had no further guidance," Harriman said, still fuming.

More indignities lay ahead. According to the White House, no government planes were available to fly Harriman's team to Paris; they would have to go on a commercial flight. For Clifford, that deliberate slight was finally too much. He took out the bunks from his Defense Department plane and flew the negotiators as far as Paris while he went on to a meeting in Brussels. Harriman had left Washington without ceremony, but Clifford timed the arrival in Paris for maximum publicity. Fifteen hundred international reporters and camera crewmen were waiting in the rain to greet him.

Just as talks were about to open, Rusk recommended resuming air strikes in the North between the 19th and 20th parallels. Clifford argued against escalation at such a sensitive moment and, although Johnson sided with him, Clifford knew that he hated to overrule the trio of Rusk, Rostow and Bus Wheeler. After Clifford won the argument, Wheeler caught him at the door. "I should have gone to law school," he said snidely, "instead of West Point."

At lunch the next week, Johnson revealed the full extent of his own doubts: "I wonder if I should have made my speech on March 31 at all."

XUAN THUY had included in his delegation other revolutionaries who had spent their adult lives fighting for independence. One was Nguyen Minh Vy, the man who had once run the Vietminh's Fifth Zone and had gone reluctantly to Hanoi to await the election of 1956. During the past twelve years, Vy had risen to become director of Hanoi's General Department of Information.

From the first sessions on May 13, any progress looked as unpromising as Rusk had predicted. With both sides trading stale accusations, the number of reporters in the hall quickly dwindled. But in Washington, Clifford remained upbeat. Polemics were to be expected, and at least the North had issued no ultimatum.

By May 21, however, Johnson was getting restless and more receptive to the urging from Rusk, Rostow and Wheeler that he move the bombing back up to the 20th parallel. "I think our force brought them to the table, not our eloquence of March 31," Johnson said sarcastically. To make his lone voice heard, Clifford was becoming strident. "We can hope only for success in Paris," he said. "We are in a war we can't win. They can't win the war militarily. We can't win the war militarily."

"I disagree," said the president, but significantly, Bus Wheeler said merely, "I disagree to some extent." Rusk was unyielding: "We will not get a solution in Paris until we prove they can't win in the South." But Johnson again put off a decision on taking the bombing further north.

When Cy Vance came back to brief Johnson on May 28, he provided Clifford with welcome reinforcement. Bombing north of the 20th parallel would lead Hanoi to break off the talks, Vance said. Xuan Thuy's delegates had lately all become a little less doctrinaire. Thuy had admitted, for example, that Tet had caused civilian casualties in Hue. It was essential now to begin private talks.

Johnson asked whether he could expect any movement in the three months before the Democratic convention. Most unlikely, Vance said. "Are they polite?" the president asked.

"Polite, proper," Vance replied. "But their words are very strong."

McNamara had been invited back for Vance's briefing; his advice was muted and cautious. Hearing about Hue, he urged that Washington release all of its intelligence data about past Communist outrages. And if bombing farther north would help at the conference table, McNamara added, do it.

WHILE JOHNSON was debating the effect of a military move on the Paris talks, the Communists acted. By the end of April, they had pulled their troops away from Khe Sanh, but Communist artillery deep in the Co Roc Mountains of Laos could keep Khe Sanh under attack. The two local U.S. commanders, General William Rosson and Lieutenant General Robert Cushman saw the base as a liability and had it all but shut down when Westmoreland showed up in Phu Bai and learned what they had done. Westmoreland could not admit that the base had no value, and fellow officers agreed that they had never seen him so angry. He overrode Rosson and Cushman, then refused to stay long enough to discuss his decision. The next day, Marines began to unpack their gear and dig out the trenches they had just filled in. When Abrams replaced Westmoreland, he shut the base down again.

By that time, the Communists were ready for their May offensive, and Khe Sanh was irrelevant to their plans. They struck instead south of the base at the town of Dong Ha. Some Politburo members had questioned the wisdom of another offensive so soon after Tet's disappointments, but the majority felt that the Paris delegates needed another show of force. "The war has entered a very fierce, complex stage of strategic offensive attacks aimed at securing final victory," the Communist resolution read. By the time the sporadic fighting around Dong Ha ended on May 30, the Americans had lost 327 dead and another 1,200 wounded. U.S. estimates put the North Vietnam losses at nearly 3,600 men. But world attention focused again on the lighter action around Saigon.

Since Tet, a sweep by more than eighty American and ARVN battalions had tried to rid the city and its surroundings of Vietcong and northern regulars. Although it was called Operation Complete Victory—Toan Thang, in Vietnamese—the battalions missed many caches of weapons that Dang's men had brought to the capital and not used during Tet. That included 100 pounds of TNT that a Vietcong taxi driver exploded on May 4 outside Saigon's broadcast studios. The blast set off the assault, and throughout the early hours, Saigon had been hit with rockets and mortar shells.

That was no one-time raid. For the next five days, the Vietcong engaged South Vietnamese Marines in Cholon, at Tan Son Nhut airfield and across a French cemetery. MACV brought in planes and helicopter gunships that razed entire city blocks and sent frightened Vietnamese running from their homes. By the time the fighting flickered out in mid-May, at least 500 civilians were dead and possibly 4,500 wounded. Many were children. Two of Ky's backers, a Saigon police official and the commander of the 5th ARVN Ranger Group, were killed by a U.S. helicopter gunship as they watched the action from the porch of a high school. Ky's loyalists swore the deaths were intentional, an American scheme to bolster Thieu.

Like Ben Tre, Saigon seemed to have been saved by its own destruction. Charles Sweet, a civilian on Ed Lansdale's staff, reported that the havoc caused by U.S. aircraft had left many Vietnamese "bitterly resentful" of the Americans. Bus Wheeler could not entirely deny Sweet's charge but said that U.S. commanders on the scene had "demonstrated a high degree of concern both for civilian casualties and property destruction." Clifford, though, asked why the army could not avoid so much civilian damage, and his question found Abrams in no mood to be diplomatic. He shot back the response of a general chagrined to be caught once again by surprise.

Abrams lived in Saigon, he wrote, and was "fully aware of the extent to which horror, destruction, sacrifice and pain have risen in this war this year.

"I have had two sons serving here," the general continued, "one of whom is here now and extending. If somehow a sensing has developed that I have been in too many wars to be concerned and sensitive to its pain or that I am too busy with plans or campaigns or something else to spend time on correcting the destruction of war, let me set the record straight. I recognize all this as my responsibility. I need no urging to look into it, investigate it or explain other ways. I live with it twenty-four hours a day."

To Clifford, Abrams's reply was rambling and emotional, and he wondered whether he was the right man for the job. He took his misgivings to the president, who agreed that Abrams must be told his tone was unacceptable. The general's resulting apology was contrite. He even allowed that his commanders had "in fact benefited from the investigation growing out of the Sweet report."

Clifford had watched Truman handle MacArthur. Convinced that Abrams now knew his place, he let him keep his job.

ON JUNE 5 AT 3:30 A.M., Washington time, Walt Rostow called the president to inform him that Robert Kennedy had been shot in the kitchen of the Ambassador Hotel in Los Angeles. The day before, Gene McCarthy had won the Oregon primary by 45 percent to Kennedy's 39 percent, but Kennedy had edged him out in California and had beaten him in South Dakota, the home state of another antiwar senator, George McGovern. Kennedy had been celebrating his victory when he was shot by Sirhan Bishara Sirhan, a twenty-four-year-old Palestinian immigrant.

Johnson talked with Ramsey Clark, the man who had replaced Katzenbach as attorney general, and ordered the Secret Service to extend protection to all candidates and their families. As Kennedy lingered near death in Good Samaritan Hospital in Los Angeles, Johnson's advisers worked to persuade him that he must make an appearance on television; merely issuing a statement would not be enough. He had spoken after the shooting of Martin Luther King, Jr. To do less now would make him look petty and vindictive.

At 10:07 P.M., with Kennedy still alive but past recovery, Johnson went before the country to hail his long-time adversary as "a young leader of uncommon energy and dedication." Johnson had been meeting with congressmen throughout the day in hopes of reviving gun-control legislation they had recently eviscerated. Now he announced the formation of a National Commission on the Causes and Prevention of Violence. But to Kennedy's partisans, the violence in Vietnam had contributed to the dangerous mood at home. The fiercest among them held Johnson more accountable for Kennedy's death than Sirhan.

At 5:01 A.M. on June 6, Robert Kennedy died and Johnson declared a day of national mourning.

FROM WASHINGTON, Rusk and Rostow had effectively brought the Paris peace talks to a standstill. The day of the California primary, Johnson received a private message from Soviet Premier Aleksei Kosygin, urging a complete halt of the bombing in North Vietnam. "My colleagues and I believe, and have grounds to believe," according to Kosygin, that an end to the bombing would lead to a breakthrough in the talks. Le Duc Tho, a senior Politburo member, had stopped over in Moscow on his way to Paris to shore up Hanoi's delegation. Although Kosygin did not say so, he had that firm assurance from Tho.

Clifford was eager to explore the offer, but Johnson was not persuaded and agreed with Rusk—who, for once, was the first to speak up. Rusk demanded that Hanoi first spell out how it would reciprocate. When Rusk's question reached Paris, Xuan Thuy responded with a puckish guarantee: Hanoi would gladly pledge not to bomb the United States.

Clifford also learned that Rostow had instructed the State Department's executive secretary, Benjamin Read, not to send to the Pentagon any sensitive telegrams from the Paris negotiations. Read protested the stratagem to Rusk, who agreed that Clifford should not be cut out of the loop and told Read to set up a private messenger service to take the wires to Clifford. But he should not tell Rostow that his orders were being disobeyed. From Read and others, Clifford heard that the jovial Rostow was now regularly disparaging him behind his back. Negative judgments on the war had become "Cliffordisms." If Rostow considered another official defeatist, the man had been "Cliffordized."

In mid-June, Clifford learned that Vance and the North Vietnamese had agreed to hold private talks and expressed his guarded optimism to reporters. This time, it was Rusk who chided him. Clifford's remarks had increased the pressure on the United States to give ground, he explained. Privately, Rusk went further: once Clifford became defense secretary, he had "lost his nerve."

Nguyen Duy Trinh, Hanoi's foreign minister, had told his delegation early in the talks that the Politburo would approve behind-the-scenes negotiations so long as the United States could not use them to sway public opinion. On June 15, Trinh authorized "contacts for probing purposes, not yet for bargaining." When Le Duc Tho arrived at the conference, his title was special adviser to Xuan Thuy, but he immediately became the North's ranking delegate.

Born Phan Dinh Khai in a northern province, Tho was in his late fifties, a graduate of the usual French jails—Hanoi prison, Son La penitentiary, Poulo Condore Island. Hardship had annealed his dedication, and underlings feared his severity. They called him "the Hammer." In 1949, he had gone to the South to serve with Le Duan, but he found the region uncongenial and returned north five years later. As he rose in Hanoi and entered the Politburo, Tho remained loyal to Le Duan and larded every ministry with men faithful to both of them.

After Tet, Tho had gone south again to reinforce COSVN and prepare for the May offensive. His presence in Paris ensured that Le Duan's wishes would be met without question. Public meetings at the Majestic Hotel would remain empty propaganda exercises. Any chance of peace would come only from contact with Tho.

Arranging for the private sessions meant overcoming suspicion on both sides, and Vance had to promise formally that he, Harriman and their aides would not arrive with concealed weapons. The meetings were to be held at three "safe houses," two owned by the North Vietnamese, one rented by the CIA in a suburb called Sceaux. Early on the evening of June 26, Vance and Phil Habib slipped out of the U.S. embassy and into an unmarked car to meet with the deputy chief of the North's delegation. On arriving for their tryst, they found French intelligence agents in brand-new overalls pretending to work on a nearby fire hydrant. The next day, Harriman called the French Foreign Ministry. "You get those damned goons away," he said. If they were not gone, he and Vance would go home and announce to the world why it was impossible to hold negotiations in Paris. The Communist delegates met the challenge another way. They sent out several members to buy lumber and hardware and built a soundproof room within their quarters where they could retire for privacy.

Despite their efforts, all the French would have learned from that first meeting was that progress was going to be as slow as Rusk could wish. Vance read to the North's delegates from typewritten instructions. As they understood the translation, he was saying, "The U.S. will stop the bombing all over the North on a day to be announced." But first came Washington's conditions: Vance said the United States was concerned about shelling from the Demilitarized Zone and about the North's massive reinforcements passing through the zone. The Communists must respect DMZ neutrality, refrain from rocket attacks on major southern cities and enter promptly into talks with the South. The Communists replied that there was nothing new in the U.S. position except its offer to set a specific date. Otherwise, whatever Vance and Habib might claim, they were still setting conditions for an end to the bombing.

That first exchange ran for more than two hours and ended after midnight. Hearing about its tenor, Clifford allowed himself a measure of optimism. At least the two sides were talking.

Bui Diem, who had been serving as South Vietnam's ambassador in Washington for eighteen months, came to Paris as a mere observer, a passive role he found humiliating for his country. The future of South Vietnam was being decided and yet no South Vietnamese was taking part. Two or three times a week, he drove to the U.S. embassy to learn what he could say about the meaningless public sessions before he met with reporters from Europe and America. He often repeated that direct negotiations between South and North would be the shortest route to peace, but he knew the Hanoi delegates would reject his offer. To the Communists, he represented a puppet government. Better to deal with the men who pulled his strings.

When Bui Diem agreed to meet with Vietnamese students living in Paris, he found most of them hostile to Thieu and Ky. Diem hammered away at one point. "Everyone knows the saying that only the one under the blanket knows what goes on in bed," he told them. "Well, I am under the blanket, so I know what goes on. And I have serious reservations about those people. But I can tell you there is a chance of working with Thieu and Ky. With the other side, there is no chance to do anything."

Each week from Tuesday to Friday, Diem argued the case for his government. But the Communists were frank about using the public meetings as a forum to build international support, and Diem was overshadowed by Mrs. Nguyen Thi Ngoc Dung from the NLF, who gained sympathy each time she took her cause to another European capital.

Fridays, Bui Diem took the TWA afternoon flight back to Washington to monitor the U.S. presidential campaign. Antiwar protests had spread from America to France. Together with demonstrators from student and labor movements, they clogged Paris streets and sometimes shut down Orly Airport. To get to America for Robert Kennedy's funeral, Bui Diem had to fly from Brussels. During one weekend stopover in Washington in mid-June, Diem was asked whether he would care to meet Richard Nixon, the likely Republican presidential nominee. Since he lost to Jack Kennedy in 1960, politics had been unrewarding for Nixon. Two years afterward, he had run for governor of California and lost to Edmund G. Brown, the liberal incumbent. For Nixon, it had been humiliating enough to seek a statewide office when he had come so close to the presidency. But to lose to Brown meant the end of his political career. The next morning, fatigued and sodden from sleeping pills, Nixon lashed out at reporters at a surreal press conference. "You won't have Nixon to kick around anymore" became a national joke, and he seemed resigned to life as a well-paid East Coast attorney. But patiently, Nixon had rebuilt his reputation. After the landslide in 1964 seemed to crush the conservative wing of his party, centrist Republicans were lining up behind his second chance at the prize.

The woman offering Bui Diem the introduction was Anna Chennault, widow of the air corps general who had once presented Ho with his autographed picture. After the war, Claire Chennault had built the Flying Tigers into an air freight company with lucrative Defense Department contracts. His wife, born to Chinese parents, had a sister living in Saigon and visited there regularly. Ky had introduced her to Bui Diem, who saw her often in Washington, where she moved easily in political circles.

As for meeting Nixon, Bui Diem said he had to think the offer over. He wanted to keep both parties committed to South Vietnam, but seeing Nixon could jeopardize his influence with the Democrats. When he finally did agree to the meeting, he told no one in Saigon so that, if necessary, Thieu could say he had not authorized it. To be doubly safe, however, Diem confided in Bill Bundy at State; he had been seeing Bundy often about progress in Paris. At his office, Bundy gave the meeting his blessing after Diem assured him that he would divulge nothing to Nixon about the Paris talks. Bill Bundy knew, as Bui Diem did not, that the CIA had him under surveillance, and the National Security Council was intercepting his cables to Saigon.

On July 12, Bui Diem flew to New York and joined Mrs. Chennault at the Hotel Pierre, where Nixon kept a suite. John Mitchell, Nixon's law partner, was also there. Washington gossip had prepared Diem to find Nixon off-putting and graceless, but he listened carefully to Diem's thoughts on the war. Diem said he expected America to withdraw from his country, but if the ARVN was to take over the fighting, a crash program was essential, especially to supply M-16 rifles. Nixon endorsed his ideas and thanked him for coming. Bui Diem left the Pierre pleased with the interview.

CLIFFORD FLEW TO SAIGON on July 14 for his first trip to the war zone since becoming defense secretary. He found that a lull in the fighting was being interpreted in one of two ways: Either the Communists were regrouping for a fall offensive in hopes of influencing the U.S. elections. Or, as Harriman and Vance cabled from Paris, the North Vietnamese were giving a tacit sign that they would respect the DMZ in exchange for total suspension of the bombing. But the Harriman cable to Johnson arrived on the same day that both Humphrey and a *New York Times* editorial recommended a complete bombing halt. Furious, Johnson told Rusk to call a press conference and warn of Communist preparations for a major new attack. When Xuan Thuy's delegates read Rusk's remarks, they asked whether the American contingent in Paris really spoke for the president these days. Publicly, Harriman kept silent, but he told his associates that Rusk had just wiped out everything they had tried to do in Paris.

In Vietnam, Clifford was depressed by the response he was getting. He told Thieu and Ky that the American people would not support the war much longer unless they saw progress. If the Paris talks failed, the ARVN would have to take over the war. From their reaction, Clifford left convinced that Thieu and Ky did not want the war to end so long as they were protected by half a million American soldiers and enjoying what Clifford called "a golden flow of money." He denounced as "shocking and outrageous" their demand for more equipment—including three to four hundred helicopters and T-39 jets for the personal use of senior South Vietnamese officials.

At the embassy, Clifford told Bunker and his deputy, Samuel Berger, that they would all be derelict if they did not use the last six months of Johnson's term to end the war honorably. But Bunker rejected his suggestion that he lean on Thieu hard enough to get serious peace talks underway.

Conferring with Johnson in Hawaii afterward, Clifford was not sure whether his approach would prevail. Thieu had also flown to Honolulu, and the two presidents met privately. Afterward, Johnson said that he had raised Clifford's points with Thieu. But Thieu had started to get more congenial advice elsewhere, along with assurances that he could safely ignore a lame-duck president.

VICE PRESIDENT HUMPHREY had been reduced to playing the double game that had wracked McNamara for so long. He needed the approval of the antiwar faction but did not dare alienate the man responsible for his nomination. When Johnson heard that Humphrey was considering even a mild veering from his policy, he denounced the vice president to his advisers as weak and disloyal. Johnson's resentment grew when he learned that Humphrey wanted the Democratic Platform Committee to draft a statement on the war that would somehow reconcile the two branches of the party.

At the Tuesday Lunch on July 24, Johnson said he planned to set up a meeting with the likely Republican nominee. "I want to sit down with Mr. Nixon to see what kind of world he really wants," Johnson said. "When he gets the nomination, he may be more responsible. He says he is for our position in Vietnam. He thinks the Democrats will go the other way."

Two days later, Johnson met with Nixon at 7 P.M. in the White House for an exploratory talk. Only Rusk and Rostow were present; Tom Johnson took notes. It proved to be a meeting of minds. Nixon said his Republican advisers wanted him to call for a complete bombing halt, but he considered bombing the "one piece of leverage you have left."

Rusk agreed. "If the North Vietnamese were not being bombed, they would have no incentive to do anything."

As he was leaving, Nixon said, "I have admired the way all of you have stood up through great fire. This is a hard time. Where was the war lost?"

It was the ultimate question, and Rusk had the answer: "In the editorial rooms of this country."

Nixon then undercut both Clifford and the negotiators in Paris. "I do not intend to advocate a bombing pause," he said.

NIXON RECEIVED his party's nomination in Miami and selected as his running mate Spiro Agnew, the governor of Maryland. In his acceptance speech, Nixon told the convention, "America is in trouble today not because her people have failed but because her leaders have failed." Johnson overlooked the rhetoric and invited Nixon and Agnew to his ranch for an official briefing with Cy Vance, who had come from Paris to answer questions. Again, the meeting was agreeable but very general. Rusk prophesied that the next American administration would see changes in the Communist world. "Mao is 75," Rusk said. "There is lots of ferment that may evolve into a non-Communist mainland."

Clifford missed the briefing but was appalled when the president told him that Nixon had promised not to criticize current policy so long as Johnson did not soften it. Clifford saw the trap Nixon had sprung. Humphrey was now saddled with an inflexible policy.

As the Democratic convention opened on August 25, Humphrey's go-betweens, including Ted Sorensen, seemed to have achieved a platform miracle. Their compromise did not call for a bombing halt with no conditions—as Hanoi and voices within Johnson's administration advocated. Nor did it insist on the guarantees that Rusk and Rostow demanded—that North Vietnam promise not to take advantage of the halt. Humphrey was proposing a bombing halt that "took into account, most importantly, the risk to American troops as well as the response from Hanoi."

It was not much of a deviation from Johnson's line, but it mollified the party's antiwar faction. Rusk said, "We can live with this, Hubert." Rostow also signed off, but with his fingers crossed. On Johnson's orders, he had already sent Abrams a secret cable asking whether the bombing continued to be worthwhile. Unaware that his reply would influence a political platform dispute, Abrams wired back defending the value of the raids. At that, Johnson called Humphrey to say he would not accept the compromise plank.

The vice president protested. "Dean Rusk approved it."

"That's not the way I hear it," Johnson said sharply. "Well, this plank just undercuts our whole policy and, by God, the Democratic party ought not to be doing that to me, and you ought not to be doing it. You've been a part of this policy."

Humphrey's instinct was to defy the president and stick with his compromise, but the platform chairman, Hale Boggs, said he would pass the word that the White House found the plank unacceptable. When Boggs showed portions of Abrams's cable to key committee members, Humphrey buckled. He gave up the fight, and the convention gave Johnson his tough plank in a Pyrrhic vote of 1,567 to 1,041.

Publicly, the president was pretending to be above the fray, even though he was controlling the convention as tightly as he had four years earlier; each morning, Humphrey's son-in-law had to get in line to get tickets for the vice president's family. To be sure that Humphrey was not planning even greater defections from his policies, Johnson ordered the FBI to tap his phones. And he sent his fellow Texan John Connally to the governors of the southern delegations to learn whether they would support an attempt to draft Johnson for a second term, after all. The president might have been using the threat as a way to keep Humphrey in line. Or he may have thought that since Nixon was endorsing much the same Vietnam policy Johnson could beat the Republicans. Or possibly he simply wanted to be asked and then say no. Reports floated among the Democrats that Richard Daley's dream ticket would be LBJ and TEK—Theodore Edward Kennedy. But Connally had to report back that, with varying degrees of tact, the southerners had all said, "No way." And Mayor Daley was having troubles of his own.

DALEY'S GRIP on his city rivaled Johnson's control of the convention. Antiwar activists had already tried to disrupt the Republican convention in Miami. When they applied for permits to demonstrate in Chicago, Daley's park officials said permission would not be given to groups that were "unpatriotic." Daley knew the demonstrators would be coming anyway. He ringed the convention amphitheater with barbed wire and put the entire 11,000-member Chicago police force on twelve-hour shifts. Some 6,000 mobilized National Guardsmen were run through special training with instructors impersonating long-haired rebels. On tap in the suburbs were 7,500 U.S. Army soldiers; those who came from the 101st Airborne were equipped with flamethrowers and bazookas. One rumor among the demonstrators claimed that 1,000 FBI agents had also come to Chicago. And those figures did not include the undercover agents who had infiltrated various hippie and antiwar groups.

Todd Gitlin, a leader in Students for a Democratic Society since the early 1960s, was apprehensive about a clash between the police and his fellow demonstrators. "Chicago May Host a Festival of Blood" ran one underground newspaper headline, and Gitlin paraphrased a popular lyric about San Francisco and flowers: "If you're going to Chicago, be sure to wear some armor in your hair."

Tom Hayden and Rennie Davis, another early SDS organizer, had first pledged not to advocate violence, and they deplored the shift toward bloody confrontation among the new SDS leaders. With the convention about to begin, the lack of city permits, a fear of the Chicago police and loud dissension within the movement's ranks threatened to cut the expected turnout from tens of thousands to three or four thousand. Hayden hoped that even the smaller numbers would panic Daley. If the mayor did not resort to repression so severe that the convention would be shut down, at least his tactics would be exposed to the world. To Gitlin, the protesters who did show up seemed to have come for nostalgia or to cap their summer's campaign against the war. They were not in Chicago because of Gene McCarthy. With no heart for running against his fellow Minnesotan, McCarthy was urging supporters to stay away.

On the Friday before the convention opened, Abbie Hoffman, Jerry Rubin and their band of political cutups called Yippies nominated a pig as their candidate for president. They turned "Pigasus" loose in the Civic Center Plaza, where Chicago police seized it and arrested Rubin and five others. On Saturday night, Yippie leaders called upon the crowd in Lincoln Park on Chicago's North Side to respect the 11 P.M. curfew. To dissipate tensions, Allen Ginsberg, the Beat poet, led a chant of "Om." When the motorcycle police arrived on the dot of eleven, Ginsberg was gone and only a handful of Yippies were arrested for refusing to leave the park.

The Yippies had planned a Festival of Life for Sunday but had been denied use of the Lincoln Park sound system. Police blocked the flatbed truck they intended to use as a stage for a rock band, and voices in the crowd began to shout insults at Daley's cops: "Pigs eat shit!" and "Kill the pigs! Fuck the pigs!" There was no way to tell whether the cries came from demonstrators or from government provocateurs who had infiltrated several of the groups. Certainly, no one knew that a strongly built blond biker in a black T-shirt and dark glasses was an undercover policeman named Robert Pierson. He was keeping Rubin under surveillance by volunteering to be his bodyguard.

By the curfew, the Yippies and other demonstrators outnumbered the 458 police two to one. But the police had tear gas and shotguns, and the Yippies had only imprecations and a few rocks and bottles. "Motherfuckers!" they shouted while the police were calling to each other, "Kill the Commies!" Before tear gas drove the crowd away, police had also attacked half a dozen reporters and photographers.

Early on the Monday afternoon of August 28, with the convention opening that evening, Hayden was taken into custody and charged with disorderly conduct, resisting arrest and obstruction. Rennie Davis led 500 protesters on a march to police headquarters with some carrying Vietcong flags, others Communism's red banner. Police taped over their identifying badges and broke up the throng with billy clubs.

Freed on bail, Hayden ditched the policemen assigned to tail him and drove by Lincoln Park, where demonstrators were promoting a rally on Tuesday billed as the Yippies' Unbirthday Party for LBJ. One of the men following Hayden, a Chicago policeman named Ralph Bell, spotted him in the crowd, tackled him, beat him and pushed him into a police car. Friends followed the car to the station and by 3 A.M., Hayden had been bailed out a second time. From then on, he wore a false beard, sunglasses, love beads and either a yellow-brimmed hat or a football helmet.

Tuesday afternoon Bobby Seale, chairman of the Black Panthers, flew in from Oakland to exhort the crowd to revolution. Following him to the microphone, Jerry Rubin endorsed Seale's call for "roasting pigs." That night, demonstrators once more flouted the curfew by going to Grant Park, across from the Conrad Hilton Hotel, where many of the convention delegates were staying. For an hour or two, the scene was idyllic, as demonstrators lay on the grass and listened to Peter, Paul and Mary, a folk trio, perform songs like "This Land Is Your Land." But at 3 A.M., 600 National Guard troops descended in full battle gear. Worried about mass arrests, Hayden took a bullhorn and urged that everyone go home.

The Mobilization rally in Grant Park on Wednesday afternoon drew the biggest crowd yet, about 10,000 people, most of them from Chicago. A young man climbed the park's flagpole, and people cried to him to lower the Stars and Stripes to half mast or fly it upside down. From the stage, the organizers shouted that he should leave the flag alone. By that time, Chicago police, marching two by two, had clubbed their way through the crowd. Rennie Davis moved toward the flagpole, and police split open his head and left him bleeding. Protesters picked up whatever was at hand and hurled it at the officers—shoes, flaming rags, sticks from their placards, chunks of park bench.

As the police drew back, Hayden caught the crowd's attention by repeating, "Rennie has been taken to the hospital and we have to avenge him." He called on the people to move out of the park and take the battle into every Chicago neighborhood. "Let us make sure," Hayden shouted, "that if our blood flows, it flows all over the city, and if we are gassed that they gas themselves! See you in the streets!"

The demonstrators were dispersed by charging police officers who waded into their midst without restraint or discipline. In about twenty minutes, the police clubbed down children, women, reporters and clergymen. Amid the wounded and bleeding, Dick Gregory, a black comedian and pacifist, told the crowd not to blame the cops. They were just following orders from Mayor Daley and "the crooks downtown," Gregory said.

As delegates in the amphitheater were rejecting the antiwar plank, Mobe organizers ignored their lack of a permit and marched down Michigan Avenue to the Hilton. It was nearly dark, but television lights illuminated the scene as the National Guard fired tear gas, which spread down the avenue and into the hotel's air-conditioning ducts. Chicago police, marching double quick, again beat anyone in their way. The crowd took up a chant: "The whole world is watching!" On their side, police were shouting, "Get out of here, you cocksuckers."

Vulgarity was not confined to the streets. During a seconding speech for Humphrey, television screens inside the convention hall began to pick up the scenes of violence. When Senator Abraham Ribicoff of Connecticut rose to nominate George McGovern, the antiwar senator from South Dakota, the podium placed him directly in front of Mayor Daley. Repelled by the bloody scenes on television, Ribicoff paused in his speech and spoke directly to the mayor: "With George McGovern, we wouldn't have Gestapo tactics on the streets of Chicago." The pandemonium in the hall spared television viewers Daley's roar of "Fuck you, you Jew son of a bitch! You lousy motherfucker! Go home!" Ribicoff may not have heard every word, but he could not miss Daley's contorted face. "How hard it is to accept the truth," he said, with a sigh. "How hard it is."

Humphrey's nomination was declared unanimous shortly before midnight, even though hundreds of delegates were shouting "No!"

The convention was ending. A march on Thursday provoked more rounds of tear gas, and nine Democratic delegates were among the several hundred arrests. At 5 A.M. Friday, ashtrays and beer cans came hurtling down from the Hilton's fifteenth floor. Hotel employees identified the rooms as those occupied by McCarthy's staff and gave police permission to clear the area. The result was a last round of indiscriminate beatings.

IN PARIS, seventeen public meetings on Avenue Kleber had dragged the peace talks into early September. Harriman proposed another private session, this one with Le Duc Tho and Xuan Thuy. The Communists accepted but gave no sign of the elation they were feeling. Among themselves, they admitted that the second wave of the General Offensive in May had accomplished little. All the same, the Communists had launched a third wave, believing that the offensive must continue until the U.S. troops were defeated. But by now, the combined NLF and PAVN forces were severely weakened, and Hanoi could no longer expect an uprising in the rural provinces. The one bright development was that under Abrams the American troops were shifting to a more defensive posture and giving up Westmoreland's tactic of search-and-destroy. From Hanoi and Paris, the Communists watched Humphrey's numbers dropping in the polls as he refused to break with Johnson over the war. By early August, the Politburo had voted this resolution: "Should the U.S. want to settle the Vietnam question in accordance with our minimal position before we win decisive victory, we should not miss the opportunity."

The United States first proposed holding the Tho-Harriman private talks on Sunday, September 8, at its small and remote villa on Boileau Street. The North Vietnamese shifted the locale to its delegates' residence in the town of Vitry-sur-Seine. Upon convening, Phil Habib opened with a conciliatory statement that "serious talks" should include Thieu's representative and that the North was welcome to invite the NLF.

The Communists conceded nothing. Xuan Thuy said his government's attitude had always been serious, whether here or in public. Le Duc Tho then spoke for nearly an hour from ten typewritten pages, blaming America and assailing its expenditure of men and ammunition. Seeing Harriman bridle, Xuan Thuy proposed a break, and Harriman instantly agreed. "I have had many things stuffed in my head," he complained.

After a half-hour respite, Tho pulled out another four pages and read about demoralized GIs, about the way this most costly of wars was draining U.S. gold reserves, about the growing American antiwar movement. Listening, Harriman fidgeted but did not interrupt. When Tho finished, the allotted time had run out. They agreed that they should try for two meetings a week.

Convening again on Thursday, September 12, Tho got a laugh by beginning, "Last time, Mr. Harriman said he had been stuffed with many things. Today, I'll continue to do so."

"Make an effort to listen, please," Xuan Thuy said fussily.

"We are a patient people," Harriman replied.

Suddenly, Tho was at his most pliant. South Vietnam could be independent and neutral. North Vietnam might even establish diplomatic relations with the United States. But first, Washington must stop unconditionally all bombing of the North, including the panhandle region closest to the DMZ. If the White House insisted on its own solution of de-Americanizing the war while retaining the South as its neocolonial property, the war would go on. "You will step up the war in South Vietnam and resume the bombing of the North," Tho said, "but anyway you will fail."

After a break, Harriman thanked Tho for his straight talk but insisted on cer-

tain concessions before the president would stop the bombing entirely. He also
threw back at Tho his earlier charges: This was not America's costliest war; it was
taking at most 3.5 percent of the country's gross national product. Korea had
taken 14 percent of the GNP in 1953, and World War II, 50 percent. But Harriman granted that the Vietnam war was an unpleasant burden. As for which side
was sure to fail, Harriman said, "You've lost 140,000 men from Tet to this day
without succeeding in seizing any city, any U.S. military base." Rubbing it in, he
added, "The so-called General Uprising has also failed."

All the same, Harriman said that the United States was ready to withdraw its
troops when Hanoi withdrew the PAVN, and he alluded to Johnson's pledge to
aid in reconstructing Indochina, including North Vietnam.

HUMPHREY HAD EMERGED from the Democratic convention 22 points behind
Nixon in the polls, and the early days of his campaign offered him no encouragement. Privately, he blamed Johnson for delaying the convention to coincide
with his birthday on August 27. A late convention might be an advantage for an
incumbent, but it was a liability for the candidate who then lost a month to organize before the traditional Labor Day kickoff. Humphrey had been Minnesota's favorite-son candidate for president as long ago as 1952. Now the violence
in Chicago had blighted what he had expected to be the happiest day of his political life. Humphrey had to admit that Nixon had looked presidential accepting
the Republican nomination in Miami and worried that he himself was appearing
fatuous. In his ebullience, Humphrey had remarked that he favored the "politics
of joy." With the war claiming new victims every day, with the assassinations of
King and Kennedy and with rioting in major American cities, it was not a season
to proclaim joy.

As the campaign progressed, Humphrey became inured to placards that
read DUMP THE HUMP or A LESSER EVIL IS STILL AN EVIL. In Seattle, his speech was
interrupted by a man with a bullhorn who bellowed, "Mr. Humphrey, you are
being accused now of complicity in the deaths of tens of thousands of Americans
and hundreds of thousands of Vietnamese." At Stanford University, a mob attacked Humphrey's car, and he was assailed even as he took a break at the Marl-
boro Music Festival in Vermont. Humphrey had enjoyed a piano recital by
Rudolf Serkin until a young woman shouted "Warmonger!" and spat in his face.

As Humphrey toured the South, audiences waved posters of George Wallace, the segregationist governor of Alabama. In running for president, Wallace
hoped to siphon away Democratic votes the way Strom Thurmond had cut into
Truman's southern support in 1948. In Boston, with Ted Kennedy at his side, the
crowd shouted insults and raised middle fingers in a gesture that even Humphrey
could not interpret as a pledge of support.

By late September, the vice president saw that he must take the gamble he
had resisted at the convention. George Ball, who was leaving his post at the

United Nations, flew to Salt Lake City to look over a speech that had been written and edited by squads of Democrats; one of them, Larry O'Brien, was now Humphrey's campaign manager. Ball pronounced the text not as strong as he would have preferred, but he called Harriman in Paris to be sure that Humphrey could not be accused of hindering the peace talks. Then Ball moved among reporters on the campaign trail to assure them that what might seem like a policy rehash was actually a significant break.

On September 30, Humphrey screwed up his nerve and called the president fifteen minutes before he was due to speak. Johnson listened to him outline what he intended to say: "As President, I would stop the bombing of North Vietnam as an acceptable risk for peace." But Humphrey also called upon the Communists to respect the DMZ, and he reserved the right to resume bombing if Hanoi showed "bad faith."

When Humphrey finished, Johnson said, "I gather you're not asking my advice."

That was true, Humphrey said, but nothing in the speech either embarrassed Johnson or imperiled the Paris talks.

"Well, you're going to give the speech anyway," Johnson said curtly. "Thanks for calling, Hubert." He hung up. Six days earlier, Johnson had told Clifford that he would respect Humphrey more if he "showed he had some balls." Now the president did not like what he had been shown.

The voters did. Flying to Nashville the next day, Humphrey found new, if tentative, respect. Amid the Wallace signs were others with variations on the same theme—IF YOU MEAN IT, WE'RE FOR YOU. In Boston, crowds were now shouting, "Humphrey's Our Man," and local candidates who had ducked having their picture taken with Humphrey were crowding the dais wherever he spoke. By October, his rising poll numbers brought him within five points of Nixon's 40 percent, and Wallace was slipping steadily.

Johnson had not approved of Humphrey choosing Ed Muskie of Maine as his vice presidential candidate. He thought the nominee should have been someone who could help the ticket in the South. But Muskie was a solid and dignified campaigner, a telling contrast with Agnew, who was blundering from gaffe to gaffe. He accused Humphrey of being "soft on Communism," then claimed not to have realized that the phrase dated back to the red-baiting days of Joe McCarthy.

In Paris, signs were also favoring the vice president. On October 11 in the town of Sceaux, negotiators met at a small house the Americans kept on Touraine Street. Although the house had only a single room, Harriman had laid in caviar and champagne, and it soon appeared that he could have reason to celebrate. Tho indicated that Hanoi might accept Saigon's participation in the talks in exchange for a complete bombing halt of the North. The conversation was entirely speculative, and both sides agreed to consult their governments. But the

North Vietnamese noticed how relieved Harriman looked as he produced the refreshments. Although an aide had bought the caviar that day in Paris, Harriman claimed expansively that it had been a gift from Chairman Kosygin. That enticement failed, however, and the North Vietnamese gravitated to the ice cream and cookies.

Two days later, Le Duc Tho received instructions from Hanoi that left him unhappy. The Politburo was now demanding that, in any four-party talks, the NLF become the chief Communist negotiating team. Tho knew that Washington would not agree to that demand, and he found it impractical as well. But this time the language was rigid. He flew the next morning to Beijing, where a special plane was waiting for his urgent flight home.

When the parties met again on Touraine Street the evening of October 15, Harriman noted Tho's absence and made a wild guess: "Perhaps Mr. Tho is going to meet Mr. Kosygin, isn't he?"

Xuan Thuy said blandly, "Yes, he is."

During these days of the U.S. election campaign, the Communist delegates were finding that Washington was more flexible than Hanoi. Harriman read from a handwritten paragraph that if South Vietnam were included in the talks "we can tell you that the order to stop all bombardments will be given within the next day or two."

But Harriman remained firm that as a proof of good faith the four-party conference must start the very next day after the bombing stopped. He said that the timing would not be too hasty since Saigon could appoint the ambassador already in France and the NLF could use the representative from its Paris information bureau.

In Hanoi, Tho was able to persuade the leadership to table the demand about the NLF. But to prevent Washington from thinking the North was too eager, Tho was told to be vague about when the expanded conference might begin. He should say only "as early as possible." Now all that remained was for Washington to notify Thieu that peace was within his grasp.

AMBASSADOR BUNKER assured the White House that Thieu would find the Paris terms acceptable but that he must be given time to inform Ky and other government officials. Bunker was unaware that Henry Kissinger had once again found a way to involve himself in the Vietnam drama. After the Republican convention, Kissinger had written to Harriman. "My dear Averell," he began, announcing that he might be in Paris around September 17. If so, he would like to pay Harriman a call. "I am through with Republican politics," Kissinger wrote. "The party is hopeless and unfit to govern."

Once in Paris, he met with Harriman, Vance and other delegates just before their first private meeting with the North Vietnamese. Daniel Davidson, a young lawyer on the team, had worked for Bill Bundy and knew Kissinger as well. He believed it when Kissinger claimed to feel repugnance for Nixon. "Three days of the week, I think I'll vote for Hubert," Kissinger said. "The other days I think I won't vote at all." But he told Davidson that whichever candidate won, he would be joining the government. Nixon would appoint Nelson Rockefeller as defense secretary, and Kissinger would become his intelligence chief in the Pentagon. As for Humphrey, Kissinger had kept up contacts with his camp until the polls pointed to victory for Nixon.

Later, Davidson could not recall any explosive information that Kissinger might have picked up from their conversation. He thought Hedrick Smith, who was covering the talks for the New York Times, probably had a better grasp of their progress than Kissinger. But when Kissinger got back to the United States, he began to call Richard Allen, Nixon's thirty-two-year-old foreign policy adviser, always using a public telephone so the Democrats would not find out. His information was vague, mostly warning that something big was afoot and Nixon should not offer any new proposals about Vietnam.

On October 12, however, Kissinger was the excited bearer of real news. He had heard from Paris that Harriman and Vance had "broken open the champagne" because the two sides had agreed to a bombing halt. Allen was on the phone immediately to John Mitchell, Nixon's campaign manager. He and Mitchell agreed that Kissinger's help had been invaluable and must be rewarded if Nixon won; Allen suggested national security adviser. But with Humphrey's rise in the polls, Kissinger wanted to ingratiate himself again with the Democrats. He sent Humphrey a letter criticizing Nixon and volunteering to serve in a Democratic administration.

Allen was also hearing from Ed Lansdale, who sent unsolicited letters on Vietnam policy. Although Lansdale genuinely favored Nixon, he had not given up his hope to go back to Vietnam one last time—as ambassador. In case Humphrey pulled ahead in the campaign's final weeks, Lansdale asked that his correspondence with Allen remain confidential. But he had no inside information to impart, only long-ignored advice. Nixon's camp saw no need for any future appointment.

In Nixon, the Republicans had nominated a man as suspicious as Lyndon Johnson and even more given to brooding over past indignities. Nixon assumed that, as he put it, Johnson intended "to throw the election to Humphrey by pulling something in Paris." But Johnson was more concerned with his own legacy than with Humphrey's future. The vice president was still being punished for his defiance in Salt Lake City and could expect no favors from the White House. To apprise Humphrey of developments in Paris, Johnson made a conference call with Nixon and George Wallace as well.

Thieu was even less willing to help Humphrey close the gap at the polls. Summoning Bunker to his office on October 17, Thieu said that he was having second thoughts about the Paris terms. Looking ahead to protracted negotiations,

Ambassador Ellsworth Bunker *(AP/Wide World Photos)*

he would not permit the NLF to be treated as a government parallel to his own. Even as the ambassador tried to reassure him, Thieu kept raising his demands. By October 21, he was insisting that the NLF participate only as part of North Vietnam's delegation. That condition was impossible for Hanoi to accept, and Thieu knew it.

At the Tuesday Lunch the next day, only Clifford seemed outraged by Thieu's intransigence. "I thought we had an agreement," he said. "There is a missing factor here. We are facing an utter debacle."

Rusk was unperturbed. "That's why we have diplomacy," he said. "We are the Department of Debacles." Rusk assured Johnson that Bunker would win Thieu over. Clifford thought to himself that the ambassador put excessive trust in Thieu's word.

BUI DIEM was the missing factor in Clifford's equation. In frequent contact with Anna Chennault, he was cabling Thieu often and on October 23 passed along what he had just heard. "Many Republican friends have contacted me and encouraged us to stand firm. They were alarmed by press reports to the effect that you had already softened your position."

A few days later, Bui Diem's cable was more explicit. "I am regularly in touch with the Nixon entourage"—Thieu would know that he meant Mrs. Chennault, John Mitchell and John Tower, the Texas Republican senator. Bui Diem was aware that he was not Mrs. Chennault's only channel to Saigon. Besides Mitchell, she stayed in close touch with Dick Allen, Nixon's foreign policy adviser, and Nguyen Van Kieu, South Vietnam's ambassador to Taiwan; Kieu was Thieu's brother.

For the American negotiators in Paris, it had come down to a matter of days. On the night of October 26, Harriman and Vance met with Xuan Thuy, who proposed a bombing halt for October 30, and the first meeting for November 6 or 7. Earlier, the Communists had set the interval at ten days. Harriman was pressing for two or three days, but the North Vietnamese said that would not allow enough time to assure their countrymen that the bombing had stopped permanently and that it was not simply a pause due to bad weather. Xuan Thuy agreed to compromise on five days. If the United States wanted to begin the second phase of talks on November 2, three days before the U.S. election, then the bombing must stop tomorrow, he said. That was clearly impossible.

Hoping to squeeze out a concession, Harriman held up his hand and calculated on the tips of his fingers. "No," he said, "it's six days, isn't it?"

"Did you count the second of November?" Xuan Thuy chided him, and everyone but Harriman joined in the laughter. He muttered, "Five days. Each day twenty-four hours. All told, 120 hours. Thank you, this is very important."

Harriman and Vance called Washington shortly before midnight, Paris time, to alert Johnson that they were sending a telegram of great importance. At the White House the next day, the president asked his advisers, "What do you think we should do?"

To Clifford's relief, Rusk said, "I think we should go ahead." Rusk, who still believed that the North Vietnamese took their orders from Moscow, ventured a bit of fancy: "I smell vodka and caviar in this proposal. The Soviets have moved into this negotiation."

The president sounded troubled. "I think this is a political move to affect this election," he said. Clifford wondered whether he truly had doubts or wanted once again to be coaxed into doing what he had already decided to do. Johnson said, "I would rather be viewed as stubborn and adamant than be seen as a tricky, slick politician. Everyone will think we're working to elect Humphrey by doing this. That is not what motivates us. I want to take it slow."

Meantime, with the election only nine days away, Johnson said he intended to bring Abrams back for consultation. Hearing that, Clifford asked himself whether, in his heart of hearts, Lyndon Johnson really wanted Humphrey to win.

When Abrams arrived at the White House, Johnson led him through carefully orchestrated questions that ended with Abrams saying that, if he were president, he would accept the Paris terms, including an end to bombing the North.

All that remained was for Bunker to report Thieu's approval. As Johnson waited for the call, he learned that an NLF delegation had left Hanoi for Paris.

It was 5 A.M. before Johnson gave up and retired to the family quarters. An hour later, Rusk heard from Saigon that Thieu had reneged on his earlier promises. He now claimed that November 2 was too soon for the first meeting of the new phase. And he had to consult again with his South Vietnamese security council. To Clifford's disgust, Bunker agreed that Washington should offer Thieu a short postponement.

Johnson knew about the Nixon camp's channels to Thieu. "It would rock the world," he remarked, "if it were said that Thieu was conniving with the Republicans."

But Rusk wanted to delay the bombing halt in order to avoid a break with Saigon. And the president seemed to blame the Democrats more than Nixon for Thieu's stalling. Johnson agreed with Rusk that Humphrey's Salt Lake City speech had scared Thieu, and he alluded angrily to a speech on October 12 at De Pauw University in which Mac Bundy had said publicly what the Wise Men had said in March: "There is no prospect of military victory against North Vietnam by any level of U.S. military force which is acceptable or desirable." Johnson had received an advance copy of Bundy's speech at the time and made no comment, but for the past two weeks he had been vitriolic about it.

Johnson had to decide whether he should still announce the bombing halt. Clifford, Abrams and Helms from the CIA all urged him to go ahead with it. Johnson's advisers wrangled for two days with little sleep, but the president remained unwilling to break openly with Thieu. Rusk proposed putting off the starting date of the new talks to November 4, one day before the election. Johnson agreed. But on October 30, Thieu flatly refused to participate in any talks with the Communists before the elections. To justify the delay, he cited a minor change in procedure and instructed Bui Diem to seek clarification from Bill Bundy in the State Department.

Bui Diem, who could imagine the president's rage, braced for a disagreeable few minutes with Bundy, although he considered him a friend. On this morning, however, Diem saw the side of Bundy that could make secretaries tremble. Not asking Diem to sit down, Bundy spoke with a coldness Diem had never heard from him. The Paris talks had nothing to do with the U.S. election, Bundy said harshly. Then he stood and turned his back on Diem as though he could not bear to look at him.

Bui Diem heard him growling as he mentioned the contacts with Nixon's advisers. "Improper," Bundy called them. "Unethical." When he finished, Diem could defend himself because he knew that Bundy would not admit to reading Diem's secret cables to Thieu. At the White House, Johnson had come to the same conclusion. His evidence against Anna Chennault and Bui Diem for obstruction came from highly sensitive surveillance by the FBI, the CIA and the

National Security Agency. However much Anna Chennault infuriated Johnson, he felt he could not reveal the evidence of her meddling on Nixon's behalf, even after John Mitchell urged her to impress on Thieu the degree of Republican support for him. Johnson decided that the surveillance had not proved a direct link to Nixon or evidence that he knew about the improper interference on his behalf. Clifford disagreed. He thought Johnson should make the affair public or at least force Nixon to back off from encouraging Thieu's resistance. Clifford was sure that was what Johnson would have done if it had been his own career at stake, not merely Humphrey's.

JOHNSON COULD WAIT no longer. He scheduled his announcement of the unconditional bombing halt for 8 P.M. on Thursday, October 31. From the Joint Chiefs, he had demanded political insurance in the form of a written statement that stopping the bombing "constitutes a perfectly acceptable military risk." Bunker was instructed to tell Thieu that Johnson was going ahead without him, and the president placed another conference call to the three candidates to give them advance notice. Nixon was angry but not surprised; Kissinger had continued to use his entrée with the Johnson administration to keep Nixon's people informed.

Johnson's draft read that "all air, naval and artillery bombardment of North Vietnam" would stop on November 1 at 8 A.M., Washington time. He added a line that on Wednesday, November 6, new and substantial talks would open in Paris, "at which the representatives of the government of South Vietnam are free to participate." In response, Thieu did Nixon one last favor by announcing that he would not be sending anyone on November 6.

With that, Johnson called Ev Dirksen to complain about what Anna Chennault and Bui Diem were up to. The next day, Nixon reached Johnson at his ranch and assured him that he had known nothing of any overtures to Thieu. Once more, Johnson did not reveal the sources of his information, but Humphrey tormented himself about his own silence. It seemed implausible that Nixon had not known about Mrs. Chennault's most recent call to Thieu. "I *wish* I could have been sure," Humphrey argued with himself. "Damn Thieu. Dragging his feet this past weekend hurt us. I wonder if that call did it. If Nixon knew. Maybe I should have blasted them anyway."

Humphrey had reason to wonder. The Harris poll showed him leading 44 to Nixon's 43. Although the Gallup poll reversed those numbers, all the surveys saw an upsurge for Humphrey. One pollster said after the election that, to win, Humphrey had needed only eight more hours before the polls opened.

Instead, Nixon received 31.7 million votes to Humphrey's 31.2 million. George Wallace drew fewer than 10 million votes, most of them from Democrats. With the margin so close, Humphrey went to bed without conceding. The next morning, Mayor Daley was on the phone urging him not to give up. He could still carry Illinois, Daley said, adding ambiguously that his state's votes were not all in. Humphrey thanked him, called Nixon and went downstairs at the Leamington Hotel in Minneapolis to admit that his dream had died. Although his words were gracious, Humphrey was thinking, "To lose to Nixon. Ye Gods!"

FOR KISSINGER, the time had come to collect for the substantial service he had performed in passing along to the Nixon camp the likely developments in Paris. Born Heinz Alfred Kissinger in Bavaria in 1923, he had been taken from Germany at age fifteen by his parents, an Orthodox Jewish schoolteacher and his gregarious wife. The Kissingers got out barely three months before Kristallnacht destroyed their temple. They settled in Manhattan at 187th Street, where Kissinger's mother supported the family as a caterer.

The boy, now Henry, excelled at George Washington High School and entered the City College of New York, thinking that accounting might provide a comfortable living. The U.S. Army drafted him in 1943, conferred American citizenship and broadened his horizons. Sent to the Counter-Intelligence Corps, he served in Germany as a sergeant in the occupying army, then entered Harvard in 1947 as a twenty-four-year-old sophomore. His 383-page undergraduate thesis, reputed to be the longest in Harvard's history also was said to have provoked the "Kissinger rule" that limited future theses to one-third that size.

Married to his teenage sweetheart, Kissinger entered Harvard's doctoral program and headed an international seminar that gave him entry to the wealthy and powerful of Cambridge and beyond. Unkind colleagues watched his incessant courting of men who could help his career and claimed that the "A" of his middle initial did not stand for "Alfred." They called him Henry Ass-Kissinger. But friends like Arthur Schlesinger, Jr., thought he was merely revealing a typical desire among refugees for approval.

Stocky, short and rumpled, Kissinger developed a humor made more droll by his persisting Bavarian accent. One epigram about academic politics became widely quoted: "The disputes are so bitter because the stakes are so small."

By 1968, Kissinger was well placed to advance himself. A consultant to Democrats, he was also on Nelson Rockefeller's payroll while the New York governor contended unsuccessfully with Nixon for the Republican nomination. After the election, there was no Mac Bundy to block Kissinger from claiming his reward from the White House. Kissinger met the president-elect for the first time on November 25 at the Pierre. He thought Nixon seemed extraordinarily nervous, as though he were the one seeking a job.

Nixon explained that he had little faith in the State Department and, like Jack Kennedy, intended to run foreign policy out of the White House. Nixon also planned to exclude the CIA from his deliberations since it was a haven for Ivy League liberals. Kissinger did not commit himself about the CIA but agreed that Johnson's Tuesday Lunches had been too informal and poorly staffed.

Given Nixon's stiffness with strangers, the interview ended inconclusively, and Kissinger flew back to Harvard in time for a 4 P.M. seminar. The next day, Rockefeller called to say that he himself would not be getting a cabinet appointment but that Nixon had inquired about how well Kissinger held up under pressure.

When John Mitchell invited him to fly back to New York, Kissinger went first to see Mac Bundy. He felt that Bundy had always patronized him, and he may have wanted to flaunt the fact that he might be occupying the seat of power Bundy had relinquished. If that was his intention, Bundy quickly deflated him. When Kissinger said he expected to be offered a position in the State Department, Bundy replied that the president-elect should really not be appointing assistant secretaries before he named his secretary of state.

By the next day, Kissinger could shrug off that slight. Puffing on his pipe, Mitchell asked directly, "What have you decided about the National Security job?"

"I did not know I had been offered it," Kissinger said.

"Oh, Jesus Christ," said Mitchell, "he has screwed up again." He led Kissinger back to Nixon. This time, Nixon made himself clear. Kissinger would succeed Bundy and Rostow as the third Cambridge professor to become the president's national security adviser.

JOHNSON'S LAST SIXTEEN WEEKS as president were bitter ones. He had gambled on securing a treaty or at least the terms that would let him leave office as a peacemaker. Thieu had denied him that consolation. Nor would Johnson be departing after another flourish he desired. He had been aiming toward a final summit with Kosygin on arms control, but Nixon told the Soviets secretly that he opposed the conference and it was not scheduled. Looking around the Oval Office, Johnson said, "I gave it up for nothing."

Both Dirksen and Joe Alsop visited Bui Diem on Johnson's behalf to insist that Thieu send a team to Paris. But Bunker was being told that it might take Saigon two months to be ready, guaranteeing that Johnson would have left office. Flying to South Vietnam, Bui Diem found the ARVN generals euphoric, convinced that in a hard-line anti-Communist like Nixon they had a steadfast friend. Diem described the antiwar mood in America to Thieu and predicted that the Republicans would also be disengaging, perhaps only more slowly than the Democrats. Thieu smiled and seemed to agree, but Diem left Saigon sure he had no policy for coping with the inevitable withdrawal.

In Paris, the Communists thought the Americans looked embarrassed when their South Vietnamese allies did not appear. They suggested that since the NLF team was now in Paris they could begin three-sided talks. But Johnson was not ready for that final rupture with Thieu. Besides, there was the question of a table. Hanoi wanted a square table with each delegation—including, if it showed up, the Saigon contingent—sitting on a side. By maintaining a semblance of NLF autonomy, that arrangement would reward Front members for their long struggle.

But since Washington had promised Saigon not to recognize the NLF, the Americans countered with a rectangle—both sets of Communists on one side, the U.S. and South Vietnamese delegates on the other. Throughout the last week of 1968, the teams debated every permutation—a round table; two arcs of a circle, opposite but not separated; opposite and separated semicircles; and six other configurations.

At the Tuesday Lunch on January 7, 1969, Johnson told Rusk, "I'm fed up with the South Vietnamese." He knew he must force the issue, as Clifford had been urging, and not rely any more on Bunker. He said, "I want these talks to start before January 20, even if we have to admit that Clark has been right all along." He instructed Rusk to warn Thieu that Washington was ready to start negotiating without him. But Rusk's cable gave Bunker the choice of conveying Johnson's message by letter or in person. Clifford had lately written to Mac Bundy that he was worn out by Vietnam but was "convinced that we have gone so far down the road that those who follow cannot turn back." He would permit no softening of Johnson's ultimatum and got him to insist on a letter.

At the same time, Washington and Hanoi accepted a Soviet suggestion for a round table with nearby rectangular tables for the secretaries. The Americans scheduled the first talk for January 18, two days before Johnson's term expired. On January 14, Harriman invited the Communist delegates to Sceaux to say goodbye. He described Cabot Lodge, who would be replacing him as head of the U.S. delegation, as an old friend of the president-elect.

Le Duc Tho said he regretted Harriman's departure. "If you had stopped bombing after two or three months of talks," Tho said, "the situation would have been different now." If Nixon and Lodge chose for some reason to protract the war, Tho added, "the fault is not ours."

At the official farewell three days later, Harriman gave each Communist delegate a paper box of matches as a souvenir. As his gifts, Xuan Thuy did somewhat better: an issue of *Vietnamese Studies* on literature for Harriman, a book about Vietnamese education for Vance. Tho said again, "De-Americanization of the war will fail, as the introduction of U.S. troops failed before." The Communists thought Harriman seemed depressed. Only a year younger than Ho, he had wanted to see Vietnam at peace in his lifetime.

But the South Vietnamese would not give Johnson even the two days he was asking. They stalled until January 25 and let Nixon reap the acclaim as peacemaker.

PART THREE

RICHARD M. NIXON AND LE DUC THO

ELEVEN

Nixon
1969

I N THE MONTHS before he left office, Lyndon Johnson wanted to provide for those aides who had proved their loyalty. Because Walt Rostow was now anathema to former colleagues in Cambridge, the president arranged an appointment for him at the University of Texas at Austin, where he could help Johnson with his memoirs. With Rusk equally unwelcome in the Ivy League, the president toyed with naming him to the U.S. Supreme Court. Earl Warren had recently resigned as chief justice, and Johnson planned to move Abe Fortas to the chief's seat, which would leave an opening.

Rusk himself had no particular plans, but he refused to fall in with Johnson's. After accepting the office of secretary of state with grave doubts about his qualifications, Rusk had shrunk the job until he was comfortable in it. For some time now, he had been boasting that he had become the doyen of foreign ministers; around the world, no one had led his country's foreign affairs longer than he. But the prospect of a court appointment revived Rusk's diffidence. He reminded Johnson that he had never completed his law degree before World War II, had never practiced law or served on any bench.

Johnson said the Constitution did not require that experience.

"True enough," Rusk said. "But the Senate would never confirm me."

"I've taken care of that," Johnson said. "I've already talked to Dick Russell, and he said you'd be confirmed easily."

When Rusk continued to object, Johnson made more inquiries and learned that Russell could not override Mississippi Senator James Eastland, chairman of the Senate's Judiciary Committee. Eastland, like Thieu, was ready to thwart Johnson and gamble on a Republican victory. He blocked the Fortas appointment, leaving Nixon free to name a more conservative chief justice. Even if Rusk had agreed, there was now no vacancy. Johnson consoled him with a Medal of Freedom, the country's highest civilian honor. On the day of Nixon's inaugural, Johnson also bestowed the medal on Clifford, Harriman, Rostow and William S. White, a Texan who, despite being a journalist, had retained Johnson's friendship for three dozen years.

The Johnsons attended Nixon's swearing-in ceremony and flew off to the ranch on *Air Force One*, lent to them by the new president. Rusk and his wife left the State Department before the ceremony. A crowd of employees had gathered to say goodbye, and Rusk offered them a three-sentence valedictory. "Eight years ago, Mrs. Rusk and I came quietly. We wish now to leave quietly. Thank you very much."

Ambassador Dobrynin gave a small farewell dinner and found Rusk fatalistic about his eight years. Mistakes had been made under both Kennedy and Johnson, Rusk said, and he was largely responsible for them. But "what's done cannot be undone." He was not going to make excuses or write his memoirs. Let history judge him.

After dinner, Dobrynin walked Rusk to his unfashionable car. Rusk was complaining that, after years of chauffeur-driven limousines, he had to learn to drive again and book his own airline tickets. Watching Rusk's old car chug off, Dobrynin considered it a symbolic end to the Johnson years.

Out of work, prospects tainted, Rusk faced the penury he had always feared. For a time, the Rockefeller Foundation bailed him out with a stipend as a "distinguished fellow," but to his family Rusk seemed to be falling apart. As vacant weeks replaced his numbing sixteen-hour days at State, he talked often about his impending death. Depressed, running a low-grade fever and suffering from a constant ache in his belly, Rusk refused to discuss his emotions with his family. But he often consulted doctors and checked himself in for tests at both Walter Reed Hospital and the Mayo Clinic in Minnesota. Doctors found nothing.

In time, a chair was created for him at the University of Georgia Law School. Roy Harris, a university regent who had run Wallace's presidential campaign, tried to block Rusk's appointment—"We don't want the university to be a haven for broken-down politicians"—but he was approved easily. Rusk settled into campus life, publishing little, teaching courses in international law and, as the years passed, collecting scores of honorary degrees. Henry Kissinger called him from time to time.

WHEN KISSINGER'S WHITE HOUSE APPOINTMENT was announced, former colleagues recalled his many cracks and insults about Nixon from the time Kissinger was still on Rockefeller's team. He had lamented Nixon's "shallowness" and claimed he had a "dangerous misunderstanding" of foreign policy. To a former Eisenhower speechwriter, Kissinger had said of Nixon's nomination: "The man is, of course, a disaster. Now the Republican Party is a disaster."

By Saturday, January 25, however, when the National Security Council held its first meeting, Kissinger's campaign was well underway to reassure Nixon of his newfound respect. He had already clashed with H. R. "Bob" Haldeman over his council staff. Believing that tradition gave him the right to pick his own aides, Kissinger quickly chose several civilians, including Morton Halperin, the deputy assistant secretary of defense who had helped to turn Clifford against the war. He also included one army colonel, Alexander Haig, who had arrived in Vietnam as a planning operator with the 1st Infantry Division eight months after the battle at Ia Drang.

Haldeman's service with Nixon went back six years—to the time he managed Nixon's losing race for governor in California. As Nixon's chief of staff, he challenged Kissinger's choices on security grounds, which Kissinger took to mean that they were either too liberal for Haldeman's taste or talked too freely to reporters. Kissinger overruled him. But he also knew that Haldeman enjoyed Nixon's confidence as few men did. At the end of the six-and-a-half-hour Security Council meeting, he went out of his way to tell Haldeman how impressed he had been by Nixon's performance. To make his gushing enthusiasm more credible, he also let Haldeman know that he had been surprised.

But Kissinger's chief rival was neither Haldeman nor John Ehrlichman, Nixon's dour assistant for domestic affairs. The threat came from William Rogers. Although he was only Nixon's third choice for secretary of state, he had first met the new president in the late 1940s and had advised him during his campaign for vice president in 1952. When Nixon lost the California governorship and moved to New York, their lopsided friendship revived—Nixon famous but Rogers handsome, well established, socially at ease. Ehrlichman wondered whether Nixon had not brought Rogers into the cabinet to redress the balance by becoming his boss. At first, Kissinger scheduled frequent meetings at State, but Secretary Rogers shared McNamara's respect for titles, Kissinger shared Jack Kennedy's predilection for brains, and each found the other man wanting.

Kissinger saw that Nixon was treating him the way Ike had once treated Nixon. As his term began, Nixon had said, "I don't trust Henry, but I can use him." Kissinger was no more than a valuable employee, while Rogers and his wife were invited to the White House family quarters for casual dinners.

Rogers believed that since he enjoyed the confidence of the president, he need not court Washington columnists or the city's established social figures. When Kissinger launched a blitz to undercut him, Rogers was unarmed.

LONG BEFORE the American public caught on, Hanoi's Politburo understood Nixon's intentions about Vietnam. During the campaign, he had claimed to know a way for ending the war honorably, which he would put into effect if he were elected. Reporters called it Nixon's "secret plan." But Hanoi saw that he had no wish to end the war. He simply intended to de-Americanize it, although his new secretary of defense had come up with a better label. Sixteen years as a Republican congressman from the Wisconsin Dells had honed Melvin Laird's political sensitivity, and he was calling the process "Vietnamization." Nguyen Duy Trinh sent the Communist delegates in Paris instructions for dealing with the Nixon White House. Americans still wanted an early end to the war, Trinh wrote, and Nixon must bow to their wishes. But in order to withdraw with honor, he might pull out U.S. troops while counting on the ARVN to implement his "neo-colonialist policies." If so, Hanoi would adopt a four-part strategy:

- Require that Washington withdraw its troops unilaterally.
- Do everything possible to sow discord between Washington and Saigon.
- Improve the status of the NLF in international eyes. Mrs. Nguyen Thi Ngoc Dung remained an effective speaker, and with the addition of Front representatives in the talks, the Communist delegation had grown to include other members with personal stories: Nguyen Khac Huynh, who as a teenager had once torn down the Japanese flag in Hanoi in 1945; Mrs. Nguyen Thi Binh and Mrs. Nguyen Thi Chon, who had survived the torture in Saigon before Tet.
- The fourth part was to go on depending on weaponry from Socialist countries and on good will from around the world, including the antiwar movement in the United States. The United States wanted to pull out its troops, and Saigon wanted them to stay. It was a contradiction ripe for exploiting.

FOR HALF A YEAR before the U.S. presidential election, William Colby had been beefing up the clandestine effort against the Vietcong called Phoenix—in Vietnamese, Chien Vich Phuong Hoang. Bob Komer had been appointed ambassador to Turkey, another recipient of Johnson's last-minute largess, but CORDS lived on. Despite Colby's presence, Phoenix was not run by the CIA, although he recruited other agents to take part. Their target was what Americans called VCI—the Vietcong infrastructure. Colby estimated its number throughout the South at well over 70,000 persons. They were the Communists who assassinated village chiefs, mined roads, collected taxes and recruited young men and women from their villages.

Colby had watched frustrated U.S. troops conducting mass screenings in a village, and he wanted to avoid the abuse and ignorant punishment that was likely to estrange the South Vietnamese even further from their government. Phoenix had been established with no forces authorized to conduct assaults against Vietcong cadres. Information from paid informers and disillusioned Vietcong would be turned over for action by the ARVN and local police. To insulate Thieu from the inevitable excesses, Provincial Reconnaissance Units of 35 or 40 men had been set up within the national police. These PRUs were the only part of the pacification program overseen by Americans.

One thing had not changed from the days of Tran Kim Tuyen: intelligence gathering remained a swamp of conflicting fiefdoms that rarely pooled information. Colby hoped to change that. Phoenix would collect information from every source and then place suspects in one of three categories: "A" were Communist Party members and other leaders; "B" were cadres with considerable responsibilities; and "C" were merely rank-and-file members. That last category would be ignored unless they took up arms to fight, since Colby thought that killing one of the "C" foot soldiers made no contribution, but "neutralizing" a member of the infrastructure did. Because informants might be motivated by the cash rewards or to settle personal grudges, Colby established a rule that all suspects' files had to include three separate identifications before they could be entered on the enemy rolls.

Colby's staff printed comic books to carry the Phoenix message to the hamlets. In one, a Mr. Ba was menaced and taxed by the Vietcong until he went to his district headquarters and announced that two Communists he had seen on a Phoenix poster were hiding in his village. "They only go out at night," Ba said in the cartoon. "If you succeed in arresting them, please keep my name secret!" The Communists were seized; one repented and was returned to his family. In the comic's final panel, Mr. Ba was receiving an award from the Phoenix Operation Committee.

Because of the disillusion among the Vietcong from failures during Tet, Phoenix sometimes succeeded in just such simplistic ways. One Vietcong defector explained that cadres had promised a revolution in seven days after Tet and had demanded money to guarantee peace and prosperity. When the General Uprising did not materialize, the Vietcong said that Tet had been only the first stage. After the second stage in May, they claimed that the government forces had been all but eliminated and August would finally see the uprising. By early 1969, however, the villagers realized there would be no third stage, and confidence in NLF promises evaporated. Saigon's statistics remained suspect, but the trend in defectors suggested that the number of persons who returned to the government's control had more than doubled after the disappointing third wave of the Communist offensive.

Phoenix's successes were seldom as antiseptic as Colby presented them, however. Spending most of his nights away from the countryside where the real work was done, Colby was surprised and distressed when a U.S. officer requested a transfer from Phoenix because he considered the program immoral.

Colby issued a directive to assure his staff that all Phoenix activities were entirely legal under both South Vietnamese and U.S. Army law. Police and soldiers were to use force against a member of the Vietcong infrastructure only as a last resort. "They are specifically not authorized to engage in assassinations," Colby wrote, but they could use reasonable force in "capturing or eliminating the VCI."

From behind that protective shield, Colby sometimes revealed his more genuine feelings about his quarry. "They were *Communists*, those people," he said, after the program ended. "Just no damn good." And reporters exposed the truth behind the way Colby's theory of Phoenix translated to practice. An American religious group spent a week touring the province interrogation centers and concluded that most prisoners had been tortured, often with electric wires to their genitals. Peter Kann told the story in the *Wall Street Journal* of one man, alleged to be a Vietcong leader, who was captured and killed in the Delta with no attempt to establish his guilt.

Colby also inherited USAID's Public Safety Program, which was responsible for police training. Americans in the field did not object to seeing Vietcong prisoners being slapped around to extract information. If a pending combat operation was involved, they tolerated more systematic abuse, including the water torture that both Thuan and Mrs. Chon had suffered under different Saigon regimes. And Colby oversaw Vietnam's prisoners. Somehow he missed the tiger cages on Con Son Island, where prisoners were still crowded into filthy cells and shackled until their limbs were paralyzed.

LESLIE GELB was finished at last. He had now worked on his Pentagon study under three defense secretaries. McNamara had initiated the project. When he left, Gelb expected first Clifford, then Laird, to become impatient and kick him and his staff out of their offices. Gelb had launched the study with half a dozen men. His staff grew until thirty men were involved in some aspect of the project, and Gelb commandeered more office space across the corridor and down the hall from the Secretary's suite. Seven thousand pages had now been bound into twenty-eight volumes, and Gelb was ready at last to deliver a set of them to McNamara at the World Bank.

From the start, the undertaking had been an unlikely one. Those angry students swarming over his car at Harvard in November 1966 had shaken McNamara more than he could admit at the time. His own questions about the war were already troubling him when the Harvard faculty pressed him for answers he did not have. Very belatedly, McNamara was recognizing that no one had ever briefed him on Vietnam's historical relations with the United States. But neither had McNamara, as he went about making life-and-death decisions, ever asked to receive such a briefing. After the scene at Harvard, he decided to get answers.

Even so, McNamara delayed more than six months before telling John McNaughton in June 1967 that he was commissioning a history of the Vietnam War. A month later, McNaughton was dead in the plane crash. The project went next to another aide, Morton Halperin, and then, when Halperin proved too busy, devolved on the very junior Gelb. Twenty-nine at the time, Gelb had been on New York Senator Jacob Javits's staff until the previous year when he joined the Pentagon's Office of International Security.

Gelb's original instructions came in the form of a hundred handwritten questions from Colonel Robert Gard, McNamara's military aide, who had sat in on the planning session with McNaughton. Ninety questions were more contemporary than historical: "Has the bombing worked?" "What about pacification?" The others were along the lines of "Could Ho have been another Tito?" The purity of Gelb's ignorance about Vietnam was almost total, but McNamara was giving him only three months to come up with the answers. Gelb collected six mid-level men on loan from elsewhere in the government, neither knowing nor caring about their political views. He himself had written speeches for Javits supporting the war and considered himself more hawk than dove.

His new staff complained that unless they collected original documents they were only going to be repeating what officials had said at press conferences. Gelb sent McNamara a memo advising him that the study would now take six months and was being organized along historical lines. McNamara replied that Gelb should make it encyclopedic and let the chips fall where they may. After that, Gelb sent him periodic summaries of progress, but McNamara did not involve himself. As the staff expanded to thirty, each member drafted one or more of the summaries, but Gelb signed all of them. He suspected that this was turning out to be no routine exercise, and some of the writers were concerned about the effect on their careers. Gelb classified each page "Top Secret—Sensitive." Despite McNamara's state of increasingly agitated distress, Gelb saw no indication that he was reading anything that was forwarded to him.

As he learned about the war, Gelb learned, too, about his staff. He considered Bob Schweitzer, assigned to write about pacification, unmistakably rightwing, and Paul Gorman, Gelb's deputy, had been a highly decorated battalion commander in Vietnam. To write the section on the year 1961, Gelb recruited Dan Ellsberg, back at the RAND Corporation after his Vietnam adventure. Gelb considered Ellsberg a passionate hawk with one of the best minds he had encountered. And yet, Ellsberg could not seem to get his assignment finished. Gelb nudged him three times, then turned it over to another staff member.

McNamara seemed to have forgotten about the project, and no other top administration officials showed much interest, either. Mort Halperin was sure that if either Rostow or the president found out, they would end it. But Bill Bundy was supplying memos to Gelb, and in the process he mentioned the study to Rusk, as did Ben Read, Rusk's executive aide. Rostow's staff was also providing papers, and the CIA handed over its National Intelligence Estimates.

Reading through them, Gelb was struck by the fact that the private remarks could be so pessimistic during the debate over increasing U.S. troops and the public statements so upbeat. Gelb himself did not favor pulling out, but he saw the war becoming a stalemate, and voicing that opinion in 1967 was enough to get one labeled a dove. George Ball had left government in September 1966 but had come back at Johnson's insistence during the spring of 1968 to replace Arthur Goldberg as ambassador to the United Nations. By then, Gelb had read Ball's compelling objections to escalation. But when a reporter on Sunday morning television asked Ball whether he had resigned in 1966 because of his disagreement with Johnson's policy, Gelb heard Ball saying no and going on to volunteer his support for the war.

Among Gelb's acquaintances, two dozen younger men in State and the White House also believed that the war was stalemated, but theirs was a decidedly minority view. Once, as they sat discussing the lessons of Vietnam, Paul Gorman walked to a blackboard and wrote, "Don't."

Clifford as defense secretary had ignored the project, and Mel Laird did not respond when Gelb sent him a distribution list for the final report. By now, Gelb, Halperin and Paul Warnke, another of McNamara's recruits to the Defense Department, realized that the study deserved its "Sensitive" stamp. After devoting eighteen months to it, Gelb could imagine the Nixon White House shredding his work under the guise of national security.

By late April, Gelb had resigned from the Pentagon and joined the Brookings Institution. Since no one had showed interest in his project, he was left to arrange distribution of the fifteen copies that had been made. For safekeeping, two copies were sent to the RAND Corporation's Washington office, where its president, Henry Rowen, had exempted the volumes from RAND's own control system for top-secret material and marked them instead as the property of Gelb, Halperin and Warnke. They agreed that access to the papers would require approval by two of the three of them.

Five copies went into Laird's Pentagon safe. One copy was sent to the Kennedy Presidential Library in Boston and the new library being built in Austin to house Johnson's papers. With Nixon's election, Bill Bundy had left government and was writing a memoir during a year arranged for him at MIT. He got a copy, and one was included in the papers Nick Katzenbach had stored at the State Department. The study also went to Paul Nitze as a former deputy secretary. Gelb delivered the volumes to Clifford's law office, where Pentagon officials had converted a closet into a "security storage area." That was commonly done as a courtesy to former secretaries of state and defense who might be asked to consult over classified data. Clifford, who still considered the project a dumb idea, did not examine what Gelb brought him. Nor did Kissinger comment when the volumes were delivered to him at the White House.

Given that pronounced apathy, Gelb was not prepared for the response when he carted the volumes to McNamara's office at the World Bank. He stepped through the door and announced what he was bringing.

"I don't want to see it!" McNamara said immediately. "Take it back!"

That was the extent of their conversation. Gelb was not even asked to sit down, and he left surprised and puzzled. McNamara still had the highest clearances, and a courtesy safe had been installed in his office. But McNamara's concern was not for security, it was for his job.

Two weeks after he left the Pentagon—which was also two weeks after Johnson took himself out of the campaign—Robert Kennedy had asked McNamara to tape a statement praising Kennedy's role in resolving the 1962 missile crisis. McNamara understood that his endorsement would wind up in a political commercial, but he had already turned Kennedy down once, and he felt affection for him. On the tape, he praised Robert Kennedy's "shrewd diplomacy." In case voters worried that the candidate was too rash or inexperienced, McNamara read from copy that claimed Kennedy had "remained calm and cool, firm but restrained, never nettled and never rattled."

When Kennedy was killed later in the year, McNamara was thankful he had not refused his last request. But the World Bank's rules were strict against its president involving himself in any country's domestic politics, and the *New York Times* had deplored McNamara's "poor judgment and poorer taste" in making the tape. His new position also required cooperation with the U.S. Congress, where Fulbright had lately accused McNamara of deliberately misleading him about the second Tonkin attack in 1964. For an unsettling moment, McNamara thought he might lose his new job.

A year had passed, but the scars remained. McNamara had succeeded in putting Vietnam behind him and Gelb was not going to contaminate his office with its detritus.

KISSINGER'S EFFORTS to undercut Bill Rogers at State turned out to have Nixon's wholehearted backing. Meeting with Dobrynin on February 17, Nixon paid Rogers a perfunctory compliment but told the Russian ambassador that he wanted all substantial matters to come to him through secret talks with Kissinger. Although Dobrynin was already accustomed to having a confidential channel to the White House, Nixon had in mind a far more active one. Four days later, Kissinger invited Dobrynin back to the White House and spelled out candidly America's terms for Vietnam. First, Nixon could not accept any settlement that looked like a military defeat. Second, he would not permit an immediate change in the Saigon government. Gradual evolution, however, would not be objectionable. Dobrynin left with a good impression of Kissinger. He seemed businesslike but not bureaucratic or dull, and he appeared to speak his mind.

Next, Kissinger moved to supplant Lodge in Paris. Lodge had begun private meetings with the North Vietnamese, but they were no more productive than Harriman's had been, and the White House had sent him no serious instructions. Kissinger asked Dobrynin to set up a secret meeting between Le Duc Tho and a special negotiator sent from Washington; Kissinger intended to be that man.

Only one Nixon appointee was playing the game even better than Kissinger. At Defense, Mel Laird knew that neither Congress nor the American people would consent to maintaining the war at its current level. He proposed cutting the number of U.S. troops by 50,000. Kissinger argued that the reduction would damage the American bargaining position in Paris, Nixon agreed and the figure was set at 25,000. But Laird knew he had won. The administration was now committed to "Vietnamization." By July of 1973, Laird intended to see in South Vietnam only the small "advisory force" that Kennedy had bequeathed to Johnson.

If the Joint Chiefs thought the new defense secretary would routinely approve the recommendations McNamara and Clifford had vetoed, Laird proved them wrong. The Chiefs called on Nixon to resume bombing the North. When Laird said that was impossible, Westmoreland, as army chief of staff, accused him of playing politics. Laird was not offended. He explained patiently to the general that American democracy rested on the give-and-take of politicians. At present, his political instincts told him that there was no support for bombing North Vietnam again. But the Chiefs still wanted air strikes against Communist positions in Cambodia, and Laird was prepared to compromise.

In early February, Abrams had cabled Bus Wheeler at the Pentagon that photographic evidence and a Vietcong deserter had finally allowed the Americans to locate COSVN, the Communist jungle headquarters, over the Cambodian border. Until then, intelligence had always put the Central Office in Laos. Abrams said sixty B-52 sorties against the Cambodian site would guarantee its destruction.

Abrams, in assuming command from Westmoreland the previous June, had quickly changed U.S. tactics. In place of attrition—killing North Vietnamese in numbers that would make them give up—Abrams had concentrated on controlling the South Vietnamese population. Rather than talking of guerrilla war versus conventional war, Abrams saw the struggle as one war, with his priority providing security for the hamlets and villages.

A return wire assured Abrams that "the highest authority" had seen his cable and was considering his request. It was vital to keep the matter secret, and Abrams need not send a briefing team to Washington. But the possibility that he might at last move against Cambodia was too exciting for restraint. Abrams dispatched two colonels to Washington for a breakfast meeting with Laird and two fellow officers. Kissinger was also on hand with Colonel Haig. The briefers explained that the sanctuary was in Base Area 353, the corner of Cambodia northwest of Saigon that protruded into South Vietnam. Americans called it the Fishhook.

Kissinger reported to Nixon that Abrams was sure no Cambodians were permitted at the base, so there would be no civilian casualties. In fact, the Joint Chiefs had concluded from aerial surveys that 1,640 Cambodians lived in the area but agreed that since they stayed away from the Vietnamese, casualties among them would be "minimal." Abrams estimated that the sixty B-52 sorties would take about an hour. Apparently, Prince Sihanouk would not protest.

A nationalist and a neutralist, Sihanouk lived like the indulgent Bao Dai but governed like the independent Souvanna Phouma. He had been crowned king in 1941, then twelve years later, with France bogged down in war with Vietnam, he had negotiated independence for Cambodia. In 1956, Sihanouk abdicated the throne to become a political leader. Then in the early 1960s he drove out of Phnom Penh the Communist insurgents called the Khmer Rouge, and their middle-class leader, Pol Pot, faded away into Cambodia's jungles. But Diem's murder alarmed Sihanouk and set him in a different direction. He broke off relations with the United States and did not pretend to mourn Jack Kennedy's assassination.

With his tacit agreement, Vietnam's Communists found sanctuaries within his borders, and Sihanouk permitted tons of their supplies to move through the port of Sihanoukville. When Americans made sporadic raids across the border, Cambodia's ministers would protest. But Sihanouk began to wonder whether his policies had become anti-American to an unwise degree. He made a symbolic overture in October 1967 by inviting Jacqueline Kennedy to visit the dazzling ruins of Angkor Wat. His gracious hospitality led to Chester Bowles, ambassador to India once again, calling on Sihanouk in January 1968. For years, Bowles had admired Sihanouk's blend of patriotism and showmanship and had once assured Kennedy that every country in Indochina needed a Sihanouk.

During their meeting, Lyndon Johnson wanted Bowles to persuade the prince to expel the North Vietnamese, and Sihanouk was receptive to the idea. He said he had no use for any Vietnamese "red, blue, north or south" and, although he could not say so publicly, he would not object to hot pursuit in unpopulated areas of his country.

That was how matters stood when Kissinger reported what Abrams's briefers had presented. In five days, Nixon would be leaving for a tour of European capitals. He put off making a decision about bombing Cambodia, but he was adamant that no word of Abrams's proposal should reach the public. The secrecy was so intense that Bus Wheeler did not inform Dr. Robert Seamans, the new secretary of the air force. If Seamans heard rumors, Wheeler was prepared to lie and deny that the raids were being considered.

THE HANOI POLITBURO understood the value to the Americans in bombing along Sihanouk's border. The past year's three dwindling Communist offensives had driven larger numbers of Vietcong and North Vietnamese troops into refuges in Cambodia. Hanoi considered the United States currently stronger on the ground and expected that, quite naturally, Washington would try to settle from its position of strength. But the Communists also saw that their disintegrating bases had been so weakened that a coalition government would be ruinous. Le Duan and the others were sure that a coalition now would suffer the fate of the premature coalition in Laos. Begun so promisingly, that neutralist government had been overthrown by American-backed forces, which led to the arrest of Prince Souphanouvong and other Pathet Lao leaders. For Hanoi, it was better to keep probing militarily while gearing up for a diplomatic offensive in late spring. Meantime, to keep the United States off balance, there must be a spring offensive.

THE DAY AFTER Nixon took office, Kissinger had assigned a chore to Dan Ellsberg, an acquaintance from Harvard now working again at RAND. Ellsberg was to circulate seventy-nine questions about the future of South Vietnam among the government's security agencies. Three weeks later, he reported the results, which were far different from the Politburo's evaluations. According to Ellsberg's information, the ARVN alone could not hold out against the Communists "in the foreseeable future." Not only did the Communists control the initiative in battle, it was far from clear that the Saigon government could survive a peaceful competition for power with the NLF. But, Ellsberg's report concluded, Hanoi probably realized that until U.S. troops were withdrawn the Communists could not attain a military victory.

As the White House weighed those judgments, the Communists launched their limited spring offensive. The date was February 22, one day before Nixon was flying to Brussels. Kissinger described it as "an act of extraordinary cynicism," even though the Americans had carried out more than a dozen ground operations in the month since Nixon took office. The new offensive was waged largely by NLF troops, not North Vietnamese regulars. Over the next month, the Communists' targets were widespread—125 of them hit by sappers, another 400 by shelling. Although the effort was put down within three weeks, 1,140 Americans and more than 1,500 ARVN were killed.

Nixon took the offensive as a personal affront. Flying to Europe on February 23, he decided to go ahead with the B-52 bombing of Cambodia. Kissinger wired Haig to join him in Brussels and to bring along Colonel Ray Sitton, known around the Pentagon as "Mr. B-52." But Laird called in his objections, and Kissinger did not want to begin the bombing while Nixon was in Europe. In Bonn the next day, Nixon agreed to a delay.

Home again in early March, Nixon was asked at a press conference, "Do you feel that you could keep American public opinion in line if this were to go on for months and even years?"

"Well, I trust that I am not confronted with that problem, when you speak of years," Nixon replied. Remembering the accusations that Johnson had not been candid about the war, he said he would tell the American people "why we are there, what our objectives are, what the costs will be and what the consequences would be if we took another course of action."

But as the Communists continued to shell Saigon, Nixon went from a White House church service to discuss with his new team the covert bombing of Cambodia. Rogers, at first opposed, was won over, and Abrams was told on March 17 that the air force could make forty-eight B-52 sorties against COSVN and twelve others away from the Cambodian border. The code name would be Breakfast, since that was where the plan had originated. Kissinger claimed later that he found the name tasteless.

U.S. SPECIAL FORCES teams had been crossing secretly into Cambodia since the early 1960s to gather intelligence and lay mines. During Johnson's last years in office, about eight hundred of those forays had been run under the code names Silver House and Daniel Boone. Like volunteers in Laos, the teams were sworn to secrecy under penalty of fines and imprisonment. When a man was killed inside Cambodia, his relatives at home were told that he had died along the border. But sending a few men into Cambodia on foot was nothing like bombing missions by America's deadliest aircraft.

The morning of March 18, a Daniel Boone team was lifted by helicopter into Base Area 353, where the B-52s had just bombed. They were told to pick up any Communist survivors, which should not be hard. Given the devastating strike, anyone still alive would be so stunned the Americans would need only to lead them by the hand to a helicopter. The team of two Americans and eleven Vietnamese set out confidently. But on landing, they learned the actual effect of the raids. One American described the scene as like poking a beehive with a stick. The Communists had not only survived, they were firing from three sides. The American radio operator and four Vietnamese were killed, the American team leader badly wounded. A second helicopter got in long enough to recover him and three of the Vietnamese. But when the next Daniel Boone team was ordered to try again, they refused. Although three men were arrested, an American lieutenant scoffed at the gesture. "You can't be court-martialled," he predicted accurately, "for refusing to violate the neutrality of Cambodia."

NONE OF THE eyewitness accounts from the ground reached Washington. Flying 30,000 feet above their targets, the pilots reported many secondary explosions, indicating that fuel and ammunition had been destroyed. Haldeman, Nixon's chief of staff, considered the bombing Kissinger's pet project and observed that he "came beaming in with the report, very productive." Secrecy held, at least for a week. Then on March 26 the *New York Times* mentioned the possibility of raids inside Cambodia but only that Abrams had requested them. Nixon's press secretary, Ronald Ziegler, assured reporters that to his knowledge no such request had reached the president's desk.

One night in mid-April, Kissinger met with Dobrynin to bluff him into pressuring the North Vietnamese to negotiate seriously. Washington would make only one more try at a settlement, Kissinger said, and Nixon had set a two-month deadline. After that, the United States would have to move. Kissinger did not say in which direction, but he had already recommended mining Haiphong Harbor.

That same night, North Korean MiGs shot down an unarmed U.S. Navy EC-121 reconnaissance plane on a spying mission forty-eight miles off the North Korean coast. Thirty-one crew members were lost. Kissinger and his staff—including Mort Halperin—wanted to bomb the MiG airbase. Laird, Rogers and Wheeler all objected that the move could lead to a second Asian ground war. Kissinger persisted, invoking a gambit that was coming to be known as the Madman Theory. If Nixon struck back against North Korea, Hanoi might say, "This guy is becoming irrational—and we'd better settle with him."

After the Security Council meeting, Kissinger tried to drum up support from other White House aides. He approached Ehrlichman, whose perpetual scowl made him even more forbidding than Haldeman, although Ehrlichman's was the livelier intelligence. When Kissinger finished his argument, Ehrlichman asked what would happen if the North Koreans responded to the bombing of their airfield by hitting an American target.

"Then it could escalate," Kissinger said.

"How far?"

"Well," Kissinger said, "it could go nuclear."

Five years earlier, Stanley Kubrick had directed a satiric movie about nuclear weapons. Even before this conversation, Ehrlichman had thought that Kissinger sometimes sounded too much like the film's crazed German scientist played by Peter Sellers. If Johnson's White House had occasionally reminded George Ball of Catch-22, Ehrlichman was thinking of Dr. Strangelove.

The next day, Nixon decided not to risk a second war, but he did accept Kissinger's argument that he must take steps to rouse the American people from their slothfulness and moral decay. In the meantime, Nixon authorized a second strike against Cambodia called Lunch.

IN AN ARMY HOSPITAL at Chu Lai three weeks before his tour in Vietnam ended, Ron Ridenhour met Michael Bernhardt from Lieutenant Calley's platoon. Ridenhour was being treated for malaria, Bernhardt for jungle rot. He had been able to stay free of the murders at My Lai, Bernhardt said, but when he spoke about them with Medina, the captain had said, "Keep your mouth shut, do you hear me?"

Ridenhour said that he was going to try to launch an investigation. Bernhardt promised that, if that happened, he would tell the truth.

Ridenhour left Vietnam on December 2, 1968, and was back in the United States the same day, welcomed home by his mother and the stepfather who had raised him until Ridenhour lit out on his own at sixteen. The family sat around their kitchen table in Phoenix and assured him how proud they were of him until

Ridenhour rebelled against their congratulations and told them about March 16 in Pinkville.

Even among his family, Ridenhour found he could not talk about My Lai without weeping. When he finished, his stepfather was in a rage. Like Medina, he said: "You better keep your mouth shut. It's none of your business. Shut up! This government will fuck with you for the rest of your life."

Over the next days, Ridenhour sought out women and men he had respected growing up—high school teachers, the leader of his Boy Scout troop. Telling him to keep quiet, they asked incredulously: Betray your friends for Vietnamese you don't even know? How could you do that? The sole exception was his high school English teacher, a Korean War veteran, who agreed that Ridenhour's information conferred an obligation on him. Write a letter to the army, the teacher suggested. Make it thorough, detailed and, above all, calm.

Ridenhour took most of that advice, except that he would not limit his letter to the army. Besides the example of Bernhardt, he had heard about a helicopter pilot who saved several lives that day. Back at his base, the man had filed a complaint that had gone nowhere, and he was later killed in combat. The army had already had its chance.

Ridenhour wrote many drafts to get his letter right. During the day, he was working at the Borden Company's Popsicle factory in Phoenix. Nights, he rewrote his three-page letter to make it as specific as he could. When he finished, a friend's secretary ran off two hundred copies. On April 2, 1969, Ridenhour went to the post office and registered the letters to make aides in the various offices take them more seriously. One letter went to his Democratic congressman, Morris Udall; the others to every official he could think of—President Nixon, Laird at the Pentagon, Fulbright, Ted Kennedy, Gene McCarthy, Barry Goldwater, Westmoreland as army chief of staff.

Ridenhour began:

Gentlemen:
It was in late April 1968 that I first heard of "Pinkville" and what allegedly happened there. I received the first report with some skepticism, but in the following month I was to hear similar stories from such a wide variety of people that it became impossible for me to disbelieve that something rather dark and bloody did indeed occur sometime in March 1968 in a village called "Pinkville" in the Republic of Vietnam.

Ridenhour explained that he had considered sending his evidence to newspapers, magazines and television stations but had "no desire to besmirch the image of the American serviceman in the eyes of the world." The appropriate body to launch an investigation was the U.S. Congress. "If you cannot, then I don't know what other course of action to take."

Udall's administrative assistant sent his copy of Ridenhour's letter to the House Armed Service Committee.

BY THE END of his presidency, Lyndon Johnson, a man who craved company all his life, had been reduced to hiding out from the demonstrators who reviled him. Nixon was temperamentally better suited to cope with the isolation of the White House—"Politics would be a helluva good business," he once remarked, "if it weren't for the goddam people." But Nixon was also given to Johnson's tidal sweeps of mood. Haldeman had come to dread being summoned to the Oval Office for hours of rehashing and rant. Nixon's litany of malefactors, already long, was constantly growing: Agnew was demanding too much of his time, for example, and Ron Ziegler, Nixon's press secretary, was not imaginative about selling the president's accomplishments. Edgar Hoover, still clinging to the directorship of the FBI, fed Nixon's appetite by sending the names of "bad guys" in the State and Defense Departments who should be transferred or fired. The New York Times, the Washington Post and the St. Louis Press Democrat were banned from the White House for printing leaked information, leaks that seemed to be coming from Kissinger's staff. Haldeman fretted about the several extreme security measures that Nixon was considering, but for now Nixon only decreed that he would hold no more meetings of the Security Council. He would confer with Kissinger alone.

AT A JUNE press conference, Nixon's competitive nature led him into a commitment that made Kissinger wince. In the journal Foreign Affairs, Clark Clifford had proposed withdrawing 100,000 American troops by the end of 1969 and all ground combat troops by the end of 1970. Because it was rare that a major architect of the war admitted to making a mistake, the article provoked an uproar; at his ranch Johnson was furious and called it self-serving. Nixon was just back from meeting with Thieu where, over Abrams's objection, he had announced the 25,000-man withdrawal. He told reporters, "I would hope that we could beat Mr. Clifford's timetable, just as I think we've done a little better than he did when he was in charge of our national defense."

Kissinger complained to Haldeman that Nixon's remarks would probably mean the collapse of the South Vietnamese government and Thieu's soldiers would turn their guns on the Americans. Worse still, Kissinger worried that Nixon might have reversed his hard-line position without informing him. He made Haldeman swear to tell him if Nixon was losing confidence in him. As he agreed, Haldeman decided that Kissinger was really quite insecure. Thieu's government did not collapse. From Washington, Nixon went on vowing to give the North Vietnamese no more warnings and then asking Dobrynin to pass along yet another threat.

July offered the president a brief respite from Vietnam when astronauts on the Apollo 11 space mission walked for the first time on the moon. Nixon reached them by telephone from the Oval Office while they faced a camera with their spacecraft and an American flag as a backdrop.

Nixon, who could sound like an aspirant to the *Guinness Book of World Records*, said, "This certainly has to be the most historic telephone call ever made from the White House." Flying to welcome the astronauts after their splashdown in the Pacific, Nixon was too euphoric to be abashed when Billy Graham, the evangelist, chided him for saying that walking on the moon had made the past week the greatest "in the history of the world since the Creation." Graham reminded the president that the birth, death and resurrection of Christ were all greater days. Nixon, ever the lawyer, told Ehrlichman to point out that he had referred to one week, not one day.

The night of the moon walk, Ted Kennedy had driven off a bridge on Chappaquiddick Island in Massachusetts, killing his twenty-eight-year-old passenger, Mary Jo Kopechne. Nixon considered the accident the end of the career of the last of the Kennedy brothers and put Ehrlichman to work on an investigation.

After greeting the astronauts, Nixon flew to Guam for a quick meeting with Thieu. Briefing reporters at the American officers club there, Nixon said that, except for a threat of a major power using nuclear weapons, the United States would expect Asian nations to handle their own military defense. Jack Kennedy had stated that same policy, and in 1964 Johnson had campaigned on it. Laird had named it Vietnamization. But when reporters called Nixon's remarks the "Guam Doctrine" and he saw the responsive chord it struck with the American people, he urged his advisers to get the policy renamed the "Nixon Doctrine." Kissinger had been kept in the dark about the statement. Miffed once again, he dismissed the doctrine as "less than meets the eye."

After Guam, Nixon made a surprise visit to South Vietnam, which pumped his blood. He spoke emotionally about how impressed he was by the American GIs he had met there. He was really fed up with the protesters and peaceniks, Nixon said, and never wanted those hippie-college types in the White House again.

From Asia, Nixon traveled to Bucharest to receive a thunderous welcome from the Rumanians. Rumanian premier Nicolae Ceaușescu had maintained friendly relations with China, and Nixon admitted that he was making the stop to needle the Russians. To Ceaușescu, Nixon delivered the same ultimatum about Vietnam that Dobrynin did not seem to be taking seriously. "We cannot indefinitely continue to have two hundred deaths a week in Vietnam and no progress in Paris," Nixon said. If the one-year anniversary of the negotiations came and went on November 1 without some movement, he would have to reevaluate U.S. policy.

In fact, since April he and Kissinger had discussed making their most generous offer. It fell short of toppling Thieu's government, but they would agree to free elections in the South. If that was rejected, Washington would stop its troop withdrawals, quarantine the North by mining its ports, even bomb its rail link to China. The plan was called Duck Hook.

Kissinger had arranged to disappear during Nixon's return flight to Washington and stay secretly in Paris to meet with the North Vietnamese. If he hoped to show up Lodge by producing a breakthrough, he was to be disappointed. Le Duc Tho did not attend the meeting, which guaranteed that it would be largely ceremonial. To translate, Kissinger was accompanied by General Vernon Walters, military attaché at the Paris embassy and accomplished in foreign languages; Mai Van Bo was on hand to translate for Xuan Thuy. They met at the Rivoli Street house of Jean Sainteny.

Kissinger spoke ingratiatingly about the bravery and dignity of the Vietnamese people and asked whether there had been any response from Ho to a private letter that Nixon sent to Paris with Sainteny the previous month. Xuan Thuy said the letter had been received and forwarded to Hanoi. Kissinger repeated Nixon's concern that November 1, 1969, would mark one full year since the bombing had stopped. To prove good faith, Washington would announce the pullout of more troops and would reduce by 10 percent the number of B-52 sorties in South Vietnam and Cambodia. Kissinger explained that from now on he would be handling the high-level channel himself, and he reported that the president was irritated that the North was now characterizing the war as "Nixon's war." Following Nixon's instructions, Kissinger assured them that if it really were Nixon's war, Nixon could not give himself the luxury of not winning.

Kissinger did not pass along another of the president's threats because he did not believe it himself. Before Kissinger stole away from *Air Force One*, Haldeman had ended a long chat with Nixon and come down the aisle to sit next to Kissinger. "You know," Haldeman said, "he actually seriously intends to visit China before the end of the second term."

Kissinger smiled. "Fat chance," he said.

ON AUGUST 30, Nixon received a letter signed by Ho. It was sympathetic to America's need "to get out of the war with honor" and sounded a mildly hopeful note if both sides would proceed with good will. The letter, dated five days earlier, had been prepared by other men, and on September 2, Ho died. It was twenty-four years to the day since he had declared Vietnam's independence. Rather than mar the anniversary celebration, the Politburo suppressed news of his death for one more day.

Only Ho's secretary knew that he had first drawn up his will in 1959 and then updated it annually to reflect the year's events. But Ho had neglected to revise the preamble, which explained its puzzling chronology. He quoted a poet from the T'ang epoch who wrote, "In all time, rare have been those who attained the age of seventy." Ho noted that, having recently celebrated his sixty-ninth birthday, he had become one of those rare people. But by the time his words were read, another decade had passed and Ho, at seventy-nine, was rarer still. He said he was looking ahead to the day he would rejoin Karl Marx, Lenin and his other revolutionary elders. He implored Vietnam's Communist leaders to remain united because he suffered whenever dissension divided the other Communist nations. At home, those who survived him must practice revolutionary morality—thrift, integrity, uprightness, total dedication to the public cause and exemplary unselfishness.

Ho warned that the struggle against American aggression might be prolonged, but he foresaw inevitable victory. "Our rivers and mountains and men will be here forever. The Yankees having been defeated, we will build up our country much finer than ever."

He asked that there be no great funeral ceremony for him. "I do not want to waste the time and money of the people," Ho wrote.

On the morning of September 9, the Politburo honored his request. A silent throng of mourners filled Hanoi's Ba Dinh Square and heard Le Duan read a funeral oration written and approved by the Politburo. Delegations from thirty nations listened under a summer sun already hot at 7 A.M. Jean Sainteny led the French delegation. No other Western nation was represented.

"Our beloved and venerated Ho Chi Minh is no more!" Le Duan read in a steady voice. "We have suffered an immense loss. Our grief is boundless," but, he added, the nation must continue to be worthy of him.

After Le Duan's ten-minute exhortation, a drum and bugle corps played patriotic numbers that included the "Internationale." The band's recital ended with music composed for Ho—"Hymn to the Leader"—and the crowd sang along. At the first words, Pham Van Dong on the platform began to sob violently. The sight released emotion through the square and people wept as they sang. The memorial had lasted thirty-five minutes.

His former comrades did not respect another of Ho's wishes. He had wanted no mausoleum, like Lenin's in Red Square, where his corpse would lie in state forever. But families from around North Vietnam had brought a sea of flowers to the Great Hall of Ba Dinh Palace to pay their final respects. The Politburo decided that burying Ho's body would deprive southerners of that same privilege when the war had ended and Vietnam was united. They set about preserving his body and designing a grand tomb to house it.

Before Ho's death, Kissinger had shrugged off Ho's letter, and Nixon termed it a "cold rebuff." Since U.S. intelligence could provide no accurate information about Ho's last months, Nixon concluded that he had controlled the Politburo up to the minute he died. On September 16, Nixon announced the withdrawal of another 35,000 men by mid-December, 1969. He hoped Ho's successors would understand that he was assuming they were not bound by Ho's response to his letter. But it was those successors who had written it.

☐

ONE DAY without warning, Vietnamese workmen appeared at Robbie Risner's cell and boarded up its windows. For the next ten months, he lived in a dark and stifling solitary confinement, the worst time of his imprisonment. At first, he thought he might lose his mind, until he found that rigorous exercise and prayer could save his sanity.

Released to a cell block called Vegas, Risner was once again caught communicating with fellow prisoners and moved to other parts of the jail—the Riviera, with more sealed doors and windows, and the Mint, with 14 inches between the bed and the far wall. The North Vietnamese finally supplied a roommate, "Swede" Larson, another lieutenant colonel, who had been held in solitary for eighteen months. Over the next two days and nights, Risner and Larson talked themselves hoarse.

Month faded into tedious month. Risner and the other prisoners watched ants and beetles on the ground and the birds nesting above their toilet. They played with the mice and rats and raised geckos to eat the swarms of mosquitoes.

With a new emphasis in Paris on the POWs, Risner saw conditions improving—new blankets, socks, extra mats, a breakfast of bread and hot water to supplement the two meals a day. But the slight relaxation presented its own problems. Young fliers being shot down now entered a prison different from the one Risner had known. Some of them seemed too willing to cooperate with their jailers; older POWs thought they were won over with candy, cigarettes and beer. Other new men seemed convinced by the constant Communist propaganda and found it hard to believe that the first prisoners could have been tortured.

Risner urged those men to adhere to the Code of Conduct, but he could not always count on compliance. One officer announced that as an American citizen, he had a right to free speech.

ON SEPTEMBER 24, 1969, more than a year after the rioting in Chicago, eight defendants stood in the court of U.S. District Judge Julius J. Hoffman to plead not guilty to charges of conspiracy and inciting violence. Except that they were all men opposed to the Vietnam War, the eight had little in common. But the antiriot provisions of the 1968 Civil Rights Act had been shaped by southern Congressmen to prosecute the "outside agitators" they blamed for the racial demonstrations in their states. Since the new act allowed federal prosecution for intent to foment a riot, the fact that several defendants had never met each other before going to Chicago would provide no defense. The prosecution had only to prove a pattern in their actions that spoke to a collective intent.

Ramsey Clark, Lyndon Johnson's last attorney general, had refused to apply the new law, but Chicago prosecutors met with John Mitchell, and got indictments in March against Tom Hayden and Rennie Davis from SDS; David Dellinger, twenty years older than the others and devoted to nonviolence; John

Froines and Lee Weiner, who had been marshals during the Mobe demonstrations; Bobby Seale, from the Black Panthers; and Jerry Rubin and the other Yippie leader, Abbie Hoffman. To their mutual relief, he was not related to the judge.

Julius Hoffman at seventy-three was tiny and tough. From the first day, he ruled gleefully against a defense team headed by William Kunstler, who had argued many civil rights cases across the South. Seale, the only black defendant, had wanted to be represented by Charles Garry, general counsel for the Panthers in San Francisco. But Garry was recovering from an emergency gall-bladder operation, and Hoffman denied his request for a six-week postponement. Seale then said he would represent himself. Hoffman ruled that he could not. For a month, they jousted. When Seale rose to speak and the judge told him to sit down, jurors could not be hustled from the courtroom fast enough to miss Seale's insults. Once they were gone, his invective continued: "This racist administration government with its Superman notions and comic book politics. We're hip to the fact that Superman never saved no black people. You got that?"

Neither the judge nor the court's marshal could force Seale to sit down before he finished: "You have did everything you could with those jive lying witnesses up there presented by these pig agents of the government to lie and say and condone some rotten racists, fascist crap by racist cops and pigs that beat people's heads—and I demand my constitutional rights."

On October 29, Judge Hoffman ordered Seale bound and gagged. A week later, he severed his charges from the case. Seale was convicted on sixteen counts of contempt of court and sentenced to four years in jail.

Convinced the defendants were being railroaded, Kunstler and his clients took revenge by playing with the decidedly unplayful judge. The Yippies oinked when police informers took the stand, and Kunstler, who was letting his hair grow longer by the week, could twirl his glasses in a way that seemed to comment on the inanity he was enduring. As he questioned Timothy Leary, testifying for the defense, Kunstler was interrupted by Thomas Foran, the chief prosecutor, who objected to Kunstler using the Yippies' first names.

Kunstler said, "Your Honor, sometimes it is hard because we work together in this case, we use first names constantly."

Judge Hoffman replied, "I know, but if I knew you that well—and I don't—how would it seem for me to say, 'Now, Billy—'"

"Your Honor, it is perfectly acceptable to me—if I could have the reverse privilege."

"I don't like it," said the judge. "I have disapproved of it before and I ask you now to refer to the defendants by their surnames."

"I was just thinking," Kunstler mused aloud, "I hadn't been called 'Billy' since my mother used that word the first time."

He had succeeded in riling Judge Hoffman. "I haven't called you that."

"It evokes some memories," Kunstler said wistfully.

Already in its third month, the trial then continued with Timothy Leary's testimony.

TWELVE DAYS BEFORE the next scheduled antiwar rally in Washington, Nixon delivered a canny address designed to undercut the demonstrators. He revealed for the first time his overture to Ho, boasted about the decline in American casualties under Abrams and promised more troop withdrawals if progress was made in Paris.

The speech was aimed at those Nixon termed the "silent majority" of Americans who expected a just peace. Nixon had asked Dean Acheson to review the text beforehand, and Acheson encouraged his former adversary to stress Vietnamization. That would rally listeners "emotionally around the flag," Acheson explained, so that their voices would drown out the small fraction of protesters. After the speech, Nixon's approval rating rose to 68 percent from the usual 50 to 60, and by a large margin the House passed a resolution of support for his Vietnam policy. For the moment, Nixon stood where Johnson had stood in 1964.

But on November 15, it was 1968 once again. Sam Brown, a divinity student in his mid-twenties and veteran of the McCarthy campaign, had persuaded antiwar protesters to move their demonstrations from the college campus into the community. He wanted to reach the same silent but concerned citizens Nixon was targeting. The first in the new round of moratoriums had been held on October 15, a month before the mass protest scheduled for Washington. The potency of U.S. public opinion had been demonstrated to Hanoi by the reaction to last year's Tet offensive, and Pham Van Dong sent a message praising the demonstrators for trying to save America's sons "from a useless death in Vietnam." A White House aide, Patrick Buchanan, wrote a speech for Vice President Agnew that implied the organizers were Hanoi's dupes and called on them to reject Dong's warm words. But Dick Gregory, the comedian, captured the mood when he told the crowd: "The President says nothing you kids do will have any effect on him. Well, I suggest he make one long-distance call to the LBJ ranch."

To herald the march the next day, the Mobilization sent thousands of protesters parading on November 14, carrying candles and placards with the names of the Americans who had died in Vietnam. Silently, they marched the nearly four miles from Arlington National Cemetery to the Mall. The only sound was the mournful beating of six drums in a funeral cadence.

Watching on television in Ehrlichman's office, Nixon joked that they should send up helicopters to blow out the marchers' candles. He stayed in front of the set for about two hours, until 11 P.M., when he remarked that it was like watching an old movie. And when police used teargas against the splinter groups that tried to march on the South Vietnamese embassy, it did seem a replay of Chicago.

On the Saturday of the march itself, the Mobilization organizers made fresher history by assembling the largest throng ever gathered in the nation's capital. No one could be sure how many hundreds of thousands took part. The government's official estimate was 250,000. From a photo count, Nixon's staff arrived at 325,000. The previous August, a music festival had drawn 400,000 young rock fans to Woodstock, a town 70 miles northwest of New York City. Some Mobe officials claimed that the Washington march had brought out "two Woodstocks."

By noon, bodies covered two-thirds of the forty-one acres around the Washington Monument. But many congressmen stayed away for fear of what extremists might do, and the speeches were predictable. Music alone redeemed the day. Pete Seeger sang, as did Woody Guthrie's son, Arlo, and John Denver and Peter, Paul and Mary. Four different touring companies performed numbers from the rock musical *Hair*. The Cleveland String Quartet played, and Mitch Miller's pop band. Leonard Bernstein, the conductor, joined Benjamin Spock on the platform. Floating over the scene were impromptu choruses of John Lennon's "Give Peace a Chance."

During one verse, Dr. Spock took the microphone and called in the direction of the White House, "Are you listening, Nixon? Are you listening?"

To Kissinger's disgust, Nixon was listening intently. When he first learned of the Mobilization, Nixon had canceled Duck Hook. That meant he would not be mining northern harbors or launching further bombing raids. Laird and Rogers had forcefully opposed Duck Hook, and members of Kissinger's own staff had doubted it would reduce Hanoi's ability to fight.

Once again, Washington's pessimism infuriated the U.S. military analysts in South Vietnam who claimed they could prove how badly the three Communist offensives of 1968 had cut into Vietcong strength. In October, Americans had recovered a forty-one-page strategy document, COSVN Resolution 9. Issued the previous July, it called for the Communists to fall back to small-unit actions. Rather than making another attempt at a total military victory, the Vietcong would disrupt Saigon's pacification program, return to selective terrorism and expand their political base against the day when the Paris talks produced a coalition government. The resolution in no way suggested capitulation, but its tone was bleak enough for even the phlegmatic Abrams to be encouraged. Maybe, Abrams said, just maybe, the initiative had passed to the ARVN.

Bus Wheeler soon punctured that fragile hope. On a trip to Saigon, he told Abrams that the discouragement among America's political leaders, past and present, was probably too ingrained to overcome. Certainly, Nixon's political problems had become more urgent lately. The *Washington Post* had exposed secret U.S. operations in Laos, and in Vietnam six Green Berets were facing court-martial for murdering a suspected Vietcong agent. Only after Kissinger persuaded the CIA not to let its agents testify against the accused men did Army Secretary Resor cancel their trial.

But another horrific story emerging from Vietnam was harder to contain. A former Chicago police reporter named Seymour Hersh had learned about a Pentagon investigation from a brother-in-law who had been drinking in Washington with an army officer. Hersh, who had served briefly as Gene McCarthy's press secretary, found a few paragraphs on the AP wire about an army lieutenant being court-martialed at Fort Benning that jibed with the information he already had. Hersh went to Benning to hear Lieutenant Calley's version at first hand and then to Claremont Men's College, where Ron Ridenhour was now studying. After Ridenhour fed him the names of Doherty, Terry and others from Charlie Company, Hersh said, "This is terrific! Give me a three-day head start."

Hersh called *Life* and *Look*, the two national photo magazines, but their editors were not interested. He gave the story instead to Dispatch News Service, a new and very junior competitor to the AP. Hersh's story ran on November 13. By the next day, public response forced an army escort from the Americal Division to lead reporters from the *New York Times*, *Newsweek* and ABC-TV to My Lai 4. They found the village deserted and overgrown with weeds. But several mounds of earth looked as though they might be mass graves.

TWELVE

SIHANOUK
1970

NORODOM SIHANOUK left Cambodia in early January 1970 with a small retinue and his wife, Monique, to take a two-month rest cure at a clinic on the French Riviera. He entrusted his government to its prime minister, Lon Nol, and first deputy, Sirik Matak. Diplomatic relations with the United States had been restored two years earlier, but Sihanouk was as frustrating for Washington to deal with as Diem had been. In place of Diem's endless monologues, Sihanouk expressed himself by making movies—nine amateurish dramas in which he and Monique sometimes appeared. When he required props, Sihanouk diverted his country's planes and helicopters to the movie set. And, like Diem, Sihanouk encouraged his armed forces to crack down on suspected enemies who were often merely farmers with valid grievances against his regime. Sihanouk never knew how many deaths his army had caused—hundreds certainly, possibly thousands.

For all his overtures to Washington, Sihanouk had worked to keep both North Vietnam and China well disposed to him. But with Sihanouk safely away, Lon Nol encouraged rioting against the presence of the North Vietnamese within Cambodia. When the North Vietnamese embassy was attacked, Sihanouk considered flying home, but his wife wanted to visit their children, who were studying in Prague and Beijing, and Sihanouk's mother sent a cable from Phnom Penh that it would not be safe for him to return.

Lon Nol used the spreading protests as proof that Sihanouk had been too lenient with Hanoi. On March 18, he persuaded the Assembly, whose members were already fed up with Sihanouk's indulgences and swollen ego, to expel him

Prince Norodom Sihanouk (*AP/Wide World Photos*)

and transfer his powers to Lon Nol. Such was the lingering reverence for the royal family, however, that Lon Nol went next to the palace, knelt at the queen mother's feet, and asked her forgiveness for overthrowing her son. In the countryside, Cambodians understood why he would feel a need for absolution. Sihanouk's popularity may have ebbed in the capital, but around Cambodia people often worshiped him for the king he once was. Farmers in the town of Kompong Cham killed one of Lon Nol's brothers, tore out his liver and brought it to a café to have it cooked and sliced before they ate it.

Heading home just before the coup, Sihanouk kept to his original itinerary and stopped in Moscow to ask for help in reducing the North Vietnamese bases inside his country. He was being driven to the Moscow airport when Kosygin told him he had just been deposed. Since Sihanouk already felt that the Russians were cool to him, he was grateful to arrive in Beijing and find Zhou Enlai as charming as ever. Sihanouk had not heard, however, the candid way that Zhou had spoken with Pham Van Dong only the day before.

Zhou told Dong that Lon Nol's coup had been supported by both Paris and Washington, with the French acting behind the scenes to protect their business interests in Cambodia. Zhou was sure he could predict the results: France would recognize Lon Nol's government but would pressure him not to attack North Vietnam's sanctuaries; he had already issued an order safeguarding the Chinese and Soviet embassies in Phnom Penh. Lon Nol would agree to the French condition in order to prevent the Communist Khmer Rouge from joining forces with Sihanouk's loyalists.

As a result of that maneuvering, Zhou assured Dong, Sihanouk could be expected to tilt toward the Soviet Union and China. "We should support Sihanouk for the time being," Zhou concluded, "and see how he will act." And if Nixon continued his actions—he had lately expanded the B-52 bombings in Laos—all of Indochina would join forces against the United States.

That plan seemed acceptable to Pham Van Dong until Zhou asked whether Hanoi would agree to meet with Lon Nol if he claimed to be endorsing Sihanouk's neutralism. "Before I came here, we discussed that," Dong replied. "We hold that negotiations would not bring any results because they would eventually fight against us. But we are not to be defeated. So what is the use of negotiations?" For now, Hanoi intended to play for time.

Receiving Sihanouk, Zhou began with elaborate expressions of admiration and support. He could assure the prince of backing from North Korea and several Arabic and African colonies. Sihanouk replied that Cambodia's ambassador in Moscow had told him that the Soviet Union was behaving very cautiously. The prospect of Eastern Europe's Socialist countries following Moscow's lead made Sihanouk frankly uneasy.

Zhou said that the Soviet Union always acted that way. But once Sihanouk, Hanoi and Beijing had issued their joint statement, "the Soviet Union will be embarrassed and have to reconsider its position."

Sihanouk, if not totally convinced, agreed to remain for the time being in Beijing and fight on against the Americans.

THE NIXON WHITE HOUSE had been unprepared for Sihanouk's ouster. Raging against the CIA headquarters, Nixon demanded, "What the hell do those clowns do out there in Langley?"

But Lon Nol and his fellow conspirators remembered the U.S. response to the coup against Diem in Saigon and had not asked for high-level pledges that Washington would back them. A sympathetic word relayed from an American agent—the sort of response Nguyen Khanh had received from Jasper Wilson in Hue in 1964—would have been more than enough encouragement.

Lon Nol's confidence was quickly rewarded. The day after the coup, Nixon sent Kissinger a note: "I want Helms to develop and implement a plan for maximum assistance to pro-U.S. elements in Cambodia." No other members of the intelligence community were to be informed. Kissinger was to handle the assignment as he had the secret Cambodian air strikes, which had long since passed through "Snack," "Dinner," "Dessert" and "Supper," and were now simply "Menu."

For Nixon, secrecy was essential because his administration recently had been caught out in a lie over Laos. When a North Vietnamese offensive early in the year threatened the government's forces, Souvanna Phouma had requested B-52 strikes. Stu Symington and others heard about the raids and labeled them part of a "secret war" in Laos. At that, Nixon decided he must admit at last to American activity there and Souvanna reluctantly agreed. Kissinger's staff wrote a statement acknowledging the bombing but denying that the war had been expanded into Laos: "No American stationed in Laos has ever been killed in ground combat operations."

Two days later, the *Los Angeles Times* reported the grisly death of a U.S. captain in Laos, and the Pentagon had to confess that 27 Americans had been killed there during the past year alone. Kissinger tried to wriggle out on a technicality: the Americans had been stationed in South Vietnam and killed only when they pursued the enemy into Laos. But Nixon saw how damaging Kissinger's lie had been and told aides, "No one cares about B-52 strikes in Laos, but people worry about our boys out there." He refused to see Kissinger for a week, even after Kissinger sent him a copy of his apology to Laird for twice putting back — over Pentagon objections — the phrase that denied combat deaths.

The affair was only the latest example of Nixon repeating the actions that had driven Johnson from office. With the fighting in Laos exposed, Nixon dropped 11 percentage points in the next Gallup poll, but given his sour view of human nature Nixon was unsurprised. His response was to identify with *Patton*, a film biography of the hard-charging general from World War II. Nixon complained that none of his aides went on the offensive as Patton did. In the gruff staccato of George C. Scott's portrayal, Nixon lectured Haldeman. The staff merely lies down, the president said. They don't radiate enthusiasm because they really don't feel it. They should see *Patton*. There was a man who inspired people. Charged them up. Haldeman and the rest had to do the same.

THE SAME DAY in February that the Chicago conspiracy trial went to the jury, Judge Hoffman began dealing out jail sentences for contempt of court. Lee Weiner got the lightest — two months and eighteen days, mostly for refusing to stand when the judge entered court. Kunstler outdid even Bobby Seale — four years and thirteen days, six months of them for calling the judge "Mr. Hoffman" instead of "Your Honor." Fifteen days of Abbie Hoffman's eight-month sentence were for laughing. One segment of Tom Hayden's one year, two months and thirteen days stemmed from his rising to protest Seale's rough treatment by his guards.

The jury split between 8 votes for guilty on both counts and 4 for acquittal. After a four-day deadlock, Weiner and Froines were acquitted, the others each found guilty of one count of the indictment.

Two days later, on February 20, the convicted men were allowed to make a statement, and they gave voice to the nation's discontent. Dellinger said that whatever unjustified punishment he faced "will be slight compared to what has happened already to the Vietnamese people, to the black people in this country, to the criminals with whom we are now spending our days in Cook County jail." Rennie Davis claimed that the suburban Chicago jury did not represent his peers. "I look to the jury that is in the streets," he said. Hayden charged that once Chicago denied permits for lawful demonstrations at the Democratic convention, "we had no choice. We had no choice in this trial. The people always do what they have to do."

Abbie Hoffman pointed to the portraits of early American revolutionaries hanging behind the judge's bench. "I know those guys on the wall. I know them better than you, I feel. I know Adams. I mean, I know all the Adams. They grew up twenty miles from my home in Massachusetts. I played with Sam Adams on the Concord Bridge. I was there when Paul Revere rode right up on his motorcycle and said, 'The pigs are coming, the pigs are coming. Right into Lexington.' I was there."

Judge Hoffman denied the men bail long enough for barbers at the Cook County Jail to cut off their hair. At a press conference, Sheriff Joseph Woods displayed Abbie Hoffman's shorn curls; his sister, Rose Mary Woods, was Nixon's long-time secretary.

Lon Nol was showing in Cambodia the kind of grit Nixon admired. He rejected a suggestion from China and North Vietnam that he pursue Sihanouk's neutral policies as their price for recognizing his government. Instead, he gave Hanoi forty-eight hours to withdraw its troops from Cambodia. The ultimatum was popular with those Cambodians who had always resented the Vietnamese, Communist or not, and 60,000 volunteers hurried to Phnom Penh to receive sketchy army training at bases around the capital. Better still for Lon Nol, Nixon sent supplies of captured weapons from CIA stockpiles. The token amounts seemed to promise that more aid would be coming.

Nixon was temporarily distracted from Indochina by a malfunction aboard *Apollo 13*'s module as it headed for the moon. The landing was aborted, and Americans waited in suspense until the astronauts landed safely. Nixon flew again to the Pacific to greet them and met in Honolulu with Admiral John McCain, who had replaced Sharp as Commander in Chief, Pacific. McCain had a more urgent stake in the war than most officers, since his son, a Navy pilot, had been shot down over the North. He had now been held for nearly five years with Robbie Risner and the other American POWs. Although the senior McCain was as diminutive as Brute Krulak, he was equally imposing, with a legendary penchant for drawing frightening maps. For Nixon, McCain produced an outline of Cambodia with China's blood-red claws already clutching half of the country. If the president was going to keep on withdrawing GIs from South Vietnam,

McCain said, he had to protect the ARVN by launching an assault on the North's sanctuaries. Impressed, Nixon brought McCain back to his residence in San Clemente, California, to repeat his performance for Kissinger, who said afterward that the pugnacious McCain reminded him less of Patton than of Popeye the Sailor Man.

On April 19, Nixon announced from San Clemente that he would speak to the nation the next day about Vietnam. Being as addicted to surprise as Lyndon Johnson, Nixon provided no details and turned away calls from Laird and Rogers. Then, allowing Kissinger to brief them by phone, Nixon deliberately misled his two senior cabinet officers. He said that he intended to reveal only a monthly rate of troop withdrawals, not an overall number.

Instead, Nixon went on the air to announce a withdrawal of 150,200 by the end of the spring of 1971. That figure might not meet Clifford's goal, but Nixon was projecting a total reduction of 265,000 men from the 549,500 he had inherited on taking office. He saw an advantage in placating his critics with a large number while keeping U.S. strength at its current level for the next two or three months while he dealt with Cambodia.

Haldeman noted with pleasure the way Nixon's apparent willingness to wind down the war had flummoxed the television commentators. He also considered Nixon's reading of the speech his best performance yet, although Hoover called from the FBI to say that Nixon had looked somewhat yellowish, rather washed out, and nothing like his healthy appearance in person. Hoover said his assistant, Clyde Tolson, thought so, too. It was a sensitive issue since Nixon's gaunt appearance in his first debate with Jack Kennedy in 1960 had seemed to lose the evening for him. Passing along Hoover's criticism, Nixon told Haldeman to do something about his lighting and makeup.

As he headed back to Washington, Nixon could not duck Laird any longer, but he instructed Kissinger to set up a back channel for dealing with Abrams and other generals so he could avoid his secretary of defense as much as possible. Nixon was not going to let Laird kill his strategy by pulling out too fast.

Kissinger, pleased to oblige, had his own frustrations. Throughout the spring, he had been irked during his secret contacts with Le Duc Tho in Paris. Kissinger took the fact that Tho had joined the anti-French movement at the age of sixteen as proof that he was a fanatic, although he had to admit that the man was always composed and well mannered. It was Tho's air of superiority that annoyed Kissinger, the sense that he was dealing with a barbarian trying to thwart North Vietnam's inevitable triumph. Attempts to charm Tho with modest jokes availed Kissinger as little as they had Jack Kennedy with Khrushchev. Tho might laugh politely, but he usually conveyed a feeling that Kissinger was wasting their time.

And it was hard for Kissinger to dispute a premise that Le Duc Tho put forward with such clarity: "Previously, with over one million U.S. and Saigon troops, you have failed. Now how can you win if you let the South Vietnamese Army fight alone and if you only give them military support?"

Meeting again in early April, Tho was at his most unyielding. He accused Washington of escalating the fighting in Laos and of staging the coup in Cambodia to bring a reactionary cabal to power. Kissinger denied CIA involvement by joking about his own success at keeping his Paris trips unknown to the agency. He despaired, Kissinger said, of convincing Tho that the United States had nothing to do with events in Phnom Penh, "although I am flattered by the high opinion he has of our intelligence services. If they knew I was here, I would tell them of his high opinion."

With the talks going nowhere, Kissinger's earlier euphoria had evaporated. He proposed another private meeting. Le Duc Tho said they should not meet again since there was nothing to discuss.

By April 22, Nixon was determined to reverse recent Communist victories in Laos and Cambodia and called on the Security Council to come up with a bold move that would preserve Lon Nol because "the only government in Cambodia in the last 25 years that had the guts to take a pro-Western and pro-American stand is ready to fall." The options were about the same as they had been for a decade: Laird and Rogers wanted to wait for further developments. Laird had already warned Nixon that politically he had to get more Americans out of Vietnam before the November congressional elections. Kissinger wanted to attack the Communist sanctuaries inside Cambodia with ARVN troops supported by American airpower. Nixon grinned as he watched his tetchy and emotional security adviser warming to the crisis in Cambodia. "Kissinger is really having fun today," Nixon told Haldeman. "He's playing Bismarck." For the time being, no one advocated the third option—adding U.S. troops to an invasion of Cambodia.

Then Spiro Agnew took the floor. For months, he had been attracting notoriety with the belligerent speeches written for him at the White House by Pat Buchanan. Nixon had chuckled as he reviewed a draft in which the vice president attacked the news media as "an unelected elite." But in recent months, Agnew had escalated to such divisive and insulting personal attacks that an alarmed Haldeman had to wrangle with Buchanan to tone down the more incendiary language.

Agnew brought that contentious spirit to the Security Council meeting. He recalled the time that Nixon had worried that antiwar demonstrators would disrupt his daughter Julie's graduation ceremonies at Smith College. To avoid attending, Nixon had fabricated a scheduling conflict, but it rankled him when Agnew said that he "damn well ought to go."

That had been bad enough for a president who needed to be the toughest man in the room. Now Agnew said that if the Cambodian sanctuaries were a threat, he was opposed to pussyfooting around. The administration should go out and attack Communist bases at two places in Cambodia—the Parrot's Beak and Fishhook. To do it, Nixon should send in American troops.

Faced with the conflicting advice, Nixon, like Kennedy and Johnson before him, split the difference. He authorized U.S. air support for Parrot's Beak if it proved necessary but held back on committing to Fishhook.

IN CAMBODIA, the Vietnamese Communists were attacking key towns and bridges, and South Vietnam's air strikes alone could not save Lon Nol's troops from surrendering their positions. Sihanouk in Beijing had allied himself with the "Cambodian Liberation Army," and the Communists now held the country's five northeastern provinces. Kissinger was sure that Cambodia could not survive a Communist offensive.

For his staff, Kissinger had recruited men who shared his former antipathy to Nixon and kept them mollified with frequent cracks about the commander in chief. "The meatball mind," Kissinger called Nixon, or "our drunken friend." Since the Security Council meeting, Nixon was staying up past midnight in the Lincoln Sitting Room, resolved to end the pussyfooting. When he told Kissinger to set up a 7:15 A.M. meeting the next morning with Richard Helms and Admiral Thomas Moorer, acting chairman of the Joint Chiefs, Kissinger reached William Watts, one of his aides, at the Jockey Club and warned him to prepare for a full day of meetings. To spur Watts on, Kissinger added, "Our peerless leader has flipped out."

Nixon called on Helms and Moorer for plans that would send American troops alongside the South Vietnamese when they raided the Parrot's Beak, and perhaps Fishhook as well. Both men heartily endorsed the idea; Rogers and Laird had not been invited to the meeting. Kissinger realized, however, that even the commander in chief should not order a military offensive without notifying his secretary of defense. He called the Pentagon and got Laird's best political advice: Don't authorize American involvement until Monday, the day Rogers was scheduled to testify before the Senate Foreign Relations Committee. That way, Rogers could truthfully deny that any Americans were involved in Cambodia.

Because Nixon did not enjoy Johnson's rapport with the Senate leadership, he left it to Kissinger to brief John Stennis of Mississippi, chairman of the Armed Services Committee. Kissinger claimed to admire Stennis and Dick Russell for their integrity and forgave them their racist votes. But even if those senators approved, Kissinger knew that sending American soldiers into Cambodia would outrage members of his own staff. He considered their objections woolly-headed since most of them agreed that, with Sihanouk now revealed as a Communist stooge, he must not be allowed to return to Cambodia. And yet they opposed adding American troops to the assault against the sanctuaries. The protesting staff members preferred to continue the Menu bombings while the ARVN alone made limited border crossings. Kissinger professed to see no moral distinction between shallow penetrations into Cambodia and deeper ones. All the same, he did not inform his staff that American troops might join the invasion. One aide, Anthony Lake, argued that GIs would inevitably be dragged in. "No," Kissinger assured him, "we'll be able to control that."

Early that same afternoon, Nixon flew to Camp David with Charles Rebozo, a Miami businessman called "Bebe." In his company, Nixon could always relax after a few of the martinis that Rebozo poured with a lavish hand. But Nixon's tolerance for liquor was low, and when he called Kissinger late Friday night, his voice sounded slurred. Kissinger signaled to William Watts to pick up an extension.

After a preamble about Kissinger's stake in making the Cambodia operation a success, Nixon said, "Wait a minute. Bebe has something to say to you." He passed the phone over to Rebozo. "The President wants you to know," Rebozo said, "if this doesn't work, Henry, it's your ass." In the background, Kissinger heard Nixon saying, "Ain't that right, Bebe?"

IN THE WEST BASEMENT on Sunday, Kissinger tried to put Watts in charge of Security Council staffing for the coming invasion. Watts begged off. He objected to the policy and would not assist in carrying it out. Kissinger snapped at him, "Your views represent the cowardice of the Eastern Establishment."

Watts moved toward Kissinger the way Peter Arnett had moved on Joe Alsop when Alsop questioned his honesty. Kissinger retreated behind his desk. On his way to write a letter of resignation, Watts ran into Alexander Haig, who told him that he could not leave. "You've just had an order from your commander in chief," Haig said. "You can't quit."

"Fuck you, Al," Watts said. "I just did."

Two other staff members, Tony Lake and Roger Morris, wrote a joint letter of resignation that set out their objections to the invasion. They said they were informing Kissinger before public reaction arose "so that it will be clear that our decision was not made after the fact and as a result of those consequences." They considered calling a news conference to protest the Cambodian offensive but decided it would hurt only Kissinger. He had persuaded them that he was the one brake on Nixon's ruthlessness. To protect him, they agreed to leave quietly.

At a meeting to unveil the coming invasion, other White House staff members were also dubious. William Safire, a speechwriter, asked whether an invasion would not violate the Nixon Doctrine.

"We wrote the goddam doctrine," Kissinger answered. "We can change it."

As the meeting ended, Haig summed up the administration's motives: "The basic substance of all this is that we have to be tough."

On Wednesday, April 29, the AP reported the ARVN offensive into Parrot's Beak. Antiwar senators asked the White House to pledge that American troops would not be involved, but a Nixon spokesman would say only that he would address the country the following night. Aware that his announcement might have the campuses roiling once more, Nixon told his secretary, Rose Mary Woods, to bring Julie and her husband David Eisenhower, Ike's grandson, to the protection of the White House.

Nixon received Buchanan's draft of the speech and stayed up working it over until 5:30 A.M. Reading the result, Haldeman found it an excellent summary of the U.S. position. Kissinger considered Nixon's language self-pitying and vainglorious but did not say so, praising instead the overwhelming merits of Nixon's case.

The U.S. attacks in the Fishhook began on April 30, at 7:30 P.M., Washington time. Ninety minutes later, Nixon stood in front of a map of Indochina to explain his decision to the American television audience. Ignoring the 14 months of Menu bombings and America's repeated guerrilla raids across the border, Nixon assured the nation that for the last five years the United States had scrupulously respected Cambodia's neutrality. Despite that restraint, he said, the North Vietnamese had launched an offensive that could overrun all of Cambodia.

Nixon promised that his response would destroy COSVN, which he described as the key control center for the Communist military staff. Once that headquarters was destroyed and the North Vietnamese were driven from their sanctuaries, the United States would withdraw. But Nixon went beyond military goals and invoked the familiar mantra of credibility. He was telling Hanoi that "we will not be humiliated. We will not be defeated." In his most vivid phrase, Nixon said that the world's most powerful nation could not act "like a pitiful, helpless giant." It was not America's power "but our will and character that is being tested tonight."

Nixon praised four of his predecessors for their toughness, three of them Democrats—Wilson in the First World War, Roosevelt in the Second, Eisenhower for ending the war in Korea and Kennedy who, "in his finest hour, made the great decision which removed Soviet nuclear missiles from Cuba."

With pugnacious self-pity, Nixon claimed that some senators had warned him that his decision in Cambodia would cost his reelection. "I would rather be a one-term President and do what I believe is right than to be a two-term President at the cost of seeing America become a second-rate power and to see this nation accept the first defeat in its proud 190-year history."

When the speech ended, Nixon was exhilarated by his performance and took congratulatory calls. Warren Burger, named chief justice the previous year, came in person to the White House to praise Nixon for his guts. It was 3 A.M. before Nixon got to bed, and the next morning he was up early. He brought in Kissinger and Ron Ziegler to review the day's public relations line. Cold steel, Nixon said. No give, nothing about negotiations. Hanoi could now choose between peace and war. Nixon wanted Ziegler to keep the emphasis on backing the boys in uniform and to sell the president's courage.

Nixon was off next on an impromptu trip to the Pentagon to find out how the Cambodian attack was going. Taking a lesson in euphemism from the way Kennedy had renamed the Cuban blockade as a quarantine, Nixon's officials were told to call the invasion of Cambodia an "incursion."

Moving through the corridors of the Pentagon, Nixon heard cheers from civilian and military men alike. His briefers assured him that the offensive was going well—194 Communists killed so far, most of them by the air strikes that had preceded the ferrying in of American troops by helicopter. Nixon spotted a wall map with four other sanctuaries marked out besides Parrot's Beak and Fishhook. He asked whether the ARVN and the U.S. troops were taking out all of them. When the Chiefs warned that Congress would object to that, Nixon was proud of his instant response: "Let me be the judge as far as the political reactions are concerned." He told them to do it. "Knock them all out so they can't be used against us again. Ever."

But, as Laird had warned Nixon might happen, COSVN had eluded them. Standing in the massive Pentagon, it was easy to imagine the Communist offices as equally centralized. But although COSVN covered a large area, with many bamboo huts and thatched roofs beneath a jungle canopy, its offices could be moved fluidly when threatened. Officers might leave behind documents or temporarily lose radio contact with their units, but even under heavy bombardment COSVN would go on functioning.

As Nixon left the Briefing Room, he was surrounded by admirers and too keyed up to be guarded with them. One woman thanked him on behalf of her husband serving in Vietnam. "You think of those kids out there," Nixon said of the soldiers, his voice thick with emotion. "I say 'kids' "—he corrected himself quickly—"I have seen them. They are the greatest."

He contrasted the servicemen with the antiwar demonstrators. "You see these bums, you know, blowing up the campuses. Listen, the boys that are on the college campuses today are the luckiest people in the world, going to the greatest universities, and here they are burning up the books, I mean storming around about the issue—I mean, you name it—get rid of the war." If the war ended, Nixon said, the demonstrators would soon be rioting over some other issue.

Back at the White House, Haldeman realized that Nixon was dead tired but still riding the crest of praise for his speech. He was glad that the president would be going to Camp David, where he could get the rest he needed. Meantime, Haldeman could report how well the polls had come out. Once again, the American people had rallied behind their commander.

AROUND THE WORLD, Nixon's incursion proved less popular. In Paris, Vernon Walters called Mai Van Bo three times on May 6 to say he had a message from Washington and wanted to arrange a meeting. But the North Vietnamese and NLF delegations announced that the U.S. actions violated the agreement of October 30, 1968. They left the conference, and Xuan Thuy and Mrs. Nguyen Thi Binh departed from Paris altogether. When he did meet with Walters, Bo received a note proposing another meeting between Kissinger and Le Duc Tho any weekend after May 16. Hanoi waited almost a month to reject that overture. "The U.S. words of peace are just empty ones," its message read.

In Phnom Penh, Lon Nol was confused by Nixon's actions. Given no advance word about the invasion, he had learned about it from the American chargé d'affaires, who had also been kept ignorant but had listened to Nixon's speech over the Voice of America. Lon Nol could overlook that slight to his authority if the invasion meant that he would be receiving vast shipments of American supplies. But although the United States would go on supplying air cover for Lon Nol's operations, Nixon did not intend to send aid on that scale. To soothe Lon Nol's anxieties, Al Haig was sent to Phnom Penh on his first major diplomatic assignment. In the spirit of the Krulak-Mendenhall trip seven years earlier, the State Department was not informed of Haig's trip. When Undersecretary of State Elliot Richardson finally heard and managed to get a man from State on the plane, Haig ignored him.

Haig landed in the Cambodian capital wearing battle fatigues. He refused to take the embassy's chief of mission with him to see Lon Nol, nor would he tell the man afterward what had transpired. But in their meeting, Lon Nol complained that, by breaking up the border sanctuaries, the Americans had pushed the Communists farther inside his country. His men could hold out now only because they had U.S. troops at their side. Haig had to inform him that Nixon intended to withdraw the Americans by the end of June. At that, Lon Nol burst into tears and went to a window to compose himself. Haig put an arm around his shoulder and promised that Nixon would give him whatever help he could—given his own political realities.

In Saigon, Abrams regretted bitterly that he could not send a U.S. division into Cambodia to follow up on this first penetration. Sitting with his officers, Abrams chafed against the restrictions from Washington. "We need to go west from where we are, we need to go north and east from where we are. And we need to do it now. It's moving and—" Abrams broke off, muttering, "goddam, goddam."

"Time to exploit," an officer said.

"Christ! It's so clear. Don't let them pick up the pieces," Abrams said. "Don't let them pick up the pieces! Just like the Germans. You give them 36 hours and, goddam it, you've got to start the war all over again."

The White House was finding that the Pentagon was its one island of support in a turbulent Washington. Senators had been aghast when they learned on May 2 that Nixon had used the Menu back channel to launch a hundred new fighter-bomber attacks against antiaircraft sites in North Vietnam. Hearing of the strikes, Fulbright said, "Good God!" Mansfield said he had a hard time believing it.

The disclosure had come from Hanoi Radio, but Kissinger saw a chance to implicate Laird and Rogers. He had stoked Nixon's fury over past leaks, but the defections among Kissinger's own staff were making Nixon suspicious. Kissinger asked the FBI to tap the phones of the two cabinet officers and their deputies.

Two days after the raids against the North were discovered, Laird announced that they had been ended. He did not inform Nixon first.

Senators John Sherman Cooper and Frank Church cosponsored a bill to cut off funds for the Cambodian invasion by June 20. George McGovern and Mark Hatfield, an Oregon Republican, went further. Their amendment to a military authorization bill would cut off all funding for U.S. operations throughout Indochina six months later.

But the most passionate response to Cambodia came on America's campuses, where students reacted even more violently than Nixon had anticipated. Stanford suffered the worst rioting in its history, and an Ohio State student was injured by a shotgun fired by a National Guardsman. At Kent State, also in Ohio, the ROTC building was burned to the ground. Afterward, sifting among the emotional rubble, one clue helped to explain why Kent State had exploded. Sihanouk had once spoken there to a respectful student audience. It was a time when *Time* regularly mocked Sihanouk as "Snookie," and the prince used his address to deplore the excesses of the American press. Later, he wrote that "my short stay at Kent somewhat consoled me for all the disappointments we have had with America and Americans."

Sounding like Nixon at the Pentagon, Ohio's Governor James Rhodes pledged to eradicate the student rioting and demonstrations. The students were worse than Nazis, Rhodes said, worse than Communists, worse than the Ku Klux Klan. "They're the worst type of people we have in America," the governor added, and he sent National Guardsmen to Kent State.

Sunday night, guardsmen and local police confined students to their dormitories, but sixty-nine students were arrested for protesting, and one girl was cut by a bayonet. Rhodes had raised the stakes. When students called a rally for noon the next day, May 4, it was as much to denounce Nixon's invasion of Cambodia as the presence of National Guardsmen on their campus.

As the demonstrators gathered, the Guard's commander ordered his troops to make them disperse by firing teargas. The students lobbed back any canister that did not explode while they shouted curses and hurled rocks and bricks. Some guardsmen were hit, and their unit withdrew to a nearby hill, provoking more jeers. Besides canisters and gas masks, the Guard had been issued M-1 rifles and told to lock and load, making them ready to fire. In the din and confusion, no one knew whether an officer had given the order or whether nervous and undertrained men set off the volley on their own. But sixty-one shots were fired into the crowd of students.

When the smoke cleared, two young men and two young women lay dead on the grass. Eight others had been wounded, and a domestic image had been added to the gallery of horrifying photographs from Vietnam. As its cover, *Newsweek* printed the picture of a young woman, Mary Ann Vecchio, bent over the body of a dead student, her mouth contorted in a scream.

From the White House, Ziegler read a statement from Nixon: "This should remind us all once again that when dissent turns to violence it invites tragedy." Nixon did not offer sympathy to the families of the dead students, and that omission made the words of the father of one victim the more poignant to an appalled nation. Allison Krause, nineteen years old, had been slain on her bucolic campus. "My child," her father told a reporter, "was not a bum."

THE KILLINGS at Kent State set off the greatest protests of the Vietnam War. In his message, Nixon had implied that the deans and faculty of the nation's universities were somehow responsible for the turmoil, and those men and women struck back. Kingman Brewster, president of Yale and a close friend of the Bundy brothers, announced that he was leading 1,000 of his faculty and students to Washington. Kissinger met with former Harvard colleagues and appealed for their sympathy. "If you only knew what I am staving off from the right," he said. The professors, with no idea that Kissinger was an architect of the Cambodian invasion, called on him to resign on principle.

Kissinger thought the protesters might menace his Washington apartment and was now sleeping in his office in the White House basement. To make that redoubt even more secure, Haig stationed a phalanx of troops there.

Two days after Kent State, two black protesters were killed on the campus of Jackson State College in Mississippi. Nixon called the college president and again did not face the issue. "What are we going to do," he asked, "to get more respect for the police from our young people?"

But with tens of thousands of distraught citizens flooding into Washington, Haldeman suspected that Nixon realized—although he would never admit it—that his "bums" remark had been badly damaging. Nixon claimed to believe that the goal of his left-wing enemies was to panic him and said he was determined not to fall into their trap. But even within his cabinet he faced dissent. From the time of the November Mobilization, Walter Hickel of Alaska, the secretary of the interior, had thought of writing a letter to the president suggesting that the young people only wanted to be heard. Now Hickel unburdened himself, invoking the youthful rebels from America's founding—Patrick Henry, Jefferson, Madison. "My point is, if we read history, it clearly shows that youth in its protest must be heard." Hickel signed his letter, "Faithfully, Wally." But when the *Washington Star* got a copy, Nixon resolved to fire Hickel as soon as the current crisis had passed. Meantime, the letter aroused Nixon's general resentment against all of his cabinet. None had called him after his speech a week ago, he complained, and no one was defending him now.

In fact, it was worse than that. The *New York Times* reported that Nixon's decisions about the war over the last two weeks had been made amid confusion and dissent and that both Rogers and Laird "had serious misgivings about the use of American troops in Cambodia." Laird denied the story and said he fully backed the invasion. Rogers said nothing. Nixon called to remind him that it was his duty to support a decision once the president made it.

On May 7, firebombs hit at least ten campuses, and governors in sixteen states called out the National Guard. Learning that the National Student Association was scheduling a day of protest for May 9, Nixon tried to lower the temperature. He called a press conference for May 8 at the odd hour of 10 P.M. He said it was to permit the students converging on Washington to hear him on their car radios. On his way to meet with reporters, Nixon said he would take absolutely no phone calls afterward. To Haldeman, that meant Nixon knew how much was at stake and was unsure about how well he would do.

Nixon told reporters that the students were saying that they wanted peace, to stop the killing and get out of Vietnam, and "I agree with everything they are trying to accomplish." But that same day, Agnew had reverted to earlier form, denouncing "choleric young intellectuals and tired, embittered elders." Nixon said he was not going to tell his vice president what to say but that his own rule was "When the action is hot, keep the rhetoric cool." A reporter asked, Then what about your "bums" remark? Nixon was ready with an explanation. He had not been talking about those who dissented, only about those who engaged in violence, burned buildings and terrorized their campuses.

As a preemptive strike, Nixon announced his plans to have most U.S. troops out of Cambodia within five weeks—by the second week in June—and all Americans out of the country by the end of June.

As the press conference ended, the mood at the White House was one of relief, and Nixon decided he would take phone calls after all. He also made them. Nixon had slipped into the exhausted but sleepless state that had accounted for his incoherent press conference when he lost the California governorship. In the three and a half hours before 2 A.M., Nixon made more than forty telephone calls. Kissinger got the largest number, eight. Haldeman lagged by only one. Nixon made a twelve-second call to Alex Johnson, now undersecretary of state, to complain about fifty junior foreign service officers who had written to oppose the invasion. "This is the President," Nixon told Johnson. "I want all those sons of bitches fired in the morning." He called Rose Mary Woods four times; Bebe Rebozo twice; two religious leaders, Norman Vincent Peale and Billy Graham. He called Nelson Rockefeller at 1 A.M.; Helen Thomas of UPI at 1:22 A.M.; Thomas Dewey, the former governor of New York, at 1:30 A.M. Nixon dozed fitfully for an hour and then began calling again. Helen Thomas got her second call at 3:50 A.M., Nixon's valet, Manolo Sanchez, at 4:22 A.M.

Hurrying to the president's office, Sanchez found Nixon at the window, watching students gather at the Washington Monument. Nixon said that the most beautiful sight in the capital was the Lincoln Memorial at night. Sanchez said he had never seen it. Nixon said, "Let's go look at it now!"

Going down to the White House lawn, the two men got a Secret Service car and driver to take them to the memorial. Eight students were there, spending the night until Saturday's rally. Nixon introduced himself, shook hands, told them about his press conference and urged them not to let their hatred of the war turn into hatred of the American system. Unprepared for the confrontation, the students said nothing.

Nixon tried again, recalling himself at their age and the mistake he had made in admiring England's Prime Minister Chamberlain for seeking peace with Hitler. As a Quaker, Nixon said, he had considered Chamberlain's opponent, Winston Churchill, to be a madman, but events had proved Churchill right.

The students still were not responding. Nixon exhorted them at length to travel while they were young. See the West, he said. San Clemente had "the greatest surfing beach in the world"—although he had to add that parts of it were closed because they were near a Marine base. Europe was fine, Nixon continued, "but it's really an older version of America." Asia was better. He hoped that sometime in his administration the students could go to China.

The number of listeners had grown to about thirty. One student cut in to say, "I hope you realize that we are willing to die for what we believe in."

Nixon said he knew that, and so was he. But better to live for what you believed in. When a contingent arrived from Syracuse University, Nixon praised their football team.

With the dawn, Nixon returned to the car, calling back a final bit of inspiration: "Remember, this is a great country, with all of its faults."

He directed the driver to go to the Capitol, where he insisted that Sanchez give a speech from the Speaker's chair. Sanchez talked about his pride in becoming an American citizen. Nixon applauded from the front row, and the cleaning women joined in.

At 5 A.M., Ehrlichman called Haldeman to say that Nixon had been spotted at the Lincoln Memorial. To find him, they dispatched a junior aide, Egil Krogh, nicknamed "Bud." By the time Haldeman caught up, Nixon was already coming out of the Capitol. Other aides had been alerted, and they joined in taking Nixon to breakfast at the Mayflower Hotel. Haldeman was relieved that Nixon would be leaving on the weekend for four days in Florida. He knew the danger signs—a crisis, no sleep, total exhaustion leading to displays of temper and bad judgment. So far, Nixon had come through his latest ordeal, but Haldeman saw the letdown coming and knew it would be monumental.

Before Florida, Nixon escaped first to Camp David. Like Johnson, he had begun to detect in his aides those doubts and insecurities he would not admit in himself. For months, Nixon had been judging Kissinger to be obsessive and paranoid and had become bored by Kissinger's constant infighting with Rogers and Laird. When the first *New York Times* story alluded to last year's bombing in Cambodia, the account had been sketchy enough that it provoked no outcry. But Nixon had been struck at the time by how emotional Kissinger became. Stamping his feet, he told Nixon, "We must crush those people!" On the phone to Laird, Kissinger said, "You son of a bitch, I know you leaked that story, and you're going to have to explain it to the president." But Nixon had never trusted the National Security Council, and he suggested that Kissinger take a hard look at his own aides.

It had been then that a panicky Kissinger called Hoover at the FBI and told him to investigate several recent leaks to prove they had not come from his office. He sent Haig to the FBI with a formal request for wiretaps on the telephones of three of his own staff—Morton Halperin, Helmut Sonnenfeldt and Daniel Davidson. Kissinger added a fourth name: Laird's military assistant, Robert Pursley. Laird regularly had his house and office phones swept for bugging equipment but had not thought to add Pursley's home number. Sonnenfeldt, like Kissinger a refugee from Nazi Germany, was a State Department officer; Davidson, a Harriman protégé, had been the man who briefed Kissinger in Paris during the 1968 campaign.

Before the wiretapping ended, the White House had ordered thirteen taps on government officials and four on journalists. Haig requested a tap on Richard Pederson, one of Rogers's confidants, which gave Kissinger access to the thinking of his two main cabinet rivals. After Tony Lake resigned over the Cambodian invasion, his phone was added to the list. The next day, Nixon took the spying operation away from Kissinger and gave it to Haldeman with instructions to decide who could see the transcripts. Kissinger did not know that John Mitchell, as attorney general, had tapped his phone for two months the previous fall. Long after the tap was removed, however, Kissinger suspected that he remained a target. Passing Haldeman in a White House corridor, he would grumble, "What do your taps tell you about me today, Haldeman?" William Safire, who was also tapped, concluded that Kissinger got a thrill out of working most closely with the same men he was spying upon most often.

Ehrlichman was approving other taps that bypassed the FBI because the bureau itself could not be trusted. He had a switch beneath his own desk so that he could record calls and conversation in his office. Kissinger was operating a dead key that allowed secretaries to make transcripts of his calls and also let aides listen in on Nixon, Laird or Rogers while Kissinger amused them by making funny faces. As the mania for bugging spread throughout the White House, Nixon had a change of heart. On taking office, he had ordered Johnson's taping system disconnected. Well into his second year in the White House, however, Nixon ordered a voice-activated taping mechanism installed in the Oval Office.

☐

IN RECENT YEARS, Dan Ellsberg had turned his private life on its head. He had come late to the spirit of the sixties but compensated with his usual passionate intensity. His marriage had dissolved before he went to Vietnam in 1965, and he was living in Malibu, working for RAND in Santa Monica and meeting regularly with a therapist.

At antiwar rallies he was hearing questions he had never raised and endorsing answers he would have disdained a few years earlier. At one rally, the simple warmth and humor of a young draft resister who was headed for prison made Ellsberg rush to the men's room and sob convulsively. By the time the army dropped charges against the six Special Forces accused of killing the South Vietnamese they suspected of being a double agent, Ellsberg knew which side he was on. He had gone from admiring the John Wayne of *Sands of Iwo Jima* to reveling in *Butch Cassidy and the Sundance Kid*, with its untrammeled heroes living beyond the law.

After winding up his assignment for Kissinger early in the Nixon administration, Ellsberg had returned to RAND in California. From Mort Halperin, he was picking up clues that perhaps Nixon intended to prolong the Vietnam war, not end it, and he wanted to read Les Gelb's documentation on its early stages. But even before Ellsberg's transformation Gelb had considered him somewhat indiscreet, and he turned Ellsberg down. Halperin intervened, a copy was made available to him, and its 7,000 pages convinced Ellsberg that he had been right: four presidents before Nixon—Truman, Eisenhower, Kennedy and Johnson—had not dealt courageously with Vietnam, and now Nixon was preparing to be the fifth.

Since the Pentagon study was restricted to the RAND premises, late each night Ellsberg put a chunk of pages in his briefcase. Passing the security desk on his way out, his stomach knotted, but the guards knew him and waved him past. Had he been stopped, he would say he was merely taking the papers to study at home and accept a mild reprimand. But his real intention would have been thwarted. Anthony Russo, a friend from Vietnam who had also turned against the war, was dating a woman with a copying machine at her office. Ellsberg went there the first night. Other times, weighed down by a pocketful of coins, he found a commercial copier. For key documents, Ellsberg was making forty or fifty copies, and the project took him much of September 1969. But early each morning, his previous day's stash was back in the RAND safe.

As he photocopied, Ellsberg was mulling over possible uses for the papers. The next summer, Kissinger invited him to visit at San Clemente, and as they chatted, Ellsberg asked whether he had a copy of the McNamara study.

Yes, said Kissinger idly. Should I look at it?

Definitely, Ellsberg said. At least look at the summaries and have someone on your staff go through the whole thing and pick out parts for you to read. It would not take long. The summaries of each volume were only two to three pages—less than two hundred pages in all.

"Do you really think we have anything to learn from that?" Kissinger asked.

Ellsberg felt his spirits sink. Nothing ever seemed to change at the National Security Council. Yes, he said. I really do. It is still relevant history.

"But you know," Kissinger protested, "we make policy very differently now."

Ellsberg was not looking for a job in the White House and did not need to be tactful. "Cambodia didn't look all that different," he said.

Kissinger hesitated. "You must understand, Cambodia was undertaken for very complicated reasons."

Ellsberg guessed what he meant. The Senate had just rejected two of Nixon's Supreme Court nominees. To his domestic opponents, Nixon had wanted to demonstrate toughness. To Hanoi, he had wanted to signal his willingness to escalate the war again.

"Henry," Ellsberg said, "there hasn't been a rotten decision on Vietnam in the last ten years that wasn't undertaken for very complicated reasons."

Kissinger mentioned a group of academics, led by Thomas Schelling of Harvard, who had come to Washington as consultants but had resigned over the Cambodia invasion. Those people, Kissinger said dismissively, knew nothing of policymaking. "They never had the clearances."

"I had the clearances," Ellsberg said.

"I know that. I am not speaking of you."

"And Bundy and Rostow had the clearances," Ellsberg persisted. "But their decisions weren't any better."

"Walt Rostow is a fool," Kissinger said.

"That may be true," Ellsberg said. "But McGeorge Bundy is no fool."

"No, he is not a fool," Kissinger granted. "But McGeorge Bundy has no sense of policy."

AFTER YEARS of treating South Vietnam as though it were a hostile country, Creighton Abrams had had enough. He scaled back the random artillery fire and decreed that he must approve the use of heavy weapons in the cities. Abrams scoffed at the way air strikes and helicopter gunships had been sent against a handful of Vietcong, and he questioned whether America's tactical airpower should be used at all in heavily populated areas. When fellow officers protested his new policies, Abrams said, "I don't want to be just out here banging up the goddam country in order to keep the *system* going." He was thinking of the Vietnamese people, he said, and ways to foster a healthy attitude toward their government.

Bus Wheeler had retired in June, succeeded as chairman of the Joint Chiefs by Admiral Thomas Moorer. The Pentagon sent General Fred Weyand to Saigon as Abrams's deputy, and on arriving Weyand asked, "What's the mission?"

"Who the hell knows?" Abrams said. "You know what has to be done. I know what has to be done. Let's get on with it."

THIRTEEN

ELLSBERG
1971

As the New Year approached, Nixon considered making 1971 the last year of America's involvement in Vietnam. Just before Christmas, he had shared his thinking with Kissinger and Haldeman. In April 1971, Nixon said, he could go to South Vietnam, tour the country and reassure Thieu about the consequences of the impending final withdrawal. Then he would come home and announce that America's role in Vietnam was over.

Kissinger strenuously protested Nixon's timetable. If U.S. combat troops came out by the end of 1971, he argued, the Communists could start trouble the following year. That meant the Nixon administration would pay the political price in the 1972 presidential election. Nixon should promise instead only that he would get American troops out by the end of 1972. That schedule would get him safely past his reelection. Nixon saw the wisdom in Kissinger's argument that guaranteeing his second term would require American soldiers to go on dying.

All the same, Nixon wanted to make a major move in 1971, and he announced that draftees would no longer be sent to Vietnam. He also began talking about an attack into Laos. It would be like the invasion of Cambodia but done secretly this time and conducted by only ARVN troops. As the plan developed, its code name became Lam Son 719, in honor of the village birthplace of Le Loi, a Vietnamese nationalist who had repelled Chinese invaders in 1428. Americans and ARVN had already adopted the name once before for successful assaults on Communist bases in the A Shau Valley.

Now, starting in late January, the ARVN would attack North Vietnamese bases along the Ho Chi Minh Trail in southern Laos. The operation would end after ninety days, when the monsoon season would wash out further maneuvers. The United States would supply helicopters, air strikes and artillery but only from the South Vietnamese side of the border.

After the Kent State killings, the Senate not only repealed the Tonkin Gulf Resolution but also voted for the Cooper-Church Amendment, withholding funds for U.S. combat troops in Cambodia or Laos. The House scuttled that measure, and a modified version had passed both chambers in December. It restructured the president's powers in Indochina but did not forbid the use of airpower.

Kissinger hoped an ARVN victory would bolster Thieu's forces against the Communist offensive predicted for 1973. By then, the U.S. election would be won and the last Americans home from the war.

But the Communists had learned from Cambodia. Since October they had been fortifying their positions, and they set up the 70B Front to run operations for three northern divisions, a total of 22,000 regulars and 640 auxiliary troops. Hanoi was not going to lose the supply lines bought at such a cost in toil and lives.

The American plan was straightforward. The 101st Airborne and the 1st Brigade of the 5th Infantry had taken over the deserted Marine base at Khe Sanh, and the ARVN would stage its assault from there. Fielding 16,000 men, the South Vietnamese would drive west from Khe Sanh along narrow Route 9, cut through the Ho Chi Minh Trail and seize the Laotian town of Tchepone, twenty-five miles from Khe Sanh. After raiding the Communist supply bases there, they would withdraw into South Vietnam.

Abrams had been concerned that Washington was pushing the ARVN too hard, but Thieu agreed to Lam Son 719 and filled in the details. Thieu estimated that the campaign would last two or three months. As always, however, the Communists had informants within the ARVN who deprived the South of any element of surprise. By now the North Vietnamese had massed 60,000 troops, the largest concentration of men in their country's history.

The ARVN offensive began at midnight on January 30, as Americans repaired the airstrip at Khe Sanh and cleared Route 9. One hundred yards from the Lao border, they posted a sign: "WARNING. NO U.S. PERSONNEL BEYOND THIS POINT."

For the ARVN, the operation started promisingly. By February 7, however, heavy clouds and rain grounded the U.S. planes that should have been taking out the Communist antiaircraft guns. Even so, the ARVN's lead units slogged down Route 9 and about five miles into Laos. They were meeting little resistance, morale ran high, and two days later the ARVN armored column could move up another half a mile.

On February 11, however, rains made the road all but unpassable. The ARVN column simply halted in its tracks, and the I Corps commander, Lieutenant General Hoang Xuan Lam, was issuing no orders to advance. Abrams learned that Thieu had directed his troops to stop for three to five days before pushing on to Tchepone. As a former tank commander, Abrams was outraged. The operation depended on speed and movement, but Thieu had adopted the thinking of Ngo Dinh Diem. Lam's men were his insurance against another coup, and Thieu had told him to be cautious and be prepared to cancel the assault once his casualties reached 3,000. With Thieu's own reelection approaching in the fall, heavy losses could undermine his campaign.

By February 16, Abrams felt he must fly to Lam's side. On the scene, he finally got the 1st ARVN Division moving west again, but Thieu was still advising Lam to take his time. Meanwhile, the Communists were massing to attack. During the last week of February, they overran the South's 39th Ranger Battalion and stepped up attacks against ARVN truck convoys on Route 9. On February 28, Lam flew to Saigon to beg for a new battle plan. Instead of occupying the enemy bases in southern Laos, he wanted the ARVN to hold the deserted town of Tchepone only briefly. Thieu agreed. "You go in there just long enough to take a piss," he told Lam, "and then leave quickly." The results might be meager, but Lam Son 719 would be declared a success.

Helicopters managed to get ARVN troops to Landing Zone Hope, less than a mile from Tchepone, but the Communist fire was unrelenting and withdrawing on foot would be costly. Lam flew again to Thieu to ask that his men be lifted out by the same helicopters. Abrams sat in on their meeting, convinced that with a little daring this could be the decisive battle of the war. Thanks to the American air support, the Communists had already lost half of their tanks and antiaircraft guns. Abrams urged that the ARVN's 2nd Infantry Division be moved from Quang Ngai province as reinforcements, which would allow the South Vietnamese to carry out their original offensive. To buttress that point, Haig had recently arrived to say that "Washington would like to see ARVN stay in Laos through April."

But Thieu understood the intention of the Cooper-Church Amendment. With the trace of a sneer, he asked, Why doesn't a U.S. division go along with them?

Abrams was overruled, and the evacuation began. It was a disaster. Television crews filmed scenes of ARVN troops, desperate to be flown out of danger, as they dangled from the landing skids of medical evacuation helicopters. For the American television viewer, Vietnamization became one more doomed fantasy. After ten years of training and costly equipment, South Vietnam's troops seemed to be no match for the Communists.

The ARVN lost 211 trucks, 96 artillery pieces, 87 combat vehicles, 54 tanks and all of its engineering machinery. A total of 107 U.S. helicopters had been destroyed, at least 544 damaged.

Casualty figures were, as usual, disputed. The Americans claimed the enemy had lost 20,000 men, half of the number that had joined the fighting. The South Vietnamese announced 7,683 ARVN casualties. *Newsweek* reporters called it closer to 9,800 and counted one of their own among the month's losses. François Sully had been killed in a helicopter on February 23. Even without crossing into Laos, the Americans had taken substantial losses, which were more reliably tallied—215 killed, 1,187 wounded.

IN WASHINGTON, Lam Son 719 was the sort of orphaned defeat Jack Kennedy once described. Bunker blamed the press for not conveying the ARVN's great military performance. Rogers had warned against the attack in late January, and Kissinger had wavered briefly. But by February 2, Kissinger had been saying that if Nixon let himself be talked out of the operation he would lose any hope of reining in the bureaucracies at State and Defense, which were already "completely out of control." Again, Kissinger's eye was on the next year's presidential election. If there was to be an outcry over invading Laos, let it come now and not in 1972. Although Kissinger had received word that Hanoi's troops were massing in Laos, he had seen that as a possible advantage. Going ahead with Lam Son 719 would allow U.S. planes to bomb them, and bombing was easier to sell to the American public than another invasion.

As the dimension of the ARVN collapse became clear, however, Kissinger complained that Abrams had misled him about the chances for success. They should pull Abrams out of there, Kissinger told Nixon. The president agreed but pointed out that Lam Son 719 had been the last of the American-directed ground operations in Indochina, anyway.

So what difference did it make?

ON MARCH 29, 1971, a day Ron Ridenhour had been awaiting for nearly three years, jurors finished deliberating over the fate of William Calley, charged with the premeditated murder of 22 villagers at My Lai. After more than seventy-nine hours, the military jury was ready to announce its verdict.

In the two years since he sent off his letter to Washington, Ridenhour had sometimes been convinced that the Pentagon and the Nixon White House were covering up his charges. Despite his suspicions, however, the Defense Department had promptly run a check on the names in Ridenhour's letter, which showed that all but one of the men had been at My Lai on March 16, 1968. The exception was the lieutenant he mentioned; Ridenhour had spelled his name "Kalley."

During the investigation, Ridenhour learned that Hugh Thompson had not been killed after all. Since My Lai, he had been shot down on five occasions, the last time badly injuring his back, but when the confusion over Calley's name was cleared up, Thompson instantly picked him out from a lineup of photographs.

The case had gone next to Colonel William V. Wilson, a forty-five-year-old Green Beret recently assigned to the inspector general's office. Wilson had read Ridenhour's letter four times. It could not be true, he thought. But if it were, he was determined to expose the coldblooded murderers. Wilson flew to Phoenix with a court reporter, read Ridenhour his rights and, after three hours of testimony, left convinced that he was telling the truth.

Ridenhour had promised not to go to the press, but as the months dragged on with no sign of progress, he often called Wilson collect to accuse him of being part of a cover-up. Ridenhour's impatience, he admitted, was making him "crazy nuts."

Two months before Sy Hersh first contacted him, Ridenhour got a call from Wilson, who sounded equally excited: Calley had been arrested. Ridenhour waited to hear about more arrests. There were none. But blame was rising up the chain of command. Medina implicated Colonel Oran K. Henderson, who had investigated the events at My Lai and not filed a report. Major General Samuel W. Koster was also said to have heard accounts of the atrocities.

Then Hersh's story broke, and for the next six months Claremont College assigned Ridenhour his own full-time public relations man. White House aides still hoped to avoid a public inquiry, but when Westmoreland heard about possible obstruction, he threatened to go directly to the president.

Handed the investigation, Lieutenant General William Peers took up the challenge gamely. Iowa-born, educated as a teacher at UCLA, Peers had served in the army for more than thirty years, with the OSS in China, with army intelligence in Korea, as commander of the 4th Infantry Division in South Vietnam's Central Highlands. Coming to know Hugh Thompson, Peers decided he had been the only brave man at My Lai that day and took him back to Vietnam in early 1970 to fly with him over the village while Thompson repeated what he could remember.

Peers's inquiry had ended that March, with 20,000 pages of testimony from more than four hundred witnesses. To his own satisfaction, Peers had established that several officers, including Henderson and Sam Koster, who was Peers's good friend, had conspired to cover up the massacre. Even the word "massacre," however, was anathema around the Pentagon. Secretary Resor also tried to avoid identifying the victims as Vietnamese women, children, babies and old men. He lobbied for the term "noncombatant casualties."

The Army's Criminal Investigation Division had judged that there was enough evidence to charge thirty GIs with serious crimes. Another fifteen were considered probably guilty but with insufficient proof against them. When Charles Hutto was found not guilty by a court-martial jury—despite his admission that he had killed unarmed villagers with his M-60 machine gun—charges were dropped against four other enlisted men.

The army prosecuted only the four officers still on active duty—Calley, Medina, Captain Eugene Kotouc and Lieutenant Thomas Willingham. Of the other officers accused by the Peers panel, Colonel Henderson was the only one put on trial. Koster, who had been named superintendent at West Point, resigned his post and left the army.

Calley's court-martial at Fort Benning took four-and-a-half months; five of the six army officers on his jury had served in Vietnam. His defense claimed that he had only obeyed a lawful order given by Medina as his superior officer. "I did not sit down and think in terms of men, women and children," Calley told the court. Since they were all classified as enemy soldiers, he added, "I do not feel wrong" about carrying out Medina's orders.

The jurors felt otherwise. Returning to court on March 29, they found Calley guilty of the premeditated murder of 22 villagers at My Lai. Two days later, they sentenced him to life in prison at hard labor.

Not all public sentiment had been outraged by the massacre. An admiring "Battle Hymn of Lt. Calley" sold 200,000 records, and at Fort Benning, recruits counted cadence with the chant "Calley! Calley! He's our man! If he can't do it, Medina can!"

Calley spent three days in the stockade before Nixon ordered him released to house arrest in his own quarters. During Medina's own trial, he celebrated his thirty-fifth birthday and was acquitted by a jury that deliberated for less than an hour. Since Medina was out of the army by the time he testified at Colonel Henderson's trial, he could safely confess that he had lied under oath to army investigators. A month after Calley's conviction, Captain Kotouc was acquitted of cutting off a Vietcong suspect's finger the day of the massacre. Henderson was also acquitted, although in a candid moment with reporters he said that the other American brigades committed atrocities like My Lai. They just did not have a Ridenhour to expose them.

IN PARIS, the peace talks had been stalled since the previous September when Kissinger had proposed withdrawing U.S. ground troops over the next twelve months. For the first time, he did not demand a similar withdrawal of northern forces from the South. It was the major concession of the talks, but the Communists had taken Kissinger's offer as no more than a ploy to give the Republicans an edge in the 1970 U.S. congressional elections.

Now, returning to the talks in late May 1971, even some members of Kissinger's staff wondered whether to allow northern troops to remain in the South was not sealing South Vietnam's fate. Richard Smyser, a foreign service officer well versed on Vietnam, warned Kissinger on the flight to Paris, "If the North Vietnamese don't withdraw, there will never be peace."

Kissinger seemed to agree but said, "We need a settlement."

For the time being, the concession would be smuggled past Saigon in vague language that pledged American troops and "all other outside forces would withdraw." To Hanoi, its soldiers, being Vietnamese, could not be regarded as an outside force.

The North was hoping for even better terms during this round of talks since America's attention had increasingly focused on the U.S. pilots being held in Hanoi. The Communists expected the agitation over the POWs to pressure Washington still further.

The North Vietnamese also weighed China's change of heart about the talks. Before the stalemate, Mao told Pham Van Dong in Beijing: "The negotiations have lasted two years. During the first year, we were anxious that you could be deceived by your adversary." But now Vietnam was fighting well, and the Chinese leadership no longer feared negotiations. Mao did not confide his own plans or his possible overtures to Hanoi's enemy.

The North next heard from the Soviet ambassador in Hanoi that Kissinger would ask only that they "respect a cease-fire during the U.S. withdrawal; plus a certain period of time—not too long—afterward." That, they were assured, was the important point. The message had come through Dobrynin in Washington, and Kissinger had not specified how long the waiting period must be. Informally, it came to be called a "decent interval" that would save face for Washington.

The Russian message concluded, "Such a process will spare the Americans the necessity to carry out a protracted and practically unfruitful negotiation about a political solution for South Vietnam when the U.S. forces have withdrawn. All these questions will directly involve only the Vietnamese."

Pham Van Dong had rejected the Soviet overture. He had been anticipating another push by Washington to win a major battle, and five days later Lam Son 719 was launched. The failure of that operation thrilled Hanoi's leaders, who described it as a "pitiful fiasco" for the United States and boasted of the way the Ho Chi Minh supply route had been enlarged. Ten times more supplies—40,000 tons—had gone south in the past year than in 1969.

By May, Hanoi no longer considered the withdrawal of U.S. troops its key issue. Le Duc Tho began to concentrate instead on getting rid of Thieu and Ky. On May 31, Kissinger met with Xuan Thuy in Paris for the first time since October. "I am here with the aim of making real progress," Kissinger began, beaming. He said Nixon had sent him to break the deadlock. "This is the last proposal," he added, unfurling seven points that incorporated past U.S. concessions: a timetable for U.S. withdrawal; the Indochinese settling among themselves the withdrawal of other outside forces, with no new outside troops to be infiltrated; a cease-fire in place with international supervision; respect of both the 1954 and 1962 Geneva Accords; release by each side of prisoners of war and civilians.

But Kissinger had also reverted to his unwillingness to talk about the politics of South Vietnam, even though Xuan Thuy pointed out that with elections in the South due soon, it was the logical time for a peaceful change. The prisoners of war were another sticking point. Xuan Thuy accused Kissinger of using them for propaganda. Kissinger replied that he would not set a deadline for troop withdrawal until the POW question had been resolved.

The North Vietnamese assumed that Kissinger had obtained Thieu's agreement to his seven points but did not know how he had described them to Saigon. The Politburo decided that if the North did not respond positively to this new initiative, Nixon would revert to Vietnamization and not try again to settle until after his 1972 reelection. By now, Hanoi's leaders had also learned about China's overtures to the United States. The Politburo resolved to go forward with the war, but with the Chinese placing their own interests above all else, the future was going to be complicated.

THE LEAD STORY in the *New York Times* on Sunday, June 13, concerned Washington's attempts to reduce friction between India and Pakistan. A front-page photograph also showed a smiling Richard Nixon at the wedding of his daughter, Tricia, in the White House Rose Garden. And there was a story about cuts in the New York City budget. Easy to ignore, despite its three-column spread, was an article with Neil Sheehan's byline: "Vietnam Archive: Pentagon Study Traces 3 Decades of Growing U.S. Involvement." The tame headline had been the conscious choice of Abe Rosenthal, the managing editor. The *Times* publisher and its lawyers were already nervous about the story. To avoid sensationalism, Rosenthal had rejected the phrase "Pentagon Papers."

For Ellsberg, the *Times*'s scoop was a letdown. In the many months since he first made copies, he had sought a better way to get the material to the public. He knew he could be tried under espionage laws, so his safest course would be to convey the volumes to a congressman with the proper security clearances. He offered them first to Fulbright, but the senator had been impressed by Nixon's early pledges to end the war. The most Fulbright would do was ask Laird to declassify the study, and Laird refused.

Ellsberg next doled out pages to historians at the Institute for Policy Studies in Washington, and in February 1970, he briefed Senator Charles Goodell, who was in favor of forcing the withdrawal of American troops. George McGovern, who was being discussed as a Democratic presidential candidate for 1972, refused to be a party to making classified documents public and advised Ellsberg to give them to the *New York Times* or the *Washington Post*. But when Ellsberg consulted lawyers, they told him that leaking to the press would be the surest way to guarantee a long prison term.

By February 1971, stymied at every turn, Ellsberg got in touch with Sheehan in the *Times* Washington bureau. They had met in Vietnam, and Ellsberg had sometimes passed along information that Sheehan had used without revealing his source. Now the two entered into an intricate negotiation. Sheehan could not commit the *Times* until its editors saw the material, but Ellsberg did not want to surrender the papers unless the *Times* promised to devote a vast amount of space to running many of the actual documents, not merely Les Gelb's summaries of them.

At the *Times*, editors were enough tantalized by Sheehan's description of the papers that they sent him to an apartment in Boston—not Ellsberg's own—where they were being stored. Ellsberg was willing to let Sheehan read through the volumes and take notes but refused to let him make copies. If the *Times* had its own set, Ellsberg lost control over them. He still hoped for a friendly congressman, whose revelations would bring the documents more attention than publishing them in a newspaper.

Sheehan knew, however, that pages Ellsberg had already distributed were making the rounds on the East Coast, and he was determined not to be scooped. The *Boston Globe* had run a teasing story on March 7 that quoted Ellsberg as saying he now realized that he had participated "in a criminal conspiracy to wage aggressive war."

Ellsberg handed Sheehan a key to the apartment and left him alone with the papers for the weekend. Sheehan immediately ignored his instructions and set out to find a copying machine. At least Ellsberg could always testify, if the worst came to pass, that he had not given copies to the *Times*.

From a pay phone, Sheehan arranged with William Kovach, the *Times* Boston correspondent, to pay $1,500 to a copy-store owner in Bedford if he would stay open all weekend; the newspaper wired the money from New York. When their copying chore was done, Sheehan and his wife, Susan, a writer for the *New Yorker* magazine, drove the carful of documents back to Washington. To wade through them, the *Times* booked a room at the Jefferson Hotel and assigned an editor, Gerald Gold, to work with Sheehan. *Times* management had not agreed yet to run the study, and its existence was known to a small number of executives. Scotty Reston was now working out of New York, and on April 20, the ranking editors gathered in his office to listen while Sheehan described what he had.

Making his presentation, Sheehan listed the major findings: that the Tonkin Gulf Resolution had been based on a nonexistent second attack; that the CIA's gloomy reporting on the war was more accurate than Westmoreland's upbeat estimates of progress; that plans for the escalation of troops had been deliberately withheld from the American public.

Sheehan warned the editors that publishing the papers would turn much of the East Coast Establishment against the *Times*, since the exposure would damage the reputations of McNamara and the Bundy brothers. Sheehan did not disclose Ellsberg's name, and he explained that the *Times* would not be getting the four volumes of the study that covered the abortive attempts to negotiate. Sheehan said that his source did not want to jeopardize the Paris peace talks.

Reston reminded the group that Foster Dulles had once given him documents from the Yalta Conference that had also been stamped "Top Secret." In this case, however, that stamp had been deliberately left off the copies before Sheehan got them. While the editors agreed unanimously that the *Times* should publish, Louis Loeb, the newspaper's lawyer from Lord, Day & Lord, was

Neil Sheehan
(AP/Wide World Photos)

adamantly opposed. The *Times* must first get the government's permission, Loeb said. It was a matter of patriotism. Beyond that, publication of classified documents was illegal, and the editors would be prosecuted and sent to jail.

After many angry exchanges, Reston said that if the *Times* did not publish the papers, he would print them in a small paper he owned on Martha's Vineyard. The final decision rested with Arthur Ochs Sulzberger, the publisher. By now, Punch Sulzberger had been running the family newspaper for eight years, and yet, even at age forty-five, he was regarded by some editors as a pleasant lightweight. Sulzberger insisted on seeing all of the copy before he made a decision. "I'm not going to jail for something I haven't read," he said.

By May, Rosenthal could put the edited version in boxes and wheel them in a shopping cart to the publisher's office on the fourteenth floor. As Sulzberger browsed through the documents, he kept his editors in suspense. Meantime, they were debating among themselves whether releasing only the summaries would expose the paper to fewer legal reprisals than printing the classified memoranda as well. They were sure that Sulzberger would prefer omitting the actual documents, but traditionally a *Times* publisher exercised his power sparingly.

Sulzberger was scheduled to leave soon for London and promised a decision on Friday, June 11. That afternoon, he surveyed his tense employees and rendered his verdict.

"I've decided you can use the documents." He paused. "But not the story."

The editors forgave his modest joke. The next evening, story and documents all appeared in the early Sunday edition. With the Pentagon Papers published at last, Sheehan and friends from the *Times* celebrated Sunday evening at an Italian restaurant in Manhattan. One of them asked what they had learned from the papers. Hedrick Smith, the reporter from the Paris talks who had been working on the project, said, "I've learned that never again will I trust any source in the government."

The others lifted their glasses in a toast.

WITH TRICIA NIXON'S wedding reception preoccupying the White House, Al Haig was the first official to spring into action when the *Times* appeared Saturday evening. Gelb and Halperin had once asked Haig to join the project, so he had a better sense than most of Nixon's staff what the Pentagon Papers involved. Haig had stayed in touch with Rostow, now teaching at the University of Texas in Austin, and called to ask what he knew about the study. Since Gelb and his crew had purposely kept their distance from him, Rostow remembered only the project's general outline, but he had a more immediate concern. "Who leaked it?"

Haig said, "We think it is a guy named Ellsberg."

"The son of a bitch!" Rostow exclaimed. "He still owes me a term paper."

Rostow was making an academic's jest. When Ellsberg was working for John McNaughton in the Pentagon, Rostow had asked him to prepare a study of the way decisions had been made during the 1962 Cuban missile episode. Rather than submit his conclusions in writing, Ellsberg had briefed Rostow in person but had never given him the paper.

After all of the soul-searching at the *Times*, Sheehan's exclusive seemed to misfire. When Haig reached Haldeman on Sunday morning, Haldeman observed that since the study blasted McNamara, Kennedy and Johnson, the Nixon administration should keep out of the matter and let the people who were embarrassed "cut each other up on it." On Capitol Hill, Senator Robert Dole of Kansas, chairman of the Republican National Committee, agreed and considered the Papers a boon for his party.

Mel Laird was headed for CBS that morning to be interviewed on *Face the Nation*. He had known that the volumes were taking up a full shelf of his wall safe and had occasionally sent an aide to consult them before Laird testified to Congress. Reading the *Times* story, he felt the Papers would not hurt Nixon and was pleased that they had come out. But after consulting with John Mitchell, Laird agreed to say, when he was asked about the Papers during his television interview, that the *Times* had endangered national security and that he had asked Mitchell's Justice Department to look into the matter. That advance planning was not necessary. During the half-hour program, not one of the twenty-seven questions concerned the Pentagon Papers.

Kissinger had been in California over the weekend. When Haig called him with the news, he was confronted by the danger to his standing with Nixon. Kissinger's involvement with the Papers went back to the beginning. Gelb had been a doctoral student when Kissinger was still teaching at Harvard, and in 1967 Gelb had invited him to the Pentagon to coax him into joining the project. Kissinger had spent a day going over the assignment with Gelb and Halperin, another of his former students. He declined a direct role, but when he got involved in the "Pennsylvania" overtures, he had read the documentation about prior negotiations with Hanoi.

Kissinger also knew that Ellsberg was not taken in by the myth that Kissinger was the one restraining influence on an unstable president. After their conversation at San Clemente, they had clashed earlier in the year at MIT. Kissinger had finished his talk when Ellsberg rose with a purposely embarrassing question: "What is your best estimate of the number of Vietnamese who will be killed in the next twelve months as a consequence of your policy?"

Kissinger began his reply by calling the question cleverly worded.

Ellsberg broke in to say he had not been trying to be clever. It was a basic consideration.

Kissinger tried to put Ellsberg on the defensive. "What other options are there?" he asked.

"I know the options game, Dr. Kissinger," Ellsberg said. "Can't you give us an answer?" The meeting broke up soon afterward.

None of that alone would be damning, but even before the tapping of his staff's telephones Kissinger knew that Nixon considered his young aides avid leakers of questionable loyalty. Just the previous month, Nixon had erupted during a leisurely ride down the Potomac on the White House yacht *Sequoia*. He was already making tentative plans for approaching China but, he said, "if those liberals on your staff, Henry, give everything to the *New York Times*, I won't be going anywhere."

That same evening, Nixon had already enjoyed both Scotch and Burgundy when his mind veered again to his enemies. "One day we will get them — we'll get them on the ground where we want them. And we'll stick our heels in, step on them hard, and twist." Nixon paid Kissinger a dubious compliment: "Henry knows what I mean," he told the other guests. "Just like you do it in the negotiations, Henry. Get them on the floor and step on them, crush them, show them no mercy."

Now the enemies were on the front page of the *New York Times*, and Kissinger had brought a few of them into the Nixon White House. He must prove his fealty by becoming even more implacable than his president. At the 7:30 A.M. staff meeting on Monday, Haldeman, Ehrlichman and the others watched a volcanic performance as Kissinger shouted, waved his arms, pounded his fist and cried for vengeance. "No foreign country will ever trust us again," he declaimed. "We might just as well turn it all over to the Soviets and get it over with."

Kissinger took his fury to the Oval Office and prodded Nixon by pushing a reliable button. If he did nothing, Kissinger warned him, "it shows that you're weak, Mr. President.

"The fact that some idiot can publish all the diplomatic secrets of this country on his own is damaging to your image as far as the Soviets are concerned," Kissinger added, "and it could destroy our ability to conduct foreign policy."

At first, suspicion also centered on Gelb and the Brookings Institution, a policy organization that the president considered hostile. As evidence began to implicate Ellsberg, Kissinger denounced him to the rapt attention of Nixon, who was intrigued by Kissinger's scabrous rumors about Ellsberg's reputed sexual practices, drug use and atrocities committed in Vietnam. Kissinger threw in that Ellsberg had "married a wealthy girl." Haldeman noted afterward that he had often heard Kissinger in a rage, sometimes so vitriolic that he had to repress a smile, but the scene Kissinger staged over the Pentagon Papers was his premier performance.

By the time the rant ended, Nixon was boiling. As he explained to his cabinet: "I get a lot of advice on PR and personality and how I've got to put on my nice-guy hat and dance at the White House, so I did it. But let me make it clear that's not my nature. We're going to go forward with Ellsberg and prosecute him."

Since the FBI and the CIA were ineffectual at plugging leaks, Nixon told Ehrlichman that he would have to remedy the lack. "I want you to set up a little group right in the White House. Have them get off their tails and find out what's going on and figure out how to stop it."

Ehrlichman sprang into action, appointing Bud Krogh and a Kissinger aide, David Young, as a Special Investigative Unit. Housed in basement quarters of the Executive Office Building, the men were nicknamed the "Plumbers" because they were supposed to stop leaks. Another Nixon aide, Charles Colson, recommended that they also hire Howard Hunt, a former CIA man. In time, a former FBI agent, G. Gordon Liddy, joined the group as well. Colson's assignment was to discredit Ellsberg by finding evidence that would support Kissinger's lurid account of his past. As Nixon kept pressing for results, Hunt and Liddy sent a team of three Cuban-American veterans of the Bay of Pigs to break into the Los Angeles office of Dr. Lewis J. Fielding, Ellsberg's psychiatrist. They found nothing.

AT MITCHELL'S JUSTICE DEPARTMENT, an assistant attorney general, Robert Mardian, asked another assistant, William Rehnquist, whether the government could prevent the *Times* from publishing more installments of the Papers. Nixon sometimes mocked Rehnquist's sideburns and pink shirts, calling him a clown and mispronouncing his name as "Renchburg." But Rehnquist had graduated first in his class at Stanford, and Nixon was forced to share the Justice Department's respect for his ability. When the attorney general's assistants agreed that the newspaper should be enjoined from publication, Mitchell got Nixon's approval to seek a prior restraint order.

Early on Tuesday afternoon, June 15, U.S. District Judge Murray I. Gurfein, newly appointed by Nixon to the bench, granted the government a temporary restraining order until 1 P.M. on Saturday. He did not require the *Times* to return the documents, however. Three parts of the series had already run. The remaining installments were held until the U.S. Supreme Court could rule on the government's motion.

WHEN THE *Times* was enjoined from printing its next article from the Pentagon Papers, Kay Graham had to decide whether to become a heroine to her *Washington Post* staff by putting her paper at risk. She took the gamble. Ben Bagdikian, a *Post* editor, had known Ellsberg from the RAND Corporation and deduced that he was the *Times*'s source. After negotiating with him by phone, Bagdikian flew to Boston on Thursday and returned with 4,000 pages of the Papers in a large box for which he bought another first-class ticket. Ellsberg extracted a pledge that the *Post* would not scoop the *Times* by picking up where its third installment had ended. Instead, he wanted the paper to go further back in the history of U.S. decision-making. The *Post*'s Friday headline read, "Documents Reveal U.S. Effort in '54 to Delay Viet Election."

At 2:45 P.M. on Saturday, Judge Gurfein accepted the *Times* argument that it had not intended to communicate vital secrets to a foreign government but had only sought "to vindicate the right of the public to know."

At the White House, Nixon received the *Times* victory bitterly. If the government's appeal was lost, he wanted White House aides at least to hang Vietnam on Johnson. They could say, "LBJ screwed up the war." Meanwhile, his administration persisted in court—through trial arguments about the *Times* in the U.S. Court of Appeals, the *Post* in District Court and the Court of Appeals and finally their joint case before the U.S. Supreme Court. On June 30, the justices ruled 6 to 3 in favor of the newspapers. The decision noted that all of the lower courts had found that the government had not met the heavy burden for justifying prior restraint. The majority said simply, "We agree."

If the Nixon White House could not punish the newspapers, Ellsberg remained a tempting substitute. Sure that government investigators were closing in, Ellsberg gave a three-hour interview to *Newsweek* and then he and his wife went into hiding. On Monday, June 28, two days before the Supreme Court ruling, he surfaced, accompanied by lawyers, and surrendered to federal authorities. Ellsberg was prepared to go to prison for life; Mitchell's Justice Department was determined to put him there. A Los Angeles grand jury indicted Ellsberg for violating the Federal Espionage Act and for the theft of government property. Tony Russo was offered full immunity if he would testify about photocopying the documents. He refused, was cited for contempt and jailed, but freed when the government reneged on an agreement to give him a transcript of his testimony before the grand jury. By December, the Justice Department revised Ellsberg's indictment to charge him with fifteen counts of espionage, conspiracy and conversion of government property. Russo was named a coconspirator. They would be tried in 1972.

BESIDES PERSONAL EMBARRASSMENT, Kissinger had another reason to deplore the furor over the Pentagon Papers. As Nixon's offhand remarks indicated, he had been considering a trip to China even before his inauguration. The implausible drama of it had immense appeal. Richard Nixon, a lifelong anti-Communist, one of Chiang Kai-shek's most reliable supporters, would turn up in Beijing with Mao at his side. By 1969, Mao had pulled back from his Cultural Revolution and was viewing America as the counterweight to an increasingly hostile Soviet Union. In June 1970, Beijing had agreed that the next time Kissinger came unobserved to Paris to meet with the North Vietnamese, he could also conduct secret talks with the Chinese ambassador. That December, Mao used Edgar Snow to convey a private invitation to Nixon to visit.

The White House, then, was less than surprised in early April when—during the 31st World Table Tennis Championship in Nagoya, Japan—the Chinese invited the U.S. team to go to China. The American Ping-Pong players arrived on April 14. Zhou Enlai greeted them and predicted that they were opening a new chapter in Chinese-American relations. After another six weeks of guarded messages, Zhou sent an invitation for a special envoy—he specifically mentioned Kissinger—or the secretary of state or the president himself.

On July 9, after a fitful night of excited anticipation, Kissinger flew the 2,500 miles from Islamabad to Beijing. For Kissinger, arriving in China was overwhelming, and he felt as though time had stood still. He ate a late lunch and then met Zhou. Kissinger made a point of shaking his hand warmly because of Dulles's rebuff in Geneva seventeen years earlier. Zhou gave a quick smile, and his charm and self-possession impressed Kissinger, who quickly learned to avoid his usual rhetorical flourishes. "Many visitors have come to this beautiful and, to us, mysterious land," Kissinger began.

Zhou stopped him. "You will find it not mysterious," he said. "When you have become familiar with it, it will not be as mysterious as before."

On Kissinger's first trip, the two men spent seventeen hours in conversation. These were not the negotiations of Paris. The great obstacle between their countries was the existence of Chiang's Taiwan, and on this trip they were not going to address that problem. They talked instead in general terms, and Zhou told about

Henry A. Kissinger
(AP/Wide World Photos)

Chinese Premier Zhou Enlai
(AP/Wide World Photos)

being confined to his office by zealous Red Guards during the height of the Cultural Revolution. He said he had doubted the need for that upheaval but that Mao had been proved right. Kissinger thought it was Zhou's way of separating himself from the debacle.

During one exchange, Zhou asked abruptly whether the summer of 1972 would be a good time for President Nixon to visit. But when it came time for a joint communiqué, the Chinese draft suggested that Nixon had requested the invitation and would come prepared to discuss Taiwan's future as a condition for normalizing relations. Kissinger rejected that language. As he was about to leave, a Chinese official hurried up with an acceptable statement. Traveling home, Kissinger cabled the code word for success—"Eureka."

On July 15, Nixon read a statement, which Beijing was releasing at the same time, announcing his forthcoming visit. He went on to reassure Japan, India, the Soviet Union and any other country that might be disconcerted by the seismic new alignment. "We seek friendly relations with all nations," Nixon said. "Any nation can be our friend without being any other nation's enemy."

At Perino's restaurant in Los Angeles that evening, Nixon and his senior aides celebrated with crab legs and Château Lafite Rothschild 1961. Even before Kissinger's trip, Nixon had assured them that they were approaching a great watershed in history, clearly the greatest since World War II. Kissinger went him one better: in its effect on the United States, Nixon's China trip would be the greatest event since the end of the Civil War.

Kissinger found a less receptive audience in Paris when he tried to use his trip to influence the Communist delegation. He finished telling of his diplomatic coup and waited for a reaction. The North Vietnamese were determined not to show their dismay. "That is your affair," Le Duc Tho said curtly. "Our fighting is our preoccupation, and that will decide the outcome for our country. What you have told us will have no influence on our fighting."

In Hanoi, reaction was even more dispirited. One high-ranking official from the Foreign Ministry came home for his customary lunch with his family just after he heard the news. Luu Doan Huynh, a member of the Vietminh since his teens, was one of those men who had turned his back on a privileged family to ally himself with the landless poor. For thirty years, dedicated to Ho's dream of independence, Huynh had studied Marx and Mao and put his faith in international Communism. Now he stared numbly at his bowl of rice.

"Daddy, Daddy," Huynh's young son cried.

"Yes?" he said, thinking about Mao's betrayal and what it meant for his country.

"Don't you see, Daddy?"

He forced himself to shake off his despair and look up. "What is it?"

"Mama's got a new haircut!"

FOURTEEN

Mao
1972

As he prepared for his trip to China, Nixon read the *Anti-Memoirs* of André Malraux, fascinated by the portraits of Mao and Zhou Enlai, men Malraux had met in China almost forty years earlier. Hoping for more insights, Nixon invited the seventy-year-old French writer to the White House, where Malraux explained what the North Vietnamese knew all too well. China, he said, had never helped any other country. "China's foreign policy is a brilliant lie! The Chinese themselves do not believe in it. They believe only in China. Only China!"

Malraux predicted that Nixon would find Mao obsessed with his own death. Five years ago, he had been afraid that Washington or Moscow would destroy China's industrial cities with nuclear weapons and set China back so far that Mao would not live to repair the damage. Now, with his own nuclear arsenal, that fear had abated. But Mao was facing his own mortality. Malraux predicted that on meeting Nixon, Mao's first thought would be, "He is so much younger than I."

Once Nixon arrived in Beijing, Mao's impatience to meet him did seem to reflect a concern with the time left to him. Bill Rogers had been stewing over protocol for the introductions, determined to avoid having Mao appear at the top of a staircase so that the president of the United States would have to climb to reach him. But Nixon's party had scarcely been installed in government guest houses when Zhou said Mao wanted to see Nixon immediately at his residence. Kissinger was aware that the secretary of state should be present at such a historic meeting, but Nixon wanted to exclude Rogers, and Kissinger would certainly not

Kissinger with President Richard M. Nixon
(Ollie Atkins/Nixon Project/National Archives)

argue on his behalf. He did get Nixon's permission to bring along Winston Lord to take notes.

Haldeman had also come to China, charged with spending $600 on a large supply of Chinese trinkets for Nixon to dole out upon his return. Just before the party left to see Mao, Haldeman was required to soothe Kissinger's hurt feelings. Nixon had already made Kissinger the butt of several jokes to Zhou, and Kissinger felt he was losing face in front of the Chinese.

The Nixon entourage drove past a red gate and through a wooded expanse to the road that led to Mao's unimposing house. The Americans were led into a study crammed with books, and Mao rose from one of a semicircle of easy chairs. To Kissinger, no one but de Gaulle radiated such intense will. Mao had suffered several strokes and seemed to expel his words with great effort. But his smile remained sly, his good humor contagious.

"Our common old friend, Generalissimo Chiang Kai-shek, doesn't approve of this," Mao said, as he took Nixon's hand in both of his own.

The previous October, the United Nations had voted 76 to 35, with 17 abstentions, to expel Chiang's Taiwan and admit Mao's government as China's only representative. The United States had expected only a vote for equal status, and Nixon remained committed to aid for Taiwan. Mao went out of his way to indicate how little the issue troubled him. "Actually," he said, through his translator, "the history of our friendship with him is much longer than the history of your friendship with him."

As Kissinger had feared, Mao and Nixon quickly achieved rapport at his expense. Mao began by mentioning Kissinger's cleverness in keeping his first trip to Beijing a secret.

"He doesn't look like a secret agent," Nixon joked, and yet Kissinger was "the only man in captivity who could go to Paris twelve times and Beijing once, and no one knew it." Except, Nixon added, with an attempt at bonhomie, "possibly a couple of pretty girls."

Kissinger, who was divorced, had burnished his reputation as the Nixon administration's Lothario by occasionally escorting Hollywood starlets, but he protested being treated as a randy adolescent. "They didn't know it," he said. "I used it as a cover."

"In Paris?" Mao asked teasingly.

Nixon wanted to keep the mood alive. "Anyone who uses pretty girls as a cover must be the greatest diplomat of all time," he said.

Mao asked, "So you often make use of your girls?"

"*His* girls, not mine," Nixon said. "It would get me into great trouble if I used girls as a cover."

"Especially during an election," Zhou said, and everyone laughed.

Mao cautioned Nixon that if the Democrats won in November, the Chinese would be dealing with them instead. "We understand," Nixon said, still jocular. "We hope we don't give you that problem."

Beneath the banter, Mao was serious when he explained that a reactionary group within his own leadership had opposed Nixon's visit. "The result was that they got in an airplane and fled abroad," Mao said. Zhou explained that the airplane, with Lin Piao aboard, had crashed in Outer Mongolia.

Mao listed the countries with right-wing governments and said he liked rightists, which led Nixon to expound on a favorite theme. "Those on the right can do what those on the left can only talk about," he said, an oblique acknowledgment that he might have savaged any Democrat who made this trip to Beijing. Later, Nixon granted to Zhou that he had held views very much like those of Foster Dulles during the Eisenhower years but that the world had changed since then.

The interview ended with Mao shuffling to the door to see them out. He said he had not been well.

Nixon protested, "But you look very good."

Mao shrugged. "Appearances are deceiving."

□

OVER THE NEXT DAYS of discussion, Nixon offered his rationale for the United States maintaining troops in Japan and claimed that a vacuum there would be as dangerous for China as for America. When talk turned to the Soviet Union, Zhou seemed to appreciate Nixon's realism. The fact that the American president had come to Beijing before scheduling a trip to Moscow meant that the Soviet leadership was "mobilizing a whole mass of their people, their followers, to curse us," Zhou said. "But let them go on. We don't care."

On the subject of Vietnam, Zhou said that of course Nixon could not resolve the problem by coming to China. "We are not in a position to settle it in talks."

IN HANOI, the North Vietnamese looked for portents in what was being revealed from Nixon's audience with Mao. "You want to bring back some of your troops to the United States," Mao had said. "Ours will not go to other countries." That seemed to mean that Washington could stop worrying about China intervening militarily in Indochina. And although Zhou reaffirmed support for North Vietnam, he distanced Beijing from Hanoi's demand that Thieu be overthrown. To Hanoi's Politburo, it was simple: Nixon had neutralized China. Next he would expect Moscow to curb North Vietnam.

The North's response was another offensive, to be launched on March 30 and centered on Quang Tri, close enough to the northern border that Hanoi could easily supply troops and matériel. Giap had opposed another new offensive, but when he was overruled by the Politburo, he was forced again, as he had done for Tet, to sign off on an attack he did not favor. This one was called "Nguyen Hue," the name that the Emperor Quang Trung had been born with. A national hero, Trung had led his army in 1789 from central Vietnam through jungles and over mountains to surprise Chinese troops near Hanoi. Now, by moving into the Central Highlands, the North would reverse the direction of the emperor's victory. If it was decisive enough, they could make the Paris peace talks irrelevant.

From surveillance and informants, American and ARVN intelligence knew that an offensive was coming. To avoid a repetition of 1968, South Vietnamese troops had been kept in their barracks until the end of this year's Tet celebration, but the holiday passed peacefully, and speculation arose that the North planned to wait until 1973, when all of the U.S. troops would be withdrawn. But early 1972 was equally tempting. The American presence was down to 140,000 men by the end of January, and half that number was due to leave by the end of April.

In mid-March, the Twentieth Plenum of the Vietnam Workers' Party Central Committee (Second Congress) passed a resolution hailing 1972 as extremely important. It called for a fundamental change in the battlefield situation in the South "so as to win a significant victory, obliging the U.S. to end the war in a losing position through a political solution that the U.S. must and can accept, but advantageous to us."

Nixon regarded any new offensive as a full-scale invasion of the South that would justify his strong reaction in an election year. After losing the vice presidency on Humphrey's ticket in 1968, Ed Muskie was now the most formidable candidate for the Democratic nomination. When Muskie played down the opening skirmishes of the Communist attack, Nixon told Haldeman to paint him as a defeatist, unconcerned with the POWs or the 70,000 U.S. troops who remained in the South. To Nixon's delight, however, George McGovern beat Muskie in Wisconsin's April 4 primary election. Nixon considered McGovern, the most outspoken peace candidate, the weakest of his possible challengers.

As with Johnson and the Tonkin Gulf attack, the new Communist offensive gave Nixon an excuse for doing what he had long wanted to do. He was assembling a huge attack force to use against northerners fighting in the South—naval guns from offshore, many conventional bombers and B-52s.

Nixon intended to justify his massive bombing by pointing to Hanoi's violation of the DMZ. He and Kissinger regarded the Communist offensive as a desperate move and expected the B-52 raids to make them yield in Paris. The problem was the air force. Nixon believed that its officers were claiming bad weather in order to avoid carrying out his orders. The weather wasn't bad, he complained to John Mitchell. "The air force isn't worth a—I mean, they won't fly."

To confirm Nixon's suspicions, Kissinger brought in Air Force General John Vogt, who denounced his colleagues as lethargic and lacking in initiative. Vogt was due to get his fourth star and an assignment to NATO headquarters, but he volunteered to give up the promotion for a chance to go to Vietnam and straighten things out. Nixon approved the idea—and promised Vogt his star anyway. Vogt was not quite satisfied. He suggested that it would strengthen his hand out there if he were to be posted not just as air commander but as deputy commander. Done, Nixon said. And bypass Abrams, Nixon added. He said that Abrams may have been a great commander in World War II, but he had forfeited the president's confidence.

Nixon was in full Patton mode. This may be the last battle to be fought by the United States Air Force, he said emotionally. This sort of war probably would never happen again. It would be tragic if the air force ended its active participation with the sort of disgraceful operation that the Pentagon seemed to be running.

I hear you loud and clear, Mr. President, Vogt assured him. I will move in and get it solved.

On April 6, U.S. fighters bombed North Vietnam again. The first attacks hit sixty miles north of the DMZ. Four days later, B-52s struck Vinh, ninety miles further north. Kissinger was urging Nixon to match Hanoi's offensive with a dramatic escalation that would send the B-52s against Hanoi and Haiphong. Laird objected. Around the Pentagon, his nickname had become "Chicken Hawk," with no question which was the dominant bird. At State, Rogers also protested and got unexpected support from Bunker and Abrams. They wanted to have all U.S. strikes flown against Hanoi's troops in the South, where the Communists looked poised to prevail. In Congress, antiwar members pointed out that bombing the North had accomplished nothing from 1965 to 1968. The military replied that this time it would be different because the Joint Chiefs and their staffs would be picking the targets.

DESPITE U.S. AIR SUPPORT, the early days of the Easter offensive were favoring the North. The South Vietnamese general staff had assigned its weakest division to the DMZ, even though a Communist offensive was known to be likely. The 3rd ARVN Division had only been activated five months earlier, and two of its regiments were dumping grounds for convicts, inept officers and recaptured deserters. The 3rd ARVN was certainly no match for the NVA's 308th Division, which had earned its name, "Iron." The 308th would be joined by the 304th NVA Division, three infantry regiments from B-5 Front—the North's corps headquarters inside the DMZ—two tank regiments and five artillery regiments with long-range Soviet-made 130-mm guns.

The ARVN corps commander was still Hoang Xuan Lam, the lieutenant general who had overseen the collapse of Lam Son 719. Not expecting an attack across the DMZ, Lam had counted on the ARVN Marines west of Quang Tri to do any fighting.

By April 1, the entire 3rd ARVN Division was retreating south, and it looked like the Laotian campaign all over again. The next day, ARVN soldiers watched their own families join the stream of refugees, and men from the 3rd's 57th Regiment joined the flight. The 56th Regiment went them one worse. Its men surrendered and turned over to the Communists all of their weapons, including twenty-two artillery pieces.

With another debacle looming, Kissinger called Dobrynin to the Map Room of the White House and denounced the Soviets for the attack since it was their weapons the NVA was using. If the offensive continued, the Soviet Union might be faced by difficult choices before the proposed summit with Nixon in Moscow, Kissinger said.

On April 6, the White House received a note from the Communist team in Paris accepting a new private meeting if the United States lived up to its past agreement to stop bombing the North. Because of the fighting at the DMZ, Kissinger dismissed the overture as insolent. But Hanoi was claiming that any action at Quang Tri had been intended only to blunt the ARVN offensive they had been expecting, one that might threaten the survival of the North.

In mid-April, one day after the Vinh bombing, Le Duc Tho and Nguyen Duy Trinh sent Xuan Thuy a message from Hanoi that the Politburo viewed the resumption of the bombing as a "very serious step of escalation, aimed at stopping the collapse of the situation in South Vietnam and putting pressure on us." They said the action showed Nixon's rash character and weak position, and predicted atrocious attacks against the North as the United States continued to lose in the South. All the same, the message continued, it would not be in Hanoi's interest to end the Paris talks. Given the détente between America and China and between America and the Soviet Union, an international conference "is not to our advantage." The Paris negotiations should merely be suspended sine die.

In Hanoi's view, the White House could put great pressure on the Soviet Union because Moscow wanted to protect the Nixon summit. The Soviet ambassador in Hanoi met individually for hours with Pham Van Dong, Nguyen Duy Trinh and Le Duan to impress on them the seriousness of what Kissinger had been telling Dobrynin: that by sending almost all of its regular forces to fight in the South, Hanoi had exposed itself to a major offensive on its own territory; that Hanoi seemed bent on overthrowing another U.S. president, which was why Nixon had ordered the bombing of Hanoi and Haiphong; that the bombing could stop if Hanoi agreed to meet secretly with Kissinger in Moscow from April 21 to 23, while he was there arranging for Nixon's summit.

Politburo members, with no wish to make the Soviets their go-between, refused the offer.

KISSINGER HAD USED the prospect of meeting Pham Van Dong in Moscow to persuade Nixon to let him make the trip. These days, he and the president had conflicting priorities. Both men overestimated Soviet influence over North Vietnam, but Nixon desperately wanted to keep South Vietnam afloat through the end of the year. It was now Kissinger, with Soviet-American relations his latest priority, who was suggesting that Nixon could be reelected whatever happened in Vietnam.

In Moscow, Kissinger told Leonid Brezhnev that the North Vietnamese must withdraw the three divisions that had crossed the DMZ for the latest offensive. But the other North Vietnamese troops could remain in the South and even regard the territory they controlled as belonging to the Provisional Revolutionary Government they had established in mid-1969. Privately, Kissinger considered even his demand that the three northern divisions withdraw a "throwaway." He did not expect to achieve in Paris what the ARVN had been unable to accomplish south of the DMZ.

While Nixon stewed with Rebozo at Camp David, Kissinger was repeating an offer that made it unlikely South Vietnam could survive a Paris agreement.

KONSTANTIN KATUSHEV, who headed the Soviet Central Committee's foreign relations commission, flew to Hanoi to pass along a message from Nixon considerably at odds with Kissinger's pliant approach in Moscow. Feeling the same pressure Johnson had faced four years earlier, Nixon wrote: "The United States would not tolerate drawn-out negotiations in a Presidential election year. If Vietnam would not compromise, the United States was prepared to expand the war to North Vietnam. . . ."

Katushev took the heat of Premier Dong's resentment: "Who allows them to threaten us? Who allows them to order us to do this and not to do that? Who allows them to tell us that the White House does not tolerate dragging on the negotiations in an election year in the United States?"

Katushev tried to be diplomatic. "Tactically," he asked, "how can you combine the fighting in South Vietnam and the negotiations at the Paris conference?"

"If we have no strong military activity," Dong explained, "they will not talk to us. We have to act to let them understand that Vietnamization will surely fail, that the puppets will undoubtedly be swept away, that there is no way to revive them."

The trick, Dong concluded, was in taking just enough action to keep the Americans at the negotiating table but not so much as to humiliate them.

But by the time Kissinger met at 10 A.M. on May 2 for his thirteenth private meeting with Le Duc Tho, humiliation seemed in the air. William Porter, the American in charge of the ceremonial public talks, had broken them off on his own initiative in March. To persuade Tho to meet again, Nixon had been forced to agree to Hanoi's demand that Porter resume those talks as well. At the same time, Communist troops had just taken Quang Tri City. Nixon sent Kissinger back to Paris but threatened him that there might not be a Moscow summit "if we're still in trouble in Vietnam."

Among themselves, the North Vietnamese observed, not sympathetically, that Kissinger had changed. Gone was the jaunty professor with his long speeches and stream of jokes. In his place was a subdued figure who seemed embarrassed. They did not know that Nixon had told him to offset the Communist victory at Quang Tri with his most severe manner. "No nonsense," Nixon had stipulated. "No niceness. No accommodations."

During the wrangling that followed, Le Duc Tho mentioned that Fulbright had agreed that Washington was using military pressure to impose its terms.

Kissinger interrupted angrily: "Our domestic discussions are no concern of yours."

Le Duc Tho overrode him. "I'm giving an example to prove that Americans share our views." He quoted Fulbright as saying that Hanoi's actions had been a natural response to Washington's undermining of the 1954 Geneva accords. Tho next cited the Pentagon Papers as proof of American aggression.

The onslaught was prolonged and brutal, but Kissinger offered no rebuttal. When he asked Tho for a counterproposal, Tho complained that waiting six months for the Americans to withdraw after agreement was reached was too long. Kissinger had already agreed that Communists could compete in an election to form a Saigon coalition and that Thieu would step down from the presidency before the new election in order to run as simply one more candidate. Tho wanted him out immediately.

Kissinger asked when Thieu should resign.

Xuan Thuy said, "Tomorrow is best."

"All other members, except Thieu, can remain in the administration, can't they?" Kissinger asked.

They could, but they had to stop oppressing the people. Political prisoners must be released and banned newspapers allowed to publish.

Kissinger twitted Xuan Thuy on that last point: "Can anybody publish a paper in North Vietnam? I ask just for my own education."

Xuan Thuy said Hanoi had "a completely different system, which it would not impose on the South."

Kissinger expressed surprise that they were not responding to the proposals he had channeled through Moscow. With some asperity, Tho said, "We have on many occasions said that if you have any question, you should talk directly to us, and we shall talk directly to you. We don't speak through a third person."

When the Communist delegates reported to Hanoi on the meeting, they got back a cautious response: "We are recording big victories but not yet big enough to compel the United States to give up Vietnam and Indochina."

If Washington proposed another meeting, Le Duc Tho should stall until Nixon returned from Moscow.

AMERICA'S ANTIWAR CONTINGENT had not been able to rally much of an outcry against the new bombings in the North or against the mining on May 8 of Haiphong Harbor. With Kissinger shifting the emphasis from Vietnam to nuclear arms control, the Russians had not protested the mines, even though their ships were damaged and their sailors killed.

The results of Dan Ellsberg's original questionnaire for Kissinger in 1969 had indicated that mining would not affect the war, since the North had many roads and waterways for transporting supplies. Laird, Rogers and Helms still agreed with that assessment, but Nixon listened instead to Spiro Agnew and John Connally, the former Texas governor now serving as treasury secretary.

Kissinger had assumed the Soviets would cancel the summit and advised Nixon, with regret, to anticipate them by withdrawing first. Kissinger also worried that escalation in Vietnam might mend the rupture between Russia and China. As he went along reluctantly with Nixon's strategy, he lamented to an aide, "I don't want to become the Walt Rostow of the administration."

When Kissinger's advice was ignored and the Moscow summit went forward, he put the best face on the coming talks. As they flew together to the Soviet Union in late May, Kissinger assured Nixon, "This has got to be one of the greatest diplomatic coups of all time."

☐

IN THE CENTRAL HIGHLANDS, Nguyen Dinh Tu, a forty-nine-year-old South Vietnamese reporter for the *Vietnamese Daily News*, was beginning to believe that his country's cause was not hopeless after all. When his newspaper sent Tu to the Democratic convention in 1968, he had come away from Chicago convinced that the United States would soon turn the fighting back to an unprepared ARVN. But now Tu was covering Vietnamese Marine units fighting to the east of Route 1 under an able three-star general, Le Nguyen Khang. To the west of the highway, Vietnamese paratroopers seemed to be equally surefooted and aggressive. As for General Lam, Tu knew him to be a good-hearted man with no technical skill or sense of strategy. His sole qualification was his loyalty to Thieu. Despite Lam's shortcomings, however, Tu noted a marked contrast between the South's soldiers during this campaign and their attitude during the Tet offensive. Then the troops had been befuddled and demoralized. Now, four years later, they were fighting with a new determination. The North Vietnamese still seemed better trained, but the southerners were displaying fierce courage. Tu told his readers, "This is their finest hour."

General Vogt had arrived in South Vietnam and was making good on his promises. Tu watched as American airpower blunted and then turned back the North's offensive. When the Communists had taken Quang Tri on May 1, they seemed capable of seizing Hue and possibly even Da Nang. Abrams had warned Thieu: "This is a battle to the death. The Communists have planned it that way and will not quit until they have been totally exhausted."

In desperation, Thieu replaced Lam with a first-rate commander, Major General Ngo Quang Truong from the Delta. Within a day, Truong established a center to coordinate the ARVN with their U.S. air support and then set about protecting Hue and retaking territory in Quang Tri province. Tu marched with Truong's men as they staged a counteroffensive that ran from late June to mid-September. At the end, the ARVN once more controlled Quang Tri City.

The Communists' attack-and-lull strategy had failed in part because the ARVN could regroup during the lulls and meet them at their next battleground. But Tu recognized that the true key to the ARVN victory was U.S. airpower. The B-52s could fly at any time, but the targeting they received from the South Vietnamese continued to be erratic, and the early massive retreats had added to the confusion. The C-130s and the other U.S. tactical aircraft and helicopter gunships were more reliable, but they were hampered by the weather. Even with their limitations, however, the planes were invaluable. When the skies clouded, the North Vietnamese advanced. When they cleared, American aircraft beat them back until the offensive collapsed.

Lieutenant General James Hollingsworth demonstrated the winning strategy during a battle for An Loc, a major ARVN installation on the road to Saigon. A tough-talking Texan much decorated in World War II, Holly Hollingsworth outlined his plan to the ARVN in the starkest terms: Their joint mission was to "Kill Cong." You hold them in one place, Hollingsworth explained, and his air-power would do the killing, a formula that saved An Loc.

Besides being a costly failure, the Easter offensive was also Giap's last campaign as his army's commander. He had developed a kidney stone and gone to Hungary for an operation, but his recovery had been slow. Although he remained national defense minister, in August the Politburo's collective leadership turned over the military high command to Giap's chief of staff, Van Tien Dung.

On the American side, a man who had come to symbolize the early days of the war was among the Easter offensive's casualties. John Vann had come back to Vietnam as the corps' senior adviser and had watched excitedly as the Vietnamese Air Force met the Communist challenge. "That's the best damn bombing I've seen in my eleven years here," he told other Americans.

On the night of June 9, Vann left Pleiku in his light observation helicopter with its pilot and another U.S. Army officer, heading for Kontum to spend the night. The helicopter crashed and burned. ARVN troops located the wreckage, and just before midnight an American officer arrived at the site to identify Vann's body.

For its official report on the incident, Pentagon analysts abandoned the antiseptic language of code names and acronyms and wrote simply, "An era had ended."

ON JULY 10, the Democrats obliged Nixon by picking his choice as their candidate for president. To boost George McGovern, the White House had been releasing false polls and indulging in other dirty tricks to derail his more formidable competitors. Once he was nominated, McGovern's liabilities looked insurmountable. Robert Kennedy had called him the most decent man in the Senate, but that was a quality American voters had not seemed to value in the last presidential election. An undeniable hero of World War II, McGovern had the high-pitched and earnest voice of a Sunday School teacher, and his antiwar speeches were igniting less enthusiasm now that Nixon had ended the draft and withdrawn most GIs from Vietnam. Lately, McGovern had antagonized many voters by saying that he would beg Hanoi for the release of America's POWs. Begging, he said, was better than bombing.

The same desperation to get out of Vietnam had been building among those American writers who had soured on Johnson and never trusted Nixon. Their frustration as they watched the war drag on had led to flights of hyperbole. In New York, Susan Sontag had written that "the white race is the cancer of the human race." From Paris, Mary McCarthy remarked that to prevent America from continuing to be self-deluded, she could countenance the "world-wide triumph of Communism." In *Harper's* magazine, David Halberstam had been drawing acid portraits of the Americans who led the country into war, and he published them in a book he called *The Best and the Brightest*. The phrase entered the language as a synonym for excellence with none of Halberstam's sardonic overtones. His conclusion about McNamara, for example, had been unsparing: "He did not serve himself nor the country well; he was, there is no kinder or gentler word for it, a fool."

Izzy Stone found a more inspiring lesson in America's failure. He asked student audiences: What is that tiny creature standing up to the fearsome might of twentieth-century technology? What is it that cannot be bombed or blasted into submission? Why, it's a man, prevailing over all of the machines of destruction! His listeners cheered, even though the man Stone glorified was a Vietcong soldier.

But to the broader electorate, Nixon's trip to Beijing had made him appear to be a more realistic peacemaker than McGovern, and when the president returned from the Moscow summit, he brought the first disarmament agreement ever negotiated with the Soviet Union. The terms of the Strategic Arms Limitations Treaty—abbreviated as SALT—set restrictions on the number of antiballistic missile defense sites, intercontinental missiles and submarine-based launchers. No limits were placed on nuclear warheads; the United States had 3,500, the Soviets 2,350.

IF NIXON COULD SCARCELY believe his luck in his opponent, troublesome loose ends remained within his own ranks. In mid-June, five employees of Nixon's Committee to Reelect the President—usually rendered as the acronym CREEP—had been caught breaking into Democratic Party headquarters at the Watergate apartment complex. At first, Haldeman thought they might squeak by without the press tracing the operation to Gordon Liddy, one of the White House Plumbers. Nixon felt confident enough to recommend attacking the Democratic Party chairman, Larry O'Brien, for malice in suggesting that there could possibly be a link between the break-in and the White House.

Now, however, the FBI's investigation was looking dangerously out of control. Patrick Gray had succeeded Hoover at the bureau, and Vernon Walters from the CIA was instructed to ward him off by claiming national security was involved. But even if Walters was successful, John Mitchell's wife had become impossible to muzzle. Martha Mitchell called Helen Thomas of UPI and vowed—before her phone was pulled from the wall—that if Mitchell didn't get his ass out of politics she was going to kick him out of the house.

All mere clouds on the horizon, and as the election drew closer, the Washington press corps seemed satisfied with Ron Ziegler's description of the Watergate break-in as a "third-rate robbery." The exceptions were a couple of junior reporters at the *Washington Post*, Bob Woodward and Carl Bernstein.

WHEN KISSINGER MET again with the North Vietnamese in Paris on July 19, he seemed conciliatory at Thieu's expense. He asked rhetorically, "If the United

States can accept governments in large countries that are not pro-American, why should it insist on a pro-U.S. government in Saigon?"

But he warned that neither side should try to impose a military solution, nor should the North attempt to influence the U.S. elections. Kissinger stressed that the Communists must not let any Democrat know the status of their negotiations. He wanted no one sabotaging Nixon as he had helped to do to Johnson in 1968.

Le Duc Tho replied that Kissinger had brought with him nothing new. After the meeting broke up, the Communists agreed that the American proposal of a four-month temporary cease-fire was merely a trick to see Nixon safely through the November elections. They were sure now that the war would continue into 1973.

By the first of August, Kissinger was sounding like Harriman as he bargained and cajoled for any sort of agreement. He promised that if Hanoi would agree to terms before September 1, the last American soldier would leave Vietnam before the end of the year. Kissinger spoke lullingly about the political future of the South. Thieu was now agreeing to resign two months before an internationally supervised election, he said. And even that resignation date might be flexible.

Le Duc Tho replied that his government was no longer concerned with Thieu's immediate resignation, but Hanoi did expect U.S. funds to heal the wounds of war. He suggested $8 billion—$4.5 billion for the North, $3.5 billion for the South. Kissinger did not respond. Instead, he tried to prevail on the Communists to make public the fact of these secret talks before the opening of the Republican convention. Tho understood that Kissinger wanted to give the appearance of momentum toward peace and refused.

In ALEXANDER HAIG, Kissinger was getting a comeuppance for years of maneuvering against Rogers and Laird. Haig's assignment to the White House had proved profitable for him. He had begun there as a colonel and, by March 1972, had been jumped to major general with a second star. Kissinger's sulks and tantrums—and, more to the point, the favorable publicity he generated—had soured Nixon on his security adviser, and Haig was adept at separating himself from his boss. West Point classmates with better academic or military records than his were annoyed by Haig's spectacular advancement. Westmoreland decided that Nixon's blatant favoritism was hurting army morale.

Haig seized his chance to exploit the sharp division between Kissinger and Nixon over the Paris talks. Nixon still harbored visions of settling the war on his own terms, which meant waiting until after his reelection to sign a treaty. Once he had crushed McGovern's antiwar faction, Nixon expected Hanoi at last to cry uncle. Kissinger, with other priorities, wanted to achieve peace before the election. Haig found ways to indicate to Nixon that he agreed with the president, and when Kissinger reported movement after his August 14 meeting in Paris, Nixon wrote in the cable's margin, "Al—it is obvious that no progress has been made and that none can be expected." He instructed Haig to rein in Kissinger until after the election.

After bending Washington's terms to get a pact, Kissinger flew with Haig to Saigon in mid-August to win Thieu's approval. The timing coincided with the last American combat unit leaving Vietnam. The U.S. Army's 3rd Battalion, 21st Infantry, was scheduled to go home on August 23. Kissinger hoped Thieu would find solace in the North dropping its demand that he step down immediately. Instead, Thieu demanded to know about a provision that northern troops would leave the South when the Americans did. It was especially important now because the Easter offensive, although it had been defeated, left the Communists in control of far more territory in the Central Highlands. Kissinger was not candid about how close the Paris talks were to a breakthrough, however, and Thieu did not press the point.

To mark North Vietnam's National Day, Hanoi did its part for McGovern by releasing three POWs to representatives of America's antiwar movement. But by now the Politburo realized that McGovern was not going to win. It became in the North's interest—and possibly Nixon's as well—to end the war before the November 7 election.

In Paris on September 15, each side chided the other for the stalemate and presented its terms in the most attractive way. When Tho accused the Americans of delaying tactics, Kissinger said, No, not at all. If they could agree on a workable timetable, they could be done by October 15. To prove his sincerity, Kissinger repeated, "We wish to end before October 15—if sooner, all the better."

The North's delegates were delighted, sure that they had manipulated Kissinger into giving them the firm deadline they wanted. After he was gone, they described themselves as glad to the bottom of their hearts.

In private conversations with Thieu, Haig had alarmed him with hints that he was being stampeded toward an undesirable settlement. And when Haig returned to Saigon alone on October 4, he indulged Thieu for four hours as he vented his resentments against Kissinger and the way he had shunted aside the South Vietnamese government. Haig forwarded that criticism of Kissinger directly to Nixon.

Watching from the sidelines, Haldeman found it strange that Kissinger still believed he had a fifty–fifty chance for an agreement with Hanoi despite the opposition Haig was reporting from Saigon. But Haldeman noted in his diary one reason for optimism: "Unlike '68, when Thieu screwed Johnson, he had Nixon as an alternative. Now he has McGovern as an alternative, which would be a disaster for him, even worse than the worst possible thing that Nixon could do to him."

By late September, Hanoi had determined to hold Kissinger to the October 15 deadline. Le Duc Tho and Xuan Thuy warned the Politburo what Haldeman had concluded: They had better try to get terms before the U.S. election. Afterward, Washington and Saigon might even renounce what they had already agreed upon. Hanoi drew up a draft treaty to present to Kissinger in early October and sent messengers with it to Moscow and Beijing. Brezhnev and Zhou Enlai each approved the terms and promised their support.

A meeting in Paris was scheduled for October 6, then put off a day so that Haig, fresh from Saigon, could join the talks. A mere six months after Haig received his second star, Nixon had bumped him past 240 senior officers to make him a four-star general and vice chief of staff of the army. Nixon laid down one condition: Haig would have to remain as Kissinger's deputy through the completion of a Paris agreement. Neither man trusted Kissinger to stand firm at the peace table without Haig at his side. For his part, Kissinger was relieved to have Haig in Paris because he no longer trusted him behind his back.

With talks seeming to enter their final phase, both sides agreed to a forum of national reconciliation that would include the NLF but give every faction veto power over all decisions. Kissinger expected that stipulation to protect Thieu during the transition to a coalition government. The haggling, while generally good humored, had edgy moments. The United States proposed seventy-five days as the time limit for withdrawal of its remaining advisers. Hanoi called for sixty. Kissinger jovially suggested sixty-seven and a half.

"For us, a few days is of no importance," Tho said coldly. "You have remained in our country for over ten years, and we still have enough force to cope with you. If you stay another seventy days more, it doesn't matter."

After a break, Kissinger surveyed the day's accomplishments and said, "You have given us a very important and fundamental document."

He proposed tying up loose ends over the next two days. He would then take the result to Nixon in Washington and to Thieu in Saigon. Kissinger would return home by way of Hanoi, and the accords could be signed in Paris on October 25 or 26.

After the meeting adjourned, Kissinger and Winston Lord shook hands solemnly and said, "We have succeeded." Even Haig was caught up in the moment. He said emotionally that the American team had saved the honor of those who had fought, suffered and lost their lives in Vietnam. The North Vietnamese delegates still worried about a trick that would postpone the signing until after the U.S. election. But when Kissinger and Haig arrived at the White House the evening of October 12, Kissinger began by saying, "Well, you've got three for three, Mr. President"—the China trip, the Soviet summit and now a Vietnam settlement.

At first Nixon was incredulous, but Kissinger opened his secret red folder and began to outline the latest terms: Thieu stays in office; a stand-in-place cease-fire by the end of October; a Council of National Reconciliation and Concord that would not jeopardize Thieu's position; total withdrawal of troops—

Americans but not North Vietnamese troops—within sixty days, and a return of the POWs within that same period. Everything was to be completed by the end of the year.

Kissinger's ebullience eased Nixon's doubts. When Kissinger broached economic aid to Vietnam, Nixon saw even that obligation as a plus. In the past, Nixon said, the Communists had refused to accept aid. Now they would be admitting the failure of their system. Haldeman watched as Nixon, "all cranked up," shrugged off the details. But Nixon kept looking over to Haig because only the week before he had called the deal unfair to Thieu. Now, although Haig pronounced the agreement a good one, he did question whether Thieu would buy it.

Still euphoric, Nixon led the group to his outer office, where Manolo had set up drinks. Nixon told him, "Bring out the good wine, my Château Lafite Rothschild, and pour it for everyone." To Haldeman, a Mormon who had finessed the unending toasts in Beijing, Nixon's gesture was the final proof that he was elated. Normally, the president drank the Lafite Rothschild and served his aides wine from California's Beaulieu Vineyards.

Over dinner, they plotted on how to break the news to Rogers. As a sop, the secretary of state would be allowed to go to Paris at the end of the month to sign the agreement with Hanoi's foreign minister. "Overall," Haldeman wrote that night in his diary, "it boils down to a super-historic night if it all holds together, and Henry is now convinced it will. He thinks that he's really got the deal. So we'll see."

FROM PARIS, Kissinger had sent a carefully worded cable to Bunker telling the ambassador only that a cease-fire might be at hand but not sending a draft of its terms. While only Hanoi and Washington had been present at the private talks, the Communists kept their NLF comrades informed at every stage. The South Vietnamese had to depend on whatever version of a day's events Kissinger chose to tell them. Since he considered all Vietnamese, northern or southern, insolent and their manner obnoxious, he was not inclined to tell Thieu's men much.

The Communists had not been above baiting Saigon's representatives about their impotence. When a journalist wrote that South Vietnam was the tail of the dog, a Saigon delegate protested in Xuan Thuy's hearing, "I'm not the tail."

"Do you really believe that?" Thuy asked smoothly. "Or is it only talk? Even you know where you're from. You know better than anyone what crack in the earth you've come from."

Thieu sensed that South Vietnam's fate had been sealed and was compensating for his powerlessness with new heights of arrogance. He had recently refused to see Bunker, directing his cousin, Hoang Duc Nha, to give the lame excuse that Thieu had injured his foot waterskiing. To stampede Thieu into accepting the agreements, Kissinger sent him one of Le Duc Tho's earlier and less accommodating proposals. He expected that when Thieu saw the actual agreement, he would be relieved enough to sign off on it.

But the speed of modern communication undid Kissinger's tactic. In a Communist command bunker in Quang Tri province, ARVN intelligence captured an accurate ten-page version of the real terms and had it flown to Saigon. Thieu read it only hours before Kissinger arrived on October 19. By now, Thieu had few cards to play but rudeness remained one of them. When Kissinger arrived at the palace, Thieu kept him waiting for fifteen minutes while photographers captured the insult for the wire services.

After Nha finally admitted him to Thieu's presence, Kissinger spoke for thirty minutes and then handed over a copy of the agreement. Unlike the captured document, it was in English. Kissinger said he did not have a Vietnamese translation. Nha, fluent in English from studying at Oklahoma State, read it through while Thieu studied Kissinger's expression and thought how badly he wanted to punch him in the mouth.

Nha whispered to Thieu, "This is not what we expected."

Throughout that first day, Kissinger attempted to gloss over the points that would alarm the South Vietnamese. Didn't the draft mention the three nations of Indochina when—with North and South Vietnam—it should have said four? A typographical error, Kissinger assured Thieu. Wouldn't the proposed Council of National Reconciliation and Concord amount, in fact, to a coalition government? "It is a miserable little council," Kissinger insisted. "It is only a consultative body." Why no mention of the North Vietnamese withdrawing from the South? Because the North would not accept those terms, Kissinger explained. "We did not want to poison the atmosphere."

Thieu and Nha listened politely.

Kissinger was due to meet with Thieu again at five o'clock the following afternoon, but Nha convinced his cousin that the Communists were poised to attack, perhaps even before the pact was signed. At 4:30 P.M., Nha called Bunker to cancel the meeting because of fresh intelligence that enemy troops were massing.

Later in the afternoon, Bunker called back and reached Nha at the home of Vice President Huong. "We are ready to leave the embassy," Bunker said.

"The palace is not ready, and we have other plans," said Nha. Angrily, Kissinger took the phone from Bunker. "This is Dr. Kissinger," he said.

"How are you?" said Nha, deliberately cheeky.

Kissinger demanded to see Thieu. Nha said he would have to wait until tomorrow.

"I am the special envoy of the President of the United States of America," Kissinger said. "You know I cannot be treated as an errand boy."

Nha was enjoying himself. "We never considered you an errand boy, but if that's what you think you are, there's nothing I can do about it."

□

THE NEXT MORNING, Kissinger handed Thieu a wire from Nixon threatening to cut off all aid to South Vietnam if he balked at signing the agreement. Thieu took the wire, smiled and passed it unread to Nha. Nixon had already sent a crasser threat to remind Thieu of the fate of Ngo Dinh Diem: Thieu should avoid an atmosphere that could lead to events "similar to those which we abhorred in 1963 and which"—Nixon added, as though he had prevented Thieu from being overthrown during the last U.S. election—"I personally opposed so vehemently in 1968."

In Washington, Nixon's second thoughts about the agreement were being fed by Haig and Westmoreland, who had retired from the army but was called to Washington for consultation. Westmoreland urged Nixon to hold off on the agreement and continue bombing the North and blockading Haiphong Harbor. In time, he said, that would force Hanoi to better terms. Do not compel Thieu to make abject concessions, Westmoreland added. That would brand him as an American puppet.

There was little chance of that. Not only was Nixon reluctant to push Thieu as far as Kissinger wanted to do, but Thieu himself would not be moved. At his last session with Kissinger, Thieu said that those whom he had regarded as friends had failed him. Kissinger bridled at Thieu's suggestion that Washington had connived against South Vietnam with the Soviets and the Chinese. "You have only one problem," Kissinger said. "President Nixon has many." He added gratuitously, "Had we wanted to see you out, there would have been many easier ways by which we could have accomplished this."

Kissinger considered the whole matter a bog and blamed Thieu for it. While he was in Saigon, Hanoi had wired to accept two last minor American points in the agreement. Without indicating his problems in Saigon, Kissinger sent back a cable over Nixon's name that assured the Communists that the agreement was now complete.

Leaving Saigon, Kissinger took a parting shot, which Thieu deflected. "This is the greatest failure of my diplomatic career," Kissinger said.

"Why?" Thieu asked. "Are you rushing to get the Nobel Prize?"

Of course, Kissinger's trip to Hanoi was now off. In his bitterness, he let Haig know that he was aware of his private conversations with Nixon. He reminded Haig that whatever he might be saying about the agreement these days, he had praised it in Paris.

The day after Kissinger left Saigon, Thieu scheduled a speech to his countrymen to explain why he would not accept the agreement. Bunker called to head him off, but Nha refused to put Thieu on the line. In his two-hour radio address, Thieu rejected a coalition by whatever name it was called and denounced the continuing presence of North Vietnamese troops in the South. He put their number at 300,000.

Once home, Kissinger found that all Nixon wanted was to slip by his reelection without a rupture with Thieu that might become a last-minute campaign issue. Despite the years of negotiation, Nixon still seemed to believe that, with American support, Saigon could go on fighting for its independence. Kissinger, however, wanted to assure Saigon that a treaty was inevitable and to reassure Hanoi it could not be derailed. As his instrument, Kissinger chose Max Frankel of the *New York Times*. In the past, he had courted Frankel, a fellow Jewish refugee from Nazi Germany, with discreet complaints about Nixon's anti-Semitism. Frankel, however, considered him a source whose value was undercut by his deceptiveness.

On October 25, Kissinger invited Frankel to the Sans Souci restaurant in Washington and allowed him to report that unnamed American officials were predicting that a cease-fire might come soon unless Saigon or Hanoi committed "a supreme act of folly." When the story appeared, Nixon complained, "I suppose now everybody's going to say that Kissinger won the election."

That same night, Radio Hanoi broadcast the terms of the agreement, along with Kissinger's cable calling it complete. In Vietnamese, French and English, the broadcast accused Saigon of torpedoing the pact. The next morning, worried that the disclosure would give his antiwar opponents new ammunition, Nixon allowed Kissinger to hold his first nationally televised press conference. Kissinger told reporters, "We believe that peace is at hand."

He pretended that it was the Hanoi delegates who had been unrealistic in ignoring Saigon's role in the settlement. Kissinger conveyed that misconception with a sonorous facility that deceived many reporters, including Scotty Reston. He called Kissinger's presentation "candid and even brilliant." Less charitable observers saw it as a crude attempt to influence the impending election.

ON ELECTION DAY, Kissinger arranged to have a handwritten note left on Nixon's pillow in his White House bedroom. Kissinger wrote that he wanted Nixon to know, before the votes were counted, what a privilege it had been to serve him. Nixon's achievement had been "to take a divided nation, mired in war, losing its confidence, wracked by intellectuals without convictions, and give it a new purpose and overcome its hesitations."

The balloting at least bore out Kissinger on the mending of a divided nation. Nixon won 60.7 percent of the vote to McGovern's 37.5 percent. He carried every state but the Kennedy bastion of Massachusetts. But for the first time in five presidential elections, the number of eligible voters who cast their ballots had dropped below 60 percent. When Nixon had run against Jack Kennedy, 64 percent had voted; against McGovern, 54 percent. And Nixon's victory did not bring a Republican majority in either Senate or House, which heartened the Communists in Hanoi. They expected Nixon's opponents in Congress to demand a quick end to the war.

Thieu had presented Washington with sixty-nine different points in the agreement that he wanted amended. Haig had been sent to Saigon to reason with him, but Thieu refused even to put his objections in their order of priority. He wanted them all presented in Paris, including his insistence that the northern troops withdraw from the South, although Kissinger had given up that requirement two years ago. Nixon replied to Thieu that his administration already considered the terms excellent but would "use maximum effort" to effect his changes.

When Kissinger returned to Paris on November 20, he went to the former house of Fernand Léger, which the painter had bequeathed to the Communist Party. Kissinger was no longer striving for secrecy, and newsmen brought tall ladders to let them photograph the house's courtyard whenever the negotiators strolled outside. Since Kissinger expected the northerners to be resentful about the delay in signing the agreement, he arrived full of smiles and bearing gifts. For Le Duc Tho, he produced a pen-and-pencil set for signing the agreement and picture books of Harvard, along with a renewed invitation to lecture at the university on Marx and Lenin. For Xuan Thuy, who was thought to enjoy horse racing, Kissinger brought a horse's head of Steuben glass.

Tho was not disarmed. "We have been deceived by the French, the Japanese and the Americans," he began, reading from a five-page statement. "But the deception has never been so flagrant as now." What sort of person, he asked Kissinger, do you think we now judge you to be?

Still beaming, Kissinger congratulated Tho on his good health. I have contributed to the unity of the two sides of Vietnam, Kissinger joked, because now both North and South hate me.

At that, both teams agreed to the terms they had reached on October 8. But during the afternoon session, Kissinger raised the objections from Thieu's list. He wanted the name of the NLF's Provisional Revolutionary Government struck from the treaty and to delete three functions of the Council of National Reconciliation and Concord, the group Kissinger had disparaged in Saigon. Kissinger also backed away from the promise of money for Vietnam. It could only be handled as part of the U.S. foreign aid package.

When Kissinger had finished, the northerners saw that he was trying to renegotiate almost the entire agreement. Kissinger cheerfully protested that the changes were not substantive, but even as he was speaking, he realized that to have presented Thieu's sixty-nine points had been a serious tactical error.

Withdrawing for the evening, the northerners reduced Thieu's list to sixteen major points. But with the U.S. election over, they felt no time constraints. If Nixon wanted to bring the POWs home for Christmas and conclude the war before his first term ended on January 19, the pressure was now on him. The next day, Tho was deliberately intransigent, while Kissinger was being pressed even harder by the three South Vietnamese officials Thieu had sent to Paris. They could not attend the talks, and Thieu had authorized them to do nothing but accept Hanoi's full capitulation on each point.

In Washington, Nixon's election victory had plunged him into one of his darker moods. He demanded immediate letters of resignation from each cabinet member and all of his staff, and he told Haldeman that the entire press corps was to be treated as enemies; Kissinger would be permitted to talk only to the columnists Rowland Evans and Robert Novak. His increasing isolation reflected Nixon's concern about the Watergate break-in. The issue may not have aroused the electorate but neither was it disappearing, and links between the arrested men and the White House were becoming harder to disguise.

In his restless mood, Nixon sent a message from Camp David that unless Le Duc Tho gave ground, he was ready to break off the talks and resume military action. Nixon was also talking to Haldeman about dumping Kissinger as soon as Vietnam was resolved. Until that time, he had Haldeman order Kissinger never to be photographed smiling with Tho. Within twenty-four hours, Nixon had reversed himself and decided that breaking off the talks was not an option because of Kissinger's ill-advised assurance that peace was at hand. It was Thieu who had to give way.

More than once, Nixon had promised Thieu that United States military force would guarantee the integrity of the Paris accords. On November 14, Nixon wrote, "You have my absolute assurance that if Hanoi fails to abide by the terms of this agreement, it is my intention to take swift and severe retaliatory action." Unaware that Nixon did not have the constitutional authority to make that pledge, Thieu was reassured by his stern words.

But when the talks broke down in mid-December, Nixon had to make good on his pledge if Thieu was ever going to accept the patently unfavorable terms from October. At that time, Kissinger had cabled the president from Saigon. "While we have a moral case for bombing North Vietnam when it does not accept our proposals, it seems to be really stretching the point to bomb North Vietnam when it has accepted our proposals and when South Vietnam has not."

But now Kissinger, already smarting from what he considered Le Duc Tho's haughty manner, welcomed the chance to exonerate Thieu and blame the stalemate on Hanoi. He told Nixon: "They're just a bunch of shits. Tawdry, filthy shits. They make the Russians look good, compared to the way the Russians make the Chinese look good when it comes to negotiating in a responsible and decent way."

Kissinger recommended large-scale bombing. Nixon wanted even more. The president said: "We will have to make the big decision to hit Hanoi and Haiphong with B-52s. Anything less will only make the enemy contemptuous."

At his most bellicose, Nixon called Admiral Moorer, chairman of the Joint Chiefs, and warned him, "I don't want any more of this crap about the fact that we couldn't hit this target or that." This was Moorer's chance, Nixon added. If

Moorer did not win this war with America's military power, Nixon would hold him responsible.

On December 17, Nixon unleashed B-52 bombers against the military targets in Hanoi and Haiphong that had been spared during the spring bombings. Called Operation Linebacker II by the air force—and the Christmas Bombing by everyone else—the campaign involved 20,000 tons of bombs dropped on the North, three-fourths of them by B-52s.

A few days later, Haiphong was seeded with aerial mines. With his reelection safely won, Nixon did not have to worry about the American people. But a Democratic Congress would be convening, ready to cut further into his powers. And the losses of B-52 aircraft were mounting. Six planes went down on December 20, 2 the next day. By the end of the operation, 15 B-52s and a total of 26 American aircraft of all types had been lost.

In Beijing, Zhou Enlai called on China's ranking expert for the most accurate figures on America's arsenal. "How many B-52s are involved over the North?" Zhou asked. "How many does the United States have all over the world? How many aircraft carriers are involved? How many jet fighters?"

On the day the bombing began, Haig conveyed Nixon's most pointed message to Thieu: the president's irrevocable intention was to proceed in Paris "preferably with your cooperation but, if necessary, alone." Nixon was preparing to tell the world that Hanoi was being punished for its intransigence, despite the fact that Le Duc Tho had only asked for a suspension of the talks while he consulted in Hanoi. Whatever Nixon claimed, the bombs were falling in the North, but their target was Thieu in Saigon.

Thieu was convinced that any cease-fire would last no more than three months. When the guerrillas resumed their assault against his government, he expected them to be clever enough not to provoke American retaliation. But when he conveyed that concern to reporters and claimed that Nixon had confronted him with an ultimatum, he gave Nixon the excuse he wanted. Professing himself "shocked," Nixon said he was now justified in breaking with Thieu and concluding a separate pact with North Vietnam.

Thieu still hoped that Nixon's earlier assurances counted for something. Calling Bui Diem to the palace, he asked him to fly to Washington. "It's late in the day," Thieu admitted, "but we still have to do everything we can. I'm asking you to explain to the gentlemen there that the problem of North Vietnam in the South is a problem of life or death for us.

"Maybe it's too late to influence them on this. I don't know. But you know the saying: As long as there is any water left, we have to scoop it."

EXCEPT FOR CHRISTMAS DAY itself, the Christmas bombing went on until December 29, the most concentrated attacks of the war. And yet the Communists considered the 1,261 civilians killed in Hanoi and 305 in Haiphong an unexpectedly small number of fatalities. Hanoi's mayor explained that two-thirds of his city's residents had already been evacuated. But Bach Mai Hospital, near a fighter-bomber airfield, was badly damaged, even though the Pentagon insisted again that all sixty-eight of its targets had been military, not civilian.

The Christmas bombing set off a revulsion worldwide, which the Hanoi delegates knew how to exploit. Pope Paul VI called the bombing "the object of daily grief." In Hamburg, the German newspaper *Die Zeit* wrote, "Even allies must call this a crime against humanity." During the long negotiations, the Communists had won sympathy throughout Europe by describing their ordeal at home. Mrs. Nguyen Thi Ngoc Dung proved superb in presenting the North's viewpoint, even in countries that recognized only South Vietnam. In Sweden, the prime minister and his cabinet officers had turned out to watch her film about chemical spraying by the Americans.

When a fifty-member delegation from the Midwest arrived in Paris to lobby for release of America's POWs, they agreed only reluctantly to listen to Mrs. Dung speak and insisted she be joined by a South Vietnamese diplomat who would expose her falsehoods. To avoid being beholden to the Communists, the Americans had showed up at the meeting with their own sandwiches. But Mrs. Dung won them over with stories about the way the war had separated her from her husband and children for fifteen years, and when she invited them to a garden buffet, they lunched as old friends. Other families of the POWs came to Paris equally belligerent and demanding to be allowed to send food to Hanoi. Mrs. Dung told them, My brother and sister-in-law have been in prison for ten years, with no information released about them. Put an end to the war. That will bring your loved ones home, and mine.

During the Christmas bombing, Mrs. Dung stepped up her speaking tour. She told about Agent Orange and other herbicides that had devastated her country and its people. It was true that General Lemnitzer's advocacy in 1962 had eventually been rewarded. The defoliation project Harriman once protested had been launched and grown steadily until, during the five years from 1965 to 1970, the U.S. Air Force had dropped more than forty-two million liters of Agent Orange in South Vietnam.

Mrs. Dung also spoke of the recent bombing in a way that reminded Europeans of the Germans destroying Holland's dikes during World War II. The parallels she drew made her audiences even more insistent that the war must end.

NIXON AND KISSINGER parried over which of them was going to explain the Christmas bombing to the American people. Neither wanted to be associated with the failure in Paris and eventually no high-level justification was offered at all. On December 22, the White House proposed stopping the bombing north of the 20th parallel if Hanoi would meet in Paris on January 3. On December 26, Nixon ordered more than one hundred bombing runs against Hanoi and

Haiphong. That afternoon, the North agreed to begin talking again on January 8. Nixon argued in his diary that Hanoi's response had been a stunning capitulation. He knew there would be doubts, however, and attributed them to his enemies. He expected the media to ask, Why was the bombing necessary? His opponents might even say that he had been forced back to the peace table by the worldwide outcry.

In fact, the bombing had accomplished nothing. Nixon was prepared to return to the October 8 terms if Kissinger could still get them. But, in ironing out the details, Nixon could always claim that the bombing had won important concessions from the North.

WITH THE LAST AMERICANS preparing to withdraw from Vietnam, Tommy Bui, living in Paris, saw a final way for Bao Dai to serve his country. During the sixteen years since Ngo Dinh Diem consolidated his power at the emperor's expense, Bui had watched Bao Dai grow deeply depressed, yet determined not to show how much he regretted his life of futility and irrelevance. When Bui laid out his plan, at least Bao Dai agreed to hear it.

Through a Japanese diplomat, Bui had received hints that Japan wanted to expand its influence in Southeast Asia by helping to end the war. Bui proposed that the Japanese finance a political office as a base for his maneuvering. To demonstrate Bao Dai's independence, the office should not be in Paris. This was a chance to prove that Bao Dai, at age fifty-nine, was no longer a French puppet.

"Look at the news coming out of Vietnam," Bui said to the former emperor. "It's the beginning of the end, and you can play a role."

"Who knows me anymore?" Bao Dai asked bitterly.

By now, familiarity had bred plain talk. "You'd be surprised," Bui said. "You're lucky that people are stupid."

Bui's plan was grandiose, but it would strap their limited resources. Bao Dai had a bit of money invested. Now Bui proposed that he should withdraw the interest and buy him a plane ticket from Paris to Saigon. Bao Dai roused himself enough to sign a document designating Bui as head of the new political office, and Bui flew off to Saigon to muster support. Systematically, he sought out dissident elements in South Vietnam and delivered the same message: Bao Dai wants to know whether he can do something for peace. He has no specific plan. But if you believe he should become active again, sign this petition asking him to come back and assist in the reconstruction of the country.

Bui got signatures from leaders of the Hoa Hao, the Cao Dai, an association of montagnards and, predictably, the Dai Viet. An underground contact also signed on behalf of the National Liberation Front; anything that weakened Thieu's position served the Vietcong. Buddhists advised Bui to seek out Bill Kohlmann, who was privately skeptical but noncommittal and agreeable enough that Bui could consider him a new ally. Bui also sent a personal message to

Thieu: To establish our credibility, he wrote, we must show hostility to your government. But in the end, we will be backing you once the Americans are gone.

Returning to Paris, Bui spread out the declarations of support in front of Bao Dai, who agreed with no great enthusiasm to fly to Hong Kong. He insisted, however, on taking along a young woman he had recently met. Bui was furious, aware that arriving on the scene with her was no way to demonstrate statesmanship. Bao Dai could not be moved. The three of them flew to Hong Kong on cheap excursion tickets that also covered one week in a hotel. When the week passed without the promised word from Tokyo, Bui returned to Paris to wait there.

Upon his arrival, he heard a radio report that former Emperor Bao Dai had pledged his firm support to the government of Nguyen Van Thieu.

More angry than surprised, Bui went to Bao Dai's Paris apartment, let himself in and rifled through the stack of mail that had accumulated. Opening the several bank statements, he found that the Thieu government had deposited funds to Bao Dai's account. The sums were not large, perhaps a total of 10,000 U.S. dollars.

When Bao Dai returned to Paris, he summoned Bui. That authorization I gave to you, the former emperor began. I want you to hand it over to Thieu's representative at the South Vietnamese embassy.

No, said Bui. I will no longer make use of it. But I won't do that.

Bao Dai never showed anger, and he was imperturbable now. But Bui's rebellion was collapsing as he spoke. He handed over the document to the last of his nation's emperors.

FIFTEEN

THO
1973

CALLING ON KISSINGER at his office on January 5, Bui Diem was not treated to his usual banter and self-mockery, and Diem plunged immediately into outlining his country's greatest concern—the continued presence of northern troops in the South. Kissinger treated the issue as passé. Thieu had agreed to the Communist presence as far back as May 1971, he said, "so it's late now to raise this again. But I will try my best."

Thieu's men should remember, Kissinger continued, that he and Nixon were their true friends. But given the mood in Congress, it was their coldblooded decision to settle for the agreement that had already been negotiated. He assured Bui Diem that the pact would allow for continued aid to the South. And, if worse came to worst, Vietnam could depend on the United States. Nixon's administration would never tolerate Hanoi's violating the agreement.

Even so, Bui Diem considered Kissinger both brusque and defensive. When he met with Alexis Johnson at the State Department, the American message became even clearer. Johnson claimed that Washington had not changed its policy on Vietnam, only its tactics. "But if your president refuses to accept the agreement once Nixon has accepted it, it will be tragic, a total break between our two peoples."

Taking the elevator from Johnson's office to Bill Rogers's on the seventh floor did not improve Bui Diem's prospects. "With the international situation prevailing right now," Rogers said, "and with pressures from Congress and public opinion, President Nixon has taken too many risks for Vietnam already. He cannot go further."

Diem toured Congress, where the two senators he considered his closest allies, George Aiken and Tower of Texas, told him to be realistic and accept the inevitable. Friendly contacts in the press—Joseph Kraft, Marvin Kalb, Chalmers Roberts—told him there was nothing left to say.

The day after talks resumed in Paris, Bui Diem played one last card and went to see Haig at his Pentagon office. Haig agreed that Thieu had not been consulted adequately—"a bad error on our part"—and offered a listless defense of Kissinger: "Your president misreads him, though part of that is Henry's fault." But if Thieu rejected the agreement, "then that will mean the abandonment of Vietnam."

OVER THE YEARS, Kissinger had felt the sting of Le Duc Tho's tongue. Once, after Tho had chastised him, Kissinger said, "Allow me to ask you one question: Do you scold your colleagues in the Central Committee the way you scold us?" But nothing in the past negotiations had prepared Kissinger for his reception by the North Vietnamese after the Christmas bombing.

When he arrived on January 8 at the house in the town of Gif-sur-Yvette, no one from the North Vietnamese delegation was at the door to greet him. He was simply allowed inside and left to find his own way to the conference room, where the North Vietnamese awaited him stonily. Ill at ease, Kissinger began to apologize. "It was not my responsibility," he began. "It was not my fault about the bombing." From the time they first met, Kissinger had resented the way Le Duc Tho treated him as Tho's student; on this day, it was as a particularly backward one.

"Under the pretext of interrupted negotiations," Tho began, "you resumed the bombing of North Vietnam, just at the moment when I reached home. You have 'greeted' my arrival in a very courteous manner! Your action, I can say, is flagrant and gross!

"You and no one else," Tho continued, "stained the honor of the United States."

Tho spoke for an hour and did not relent. At one point, Kissinger asked that he talk less loudly so that the reporters gathered outside would not hear. Tho ignored him. "For more than ten years," Tho said, "America has used *violence* to beat down the Vietnamese people—napalm, B-52s. But you don't draw any lessons from your failures. You continue the same policy! *Ngu xuan! Ngu xuan! Ngu xuan!*"

When Tho finished banging the table, the Vietnamese translator looked at the floor, unwilling to translate that last word. Members of the U.S. delegation had to supply what Tho had repeated: "Stupid! Stupid! Stupid!"

Kissinger was subdued. He justified the B-52 bombings by Hanoi's conduct in December, which had made Washington believe that the North was refusing to settle. Tho called the bombings therapy for Saigon and went on with his denunciation. "You've spent billions of dollars and many tons of bombs when we have a text ready to sign."

Kissinger tried to counter Tho's earlier outburst. "I have heard many adjectives in your comments," he said. "I propose that you should not use them."

Tho said, "I have used those adjectives with a great deal of restraint already. The world opinion, the U.S. press and U.S. political personalities have used harsher words."

Kissinger said nothing.

When bargaining got underway, Kissinger put forth Saigon's demand for the withdrawal of the North Vietnamese troops, but he did not protest when Tho rejected that condition. Tho said that only two major hurdles remained. The North no longer wanted to recognize the DMZ since Hanoi had always considered Vietnam one country. Tho said no concession on that point was possible. And Washington wanted to allow only civilians to pass through the zone in hopes of barring more troops or equipment from going south. After much bickering, Kissinger agreed to delay a decision on the matter and accept the unwieldy phrase that "among the questions to be negotiated there is the question of the modalities for civilian movement across the provisional military demarcation line." The new pact would also respect the 1962 Geneva agreements on Laos and Cambodia.

A sentence that called for the withdrawal of foreign forces blurred Thieu's objection so thoroughly that Kissinger could claim that it covered North Vietnamese troops, while Hanoi could insist that any Vietnamese on Vietnam soil could not be considered a foreigner.

Beyond the written terms, Le Duc Tho gave a spoken pledge that a cease-fire in Laos would follow Vietnam's within fifteen days. But Tho said that Hanoi could not offer a similar guarantee about the Khmer Rouge in Cambodia.

By now, Lon Nol held little more than the capital, Phnom Penh. Kissinger was skeptical that Tho was telling him the truth about Hanoi's lack of influence over Pol Pot, the Cambodian Communist leader. But when a North Vietnamese Politburo member had recently urged Pol Pot to accept the cease-fire being worked out in Paris, Pol Pot had replied that the Lon Nol regime was on its last legs and rejected the suggestion scornfully.

As their meeting broke up, Kissinger became self-consciously jovial and made an appeal to Le Duc Tho. "We must forget all that has happened," Kissinger said. "When we walk out, we must be smiling."

Working out the final language proved as contentious as agreeing on a shape for the table. But on the night of January 9, Kissinger called to wish Nixon a happy sixtieth birthday and tell him that the talks had reached a breakthrough. Nixon wondered whether Kissinger was being overly enthusiastic again but agreed to tell no one — not Rogers, Laird, Haig or Abrams.

On January 10, negotiations hit an unexpected snag over the POWs.

Kissinger had demanded the release of all captive Americans upon signing the agreement, but he pledged only to urge the return of the majority of Saigon's prisoners within sixty days.

"I cannot accept your proposal," said Tho. "I completely reject it." All prisoners must be exchanged at the same time. Otherwise, the North risked not getting back its men and women.

To arrange that would be hard, Kissinger said.

Le Duc Tho's temper flared. "You have never been a prisoner," he said with the authority of a man who had known Poulo Condore. "You don't understand suffering. It's unfair."

Kissinger seemed to be listening sympathetically. "You are not satisfied," he said. "I am not totally satisfied. We must try to find a consensus."

In the end, Hanoi settled for a protocol that committed the United States to use "its maximum influence" to secure the release of political prisoners in South Vietnam within sixty days of signing the agreement and all detainees within ninety days.

By January 13, Kissinger was back in Washington with an agreement ready to sign and annoyed that the White House was playing down his contribution. Nixon still blamed Kissinger, not without reason, for a Scotty Reston column at the time of the Christmas bombing that suggested Kissinger had opposed the B-52 raids and might even resign to write a book about the Paris talks. Such a book, according to Reston, "would probably be highly embarrassing to Mr. Nixon."

Kissinger flatly denied that he had spoken with Reston until the log of his telephone calls caught him out. "Yes," Kissinger admitted, he did have a conversation with the columnist, "but that was only on the telephone."

For Nixon, it was just one more indignity. Kissinger's recent interview with Oriana Fallaci, an Italian journalist, had boomeranged when Kissinger resurrected the image he had once used about Lyndon Johnson, this time painting himself as "the cowboy who rides all alone into town with his horse and nothing else." Kissinger said that the "amazing romantic character suits me precisely because to be alone has always been part of my character."

Reprinted throughout the world, his grandiose self-portrait amused everyone but Kissinger and a president shunted to the role of loyal sidekick. Kissinger wanted to deny the whole embarrassment, but Fallaci had his remarks on tape. *Time* then crowned Nixon's chagrin by naming both the president and Kissinger the magazine's Co–Men of the Year for 1972.

At midnight on the thirteenth, Kissinger went to see Nixon at the White House. He still considered the president ruthless and devious in promoting his reputation, but at this moment he was feeling what he considered an odd tenderness toward the man. He decided that Nixon was entitled, after all, to his hour of triumph in the limelight.

Haig next flew with the document to Saigon for Thieu's signature. Nixon was itching for a showdown. "Brutality is nothing," he boasted to Kissinger. "You have never seen it if this son-of-a-bitch doesn't go along, believe me."

But Thieu held out for a bit even after other firm allies, including Senators Stennis and Goldwater, announced publicly that blocking the agreement would jeopardize Thieu's relations with Washington. On January 21, he gave in.

The next day, back in Paris, Kissinger learned that Lyndon Johnson had died. He saw it as symbolic that Johnson's life should end at the same time as the war that had driven him from office. Kissinger might have reflected, too, on the fact that the terms he had accepted in Paris did not differ greatly from what the United States could have achieved at the end of Johnson's presidency. Nixon's determination to preserve Thieu in office, at least through his own re-election, had cost 20,533 American lives in the four years from 1969 to 1972. About 107,000 ARVN soldiers died during that time, and perhaps five times that number of North Vietnamese and Vietcong troops. Civilian casualties were impossible to estimate. They may have run to a million men, women and children.

Le Duc Tho asked for a last-minute assurance about the economic aid the North had been promised, but Kissinger considered his request obnoxious and replied that it would depend on the U.S. Congress and on Hanoi's observing the Paris agreements.

At 12:45 P.M. on January 23, Le Duc Tho and Kissinger initialed the final text. The war was over. More correctly, the American war was over.

ON MARCH 28, Nixon brought home the last of the 25,000 U.S. soldiers, and the Communists released nearly 600 prisoners of war. Throughout the past year, Robbie Risner and his fellow POWs had designated certain prisoners to monitor the Voice of Vietnam broadcasts and winnow out legitimate news from Communist propaganda. Last October 26, the broadcast had announced the Kissinger-Tho agreement in Paris, and for a moment Risner and the others thought they would be going home in sixty days. At the end of the broadcast, the Vietnamese announcer said, "The United States was supposed to have been in Hanoi to initial this today. On the twenty-eighth they were supposed to go to Paris to sign it." But, he added, the United States had gone back on its word.

On December 18, Risner had been lying on his bunk when he heard far-off engines. Hanoi had not been bombed for a long time, and yet three squadrons, perhaps four, seemed to be heading toward the city. As the ground shook and plaster fell from the ceiling, the Americans cheered and clapped each other on the back. By the next night, it was established that the planes were B-52s, and Risner detected a change in the prison guards. While they had shouted defiantly at the fighter planes, they seemed to feel powerless against B-52s flying at such great height. But the bigger planes were also vulnerable. Hanoi captured 31 more airmen, and another 93 were officially listed as missing.

Initialing the Paris accord, January 24, 1973. From left: Nguyen Co Thach, North Vietnam's vice minister for foreign affairs; Xuan Thuy; Nguyen Dinh Phuong, interpreter; Le Duc Tho, special adviser to North Vietnam's delegation; Kissinger *(AP/Wide World Photos)*

When the Paris agreement was signed, prisoners were given a copy, along with the protocols that called for their release within sixty days. As that day approached, the North Vietnamese began trucking groups of prisoners to Hanoi's War Museum. They wanted to show the Americans photographs of the carnage from the bombing. When Risner refused to go, the camp commander railed at him: "Look, you are going, and you are going to see what President Nixon has done to the Vietnamese people. You are going to see the instruments of death that he has used. And you are going to see the death and destruction we have suffered."

Risner was forced onto a bus along with others who had refused and was dragged inside the museum. The Americans stared at the floor or ceiling. When guards pushed their heads toward the exhibits, they closed their eyes. The next group resisted even more strenuously, and the tours were canceled.

On the day the prisoners were to be set free, they were lined up in the order they had been captured. Guards brought them brightly colored sweaters, which the men refused to wear. They did accept jackets, though, since the winter air was cold. Each of four groups numbered about 120 men. Ev Alvarez was number one, Risner number twenty-seven. As he waited, he thought of men who had not survived in prison; he could name at least four.

At the airstrip, Risner watched the landing of three C-141s with red crosses painted on their tails. The prisoners were marched in columns of two past a U.S. representative to salute and board the plane. Only after they were airborne did the men cheer and kiss the nurses who had come along on the flight.

At Clark Air Force Base, amid a throng of American flags and banners, Risner was the first off his plane. Admiral Noel Gayler, Commander in Chief, Pacific, shook his hand, and General Joseph Moore, commander of the Thirteenth Air Force, said, "Welcome home, Robbie." Risner had waited seven and a half years to hear it.

NEWS OF THE PARIS AGREEMENT gave a moment of hope to the highest-ranking Communist in custody in the South. A former deputy minister in Hanoi, Nguyen Van Tai had slipped into South Vietnam ten years earlier to run the counterespionage operation against the Americans. He had been captured in December 1970 during an ARVN dragnet in Saigon but refused to admit his identity or divulge any information.

After the standard beatings and electrodes wired to his testicles, frustrated ARVN investigators had turned to CIA specialists, who built for Tai an antiseptic white cell, bare except for an open-hole toilet and a television camera to record his every action. The guards discovered that Tai held a common Vietnamese belief that his blood vessels contracted in the cold, and they pumped in frigid air to unnerve him.

Despite his discomfort, Tai remained silent until Frank Snepp arrived in October 1972 to take over his interrogation. Young, handsome, entirely self-assured, Snepp had come to the CIA from North Carolina by way of Columbia University's School of International Affairs. He had joined the agency to avoid Vietnam, but once he was hired, Snepp's diligence and manner rankled his coworkers, and they volunteered him for duty in Saigon. Beginning in 1969, Snepp spent two years there at a desk, analyzing intelligence reports. He returned to CIA headquarters in Langley with a reputation for being savvy about Hanoi politics.

Snepp knew that Tai had a value for the CIA beyond his information. Tran Bach Dang, the Saigon Communist who planned Tet in the capital, had once offered a trade. To get back Tai and Le Van Hoai, an NLF labor organizer, the Communists would release Douglas Ramsey, a State Department official captured in 1966. After much debate, the U.S. embassy agreed to release only Hoai. Tai was deemed too valuable and, as a CIA coworker explained to Snepp, Ramsey was "no more than a Foreign Service officer."

The Communists rejected the deal, and negotiations were allowed to die. Snepp was cynical about being assigned to the case. He understood that his CIA superiors were determined to break Tai in order to justify their decision not to bargain for Ramsey. If he failed, Snepp thought, they would blame the whole affair on him, the kid.

Back in South Vietnam, Snepp was hurried to Tai's frigid cell. He found a small but compact man who had kept fit with hours of calisthenics. Tai still claimed to be a simple farmer, but he snatched up the books of French poetry Snepp left with him and used an English grammar to teach himself phrases. Snepp came to like Tai but considered his reasons entirely pragmatic for wearing him down psychologically rather than pummeling him or searing his genitals. Psychology, he thought, worked better.

At least twice a day, Snepp questioned Tai for two and three hours at a time, often at odd hours, hoping to disorient him. Tai's only lapse came when Snepp asked if he did not miss his wife and children. After ten years, Tai said, he could not bear to think about them. "The only way I can survive this is by putting all such hope aside. Then there are no disappointments."

By early January, Snepp felt that he had Tai near collapse. From Washington, the CIA was cheering him on, although ARVN intelligence recommended reverting to torture. It was then that news arrived about the Paris agreements, and the interrogation stopped.

On February 1, Snepp told Tai the terms. "If what you tell me is true," Tai said, "this is the happiest day of my life."

The Saigon authorities rebuked Snepp for informing Tai of the agreement. They said that since Tai had never acknowledged his identity, the prisoner exchange would not apply to him. Snepp was removed from the case, and Tai, shivering in his cell, was returned to his South Vietnamese guards.

ROBBIE RISNER'S rebellious attitude in prison had guaranteed that he would not meet Jane Fonda when she arrived in Hanoi the previous summer. The actress spoke with other prisoners, however, and broadcast a message of peace to the American soldiers still stationed in Vietnam. For photographers, she posed cheerily next to an antiaircraft gun of the sort that was shooting down U.S. pilots. Outraged Americans remembered Tokyo Rose, whose broadcasts had attempted to demoralize GIs during World War II, and denounced the actress as "Hanoi Jane."

Jane Fonda's visit carried extra freight both artistically and erotically because her role in the film *Klute* had won her an Academy Award in 1971 as Best Actress, and her near-naked poster for *Barbarella* was a favorite GI pinup.

Given her condemnation of the war, the actress objected when the POWs returned home to a hero's welcome. As Risner and others spoke of being brutally tortured from 1965 to 1969, she called them "hypocrites and liars." The war still generated high emotion, but that remark was too harsh and she soon edged away from it. She allowed that she was "quite sure that there were incidents of torture," but the pilots had probably suffered at the hands of "the people whose homes and families they were bombing and napalming." She could not believe that torture had been prison policy.

The public outcry did not fade, and the actress was forced to clarify her position again. In a letter to the *Los Angeles Times*, she lamented the fact that the "600 strong, healthy-looking POWs"—men who had cheered the B-52 Christmas bombings—were diverting attention from those American veterans who spoke out against the atrocities in Vietnam. As willing agents in an obscene war, she added, the "military, elite, career officers" deserved no sympathy.

HEARING AT FIRST HAND what the American prisoners had endured in Hanoi set off a new revulsion against the entire Vietnam involvement. Even before the Paris agreement, Democrats in the House had voted two-to-one on January 2 to cut off all funds for military operations once the American POWs were released. Two days later, Senate Democrats passed a similar resolution by a margin of three to one. Given that mood in Congress, Nixon would be depending on his personal prestige to win the reconstruction money of Kissinger's final promise— $3.25 billion over a five-year period. And Nixon's prestige was never higher. In the week after the Paris agreement was signed, Gallup showed his approval rating at 68 percent. But when asked how the United States should respond if Hanoi again attacked South Vietnam, 50 percent opposed sending even military aid. Resistance to resuming the U.S. bombing was stronger still—71 percent were against it.

Kissinger's triumphal tour of Asia could not include Saigon because Thieu hated him. Nor could he stop in Phnom Penh, where the fighting continued. Although Lon Nol was now asking for a cease-fire, Pol Pot refused. His Khmer Rouge had bolstered their strength to more than 40,000 men, far outnumbering the few thousand North Vietnamese troops who remained in Cambodia. With complete victory in sight, Pol Pot had no reason to defer to Hanoi or Beijing or Moscow.

In Laos, Souvanna Phouma accepted the Paris cease-fire, even though he knew that North Vietnam would not give up control of the Ho Chi Minh Trail. Stopping in Vientiane, Kissinger assured Souvanna that the United States had not done so much in Southeast Asia only to let its friends down.

To bail out Lon Nol, Nixon resumed bombing in Cambodia early in February. Throughout all of 1972, American B-52s had dropped nearly 37,000 tons of bombs on the country. Now, in the three months from March through May of 1973, the tonnage rose to 95,000, plus another 15,000 tons dropped each month by fighter-bombers. Public apathy and restrictions on reporting from the scene combined to keep the bombing from igniting new debate.

□

As a sop for signing off on the Paris agreement, Nixon arranged in April for Nguyen Van Thieu to make his first visit to the United States. True, Nixon only received him at San Clemente, not in the Oval Office. And true, Nixon once again reassured him only in private that he could count on the United States if the Paris agreement was grossly violated. The public statement was far more tepid.

Thieu had only a sketchy knowledge of an inquiry by Senator Sam Ervin's select committee into the Watergate scandal, and when Spiro Agnew hosted a formal dinner party in his honor, Thieu was unaware that the vice president was under investigation for bribery. Flying back to Saigon in a chartered 707 jet, Thieu considered his trip a complete success.

If Thieu felt more confident, Lon Nol had also taken heart. The B-52s had saved his regime, even though crowds of Cambodian farmers were flooding into Phnom Penh and other towns where they hoped to be safe from the bombing. Lon Nol cracked down on dissidents and locked up Sirik Matak, his partner in the coup against Sihanouk. Haig was sent as the army's vice chief of staff to persuade Lon Nol that his government should be more democratic.

Almost by accident, Secretary Rogers finally learned of the scope of the bombings in Cambodia. He cobbled together a defense of the State Department's role and headed for Capitol Hill on the morning of April 30. During the drive, an aide remarked, "This will be hot."

"No," Rogers told him, "the President is about to make a statement which will far overshadow this."

Rogers knew that the 1972 Watergate break-in was about to claim its most prominent scapegoats. That evening, Nixon planned to announce the resignations of Haldeman and Ehrlichman. Also forced out was Richard Kleindienst, the man who had replaced John Mitchell as attorney general when Mitchell left to run Nixon's reelection campaign. During the month of April, Nixon had been working to ease out his two key advisers, but he also wanted to boost their spirits. On Easter Day, Nixon had called from Key Biscayne to tell Haldeman: "Just remember you're doing the right thing. That's what I used to think when I killed some innocent children in Hanoi."

Haldeman and Ehrlichman preferred a leave of absence over resignation. Nixon turned to Ron Ziegler to convey to them that a leave was not sufficient. Both would surely be cleared, Nixon said. In the meantime, they had to resign.

When they continued to balk, Nixon took them to Camp David on Sunday, April 29. He began his remarks by saying that he was not a publicly religious man, but he had been praying on his knees every night since he became president. He had prayed over this decision, one of the hardest he had ever made. After that preamble, Nixon said that he was the guilty one for launching Chuck Colson on his illicit projects. He would probably have to resign the presidency. Nixon paused long enough to let Haldeman talk him out of quitting.

Ehrlichman proved harder to oust, but by 6 P.M. Nixon had in hand the letters he wanted. The next evening, Haldeman listened to the president as he announced the resignations and called the White House afterward to advise Nixon that he now had Watergate behind him and should keep it that way. Nixon seemed to be feeling sorry mostly for himself. He asked Haldeman whether he would check around, as he had always done in the past, to sample reaction to the speech. Haldeman said, no, he didn't think he could do that.

NEARING EIGHTY when the Paris agreement was signed, Ellsworth Bunker had been ambassador in Saigon since Johnson appointed him in 1967. He had ridden out accusations of meddling in South Vietnam's elections in 1971 with his open support of Thieu, and he had tried unsuccessfully to bribe Big Minh to enter that year's presidential race to give it the look of a real contest. The heir to a sugar fortune, Bunker came from the generation that assumed American policy was always right, and when he left Saigon he turned the embassy over to a successor no more given to self-doubt. Graham Martin, considered one of Harriman's protégés, had served in the mid-1960s as ambassador to Thailand. But while he could be as cantankerous as Harriman, Martin lacked his patron's political instincts, even though his mission in Saigon would involve guiding Thieu through the pitfalls ahead.

FIRING KLEINDIENST set off a shuffle within Nixon's cabinet. Laird had been increasingly frozen out of decisions by the president and Kissinger and deliberately not told about the Christmas bombing and the resumption of air strikes in Cambodia. When Laird resigned, Nixon replaced him briefly with Elliot Richardson before moving Richardson to the attorney general's office and naming his CIA director, James Schlesinger, to head the Defense Department. Schlesinger had always taken a hard line against the Communists, but the Paris peace agreement limited the Pentagon's options. U.S. Army officers who remained in South Vietnam could no longer advise ARVN units, which meant that the chief duty of John Murray, the major general in command, was to distribute the equipment that had been rushed to South Vietnam the previous year.

A program called Enhance during the summer of 1972 had replaced ARVN losses from the Easter offensive with tanks, anti-tank missiles and long-range 175-mm guns. During several weeks that autumn, Enhance Plus had tried to prepare South Vietnam's air force for the battles to come by sending nine squadrons of planes and nearly 100,000 tons of other equipment before the Paris accords would prohibit such shipments. But Murray had expected Congress to keep voting whatever funds the South required. He was unprepared when the Senate

Armed Services Committee cut South Vietnam's appropriation for fiscal 1974 from $1.6 billion to little more than $1 billion. Senators could justify the cuts by pointing to Ambassador Martin's encouraging reports, and Kissinger had assured Ted Kennedy, who was leading a move to cut the appropriation still further, that the Paris agreement was not working badly since ARVN casualties were down by two-thirds.

LIKE MCNAMARA in the mid-1960s, Kissinger wanted to disassociate himself from policies that his liberal acquaintances in Cambridge and Georgetown found repellent. Kissinger would defend the bombing in Cambodia as necessary to save American lives, but he would also denounce the White House wiretaps and claim that he himself had been their main target. He was persuasive in denying knowledge of the Watergate crimes and in portraying himself as an unsullied victim of Nixon's thuggish inner circle. Kissinger could say that he had known nothing about rifling files in the office of Ellsberg's psychiatrist, and expect his listeners to be unaware that it was his salacious rumors about Ellsberg that helped prompt the break-in.

For months, Kissinger had been waiting nervously for Nixon to get rid of Rogers and give him the title of secretary of state. His only competition was Kenneth Rush, a deputy secretary at the Pentagon, who had been promised the job by John Mitchell. But Rogers was not going gently. First, he had wanted to stay until the Paris agreements were signed; and besides, he did not want to give Kissinger the satisfaction of forcing him out.

When Kissinger learned that Rogers would not be leaving until June at the earliest, he began to shout: "And now he's hanging on just like I said he would. Piece by piece. Bit by bit. He stays on and on and on!" As his tantrum subsided, Kissinger sighed. "He will be with me forever—because he has this President wrapped around his little finger."

It was not until August 21 that Nixon invited Kissinger for a swim at San Clemente and told him the good news: "I would like to nominate you for Secretary of State tomorrow." With Watergate threatening to submerge him, Nixon had not held a press conference in five months. As a result, when he announced the appointment, reporters had no questions about Kissinger, only about Nixon's legal difficulties. At his own news conference, however, the new secretary of state was pressed to talk about the secret bombing in Cambodia, the effect of Watergate on foreign affairs and his own role in the wiretapping. Kissinger fielded the questions deftly and capped his appearance with the sort of quip journalists found irresistible.

A reporter asked, "Do you prefer to be called Mr. Secretary or Dr. Secretary?"

"I don't stand on protocol," Kissinger replied smoothly. "If you just call me Excellency, it will be okay."

☐

KISSINGER WAS SOON CAST in a drama of high statecraft. Spiro Agnew was leaving the vice presidency, and under the law his letter of resignation went to the secretary of state. A minute after he delivered the one-sentence note to Kissinger on October 10, Agnew appeared before a district judge in Baltimore to plead no-contest to one charge of evading income tax on the bribe money he had taken as governor. He was fined $10,000 and put on three years' probation.

Two days later, Nixon nominated Gerald Ford as Agnew's successor. A football star at the University of Michigan, Ford had been hired by Yale to coach undergraduate teams, then managed to slip into the Yale Law School, where he surprised fellow students by graduating in the upper third of the class. As a politician, Ford had one specific ambition. He hoped his decency and bluff Midwestern manner would one day make him Speaker of the House, but the Democrats had thwarted him by retaining control of the Congress. Ford obliged Lyndon Johnson by serving on the commission that investigated Jack Kennedy's assassination, and he supported the Vietnam War. But when he opposed a bombing pause, Johnson struck back with a phrase that had dogged Ford ever since. The president told reporters that Ford must have played football without a helmet. Why, Johnson cracked, he can't walk a straight line and chew gum at the same time.

Nixon would have preferred to name John Connally as vice president. But Connally had switched parties to become a Republican, and Nixon was persuaded that Congress might refuse to confirm him. Ford presented no such problem. Once nominated, however, he had to endure speculation that Nixon was counting on Ford's dim wattage as insurance against impeachment. *Newsweek* reported that when Nelson Rockefeller visited the Oval Office, Nixon had said scornfully, "Can you see Gerald Ford sitting in this chair?"

Ford was mad enough to ask Nixon about it. "Of course I never said anything like that," Nixon told him. "It's just a story that our enemies made up."

Ford wanted to believe him.

THE SAME DAY that Nixon nominated Ford as vice president, the Court of Appeals ordered him in a 5-to-2 vote to turn over his White House tapes to Judge John J. Sirica, who was hearing the case against defendants in the Watergate break-in. Archibald Cox, the special prosecutor investigating the affair, had sued to obtain the tapes, and Nixon was fed up with him. Haig had replaced Haldeman at the White House, and he called Elliot Richardson at the Justice Department to demand that Cox make no further effort to procure tapes, notes or memoranda. But Cox, a professor at the Harvard Law School who had served as Robert Kennedy's solicitor general, could not be bullied. On Saturday, October 20, he told reporters at the National Press Club that he would not accept Nixon's attempt to hamper his inquiry.

An hour later, Haig called Richardson again and told him to fire Cox.

"Well, I can't do that," Richardson said. "I guess I'd better come over and resign."

Haig next called William Ruckelshaus, the deputy attorney general, who also demurred. "Your commander in chief has given you an order," Haig said. "You have no alternative."

The two civilians saw their duty differently. Finally, the current solicitor general, Robert Bork, said he was willing to fire Cox. He was designated acting attorney general, and Cox was dismissed, along with Ruckelshaus, who was not given Richardson's option of resigning.

Termed the "Saturday Night Massacre," the firings outraged the country. The president of the American Bar Association said Nixon had tried to "abort the established process of justice," and House Republicans weakened in their defense of Nixon against impeachment. The next Tuesday, with Judge Sirica ready to cite Nixon for contempt, the White House abruptly agreed to surrender the tapes.

A group of Nixon loyalists in the Senate came to the White House for drinks some time later, and Richard Schweiker of Pennsylvania asked, "Mr. President, are there going to be any more surprises about the tapes?"

"No," said Nixon. "Absolutely not."

IN MID-OCTOBER, the Nobel Committee of the Norwegian Parliament awarded Kissinger and Le Duc Tho the 1973 Nobel Peace Prize for bringing "their talent and good will to bear in order to obtain a peace agreement." Learning of the honor, George Ball remarked to the *Washington Post* that "the Norwegians must have a sense of humor." Le Duc Tho declined the award because the Paris agreement was not being honored.

Kissinger regarded Tho's refusal as "another insolence by North Vietnam." He himself was happy to accept, but because his presence at the ceremony might provoke a massive antiwar demonstration, Kissinger did not go to Norway. Instead, he sent an acceptance statement to be read by the U.S. ambassador, and even that man had to slip in through a side door at the University of Oslo.

IN LATE OCTOBER, Tom Hayden and his fellow defendants went back to Chicago for a new trial on the contempt charges from their conspiracy trial. Hayden had reason to be hopeful, since the courts in recent months were ruling regularly against the Nixon White House. In November 1972, the U.S. Court of Appeals for the Seventh Circuit had reversed the conspiracy convictions because of the "demeanor of the judge and prosecutors." The case against Daniel Ellsberg was thrown out when the presiding judge learned of the break-in at his psychiatrist's office.

After five weeks, the new judge in the retrial, Edward Gignoux, dismissed

146 of Julius Hoffman's 159 contempt citations, and Hayden was free to go. His file at the FBI noted that he had married Jane Fonda in January and quoted from the *Los Angeles Times* that the ceremony "included poetry, Vietnamese music and a vow to keep their sense of humor."

ON NOVEMBER 7, Congress overrode Nixon's veto of the War Powers Resolution and required the president to report any commitment of troops to the Speaker of the House and the president pro tem of the Senate. The act had loopholes but none broad enough to let Nixon live up to the pledges made to Thieu in Paris and San Clemente.

SIXTEEN

THIEU
1974

A s 1974 OPENED, Hanoi's generals drew up a tally sheet. The previous year had begun disastrously for them. Their troops had been worn out and demoralized by the failure of the Easter offensive. Some Vietcong villagers were obeying the cease-fire order even as Thieu seized land and planned ways to win an election. The Communists had no doubt that he would be as ruthless in rooting them out as Diem had been in the late 1950s. But as the year progressed, Hanoi made striking gains in Ben Tre and My Tho. The ARVN also continued to do well, taking back about four hundred hamlets and setting up seven hundred new military posts. Stepped-up U.S. military aid had allowed Saigon to increase its forces substantially.

From Hanoi, General Hoang Van Thai estimated that the ARVN could now fight a small war, even a medium-sized one. But by itself South Vietnam's army could not cope with a major offensive. If the North repeated an attack as large as the one in 1972—and if the Americans did not return to provide air support—Saigon's forces would crumble.

General Thai was in Hanoi unwillingly. At sixty-eight, his service dated back to the armed propaganda teams that Giap had formed even before he created the People's Army of Vietnam. The son of a peasant family from Thai Binh province, Thai left Hanoi in 1965 to head the 5th Military Command, which directed Communist activities in the northern third of South Vietnam. He had been content in the job until he was called north for the major reevaluation of 1973. During that stay, doctors discovered a thrombosis and a kidney stone that required an operation. Upset that he might miss the war's climax, Thai was consoled by fellow officers. Go and look after yourself, they told him; the fight will be long.

Sent to East Germany for three months, he returned in November, in time to join in the planning for 1974. Thai was prepared to return to his headquarters in the South in January; he had already shipped down his Tet gifts so he could travel lightly when Le Duc Tho informed him that the Politburo was keeping him in Hanoi. A medical council said that his cardiovascular system had not stabilized.

"Please let me go," Thai pleaded, "and I promise to be very careful about my health."

Tho refused and Thai knew further argument was futile. Tran Van Tra had already been named to replace him. Leaving Tho's office, Thai spent the next three hours writing an eight-page letter to Giap about conditions in the South. Giap responded by making Thai first deputy chief of the general staff and putting him in charge of getting supplies to the B-2 front. But another general, Van Tien Dung, would be leading the North Vietnamese troops into battle. Thai resolved to put aside personal grievances and get to work.

The job was immense. Using Soviet and Chinese bulldozers and earth movers, labor battalions had widened the existing roads south to fashion a highway from Quang Tri, just over the DMZ, all the way down to the Mekong Delta. The result gave the Communists 12,000 miles of roadway and a 3,000-mile pipeline to carry oil from Quang Tri to their headquarters at Loc Ninh, seventy-five miles northwest of Saigon. From that base, radio equipment let field commanders communicate instantly with Hanoi.

While the Nixon administration was unraveling in Washington, Nguyen Van Thieu faced a different challenge. Although the United States had rushed weaponry and aircraft to him as part of the two Enhance shipments, Thieu knew that without American airpower to deter the Communists their forces were certain to become bolder. And yet, now that he was on his own, Thieu seemed drained of all initiative. For months after his trip to the United States, he had insisted that Nixon's clear signals of backing meant that he was dealing from a position of strength. When Bui Diem urged a serious reform of his government, Thieu listened, nodded and did nothing.

Nor would he reach out to broaden his administration—the goal in South Vietnam of every American policy-maker for twenty years. Whenever Thieu could be made to focus on his problems, he claimed to be waiting to make changes in his government until the U.S. Congress increased his military and economic aid. Other Vietnamese tried to make him understand the realities in Washington. Thieu ignored them. His prime minister, Tran Thien Khiem, was no help—as inert as Rusk, as removed from decision-making as Rogers.

But by March, Thieu started to realize what the Watergate hearings coulu mean and sent Bui Diem to Washington again to evaluate the effect of Nixon's impeachment on Saigon. Bui Diem met with Vice President Gerald Ford, who was cordial but could offer no reassurance.

IN THE NORTH, General Thai's staff was hearing that ARVN morale was especially low in the Mekong Delta. His analysts were also concluding that the political strife in America meant Washington could no longer intervene freely to save Thieu. Over the past year, North Vietnam had sent south nearly 100,000 troops, but military supplies for them remained inadequate. Even so, one fact remained irrefutable: the North must take the country in the next few years. Le Duan made the point often and forcefully that a prolonged war would be disastrous. He asked that Thai and his top aides travel by separate cars to Do Son beach, near Haiphong, where Le Duan was on vacation.

Arriving on July 21, they realized that Le Duan was more eager than ever for a showdown in the South. He said that the United States was no longer the only country trying to gain influence in Indochina. Without mentioning China, he exhorted his military audience to unite the country as soon as possible. "A unified Vietnam with a population of 50 million would not be an easy target for any prospective invader or interventionists," Le Duan concluded. "We must organize to deal stunning blows that will wipe out the enemy forces in big chunks."

Reviewing the political situation, Le Duan recalled that during Ngo Dinh Diem's years in power, the Saigon government had been stronger than the Communists because "we had withdrawn our forces under the Geneva Agreement." When the Americans stepped in to replace Diem, the enemy remained strong. But now the Americans had gone home and the enemy had not been this weak since 1954. If Nixon was driven from office, Le Duan speculated that Ford "might seek some sort of arrangement with us."

The general staff drew up a detailed plan: Destroy 1,000 enemy posts in the Mekong Delta before the year was out, and add 10,000 Communist troops in Ben Tre and Tra Vinh. Extend the rear guard along Highway 14 and expand the contested areas around Saigon. Fight Thieu's pacification program and continue NVA training for possible large-scale fighting.

A severe problem was the lack of artillery shells. At the moment, the Communist forces had only 100,000 of them. Men were being told to recover shell casings that the munition workshops could then recycle. The generals asked Le Duan to request emergency aid from other Socialist countries.

Le Duan was not optimistic. "Obviously, China is exerting pressure on us," he said. But even though China wanted to end the fighting, Hanoi would ask Beijing for more aid. Meantime, however, they had better expect to keep using recycled shells.

General Thai told Le Duan that if they achieved their goals in 1975 "then in

Le Duan
touring North Vietnam's farms
(Archive Photos)

1976, we could move much faster to deal the final blow in just a few months." That would compel the South to accept a tripartite government and "would smooth the way towards reunification of the country in two or three years."

Le Duan was enthusiastic. "It would be marvelous," he said, "if we could win in a few years."

KISSINGER SEEMED TO understand that the end of Nixon's presidency was near and was staying out of Washington as much as he could. In the ten months since the Saturday Night Massacre, he had traveled 196,000 miles overseas in trips to twenty-eight countries. But by mid-July, new and damaging White House tapes had convinced him that Nixon would have to resign. On August 6, Kissinger confronted the president in the Oval Office to say that an impeachment trial would paralyze the nation's foreign policy. Nixon made no direct reply. That evening, he called Kissinger to say he was cutting off all military aid to Israel.

As Nixon's chief of staff, Haig called Kissinger at the State Department on August 7 and asked him to hurry right over. Nixon was alone when he arrived. He said that he intended to announce his resignation the next night, effective at noon on Friday, August 9. As Nixon mused aloud about how the news would strike Mao and Brezhnev, Kissinger said, "History will treat you more kindly than your contemporaries."

Nixon was realistic. "It depends on who writes the history."

That evening, as Kissinger was having dinner at home with Joe Alsop, Nixon called, said he was alone and asked Kissinger to stop by again. At the White House, Kissinger found Nixon listening to Russian classical music and brooding over his disgrace. Kissinger hoped to cheer him by recounting his contributions to peace — the summits, the invasion of Cambodia, the mining of Haiphong Harbor. Amid mutual pledges of support, the two men collapsed in tears. After an hour and a half, Kissinger was about to leave when Nixon asked him to join in dropping to his knees to pray. Kissinger obliged him and comforted him as Nixon sobbed about his fate. Back at his office, Kissinger told aides, "He is truly a tragic figure."

One reason for the past three American presidents to wage war in Vietnam had been to ensure a second term, a term that none of the three was destined to complete.

AT NOON ON AUGUST 9, Gerald Ford became president. Hearing of Nixon's resignation, Thieu was deeply shaken, but within a day he was exuding hope again. As a first priority, Ford had written to remind him of America's bipartisan foreign policy. Past commitments made by the United States, Ford wrote, "are still valid and will be fully honored in my administration."

Thieu soon learned how little Ford could deliver. Congress cut Nixon's final $1 billion aid package for South Vietnam to $700 million. By the time the appropriation moved through the Defense Department, it was down to $400 million.

Just as the flood of dollars became a trickle, Thieu was belatedly assailed for corruption by a Catholic priest who was exposing the rot in the Saigon government. Washington had recognized the problem for years but played down its importance for fear of offending whichever Vietnamese was in power. Ky claimed to have resisted bribes when he was premier. He said a Buddhist monk had offered him a million dollars in cash to license a Japanese automobile factory; the deal included three hundred cars for Ky to distribute to his friends. Ky refused but said his wife had reproached him for being too hasty. His story reinforced an impression that it was the generals' wives who were most vulnerable to temptation. One anecdote floating through Saigon concerned wives who demanded 100,000 piasters to keep a young man out of the draft. Playing high-stakes poker, one woman was supposed to have called, "I'll raise you a soldier."

The chief of police of Cholon was notorious for selling military exemptions for the sons of Chinese merchants, and some American GIs learned that they could unload merchandise from the PX at a healthy profit. Bribery, the black market, manipulation of rice prices—all had demoralized the Vietnamese people and increased Thieu's unpopularity. A survey by his political enemies estimated that the generals' wives had skimmed off $500 million.

Knowledgeable men around Thieu said he had been relatively honest until the Paris agreement. Then, foreseeing a bleak future, he had turned to the security of money. Thieu's wife was singled out for using her position at a Saigon charity hospital to import items free of customs tax and sell them at a profit. For the Saigonese, the proof was that Thieu's family, with its modest holdings before he took office, had bought a villa on Cong Ly Street for 92 million piasters—about $400,000. Equally damaging reports implicated Premier Khiem's wife. Not that the generals always entrusted corruption to their women. A two-star general in I Corps at the DMZ was discovered to be selling government rice to the Communists.

An exception to the prevailing greed was General Ngo Quang Truong, who commanded the Central Highlands. He and his family lived simply. When Truong learned that profiteers were contacting his wife, he put an end to it. But Truong's staff could admire his honesty, praise his skill during the Easter offensive and still worry about the challenges ahead.

Thieu's chief antagonist, the priest named Tran Huu Thanh, had been closely allied with Diem. His People's Anticorruption Movement attracted a following with attacks on Thieu, his wife and many other officials. With workers and farmers suffering from the worldwide effect of runaway oil prices, outrage at anyone who was bilking the government spread quickly and reinforced resentment over the government's repressive policies. The result was turmoil in the streets when Thieu could least afford it.

After suffering many slights at the hands of Thieu's cousin, the embassy had pried Hoang Duc Nha from an official role at the palace, but he remained close to Thieu. Nha recommended a television speech that would calm and reassure the nation, and Bui Diem began to draft it. As he had told students in Paris, he had little good to say about Thieu or the men around him. Still, his country was at war, and Thieu, taciturn and bullheaded as he might be, was the South's leader.

For Thieu's opening statement, Bui Diem wrote, "Although I do not admit the veracity of all the specific allegations made by Father Thanh and the opposition, I do recognize the existence of corruption, and I do recognize the necessity of dealing with it."

Bui Diem handed in his draft and heard nothing more until he turned on his television at the appointed hour. Thieu was there, raging against the Communists as shrilly as his low energy allowed him. They were behind all of the discontent, he insisted.

It was a speech Ngo Dinh Diem might have given. Bui Diem thought, Thieu has not truly grasped what has happened with Nixon in the United States or what is happening to him in his own country.

Autumn seemed to be imploding. As South Vietnamese families scrambled to eat, political demonstrations disrupted Saigon's street life. Isolated in the modern Independence Palace that had replaced Diem's Gia Long Palace in the mid-1960s, Thieu struggled to hold on to the power slipping through his fingers.

WILLIAM CALLEY was free from confinement thanks to a benevolent civil ruling from a judge in Columbus, Georgia. Calley rented an apartment in town and drove through the streets in a white Mercedes given to him by a local supporter. When the U.S. Circuit Court in New Orleans overturned the judge's ruling, Calley was returned to custody for a few months until the secretary of the army ordered him paroled.

In subsequent legal maneuvering, the U.S. Supreme Court upheld Calley's conviction, but he remained free. At the age of thirty-two, he married a young woman who met him at about the time he was charged with mass murder. When a proposed lecture tour did not prove profitable, Calley went to work in his father-in-law's Columbus jewelry store.

FOR THE FIRST MONTH of his presidency, Gerald Ford felt badgered by questions about Nixon's future, and he resolved to end them. Haig had raised the possibility of a presidential pardon for Nixon on August 1, while Ford was still vice president, laying out several scenarios that might induce Nixon to resign. "It's my understanding from a White House lawyer," Haig had said, "that a President does have the authority to grant a pardon even before criminal action has been taken against an individual."

Ford did not commit himself at the time, but in September he signed "a full, free and absolute pardon unto Richard Nixon for all offenses against the United States which he, Richard Nixon, has committed or taken part in during the period from January 20, 1969, through August 9, 1974."

Nixon had been undone by attempting to cover up the crimes associated with Watergate. Now many Americans suspected another cover-up—that Ford had worked out this secret deal before Nixon left office. Ford's own new press secretary, a longtime friend, resigned over the pardon.

Ford defended his decision with an eloquent statement about hoping to end "years of bitter controversy and divisive national debate." But as he traveled around the country, demonstrators shouted, "Jail Ford! Jail Ford!" In one week, his favorable rating in the Gallup poll dropped from 71 to 49 percent. Ford responded by separating himself whenever possible from Nixon's tainted legacy. On the death of Creighton Abrams, Haig asked to replace him as army chief of staff. Ford thought his closeness to Nixon made him difficult to confirm by the Senate and sent him instead to head NATO.

James Schlesinger and Mel Laird had been encouraging Ford to work out an amnesty program for the Vietnam War's 50,000 draft dodgers and deserters.

On September 16, Ford announced the creation of a Presidential Clemency Board that would determine whether a man who evaded the draft met three conditions for forgiveness: he had to surrender to a U.S. attorney before January 31, 1975, pledge allegiance to America and agree to two years of alternative service. Deserters would be required to return for two years to their military branch.

Even though the men were being asked to earn a pardon that Nixon had been freely given, the public response was favorable. Ford could begin to believe what he had said upon being sworn into office by Chief Justice Burger: "My fellow Americans, our long national nightmare is over." But although Nixon was gone, the war in Vietnam could not be terminated as neatly as his presidency.

PART FOUR

Le Duan
and
Gerald R. Ford

SEVENTEEN

LE DUAN
1975

A SPY PLANTED among Thieu's advisers told the Communists that the ARVN would be concentrating its forces in the military district around Saigon and would not reinforce the government troops in the Central Highlands. Armed with that information, Hanoi's generals secretly sent their 316th Division to prepare for an attack on Ban Me Thuot. A few days later, they added the capital of Phuoc Long province to the plan. They felt no qualms about violating the Paris agreement since Thieu's army had launched many attacks against their forces since early 1973. An American study bore out the Communists' claim. In the highlands and around Saigon, ARVN soldiers were firing sixteen times more rounds of ammunition than the Communist troops. As Hanoi saw it, the "Nixon Doctrine" remained committed to keeping Thieu in power.

The Communists also pointed to the two phases of the postagreement Enhance shipments. By Hanoi's reckoning, they amounted to nearly 700 new aircraft, 500 artillery pieces and 400 tanks and armored carriers. And Thieu had announced a "1974–1979 Armed Forces Development Plan," aimed at eradicating Communist strength in the South. On the Communist side, however, Soviet supplies sent by sea to them since late December had increased fourfold.

In the South, Saigon's leaders viewed Enhance as one more of America's empty promises. They complained that the equipment was secondhand and that many of the C-130s and F-5s coming from South Korea and Taiwan were not airworthy. Even with the functioning aircraft, Saigon's pilots had begun to fly their bombers at higher altitudes. That reduced their risk but also the likelihood of hitting their targets. A squadron leader told Ky, "Frankly, you know, now I drop a bomb at 35,000 feet because I don't want to go down and be hit by Communist anti-aircraft. What for?"

On January 6, 1975, the Communists took the town of Phuoc Long and held their breath. This was the first time they had occupied an entire province. The ARVN may have launched many small attacks since the Paris treaty, but at Phuoc Long the North Vietnamese were openly violating the cease-fire.

Thieu told his cabinet that it was not impossible to retake Phuoc Long but, militarily, it was not worth the price. A South Vietnamese air force commander had already reported losing some twenty planes to Communist antiaircraft and missile fire. General Cao Van Vien, the chairman of Thieu's joint chiefs, warned him that both the Communists and his own people would take Thieu's decision as proof of ARVN's weakness.

Vien was right about the Communists' reaction. They watched the USS *Enterprise*, a nuclear carrier from the Seventh Fleet, as it sailed from the Philippines to the Vietnam coast, and they heard that in Okinawa, America's 3rd Marine Battalion had been put on alert. But then Defense Secretary Schlesinger undercut those gestures by reassuring Americans about the Communist assault on Phuoc Long. "I am not at this time anticipating a major country-wide offensive of the type of 1972," he said.

To Hanoi, opportunity beckoned. They might even be able to possess the entire country well ahead of their most sanguine timetable. Two days after the North Vietnamese took Phuoc Long, Le Duan excited a session of the Political Bureau by pointing to the map behind him and saying, "We must strike the strategic blow in 1975." Before the rainy season, he wanted the North to seize Ban Me Thuot, the capital of Darlac province, and then the territory from Hue to Da Nang.

Le Duc Tho joined the central military committee as its members were deciding where to strike next. The generals realized that Tho's presence meant that the Politburo was uneasy because they had not yet spelled out their plans. Giap agreed that Ban Me Thuot should be the target, but he wanted distracting feints in the northern sector of Tay Ninh.

For some time, Giap had been too frail to conduct a ground offensive, and the Politburo had turned again to its youngest member, General Van Tien Dung, the fifty-eight-year-old defense minister. His code name would be "Tuan." As Dung headed south, each Politburo member embraced him, wrung his hand and wished him a safe trip and a great victory.

On February 5, Dung flew from Hanoi to Dong Hoi field in an AN-24 airplane and drove over badly rutted roads to Quang Tri. He proceeded by boat along the Ben Hai River and arrived finally at the headquarters of the 559th Division; as the name suggested, it had been formed in May 1959. Too keyed up to sleep, Dung reviewed his plans. He intended to smash Ban Me Thuot like a bolt of lightning. But would its defenses collapse?

General Van Tien Dung
(Vietnam News Agency)

The next day, touring the base, he encountered Vanguard Youth girls who clustered around his car to giggle and complain, "Oh, Commander, it's nearly Tet and we haven't got any letters from home yet." Dung had come prepared. He passed out a few hundred hair clips to mollify the women and cigarettes for the truckdrivers who had brought ammunition south. Dung watched as five hundred other troop trucks from the 316th Division went south, the first time the Communists had been able to send an entire division on wheels. The men were waving their hats and singing. Dung saw their procession as a great waterfall rushing toward the front.

The ARVN had two regular divisions in all of Central Vietnam's II Corps, and those men were occupied with defending the lowland provinces where most southerners lived. The Communists had sent five divisions into the area. With their other units, they were fielding 36,000 regulars out of their total in the South of 75,000 to 80,000 troops.

On the night of March 9, Dung felt that waiting for the hour to strike was like waiting for midnight on New Year's Eve. At 2 A.M., he launched his attack on the ARVN's rear 23rd Division. Despite the South's bombers and infantry, the Communists swept through Darlac province. By early on March 11, they had captured the province chief and learned that most officers of the ARVN division had fled.

General Pham Van Phu, the ARVN's corps commander, did not want to send troops away from his headquarters in Pleiku. When the scope of the Communist attack became clear, he made no counterattack and used his Ranger reinforcements instead to prepare the evacuation of women and children while he moved his own family to Nha Trang. Lifted into the area, ARVN immediately began to desert, throwing away their uniforms and weapons, disguising themselves as civilians and joining their families in the comparative safety of Nha Trang.

By 10:30 A.M. on March 11, the Communists had achieved total victory in just over thirty-two hours. "What joy!" an officer told Dung, recalling that in 1968 they had been able to seize only Ban Me Thuot's radio transmitter in the three days before they were forced to pull out.

One of the captured ARVN officers told Dung's interrogators obligingly, "If you strike Nha Trang now, it would be to your advantage because they are in a panic." He also volunteered a thorough rundown of ARVN strength in the region, blithely dismissing the defenses at an immense port the Americans had built at Cam Ranh Bay: "Since the Americans pulled out, they've been short of sandbags, barbed wire, cement and vehicles. It's a very fragile situation."

Dung wired Giap, proposing to surround and wipe out Pleiku. For now, he would only isolate Kontum and deal with it later. As his telegram went out, Le Duan in Hanoi was already suggesting that they build on the stunning victory at Ban Me Thuot and consider it the opening battle of a large general offensive. Until now, more cautious men in the Politburo had worried that such rashness would bring back the Americans. Now Le Duan could reassure them. The offensive could go forward a full year ahead of time.

On the afternoon of March 12, Dung heard that Giap, Le Duan and Le Duc Tho all endorsed his plan for Pleiku and Kontum. Moving against Saigon might come next. They also approved his suggestion that this campaign be named for Ho Chi Minh.

MAL BROWNE had been expelled from South Vietnam in 1972 for writing some of the earliest stories about corruption in the Thieu regime, including an article that exposed the Vietnamese War Veterans Agency for demanding kickbacks from war widows before providing coffins for their husbands. Browne left for a posting in Belgrade, expecting never to return. But he was now working at the *New York Times* and his editors wanted their most experienced reporters on the scene. The prevailing uncertainty had also convinced Saigon's Defense Ministry that any American might soon become a useful contact, and in early March Browne was allowed back into the country.

By the end of the month, Browne saw that the South was in grave trouble.

The Communists now controlled everything north of Ban Me Thuot and were not stopping there. Browne thought the *Times*'s current bureau chief, James Markham, seemed oblivious to the impending disaster. Markham's wife and children were still with him in Saigon, and he was passing off the danger as critical but hardly as desperate as Browne claimed. The two argued until tempers rose on both sides and they agreed to break for lunch to cool off.

Browne had been more persuasive than he guessed. After his meal, he went back to the *Times*'s office and found Markham gone. He had left behind everything he owned and taken off for Hong Kong with his family. Browne was now in charge of the bureau, and hour by hour he felt the government disintegrating. Flying to Da Nang, he discovered the Vietnamese staff at the U.S. consulate in tears. Their American employers had promised to help them, but now they were all gone.

THIEU WATCHED fatalistically as the highlands collapsed. He ordered General Phu to retake Ban Me Thuot at any cost. Instead, Phu abandoned his Pleiku headquarters and joined his family in Nha Trang. Thieu learned that his orders had been defied but took no further action. At the American mission, Frank Snepp was among those who considered that passivity a fatal blunder, but Thieu's priority remained keeping troops around Saigon to protect himself against a coup.

Despite the alarm among many Americans, Thieu was getting no useful intelligence about the highlands from the CIA. Eighteen months earlier, its agent in Nha Trang had pocketed money earmarked for setting up a network of informants. Auditors discovered the embezzlement, and the man was sent home to Langley and early retirement. To avoid embarrassing the agency, he left with full pension and benefits. The incident helped to explain why Bill Colby had assured the White House earlier in the year that the CIA's latest National Intelligence Estimate foresaw no general offensive in 1975.

In the Delta, the CIA was doing far better. For several years, the agency could count on an informant within COSVN who would meet periodically with Snepp at a safe house in Tay Ninh. Snepp knew that the man—code name T. U. Hackle—explained his absences to the Communists by claiming to have infiltrated the South Vietnamese police, and Snepp had to be wary that he might be feeding the Americans false information. But the agency was also receiving secondhand but reliable reports out of Hanoi by way of a European intelligence service. By cross-checking the two sources, Snepp became convinced that the Communists had now decided to go for broke. For them, there would be no coalition, no decent interval. They would possess all of Vietnam before the rainy season.

Neither Ambassador Martin nor Tom Polgar, the Saigon CIA chief, could accept Snepp's cheerless evaluations. Both men liked young Snepp, who was dating Martin's daughter, but they omitted his predictions from the intelligence estimates being sent to Washington. Within the CIA Saigon office, however, other agents shared Snepp's view and were stocking up on C-rations and drinkable water, along with arms and ammunition in case they had to defend themselves as George Jacobson had done within the embassy compound during Tet of 1968. And yet Polgar declined to draw up an evacuation schedule based on the possibility of the South collapsing. It was not going to come to that.

Thieu ignored the bad news from the highlands and appointed General Nguyen Van Toan as the new regional commander for the Saigon area. Toan was Graham Martin's choice, although the man had distinct liabilities. To oblige the Americans, Toan had covered up the massacre at My Lai, and in 1972 he had taken the credit when John Vann's strategy saved Kontum. Several months before Thieu picked him, Toan had been removed from his command for ineptness and corruption.

Martin reassured Thieu about Toan's bad reputation. Ulysses S. Grant had one, too, the ambassador said. "But he won the American Civil War for Mr. Lincoln, didn't he? That's what Toan will do for you." For Thieu, Toan had one overriding virtue: he would stage no coups.

Thieu was newly realistic about U.S. air support in the future. With the ARVN troops gone from Kontum and Pleiku, he decided to sacrifice the mountainous west of his country but continued to resist forming a coalition with the Communists. Thieu was also ready to abandon Hue but wanted to hold the port of Da Nang. It could provide the site for a Normandy Beach–type landing if President Ford should change his mind and bail out Thieu with U.S. troops. The BBC, however, was predicting that Communist troops could march down Route 1 from Ban Me Thuot and reach the outskirts of Saigon in two to three weeks.

Thieu's advisers urged him to make public Nixon's secret assurances that the United States would "respond with full force should the settlement be violated by North Vietnam." Thieu remained reluctant to break his oath of secrecy. Instead, he said, "I still think Ford can do something to help us if he really understands the situation." Ignoring Voice of America bulletins about the congressional votes against further aid, Thieu told aides to draft a dramatic appeal to Ford.

IN THE JUNGLE, North Vietnam's General Dung was puzzled one noon when his communications line to headquarters abruptly broke off. He heard no bombing, only a low thudding through the spring grass. It proved to come from a herd of wild elephants, disturbed by the artillery shelling and thundering toward Dung's headquarters as they headed for the Cambodian border. Dung ordered his men not to shoot and joked that the beasts must be spared despite their low level of political consciousness. If the herd came too near, the troops were to retreat to their reinforced bunkers. He assured them, "There's nothing wrong with running from elephants."

Dung was meeting few other obstacles. On March 25, his men flew their revolutionary flag over Hue for the first time in the seven years since the Tet offensive. At Hao Cam training center near Da Nang, 3,000 ARVN recruits either defected to Dung's troops or fled to their homes. Again, in less than a day and a half, the Communists had scattered the tens of thousands of ARVN troops in Da Nang and taken over the South's second-largest city.

The ARVN commander, honest but inept Ngo Quang Truong, flew by helicopter to a warship and then to a Saigon hospital. The Communists' next target was Tay Ninh. By cutting Route 22, Dung's men isolated the province capital and left it vulnerable to assault when the time was right. As his 968th Division and 3rd Division got to Qui Nhon, Dung finally witnessed a general uprising. The city's people stopped Thieu's ships from entering the port to pick up the thousands of ARVN troops milling around on the beach.

For Communist soldiers who had been hiding in the mountains, the sight of the ocean was the most emotional moment of their war. Colonel Dang Vu Hiep had been confined to the highlands in western Kontum province from the time of the 1965 Pleiku attack and the battle of Ia Drang. He saw the sea and began to cry. Looking around, he found his men crying with him.

ON EASTER SUNDAY, March 30, Saigon's deputy premier made the official admission: "It is lost. The Communists have taken Da Nang." From Palm Springs, Ford's press secretary quoted him as calling the news an "immense human tragedy." Fewer than 70,000 of the 3 million Vietnamese in I Corps escaped, most of them by sea. The American consulate in Hue could not estimate how many of its five hundred employees got out. The CIA roster was about the same size, and agents guessed that fewer than half of their Vietnamese employees had escaped.

Dung's delay in occupying Nha Trang when he clearly had the capability had puzzled the CIA station in Saigon, but by early April analysts saw that he was simply heading toward more strategic targets. Polgar and Martin listened with interest when Mrs. Nguyen Thi Binh, foreign minister for the Provisional Revolutionary Government, said in Algeria that if Big Minh was ready to negotiate for peace, her PRG was prepared to meet with him. First, though, Thieu had to resign.

Thieu's desperate letter to Ford had not conveyed to the president how fast the Communists were foreclosing, and Ford sent General Weyand to Saigon on another fact-finding mission. Tall, rugged, balding, Weyand had replaced Abrams as MACV commander in June 1972. The following March, he had left South Vietnam with the last American soldiers and was now the Army's chief of staff.

The general arrived with George Carver and Ted Shackley, Polgar's predecessor, as well as Erich Von Marbod, a Pentagon deputy in charge of logistical support for South Vietnam. Von Marbod, who had been coming to Saigon for the past two years, was skeptical about the frantic speed behind Vietnamization. He called it "like getting nine women pregnant in order to have a baby in a month."

After Weyand's team had assessed the situation, he met with Thieu on April 3. The day had begun badly for Thieu. Prime Minister Tran Thien Khiem had resigned, brought down the cabinet and begun shipping everything he owned to Paris and Taipei. Then Thieu heard that Ford had criticized him from Palm Springs for withdrawing from the highlands. Ford also told reporters that Washington was considering the evacuation of the 6,000 Americans who remained in South Vietnam.

In his meeting with Thieu, Shackley shifted the discussion away from military aid. The real need, he said, was for them to rally American public opinion to Saigon's cause. "The refugee problem can be used to generate sympathy," Shackley said. George Carver was no more helpful. He thought Thieu should concentrate on telling the world that he had been invaded. Invite representatives from the World Council of Churches to Saigon and let them see the suffering the North was causing. Meanwhile, try to undermine morale in North Vietnam.

Ambassador Martin, as chairman of the meeting, saw that the Vietnamese had become restless. He was still sure that Washington would send military aid and asked Von Marbod when it would arrive. He was told that supplies would come as soon as they could be appropriated from Okinawa and South Korea.

When Weyand's turn came to speak, he made a promise to Thieu: "We will get you the assistance you need and will explain your needs to Congress." But when the Vietnamese asked—in an elaborately indirect way—for a resumption of B-52 raids, Weyand did not commit himself. Before he left Washington, James Schlesinger had warned him not to overpromise. "It is all coming down," the defense secretary had said.

After the Americans left, Thieu's advisers pleaded with him once again to go on television and reveal Nixon's secret commitments. No, said Thieu, the country was now in Weyand's hands.

GENERAL DUNG remembered his counterpart, Fred Weyand, as the man who had lowered and then furled the American flag as he withdrew from South Vietnam. Informants told him now that Weyand had urged the ARVN to strengthen their defense line at Phan Rang, south of Cam Ranh Bay, in order to keep the Communists away from Saigon. Weyand had advised them to hold out for another two months, until the start of the rainy season in early June. Dung was undaunted. His men felt invulnerable from victories that had come as easily as splitting bamboo. But he did not underestimate the obstinacy and desperation that would go into the ARVN's defense of Saigon. For Dung, it loomed as the final test between revolution and counterrevolution.

Le Duc Tho went south for an inspection tour and wrote a few lines of poetry for Le Duan. "You warned: Go out and come back in victory," his poem began. It ended, "The time of opportunity has arrived."

At Dong Ha, the Communist forces split for their push to the south, one branch traveling east and west of the Truong Son Mountains, the other down Route 1, south of Qui Nhon. Dung was gratified when townspeople first gaped, then cheered, as his artillery, missiles and tanks plowed down roads thick with red dust. The weapons were followed by thousands of trucks and buses. Dung was sure the people had never imagined that Uncle Ho's soldiers would have so many vehicles or that his soldiers would be so cheerful and handsome. He heard villagers describe the rockets being carried on trucks as "airplanes without wings."

On April 13, the Communists arrived at Phan Rang, ready to take on the ARVN's III Corps, whose officers were promising to defend the base to the death. Dung's men sought to live up to the slogan they wore on their helmets: "Lightning Speed and Daring." But two days of heavy fighting won the Communists only the territory surrounding the town's perimeters. Then, early on April 16, they attacked the military base and the town's center from three directions. Routing the ARVN, they captured the III Corps commander, Major General Nguyen Vinh Nghi, and his senior officers. The Communists also seized some forty planes in prime condition. Dung called for pilots to be rushed down from the North and begin practicing with the A-37 and F-5 fighters.

AT TAN SON NHUT, an Air Force C-5A Galaxy, the world's biggest jet transport, arrived with supplies already in the pipeline. For their return trip, the pilots planned an evacuation called Operation Babylift. Orphans were bundled aboard with wristbands that would direct some of them to New York, others to New Jersey.

The plane had barely taken off when an explosion brought it crashing down in a paddy south of the airstrip. Covered with mud, the small bodies had to be hosed down to determine whether they were alive or dead. Two hundred babies were killed. All but one of 43 American adults also died, most of them women who were on board to care for the infants.

ON TUESDAY, APRIL 8, First Lieutenant Nguyen Thanh Trung, a Communist double agent, flew an F-5E jet over Thieu's palace. In three bombing passes, Trung struck only a corner of the building. One official was hurt; Thieu escaped injury. From the embassy roof, Snepp watched Trung's plane roar away and realized how badly prepared the Americans in Saigon would be if they came under enemy fire. He deplored the discrepancy between the intelligence he was receiving and the reassurances from Martin and Polgar. But Polgar had shipped his wife and household goods out of the country the first week in April, a decision that undercut his brave words. Polgar's prudence annoyed the ambassador, who considered it bad for South Vietnamese morale. But even with his wife gone, Polgar continued to insist that a negotiated settlement was still possible with the advancing Communist troops.

Big Minh got word to his brother in the PRG that he would be willing to replace Thieu and work out a settlement. From the mid-fifties, Minh remembered Nguyen Huu Tho, still active in the National Liberation Front, and was sure Tho was a southerner before he was a Communist. But Snepp knew that the Communists had absolutely ruled out a coalition, that what they were saying was only a ruse to lull the South Vietnamese. When he wrote out that analysis, however, both Polgar and Martin found it "too alarmist." Martin ordered Alan Carter, the information chief in Saigon, to overcome Carter's own sense of impending catastrophe and film a video that would assure the Vietnamese that there was no danger of a Communist invasion and that the Americans were determined to stay.

In Washington, Kissinger resisted James Schlesinger and General George Brown, Ford's chairman of the Joint Chiefs, when they demanded that Washington speed up the American withdrawal. Kissinger claimed that evacuation would undercut Thieu. When Colby joined in questioning Martin's confident reports, Kissinger snapped at the three of them, You're just trying to cover your asses.

By April 10, three North Vietnamese divisions were pouring artillery and rockets on the town of Xuan Loc, thirty-eight miles from Saigon. The next night, 25,000 ARVN troops drove the Communists back. In approving the Communist assault, Tran Van Tra had underestimated the resistance now that his forces were threatening Saigon itself. Tra told the Communist commanders near Xuan Loc not to persist in attacking the ARVN head-on. Instead, they should strike outer perimeters, where ARVN defenses were weakest, while they shut down Bien Hoa airfield with long-range artillery. The shelling would deprive the South Vietnamese air force of a takeoff point.

While that operation was underway, Dung moved the eastern wing of his troops down Route 1. On April 20, he surrounded Xuan Loc and blasted his way into the city while the ARVN fled down Route 2 toward Ba Ria. Dung had opened an eastern gateway to Saigon. But to set up a strike base southwest of the capital, Dung had to revert to the war's earliest methods. His men needed tens of thousands of artillery shells, which could only be carried on their shoulders or in small boats. There was also the question of getting his weapons into position. Few roads were suitable for motorized artillery, and Dung had to build bridges and commandeer ferries for moving his equipment. He hoped the large-scale operation would go undetected until he could strike.

After bombing the palace, Lieutenant Trung had been teaching northern pilots to fly the many captured U.S. A-37s. Dung had not yet decided how to use them for the final assault on Saigon. He was counting more on sixty special action squads to rise up within the city—armed cells of the kind that had attacked the Brinks Hotel and sunk ships in the Saigon River.

To the east, Dung's troops had totally cut Route 1 and could do the same with Route 15. To the west and southwest, his forces were nearing Route 4, Saigon's artery to the Mekong Delta. To the southeast, his 4th Army Corps had moved from Xuan Loc to Trang Bom. In the north, Dung had a secure zone that extended up to Phuoc Long.

The Paris agreement had set up a joint military commission of Communists and ARVN, but Thieu had confined its members to quarters at Tan Son Nhut. Dung received a telegram from his men urging that he not worry about them when he trained his artillery on the airfield. They were not only prepared to sacrifice their lives for the revolution, they said, "We would consider it an honor."

In drawing up plans for their assault on Saigon, Dung's officers had little to guide them. Only after they overran Ban Me Thuot had the northerners possessed an accurate map of the capital. Before that, they had been depending on scattered reports from the Communist attacks during the Tet of 1968. Now at B-2 headquarters, Dung was consulting every possible guide, including maps of the city printed for tourists. He and his commanders were awaking and sleeping with images of Saigon's topography, memorizing the names of streets and the locations of bridges. They knew they lacked a sense of the landscape—of colors and architecture—but within a few days they were able to plot maneuvers through Saigon streets without first laying out their maps across a table.

By cable, the Politburo consulted with Dung about his two major military decisions—how to attack and where. Dung wanted to smash ARVN capacity at every level but without destroying the lives and property of the 3.5 million Saigonese the North had come to liberate. He remembered what Ho had said: "The puppet soldiers are also sons of Vietnam."

NOT FOR THE FIRST TIME, American patience was running out with Nguyen Van Thieu. Kissinger had successfully blocked General Weyand's recommendation that Thieu be supported with renewed U.S. air strikes. "If you do that," Kissinger assured Ford in Palm Springs, "the American people will take to the streets again." After that meeting, Kissinger drove with Ron Nessen, Ford's current press secretary, to a briefing with reporters. On the way, his anger with Thieu boiled over. "Why don't those people die fast?" Kissinger exclaimed. "The worst thing that could happen would be for them to linger on."

Meeting with reporters, Kissinger appealed for an end to placing blame for the tragedy that was underway. "For God's sake," he said, "we ought to stop talking as if one side had the monopoly of wisdom, morality and insight."

Thieu, convinced at last that he would not be receiving more aid, devised a final plan. An ARVN division would block the Communists in Saigon while

Thieu moved to the Mekong Delta and held on to its population centers and rice supply. But Kissinger had already told Martin that he must get all the Americans out "fast and now." Kissinger said there was no support for evacuating any Vietnamese.

To ensure total secrecy, Martin typed out his own reply. The ARVN could hold the approaches to Saigon "for quite a while," he wrote, "and I still doubt that Hanoi desires a frontal smash at Saigon for a multitude of reasons." All the same, Martin was aware that Thieu had to resign and was prepared to tell him, as a friend, that his place in history would be better assured if he did not try to stay on any longer.

After Kissinger approved that message, the ambassador paid a call on Thieu on Sunday evening, April 20. Their dialogue was as dispirited as Diem's last call to Lodge.

"I believe that in a few days your generals will come to tell you to step down," Martin said.

Thieu asked, "If I step down, will military aid come?"

Martin's answer came entirely from his own hopes, not from the cables out of Washington. "I cannot promise you," he said, "but there may be a chance."

Thieu said, "I will do what's best for my country."

The next day, looking for a show of support, Thieu called together his generals. When he asked whether they regarded him as an obstacle to peace, none spoke up. Thieu weighed their silence and said he would resign.

GENERAL DUNG heard with satisfaction that Lon Nol had fled Phnom Penh, leaving by way of the Pentagon's Operation Eagle Pull, which had been set up to evacuate Americans from Cambodia. The U.S. ambassador, John Gunther Dean, left with him, carrying the American flag that had just been lowered at the embassy. Twelve hundred Cambodians had already left the country. Then for one hour, large CH-53 helicopters landed in groups of three and took out 82 Americans, another 159 Cambodians and 35 citizens of other countries. There was no panic.

Sydney Schanberg of the New York Times was among the newsmen who elected to stay behind. When the ambassador invited Sirik Matak to leave, the former prime minister sent back a stinging refusal. He could not depart in so cowardly a fashion, Matak wrote. He had never believed that the United States would abandon people who had chosen liberty. He concluded, "I have only committed the mistake of believing in the Americans."

Dung assumed that the evacuation of Cambodia was a practice run for pulling out of South Vietnam. An informant had brought him Defense Minister Don's statement that he was now calculating the South's existence by only the day or week, not even by the month. That report spurred on Dung's men, as did the news of the transport plane crashing with the orphans aboard. The northerners considered the orphans kidnap victims and wanted to prevent more babies from being flown out of the country.

At their base, Dung listened with Le Duc Tho and other officers as Thieu made a two-hour resignation address to the nation. Thieu's supporters considered it the best speech he had made during his eight years in power. It was certainly the most spirited. "You have let our combatants die under a hail of shells," Thieu said in his long reproach to the American government. "This is an inhumane act by an inhumane ally."

Dung had only scorn for Thieu's farewell. The man was a miserable betrayer of the Vietnamese nation who was guilty of bloody crimes against his people. When Tran Van Huong succeeded Thieu as president, Dung saw no improvement. A savage military traitor was being replaced by a crafty civilian one.

Dung regarded CIA men like Polgar, Snepp and the rest as poisonous snakes, forever slippery as they spied and spread rumors. But it was the CIA that was now giving the White House more accurate information than either the Pentagon or the State Department. From April 19, Colby had been predicting that "South Vietnam faces total defeat—and soon." He also repeated in Washington Snepp's appraisal that the Communists were no longer interested in negotiating.

On April 22, Le Duan cabled Dung on behalf of the Politburo: "If we grasp this great opportunity firmly, our total victory is sure." Dung prepared a fresh map with red markings to indicate the direction of his attacks on Saigon. Dung, Le Duc Tho and Pham Hung, the ranking political officer, all signed the map. They agreed that their signatures were sealing the fate of Saigon's reactionary traitors.

GENERAL HOMER SMITH felt more urgency than Ambassador Martin about getting friendly South Vietnamese out of the country. Martin had resisted reducing the number of Americans in Saigon to 1,100, and he had argued against using the freighters standing by in the Saigon River to carry boatloads of Vietnamese to Vung Tau and then the open seas. At the same time, Martin was rigid in defining which Vietnamese qualified as legitimate dependents. Since he excluded common-law wives and their children, many American civilians were refusing to leave.

General Smith came up with a solution that Martin did not like but did not forbid. On his way out of the embassy, Smith stopped at a secretary's desk and dictated a simple "Affidavit of Support." It called for the name of the Vietnamese to be evacuated, the name of an American guaranteeing to be financially responsible and the embassy's seal. Eva Kim, a secretary in Martin's office, typed the form on a stencil and ran off thousands of copies, which Smith's staff began distributing that same afternoon.

Using a back channel, Martin told Kissinger that he opposed a mass evacuation of Vietnamese and wanted the ships in Saigon Harbor withdrawn. Still minimizing the immediate threat, Martin accused his colleagues in Saigon and Washington of caring mostly about their reputations. He complained that the only "ass which isn't covered is mine."

Kissinger repeated his instructions to cut back the American community as soon as possible and added a note of cheerless consolation: "When this thing is finally over, I'll be hanging several yards higher than you."

Even with General Smith's attempt to cut through the bureaucracy, processing the Vietnamese was chaotic. The American officials' demand to see an exit visa from the South Vietnamese government was enriching the black marketeers, as prices for a bogus marriage certificate or adoption papers jumped from $70 to more than $1,000. Desperate, some Americans drew up an alternative form that read, "I have lost my paperwork but I am an American dependent" or "This is my legally adopted child." At first, Vietnamese consular clerks rejected those makeshift papers but relented when the Americans promised to get the clerks' families out as well.

Hundreds of Vietnamese were jamming the streets around the embassy compound with extended families of fifty or sixty people. U.S. officials told them to cut the number to ten or fifteen. Heads of the families begged the Americans to make the decision. Doing it themselves was too painful.

GENERAL CHARLES TIMMES was the seventies version of Lou Conein, a CIA man serving as liaison with the ARVN generals. As Thieu was leaving office, Polgar sent Timmes to ask Big Minh whether he would take charge and negotiate a peace with the North Vietnamese if President Huong could be elbowed aside. Minh nodded. He could deal with the Communists, he said, and would start by sending his representative to Paris immediately to open talks. Timmes pulled out a thousand dollars in crisp bills from his briefcase to cover travel expenses.

Thieu proved easily disposable. Huong named him as special emissary to Taiwan to pay belated respects to Chiang Kai-shek, who had died on April 5. At 8:30 P.M. on April 25, Snepp drove a limousine to the Air America terminal at Tan Son Nhut with Thieu in the backseat amid a miasma of Scotch whiskey fumes. When aides had carefully deposited his bags in the trunk, Snepp took a noticeable clinking for the sound of gold bars. Polgar and Martin were also present at the tarmac for strained goodbyes.

Days later in Taiwan, Anna Chennault relayed a message for Thieu that she said came from Gerald Ford. She had been asked to tell him that his family was welcome in the United States but, given the antiwar sentiment in America, Thieu should go into exile elsewhere.

"It is so easy to be an enemy of the United States," Thieu said, smiling wanly, "but so difficult to be a friend."

☐

ON APRIL 28, Big Minh took over from Huong. To prove his good faith to the North Vietnamese, he asked that Martin evacuate all Americans the next day. But at dusk that afternoon, five A-37 Dragonfly jets flew over the Tan Son Nhut airstrip. When the control tower asked them to identify their squadron, a pilot answered, "American-made planes here."

It was an honest answer, since the planes had been captured at Phan Rang. Now flown by North Vietnamese MiG pilots, they made a pass over the main runway and destroyed three AC-119 gunships and several C-47s before flying off again. But the runway was still usable. Two hours later, two C-130s—each with 180 Americans and Vietnamese aboard—began the evacuation Minh was demanding. Ambassador Martin estimated that 60 was the maximum number of flights the C-130s could make the next day. He announced also that he and twenty members of his staff would stay on for a day or two past Minh's deadline. He felt that his mild defiance would lend dignity to the American departure.

COLONEL TA MINH KHAM expected that his years in the jungle would soon be crowned with success. On April 29, his men seized the town of Cu Chi west of Saigon, and at 3:30 P.M. Kham went to the post office in his National Liberation Army uniform but without insignia or rank. He asked the woman on duty, "Can I get through to Saigon?"

She said he could and connected the line.

The operator who answered at the Saigon exchange was breathing heavily. Kham thought she seemed frightened.

"I am with the Liberation Army troops," he said. "Can you tell me whether the police station or the military headquarters in Saigon has contacted you?"

"No," said the woman. "Not for the past three days."

As Kham was talking, his scouts returned from the headquarters of the 25th ARVN Division. The boardroom was deserted, they said, but they had found cups of warm coffee on the table. Just then, an old woman had caught sight of the ARVN commander, Major General Ly Tong Ba, hiding in a nearby rice field.

"*Cac con!*" the woman cried to Kham's men. "*Cac con!* Come and catch him!"

They rushed out and captured Ba alive. Their news pleased Kham, particularly when he heard that a South Vietnamese woman had called his men *con*. It was a warm way of saying "my children."

THE MORNING OF APRIL 29, General Timmes drove in an embassy limousine to call on Big Minh at Independence Palace. Timmes asked if there were anything more he could do. Minh shook his head. The French ambassador, due at the palace soon, claimed that the Chinese opposed North Vietnam's total control of Indochina and would pressure Hanoi into forming a coalition. Hanoi would agree because the North did not have an efficient structure for governing the South. Timmes received that analysis skeptically but said he would pass it along to Martin.

At about that time, Tran Van Don, no longer defense minister, went to the ARVN general staff headquarters. During the raucous debates of recent days, Don had thought that he, not Minh, might end up as president, and he had been negotiating privately with an NLF contact. Then Minh had been named after all, and at headquarters Don learned that Ky had surveyed enemy positions from his helicopter, concluded that the situation was hopeless and taken off for a U.S. carrier with the Seventh Fleet.

At 11:30 A.M., Don attended the installation of a new cabinet thrown together by the prime minister, Vu Van Mau. Afterward, Don called a friend at the U.S. embassy, who told him that all of the Americans were getting out. "If you want to go yourself," the man told him, "be at the embassy before 2 P.M. this afternoon."

On the spot, Don decided to leave. Whatever chances Minh claimed to have for survival, Don knew that Minh was not prepared to stake his family on them. Five days earlier, Minh had sent away his daughter and grandchildren. Now, as he prepared to receive the Communists, Minh also got his son-in-law and nephew out of the country. Minh's wife ignored his urging and refused to go with them.

Bui Diem had come back reluctantly from Washington earlier in the month because of an appeal from Bob Shaplen, the *New Yorker* correspondent. Calling from Hong Kong, Shaplen had persuaded him that it was his patriotic duty to return to Saigon and make Thieu face facts. But as Thieu hung on, Bui Diem turned instead to convincing his ninety-year-old mother that she and his sister must leave Saigon. Graham Martin offered to help, and when Diem called to say they were ready, the ambassador got the three of them on a navy plane to Bangkok and then a commercial flight to Washington.

Bui Diem was leaving with a few suitcases and a small bag of photographs: they showed him posing over the years with Lyndon Johnson, Dean Rusk, Cabot Lodge, Max Taylor, Averell Harriman, Walt Rostow, Ellsworth Bunker, William Bundy, Richard Nixon, and Henry Kissinger. Bui Diem was leaving for permanent exile with a gallery of the Americans who had vowed to protect his country.

Despite the heavy shelling at Tan Son Nhut, Ambassador Martin insisted that the Americans and the high-risk Vietnamese be taken out by fixed-wing aircraft rather than by helicopters. But Colby had confirmed that a Communist takeover was inevitable by the next day, April 30, and before noon on the twenty-ninth, Kissinger got through to Martin on a secure line. The ambassador finally agreed to Option IV, or "Frequent Wind"—evacuation by helicopter. Kissinger promised that the first of them would arrive within one hour. At Armed Services Radio in Saigon, disk jockeys played "White Christmas," the code for a full-scale evacuation. They played it several times, then put on a long tape of marches by John Philip Sousa and joined the exodus to Tan Son Nhut.

Embassy staff leaving the compound had to push through hundreds of Vietnamese massed at the gates and begging for deliverance. Several U.S. Marines carried canvas bags into the courtyard containing more than $2 million in cash—the embassy's emergency funds—that Martin had ordered destroyed to keep the money out of Communist hands. The Marines took the bags to metal cans at the far end of the compound, doused them with gasoline and set them on fire. Before all of the money could burn, an aide ran out shouting that Martin had changed his mind. The Marines salvaged some charred bills, but helicopter rotors scattered most of the money. One embassy official managed to scoop up $80,000 and slip it to his Vietnamese girl friend as she flew out of the country.

Far greater wealth remained behind at South Vietnam's Central Bank in its office near the Saigon River. After the 1945 revolution, the Vietminh leaders in Hanoi had regretted not confiscating the assets of the French bureau in Hanoi that issued the country's currency. Graham Martin was sure the Communists would not repeat their oversight and would head at once for the nation's gold supply. Martin asked the State Department to arrange insurance that would cover transferring the gold to a bank in Geneva or to the Federal Reserve in New York. Washington moved sluggishly, and by the time policies were in place—insuring $60 million in gold valued at twice that amount—Thieu had resigned and no South Vietnamese would take responsibility for the transfer. The gold, crated and ready for shipping, remained at the Central Bank.

BILL KOHLMANN was contacting his Vietnamese assets to discuss their plans for escape. He had now known Nguyen Dinh Tu, the war correspondent, for twelve years and invited him to his apartment for lunch. Tu said he realized the war was lost when Thieu chose not to defend Ban Me Thuot. Neither he nor Kohlmann doubted what lay in store for Saigon. Tu said his publisher, a Vietnamese senator named Dang Van Sung, had ordered him to leave when Sung did, but Tu had refused. Unlike other journalists who had tried to protect themselves with a pen name, Tu had signed his anti-Communist dispatches and knew he would not be hard to find. But, he explained to Kohlmann, I'm a reporter. I must stay to report on the North Vietnamese entering Saigon.

Other Vietnamese were clamoring to get out, however, and they learned before Kohlmann did that helicopters would be landing on the roof of his apartment building across from the Continental Hotel. Given the chaotic mob at the embassy, several of his contacts preferred to leave from there.

Kohlmann arranged flights for the wife, four children and nephew of his most steadfast recruit, Tran Quang Thuan, but Thuan himself was staying until the last possible moment. Hoping that the Communists were still open to compromise, Saigon's Assembly and Senate had combined into one body and had chosen Thuan to investigate a possible coalition. Bill Kohlmann had never leaned on him, never asked him to violate his political principles, and Thuan had met over the years with so many other Americans that he doubted the Communists knew about his alliance with the CIA.

As for Tri Quang, he was so notoriously independent that suspicion about his CIA connection was unlikely. Certainly, the agency funds he had accepted had never led him to do America's bidding. All the same, Thuan went to An Quang pagoda to offer the monk a chance to leave. Tri Quang looked dispirited but was adamant about staying on. "We are going to suffer a lot," he predicted, "but still I cannot go. I will take my chances."

By that time, every scrap of information indicated that Thuan had no role in his country's future. After a day of edgy waiting, he and a group of his political allies were flown by helicopter to the *Midway*. His family would be awaiting him in a refuge center, but Thuan did not know where. He had the clothes on his back and $813 in American bills.

TRAN KIM TUYEN had been jailed or under house arrest for the twelve years since Diem was overthrown. Tried on the same charges that led to the execution of Diem's brother Can, he had remained in prison until Thieu's brother arranged for confinement to his house. Despite a police agent stationed outside his door, life was not onerous. His wife Jackie was allowed to teach in a high school, and Tuyen received old friends such as Bob Shaplen and wrote political columns under an assumed name.

As South Vietnam's defenses began to crack, the British ambassador in Singapore arranged for Jackie and three of their children to fly to England and join their eldest son, who was studying at Cambridge. But even with them gone, Tuyen could not conceive of the crash coming so suddenly.

On April 29, his niece's husband, an ARVN major, came to say, "Uncle, the Communists are arriving at the motorway. What do we do now?"

Tuyen called Kohlmann, but he had already left for the embassy since he would need a less taxing way to get aboard a helicopter than by precarious stairs lowered to the top of his building. When Tuyen could rouse no one else, he put through a call to Shaplen at the Continental Hotel, who told him to come there and fly out with the journalists. Tuyen's police agent was still following him when he got to the hotel.

Buses were waiting to take the reporters to the defense attaché's airstrip at Tan Son Nhut, but once there, a U.S. Marine checked his list and found only Shaplen's name, not Tuyen's. From the airstrip, Shaplen called the embassy for an emergency authorization. All the lines were busy. The pilots announced that they were leaving. "Now I have to go," Shaplen said. He pressed his Continental key and 50,000 Vietnamese piasters into Tuyen's hand.

Back at the hotel, Tuyen ran into An, working these days for *Time* but ready to reveal his rank in the North Vietnamese army. An drove Tuyen twice to the embassy. The second time the mob was even larger and more frenzied. A former politician who recognized Tuyen shouted to him: "Why bother to leave? You've been out of politics for ten years already! You're in no danger!"

An knew better. "You must leave," he insisted, and took Tuyen back to his own house to think of a plan. At dusk, An's phone rang. A reporter for the *Christian Science Monitor* was calling from the embassy. No one could get inside anymore, he said, but the ambassador had told him a CIA helicopter would be landing on the roof of an apartment building near the Continental. Excitedly, An repeated the message to Tuyen and they raced there.

An had already sent his wife and children to America until he could see how deadly the battle over Saigon might become. He would stay on, reveal his commission in the NVA and bring them back to Vietnam when it was safe again.

At the last moment, Tuyen was pulled onto a helicopter as it rose above the city.

"What do I do now?" he asked himself. "Where is my family? What will happen to us?"

HAVING A VIETNAMESE WIFE made Mal Browne more aware of the blatant racism that marked the panic at the embassy. He watched as even Vietnamese with U.S. passports were turned away at the gates while any white face was pulled inside. Air Vietnam's last commercial flight had left for Hong Kong on April 28, carrying Browne's wife, Le Lieu, her two brothers and their children. To evacuate the *New York Times* staff, Browne and another reporter took turns loading up a car with Vietnamese families and driving as close as they could get to the private landing strip of the CIA's Air America. To ease past Vietnamese guards, the Americans put on ties, showed an airline ticket sticking out of their pockets and said, We big noses—Vietnamese slang for Westerners—are leaving and these friends have come to see us off. That got them as far as the terminal waiting room. From there, the Vietnamese dashed the 500 feet to the Air America compound and within hours were on their way to Guam.

Browne was impressed by the fact that executives from CBS Television had come from New York to spend the last week methodically getting their Vietnamese employees out of the country. He regretted that the *New York Times* was not showing the same concern. Hearing that the embassy was being evacuated, however, the publisher ordered Browne and the other reporter, Fox Butterfield, to leave the country. They boarded a bus for Tan Son Nhut and waited four hours in a bunker for the Chinook helicopter that took them out. Later in the night, a Communist shell hit a nearby gymnasium and killed the 20 Vietnamese who had huddled there to wait.

From the air, Browne looked down on the Seventh Fleet arrayed off Vietnam's shore. There were not ships enough to carry off all of the helicopters. U.S. crews were pitching the choppers over the side to keep them from the Communists, and Vietnamese sampans had been set on fire. The smoke and confusion below him looked like a scene by Brueghel.

Ambassador Graham Martin departs Saigon *(UPI/Corbis-Bettmann)*

INSIDE THE EMBASSY COMPOUND, CIA agents were burning the thousands of laminated name cards that had been intended as seat tickets for high-risk Vietnamese. Martin's reluctance to order an evacuation meant that the tickets had not been distributed, and now those collaborators were being left to face the Communists alone. When Snepp caught sight of Martin, he thought the ambassador looked like a walking corpse. Martin was taking strong doses of antibiotics for pneumonia, but he insisted on going personally to his residence for his wife. He could not be dissuaded, even after the sight of his limousine set off a new clamor from the mob at the gates. Martin slipped out a back entrance on foot, walked the four blocks to his house and collected his wife. He took away only an overnight case and a favorite antique model of a Chinese pagoda. Back at the embassy, he went through a connecting passage and presented the model to the French ambassador, who was trying to broker a last-minute deal between the Communists and Big Minh.

Martin's wife was led to the embassy roof and flown off in an Air America helicopter to the USS *Denver* with the Seventh Fleet. Soon afterward, Kissinger called to say that even the bitter-enders were ordered to leave Saigon that day and that he specifically meant Martin.

General Pham Van Phu, who had doomed his highland troops to ignominy

South Vietnamese
scaling the walls of the
U.S. embassy in Saigon,
April 29, 1975
(AP/Wide World Photos)

and defeat, showed up at the U.S. defense attaché's compound to ask for help in getting his family out. That accomplished, Phu went into another room and shot himself.

From the CIA office, a senior American agent called the Saigon authorities to suggest that they attend to one loose end before the Communists arrived. Nguyen Van Tai, the North Vietnamese agent Snepp had interrogated, should be made to disappear.

The instructions were simple: Lead Tai from solitary confinement, herd him onto a plane and take him ten thousand feet above the South China Sea. Open the plane door. Push Tai out.

AT THE CIA LIVING QUARTERS in the Duc Hotel, more than a hundred Vietnamese who were depending on the agency to save them heard accidentally from a two-way radio that Polgar was evacuating only Americans. As they called frantically to the embassy—"Save me! I'm Mr. Hai, the cook"—CIA agents and secretaries urged them to go back to their homes. Buses and helicopters would come for them there.

But there were no buses, and the helicopters were reserved for Americans. Looking on, Snepp was as ashamed of his employer as Browne had been of his. Callous and ignominious, he thought. One day, if he survived, he promised himself he would write an internal review for headquarters at Langley, exposing how Kissinger, Martin, Polgar and the others had botched a potentially orderly withdrawal and betrayed thousands of loyal allies. Until that time came, Snepp had to listen to the screaming of the Vietnamese, crowded three deep around the embassy walls. Convoys could no longer get through that human barricade. In the confusion, barges were sailing off from the docks with far fewer Vietnamese than they might have carried.

Caught outside, Keyes Beech, a correspondent for the *Chicago Sun-Times*, was trying to climb over the embassy wall when a Vietnamese teenager grabbed his sleeve. "You adopt me and take me with you, and I'll help you," the boy shouted. "If you don't, you don't go."

Beech said he would adopt him. At that moment, he would have said anything. Just then, American Marines appeared on the wall, kicking away the Vietnamese who were nearing the top. "Help me," Beech cried. A Marine spotted him, reached down and pulled him out of the mob. A respected correspondent during the Korean War, Beech came from the generation that trusted embassy officials and did not expect them to lie. Snepp had counted on that trust to get the CIA's slant on stories into print. Now he saw Beech inside the embassy compound and atoned slightly by bringing him a soda from the medical refrigerator.

By afternoon, an open bar in Martin's office and another in Polgar's had drawn the last American employees and newsmen, all celebrating the fact that the Communists were apparently letting the evacuation continue unhindered. The only scare came at 6 P.M. when a rocket seemed to explode nearby. It turned out to be the gas tank of a Volkswagen parked outside the gates.

Shortly after 9 P.M., George McArthur, a reporter for the *Los Angeles Times*, lifted the ambassador's black poodle, Nit Noy, into a CH-47 helicopter on the embassy pad. A little later, Snepp and the other CIA agents flew out with General Timmes to the *Denver* in the South China Sea.

At 11:30 P.M., U.S. Army demolition experts moved through the embassy setting off delayed-action thermite bombs to blow up the communications satellite terminal and its antenna dish. Kissinger called to find out how many Americans were left to be airlifted out. Martin did not have the figure and made one up — 726.

All right, Kissinger said, but after that, "I want you heroes to come home."

Colby's final cable to Polgar was more effusive: "Thousands of Vietnamese owe their lives and future hopes to your efforts, your Government has profited immensely from the accuracy and breadth of your reporting and your country will one day learn with admiration of the way you represented its best instinct and ideas."

It was nearly 5 A.M. when Martin was cajoled into boarding a helicopter. The 400 Vietnamese, Koreans and Filipinos inside the embassy were assured that more CH-53s would be coming back for them, but when a final one did land within the compound, it was to pick up Polgar and the last of the Americans. President Ford had ordered the airlift ended.

At 7:53 A.M. on April 30, the American Marines who had been securing the helicopter pad on the ground ran up the stairs to the roof, throwing gas grenades behind them to stop the terrified Vietnamese in the courtyard from chasing after them. The last Marine jumped into an escape helicopter as a few Vietnamese threw themselves, too late, at its struts.

As a MILITARY MAN, General Dung admired the logistics of the evacuation. Seventy helicopters and 865 Marines made 630 flights in 18 hours and took out 1,373 Americans, 5,595 South Vietnamese and 815 persons from other countries. Nearly 2,100 persons had been lifted out from the embassy compound alone. As the Americans had surmised, the Communists had resolved to let the evacuation proceed unmolested. They had rendered Tan Son Nhut unusable for most fixed-wing aircraft, but otherwise Dung and his colleagues wanted to inherit Saigon, not destroy it.

Dung found the clear and cool dawn of April 30 extraordinarily beautiful. He had boxed in the ARVN 5th and 25th Divisions so that they could not pull back into Saigon. By 9:25 A.M. ARVN commanders were reporting that Saigon was now totally cut off by Dung's troops, and yet Dung heard that Minh was convening his new ministers at Independence Palace at 10 A.M.

An announcer on Saigon Radio proposed a cease-fire "to discuss the transfer of power." But Dung's political cadres kept prodding their soldiers through the city's streets by calling: "Keep up the attack! There won't be any ceasefire. This is a once-in-a-thousand-years chance."

NGUYEN DINH TU was on hand to observe the Communist troops entering Saigon but had found no outlet for his account of their victory before he was identified and led away to jail. Neil Davis, an Australian correspondent for NBC, had also stayed behind and was pacing the palace grounds as he awaited the North Vietnamese. Since 1964, Davis had been covering the war with wry detachment and an affection for Vietnamese of all political stripes. He had given thousands of dollars from his salary to orphans and war victims. Tran Tha Sa, a lame eleven-year-old who sold cigarettes on the Saigon streets, never knew that Davis had paid to send her to Germany for operations that mended her crippled leg.

After the Paris agreement, Davis had arranged to film a Vietcong unit in the Delta, but on this morning he did not expect his impartial sympathies to protect him. He was tall and very blond and today, particularly, he did not wish to be mis-

A North Vietnamese tank crashes through the gates of Independence Hall in Saigon, April 30, 1975 (*EUPRA GmbH./Time Inc. Picture Collection*)

taken for an American. Hearing noises outside the palace gates, Davis hoisted his 15-pound camera to his shoulder and ran to the scene just as Communist tank number 843 smashed through the iron grillwork.

From the corner of the eye not pressed to his camera, Davis saw a Communist soldier racing toward him and shouting, "Stop! Stop! Hands up!"

I've been covering this war for eleven years, Davis told himself. I'm not going to stop filming now. The soldier reached Davis's side and poked him with his rifle. Davis shut off the camera, lifted it above his head and spoke the Vietnamese phrase he had been rehearsing: "Welcome to Saigon, comrade. I've been waiting for you!"

The soldier scowled. "You are American?"

"No, no, no! I'm an Australian."

At that, the soldier's eyes looked past Davis to the spectacle of ARVN troops coming out of the palace with their hands up. The North Vietnamese waved his rifle dismissively, and Davis went back to filming one last shot of the South Vietnamese flag flying over the palace before it was torn down.

OFFICERS FROM Dung's 2nd Army Corps rushed upstairs in the palace to the room where Minh and his cabinet awaited them. It fell to a journalist not only to record the scene but to play the leading role. Colonel Bui Tin was deputy editor of *Quan Doi Nhan Dan*, the North Vietnamese Army newspaper. He had arrived in one of the tanks, but until he reached Minh's conference room, he had not realized that he was the ranking officer.

Big Minh addressed him: "I have been waiting since early this morning to transfer power to you."

"There is no question of your transferring power," Bui Tin replied. "Your power has crumbled. You cannot give up what you do not have."

From beyond the window came a burst of gunfire. Bui Tin saw Minh's ministers flinch. "Our men are merely celebrating," he assured them. "You have nothing to fear. Between Vietnamese, there are no victors and no vanquished. Only the Americans have been beaten. If you are patriots, consider this a moment of joy. The war for our country is over."

To lessen the tension, Bui Tin attempted a bit of small talk. "Do you still play tennis?" he asked Big Minh, and then drew him out about his orchid collection. He teased Vu Van Mau about having long hair. Had he not vowed to wear it short as long as Thieu remained president?

Big Minh laughed and said it was no wonder Bui Tin's comrades had won the war. They seemed to know everything.

As another northern officer took Minh to the Saigon Radio station to read his surrender statement over the air, Bui Tin moved into Thieu's office, found a desk and sat down to write the story for his newspaper.

At 11:30 A.M., the revolutionary flag was flying over the palace, and the Communist troops were flocking there. At Dung's headquarters, his officers were shouting and jumping up and down, embracing and boosting each other up on their shoulders to be carried around the room. Dung lighted a cigarette. Beside him, one of his generals said, "Now if these eyes close, my heart will be at rest."

AFTER THE 1973 AGREEMENT, Nguyen Thi Chon, who had survived torture in Saigon before Tet, had stayed on in the Paris office that was monitoring violations of its terms. When word of the liberation of Saigon reached her delegation, each member bought a red rose and marched to the South Vietnamese embassy. Jubilant Frenchmen joined them until there was a throng descending on the building. The South Vietnamese had fled. Mrs. Chon joined the crowd as it pressed inside to celebrate victory in the lair of her former enemy.

IN HANOI, Mrs. Dung had been keeping a radio to her ear for a month. Now, hearing firecrackers explode in the streets, she could believe that the war might truly be over. She was thrilled that Saigon had not been destroyed and wondered about the mother she had not seen for twenty years. On her speaking tours of Europe on behalf of the NLF, she had always been able to count on a murmur of sympathy when she mentioned that she had received no word about her children since 1954. Now the country would be united and her family with it. Ever since the peace agreement of 1973, she had been holding her feelings in check. At this moment, they all burst forth. Everything was marvelous! From this day forward there would be no more fighting among Vietnamese!

WHEN THE CHEERS and joyous tears faded at General Dung's headquarters, he consulted Le Duc Tho and his commanders about the massive job facing them. Was Saigon's water running and its electricity working? How would they feed the hungry and put the unemployed to work? Beginning today, they must cope with a defeated and disbanded army of nearly 1 million soldiers, and they had no civic administration in place. The days ahead would be daunting.

But tomorrow was May 1, International Communism's Labor Day. It was also Dung's birthday. On the table before him was his best gift, a cable of congratulations from Hanoi that summed up thirty years of misery and sacrifice: "Political Bureau is most happy."

NGUYEN KHAC HUYNH had gone Mrs. Dung one better and listened to two radios. In his Hanoi office, he picked up Big Minh's remarks from a Saigon broadcast but waited for official confirmation over the Voice of Vietnam. When it came, he joined the others in his office in cheering and pounding his hand on his desk, then hurried to Mrs. Nguyen Thi Binh to share the celebration with her.

Huynh had told aides in the protocol division to find champagne, and everyone now drank a toast to independence and freedom. Huynh stopped at home to tell his wife and children the news but found himself drawn to the street to share his happiness on the crowded sidewalks.

Thirty years had passed since he first felt this same elation, and he was sure that he would not sleep tonight. His country had defeated the Japanese in 1945, the French in 1954, and now the Americans in 1975. The difference was that today the war for independence was truly over.

In that, Huynh was right. He did not foresee his country's future. He could not predict the reeducation gulags, the slaughter in Cambodia, the border war between Vietnam and China or the families drowning at sea as they tried to flee a united Vietnam. But on April 30, 1975, one judgment was possible about the war just ended:

North Vietnam's leaders had deserved to win. South Vietnam's leaders had deserved to lose. And America's leaders, for thirty years, had failed the people of the North, the people of the South, and the people of the United States.

CHRONOLOGY

7th Century B.C.
By the Dong Son archeological era, Vietnamese who first call themselves the Lac are populating the Red River Delta.

208 B.C.
The first emperor of Vietnam, a rebel Chinese general named Trieu Da, conquers the kingdom of Au Lac in the northern mountains of Vietnam and makes it his capital.

111 B.C.
The Han dynasty takes over the kingdom and brings it under Chinese military control, although administered through local officials called Lac lords.

A.D. 40
The Trung sisters, wives of local leaders put to death for resisting Han authority, lead a tax rebellion that ultimately fails but makes them martyrs in the cause of independence.

10th Century A.D.
After centuries of Chinese domination, a Vietnamese named Ngo Quyen seizes upon the collapse of China's T'ang dynasty to declare the independence of a kingdom called Nam Viet, or Southern Viet.

1225
After two centuries of stability under a dynasty founded by Ly Thai To, vigorous new rulers, the Tran, replace it. But early in the fifteenth century, it, too, has declined, and a Chinese dynasty, the Ming, again brings Vietnam under China's control.

1426
The military campaign of Le Loi, the son of a rich landowner, succeeds in forcing China to evacuate. Le's dynasty wrenches the southern sections of Vietnam from the Angkor empire. But by the end of the sixteenth century, the dynasty has lost its force, and civil war in Vietnam leads to a division between the Trinh family in the north and the Nguyen family in the south.

1627
A French Jesuit missionary, Alexandre de Rhodes, converts Vietnam's spoken language into the Roman alphabet and praises the country's riches to the French.

1772
After a century of occasional rural rebellion, a full-scale peasant revolt is mounted by three brothers from the southern village of Tay Son, who unseat the Nguyens and go on to conquer the North.

1802
Nguyen Anh of the former ruling family defeats the last of the Tay Son rulers and indicates his plan to reunite the country by making the central city of Hue his capital. Pigneau de Behaine, a French missionary and soldier of fortune, helps Nguyen Anh to gain support from France. Anh becomes Emperor Gia Long.

1847
French troops battle with Vietnamese mandarins in Tourane, the city later called Da Nang. Tu Duc takes the throne vowing to eliminate Christianity from his realm. But fifteen years later, with the French occupying Saigon, Tu Duc agrees to turn over three southern provinces to France.

1863
French troops take over Cambodia and after some setbacks have also taken most of the Vietnamese empire. In 1879, France names its first civilian governor of Cochin China. Four years later, treating Cochin China as a colony, Paris claims Annam and Tonkin as its protectorate.

1890
Ho Chi Minh is born in central Vietnam; in 1911, he will leave Vietnam for the West.

1918
Calling himself Nguyen Ai Quoc, Ho goes to Paris and stays seven years.

1919
Ho fails in his attempt at the Versailles peace talks for an audience with American President Woodrow Wilson to petition for self-determination in Vietnam.

1920
December: Ho joins the new French Communist Party. He travels to Moscow four years later and then to China as assistant and translator for the Soviet representative Mikhail Borodin.

1930
Ho unites various Asian factions to form the Indochinese Communist Party in Hong Kong.

1932
The French allow Bao Dai, the schoolboy named emperor of Vietnam seven years earlier, to return from Paris and take the throne.

1940
June: The German Army takes France. Three months later, Japan invades Indochina but does not overthrow the French colonial government.

1941
Ho returns secretly to Vietnam for the first time in thirty years and creates the Vietminh to struggle against both France and Japan.

1944
Vo Nguyen Giap, from a poor family in Quang Binh province, forms the Vietminh Army to turn the guerrilla forces into regular soldiers.

1945
March 9: Japanese seize control of the French government in Indochina. Two days later, the Japanese permit Bao Dai to proclaim independence from France.

1945

April 12: Franklin Roosevelt dies and Harry Truman becomes president.

May 8: Germany surrenders to the Allied forces.

July: At the Potsdam Conference, the Allies agree that Britain will disarm the Japanese in South Vietnam, and that Chinese Nationalists will do the same north of the 16th parallel.

August 15: After the U.S. drops atomic bombs on Hiroshima and Nagasaki, Japan surrenders unconditionally and three days later transfers control of Indochina to the Vietminh.

September 2: Ho declares Vietnam's independence and the formation of the Democratic Republic of Vietnam (DRV), which includes the entire country. He dissolves the Indochinese Communist Party on November 11 to form a broader coalition with the nationalists.

1946

March 6: France recognizes the DRV as a free state within the French Union.

September 14: Ho signs an agreement in Paris with the French overseas affairs minister that is purposely vague about Vietnam's political future.

November 23: Responding to a jurisdictional dispute with the Vietminh, French troops open fire on civilians at Haiphong harbor. In response, the Vietminh launch the French-Indochina War on December 19 with attacks on French troops in northern and central Vietnam.

1949

October 1: Mao Zedong proclaims the creation of the People's Republic of China.

1950

February 7: The United States and Great Britain extend recognition to Vietnam under Bao Dai.

June 25: The Korean War begins when Kim Il Sung of North Korea launches his attack on South Korea and seizes its capital at Seoul.

1951

April 11: General Douglas MacArthur is relieved of his command for challenging Truman's conduct of the Korean War.

1952

November 4: Retired General Dwight Eisenhower wins the U.S. presidential election for the Republicans, with Senator Richard M. Nixon of California as his vice president.

1953

Giap marches North Vietnamese troops to the Laotian royal capital of Luang Prabang and installs Souphanouvong, a leftist prince, as head of the Government of the Free Laotian, the Pathet Lao.

1954

May 8: The French base at Dien Bien Phu falls to Giap's troops after a siege that began on March 13. The same day, the Geneva conference on Indochina opens in Switzerland with Great Britain and the Soviet Union as cochairmen.

July 7: Former Emperor Bao Dai appoints Ngo Dinh Diem as premier of the forthcoming nation in southern Vietnam to be called the Republic of Vietnam.

July 20 and 21: Agreements are signed in Geneva that partition Vietnam along the 17th parallel, creating the Democratic Republic of Vietnam in the north, with Hanoi as its capital, and the Republic of South Vietnam, with Saigon as its capital. The agreements restrict foreign military bases and personnel in the country and stipulate countrywide elections to unify Vietnam by July 20, 1956. The United States does not sign but promises to refrain from threat or use of force to disturb the agreements. Washington also endorses the promise of free elections supervised by the United Nations.

1955

January 1: Direct U.S. assistance to South Vietnam begins, and on February 12 the U.S. Military Assistance Advisory Group (MAAG) takes over the training of Diem's army.

February 19: The Southeast Asia Collective Defense Treaty (SEATO) takes effect.

July 20: Diem's government rejects North Vietnam's invitation to plan for the unification elections, claiming that the North's vote will not be a free one.

October 23: South Vietnam's national referendum replaces Bao Dai as head of state with Ngo Dinh Diem as president.

1956

October 26: Diem's government produces South Vietnam's first constitution and creates a National Assembly.

1958

January 4: A large band of former Vietminh guerrillas protest Diem's crackdown on dissidents with an attack on a rubber plantation north of Saigon.

1959

January: The Hanoi Politburo passes Resolution 15, making the struggle against Diem in the South military as well as political.

1960

April 17: North Vietnam protests to Britain and the Soviet Union a U.S. increase in MAAG advisers. Washington announces on May 5 that the increase from 327 persons to 685 of MAAG personnel is at the request of Diem's government.

September: Le Duan, a militant Communist from the South, becomes first secretary of the Lao Dong (workers') party in Hanoi.

November 11: A military coup against Diem is foiled by his loyalists. The U.S. State Department suggests that Diem should implement radical reforms within his government and take energetic action against corruption.

December 10: Hanoi announces formation of the National Liberation Front of South Vietnam, along with a ten-point declaration that calls for the overthrow of Diem and unification of the two halves of the county. The NLF's military guerrillas are popularly called the Vietcong.

1961

January 20: John F. Kennedy is sworn in as president of the United States.

April 17: Fifteen hundred Cuban exiles, financed by the U.S. Central Intelligence Agency, are defeated in their attempt at the Bay of Pigs to overthrow Cuban leader Fidel Castro.

May 11–13: Vice President Lyndon Johnson, visiting Vietnam, announces increased American aid for Diem's government.

May 16: A fourteen-nation conference on neutrality for Laos opens in Geneva.

October 18: Diem proclaims a state of emergency due to flooding in South Vietnam. On the same day, a U.S. delegation headed by General Maxwell Taylor and White House aide Walt Rostow arrive in Saigon on a fact-finding mission.

November 16: President Kennedy agrees to increase military aid to South Vietnam but rejects Taylor's private recommendation that he send American troops to the Mekong Delta.

1962

February 7: The 300 men of two U.S. Army air-support companies arrive in South Vietnam, raising the number of U.S. military personnel in the country to 4,000. The following day, the former MAAG office is upgraded to "U.S. Military Assistance Command, Vietnam" (MACV) under the command of four-star General Paul Harkins.

February 27: Two South Vietnamese air force planes bomb the Presidential palace in Saigon, slightly injuring Madame Ngo Dinh Nhu, Diem's sister-in-law.

October 22: President Kennedy announces a "quarantine" of Cuba because the Soviets have introduced nuclear missiles to the island. Six days later, Premier Khrushchev announces that the missiles will be removed.

1963

January 2: In Ap Bac, a village in the Mekong Delta, 200 Vietcong soldiers stand their ground in the first stand-and-fight battle of the American phase of the Vietnam War. They hold off 2,000 ARVN troops, shoot down 5 helicopters and kill 3 American advisers.

May 8: A protest in Hue by Buddhists against restrictions on flying their flag is broken up by South Vietnamese government troops who kill 12 persons, some of them children.

June 3: Diem imposes martial law in Hue to quell persisting Buddhist demonstrations. Eight days later, Thich Quang Duc, a Buddhist monk, publicly burns himself to death in Saigon.

June 27: Kennedy appoints Henry Cabot Lodge to replace Frederick Nolting as ambassador to South Vietnam.

August 21: Hundreds of Diem's police and army troops raid the Xa Loi pagoda in Saigon and other pagodas throughout the country.

August 24: With President Kennedy, Secretary of State Rusk, Secretary of Defense McNamara and CIA Director John McCone away from Washington, State Department officials Roger Hilsman and Averell Harriman obtain the president's approval for a cable to Lodge that seems to authorize a military coup against Diem.

November 1: South Vietnamese generals led by Duong Van "Big" Minh oust President Diem and his brother Nhu from power; Diem and Nhu are killed the next day.

November 22: John F. Kennedy is assassinated in Dallas, Texas, and Lyndon B. Johnson becomes President.

1964

January 30: General Nguyen Khanh launches a second coup, replaces Big Minh in command of South Vietnam and takes four fellow generals into custody.

June 23: President Johnson announces the appointment of General Taylor to replace Lodge as U.S. ambassador to South Vietnam.

July 27: Johnson informs Robert Kennedy that he will not be selected as the president's running mate in November.

August 2: North Vietnamese patrol boats fire torpedoes at the USS *Maddox*, an American destroyer, in the Gulf of Tonkin. Two days later, a similar attack is erroneously reported.

August 5: Johnson launches retaliatory U.S. bombing strikes against a North Vietnamese oil depot and four naval bases.

August 7: The U.S. Congress approves a joint resolution called informally the Tonkin Gulf Resolution, which authorizes the president to take "all necessary measures to repel any armed attacks against the forces of the United States and to prevent further aggression." Senators Wayne Morse of Oregon and Ernest Gruening of Alaska are the only members of Congress to vote against the resolution.

October 5: Undersecretary of State George Ball sends copies to the president's chief advisers of his sixty-seven-page memorandum in favor of negotiations.

October 14: Nikita Khrushchev is removed from power in Moscow and replaced by Leonid Brezhnev and Aleksei Kosygin.

November 3: Lyndon Johnson and Hubert Humphrey are elected president and vice president in the greatest sweep of the electoral college since 1936. Robert Kennedy is elected to the U.S. Senate from New York.

1965

February 7: Vietcong guerrillas fire on the U.S. base at Pleiku, killing 8 Americans, wounding 126 and destroying 10 U.S. planes. The attack coincides with the first trip to South Vietnam by McGeorge Bundy, the president's national security adviser. On February 7 and 8, U.S. retaliatory air strikes called "Flaming Dart" are launched against North Vietnamese installations.

February 19: A series of competing coups and political crises begin that result in Air Vice Marshal Nguyen Cao Ky taking control of South Vietnam and Nguyen Khanh being sent out of the country.

March 2: The United States begins "Rolling Thunder," the systematic bombing of North Vietnam that continues, except for several pauses, until October 31, 1968.

March 8: Over Ambassador Taylor's objections, Johnson sends two U.S. Marine battalions to guard the American base at Da Nang. They are the first U.S. combat troops stationed in South Vietnam.

March 30: Vietcong set off a bomb at the U.S. embassy in Saigon, killing 2 Americans and 20 Vietnamese.

April 7: In a speech at Johns Hopkins University in Baltimore, Johnson proposes allotting billions of U.S. dollars to develop dams and other projects in Indochina if the North Vietnamese will agree to negotiate on his terms.

April 8: Pham Van Dong, North Vietnam's Prime Minister, presents Four Points that Washington must accept before peace talks can begin.

April 8 and 9: Ho meets secretly with Mao in Beijing and agrees that China will not send combat troops unless the United States invades North Vietnam. Mao is also planning his Great Proletarian Cultural Revolution.

April 24: Rebels in the Dominican Republic overthrow their pro-American dictator. Johnson says he is sending U.S. Marines and airborne troops to protect American citizens.

May 12: Johnson orders the first pause in the bombing of North Vietnam to test the Communist reaction.

June 11: Fellow generals choose Air Vice Marshal Nguyen Cao Ky to become South Vietnam's prime minister.

July 8: Lodge is named U.S. ambassador to South Vietnam for the second time.

July 28: Johnson approves the request of the commander of U.S. troops in South Vietnam, General William Westmoreland, for forty-four more U.S. combat battalions in South Vietnam.

November 14–17: Regular troops from the North Vietnam People's Army of Vietnam meet U.S. soldiers from the 1st and 7th Cavalry in the first large-scale conventional battle of the war.

December 25: Johnson again suspends bombing of the North to persuade Hanoi to negotiate. Bombing is resumed January 31, 1966.

1966

February 5: Johnson meets in Honolulu with Ky and General Nguyen Van Thieu to urge domestic reforms in South Vietnam.

March 23: Ky's troops seize Da Nang to end two weeks of Buddhist demonstrations.

December: Harrison Salisbury of the *New York Times* files dispatches from Hanoi that describe the casualties inflicted by U.S. bombs on North Vietnamese civilians.

1967

April 27: Westmoreland argues for another 200,000 U.S. troops to be sent to South Vietnam, in addition to the 470,000 Johnson has already approved. Johnson agrees only to 47,000 more troops and sets a ceiling of 525,000.

May 1: Ellsworth Bunker replaces Lodge as ambassador in Saigon.

August 25: McNamara tells a Senate committee that expanded bombing of North Vietnam would not be effective.

September 3: Thieu is elected president of South Vietnam with Ky as vice president.

September 29: In a speech in San Antonio, Texas, Johnson promises to stop bombing the North if Hanoi will enter into "productive discussions." Two months later, Hanoi's foreign minister says the North will talk once the bombing ends.

1968

January 23: North Koreans seize the U.S. intelligence ship *Pueblo* off the coast of the Korean peninsula.

January 31: Communists launch their ambitious Tet offensive, which does not lead to the general uprising in the South that Hanoi had hoped for but which does shake American confidence that the war is being won.

March 12: Senator Eugene McCarthy of Minnesota, a critic of the war, runs strongly against Johnson in the New Hampshire Democratic presidential primary election.

March 16: Senator Robert Kennedy announces he will challenge Johnson for the Democratic nomination. The same day, U.S. Lieutenant William Calley's Charlie Company of the 11th Infantry Brigade enters the village of My Lai 4 and massacres Vietnamese who live there.

March 25: Senior policy experts called the "Wise Men" advise Johnson not to escalate the war further.

March 31: In a speech to the nation, Johnson says he will halt much of the bombing of the North and agree to negotiations with Hanoi. He adds that he will not be a candidate for re-election.

April 4: Civil rights leader Martin Luther King, Jr., is assassinated in Memphis, Tennessee.

June 5: Robert Kennedy is assassinated in Los Angeles on the night he wins the California Democratic presidential primary.

August: Antiwar protesters and police clash in the streets of Chicago as the Democratic Party Convention nominates Hubert Humphrey for president.

November 5: The Republican ticket of Richard Nixon and Spiro Agnew wins the U.S. presidential election.

1969

January 25: The Saigon regime agrees to join the Paris peace talks, along with representatives from the National Liberation Front. The talks, limited to Washington and Hanoi, have been underway with no progress since mid-May 1968.

March 18: Nixon and his national security adviser, Henry Kissinger, begin a secret bombing campaign against Communist bases in Cambodia.

June 8: Nixon announces the withdrawal of 25,000 U.S. troops from South Vietnam.

September 2: Ho Chi Minh dies at seventy-nine.

December 31: American troop strength in South Vietnam has been reduced to 475,200.

1970

February 18: A Chicago jury finds all but two of the defendants from the 1968 rioting at the Democratic Convention—including Tom Hayden and Abbie Hoffman—guilty on one count of conspiracy.

March 18: Prince Norodom Sihanouk is deposed as head of Cambodia's government by Prime Minister Lon Nol and First Deputy Sirik Matak.

May 4: Members of the Ohio National Guard kill four Kent State University students during campus riots over Nixon's decision in April to send U.S. troops into Cambodia.

December 31: American troop strength in South Vietnam has been reduced to 334,600.

1971

January 30: South Vietnam crosses the Laotian border to attack a Communist stronghold. Called Lam Son 719, the operation is easily defeated by Communist troops.

March 29: An Army court-martial finds William Calley guilty of the premeditated murder of 22 villagers at My Lai. After Calley spends three days in a stockade, Nixon releases him to house arrest in his own quarters.

June 13: The New York Times begins to publish the Pentagon Papers, the Defense Department study of Vietnam policy provided to the paper by former Pentagon analyst Daniel Ellsberg. On June 28, Ellsberg surrenders to federal authorities to stand trial for violating the Federal Espionage Act and stealing government property.

December 31: American troop strength has been reduced to 156,800.

1972

February 21: Nixon and Kissinger arrive in China to meet with Mao and Zhou Enlai, the Chinese premier.

June 17: Five men linked to the White House and Nixon's reelection campaign are arrested for breaking into the Democratic National Committee's office at the Watergate complex in Washington.

October 8: Kissinger and Hanoi's chief representative in Paris, Le Duc Tho, reach agreement on peace terms, which Thieu in Saigon resists.

November 7: Nixon easily defeats Senator George McGovern in the presidential election.

December 18: Nixon resumes bombing near Hanoi and Haiphong for eleven days, claiming that the Communists are refusing to negotiate.

December 31: American troop strength has been reduced to 24,000.

1973

January 23: Kissinger and Le Duc Tho initial a peace agreement, which is signed in Paris on January 27. The war will continue between North and South Vietnam.

March 29: The last U.S. combat troops leave South Vietnam, and the last American prisoners of war are released in Hanoi three days later.

June 24: Graham Martin replaces Ellsworth Bunker as ambassador to South Vietnam.

August 22: Nixon appoints Kissinger to replace William Rogers as secretary of state.

October 10: Spiro Agnew resigns in a bribery scandal, and Nixon nominates Congressman Gerald Ford to replace Agnew as vice president.

October 23: Kissinger and Le Duc Tho are awarded the Nobel Peace Prize, which Tho rejects because fighting continues in Vietnam.

1974

May 9: The House Judiciary Committee begins impeachment hearings against Nixon on charges growing out of the Watergate break-in.

July 21: North Vietnam's generals tell Le Duan that they might be able to win the war in 1976.

August 9: Nixon resigns the presidency and is succeeded by Ford, who pardons him on September 8 for any federal crimes Nixon might have committed.

1975

March 11: Communist troops led by Hanoi General Van Tien Dung take Ban Me Thuot in South Vietnam's Central Highlands.

March 15: Thieu orders South Vietnam's northern provinces abandoned, then reverses himself five days later; the Communists take Hue on March 25.

March 30: Dung's forces take Da Nang, and the next day Hanoi authorizes his army to march on to Saigon.

April 13: The United States evacuates the last of its personnel from Cambodia.

April 17: The Communist Khmer Rouge troops seize control of Phnom Penh.

April 25: Thieu leads an evacuation of Saigon by high-ranking southern officials as North Vietnamese troops advance on the city.

April 28: General Duong Van Minh once again becomes South Vietnam's chief of state.

April 29: The last Americans in Saigon, including Ambassador Martin, leave by helicopter as throngs of Vietnamese surround the U.S. embassy begging to escape.

April 30: Dung's troops smash through the gates of Independence Palace in Saigon, and Colonel Bui Tin accepts Big Minh's surrender. In Hanoi and Paris, veteran Communist officials celebrate their country's independence and unity.

NOTES

Abbreviations

FRUS: *Foreign Relations of the United States* (Washington, D.C.)
JFK Library: John F. Kennedy Library (Boston, MA)
LBJ Library: Lyndon B. Johnson Library (Austin, TX)
OH: Oral History

one: Kennedy and Ho (1960)

27 Eisenhower's mood: Ambrose, *Eisenhower*, 531.
28 Kennedy's hat: *New York Times*, Dec. 7, 1960, 46.
28 Ball's agenda: JFK Library, POF-Box 29A.
29 "an enormous amount of charm": Lasky, 317.
29 "a serious, earnest": Ambrose, *Eisenhower*, 531.
29 "I pray": Ibid.
29 Clifford background: Clifford, 314.
30 Clifford's memorandum: JFK Library, Pre-Presidential Task Force; Boxes 1071–75, Clifford, "Memorial on Transition," 4.
30 Not knowing people who could help JFK *be* President: JFK Library, Acheson OH, 6.
30 Dulles and James Bond: JFK Library, Allen Dulles OH, 16.
32 "happiness" as rice field: Fenn, 16.
33 "Being a mandarin": Lacouture, 14.
33 Ho's father fired: Fenn, 17.
33 a rebellious mandarin: His name was Phan Boi Chau. Lacouture, 16.
33 Ho's trip to New York: Fenn, 25–26.
34 Overseas Workers: Lacouture, 18.
34 "If you would like a lifetime memento": Fenn, 28.
34 "Whether soup salesmen": Ibid., 30.
35 "Dear martyrs": Lacouture, 31.
35 "What are we going to do": Ibid., 43.
36 "Nguyen O Phap": Halberstam, *Ho*, 23.
36 "Peasants believe": Karnow, *Vietnam*, p. 123.
36 "Died in the Hong Kong gaol": Fenn, 57.
37 Lovett recommends McNamara: JFK Library, Lovett OH, 15.
37 Acheson on Lovett: JFK Library, Acheson OH, 7.
37 Robert Kennedy as campaign manager: JFK Library, David Powers OH, 4.
38 Shriver calls on McNamara: Shapley, 83.
38 JFK sounds out Bowles: JFK Library, Bowles OH, 14.

40   McNamara's fibs: Shapley, 85.
40   McNamara admires *Profiles:* Ibid., 84.
41   Kennedy's authorship: Examined in Parmet *(Profiles,* 320–333 and *While England Slept,* 68–78).
41   Bell reads McNamara's note: JFK Library, Bell OH, 16.
42   "Could you tell us": JFK Library, Pre-Presidential, Press Secretary's Transcripts, Box 1060.
42   Stevenson with Lippmann: JFK Library, Lippmann OH, 4.
42   Lippmann suggests Bundy: Ibid.
43   "I'm not going to become": JFK Library, Bowles OH, 15.
43   JFK ready to name Fulbright: JFK Library, Rusk OH, 2.
43   Rusk's misgivings: Ibid., 2–3.
44   McNamara and Kennedy on FDR, Jr.: McNamara, *In Retrospect,* 18–19.
45   "The first capitalist": Terrill, 39.
45   Mao impressed by George Washington: Ibid., 40; Marrin, 15.
45   Mao's petition against headmaster: Terrill, 45.
45   Mao's snobbery: Archer, 15.
45   Mao's courses: Ibid., 16.
45   Makeup of Chinese Communist Party: Ibid., 22.
46   When peasants sneezed: Ibid., 36.
46   Mao designed flag: Salisbury, March, 22.
46   Long March statistics: Ibid., 2.
46   "Divide the land": Terrill, 160.
46   "Enemy advances, we retreat": Ibid., 138–39; Archer, 62.
46   "Political power grows": Terrill, 173.
47   Mao and Edgar Snow: Ibid., 175.
47   Ho's difficulties in Soviet Union: Author's interviews, Hanoi, August 1999; Sophia Quinn-Judge in "Ho Chi Minh: New Perspectives from the Comintern Files" (171–187), published in *Vietnam: Sources et Approches* (Aix-en Provence, France, 1996) provides supporting details of Ho's travails in the Soviet Union based on her research at Moscow's former Institute of Marxism-Leninism, now the Russian Center for the Preservation and Study of Documents of Modern History. Quinn-Judge also suggests (173) that Ho was married in the 1930s to a fellow revolutionary, Nguyen Thi Minh Khai.
47   Ho's lessons in verse: Lacouture, 65.
48   Eisenhower and Washington: Eisenhower, 41.
49   "Well, when you come down to it": *New York Times,* Jan. 18, 1960.
49   Second JFK trip to White House: JFK Library, Memorandum of subject for discussion at meeting of President Eisenhower and Senator Kennedy on Thursday, Jan. 19, 1961, POF Box 292.
50   Eisenhower questions morale: Schlesinger, *Thousand Days,* 148.
51   Giap's response to Ho: Giap, *Unforgettable Days,* 46.
51   "Look, there are a lot of books": Bui Diem, 13.
52   Le Duan and Giap's wife: Author's interview, Hanoi, August 1999.
52   The name "Ho Chi Minh": Fenn, 70n.
53   Ho's routine: Giap, 55.
53   "he who pays": Ibid., 57.
53   "I didn't read them": Ibid.
53   "You are a very naughty boy": Ky, 15.
54   "Like you": Ho, *Prison Diary,* 79.
54   "Under the pestle": Ibid., 157.
54   "I am thinking of my friends": Lacouture, 79.
54   "Stealth, continual stealth": *Souvenirs sur Ho Chi Minh,* 201–2; cited in Lacouture, 89.
55   Donovan plans to kidnap kaiser: Currey, *Lansdale,* 18.

55 "Take your pick": Fenn, 79.
55 "Don't think for a moment": E. Roosevelt, 114.
55 Churchill on China and India: Schaller, 169.
56 Roosevelt to de Gaulle: Tonnesson, 167.
56 "French blood shed on the soil": de Gaulle, III, 163–64.
56 "France has milked it": United States–Vietnam Relations, 1945–1967 (Pentagon Papers), vol. 1, A-14.
56 "over which flew the French flag in 1939": Ibid., A-13.
56 Roosevelt leaves Vietnam for post-war: Ibid., A-15.
56 James Roosevelt's reaction to his father: J. Roosevelt, 354–56.
56 never "consent to forty or fifty": FRUS, Conference at Malta and Yalta, 844.
57 "dear old Winston": Freidel, 596.
57 Truman on Yalta: Gravel, Pentagon Papers, 2.
57 Bui Toan Minh: Author's interviews, Southern California, 1998–99.
58 OSS supplies and training: Letter to author from Seymour Topping, March 17, 2000.
58 Patti's premonition: Patti, 129.
58 "within no less than five years": Lacouture, 96.
58 U.S. "as a champion of democracy": Tonnesson, 378.
59 "the Viet-American Army": Ibid., 391.
59 "All men are created equal": Fenn, 90.
60 "The war is finished.": Ibid., 83.
60 Rusk and Ho: Rusk, 113.
60 Rusk on Cecil Rhodes: Ibid., 65.
61 "We cannot trust Ho.": Fenn, 92.
61 George Marshall and Bao Dai: Author's interviews, Bui Tuong Minh, Southern California, 1998–99.
62 "It is better to sniff": Author's interview, Bellagio, Italy, July 1998.
62 "You know very well": Lacouture, 134.
62 "I swear I have not betrayed you": Ibid., 136.
62 Ho protests a "misunderstanding": Buttinger, Vietnam: Political, 250.
62 Ho as Gandhi: Fenn, 98.
63 "Time spent in jail": Lacouture, 147.
63 "You would kill ten of my men": Ibid., 171.
63 "Don't let me go back empty-handed": Ibid., 154.
63 Vietminh 100,000 strong: Buttinger, Vietnam: Political, 261.
63 "a harsh lesson": Chaffard, 70–74.
63 "If these dirty peasants": Buttinger, Vietnam: Dragon, I, 431.
63 Possibly 1,000 civilians killed: Karnow, Vietnam, 157.
64 "Our resistance will be long": Fenn, 102.
64 "policy of appeasement": Cray, 572.
64 "People have said you were a modern": Ibid., 582.
64 Stilwell's view of Chiang: Marin, 164.
64 "our quartermaster": Terrill, 216.
64 Communist victory: Topping (Journey, 54–55) notes Stalin's attempt to persuade Mao to stop his armies at the Yangtze and leave the south of China to the Nationalists. In 1962, Mao recalled that the Soviets feared he would become another Tito.
65 Rusk on avoiding World War II: JFK Library, Rusk OH, 39.
65 "Mousie Dung": Rusk, 155.
65 Acheson muzzles Rusk: Ibid., 423.
66 Background of Nguyen Thi Ngoc Dung: Author's interviews, Ho Chi Minh City, 1998–99.
68 Stalin withdraws advisers: Khrushchev, Glasnost, 146.
68 Stalin's autograph: Ibid., 155.

68   Stalin sends half a ton of quinine: Ibid., 156.
68   Truman at Valley Forge: Gardner, *Approaching*, 89.
68   Topping (*Journey*, 168–69) writes that on October 3, 1950, Zhou Enlai formally warned
      K. M. Pannikar, India's ambassador in Beijing, that China would intervene if American
      troops crossed the 38th parallel. New Delhi forwarded the warning to the State Depart-
      ment in Washington. The U.S. 1st Cavalry Division crossed the parallel on October 7,
      and on October 25, Chinese troops went into action.
68   Mood of Chinese leaders: Author's interview, Beijing, 1995.
69   MacArthur requests nuclear bombs: Thomson, *Sentimental*, 246.
69   G-2 report: Gardner, *Approaching*, 106.
69   Kennedy's Addison's disease: Parmet, 190–92.
70   Kennedy with Toppings: Author's interview, Seymour Topping, Los Angeles, October
      1999; also, Topping, *Journey*, 142.
70   "In Indochina, we have allied": Hilsman, 99.
70   "some people of colored origin": Parmet, 228.
70   "that every country is entitled": Ibid., 227.
70   JFK on Lattimore and Fairbank: Kattenburg (314) cites *Congressional Record*, House,
      Jan. 25, 1949, 532–33.
70   Acheson on oldest ally: JFK Library, Acheson OH, 1.
70   33,000 Americans killed: Thomson, *Sentimental*, 249.
70   Acheson on "Soviet imperialism": Acheson, 271.
71   Acheson on smoke machine: Thomson, *Sentimental*, 230.
71   "holds a Ph.D.": Ambrose, *Nixon*, 297.
71   "Who lost Vietnam?": Ambrose, *Eisenhower*, 358.
72   Rusk testified for Service and Davies: Rusk, 159.
72   Rusk on Alger Hiss: Ibid., 135.
72   "infinite capacity to adjust": Ibid., 423.
72   "We have granted Viet Nam": Fall, *Two Vietnams*, 221.
72   "Not unless our automobiles": Gardner, *Approaching*, 248.
72   Patti's impression of Giap: Ibid., 208.
72   180 miles in six weeks: Fall, *Two Vietnams*, 119.
73   Giap sets up government of Pathet Lao: Patti, 416.
73   Navarre's plans: Davidson, 178.
74   Lt. Gen. John "Iron Mike" O'Daniel: Fall, *Street*, 318.
74   "Never fight on a terrain which looks like": Roy, 298.
74   Chinese aid diverted from Korea: Macdonald, 94.
74   Chen Geng at Dien Bien Phu: Author's interview, Beijing, May 1995.
74   Six hundred trucks: Davidson, 214.
74   Co's background: Author's interview, Tran Quang Co, Hanoi, May 1998.
75   Hiep's background: Author's interview, Dang Vu Hiep, Hanoi, May 1998.
76   French troops at 16,000: Giap, *Military Art*, 139.
76   "butterfly bombs": Ibid., 137n.
77   Chen complains about Giap: Author's interview, Beijing, May 1995.
78   "You boys must be crazy": Ambrose, *Eisenhower*, 363.
78   "I want you to carry": Ibid., 369.
78   Final assault: Giap, *Military Art*, 138.
79   Huynh's response to French defeat: Author's interview, Nguyen Khac Huynh, Hanoi,
      May 1998.
79   Zhou says he came to make peace: Karnow, *Vietnam*, 201.
80    $2 billion, 75 percent of French costs: Hilsman, 100.
80   "He has double crossed us": Karnow, *Vietnam*, 205.

TWO: DIEM (1960)

81 Tommy Bui and Bao Dai: Author's interviews, Bui Tuong Minh, Southern California, 1998–99.

83 Diem meets with Giap: Shaplen, 109.

84 "You are a criminal": The dialogue, recalled by Diem fifteen years later, appears in Karnow, *Vietnam*, 216–17. Higgins, *Nightmare*, 157–58, offers a slightly different version.

84 Nguyen Ngoc Bich's background: Author's interview, Chester Cooper, Washington, D.C., Feb. 24, 1999.

85 Vy's resettlement: Author's interview, Nguyen Minh Vy, Hanoi, May 1999.

86 Rusk's response to SEATO: Rusk, 427.

87 Tuyen background: Author's interviews, Tran Kim Tuyen, Cambridge, England, March 12, 14, 17, 1996.

88 "For limited service only": Currey, *Lansdale*, 18.

88 "Filipinos and I fell in love": Ibid., 34.

89 "the look in your eyes": Ibid., 42.

89 "Colonel, Colonel": Warner, 103–4.

89 Lansdale's black propaganda: Currey, *Lansdale*, 107.

89 "It's not enough to be *against*": Ibid., 111.

90 "I am Diem": Shaplen, 103.

91 "The prime minister has asked me": Author's interviews, Tuyen.

91 Tuyen and refugee resettlement: Ibid.

91 Tuyen and fake Communist magazine: Ibid.

92 Cao Dai background: FitzGerald, 71.

92 Nhu more sympathetic than Diem: Author's interviews, Tuyen.

93 Sabotage in Hanoi: Lansdale's Team Report, doc. 15, *Pentagon Papers* (NYT), 53–66.

93 Lansdale's bribes: FitzGerald, 99.

93 "back pay": Currey, *Lansdale*, 173.

93 Lansdale arranges Philippine junket: Ibid., 181.

94 red and green ballots: Ibid., 180.

94 opposition voters beaten: Karnow, *Vietnam*, 223.

94 election results: Currey, *Lansdale*, 189.

94 35 million landowners: Marrin, 192.

94 2 million landlords executed: Ibid.

94 Truong Chinh background: Author's interviews, Hanoi, May 1998; Critchfield, 190.

95 Famine averted: Fall, *Two Vietnams*, 153.

96 Farmers neglected chores: Honey, 46.

96 "Comrade Chiem": Elliott, 17.

96 Diem's land program: King, 245.

96 North not prepared to absorb South Vietnam: Author's interviews, Hanoi, June 1995.

97 "Let a hundred flowers": Fall, *Two Vietnams*, 188.

97 Intellectuals' Revolt: Lacouture (210) cites "The Economy of North Vietnam," *China Quarterly*, Winter 1962, 85.

97 Guilty of reading *Le Monde*: Fall, *Two Vietnams*, 190.

97 "Rectification of Errors": Elliott (26) cites *Nhan Dan*, July 18, 1959.

97 "by sincerity alone": Ibid.

97 meat coupons only distributed: Elliott, 32.

97 Three-fourths in cooperatives: King, 241.

97 "Worse still, torture": Karnow, *Vietnam*, 226.

97 "What could they possibly do": Lacouture (216) quotes Ho speaking to General Salan in late 1946.

98 Tuyen and American mission: Author's interviews, Tuyen.

98 The elderly mandarin who refused to deal with Americans: His name was Vu Tien Huan. Ibid.

99   Dang sees beheading: Author's interview, Tran Bach Dang, Ho Chi Minh City, May 1998.
100   "If a son is mistreated": Karnow, *Vietnam*, 232.
100   North Vietnam's activities in the South: Author's interviews, Hanoi, 1995–99.
101   "Two Tour Base" battle: Author's interview, Ta Minh Kham, Ho Chi Minh City, May 1998. Two Tours Battle results: Vietcong claimed 55 VC killed, 20 wounded; Kham claims 200 ARVN killed, 500 wounded, 200 of them seriously. McNamara, *Argument*, 30, reports U.S. claiming 23 ARVN killed. Whatever the figures, Lt. Gen. Samuel Williams of MAAG called Two Tours "a severe blow to the South Vietnamese army and an indication of the VC ability to stage large-scale and well planned attacks." The quotation is cited in Robert McMahon, Jr., ed., *Major Problems in the History of the Vietnam War: Documents and Essays*, 2nd ed., (Lexington, Mass., 1995), 321.
102   Nguyen Huu Tho as dedicated Communist: Author's interviews, Hanoi, 1995–96; Tho's background: *New York Times Magazine*, April 7, 1968, 29. Brigham (16–17) supplies background of two other NCF officials, Huynh Tan Phat, an architect, and Nguyen Van Hieu, a journalist.
103   Cu Chi tunnels: Author's observation, May 1996; *The Document Album of Cu Chi—1960–1965* (Ho Chi Minh City, 1990).
104   Durbrow intervenes against Tuyen: Author's inteviews, Tuyen.
105   Mrs. Nguyen Thi Dinh: Author's interviews, Ho Chi Minh City, May 1998; also, Kristen Peltzer, "Love, War and Revolution: Reflections of the Memoirs of Nguyen Thi Dinh" in Werner and Huynh, 95–109.
107   Caravelle Manifesto: Bui Diem, 94.
108   1960 failed coup: Author's interviews, Tuyen.
109   "Be calm": Fall, *Two Vietnams* (246) cites *Journal d'Extrême-Orient*, November 12, 1960.
110   Colby lies to Nhu: Colby, 164.

THREE: BOWLES (1961)

112   "That's all right," Rostow told Kennedy: Author's interview, Walt W. Rostow, Austin, Texas, December 18, 1975.
113   "You ought to read this": Ibid.
114   "This is the worst one we've got": Ibid.
114   The cost would run about $40 million: FRUS, *Vietnam*, 1961, 13.
114   Parsons on larger army: Ibid., 14.
115   Diem believed Americans involved in plot: JFK Library, NS Files, Vietnam, Country Series, Top Secret. Prepared for McG. Bundy by Rostow.
115   JFK expects to be better off: FRUS, *Vietnam*, 1961, 19.
115   McNamara on need for new measures: Ibid.
116   "that horrible book": JFK Library, Parsons OH, 23.
116   "Not a team player": FRUS, *Vietnam*, 1961, 19.
116   "Dear Friend": Ibid., 20–23.
116   Kennedy authorizes increase in aid: Ibid., 26–27.
117   "He may have been good": JFK Library, National Security File, Vietnam, Box 193, WWR to JFK, April 15, 1961.
117   "We must go with Nolting": Ibid.
118   "Perhaps the way things are going": JFK Library, Nolting OH, II, 1970, 30.
118   "Well, Mr. Prime Minister": JFK Library, Parsons OH, 29–30.
120   "He's making a goddamned ass": Abramson, 571.
120   "Averell's hearing is atrocious": Ibid.
120   Laotians at water festival: Rusk, 428.
121   "Don't worry": McNamara, *In Retrospect*, 20.
121   "Mr. Secretary, you have been here": Ibid., 21.
122   "There is no doubt": Fairlee, *Promise*, 21, 24.

122   "Kennedy Defense Study": *New York Times*, Feb. 7, 1961, 1.
122   Dirksen calls for new elections: McNamara, *In Retrospect*, 21.
122   "Oh, come on, Bob": Ibid.
122   "Well, they are hazardous": Kennedy, *Press Conferences*, Feb. 8, 1961, 24.
122   "What we should be saying": *Time*, May 19, 1961, 21.
123   Plain of Jars: Hilsman, 95n.
124   Kennedy asks about plane speeds: JFK Library, Graham Parsons OH, 26.
124   "We can get them in": Hilsman, 128.
124   Rostow argued for troops: Schlesinger, *Thousand Days*, 302.
124   "If we are given the right": Ibid., 307.
124   John Kennedy thinking of neutralized Laos: JFK Library, Robert Kennedy OH, 609.
124   "Soviet planes, I regret to say": Kennedy, *Press Conferences*, March 23, 1961, 67.
125   "Mr. President, there appears to be": Ibid., 71.
125   "the American people are entitled": Schlesinger, *Thousand Days*, 249.
125   "The Castro regime is a thorn": Ibid., 228.
126   "I suggest that you personally": Bowles, 328.
127   "did not stand a snowball's chance": Rusk, 210.
127   Kennedy called Rusk: *Newsweek*, May 1, 1961, 27.
127   "somewhat deviously": *Time*, April 28, 1961, 11.
127   "way, way down": *Time*, May 5, 1961, 14.
127   "Dulles is a man": Ibid.
127   "the time has come": Ibid.
127   Khrushchev on Laos as a ripe apple: Schlesinger, *Thousand Days*, 304.
128   Harriman's trip to Laos: JFK Library, Harriman OH.
128   Eisenhower never let Nixon into living quarters: JFK Library, Onassis OH, 1.
129   "I just want you to know": JFK Library, O'Donnell OH, I, 24–25.
129   "I can't afford": Ibid., 26.
130   Johnson in Taipei: JFK Library, Cline OH, 4–5.
130   "*Van tue!* Long life!": *Time*, May 19, 1961, 20.
130   Lansdale's warning: *FRUS, Vietnam*, 1961, 121.
131   Diem response to JFK letter: Ibid., 132.
131   Johnson and Madame Nhu: JFK Library, Robert Kennedy OH, 85, 613.
131   "who would fight Communism": *Time*, May 19, 1961, 20.
131   "*C'est magnifique!*": Ibid.
131   "the Winston Churchill of Asia": Karnow, *Vietnam*, 214.
131   Tuyen's reaction: Author's interviews, Tuyen.
132   "Shit," the vice president said: Karnow, *Vietnam*, 214.
132   Rusk predicted failure: Abramson, 584.
132   "If we have to fight": Rusk, 430.
132   Harriman and "Parkinson's Law": JFK Library, Harriman OH, 64.
132   Harriman on staff reports: JFK Library, Sullivan OH, 14.
132   Harriman cuts delegation: JFK Library, Harriman OH, 65.
132   Proposed meeting with Chen Yi: Ibid., 67.
133   Harriman in a rage: Abramson, 585.
133   Chen Yi returns to Beijing: JFK Library, Harriman OH, 67.
133   Sino-Soviet break: Sullivan cites Mose Harvey, Soviet specialist on the Policy Planning Board, and other middle-level State Department officials as denying the break. JFK Library, Sullivan OH, 16.
133   Soviet-Hanoi disagreements: Dommen, 79–81; author's interviews, Hanoi, 1995–96.
134   de Gaulle on Indochina: JFK Library, Rusk OH, 29.
134   Kennedy and amphetamines: Thomas Reeves, 295.
134   "all give and no take": Collier and Horowitz, 277. Had his encounter with Khrushchev discomfited him less, Kennedy might have said "all take and no give."
134   Khrushchev on Kennedy: Khrushchev, *Remembers*, 458.
135   Georgetown gossip: Author's interview, W. W. Rostow, Austin, Tex., Dec. 18, 1995.

135   Khrushchev warning about guerrilla war: Schlesinger, *Thousand Days*, 329.
136   "solemn, although confident": *New York Times*, June 15, 1961, 1.
136   "rates more highly": Ibid., 12.
136   "Now we have a problem": Karnow, *Vietnam*, 248.
136   Rusk's and Sorensen's drafts: Rusk, 222.
136   Rostow's view on Berlin: Author's interview, W. W. Rostow, Austin, Tex., Dec. 18, 1995.
137   "to put it crudely": Schlesinger, *Thousand Days*, 349.
137   McNamara argues both sides of national emergency: Author's interview, Theodore Sorensen, New York City, Feb. 12, 1998.
137   "Life," he told reporters: Kennedy, *Press Conferences*, March 21, 1962, 253.
138   "You know, Khrushchev is going to build": Author's interview, W. W. Rostow, Austin, Tex., Dec. 18, 1995.
138   Kennedy and Thuan: *FRUS, Vietnam*, 1961, 174.
138   700 American advisers: *Dictionary of the Vietnam War*, 288.
139   "What do I do": J. Taylor, 248.
139   Lansdale recommends delaying increase: *FRUS, Vietnam*, 1961, 237.
139   "badly in need": Ibid., 238.
139   Couve de Murville: Ibid., 268.
140   Kennedy and Bowles, mid-July 1961: Bowles, 353.
140   Salinger on Bowles: Ibid., 355.
140   Bowles's Vietnam memorandum: *FRUS, Vietnam*, 1961, 322.
141   "a major commitment of U.S. troops": Ibid.
141   Ho at Chinese Embassy: Author's interview, Beijing, 1975.
142   Ho and apple: Lacouture, 217.
142   "putting the Party's interests": Ho, *Articles and Speeches*, 203.
143   Le Duan's suspicion of Russians: Lacouture, 252; author's interviews, Hanoi, 1995–99.
143   Viet Cong growing at 1,500 a month: *FRUS, Vietnam*, 1961, 484.
143   Victories in Phuoc Thanh and Darlac: Karnow, *Vietnam*, 251.
143   Ho questions Kennedy's choices: Author's interviews, Hanoi, 1995–96.
144   "Well, we are going to wait": Kennedy, *Press Conferences*, 150.
144   "damaging letdown": *FRUS, Vietnam*, 1961, 362.
144   Lemnitzer's telegram: Ibid., 362–63.
144   Rostow's assignment: Author's interview, W. W. Rostow, Austin, Tex., Dec. 18, 1995.
144   Lansdale to General Williams: Newman, 131.
145   "You'll simply be 'working party' ": Currey, *Lansdale*, 236.
145   "That's not my subject": Ibid., 237.
145   Tuyen's secret meeting: JFK Library, CIA report, NSF Box 194, Oct. 16 to Oct. 19, 1961.
145   Mission sees flood damage: Kinnard, 96; John Taylor, 250.
145   "ostensibly for guard duty": *FRUS, Vietnam*, 1961, 383.
145   "I might be there for dinner": Currey, *Lansdale*, 237.
146   Lansdale on Taylor: Ibid.
146   "Have you reached the point": Ibid., 238.
147   Rostow's prisoner interviews: Author's interview, W. W. Rostow, Austin, Tex., Dec. 15, 1995.
147   Minh's opinions: *FRUS, Vietnam*, 1961, 396–98.
147   Nhu's remarks to Lansdale: Ibid., 411–16.
148   Rostow on Nhu: Rostow, 276–77; author's interview, W. W. Rostow, Austin, Tex., Dec. 14, 1995.
148   "As representative of the Joint Chiefs": *FRUS, Vietnam*, 1961, 426–27.
149   Taylor's evaluation of McGarr: JFK Library, Taylor OH, Jan. 9, 1969, 14.
149   "These men you have met talk well": Rostow, *Diffusion*, 277.
149   Diem welcomed Taylor's idea: *FRUS, Vietnam*, 1961, 478.
149   Rusk on sending troops: Rusk, 432.
149   Alsop's criticism: Halberstam, *Best*, 204.

150   Kennedy's instructions to Taylor: Newman, 136.
150   "No. No. NO!": *FRUS, Vietnam, 1961*, 432, 4n.
150   "The President requests": Ibid., 443.
150   Mansfield's memorandum: Ibid., 468.
150   "one of high career risk": Ibid., 469.
150   "We will have achieved": Ibid., 470.
151   "a new country": Ibid., 478.
151   estimates of Communist strength: Ibid., 486.
151   "There is no need for fatalism": Ibid., 478–79.
151   U.S. troops to raise morale: Ibid., 481.
151   "from advice to limited": Ibid.
151   "any errors, therefore": Shapley, 116.
151   McNamara on warning North Vietnam: *FRUS, Vietnam, 1961*, 560.
152   Dulles warning on USSR and China: Ibid., 607.
152   "Laos was never really ours": Ibid., 606.
152   "within five years": Ball, 366.
152   "George, you're just crazier": Ibid.
153   "We're heading hell-bent": Ibid., 367.
153   Kennedy makes a rather strong case: *FRUS, Vietnam, 1961*, 608.
153   Kennedy faults every proposal: Ibid., 610.
154   SEATO Plan 5: Ibid., 243.
155   "If this doesn't work": Rostow, *Diffusion*, 278.
155   "The troops will march in": Schlesinger, *Thousand Days*, 476.
155   "would go beyond permissible": *FRUS, Vietnam, 1961*, 634.
155   Rusk on McConaughy's house: Bowles, 362.
156   Acheson's speech: Ibid., 627.
157   Acheson and Louis Johnson not speaking: Ball, 368.
157   McNamara volunteers to oversee Vietnam: Shapley, 133.
157   "naturally embarrassing": *FRUS, Vietnam, 1961*, 611.
157   Diem on George Marshall: Ibid., 692.

FOUR: BIGART (1962)

159   "a grim signal of the extent": Wyatt, 66.
160   Bigart briefs Kennedy in 1951: Prochnau, 82.
161   "It looks as though": Wyatt, 86; Browne, *New Face*, 1–8.
161   Thao was Viet Cong: Karnow, *Vietnam*, 38.
162   "Look at that carrier!": Ibid., 254.
162   "Mr. President, are American troops": Kennedy, *Press Conferences*, 177.
162   Nolting's testimony: Prochnau, 40–41.
163   "I am an optimist": Karnow, *Vietnam*, 258.
163   Cu bombing raid: Author's interviews, Tuyen.
164   Fishel in Vietnam: *FRUS, Vietnam, 1962*, 148–52.
165   "We've got twenty Vietnams": Karnow, *Vietnam*, 248.
165   Robert Kennedy impressed by French troops: Schlesinger, *RFK*, II, 734.
165   "greatly hated": Schlesinger, *RFK*, I, 96.
165   RFK says U.S. in Vietnam to win: *FRUS, Vietnam, 1962*, 230n.
165   "Perhaps it adds up": Prochnau, 211.
165   Felt's ban on reporters: Wyatt, 91.
165   Sochurek got special access: *FRUS, Vietnam, 1962*, 123.
165   "If the NY Times cannot": Wyatt, 77.
166   Cottrell on civilian casualties: *FRUS, Vietnam, 1962*, 126.
166   Harriman's memo to Rowan: Ibid., 124n.

166   Headed for a major domestic furor: Ibid., 129.

166   "We do not want news reports": Ibid., 130.

166   "proof enough that the press boys": Ibid., 131.

166   playing God: Ibid., 176–77.

166   Cable 1006: Ibid., 158–60.

166   "undesirable dispatches": Ibid., 159–60.

166   Bigart's report on Cai Ngai: Prochnau, 46.

167   "How ca-ca-can a fact": Malcolm Browne, "Fighting Words," *New York Times Book Review*, April 11, 1993, 13.

170   Ho's austerity: Author's interviews, Beijing, 1995.

171   Tuyen's letter to Nhu: Author's interviews with Tuyen, March 1996.

172   Nolting-Diem interview: *FRUS, Vietnam*, 1962, 253.

172   Nolting's explicit instructions: Ibid., 279.

172   "Sully has been here too long": Ibid., 281.

172   Poor Man's 707: McNamara, *In Retrospect*, 44.

172   Galbraith on Diem's odds: *Pentagon Papers (NYT)*, IV, Bl, 140.

172   "Incidentally, who is the man": Newman, 236.

173   Winterbottom's estimates: Ibid., 192.

173   Winterbottom's erratic behavior: Ibid., 196.

173   "Well, ah," Winterbottom said: Ibid., 224.

174   Dowling and Harris's estimate: Ibid., 244.

174   16,305 Vietcong: Ibid., 247.

174   Briefer's misleading statistics: *FRUS, Vietnam*, 1962, 385; Newman (250) uses a sports analogy. The briefing was like an announcer reporting the score for a game by giving the points of one team for the entire game and only the second half's points for the other team.

174   200 Vietcong offensives: Newman, 251.

174   "doubtless because of dynamic": *FRUS, Vietnam*, 1962, 383.

175   Harkins admits duress: Ibid., 381.

175   Thao and Vietcong attacks: Prochnau, 76; Shapley, 149.

176   "I've seen nothing but progress": Sheehan, *Lie*, 289.

176   Security checks at new hamlets: Shapley, 151.

176   Bigart-McNamara exchange: Wyatt, 100.

177   Sullivan's attitude about boundaries: JFK Library, Sullivan OH, 4.

177   Harriman's performance: Ibid., 18.

177   Sullivan never trusted Phoumi: Ibid., 25.

178   "What the hell is going on": Ibid., 24.

178   "But try to impress on everyone": Hilsman, 145.

178   *New York Times* report: Ibid.

178   Politburo analysis: Author's interviews, Hanoi, 1995–96.

179   "We can wipe Tchepone off the face": Shapley, 159–60.

179   Souvanna's deadline: Hilsman, 150.

179   "Well, we'll go along": Ibid., 153.

180   Harriman got Kennedy's approval: Abramson, 605.

180   Harriman on Roosevelt: *FRUS, Vietnam*, 1962, 543–46.

180   Khiem's aide troubled by his rigidity: Author's interview, Hanoi, May 1998.

181   William Kohlmann: Author's interviews, Southern California, 1994–99.

183   Ta Minh Kham: Author's interviews, Ho Chi Minh City, 1996–99.

184   Vietcong ambushes in 1962: Fall, *Street*, 351.

184   American captain and lieutenant killed: They were Capt. Walter P. McCarthy and 1st Lt. William F. Train III; ibid., 354.

184   Special Forces training: Kelly, *Berets*, 14.

184   Training the Civilian Irregular Defense Group: Ibid., 6.

185   crossbows seized: Ibid., 20.

185 Americans take charge: Ibid., 40.
186 Sorensen-Dobrynin exchange: Dobrynin, 67–68.
186 U.S. and Soviet missile strength: Shapley, 168; Dobrynin, 73n.
186 Khrushchev relished giving America its own medicine: Khrushchev, *Remembers*, 494.
186 First photographs of missiles: Hilsman, 180; Shapley, 166.
187 "Those things we've been worrying about": Bird, *Color*, 226.
187 "It makes no great difference": Hilsman, 195.
187 Rusk leaves George Ball: Rusk, 231.
188 "You're in a pretty bad fix": May and Zelikow, 182.
188 "You're in with me": Sheldon M. Stern, "What JFK Really Said," *The Atlantic Monthly*, May 2000, 122. The quality of the tape (31.2) being very poor, Stern, a retired historian from the JFK Library, takes issue with the May and Zelikow transcript, which renders Kennedy's response as "(Kennedy makes an unclear, joking, reply.)."
188 "You pulled the rug": May and Zelikow, 188.
188 Acheson argues for strikes: Shapley, 174.
188 Proportion killed in Civil War: Blight et al., 184.
188 "I don't want to see": Hilsman, 203.
189 Sylvester lies about missiles: Shapley, 174.
189 "By this time tomorrow": Ibid., 207.
189 Pentagon had prepared 500 sorties: Ibid., 174.
189 Dobrynin on captains' instructions: Dobrynin, 82.
189 Rusk's response: Rusk, 232.
190 "It isn't the first step": R. Kennedy, 98.
190 "spoiling for a fight": Dobrynin, 87.
190 Who knows? Bobby said, I might: Ibid., 90.
190 "Which two would you get rid of?": Author's interview, Robert McNamara, Los Angeles, May 28, 1999.
190 Admiral Anderson tells McNamara to leave Naval Operations: McMaster, 30; Shapley, 177; Bird, *Color*, 237.
191 Harkins's meeting with Diem: FRUS, *Vietnam*, 1962, 622–33.
192 Diem's strategy to avoid losses: Newman, 289.
192 Diem agreed halfheartedly: FRUS, *Vietnam*, 1962, 633.
193 Harriman's instructions to Nolting: Ibid., 693–96.
193 Lemnitzer's complaint: Ibid., 611.
194 Fall quotes Chinh: *Newsweek*, Sept. 20, 1962, 40–41.
194 Madame Nhu seeks Sully's expulsion: Mecklin, 132.
194 Mecklin's estimate of Sully: Ibid., 133.
194 "your crazy freedoms": Ibid., 136.
194 Robinson expelled: Ibid., 137.
195 Madame Nhu and reporters: FRUS, *Vietnam*, 1962, 724.
195 Mecklin on expulsions: Ibid., 725.
196 Halberstam and Gullion: Halberstam, *Quagmire*, 17.
196 "a neutral bystander": Mecklin, 139.
196 Mecklin on Cable 1006: Ibid., 149.

FIVE: LODGE (1963)

198 Cao's parade and promotion: Sheehan, *Lie*, 79–90.
198 Colonel Dam: Ibid., 20.
199 Description of Ap Bac: *Newsweek*, Jan. 14, 1963, 34.
199 Civil Guard provokes attack: Sheehan, *Lie*, 212.
200 Vietcong method of hitting helicopters: Author's interview, Ta Minh Kham, Ho Chi Minh City, May 1996.

200   "After napalm, rockets": *Newsweek*, Jan. 14, 1963, 34.

201   "I don't take orders": Sheehan, *Lie*, 228.

201   Ba knocked down by gun barrel: Ibid., 253.

202   "It is not prudent": Ibid., 259.

202   "Under this blue cloth": Pike, *Viet Cong*, 131.

202   Matagulay released: *Newsweek*, Jan. 21, 1963, 46.

203   Kham on Vietcong diet: Author's interview, May 1996.

203   New York printers' strike: The strike ran 114 days.

203   "with their little feet": Halberstam, *Quagmire*, 155.

203   Browne on Vann: Browne, *Muddy*, 215.

203   "a miserable damn performance": Sheehan, *Lie*, 277.

204   Madame Nhu on Vann: Ibid., 278.

204   "So you're Sheehan": Prochnau, 240.

204   "There are times": Hammond (34) cites *Washington Post*, Jan. 10 and 11, 1963.

205   "Yes, I consider it a victory": Halberstam, *Quagmire*, 158.

205   Bundy vetoes job for Kissinger: Forrestal interview, Halberstam archive, Boston University.

205   "Mike, you're talking well": Ibid.

206   "Have you thought that out?": Ibid.

206   "You will be my emissary": Ibid.

206   Sidey and Kennedy: JFK Library, Sidey OH, 6–9.

207   "legs are a soldier's chief weapon": Hammond, 33.

207   "Why do we have such a bad press": FRUS, *Vietnam*, Jan.–Aug. 1963, 95.

207   average age twenty-seven: Ibid., 98–99.

207   "irresponsible, sensationalized": Mecklin, 148.

207   "I hope the son-of-a-bitch dies": Prochnau, 300.

208   Nhu's interpretation of Mansfield report: FRUS, *Vietnam*, Jan.–Aug. 1963, 124.

208   "I got angry with Mike": O'Donnell and Powers, *Johnny*, 16; Francis X. Winters in *The Year of the Hare* (Athens, Ga., 1997), 232, cites a letter to Winters from Mansfield confirming O'Donnell's account.

208   "But I don't care": Ibid.

208   "We don't have a prayer": Logevall (38–39) cites LBJ Library, Bartlett OH.

209   Luce–Joe Kennedy dinner: JFK Library, Luce OH.

209   "That's for the second term": O'Donnell and Powers, *Johnny*, 16.

209   "But I also believe that we must examine": Schlesinger, *Thousand Days*, 769. Kennedy delivered the speech on June 10, 1963, at the American University commencement. Schlesinger (722) quotes Khrushchev as telling Harriman in Moscow that it was "the greatest speech by any American president since Roosevelt."

210   "If you don't level": Mecklin, 150.

210   Kennedy's doubts to Salinger: Prochnau, 302.

210   Diem fires Tuyen: Author's interviews, Tuyen, March 1996.

211   "Send an official telegram": Ibid.

211   Two children crushed to death: FRUS, *Vietnam*, Jan.–Aug. 1963, 277n.

211   Palace explanation for deaths: Gravel, *Pentagon Papers*, 225–36, cited by Gettleman et al., 217.

211   The final five Buddhist demands: These were the right to fly religious flags on church holidays; equal legal footing with the Catholics; prompt action against violations of religious freedom; an end to arbitrary arrests of Buddhists; acknowledgment of government guilt for the May 8 shooting: FRUS, *Vietnam*, Jan.–Aug. 1963, 287.

211   Quang's instructions: Ibid., 285.

212   "All these things I already do": Author's interviews, Tuyen, March 1996.

213   "A silly mistake": Ibid.

213   Thuan's background: Author's interviews, Tran Quang Thuan, Los Angeles, 1997–2000.

214   Description of monk burning: Browne, *Muddy*, 9–11.

216   Mecklin understood: Mecklin, 157.

216 "Let them burn!" Wyatt, 112.
216 "If Diem does not take prompt": FRUS, Vietnam, Jan.–Aug. 1963, 383.
217 "Cabot, I'd like to persuade": William J. Miller, 334.
218 Ike on Kennedy's GOP appointments: Ibid., 335.
219 "Get back, get back": Wyatt, 117.
219 Arnett's photo: Arnett, 95.
219 Trueheart's response: FRUS, Vietnam, Jan.–Aug. 1963, 471.
219 Diem drops charges: Hilsman, 479.
219 Village named for Nolting: Mecklin, 179.
219 Four monks burn to death: Hilsman, 482.
220 Hilsman observes Nolting: Ibid.
220 "This is the first time that you": LBJ Library, Nolting OH, November 11, 1982.
220 Rusk and McCone about leaks: Mecklin, 184–85.
220 "I suppose that these are the worst": JFK Library, Lodge OH, 36.
220 police escort for press: Mecklin, 240.
220 "Where are the gentlemen": Wyatt, 125.
220 "Our old mandarin": Mecklin, 190.
221 Lodge greets Buddhists: William J. Miller, 341.
221 Tuyen exiled: Author's interviews, Tuyen, March 1996.
222 Boy Scout with brass knuckles: Author's interview, James Thomson, Cambridge, Mass., 1995.
222 "I don't think Roger agrees with you": Ibid.
223 Diem's threat to Madame Nhu: FRUS, Vietnam, 1963, 644.
223 Ball on golf course: Ball, 371.
224 "I don't know about that last sentence": DiLeo (60) cites TELCON, Ball and the president, Aug. 21, 1963, Papers of George W. Ball.
224 "You may also tell": FRUS, Vietnam, Jan.–Aug. 1963, 628–29.
224 cable cleared with Forrestal: Ball, 372.
224 "we are prepared to have Diem": FRUS, Vietnam, Jan.–Aug. 1963, 634.
225 Hilsman and Hensley: Hilsman, 489.
225 Lodge and VOA broadcast: FRUS, Vietnam, Jan.–Aug. 1963, 636.
225 "Paul": Mecklin, 194.
225 Taylor on Bundy: FRUS, Vietnam, Jan.–Aug. 1963, 631.
226 Halberstam as a twenty-eight-year-old: Ibid., 638.
226 Hilsman on Nhu loyalists: Ibid., 639, n. 5.
226 Hilsman says outcome horrible to contemplate: Ibid., 641.
227 "a jumpy answer": Ibid., 660.
227 Nolting on Diem, Nhu: FRUS, Vietnam, Jan.–Aug. 1963, 662.
228 "The way things are going": Hilsman, 491.
228 "quit being a goddamned fool": Abramson, 622.
228 Harriman to Nolting: Hilsman, 492.
228 Kennedy speaks up for Nolting: Abramson, 622.
228 Ball's position: FRUS, Vietnam, Aug.–Dec. 1963, 4; and Ball, 373.
229 "Authorities are now": FRUS, Vietnam, Jan.–Aug. 1963, 675.
229 "Averell Harriman is one sharp": Ibid., Aug.–Dec. 1963, 14.
229 Bundy's Newsweek cover: March 4, 1963.
230 "Though war is evil": Time, June 25, 1965.
230 Bundy at Normandy: Newsweek, March 4, 1963, 22.
232 "First," Kennedy said: Ibid., 23.
232 Maneli's experiences: Maneli, 136–37.
232 Maneli's report to Warsaw: Ibid., 125.
232 "We can come to any": Ibid., 128.
233 Chinese ambassador's reaction: Ibid., 130–31.
233 French ambassador's warning: Ibid., 140–41.
233 Nhu and Vietnamese generals: FRUS, Vietnam, Aug.–Dec. 1963, 91.

234 Nhu advises "No comment": Ibid.
234 "When we go, we must go to win": Ibid., 35.
235 "pushing a piece of spaghetti": Karnow, *Vietnam*, 290.
235 Nhu to Lodge: *FRUS, Vietnam*, Aug.–Dec. 1963, 85.
235 Nhu about Maneli: Maneli, 144–45.
235 Kattenburg in Vietnam and Washington: Author's telephone interview, Paul Kattenburg, 1997.
236 "it was tragic" to "it should be": *FRUS, Vietnam*, Aug.–Dec. 1963, 71, n. 5.
236 Kattenburg's reactions: Author's interview.
237 Johnson against a coup: *FRUS, Vietnam*, Aug.–Dec. 1963, 74.
238 "In the final analysis": *Public Papers of the President of the United States: John F. Kennedy*, 1963, 650–53.
239 RFK's opinion: *FRUS, Vietnam*, Aug.–Dec. 1963, 118.
239 Rusk's rebuttal: Ibid.
240 Krulak on plane in ninety minutes: Hilsman, 501.
240 Hilsman has plane held: Sheehan, *Lie*, 365.
240 Krulak and Mendenhall return: *FRUS, Vietnam*, Aug.–Dec. 1963, 161.
240 "Looks like you don't brief": Sheehan, *Lie*, 341.
241 Politburo response: Author's interviews, Hanoi; and Robert Brigham, paper, Washington, D.C., April 15, 1997.
243 "Paul D. Harkins should be": Sheehan, *Lie*, 351.
243 "We are not interested": Maneli, 160.
243 "Reporters here": Prochnau, 350.
243 "If you mention": Wyatt, 122.
244 "Assume you keeping material": Prochnau, 417.
244 "a fragile, exciting beauty": Wyatt, 121.
244 Kennedy's ratings drop: Schlesinger, *Thousand Days*, 826.
245 Lansdale meeting with Kennedy: Daniel Ellsberg, unpublished memoir. Lansdale told him the story in South Vietnam; McNamara in a 1997 author's interview said he did not recall the incident.
245 McNamara draws on Phillips's report: Shapley, 260.
246 Honey's briefing: *FRUS, Vietnam*, Aug.–Dec. 1963, 293–95.
246 "acting like little soldiers": Mecklin, 234.
247 Taylor's report: *FRUS, Vietnam*, Aug.–Dec. 1963, 328–30.
247 "In summary": Ibid., 327.
247 Kennedy on troop withdrawal schedule: Ibid., 350–52.
248 "set in concrete": McNamara, *In Retrospect*, 80.
248 Sheehan on Richardson: *FRUS, Vietnam*, Aug.–Dec. 1963, 384.
248 Funding cut for Tung: Ibid., 361–63.
248 *Times of Vietnam*: Mecklin, 230.
249 "We must not lose": Hilsman, 513.
249 Nhu compares Negroes and Buddhists: Mecklin, 244.
249 "would make traitors": *FRUS, Vietnam*, Aug.–Dec. 1963, 485.
249 Lodge argues against Harkins's role: Ibid., 486.
249 RFK on coup: Ibid., 470.
250 "We do not accept": Ibid., 500. The cable was sent October 30, 1963, 5:49 P.M. EST.
250 Thuan in captivity: Author's interview, Tran Quang Thuan, Los Angeles, Jan. 31, 1997.
251 "civil disturbance": Mecklin, 254.
251 "become more mysterious": Ibid., 249.
251 Don tells Conein about coup: *FRUS, Vietnam*, Aug.–Dec. 1963, 480.
251 "There's an old saying here": William J. Miller, 350.
251 Discussion of coup groups: *FRUS, Vietnam*, Aug.–Dec. 1963, 503.
251 Nhu's false coup: Mecklin, 234.
252 Lodge on rumors of his assassination: *FRUS, Vietnam*, Aug.–Dec. 1963, 517.

252 Diem's response: Ibid.
253 Generals' ultimatum to Diem: Ibid., 511.
253 Diem-Lodge conversation: Ibid., 513.
254 Kohlmann during coup: Author's interview, William Kohlmann, Southern California, 1997.
254 rebels at the palace: Arnett, 114–15.
254 "Nhu was dickering": FRUS, Vietnam, Aug.–Dec. 1963, 521.
255 Washington vetoes Tri Quang: Ibid., 520.
255 "they were reporting to headquarters": Ibid.
255 "We are no longer a republic": Ibid., 534.
255 The Chinese businessman: His name was Cao Xuan Vy.
255 Minh to Conein about killing Diem: Don, 97.
256 "Best estimate this time": FRUS, Vietnam, Aug.–Dec. 1963, 527, n. 2.
256 McNamara quotes son: Shapley, 216.
256 Kennedy called committee chairman: Bradlee, 157.
256 Hilsman on suicides: JFK Library, President's Office File, Meeting Recordings, Tape A/55, Nov. 2, 1963 to Nov. 7, 1963.
257 "Mission accomplie": Don, 111.
257 Cao in Can Tho: Halberstam, Quagmire, 291.
257 "Do you believe": Higgins, 224.
258 Can's fate: Don, 113.
258 Diem's fifty jails: Shaplen, 157.
258 "Lodge is so popular": JFK Library, President's Office File, Meeting Recordings, Tape A/55, Nov. 2, 1963 to Nov. 7, 1963.
259 "Come up here and take a rest": Prochnau, 456.
260 Lodge and the generals: FRUS, Vietnam, Aug.–Dec. 1963, 546–47.
260 Tuyen's remark about Vietnam: Karnow, Vietnam, 280.
260 Tuyen's experiences: Author's interviews, Tuyen, March 1996.
261 Bundy on suicide: FRUS, Vietnam, Aug.–Dec. 1963, 556.
261 de Gaulle's predictions: Ibid., 568–69.
261 Rusk's testimony: Ibid., 573.
261 "certain that the ground": Ibid., 577.
262 "a dazzling display": Forrestal memo, Nov. 13, 1963, JFK Library, NSF, Country File, Vietnam, Box 204.
262 Forrestal on McNamara's interruptions: FRUS, Vietnam, Aug.–Dec. 1963, 593–94.
262 Cooper compares Bundy and McNamara: Author's interview, Chester Cooper, Washington, D.C., Feb. 1999.
262 "I even want to think about whether": Schlesinger, RFK, II, 722.
262 Lodge's views on democracy: FRUS, Vietnam, Aug.–Dec. 1963, 609.
263 "Mr. Secretary, it isn't gonna": Newman, 435.
263 Colby wondered about first step: Ibid.
263 goal of bringing Americans home: JFK press conference, Nov. 12, 1963.
263 Bundy on McNamara at meetings: FRUS, Vietnam, Aug.–Dec. 1963, 625.
264 "If anybody really wanted to shoot": Warren Commission Report, New York Times edition, xxxvii.
264 "Mr. President, you can't say": Ibid., xxxiii.
265 Dialogue at budget meeting: Shapley, 271–72; McNamara, In Retrospect, 90.
265 Taylor's naps: John Taylor, 289.
265 "We have a new president": Rusk, 296.
266 Bundy in Oval Office: McGeorge Bundy, personal memorandum, Bundy archive.
266 McNamara at Andrews: Shapley, 275.
267 "My own hunch": McGeorge Bundy memo to LBJ, Nov. 3, 1963, LBJ Library, NSF, Country File, Vietnam, Box 1.
267 CIA briefing: Johnson, Vantage, 22.

267   Lodge disclaims deaths: *FRUS, Vietnam*, Aug.–Dec. 1963, 635.
268   Johnson on Vietnam strategy: Ibid.
268   McCone's reaction: Ibid., 637.
268   Johnson-Moyers dialogue: Moyers, "Flashbacks," *Newsweek*, Feb. 10, 1975, 76.
269   Johnson ends restriction on sabotage: Newman, 466.
269   Johnson suspects Vietnam reporting: Johnson, *Vantage*, 63.
269   McNamara's airport optimism: Karnow, 325.
270   "Who's in charge here?": Don, 133.
270   Minh on speeches: *FRUS, Vietnam*, Aug.–Dec. 1963, 708.
270   situation is "very disturbing": Ibid., 732.
270   "Vietcong progress has been great": Ibid., 733.
271   "Indecisive and drifting": Ibid., 732.
271   Minh prefers orchids: Karnow, *Vietnam*, 324.
271   "watch the situation very carefully": *FRUS, Vietnam*, Aug.–Dec. 1963, 735.
271   Johnson's disrespect for Chiefs: McMaster, 52–53.
271   "Just let me get elected": Karnow, *Vietnam*, 326.
272   Johnson disturbed by caricatures: LBJ Library, Tape K6312.01, Dec. 1, 1963.
272   "Could I drop by": Ibid.
272   "I just hear that sweet voice": Ibid., Dec. 2, 1963.
272   RFK resentments: Schlesinger, *RFK*, II, 654–56.

SIX: KHANH (1964)

275   Khanh-Wilson conversation: *FRUS, Vietnam*, 1964, 30.
275   de Gaulle's policies: Shaplen, 232.
276   Khanh's rumors: *FRUS, Vietnam*, 1964, 36.
276   Lodge promises to share information: Ibid., 39.
276   "I do not know anyone": JFK Library, Bundy memo: LBJ Library, NSF, Country File, Vietnam, Box 1.
277   Khanh raised by actress: Karnow, *Vietnam*, 336.
278   Lodge's instructions to Nes: LBJ Library, Nes OH, 9.
278   "Oh," Khiem said: Karnow, *Vietnam*, 336.
278   Don's experiences: Don, 122–24.
278   Don's reactions: Ibid., 133.
279   "If we could have neutralization": *FRUS, Vietnam*, 1964, 56.
279   Khanh "should treat deposed members": Ibid., 52.
280   De Silva's prediction: Ibid., 66.
280   Mansfield on Vietnam: Olson, 129.
280   Fulbright's two choices: Dallek, 105.
280   "Bob," Johnson said: McNamara, *In Retrospect*, 112.
281   Jack Kennedy coached in German: Richard Reeves, 536.
281   "Vietnam, go to sleep!": Don, 126.
281   McNamara's doubts: McNamara, *In Retrospect*, 113.
281   Nes's predictions: *FRUS, Vietnam*, 1964, 91.
281   Joint Chiefs' recommendations: Ibid., 111.
282   Rostow's recommendation: Ibid., 105.
282   Pentagon bombing plans: Ibid., 363–65.
282   "Hickenlooper said they had to stand": LBJ Library, Tape WH6405.10, Side A, 31519–21, May 27, 1964.
282   "I think that's good thinking": Ibid., Tape WH6405.11, Side A, 3539–40, May 27, 1964.
283   LBJ-Russell conversation: Ibid., Tape WH6405.10, Side A, 31519–21, May 27, 1964.
284   Gallup poll: Dallek, 106.
284   Lodge on need for high commissioner: *FRUS, Vietnam*, 1964, 346.

285   "McNamara's War": McNamara, *In Retrospect*, 118.

286   Greene and LeMay strategies: *FRUS, Vietnam*, 1964, 149–50, n. 3.

286   McCone's recommendation: Ibid., 164, n. 18.

286   Hilsman's recommendation: Ibid., 178.

287   Bundy-LBJ conversation: LBJ Library, Tape WH6405.10, Side B, 3522–23, May 27, 1964.

288   "then it must be because we can't read": Ibid.

288   "What John F. Kennedy started": Steel, 547.

289   "Well, what's the French plan?": Ibid., 549.

289   Ball's report to Rusk: *FRUS, Vietnam*, 1964, 401.

290   Sullivan's instructions to Seaborn: Ibid., 352–55.

290   Politburo reaction: McNamara's Hanoi conference, 1997.

290   William Bundy's Congressional resolution: *FRUS, Vietnam*, 1964, 356–58.

290   Don's trial at Dalat: Don, 126.

291   CIA and neutralist suspicions: Author's interview, William Kohlmann, Southern California, 1997–99.

292   Westmoreland's response to Khanh and McNamara: Westmoreland, 64.

292   McNamara's description of Westmoreland: McNamara, *In Retrospect*, 21.

292   Khanh's flight: Westmoreland, 65.

294   "I don't need that little runt to win": Dallek, 139.

294   "I remember well your saying": *FRUS, Vietnam*, 1964, 522.

294   "Bobby's a very controversial man": LBJ Library, Tape WH6406.09, Side B, 3761–62, June 17, 1964.

294   LBJ-Bundy on Vietnam ambassador: LBJ Library, Tape WH6406.09, Side A, 3748, June 16, 1964.

295   Gilpatric's reputation: Shapley, 205–17.

296   LBJ and McNamara on Vietnam ambassador: Ibid.

296   Pentagon cool to multinational force: *FRUS, Vietnam*, 1964, 526.

296   Gallup poll on U.N. army: Dallek, 147.

296   Rusk-Alphand exchange: *FRUS, Vietnam*, 1964, 533–37.

297   "We won't abandon Saigon": LBJ Library, Tape WH6406.10, Side A, June 17, 1964.

297   "I could have helped you": Shesol, 207.

297   "A large part of the reason": Schlesinger, *RFK*, II, 691.

297   LBJ-Clifford exchange: Dallek, 142.

298   "Sorry I took so many of you": Shesol, 209.

298   "that damned albatross": Dallek, 142.

299   "He tells so many lies": Schlesinger, *RFK*, II, 692.

299   First *Maddox* reports: *FRUS, Vietnam*, 1964, 589.

299   Ky's boasting: Ibid., 577, n. 3.

299   LBJ twits Wheeler: Author's telephone interview, Thomas Hughes, Sept. 29, 1999.

300   "falsified version": *FRUS, Vietnam*, 1964, 589.

300   Giap's instructions: McNamara's Hanoi Conference, 1997.

300   LBJ press conference: *FRUS, Vietnam*, 1964, 597.

300   Range of U.S. guns: Ibid., 602.

300   "Such an attitude": Ibid., 593.

300   Khanh was "kicking up": Ibid., 602.

300   "The damned fool just ought to": LBJ Library, Tape, Aug. 4, 1964.

301   *Maddox* reports ships disappeared: *FRUS, Vietnam*, 1964, 604.

301   McNamara prepares options: Ibid., 605.

301   "Review of action makes many reported": Ibid., 609; McNamara, *In Retrospect*, 133.

301   "whether or not the objective": Beschloss, *Taking Charge*, 494.

301   "bombing the hell out of the Vietnamese": LBJ Library, Tape, Aug. 4, 1964.

301   "Certain that the original ambush": McNamara, *In Retrospect*, 133.

302   Rusk and McCone reactions: *FRUS, Vietnam*, 1964, 611.

302 "Mr. President, I urge you" and Johnson's response: Ball, 379–80.
302 LBJ with Congressional leaders: *FRUS, Vietnam*, 1964, 615.
303 "We are trying to get across": Ibid.
303 Hickenlooper's opinion: Ibid., 617.
303 Johnson's remarks: Ibid., 618.
303 Mansfield's response: Ibid., 620.
304 "I will support it": Ibid., 621.
304 Johnson waits to make announcement: LBJ Library, Tape, Aug. 4, 1964, 9:15 P.M.
304 "I'd sure as hell hate to have": Ibid.
304 Johnson goes on the air: *FRUS, Vietnam*, 1964, 626.
304 Reston's praise: *New York Times*, Aug. 6, 1964, 8.
304 I. F. Stone's response: Stone, *Torment*, 198.
305 "You know that resolution": Dallek, 150.
305 Bundy's "Don't": Author's interview, Francis Bator, Cambridge, Mass., June 18, 1998.
306 "see things in their complexity": DiLeo, 27.
306 "a terrifyingly open-ended": Ball, 380.
306 Johnson calls for roll call: Johnson, *Vantage*, 118.
306 "Are we now giving": *Congressional Record*, Aug. 6, 1964, 17825.
306 "present" votes: LBJ Library, Tape, Aug. 6, 1964, 12:46 P.M.
307 "War cannot be declared": *Congressional Record*, Aug. 7, 1964, 17858.
307 "He's just no good": LBJ Library, Tape, Aug. 7, 1964, 3:01 P.M.
307 Foreman's criticism: Beschloss, *Taking Charge*, 507, n. 5.
307 "little shitass": LBJ Library, Tape, Aug. 7, 1964, 3:01 P.M.
307 "Hell, those dumb, stupid sailors": Ball, 379.
307 "tell Rostow to button his lip": Author's interview, James Thomson, Nov. 11, 1995.
307 Khanh with Alden Sibley: *FRUS, Vietnam*, 1964, 665–66.
308 Seaborn in Hanoi: Ibid., 653, n. 2.
308 Khanh's "state of urgency": *Time*, Aug. 14, 1964, 20.
308 "Our candidate is Khanh": *FRUS, Vietnam*, 1964, 708.
308 anti-Catholic activity in Da Nang: *Time*, Sept. 4, 1964, 39.
309 Oanh's statements on Khanh: Ibid., 34; Westmoreland, 72.
309 Khanh offers Don and others positions: Don, 130.
309 Teletype conference with Washington: *FRUS, Vietnam*, 1964, 764.
309 Colonel Homan and Scotch: Westmoreland, 74.
310 Taylor's warning to Minh and Khanh: *FRUS, Vietnam*, 1964, 772.
310 "as a parting shot": Ibid.
310 "Mr. President," said Rusk: LBJ Library, Tape, Aug. 17, 1964, 8:10 P.M.
310 Robert Kennedy's candidacy: Shesol, 212–13.
311 Mississippi Freedom Democratic Party: Merle Miller, 392.
311 Johnson at convention: Dallek, 167.
311 Johnson's acceptance speech: Merle Miller, 393.
311 "look for a scapegoat": Johnson, *Vantage*, 94.
311 "How many applauses?": Beschloss, *Taking Charge*, 543.
312 "When he shall die": Shakespeare, *Romeo and Juliet*, Act III, scene 2.
312 The Lao political front: Called the Neo Lao Hak Sat.
312 not "take a single needle and thread": *77 Conversations*, 68.
313 Mao with Sihanouk: Ibid., 71–73.
313 Mao predicts Chiang expelled from United Nations: *77 Conversations*, 71. The expulsion occurred in 1971.
313 China gives half a billion: The estimate—from 1955 to 1965—comes from Soviet analysts with no motive to inflate the figure. *77 Conversations*, 16.
313 "fight for one hundred years": Ibid., 74.
314 "You beat the French": Ibid., 76.

314 Khrushchev's attitude toward Mao: *Khrushchev Remembers*, 462–67.
314 "Chiang Kai-shek wants the United States to use the bomb": Li Zhisu, 262.
314 "The relationship between politics and numbers": Short, 480.
315 Famine kills perhaps thirty million Chinese: Ibid., 505n.
315 Le Duan's policy changes: Author's interviews, Hanoi, 1996–99.
315 Ball dictates arguments: DiLeo, 65.
315 Ball's secrecy: Ball, 380.
315 Ball's background: DiLeo, 1–2.
316 Ball's lack of rapport with JFK: JFK Library, Joseph Alsop OH, 96.
316 Ball on Robert Kennedy: DiLeo, 142.
316 LBJ on Ball as schoolteacher: Ball, 377–78.
317 Ball's memorandum: Ibid., 383.
317 McNamara's reaction: DiLeo, 103; LBJ Library, Ball OH, July 8, 1971.
317 Rusk's reaction: DiLeo, 111.
318 Ball and Reston: Ibid., 122.
318 "a general petering out": Bird, *Color*, 290.
318 Bill Bundy on de Gaulle: Author's interviews, William Bundy, Princeton, New Jersey, 1998–99.
318 Pentagon war games: Bird, *Color*, 292.
319 Bill Bundy on a Communist South Vietnam: Ibid., 293.
319 Taylor picks Phuc Yen airfield: *FRUS, Vietnam, 1964*, 824.
319 "Old beyond his years": Ibid., 858.
319 Huong's appointment: *New York Times*, Oct. 3, 1964, 9.
319 Rusk's cable about American elections: *FRUS, Vietnam, 1964*, 878.
320 Results of 1964 election: Dallek, 184.
320 Republican state losses: Merle Miller, 402.
320 Politburo and NLF evaluations: Author's interviews, Hanoi, May 1998.
320 poetical view of Lao trails: Author's interview, Nguyen Khac Huyen, Hanoi, May 18, 1998.
322 "It seems to me": James Thomson, "How Could Vietnam Happen?" *Atlantic Monthly*, April 1968, 51.
322 William Bundy's reversal: Bird, *Color*, 295.
322 "Admiral Mustin didn't like it": Ellsberg, unpublished memoir.
322 "no hurry": Bird, *Color*, 296.
323 Khanh calls for expanded war: *New York Times*, Nov. 7, 1964, 4.
323 Ky's advice: Westmoreland, 73.
323 "completely dismayed the staunchest": Ibid., 93.
323 Don's reaction to Taylor: Don, 138.
323 "have had an effect": *FRUS, Vietnam, 1964*, 998.
323 Khanh dissolves council: Don, 138–39.
324 It had been a wasted dinner: *FRUS, Vietnam, 1964*, 1053.
324 "calculated asperity": Westmoreland, 94.
324 Khanh-Taylor dialogue: *FRUS, Vietnam, 1964*, 1021–23.
324 "You *have* to punish the Young Turks": Author's interview, Nguyen Khanh, Lubbock, Texas, April 16, 1999.
325 Taylor seeks travel funds: *FRUS, Vietnam, 1964*, 1023, n. 5.
325 Young Turks' quandary: Don, 140.
325 Ky's complaint to reporter: *FRUS, Vietnam, 1964*, 1055.
325 "to carry out the policy of any": *New York Times*, Dec. 23, 1964, 1.
326 Khanh asked for anti-American demonstrations: Ibid., Dec. 24, 1964, 1.
326 Lansdale's recommendation: *FRUS, Vietnam, 1964*, 1040.
326 Conein and Khanh: Author's interview, Ho Chi Minh City, May 1998.
326 General Francis Brink: Westmoreland, 89.
327 Nguyen Thanh Xuan's mission: Karnow, *Vietnam*, 408–9.

327   Brink casualties: *FRUS, Vietnam,* 1964, 1049.
327   "Hanoi will get word": Ibid., 1043.
327   "give this signal a very mixed": Ibid., 1051.
327   Target 36: Ibid.
327   Wheeler's recommendation: Ibid., 1050.
328   It was Winston Churchill: Ibid., 1052.
328   widow v. Dempsey: Dallek, 242.
328   "They hate this stuff": Halberstam, *Best,* 605–6, 614–15.
328   Alsop column: Dallek, 244.
328   "I simply do not understand": *FRUS, Vietnam,* 1964, 1058.
328   "the most sensitive, persistent": Ibid.
329   "I am ready to look with great favor": Ibid., 1059.
329   "disengage ourselves": Ibid., 1062.
329   McNamara brushes aside Taylor: McNamara, *In Retrospect,* 164.
329   Kham's view of battle: Author's interviews, Ho Chi Minh City, 1996–99.
331   U.S. losses in battle: *FRUS, Vietnam,* 1965, 29.
331   "showed they were capable": *New York Times,* Jan. 3, 1965, 1.

SEVEN: BALL (1965)

333   "What we want to say": *FRUS, Vietnam,* 1965, 95.
333   "They feel that we": Ibid., 96.
333   "The first option": Ibid.
334   "Bob and I do not think": Ibid., 97.
334   LBJ's reverence for education: Merle Miller, 407.
334   Johnson sees dilemma as two women: Kearns, 251–52.
334   "offer a priceless advantage": Dallek, 247.
334   Delay of DeSoto patrols: *FRUS, Vietnam,* 1965, 123.
335   Hiep's planning: Author's interview, Dang Vu Hiep, Hanoi, May 1998.
335   "I know a damn good": LBJ Library, Confidential File, undated memorandum to Mc-George Bundy.
335   Hertz kidnapping: Cooper, 257.
335   Bundy-Khanh meeting: *FRUS, Vietnam,* 1965, 153.
336   Thuan on Ngo brothers' murders: Author's interview, Tran Quang Thuan, Los Angeles, Jan. 6, 1998.
336   "sharp confrontation": Bird, *Color,* 306.
336   Bundy found the Buddhists opaque: Cooper, 257.
337   Pleiku casualties: *Dictionary of the Vietnam War,* 372; Kutler, *Encyclopedia,* 439–40.
337   Westmoreland on Bundy: Westmoreland, 115.
337   Westmoreland and base security: Ibid., 115–16.
337   LBJ reads projected casualties: *FRUS, Vietnam,* 1965, 156.
337   Ball's evaluation of meeting: Ball, 389.
338   Thompson on Kosygin's visit: Ibid., 390.
338   "We are not now": *FRUS, Vietnam,* Jan.–June 1965, 157.
338   Mansfield on war with China: Johnson, *Vantage,* 125.
338   Bill Bundy's response to Mansfield: Gibbons, III, 61–64.
338   "We have kept our gun": Johnson, *Vantage,* 124–25.
338   "If those guys would only": Cooper, 259.
338   Khanh's reaction to retaliation: Westmoreland, 116.
338   Bundy looks stricken: Bird, *Color,* 307.
338   Cooper on Bundy: Author's interview, Chester Cooper, Washington, D.C., Feb. 19, 1997.
339   LBJ orders dependents evacuated: *FRUS, Vietnam,* 1965, 161; Westmoreland, 118.

339   U.S. bombing results: *FRUS, Vietnam*, 1965, 167.
339   Gerald Ford's question: Ibid., 168.
339   Ky's bombing raid: Ky, 58.
339   Bundy memorandum: *FRUS, Vietnam*, 1965, 175–77.
340   94 targets identified: Johnson, *Vantage*, 128.
341   Ball on military's Catch-22: Ball, 389.
341   Qui Nhon bombing: Author's observation, 1965.
341   Qui Nhon as site of largest U.S. casualties: Westmoreland, 117; he identifies the Korean doctor as Captain Un Sup Kim.
        Although Johnson's "More Flags Program" never produced the support he sought, several nations supplied troops. At the peak year of 1968, South Korea put nearly 50,000 infantrymen and Marines into South Vietnam, the largest number sent by any U.S. ally.
        Four signatories to SEATO also supplied troops: Australia provided a 30-member training team as early as 1962; its highest number came in 1969 with 7,672. New Zealand dispatched a nominal thousand soldiers and artillery support forces. The Philippines sent 2,000 combat engineers in February 1966. By 1969, Thailand had a total approaching 12,000 combat soldiers. To avoid retaliation by China, Taiwanese advisers from their first arrival in 1964 were limited to medicine, agriculture and engineering.
342   contradictory messages about sites: Westmoreland, 117.
342   LBJ does not tell congressional leaders: *FRUS, Vietnam*, 1965, 225.
342   "further direct provocations": Westmoreland, 117.
342   LBJ rejects explaining policy: Bird, *Color*, 308.
342   Thompson and Dobrynin: *FRUS, Vietnam*, 1965, 173, and n. 2.
342   "what was to be gained": Ibid., 230.
342   "why don't you run Malaysia": Ibid., 231.
343   "I'm finally working": Author's interview, James Thomson, Cambridge, Mass., Oct. 11, 1995.
343   Thomson's memo to Cooper: *FRUS, Vietnam*, 1965, 228–29.
343   Dodd and Dirksen speeches: Bird, *Color*, 309.
343   Bundy hears out Thomson: Ibid., 299.
343   "For us to shoulder": "Inheritor of a Wretched War," *New York Times Sunday Magazine*, Nov. 1964.
343   "Any true professional": Ibid.
343   Taylor presses for bombing: Westmoreland, 118.
344   Joint Chiefs' targets: Gibson, 324.
344   Choice of fighter-bombers: Westmoreland, 119.
344   Joint Chiefs prepare for more bombing: Gibson, 325.
344   Westmoreland's view of bombing: Westmoreland, 119.
344   Le Duan's plan for victory: Duiker, *Road*, 261–62; author's interviews, Hanoi, 1996–99.
345   "Let's act, then see": Duiker, *Road*, 261–62.
345   Kennedy to Guthman: Author's interview, Edwin Guthman, Los Angeles, Nov. 30, 1998.
345   "We must understand": Guthman, 319.
345   Politics delay Rolling Thunder: Ky, 57.
346   "If you can't get tougher": Ibid., 60.
346   Ky's divorce and marriage: Ibid., 71.
346   "I know what you mean": Ibid., 60.
346   "I think something has happened": Ibid., 61.
346   Khanh chased through Saigon: Don, 140.
346   "I don't think I can": Ky, 61.
346   "You have my full authority": Ibid., 62.
347   "Well, Ky,": Ibid., 63.
347   "I think the time has come": Don, 141.
347   Friend's epitaph for Thao: Tang, 62.

348   "If Da Nang needs better protection": *FRUS, Vietnam*, 1965, 347.
348   "White-faced soldier": Ibid., 348.
348   Westmoreland's request: Ibid., 394, n. 3.
348   Mao's aid for Vietnam: Parker, 44.
348   Chinese claim not undercutting: *New York Times*, April 2, 1965, 16.
348   RPG-2s come by sea: Parker, 61.
349   Mao on not joining war: Ibid., 57.
349   "as long as China itself": *New York Times*, Feb. 12, 1965, 1.
349   Mao's prediction: Parker, 51.
349   Eisenhower's views: *FRUS, Vietnam*, 1965, 298–301.
349   McNaughton's memo: Ibid., 427–32.
350   Hiep's reaction to landing: Author's interview, Dang Vu Hiep, Hanoi, May 15, 1998.
350   Westmoreland on nuclear shells: Westmoreland, 125.
351   battalions' name changed: Ibid., 126.
351   "Do you know my terms": Ibid., 125.
351   Westmoreland requests third battalion: *FRUS, Vietnam*, 1965, 454.
351   Taylor's memo on Westmoreland request: Ibid., 456.
351   U.S. planes allowed to bomb in the South: *FRUS, Vietnam*, Jan.–June 1965, 379.
352   Embassy casualties: Ibid., 494.
352   Harold Johnson's recommendations: McNamara, *In Retrospect*, 177.
352   Sharp and Joint Chiefs' requests: Ibid., 179.
352   Rusk, McNamara, Bundy's successful argument: Ibid.
352   change in U.S. role: Ibid.
352   "should be understood as being": Bird, *Color*, 312.
352   LBJ's response to protests: Johnson, *Vantage*, 132.
352   "as soon as possible": Ibid., 133.
353   "bigger and more imaginative": Bird, *Color*, 315.
353   "Walter," said the president: Ibid., 318.
353   "I'm not just going": Ibid.
354   "Bomb, bomb, bomb!": Dallek, 254.
354   "more ideas, and more horsepower": Ibid., 256.
354   Kennedy-Johnson exchange about Rusk: Shesol, 297.
354   "Light at the end": Dallek, 255.
354   Bundy on South Vietnam as nation: Bird, *Color*, 327.
354   "We must stay": Berman, *Planning*, 9.
354   "The vast Mekong River": Dallek, 261.
355   "Ho will never be able": Ibid.
355   Politburo had been preparing Dong's speech: Author's interviews, Hanoi, 1996–99.
355   Politburo's Four Points: *FRUS, Vietnam*, 1965, 544–45.
355   Politburo prepared to negotiate: McNamara's conference, Hanoi, June 1997.
356   Mao agrees to send support troops: Author's interviews, Hanoi, 1996–99.
356   Ball on Dong's response: *FRUS, Vietnam*, 1965, 587.
356   "full of lies": Johnson, *Vantage*, 134.
356   "noisy propaganda": Ibid.
356   Hayden's aspirations: Author's interview, Tom Hayden, Los Angeles, Dec. 9, 1999.
356   Port Huron statement: Hayden, 93–96.
357   "issues arise together": Gitlin, 103.
357   "I must say to you": Ibid., 177.
357   "We Won't Go" petitions: Ibid., 180.
357   SDS slogans: Ibid., 183.
357   "I do not believe": Bird, *Color*, 317.
357   "We must name that system": Gitlin, 184.
358   "if your letter came to me for grading": Bird, *Color*, 318.
358   Bundy rules out Morganthau: Ibid.

358   Bundy's "freedom vs. Castro": Dallek, 264.
358   "We are trying to stop": Ibid., 263.
359   "has turned in a terrible record": Bird, *Color*, 318.
360   "we are in danger": Merle Miller, *Lyndon*, 422.
360   "Let these words": Ibid., 423.
361   "Some of them insult me": Dallek, 281.
361   "just be available": Currey, *Lansdale*, 291.
361   "And I don't think": J. Taylor, 311.
361   "Max has been gallant": LBJ Library, McG. Bundy memo to LBJ, March 1965, NSF, "Deployment of US Forces to Vietnam," cited in J. Taylor, 312.
362   Ky appreciates buffet: Ky, 64.
363   "I resign": Ibid., 65.
363   "Why is my dear friend Quat": Ibid.
363   "No, no, no!": Ibid., 67.
363   "I am ready to accept": Ibid., 68.
363   Dodd wins Lansdale a position: Currey, *Lansdale*, 292.
364   "Go with me": Ibid.
364   *Newsweek* on Lansdale: Ibid., 293.
364   Lansdale as miracle worker: Ibid.
364   Ellsberg's background: Ellsberg, unpublished memoir.
364   Ellsberg's view of Lansdale: Currey, *Lansdale*, 296.
364   Ellsberg and documents: Ibid., 297.
365   Ho's call to Vietnamese: McNamara, *In Retrospect*, 198.
365   Children's response to countryside: Author's interview, Nguyen Dinh Phuong, Bellagio, Italy, July 1998.
365   "just as we say any settlement": Kahin, 328.
365   "the third of those four points": Rusk, 460.
365   Politburo approach to unity: McNamara, *Argument*, 148.
365   Washington's advice to Westmoreland: Westmoreland, 131–32.
365   "I'm sure you realize": Ibid., 139.
366   Westmoreland unhappy with LBJ's evasion: Ibid., 135.
366   McNamara on troop requests: Ibid., 142.
366   Ball's memo: Ball, 395.
366   "I told McNamara": *FRUS, Vietnam*, June–Dec. 1965, 33.
366   "Look," Deputy Secretary Ball would say: DiLeo, 99.
367   Ball teases McNamara: Ball, 174.
367   Bundy arranges debate: Bird, *Color*, 320. Gordon Goldstein, who worked with Bundy on his memoirs, says Bundy told him the initiative came from Friendly. Author's telephone interview, July 28, 2000.
367   "Do you see this?" Ibid., 323.
367   Moyers to Goodwin: Ibid., 324.
368   Johnson on liberals: Dallek, 281.
368   "Try to be tonight": Bird, *Color*, 321.
368   "I am forced to conclude": Ibid.
368   "my debater": Ibid., 325.
369   Moyers sent to fire Bundy: Moyers, LBJ Staff Roundtable Discussion, Austin, Texas, May 12, 1999.
369   "Suppose I wanted to get out of government": McGeorge Bundy interview with Fredrik Logevall, New York City, April 15, 1994.
369   "well aware that we place": *FRUS, Vietnam*, June–Dec. 1965, 47.
369   Bundy to Ball, Ibid., 49.
370   "the tide almost certainly": Berman, *Planning*, 79.
370   "easier to identify": Ibid., 80.
370   "press the Chinese": Ibid., 81.
370   "Even though casualties": Ibid.

370 "My first reaction": FRUS, Vietnam, June–Dec. 1965, 90.
370 "But this is a slippery slope": Ibid.
370 "The paper also omits": Ibid.
370 "If it is to get to the conference": Ibid.
371 Bundy presses McNamara to resist: Ibid., 334.
371 "This could be a quagmire": Clifford, 410.
371 "the Communist world would draw": McNamara, In Retrospect, 195.
371 Bill Bundy's middle way: Bird, Color, 334.
371 "I find that both Rusk": FRUS, Vietnam, June–Dec. 1965, 116.
372 "So they would tend to cluster": Ibid., 117.
372 "My hunch is": Ibid.
372 Bundy's paper on France and U.S.: Ibid., 79.
372 "would quickly succumb": Ibid., 81.
372 "France was never united": Ibid., 82.
372 "they have stimulated extensive": Ibid., 83.
372 Harris poll results: Ibid., 84.
373 Ball's wire to Saigon embassy: Ibid., 123.
373 Westmoreland's plans through 1966: Ibid., 118–19.
373 "We are about to get our noses": Bird, Chairman, 576.
373 Arthur Dean's objection to negotiating: McNamara, In Retrospect, 197.
374 "The mustache": Bird, Chairman, 578.
374 "We know ourselves," Johnson to McNamara: LBJ Library, Tape 6507.02, July 14, 1965, 6:15 P.M.
374 "Almost surely": McNamara, In Retrospect, 201.
374 Chinese engineers arrive in North: Author's interviews, Hanoi, 1996–99.
375 "Speaking in human terms": FRUS, Vietnam, June–Dec. 1965, 147.
375 "You just cannot believe": Ibid., 148.
375 "This is a monstrous statement": Ibid., 149.
376 Kosygin on Ho: Ibid., 152.
376 "people with the noise of bombs": Ibid.
376 Westmoreland's estimates: Westmoreland, 142.
376 Thieu briefs McNamara: FRUS, Vietnam, June–Dec. 1965, 160.
377 Vance's cable to McNamara: Ibid., 162–63.
377 Dialogue at July 21 meeting: Ibid., 190–91.
377 "If so, I'd like to hear from them": Ibid.
378 "But let me be clear": Ibid. In Ball's memoir (399–403), he recapitulates the arguments in detail but omits his promise to support whatever decision Johnson reaches.
378 "Can we make a case": FRUS, Vietnam, June–Dec. 1965, 190–91.
378 "I don't think we ought": Ibid., 193.
379 Raborn on task force: Ibid., 195.
379 "No great captain in history": Ball, 400–401.
379 "That's the key question": Ibid., 401.
379 "I think we have underestimated": FRUS, Vietnam, June–Dec. 1965, 194.
379 "The world, the country": Ball, 402.
379 Clark Clifford invited: FRUS, Vietnam, June–Dec. 1965, 210n.
379 Admiral McDonald's remarks: Ibid., 210.
380 Wallace Greene's recommendation: Ibid., 214.
380 "It can't be helped.": Ibid., 216.
380 Johnson's civilian casualty figures: Ibid.
380 "But if you make a commitment": Ibid.
380 Ford on calling up the reserves: Ibid., 217.
381 Ball on Clifford: Ball, 402–403.
381 Clifford's notes: Clifford, 413–14.
381 "This war is like a prize fight": Ibid., 415.
381 Ball and Clifford: Ibid., 415. Ball (402) calls their meeting place the Fish Room.

382   "George, don't pay any attention": Clifford, 417.
382   Clifford on McNamara: Ibid.
382   Goldberg leaves U.S. Supreme Court: Dallek, 234.
383   "I hate this war": Clifford, 420.
383   Johnson increases draft: *FRUS, Vietnam*, June–Dec. 1965, 273.
383   "instruct officials and spokesmen": Ibid., 221.
384   "when the figures would be firmer": Dallek, 276.
384   "Goddammit, Bob, that's what's wrong": McNamara, *In Retrospect*, 205.
384   "drowned in the wasteful ravages": Dallek, 276.
384   "press conference came alive": Berman, *Planning*, 151.
385   "If you have a mother-in-law": Dallek, 277.
385   Safer's Cam Ne report: Wyatt, 145.
385   "Frank, are you trying to fuck me?": Halberstam, *Powers*, 490.
385   Buchwald on Goldwater: Buchwald, 1–2.
386   XYZ overture: Herring, *Secret*, 8ff.
386   "could wait some time": Herring, *Secret*, 101.
387   Training of Kinnard's men: Perry, 156.
387   22 pounds of food: Schulzinger, 185.
387   porters on bicycles and horses: Moore and Galloway, 52.
387   Kham's reflections on Americans: Author's interview, Ta Minh Kham, Ho Chi Minh City, June 25, 1997.
388   Lieutenant Colonel Risner: The Risner sections combine material from his memoir with a telephone interview, Austin, Texas, July 19, 1999.
388   Risner's bailout: Risner, 9–11.
389   Risner moved to the Zoo: Ibid., 69.
390   Camp commander and *Time* cover: Ibid., 70.
390   "Lord," he said: Ibid., 89.
390   Risner tortured with ropes: Ibid., 93.
391   Risner modifies Code of Conduct: Author's interview, Risner.
391   "I shrivel up inside": Ibid.
391   Clifford's trip to Saigon: Clifford, 426–29.
392   Ky's reaction to Kissinger: Ky, 85.
392   Tri Quang on bombing: Author's interview. Higgins (285) passes along a British report that Tri Quang gave similar advice to Taylor and then told the French he had only done it to lull the Americans.
393   "I am depressed and shaken": Clifford, 432.
393   Kissinger compares Johnson to Gary Cooper, *Time*, Nov. 19, 1965, 31.
393   "cling to their belts": Author's interview, Ta Minh Kham.
394   Johnson calls McCloy "yellow": Isaacson and Thomas, 648.
394   Wyzanski mentions future posts: Bird, *Color*, 343.
394   Ford Foundation monies: McNamara, *In Retrospect*, 325.
394   Bundy not suffering fools: Bird, *Color*, 344.
394   "a smart kid, period": Ibid.
394   Norman Morrison: Hendrickson, 188–89.
395   McNamara's reaction: McNamara, *In Retrospect*, 216.
395   "make sense only if they are": Ibid., 217.
395   Moore's questions: Author's telephone interview, Harold G. Moore, Auburn, Ala., April 16, 2000.
395   Operations officer picks "X-Ray": Moore and Galloway, 51.
396   Termite mounds: Author's telephone interview, Joseph L. Galloway, Washington, D.C., April 19, 2000.
398   "They're PAVN!": Capt. Ramon A. (Tony) Nadal was the officer. Moore and Galloway, 78.
398   running into a wall of lead: Ibid.
398   Moore's command to Hueys: Ibid., 36.
398   practice against straw dummies: Moore and Galloway (122) quote Bill Beck.

400   Vietnamese look like little trees: Moore and Galloway, 146.

400   Dennis Deal's reflection: Ibid., 185.

400   Moore ordered back to Saigon: Author's interview, Harold G. Moore, April 16, 2000.

401   Moore's casualty estimates: Ibid., 199.

401   Smith's account: *Saturday Evening Post*, Jan. 28, 1967, reprinted in *Reporting Vietnam*, pt. I, *American Journalism 1959–1969*; and author's telephone interview, Washington, D.C., Sept. 17, 1999.

405   Bird's initial account: Santoli, 34–43. Bird admits the truth: Author's interview with Bird in New York, October 27, 2001.

407   Johnson talks of resigning: Dallek, 522.

408   "preparatory to knocking hell": Ibid., 341.

408   "We have stopped losing": McNamara, *In Retrospect*, 222.

408   "We're getting deeper and deeper": FRUS, *Vietnam*, June–Dec. 1965, 620.

408   "He wants to let the Commies in": Ibid., 621.

408   "It comes ahead of poverty": Ibid.

408   Rusk and Hungary's foreign minister: Ibid., 431.

409   McNamara polls congressmen: Ibid., 634–35.

409   "I was in charge of bombing surveys": Ibid., 645.

410   "I can take on the Chiefs": Ibid., 646.

410   "I know exactly what the arguments": Ibid., 647.

410   "The weakest link in our armor": Ibid.

410   Stevenson-Sevareid interview: Ibid., 572–74.

411   "You must think of the morale": Ibid., 660.

411   "The greatest danger of leaks": Ibid., 663. A slightly different version appears in Clifford, 435.

411   "Magnificent—to sum up": Clifford, 436.

412   "We'll take the pause": Dallek, 344.

412   U.S. diplomatic offensive: McNamara, *In Retrospect*, 226–27.

412   Ho relinquishes control and muses on successors: Author's interviews, Hanoi, 1995–99.

413   Le Duan criticizes Beijing: Hoang Van Hoan, 328.

413   Rusk's Fourteen Points: FRUS, *Vietnam*, June–Dec. 1965, 706–7.

413   Hanoi's rejoinder to points: McNamara, *Argument*, 234.

414   Zhou Enlai's warning: 77 *Conversations*, 92, n. 39.

EIGHT: SALISBURY (1966)

416   Tito's advice: FRUS, *Vietnam*, 1966, 5.

416   de Gaulle sneers at peace feelers: Ibid.

416   "the lines are nearly all out": Ibid.

416   Bo in Paris: Herring, *Secret*, 110.

417   McNamara challenges Chiefs on pause: McNamara, *In Retrospect*, 227.

417   "Every day makes a difference": Dallek, 348.

417   Ball on Foreign Relations Committee: Ibid.

417   Russell on casualties: Ibid., 349.

417   Polling on bombing pause: Ibid., 350.

417   McNamara on New Year's Eve: Author's interview, Ben Bradlee, Washington, D.C., Feb. 23, 1999.

418   McNamara at Schlesinger's: Bird, *Color*, 345.

418   McNamara with Wise Men: Clifford, 437.

418   U.S. bombs dropped on Vietnam: McNamara, *In Retrospect*, 228.

418   "We must fight the war where": Clifford, 437.

418   "Get this to Rusk": LBJ Library, Confidential File ND 19/CO230, Box 71.

418   Valenti on Steinbeck: Ibid.

419 Gavin in *Harper's:* The February 1966 issue was released on Jan. 16.

419 Wheeler to McNamara on enclaves: *FRUS, Vietnam,* 1966, 196–201.

419 Senate Hearings: *The Vietnam Hearings* (New York, 1966), 109. All three networks had begun showing the hearings, but by the time Kennan testified, CBS had returned to its scheduled reruns of *I Love Lucy* and *The Real McCoys.* The network's chief of news, Fred W. Friendly, resigned in protest: Zaroulis and Sullivan, 73.

419 Morse-Taylor exchange: United States, *The Vietnam Hearings,* 187.

420 "a very, very disastrous break": LBJ Library, Confidential File ND 19/CO230.

420 Ward Just's report: *Washington Post,* Feb. 27, 1966, 18.

420 "if something happened to Ky": *FRUS, Vietnam,* 1966, 204.

420 "General," he told Westmoreland: Westmoreland, 159.

420 "I hope you don't pull a MacArthur": Ibid.

421 Ky about Taylor: Ky, 82.

421 Ky knew how to talk: *FRUS, Vietnam,* 1966, 218.

421 "In paragraph two": Ky, 83.

421 *"Ong ay noi cai gi the?":* Bui Diem, 162.

421 "Come into my bedroom": Ky, 83.

422 Bundy sees "fantastic" progress: Dallek, 355.

422 LBJ meets with neither Gavin nor Kennan: *FRUS, Vietnam,* 1966, 235–37.

422 Johnson finds Church effective: Ibid., 221.

422 Robert Kennedy breaks with LBJ: Shesol, 285.

422 "I don't think anyone has ever suggested": Ibid., 290.

423 "I'm not their Wayne Morse": Ibid., 293.

423 "danger to one man's life, as such": Bird, *Color,* 347.

423 Rostow on nuclear confrontation: Ibid., 348.

424 "They're saying this is the Yalu": Author's telephone interview, Jack Smith, Washington, D.C., Sept. 17, 1999.

424 Le Duan in China: *77 Conversations,* 94–98.

425 "The Buddhists are crucial": *FRUS, Vietnam,* 1966, 418.

426 "And if the Americans do leave": Ky, 92.

426 Ky-Walt confrontation: Ibid., 97–98.

427 CIA assessment of U.S. bombing: LBJ Library, "An Appraisal of the Bombing of North Vietnam Through 14 May," Intelligence memorandum, Directorate; ibid., through June 14.

427 Kintner's reports to Johnson: LBJ Library, Confidential File, April–May 1966, Box 7 (Goldwater, May 15, 1966; Kennedy, April 28, 1966).

427 Galbraith's letters to Johnson: LBJ Library, Letter 1, Confidential File, April, May, Box 71; Letters 2 and 3, CF ND 19/CO 312.

428 "If you have to fart": Terrill, 329.

429 Ding's mother as "bad element": Steven Mufson, "Recalling 30 Years of Madness," *International Herald Tribune,* May 17, 1996, 2.

429 Lodge at the embassy: LBJ Library, Confidential File, ND19/CO312, July–Dec. 1966.

429 "Quite an unusual enemy": Ibid.

430 Democratic primary elections: Ibid.

430 Ellsberg with McNamara: Ellsberg, unpublished memoirs.

431 McNamara's children: Shapley, 380–81.

431 "Okay, fellas," and McNamara's talk to student crowd: Ibid., 377.

431 McNamara rationalizes his taunt: McNamara, *In Retrospect,* 255.

432 Skybolt controversy: Shapley, 241–43.

432 McNamara considers study of war: McNamara, *In Retrospect,* 256.

432 "I would like to keep in touch": LBJ Library, Confidential File ND19/CO312, July–Dec. 1966, letter to Rep. Jonathan Bingham, Sept. 22, 1966.

432 Symington to Rostow: Ibid.

433 "I know at least one more fellow": Ibid.

433   Salisbury in Hanoi: Salisbury, *Behind*, 10ff.
434   "Imagine!": Ibid., 67.
435   Salisbury in Nam Dinh: *New York Times*, Dec. 17, 1966, 1; Dec. 31, 1966, 3. William Baggs, in North Vietnam as a director of the Center for the Study of Democratic Institutions in Santa Barbara, California, went to Nam Dinh ten days after Salisbury left the country and confirmed his reports: *New York Times*, Jan. 20, 1967, 3.
435   Salisbury's interview with Pham Van Dong: *New York Times*, Jan. 4, 1967, 2.
435   "The party secretary's name": Ibid., Jan. 16, 1967, 1.
436   Howard K. Smith's "careless, erratic": Ibid., Jan. 19, 1967, 3.
436   Baldwin quotes Pentagon: Ibid., Dec. 30, 1966, 1.
436   *Times* editorial: Ibid., Jan. 2, 1967, 12.
436   I. F. Stone on Salisbury's reports: Stone, *Torment*, 395.
437   Salisbury on reporters upsetting people: Author's telephone interview, Stefan Salisbury, Philadelphia, Feb. 3, 1999.

NINE: McNAMARA (1967)

438   "Our air strikes on the railyard": Sharp, 122–23.
438   "The restrictions should be removed": Ibid., 124.
438   Rostow on McNamara's family: Author's interview, Walt Rostow, Austin, Texas, Dec. 15, 1995.
439   Thanh's trip to Hanoi and Politburo debate: "Tet: The 1968 General Offensive and General Uprising" by General Tran Van Tra in Werner and Huynh, 37–41.
440   Giap's response: Author's interviews, Hanoi, 1995–99.
440   effects of bombing the dikes: Davidson, 438.
440   Vietcong preparations; mockup of U.S. Embassy: Author's interview, Dr. Dang Vu Hiep, Ho Chi Minh City, May 1997.
441   "L.B.J. wanted you out": Currey, *Lansdale*, 315.
441   "just as proudly as I looked": Ky, 99.
442   Westmoreland's request: McNamara, *In Retrospect*, 264–65.
442   alternative to annihilation: Westmoreland, 217.
442   Westmoreland's estimates: McNamara, *In Retrospect*, 265.
443   "When we add divisions": Ibid.
443   Samuel Adams disputes army figures: LBJ Library, Samuel A. Adams OH, Sept. 20, 1984, 4–8. On January 23, 1982, CBS broadcast a 90-minute documentary, "The Uncounted Enemy: A Vietnam Deception," for which Adams had been a consultant. Westmoreland filed a suit for well over a hundred million dollars on September 13, 1982, against the network, the producer, the reporter and Adams. The trial opened on October 31, 1984, and went on until a settlement was reached on February 19, 1985. Westmoreland discontinued his suit; CBS issued a statement that the network respected "General Westmoreland's long and faithful service to his country and never intended to assert, and does not believe, that General Westmoreland was unpatriotic or disloyal in performing his duties as he saw them."
443   "The bombing campaign": McNamara, *In Retrospect*, 265.
443   "From the military standpoint, it was fine": Westmoreland, 229.
444   "the hour is growing very, very late": Barrett, *Vietnam Papers*, 417.
444   "an officer of the United States": Ibid., 418.
444   "All that I can say": Ibid., 419–20.
444   Katzenbach moves to State: Author's interview, Robert McNamara, Washington, D.C., Feb. 23, 1999.
445   McNamara and George Woods: Shapley, 414.
445   Offer was "appealing": McNamara, *In Retrospect*, 312.
446   "The Vietnam war is unpopular": Ibid., 266.

446 "The picture of the world's greatest": Ibid., 270.

447 Joint Chiefs' protest: Barrett, *Vietnam Papers*, 429.

447 "a figleaf for withdrawal": Shapley, 421.

447 "Nothing you could do": Barrett, *Vietnam Papers*, 431.

447 Westmoreland's reaction: Westmoreland, 230.

447 Nguyen Chi Thanh's heart attack: Author's interviews, Hanoi, 1995–99.

447 Giap's convalescence: Ibid.

448 "Wipe the sweat off": Risner, 165.

449 Mary McCarthy in Hanoi: Ibid., 174–75. In her book, *The Seventeenth Degree* (New York, 1974), Mary McCarthy characterized Risner as a "widely admired hardliner and Nixon zealot" and was unflattering about his physical appearance. In a review of Risner's *The Passing of the Night* in the March 7, 1974, issue of *The New York Review of Books*, she attacked his "naive sense of his own importance" and his "primitive vanity," although she granted that his behavior on the day they met had been "consonant with his having been tortured." McCarthy was sure, however, that Pham Van Dong, whom she had also interviewed, was too perceptive and intelligent not to find torture "morally repugnant." She concluded that "the full truth of whatever went on in the camps is not yet known." A recent biographer (Kiernan, 603–4) has noted that while Mary McCarthy's recent nonfiction had not been commercially successful, the paperback edition of Risner's book had sold hundreds of thousands of copies.

449 "The North Vietnamese genuinely care": Sontag, 71.

449 Johnson with congressional chairmen: Barrett, *Vietnam Papers*, 452–53.

450 Mansfield changes the subject: Ibid., 453.

450 "Margy got my ulcer": Author's interview, Robert McNamara, Washington, D.C., Feb. 23, 1999; Shapley, 426.

451 "You know, he's a fine man": Ibid., 427.

451 McNamara not tempted to kill himself: Author's interview, Robert McNamara, Washington, D.C., Feb. 23, 1999.

451 "Pennsylvania" peace overture: Cooper, 364–68; Cooper's *The Last Crusade* sets out in detail the many unsuccessful attempts to launch negotiations.

452 "I can't send this": Author's interview, Chester Cooper, Washington, D.C., Feb. 24, 1999.

452 "Where shall I live when I next come": Herring, *Secret*, 722.

452 "He is an old man": Ibid.

453 Hanoi is too dangerous for visitors: Ibid., 730.

453 "I am not worried": McNamara, *In Retrospect*, 284.

453 McNamara's eight-page statement: *New York Times*, Aug. 26, 1967, 4.

453 McNamara's testimony on targets: Shapley, 429.

453 "I am wondering whether or not": McNamara, *In Retrospect*, 290.

454 "I think it is a statement": *Washington Post*, Aug. 26, 1967, 5.

454 McNamara's opinion of Thurmond: Author's interview, Robert McNamara, Washington, D.C., Feb. 23, 1999.

454 "I think from what you have heard": Shapley, 430.

454 "He says if you are right": Ibid., 431.

454 Other officers' view of Wheeler: Ibid., 432.

454 Chiefs' response to resigning: Ibid., 433.

455 Dzu's strategy: Karnow, *Vietnam*, 452.

456 "I still belong": Ky, 156.

457 "underground politburo": Ibid., 157.

457 Votes for Don: Don, 174.

457 U.S. embassy intervenes with Thieu: Karnow, *Vietnam*, 452.

457 Ky could have won larger vote: Ky, 157.

457 "Bo said something like": Barrett, *Vietnam Papers*, 481.

457 "If the bombing isn't having": Ibid., 482.

458   Francis Bator's reaction to Johnson: Author's interview, Cambridge, Mass., Oct. 18, 1996.
458   "You must not go down": Barrett, *Vietnam Papers*, 482.
458   Rusk's fatigue: Author's interview, William Bundy, Princeton, N.J., Oct. 9, 1998; McNamara interview, Washington, D.C., Feb. 23, 1999.
459   "I know this bombing": Barrett, *Vietnam Papers*, 485.
459   SDS opposed any march: Zaroulis and Sullivan, 136.
459   Calvert on sedition: Farrell, *Spirit*, 197.
459   Abbie Hoffman: Zaroulis and Sullivan, 136.
460   "Hell, no!": Ibid., 137.
460   "no significant evidence": Dallek (489) cites LBJ Library, Helms to President, November 15, 1967, NSF, Intelligence File.
460   Rusk on Helms's report: Powers, *Secrets*, 246.
460   McNamara muses on the march: Shapley, 435–36.
461   "would be dangerous": Clifford, 457.
461   "How do we get this conclusion": Barrett, *Vietnam Papers*, 515–22.
461   McNamara notes absences: McNamara, *In Retrospect*, 306.
461   McNamara assures George Allen: Shapley, 422.
462   Bill Bundy on food and drink: Isaacson and Thomas, 698–99.
462   Harriman's relations with Johnson: Author's interview, Chester Cooper, Washington, D.C., Feb. 24, 1999; Isaacson and Thomas, 681.
462   "No matter what we do": Barrett, *Vietnam Papers*, 529.
462   "the end of the road": Ibid., 527.
462   Response to McNamara's memo: McNamara, *In Retrospect*, 310.
463   Rostow on Hanoi: Barrett, *Vietnam Papers*, 524.
463   "McNamara, McNamara, McNamara": Shesol, 393.
464   "It is absolutely horrible": National Security Archives, George Washington University, Washington, D.C., "Account of events prepared for McNamara's *In Retrospect*"; chronology prepared at Lyndon Johnson's behest by Rainer B. Steckman, personal assistant to Woods.
465   Kennedy in Manhattan: Shesol, 394.
465   Kennedy's response to headline: Schlesinger, *RFK*, II, 859.
465   Experiences of Mrs. Chon: Author's interview, Nguyen Thi Chon, Ho Chi Minh City, May 22, 1998.
467   "We have got our opponents": LBJ Library National Security File: Congressional Briefings on Vietnam, November 16, 1967.
467   "I think it's the beginning": Westmoreland, 313.

TEN: CLIFFORD (1968)

468   abbreviated to TCK-TKN: Davidson, 441.
469   General Tran Van Tra's plans: Werner and Huynh, 63.
469   Dang's history and plans for Tet: Author's interview, Ho Chi Minh City, May 25, 1996.
469   McNamara eases bombing halt: Braestrup, I, 75n.
469   Westmoreland on television: Ibid., 36.
470   Discrepancy in VC calendars: Werner and Huynh, 45.
471   25 of Saigon's MPs on duty: Braestrup, I, 79.
471   Zorthian hears of attack: Ibid., 87.
471   Johnson's Tuesday Lunch disrupted: Clifford, 472–73.
472   "This could be very bad": Ibid.
472   Bunker at Lansdale's house: Currey, *Lansdale*, 318.
472   "The Vietcong sent in a few": Braestrup, *Big Story*, Vol. 1, 91n.
473   "My God, yes": Arnett, 243–44.

473   "The Vietcong seized part": Braestrup, I, 94.

474   Jacobson and Vietcong: Arnett, 244.

474   "the enemy's well-laid plans": Ibid.

474   "Christ," John Vann told: Ibid., 231.

474   Statistics on Tet offensive: Wyatt, 181. Arnett (253) has thirty-six provincial hit and sixty-four district centers.

474   mass graves: Arnett, 247.

475   "It became necessary to destroy": Ibid., 255.

475   "Peter, go back and sit": Ibid., 258.

475   Loan shoots Vietcong: Braestrup, I, 460.

475   "They killed many Americans": Arnett, 251.

475   "Damn": Ibid.

475   *Daily News* and *Times* use of photo: Braestrup, I, 462.

475   American intelligence breakdown: Oberdorfer, reprinted in *Reporting Vietnam*, I, 565.

477   Manhard and Miller: Ibid.

477   Vietcong treatment of priests: Ibid., 566.

477   Quang criticized by Hanoi: Bui Tin, 63.

478   "What makes the North Vietnamese fight": Barrett, *Vietnam Papers*, 597.

478   "very strange contradiction": Ibid.

478   "If this is a failure": Clifford, 475.

478   "a Dien Bien Phu": Braestrup, I, 344.

478   Johnson has model set up: Westmoreland, 316.

478   Wheeler-Westmoreland exchange: Braestrup, I, 344–45, n. 13.

479   Vietcong do not attack water supply: George R. Vickers, "U.S. Military Strategy and the Vietnam War," in Werner and Huynh, 120.

479   Khe Sanh's placement: Tuohy, 126–27.

479   U.S. Marine losses: John Wheeler, AP dispatch, quoted in *Reporting Vietnam*, I, 577.

480   "Yea, though we walk": Tuohy, 129.

480   Johnson opposes using force over Pueblo: Dallek, 514.

480   Jack Kennedy on Gene McCarthy: Schlesinger, *RFK*, II, 864.

480   McCarthy on Robert Kennedy: Ibid., 868–69.

480   "would not oppose Lyndon Johnson": Dallek, 525.

480   McCarthy poll: Ibid., 526.

480   casualty figures: Clifford, 479.

480   Westmoreland's oblique cable: Ibid., 477.

481   Westmoreland talks of opportunity: Westmoreland, 352.

481   Rusk and McNamara agree to increase: Barrett, *Vietnam Papers*, 606.

481   "Westy said he *could* use": Ibid., 608.

481   Wheeler meets with Westmoreland: Westmoreland, 353.

481   Wheeler changes quarters: Ibid., 354.

482   Wheeler puts chance at fifty-fifty: Ibid., 356.

482   "The offensive has by no means": Clifford, 481.

482   Black paratroopers: Barrett, *Vietnam Papers*, 621.

482   "Practically every period": Ibid., 619.

483   McCarthy calls for national debate: Merle Miller, 504.

483   "Children's Crusade": Zaroulis and Sullivan, 157.

483   McCarthy campaigners' schedule: Gitlin, 297.

483   "The Democratic Party in 1964": Ibid., 299.

483   Sheehan and Smith: Clifford, 499–500.

483   Rusk and Fulbright: Rusk, 478.

483   Church and Symington: Zaroulis and Sullivan, 156.

484   Johnson's write-in vote: Merle Miller, 506.

484   Johnson on Civil Rights Act: Ibid., 505.
484   "Every son-of-a-bitch": Shesol, 417.
484   New Hampshire voters "dissatisfied": Zaroulis and Sullivan, 157.
484   Schlesinger's gambit: Schlesinger, *RFK*, II, 886.
485   "Clifford is not the hawk": Clifford, 503.
485   "You know, maybe Robert Kennedy": Shesol, 419.
485   "But how do I know": Barrett, *Vietnam Papers*, 670.
485   Kennedy sets his conditions: Ibid., 672.
485   Clifford's response: Ibid., 673.
486   Johnson's reaction: Clifford, 505.
487   "We both know": Barrett, *Vietnam Papers*, 669.
487   Clifford labels Wise Men: Ibid., 684.
487   "You tell the President": Isaacson and Thomas, 687.
488   Westmoreland promoted: Westmoreland, 361.
488   reaction to Johnson's speech: Barrett, *Vietnam Papers*, 702.
488   "If we get tagged": Ibid., 700.
488   McPherson's warning to Johnson: Ibid., 680.
489   Goldberg-DePuy exchange: Clifford, 513.
489   Clifford-Habib exchange: Ibid.
490   Johnson-Wheeler exchange: Barrett, *Vietnam Papers*, 707.
490   Rostow calls briefings rigged: Clifford, 513.
490   Johnson's appearance: Isaacson and Thomas, 695.
491   "We need more money": Clifford, 516.
491   Harriman attends the lunch: Isaacson and Thomas, 701.
491   "Mr. President": Barrett, *Vietnam Papers*, 713.
491   "Then what in the name of God": Clifford, 517.
492   "Let's get one thing clear!": Isaacson and Thomas, 695.
492   "No, no, no!": Bird, *Color*, 369; Clifford, 516–18.
492   "The picture I get": Barrett, *Vietnam Papers*, 715.
492   "The issue is not that stated by Fortas": Ibid.
492   "Tet really set us back": Johnson, *Vantage*, 418.
493   "Let's get 'peace' out": Clifford, 509.
493   "What the President needs": Ibid., 520.
493   "We've won!": Ibid., 521.
493   Busby prepares paragraphs: Johnson, *Vantage*, 429.
493   "Accordingly, I shall not seek": Ibid., 435; the entire speech: *Public Papers of the Presidents of the United States: Lyndon Johnson, 1968–69*, vol. I (Washington, D.C., 1970), 470.
494   "as it is that Dean Rusk will turn": Johnson, *Vantage*, 433.
494   "can't be better than a million": Ibid.
494   Johnson's grandmother's stroke: Ibid., 425.
494   Hoover predicts race riots: Ibid., 426.
494   11 P.M. press conference: Clifford, 523.
494   "I was never surer": Ibid., 524.
495   Kennedy and McCarthy's responses: Schlesinger, *RFK*, II, 907.
495   "You fellows won't have me": Ibid., quotes Sam Johnson, *My Brother Lyndon* (New York, 1969), 251–52.
495   Ridenhour's background and early Vietnam experiences: Author's interviews, Ron Ridenhour, New Orleans, Nov. 30, 1994, Dec. 4, 1997.
496   Sergeant Cox killed and aftermath: Bilton and Sim, 92.
497   "It's a tough war, Chaplain": Ibid., 95.
497   Medina interprets Barker's orders: Ibid., 99.
498   Calley at Jungle Warfare School: Ibid., 54.
499   Conti and Calley: Ibid., 113.

499   "Take care of them": Ibid., 119.

501   Roschevitz: Ibid., 131.

501   "I'm the boss here": Author's interview, Hugh Thompson, New Orleans, La., Nov. 31, 1994; Goldstein, Marshall and Schwartz, 503.

502   Child rescued and flown to Quang Ngai: Bilton and Sim, 140–41.

502   "Then we finished": Author's interviews, Ron Ridenhour, New Orleans, La., Nov. 30, 1994, Dec. 4, 1997.

503   "one of our most distinguished": Abramson, 657.

503   Politburo's gleeful reaction: Author's interview, Nguyen Khac Huynh, Hanoi, Aug. 10, 1999.

503   "progressive public opinion": Loi, 16.

503   "In the negotiations, Governor Harriman": Clifford, 531.

503   Zhou Enlai and Pham Van Dong: 77 *Conversations*, 126–29.

504   "I would like to be able to tell": Abramson, 658.

505   Xuan Thuy background: Author's interviews, Hanoi, 1995–99; Loi, 17.

506   Rusk's lectures on Communists: Clifford, 533, 536.

506   Clifford flies Harriman to Paris: Abramson, 660.

506   "I should have gone to law school": Clifford, 539.

506   "I wonder if I should have made": Ibid.

506   Clifford upbeat: Barrett, *Vietnam Papers*, 748.

507   "We can hope only for success": Ibid., 751–52.

507   "We will not get a solution": Ibid., 752.

507   "Are they polite?": Ibid., 754.

507   McNamara's advice: Ibid.

507   Westmoreland on maintaining Khe Sanh: Spector, 129.

507   "The war has entered a very fierce": Ibid., 144.

508   Communist raid on Saigon: Ibid., 162.

508   Two Ky supporters killed: Ibid., 164.

508   "demonstrated a high degree of concern": Barrett, *Vietnam Papers*, 775.

508   Abrams's response: Ibid., 756.

509   Clifford's reaction to Abrams's cable: Clifford, 542–43.

509   "in fact benefited": Ibid.

509   Johnson extends Secret Service protection: Merle Miller, 520.

509   Kennedy loyalists blame Johnson: Shesol, 458.

509   "My colleagues and I believe": Clifford, 547.

510   Xuan Thuy's puckish offer: Abramson, 661.

510   Rostow disparages Clifford: Clifford, 548.

510   "lost his nerve": Abramson, 665.

510   "contacts for probing": Loi, 19.

510   "the Hammer": Ibid., 20.

511   "You get those damned goons": Abramson, 665.

511   Vance's conditions: Clifford, 549.

511   Bui Diem in Paris: Diem, 231.

511   "Everyone knows the saying": Ibid., 232.

512   Bui Diem and Anna Chennault: Ibid., 235–36.

512   Diem followed and cables intercepted: Ibid., 236.

512   Diem's meeting with Nixon: Ibid., 237.

513   Johnson orders a Rusk press conference: Abramson, 666.

513   Clifford warns Thieu and Ky: Clifford, 551.

513   "a golden flow of money": Ibid.

513   "shocking and outrageous": Ibid.

513   Johnson denounces Humphrey: Ibid., 563.

514   "I want to sit down": Barrett, *Vietnam Papers*, 769.

514   "one piece of leverage": Ibid.

514   "I do not intend to advocate": Ibid., 770.
514   "America is in trouble": Lukas, *Nightmare*, 567.
514   "Mao is 75": Barrett, *Vietnam Papers*, 771.
514   Clifford sees Nixon's trap: Clifford, 563.
514   "took into account, most importantly": Dallek, 575.
515   Johnson rejects platform compromise: Clifford, 564.
515   "Dean Rusk approved it": Humphrey, 389.
515   platform vote: Dallek, 575.
515   Humphrey's son-in-law: Solberg, *Humphrey*, 341.
515   FBI taps Humphrey's phones: Dallek, 576.
515   "unpatriotic" groups denied permit: Gitlin, 323.
515   variety of troops in Chicago: Ibid.
516   "If you're going to Chicago": Ibid., 324.
516   Hayden's strategy: Ibid.
516   "Pigasus": Zaroulis and Sullivan, 184.
516   Ginsberg in Lincoln Park: Ibid.
516   Robert Pierson, undercover policeman: Ibid., 185.
517   clash between Yippies and police: Ibid., 186.
517   Ralph Bell beats Hayden: Hayden, 307.
517   riot at flagpole: Zaroulis and Sullivan, 190.
518   "Let us make sure": Hayden, 318.
518   "the crooks downtown": Zaroulis and Sullivan, 191.
518   Daley to Ribicoff: Hayden, 320.
518   police clear McCarthy's suite: Zaroulis and Sullivan, 198.
518   Hanoi's judgment of war in the South: Loi, 26.
519   "Should the U.S. want to settle": Ibid., 27.
519   "I have had many things stuffed": Ibid., 29.
519   "We are a patient people": Ibid., 30.
519   "You will step up the war": Ibid., 31.
520   "You've lost 140,000 men": Ibid., 32.
520   Harriman renews reconstruction pledge: Ibid., 34.
520   Humphrey blames Johnson for late convention: Humphrey, 396.
520   "A Lesser Evil": Wicker, *One*, 356.
521   "Mr. Humphrey, you are": Garrettson, 197.
521   "bad faith": Clifford, 572n.
521   "I gather you're not asking": Humphrey, 403.
521   "showed he had some balls": Clifford, 571.
521   "If you mean it": Humphrey, 403.
521   poll results: Wicker, *One*, 359.
521   "soft on Communism": Ibid., 363.
522   caviar as Kosygin's gift: Loi, 46.
522   Vietnamese prefer ice cream: Abramson, 666.
522   "Yes, he is": Loi, 49.
522   "we can tell you": Ibid.
522   "as early as possible": Ibid., 52.
522   "I am through with Republican politics": Kimball (57–58) cites letter, Kissinger to Harriman, August 15, 1968, folder: Henry Kissinger, Box 481, Harriman Papers, Manuscript Division, Library of Congress.
523   "Three days of the week": Author's telephone interview, Daniel Davidson, Washington, D.C., Dec. 5, 1999.
523   Kissinger's calls to Allen: Author's telephone interview, Richard Allen, Washington, D.C., November 4, 1999. In a letter to the author dated March 9, 2000, Kissinger responded to a question about his telephone calls to Richard Allen. Kissinger wrote, "With respect to your second question, my recollection and Dick Allen's differ, as I have re-

peatedly explained. You no doubt know that Bill Bundy, in his highly critically book *The Tangled Web*, affirms that I possessed no inside information."

523 "broken open the champagne": Isaacson, *Kissinger*, 132.
523 Kissinger's overture to Humphrey: Ibid., 133.
523 Lansdale's letters to Allen: Currey, *Lansdale*, 327.
523 "to throw the election": Clifford, 577.
523 conference call to three candidates: Ibid.
524 "I thought we had an agreement": Ibid., 575.
524 "Many Republican friends": Bui Diem, 244.
525 "I am regularly in touch": Ibid.
525 Harriman counts days and hours: Loi, 56.
525 "I think we should go ahead": Clifford, 580.
525 "I think this is a political move": Ibid.
525 Clifford asked himself: Ibid., 581.
526 Clifford's response to postponement: Ibid., 587.
526 "It would rock the world": Ibid.
526 "There is no prospect": Cooper, 404.
526 Johnson first made no comment on Bundy's speech: Ibid.
526 Johnson vitriolic: Clifford, 589n.
526 Rusk delays talks until November 4: Ibid., 590.
526 W. Bundy–Bui Diem interview: Bui Diem, 241.
527 Clifford's reaction to meddling: Clifford, 584.
527 "constitutes a perfectly acceptable": Ibid., 592.
527 Kissinger's role: Nixon, 322–24.
527 "all air, naval and artillery bombardment": Cooper, 404.
527 "at which the representatives": Clifford, 593.
527 "I *wish* I could have been": Humphrey, 8–9.
527 Daley's call to Humphrey: Ibid., 13.
528 "To lose to Nixon": Ibid.
528 Kissingers leave Germany: Isaacson, 28.
528 Kissinger's education: Ibid., 38.
528 Kissinger's thesis: Ibid., 65.
528 Kissinger's middle initial: Ibid., 79.
528 Schlesinger's evaluation: Ibid., 31.
528 "The disputes are so bitter": Ibid., 72.
528 Kissinger finds Nixon nervous: Kissinger, *White House*, 11.
529 Kissinger-Bundy exchange: Ibid., 14.
529 "Oh, Jesus Christ": Ibid.
529 Kissinger's title: Ibid., 15.
529 Soviet summit not scheduled: Clifford, 599.
529 "I gave it up for nothing": Author's interview, Francis Bator, Cambridge, Mass., Nov. 11, 1998.
529 Dirksen and Alsop call on Diem: Bui Diem, 245.
529 Table debate: Loi, 69.
530 "I'm fed up": Clifford, 605.
530 "convinced that we have gone": Ibid.
530 "If you had stopped": Loi, 71.
530 "De-Americanization of the war": Ibid., 73.

ELEVEN: NIXON (1969)

533 "True enough": Rusk, 603.
534 Medal of Freedom recipients: Johnson, *Vantage*, 567.

534   "Eight years ago, Mrs. Rusk": Rusk, 604.

534   Rusk would not write memoirs: Rusk relented and in 1990 published *As I Saw It*, as told to his son, Richard Rusk, and edited by Daniel S. Papp.

534   Dobrynin on Rusk: Dobrynin, 188.

534   Rusk's ailments: Rusk, 595.

534   "We don't want the university": Ibid., 596.

534   Kissinger's remarks about Nixon: Isaacson, 127.

535   Kissinger's staff: Kissinger, *White House* (24), lists his core appointees as Winston Lord, Lawrence Eagleburger, Helmut Sonnenfeldt, William Hyland, Harold Saunders, Peter Rodman and Alexander Haig.

535   Halperin helped turn Clifford: Karnow, *Vietnam*, 587.

535   Haig in South Vietnam: Morris, *Haig*, 69.

535   Ehrlichman on Rogers and Nixon: Isaacson, 196.

535   "I don't trust Henry": Ibid., 142.

536   "neo-colonialist policies": Loi, 75.

536   Hanoi's strategy: Ibid.

536   Komer's appointment: Grant, 302; Congress did not confirm Komer as ambassador, partially because of his involvement with Phoenix.

536   CIA agents in Phoenix: Colby and Forbath, 269.

536   organization of Phoenix: Ibid.

537   PRU organization: Moyar, 38.

537   "They only go out at night": Valentine, 435.

537   Villager disillusioned with uprising: Moyar, 205.

537   Statistics on defectors from NLF: Ibid., 240.

537   Officer considers Phoenix immoral: Colby and Forbath, 270.

538   "They are specifically not authorized": Ibid., 271.

538   American religious team: Joseph Treaster, "The Phoenix Murders," *Penthouse*, Dec. 1975.

538   Kann's story: Colby and Forbath, 276.

538   Americans witness abuse: Moyar, 102.

538   Tiger cages: Colby and Forbath, 277.

538   Background of Gelb's study: Author's interview, Leslie Gelb, New York, Oct. 8, 1998.

540   Courtesy safe for Clifford: Rudenstine, 31.

540   Clifford thinks project is dumb idea: Clifford, 611.

540   "I don't want to see it!": Gelb interview, Oct. 8, 1998.

541   Robert Kennedy's "shrewd diplomacy": Shapley, 466.

541   McNamara thankful he obliged RFK: Author's interview, Robert McNamara, Washington, D.C., Feb. 23, 1999.

541   Fulbright attacks McNamara: Shapley, 467.

541   Nixon's terms to Dobrynin: Dobrynin, 200.

541   Lodge in Paris: W. Bundy, 61.

542   Laird's troop reduction: Author's telephone interview, Melvin Laird, Washington, D.C., Jan. 31, 1999.

542   Laird's 1973 projection: W. Bundy, 65.

542   Laird explains politics to Westmoreland: Laird interview, Jan. 31, 1999.

542   Abrams on COSVN: Shawcross, 19–20.

542   Abrams's new strategy on war: Sorley, 19.

542   Breakfast briefing on Cambodia: Ibid., 21.

542   Chiefs estimate "minimal" civilian casualties: Ibid., 29.

543   Sihanouk and Bowles: W. Bundy, 71.

543   Wheeler and Seamans: Shawcross, 29.

543   Politburo strategy: Loi, 85.

544   "in the foreseeable future": Kimball, 94.

544 "an act of extraordinary cynicism": Ibid., 128.
544 "Mr. B-52": Ibid., 125.
544 "Do you feel that you could keep": Ambrose, *Nixon*, 258.
545 Kissinger deplores name "Breakfast": Kissinger, *White House*, 247.
545 "Silver House," "Daniel Boone": M. Young, 218.
545 "You can't be court-martialled": Shawcross, 26.
545 "came beaming in": Haldeman, *Diaries*, 41.
545 Kissinger with Dobrynin: Ibid., 50.
546 "This guy is becoming irrational": Kimball, 143.
546 Kissinger as Dr. Strangelove: Isaacson, 181.
546 Kissinger on America's moral decay: Haldeman, *Diaries*, 52.
546 Ridenhour at home: Author's interviews, Ron Ridenhour, New Orleans, Nov. 30, 1994, Dec. 4, 1997.
547 Ridenhour's letter: Bilton and Sim, 220.
548 "Politics would be": *Los Angeles Times*, Apr. 24, 1994, M1.
548 Agnew demanding time: Haldeman, *Diaries*, 53.
548 Ziegler not imaginative: Ibid., 58.
548 Hoover's list of "bad guys": Ibid., 57.
548 Newspapers banned: Ibid., 60.
548 "I would hope that we could": Clifford, 608-9.
548 Kissinger's reaction to Nixon: Haldeman, *Diaries*, 65.
548 Haldeman on Kissinger: Ibid., 66.
549 Nixon–Billy Graham exchange: Ambrose, *Nixon*, 285.
549 Nixon wants Ted Kennedy investigated: Haldeman, *Diaries*, 73.
549 "less than meets the eye": Kissinger, *White House*, 225.
549 Nixon's response to South Vietnam trip: Haldeman, *Diaries*, 77.
549 Nixon's threat to Ceauşescu: Kissinger, *White House*, 280.
550 Plans for quarantine of the North: Ibid.; Kimball, 159.
550 Nixon's letter to Ho: Loi, 98.
550 "Nixon's war": Ibid., 100.
550 "You know," Haldeman said: Ambrose, *Nixon*, 287.
550 "to get out of the war with honor": Kimball, 158.
550 Politburo suppresses news of Ho's death: Author's interviews, Hanoi, 1995–99.
550 Ho's will: Author's interview, Nguyen Dinh Phuong, Hanoi, Aug. 10, 1999.
551 "Our rivers and mountains": Sainteny, 169.
551 Ho's funeral: Ibid., 171.
551 "Our beloved and venerated Ho": Le Duan, funeral oration from *This Nation and Socialism Are One* (Chicago, 1976), 215–19.
551 Ho's mausoleum: Author's interviews, Hanoi.
551 "cold rebuff": Kimball, 158.
551 Nixon's hope for new leadership: Ibid., 162.
552 Risner's cell boarded up: Risner, 191.
552 Risner with mice, rats, geckos: Ibid., 196–97.
552 Later POWs act differently: Author's telephone, interview, Robinson Risner, Austin, Texas, July 18, 1999.
553 "This racist administration": Clavir and Spitzer, 136.
553 Kunstler–Julius Hoffman exchange: Ibid., 335.
554 "emotionally around the flag": W. Bundy, 82.
554 Sam Brown's strategy: Karnow, *Vietnam*, 598.
554 "from a useless death in Vietnam": Ibid.
554 Agnew's response: Ibid., 599.
554 "The President says nothing": Ambrose, *Nixon*, 312.
554 Mobilization march from Arlington: Kimball, 175.
554 Nixon jokes about using helicopters: Haldeman, *Diaries*, 108.

555   Crowd estimates: Ibid.; Zaroulis and Sullivan, 260.
555   Opposition to Duck Hook: Kimball, 164.
555   Abrams and COSVN Resolution 9: Sorley, 157.
555   Special Forces charged with murder: Ibid., 165.
555   Kissinger persuades CIA: Ibid.
556   "This is terrific": Author's interview, Ron Ridenhour, New Orleans.
556   Reporters taken to My Lai: Bilton and Sim, 255.

TWELVE: SIHANOUK (1970)

557   Sihanouk's movies and crackdowns: Osborne, *Sihanouk*, 190.
557   Cambodia deaths: Ibid., 192.
557   Sihanouk does not return immediately: Kissinger, *White House*, 462.
558   Lon Nol with queen mother: Shawcross, 128.
558   Fate of Lon Nol's brother: Isaacson, 257.
559   "We should support Sihanouk": 77 *Conversations*, 160.
559   "Before I came here, we discussed": Ibid., 162.
559   "the Soviet Union will be embarrassed": Ibid., 163.
559   "What the hell do those clowns": Isaacson, 257.
559   "I want Helms to develop": Ibid., 258.
560   "No American stationed in Laos": *New York Times*, March 7, 1970, 1.
560   Pentagon on Americans killed in Laos: Ambrose, *Nixon*, 336.
560   Kissinger's explanation: Kissinger, *White House*, 456.
560   "No one cares about B-52 strikes": Ambrose, *Nixon*, 336.
560   Nixon drops 11 points in poll: Haldeman, *Diaries*, 138.
560   Nixon on "Patton": Ibid., 147.
560   Chicago Seven sentenced: Hayden, 407.
561   Cambodians volunteer for army: W. Bundy, 152.
561   Nixon sends CIA captured weapons: Ibid.
561   McCain's map: Shawcross, 136.
562   Kissinger on McCain: Kissinger, *White House*, 480.
562   Haldeman on Nixon's speech: Haldeman, *Diaries*, 153.
562   Hoover on Nixon's appearance; Oudes, 120.
562   Kissinger's attitude toward Tho: Kissinger, *White House*, 442.
562   "Previously, with over one million": Loi, 119.
563   Tho's accusation about Cambodia: Ibid., 136.
563   "although I am flattered": Isaacson, 258.
563   "the only government in Cambodia": Ibid., 260.
563   "Kissinger is really having fun": Haldeman, *Diaries*, 153.
563   "an unelected elite": Ibid., 107.
563   "damn well ought to go": Isaacson, 261; the NSC meeting was April 22, 1970.
563   Agnew's recommendations: Kissinger, *White House*, 491.
564   Nixon's decision: Ibid., 492.
564   Communists control five provinces: Loi, 140.
564   Kissinger thinks Cambodia cannot survive: Kissinger, *White House*, 493.
564   Kissinger insults Nixon to aides: Isaacson, 145.
564   "Our peerless leader has flipped": Ibid., 263.
565   "No," Kissinger assured him: Ibid.
565   "Your views represent the cowardice": Shawcross, 145.
565   Haig-Watts exchange: Ibid.
565   "so that it will be clear": Ibid.
565   Lake and Morris's reason for keeping silent: M. Young, 247.
565   "We wrote the goddam doctrine": Shawcross, 145.

565   "The basic substance": Ibid.
566   Nixon calls the young Eisenhowers to White House: Ambrose, *Nixon*, 343–44.
566   Haldeman's reaction to speech: Haldeman, *Diaries*, 158.
566   Kissinger's reaction to speech: Kissinger, *White House*, 505.
566   Nixon's speech: Kimball, 211.
566   "pitiful, helpless giant": Ambrose, *Nixon*, 345.
566   "I would rather be a one-term": Ibid. (346) cites *Public Papers of the President* (1970), 405–410.
566   Burger calls on Nixon: Ambrose, *Nixon*, 346.
567   "Let me be the judge": Nixon, 454.
567   "You see these bums": Ambrose, *Nixon*, 348.
567   Haldeman's reaction: Haldeman, *Diaries*, 158.
568   "The U.S. words of peace": Loi, 144.
568   Lon Nol kept ignorant: M. Young, 248.
568   Limits to Lon Nol's aid: W. Bundy, 156–57.
568   Haig with Lon Nol: Morris, *Haig*, 143–45.
568   "We need to go west": Sorley (204) cites recording, Intelligence Update, 3MM1970, ASC.
568   Senate reaction to bombing North Vietnam: Ambrose, *Nixon*, 349–50.
569   Kissinger has Laird and Rogers wiretapped: Hersh, *Price*, 193–94.
569   Laird announces strikes end: Ambrose, *Nixon*, 350.
569   Hatfield-McGovern amendment: Kimball, 221.
569   Student rioting: Zaroulis and Sullivan, 319.
569   "my short stay at Kent": Shawcross, 153.
569   "They're the worst": Ibid., 153.
569   Students arrested at Kent State, Zaroulis and Sullivan, 319.
569   Guard issued M-1s: Ibid., 320.
570   "This should remind us": Ambrose, *Nixon*, 351.
570   "If you only knew": Ibid., 357.
570   Kissinger sleeps in office: Isaacson, 269.
570   Haig brings in troops: Shawcross, 153.
570   "What are we going to do": Young, 248.
570   Haldeman on "bums" remark: Haldeman, *Diaries*, 161.
570   Nixon believed enemies trying to panic him: Ibid.
570   Hickel's letter: Zaroulis and Sullivan, 321–22.
570   Nixon decides to fire Hickel: Haldeman, *Diaries*, 161.
570   Nixon on his cabinet: Ibid.
571   "had serious misgivings": Ambrose, *Nixon*, 351.
571   firebombs on campus: *New York Times*, May 6, 1970.
571   Nixon to take no phone calls: Haldeman, *Diaries*, 162.
571   "I agree with everything": Ambrose, *Nixon*, 353.
571   "choleric young intellectuals": Ibid.
571   "When the action is hot": Ibid., 354.
571   Nixon explains "bums" remark: Ibid.
571   Nixon's phone calls: Ibid., 354–55; Isaacson, 270.
572   "Let's go look at it": Ambrose, *Nixon*, 355.
572   Nixon at Lincoln Memorial: Price, 170–74; Safire, 204–8; Nixon, 459–66.
572   Sanchez in Capitol: Ambrose, *Nixon*, 356.
572   Haldeman on Nixon's moods: Haldeman, *Diaries*, 163.
573   Nixon's view of Kissinger: Ibid., 139.
573   "You son of a bitch": Isaacson, 213.
573   Kissinger orders wiretaps: Ibid., 216–17.
573   Kissinger taps Pederson: Ibid., 221.
573   Safire on taps: Safire, 169.

573 FBI not trusted: Isaacson, 229.
573 Kissinger makes faces: Ibid., 230.
574 Ellsberg's transformation and photo copies of Pentagon Papers: Author's interviews,
     Daniel Ellsberg, Washington, D.C., 1997–99; Rudenstine, 40–41.
574 Kissinger and Ellsberg at San Clemente: Ellsberg, unpublished memoir.
575 "I don't want to be just out here banging up": Sorley, 220.
575 "Who the hell knows?": Ibid., 216.

THIRTEEN: ELLSBERG (1971)

576 Kissinger protests 1971 pullout: Haldeman, *Diaries*, 223. In a letter dated March 9, 2000,
     Kissinger responded to a question from the author about the December 15, 1970, con-
     versation. Kissinger wrote, "Your third question implies that Nixon had a plan to with-
     draw rapidly from Vietnam. You will find no reference to any such thought in any of his
     many memos to me, in the NSC files, or in the recollections of participants. I cannot re-
     construct at this remove what Bob Haldeman claimed."
577 Hanoi's troop strength: The units were the 304th, 308th and 320th NVA Divisions: Sor-
     ley, 248.
577 Plan for ARVN invasion: Summers, *Almanac*, 224.
577 Thieu filled in details for Lam Son, 719: Sorley, 234.
577 Communists massed 60,000 troops: Ibid. (243) cites *History of the People's Army of Viet-
     nam*, II (Hanoi, 1994), 374ff.
577 "WARNING. NO U.S. PERSONNEL": Sorley, 244.
577 ARVN column halted: Davidson, 645.
578 Thieu orders column to stop: Sorley, 247.
578 "You go in there just long enough": Kimball, 246.
578 "Washington would like to see ARVN": Sorley, 255.
578 ARVN troops cling to skids: Davidson, 645.
578 Material and equipment losses: Sorley, 262; Davidson (650) puts them somewhat
     higher.
578 ARVN casualties: Davidson, 650.
579 Sully killed: *Dictionary*, Leepson, 382.
579 Bunker blames the press: Sorley, 266.
579 Kissinger promotes Lam Son, 719: Haldeman, *Diaries*, 239.
579 Nixon and Kissinger on Abrams: Ibid., 259.
579 Ridenhour awaits verdict: Author's interviews, Ron Ridenhour, New Orleans, La., Nov.
     30, 1994, Dec. 4, 1997.
581 Kissinger's concession on North Vietnamese troops: Loi, 151. In a letter dated March 9,
     2000, Kissinger responded to questions sent to him by fax by the author on January 30,
     2000. Kissinger began, "Thank you for your courteous offer to permit me to partici-
     pate in my assassination, which reached my office while I was in Asia. Here are my
     answers."
         The author's first questions were these: "When did the United States first drop its de-
     mand that North Vietnamese troops leave South Vietnam? When was President
     Nguyen Van Thieu first advised that the demand had been dropped? What was the rea-
     son for dropping it?"
         Kissinger wrote, "I am enclosing the text of President Nixon's speech of January 25,
     1972, setting forth our final peace proposal. You will note that it omits withdrawal of
     North Vietnamese forces. Obviously President Thieu had approved the text, which was
     also published. These provisions are almost verbatim in the final agreement.
         "Our reason can easily be found by reviewing the back-issues of your former newspa-
     per. [Kissinger refers to the *New York Times*, where the author worked as a reporter in the
     mid-1960s.] We judged that congressional and public pressures made it imperative to go

to the outer limit of flexibility. We believed also that the provisions for non-infiltration and non-reinforcement would have led to the atrophying of North Vietnamese forces *provided* the agreement was being enforced. This, as you know, Congress prevented."

Kissinger attached Nixon's January 25, 1972, speech as printed in *Public Papers of the President, Richard Nixon, 1972*, 100–106. The speech does omit mention of North Vietnamese troops in South Vietnam. A note following the speech outlined the text of the U.S.–South Vietnam peace proposal released the same day, which also did not refer to the question of North Vietnamese troops in the South. But Point 5 read, "The problems existing among the Indochinese countries will be settled by the Indochinese parties on the basis of mutual respect for independence, sovereignty, territorial integrity, and non-interference in each other's affairs. Among the problems that will be settled is the implementation of the principle that all armed forces of the countries of Indochina must remain within their national frontiers."

581   Smyser warns Kissinger: Isaacson, 332.
582   "The negotiations have lasted": Loi, 154.
582   "pitiful fiasco": Ibid., 161.
582   debate over POWs: Ibid., 171.
583   North Vietnamese learn of China's overtures: Ibid., 168.
583   *Times* treatment of Pentagon Papers: Salisbury, *Without*, 213.
583   Fulbright and Laird with Pentagon Papers: Rudenstine, 43.
583   Goodell and McGovern responses: Ibid., 45.
583   Ellsberg and Sheehan negotiate: Ibid., 47.
584   Ellsberg seeks to maintain control: Salisbury, *Without*, 97.
584   "in a criminal conspiracy to wage": Ibid., 98.
584   Sheehan's presentation to editors: Ibid., 121.
584   Loeb opposed to publishing: Ibid., 127.
585   Reston's ultimatum: Ibid., 136.
585   "I'm not going to jail": Frankel, 328.
586   "I've decided you can use": Ibid., 331.
586   "I've learned that never again": Salisbury, *Without*, 194.
586   Haig-Rostow exchange: Ibid., 210.
586   Ellsberg's paper for Rostow: Ibid., 210–11.
586   "cut each other up on it": Haldeman, *Diaries*, 300.
586   Laird's reaction: Salisbury, *Without*, 233.
587   Laird not questioned on Papers: Rudenstine, 69.
587   Kissinger's involvement with Papers: Ibid., 70.
587   Ellsberg-Kissinger exchange at MIT: Isaacson, 329.
587   Nixon on the *Sequoia*: Ibid., 328.
588   "No foreign country will ever trust": Ibid., 329.
588   "it shows that you're weak, Mr. President": Haldeman, *Ends*, 110.
588   Haldeman on Kissinger's performance: Ibid., 111. In a letter to the author dated March 9, 2000, Kissinger responded to a question about the accuracy of John Ehrlichman's account of Kissinger's remarks, as quoted by Walter Isaacson on page 329 of his biography *Kissinger*. Kissinger wrote, "There is no reference to any such allegations regarding Daniel Ellsberg in any of the Nixon tapes on the Pentagon Papers that have been published. You may want to consider the possibility that something critical of me is untrue."
588   "I get a lot of advice": Haldeman, *Diaries*, 311.
588   "I want you to set up": Haldeman, *Ends*, 112.
588   the "Plumbers": Ibid.
589   Gurfein's ruling: Rudenstine, 107.
589   "to vindicate the right": Salisbury, 312.
589   "LBJ screwed up the war": Ibid., 314.
589   "We agree": Ibid., 334.
590   Ellsberg indicted: Rudenstine, 341.

590   Kissinger and Chinese ambassador: Loi, 167.
590   Zhou Enlai and U.S. Ping-Pong team: Kissinger, *White House*, 710.
590   "Many visitors have come": Ibid., 746.
591   Zhou on Cultural Revolution: Ibid., 750–51.
591   problems in joint communiqué: Ibid., 751–52.
591   Nixon reads statement: Ibid., 760.
592   Perino's menu: Ibid.
592   "That is your affair": Author's interview, Nguyen Dinh Phuong, Hanoi, Aug. 16, 1998.
592   Huynh at lunch: Author's interview, Luu Doan Huynh, Hanoi, June 3, 1995.

FOURTEEN: MAO (1972)

593   Nixon invites Malraux: Nixon, 557.
593   "China's foreign policy": Ibid.
593   "He is so much younger": Ibid., 558.
593   Rogers's concern about staircase: Ibid., 560.
593   Nixon and Kissinger exclude Rogers: Kissinger, *White House*, 1057.
594   Haldeman and the jokes about Kissinger: Haldeman, *Diaries*, 413.
594   Kissinger's response to Mao: Kissinger, *White House*, 1059.
594   "Our common old friend": Nixon, 561.
595   "Actually," he said: Ibid.
595   Jokes about Kissinger's girlfriends: Ibid., 561–62.
595   "We understand": Ibid., 562.
595   Lin Piao's plane crash: Kissinger, *White House*, 1061.
596   "mobilizing a whole mass": Nixon, 568.
596   "We are not in a position": Ibid.
596   "You want to bring back": Loi, 216.
596   Zhou separates China's position from Hanoi's: Ibid., 217.
596   Politburo's judgment: Ibid., 218.
596   "Nguyen Hue" offensive: Truong, *Easter*, 9.
596   "so as to win a significant": Loi, 218–19.
597   Muskie painted as defeatist: Haldeman, *Diaries*, 435.
597   Nixon's goal in B-52 raids: Ibid.
597   "The Air Force isn't worth a—": S. Hersh, *Price*, 506.
597   Nixon's interview with Vogt: Ibid., 436.
597   Debate over bombing: Davidson, 704.
598   Makeup of 3rd ARVN Division: Ibid., 680.
598   Lam's strategy: Ibid., 681.
598   Performance of 3rd ARVN: Ibid., 683.
598   Kissinger with Dobrynin: Kissinger, *White House*, 1114.
598   Kissinger calls overture insolent: Ibid., 1115.
598   North's justification for offensive: Loi, 219.
599   "is not to our advantage": Ibid., 220.
599   Kissinger repeats concession to Brezhnev: Kissinger, *White House*, 1147.
599   troop condition as "throwaway": Ibid.
599   Russia's envoys in Hanoi: Loi, 226.
600   Dong's strategy: Ibid.
600   Nixon's threat to cancel summit: S. Hersh, *Price*, 516.
600   Changes in Kissinger: Loi, 227.
600   "No nonsense": S. Hersh, *Price*, 516.
600   "I'm giving an example": Loi, 229. Rather than Loi's account, quoting Fulbright on the
       Geneva accords, Kissinger (*White House*, 1170) quotes Tho as saying that Hanoi's actions
       had been "a direct response to your sabotage of the Paris Conference."

601   "Tomorrow is best": Loi, 231.
601   "All other members, except Thieu": Ibid.
601   "Can anybody publish a paper": Kissinger, *White House*, 1172.
601   "We have on many occasions": Loi, 232.
601   "We are recording big victories": Ibid., 233.
601   Kissinger's policy with Soviets: Isaacson, 424–25.
601   "I don't want to become the Walt Rostow": S. Hersh, *Price*, 523.
601   "This has got to be": Isaacson, 424.
602   Tu's reporting: Author's telephone interview, Nguyen Dinh Tu, Alexandria, Va., Oct. 5, 1999.
602   "This is a battle to the death": Sorley, 330–31.
602   Hollingsworth's strategy: Ibid., 700.
603   Death of John Vann: Liebchen, 83.
603   McGovern begs for POWs: Haldeman, *Diaries*, 478.
603   "the white race is the cancer": Vogelgesang, 175. "Sontag later withdrew the remark, calling it a slur on cancer patients. . . ." Christopher Hitchens, "Signature Sontag," *Vanity Fair*, March 2000, 245.
603   Mary McCarthy quote: Vogelgesang, 138.
604   Halberstam on McNamara: Halberstam, *Best*, 306.
604   Stone on man prevailing: *I. F. Stone's Weekly*, documentary narrated by Tom Wicker.
604   Liddy, Walters, Martha Mitchell: Haldeman, *Diaries*, 475.
604   "If the United States can accept": Loi, 246.
605   Democrats not to be informed: Ibid., 252–53.
605   Kissinger's August 1 proposals: Ibid., 261.
605   Tho suggests reparations: Ibid., 264.
605   Tho refuses to make talks public: Ibid., 268.
605   Westmoreland on Haig: Westmoreland, 388.
605   Nixon's plan for postelection: Isaacson, 441.
606   "Al—it is obvious": Ibid., 441–42.
606   Kissinger with Thieu: Ibid., 444.
606   "We wish to end before October 15": Ibid., 289.
606   North Vietnamese glad about deadline: Ibid.
606   Haig alarms Thieu: Morris, *Haig*, 200.
606   Haldeman's observation: Haldeman, *Diaries*, 512.
606   "Unlike '68": Ibid., 517.
606   Tho and Thuy's report to Politburo: Loi, 299.
607   Terms sent to Moscow and Beijing: Ibid., 306.
607   Haig's promotion: Morris, *Haig*, 201.
607   Nixon's condition for Haig: Isaacson, 442.
607   Kissinger on Haig: Ibid., 447.
607   forum of reconciliation: Loi, 319.
607   Kissinger's timetable: Ibid., 317.
607   "We have succeeded": Ibid.
607   "Well, you've got three": Haldeman, *Diaries*, 515.
607   Summary of peace terms: Ibid., 515–16.
608   "all cranked up": Ibid., 516.
608   Haldeman on Nixon's wine: Ibid.
608   "Overall," it boils down: Ibid., 517.
608   Kissinger's cable to Bunker: Isaacson, 450.
608   Kissinger considers Vietnamese insolent: Kissinger, *White House*, 1467.
608   "I'm not the tail": Author's interview, Nguyen Thi Ngoc Dung, Ho Chi Minh City, May 26, 1996.
608   Thieu's excuse to Bunker: Isaacson, 449.
608   Kissinger sends earlier draft: Ibid., 451.

609   Thieu keeps Kissinger waiting: Hung and Schecter, 85.
609   Thieu wants to punch Kissinger: Ibid., 88.
609   Nha-Kissinger dialogue: Ibid. (100) cites Schecter interview with Nha, July 23, 1985.
610   "similar to those which we abhorred": Ibid., 74.
610   Westmoreland's advice: Westmoreland, 394.
610   "You have only one problem": Kissinger, *White House*, 1385–86.
610   Kissinger assures Hanoi on agreement: Isaacson, 454.
610   Kissinger chides Haig: Ibid.
610   Nha rebuffs Bunker: Hung and Schecter, 110.
611   Kissinger and Frankel: Frankel, 316–18.
611   "a supreme act of folly": Isaacson, 458.
611   "I suppose now everybody's": S. Hersh, *Price*, 604.
611   "candid and even brilliant": Isaacson, 459.
611   "to take a divided nation": Ambrose, *Nixon*, 651.
611   Voter turnout: Ibid.
611   Hanoi's reaction to vote: Loi, 353.
612   Thieu's sixty-nine demands: Kissinger, *White House*, 1412.
612   Meeting at Leger's house: Loi, 357.
612   Kissinger's gifts for Tho: Ibid.
612   Gift for Xuan Thuy: Kissinger, *White House*, 1417.
612   "We have been deceived": Loi, 358.
612   Kissinger's joke about unity: Ibid.
612   Northern response to renegotiation: Ibid., 362.
612   Kissinger sees his error: Kissinger, *White House*, 1417.
612   Tho deliberately intransigent: Loi, 364.
613   Nixon's approach to press: Haldeman, *Diaries*, 532.
613   Nixon ready to break off talks: Kissinger, *White House*, 1419.
613   Nixon thinks of dumping Kissinger: Haldeman, *Diaries*, 537.
613   "You have my absolute": W. Bundy, 361.
613   "While we have a moral case": *New York Times*, Apr. 30, 2000, Week in Review, section 7, quotes Kissinger cable of Oct. 22, 1972.
613   "They're just a bunch of shits": Nixon, 733.
613   "I don't want any more of this crap": Ibid., 734.
614   B-52 losses: Ibid., 737.
614   Zhou Enlai requests figures: Author's interview, Beijing, 1995.
614   "preferably with your cooperation": Kimball, 361.
614   Nixon "shocked": Nixon, 737.
614   "It's late in the day": Bui Diem, 308.
614   Christmas bombing casualties: Herz, 55.
615   "Even allies must call": Isaacson, 471.
615   Mrs. Dung's appearances: Author's interviews, Nguyen Thi Ngoc Dung, Ho Chi Minh City, May 26, 1998, Aug. 24, 1999.
615   Agent Orange dropped in Vietnam: Young and Reggiani, 3. Their book (3) also reports that during the five years from 1965 to 1970, some 2½ million U.S. servicemen and American allies from Australia, New Zealand and South Korea served one-year terms in South Vietnam.
        Ongoing U.S. government studies, required by Congress since 1991, have "found sufficient evidence of an association with herbicides" in four diseases: soft-tissue sarcoma, non-Hodgkin's lymphoma, Hodgkin's disease and chloracne (in genetically susceptible individuals). "Limited/suggestive evidence of an association" appeared in seven ailments, including respiratory and prostate cancers and multiple myeloma (*Veterans and Agent Orange*, 6).
616   Nixon's strategy: Nixon, 741–43.
616   Bui–Bao Dai incident: Author's interview, Nov. 6, 1999.

FIFTEEN: THO (1973)

618 "so it's late now to raise": Bui Diem, 309.
618 Kissinger's promise to Bui Diem: Ibid., 310.
618 "But if your president refuses": Ibid., 311.
618 "With the international situation": Ibid.
619 "then that will mean the abandonment": Ibid., 313.
619 "Allow me to ask you": Author's interview, Ho Chi Minh City, 1998.
619 January 8 meeting; In Kissinger's *White House Years* (1463), he presents the January 8, 1973, meeting very differently from the recollection of Communist delegates present that day. Kissinger grants that no Vietnamese greeted him at the door. "All this evoked many self-satisfied media stories of a chilly atmosphere after our bombing. In fact, relations on the inside, out of sight of the press, were rather warm."
619 "It was not my responsibility": Author's interview, Nguyen Co Thach, Hanoi, June 1997.
619 "Under the pretext": Loi, 424.
619 Kissinger asks Tho to lower his voice: S. Hersh, *Price*, 632.
619 "*Ngu xuan!*": Author's interviews, Nguyen Khac Huynh, Hanoi, Aug. 19 and 21, 1999.
620 "among the questions": Loi, 428.
620 Hanoi and the Khmer Rouge: W. Bundy, 366.
621 Kissinger-Tho exchange on prisoners: Loi, 429.
621 Kissinger and Reston: Isaacson, 473.
621 Kissinger and Fallaci: Ibid., 477–78.
621 Kissinger about Nixon: Kissinger, *White House*, 1468.
622 "Brutality is nothing": Ibid., 1469.
622 Kissinger about Johnson's death: Ibid., 1472.
622 Casualty figures 1969–72: Kutler, *Encyclopedia*, 289; S. Hersh, *Price*, 628n.
622 Risner awaits release: Risner, 248.
624 Snepp, background and interrogation of Tai: Author's interviews, Frank Snepp, Los Angeles, 1995–99.
625 Jane Fonda on POWs: Howes, 53–54.
626 Poll figures on Vietnam War: W. Bundy, 373.
626 Kissinger's pledge to Souvanna: Ibid.
626 Tonnage dropped in Cambodia: Shawcross, 272.
627 Thieu's trip to the United States: Bui Diem, 319–20.
627 Haig's mission to Lon Nol: Shawcross, 275.
627 "This will be hot": Ibid., 277.
627 "Just remember": Haldeman, *Diaries*, 653.
627 Ziegler's message from Nixon: Ibid., 671.
628 Nixon's request to Haldeman: Ibid., 675.
629 Kissinger denies role in Ellsberg case: Kissinger, *Upheaval*, 115.
629 Kenneth Rush promised State: S. Hersh, *Price*, 611.
629 "And now he's hanging on": Ibid., 612.
629 "I don't stand on protocol": Kalb and Kalb, 447.
630 Agnew's plea and sentence: Lukas, *Nightmare*, 412.
630 Ford walking and chewing gum: G. Ford, 84.
630 "Can you see Gerald Ford sitting?": Ibid., 122.
631 "Well, I can't do that": Lukas, *Nightmare*, 436.
631 "abort the established processes": Ibid., 441
631 "Mr. President, are there going to be": Ibid., 452. On August 5, 1974, a tape of three of Nixon's conversations from June 23, 1972, was made public and became known as "the smoking gun." They revealed Nixon conspiring with Haldeman to call off FBI and CIA investigations into Watergate by claiming the break-in involved national security dating back to Kennedy's Cuban invasion.

Nixon had instructed Haldeman to say, "The President's belief is that this is going to open the whole Bay of Pigs up again." (Kutler, *Abuse*, 69.)

With the tape released, Nixon admitted to reporters that it was "at variance with certain of my previous statements" about being ignorant of any cover-up. (Lukas, *Nightmare*, 556.)

With that admission, Nixon's last congressional and public support evaporated.

631   "the Norwegians must have": Kissinger, *Upheaval*, 372.
631   "another insolence": Ibid.
631   U.S. ambassador in Oslo: Ibid., 373.
631   Hayden in court: Hayden, 452.
632   "included poetry, Vietnamese music": Ibid., 454.

SIXTEEN: THIEU (1974)

633   General Thai's health problems: Thai, 82.
634   Thai resolved to get to work: Ibid., 86.
635   "A unified Vietnam with a population": Ibid., 118.
635   "Obviously, China is exerting": Ibid., 123.
636   "It would be marvelous": Ibid.
636   Kissinger's foreign travel: Isaacson, 595.
637   "History will treat you more kindly": Ibid., 597.
637   "He is truly a tragic figure": Ibid., 599.
637   "are still valid": Bui Diem, 326.
637   Ky rejects bribe: Ky, 101.
637   "I'll raise you a soldier": Ibid., 105.
638   Estimate of $500 million: Don, 237.
638   General sells rice to Communists: Ibid., 236.
638   Staff judgment on General Truong: Ibid., 238.
638   Bui Diem's reaction to Thieu's speech: Bui Diem, 328–29.
639   Calley's apartment and Mercedes: Bilton and Sim, 355.
639   "It's my understanding": G. Ford, 4.
639   "a full, free and absolute pardon": Ibid., 178.
639   "Jail Ford!": Ibid., 179.
640   Ford's amnesty terms: Ibid., 182.
640   "My fellow Americans, our long": Ibid., 41.

SEVENTEEN: LE DUAN (1975)

643   Hanoi spy in Thieu's camp: Snepp, *Decent*, 134.
643   Communist justification for offensive: Dung, 7.
643   Ratio of ARVN rounds to Communists: Kutler, *Encyclopedia*, 366.
643   Enhance shipments: Dung, 8.
643   Russian arms increase: Snepp, *Decent*, 138.
643   Complaints about Enhance: Hosmer et al., 32.
644   "Frankly, you know": Ibid., 148.
644   Open violation of Paris agreement: Ibid., 161.
644   Thieu on military value of Phuoc Long: Ibid.
644   Air Force commander on his losses: Ibid., 162.
644   "We must strike the strategic blow": Dung, 24.
644   Dung's send-off: Ibid., 27.
644   Dung's strategy: Ibid., 40.
645   Dung passes 316th Division: Ibid., 41.

645 Dung captures Darlac province chief: Ibid., 69.
646 ARVN exodus from Ban Me Thuot: Hosmer et al., 171–72.
646 "If you strike Nha Trang": Dung, 71.
646 "Since the Americans pulled out": Ibid.
646 Politburo concerned about Americans returning: Snepp, *Decent*, 137.
646 Le Duan suggests large offensive: Dung, 73.
646 Dung's plan endorsed: Ibid, 78.
646 Mal Browne's return to Vietnam: Author's interview, Malcolm Browne, New York City, April 10, 1998.
647 CIA agent's embezzlement: Snepp, *Decent*, 178.
647 Colby's prediction for 1975: Ibid., 143.
647 T. U. Hackle: Author's interviews, Frank Snepp, Los Angeles, 1995–99.
648 Polgar and lack of evacuation plan: Snepp, *Decent*, 153.
648 Martin on U. S. Grant: Ibid., 155.
648 Thieu resists coalition: Hung and Schecter, 269.
648 Thieu hears BBC predictions: Ibid., 270.
648 "respond with full force": Nixon's letter dated January 15, 1973; Ibid., 392.
648 "I still think Ford can do": Ibid., 279.
648 "There's nothing wrong with running": Dung, 83.
649 Communist flag over Hue: Ibid., 103.
649 ARVN recruits defect: Ibid., 109.
649 Truong to Saigon hospital: Ibid., 110.
649 Hiep and his men weep: Author's interview, Colonel Dang Vu Hiep, Hanoi, May 15, 1998.
649 "It is lost": Snepp, *Decent*, 259; Saigon's deputy premier was Phan Quang Dan.
649 "immense human tragedy": Ibid.
649 Mrs. Binh in Algeria: Ibid., 273.
649 Weyand's mission to Saigon: Hung, 290.
650 "like getting nine women pregnant": Snepp, *Decent*, 296.
650 Tan Thien Khiem resigns: Ibid., 298.
650 Ford discusses evacuation: Ibid.
650 Martin sees Vietnamese grow restless: Ibid., 299.
650 supplies from Okinawa, South Korea: Ibid., 300.
650 "It is all coming down": Ibid., 302.
650 Dung hears Weyand's advice: Dung, 125.
650 Dung's view of final test: Ibid., 127.
651 "You warned: Go out and come back": Ibid., 129.
651 Communist forces split: Ibid., 134.
651 "airplanes without wings": Ibid., 135.
651 Nghi captured: Ibid., 140.
651 Hanoi pilots rushed south: Ibid., 142.
651 Babylift crash: Snepp, *Decent*, 304.
651 Snepp's reflections: Ibid., 317.
652 Minh on Nguyen Huu Tho: Ibid., 321.
652 "too alarmist": Ibid., 327.
652 Carter's tape to Vietnamese: Ibid., 330.
652 Kissinger opposes evacuation: Ibid., 331.
652 The three NVA divisions at Xuan Loc: the 6th, 7th and 341st.
652 Tran Van Tra's revised strategy: Dung, 167.
652 Dung transports artillery shells: Ibid., 169–70.
653 "We would consider it an honor": Ibid., 175.
653 Dung studies Saigon maps: Ibid., 179.
653 "The puppet soldiers": Ibid., 181.
653 "If you do that": Hung and Schecter, 304.

653   "Why don't those people die": Nessen, 98.
653   "For God's sake": Ibid.
653   Thieu plans move to Delta: Hung and Schecter, 323.
654   evacuate Americans "fast and now": Ibid., 328.
654   Martin's cable to Kissinger: Ibid.
654   Thieu-Martin dialogue: Ibid., 300.
654   Thieu with ARVN generals: Ibid., 331.
654   "I have only committed the mistake": Snepp, *Decent*, 339.
654   Don's estimate of the South's future: Dung, 199.
655   Dung on Thieu and Huong: Ibid., 203.
655   Dung on CIA agents: Ibid., 205.
655   "South Vietnam faces total defeat": Snepp, *Decent*, 384n.
655   "If we grasp this great opportunity": Dung, 209.
655   Signing of the invasion map of Saigon: Ibid., 210.
655   "Affidavit of Support": Snepp, *Decent*, 386.
656   "When this thing is finally over": Ibid., 387.
656   "I have lost my paperwork": Ibid., 388.
656   Extended families of fifty or sixty: Ibid., 389.
656   Timmes and Minh: Ibid., 395.
656   Snepp drives Thieu to airport: Ibid., 436.
656   "It is so easy to be an enemy": Hung and Schecter, 333.
657   Minh asks Martin to evacuate Americans: Ibid., 342.
657   A-37 raid on Tan Son Nhut: Ibid., 344.
657   Martin vows to stay on: Ibid.
657   Kham at post office: Author's interview, Colonel Ta Minh Kham, Ho Chi Minh City,
       May 28, 1996.
658   "If you want to go yourself": Don, 251.
658   Minh sends out his family: Ibid., 252.
658   Bui Diem's bag of photographs: Bui Diem, 333.
658   "Frequent Wind": Snepp, *Decent*, 490.
659   Burning of $2 million: Ibid., 491.
659   South Vietnam's gold reserves: Hung and Schecter, 334–35.
659   Nguyen Tu refuses to leave: Author's telephone interview, Nguyen Dinh Tu, Alexan-
       dria, Va., Oct. 5, 1999. Tu spent a total of thirteen years in a Communist prison and a
       reeducation camp. For the first three weeks after the North Vietnamese took Saigon, he
       was held in the city's Chi Hoa prison, where guards broke his teeth with their rifle butts,
       attempting to get him to confess to being an American agent. Tu spent much of the next
       years in solitary confinement until he was sent in the summer of 1985 to a reeducation
       camp in Tuy Hoa province in the forests of central Vietnam. There prisoners planted
       rice and made bricks.
          Released in 1988, Tu found himself under constant surveillance and fled by sea to
       Hong Kong in July 1989. The British held him in a detention camp until friendly jour-
       nalists appealed to the Bush administration. Tu flew to the United States on February 14,
       1990.
660   Tri Quang declines to leave: Author's interviews, Tran Quang Thuan, Los Angeles,
       1997–99.
660   Tuyen's recent history and evacuation: Author's interviews, Tran Kim Tuyen, Cam-
       bridge, England, March 1996.
661   Mal Browne's evacuation: Author's interview, Malcolm Browne, New York City, April
       10, 1998.
662   Laminated seat tickets burned: Snepp, *Decent*, 497.
662   Graham Martin's activities: Ibid., 499.
663   Phu's suicide: Ibid., 504.
663   Tai thrown out of plane: Ibid., 38. In an e-mail to the author from Hanoi in 2001, Nguyen

Van Tai confirmed that ARVN authorities had been prepared to throw him to his death from a plane but confusion in Saigon as North Vietnamese forces approached had thwarted the plan, and Tai was able to return to North Vietnam.

663 Vietnamese at Duc Hotel: Ibid., 519.
664 Barges sail with few Vietnamese: Ibid., 524.
664 Beech at embassy walls: Ibid., 525–26.
664 Volkswagen gas tank explodes: Ibid., 535.
664 Poodle evacuated: Ibid., 545.
664 Polgar, Snepp leave by helicopter: Ibid., 548.
664 "I want you heroes": Ibid., 554.
664 "Thousands of Vietnamese owe": Ibid., 557.
665 last American Marines leave: Ibid., 562.
665 evacuation statistics: Ibid., 563; Dung, 235.
665 Dung on April 30: Dung, 236.
665 Neil Davis background and at palace: Bowden, 337–38. On September 9, 1985, Davis was killed by gunfire during an attempted coup d'état in Bangkok.
667 Minh–Bui Tin exchange: Dung, 242; Karnow, *Vietnam*, 669.
667 Bui Tin's small talk: Bui Tin, 88.
667 Mrs. Chon in Paris: Author's interview, Nguyen Thi Chon, Hanoi, May 22, 1998.
667 Mrs. Dung's reaction to peace: Author's interview, Mrs. Nguyen Thi Ngoc Dung, Ho Chi Minh City, May 20, 1998.
668 "Political Bureau is most happy": Dung, 246.
668 Huynh's reaction: Author's interview, Nguyen Khac Huynh, Hanoi, May 13, 1998.

BIBLIOGRAPHY

Ablin, David A., and Marlowe Hood, eds. *The Cambodian Agony.* Armonk, N.Y., 1987.
Abramson, Rudy. *Spanning the Century: The Life of W. Averell Harriman.* New York, 1992.
Acheson, Dean. *Present at the Creation.* New York, 1987.
Adler, Renata. *Reckless Disregard.* New York, 1986.
Ambrose, Stephen E. *Eisenhower: Soldier and President.* New York, 1990.
——. *Nixon: The Triumph of a Politician 1962–72.* New York, 1989.
An, Tai Sung. *The Vietnam War.* Cranbury, N.J., 1998.
Appy, Christian G. *Working-Class War.* Chapel Hill, N.C., 1993.
Archer, Jules. *Mao Tse-Tung.* New York, 1972.
Arnett, Peter. *Live from the Battlefield.* New York, 1994.
Ashmore, Harry S., and William Baggs. *Mission to Hanoi.* New York, 1968.
Ball, George W. *The Past Has Another Pattern.* New York, 1982.
Bao Ninh. *The Sorrow of War.* Translated by Frank Palmos. London, 1994.
Baritz, Loren. *Backfire.* New York, 1985.
Barrett, David M. *Uncertain Warriors: Lyndon Johnson and His Vietnam Advisers.* Lawrence,
    Kans., 1993.
——, ed. *Lyndon B. Johnson's Vietnam Papers.* Austin, Tex., 1997.
Bator, Viktor. *Vietnam: A Diplomatic Tragedy.* Dobbs Ferry, N.Y., 1965.
Bergerud, Eric. *Red Thunder, Tropic Lightning.* Boulder, Colo., 1993.
Berman, Edgar. *Hubert.* New York, 1979.
Berman, Larry. *Lyndon Johnson's War.* New York, 1989.
——. *Planning a Tragedy.* New York, 1982.
Berval, René de. *Kingdom of Laos.* Saigon, 1959.
Beschloss, Michael R. *Kennedy and Roosevelt.* New York, 1980.
——. *Taking Charge: The Johnson White House Tapes, 1963–1964.* New York, 1997.
Bigart, Homer. *Forward Positions.* Betsy Wade, ed. Fayetteville, Ark., 1992.
Bilton, Michael, and Kevin Sim. *Four Hours in My Lai.* New York, 1992.
Bird, Kai. *The Chairman.* New York, 1992.
——. *The Color of Truth.* New York, 1998.
Blight, James G., Joseph S. Nye, Jr., and David A. Welch. "The Cuban Missile Crisis Revis-
    ited." *Foreign Affairs,* Fall 1987.
Blumenfeld, Ralph, and the Staff and Editors of the *New York Post. Henry Kissinger.* New York, 1974.
Bosiljevac, T. L. *SEALs.* New York, 1991.
Bowden, Tim. *One Crowded Hour.* Sydney, 1987.
Bowles, Chester. *Promises to Keep.* New York, 1971.
Bradlee, Benjamin C. *Conversations with Kennedy.* New York, 1975.
Braestrup, Peter. *Big Story.* 2 vols. Boulder, Colo., 1977.
Brigham, Robert K. *Guerrilla Diplomacy: The NLF's Foreign Relations and the Viet Nam War.*
    Ithaca, N.Y., 1999.
Brown, Weldon A. *Prelude to Disaster.* Port Washington, N.Y., 1975.

Browne, Malcolm. *Muddy Boots and Red Socks*. New York, 1993.
———. *The New Face of War*. New York, 1968.
Buchwald, Art. *Son of the Great Society*. London, 1967.
Bui Diem, with David Chanoff. *In the Jaws of History*. Boston, 1987.
Bui Tin. *Following Ho Chi Minh*. Translated by Judy Stowe and Do Van. Honolulu, 1995.
Bundy, William. *A Tangled Web*. New York, 1998.
Burchett, Wilfred G. *Vietnam North*. New York, 1966.
Burr, William, ed. *The Kissinger Transcripts*. New York, 1998.
Buttinger, Joseph. *Vietnam: A Dragon Embattled*. 2 vols. New York, 1967.
———. *Vietnam: A Political History*. New York, 1968.
Caldwell, Dan, ed. *Henry Kissinger*. Durham, N.C., 1983.
Califano, Joseph A., Jr. *The Triumph and Tragedy of Lyndon Johnson*. New York, 1991.
Capps, Walter H. *The Unfinished War*. Boston, 1990.
Castle, Timothy N. *One Day Too Long*. New York, 1999.
Chaffard, Georges. *Les Carnets secrets de la décolonisation*. Paris, 1965.
Chandler, David P. *Brother Number One*. Boulder, Colo., 1992.
Chang, Pao-Min. *Kampuchea Between China and Vietnam*. Singapore, 1985.
Chanoff, David, and Doan Van Toai. *Vietnam*. London, 1996.
Chapuis, Oscar. *A History of Vietnam*. Westport, Conn., 1995.
Chi, Hoang Van. *From Colonialism to Communism: A Case History of North Vietnam*. New York, 1964.
Clavir, Judy, and John Spitzer, ed. *The Conspiracy Trial*. Indianapolis, 1970.
Clifford, Clark, with Richard Holbrooke. *Counsel to the President*. New York, 1991.
Colby, William, and Peter Forbath. *Honorable Men: My Life in the CIA*. New York, 1978.
Collier, Peter, and David Horowitz. *The Kennedys: An American Drama*. New York, 1984.
Cooper, Chester L. *The Lost Crusade*. New York, 1970.
Corn, David. *Blond Ghost*. New York, 1994.
Craig, Gordon A., and Francis L. Lowenheim. *The Diplomats 1939–1979*. Princeton, N.J., 1994.
Cray, Ed. *General of the Army*. New York, 1990.
Critchfield, Richard. *The Long Charade*. New York, 1968.
Currey, Cecil B. *Edward Lansdale*. Boston, 1988.
———. *Victory at Any Cost*. Washington, D.C., 1997.
Dallek, Robert. *Flawed Giant: Lyndon Johnson and His Times 1961–1973*. New York, 1998.
Davidson, Phillip B. *Vietnam at War*. Oxford, 1988.
Davis, James Kirkpatrick. *Assault on the Left*. Westport, Conn., 1997.
Dawson, Alan. *55 Days: The Fall of Saigon*. Englewood Cliffs, N.J., 1997.
De Gaulle, Charles. *War Memoirs*. New York, 1967.
Dellums, Ronald V. *The Dellums Committee Hearings on War Crimes in Vietnam*. Edited by The Citizens Commission of Inquiry. New York, 1972.
Dictionary of the Vietnam War. Edited by Marc Leepson, with Helen Hannaford. New York, 1999.
Dictionary of the Vietnam War. Edited by James Olson. New York, 1987.
DiLeo, David L. *George Ball, Vietnam, and the Rethinking of Containment*. Chapel Hill, N.C., 1991.
Dobrynin, Anatoly. *In Confidence*. New York, 1995.
Dommen, Arthur J. *Laos*. Boulder, Colo., 1985.
Don, Tran Van. *Our Endless War*. San Rafael, Calif., 1978.
Dong, Pham Van. *Selected Writings*. Hanoi, 1977.
Doyle, Edward, and Samuel Lipsman, ed. *Setting the Stage*. Boston, 1981.
Duiker, William J. *The Communist Road to Power in Vietnam*. New York, 1996.
———. *Ho Chi Minh*. New York, 2000.
———. *U.S. Containment Policy and the Conflict in Indochina*. Stanford, Calif., 1994.
Dung, Van Tien. *Our Great Spring Victory*. Translated by John Spragens, Jr. New York, 1977.
Eisenhower, Dwight D. *At Ease: Stories I Tell to Friends*. New York, 1988.

Elliott, David W. P. *Political Integration in North Vietnam: The Cooperativization Period.* New York, 1974.

Ellsberg, Daniel. *Papers on the War.* New York, 1972.

Emerson, Gloria. *Winners and Losers.* New York, 1976.

Epstein, Jason. *The Great Conspiracy Trial.* New York, 1970.

Fairbank, John King. *The Great Chinese Revolution 1800–1985.* New York, 1986.

Fairlee, Henry. *The Kennedy Promise.* Garden City, N.Y., 1973.

Falk, Richard. *Appropriating Tet.* Princeton, N.J., 1988.

———. *What's Wrong with Henry Kissinger's Foreign Policy.* Princeton, N.J., 1974.

Fall, Bernard B. *Street Without Joy.* 1961. Reprint, Mechanicsburg, Pa., 1989.

———. *The Two Vietnams.* New York, 1964.

Fang, Percy Jucheng, and Lucy Guinong J. Fang. *Zhou Enlai: A Profile.* Beijing, 1986.

Farrell, James J. *The Spirit of the Sixties.* New York, 1997.

Fay, Paul B. *The Pleasure of His Company.* New York, 1966.

Fenn, Charles. *Ho Chi Minh.* New York, 1973.

Fifield, Russell H. *The Diplomacy of Southeast Asia: 1945–1958.* New York, 1958.

Fishel, Wesley R., ed. *Vietnam: Anatomy of a Conflict.* Itasca, Ill., 1968.

FitzGerald, Frances. *Fire in the Lake.* New York, 1972.

Ford, Gerald R. *A Time to Heal.* New York, 1979.

Ford, Harold P. *CIA and the Vietnam Policymakers: Three Episodes, 1962–1968.* Washington, D.C., 1998.

Ford, Ronnie E. *Tet 1968: Understanding the Surprise.* London, 1995.

Foreign Relations of the United States, Vietnam. Edited by John P. Glennon. Washington, D.C., 1988– .

Frankel, Max. *The Times of My Life.* New York, 1999.

Freidel, Frank. *Franklin D. Roosevelt.* Boston, 1990.

Gaiduk, Ilya V. *The Soviet Union and the Vietnam War.* Chicago, 1996.

Galbraith, John Kenneth. *Name-Dropping.* Boston, 1999.

Gardner, Lloyd C. *Approaching Vietnam.* New York, 1988.

———. *Pay Any Price.* Chicago, 1995.

Garrettson, Charles Lloyd, III. *Hubert H. Humphrey.* New Brunswick, N.J., 1993.

Gelb, Leslie H., with Richard K. Betts. *The Irony of Vietnam: The System Worked.* Washington, D.C., 1979.

Gettleman, Marvin E., et al., eds. *Vietnam and America.* New York, 1995.

Giap, Vo Nguyen. *The Military Art of People's War.* Edited by Russell Stetler. New York, 1970.

———. *Unforgettable Days.* Hanoi, 1975.

Gibbons, William Conrad. *The U.S. Government and the Vietnam War.* 4 vols. Princeton, N.J., 1986–95.

Gibson, James William. *The Perfect War.* Boston, 1986.

Gilbert, Marc Jason, and William Head, ed. *The Tet Offensive.* Westport, Conn., 1996.

Gitlin, Todd. *The Sixties.* New York, 1987.

Goldstein, Joseph, Burke Marshall and Jack Schwartz. *The My Lai Massacre and Its Cover-up: Beyond the Reach of the Law?* New York, 1976.

Goodwin, Doris Kearns. *Lyndon Johnson and the American Dream.* New York, 1976.

Goodwin, Richard. *Remembering America.* Boston, 1988.

Grant, Zalin. *Facing the Phoenix.* New York, 1991.

Gravel, Mike, ed. *Pentagon Papers: The Defense Department History of United States Decision Making on Vietnam,* Senator Gravel Edition. Boston, 1971.

Greene, Graham. *The Quiet American.* London, 1955.

Greene, John Robert. *The Presidency of Gerald R. Ford.* Lawrence, Kans., 1995.

Greenstein, Fred, and Richard Immerman. "What Did Eisenhower Tell Kennedy About Indochina?" *Journal of American History,* September 1992.

Gruening, Ernest, and Herbert Wilton Beaser. *Vietnam Folly.* Washington, D.C., 1968.

Gunn, Geoffrey C. *Rebellion in Laos.* Boulder, Colo., 1990.

Guthman, Edwin. *We Band of Brothers.* New York, 1972.
Halberstam, David. *The Best and the Brightest.* New York, 1971.
——. *Ho.* New York, 1971.
——. *The Making of a Quagmire.* 1964. Reprint, edited with an introduction by Daniel J. Singal. New York, 1988.
——. *The Powers That Be.* New York, 1979.
——. *The Reckoning.* New York, 1986.
Haldeman, H. R. *The Haldeman Diaries.* New York, 1994.
——. *The Ends of Power.* New York, 1978.
Hallin, Daniel C. *The "Uncensored War."* Berkeley, Calif., 1989.
Hamilton, Nigel. *JFK: Reckless Youth.* New York, 1992.
Hammer, Ellen J. *A Death in November.* New York, 1987.
Hammond, William M. *The Military and the Media, 1962–1968.* Washington, D.C., 1988.
Han Suyin. *The Morning Deluge: Mao Tsetung and the Chinese Revolution.* Boston, 1972.
Hayden, Tom. *Reunion.* New York, 1988.
Hendrickson, Paul. *The Living and the Dead.* New York, 1996.
Herr, Michael. *Dispatches.* New York, 1977.
Herring, George. *LBJ and Vietnam.* Austin, Tex., 1994.
——. *The Secret Diplomacy of the Vietnam War: The Negotiating Volumes of the Pentagon Papers.* Austin, Tex., 1983.
Hersh, Burton. *The Old Boys: The American Elite and the Origins of the CIA.* New York, 1992.
Hersh, Seymour M. *The Dark Side of Camelot.* New York, 1997.
——. *The Price of Power.* New York, 1983.
Herz, Martin F. *The Prestige Press and the Christmas Bombing, 1972.* Washington, D.C., 1980.
Higgins, Marguerite. *Our Vietnam Nightmare.* New York, 1965.
Hilsman, Roger. *To Move a Nation.* New York, 1967.
Hoan, Hoang Van. *A Drop in the Ocean.* Beijing, 1988.
Ho Chi Minh. *Prison Diary.* Translated by Dang The Binh. Hanoi, 1994.
——. *Selected Articles and Speeches, 1920–1967.* Edited by Jack Woddis. London, 1969.
——. *Selected Writings (1920–1969).* Hanoi, 1973.
Honey, P. J. *Communism in North Vietnam.* Westport, Conn., 1963.
Hoopes, Townsend. *The Limits of Intervention.* New York, 1987.
Hosmer, Stephen T., Konrad Kellen and Brian M. Jenkins. *The Fall of South Vietnam.* New York, 1980.
Howes, Craig. *Voices of the Vietnam POWs.* New York, 1993.
Humphrey, Hubert H. *The Education of a Public Man.* Edited by Norman Sherman. Garden City, N.Y., 1976.
Hung, Nguyen Tien, and Jerrold L. Schecter. *The Palace File.* New York, 1986.
Huyen, N. Khac. *Vision Accomplished? The Enigma of Ho Chi Minh.* New York, 1971.
Isaacson, Walter. *Kissinger.* New York, 1992.
Isaacson, Walter, and Evan Thomas. *The Wise Men.* New York, 1986.
Jensen-Stevenson, Monika, and William Stevenson. *Kiss the Boys Goodbye.* New York, 1990.
Johnson, Lyndon B. *Lyndon B. Johnson's Vietnam Papers.* Edited by David M. Barrett. College Station, Tex., 1997.
——. *The Vantage Point.* New York, 1971.
Kahin, George M. *Intervention.* New York, 1986.
Kaiser, David. *American Tragedy.* Cambridge, Mass., 2000.
Kalb, Marvin, and Bernard Kalb. *Kissinger.* Boston, 1974.
Kaplan, Morton A., et al. *Vietnam Settlement: Why 1973, Not 1969.* Washington, D.C., 1973.
Karnow, Stanley. "Spook." *New York Times Sunday Magazine,* Jan. 3, 1999, 34.
——. *Vietnam: A History.* New York, 1983.
Katsiaficas, George, ed. *Vietnam Documents: American and Vietnamese Views of the War.* Armonk, N.Y., 1992.

Kattenburg, Paul M. *The Vietnam Trauma in American Foreign Policy, 1945–75.* New Brunswick, Conn., 1980.

Kearns, Doris. *Lyndon Johnson and the American Dream.* New York, 1976.

Kelly, Francis J. *The Green Berets in Vietnam, 1961–71.* McLean, Va., 1991.

——. *U.S. Army Special Forces, 1961–1971.* Washington, D.C., 1973.

Kennedy, John F. *The Kennedy Presidential Press Conferences.* New York, 1978.

——. *Public Papers of the Presidents of the United States: John F. Kennedy.* Washington, D.C., 1961–63.

——. *The Kennedy Wit.* Edited by Bill Adler. New York, 1991.

Kennedy, Robert. *Thirteen Days.* New York, 1969.

Khrushchev, Nikita. *The Glasnost Tapes.* Edited and translated by Jerrold L. Schecter, with Vyachesla V. Luchkov. Boston, 1990.

——. *Khrushchev Remembers.* Edited and translated by Strobe Talbott. Boston, 1970.

Kiernan, Frances. *Seeing Mary Plain: A Life of Mary McCarthy.* New York, 2000.

Kimball, Jeffrey. *Nixon's Vietnam War.* Lawrence, Kans., 1998.

King, Russell. *Land Reform.* Boulder, Colo., 1977.

Kinnard, Douglas. *The Certain Trumpet.* McLean, Va., 1991.

Kissinger, Henry. *White House Years.* Boston, 1979.

——. *Years of Renewal.* New York, 1999.

——. *Years of Upheaval.* Boston, 1982.

Komer, Robert W. *Bureaucracy at War.* Boulder, Colo., 1986.

Krohn, Charles A. *The Lost Battalion.* Westport, Conn., 1993.

Kutler, Stanley I., ed. *Abuse of Power: The New Nixon Tapes.* New York, 1997.

——, ed. *Encyclopedia of the Vietnam War.* New York, 1996.

Ky, Nguyen Cao. *Twenty Years and Twenty Days.* New York, 1976.

Lacouture, Jean. *Ho Chi Minh.* Translated by Peter Wiles. New York, 1968.

Lasky, Victor. *JFK: The Man and the Myth.* New York, 1963.

Le Duan. *On Some Present International Problems.* Hanoi, 1964.

——. *Selected Writings.* Hanoi, 1977.

——. *This Nation and Socialism Are One.* Edited by Tran Van Dinh. Chicago, 1976.

Leckie, Robert. *The Wars of America.* Vol. 2. New York, 1993.

Leepson, Marc, with Helen Hannaford, eds. *Dictionary of the Vietnam War.* New York, 1999.

Lewy, Guenter. *America in Vietnam.* Oxford, 1978.

Li Jui. *The Early Revolutionary Activities of Comrade Mao Tse-Tung.* Translated by Anthony W. Sariti. White Plains, N.Y., 1977.

Li, Tana, and Anthony Reid, eds. *Southern Vietnam Under the Nguyen.* Canberra, Australia, 1993.

Li, Zhisui. *The Private Life of Chairman Mao.* Translated by Tai Hung-Chao. New York, 1994.

Liebchen, Peter A. *Kontum: Battle for the Central Highlands, 30 March–10 June, 1972.* San Francisco, 1972.

Lincoln, Evelyn. *Kennedy and Johnson.* New York, 1968.

Lind, Michael. *Vietnam: The Necessary War.* New York, 1999.

Linh, Nguyen Van. *Vietnam: Urgent Problems.* Hanoi, 1988.

Lodge, Henry Cabot. *As It Was.* New York, 1976.

Logevall, Fredrik. *Choosing War.* Berkeley, Calif., 1999.

Loi, Luu Van, and Nguyen Anh Vu. *Le Duc Tho–Kissinger Negotiations in Paris.* Hanoi, 1996.

Lowenheim, Francis L., Harold D. Langley and Manfred Jonas, eds. *Roosevelt and Churchill: Their Secret Wartime Correspondence.* New York, 1975.

Loye, J. F., Jr., et al. *Lam Son 719.* Christiansburg, Va., n.d.

Lukas, J. Anthony. *The Barnyard Epithet and Other Obscenities.* New York, 1970.

——. *Nightmare.* Athens, Ohio, 1999.

Macdonald, Peter. *Giap.* New York, 1993.

MacGarrigle, George. *Taking the Offensive: October 1966 to October 1967.* Washington, D.C., 1998.

Mahony, Phillip. *From Both Sides Now*. New York, 1998.

Mai, Huu. *Ong Co Van*. 3 vols. Hanoi, 1995.

Maneli, Mieczyslaw. *War of the Vanquished*. Translated by Maria de Gorgey. New York, 1971.

Marr, David G. *Vietnamese Tradition on Trial, 1920–1945*. Berkeley, Calif., 1981.

Marrin, Albert. *Mao Tse-Tung and His China*. New York, 1989.

May, Ernest R., and Philip D. Zelikow, eds. *The Kennedy Tapes*. Cambridge, Mass., 1997.

McAlister, John T., Jr. *Vietnam: The Origins of Revolution*. New York, 1969.

McConnell, Malcolm. *Inside Hanoi's Secret Archives*. New York, 1995.

McMaster, H. R. *Dereliction of Duty*. New York, 1997.

McNamara, Robert, with James Blight, Robert Brigham, Thomas Biersteker and Col. Herbert Schandler. *Argument Without End*. New York, 1999.

———. *In Retrospect*. New York, 1995.

McPherson, Harry. *A Political Education*. Boston, 1972.

Mecklin, John. *Mission in Torment*. Garden City, N.Y., 1965.

Meshad, Shad. *Captain for Dark Mornings*. Playa del Rey, Calif., 1982.

Meyerson, Harvey. *Vinh Long*. Boston, 1970.

Miller, Merle. *Lyndon*. New York, 1980.

Miller, William J. *Henry Cabot Lodge*. New York, 1967.

Milton, David, and Nancy Dall Milton. *The Wind Will Not Subside: Years in Revolutionary China, 1964–1969*. New York, 1976.

Minh, Ho Chi. *Selected Writings*. Hanoi, 1973.

Moore, Harold G., and Joseph L. Galloway. *We Were Soldiers Once—and Young*. New York, 1992.

Morris, Roger. *Haig: The General's Progress*. New York, 1982.

———. *Richard Milhous Nixon*. New York, 1990.

Moss, George Donelson, ed. *A Vietnam Reader*. New York, 1991.

Moyar, Mark. *Phoenix and the Birds of Prey*. Annapolis, Md., 1997.

Murphy, Edward F. *Dak To*. Novato, Calif., 1993.

Nessen, Ron. *It Sure Looks Different from the Inside*. New York, 1978.

Newman, John M. *JFK and Vietnam*. New York, 1992.

Nixon, Richard. *RN*. New York, 1990.

Oberdorfer, Don. *Tet*. New York, 1984.

O'Donnell, Kenneth P., and David F. Powers, with Joseph McCarthy. *Johnny, We Hardly Knew Ye*. New York, 1972.

Olson, Gergory A. *Mansfield and Vietnam*. East Lansing, Mich., 1995.

O'Nan, Stewart, ed. *The Vietnam Reader*. New York, 1998.

O'Neill, Robert J. *General Giap*. New York, 1969.

Osborne, Milton. *Before Kampuchea*. London, 1979.

———. *Sihanouk*. Honolulu, 1994.

O'Toole, G. J. A. *Honorable Treachery*. New York, 1991.

Oudes, Bruce, ed. *From the President: Richard Nixon's Secret Files*. New York, 1988.

Page, Tim. *Page After Page*. New York, 1989.

Page, Tim, and John Pimlott, eds. *Nam, The Vietnam Experience, 1965–75*. New York, 1990.

Palmer, Dave Richard. *Summons of the Trumpet*. San Rafael, Calif., 1978.

Parker, F. Charles, IV. *Vietnam: Strategy for a Stalemate*. New York, 1989.

Parmet, Herbert S. *Jack: The Struggles of John F. Kennedy*. New York, 1980.

Patti, Archimedes L. *Why Vietnam?* Berkeley, Calif., 1980.

The Pentagon Papers as Published by the New York Times. Based on investigative reporting by Neil Sheehan et al. New York, 1971.

Pentagon Papers Case Collection. Edited by Ann Fagan Ginger. Berkeley, Calif., 1975.

Perry, Mark. *Four Stars*. Boston, 1989.

Phathanothai, Sirin. *The Dragon's Pearl*. New York, 1994.

Pike, Douglas. *History of Vietnamese Communism, 1925–1976*. Stanford, Calif., 1978.

———. *PAVN: People's Army of Vietnam*. Novato, Calif., 1986.

——. *Viet Cong*. Cambridge, Mass., 1967.

——. *War, Peace and the Viet Cong*. Cambridge, Mass., 1969.

Pilger, John, and Anthony Barnett. *Aftermath: The Struggle of Cambodia and Vietnam*. London, 1982.

Pimlott, John. *Vietnam: The Decisive Battles*. New York, 1990.

Porter, Gareth. *A Peace Denied*. Bloomington, Ind., 1975.

——. *Vietnam: The Politics of Bureaucratic Socialism*. Ithaca, N.Y., 1993.

Powers, Thomas. *The Man Who Kept the Secrets*. New York, 1979.

——. *The War at Home*. New York, 1973.

Prados, John. *The Hidden History of the Vietnam War*. Chicago, 1995.

Pratt, John Clark, ed. *Vietnam Voices*. New York, 1984.

Price, Raymond. *With Nixon*. New York, 1977.

Prochnau, William. *Once Upon a Distant War*. New York, 1995.

Raskin, Marcus G., and Bernard B. Fall. *The Vietnam Reader*. New York, 1965.

Reeves, Richard. *President Kennedy*. New York, 1993.

Reeves, Thomas C. A *Question of Character*. Rocklin, Calif., 1992.

Report of the Warren Commission on the Assassination of President Kennedy, New York Times. New York, 1964.

Reporting Vietnam. 2 vols. New York, 1998.

Risner, Robinson. *The Passing of the Night*. New York, 1973.

Roosevelt, Elliott. *As He Saw It*. New York, 1946.

Roosevelt, James, and Sidney Shalett. *Affectionately, FDR*. New York, 1959.

Rostow, W. W. *The Diffusion of Power*. New York, 1972.

——. *Getting from Here to There*. New York, 1978.

Roy, Jules. *The Battle of Dien Bien Phu*. Translated by Robert Baldick. New York, 1965.

Rudenstine, David. *The Day the Presses Stopped*. Berkeley, Calif., 1996.

Rusk, Dean. *As I Saw It*. As told to Richard Rusk, Daniel S. Papp, ed. New York, 1990.

Safer, Morley. *Flashbacks*. New York, 1990.

Safire, William. *Before the Fall*. Garden City, N.Y., 1975.

Sainteny, Jean. *Ho Chi Minh and His Vietnam*. Translated by Herma Briffault. Chicago, 1972.

Salisbury, Harrison E. *Behind the Lines—Hanoi*. New York, 1967.

——. *The Long March*. New York, 1985.

——. *Without Fear and Favor*. New York, 1980.

——, ed. *Vietnam Reconsidered*. New York, 1984.

Santoli, Al. *Everything We Had*. New York, 1981.

Schaffer, Howard B. *Chester Bowles: New Dealer in the Cold War*. Cambridge, Mass., 1993.

Schalk, David L. *War and the Ivory Tower*. New York, 1991.

Schlesinger, Arthur, Jr. *Robert Kennedy and His Times*. 2 vols. Boston, 1978.

——. *A Thousand Days*. New York, 1965.

Schultz, John. *Motion Will Be Denied*. New York, 1972.

Schulzinger, Robert D. A *Time for War*. New York, 1997.

77 Conversations Between Chinese and Foreign Leaders on the Wars in Indochina, 1964–1977. Edited by Odd Arne Westad et al. Washington, D.C., 1998.

Shaplen, Robert. *The Lost Revolution*. New York, 1965.

Shapley, Deborah. *Promise and Power*. Boston, 1993.

Sharp, U. S. Grant. *Strategy for Defeat*. Novato, Calif., 1978.

Sharp, U. S. Grant, and William C. Westmoreland. *Report on the War in Vietnam*. Washington, D.C., 1969.

Shawcross, William. *Sideshow*. New York, 1979.

Sheehan, Neil. *After the War Was Over*. New York, 1992.

——. *A Bright Shining Lie*. New York, 1988.

Shesol, Jeff. *Mutual Contempt*. New York, 1997.

Short, Philip. *Mao*. New York, 1999.

Siao-Yu. *Mao Tse-Tung and I Were Beggars*. Syracuse, N.Y., 1956.

Simpson, Howard R. *Dien Bien Phu*. Washington, D.C., 1994.

Sinke, Ralph E. G., Jr. *Don't Cry for Us*. Dale City, Va., 1984.

Smith, George E. *P.O.W.: Two Years with the Vietcong*. Berkeley, Calif., 1971.

Smith, R. B. *An International History of the Vietnam War*. London, 1983.

Snepp, Frank. *Decent Interval*. New York, 1977.

——. *Irreparable Harm*. New York, 1999.

Snow, Edgar. *The Long Revolution*. New York, 1971.

——. *Red Star over China*. 1937. Reprint, New York, 1968.

Solberg, Carl. *Hubert Humphrey*. New York, 1984.

Sontag, Susan. *Trip to Hanoi*. New York, 1968.

Sorensen, Theodore C. *Decision Making in the White House*. New York, 1963.

——. *Kennedy*. New York, 1965.

Sorley, Lewis. *A Better War*. New York, 1999.

Spector, Ronald H. *After Tet*. New York, 1993.

Spence, Jonathan. *Mao Zedong*. New York, 1999.

Stavins, Ralph, Richard J. Barnet and Marcus G. Raskin. *Washington Plans an Aggressive War*. New York, 1971.

Steel, Ronald. *Walter Lippmann and the American Century*. New York, 1980.

Stone, I. F. *In a Time of Torment*. New York, 1968.

——. *Polemics and Prophecies*. Boston, 1970.

Summers, Harry G., Jr. *On Strategy*. Novato, Calif., 1984.

——. *Vietnam War Almanac*. New York, 1985.

Tana, Li, and Anthony Reid, eds. *Southern Vietnam under the Nguyen*. Canberra, 1993.

Tang, Truong Nhu, with David Chanoff and Doan Van Toai. *A Vietcong Memoir*. San Diego, 1985.

Taylor, John M. *General Maxwell Taylor*. New York, 1989.

Taylor, Maxwell D. *Responsibility and Response*. New York, 1967.

terHorst, Jerald F. *Gerald Ford and the Future of the Presidency*. New York, 1974.

Terrill, Ross. *Mao*. New York, 1980.

Thai, Hoang Van. *How South Vietnam Was Liberated*. Hanoi, 1996.

Thao, Hoang Minh. *The Victorious Tay Nguyen Campaign*. Hanoi, 1979.

Thomson, James. "How Could Vietnam Happen?" *Atlantic Monthly*, April 1968.

——. *Sentimental Imperialists*, with Peter W. Stanley and John Curtis Perry. New York, 1981.

——. *While China Faced West*. Cambridge, Mass., 1969.

Tonnesson, Stein. *The Vietnamese Revolution of 1945*. London, 1991.

Topping, Seymour. *Journey Between Two Chinas*. New York, 1972.

Tornquist, David. *Vietnam Then and Now*. London, 1991.

Truong Chinh. *The Resistance Will Win*. Hanoi, 1966.

Truong, Ngo Quang. *The Easter Offensive of 1972*. Washington, D.C., 1980.

Tuohy, William. *Dangerous Company*. New York, 1987.

Turley, G. H. *The Easter Offensive*. Annapolis, Md., 1985.

Ungar, Sanford J. *The Papers & The Papers*. New York, 1972.

U.S. Department of the Air Force. *The 1972 Invasions of Military Region I: Fall of Quang Tri and Defense of Hue*. Christiansburg, Va., n.d.

U.S. Department of the Army. *U.S. Army Special Forces, 1961–1971*. Washington, D.C., 1972.

U.S. Senate Committee on Foreign Relations. *Vietnam Commitments, 1961*. Washington, D.C., 1972.

United States–Vietnam Relations, 1945–1967 (Pentagon Papers). 12 vols. Washington, D.C., 1971.

——. *The Vietnam Hearings*. Introduction by J. William Fulbright. New York, 1966.

Unsigned. *Initial Failure of the U.S. "Limited War."* Hanoi, 1967.

Valenti, Jack. *A Very Human President*. New York, 1975.

Valentine, Douglas. *The Phoenix Program*. New York, 1990.

Vandiver, Frank E. *Shadows of Vietnam*. College Station, Tex., 1997.

Veterans and Agent Orange, Update 1996. Institute of Medicine. Washington, D.C., 1996.

Vien, Nguyen Khac, and Phong Hien. *American Neo-Colonialism in South Vietnam (1954–1975): Socio-Cultural Aspects.* Hanoi, n.d.

——. *Tradition and Revolution in Vietnam.* Berkeley, Calif., 1974.

Vogelgesang, Sandy. *Long Dark Night of the Soul.* New York, 1974.

Walters, Vernon A. *Silent Missions.* New York, 1978.

Warbey, William. *Ho Chi Minh.* London, 1972.

Warner, Denis. *Certain Victory: How Hanoi Won the War.* Kansas City, 1977.

Werner, Jayne S., and Luu Doan Huynh, eds. *The Vietnam War: Vietnamese and American Perspectives.* Armonk, N.Y., 1993.

Westmoreland, William. *A Soldier Reports.* New York, 1989.

White, Theodore. *The Making of the President, 1972.* New York, 1973.

——. *The Making of the President, 1960.* New York, 1961.

——. *The Making of the President, 1968.* New York, 1969.

——. *The Making of the President, 1964.* New York, 1965.

Wicker, Tom. *One of Us: Richard Nixon and the American Dream.* New York, 1991.

——. "The Wrong Rubicon." *Atlantic Monthly,* May 1968.

Wilson, Dick. *Zhou Enlai.* New York, 1984.

——, ed. *Mao Tse-Tung in the Scales of History.* Cambridge, 1977.

Wirtz, James J. *The Tet Offensive.* Ithaca, N.Y., 1991.

Wyatt, Clarence R. *Paper Soldiers.* New York, 1993.

Yarborough, Colonel Tom. *Danang Diary.* New York, 1990.

Young, A. L., and G. M. Reggiani, eds. *Agent Orange.* Amsterdam, 1988.

Young, Marilyn. *The Vietnam Wars, 1945–1990.* New York, 1991.

Zaroulis, Nancy, and Gerald Sullivan. *Who Spoke Up?* Garden City, N.Y., 1984.

Zasloff, Joseph J. *The Pathet Lao.* Lexington, Mass., 1973.

ACKNOWLEDGMENTS

WHEN I FIRST CONSIDERED writing this book, I asked a dozen alert and talented students in my journalism class to identify several names from the Vietnam era. Since they had not been born when the American troops withdrew from the country, I was not entirely surprised that they didn't know Dean Rusk, McGeorge Bundy or even William Westmoreland. The one name that proved familiar to them was Robert McNamara. Three students said that he had dynamited the *Los Angeles Times* building in 1910.

They had confused the former secretary of defense with one of the McNamara brothers from a celebrated labor dispute with the newspaper. It struck me then that our students might be graduating with a better grasp of journalism history than of a critical event in America's recent past.

Certainly, there were already many first-rate books about aspects of the Vietnam War to enlighten them. But the authors were often arguing for their point of view or defending an overarching thesis. Vietnam had never been that simple to me.

Some books presented counter-factuals, history's "what-ifs?" What would Kennedy have done if he had lived? What difference would it have made if Johnson's closest advisers had warned against escalation? What would the war's outcome have been if Richard Nixon had not been forced to resign? Such speculation can be provocative, but I did not want to indulge in it. My goal was simply a straightforward narrative that would let readers draw their own conclusions. Because I began the book with no theory to prove, I wrote its final paragraph only after reliving the events that led to April 30, 1975.

My own introduction to Vietnam came in 1964, when the *New York Times* sent me as a correspondent to Southeast Asia. The following year, Peter Grose, the *Times*'s Saigon bureau chief, was transferred to Moscow and I replaced him. When I told the paper's executives later that I was quitting to write a novel, the editor of the Sunday magazine suggested I sum up my fourteen months in Southeast Asia.

The piece, which ran on September 19, 1965, ended this way:

> I ask myself these questions as I leave Vietnam: If one nation begins an ugly and inhuman war, does national honor require resisting even more brutally? But, then, why shouldn't America pursue a war on its terms rather than follow rules that can only lead to failure? Won't, perhaps, the Communists be intimidated by American strength and draw back from aggression before the South Vietnamese suffer even more misery?
>
> If the United States can win in Vietnam only by American bombers and American troops, has the country's leadership learned anything at all

about guerrilla war? Will the desperation over South Vietnam seem justified 15 years from now? Will the South Vietnamese peasant be better off under today's Premier Nguyen Cao Ky, or his successor, than under Ho Chi Minh?

Will Thailand be reassured by a victory in Vietnam if it is achieved at a great cost to the civilian population? Is the United States compounding mistakes in its policy toward China that it must one day redress? Or is the next generation of China's leaders learning that wars of liberation are too costly? Finally, is the United States now helping the people of South Vietnam more than it is hurting them? I don't know.

I returned twice to South Vietnam on two-month freelance assignments for the *Times Magazine*, once in 1968 to write about the aftermath of the Tet offensive, and again in 1970 to report on the American invasion of Cambodia.

Even before 1964, I had known several participants in the Vietnam story. McGeorge Bundy asked me to be his assistant in August 1956, when he was dean of the Harvard College faculty. I joined him for a few months until I was drafted in December. Seven years later, Harrison Salisbury, then the *New York Times* national editor, hired me as a reporter.

During my three assignments in South Vietnam, I observed at close range many of the other figures: Khanh, Ky and Thieu; Max Taylor and Ellsworth Bunker; Westmoreland and Abrams; and, during one of his whirlwind tours, Secretary McNamara.

I also came to know the outstanding reporters based in Saigon; the book is dedicated to one of them. Given the debate over press coverage, it has been gratifying to hear Barry Zorthian, once the chief U.S. spokesman in Saigon, conclude that, despite some inaccuracies and distortions in coverage during the years before Tet, more often than not the press had been more accurate in portraying the war than the government's public reports had been.

When I flew out of Saigon for the last time in 1970, I did not imagine that one day I'd be surrounded by stacks of top-secret documents in the presidential libraries in Boston and Austin. Nor did I anticipate making five trips in the 1990s to Hanoi and Ho Chi Minh City and being warmly received by Vietcong officers and lifelong Communist politicians.

The end notes identify most of the men and women I have interviewed, and I thank them all for their time and patience. Many scholars also have helped me to understand aspects of the era, among them James Blight and janet Lang of Brown University; Robert Brigham of Vassar College; Fredrik Logevall of the University of California at Santa Barbara; and Gordon Goldstein, who is editing McGeorge Bundy's memoirs for Yale University Press. Friends have read portions of the manuscript, catching errors and suggesting improvements: Goldstein and Seymour Topping in New York, Sue Horton and Charles Fleming in Los Angeles. Any mistakes that have persisted are entirely mine. I am grateful to Dean Geoffrey Cowan of the Annenberg School for Communication at the University of Southern California for approving a sabbatical leave during the writing of the book.

The Foreign Press Centers in Hanoi and Ho Chi Minh City provided gifted young translators, including Mai Thu Ha, Phan Thu Hang, Trinh Tu Lan and Luu Lan Phuong.

In Beijing, Shanghai and Vietnam, some men and women were willing to speak with me but adamant about my not using their names. Shortly before publication, I asked them to reconsider and received word that the repercussions for them still could be severe. It was one more reminder about modern-day life in China and Vietnam. The men and women of North Vietnam and the Vietcong who appear in these pages impressed me deeply with their dedication to the independence and unity of their country. But they marched under the one banner they thought promised success, and the future has not turned out as many in their crusade envisioned it.

South Vietnam's cause of freedom and democracy, which seldom attracted comparable leaders, was betrayed by ineptitude and greed. On both sides, the actual fighting fell to men and women who were often uncommonly brave. On both sides, civilians suffered unforgivably.

Another point about sources: I am grateful to the men and women of U.S. intelligence agencies who helped me, and several of them are named in the text. All of them scrupulously observed the oath they had once signed. They might reveal details of their personal lives, but they gave away nothing sensitive about their work. Their Vietnamese contacts had not taken similar vows, however, and often spoke freely.

I expect that future writers on the war will agree with me that our greatest single debt is to the devoted scholars who are in the process of compiling the Vietnam volumes of *Foreign Relations of the United States*. Led by John P. Glennon, Glenn W. LaFantasie and David S. Patterson, those men and women are producing a comprehensive and unbiased collection of the U.S. government's essential documents.

Although I can't list all of the other resources I found valuable, I hope my brief summaries drawn from several of them will lead readers back to books that deserve to be read in full: Robinson Risner's *The Passing of the Night*, Harold G. Moore and Joseph Galloway's *We Were Soldiers Once—and Young*, and Frank Snepp's *Decent Interval*. Jack Smith's account of the battle at Ia Drang gains its power from being written as a letter to a buddy back home. Only at his parents' urging did Smith offer it to the *Saturday Evening Post*.

Richard Holbrooke ably assisted Clark Clifford on *Counsel to the President*, which reflects Clifford's impressive career. *Reunion* by Tom Hayden and the memoirs soon to be published by Daniel Ellsberg deal with extraordinary events by two men who helped to shape their times. Stephen Ambrose has given us detailed and persuasive portraits of Eisenhower and Nixon, Arthur Schlesinger, Jr., of John and Robert Kennedy.

Both David Halberstam's *The Best and the Brightest* and Frances FitzGerald's *Fire in the Lake* were published when passions over the war ran high. Neither writer could enjoy the ease of a presidential library and had to rely instead on the best sort of reportorial acumen and energy. As for *A Bright Shining Lie*, from the time it was published in 1988, I have urged that anyone trying to understand America's role in Vietnam begin with Neil Sheehan. And every bookshelf on the war must include Stanley Karnow's *Vietnam: A History*.

Writers often thank their agents and editors but none with more reason or gratitude than I thank mine. For thirty-five years, Lynn Nesbit of Janklow & Nesbit has been placing my work with great skill and good humor. For twenty-two years, Alice Mayhew has offered me inspiration and friendship; I never forget how lucky I am. The contributions of her colleagues at Simon & Schuster have been uniformly superb: the editing of Roger Labrie; the page design by Edith Fowler; the photographs selected by Natalie Goldstein; the extraordinary copyediting by Fred Wiemer and overseen by Jennifer Thornton; the maps of Jeffrey L. Ward; the jacket design of Henry Sene Yee and the art direction of Michael Accordino.

INDEX

Page numbers in *italics* refer to illustrations.